10-3A Depreciation expense, balance Dec. 31, 19X5, before closing, $7,688
10-4A No check figure
10-5A Cost of new truck, $18,578
10-6A No check figure
10-1B Depr.: Land improve., $2,277; Office bldg., $16,936; Storage bldg., $1,065; Furniture, $14,625
10-2B Depr. for 19X5: SL, $15,750; UOP, $11,250; DDB, $414; SYD, $5,250
10-3B Depreciation expense, Dec. 31, 19X3, balance before closing, $2,683
10-4B No check figure
10-5B Cost of new truck, $16,807
10-6B No check figure
DP Net income, Frycer Company $38,000 more than Bergdahl Company
FSP No check figure

11-1A No check figure
11-2A No check figure
11-3A Total liabilities, $283,926
11-4A Salary Expense, $10,170
11-5A Total annual cost for employee, $58,682
11-6A 3. Cash payment, $12,889; 4. Cash payment, $11,788
11-7A Net pay, $1,740
11-1B No check figure
11-2B No check figure
11-3B Total liabilities, $317,035
11-4B Wage Expense, $15,639
11-5B Total annual cost for employee, $68,274
11-6B 3. Cash payment, $55,545; 4. Cash payment, $40,264
11-7B Net pay, $1,480
DP No check figure
FSP No check figure

12-1A No check figure
12-2A No check figure
12-3A No check figure
12-4A Gross profit, installment method, $18,000
12-5A Net income, year 3, $60,200
12-6A Income, 19X8, percentage-of-completion method, $854,000
12-7A Correct net income, 19X5, $42,100
12-1B No check figure
12-2B No check figure
12-3B No check figure
12-4B Gross profit, installment method, $204,900
12-5B Net income, year 3, $105,830
12-6B Income, 19X6, percentage-of-completion method, $942,000
12-7B Correct net income, 19X9, $47,700
DP Net income, $27,800
FSP No check figure

13-1A Total assets, $152,620
13-2A 1.d. Warner, $30,000; Deitmer, $27,000; Mullaney, $24,000

13-3A 4. Lake's capital at ⅛ interest, $30,000; 5. Lake's capital at 15% interest, $34,500
13-4A 5. Debit Golden, Capital, $29,000
13-5A 1.d. Disbursement of cash to partners: Yagoda, $3,100; Kelly, $2,400; Dobbs, $0
13-6A Disbursements to: Morales, $6,000; Goldberg, $8,000
13-1B 2. Total assets, $111,600
13-2B 1.d. Hogan, $42,500; Stanford, $37,500; Reichlin, $52,000
13-3B 3. Newton's capital at ⅛ interest, $60,000; 5. Newton's capital at 10% interest, $34,000
13-4B 5. Debit Herron, Capital, $60,600
13-5B 1.d. Disbursement of cash to partners: Monet, $0; Dixon, $14,625; Palma, $5,375
13-6B Disbursements: Bell, $2,625; Pastena, $1,375
DP No check figure

14-1A Total stockholders' equity, $91,000
14-2A Total stockholders' equity: Lopez, $155,000; Monroe, $585,000
14-3A Total stockholders' equity, $221,570
14-4A Total yearly pref. dividends to pay to avoid paying dividends in arrears, $22,500,000
14-5A 2. 19X3 dividends: Preferred, $2,000; Common, $32,000
14-6A Book value per share: Preferred, $28.20; Common, $7.16
14-7A Total assets, $683,000
14-1B Total stockholders' equity, $177,500
14-2B Total stockholders' equity: Baker, $94,000; Wang, $397,000
14-3B Total stockholders' equity, $324,320
14-4B Total yearly pref. dividends to pay to avoid paying dividends in arrears, $212,080
14-5B 2. 19X3 dividends: Preferred, $42,500; Common, $222,500
14-6B Book value per share: Preferred, $56.45; Common, $4.80
14-7B Total assets, $378,000
DP Total stockholders' equity: Plan 1, $405,200; Plan 2, $380,200
FSP No check figure

15-1A No check figure
15-2A Total stockholders' equity, Dec. 31, 19X2, $808,700
15-3A Total stockholders' equity, Dec. 31, 19X6, $321,500; Total stockholders' equity, Dec. 31, 19X7, $339,600
15-4A Earnings per share, $3.25; Total stockholders' equity, Sept. 30, 19X6, $618,000
15-5A Retained Earnings balance, Dec. 31, 19X3, $114,000; Earnings per share, $.30
15-6A 2. Debit to Retained Earnings, $28.3 mil.; 4. Treasury Stock, ending bal-

ance, $222.2 mil.; 7. Earnings per share, $1.95
15-7A Earnings per share for net income, $.97
15-1B No check figure
15-2B Total stockholders' equity, Dec. 31, 19X4, $561,400
15-3B Total stockholders' equity, Dec. 31, 19X8, $443,000; Total stockholders' equity, Dec. 31, 19X9, $513,000
15-4B Total stockholders' equity, June 30, 19X5, $509,000
15-5B Retained Earnings balance, June 30, 19X4, $94,000; Earnings per share, $2.85
15-6B 2. Debit to Retained Earnings, $1.3 mil.; 4. Treasury Stock, ending balance, $213.5 mil.; 7. Earnings per share, $4.46
15-7B Earnings per share for net income, $2.89
DP No check figure
FSP No check figure

16-1A 2. Interest Expense, $112,500
16-2A Interest expense for one year, $54,500
16-3A 3. Dec. 31, 19X3, bond carrying value, $105,262
16-4A Sept. 30, X5, debenture carrying value, $108,958
16-5A Dec. 31 Interest Expense, Dr. $43,500 (on bonds); Dr. $7,290 (on lease liability)
16-6A Pension liability, $55,000
16-7A 2. Long-term investment in bonds, $486,350; 3. Short-term investment in bonds, $485,000
16-1B 2. Interest Expense, $80,000
16-2B Interest expense for one year, $25,950
16-3B 3. Dec. 31, 19X3, bond carrying value, $45,128
16-4B July 31, X5, debenture carrying value, $166,350
16-5B Dec. 31 Interest Expense, Dr. $93,000 (on bonds); Dr. $10,230 (on lease liability)
16-6B Pension liability is not reported on the balance sheet
16-7B Dec. 31, Cr. $600 Long-term Investment
DP Plan A EPS, $1.26; Plan B EPS, $1.29; Plan C EPS, $1.05
FSP No check figure

PV-1 3. $112,472; 4. $89,364
PV-2 Dec. 31, 19X2, bond carrying value, $476,049
PV-3 Dec. 31, 19X2, bond carrying value, $4,584,909
PV-4 Dec. 31 Depr. Exp., $3,562; Interest Exp., $2,619
PV-5 Cost (present value) of bond investment, $462,350

(continued on back cover)

ACCOUNTING

PRENTICE HALL SERIES IN ACCOUNTING
Charles T. Horngren, Consulting Editor

ACCOUNTING

Charles T. Horngren
Stanford University

Walter T. Harrison, Jr.
Baylor University

Prentice Hall
A Division of Simon & Schuster
Englewood Cliffs, New Jersey 07632

Library of Congress Cataloging-in-Publication Data

Horngren, Charles T.
  Accounting.

  Includes index.
  1. Accounting. 2. Managerial accounting.
I. Harrison, Walter T. II. Title.
HF5635.H8125   1989   657   88-28851
ISBN 0-13-705519-6

Production editor: Esther S. Koehn
Development editor: Stephen Deitmer
Acquisitions editor: Joseph Heider
Interior and cover design: Linda Conway
Cover art: France: 30th Salon de la Jeune Sculpture, Paris;
  © Robert Clark 1980
Manufacturing buyer: Ed O'Dougherty

For our wives, Joan and Nancy

© 1989 by Prentice Hall, Inc.
A Division of Simon & Schuster
Englewood Cliffs, New Jersey 07632

FOURTH PRINTING
Printed in the United States of America
10 9 8 7 6 5 4

ISBN 0-13-705519-6

Prentice Hall International (UK) Limited, *London*
Prentice Hall of Australia Pty. Limited, *Sydney*
Prentice Hall Canada Inc., *Toronto*
Prentice Hall Hispanoamericana, S.A., *Mexico*
Prentice Hall of India Private Limited, *New Delhi*
Prentice Hall of Japan, Inc., *Tokyo*
Simon & Schuster Asia Pte. Ltd., *Singapore*
Editora Prentice Hall do Brasil, Ltda., *Rio de Janeiro*

Contents

22 Manufacturing Accounting and Job Order Costing 855

23 Process Costing, Operation Costing, and Joint Products 897

24 Flexible Budgets and Standard Costs 935

The Class-Test Edition

To ensure that we have delivered to you a completely error-free text, we extended the development process of **Accounting** and established the *Prentice Hall Class-Testing Program*. Over sixty community colleges and universities—listed below—participated. Instructors at these educational institutions taught their students from our limited first printing of **Accounting**. *Each chapter* of Accounting has been thoroughly checked by your colleagues and their students. Any errors found by instructors or students and sent to Prentice Hall have been corrected in this second printing—the *Class-Test Edition*. Copies of the limited first printing have been destroyed. We guarantee that all orders placed for Fall 1989 classes have been filled with copies of the *Class-Test Edition* of **Accounting**.

The authors and the publisher wish to thank the following people—your colleages and their students—for participating in the *Prentice Hall Class-Testing Program*.

Fred Baird and his students
Austin Community College

Gordon Bell and his students
Florida Atlantic University

Walter Berry and his students
Old Dominion University

Allen B. Bess and his students
University of Evansville

Earl Biggett and his students
Edison Community College

David Blummer and his students
West Virginia Northern Community College

Arthur Braza and his students
Dean Junior College

Philip Brown and his students
Harding University

Charles Buckley and his students
University of Scranton

Sarah Brown and her students
University of North Alabama, University Station

Eric Carlsen and his students
Kean College

Ray Carreon and his students
Fullerton College

Barbara Carter and her students
Pensacola Junior College

Matthew Coyne and his students
Dominican College

Billie Cunningham and her students
Collin County Community College

Deborah Davis and her students
Hampton University

Larry C. Davis and his students
Southwest Virginia Community College

Fred Dial and his students
Stephen F. Austin University

David Doran and his students
West Virginia University

Steve Driver and his students
Horry-Georgetown Technical College

William Eberle and his students
Community College of Philadelphia

Anthony Falgioni and his students
State University of New York, Fredonia

Russell Ferrara and his students
Bryant College

Patrick J. Flynn and his students
Baldwin Wallace College

Marilyn Fuller and her students
Paris Junior College

Mohammed Gaber and his students
State University of New York, Plattsburgh

Lucille Genduso and her students
Nova University

James Genseal and his students
Joliet Junior College

Joyce Griffin and her students
Kansas City Community College

Tom Harrison and his students
Baylor University

Ruby Hayes and her students
Virginia State University

Delmer Hylton and his students
Wake Forest University

George Johnson and his students
Norfolk State University

Becky Jones and her students
Baylor University

Mike Kalphat and his students
Barry University

James Krause and his students
University of Tampa

Ken Larson and his students
Adelphi University

Joan Lawrence and her students
Fairmont State College

Carl Leggett and his students
Valdosta State College

Larry Lipner and his students
Barry University

Ken Mark and his students
Kansas City Community College

Frances McNair and her students
Mississippi State University

Tony Merlonghi and his students
Napa Valley College

Patty Mills and her students
Indiana State University

Bill Nalepka and his students
University of Arkansas

Lee Nicholas and his students
University of Northern Iowa

William Olson and his students
Wagner College

Ed Pauley and his students
West Virginia State College

Grace Peng and her students
Muskingum Area Technical College

Ida Pound and her students
College of Alemeda

Fabiola Rubio and his students
El Paso Community College

Dan Rutz and his students
West Virginia Institute of Technology

Wallace Satchell and his students
St. Phillips College

Walter Schimpf and his students
Dowling College

David Schmedel and his students
Amarillo College

William Shaver and his students
J. Sargeant Reynolds Community
College

Lee E. Stokes and his students
Wake Forest University

Norman Sunderman and his students
Angelo State University

Robin Turner and her students
University of North Carolina,
Greensboro

James Walden and his students
Sinclair Community College

Bea Wallace and her students
University of Texas

Connie Wedemeyer and her students
McClennan Community College

David Weiner and his students
University of San Francisco

Betsy Willis and her students
Baylor University

The Business Context of

ACCOUNTING

To enhance our presentation of accounting, we set out to create a business context for the student. As accounting educators, we know that students benefit from perceiving accounting as more than mere numbers set apart from the rest of their lives and education. We have constructed this business context in two ways.

(1) As often as possible, we have integrated real-world companies and their data into our text and assignment material. Students reading about companies familiar to them find the material more interesting and also develop a deeper appreciation for accounting's importance in today's business world. We have not used boxes to set aside this real-world material. Our references to the world of business are woven into our text narrative.

(2) When information drawn from real companies would be too advanced for introductory students, we have illustrated the accounting point at hand by using realistic examples, building a framework of relevance that makes learning the topic more inviting for the student.

The following list presents only a sampling of how our narrative creates a business context in Chapter 1, *Accounting and Its Environment,* and Chapter 22, *Manufacturing Accounting and Job Order Costing.* These two chapters contain many other realistic business examples. We invite readers to examine these two chapters and other chapters to see how we incorporate the world of business throughout the entire book.

Chapter 1

p.1. A student's decision about which college to attend depends in part on accounting information, including the costs and benefits of various education choices.

p. 2. Investors and creditors use accounting information reported in *The Wall Street Journal, Business Week, Forbes,* and *Fortune.*

p. 4. Private accountants may work for a local department store, the McDonald's restaurant chain, or the Eastman Kodak Company.

p. 5. Price Waterhouse estimated that it took 630,720 hours—72 years of nonstop work—to complete one audit.

p. 7. Procter & Gamble and General Electric are leaders in budgeting. Motorola, Bank of America, and 3M Company have internal auditors.

p. 9. To illustrate the entity concept, the income from Mazzio's personal business dealings is distinguished from his pizzeria's operations.

p. 12. Gary Lyon, CPA, is introduced. His accounting practice is used to illustrate proprietorships throughout Chapters 1 through 4.

p. 20. Campus Apartment Locators, owned by Jill Smith, is the subject of a *Summary Problem for Your Review,* which asks students to record transactions and prepare financial statements.

p. 25. In Exercise 1-2, students use the accounting equation to analyze the first month's events for the medical practice of Gloria Hill, M.D.

p. 26. Exercise 1-5 uses the business of Fadal Travel Agency to focus on income statement preparation.

p. 27. Stevens Interiors in Problem 1-1A provides the data with which students analyze transactions and prepare financial statements.

p. 28. In Problem 1-2A, Zane Jones, attorney, opens up his own law office. Students are tested on the entity concept, transaction analysis, and the accounting equation using his business.

p. 36. The *Decision Problem* centers on whether to loan money to Butler Department Store or to Nielsen Home Decorators.

p. 37. The *Financial Statement Problem* requires students to turn to the actual balance sheet of Gulf+Western Inc., which appears in Appendix C, and asks them to write the accounting equation at October 31, 1987. Many chapters feature a *Financial Statement Problem*, which ties the chapter's topic directly to Gulf+Western's actual financial statements.

Chapter 22

p. 855. The Sportster, a merchandiser, specializes in athletic shoes. How do we account for the companies—Nike, Reebok, Adidas—that manufacture the shoes The Sportster sells? The process of converting materials—cloth, rubber, and plastic for athletic shoes—into finished products makes it more difficult to measure a manufacturer's inventory cost than The Sportster's inventory cost.

p. 856. Nike managers, using cost data, may learn that the company is losing money on children's shoes and decide to drop that product line.

p. 857. *Raw materials* for Bethlehem Steel include iron ore, coal, and chemicals. . . . For a petroleum refiner, *work in process* is the crude oil being distilled into gasoline. . . . Procter & Gamble manufactures soap and toothpaste, which it sells as *finished goods* to K mart and other stores.

p. 858. For General Motors, *direct labor* is the pay to employees who work on production lines manufacturing automobiles. The efforts of these persons can be traced directly to finished goods.

p. 863. Ramirez Furniture Company produces recliner chairs for sale to Macy's in New York City. This example looks in detail at the costs of the lumber, padding, upholstery fabric, nails, thread, and other materials, plus the labor and overhead costs, incurred in manufacturing a job order of 10 recliners. As materials, labor, and overhead are added, the text builds the job cost record sequentially, ending in the complete document on p. 872.

p. 885. In Problem 22-3A, students prepare Stride-Rite's statement of cost of goods manufactured for their brown leather Top-Sider shoe. They also compute cost of goods sold and cost of materials purchased.

p. 886. In Problem 22-5A, students prepare a job cost record for the Maxell Magnetic Tape Company, which manufacturers diskettes.

p. 894. MultiMedia, Inc., is experimenting with a new laser technology for manufacturing telephones. The goal is to lower product cost and selling price in the hope of capturing a larger market share. The *Decision Problem* directs students to compare cost per unit at present to expected unit cost using the new technology to decide whether to proceed with the new process.

p. 895. In the *Financial Statement Problem*, students use the Gulf+Western financial statements and related notes to identify specific jobs, direct materials, direct labor, and overhead cost of the company. Also, students determine how much Gulf+Western could afford to pay former President Reagan to star in a movie about this presidency and still earn a target net income.

Preface

Accounting provides full introductory coverage of both financial and management accounting. We have written the book for use throughout a two-semester or three-quarter sequence of accounting courses.

In content and emphasis, instructors will find that **Accounting** is in the mainstream for courses in introductory accounting. This book focuses on the most widely used accounting theory and practice. This text and its supplements supply the most effective tools available for learning fundamental accounting concepts and procedures.

Clarity and Accuracy

Two themes have directed our writing of this text—*clarity* and *accuracy.* We believe that we have produced the clearest prose, learning objectives, exhibits, definitions, and assignment material for courses in principles of accounting. Students will find this book easy to study. We have assumed that students have no previous education in accounting or business.

The contributions of technical reviewers, general reviewers, and class testers and their students have guided us in writing an accurate text. We and the publishers have sought input on our work from an unprecedented number of accounting educators and students in order to publish a book that meets your strict demands for accuracy.

Distinctive Features

Accounting offers many features that make this text special and superior.

1. **Accounting** has more—and better—exercises and problems than the leading competitors. Exercises and problems tie directly with the text in terminology, setup, and difficulty level. They progress from simple to complex, from short to long.
2. The emphasis on real-world examples promotes student interest.
3. The four-color design enlivens and eases learning. A strong program of visual features—exhibits and tables—helps reinforce the text. Note that the two-tone beige color in exhibits denotes financial statements. The green color in exhibits is used with ledgers, journals, work sheets, and the like. The learning objectives appear with a purple tint at the chapter's opening and in the text. Key headings appear in blue.
4. An up-to-the-minute chapter on the statement of cash flows, Chapter 18, presents a framework for understanding both the concepts and procedures underlying the statement and its preparation.

5. A separate chapter, Chapter 28, provides a thorough introduction to computers as they apply to accounting, including discussion of general ledger software programs, spreadsheets, and Lotus 1-2-3. The chapter offers students hands-on instruction in the preparation of accounting documents. In addition, the text addresses the role of computers in accounting within appropriate chapters. For example, Chapter 9, Merchandise Inventory, and Chapter 21, Cost-Volume-Profit Relationships and the Contribution Margin Approach to Decision Making, contain discussions of the role of the computer in those accounting areas.

6. Management accounting chapters follow an improved, more logical order. Chapter 20 begins our study of management accounting by explaining how budgets are prepared. Chapter 21 introduces a model of cost-volume-profit relationships, an important planning tool of managers. Our first two chapters on management accounting are confined to nonmanufacturing organizations. In this way, we can explore two major tools (budgets and the cost-volume-profit model) without contending with the many new terms associated with manufacturing organizations. Chapters 22 and 23 describe manufacturing accounting systems. Chapters 24, 25, and 26 pursue management accounting tools in more depth. We want students to recognize that management accounting applies to all kinds of organizations, not just to manufacturing companies.

7. Appendix A: Mathematical Presentations, presents the mathematical operations essential to accounting. Students may refer to this appendix to refresh their knowledge of necessary math skills.

8. Appendix B: Reversing Entries, offers instructors the opportunity to teach reversing entries. This appendix is presented in a standard text chapter format, complete with learning objectives and assignment material.

Chapter Organization

1. Each chapter begins with *Learning Objectives*, which also appear in the margin, keyed to the relevant chapter material.

2. Most chapters offer two *Summary Problems for Your Review*. Each *Summary Problem* includes its fully worked-out solution. These features, which generally appear at the halfway point and at the end of each chapter, provide students with immediate feedback and serve as key review aids.

3. Each chapter presents three important tools for student review. A text *Summary* recaps the chapter discussion. *Self-Study Questions* allow students to test their understanding of the chapter. The text that supports the answer is referenced by page number, and the answers appear on the last page of the chapter. *Accounting Vocabulary* presents the key terms introduced in the chapter, referenced by page number. A complete Glossary, also with terms keyed by page number, appears at the end of the book.

4. *Assignment Material* is more varied and plentiful than in competing texts. *Questions* (covering the major definitions, concepts, and procedures) may be assigned as homework or used to promote in-class discussion. **Accounting** has more exercises and more problems than the competitors. *Exercises*, identified by topic area, cover the full spectrum of the chapter text. These "short problems" allow instructors to cover a wide range of topics in a limited time. *Problems*, also identified by topic area, come in A and B sets. The two sets allow instructors to vary assignments from term to term and to solve the A or B problem in class and assign the related problem for homework. Those exercises and problems that can be solved using the Lotus® 1-2-3 or Microsoft Excel templates are designated by a computer disk.

5. Each chapter presents a *Decision Problem*, which helps students to develop critical thinking skills. Analysis, interpretation, and determining a course of action are ordinarily required.

6. Most chapters feature a *Financial Statement Problem*. In these problems, the chapter's subject matter is directly linked to the actual financial statements of Gulf+Western Inc., which appears in Appendix C. As students progress through the course, they will grow increasingly comfortable with the real-world financial report of a large company.

The Supplements Package _____

We have a far-reaching, highly developed package of teaching and learning tools to supplement the text. A team of twenty-seven contributors, five editors, five coordinators, and dozens of reviewers devoted hundreds of hours to perfecting the supplements. The coordinators are professional accounting teachers who worked with the contributors and editors to ensure maximum instructional value, accuracy, and consistency with the text and within the supplements package. All of the supplements are uniquely useful, and fuller descriptions of them are available in the *Annotated Instructor's Edition* and from the publisher's representatives.

Resources for the Instructor _____

Annotated Instructor's Edition
Solutions Manuals (Volume I, Chapters 1–13 and Appendix B; Volume II, Chapters 12–28)
Test Bank and Achievement Tests
Prentice Hall Test Generator Version 3.0
Telephone Test-Preparation Service
Solutions & Teaching Transparencies
Electronic Transparencies
Instructor's Resource Package

Resources for the Student _____

Study Guide with Demonstration and Practice Problems (Volume I, Chapters 1–13; Volume II, Chapters 12–28)
Working Papers (Volume I, Chapters 1–13; Volume II, Chapters 12–28)
Videos
Manual and Computerized Practice Sets
Software Packages

Acknowledgments _____

The authors and publisher wish to thank our many reviewers, whose contributions have meant so much to this project:

Neal Adkins
Marshall University

Harold Averkamp
University of Wisconsin, Whitewater

James Barnhart
Ball State University

Martin Batross
Franklin University

Deborah Boswell
University of North Carolina, Greensboro

David Bourque
Middlesex College

Nancy Boyd
Middle Tennessee State University

Lloyd Buckwell, Jr.
Indiana University, Northwest

Eric Carlson
Kean College

Janet Cassagio
Nassau Community College

Judith Cassidy
Louisiana State University

Leo Chiantelli
Shasta College

Judith Considine
Rutgers University, New Brunswick

James F. Cook
University of Texas at Arlington

Judith Cook
Grossmont Community College

Pauline Corn
Virginia Polytechnic Institute

Art Croisette
Saddleback College

Joyce Dean
Baylor University

Walter Doehring
Genesee Community College

Kathy Dow
Boston University

William Enderlein
Golden Gate University

Richard Fern
Eastern Kentucky University

Joseph Ford
Mesa Community College

Louis H. Gilles
USC — Coastal Carolina College
(Retired)

Max Godwin
Southwest Texas State University

Edward Gordon
Triton College

Diane Green
Sam Houston State University

Don Green
State University of New York,
Farmingdale

Raymond Green
Texas Tech University

B. B. Griffith
Odessa College

Nancy Grzesik
Chesapeake Business Institute

Larry Hagler
Mississippi State University

Gloria Halpern
Montgomery College, Rockville

Gaylon Halverson
University of Northern Iowa

Joseph Hampton
American University

Dorothy Dean Harris
J. Sargeant Reynolds Community College,
Parham

Linda Herrington
Community College of Allegheny County

Carl High
New York City Technical College

George Holdren
University of Nebraska, Lincoln

Cynthia Holloway
Tarrant County Junior College

W. Clyde Hopkins
Memphis State University

Fred A. Jacobs
Georgia State University

Letha Jeanpierre
DeAnza College

Becky Jones
Baylor University

Edward Kelly
Delaware Technical and Community
College

Sandra Knecht
Florida Community College

Anthony Krzystofik
University of Massachusetts, Amherst

Kris Lawyer
North Carolina State University

Albert Lew
Wright State University

Dale Martin
Wake Forest University

Dianna Matthew
Ball State University

Emily Miklis
Cuyahoga Community College

Helen Miller
Baylor University

Michael Milliren
Milwaukee Area Technical College

John Minch
Cabrillo College

Jane Murden
University of North Carolina, Greensboro

Ravi C. Narayan
Northern Virginia Community College

Lois Anne New
Sam Houston State University

Mary Ann Prater
Clemson University

Agnes Price
University of North Carolina, Greensboro

Patrick Reihing
Nassau Community College

Arthur T. Roberts
University of Baltimore

Scott Sandstrom
College of the Holy Cross

Nathan Schmukler
C. W. Post

Janice Shields
University of Maine, Orono

Paul J. Shinal
Cayuga Community College

Ben Shlaes
Des Moines Area Community College

Robert Spear
University of North Carolina, Charlotte

Beverly Terry
Central Piedmont Community College

Phyllis Webster
University of North Carolina, Greensboro

Robert Wennagel
College of the Mainland

Betsy Willis
Baylor University

Deanne Winiarski
Western Carolina University

Ray Winn
El Paso Community College

Among the many people at Prentice Hall who helped to publish this book are Linda Albelli, Sara Colacurto, Linda Conway, Stephen Deitmer, Lisa Garboski, Deborah Garvin, Jackie Hartwick, Joseph Heider, Irene Hess, Jeanne Hoeting, Dennis Hogan, Joanne Jimenez, Gary June, Esther Koehn, Susanna Lesan, Raymond Mullaney, Asha Rohra, Susan Seuling, Beth Stoll, Jacqueline Vernaglia, and Julie Warner. The authors also wish to thank Fred Hulme and Susan Lanier for their assistance with the chapter Accounting with Computers. Elsie Young likewise deserves our thanks.

Charles T. Horngren
Stanford, California, November 1988

Walter T. Harrison, Jr.
Waco, Texas, November 1988

Accounting and
Its Environment

Accounting has been called "the language of business." Perhaps a better term is "the language of financial decisions." The better you understand the language, the better you can manage the financial aspects of living. Personal financial planning, investments, loans, car payments, income taxes, and many other aspects of daily life are based on accounting. A recent survey indicates that business managers believe it is more important for college students to learn accounting than any other subject. Other surveys show that persons trained in accounting and finance make it to the top of their organizations in greater numbers than persons trained in any other field. Indeed, accounting is an important subject.

Decisions and Accounting

Do you make decisions that have a financial impact? Your answer is undoubtedly yes. Regardless of your roles in life — student, head of household, investor, manager, politician — you will find a knowledge of accounting helpful. The major purpose of this book is to help you learn to use accounting information to make informed decisions. Individuals who can do so have a great advantage over those who cannot.

As a student you must decide whether to attend a community college, a four-year college, or a university. And how are you going to finance your education? To make these decisions you weigh the costs and benefits of the various educational choices. These decisions are largely accounting matters. Accounting is also used to form a financial picture of businesses that range from a corner pharmacy to giant companies such as IBM and General Motors. Being able to understand their financial statements will help you make wise investment decisions.

OBJECTIVE 1
Define Accounting

What Is Accounting?

Accounting is the system that measures business activities, processes that information into reports, and communicates these findings to decision makers. **Financial statements** are the documents that report on an individual's or an organization's business in monetary amounts.

Is our business making a profit? Should we start up a new line of women's clothing? Are sales strong enough to warrant opening a new branch outlet? The most intelligent answers to business questions like these use accounting information. Decision makers use the information to develop sound business plans. As new programs affect the business's activities, accounting takes the company's financial pulse beat. The cycle continues as the accounting system measures the results of activities and reports the results to decision makers.

Bookkeeping is a procedural element of accounting as arithmetic is a procedural element of mathematics. Increasingly, people are using computers to do much of the detailed bookkeeping work at all levels — in households, business, and organizations of all types. Exhibit 1-1 illustrates the role of accounting in business.

OBJECTIVE 2
Identify users of
accounting information

Users of Accounting Information

Most of the material in this book describes business situations, but the principles of accounting apply to the financial considerations of individuals as well. The following sections discuss the range of people and groups who use accounting information.

Individuals.   People use accounting information in day-to-day affairs to manage their bank accounts, to evaluate job prospects, to make investments, and to decide whether to rent or to buy a house.

Businesses.   Managers of businesses use accounting information to set goals for their organizations, to evaluate their progress toward those goals, and to take corrective action if necessary. Decisions based on accounting information may include which building and equipment to purchase, how much merchandise inventory to keep on hand, and how much cash to borrow.

Investors and Creditors.   Investors provide the money that businesses need to begin operations. To decide whether to help start a new venture, potential investors evaluate what income they can reasonably expect on their investment. This means analyzing the financial statements of the new business. Those people who do invest monitor the progress of the business by analyzing the company's financial statements and by keeping up with its developments in the business press — for example, *The Wall Street Journal, Business Week, Forbes,* and *Fortune.* Accounting reports are a major source of information for the business press.

EXHIBIT 1-1 *The Accounting System: The Flow of Information*

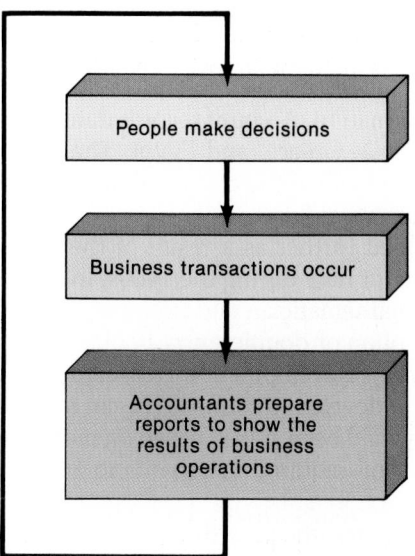

Before making a loan, potential lenders determine the borrower's ability to meet scheduled payments. This evaluation includes a projection of future operations, which is based on accounting information.

Government Regulatory Agencies.   Most organizations face government regulation. For example, the Securities and Exchange Commission (SEC), a federal agency, requires businesses to disclose certain financial information to the investing public. The SEC, like many government agencies, bases its regulatory activity in part on the accounting information it receives from firms.

Taxing Authorities.   Local, state, and federal governments levy taxes on individuals and businesses. The amount of the tax is figured using accounting information. Businesses determine their sales tax based on their accounting records that show how much they have sold. Individuals and businesses compute their income tax based on how much money their records show they have earned.

Nonprofit Organizations.   Nonprofit organizations — such as churches, most hospitals, government agencies, and colleges, which operate for purposes other than to earn a profit — use accounting information in much the same way that profit-oriented businesses do. Both profit organizations and nonprofit organizations deal with budgets, payrolls, rent payments, and the like — all from the accounting system.

Other users.   Employees and labor unions may make wage demands based on the accounting information that shows their employer's reported income. Consumer groups and the general public are also interested in the amount of income that businesses earn. For example, during times of fuel shortages consumer groups have charged that oil companies have earned "obscene profits." On a more positive note, newspapers report "improved profit pictures" of companies as the nation emerges from an economic recession. Such news, based on accounting information, is related to our standard of living.

The Development of Accounting Thought _____

Accounting has a long history. Some scholars claim that writing arose in order to record accounting information. Account records date back to the ancient civilizations of China, Babylonia, Greece, and Egypt. The rulers of these civilizations used accounting to keep track of the cost of labor and materials used in building structures like the great pyramids.

Accounting developed further as a result of the information needs of merchants in the city-states of Italy during the 1400s. In that commercial climate the monk Luca Pacioli, a mathematician and friend of Leonardo da Vinci, published the first known description of double-entry bookkeeping in 1494.

The pace of accounting development increased during the Industrial Revolution as the economies of developed countries began to mass-produce goods. Until that time, merchandise had been priced based on managers' hunches about cost, but increased competition required merchants to adopt more sophisticated accounting systems.

In the nineteenth century, the growth of corporations, especially those in the railroad and steel industries, spurred the development of accounting. Corporation owners—the stockholders—were no longer necessarily the managers of their business. Managers had to create accounting systems to report to the owners how well their businesses were doing.

The role of government has led to still more accounting developments. When the federal government started the income tax, accounting supplied the concept of "income." Also, government at all levels has assumed expanded roles in health, education, labor, and economic planning. To ensure that the information that it uses to make decisions is reliable, the government has required strict accountability in the business community.

OBJECTIVE 3
Identify different aspects of the accounting profession

The Accounting Profession _____

Positions in the field of accounting may be divided into several areas. Two general classifications are *public accounting* and *private accounting*. **Public accountants** are those who serve the general public and collect professional fees for their work, much as doctors and lawyers do. Their work includes auditing, income tax planning and preparation, and management consulting. These specialized accounting services are discussed in the next section. Public accountants are a small fraction (about 10 percent) of all accountants. Those public accountants who have met certain professional requirements are designated as **Certified Public Accountants (CPAs).**

Private accountants work for a single business, such as a local department store, the McDonald's restaurant chain, or the Eastman Kodak Company. Charitable organizations, educational institutions, and government agencies also employ private accountants. The chief accounting officer usually has the title of controller, treasurer, or chief financial officer. Whatever the title, this person usually carries the status of vice-president.

Some public accountants pool their talents and work together within a single firm. Most public accounting firms are also called *CPA firms* because most of their professional employees are CPAs. CPA firms vary greatly in size. Some are small businesses, and others are medium-sized partnerships. The largest CPA firms are worldwide partnerships with over 2,000 partners. Such huge firms are necessary because some of their clients are so large and their operations are so complex. For instance, Price Waterhouse, one of the eight largest American CPA firms, has reported that its annual audit of one particular client would take one accountant 630,720 hours of effort—that equals 72 years of nonstop work! Another Price Waterhouse client owns 300 separate corporate entities. All their records are combined into a single set of financial statements. Such time-consuming tasks make a large staff of accountants a necessity.

The eight largest American accounting firms, often called the Big Eight, are, in alphabetical order,

Arthur Andersen & Co.
Coopers & Lybrand
Deloitte & Touche

Ernst & Young
Peat Marwick Main & Co.
Price Waterhouse & Co.

Although these firms employ only about 12 percent of the 200,000 CPAs in the United States, they audit the financial statements of approximately 85 percent of the 2,600 largest corporations. The top partners in large accounting firms earn about the same amount as the top managers of other large businesses.

Exhibit 1-2 shows the accounting positions within public accounting firms and other organizations. Of special interest in the exhibit is the upward movement of accounting personnel, as the arrows show. In particular, note how accountants may move from positions in public accounting firms to similar or higher positions in industry and government. This is a frequently traveled career path. Because accounting deals with all facets of an organization—such as purchasing, manufacturing, marketing, and distribution—it provides an excellent basis for gaining broad business experience.

Accounting Organizations and Designations _____

The position of accounting in today's business world has created the need for control over the professional, educational, and ethical standards for accountants. The *American Institute of Certified Public Accountants (AICPA)* is the national

EXHIBIT 1-2 *Accounting Positions within Organizations*

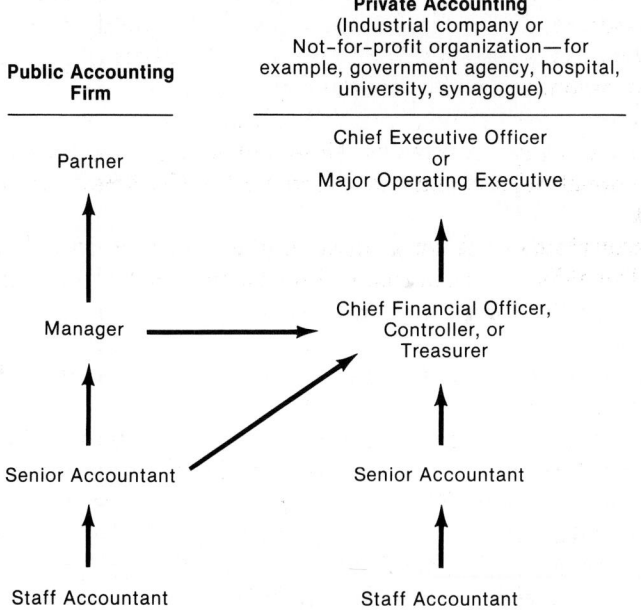

professional organization of CPAs. A CPA is a professional accountant who earns this title through a combination of education, qualifying experience, and an acceptable score on a written national examination that takes approximately three days. The AICPA prepares and grades the examination and gives the results to the individual states, which then issue licenses that enable qualifying people to practice accounting as CPAs. CPAs must also be of high moral character and must conduct their professional practices according to a code of professional conduct. Other nations have similar arrangements, but some use the designation *Chartered Accountant* in place of *Certified Public Accountant.*

The AICPA also develops accounting and auditing principles. The Auditing Standards Board of the AICPA formulates generally accepted auditing standards, which govern the way CPAs perform audits. The AICPA publishes a monthly professional journal, the *Journal of Accountancy.*

State societies of CPAs are professional organizations, much like the AICPA, whose jurisdictions are limited to their respective states. Each state has a state board of accountancy, which administers the state laws that regulate the practice of accounting within its borders. State boards of accountancy, not the AICPA, issue CPA certificates to qualifying individuals.

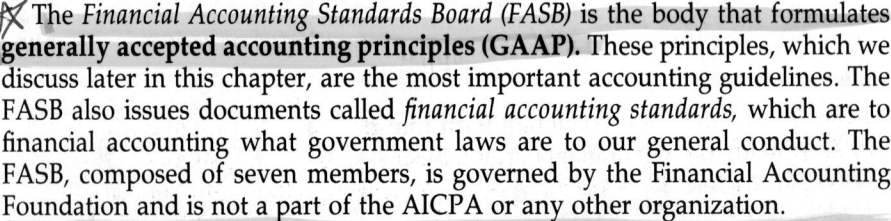

The *Financial Accounting Standards Board (FASB)* is the body that formulates **generally accepted accounting principles (GAAP).** These principles, which we discuss later in this chapter, are the most important accounting guidelines. The FASB also issues documents called *financial accounting standards,* which are to financial accounting what government laws are to our general conduct. The FASB, composed of seven members, is governed by the Financial Accounting Foundation and is not a part of the AICPA or any other organization.

The *National Association of Accountants (NAA)* focuses on the practice of management accounting, the branch of accounting that is designed to help manage a business. A *CMA* — Certified Management Accountant — earns this designation much as a CPA does but under the direction of the NAA. The NAA publishes the journal *Management Accounting.*

Like the NAA, the *Financial Executives Institute (FEI)* is active in management accounting. The FEI's journal is the *Financial Executive.*

The *CIA* — Certified Internal Auditor — receives this designation from the *Institute of Internal Auditors (IIA).* This organization publishes the journal *The Internal Auditor.*

The *American Accounting Association (AAA)* focuses on the academic and research aspects of accounting. A high percentage of its members are professors. The AAA publishes a quarterly journal, *The Accounting Review.*

The *Securities and Exchange Commission (SEC)* is an agency of the United States government with the legal power to set and enforce accounting and auditing standards. The SEC has delegated much of this authority to the private sector (through the FASB and the AICPA).

The *Internal Revenue Service (IRS),* another federal agency, has the responsibility of enforcing the tax laws and of collecting the revenue needed to finance the operations of the government. Since it focuses primarily on taxes, the IRS's main impact is on taxation.

Specialized Accounting Services

Because accounting affects people in many different fields, public accounting and private accounting include specialized services.

Public Accounting

Auditing is the accounting profession's most significant service to the public. An audit is the independent examination that assures the reliability of the accounting reports that management prepares and submits to investors, creditors, and others outside the business. In carrying out an audit, CPAs from outside a business examine the business's financial statements. If the CPAs believe that these documents are a fair presentation of the business's operations, the CPAs give a professional opinion stating that the firm's financial statements are in accordance with generally accepted accounting principles, which is the standard. Why is the audit so important? Creditors considering loans want assurance that the facts and figures the business submits are reliable. Stockholders, who have invested in the business, need to know that the financial picture management shows them is complete. Government agencies need accurate information from businesses.

Tax accounting has two aims: complying with the tax laws and minimizing taxes to be paid. Because income tax rates range as high as 28 percent for individuals and 34 percent for corporations, reducing income tax is an important management consideration. Tax work by accountants consists of preparing tax returns and planning business transactions in order to minimize taxes. CPAs advise individuals on what types of investments to make and on how to structure their transactions.

Management consulting is the catchall term that describes the wide scope of advice CPAs provide to help managers run a business. As CPAs conduct audits, they look deep into a business's operations. With the insight they gain, they often make suggestions for improvements in the business's management structure and accounting systems. (We discuss these areas of accounting in the next section.) Management consulting is the fastest-growing service provided by accountants.

Private Accounting

Cost accounting analyzes a business's costs to help managers control expenses. Traditionally, cost accounting has emphasized manufacturing costs, but it is increasingly concerned with the cost of selling the goods. Good cost accounting records guide managers in pricing their products to achieve greater profits. Also, cost accounting information shows management when a product is not profitable and should be dropped.

Budgeting sets sales and profit goals and develops detailed plans—called budgets—for achieving those goals. Many companies regard their budgeting activities as one of the most important aspects of their accounting systems. Some of the most successful companies in the United States have been pioneers in the field of budgeting—Procter & Gamble and General Electric, for example.

Information systems design identifies the organization's information needs, both internal and external. It then develops and implements the system to meet those needs. Accounting information systems help control the organization's operations. Flow charts and manuals that describe the various functions of the business and the placement of responsibility with specific employees are parts of system design.

Internal auditing is performed by a business's own accountants. Many large organizations—Motorola, Bank of America, and 3M among them—maintain a staff of internal auditors. These accountants evaluate the firm's own accounting and management systems. Their aim is to improve operating efficiency and to ensure that employees and departments follow management's procedures and plans.

EXHIBIT 1-3 *Accounting*

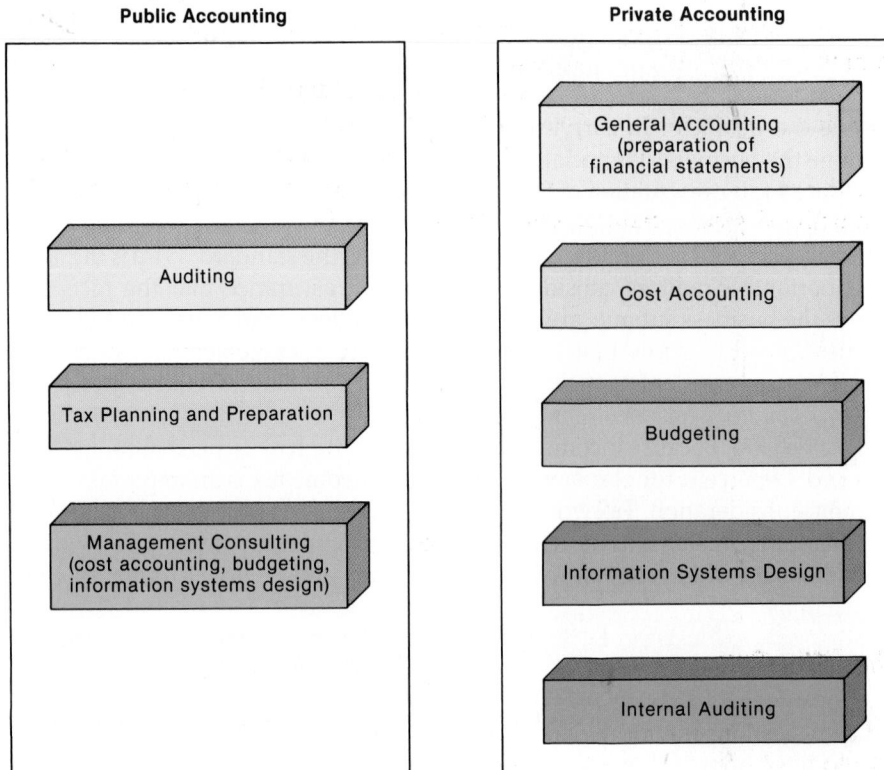

Exhibit 1-3 summarizes these accounting specializations. They may also be grouped under the headings financial accounting and management accounting.

Financial accounting provides information to people outside the firm. Creditors and stockholders, for example, are not part of the day-to-day management of the company. Likewise, government agencies, such as the SEC, and the general public are external users of a firm's accounting information. Chapters 2 through 19 of this book deal primarily with financial accounting.

Management accounting generates confidential information for internal decision makers, such as top executives, department heads, college deans, and hospital administrators. Chapters 20 through 26 cover management accounting.

OBJECTIVE 4

Identify the three different types of business organizations

Types of Business Organizations

Businesses take one of three forms of organization, and in some cases the accounting procedures depend on the organization form. Therefore, you should understand differences between a proprietorship, a partnership, and a corporation.

A **proprietorship** has a single owner, called the proprietor, who is usually also the manager. Proprietorships tend to be small retail establishments and individual professional businesses, such as those of physicians, attorneys, and accountants. From the accounting viewpoint each proprietorship is distinct from its proprietor. Thus the accounting records of the proprietorship do *not* include records of the proprietor's personal affairs.

A **partnership** joins two or more individuals together as co-owners. Each owner is a partner. Many retail establishments, as well as some professional organizations of physicians, attorneys, and accountants, are partnerships. Most partnerships are small and medium-sized, but some are gigantic, running to 2,000 partners. Accountants treat the partnership as a separate organization, distinct from the personal affairs of each partner.

A **corporation** is a business owned by **stockholders.** The business becomes a corporation when the state approves its articles of incorporation. A corporation is a legal entity, an "artificial person" that conducts its business in its own name. Like the proprietorship and the partnership, the corporation is also an organization with existence separate from its owners.

Accounting Concepts and Principles

Accounting practices rest on certain guidelines. The rules that govern how accountants measure, process, and communicate financial information fall under the heading GAAP, which stands for generally accepted accounting principles. Among these rules are the *entity concept*, the *reliability principle*, and the *cost principle*.

The Entity Concept

OBJECTIVE 5

Apply accounting concepts and principles to business situations

The most basic concept in accounting is that of the **entity.** An accounting entity is an organization or a section of an organization that stands apart from other organizations and individuals as a separate economic unit. From an accounting perspective, sharp boundaries are drawn around each entity so as not to confuse its affairs with those of other entities.

Consider Mazzio, a pizzeria owner whose bank account shows a $20,000 balance at the end of the year. Only half of that amount—$10,000—grew from the business's operations. The other $10,000 arose from the sale of the family motorboat. If Mazzio follows the entity concept, he will account for the money generated by the business—one economic unit—separately from the money generated by the sale of an item belonging not to the business but to himself—a second economic unit. This separation makes it possible to view the business's operating result clearly. The owner knows that the pizzeria did not bring in much money. To make the pizzeria more profitable, Mazzio probably must make some operating changes.

Suppose he disregards the entity concept and treats the full $20,000 amount as income from the pizzeria's operations. He will be misled into believing that the business has performed twice as well as it has. The steps needed to improve the business will likely not be taken.

Consider GM, a huge organization made up of its Chevrolet, Buick, Oldsmobile, Cadillac, and Pontiac divisions. GM management considers each division as a separate accounting entity, and the following example shows why. Suppose sales in the Buick division are dropping drastically. GM would do well to come up with an immediate solution to the problem. But if sales figures from all five divisions are treated as a single lump-sum amount, then management will not even know the company is not selling enough Buicks.

Other accounting entities include professional organizations such as a law firm, a doctor's practice, a hospital, a church or synagogue, a college or university, and a family household. Each entity may have a number of subentities. For example, universities have various colleges like law and business as subentities. Each subentity should be accounted for separately.

In summary, business transactions should not be confused with personal transactions. Similarly, the transactions of different entities should not be accounted for together. Each entity should be evaluated separately.

The Reliability (or Objectivity) Principle

Accounting records and statements are based on the most reliable data available so that they will be as accurate and as useful as possible. This is the *reliability principle.* Reliable data are verifiable. They may be confirmed by any independent observer. Ideally, then, accounting records are based on information that flows from activities that are documented by objective evidence. Without the reliability principle, also called the objectivity principle, accounting records would be based on whims and opinions and would be subject to dispute.

Suppose that you start a stereo shop, and in order to have a place for operations, you transfer a small building to the business. You believe the building is worth $55,000. To confirm its value, you hire two real estate professionals, who appraise the building at $47,000. Is $55,000 or $47,000 the more reliable estimate of the building's value? The real estate appraisal of $47,000 is, because it is supported by independent, objective observation.

The Cost Principle

The *cost principle* states that assets and services that are acquired should be recorded at their actual cost (also called historical cost). Even though the purchaser may believe the price paid is a bargain, the item is recorded at the price paid in the transaction.

Suppose your stereo shop purchases some stereo equipment from a supplier who is going out of business. Assume you get a good deal on this purchase and pay only $2,000 for merchandise that would have cost you $3,000 elsewhere. The cost principle requires you to record this merchandise at its actual cost of $2,000, not the $3,000 that you believe the equipment to be worth.

The cost principle also holds that the accounting records should maintain the historical cost of an asset for as long as the business holds the asset. Why? Because cost is a reliable measure. Suppose your store holds the stereo equipment for six months. During that time, stereo prices increase, and the equipment can be sold for $3,500. Should its accounting value—the figure "on the books"—be the actual cost of $2,000 or the current market value of $3,500? According to the cost principle, the accounting value of the equipment remains at actual cost, $2,000.

As we continue to explore accounting, we will discuss other principles that guide accountants.

OBJECTIVE 6
Use the accounting equation to describe an organization

The Accounting Equation

Accountants measure business activities and process those data to turn out financial statements. Their basic tool is the accounting equation. The accounting equation shows the equality of assets and claims to assets, called equities:

$$ \text{ASSETS} = \text{EQUITIES} $$

Assets are the economic resources a business owns that are expected to be of benefit in the future. Cash, office supplies, merchandise, furniture, land, and building are examples.

Equities are the legal and economic claims to the assets. For example, a creditor who has loaned money to a business has a claim—a legal right, in fact—to a part of the assets until the business pays the debt. Also, the owner of the business has a claim to those assets that he or she has invested in the business. Equities logically divide into two categories: claims owing to people outside the business (the creditors), and claims held by people inside the business (those who own it).

"Outsider" claims. These are economic obligations—debts—payable to outsiders, and they are called **liabilities.** Debts owed to banks and lenders, for example, are liabilities. These outside parties are called *creditors.*

"Insider" claims. These claims belong to the owner of the business, and they are called **owner's equity,** or **capital.**

Adding these two categories—liabilities and owner's equity—to the accounting equation gives us:

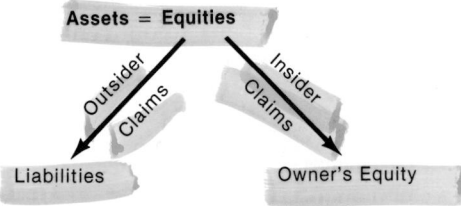

Liabilities plus owner's equity equals total equities, so we can express the accounting equation in its most common form and the one that we will use throughout the book:

ASSETS = LIABILITIES + OWNER'S EQUITY

Let's take a closer look at the elements that make up the accounting equation. Suppose you run a business that supplies meat to fast-food restaurants. Some customers may pay you in cash when you deliver the meat. Cash is an asset. Other customers may buy on credit and promise to pay you within a certain time after delivery. This promise is also an asset because it is an economic resource that will benefit you in the future when you receive cash from the customer. This promise is called an **account receivable.** If the promise that entitles you to receive cash in the future is written out, it is called a **note receivable.** All receivables are assets.

The fast-food restaurant's promise to pay you for the meat it purchases on credit creates a debt for the restaurant. This liability is an **account payable,** which means that the debt is not written out. Instead it is backed up by the reputation and the credit standing of the restaurant and its owner. A written promise of future payment is called a **note payable.** All payables are liabilities.

Owner's equity is the amount of the assets that remains after subtracting liabilities. A rearrangement of the accounting equation shows this relationship:

ASSETS − LIABILITIES = OWNER'S EQUITY

Accounting for Business Transactions _____

In accounting terms, a **transaction** is any event that *both* affects the financial position of the business entity *and* may be reliably recorded. Many events may affect a company, including (1) elections, (2) economic booms and recessions, (3) purchases and sales of merchandise inventory, (4) payment of rent, (5) collection of cash from customers, and so on. However, the accountant records only events with effects that can be measured reliably as transactions.

Which of the above five events would the accountant record? The answer is events (3), (4), and (5) because their dollar amounts can be measured reliably. Dollar effects of elections and economic trends cannot be measured reliably, so they would not be recorded even though they may affect the business more than events (3), (4), and (5).

To illustrate accounting for business transactions, let's assume that Gary Lyon has recently become a CPA and opens his own accounting practice. Because the business has a single owner, it is called a proprietorship.

We now consider eleven events and analyze each in terms of its effect on the accounting equation of Gary Lyon's accounting practice. Transaction analysis is the essence of accounting.

Transaction 1.   Gary Lyon invests $50,000 of his money to begin the business. Specifically, he deposits $50,000 in a bank account entitled Gary Lyon, CPA. The effect of this transaction on the accounting equation of the business entity is

Assets		Liabilities +	Owner's Equity	Type of Owner's Equity Transaction
Cash	=		Gary Lyon, Capital	
(1) +50,000			+50,000	Owner investment

OBJECTIVE 7

Use the accounting equation to analyze business transactions

The first transaction increases both the assets, in this case Cash, and the owner's equity of the business, Gary Lyon, Capital. The transaction involves no liabilities of the business because it creates no obligation for Lyon to pay an outside party. To the right of the transaction we write "Owner investment" to keep track of the reason for the effect on owner's equity.

Note that the amount on the left side of the equation equals the amount on the right side. This equality must hold for every transaction.

Transaction 2.   Lyon purchases land for a future office location, paying cash of $20,000. The effect of this transaction on the accounting equation is

Assets			Liabilities + Owner's Equity	Type of Owner's Equity Transaction
Cash + Land		=	Gary Lyon, Capital	
(1) 50,000			50,000	Owner investment
(2) −20,000 + 20,000				
Bal. 30,000 20,000			50,000	
50,000			50,000	

The cash purchase of land increases one asset, Land, and decreases another asset, Cash, by the same amount. After the transaction is completed, Lyon's business has cash of $30,000, land of $20,000, no liabilities, and owner's equity of $50,000. Note that the sums of the balances (which we abbreviate Bal.) on each side of the equation are equal. This equality must always exist.

Transaction 3.   Lyon buys stationery and other office supplies, agreeing to pay $500 within thirty days. This transaction increases the assets and the liabilities of the business. Its effect on the accounting equation is

	Assets				Liabilities + Owner's Equity		
	Cash	Office + Supplies +	Land		Accounts Payable +	Gary Lyon, Capital	
Bal.	30,000		20,000			50,000	
(3)		+500		=	+500		
Bal.	30,000	500	20,000		500	50,000	
		50,500				50,500	

The asset affected is office supplies, and the liability is called an account payable. The term *payable* signifies a liability. Since Lyon is obligated to pay $500 in the future, but signs no formal promissory note, we record the liability as an Account Payable, not as a Note Payable. We say that purchases supported by the general credit standing of the buyer are made on *open account*.

Transaction 4.   The purpose of business is to increase assets and owner's equity through **revenues,** which are amounts earned by delivering goods or services to customers. Revenues increase owner's equity because they increase the business's assets but not its liabilities. As a result, the owner's interest in the assets of the business increases.

Exhibit 1-4 shows that owner investments and revenues increase the owner's equity of the business.

The exhibit also indicates the types of transactions that decrease owner's equity. Owner withdrawals are those amounts removed from the business by the owner. Withdrawals are the opposite of owner investments. Expenses are the cost of doing business and are the opposite of revenues. Our illustration will also show how to account for expenses and withdrawals. Gary Lyon earns service revenue by providing professional accounting services for his clients. Assume he earns $5,500 and collects this amount in cash. The effect on the accounting equation is an increase in the asset Cash and an increase in Gary Lyon, Capital, as follows:

	Assets				Liabilities +	Owner's Equity	Type of Owner's Equity Transaction
	Cash	Office + Supplies +	Land		Accounts Payable +	Gary Lyon, Capital	
Bal.	30,000	500	20,000		500	50,000	
(4)	+ 5,500			=		+ 5,500	Service revenue
Bal.	35,500	500	20,000		500	55,500	
		56,000				56,000	

This revenue transaction caused the business to grow, as shown by the increase in total assets and total equities.

Transaction 5.   Lyon performs services for a client who does not pay immediately. In return for his accounting services, Lyon receives the client's promise to pay the $3,000 amount within one month. This promise is an asset to Lyon, an account receivable because he expects to collect the cash in the future. In accounting, we say that Lyon performed this service *on account.* When the business performs service for a client or a customer, the business earns revenue regardless of whether it receives cash immediately or expects to collect cash later. This

EXHIBIT 1-4 *Transactions That Increase and Decrease Owner's Equity*

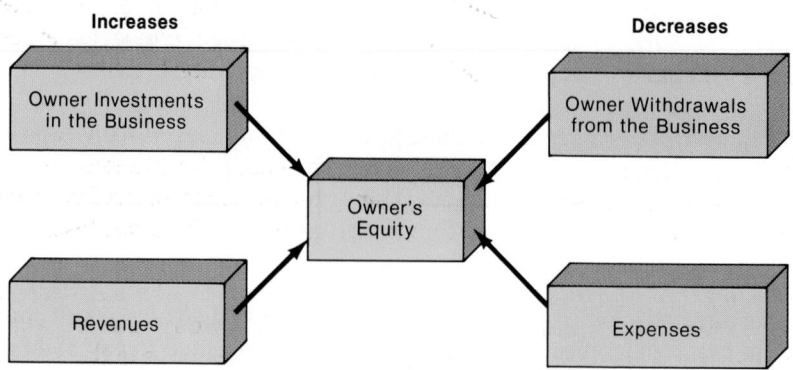

$3,000 of service revenue is as real to Lyon's business as the $5,500 of revenue that he collected immediately in the preceding transaction. Lyon records an increase in the asset accounts receivable and an increase in owner's equity as follows:

		Assets				Liabilities +	Owner's Equity	Type of Owner's Equity Transaction
	Cash	+ Accounts Receivable	+ Office Supplies	+ Land	=	Accounts Payable +	Gary Lyon, Capital	
Bal.	35,500	0	500	20,000		500	55,500	
(5)		+3,000					+ 3,000	Service revenue
Bal.	35,500	3,000	500	20,000		500	58,500	
		59,000					59,000	

Again, this revenue transaction caused the business to grow.

Transaction 6.   In earning revenue a business incurs expenses. **Expenses** are decreases in owner's equity that occur in the course of delivering goods or services to clients. Expenses decrease owner's equity because they use up the business's assets. Expenses include office rent, salaries paid to employees, newspaper advertisements, and utility payments for light, electricity, gas, and so forth. During the month, Lyon pays $2,700 in cash expenses: office rent, $1,100; employee salary, $1,200 (for a part-time assistant); and total utilities, $400. The effect on the accounting equation is

		Assets				Liabilities +	Owner's Equity	Type of Owner's Equity Transaction
	Cash	+ Accounts Receivable	+ Office Supplies	+ Land	=	Accounts Payable +	Gary Lyon, Capital	
Bal.	35,500	3,000	500	20,000		500	58,500	
(6)	− 2,700						− 1,100	Rent expense
							− 1,200	Salary expense
							− 400	Utilities expense
Bal.	32,800	3,000	500	20,000		500	55,800	
		56,300					56,300	

Because expenses have the opposite effect of revenues, they cause the business to shrink, as shown by the smaller amounts of total assets and total equities.

Each expense should be recorded in a separate transaction. Here, for simplicity, they are recorded together. Note that even though the figure $2,700 does not appear on the right-hand side of the equation, the three individual expenses add up to a $2,700 total. As a result, the "balance" of the equation holds, as we know it must.

Businesspeople, Gary Lyon included, run their businesses with the objective of taking in more revenues than they pay out in expenses. An excess of total revenues over total expenses is called **net income, net earnings,** or **net profit.** If total expenses are greater than total revenues, the result is called a **net loss.**

Transaction 7.   Lyon pays $400 to the store from which he purchased $500 worth of office supplies in Transaction 3. In accounting, we say that he pays $400 *on account.* The effect on the accounting equation is a decrease in the asset Cash and a decrease in the liability Accounts Payable as follows:

		Assets					Liabilities +	Owner's Equity
	Cash	+ Accounts Receivable	+ Office Supplies	+ Land		=	Accounts Payable +	Gary Lyon, Capital
Bal.	32,800	3,000	500	20,000			500	55,800
(7)	− 400						−400	
Bal.	32,400	3,000	500	20,000			100	55,800
		55,900					55,900	

The payment of cash on account has no effect on the asset Office Supplies because the payment does not increase or decrease the supplies available to the business.

Transaction 8.   Lyon remodels his home at a cost of $30,000, paying cash from his personal funds. This event is a *nonbusiness* transaction. It has no effect on Lyon's accounting practice and therefore is not recorded by the business. It is a transaction of the Gary Lyon *personal* entity, not the Gary Lyon, CPA, *business* entity. We are focusing now solely on the business entity, and this event does not affect it. This transaction illustrates an application of the *entity concept.*

Transaction 9.   In Transaction 5, Gary Lyon performed service for a client on account. Lyon now collects $1,000 from the client. We say that Lyon collects the cash *on account.* Lyon will record an increase in the asset Cash. Should he also record an increase in service revenue? No, because Lyon already recorded the revenue when he earned it in Transaction 5. The phrase "collect cash on account" means to record an increase in Cash and a decrease in the asset Accounts Receivable. The effect on the accounting equation is

		Assets					Liabilities +	Owner's Equity
	Cash	+ Accounts Receivable	+ Office Supplies	+ Land		=	Accounts Payable +	Gary Lyon, Capital
Bal.	32,400	3,000	500	20,000			100	55,800
(9)	+ 1,000	−1,000						
Bal.	33,400	2,000	500	20,000			100	55,800
		55,900					55,900	

Total assets are unchanged from the preceding transaction's total. Why? Because Lyon merely exchanged one asset for another. Also, total equities are unchanged.

Transaction 10. An individual approaches Lyon about selling a parcel of the land owned by the Gary Lyon, CPA, entity. Lyon and the other person agree to a sale price of $6,000, which is equal to Lyon's cost of the land. Lyon's business sells the land and receives $6,000 cash, and the effect on the accounting equation is

	Assets				=	Liabilities +	Owner's Equity
	Cash	+ Accounts Receivable	+ Office Supplies +	Land		Accounts Payable +	Gary Lyon, Capital
Bal.	33,400	2,000	500	20,000		100	55,800
(10)	+ 6,000			− 6,000			
Bal.	39,400	2,000	500	14,000		100	55,800

55,900   55,900

Transaction 11. Lyon withdraws $2,100 cash from the business for personal use. The effect on the accounting equation is

	Assets				=	Liabilities +	Owner's Equity	Type of Owner's Equity Transaction
	Cash	+ Accounts Receivable	+ Office Supplies +	Land		Accounts Payable +	Gary Lyon, Capital	
Bal.	39,400	2,000	500	14,000		100	55,800	
(11)	− 2,100						− 2,100	Owner withdrawals
Bal.	37,300	2,000	500	14,000		100	53,700	

53,800   53,800

Lyon's withdrawal of $2,100 in cash decreases the asset Cash and also the owner's equity of the business.

Does this withdrawal decrease the business entity's holdings? The answer is yes because the cash withdrawn is no longer available for business use after Lyon spends it on food, clothing, home mortgage payments, and so on. The withdrawal does *not* represent a business expense, however, because the cash is used for personal affairs unrelated to the business. We record this decrease in owner's equity as Withdrawals. Another acceptable title is Drawing.

Evaluating Business Transactions _____

Exhibit 1-5 summarizes the 11 preceding transactions. Panel A of the exhibit lists the details of the transactions, and Panel B presents the analysis. As you study the exhibit, note that every transaction maintains the equality:

ASSETS = LIABILITIES + OWNER'S EQUITY

EXHIBIT 1-5 *Analysis of Transactions of Gary Lyon, CPA*

Panel A—Details of transactions

1. Lyon invested $50,000 cash in the business.
2. Paid $20,000 cash for land.
3. Purchased $500 of office supplies on account payable.
4. Received $5,500 cash from clients for accounting service revenue earned.
5. Performed accounting service for a client on account, $3,000.
6. Paid cash expenses: rent, $1,100; employee salary, $1,200; utilities, $400.
7. Paid $400 on the account payable created in Transaction 3.
8. Remodeled his personal residence. This is not a business transaction.
9. Received $1,000 on the account receivable created in Transaction 5.
10. Sold land for cash equal to its cost of $6,000.
11. Withdrew $2,100 cash for personal living expenses.

Panel B—Analysis of transactions

	Cash	+ Accounts Receivable	+ Office Supplies +	Land	=	Accounts Payable +	Gary Lyon, Capital	Type of Owner's Equity Transaction
(1)	+50,000						+50,000	Owner investment
Bal.	50,000						50,000	
(2)	−20,000			+20,000				
Bal.	30,000			20,000			50,000	
(3)			+500			+500		
Bal.	30,000		500	20,000		500	50,000	
(4)	+ 5,500						+ 5,500	Service revenue
Bal.	35,500		500	20,000		500	55,500	
(5)		+3,000					+ 3,000	Service revenue
Bal.	35,500	3,000	500	20,000		500	58,500	
(6)	− 2,700						− 1,100	Rent expense
							− 1,200	Salary expense
							− 400	Utilities expense
Bal.	32,800	3,000	500	20,000		500	55,800	
(7)	− 400					−400		
Bal.	32,400	3,000	500	20,000		100	55,800	
(8)	Not a business transaction							
(9)	+ 1,000	−1,000						
Bal.	33,400	2,000	500	20,000		100	55,800	
(10)	+ 6,000			− 6,000				
Bal.	39,400	2,000	500	14,000		100	55,800	
(11)	− 2,100						− 2,100	Owner withdrawal
Bal.	37,300	2,000	500	14,000		100	53,700	

53,800 = 53,800

Financial Statements

The analysis of the transactions complete, what is the next step in the accounting process? How does an accountant present the results of the analysis? We now look at the **financial statements.** These business documents report financial information about the entity to persons and organizations outside the business.

The primary financial statements are the (1) balance sheet, (2) income statement, (3) statement of owner's equity, and (4) statement of cash flow. In this chapter, we discuss and illustrate the first three statements. We cover the statement of cash flow in Chapter 18.

The **balance sheet** lists all the *assets, liabilities,* and *owner's equity* of an entity as of a specific date, usually the end of a month or a year. The balance sheet is like a snapshot of the entity. For this reason, it is also called the **statement of financial position.**

The **income statement** presents a summary of the *revenues* and *expenses* of an entity for a specific period of time, such as a month or a year. The income statement, also called the **statement of operations,** is like a moving picture of the entity's operations during the period. The income statement holds perhaps the most important single piece of information about a business—its net income, which is revenues minus expenses. If expenses exceed revenues, the result is a net loss for the period.

The **statement of owner's equity** presents a summary of the changes that occurred in the owner's equity of the entity during a specific time period, such as a month or a year. Increases in owner's equity arise from investments by the owner and net income earned during the period. Decreases result from withdrawals by the owner and from a net loss for the period. Net income or net loss comes directly from the income statement. Investments and withdrawals by the owner are capital transactions between the business and its owner, so they do not affect the income statement.

Each financial statement has a heading, which gives the name of the business —in our discussion, Gary Lyon, CPA, the name of the particular statement, and the date or time period covered by the statement. A balance sheet taken at the end of year 19X4 would be dated December 31, 19X4. A balance sheet prepared at the end of March 19X7 is dated March 31, 19X7.

An income statement or a statement of owner's equity covering an annual period ending in December 19X5 is dated For the Year Ended December 31, 19X5. A monthly income statement or statement of owner's equity for September 19X9 has in its heading For the Month Ended September 30, 19X9, Month Ended September 30, 19X9, or For the Month of September 19X9.

Exhibit 1-6 illustrates all three statements. Their data come from the transaction analysis in Exhibit 1-5. We are assuming the transactions occurred during the month of April 19X1. Study the exhibit carefully, because it shows the relationships among the three financial statements.

Observe the following in Exhibit 1-6:

1. The *income statement* for the month ended April 30, 19X1
   a. Reports all *revenues* and all *expenses* during the period. Revenues and expenses are reported only on the income statement.
   b. Reports *net income* of the period if total revenues exceed total expenses, as in the case of Gary Lyon's accounting practice for April. If total expenses exceed total revenues, the result is a net loss.
2. The *statement of owner's equity* for the month ended April 30, 19X1
   a. Opens with the owner's capital balance at the beginning of the period.

EXHIBIT 1-6   *Financial Statements of Gary Lyon, CPA*

Gary Lyon, CPA
Income Statement
Month Ended April 30, 19X1

Revenues:		
Service revenue		$8,500
Expenses:		
Salary expense	$ 1,200	
Rent expense.	1,100	
Utilities expense	400	
Total expenses		2,700
Net income.		$5,800

Gary Lyon, CPA
Statement of Owner's Equity
Month Ended April 30, 19X1

①

Gary Lyon, capital, April 1, 19X1	$ 0
Add: Investments by owner	50,000
Net income for the month	5,800
	55,800
Less: Withdrawals by owner.	2,100
Gary Lyon, capital, April 30, 19X1	$53,700

Gary Lyon, CPA
Balance Sheet
April 30, 19X1

②

Assets		**Liabilities**	
Cash	$37,300	Accounts payable.	$ 100
Accounts receivable	2,000	**Owner's Equity**	
Office supplies	500		
Land	14,000	Gary Lyon, capital	53,700
		Total liabilities and	
Total assets	$53,800	owner's equity	$53,800

---

   b. Adds *investments by the owner* of the business and also adds *net income* (or
      subtracts *net loss*, as the case may be). Net income (or net loss) comes
      directly from the income statement, which includes the effect of all the
      revenues and all the expenses for the period (see the first arrow).
   c. Subtracts *withdrawals by the owner.*
   d. Ends with the owner's capital balance at the end of the period.
3. The *balance sheet* at April 30, 19X1, the end of the period
   a. Reports all *assets,* all *liabilities,* and *owner's equity* of the business at the end
      of the period. No other statement reports assets and liabilities.

b. Balances. That is, total assets equal the sum of total liabilities plus total owner's equity. This balancing feature gives the balance sheet its name. It is based on the accounting equation.
c. Reports the owner's ending capital balance, taken directly from the statement of owner's equity (see the second arrow).

Summary Problem for Your Review

Jill Smith opens an apartment-locator business near a college campus. She is the sole owner of the proprietorship, which she names Campus Apartment Locators. During the first month of operations, May 19X1, Smith engages in the following transactions:

a.   Smith invests $20,000 of personal funds to start the business.
b.   She purchases on account office supplies costing $350.
c.   Smith pays cash of $8,000 to acquire a lot next to the campus. She intends to use the land as a future building site for her business office.
d.   Smith locates apartments for clients and receives cash of $1,900.
e.   She pays $100 on the account payable she created in transaction b.
f.   She pays $2,000 of personal funds for a vacation for her family.
g.   She pays cash expenses for office rent, $400, and utilities, $100.
h.   The business sells office supplies to another business for its cost of $150.
i.   Smith withdraws cash of $1,200 for personal use.

Required

1.   Record the preceding transactions in terms of their effects on the accounting equation of Campus Apartment Locators. Use Exhibit 1-5 as a guide, but show balances only after the last transaction.
2.   Prepare the income statement, statement of owner's equity, and balance sheet of the business after recording the transactions. Use Exhibit 1-6 as a guide.

SOLUTION TO REVIEW PROBLEM

Panel A.   Details of transactions

a.   Smith invested $20,000 cash to start the business.
b.   Purchased $350 of office supplies on account.
c.   Paid $8,000 to acquire land as a future building site.
d.   Earned service revenue and received cash of $1,900.
e.   Paid $100 on account.
f.   Paid for a personal vacation, which is not a business transaction.
g.   Paid cash expenses for rent, $400, and utilities, $100.
h.   Sold office supplies for cost of $150.
i.   Withdrew $1,200 cash for personal use.

Panel B.   Analysis of transactions

	Assets				Liabilities +	Owner's Equity	Type of Owner's Equity Transaction
	Cash	+ Office Supplies +	Land		Accounts Payable +	Jill Smith, Capital	
(a)	+20,000					+20,000	Owner investment
(b)		+350			+350		
(c)	− 8,000		+8,000				
(d)	+ 1,900					+ 1,900	Service revenue
(e)	− 100			=	−100		
(f)	Not a business transaction						
(g)	− 500					− 400	Rent expense
						− 100	Utilities expense
(h)	+ 150	−150					
(i)	− 1,200					− 1,200	Owner withdrawal
Bal.	12,250	200	8,000		250	20,200	

20,450   20,450

Financial Statements of Campus Apartment Locators

Campus Apartment Locators
Income Statement
Month Ended May 31, 19X1

Revenues:		
Service revenue		$1,900
Expenses:		
Rent expense	$400	
Utilities expense.	100	
Total expenses		500
Net income		$1,400

Campus Apartment Locators
Statement of Owner's Equity
Month Ended May 31, 19X1

Jill Smith, capital, May 1, 19X1	$ 0
Add: Investments by owner.	20,000
Net income for the month.	1,400
	21,400
Less: Withdrawals by owner	1,200
Jill Smith, capital, May 31, 19X1	$20,200

Campus Apartment Locators
Balance Sheet
May 31, 19X1

Assets		Liabilities	
Cash.	$12,250	Accounts payable	$ 250
Office supplies.	200	**Owner's Equity**	
Land.	8,000		
		Jill Smith, capital	20,200
		Total liabilities	
Total assets	$20,450	and owner's equity	$20,450

Summary

Accounting is a system for measuring, processing, and communicating financial information. As the "language of business," accounting helps a wide range of decision makers.

Accounting dates back to ancient civilizations, but its importance to society has been greatest since the Industrial Revolution. Today, accountants serve as CPAs, CMAs, or CIAs in all types of organizations. They offer many specialized services for industrial companies, including general accounting, cost accounting, budgeting, system design, and internal auditing. CPAs in public practice deal with auditing, tax planning and preparation, and management consulting.

The three basic forms of business organization are the proprietorship, the partnership, and the corporation. Whatever the form, accountants use the entity concept to keep the business's records separate from the personal records of the people who run it.

Generally accepted accounting principles—GAAP—guide accountants in their work. Among these guidelines are the entity concept, the reliability principle, and the cost principle.

In its most common form, the accounting equation is

$$\text{ASSETS} = \text{LIABILITIES} + \text{OWNER'S EQUITY}$$

Transactions affect a business's assets, liabilities, and owner's equity. Therefore, transactions are analyzed in terms of their effect on the accounting equation.

The *financial statements* communicate information for decision making by the entity's managers, owners, and creditors and by government agencies. The *income statement* presents a moving picture of the entity's operations in terms of revenues earned and expenses incurred during a specific period. Total revenues minus total expenses equal net income. Net income or net loss answers the question, How much income did the entity earn, or how much loss did it incur during the period? The *statement of owner's equity* reports the changes in owner's equity during the period. The *balance sheet* provides a photograph of the entity's financial standing in terms of its assets, liabilities, and owner's equity at a specific time. It answers the question, What is the entity's financial position?

Self-Study Questions

Test your understanding of the chapter by marking the best answer for each of the following questions:

1. To become a CPA, a person must *(p. 6)*
   a. Graduate from college with a master's degree
   b. Obtain four years of accounting experience
   c. Pass a national examination
   d. Pass an accounting examination that differs from state to state

2. The organization that formulates generally accepted accounting principles is *(p. 6)*
   a. American Institute of Certified Public Accountants (CPAs)
   b. Internal Revenue Service
   c. Financial Accounting Standards Board
   d. National Association of Accountants

3. Which of the following forms of business organization is an "artificial person" and must obtain legal approval from a state to conduct business? *(p. 9)*
   a. Law firm   c. Partnership
   b. Proprietorship   d. Corporation

4. The economic resources that a business owns and expects to be useful to the enterprise are called *(p. 10)*

    a. Assets   c. Owner's equity
    b. Liabilities   d. Receivables

5. A business has assets of $140,000 and liabilities of $60,000. How much is its owner's equity? *(p. 11)*
    a. $0   c. $140,000
    b. $80,000   d. $200,000

6. The purchase of office supplies (or any other asset) on account will *(p. 13)*
    a. Increase an asset and increase a liability
    b. Increase an asset and increase owner's equity
    c. Increase one asset and decrease another asset
    d. Increase an asset and decrease a liability

7. The performance of service for a customer or client and immediate receipt of cash will *(p. 13)*
    a. Increase one asset and decrease another asset
    b. Increase an asset and increase owner's equity
    c. Decrease an asset and decrease a liability
    d. Increase an asset and increase a liability

8. The payment of an account payable (or any other liability) will *(p. 15)*
    a. Increase one asset and decrease another asset
    b. Decrease an asset and decrease owner's equity
    c. Decrease an asset and decrease a liability
    d. Increase an asset and increase a liability

9. The business document that reports assets, liabilities, and owner's equity is called the *(p. 18)*
    a. Financial statement   c. Income statement
    b. Balance sheet   d. Statement of owner's equity

10. The financial statements that are dated for a time period (rather than a specific time) are the *(p. 18)*
    a. Balance sheet and income statement
    b. Balance sheet and statement of owner's equity
    c. Income statement and statement of owner's equity
    d. All financial statements are dated for a time period.

Answers to the Self-Study Questions are at the end of the chapter.

Accounting Vocabulary

Accounting, like many other subjects, has a special vocabulary. It is important that you understand the following terms. They are explained in the chapter and also in the glossary at the end of the book.

accounting *(p. 2)*, account payable *(p. 11)*, account receivable *(p. 11)*, asset *(p. 10)*, auditing *(p. 7)*, balance sheet *(p. 18)*, budgeting *(p. 7)*, capital *(p. 11)*, certified public accountant (CPA) *(p. 4)*, corporation *(p. 9)*, cost accounting *(p. 7)*, entity *(p. 9)*, equities *(p. 11)*, expense *(p. 14)*, financial accounting *(p. 8)*, financial statements *(p. 18)*, generally accepted accounting principles (GAAP) *(p. 6)*, income statement *(p. 18)*, information systems design *(p. 7)*, internal auditing *(p. 7)*, liability *(p. 11)*, management accounting *(p. 8)*, net earnings *(p. 15)*, net income *(p. 15)*, net loss *(p. 15)*, net profit *(p. 15)*, note payable *(p. 11)*, note receivable *(p. 11)*, owner's equity *(p. 11)*, partnership *(p. 8)*, private accountant *(p. 4)*, proprietorship *(p. 8)*, public accountant *(p. 4)*, revenue *(p. 13)*, statement of financial position *(p. 18)*, statement of operations *(p. 18)*, statement of owner's equity *(p. 18)*, stockholder *(p. 9)*, transaction *(p. 11)*.

ASSIGNMENT MATERIAL _____

Questions

1. Distinguish between accounting and bookkeeping.
2. Identify five users of accounting information and explain how they use it.
3. Where did accounting have its beginning? Who wrote the first known description of bookkeeping? In what year?
4. Name two important reasons for the development of accounting thought.
5. Name three professional titles of accountants. Also give their abbreviations.
6. What organization formulates generally accepted accounting principles? Is this organization a government agency?
7. Name the three principal types of services provided by public accounting firms.
8. How do financial accounting and management accounting differ?
9. Give the name(s) of the owner(s) of a proprietorship, a partnership, and a corporation.
10. Why is the entity concept so important to accounting?
11. Give four examples of accounting entities.
12. Briefly describe the reliability principle.
13. What role does the cost principle play in accounting?
14. If *assets = liabilities + owner's equity*, then how can *liabilities* be expressed?
15. Explain the difference between an account receivable and an account payable.
16. What role do transactions play in accounting?
17. What is a more descriptive title for the balance sheet?
18. What feature of the balance sheet gives this financial statement its name?
19. What is another title of the income statement?
20. Which financial statement is like a snapshot of the entity at a specific time? Which financial statement is like a moving picture of the entity's operations during a period of time?
21. What information does the statement of owner's equity report?
22. Give two synonyms for the owner's equity of a proprietorship.
23. What piece of information flows from the income statement to the statement of owner's equity? What information flows from the statement of owner's equity to the balance sheet?

Exercises

Exercise 1-1   *Transaction analysis*

Indicate the effects of the following business transactions on the accounting equation. Transaction *a* is answered as a guide.

a. Paid $90 cash to purchase office supplies.

> *Answer:* Increase asset (Office Supplies)
>   Decrease asset (Cash)

b. Performed legal service for a client and received cash of $2,000.
c. Paid monthly office rent of $700.
d. Invested cash of $1,800 in the business.
e. Performed legal service for a client on account, $650.
f. Purchased on account office furniture at a cost of $500.

g. Received cash on account, $400.

h. Paid cash on account, $250.

i. Sold land for $12,000, which was our cost of the land.

Exercise 1-2 *Transaction analysis; accounting equation*

Gloria Hill opens a medical practice to specialize in child care. During her first month of operation, January, her practice, entitled Gloria Hill, M.D., experienced the following events:

Jan. 6	Hill invested $135,000 in the business by opening a bank account in the name of Gloria Hill, M.D.
9	Hill paid cash for land costing $90,000. She plans to build an office building on the land.
12	She purchased medical supplies for $2,000 on account.
15	On January 15, Hill officially opened for business.
15–31	During the rest of the month she treated patients and earned service revenue of $6,000, receiving cash.
15–31	She paid cash expenses: employee salaries, $1,400; office rent, $1,000; utilities, $300.
28	She sold supplies to another physician for cost of $500.
31	She paid $1,500 on account.

Required

Analyze the effects of these events on the accounting equation of the medical practice of Gloria Hill, M.D. Use a format similar to that of Exhibit 1-5 in the chapter, with headings for Cash; Supplies; Land; Accounts Payable; and Gloria Hill, Capital.

Exercise 1-3 *Accounting equation*

Compute the missing amount in the accounting equation of each of the following three entities:

	Assets	Liabilities	Owner's Equity
Entity A	$?	$41,800	$26,400
Entity B	85,900	?	34,000
Entity C	63,700	29,800	?

Exercise 1-4 *Business organization, balance sheet*

Presented below are the balances of the assets and liabilities of Stark Delivery Service as of September 30, 19X2. Also included are the revenue and expense figures of the business for September.

Delivery service revenue	$3,500	Delivery equipment	$9,500
Accounts receivable	900	Supplies	600
Accounts payable	750	Note payable	5,000
D. Stark, capital	?	Rent expense	500
Salary expense	1,000	Cash	650

Required

1. What type of business organization is Stark Delivery Service? How can you tell?

2. Prepare the balance sheet of Stark Delivery Service as of September 30, 19X2. Not all amounts are used. Recall that only assets, liabilities, and owner's equity appear on the balance sheet.

Exercise 1-5 *Income statement*

Presented below are the balances of the assets, liabilities, owner's equity, revenues, and expenses of Fadal Travel Agency at December 31, 19X3, the end of its first year of business. During the year W. Fadal, the owner, invested $20,000 in the business.

Note payable	$30,000	Office furniture	45,000
Utilities expense	5,800	Rent expense	21,000
Accounts payable	3,300	Cash	3,600
W. Fadal, capital	27,100	Office supplies	4,800
Service revenue	108,000	Salary expense	29,000
Accounts receivable	9,000	Salaries payable	2,000
Supplies expense	4,000	Property tax expense	1,200

Required

1. Prepare the income statement of Fadal Travel Agency for the year ended December 31, 19X3. Not all amounts are used. Recall that only revenues and expenses appear on the income statement.
2. What was the amount of the proprietor's withdrawals during the year?

Exercise 1-6 *Business transactions*

For each of the following items, give an example of a business transaction that has the described effect on the accounting equation:

a. Increase an asset and increase owner's equity.
b. Increase an asset and increase a liability.
c. Increase one asset and decrease another asset.
d. Decrease an asset and decrease owner's equity.
e. Decrease an asset and decrease a liability.

Exercise 1-7 *Business organization, transactions, and net income*

The analysis of the transactions that United Rentals engaged in during its first month of operations follows. The company buys equipment that it rents out to earn rent revenue. The owners of the business made only one investment to start the business and no withdrawals.

	Cash	+	Accounts Receivable	+	Rental Equipment	=	Accounts Payable	+	Partners' Capital
a.	+65,000								+65,000
b.					+100,000		+100,000		
c.	+ 1,600								+ 1,600
d.			+150						+ 150
e.	−10,000						− 10,000		
f.			+850						+ 850
g.	+ 150		−150						
h.	− 2,000								− 2,000

Required

1. What type of business organization is United Rentals? How can you tell?
2. Describe each transaction.
3. If these transactions fully describe the operations of United Rentals during the month, what was the amount of net income or net loss?

Exercise 1-8 *Accounting equation*

Milstead Supply balance sheet data, at May 31, 19X2, and June 30, 19X2, were as follows:

	May 31, 19X2	June 30, 19X2
Total assets	$150,000	$195,000
Total liabilities	109,000	131,000

Required

Below are three assumptions about investments and withdrawals by the owner of the business during June. For each assumption, compute the amount of net income or net loss of the business during June 19X2.

a. The owner invested $25,000 in the business and made no withdrawals.
b. The owner made no additional investments in the business but withdrew $12,000 for personal use.
c. The owner invested $8,000 in the business and withdrew $12,000 for personal use.

Exercise 1-9 *Transaction analysis*

Bliss Stone Masonry, a proprietorship, recorded the following events. State whether each event (1) increased, (2) decreased, or (3) had no effect on the total assets of the business. Identify any specific asset affected.

a. Paid cash on accounts payable.
b. Purchased machinery and equipment for a manufacturing plant; signed a promissory note in payment.
c. Performed service for a customer on account.
d. Bliss, the owner, withdrew cash from the business for personal use.
e. Received cash from a customer on account receivable.
f. Bliss used personal funds to purchase a swimming pool for his home.
g. Sold land for a price equal to the cost of the land; received cash.
h. Borrowed money from the bank.
i. Cash purchase of land for a future building site.
j. Bliss increased his cash investment in the business.

Problems   (Group A)

Problem 1-1A *Transaction analysis, accounting equation, financial statements*

Margaret Stevens owns and operates an interior design studio called Stevens Interiors. The following amounts summarize the financial position of her business on August 31, 19X2:

	Assets		=	Liabilities	+	Owner's Equity
Cash +	Accounts Receivable +	Land	=	Accounts Payable +		Margaret Stevens, Capital
Bal. 1,250	1,500	12,000		8,000		6,750

During September 19X2 the following events occurred:

a. Stevens inherited $15,000 and deposited the cash in the business bank account.
b. Performed services for a client and received cash of $700.
c. Paid off the beginning balance of accounts payable, $8,000.
d. Purchased supplies on account, $500.
e. Collected cash from a customer on account, $800.
f. Invested personal cash of $1,000 in the business.
g. Consulted on the interior design of a major office building and billed the client for services rendered, $2,000.
h. Recorded the following business expenses for the month:
1. Paid office rent—$900.
2. Paid advertising—$100.
i. Sold supplies to another business for $150, which was the cost of the supplies.
j. Withdrew cash of $1,800 for personal use.

Required

1. Record the effects of the above transactions on the accounting equation of Stevens Interiors. Adapt the format of Exhibit 1-5. You need to add a column for Supplies.
2. Prepare the income statement of Stevens Interiors for the month ended September 30, 19X2. List expenses in decreasing order by amount.
3. Prepare the statement of owner's equity of Stevens Interiors for the month ended September 30, 19X2.
4. Prepare the balance sheet of Stevens Interiors at September 30, 19X2.

Problem 1-2A   *Entity concept, transaction analysis, accounting equation*

Zane Jones practiced law with a large firm, a partnership, for five years after graduating from law school. Recently he resigned his position to open his own law office, which he operates as a proprietorship. The name of the new entity is Zane Jones, Attorney.

Jones recorded the following events during the organizing phase of his new business and its first month of operations. Some of the events were personal and did not affect his law practice. Others were business transactions and should be accounted for by the business.

May 4 Jones received $50,000 cash from his former partners in the law firm from which he resigned.
May 5 Jones deposited $50,000 cash in a new business bank account, entitled Zane Jones, Attorney.
May 6 Jones paid $300 cash for letterhead stationery for his new law office.
May 7 Jones purchased office furniture for his law office. Jones agreed to pay the account payable, $5,000, within six months.
May 10 Jones sold 500 shares of IBM stock, which he and his wife had owned for several years, receiving $75,000 cash from his stockbroker.
May 11 Jones deposited the $75,000 cash from sale of the IBM stock in his personal bank account.
May 12 A representative of a large company telephoned Jones and told him of the company's intention to transfer its legal business to the new entity of Zane Jones, Attorney.
May 29 Jones finished court hearings on behalf of a client and submitted his bill for legal services, $4,000. Jones expected to collect from this client within two weeks.
May 30 Jones paid office rent expense, $1,000.
May 31 Jones withdrew $2,500 cash from the business for personal living expenses.

Required

1. Classify each of the preceding events as one of the following:
a. Personal transaction *not* to be accounted for by the proprietorship of Zane Jones, Attorney.

b. Business transaction to be accounted for by the proprietorship of Zane Jones, Attorney.
    c. Business-related event but *not* a transaction to be accounted for by the proprietorship of Zane Jones, Attorney.
2. Analyze the effects of the above events on the accounting equation of the proprietorship of Zane Jones, Attorney. Use a format similar to Exhibit 1-5.

Problem 1-3A   *Balance sheet*

The bookkeeper of Dorman Home Builders prepared the balance sheet of the company while the accountant was ill. The balance sheet contains numerous errors. In particular, the bookkeeper knew that the balance sheet should balance, so he plugged in the owner's equity amount needed to achieve this balance. However, the owner's equity amount is not correct. All other amounts are accurate.

Dorman Home Builders
Balance Sheet
Month Ended July 31, 19X3

Assets		Liabilities	
Cash	$ 2,000	Accounts receivable	$ 3,000
Office supplies	1,000	Service revenue	35,000
Land	22,000	Property tax expense	800
Advertising expense	500	Accounts payable	8,000
Office furniture	10,000	**Owner's Equity**	
Note payable	16,000		
Rent expense	4,000	Owner's equity	8,700
Total assets	$55,500	Total liabilities	$55,500

Required

1. Prepare the correct balance sheet as of July 31, 19X3. Compute total assets and total liabilities. Then take the difference to determine correct owner's equity.
2. Identify the accounts listed above which should *not* be presented on the balance sheet and state why you excluded them from the correct balance sheet you prepared for Requirement 1.

Problem 1-4A   *Business transactions and analysis*

Larkin Company was recently formed. The balance of each item in the company's accounting equation is shown below for May 10 and for each of nine following business days.

	Cash	Accounts Receivable	Supplies	Land	Accounts Payable	Owner's Equity
May 10	$ 6,000	$4,000	$1,000	$ 8,000	$4,000	$15,000
11	11,000	4,000	1,000	8,000	4,000	20,000
12	6,000	4,000	1,000	13,000	4,000	20,000
15	6,000	4,000	3,000	13,000	6,000	20,000
16	5,000	4,000	3,000	13,000	5,000	20,000
17	8,000	1,000	3,000	13,000	5,000	20,000
18	16,000	1,000	3,000	13,000	5,000	28,000
19	13,000	1,000	3,000	13,000	2,000	28,000
22	12,000	1,000	4,000	13,000	2,000	28,000
23	8,000	1,000	4,000	13,000	2,000	24,000

Required

Assuming a single transaction took place on each day, describe briefly the transaction that was most likely to have occurred, beginning with May 11. Indicate which accounts were affected and by what amount. No revenue or expense transactions occurred on these dates.

Problem 1-5A *Balance sheet, entity concept*

Jan Gibson is a realtor. She buys and sells properties on her own, and she also earns commission as a real estate agent for buyers and sellers. She organized her business as a proprietorship on November 24, 19X4. Consider the following facts as of November 30, 19X4:

a. Gibson owed $100,000 on a note payable for some undeveloped land that had been acquired by her business for a total price of $160,000.
b. Gibson's business had spent $15,000 for a Century 21 real estate franchise, which entitled her to represent herself as a Century 21 agent. Century 21 is a national affiliation of independent real estate agents. This franchise is a business asset.
c. Gibson owed $120,000 on a personal mortgage on her personal residence, which she acquired in 19X1 for a total price of $170,000.
d. Gibson had $10,000 in her personal bank account and $12,000 in her business bank account.
e. Gibson owed $1,800 on a personal charge account with Neiman-Marcus Specialty Department Store.
f. Gibson acquired business furniture for $17,000 on November 25. Of this amount, her business owed $6,000 on open account at November 30.
g. Office supplies on hand at the real estate office totaled $1,000.

Required

1. Prepare the balance sheet of the real estate business of Jan Gibson, Realtor, at November 30, 19X4.
2. Identify the personal items given in the preceding facts that would not be reported on the balance sheet of the business.

Problem 1-6A *Income statement, statement of owner's equity, balance sheet*

Presented below are the amounts of (a) the assets and liabilities of Johnson Service Company as of December 31 and (b) the revenues and expenses of the company for the year ended on that date. The items are listed in alphabetical order.

Accounts payable	$ 19,000	Note payable	85,000
Accounts receivable	12,000	Property tax expense	4,000
Advertising expense	11,000	Rent expense	23,000
Building	180,000	Salary expense	53,000
Cash	10,000	Salaries payable	1,000
Furniture	20,000	Service revenue	200,000
Interest expense	9,000	Supplies	3,000
Land	65,000		

The beginning amount of Ray Johnson, Capital, was $150,000, and during the year Johnson withdrew $65,000 for personal use.

Required

1. Prepare the income statement of Johnson Service Company for the year ended December 31 of the current year.

2. Prepare the statement of owner's equity of the company for the year ended December 31.
3. Prepare the balance sheet of the company at December 31.

Problem 1-7A *Transaction analysis for an actual company*

A recent balance sheet of Levi Strauss & Company, the world's largest seller of jeans and casual pants, is summarized as follows, with amounts in thousands. For example, Cash of $263,389,000 is presented as $263,389.

Levi Strauss & Company
Balance Sheet
November 25, 19XX
(thousands)

Assets		Liabilities	
Cash....................	$ 263,389	Notes payable	$ 83,361
Accounts receivable........	339,798	Accounts payable	229,453
Merchandise inventories....	387,660	Other liabilities	300,847
Property, plant, and equip...	330,455	Total liabilities	613,661
Other assets	99,800		
		Owner Equity...............	807,441
		Total liabilities and owner	
Total assets.............	$1,421,102	equity	$1,421,102

During December, the company had the following transactions and events (amounts in thousands):

a. Received cash investments from owners, $18.
b. Received special equipment from an owner as an investment in the company. The value of the equipment was $40.
c. Borrowed cash, signing a note payable, $100.
d. Purchased equipment for cash, $125.
e. Purchased inventories on account, $90.
f. Paid cash on account (to reduce accounts payable), $54.
g. Sold equipment to another company on account, $14. The equipment had cost $14.
h. Discovered that the president of the United States was going to wear Levi blue jeans while giving his State of the Union address next January.
i. Collected cash on account from customers, $84.

Required:

1. Showing all amounts in thousands, analyze the December transactions of Levi Strauss. Use a format similar to Exhibit 1-5.
2. Prove that assets = liabilities + owner equity after analyzing the transactions.

(Group B)

Problem 1-1B *Transaction analysis, accounting equation, financial statements*

Maury Cheng owns and operates an interior design studio called Cheng Designers. The following amounts summarize the financial position of his business on April 30, 19X5:

	Assets			=	Liabilities	+	Owner's Equity
Cash	+	Accounts Receivable	+	Land	=	Accounts Payable	+	Maury Cheng, Capital

	Cash	+	Accounts Receivable	+	Land	=	Accounts Payable	+	Maury Cheng, Capital
Bal.	720		2,240		23,100		4,400		21,660

During May 19X5 the following events occurred:

a. Cheng received $12,000 as a gift and deposited the cash in the business bank account.
b. Paid off the beginning balance of accounts payable, $4,400.
c. Performed services for a client and received cash of $1,100.
d. Collected cash from a customer on account, $750.
e. Purchased supplies on account, $120.
f. Consulted on the interior design of a major office building and billed the client for services rendered, $5,500.
g. Invested personal cash of $1,700 in the business.
h. Recorded the following business expenses for the month:
   1. Paid office rent—$1,200.
   2. Paid advertising—$860.
i. Sold supplies to another interior designer for $80, which was the cost of the supplies.
j. Withdrew cash of $2,400 for personal use.

Required

1. Record the effects of the above transactions on the accounting equation of Cheng Designers. Adapt the format of Exhibit 1-5. You need to add a column for Supplies.
2. Prepare the income statement of Cheng Designers for the month ended May 31, 19X5. List expenses in decreasing order by amount.
3. Prepare the statement of owner's equity of Cheng Designers for the month ended May 31, 19X5.
4. Prepare the balance sheet of Cheng Designers at May 31.

Problem 1-2B *Entity concept, transaction analysis, accounting equation*

Rhonda Sperry practiced law with a large firm, a partnership, for ten years after graduating from law school. Recently she resigned her position to open her own law office, which she operates as a proprietorship. The name of the new entity is Rhonda Sperry, Attorney and Counselor.

Sperry recorded the following events during the organizing phase of her new business and its first month of operations. Some of the events were personal and did not affect the law practice. Others were business transactions and should be accounted for by the business.

July 1 Rhonda sold 1,000 shares of Procter & Gamble stock, which she had owned for several years, receiving $88,000 cash from her stockbroker.
July 2 Rhonda deposited the $88,000 cash from sale of the Procter & Gamble stock in her personal bank account.
July 3 Rhonda received $135,000 cash from her former partners in the law firm from which she resigned.
July 5 Rhonda deposited $130,000 cash in a new business bank account entitled Rhonda Sperry, Attorney and Counselor.
July 6 A representative of a large company telephoned Rhonda and told her of the company's intention to transfer its legal business to the new entity of Rhonda Sperry, Attorney and Counselor.
July 7 Rhonda paid $550 cash for letterhead stationery for her new law office.

July 9 Rhonda purchased office furniture for the law office, agreeing to pay the account payable, $11,500, within three months.

July 23 Rhonda finished court hearings on behalf of a client and submitted her bill for legal services, $2,100. She expected to collect from this client within one month.

July 30 Rhonda paid office rent expense, $1,900.

July 31 Rhonda withdrew $3,000 cash from the business for personal living expenses.

Required

1. Classify each of the preceding events as one of the following:
   a. Personal transaction *not* to be accounted for by the proprietorship of Rhonda Sperry, Attorney and Counselor.
   b. Business transaction to be accounted for by the proprietorship of Rhonda Sperry, Attorney and Counselor.
   c. Business-related event but *not* a transaction to be accounted for by the proprietorship of Rhonda Sperry, Attorney and Counselor.
2. Analyze the effects of the above events on the accounting equation of the proprietorship of Rhonda Sperry, Attorney and Counselor. Use a format similar to Exhibit 1-5.

Problem 1-3B   *Balance sheet*

The bookkeeper of Reynolds Construction Company prepared the balance sheet of the company while the accountant was ill. The balance sheet contains numerous errors. In particular, the bookkeeper knew that the balance sheet should balance, so he plugged in the owner's equity amount needed to achieve this balance. However, the owner's equity amount is not correct. All other amounts are accurate.

Reynolds Construction Company
Balance Sheet
Month Ended October 31, 19X7

Assets		Liabilities	
Cash	$ 1,400	Notes receivable	$11,000
Advertising expense	300	Interest expense	2,000
Land	31,600	Office supplies	800
Salary expense	2,200	Accounts receivable	1,600
Office furniture	4,700	Note payable	20,000
Accounts payable	3,000	**Owner's Equity**	
Utilities expense	1,100		
		Owner's equity	8,900
Total assets	$44,300	Total liabilities	$44,300

Required

1. Prepare the correct balance sheet as of October 31, 19X7. Compute total assets and total liabilities. Then take the difference to determine correct owner's equity.
2. Identify the accounts listed above that should *not* be presented on the balance sheet and state why you excluded them from the correct balance sheet you prepared for Requirement 1.

Problem 1-4B   *Business transactions and analysis*

Kluzewski Company was recently formed. The balance of each item in the company's accounting equation is shown below for February 8 and for each of nine following business days.

	Cash	Accounts Receivable	Supplies	Land	Accounts Payable	Owner's Equity
Feb. 8	$3,000	$7,000	$ 800	$11,000	$3,800	$18,000
12	5,000	7,000	800	11,000	3,800	20,000
14	6,000	6,000	800	11,000	3,800	20,000
17	6,000	6,000	1,100	11,000	4,100	20,000
19	3,000	6,000	1,100	11,000	4,100	17,000
20	1,900	6,000	1,100	11,000	3,000	17,000
22	7,900	6,000	1,100	5,000	3,000	17,000
25	7,000	6,000	1,100	5,000	2,100	17,000
26	6,800	6,000	1,300	5,000	2,100	17,000
28	1,700	6,000	1,300	10,100	2,100	17,000

Required

Assuming a single transaction took place on each day, describe briefly the transaction that was most likely to have occurred, beginning with February 12. Indicate which accounts were affected and by what amount. No revenue or expense transactions occurred on these dates.

Problem 1-5B   *Balance sheet, entity concept*

Drew Beaty is a realtor. He buys and sells properties on his own, and he also earns commission as a real estate agent for buyers and sellers. He organized his business as a proprietorship on March 10, 19X2. Consider the following facts as of March 31, 19X2:

a. Beaty had $5,000 in his personal bank account and $9,000 in his business bank account.
b. Office supplies on hand at the real estate office totaled $1,000.
c. Beaty's business had spent $15,000 for an Electronic Realty Associates (ERA) franchise, which entitled him to represent himself as an ERA agent. ERA is a national affiliation of independent real estate agents. This franchise is a business asset.
d. Beaty owed $38,000 on a note payable for some undeveloped land that had been acquired by his business for a total price of $70,000.
e. Beaty owed $65,000 on a personal mortgage on his personal residence, which he acquired in 19X1 for a total price of $90,000.
f. Beaty owed $950 on a personal charge account with Sears, Roebuck and Co.
g. He had acquired business furniture for $12,000 on March 26. Of this amount, Beaty's business owed $6,000 on open account at March 31.

Required

1. Prepare the balance sheet of the real estate business of Drew Beaty, Realtor, at March 31, 19X2.
2. Identify the personal items given in the preceding facts that would not be reported on the balance sheet of the business.

Problem 1-6B   *Income statement, statement of owner's equity, balance sheet*

Presented below are the amounts of (a) the assets and liabilities of Bryant Repair Service as of December 31 and (b) the revenues and expenses of the company for the year ended on that date. The items are listed in alphabetical order.

Accounts payable	$ 14,000	Note payable	31,000
Accounts receivable	6,000	Property tax expense	2,000
Building	18,000	Rent expense	14,000
Cash	4,000	Salary expense	38,000
Equipment	26,000	Service revenue	110,000
Interest expense	4,000	Supplies	13,000
Interest payable	1,000	Utilities expense	3,000
Land	8,000		

The beginning amount of Mike Bryant, Capital, was $12,000, and during the year Bryant withdrew $32,000 for personal use.

Required

1. Prepare the income statement of Bryant Repair Service for the year ended December 31 of the current year.
2. Prepare the statement of owner's equity of the company for the year ended December 31.
3. Prepare the balance sheet of the company at December 31.

Problem 1-7B   *Transaction analysis for an actual company*

A recent balance sheet of Xerox Corporation, the manufacturer of copiers and other office equipment, is summarized as follows, with amounts in thousands. For example, Cash of $266,600,000 is presented as $266,600.

Xerox Corporation
Balance Sheet
December 31, 19XX
(thousands)

Assets		Liabilities	
Cash.	$ 266,600	Notes payable	$1,985,500
Accounts receivable.	1,466,900	Accounts payable	390,300
Merchandise inventories. . . .	1,469,800	Other liabilities	2,107,600
Land, buildings, and equip. .	2,659,700	Total liabilities	4,483,400
Other assets	3,953,700		
		Owner Equity.	5,333,300
		Total liabilities	
Total assets.	$9,816,700	and owner equity.	$9,816,700

During January, the company had the following transactions and events (amounts in thousands):

a. Received cash investment from owners, $37.
b. Purchased inventories on account, $400.
c. Paid cash on account (to reduce accounts payable), $136.
d. Sold inventory to another company on account, $670. The equipment had cost $670.
e. Learned that a national television news program would show members of Congress using Xerox copy machines as part of a senate investigation. The value of this advertisement to the company is estimated to be $1,000.

f. Borrowed cash, signing a note payable, $550.
g. Purchased equipment for cash, $380.
h. Collected cash on account from customers, $289.
i. Received special equipment from an owner as an investment in the company. The value of the equipment was $119.

Required

1. Showing all amounts in thousands, analyze the January transactions of Xerox. Use a format similar to Exhibit 1-5.
2. Prove that assets = liabilities + owner equity after analyzing the transactions.

Decision Problem

Using Financial Statements to Evaluate a Request for a Loan

The proprietors of two businesses, Butler Department Store and Susan Nielsen Home Decorators, have sought business loans from you. To decide whether to make the loans, you have requested their balance sheets.

Butler Department Store
Balance Sheet
August 31, 19X4

Assets		Liabilities	
Cash	$ 1,000	Accounts payable	$ 12,000
Accounts receivable	14,000	Note payable	18,000
Merchandise inventory	85,000	Total liabilities	30,000
Store supplies	500		
Furniture and fixtures	9,000	**Owner's Equity**	
Building	90,000		
Land	14,000	Roy Butler, capital	183,500
		Total liabilities and	
Total assets	$213,500	owner's equity	$213,500

Susan Nielsen Home Decorators
Balance Sheet
August 31, 19X4

Assets		Liabilities	
Cash	$11,000	Accounts payable	$ 3,000
Accounts receivable	4,000	Note payable	18,000
Office supplies	1,000	Total liabilities	21,000
Office furniture	6,000	**Owner's Equity**	
Land	19,000		
		Susan Nielsen, capital	20,000
		Total liabilities and	
Total assets	$41,000	owner's equity	$41,000

Required

1. Based solely on these balance sheets, which entity would you be more comfortable loaning money to? Explain fully, citing specific items and amounts from the balance sheets.
2. In addition to the balance sheet data, what other financial statement information would you require? Be specific.

Financial Statement Problem

Identifying Items from a Company's Financial Statements

This and similar problems in succeeding chapters focus on the financial statements of an actual company (Gulf+Western Inc.). As each problem is solved, readers gradually strengthen their understanding of actual financial statements in their entirety.

Refer to the Gulf+Western financial statements in Appendix C, and answer the following questions.

1. How much in cash (including cash equivalents) did Gulf+Western have on October 31, 1987?
2. What were total assets at October 31, 1987? At October 31, 1986?
3. Write the company's accounting equation at October 31, 1987, by filling in the dollar amounts:

ASSETS = LIABILITIES + OWNER EQUITY

4. Identify total revenues and net revenues for the year ended October 31, 1987. (Net revenues means total revenues after certain subtractions.)
5. How much net income (net earnings) did Gulf+Western experience for the year ended October 31, 1987?

Answers to Self-Study Questions

1. c	3. d	5. b	7. b	9. b
2. c	4. a	6. a	8. c	10. c

2

Recording Business Transactions

Chapter 1 illustrates how to account for business transactions by analyzing their effects on the accounting equation. That approach emphasizes accounting concepts, but it becomes unwieldy in day-to-day business if many transactions occur. In large businesses—such as a chain of department stores—hundreds or even thousands of transactions occur hourly. In practice, then, accountants use a different approach to handle accounting information. This chapter focuses on processing accounting information as it is actually done in practice.

The Account

OBJECTIVE 1
Define and use all new terms in the chapter

The basic summary device of accounting is the **account.** This is the detailed record of the changes that have occurred in a particular asset, liability, or owner's equity during a period of time. Each account appears on its own page. For convenient access to the information in the accounts the pages are grouped together in a single book called the **ledger.** When you hear reference to "keeping the books" or "auditing the books," the word *books* refers to the ledger. The ledger may be a bound book, a loose-leaf set of pages, or a computer record.

In the ledger, the accounts are grouped in three broad categories, based on the accounting equation:

$$\text{ASSETS} = \text{LIABILITIES} + \text{OWNER'S EQUITY}$$

Assets

Those economic resources that will benefit the business in the future are *assets*. The following asset accounts are common to many firms.

Cash. The Cash account shows the cash effects of a business's transactions. Cash means money and any medium of exchange that a bank accepts at face value. Cash includes currency, coins, money orders, certificates of deposit, and checks. The Cash account includes these items whether they are kept on hand, in a safe, in a cash register, or in a bank.

Notes Receivable. A business may sell its goods or services in exchange for a promissory note, which is a written pledge that the customer will pay the business a fixed amount of money by a certain date. The Notes Receivable account is a record of the promissory notes that the business expects to collect in cash.

Accounts Receivable. A business may sell its goods or services in exchange for an oral or implied promise for future cash receipt. Such sales are made on credit (on account). The Accounts Receivable account includes these amounts.

Prepaid Expenses. A business often pays certain expenses in advance. Prepaid expenses are assets because they will be of future benefit to the business. The ledger holds a separate asset account for each prepaid item. Prepaid Rent and Prepaid Insurance are prepaid expenses that occur often in business. Office Supplies are also accounted for as prepaid expenses.

Land. The Land account is a record of the land that a business owns.

Building. A business's buildings — office, warehouse, garage, and the like — appear in the Building account.

Equipment, Furniture and Fixtures. A business has a separate asset account for each type of equipment — Office Equipment and Store Equipment, for example. The Furniture and Fixtures account shows the cost of this asset. Other asset categories and accounts will be discussed as needed. For example, many businesses have an Investments account for their investments in other companies.

Liabilities

Recall that a *liability* is a debt. A business generally has fewer liability accounts than asset accounts because a business's liabilities can be summarized under relatively few categories.

Notes Payable. This account is the opposite of the Notes Receivable account. Notes Payable records the amounts that the business must pay because it signed a promissory note to purchase goods or services.

Accounts Payable. This account is the opposite of the Accounts Receivable account. The oral or implied promise to pay off debts arising from credit purchases of goods appears in the Accounts Payable account. Such a purchase is said to be made on account. Other liability categories and accounts are added as needed. Taxes Payable, Wages Payable, and Salary Payable are accounts that appear in many ledgers.

Owner's Equity

The claim that the owner has on the assets of the business is called *owner's equity.* In a proprietorship or a partnership, owner's equity is often split into separate accounts for the owner's capital balance and the owner's withdrawals.

Capital. This account shows the owner's claim to the assets of the business. After total liabilities are subtracted from total assets, the remainder is the owner's capital. The balance of the capital account equals the owner's investments in the business plus its net income and minus net losses and owner withdrawals. In addition to the capital account, the following accounts also appear in the owner's equity section of the ledger.

Withdrawals. When the owner withdraws cash or other assets from the business for personal use, its assets and its owner's equity both decrease. The amounts taken out of the business appear in a separate account entitled Withdrawals, or Drawing. If withdrawals were recorded directly in the capital account, the amount of owner withdrawals would be merged with owner investments. To separate these two amounts for decision making, businesses use a separate account for Withdrawals. This account shows a *decrease* in owner's equity.

Revenues. The increase in owner's equity from delivering goods or services to customers or clients is called *revenue.* The ledger contains as many revenue accounts as needed. Gary Lyon's accounting practice would have a Service Revenue account for amounts earned by providing accounting service for clients. If the business loans money to an outsider, it will also need an Interest Revenue account. If the business rents a building to a tenant, it will need a Rent Revenue account. Increases in revenue accounts are *increases* in owner's equity.

Expenses. The cost of operating a business is called *expense.* Expenses have the opposite effect of revenues, so they decrease owner's equity. A business needs a separate account for each category of its expenses, such as Salary Expense, Rent Expense, Advertising Expense, and Utilities Expense. Expense accounts are decreases in owner's equity.

Exhibit 2-1 shows how asset, liability, and owner's equity accounts can be grouped into the ledger. Typically, each account occupies a separate sheet.

Double-Entry Bookkeeping

Accounting is based on double-entry bookkeeping, which means that accountants record the *dual effects* of a business transaction. We know that each transaction affects two accounts. For example, Gary Lyon's $50,000 cash investment in his accounting practice increased both the Cash account and the Capital account of the business. It would be incomplete to record only the increase in the entity's cash without recording the increase in its owner's equity.

Consider a *cash purchase of supplies.* What are the dual effects of this transaction? The purchase (1) decreases cash and (2) increases supplies. A *purchase of supplies on credit* (1) increases supplies and (2) increases accounts payable. A *cash payment on account* (1) decreases cash and (2) decreases accounts payable. All transactions have at least two effects on the entity.

EXHIBIT 2-1 *The Ledger (Asset, Liability, and Owner's Equity Accounts)*

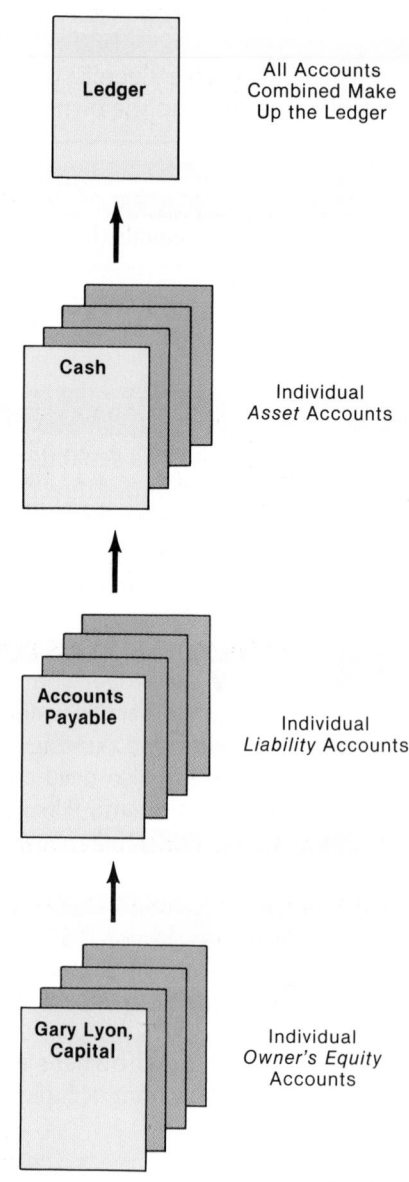

The T-Account

How do accountants record business transactions in the accounts? The account format used for most illustrations in this book is called the T-account. It takes the form of the capital letter "T." The vertical line in the letter divides the account into its left and right sides. The account title rests on the horizontal line. For example, the Cash account of a business appears in the following T-account format:

Cash	
Left side *Debit*	**Right side** *Credit*

The left side of the account is called the **debit** side, and the right side is called the **credit** side. Often beginners in the study of accounting are confused by the words *debit* and *credit*. To become comfortable using them, simply remember this:

✓ **debit = left side**

✓ **credit = right side**

Even though *left side* and *right side* are more descriptive, *debit* and *credit* are too deeply entrenched in accounting to avoid using.[1]

Increases and Decreases in the Accounts

The type of an account determines how increases and decreases in it are recorded. Increases in *assets* are recorded in the left (the debit) side of the account. Decreases in assets are recorded in the right (the credit) side of the account. Conversely, increases in *liabilities* and *owner's equity* are recorded by *credits*. Decreases are recorded by debits.

This pattern of recording debits and credits is based on the accounting equation:

ASSETS = LIABILITIES + OWNER'S EQUITY

Notice that assets are on the opposite side of the equation from liabilities and owner's equity. This explains why increases and decreases in assets are recorded in the opposite manner from liabilities and owner's equity. It also explains why liabilities and owner's equity follow the same pattern: they are on the same side of the equal sign. Exhibit 2-2 shows the relationship between the accounting equation and the rules of debit and credit.

To illustrate the ideas diagrammed in Exhibit 2-2, reconsider the first transaction from the preceding chapter. Gary Lyon invested $50,000 in cash to begin his accounting practice. Which accounts of the business are affected? By what amounts? On what side (debit or credit)? The answer is that Assets and Capital would increase by $50,000, as the following T-accounts show.

Assets	=	Liabilities	+	Owner's Equity
Cash				Gary Lyon, Capital
Debit for Increase, 50,000				Credit for Increase, 50,000

EXHIBIT 2-2 *Accounting Equation and the Rules of Debit and Credit*

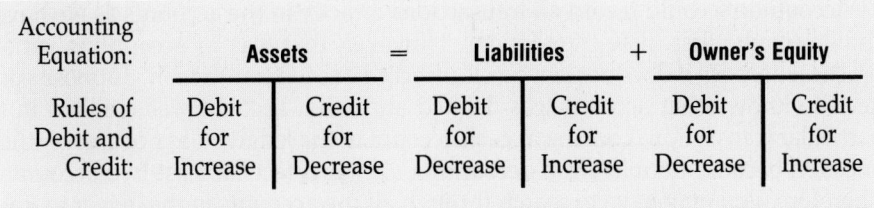

Accounting Equation:	Assets		=	Liabilities		+	Owner's Equity	
Rules of Debit and Credit:	Debit for Increase	Credit for Decrease		Debit for Decrease	Credit for Increase		Debit for Decrease	Credit for Increase

---

[1] The words *debit* and *credit* have a Latin origin (*debitum* and *creditum*). Pacioli, the Italian monk who wrote about accounting in the fifteenth century, used these terms.

The amount remaining in an account is called its *balance.* This initial transaction gives Cash a $50,000 debit balance and Gary Lyon, Capital a $50,000 credit balance.

OBJECTIVE 2

Apply the rules of debit and credit

The second transaction is a $20,000 cash purchase of land. This transaction affects two assets: Cash and Land. It decreases Cash (a credit) and increases Land (a debit), as shown in the T-accounts:

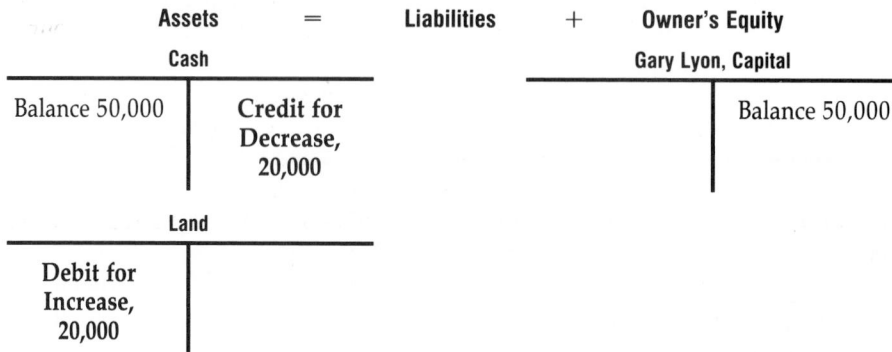

After this transaction, Cash has a $30,000 debit balance ($50,000 debit balance − $20,000 credit amount), Land's debit balance is $20,000, and the Capital account has a $50,000 credit balance.

Transaction 3 is a $500 purchase of office supplies on account. This transaction increases the asset Office Supplies and the liability Accounts Payable, as shown in the following accounts:

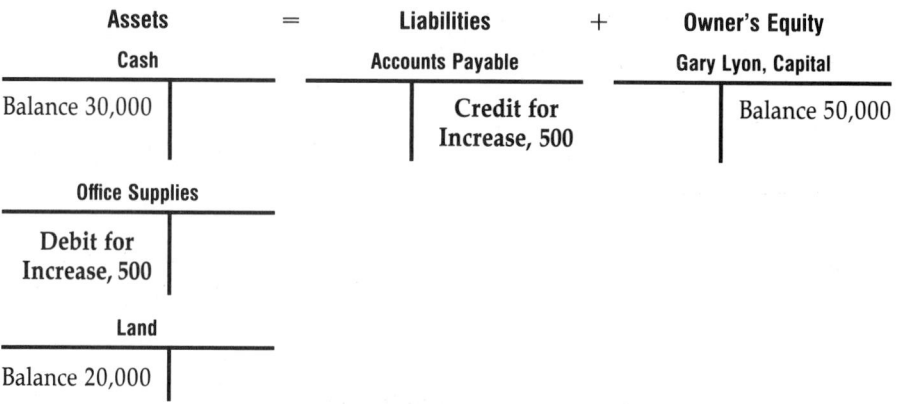

Accountants create accounts as needed. The process of writing a new T-account in preparation for recording a transaction is called *opening the account.* For Transaction 1, we opened the Cash account and the Gary Lyon, Capital account. For Transaction 2, we opened the Land account, and for Transaction 3, Office Supplies and Accounts Payable.

Accountants could record all transactions directly in the accounts as we have shown for the first three transactions. However, that way of accounting is not practical because it does not leave a clear record of each transaction. Suppose you need to know what account was debited and what account was credited in a particular transaction. Looking at each account in the ledger does not answer this question because double-entry accounting always affects at least two accounts. Therefore, you may have to search through all the accounts in the ledger to find both sides of a particular transaction. To avoid this waste of time, accountants keep a record of each transaction and then transfer this information into the accounts.

The Debit-Credit Language of Accounting

As we have seen, *debit* means "left side" and *credit* means "right side." We say "Debit Cash for $1,000," which means to place $1,000 on the left side of the cash account. We record "a $500 debit to Accounts Payable" by entering the $500 in the left side of this account, which signals a decrease in a liability. When we speak of "crediting a liability account for $750," we mean to increase the account's balance by recording $750 on the right side of the account.

In everyday conversation, we sometimes use the word *credit* in a sense that is different from its technical accounting meaning. For example, we may praise someone by saying, "She deserves credit for her good work." In your study of accounting forget this general use. Remember that *debit means left side* and *credit means right side.* Whether an account is increased or decreased by a debit or credit depends on the type of account (see Exhibit 2-2).

Recording Transactions in Journals

In actual practice, accountants record transactions first in a book called the **journal.** A journal is a chronological record of the entity's transactions. In this section, we describe the recording process and illustrate how to use the journal and the ledger.

The recording process follows these five steps:

1. Identify the transaction from source documents, such as bank deposit slips, sales receipts, and check stubs.
2. Specify each account affected by the transaction and classify it by type (asset, liability, or owner's equity).
3. Determine whether each account is increased or decreased by the transaction.
4. From the rules of debit and credit, determine whether to debit or credit the account.
5. Enter the transaction in the journal, including a brief explanation for the journal entry. It is customary to write the debit side of the entry first and the credit side next.

We have discussed steps 1, 2, 3, and 4. Step 5, "Enter the transaction in the journal," means to write the transaction in the journal. This step is also called "making the journal entry," "preparing the journal entry," or "journalizing the transaction." A major part of learning accounting is learning how to make journal entries.

Let's apply the five steps to journalize the first transaction of the accounting practice of Gary Lyon, CPA — the $50,000 cash investment in the business.

OBJECTIVE 3
Record transactions in the journal

Step 1. The source documents are the bank deposit slip and Lyon's $50,000 check, which is drawn on his personal bank account.

Step 2. *Cash* and *Gary Lyon, Capital* are the accounts affected by the transaction. Cash is an asset account, and Gary Lyon, Capital is an owner's equity account.

Step 3. Both accounts increase by $50,000. Therefore, debit Cash: it is the asset account that is increased. Also, credit Gary Lyon, Capital: it is the owner's equity account that is increased.

Step 4. Debit Cash to record an increase in this asset account. Credit Gary Lyon, Capital to record an increase in this account.

Step 5. The journal entry is

Date	Accounts and Explanation	Debit	Credit
Apr. 2	Cash	50,000	
	Gary Lyon, Capital		50,000
	Initial investment by owner.		

Note that the journal entry includes (a) the date of the transaction, (b) the title of the account debited (placed flush left) and the title of the account credited (indented slightly), (c) the dollar amounts of the debit (left) and credit (right)—dollar signs are omitted in the money columns, and (d) a short explanation of the transaction.

A helpful hint: To get off to the right start when analyzing a transaction, you should first pinpoint its effects (if any) on cash. Did cash increase or decrease? Then find its effect on other accounts. Typically, it is much easier to identify the effect of a transaction on cash than to identify the effect on other accounts.

The journal offers information that the ledger's T-accounts do not provide. Each journal entry shows the complete effect of a business transaction. Let's examine Gary Lyon's initial investment. The Cash account shows a single figure, the $50,000 debit. We know that every transaction has a credit, so in what account will we find the corresponding $50,000 credit? In this simple illustration, we know that the Capital account holds this figure. But imagine the difficulties an accountant would face trying to link debits and credits for hundreds of daily transactions—without a separate record of each transaction. The journal answers this problem and presents the full story for each transaction.

The journal can be a loose-leaf notebook, a bound book, or a computer listing. Exhibit 2-3 shows how a journal page might look with the first transaction entered.

In these introductory discussions we temporarily ignore the date of each transaction in order to focus on other details.

Posting from the Journal to the Ledger

Posting means transferring the amounts from the journal to the appropriate accounts in the ledger. Debits in the journal are posted as debits in the ledger, and credits in the journal as credits in the ledger. The initial investment transaction of Gary Lyon is posted to the ledger as shown in Exhibit 2-4.

EXHIBIT 2-3 The Journal

			Page 6
	Journal		
Date	Accounts and Explanation	Debit	Credit
Apr. 2	Cash	50,000	
	Gary Lyon, Capital		50,000
	Initial investment by owner.		

EXHIBIT 2-4 *Journal Entry and Posting to the Ledger*

Panel A—Journal Entry:

Accounts and Explanation	Debit	Credit
Debit: Cash	50,000	
Credit: Gary Lyon, Capital		50,000
Initial investment by owner.		

Panel B—Posting to the Ledger:

Cash

50,000

Gary Lyon, Capital

50,000

Flow of Accounting Data

Exhibit 2-5 summarizes the flow of accounting data from the business transaction
to the ledger.

EXHIBIT 2-5 *Flow of Accounting Data*

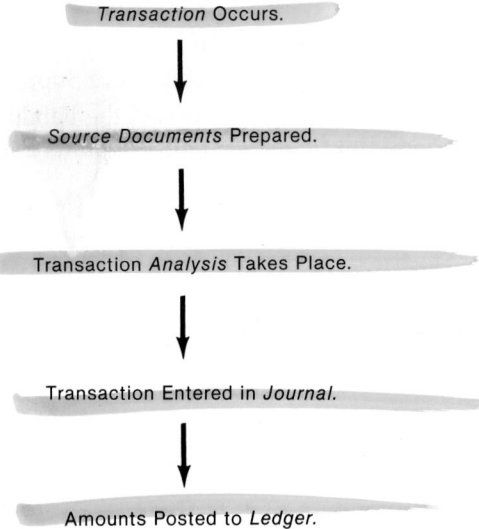

Transaction Occurs.

Source Documents Prepared.

Transaction *Analysis* Takes Place.

Transaction Entered in *Journal.*

Amounts Posted to *Ledger.*

Illustrative Problem

In this section, we illustrate transaction analysis, journalizing, and posting. We continue the example of Gary Lyon, CPA, and account for six of his early transactions.

Transaction Analysis, Journalizing, and Posting

1. *Transaction:* Lyon invested $50,000 to begin his accounting practice.

   Analysis: Lyon's investment in the business increased its asset cash; to record this increase, debit Cash.

   His investment also increased the owner's equity of the entity; to record this increase, credit Gary Lyon, Capital.

   Journal Entry:
   ```
   Cash ................................  50,000
        Gary Lyon, Capital ................          50,000
   Initial investment by owner.
   ```

   Ledger Accounts:

Cash		Gary Lyon, Capital	
(1) 50,000			(1) 50,000

2. *Transaction:* He paid $20,000 cash for land as a future office location.

   Analysis: The purchase increased the entity's asset land; to record this increase, debit Land.

   The purchase decreased cash; therefore, credit Cash.

   Journal Entry:
   ```
   Land ................................  20,000
        Cash ...........................          20,000
   Paid cash for land
   ```

   Ledger Accounts:

Cash		Land	
(1) 50,000	(2) 20,000	(2) 20,000	

3. *Transaction:* He purchased $500 office supplies on account payable.

   Analysis: The credit purchase of office supplies increased this asset; to record this increase, debit Office Supplies.

   The purchase also increased the liability accounts payable; to record this increase, credit Accounts Payable.

   Journal Entry:
   ```
   Office Supplies .........................  500
        Accounts Payable..................          500
   Purchased office supplies on account.
   ```

   Ledger Accounts:

Office Supplies		Accounts Payable	
(3) 500			(3) 500

4. *Transaction:* He paid $400 on the account payable created in the preceding transaction.

Analysis: The payment decreased the asset cash; therefore, credit Cash. The payment also decreased the liability, accounts payable; to record this decrease, debit Accounts Payable.

Journal Entry:

Accounts Payable. 400
     Cash 400
Paid cash on account.

Ledger Accounts:

Cash				Accounts Payable		
(1)	50,000	(2)	20,000	(4) 400	(3)	500
		(4)	400			

5. *Transaction:* He remodeled personal residence. This is not a business transaction of the accounting practice, so no journal entry is made.

6. *Transaction:* Lyon withdrew $2,100 cash for personal living expenses.

    Analysis: The withdrawal decreased the entity's cash; therefore, credit Cash.

    The transaction also decreased the owner's equity of the entity and must be recorded by a debit to an owner's equity account. Decreases in the owner's equity of a proprietorship that result from owner withdrawals are debited to a separate owner's equity account entitled Withdrawals. Therefore, debit Gary Lyon, Withdrawals.

Journal Entry:

Gary Lyon, Withdrawals 2,100
    Cash 2,100
Withdrawal of cash by owner.

Ledger Accounts:

Cash				Gary Lyon, Withdrawals	
(1)	50,000	(2)	20,000	(6)	2,100
		(4)	400		
		(6)	2,100		

As each journal entry is posted to the ledger, it is keyed by date or by transaction number. In this way, a trail is provided through the accounting records so that any transaction can be traced from the journal to the ledger and, if need be, back to the journal. This linking allows the accountant to locate efficiently any information needed.

Ledger Accounts after Posting

We next illustrate how the accounts look when the amounts of the preceding transactions have been posted. The accounts are grouped under the accounting equation's headings.

Note that each account has a balance figure. This amount is the difference between the account's total debits and its total credits. For example, the balance in the Cash account is the difference between the debits, $50,000, and the credits, $22,500 ($20,000 + $400 + $2,100). Thus the balance figure is $27,500. The balance amounts are not journal entries posted to the accounts, so we set an account balance apart by horizontal lines.

If the sum of an account's debits is greater than the sum of its credits, that account has a debit balance, as the Cash account does here. If the sum of its credits is greater, that account has a credit balance, as Accounts Payable does.

Assets	=	Liabilities	+	Owner's Equity

Cash

(1) 50,000	(2) 20,000
	(4) 400
	(6) 2,100
Bal. 27,500	

Office Supplies

(3) 500	
Bal. 500	

Land

(2) 20,000	
Bal. 20,000	

Accounts Payable

(4) 400	(3) 500
	Bal. 100

Gary Lyon, Capital

	(1) 50,000
	Bal. 50,000

Gary Lyon, Withdrawals

(6) 2,100	
Bal. 2,100	

Trial Balance

A **trial balance** is a list of all accounts with their balances. It provides a check on accuracy by showing whether the total debits equal the total credits. A trial balance may be taken at any time the postings are up to date. Exhibit 2-6 is the trial balance of the general ledger of Gary Lyon's accounting practice after the first six transactions have been journalized and posted.

The word *trial* is well chosen. The list is prepared as a *test* of the accounts' balances. The trial balance shows the accountant whether the total debits and total credits are equal. In this way it may signal accounting errors. For example, if only the debit (or only the credit) side of a transaction is posted, the total debits will not equal the total credits. If a debit is posted as a credit or vice versa, debits and credits will be out of balance. For example, if the $500 debit in Office Supplies

OBJECTIVE 5
Prepare a trial balance

EXHIBIT 2-6   *Trial Balance*

Gary Lyon, CPA
Trial Balance
April 30, 19X1

Account Titles	Balance Debit	Balance Credit
Cash..........................	$27,500	
Office supplies....................	500	
Land..........................	20,000	
Accounts payable		$ 100
Gary Lyon, capital.................		50,000
Gary Lyon, withdrawals.............	2,100	
Total	$50,100	$50,100

is incorrectly posted as a credit, total debits will be $49,600 and total credits will be $50,600. The trial balance alerts the accountant to such errors in posting.

Some errors may not be revealed by the trial balance. For example, a $1,000 cash payment for supplies may be credited to Accounts Payable instead of to Cash. This error would cause both Cash and Accounts Payable to be overstated, each by $1,000. However, because an asset and a liability are overstated by the same amount, the trial balance would still show debits equal to credits. Also, if an accountant erroneously recorded a $5,000 transaction at only $500, the trial balance would show no error. However, total debits and total credits would both be understated by $4,500 (that is, $5,000 − $500).

Summary Problem for Your Review

On August 1, 19X5, Liz Shea, opens a business that she names Shea's Research Service. She will be the sole owner of the business, so it will be a proprietorship. During the entity's first ten days of operations, the following transactions take place:

a. To begin operations, Shea deposits $50,000 of personal funds in a bank account entitled Shea's Research Service.

b. Shea pays $40,000 cash for a small house to be used as an office. (Debit an asset account entitled Building.)

c. Shea purchases $250 in office supplies on credit (that is, on account).

d. Shea pays cash of $6,000 for office furniture. (Debit Office Furniture.)

e. Shea pays $150 on the account payable she created in transaction *c*.

f. Shea withdraws $1,000 cash for personal use.

Required

1. Prepare the journal entries to record these transactions. Key the journal entries by letter.
2. Post the entries to the ledger.
3. Prepare the trial balance of Shea's Research Service at August 10, 19X5.

SOLUTION TO REVIEW PROBLEM

Requirement 1

ACCOUNTS and EXPLANATION	Debit	Credit
a. Cash	50,000	
Liz Shea, Capital		50,000
Initial investment by owner.		
b. Building	40,000	
Cash		40,000
Purchased building for an office.		
c. Office Supplies	250	
Accounts Payable		250
Purchased office supplies on account.		

d. Office Furniture 6,000
      Cash   6,000
      Purchased office furniture.

e. Accounts Payable. 150
      Cash   150
      Paid cash on account.

f. Liz Shea, Withdrawals. 1,000
      Cash   1,000
      Withdrew cash for personal use.

Requirement 2

Assets

Cash				Office Supplies	
(a) 50,000	(b) 40,000		(c) 250		
	(d) 6,000		Bal. 250		
	(e) 150				
	(f) 1,000				
Bal. 2,850					

Office Furniture			Building	
(d) 6,000			(b) 40,000	
Bal. 6,000			Bal. 40,000	

Liabilities

Owner's Equity

Accounts Payable			Liz Shea, Capital		Liz Shea, Withdrawals	
(e) 150	(c) 250		(a) 50,000	(f) 1,000		
	Bal. 100		Bal. 50,000	Bal. 1,000		

Requirement 3

Shea's Research Service
Trial Balance
August 10, 19X5

Account Title	Balance	
	Debit	Credit
Cash	$ 2,850	
Office supplies	250	
Office furniture	6,000	
Building	40,000	
Accounts payable.		$ 100
Liz Shea, capital.		50,000
Liz Shea, withdrawals.	1,000	
Total	$50,100	$50,100

Details of Journals and Ledgers

In order to focus on the main points of journalizing and posting, we purposely omitted certain essential data. In actual practice, the journal and the ledger provide additional details that create a "trail" through the accounting records for future reference. For example, an accountant may need to verify the date of a transaction or to determine whether a journal entry has been posted to the ledger. Let's take a closer look at the journal and the ledger.

Journal.   Exhibit 2-7, Panel B, presents the journal format most often used by accountants. The top of the journal holds the journal title. Note also that the journal page number appears in the upper-right corner.

As the column headings indicate, the *journal* displays the following information:

1. The *date,* which is most important because it indicates when the transaction occurred. The year appears first. It is not necessary to repeat it for each journal entry. The year appears only when the journal is started or when the year has changed. Note that the year appears with an X in the third column. We present the year in this way because the dates we choose are for illustration only. Thus 19X1 is followed by 19X2, and so on. We will use this format throughout the book. Like the year, the month is entered only once. The second date column shows the day of the transaction. This column is filled in for every transaction.

2. The *account title* and explanation of the transaction. You are already familiar with this presentation from Exhibit 2-3.

3. The *posting reference,* abbreviated Post. Ref. How this column helps the accountant becomes clear when we discuss the details of posting.

4. The *debit* column, which shows the amount debited.

5. The *credit* column, which shows the amount credited.

Ledger.   Exhibit 2-7, Panel C, presents the *ledger* in T-account format. Each account has its own page in the ledger. Our example shows Gary Lyon's Cash account. This account maintains the basic format of the T-account but offers more information.

The account title appears at the top of the page. Note also the account number at the upper-right column. Each account has its own identification number. We will look later at how accountants assign account numbers.

The column headings identify the ledger account's features.

1. The date.

2. The item column. This space is used for any special notation.

3. The journal reference column, abbreviated Jrnl. Ref. The importance of this column becomes clear when we discuss the mechanics of posting.

4. The debit column, with the amount debited.

5. The credit column, with the amount credited.

Posting

We know that posting means moving information from the journal to the ledger accounts. But how do we handle the additional details that appear in the journal and the ledger formats that we have just seen? Exhibit 2-7 illustrates the steps in

EXHIBIT 2-7 *Details of Journalizing and Posting*

Panel A—Illustrative Transactions

Date	Transaction
April 2, 19X1	Gary Lyon invested $50,000 in his accounting practice.
3	Paid $500 cash for office supplies.

Panel B—Journal

Page 1

Date	Accounts and Explanation	Post Ref.	Debit	Credit
19X1				
Apr. 2	Cash	11	50,000	
	Gary Lyon, Capital	31		50,000
	Initial investment			
3	Office Supplies	13	500	
	Cash	11		500
	Purchased office supplies.			

① ② ③ ④

Panel C—Ledger

Cash   Account No. 11

Date	Item	Jrnl. Ref.	Debit	Date	Item	Jrnl. Ref.	Credit
19X1				19X1			
Apr. 2		J.1	50,000	Apr. 3		J.1	500

Office Supplies   Account No. 13

Date	Item	Jrnl. Ref.	Debit	Date	Item	Jrnl. Ref.	Credit
19X1							
Apr. 3		J.1	500				

Gary Lyon, Capital   Account No. 31

Date	Item	Jrnl. Ref.	Debit	Date	Item	Jrnl. Ref.	Credit
				19X1			
				Apr. 2		J.1	50,000

full detail. Panel A lists the first two transactions of Gary Lyon, CPA; Panel B presents the journal; and Panel C shows the ledger.

Since the flow of accounting data moves from the journal to the ledger, the accountant first records the journal entry, as shown in Panel B. The transaction data are given in Panel A, except for the Post. Ref. number. Let's trace the arrows to follow the details of posting.

Arrow 1 traces the date, Apr. 2, 19X1, from the journal to the ledger account Cash.

Arrow 2 begins at the journal's page number, Page 1, and ends in the journal reference column, Jrnl. Ref. of the ledger. The *J.1* entry in that column stands for "Journal (page) 1." Why bother with this detail? If an accountant is using the Cash account and needs to locate the original journal entry, the journal page number tells where to look.

Arrow 3 indicates that the accountant posts the debit figure—$50,000 in this journal entry—as a debit figure in the account.

Arrow 4 points to a posting detail. Once the accountant has posted a dollar figure to the appropriate account, that account's number is entered in the journal's Post. Ref. column. This step indicates that the information for that account has been posted from the journal to the ledger. A blank Post Ref. column for a journal entry means that the entry has not yet been posted to the ledger account.

Having performed these steps for the debit entry, the accountant then posts the credit entry to the ledger. After posting, the accountant draws up the trial balance, as we discussed earlier.

Four-Column Account Format

The ledger accounts illustrated in Exhibit 2-7 are in two-column T-account format, with the debit column placed left and the credit column placed right. The T-account clearly distinguishes debits from credits and is often used for illustrative purposes that do not require much detail.

Another standard format has four amount columns, as illustrated for the Cash account in Exhibit 2-8. The first pair of amount columns are for the debit and credit amounts, and the second pair of amount columns are for the account's balance. This four-column format keeps a running balance in the account and for this reason is used more often in actual practice.

In the exhibit, Cash has a debit balance of $50,000 after the first transaction is posted and a debit balance of $49,500 after the second transaction.

EXHIBIT 2-8 *Account in Four-Column Format*

Account Cash					Account No. 11	
		Jrnl. Ref.	Debit	Credit	Balance	
Date	Item				Debit	Credit
19X1						
Apr.2		J.1	50000		50000	
3		J.1		500	49500	

Chart of Accounts

As you know, the general ledger contains the business's accounts grouped under the headings Assets, Liabilities, Owner's Equity, Revenues, and Expenses. To keep track of their accounts, organizations have a **chart of accounts,** which lists all the accounts and their account numbers. These account numbers are used as posting references, as illustrated by arrow 4 in Exhibit 2-7. It is easier to write the account number, 11, in the posting reference column of the journal than to write the account title, Cash. Also, this numbering system makes it easy to locate individual accounts in the ledger.

Assets are usually numbered beginning with 1, liabilities with 2, owner's equity with 3, revenues with 4, and expenses with 5. The second digit in an account number indicates the position of the individual account within the category. For example, Cash may be account number 11, which is the first asset account. Accounts Receivable may be account number 12, the second asset account. Accounts Payable may be account number 21, the first liability account. All accounts are numbered using this system.

Many organizations have so many accounts that they use three- or four-digit account numbers. For example, account number 101 may be Cash on Hand, account number 102 may be Cash on Deposit in First National Bank, and account number 103 may be Cash on Deposit in Lakewood Bank.

The chart of accounts for Gary Lyon, CPA, appears in Exhibit 2-9. Notice that the account numbers jump from 13 to 17. Gary Lyon realizes that later he may need to add other supplies accounts—for example, Tax Forms Supplies. Any additional supplies account would logically appear after Office Supplies, and Tax Forms Supplies might be account number 14.

Normal Balances of Accounts

Accountants speak of an account's *normal balance,* which refers to the side of the account—debit or credit—where *increases* are recorded. This term also refers to the usual balance—debit or credit—in the account. For example, Cash and all

EXHIBIT 2-9 *Chart of Accounts—Accounting Practice of Gary Lyon, CPA*

Balance Sheet Accounts:

Assets	Liabilities	Owner's Equity
11 Cash	21 Accounts Payable	31 Gary Lyon, Capital
12 Accounts Receivable	22 Notes Payable	32 Gary Lyon, Withdrawals
13 Office Supplies		
17 Office Furniture		
19 Land		

Income Statement Accounts:

Revenues	Expenses
41 Service Revenue	51 Rent Expense
	52 Salary Expense
	53 Utilities Expense

EXHIBIT 2-10   *Normal Balances of Balance Sheet Accounts*

Assets	=	Liabilities	+	Owner's Equity
Normal Bal. Debit		Normal Bal. Credit		Normal Bal. Credit

other assets usually have a debit balance, so assets are *debit-balance* accounts. On the other hand, liabilities and owner's equity usually have a credit balance, so they are *credit-balance* accounts. Exhibit 2-10 illustrates the normal balances of assets, liabilities, and owner's equity.

An account that normally has a debit balance may occasionally have a credit balance. This indicates a negative amount of the item. For example, Cash will have a temporary credit balance if the entity overdraws its bank account. Similarly, the liability Accounts Payable—normally a credit balance account—will have a debit balance if the entity overpays its account. In other instances, the shift of a balance amount away from its normal column indicates an accounting error. For example, a credit balance in Office Supplies, Office Furniture, or Buildings indicates an error because negative amounts of these assets cannot exist.

As we have explained, owner's equity usually contains several accounts. In total, these accounts show a normal credit balance for the owner's equity of the business. Each individual owner's equity account has a normal credit balance if it represents an *increase* in owner's equity (for example, the Capital account). However, if the individual owner's equity account represents a *decrease* in owner's equity, the account will have a normal debit balance (for example, the Withdrawals account).

Additional Owner's Equity Accounts: Revenues and Expenses

The owner's equity category includes two additional types of accounts: revenues and expenses. As we have discussed, **revenues** are increases in owner's equity that result from delivering goods or services to customers. **Expenses** are decreases in owner's equity due to the cost of operating the business. Therefore, the accounting equation may be expanded as follows:

ASSETS = LIABILITIES + OWNER'S EQUITY

(CAPITAL − WITHDRAWALS) + (REVENUES − EXPENSES)

Revenues and expenses appear in parentheses because their impact on the accounting equation arises from their effect on owner's equity. If revenues exceed expenses, the net effect—revenues minus expenses—is net income, which increases owner's equity. If expenses are greater, the net effect is a net loss, which decreases owner's equity.

We can now express the *rules of debit and credit* in final form as shown in Exhibit 2-11, Panel A. Panel B shows the *normal balances* of the five types of accounts.

EXHIBIT 2-11   *Rules of Debit and Credit and Normal Balances of Accounts*

Panel A—Rules of Debit and Credit:

Assets		=	Liabilities		+	Capital	
Debit for Increase	Credit for Decrease		Debit for Decrease	Credit for Increase		Debit for Decrease	Credit for Increase

Withdrawals

Debit for Increase	Credit for Decrease

Revenues

Debit for Decrease	Credit for Increase

Expenses

Debit for Increase	Credit for Decrease

Panel B—Normal Balances:

Assets	Debit	
Liabilities		Credit
Owner's equity-overall		Credit
Capital		Credit
Withdrawals	Debit	
Revenue		Credit
Expenses	Debit	

All of accounting is based on these five types of accounts. You should become very familiar with the related rules of debit and credit and the normal balances of accounts.

Typical Account Titles

Thus far we have dealt with a limited number of transactions and accounts to introduce key concepts. Actual businesses engage in more transactions, requiring more accounts. Additional transactions are recorded in the same manner, with accounts added to the analysis as needed. The following summary describes some of the more common accounts grouped by financial statement and account category. As you work exercises and problems in this and future chapters, you will find these descriptions useful.

Income Statement—Revenues and Expenses

Revenues

Service revenue: Revenue earned by performing a service (accounting service by a CPA firm, laundry service by a laundry, and so forth).

Sales revenue: Revenue earned by selling a product (sales of hardware by a hardware store, food by a grocery store, and so forth).

Expenses

Rent expense: Expense for office rent and the rental of office equipment or the rental of any other business asset.

Salary or wage expense: Expense of having employees work for the business.

Utilities expense: Expense of using electricity, water, gas, and other items provided by utility companies.

Supplies expense: Expense of using supplies such as stationery, stamps, paper clips, staples, and so forth.

Advertising expense: Expense of advertising the business.

Interest expense: Expense of using borrowed money.

Property tax expense: Expense for property tax on business land and buildings.

Balance Sheet—Assets, Liabilities, and Owner's Equity

Assets

Cash: Money on hand and in the bank

Accounts receivable: Claim on open account against the cash of a client or a customer. (Open account means that no promissary note exists to support the receivable.)

Note receivable: Claim against the cash of another party, supported by a promissory note signed by the other party. *(All receivables are assets, and any account with* receivable *in its title is an asset.)*

Merchandise inventory: Merchandise that an entity sells in its business (such as clothing by a department store, stereos by a stereo shop, and so forth).

Office supplies: Stationery, stamps, paper clips, staples, and so forth.

Office furniture: Desks, chairs, file cabinets, and so forth.

Office equipment: Typewriters, calculators, and other equipment used in a business office. A business may have other types of equipment, such as delivery equipment or store equipment.

Building: Building used in a business.

Land: Land on which a business building stands.

Liabilities

Account payable: Liability to pay cash to another party on open account.

Note payable: Liability to pay cash to another party, supported by a signed promissory note.

Salary or wage payable: Liability to pay an employee for work. *(Most liabilities have the word* payable *in the account title, and any account with* payable *in its title is a liability.)*

Owner's Equity

Gary Lyon, Capital: The interest of the owner of the business in its assets. (This account title bears the name of the owner.)

Gary Lyon, Withdrawals: The owner's withdrawals of assets from the business for personal use.

Illustrative Problem _____

Let's account for the revenues and expenses of the accounting practice of Sara Nichols, Attorney for the month of July 19X1. We follow the same steps illustrated earlier: analyze the transaction, journalize, post to the ledger, and prepare the trial balance. Revenue accounts and expense accounts work just like asset, liability, and owner's equity accounts. Each revenue and each expense account has its own page in the ledger and its own identifying account number.

Transaction Analysis, Journalizing, and Posting

OBJECTIVE 6

Record revenues and expenses

1. *Transaction:* Sara Nichols invested $10,000 cash in a business bank account to open her law practice.

   Analysis: The asset cash is increased; therefore debit Cash.
   The owner's equity of the business increased; therefore, credit Sara Nichols, Capital

   Journal Entry:
   Cash 10,000
       Sara Nichols, Capital 10,000
   Invested cash in the business.

   Ledger Accounts:

Cash		Sara Nichols, Capital	
(1) 10,000			(1) 10,000

2. *Transaction:* Nichols performed service for a client and collected $3,000 cash.

   Analysis: The asset cash is increased; therefore, debit Cash.
   The revenue service revenue is increased; credit Service Revenue.

   Journal Entry:
   Cash 3,000
       Service Revenue 3,000
   Performed service and received cash.

   Ledger Accounts:

Cash		Service Revenue	
(1) 10,000			(2) 3,000
(2) 3,000			

3. *Transaction:* Nichols performed service for a client and billed the client for $500 on account receivable. This means the client owes the business $500 even though the client signed no formal promissory note.

   Analysis: The asset accounts receivable is increased; therefore, debit Accounts Receivable.
   The revenue service revenue is increased; credit Service Revenue.

   Journal Entry:
   Accounts Receivable 500
       Service Revenue 500
   Performed service on account.

Ledger
Accounts:

Accounts Receivable		Service Revenue	
(3) 500			**(2) 3,000**
			(3) 500

4. *Transaction:* Nichols performed accounting service of $700 for a client, who paid $300 cash immediately. Nichols billed the remaining $400 to the client on account receivable.

  Analysis: The assets cash and accounts receivable are increased; therefore, debit both of these asset accounts.

  The revenue service revenue is increased; credit Service Revenue for the sum of the two debit amounts.

  Journal
  Entry:

  Cash 300
  Accounts Receivable 400
      Service Revenue........................ 700
  Performed service for cash and on account.

  Note: Because this transaction affects more than two accounts at the same time, the entry is called a *compound entry*. No matter how many accounts a compound entry affects—there may be any number—total debits must equal total credits.

Ledger
Accounts:

Cash		Accounts Receivable	
(1) 10,000		**(3) 500**	
(2) 3,000		**(4) 400**	
(4) 300			

Service Revenue	
	(2) 3,000
	(3) 500
	(4) 700

5. *Transaction:* Nichols paid the following cash expenses: office rent, $900; employee salary, $1,500; and utilities, $500.

  Analysis: The following expenses are increased: Rent Expense, Salary Expense, and Utilities Expense. They should each be debited.

  The asset cash is decreased; therefore, credit Cash for the sum of the three expense amounts.

  Journal
  Entry:

  Rent Expense 900
  Salary Expense........................... 1,500
  Utilities Expense......................... 500
      Cash 2,900
  Paid cash expenses.

Ledger
Accounts:

Cash		Rent Expense	
(1) 10,000	**(5) 2,900**	**(5) 900**	
(2) 3,000			
(4) 300			

Salary Expense		Utilities Expense	
(5) 1,500		**(5) 500**	

6. *Transaction:* Nichols received a telephone bill for $120 and will pay this expense next week.

   Analysis: Utilities expense is increased; therefore, debit this expense. The liability accounts payable is increased; credit this account.

   Journal Entry:

   Utilities Expense............................ 120
       Accounts Payable....................... 120
   Received utility bill.

   Ledger Accounts:

Accounts Payable				Utilities Expense		
		(6)	120	(5)	500	
				(6)	120	

7. *Transaction:* Nichols collected $200 cash from the client established in Transaction 3.

   Analysis: The asset cash is increased; therefore, debit Cash.

   The asset accounts receivable is decreased; therefore, credit Accounts Receivable.

   Journal Entry:

   Cash 200
       Accounts Receivable 200
   Received cash on account.

   Note: This transaction has no effect on revenue; the related revenue is accounted for in transaction 3.

   Ledger Accounts:

Cash				Accounts Receivable			
(1)	10,000	(5)	2,900	(3)	500	(7)	200
(2)	3,000			(4)	400		
(4)	300						
(7)	200						

8. *Transaction:* Nichols paid the telephone bill that was received and recorded in transaction 6.

   Analysis: The liability accounts payable is decreased; therefore, debit Accounts Payable.

   The asset cash is decreased; credit Cash.

   Journal Entry:

   Accounts Payable........................... 120
       Cash 120
   Paid cash on account.

   Note: This transaction has no effect on expense because the related expense was recorded in transaction 6.

   Ledger Accounts:

Cash				Accounts Payable			
(1)	10,000	(5)	2,900	(8)	120	(6)	120
(2)	3,000	(8)	120				
(4)	300						
(7)	200						

9. *Transaction:* Nichols withdrew $1,100 cash for personal use.

Analysis: The withdrawal decreased owner's equity; therefore, debit Sara
Nichols, Withdrawals.

The asset cash decreased; credit Cash.

Journal   Sara Nichols, Withdrawals 1,100
Entry: Cash   1,100
Withdrew for personal use.

Ledger
Accounts:

Cash				Sara Nichols, Withdrawals	
(1)	10,000	(5)	2,900	**(9)**	**1,100**
(2)	3,000	(8)	120		
(4)	300	**(9)**	**1,100**		
(7)	200				

Ledger Accounts After Posting

Assets

Cash				Accounts Receivable			
(1)	10,000	(5)	2,900	(3)	500	(7)	200
(2)	3,000	(8)	120	(4)	400		
(4)	300	(9)	1,100	Bal.	700		
(7)	200						
Bal.	9,380						

Liabilities

Accounts Payable			
(8)	120	(6)	120
		Bal.	0

Owner's Equity

Sara Nichols, Capital				Sara Nichols, Withdrawals			
		(1)	10,000	(9)	1,100		
		Bal.	10,000	Bal.	1,100		

Owner's Equity

Revenue

Service Revenue			
		(2)	3,000
		(3)	500
		(4)	700
		Bal.	4,200

Expenses

Rent Expense		Salary Expense		Utilities Expense	
(5)	900	(5)	1,500	(5)	500
Bal.	900	Bal.	1,500	(6)	120
				Bal.	620

Trial Balance

Sara Nichols, Attorney
Trial Balance
July 31, 19X1

Account Title	Balance	
	Debit	Credit
Cash.........................	$ 9,380	
Accounts receivable	700	
Accounts payable		$ 0
Sara Nichols, capital.....................		10,000
Sara Nichols, withdrawals	1,100	
Service revenue........................		4,200
Rent expense..........................	900	
Salary expense........................	1,500	
Utilities expense	620	
Total...........................	$14,200	$14,200

Analytical Use of Accounting Information _____

OBJECTIVE 7

Analyze transactions
without a journal

What dominates the accountant's analysis of transactions: the accounting equation, the journal, or the ledger? The *accounting equation* is most fundamental. In turn, the ledger is more useful than the journal in providing an overall model of the organization. Accountants and other businesspersons must often make quick decisions without the benefit of a complete accounting system: journal, ledger, accounts, and trial balance. For example, the owner of a company may be negotiating the purchase price of another business. For a quick analysis of the effects of transactions, accountants often skip the journal and go directly to the ledger. They compress transaction analysis, journalizing, and posting into one step. This type of analysis saves time that may be the difference between a good business decision and a lost opportunity.

Let's take an example to see how it works. For instance, the first revenue transaction—Sara Nichols performed accounting service for a client and collected cash of $3,000—may be analyzed be debiting the Cash account and crediting the Service Revenue account directly in the ledger in the following manner:

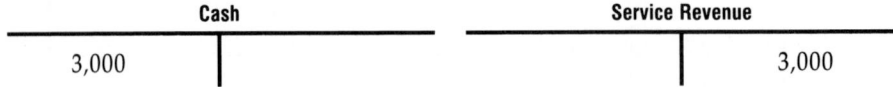

Cash		Service Revenue	
3,000			3,000

With this short cut, the accountant can see immediately the effect of the transaction on both the entity's cash and its service revenue. Modern computer-assisted accounting systems often have this "journal-less" feature. These systems can also produce the essential data for individual transactions, such as the date, the transaction amount, and the accounts affected.

Summary Problem for Your Review

The trial balance of Tomassini Computer Service Center on March 1, 19X2, lists the entity's assets, liabilities, and owner's equity on that date.

Account Title	Balance	
	Debit	Credit
Cash..................................	$26,000	
Accounts receivable	4,500	
Accounts payable		$ 2,000
L. Tomassini, capital....................		28,500
Total...........................	$30,500	$30,500

During March the business engaged in the following transactions:

1. Tomassini borrowed $45,000 from the bank. He signed a note payable in the name of the business.
2. He paid cash of $40,000 to a real estate company to acquire land.
3. He performed service for a customer and received cash of $5,000.
4. He purchased supplies on credit, $300.
5. He performed customer service and earned revenue on account, $2,600.
6. He paid $1,200 on account.
7. He paid the following cash expenses: salaries, $3,000; rent, $1,500; and interest, $400.
8. He received $3,100 on account.
9. He received a $200 utility bill that will be paid next week.
10. Tomassini withdrew $1,800 for personal use.

Required

1. Open the following accounts, with the balances indicated, in the ledger of Tomassini Computer Service Center. Use the T-account format.

    Assets—Cash, $26,000; Accounts Receivable, $4,500; Supplies, no balance; Land, no balance

    Liabilities—Accounts Payable, $2,000; Note Payable, no balance

    Owner's Equity—Larry Tomassini, Capital, $28,500; Larry Tomassini, Withdrawals, no balance

    Revenues—Service Revenue, no balance

    Expenses—(none have balances) Salary Expense, Rent Expense, Utilities Expense, Interest Expense

2. Journalize the preceding transactions. Key journal entries by transaction number.
3. Post to the ledger.
4. Prepare the trial balance of Tomassini Computer Service Center at March 31, 19X2.
5. Compute the net income or net loss of the entity during the month of March. List expenses in order from the largest to the smallest.

SOLUTION TO REVIEW PROBLEM

Requirement 1

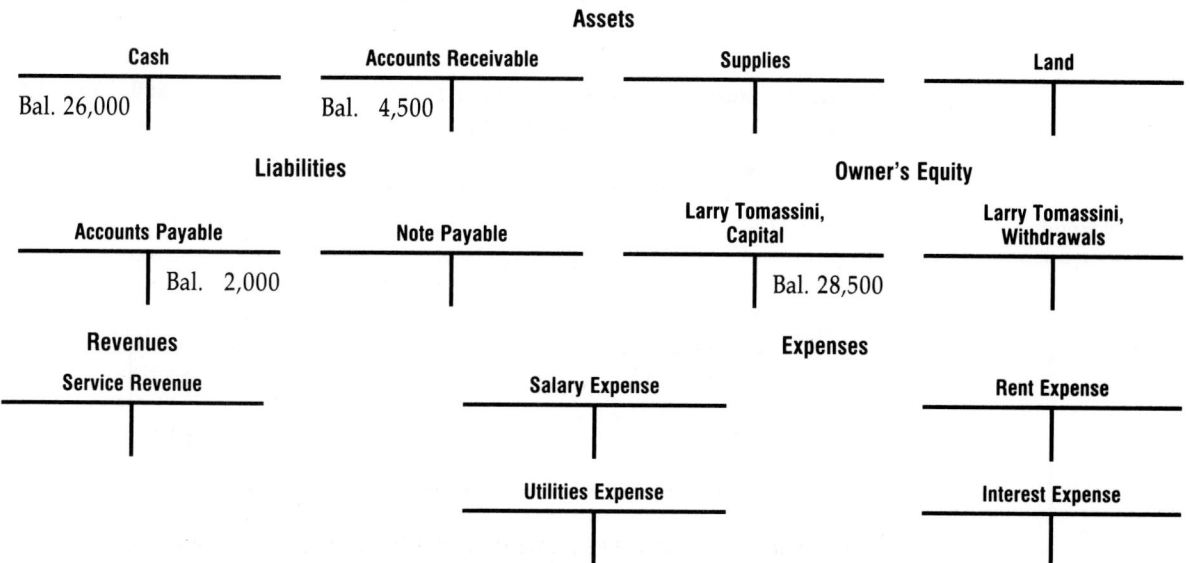

Requirement 2

	Accounts and Explanation	Debit	Credit
1.	Cash...	45,000	
	Note Payable..		45,000
	Borrowed cash on note payable.		
2.	Land..	40,000	
	Cash...		40,000
	Purchased land for cash.		
3.	Cash...	5,000	
	Service Revenue		5,000
	Performed service and received cash.		
4.	Supplies..	300	
	Accounts Payable		300
	Purchased supplies on account.		
5.	Accounts Receivable...	2,600	
	Service Revenue		2,600
	Performed service on account.		
6.	Accounts Payable	1,200	
	Cash...		1,200
	Paid on account.		
7.	Salary Expense	3,000	
	Rent Expense..	1,500	
	Interest Expense	400	
	Cash...		4,900
	Paid cash expenses.		
8.	Cash...	3,100	
	Accounts Receivable.....................................		3,100
	Received on account.		
9.	Utilities Expense	200	
	Accounts Payable		200
	Received utility bill.		
10.	Larry Tomassini, Withdrawals...........................	1,800	
	Cash...		1,800
	Withdrew for personal use.		

Requirement 3

Assets

Cash			
Bal. 26,000	(2)	40,000	
(1) 45,000	(6)	1,200	
(3) 5,000	(7)	4,900	
(8) 3,100	(10)	1,800	
Bal. 31,200			

Accounts Receivable		
Bal. 4,500	(8)	3,100
(5) 2,600		
Bal. 4,000		

Supplies	
(4) 300	
Bal. 300	

Land	
(2) 40,000	
Bal. 40,000	

Liabilities

Accounts Payable

(6)	1,200	Bal.	2,000
		(4)	300
		(9)	200
		Bal.	1,300

Note Payable

| | | (1) | 45,000 |
| | | Bal. | 45,000 |

Owner's Equity

Larry Tomassini, Capital

| | | Bal. | 28,500 |

Larry Tomassini, Withdrawals

| (10) | 1,800 | |
| Bal. | 1,800 | |

Revenues

Service Revenue

		(3)	5,000
		(5)	2,600
		Bal.	7,600

Expenses

Salary Expense

| (7) | 3,000 | |
| Bal. | 3,000 | |

Rent Expense

| (7) | 1,500 | |
| Bal. | 1,500 | |

Utilities Expense

| (9) | 200 | |
| Bal. | 200 | |

Interest Expense

| (7) | 400 | |
| Bal. | 400 | |

Requirement 4

Tomassini Computer Service Center
Trial Balance
March 31, 19X2

Account Title	Debit	Credit
Cash	$31,200	
Accounts Receivable	4,000	
Supplies	300	
Land	40,000	
Accounts Payable		$ 1,300
Note Payable		45,000
Larry Tomassini, Capital		28,500
Larry Tomassini, Withdrawals	1,800	
Service Revenue		7,600
Salary Expense	3,000	
Rent Expense	1,500	
Utilities Expense	200	
Interest Expense	400	
Total	$82,400	$82,400

Requirement 5   Net income for the month of March

Revenues:		
Service revenue		$7,600
Expenses:		
Salary expense.	$3,000	
Rent expense	1,500	
Interest expense.	400	
Utilities expense.	200	
Total expenses.		5,100
Net income		$2,500

Summary

The *account* can be viewed in the form of the letter "T." The left side of each account is its *debit* side. The right side is its *credit* side. The *ledger,* which contains a record for each account, groups and numbers accounts by category in the following order: assets, liabilities, owner's equity, revenues, and expenses.

Assets and *expenses* are increased by debits and decreased by credits. *Liabilities, owner's equity,* and *revenues* are increased by credits and decreased by debits. The side—debit or credit—of the account in which increases are recorded is that account's normal balance. Thus the normal balance of assets and expenses is a debit, and the normal balance of liabilities, owner's equity, and revenues is a credit. Withdrawals, which decreases owner's equity, normally has a debit balance. *Revenues,* which are increases in owner's equity, have a normal credit balance. *Expenses,* which are decreases in owner's equity, have a normal debit balance.

The accountant begins the recording process by entering the transaction's information in the *journal,* a chronological list of all the business's transactions. The information is then posted—transferred—to the *ledger* accounts. Posting references are used to trace amounts back and forth between the journal and the ledger. Businesses list their account titles and numbers in a chart of accounts.

The *trial balance* is a summary of all the account balances in the ledger. When *double-entry accounting* has been done correctly, the total debits and the total credits in the trial balance are equal.

We can now trace the flow of accounting information through these steps:

Business Transaction → Source Documents → Journal Entry → Posting to Ledger → Trial Balance

Self-Study Questions

Test your understanding of the chapter by marking the best answer for each of the following questions.

1. An account has two sides called the *(p. 42)*
   a. Debit and credit
   b. Asset and liability
   c. Revenue and expense
   d. Journal and ledger

2. Increases in liabilities are recorded by *(p. 43)*
   a. Debits
   b. Credits

3. Why do accountants record transactions in the journal? *(p. 45)*
   a. To ensure that all transactions are posted to the ledger
   b. To ensure that total debits equal total credits
   c. To have a chronological record of all transactions
   d. To help prepare the financial statements
4. Posting is the process of transferring information from the *(p. 46)*
   a. Journal to the trial balance   c. Ledger to the financial statements
   b. Ledger to the trial balance   d. Journal to the ledger
5. The purchase of land for cash is recorded by a *(p. 48)*
   a. Debit to Cash and a credit to Land
   b. Debit to Cash and a debit to Land
   c. Debit to Land and a credit to Cash
   d. Credit to Cash and a credit to Land
6. The purpose of the trial balance is to *(p. 50)*
   a. Indicate whether total debits equal total credits
   b. Ensure that all transactions have been recorded
   c. Speed the collection of cash receipts from customers
   d. Increase assets and owner's equity
7. What is the normal balance of the Accounts Receivable, Office Supplies, and Rent Expense accounts? *(p. 58)*
   a. Debit   b. Credit
8. A business has Cash of $3,000, Notes Payable of $2,500, Accounts Payable of $4,300, Service Revenue of $7,000, and Rent Expense of $1,800. Based on these data, how much are its total liabilities? *(p. 59)*
   a. $5,500   c. $9,800
   b. $6,800   d. $13,800
9. The earning of revenue that is not received in cash is recorded by a *(pp. 60, 61)*
   a. Debit to Cash and a credit to Revenue
   b. Debit to Accounts Receivable and a credit to Revenue
   c. Debit to Accounts Payable and a credit to Revenue
   d. Debit to Revenue and a credit to Accounts Receivable
10. The account credited for a receipt of cash on account is *(p. 62)*
    a. Cash   c. Service Revenue
    b. Accounts Payable   d. Accounts Receivable

Answers to the Self-Study Questions are at the end of the chapter.

Accounting Vocabulary

account *(p. 39)*,   chart of accounts *(p. 56)*,   credit *(p. 43)*,   debit *(p. 42)*,   journal *(p. 45)*,   ledger *(p. 39)*,   posting *(p. 46)*,   trial balance *(p. 50)*.

ASSIGNMENT MATERIAL _____

Questions

1. Name the basic summary device of accounting. What letter of the alphabet does it resemble, and what are its two sides called?
2. Is the following statement true or false? Debit means decrease and credit means increase. Explain your answer.
3. Write two sentences that use the term *debit* in different ways.

4. What are the three *basic* types of accounts? Name two additional types of accounts. To which one of the three *basic* types are these two additional types of accounts most closely related?

5. Suppose you are the accountant for Smith Courier Service. Keeping in mind double-entry bookkeeping, identify the *dual effects* of Mary Smith's investment of $10,000 cash in her business.

6. Briefly describe the flow of accounting information. (Hint: See the diagram in the chapter summary.)

7. To what does the *normal balance* of an account refer?

8. Complete the table by indicating the normal balance of the five types of accounts.

Account Type	Normal Balance
Assets	_____
Liabilities	_____
Capital	_____
Revenues	_____
Expenses	_____

9. What does posting accomplish? Why is it important? Does it come before or after journalizing?

10. Label each of the following transactions as increasing owner's equity (+), decreasing owner's equity (−), or as having no effect on owner's equity (0). Write the appropriate symbol in the space provided.

  _____ a. Investment by owner
  _____ b. Revenue transaction
  _____ c. Purchase of supplies on credit
  _____ d. Expense transaction

  _____ e. Cash payment on account
  _____ f. Withdrawal by owner
  _____ g. Borrowing money on a note payable
  _____ h. Sale of services on account

11. What four steps does posting include? Which step is the fundamental purpose of posting?

12. Rearrange the following accounts in their logical sequence in the ledger:

  Notes Payable
  Accounts Receivable
  Sales Revenue

  Cash
  Jane East, Capital
  Salary Expense

13. What is the meaning of the statement, Accounts Payable has a credit balance of $1,700?

14. Jack Brown Campus Cleaners launders the shirts of customer Bobby Baylor, who has a charge account at the cleaners. When Bobby picks up his clothes and is short on cash, he charges it. Later, when he receives his monthly statement from the cleaners, Bobby writes a check on Dear Old Dad's bank account and mails the check to Jack Brown. Identify the two business transactions described here. Which transaction increases Jack Brown's owner's equity? Which transaction increases Jack Brown's cash?

15. Explain the difference between the ledger and the chart of accounts.

16. Why do accountants prepare a trial balance?

17. What is a compound journal entry?

18. The accountant for Bower Construction Company mistakenly recorded a $500 purchase of supplies on account as a $5,000 purchase. He debited Supplies and credited Accounts Payable for $5,000. Does this error cause the trial balance to be out of balance? Explain your answer.

19. What is the effect on total assets of collecting cash on account from customers?

20. What is the advantage of analyzing and recording transactions without the use of a journal? Describe how this "journal-less" analysis works.

Exercises

Exercise 2-1 *Analyzing transactions*

Analyze the following transactions in the manner shown for the October 1 transaction:

Oct. 1 Paid monthly rent expense of $700. (Analysis: The expense rent expense is increased; therefore, debit Rent Expense. The asset cash is decreased; therefore credit Cash.)

 4 Received $350 cash on account from a customer.
 8 Performed service on account for a customer, $1,100.
 12 Purchased office furniture on account, $620.
 19 Sold for $19,000 land that had cost this same amount.
 24 Purchased building for $48,000; signed a note payable.
 27 Paid the liability created on October 12.

Exercise 2-2 *Journalizing transactions*

Garner Service Company engaged in the following transactions during March 19X3, its first month of operations:

Mar. 1 Lynn Garner invested $40,000 of cash to start the business.
 2 She purchased supplies of $200 on account.
 4 She paid $15,000 cash for land to use as a future building site.
 6 She performed service for customers and received cash, $2,000.
 9 She paid $100 on accounts payable.
 17 She performed service for customers on account, $1,600.
 23 She received $1,200 cash from customer on account.
 31 She paid the following expenses: salary, $1,200; rent, $500.

Required

Record the preceding transactions in the journal of Garner Service Company. Key transactions by date and include an explanation for each entry, as illustrated in the chapter. Use the following accounts: Cash; Accounts Receivable; Office Supplies; Land; Accounts Payable; Lynn Garner, Capital; Service Revenue; Salary Expense; Rent Expense.

Exercise 2-3 *Posting to the ledger and preparing a trial balance*

1. After journalizing the transactions of Exercise 2-2, post the entries to the ledger, using T-account format. Key transactions by date as in the following example. Label the balance of each account *Bal.*

Lynn Garner, Capital	
	Mar. 1 40,000

2. Prepare the trial balance of Garner Service Company at March 31, 19X3.

Exercise 2-4 *Describing transactions and posting*

The journal of Scholes Company appears at the top of the next page.

Required

1. Describe each transaction. Example: Aug. 5 — Cash sale.
2. Post the transactions to the ledger using the following account numbers: Cash, 11; Accounts Receivable, 12; Supplies, 13; Accounts Payable, 21; Sales Revenue, 41; Rent

Journal   **Page 5**

Date	Accounts and Explanation	Post Ref.	Debit	Credit
Aug. 5	Cash......................................		850	
	Sales Revenue			850
9	Supplies..................................		270	
	Accounts Payable			270
11	Accounts Receivable		2,100	
	Sales Revenue			2,100
14	Rent Expense...........................		900	
	Cash...................................			900
22	Cash......................................		1,400	
	Accounts Receivable			1,400
25	Advertising Expense		350	
	Cash...................................			350
27	Accounts Payable		270	
	Cash...................................			270
31	Utilities Expense		220	
	Accounts Payable			220

Expense, 51; Advertising Expense, 52; Utilities Expense, 53. Use dates, journal references, and posting references as illustrated in Exhibit 2-7. You may write the account numbers as posting references directly in your book unless directed otherwise by your instructor.

3. Compute the balance in each account after posting. The first debit amount of $850 is posted to Cash as an example:

Cash

Aug. 5   J.5   850 |

Exercise 2-5   *Preparing a trial balance*

The accounts of Norman Realty Company are listed below with their normal balances at September 30, 19X4. The accounts are listed in no particular order.

Account	Balance
Ken Norman, capital	$48,800
Advertising expense......................	650
Accounts payable........................	1,300
Sales commission revenue.................	16,000
Land	23,000
Note payable	25,000
Cash	7,000
Salary expense	3,000
Building.................................	45,000
Rent expense............................	2,000
Ken Norman, withdrawals	4,000
Utilities expense	400
Accounts receivable	5,500
Supplies expense	300
Supplies	250

Required

Prepare the company's trial balance at September 30, 19X4, listing accounts in proper sequence, as illustrated in the chapter. Supplies comes before Building and Land. List the expense with the largest balance first, the expense with the next largest balance second, and so on.

Exercise 2-6 *Journalizing transactions*

The first five transactions of Hoyt Repair Service have been posted to the company's accounts as follows:

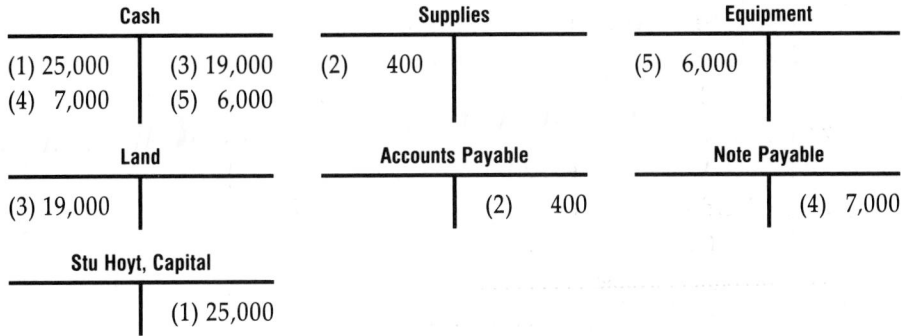

Cash		Supplies		Equipment	
(1) 25,000	(3) 19,000	(2) 400		(5) 6,000	
(4) 7,000	(5) 6,000				

Land		Accounts Payable		Note Payable	
(3) 19,000			(2) 400		(4) 7,000

Stu Hoyt, Capital	
	(1) 25,000

Required

Prepare the journal entries that served as the sources for the five transactions. Include an explanation for each entry as illustrated in the chapter.

Exercise 2-7 *Preparing a trial balance*

Prepare the trial balance of Hoyt Repair Service at September 30, 19X4, using the account data from the preceding exercise.

Exercise 2-8 *Correcting errors in a trial balance*

The trial balance of Walker Enterprises at November 30, 19X9, does not balance:

Cash.....................................	$ 6,000	
Accounts receivable	2,000	
Supplies...............................	600	
Land..................................	46,000	
Account payable		$ 3,000
Claudia Walker, capital.................		42,000
Service revenue........................		6,500
Salary expense........................	1,700	
Rent expense.........................	800	
Utilities expense	300	
Total................................	$57,400	$51,500

Investigation of the accounting records reveals that the bookkeeper:

1. Recorded a cash revenue transaction by debiting Cash for the correct amount of $5,000 but failed to record the credit to Service Revenue.
2. Posted a $1,000 credit to Accounts Payable as $100.
3. Did not record utilities expense or the related account payable in the amount of $200.
4. Understated Cash and Claudia Walker, Capital, by $400 each.

Required

Prepare the correct trial balance at November 30, complete with a heading. Journal entries are not required.

Exercise 2-9   *Recording transactions without a journal*

Open the following T-accounts: Cash; Accounts Receivable; Office Supplies; Office Furniture; Accounts Payable; Lisa Lenski, Capital; Lisa Lenski, Withdrawals; Service Revenue; Salary Expense; Rent Expense.

Record the following transactions directly in the T-accounts without using a journal. Use the letters to identify the transactions.

a. Lisa Lenski opened an accounting firm by investing $10,000 cash and office furniture valued at $7,400.
b. Paid monthly rent of $1,500.
c. Purchased office supplies on account, $800.
d. Paid employee salary, $1,800.
e. Paid $400 of the account payable created in *c.*
f. Performed accounting service on account, $1,700.
g. Withdrew $2,000 for personal use.

Exercise 2-10   *Preparing a trial balance*

After recording the transactions in Exercise 2-9, prepare the trial balance of Lisa Lenski, CPA, at May 31, 19X7.

Problems   *(Group A)*

Problem 2-1A   *Analyzing and journalizing transactions*

Paramount Theater Company owns movie theaters in the shopping centers of a major metropolitan area. Its owner, Robert Preston, engaged in the following business transactions:

Dec. 1   Preston invested $100,000 personal cash in the business by depositing this amount in a bank account entitled Paramount Theater Company.
      2   Paid $55,000 cash to purchase land for a theater site.
      5   Borrowed $300,000 from the bank to finance the construction of the new theater. Preston signed a note payable to the bank in the name of Paramount Theater Company.
      7   Received $20,000 cash from ticket sales and deposited this amount in the bank. (Label the revenue as Sales Revenue.)
     10   Purchased supplies for the older theaters on account, $1,700.
     15   Paid theater employee salaries, $2,800, and rent on a theater building, $1,800.
     15   Paid property tax expense on theater building, $1,200.
     16   Paid $800 on account.
     17   Withdrew $2,000 from the business to take his family to a nearby resort.

Paramount uses the following accounts: Cash; Supplies; Land; Accounts Payable; Notes Payable; Robert Preston, Capital; Robert Preston, Withdrawals; Sales Revenue; Salary Expense; Rent Expense; Property Tax Expense.

Required

1. Prepare an analysis of each business transaction of Paramount Theater Company, as shown for the December 1 transaction:

Dec. 1   The asset Cash is increased. Increases in assets are recorded by debits; therefore, debit Cash.

The owner's equity of the entity is increased. Increases in owner's equity are recorded by credits; therefore, credit Robert Preston, Capital.

2. Prepare the journal entry for each transaction. Explanations are not required.

Problem 2-2A   *Journalizing transactions, posting to T-accounts and preparing a trial balance*

Gwen Kraft opened a law office on September 3 of the current year. During the first month of operations, the business completed the following transactions:

Sep. 3   Kraft transferred $25,000 cash from her personal bank account to a business account entitled Gwen Kraft, Attorney.

4   Purchased supplies, $200, and furniture, $1,800, on account.

6   Performed legal services for a client and received $1,000 cash.

7   Paid $15,000 cash to acquire land for a future office site.

10   Defended a client in court, billed the client, and received his promise to pay the $900 within one week.

14   Paid for the furniture purchased September 4 on account.

15   Paid the secretary's salary, $600.

16   Paid the telephone bill, $120.

17   Received partial payment from client on account, $700.

20   Prepared legal documents for a client on account, $800.

24   Paid the water and electricity bills, $110.

28   Received $1,500 cash for assisting a client sell real estate.

30   Paid secretary's salary, $600.

30   Paid rent expense, $500.

30   Withdrew $2,000 for personal use.

Required

Open the following T-accounts: Cash; Accounts Receivable; Supplies; Furniture; Land; Accounts Payable; Gwen Kraft, Capital; Gwen Kraft, Withdrawals; Service Revenue; Salary Expense; Rent Expense; Utilities Expense.

1. Record each transaction in the journal, using the account titles given. Key each transaction by date. Explanations are not required.
2. Post the transactions to the ledger, using transaction dates as posting references in the ledger. Label the balance of each account *Bal.,* as shown in the chapter.
3. Prepare the trial balance of Gwen Kraft, Attorney, at September 30 of the current year.

Problem 2-3A   *Journalizing transactions, posting to accounts in four-column format, and preparing a trial balance*

The trial balance of the accounting practice of Rob Cheng, CPA, at February 14, 19X3, is shown at the top of the next page.

During the remainder of February, Cheng completed the following transactions:

Feb. 15   Cheng collected $2,000 cash from a client on account.

16   Performed tax services for a client on account, $700.

18   Paid utilities, $300.

20   Paid on account, $1,000.

21   Purchased supplies on account, $100.

21   Withdrew $1,200 for personal use.

21   Paid for a swimming pool for private residence, using personal funds, $13,000.

22   Received cash of $2,100 for audit work just completed.

28   Paid rent, $800.

28   Paid employees' salaries, $1,600.

Rob Cheng, CPA
Trial Balance
February 14, 19X3

Account Number	Account	Debit	Credit
11	Cash......................................	$ 4,000	
12	Accounts receivable	11,000	
13	Supplies.....................................	800	
14	Land..	18,600	
21	Accounts payable		$ 3,000
31	Rob Cheng, capital		29,000
32	Rob Cheng, withdrawals	1,200	
41	Service revenue..............................		6,200
51	Salary expense..............................	1,600	
52	Rent expense................................	800	
53	Utilities expense	200	
	Total.......................................	$38,200	$38,200

Required

1. Record the transactions that occurred during February 15 through 28 in *page* 3 of the journal. Include an explanation for each entry.

2. Open the ledger accounts listed in the trial balance, together with their balances at February 14. Use the four-column account format illustrated below. Enter *Bal.* (for previous balance) in the Item column, and place a check mark (✓) in the journal reference column for the February 14 balance, as illustrated for Cash:

Account Cash   Account No. 11

Date	Item	Jrnl. Ref.	Debit	Credit	Balance Debit	Balance Credit
Feb. 14	Bal.	✓			4,000	

Post the transactions to the ledger, using dates, account numbers, journal references, and posting references.

3. Prepare the trial balance of Rob Cheng, CPA, at February 28, 19X3.

Problem 2-4A   *Journalizing, posting to T-accounts, and preparing a trial balance*

Flaten Delivery Service completed the following transactions during its first month of operations:

a. Dick Flaten, the proprietor of the business, began operations by investing $5,000 cash and a truck valued at $10,000 in the business.

b. Paid $200 cash for supplies.

c. Used a company credit card to purchase $50 fuel for the delivery truck. (Credit Accounts Payable).

d. Performed delivery services for a customer and received $600 cash.

e. Completed a large delivery job, billed the customer $2,000, and received a promise to be paid the $2,000 within one week.
f. Paid employee salary, $800.
g. Received $900 cash for performing delivery services.
h. Purchased fuel for the truck on account, $40.
i. Received $2,000 cash from a customer on account.
j. Paid for advertising in the local newspaper, $170.
k. Paid utility bills, $100.
l. Purchased fuel for the truck, paying $30 with a company credit card.
m. Performed delivery services on account, $200.
n. Paid for repairs to the delivery truck, $110.
o. Paid employee salary, $800, and office rent, $200.
p. Paid $120 on account.
q. Withdrew $1,900 for personal use.

Required

1. Record each transaction in the journal, using the account titles given. Key each transaction by letter. Explanations are not required.
2. Open the following T-accounts: Cash; Accounts Receivable; Supplies; Delivery Truck; Accounts Payable; Dick Flaten, Capital; Dick Flaten, Withdrawals; Delivery Service Revenue; Salary Expense; Rent Expense; Advertising Expense; Fuel Expense; Repair Expense; Utilities Expense. Post the transactions to the ledger, keying transactions by letter. Label the balance of each account *Bal.*, as shown in the chapter. However, if an account has only one entry, it is not necessary to label the balance separately. If an account has a zero balance after posting, draw double underlines under the posted amounts.
3. Prepare the trial balance of Flaten Delivery Service, using the current date.

Problem 2-5A   *Correcting errors in a trial balance*

The following trial balance does not balance:

Family Counseling Services
Trial Balance
June 30, 19X2

Cash.	$ 2,000	
Accounts receivable	10,000	
Supplies.	900	
Office furniture	3,600	
Land.	26,000	
Accounts payable		$ 4,000
Note payable.		14,000
Lisa Vivaldi, capital.		22,000
Lisa Vivaldi, withdrawals.	2,000	
Counseling service revenue		6,500
Salary expense.	1,600	
Rent expense	1,000	
Advertising expense	500	
Utilities expense	300	
Property tax expense.	100	
Total.	$48,000	$46,500

The following errors were detected:

a. The cash balance is understated by $300.
b. Property tax expense of $500 is omitted from the trial balance.
c. Land should be listed in the amount of $25,000.
d. A $200 purchase of supplies on account was neither journalized nor posted.
e. A $2,800 credit to Counseling Service Revenue was not posted.
f. Rent expense of $200 was posted as a credit rather than a debit.
g. The balance of Advertising Expense is $600, but it was listed as $500 on the trial balance.
h. A $300 debit to Accounts Receivable was posted as $30.
i. The balance of Utilities Expense is overstated by $70.
j. A $400 debit to the Withdrawal account was posted as a credit to Lisa Vivaldi, Capital.

Required

Prepare the correct trial balance at June 30. Journal entries are not required.

Problem 2-6A   *Recording transactions directly in the ledger, preparing a trial balance*

Peg Howison started a consulting service and during the first month of operations completed the following selected transactions:

a. Howison began the business with an investment of $15,000 cash and a building valued at $75,000.
b. Borrowed $30,000 from the bank; signed a note payable.
c. Purchased office supplies on account, $1,300.
d. Paid $18,000 for office furniture.
e. Paid employee salary, $2,200.
f. Performed consulting service on account for client, $2,100.
g. Paid $800 of the account payable created in *c*.
h. Received a $900 bill for advertising expense that will be paid in the near future.
i. Performed consulting service for customers and received cash, $1,600.
j. Received cash on account, $1,200.
k. Paid the following cash expenses:
   (1) Rent on land, $700.
   (2) Utilities, $400.
l. Withdrew $3,500 for personal use.

Required

1. Open the following T-accounts: Cash; Accounts Receivable; Office Supplies; Office Furniture; Building; Accounts Payable; Note Payable; Peg Howison, Capital; Peg Howison, Withdrawals; Service Revenue; Salary Expense; Advertising Expense; Rent Expense; Utilities Expense.
2. Record the following transactions directly in the T-accounts without using a journal. Use the letters to identify the transactions.
3. Prepare the trial balance of Howison Consulting Service at June 30, 19X3.

(Group B)

Problem 2-1B   *Analyzing and journalizing transactions*

Roland Marks practices medicine under the business title Roland Marks, M.D. During April his medical practice engaged in the following transactions:

Apr. 1   Marks deposited $50,000 cash in the business bank account.

5   Borrowed $20,000 from the bank for business use. Marks signed a note payable to the bank in the name of the business.

9   Paid $25,000 cash to purchase land for an office site.

10   Purchased supplies on account, $1,200.

19   Paid $1,000 on account.

30   Revenues earned during the month included $6,000 cash and $5,000 on account.

30   Paid employee salaries ($2,400), office rent ($1,500), and utilities ($400).

30   Paid monthly rent on medical equipment, $700.

30   Withdrew $4,000 from the business to take his family on a trip.

Marks's business uses the following accounts: Cash; Accounts Receivable; Supplies; Land; Accounts Payable; Notes Payable; Roland Marks, Capital; Roland Marks, Withdrawals; Service Revenue; Salary Expense; Rent Expense; Utilities Expense.

Required

1. Prepare an analysis of each business transaction of Roland Marks, M.D., as shown for the April 1 transaction:

Apr. 1   The asset Cash is increased. Increases in assets are recorded by debits; therefore, debit Cash.

The owner's equity is increased. Increases in owner's equity are recorded by credits; therefore, credit Roland Marks, Capital.

2. Prepare the journal entry for each transaction. Explanations are not required.

Problem 2-2B   *Journalizing transactions, posting to T-accounts, and preparing a trial balance*

Nancy Katz opened a law office on January 2 of the current year. During the first month of operations the business completed the following transactions:

Jan. 2   Katz deposited $45,000 cash in a business bank account entitled Nancy Katz, Attorney.

3   Purchased supplies, $300, and furniture, $2,100, on account.

4   Performed legal services for a client and received cash, $1,500.

7   Paid cash to acquire land for a future office site, $22,000.

11   Defended a client in court, billed the client, and received his promise to pay the $800 within one week.

15   Paid secretary salary, $650.

16   Paid for the furniture purchased January 3 on account.

17   Paid the telephone bill, $110.

18   Received partial payment from client on account, $400.

19   Prepared legal documents for a client on account, $600.

22   Paid the water and electricity bills, $130.

29   Received $1,800 cash for helping a client sell real estate.

31   Paid secretary salary, $650.

31   Paid rent expense, $700.

31   Withdrew $2,200 for personal use.

Required

Open the following T-accounts: Cash; Accounts Receivable; Supplies; Furniture; Land; Accounts Payable; Nancy Katz, Capital; Nancy Katz, Withdrawals; Service Revenue; Salary Expense; Rent Expense; Utilities Expense.

1. Record each transaction in the journal, using the account titles given. Key each transaction by date. Explanations are not required.

2. Post the transactions to the ledger, using transaction dates as posting references in the ledger. Label the balance of each account *Bal.* as shown in the chapter.
3. Prepare the trial balance of Nancy Katz, Attorney, at January 31 of the current year.

Problem 2-3B   *Journalizing transactions, posting to accounts in four-column format and preparing a trial balance*

The trial balance of the accounting practice of Ralph Cohen, CPA, at November 15, 19X3, was

Ralph Cohen, CPA
Trial Balance
November 15, 19X3

Account Number	Account	Debit	Credit
11	Cash	$ 5,000	
12	Accounts receivable	8,000	
13	Supplies	600	
14	Land	38,000	
21	Accounts payable..............		$ 4,400
31	Ralph Cohen, capital		45,000
32	Ralph Cohen, withdrawals	2,100	
41	Service revenue		7,100
51	Salary expense	1,800	
52	Rent expense	700	
53	Utilities expense..............	300	
	Total	$56,500	$56,500

During the remainder of November, Cohen completed the following transactions:

Nov. 16   Collected $4,000 cash from a client on account.
    17   Performed tax services for a client on account, $1,200.
    19   Paid utilities, $200.
    21   Paid on account, $2,600.
    22   Purchased supplies on account, $200.
    23   Withdrew $2,100 for personal use.
    23   Paid for the renovation of private residence, $55,000.
    24   Received $1,900 cash for audit work just completed.
    30   Paid rent, $700.
    30   Paid employees' salaries, $1,800.

Required

1. Record the transactions that occurred during November 16 through 30 in page 6 of the journal. Include an explanation for each entry.
2. Post the transactions to the ledger, using dates, account numbers, journal references, and posting references. Open the ledger accounts listed in the trial balance together with their balances at November 15. Use the four-column account format illustrated below. Enter *Bal.* (for previous balance) in the Item column, and place a check mark (✓) in the journal reference column for the November 15 balance, as illustrated for Cash:

Account Cash   **Account No. 11**

Date	Item	Jrnl. Ref.	Debit	Credit	Balance Debit	Balance Credit
Nov. 15	Bal.	✓			5,000	

3. Prepare the trial balance of Ralph Cohen, CPA, at November 30, 19X3.

Problem 2-4B *Journalizing, posting to T-accounts, and preparing a trial balance*

Marquardt Delivery Service began operations during May of the current year. During a short period thereafter, the entity engaged in the following transactions:

a. Rube Marquardt, the owner, deposited $3,500 cash in a bank account entitled Marquardt Delivery Service and also invested in the business a delivery truck valued at $8,000.
b. Purchased $40 fuel for the delivery truck, using a business credit card.
c. Paid $100 cash for supplies.
d. Completed a delivery job and received cash, $700.
e. Performed delivery services on account, $3,200.
f. Purchased advertising leaflets for cash, $200.
g. Paid the office manager salary, $950.
h. Received $1,000 cash for performing delivery services.
i. Received cash from customer on account, $1,800.
j. Purchased used office furniture on account, $600.
k. Paid office utility bills, $120.
l. Purchased $70 fuel on account for the truck.
m. Completed a delivery job and received the customer's promise to pay the amount due, $500, within ten days.
n. Paid cash to creditor on account, $200.
o. Paid $250 for repairs to the delivery truck.
p. Paid office manager the salary of $950 and office rent of $250.
q. Withdrew $1,700 for personal use.

Required

1. Record each transaction in the journal, using the account titles given. Key each transaction by letter. Explanations are not required.
2. Open the following T-accounts: Cash; Accounts Receivable; Supplies; Delivery Truck; Office Furniture; Accounts Payable; R. Marquardt, Capital; R. Marquardt, Withdrawals; Delivery Service Revenue; Salary Expense; Rent Expense; Repair Expense; Advertising Expense; Utilities Expense; Fuel Expense. Post the transactions to the ledger, keying transactions by letter. Label the balance of each account *Bal.* as shown in the chapter. However, if an account only has one entry, it is not necessary to label the balance separately.
3. Prepare the trial balance of Marquardt Delivery Service, using the current date.

Problem 2-5B *Correcting errors in a trial balance.*

The trial balance on the following page does not balance.

The following errors were detected:

a. The cash balance is overstated by $400.
b. Office maintenance expense of $200 is omitted from the trial balance.

Jackson Management Consulting
Trial Balance
October 31, 19X1

Cash..................................	$ 3,800	
Accounts receivable	2,000	
Supplies.............................	500	
Office furniture	2,300	
Land................................	46,800	
Accounts payable		$ 2,000
Note payable.........................		18,300
Pamela Jackson, capital.		32,100
Pamela Jackson, withdrawals.............	3,700	
Consulting service revenue.		4,900
Salary expense........................	1,000	
Rent expense.........................	600	
Advertising expense	400	
Utilities expense	200	
Property tax..........................	100	
Total................................	$61,400	$57,300

c. Rent expense of $200 was posted as a credit rather than a debit.

d. The balance of Advertising Expense is $300, but it is listed as $400 on the trial balance.

e. A $600 debit to Accounts Receivable was posted as $60.

f. The balance of Utilities Expense is understated by $60.

g. A $500 debit to the withdrawal account was posted as a credit to Pamela Jackson, Capital.

h. A $100 purchase of supplies on account was neither journalized nor posted.

i. A $4,800 credit to Consulting Service Revenue was not posted.

j. Office furniture should be listed in the amount of $1,300.

Required

Prepare the correct trial balance at October 31. Journal entries are not required.

Problem 2-6B   *Recording transactions directly in the ledger, preparing a trial balance*

Jack Montague started a cable television service and during the first month of operations completed the following selected transactions:

a. Montague began the business with an investment of $30,000 cash and a building valued at $65,000.

b. Borrowed $25,000 from the bank; signed a note payable.

c. Paid $32,000 for transmitting equipment.

d. Purchased office supplies on account, $400.

e. Paid employee salary, $1,300.

f. Received $500 for cable TV service performed for customers.

g. Sold cable service to customers on account, $2,300.

h. Paid $100 of the account payable created in *d*.

i. Received a $600 bill for utility expense that will be paid in the near future.

j. Received cash on account, $1,100.

k. Paid the following cash expenses:
   (1) Rent on land, $1,000.
   (2) Advertising, $800.
l. Withdrew $2,600 for personal use.

Required

1. Open the following T-accounts: Cash; Accounts Receivable; Office Supplies; Transmitting Equipment; Building; Accounts Payable; Note Payable; Jack Montague, Capital; Jack Montague, Withdrawals; Service Revenue; Salary Expense; Rent Expense; Advertising Expense; Utilities Expense.
2. Record the following transactions directly in the T-accounts without using a journal. Use the letters to identify the transactions.
3. Prepare the trial balance of Montague Cable TV Service at January 31, 19X7.

Decision Problem

Recording Transactions Directly in the Ledger, Preparing a Trial Balance, and Measuring Net Income or Loss

You have been requested by a friend named Milton Abel to give advice on the effects that certain business transactions will have on the entity he plans to start. Time is short, so you will not be able to do all the detailed procedures of journalizing and posting. Instead, you must analyze the transactions without the use of a journal. Abel will continue the business only if he can expect to earn monthly net income of $2,750. Assume the following transactions have occurred:

a. Abel deposited $6,000 cash in a business bank account.
b. Borrowed $4,000 cash from the bank and signed a note payable due within one year.
c. Paid $300 cash for supplies.
d. Purchased advertising in the local newspaper for cash, $800.
e. Purchased office furniture on account, $1,500.
f. Paid the following cash expenses for one month: secretary salary, $1,400; office rent, $400; utilities, $300; interest, $50.
g. Earned revenue on account for one month, $3,300.
h. Earned revenue and received $2,500 cash.
i. Collected cash from customers on account, $1,500.
j. Paid on account, $1,000.

Required

1. Open the following T-accounts: Cash; Accounts Receivable; Supplies; Furniture; Accounts Payable; Notes Payable; Milton Abel, Capital; Service Revenue; Salary Expense; Advertising Expense; Rent Expense; Utilities Expense; Interest Expense.
2. Record the transactions directly in the accounts without using a journal. Key each transaction by letter.
3. Prepare a trial balance at the current date. List expenses with the largest first, the next largest second, and so on. The business name will be Abel Apartment Locators.
4. Compute the amount of net income or net loss for this first month of operations. Would you recommend that Abel continue in business?

Financial Statement Problem

Journalizing Transactions

This problem helps to develop skill in recording transactions by using an actual company's account titles. Refer to the Gulf+Western financial statements in Appendix C. Assume Gulf+Western completed the following selected transactions during August 1987:

Aug. 5   Earned revenues on account, $40,000.

9   Borrowed $500,000 by signing a note payable (long-term debt).

12   Purchased equipment on account, $70,000.

17   Paid $120,000, which represents payment of a $100,000 current maturity of long-term debt, plus interest expense of $20,000.

19   Earned revenues and immediately received cash of $16,000.

22   Collected the cash on account that was earned on August 5.

24   Paid rent of $14,000 for three months in advance.

28   Received a home-office electricity bill for $1,000, which will be paid in September (this is a general and administrative expense).

30   Paid off half the account payable created on August 12.

Required

Journalize these transactions using the following account titles taken from the financial statements of Gulf+Western: Cash; Trade Receivables; Prepaid Expenses; Equipment; Current Maturities of Long-term Debt; Trade Accounts Payable; Long-Term Debt; Revenues; Selling, General, and Administrative Expenses; Interest Expense. Explanations are not required.

Answers to Self-Study Questions

1. a	5. c	8.	b ($6,800 = $2,500 + $4,300)
2. b	6. a	9.	b
3. c	7. a	10.	d
4. d			

3

Measuring Business Income: The Adjusting Process

LEARNING OBJECTIVES
After studying this chapter, you should be able to

1 Distinguish accrual-basis accounting from cash-basis accounting

2 Explain and apply the revenue and matching principles

3 Make the typical adjusting entries at the end of the accounting period

4 Prepare an adjusted trial balance

5 Prepare the financial statements from the adjusted trial balance

The primary goal of business is to earn a profit. By providing food and other goods at a reasonable price, a grocery store benefits its customers. The benefit to the store owner is the excess of the business's revenues over its expenses—net income. Gary Lyon, the CPA whose accounting practice we discussed in the earlier chapters, earns business income by providing accounting services for clients. Regardless of the type of activity, the profit motive increases the owner's drive to carry on the business.

At the end of each accounting period, the accountant prepares the entity's financial statements. The period may be a month, three months, six months, or a full year. Whatever the length of the period, the end accounting product is the same, the financial statements. And the most important single amount in these statements is the net income or net loss—the profit or loss—for the period. A double-entry accounting system produces not only the income statement but the other financial statements as well.

An important step in financial statement preparation is the trial balance that we discussed in Chapter 2. The trial balance includes the effects of the transactions that occurred during the period—the cash collections, purchases of assets, payments of bills, sales of assets, and so on. To measure its income properly, however, a business must do some additional accounting at the end of the period to bring the records up to date before preparing the financial statements. This process is called *adjusting the books,* and it consists of making special entries called *adjusting entries.* This chapter focuses primarily on these adjusting entries to help you better understand the nature of business income.

Accountants have devised concepts and principles to guide the measurement of business income. Chief among these are the concepts of accrual accounting, the accounting period, the revenue principle, and the matching principle. In this chapter, we apply these concepts and principles to measure the income and prepare the financial statements of Gary Lyon's business for the month of April.

Accrual-Basis Accounting versus Cash-Basis Accounting

OBJECTIVE 1

Distinguish accrual-basis accounting from cash-basis accounting

There are two widely used bases of accounting: the accrual basis and the cash basis. In **accrual-basis accounting,** an accountant recognizes the impact of a business event as it occurs. When the business performs a service, makes a sale, or incurs an expense, the accountant enters the transaction into the books, whether or not cash has been received or paid. In **cash-basis accounting,** however, the accountant does not record a transaction until cash is received or paid. GAAP requires that a business use the accrual basis. This means that the accountant records revenues as they are *earned* and expenses as they are *incurred*—not necessarily when cash changes hands.

Using accrual-basis accounting, Gary Lyon records revenue when he performs services for a client on account. Lyon has earned the revenue at that time because his efforts have generated an account receivable, a legal claim against the client for whom he did the work. By contrast, if Gary Lyon used cash-basis accounting, he would not record revenue at the time he performed the service. He would wait until he received cash.

Why does GAAP require that businesses use the accrual basis? What advantage does accrual-basis accounting offer? Suppose Gary Lyon's accounting period ends after he has earned the revenue but before he has collected the money due him. If he used the cash-basis method, his financial statements would not include this revenue or the related account receivable. As a result, the financial statements would be misleading. Revenue and the asset Accounts Receivable would be understated, and thus his business would look less successful than it actually is. If he wants to get a bank loan to expand his practice, the understated revenue and asset figures might hurt his chances.

Gary Lyon, using accrual-basis accounting, treats expenses in a like manner. For instance, salary expense includes amounts paid to employees plus any amount owed to employees but not yet paid. Lyon's use of the employee's service, not the payment of cash to the employee, brings about the expense. Under cash-basis accounting, Lyon would record the expense only when he actually paid the employee.

Suppose Gary Lyon owes his secretary a salary and the financial statements are drawn up before Lyon pays. Expenses and liabilities would be understated, so the business would look more successful than it really is. This incomplete information would not provide an accurate accounting to potential creditors.

As these examples show, accrual accounting provides more complete information than does cash-basis accounting. This is important because the more complete the data, the better equipped decision makers are to reach intelligent conclusions about the firm's financial health and future prospects. Three concepts used in accrual accounting are the accounting period, the revenue principle, and the matching principle.

The Accounting Period

The only way to know for certain how successfully a business has operated is to close its doors, sell all its assets, pay the liabilities, and return any leftover cash to the owner. This process, called liquidation, is the same as going out of business. Obviously, it is not practical for accountants to measure business income in this manner. Instead, businesses need periodic reports on their progress. Accountants slice time into small segments and prepare financial statements for specific periods. Until a business liquidates, the amounts reported in its financial statements must be regarded as estimates.

The most basic accounting period is one year, and virtually all businesses prepare annual financial statements. For about 60 percent of large companies in a recent survey, the annual accounting period runs the calendar year from January 1 through December 31. Other companies use what is called a *fiscal year,* which ends on some date other than December 31. The year-end date is usually the low point in business activity for the year. Depending on the type of business, the fiscal year may end on April 30, July 31, or some other date. Retailers are a notable example. Traditionally, they have used a fiscal year ending on January 31 because the low point in their business activity has followed the after-Christmas sales during January.

Companies cannot wait until the end of the year to gauge their progress. The manager of a business wants to know how well the business is doing each month, each quarter, and each half year. Outsiders such as lenders also demand current information about the business. So companies also prepare financial statements for *interim* periods, which are less than a year. Monthly financial statements are common, and a series of monthly statements can be combined for quarterly and semiannual periods. Most of the discussions in this book are based on an annual accounting period. However, the procedures and statements can also be applied to interim periods as well.

Revenue Principle

The **revenue principle** tells accountants (1) *when* to record revenue and (2) the *amount* of revenue to record. When we speak of "recording" something in accounting, the act of recording the item naturally leads to posting to the ledger accounts and preparing the trial balance and the financial statements. Although the financial statements are the end product of accounting and what accountants are most concerned about, our discussions often focus on recording the entry in the journal because that is where the accounting process starts.

The general principle guiding *when* to record revenue says to record revenue when, but not before, it has been earned. In most cases, revenue is earned when the business has delivered a completed good or service to the customer. The business has done everything required by the agreement, including transferring the item to the customer. Two situations that provide guidance on when to record revenue follow. The first situation illustrates when *not* to record revenue. Situation 2 illustrates when revenue should be recorded.

Situation 1—Do not record revenue. A client of another CPA expresses her intention to transfer her tax work to Gary Lyon. Should Lyon record any revenue based on this intention? The answer is no because no transaction has occurred.

Situation 2—Record revenue. Next month Gary Lyon consults with this client and tailors a business plan to her goals. After transferring the business plan to the client, Lyon should record revenue. If the client pays for this service immediately, Lyon will debit Cash. If the service is performed on account, Lyon will debit Accounts Receivable. In either case, Lyon should record revenue by crediting the Service Revenue account.

The general principle guiding the *amount* of revenue says to record revenue equal to the cash value of the goods or the service transferred to the customer. Suppose that in order to obtain a new client, Gary Lyon performs accounting

OBJECTIVE 2

Explain and apply the revenue and matching principles

service for the price of $500. Ordinarily, Lyon would have charged $600 for this service. How much revenue should Lyon record? The answer is $500 because that was the cash value of the transaction. Lyon will not receive the full value of $600, so that is not the amount of revenue to record. He will receive only $500 cash, and that pinpoints the amount of revenue earned.

Matching Principle

The **matching principle** is the basis for recording expenses. Recall that expenses, such as rent, utilities, and advertising, are the costs of operating a business. Expenses are the costs of assets that are used up in the earning of revenue. The matching principle directs accountants (1) to identify all expenses incurred during the accounting period, (2) to measure the expenses, and (3) to "match" them against the revenues earned during that same span of time. To "match" expenses against revenues means to subtract the expenses from the revenues in order to compute net income or net loss.

There is a natural link between revenues and some types of expenses. Accountants follow the matching principle by first identifying the revenues of a period and the expenses that can be linked to particular revenues. For example, a business that pays sales commissions to its sales persons will have commission expense if the employees make sales. If they make no sales, the business has no commission expense.

Other expenses are not so easy to link with particular sales. Monthly rent expense occurs, for example, regardless of the revenues earned during the period. The matching principle directs accountants to identify these types of expenses with a particular time period, such as a month or a year. If Gary Lyon employs a secretary at a monthly salary of $1,900, the business will record salary expense of $1,900 each month.

Because financial statements appear at definite intervals, there must be some cutoff date for the necessary information. Most entities engage in so many transactions that some are bound to spill over into more than a single accounting period. Gary Lyon prepares monthly statements for his business at April 30. How does he handle a transaction that begins in April but ends in May? How does he bring the accounts up to date for preparing the financial statements? To answer these questions, accountants use adjusting entries.

Adjustments to the Accounts

At the end of the period, the accountant prepares the financial statements. This end-of-the-period process begins with the trial balance that lists the accounts and their balances after the period's transaction's have been recorded in the journal and posted to the accounts in the ledger. Exhibit 3-1 is the trial balance of Gary Lyon's accounting practice at April 30, 19X1.

This *unadjusted* trial balance includes some new accounts that will be explained in this section. It lists most, but not all, of the revenue and the expenses of Lyon's accounting practice for the month of April. These trial balance amounts are incomplete because they omit certain revenue and expense transactions that affect more than one accounting period. That is why it is called an *unadjusted* trial

EXHIBIT 3-1 *Unadjusted Trial Balance*

Gary Lyon, CPA Unadjusted Trial Balance April 30, 19X1		
Cash	$24,800	
Accounts receivable	2,250	
Supplies	700	
Prepaid rent	3,000	
Furniture	16,500	
Accounts payable		$13,100
Unearned service revenue		450
Gary Lyon, capital		31,250
Gary Lyon, withdrawals	3,200	
Service revenue		7,000
Salary expense	950	
Utilities expense	400	
Total	$51,800	$51,800

balance. In most cases, however, we refer to it simply as the trial balance, without the "unadjusted" label.

Under the cash basis of accounting, there would be no need for adjustments to the accounts because all April cash transactions would have been recorded. The accrual basis requires adjusting entries at the end of the period in order to produce correct balances for the financial statements. To see why, consider the Supplies account in Exhibit 3-1.

Lyon's accounting practice uses supplies in providing accounting services for clients during the month. This reduces the quantity of supplies on hand and thus constitutes an expense, just like salary expense or rent expense. Gary Lyon does not bother to record his daily expense, and it is not worth his while to record supplies expense more than once a month. It is time consuming to make hourly, daily, or even weekly journal entries to record the expense for the use of supplies. So how does he account for supplies expense?

By the end of the month, the Supplies balance is not correct. The balance represents the amount of supplies on hand at the start of the month plus any supplies purchased during the month. This balance fails to take into account the supplies used (supplies expense) during the accounting period. It is necessary, then, to subtract the month's expenses from the amount of supplies listed on the trial balance. The resulting new adjusted balance measures the cost of supplies that are still on hand at April 30. This is the correct amount of supplies to report on the balance sheet. Adjusting entries in this way will bring the accounts up to date.

Adjusting entries assign revenues to the period in which they are earned and expenses to the period in which they are incurred. They are needed (a) to measure properly the period's income and (b) to bring related asset and liability accounts to correct balances for the financial statements. For example, an adjusting entry is needed to transfer the amount of supplies used during the period from the asset account Supplies to the expense account Supplies Expense. The adjusting entry updates both the Supplies asset account and the Supplies Expense account. This achieves accurate measures of assets and expenses. Adjusting entries, which are the key to the accrual basis of accounting, are made before preparing the financial statements.

The end-of-period process of updating the accounts is called *adjusting the accounts, making the adjusting entries,* or *adjusting the books.* Adjusting entries can be divided into five categories:

1. Prepaid expenses
2. Depreciation
3. Accrued expenses
4. Accrued revenues
5. Unearned revenues

Prepaid Expenses

Prepaid expenses is a category of miscellaneous assets that typically expire or are used up in the near future. Prepaid rent and prepaid insurance are examples of prepaid expenses. They are called prepaid expenses because they are expenses that are paid in advance. Salary expense and utilities expense, among others, are *not* prepaid expenses because they are not paid in advance.

Prepaid Rent. Landlords usually require tenants to pay rent in advance. This prepayment creates an asset for the renter because that person has purchased the future benefit of using the rented item. Suppose Gary Lyon prepays three months' rent on April 1, 19X1, after negotiating a lease for his business office. If the lease specifies monthly rental amounts of $1,000 each, the entry to record the payment for three months is a debit to the asset account, Prepaid Rent, as follows:

Apr. 1	Prepaid Rent ($1,000 × 3)............................	3,000	
	Cash		3,000
	Paid three months' rent in advance.		

After posting, Prepaid Rent appears as follows:

Prepaid Rent	
Apr. 1 3,000	

The trial balance at April 30, 19X1, lists Prepaid Rent as an asset with a debit balance of $3,000. Throughout April, the Prepaid Rent account maintains this beginning balance as shown in Exhibit 3-1.

At April 30 Prepaid Rent should be adjusted to remove from its balance the amount of the asset that has *expired,* which is one month's worth of the prepayment. By definition, the amount of an asset that has expired is *expense.* The adjusting entry transfers one-third, or $1,000 ($3,000 × $\frac{1}{3}$), of the debit balance from Prepaid Rent to Rent Expense. The debit side of the entry records an increase in Rent Expense, and the credit records a decrease in the asset Prepaid Rent.

OBJECTIVE 3

Make the typical adjusting entries at the end of the accounting period

Apr. 30	Rent Expense ($3,000 × $\frac{1}{3}$)	1,000	
	Prepaid Rent		1,000
	To record rent expense.		

After posting, Prepaid Rent and Rent Expense appear as follows:

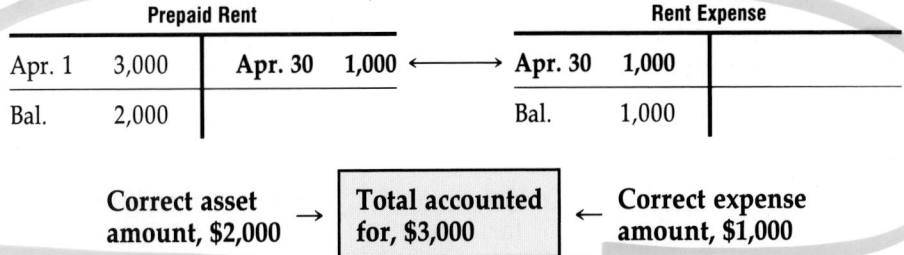

Prepaid Rent				Rent Expense	
Apr. 1	3,000	Apr. 30	1,000 ⟷ →	Apr. 30	1,000
Bal.	2,000			Bal.	1,000

Correct asset amount, $2,000 → | **Total accounted for, $3,000** | ← **Correct expense amount, $1,000**

The full $3,000 has been accounted for: two thirds is asset, and one-third is expense. This is correct because two thirds of the asset remains for future use, and one third of the prepayment has expired. Recording this expense illustrates the matching principle. The same analysis applies to a prepayment of three months' insurance premiums. The only difference is in the account titles, which would be Prepaid Insurance and Insurance Expense instead of Prepaid Rent and Rent Expense. This adjusting entry illustrates the matching principle.

Supplies.   Supplies are accounted for in the same way as prepaid expenses. On April 2 Gary Lyon paid cash of $700 for office supplies:

Apr. 2	Supplies	700	
	Cash		700
	Paid cash for supplies.		

Assume that Lyon purchased no additional supplies during April. The April 30 trial balance, therefore, lists Supplies with a $700 debit balance, as shown in Exhibit 3-1.

During April, Lyon used supplies in performing services for clients. The cost of the supplies used is the measure of *supplies expense* for the month.

Lyon does not keep a continuous record of supplies used each day or each week during April. To keep these detailed records would be impractical. Instead, to measure his firm's supplies expense during April, Gary Lyon counts the supplies on hand at the end of the month. This is the amount of the asset still available to the business. Assume the count indicates that supplies costing $400 remain. Subtracting the entity's $400 supplies on hand at the end of April from the cost of supplies available during April ($700) measures supplies expense during the month ($300).

Cost of asset available during the period	−	Cost of asset on hand at the end of the period	=	Cost of asset used (expense) during the period
$700	−	$400	=	$300

The April 30 adjusting entry to update the Supplies account and to record the supplies expense for the month debits the expense and credits the asset as follows:

Apr. 30	Supplies Expense ($700 − $400).......................	300	
	Supplies		300
	To record supplies expense.		

After posting, the Supplies and Supplies Expense accounts appear as follows:

Supplies					Supplies Expense		
Apr. 2	700	Apr. 30	300	⟷	Apr. 30	300	
Bal.	400				Bal.	300	

Correct asset → Total accounted ← Correct expense
amount, $400   for, $700   amount, $300

The Supplies account then enters the month of May with a $400 balance, and the adjustment process is repeated each month.

Depreciation and Plant Assets

The logic of the accrual basis is probably best illustrated by how businesses account for plant assets. **Plant assets** are long-lived assets, such as land, buildings, furniture, machinery, and equipment used in the operations of the business. As one accountant said, "All assets but land are on a march to the junkyard." That is, all plant assets but land decline in usefulness as they age. This decline is an *expense* to the business. Accountants systematically spread the cost of each plant asset, except land, over the years of its useful life. This process is called the recording of **depreciation.** The concept underlying accounting for plant assets and depreciation expense is the same as for prepaid expenses. In both cases the business purchases an asset that wears out. As the asset is used, more and more of its cost is transferred from the asset account to the expense account. The only difference between prepaid expenses and plant assets is the length of time it takes for the asset to lose its usefulness. Prepaid expenses usually expire within a year. Most plant assets remain useful for a number of years.

Consider Gary Lyon's accounting practice. Suppose that on April 3 Lyon purchased furniture on account for $16,500:

Apr. 3	Furniture	16,500	
	Accounts Payable		16,500
	Purchased office furniture on account.		

After posting, the Furniture account appears as follows:

Furniture	
Apr. 3 16,500	

Using cash-basis accounting, Gary Lyon would enter in the ledger the entire $16,500 as an expense for April. As a result, his financial statements for that month would be extremely misleading. Income would be significantly understated. Also, the cash-basis approach fails to take into consideration that the asset will be of benefit to Lyon's business in future accounting periods.

In accrual-basis accounting, an asset is recorded when the furniture is acquired. Then, a portion of the asset's cost is transferred from the asset account to Depreciation Expense each period that the asset is used. This method matches the asset's expense to the revenue of the period, which is an application of the matching principle. We discuss how accountants determine the amount of depreciation for each accounting period in Chapter 10. For now, we need concern ourselves only with the accounts involved in recording depreciation.

Let's assume the depreciation for the month of April is $275, computed by dividing the asset's cost by its useful life. Depreciation expense for April is recorded by the following entry:

Apr. 30	Depreciation Expense	275	
	Accumulated Depreciation–Furniture		275
	To record depreciation on furniture.		

You may be wondering why Accumulated Depreciation is credited instead of Furniture. The reason is that the original cost of the plant asset is an objective measurement, and that figure remains in the original asset account as long as the business uses the asset. Accountants may refer to that account if they need to know how much the asset cost. This information may be useful in a decision about whether to replace the furniture and the amount to pay. The amount of depreciation, however, is an *estimate*. Accountants use the **Accumulated Depreciation** account to show the cumulative sum of all depreciation expense from the date of acquiring the asset.

Accumulated Depreciation is a **contra asset** account, which means an asset account with a credit balance. A **contra account** has two distinguishing characteristics: (1) it always has a companion account, and (2) its normal balance is opposite that of the companion account. In this case, Accumulated Depreciation accompanies Furniture. It appears in the ledger directly after Furniture. Furniture has a debit balance, and therefore Accumulated Depreciation has a credit balance. All contra asset accounts have credit balances.

A business carries an accumulated depreciation account for each depreciable asset. If a business has a building and a machine, for example, it will carry the accounts Accumulated Depreciation–Building, and Accumulated Depreciation–Machine.

After posting the depreciation entry, the Furniture, Accumulated Depreciation, and Depreciation Expense accounts are

Furniture		Accumulated Depreciation Furniture		Depreciation Expense	
Apr. 3 16,500			Apr. 30 275	Apr. 30 275	
Bal. 16,500			Bal. 275	Bal. 275	

The balance sheet shows the relationship between Furniture and Accumulated Depreciation. The balance of Accumulated Depreciation is subtracted from the balance of Furniture. The net amount of a plant asset (cost minus accumulated depreciation) is called its **book value,** as shown below for Furniture.

Plant Assets:

Furniture.................................	$16,500
Less Accumulated depreciation.............	275
Book value	$16,225

Because Accumulated Depreciation is subtracted from its companion account to determine the asset's book value, Accumulated Depreciation is also called a *valuation* account.

Suppose Lyon's accounting practice owns a building that cost $48,000 and on which annual depreciation is $2,400. The amount of depreciation for one month

EXHIBIT 3-2 *Plant Assets on the Balance Sheet (April 30)*

Plant assets:		
Furniture	$16,500	
Less Accumulated depreciation....	275	$16,225
Building	48,000	
Less Accumulated depreciation....	200	47,800
Book value of plant assets...........		$64,025

would be $200 ($2,400/12), and the entry to record depreciation for April is

Apr. 30	Depreciation Expense–Building	200	
	Accumulated Depreciation–Building		200
	To record depreciation on building.		

The balance sheet at April 30 would report Lyon's plant assets as shown in Exhibit 3-2. Now, however, let's return to Gary Lyon's actual situation.

Accrued Expenses

Businesses often incur expenses before they pay cash because payment is not due until later. Consider an employee's salary. The employer's salary expense and salary payable grow as the employee works, so the liability is said to *accrue.* Another example is interest expense on a note payable. Interest accrues as the clock ticks. The term **accrued expenses** refers to an expense that the business has incurred but has not yet paid.

It is time consuming to make hourly, daily, or even weekly journal entries to accrue expenses. Consequently, the accountant waits until the end of the period. Then an adjusting entry brings each expense (and related liability) up to date just before the financial statements are prepared.

Salary Expense. Most companies pay their employees at set times. Suppose Gary Lyon pays his employee a monthly salary of $1,900, half on the 15th and half on the last day of the month. Here is a calendar for April that has paydays circled:

APRIL

Sun.	Mon.	Tue.	Wed.	Thur.	Fri.	Sat.
					1	2
3	4	5	6	7	8	9
10	11	12	13	14	(15)	16
17	18	19	20	21	22	23
24	25	26	27	28	29	(30)

Assume that if either payday falls on a weekend, Lyon pays the employee on the following Monday. During April Lyon paid his employee's first half-month salary of $950 on Friday, April 15, and recorded the following entry:

Apr. 15	Salary Expense.....................................	950	
	Cash		950
	To pay salary.		

After posting, the Salary Expense account is

Salary Expense	
Apr. 15 950	

The trial balance at April 30 (Exhibit 3-1) includes Salary Expense, with its debit balance of $950. Because April 30, the second payday of the month, falls on a Saturday, the second half-month amount of $950 will be paid on Monday, May 2. Without an adjusting entry, this second $950 amount is not included in the April 30 trial balance amount for Salary Expense. Therefore, at April 30 Lyon adjusts for additional *salary expense* and *salary payable* of $950 by recording an increase in each of these accounts as follows:

Apr. 30	Salary Expense......................................	950	
	Salary Payable..................................		950
	To accrue salary expense.		

After posting, the Salary Expense and Salary Payable accounts appear as follows:

Salary Expense			Salary Payable		
Apr. 15	950			**Apr. 30**	**950**
Apr. 30	**950**			Bal.	950
Bal.	1,900				

The accounts at April 30 now contain the complete salary information for the month. The expense account has a full month's salary, and the liability account shows the portion that the business still owes.

Lyon will record the payment of this liability on May 2 by debiting Salary Payable and crediting Cash for $950. This payment entry does not affect April or May expenses because the April expense was recorded on April 15 and April 30. May expense will be recorded in a like manner. All accrued expenses are recorded with similar entries—a debit to the appropriate expense account and a credit to the related liability account.

Accrued Revenues

Businesses often earn revenue before they receive the cash because payment is not due until later. A revenue that has been earned but not yet received in cash is called an **accrued revenue**. Assume Gary Lyon is hired on April 15 by Guerrero Construction Company to perform services on a monthly basis. Under this agreement, Guerrero will pay Lyon $500 monthly, with the first payment on May 15. During April, Lyon will earn half a month's fee, $250. On April 30 he makes the following adjusting entry to record an increase in Accounts Receivable and Service Revenue:

Apr. 30	Accounts Receivable ($500 X ½)	250	
	Service Revenue................................		250
	To accrue service revenue.		

Recall that Accounts Receivable has an unadjusted balance of $2,250, and the

Service Revenue unadjusted balance is $7,000 (Exhibit 3-1). Posting this adjusting entry has the following effects on these two accounts:

Accounts Receivable			Service Revenue		
	2,250				7,000
Apr. 30	250			Apr. 30	250
Bal.	2,500			Bal.	7,250

This adjusting entry illustrates accrual accounting and the revenue principle in action. Without the adjustment, Lyon's financial statements would be misleading. All accrued revenues are accounted for similarly — by debiting a receivable and crediting a revenue.

Unearned Revenues

Some businesses collect cash from customers in advance of doing work for the customer. This creates a liability called **unearned revenue.** The liability arises because the business receiving cash in advance is obligated to provide a product or a service in the future. Only when the job is completed will the business have earned the revenue. Suppose Baldwin Computing Service Center engages Lyon's services, agreeing to pay him $450 monthly, beginning immediately. If Baldwin makes the first payment on April 20, Lyon records this increase in the business's liabilities by recording:

Apr. 20	Cash	450	
	Unearned Service Revenue		450
	Received revenue in advance.		

After posting, the liability account appears as follows:

Unearned Service Revenue		
	Apr. 20	450

Unearned Service Revenue is a liability because it represents Lyon's obligation to perform service for the client. The April 30 unadjusted trial balance (Exhibit 3-1) lists this account with a $450 credit balance prior to the adjusting entries. During the last 10 days of the month, Lyon will have earned one third (10 days divided by April's total 30 days) of the $450, or $150. Therefore, he makes the following adjustment to decrease the liability, Unearned Service Revenue, and to record an increase in Service Revenue:

Apr. 30	Unearned Service Revenue ($450 × $\frac{1}{3}$)	150	
	Service Revenue.		150
	To record unearned service revenue that has been earned.		

This adjusting entry shifts $150 of the total amount from the liability account to the revenue account. After posting, the balance of Service Revenue is increased by $150 and the balance of Unearned Service Revenue has been reduced to $300:

Unearned Service Revenue				Service Revenue		
Apr. 30	**150**	Apr. 21	450			7,000
					Apr. 30	250
		Bal.	300		**Apr. 30**	**150**
					Bal.	7,400

Correct liability → Total accounted ← Correct revenue
amount, $300   for, $450   amount, $150

Accounting for all types of revenues that are collected in advance follows the same pattern.

Summary of the Adjusting Process

Because one purpose of the adjusting process is to measure business income properly, each adjusting entry affects at least one income statement account—a revenue or an expense. The other side of the entry—a debit or a credit, as the case may be—is to a balance sheet account—an asset or a liability. This step updates the accounts for preparation of the balance sheet, which is the second purpose of the adjustments. No adjusting entry debits or credits Cash because the cash transactions are recorded earlier in the period. The end-of-period adjustment process is reserved for the noncash transactions that are required by accrual accounting. Exhibit 3-3 summarizes the adjusting entries.

Appendix B at the end of the book covers the adjusting process in more detail. It also discusses and illustrates an optional category of accounting entries known as reversing entries.

Posting the Adjusting Entries _____

Exhibit 3-4 summarizes the adjusting entries of Lyon's business at April 30. Panel A of the exhibit briefly describes the data for each adjustment, Panel B gives the adjusting entries, and Panel C shows the accounts. The adjustments are keyed by letter.

EXHIBIT 3-3 *Summary of Adjusting Entries*

Adjusting Entry	Type of Account Debited	Type of Account Credited
Prepaid expense, supplies	Expense	Prepaid expense, supplies
Depreciation	Expense	Accumulated depreciation
Accrued expenses	Expense	Payable
Accrued revenues	Receivable	Revenue
Unearned revenues	Unearned revenue	Revenue

Adapted from Beverly Terry.

EXHIBIT 3-4 *Journalizing and Posting the Adjusting Entries*

Panel A—Information for Adjustments at April 30, 19X1

a. Accrued service revenue, $250.
b. Supplies on hand, $400.
c. Prepaid rent expired, $1,000.
d. Depreciation on furniture, $275.
e. Accrued salary expense, $950.
f. Amount of unearned service revenue that has been earned, $150.

Panel B—Adjusting Entries

a. Accounts Receivable... 250
       Service Revenue 250
   To accrue service revenue.

b. Supplies Expense 300
       Supplies.. 300
   To record supplies used.

c. Rent Expense... 1,000
       Prepaid Rent 1,000
   To record rent expense.

d. Depreciation Expense 275
       Accumulated Depreciation.................................... 275
   To record depreciation on furniture.

e. Salary Expense 950
       Salary Payable 950
   To accrue salary expense.

f. Unearned Service Revenue 150
       Service Revenue 150
   To record unearned revenue that has been earned.

Panel C—Ledger Accounts

Assets

Cash		Accounts Receivable		Supplies	
Bal. 24,800		2,250		700	(b) 300
		(a) 250		Bal. 400	
		Bal. 2,500			

Prepaid Rent		Furniture		Accumulated Depreciation	
3,000	(c) 1,000	Bal. 16,500			(d) 275
Bal. 2,000					Bal. 275

Liabilities

Accounts Payable		Salary Payable		Unearned Service Revenue	
	Bal. 13,100		(e) 950	(f) 150	450
			Bal. 950		Bal. 300

Owner's Equity

Gary Lyon, Capital

	Bal. 31,250

Gary Lyon, Withdrawals

Bal. 3,200	

Revenues

Service Revenue

	7,000
	(a) 250
	(f) 150
	Bal. 7,400

Expenses

Rent Expense

(c) 1,000	
Bal. 1,000	

Salary Expense

950	
(e) 950	
Bal. 1,900	

Supplies Expense

(b) 300	
Bal. 300	

Depreciation Expense

(d) 275	
Bal. 275	

Utilities Expense

Bal. 400	

Adjusted Trial Balance

This chapter began with the trial balance before any adjusting entries—the unadjusted trial balance (Exhibit 3-1). After the adjustments are journalized and posted, the accounts appear as shown in Exhibit 3-4, Panel C. A useful step in preparing the financial statements is to list the accounts, along with their adjusted balances, on an **adjusted trial balance.** This document has the advantage of listing all the accounts and their adjusted balances in a single place. Exhibit 3-5 shows the preparation of the adjusted trial balance.

Each amount on the adjusted trial balance is computed by combining the amounts from the unadjusted trial balance and the adjustments. For example, Accounts Receivable starts with a debit balance of $2,250. Adding the $250 debit amount from adjusting entry *a* gives Accounts Receivable an adjusted balance of $2,500. Supplies begins with a debit balance of $700. After the $300 credit adjustment, its adjusted balance is $400. More than one entry may affect a single account, as is the case for Service Revenue. If accounts are unaffected by the adjustments, they show the same amount on both trial balances. This is true for Cash, Furniture, Accounts Payable, and the Owner's Equity accounts.

OBJECTIVE 4
Prepare an adjusted trial balance

Preparing the Financial Statements from the Adjusted Trial Balance

The April financial statements of Gary Lyon, CPA, can be prepared from the information on the adjusted trial balance. The income statement comes from the revenue and expense accounts. The balance sheet reports the assets, liabilities, and owner's equity. The statement of owner's equity shows the reasons for the

EXHIBIT 3-5 *Preparation of Adjusted Trial Balance*

Gary Lyon, CPA
Preparation of Adjusted Trial Balance
April 30, 19X1

Account Title	Trial Balance Debit	Trial Balance Credit	Adjustments Debit		Adjustments Credit		Adjusted Trial Balance Debit	Adjusted Trial Balance Credit
Cash	24,800						24,800	
Accounts receivable	2,250		(a)	250			2,500	
Supplies	700				(b)	300	400	
Prepaid rent	3,000				(c)	1,000	2,000	
Furniture	16,500						16,500	
Accumulated depreciation					(d)	275		275
Accounts payable		13,100						13,100
Salary payable					(e)	950		950
Unearned service revenue		450	(f)	150				300
Gary Lyon, capital		31,250						31,250
Gary Lyon, withdrawals	3,200						3,200	
Service revenue		7,000			(a)	250		7,400
					(f)	150		
Rent expense			(c)	1,000			1,000	
Salary expense	950		(e)	950			1,900	
Supplies expense			(b)	300			300	
Depreciation expense			(d)	275			275	
Utilities expense	400						400	
	51,800	51,800	2,925		2,925		53,275	53,275

EXHIBIT 3-6 *Preparing the Financial Statements from the Adjusted Trial Balance*

Account Title	Adjusted Trial Balance Debit	Adjusted Trial Balance Credit	
Cash	24,800		
Accounts receivable	2,500		
Supplies	400		
Prepaid rent	2,000		
Furniture	16,500		Balance Sheet
Accumulated depreciation		275	
Accounts payable		13,100	
Salary payable		950	
Unearned service revenue		300	
Gary Lyon, capital		31,250	Statement of
Gary Lyon, withdrawals	3,200		Owner's Equity
Service revenue		7,400	
Rent expense	1,000		
Salary expense	1,900		
Supplies expense	300		Income Statement
Depreciation expense	275		
Utilities expense	400		
	53,275	53,275	

change in the owner's capital during the period. Exhibit 3-6 shows how the accounts are distributed from the adjusted trial balance to these three financial statements.

Financial Statements

The accounts and the amounts for the income statement and the balance sheet may be taken from the adjusted trial balance. The adjusted trial balance also provides the data for the statement of owner's equity. Exhibits 3-7, 3-8, and 3-9 illustrate these three financial statements, best prepared in the order shown: the income statement first, followed by the statement of owner's equity and last, the balance sheet. The essential features of all financial statements are (1) the name of the entity, (2) the title of the statement, (3) the date or the period covered by the statement, and (4) the body of the statement.

It is customary to list expenses in descending order by amount, as shown in Exhibit 3-7. However, Miscellaneous Expense, a catch-all account for expenses that do not fit another category, is usually reported last regardless of its amount.

Relationships among the Three Financial Statements _____

The arrows in Exhibits 3-7, 3-8, and 3-9 illustrate the relationship among the income statement, the statement of owner's equity, and the balance sheet.

1. The income statement reports net income or net loss, figured by subtracting expenses from revenues. Because revenues and expenses are owner's equity accounts, their net figure is then transferred to the statement of owner's equity. Note that net income in Exhibit 3-7, $3,525, increases owner's equity in Exhibit 3-8. A net loss would decrease owner's equity.

2. Capital is a balance sheet account, so the ending balance in the statement of owner's equity is transferred to the balance sheet. This amount is the final balancing element of the balance sheet. To solidify your understanding of this relationship, trace the $31,575 figure from Exhibit 3-8 to Exhibit 3-9.[1]

Microcomputers and the Accounting Process _____

Computers have been used by large businesses for years to account for their transactions. Until recently, most computers were bulky and expensive, and only large organizations could afford them. In recent years, small, more affordable microcomputers have caused a revolution in the computer industry. The term

---

[1] You may be wondering why the total assets on the balance sheet ($45,925 in Exhibit 3-9) do not equal the total debits on the adjusted trial balance ($53,275 in Exhibit 3-6). Likewise, the total liabilities and owner's equity do not equal the total credits on the adjusted trial balance. The reason for these differences is that Accumulated Depreciation and Owner Withdrawals are *subtracted* from their related accounts on the balance sheet but *added* in their respective columns on the adjusted trial balance.

OBJECTIVE 5

Prepare the financial statements from the adjusted trial balance

EXHIBIT 3-7 *Income Statement*

Gary Lyon, CPA
Income Statement
For the Month Ended April 30, 19X1

Revenue		
Service revenue................................		$7,400
Expenses:		
Salary expense.................................	$1,900	
Rent expense..................................	1,000	
Utilities expense..............................	400	
Supplies expense..............................	300	
Depreciation expense.........................	275	
Total expenses...........................		3,875
Net income.....................................		$3,525

EXHIBIT 3-8 *Statement of Owner's Equity*

Gary Lyon, CPA
Statement of Owner's Equity
For the Month Ended April 30, 19X1

Gary Lyon, capital, April 1, 19X1.............................	$31,250
Add: Net income...	3,525
	34,775
Less: Withdrawals...	3,200
Gary Lyon, capital, April 30, 19X1..........................	$31,575

①

EXHIBIT 3-9 *Balance Sheet*

Gary Lyon, CPA
Balance Sheet
April 30, 19X1

②

Assets			Liabilities		
Cash................		$24,800	Accounts payable......		$13,100
Accounts receivable....		2,500	Salary payable........		950
Supplies.............		400	Unearned service		
Prepaid rent..........		2,000	revenue............		300
Furniture............	$16,500		Total liabilities........		14,350
Less Accumulated					
depreciation....	275	16,225	**Owner's Equity**		
			Gary Lyon, capital.....		31,575
			Total liabilities and		
Total assets..........		$45,925	owner's equity......		$45,925

microcomputer simply means "small computer." Like the bigger computers, these machines handle electronically much of the work done by hand in the past. Their prices continue to fall, enabling more and more small businesses to own one. Names like Apple (a leading microcomputer company), IBM PC (International Business Machines Personal Computer), TRS (a line of Radio Shack microcomputers), and Epson have become almost household words.

Whether a system is manual, as we have illustrated so far, or computerized, the steps in the accounting process are essentially the same: journalize transactions, post to the ledger, prepare the trial balance, make the adjustments, and present the financial statements. Computers can perform mathematical operations fast and error free. This ability comes in handy for such routine tasks as recording cash receipts and cash payments and keeping track of accounts receivable and accounts payable. Posting, which requires no analysis, is also well suited for a computer. The computer can be programmed to print the trial balance and the financial statements. Having the machine do these routine jobs saves time and money.

What are a computer's limits? Computers are not people, so they cannot think. The adjusting entries illustrate the need for the type of analysis that requires the human touch. At the end of the period, the office manager may count the supplies on hand. The accountant then makes the necessary entry to adjust the Supplies and Supplies Expense accounts. A computer cannot perform these operations. It takes a human to count assets on hand and to enter the data for the adjustments. If the system is computerized, the machine takes over and does the posting and statement preparation. In a manual system, these steps are done by hand.

It may be economical to use a computer for some of the adjusting entries. Depreciation, for example, is often a routine computation that a computer performs well. But it takes a human to do the thinking and to program the machine to make the calculations. As we progress through the study of accounting, we will be discussing computer applications that fit the topics under discussion.

Summary Problem for Your Review

The trial balance of State Service Company at December 31, 19X1, which is the end of its year-long accounting period, is presented on the following page.

Data needed for the adjusting entries include:

a. Supplies on hand at year's end, $2,000.
b. Depreciation on furniture and fixtures, $20,000.
c. Depreciation on building, $10,000.
d. Salaries owed but not yet paid, $5,000.
e. Accrued service revenue, $12,000.
f. Of the $45,000 balance of unearned service revenue, $32,000 was earned during the year.

Required

1. Open the ledger accounts with their unadjusted balances. Show dollar amounts in thousands, as shown on the next page for Accounts Receivable:

State Service Company
Trial Balance
December 31, 19X1

Cash	$ 198,000	
Accounts receivable............................	370,000	
Supplies	6,000	
Furniture and fixtures	100,000	
Accumulated depreciation–furniture and fixtures.........		$ 40,000
Building	250,000	
Accumulated depreciation–building		130,000
Accounts payable................................		380,000
Salary payable		
Unearned service revenue.........................		45,000
Capital		293,000
Owner's withdrawals............................	65,000	
Service revenue		286,000
Salary expense.................................	172,000	
Supplies expense		
Depreciation expense–furniture and fixtures.............		
Depreciation expense–building		
Miscellaneous expense............................	13,000	
Total	$1,174,000	$1,174,000

Accounts Receivable

370 |

2. Journalize State Service Company's adjusting entries at December 31, 19X1. Key entries by letter as in Exhibit 3-4.

3. Post the adjusting entries.

4. Write the trial balance on a sheet of paper, enter the adjusting entries, and prepare an adjusted trial balance, as shown in Exhibit 3-5.

5. Prepare the income statement, the statement of owner's equity, and the balance sheet. Draw the arrows linking the three statements together.

SOLUTION TO REVIEW PROBLEM

Requirements 1 and 3

Assets

Cash		Accounts Receivable		Supplies			Furniture and Fixtures	
Bal. 198		370		6	(a)	4	Bal. 100	
		(e) 12						
		Bal. 382		Bal. 2				

Accumulated Depreciation-Furniture and Fixtures

			40
		(b)	20
		Bal.	60

Building

Bal.	250	

Accumulated Depreciation-Building

			130
		(c)	10
		Bal.	140

Liabilities

Accounts Payable

		Bal.	380

Salary Payable

		(d)	5
		Bal.	5

Unearned Service Revenue

(f)	32		45
		Bal.	13

Owner's Equity

Capital

		Bal.	293

Owner's Withdrawals

Bal.	65	

Revenues

Service Revenue

			286
		(e)	12
		(f)	32
		Bal.	330

Expenses

Salary Expense

	172	
(d)	5	
Bal.	177	

Supplies Expense

(a)	4	
Bal.	4	

Depreciation Expense-Furniture and Fixtures

(b)	20	
Bal.	20	

Depreciation Expense-Building

(c)	10	
Bal.	10	

Miscellaneous Expense

Bal.	13	

Requirement 2

	19X1			
a.	Dec. 31	Supplies Expense ($6,000 − $2,000)	4,000	
		Supplies.		4,000
		To record supplies used.		
b.	31	Depreciation Expense-Furniture and Fixtures	20,000	
		Accumulated Depreciation–Furniture and Fixtures		20,000
		To record depreciation expense on furniture and fixtures.		

c.	Dec. 31	Depreciation Expense-Building	10,000	
		Accumulated Depreciation – Building		10,000
		To record depreciation expense on building.		
d.	31	Salary Expense	5,000	
		Salary Payable		5,000
		To accrue salary expense.		
e.	31	Accounts Receivable.	12,000	
		Service Revenue		12,000
		To accrue service revenue.		
f.	31	Unearned Service Revenue	32,000	
		Service Revenue		32,000
		To record unearned service revenue that has been earned.		

Requirement 4

State Service Company
Preparation of Adjusted Trial Balance
December 31, 19X1
(amounts in thousands)

	Trial Balance		Adjustments		Adjusted Trial Balance	
	Debit	Credit	Debit	Credit	Debit	Credit
Cash	198				198	
Accounts receivable	370		(e) 12		382	
Supplies	6			(a) 4	2	
Furniture and fixtures	100				100	
Accumulated depreciation – furniture and fixtures		40		(b) 20		60
Building	250				250	
Accumulated depreciation — building		130		(c) 10		140
Accounts payable		380				380
Salary payable				(d) 5		5
Unearned service revenue		45	(f) 32			13
Capital		293				293
Owner's withdrawals	65				65	
Service revenue		286		(e) 12		330
				(f) 32		
Salary expense	172		(d) 5		177	
Supplies expense			(a) 4		4	
Depreciation expense — furniture and fixtures			(b) 20		20	
Depreciation expense — building			(c) 10		10	
Miscellaneous expense	13				13	
	1,174	1,174	83	83	1,221	1,221

Requirement 5

**State Service Company
Income Statement
For the Year Ended December 31, 19X1
(amounts in thousands)**

Revenues:

    Service revenue.......................... $330

Expenses:

    Salary expense $177

    Depreciation expense–furniture & fixtures.... 20

    Depreciation expense–building............. 10

    Supplies expense....................... 4

    Miscellaneous expense 13

        Total expenses...................... 224

Net income $106

**State Service Company
Statement of Owner's Equity
For the Year Ended December 31, 19X1
(amounts in thousands)**

Capital, January 1, 19X1 .... $293

Add: Net income 106

         399

Less: Withdrawals 65

Capital, December 31, 19X1 .... $334

**State Service Company
Balance Sheet
December 31, 19X1
(amounts in thousands)**

Assets

Cash...............................		$198
Accounts receivable		382
Supplies.............................		2
Furniture and fixtures	$100	
Less Accumulated depreciation..	60	40
Building	250	
Less Accumulated depreciation..	140	110
Total assets		$732

Liabilities

Accounts payable	$380
Salary payable............	5
Unearned service revenue ..	13
Total liabilities............	398

Owner's Equity

Capital.................	334
Total liabilities and owner's equity.........	$732

Summary

In *accrual-basis* accounting, business events are recorded as they affect the entity. In *cash-basis accounting,* only those events that affect cash are recorded. The cash basis omits important events such as purchases and sales of assets on account. It also distorts the financial statements by labeling as expenses those cash payments that have long-term effects, like the purchases of buildings and equipment. Some small organizations use cash-basis accounting, but the generally accepted method is the accrual basis.

Accountants divide time into definite periods—such as a month, a quarter, and a year—to report the entity's financial statements. The year is the basic *accounting period,* but companies prepare financial statements as often as they need the information. Accountants have developed the *revenue principle* to determine when to record revenue and the amount of revenue to record. The *matching principle* guides the accounting for expenses.

Adjusting entries are a result of the accrual basis of accounting. These entries, made at the end of the accounting period, update the accounts for preparation of the financial statements. One of the most important pieces of accounting information is net income or net loss, and the adjusting entries help to measure the *net income* of the period.

Adjusting entries can be divided into five categories: *prepaid expenses, depreciation, accrued expenses, accrued revenues,* and *unearned revenues.* To prepare the *adjusted trial balance,* enter the adjusting entries next to the *unadjusted trial balance.* This document can be used to prepare the income statement, the statement of owner's equity, and the balance sheet.

These three financial statements are related as follows: Income, shown on the *income statement,* increases owner's equity, which also appears on the *statement of owner's equity.* The ending balance of capital is the last amount reported on the *balance sheet.*

Computers can aid the accounting process in a number of ways, chiefly by performing routine operations. Many adjusting entries, however, require analysis that is best done manually, without the computer.

Self-Study Questions

Test your understanding of the chapter by marking the best answer for each of the following questions.

1. Accrual-basis accounting *(p. 86)*
   a. Results in higher income than cash-basis accounting
   b. Leads to the reporting of more complete information than does cash-basis accounting
   c. Is not acceptable under GAAP
   d. Omits adjusting entries at the end of the period
2. Under the revenue principle, revenue is recorded *(p. 87)*
   a. At the earliest acceptable time
   b. At the latest acceptable time
   c. After it has been earned, but not before
   d. At the end of the accounting period
3. The matching principle provides guidance in accounting for *(p. 88)*
   a. Expenses   c. Assets
   b. Owner's equity   d. Liabilities
4. Adjusting entries *(p. 89)*
   a. Assign revenues to the period in which they are earned
   b. Help to properly measure the period's net income or net loss
   c. Bring asset and liability accounts to correct balances
   d. All of the above
5. A law firm began November with office supplies of $160. During the month, the firm purchased supplies of $290. At November 30 supplies on hand total $210. Supplies expense for the period is *(p. 91)*

a. $210
b. $240

c. $290
d. $450

6. A building that cost $120,000 has accumulated depreciation of $50,000. The book value of the building is *(p. 93)*
   a. $50,000
   b. $70,000

   c. $120,000
   d. $170,000

7. The adjusting entry to accrue salary expense *(p. 95)*
   a. Debits Salary Expense and credits Cash
   b. Debits Salary Payable and credits Salary Expense
   c. Debits Salary Payable and credits Cash
   d. Debits Salary Expense and credits Salary Payable

8. A business received cash of $3,000 in advance for revenue that will be earned later. The cash receipt entry debited Cash and credited Unearned Revenue for $3,000. At the end of the period, $1,100 is still unearned. The adjusting entry for this situation will *(p. 96)*
   a. Debit Unearned Revenue and credit Revenue for $1,900
   b. Debit Unearned Revenue and credit Revenue for $1,100
   c. Debit Revenue and credit Unearned Revenue for $1,900
   d. Debit Revenue and credit Unearned Revenue for $1,100

9. The links between the financial statements are *(p. 102)*
   a. Net income from the income statement to the statement of owner's equity
   b. Ending capital from the statement of owner's equity to the balance sheet
   c. Both of the above
   d. None of the above

10. Accumulated Depreciation is reported on the *(p. 102)*
    a. Balance sheet
    b. Income statement

    c. Statement of owner's equity
    d. Both a and b

Answers to the self-study questions are at the end of the chapter.

Accounting Vocabulary

accrual-basis accounting *(p. 86)*, accrued expense *(p. 94)*, accrued revenue *(p. 95)*, accumulated depreciation *(p. 93)*, adjusted trial balance *(p. 99)*, adjusting entry *(p. 89)*, book value of a plant asset *(p. 93)*, cash-basis accounting *(p. 86)*, contra account *(p. 93)*, contra asset *(p. 93)*, depreciation *(p. 92)*, matching principle *(p. 88)*, plant asset *(p. 92)*, prepaid expense *(p. 90)*, revenue principle *(p. 87)*, unearned revenue *(p. 96)*.

Assignment Material _____

Questions

1. Distinguish the accrual basis of accounting from the cash basis.
2. How long is the basic accounting period? What is a fiscal year? What is an interim period?
3. What two questions does the revenue principle help answer?
4. Briefly explain the matching principle.
5. What is the purpose of making adjusting entries?
6. Why are adjusting entries made at the end of the accounting period, not during the period?
7. Name five categories of adjusting entries and give an example of each.
8. Do all adjusting entries affect the net income or net loss of the period? Include in your answer the definition of an adjusting entry.
9. Why does the balance of Supplies need to be adjusted at the end of the period?

10. Manning Supply Company pays $1,800 for an insurance policy that covers three years. At the end of the first year, the balance of its Prepaid Insurance account contains two elements. What are the two elements, and what is the correct amount of each?

11. The title Prepaid Expense suggests that this type of account is an expense. If so, explain why. If not, what type of account is it?

12. What is a contra account? Identify the contra account introduced in this chapter, along with the account's normal balance.

13. The manager of a Quickie-Pickie convenience store presents his entity's balance sheet to a banker to obtain a loan. The balance sheet reports that the entity's plant assets have a book value of $135,000 and accumulated depreciation of $65,000. What does *book value* of a plant asset mean? What was the cost of the plant assets?

14. Give the entry to record accrued interest revenue of $800.

15. Why is an unearned revenue a liability? Use an example in your answer.

16. Identify the types of accounts (assets, liabilities, and so on) debited and credited for the five types of adjusting entries.

17. What purposes does the adjusted trial balance serve?

18. Explain the relationship among the income statement, the statement of owner's equity, and the balance sheet.

19. Bellevue Company failed to record the following adjusting entries at December 31, the end of its fiscal year: (a) accrued expenses, $500; (b) accrued revenues, $850; and (c) depreciation, $1,000. Did these omissions cause net income for the year to be understated or overstated and by what overall amount?

20. Identify several accounting tasks for which it is efficient to use a microcomputer. What is the basic limitation on the use of a computer?

Exercises

Exercise 3-1 *Applying accounting concepts and principles*

Identify the accounting concept or principle that gives the most direction on how to account for each of the following situations:

a. The owner of a business desires monthly financial statements to measure the progress of the entity on an ongoing basis.

b. Expenses of the period total $4,900. This amount should be subtracted from revenue to compute the period's income.

c. Expenses of $650 must be accrued at the end of the period to properly measure income.

d. A customer states her intention to shift her business to a travel agency. Should the travel agency record revenue based on this intention?

Exercise 3-2 *Journalizing adjusting entries*

Journalize the entries for the following adjustments at December 31, the end of the accounting period.

a. Employee salaries owed, $3,600

b. Prepaid insurance expired, $450

c. Interest revenue accrued, $5,000

d. Unearned service revenue earned, $800

e. Depreciation, $6,200

Exercise 3-3 *Analyzing the effects of adjustments on net income.*

Suppose the adjustments required in Exercise 3-2 were not made. Compute the overall overstatement or understatement of net income as a result of the omission of these adjustments.

Exercise 3-4   *Allocating prepaid expense to the asset and the expense*

Compute the amounts indicated by question marks for each of the following Prepaid Rent situations. Consider each situation separately.

	Situation			
	1	**2**	**3**	**4**
Beginning Prepaid Rent	$ 900	$ 600	$ 300	$500
Payments for Prepaid Rent during the year	1,100	?	700	?
Total amount to account for	2,000	1,500	1,000	?
Ending Prepaid Rent	?	500	200	800
Rent Expense	1,600	1,000	?	300

Exercise 3-5   *Recording adjustments in T-accounts*

The accounting records of Manny Fernandez, Tailor, include the following unadjusted balances at May 31: Accounts Receivable, $1,200; Supplies, $600; Salary Payable, $0; Unearned Service Revenue, $400; Service Revenue, $5,100; Salary Expense, $1,200; Supplies Expense, $0.

Fernandez's accountant develops the following data for the May 31 adjusting entries:

a.   Supplies on hand, $200.
b.   Salary owed to employee, $100.
c.   Service revenue accrued, $350.
d.   Unearned service revenue that has been earned, $250.

Open the foregoing T-accounts and record the adjustments directly in the accounts, keying each adjustment amount by letter. Show each account's adjusted balance. Journal entries are not required.

Exercise 3-6   *Adjusting the accounts*

Complete the following adjusted trial balance by entering the adjustment amounts directly in the adjustment columns of the text. Service Revenue is the only account affected by more than one adjustment.

Austin Hill Travel Agency
Preparation of Adjusted Trial Balance
October 31, 19X2

Account Title	Trial Balance		Adjustments		Adjusted Trial Balance	
	Debit	**Credit**	**Debit**	**Credit**	**Debit**	**Credit**
Cash	3,000				3,000	
Accounts receivable	6,500				6,950	
Supplies	1,040				800	
Office furniture	19,300				19,300	
Accumulated depreciation		11,060				11,320
Salary payable						600
Unearned revenue		900				690
Capital		16,340				16,340
Owner's withdrawals	6,200				6,200	
Service revenue		11,830				12,490
Salary expense	2,690				3,290	
Rent expense	1,400				1,400	
Depreciation expense					260	
Supplies expense					240	
	40,130	40,130			41,440	41,440

Exercise 3-7 *Journalizing adjustments*

Make journal entries for the adjustments that would complete the preparation of the adjusted trial balance in Exercise 3-6. Include explanations.

Exercise 3-8 *Preparing the financial statements*

Refer to the adjusted trial balance in Exercise 3-6. Prepare Austin Hill Travel Agency's income statement and statement of owner's equity for the three months ended October 31, 19X2, and its balance sheet on that date. Draw the arrows linking the three statements.

Exercise 3-9 *Preparing the financial statements*

The accountant for Patrick Beckham, M.D., has posted adjusting entries *a* through *e* to the accounts at September 30, 19X2. All the revenues and expenses of the entity are listed here in T-account form.

Accounts Receivable			
23,000			
(e) 3,500			

Supplies			
4,000	(a)	2,000	

Accumulated Depreciation – Furniture			
		5,000	
	(b)	3,000	

Accumulated Depreciation – Building		
	33,000	
(c)	6,000	

Salaries Payable		
	(d)	1,500

Service Revenue		
	135,000	
	(e)	3,500

Salary Expense	
28,000	
(d) 1,500	

Supplies Expense	
(a) 2,000	

Depreciation Expense – Furniture	
(b) 3,000	

Depreciation Expense – Building	
(c) 6,000	

Required

Prepare the income statement of Patrick Beckham, M.D., for the year ended September 30, 19X2. List expenses in order from the largest to the smallest.

Exercise 3-10 *Preparing the statement of owner's equity*

A. B. Leewright Company began the year with capital of $85,000. On July 9 the owner invested $12,000 cash in the business. On September 26 he transferred to the company land valued at $19,000. The income statement for the year ended September 30, 19X5, reported a net loss of $28,000. During this fiscal year, the owner withdrew $1,500 monthly for personal use. Prepare the company's statement of owner's equity for the year ended September 30, 19X5.

Problems *(Group A)*

Problem 3-1A *Journalizing adjusting entries*

Journalize the adjusting entry needed on December 31, end of the current account period, for each of the following independent cases affecting Willis Engineering Company.

a. Each Friday Willis pays its employees for the current week's work. The amount of the payroll is $2,500 per day for a five-day work week. The current accounting period ends on Thursday.

b. Willis has received notes receivable from some clients for professional services. During the current year, Willis has earned accrued interest revenue of $8,575, which will be received next year.

c. The beginning balance of Engineering Supplies was $3,800. During the year the entity purchased supplies costing $12,530, and at December 31 the inventory of supplies on hand is $2,970.

d. Willis is conducting tests of the strength of the steel to be used in a large building, and the client paid Willis $27,000 at the start of the project. Willis recorded this amount as Unearned Engineering Revenue. The tests will take several months to complete. Willis executives estimate that the company has earned two-thirds of the total fee during the current year.

e. Depreciation for the current year includes: Office Furniture, $4,500; Engineering Equipment, $6,360; Building, $3,790. Make a compound entry.

f. Details of Prepaid Insurance are shown in the account:

Prepaid Insurance

Jan. 1 Bal. 2,400	
Apr. 30 3,600	
Oct. 31 3,600	

Willis pays semiannual insurance premiums (the payment for insurance coverage is called a *premium*) on April 30 and October 31. At December 31, $2,400 of the last payment is still in force.

Problem 3-2A *Preparing the financial statements from an adjusted trial balance*

The adjusted trial balance of Sommerfeld Engineering Services at December 31, 19X8 follows:

Sommerfeld Engineering Services
Adjusted Trial Balance
December 31, 19X8

Cash	$ 8,340	
Accounts receivable....................................	41,490	
Prepaid rent..	1,350	
Supplies	970	
Equipment	55,690	
Accumulated depreciation–equipment		$ 7,240
Office furniture......................................	24,100	
Accumulated depreciation–office furniture		18,670
Accounts payable.....................................		13,600
Unearned service revenue..............................		4,520
Interest payable		2,130
Salaries payable		930
Note payable		40,000
Lou Sommerfeld, capital		36,380
Lou Sommerfeld, withdrawals	48,000	
Service revenue		197,790
Depreciation expense–equipment	11,300	
Depreciation expense–office furniture	2,410	
Salary expense.......................................	102,800	
Rent expense	12,000	
Interest expense	4,200	
Utilities expense.....................................	3,770	
Insurance expense	3,150	
Supplies expense	1,690	
Total	$321,260	$321,260

Required

Prepare Sommerfeld's 19X8 income statement, statement of owner's equity, and balance sheet. List expenses in decreasing order on the income statement and show total liabilities on the balance sheet. Draw the arrows linking the three financial statements.

Problem 3-3A   *Preparing an adjusted trial balance and the financial statements*

The unadjusted trial balance of Bette Kurtz, Consulting Psychologist, at October 31, 19X2, and the related month-end adjustment data follow:

Bette Kurtz, Consulting Psychologist
Trial Balance
October 31, 19X2

Cash	$16,300	
Accounts receivable	8,000	
Prepaid rent	4,000	
Supplies	600	
Furniture	12,000	
Accumulated depreciation		$ 3,000
Accounts payable		2,800
Salary payable		
Bette Kurtz, capital		33,000
Bette Kurtz, withdrawals	3,600	
Consulting service revenue		7,400
Salary expense	1,400	
Rent expense		
Utilities expense	300	
Depreciation expense		
Supplies expense		
Total	$46,200	$46,200

Adjustment data:

a. Prepaid rent expired during the month, $1,000.
b. Supplies on hand at October 31, $400.
c. Depreciation on furniture for the month, $250.
d. Accrued salary expense at October 31, $300.
e. Accrued consulting service revenue at October 31, $1,000.

Required

1. Write the trial balance on a sheet of paper, using as an example Exhibit 3-5, and prepare the adjusted trial balance of Bette Kurtz, Consulting Psychologist, at October 31, 19X2. Key each adjusting entry by letter.
2. Prepare the income statement, the statement of owner's equity, and the balance sheet. Draw the arrows linking the three financial statements.

Problem 3-4A   *Analyzing and journalizing adjustments*

Song Kim Sales Company's unadjusted and adjusted trial balances at December 31, 19X0, are shown on the following page.

Required

Journalize the adjusting entries that account for the differences between the two trial balances. The only account affected by more than one adjustment is Commission Revenue.

Song Kim Sales Company
Adjusted Trial Balance
December 31, 19X0

Account Title	Trial Balance Debit	Trial Balance Credit	Adjusted Trial Balance Debit	Adjusted Trial Balance Credit
Cash	3,620		3,620	
Accounts receivable	11,260		12,090	
Supplies	1,090		780	
Prepaid insurance	2,200		1,330	
Office furniture	21,630		21,630	
Accumulated depreciation		8,220		10,500
Accounts payable		6,310		6,310
Salary payable				960
Interest payable				350
Note payable		12,000		12,000
Unearned commission revenue		1,440		960
Song Kim, capital		13,010		13,010
Song Kim, withdrawals	29,370		29,370	
Commission revenue		72,890		74,200
Depreciation expense			2,280	
Supplies expense			310	
Utilities expense	4,960		4,960	
Salary expense	26,660		27,620	
Rent expense	12,200		12,200	
Interest expense	880		1,230	
Insurance expense			870	
	113,870	113,870	118,290	118,290

Problem 3-5A *Journalizing and posting adjustments to T-accounts; preparing the adjusted trial balance and the financial statements*

The trial balance of Conrad Realty at August 31 of the current year and the data needed for the month-end adjustments follow.

Adjustment data:

a. Prepaid rent still in force at August 31, $900.
b. Supplies used during the month, $300.
c. Depreciation for the month, $400.
d. Accrued advertising expense at August 31, $110. (Credit Accounts Payable.)
e. Accrued salary expense at August 31, $550.
f. Unearned commission revenue still unearned at August 31, $1,670.

Conrad Realty
Trial Balance
August 31, 19XX

Cash	$ 2,200	
Accounts receivable	23,780	
Prepaid rent	2,420	
Supplies	1,180	
Furniture	19,740	
Accumulated depreciation		$ 3,630
Accounts payable		2,410
Salary payable		
Unearned commission revenue		2,790
Lou Conrad, capital		39,510
Lou Conrad, withdrawals	4,800	
Commission revenue		11,700
Salary expense	3,800	
Rent expense		
Utilities expense	550	
Depreciation expense		
Advertising expense	1,570	
Supplies expense		
Total	$60,040	$60,040

Required

1. Open T-accounts for the accounts listed in the trial balance, inserting their August 31 unadjusted balances.
2. Journalize the adjusting entries and post them to the T-accounts. Key the journal entries and the posted amounts by letter.
3. Prepare the adjusted trial balance.
4. Prepare the income statement, the statement of owner's equity, and the balance sheet. Draw the arrows linking the three financial statements.

Problem 3-6A *Journalizing and posting adjustments to four-column accounts; preparing the adjusted trial balance and the financial statements*

The trial balance of King Carpet Cleaners at May 31, 19X3, and the data needed to make the year-end adjustments follow.

Adjustment data:

a. At May 31 the business has earned $1,000 service revenue that has not yet been recorded.
b. Supplies used during the year totaled $5,650.
c. Prepaid rent still in force at May 31 is $330.
d. Depreciation for the year is $3,100.
e. King cleans the carpets of a large apartment complex that pays him in advance. At May 31 the entity has earned $3,600 of the unadjusted balance of Unearned Service Revenue.
f. At May 31 the business owes its employees accrued salaries of $1,300.

King Carpet Cleaners
Trial Balance
May 31, 19X3

Account No.			
101	Cash...................................	$ 3,260	
112	Accounts receivable	4,700	
127	Supplies.................................	7,700	
129	Prepaid rent.............................	1,430	
143	Cleaning equipment	28,300	
154	Accumulated depreciation		$ 12,550
211	Accounts payable		4,240
221	Salary payable.............................		
243	Unearned service revenue		5,810
301	Thomas King, capital		7,080
311	Thomas King, withdrawals....................	34,800	
401	Service revenue............................		80,610
511	Salary expense	28,800	
513	Depreciation expense		
515	Supplies expense...........................		
519	Rent expense..............................		
521	Utilities expense	1,300	
	Total.....................................	$110,290	$110,290

Required

1. Open the accounts listed in the trial balance, inserting their May 31 unadjusted balances. Use four-column accounts. Date the balances of the following accounts as of May 1: Supplies, Prepaid Rent, Accumulated Depreciation, and Unearned Service Revenue.
2. Journalize the adjusting entries, using page 7 of the journal.
3. Post the adjusting entries to the ledger accounts, using all posting references.
4. Prepare the adjusted trial balance at May 31.
5. Prepare the income statement, the statement of owner's equity, and the balance sheet. Draw the arrows linking the three financial statements.

(Group B)

Problem 3-1B *Journalizing adjusting entries*

Journalize the adjusting entry needed on December 31, end of the current accounting period, for each of the following independent cases affecting Enfield Air Conditioning Contractors.

a. Enfield pays its employees each Friday. The amount of the weekly payroll is $1,800 for a five-day work week, and the daily salary amounts are equal. The current accounting period ends on Monday.
b. Enfield has loaned money, receiving notes receivable. During the current year the entity has earned accrued interest revenue of $1,673 that it will receive next year.
c. The beginning balance of Supplies was $2,680. During the year the entity purchased supplies costing $8,180, and at December 31 the inventory of supplies on hand is $2,150.

d. Enfield is installing the air-conditioning system in a large building, and the owner of the building paid Enfield $12,900 at the start of the project. Enfield recorded this amount as Unearned Service Revenue. The installation will take several weeks to complete. Les Enfield, the owner, estimates that the company has earned one fourth of the total fee during the current year.

e. Depreciation for the current year includes: Office Furniture, $650; Equipment, $3,850; Trucks, $10,320. Make a compound entry.

f. Details of Prepaid Rent are shown in the account:

Prepaid Rent

Jan. 1 Bal.	600	
Mar. 31	1,200	
Sep. 30	1,200	

Enfield pays office rent semiannually on March 31 and September 30. At December 31 $600 of the last payment is still an asset.

Problem 3-2B *Preparing the financial statements from an adjusted trial balance*

The adjusted trial balance of Gillen Tax Service at December 31, 19X6, is as follows:

**Gillen Tax Service
Adjusted Trial Balance
December 31, 19X6**

Cash	$ 3,320	
Accounts receivable	11,920	
Supplies	2,300	
Prepaid rent	600	
Office equipment	23,180	
Accumulated depreciation – office equipment		$ 6,350
Office furniture	17,680	
Accumulated depreciation – office furniture		4,870
Accounts payable		3,640
Property tax payable		1,100
Interest payable		830
Unearned service revenue		620
Note payable		30,500
Monica Gillen, capital		6,090
Monica Gillen, withdrawals	44,000	
Service revenue		124,880
Depreciation expense – office equipment	6,680	
Depreciation expense – office furniture	2,370	
Salary expense	39,900	
Rent expense	14,400	
Interest expense	3,100	
Utilities expense	2,670	
Insurance expense	3,810	
Supplies expense	2,950	
Total	$178,880	$178,880

Required

Prepare Gillen's 19X6 income statement, statement of owner's equity, and balance sheet. List expenses in decreasing order on the income statement and show total liabilities on the balance sheet. Draw the arrows linking the three financial statements.

Problem 3-3B *Preparing an adjusted trial balance and the financial statements*

The unadjusted trial balance of Jack Ochs, Attorney, at July 31, 19X2, and the related month-end adjustment data are as follows:

Jack Ochs, Attorney		
Trial Balance		
July 31, 19X2		
Cash	$14,600	
Accounts receivable	11,600	
Prepaid rent	3,600	
Supplies	800	
Furniture	16,000	
Accumulated depreciation		$ 4,000
Accounts payable		3,150
Salary payable		
Jack Ochs, capital		38,650
Jack Ochs, withdrawals	5,000	
Legal service revenue		8,750
Salary expense	2,400	
Rent expense		
Utilities expense	550	
Depreciation expense		
Supplies expense		
Total	$54,550	$54,550

Adjustment data:

a. Prepaid rent expired during the month, $900.
b. Supplies on hand at July 31, $500.
c. Depreciation on furniture for the month, $350.
d. Accrued salary expense at July 31, $200.
e. Accrued legal service revenue at July 31, $700.

Required

1. Write the trial balance on a sheet of paper similar to Exhibit 3-5 and prepare the adjusted trial balance of Jack Ochs, Attorney, at July 31, 19X2. Key each adjusting entry by letter.
2. Prepare the income statement, the statement of owner's equity, and the balance sheet. Draw the arrows linking the three financial statements.

Problem 3-4B *Analyzing and journalizing adjustments*

Maddux Service Company's unadjusted and adjusted trial balances at April 30, 19X1, are as follows:

Maddux Service Company
Adjusted Trial Balance
April 30, 19X1

Account Title	Trial Balance		Adjusted Trial Balance	
	Debit	Credit	Debit	Credit
Cash	8,180		8,180	
Accounts receivable	6,360		6,540	
Interest receivable			50	
Note receivable	4,100		4,100	
Supplies	980		290	
Prepaid rent	1,440		720	
Building	66,450		66,450	
Accumulated depreciation		14,970		16,070
Accounts payable		6,920		6,920
Wages payable				220
Unearned service revenue		670		110
Debra Maddux, capital		60,770		60,770
Debra Maddux, withdrawals	3,600		3,600	
Service revenue		9,940		10,680
Interest revenue				50
Wage expense	1,600		1,820	
Rent expense			720	
Depreciation expense			1,100	
Insurance expense	370		370	
Supplies expense			690	
Utilities expense	190		190	
	93,270	93,270	94,820	94,820

Required

Journalize the adjusting entries that account for the differences between the two trial balances. The only account affected by more than one adjustment is Service Revenue.

Problem 3-5B *Journalizing and posting adjustments to T-accounts; preparing the adjusted trial balance and the financial statements*

The trial balance of Impala Realty at October 31, 19X2, and the data needed for the month-end adjustments follow.

Adjustment data:

a. Prepaid rent still in force at October 31, $650.
b. Supplies used during the month, $440.
c. Depreciation for the month, $700.
d. Accrued advertising expense at October 31, $320. (Credit Accounts Payable.)
e. Accrued salary expense at October 31, $180.
f. Unearned commission revenue still unearned at October 31, $2,000.

Required

1. Open T-accounts for the accounts listed in the trial balance, inserting their October 31 unadjusted balances.

Impala Realty
Trial Balance
October 31, 19X2

Cash	$ 1,460	
Accounts receivable	14,750	
Prepaid rent	3,100	
Supplies	780	
Furniture............................	22,370	
Accumulated depreciation		$11,640
Accounts payable......................		1,940
Salary payable		
Unearned commission revenue		2,290
Ellie Taft, capital......................		24,140
Ellie Taft, withdrawals..................	2,900	
Commission revenue		8,580
Salary expense	2,160	
Rent expense..........................		
Utilities expense	340	
Depreciation expense...................		
Advertising expense....................	730	
Supplies expense		
Total	$48,590	$48,590

2. Journalize the adjusting entries and post them to the T-accounts. Key the journal entries and the posted amounts by letter.
3. Prepare the adjusted trial balance.
4. Prepare the income statement, the statement of owner's equity, and the balance sheet. Draw the arrows linking the three financial statements.

Problem 3-6B *Journalizing and posting adjustments to four-column accounts; preparing the adjusted trial balance and the financial statements*

The trial balance of Apartment Cleaning Service at July 31, 19X3, and the data needed to make the year-end adjustments are as follows:

Adjustment data:

a. At July 31 the business has earned $1,420 of service revenue that has not yet been recorded.
b. Supplies used during the year totaled $3,060.
c. Prepaid rent still in force at July 31 is $1,040.
d. Depreciation for the year is $3,730.
e. The entity cleans the carpets of a large apartment complex that pays in advance. At July 31 the entity has earned $2,210 of the unadjusted balance of Unearned Service Revenue.
f. At July 31 the business owes its employees accrued salaries of $1,780.

Required

1. Open the accounts listed in the trial balance, inserting their July 31 unadjusted balances. Use four-column accounts. Date the balances of the following accounts as of July 1: Supplies, Prepaid Rent, Accumulated Depreciation, and Unearned Service Revenue.

Apartment Cleaning Service
Trial Balance
July 31, 19X3

Account No.			
101	Cash......................................	$ 2,110	
121	Accounts receivable	6,200	
131	Supplies...................................	3,400	
133	Prepaid rent...............................	1,890	
141	Cleaning equipment	36,200	
151	Accumulated depreciation		$ 14,360
201	Accounts payable		6,410
211	Salary payable..............................		
221	Unearned service revenue		3,110
301	Alvin McKay, capital		14,310
302	Alvin McKay, withdrawals.....................	40,100	
401	Service revenue.............................		91,060
501	Salary expense	32,150	
504	Depreciation expense		
506	Supplies expense............................		
509	Rent expense...............................	6,000	
511	Utilities expense	1,200	
	Total..	$129,250	$129,250

2. Journalize the adjusting entries, using page 4 of the journal.
3. Post the adjusting entries to the ledger accounts, using all posting references.
4. Prepare the adjusted trial balance at July 31.
5. Prepare the income statement, the statement of owner's equity, and the balance sheet. Draw the arrows linking the three financial statements.

Decision Problem

Valuing a Business Based on its Net Income

Slade McQueen has owned and operated McQueen Medical Systems, a management consulting firm for physicians, since its beginning ten years ago. From all appearances the business has prospered. McQueen lives in the fast lane—flashy car, home located in an expensive suburb, frequent trips abroad, and other signs of wealth. In the past few years, you have become friends with him and his wife through weekly rounds of golf at the country club. Recently, he mentioned that he has lost his zest for the business and would consider selling it for the right price. He claims that his clientele is firmly established and that the business "runs on its own." According to McQueen, the consulting procedures are fairly simple and anyone could perform the work.

Assume you are interested in buying this business. You obtain its most recent monthly trial balance, which follows. Assume that revenues and expenses vary little from month to month and April is a typical month.

Your investigation reveals that the trial balance does not include the effects of monthly revenues of $1,100 and expenses totaling $2,100. If you were to buy McQueen Medical Systems, you would hire a manager so you could devote your time to other duties. Assume that this person would require a monthly salary of $2,000.

McQueen Medical Systems
Trial Balance
April 30, 19XX

Cash.	$ 7,700	
Accounts receivable.	4,900	
Prepaid expenses.	2,600	
Plant assets	252,300	
Accumulated depreciation		$189,600
Land.	138,000	
Accounts payable		11,800
Salary payable.		
Unearned consulting revenue.		56,700
Slade McQueen, capital		148,400
Slade McQueen, withdrawals.	9,000	
Consulting revenue.		12,300
Salary expense.	3,400	
Rent expense		
Utilities expense.	900	
Depreciation expense		
Supplies expense.		
Total.	$418,800	$418,800

Required

1. Is this an unadjusted or an adjusted trial balance? How can you tell?
2. Assume that the most you would pay for the business is thirty times the monthly net income you could expect to earn from it. Compute this possible price.
3. McQueen states that the least he will take for the business is his ending capital. Compute this amount.
4. Under these conditions, how much should you offer McQueen? Give your reason.

Financial Statement Problem

This problem uses the notes to the financial statements in Appendix C. The notes are needed to avoid cluttering the financial statements (the balance sheet, for example) with excessive detail.

Journalizing and Posting Transactions, and Tracing Account Balances to the Financial Statements

Note J in the Gulf+Western financial statements in Appendix C gives details of these balance sheet items: prepaid expenses, and accrued expenses and other liabilities. In Note J, "Other" among the prepaid expenses includes prepaid rent, prepaid insurance, and supplies. "Accrued compensation and other employee benefit related items" is a liability similar to salary payable. "Unexpired subscriptions and advance subscription payments" are liabilities for unearned subscription revenue, which is like unearned service revenue as discussed in this chapter.

Gulf+Western's accounting year is called a *fiscal year* because it ends on a date other than December 31.

Required

1. Open T-accounts for Other Prepaid Expenses, Accrued Compensation Payable, and Unexpired Subscriptions. For each account, insert Gulf+Western's actual October 31, 1986, balance (in millions) from Note J. (Example: Other Prepaid Expenses, $150.3).

2. Journalize the following for fiscal year 1987. Key entries by letter. Explanations are not required.

   Cash transactions (amounts in millions):
   a. Paid prepaid expenses, $73.4.
   b. Paid the October 31, 1986, accrued compensation payable.
   c. Received $19.8 cash for unexpired subscriptions.

   Adjustments at October 31, 1987 (amounts in millions):
   d. Prepaid expenses expired, $40.5. (Debit General and Administrative Expense.)
   e. Accrued compensation payable, $77.7. (Debit Selling Expense.)
   f. Unexpired subscription revenue earned, $15.8. (Credit Subscription Revenue).

3. After these entries are posted, show that the balances in the three accounts opened in Requirement 1 agree with their October 31, 1987, amounts in Note J. Key posted amounts by letter.

Answers to Self-Study Questions

1. b
2. c
3. a
4. d
5. b ($160 + $290 − $210 = $240)
6. b ($120,000 − $50,000 = $70,000)
7. d
8. a ($3,000 received − $1,100 unearned = $1,900 earned)
9. c
10. a

4

Completing the Accounting Cycle

LEARNING OBJECTIVES

After studying this chapter, you should be able to

1 Give an overview of the accounting cycle

2 Prepare a work sheet

3 Use the work sheet to complete the accounting cycle

4 Close the revenue, expense, and withdrawal accounts

5 Classify assets and liabilities as current or long-term

6 Correct typical accounting errors

7 Explain how a microcomputer spreadsheet can be used in accounting

---

You have studied how accountants journalize transactions, post to the ledger accounts, prepare the trial balance and the adjusting entries, and draw up the financial statements. One major step remains to complete the accounting cycle — closing the books. This chapter illustrates the closing process for Gary Lyon's accounting practice at April 30, 19X1. It also shows how to use two additional accounting tools that are optional. One of these optional tools is the accountant's work sheet. Building upon the adjusted trial balance, the work sheet leads directly to the financial statements, which are the focal point of financial accounting. The chapter also presents an example of an actual balance sheet to show how companies classify assets and liabilities in order to provide meaningful information for decision making.

Overview of the Accounting Cycle

The **accounting cycle** is the process by which accountants produce an entity's financial statements for a specific period of time. For a new business, the cycle begins with setting up (opening) the ledger accounts. Gary Lyon started his accounting practice from scratch on April 1, 19X1, so the first step in the cycle was to open the accounts. After a business has operated for one period, however, the account balances carry over from period to period. Therefore, the accounting cycle usually starts with the account balances at the beginning of the period, as shown in Exhibit 4-1. The exhibit highlights the new steps that we will be discussing in this chapter.

EXHIBIT 4-1   *The Accounting Cycle*

During the period	1. Start with the account balances in the ledger at the beginning of the period.
	2. Analyze and journalize transactions as they occur.
	3. Post journal entries to the ledger accounts.
End of the period	4. Compute the unadjusted balance in each account at the end of the period.
	5. Enter the trial balance on the work sheet, and complete the work sheet.*
	6. Using the work sheet as a guide,
	a. Prepare the financial statements.
	b. Journalize and post the adjusting entries.
	c. Journalize and post the closing entries.
	7. Prepare the postclosing, or afterclosing, trial balance. This trial balance becomes step 1 for the next period.

* Optional

The accounting cycle is divided into work that is performed during the period —journalizing transactions and posting to the ledger—and work performed at the end of the period to prepare the financial statements. A secondary purpose of the end-of-period work is to get the accounts ready for recording the transactions of the next period. The greater number of individual steps at the end of the period may imply that most of the work is done at the end. Nevertheless, the recording and posting during the period takes far more time than the end-of-period work. Some of the terms in Exhibit 4-1 may be unfamiliar, but they will become clear by the end of the chapter.

The Accountant's Work Sheet

Accountants often use a **work sheet,** a columnar document that is designed to help move data from the trial balance to the finished financial statements. The work sheet provides an orderly way to compute net income and arrange the data for the financial statements. By listing all the accounts and their unadjusted balances, it helps the accountant identify the accounts needing adjustment. Although it is not essential, the work sheet is helpful because it brings together in one place the effects of all the transactions of a particular period. The work sheet aids the closing process by listing the adjusted balances of all the accounts. It also helps the accountant discover potential errors.

The work sheet is not part of the ledger or the journal, nor is it a financial statement. Therefore, it is not part of the formal accounting system. Instead, it is a summary device that exists for the accountant's convenience.

Exhibits 4-2 through 4-6 illustrate the development of a typical work sheet for the business of Gary Lyon, CPA. The heading at the top names the business, identifies the document, and states the accounting period. A step-by-step description of its preparation follows. Observe that steps 1 through 4 use the adjusted trial balance that was introduced in Chapter 3. Only step 5 is entirely new.

Steps introduced in Chapter 3 to prepare the adjusted trial balance:

1. Write the account titles and their unadjusted ending balances in the Trial Balance columns of the work sheet and total the amounts.
2. Enter the adjustments in the Adjustments columns and total the amounts.
3. Compute each account's adjusted balance by combining the trial balance and adjustment figures. Enter the adjusted amounts in the Adjusted Trial Balance columns.
4. Extend the asset, liability, and owner's equity amounts from the Adjusted Trial Balance to the Balance Sheet columns. Extend the revenue and expense amounts to the Income Statement columns. Total the statement columns.

New step introduced in this chapter:

5. Compute net income or net loss as the difference between total revenues and total expenses on the income statement. Enter net income or net loss as a balancing amount on the income statement and on the balance sheet and compute the adjusted column totals.

1. Write the account titles and their unadjusted ending balances in the Trial Balance columns of the work sheet and total the amounts. Of course, total debits should equal total credits as shown in Exhibit 4-2. The account titles and balances come directly from the ledger accounts before preparing the adjusting entries. If the business uses a work sheet, there is no need for a separate trial balance. It is written directly onto the work sheet, as shown in the exhibit. Accounts are grouped on the work sheet by category and are usually listed in the order they appear in the ledger. By contrast, their order on the financial statements follows a different pattern. For example, the expenses on the work sheet in Exhibit 4-2 indicate no particular order. But on the income statement, expenses are ordered by amount with the largest first (see Exhibit 4-7).

Accounts may have zero balances (for example, Depreciation Expense). All accounts are listed on the trial balance because they appear in the ledger. Electronically prepared work sheets list all the accounts, not just those with a balance.

2. Enter the adjusting entries in the Adjustments columns and total the amounts. Exhibit 4-3 includes the April adjusting entries. These are the same adjustments that were illustrated in Chapter 3 to prepare the adjusted trial balance.

How does the accountant identify the accounts that need to be adjusted? By scanning the trial balance. Cash needs no adjustment because all cash transactions are recorded as they occur during the period. Consequently, Cash's balance is up to date.

Accounts Receivable is listed next. Has Gary Lyon earned revenue that he has not yet recorded? The answer is yes. Lyon provides professional service for a client who pays a $500 fee on the 15th of each month. At April 30 Lyon has earned half of this amount, $250, which must be accrued. To accrue this service revenue, Lyon debits Accounts Receivable and credits Service Revenue on the work sheet in Exhibit 4-3. A letter is used to link the debit and the credit of each adjusting entry. By moving down the trial balance, Lyon identifies the remaining accounts needing adjustment. Supplies is next. The business has used supplies during April, so Lyon debits Supplies Expense and credits Supplies. The other adjustments are analyzed and entered on the work sheet as shown in the exhibit.

The process of identifying accounts that need to be adjusted is aided by listing the accounts in their proper sequence. However, suppose one or more accounts is omitted from the trial balance. It can always be written below the first column

EXHIBIT 4-2

Gary Lyon, CPA
Work Sheet
For the Month Ended April 30, 19X1

Account Title	Trial Balance		Adjustments		Adjusted Trial Balance		Income Statement		Balance Sheet	
	Debit	Credit	Debit	Credit	Debit	Credit	Debit	Credit	Debit	Credit
Cash	24,800									
Accounts receivable	2,250									
Supplies	700									
Prepaid rent	3,000									
Furniture	16,500									
Accumulated depreciation										
Accounts payable		13,100								
Salary payable										
Unearned service revenue		450								
Gary Lyon, capital		31,250								
Gary Lyon, withdrawals	3,200									
Service revenue		7,000								
Rent expense										
Salary expense	950									
Supplies expense										
Depreciation expense										
Utilities expense	400									
	51,800	51,800								

EXHIBIT 4-3

Gary Lyon, CPA
Work Sheet
For the Month Ended April 30, 19X1

Account Title	Trial Balance Debit	Trial Balance Credit	Adjustments Debit	Adjustments Credit	Adjusted Trial Balance Debit	Adjusted Trial Balance Credit	Income Statement Debit	Income Statement Credit	Balance Sheet Debit	Balance Sheet Credit
Cash	24,800									
Accounts receivable	2,250		(a) 250							
Supplies	700			(b) 300						
Prepaid rent	3,000			(c) 1,000						
Furniture	16,500									
Accumulated depreciation				(d) 275						
Accounts payable		13,100								
Salary payable				(e) 950						
Unearned service revenue		450	(f) 150							
Gary Lyon, capital		31,250								
Gary Lyon, withdrawals	3,200									
Service revenue		7,000		(a) 250 (f) 150						
Rent expense			(c) 1,000							
Salary expense	950		(e) 950							
Supplies expense			(b) 300							
Depreciation expense			(d) 275							
Utilities expense	400									
	51,800	51,800	2,925	2,925						

totals—$51,800. Assume that Supplies Expense was accidentally omitted and thus did not appear on the trial balance. When the accountant identifies the need to update the Supplies account, he or she knows that the debit in the adjusting entry is to Supplies Expense. In this case, the accountant can write Supplies Expense on the line beneath the amount totals and enter the debit adjustment—$300—on the Supplies Expense line. Keep in mind that the work sheet is not the finished version of the financial statements, so the order of the accounts on the work sheet is not critical. When the accountant prepares the income statement, Supplies Expense can be listed in its proper sequence.

After the adjustments are entered on the work sheet, the amount columns should be totaled to see that total debits equal total credits. This provides some assurance that each debit adjustment is accompanied by an equal credit.

3. Compute each account's adjusted balance by combining the trial balance and adjustment figures. Enter the adjusted amounts in the Adjusted Trial Balance columns. Exhibit 4-4 shows the work sheet with the adjusted trial balance added.

This step is performed as it was in Chapter 3. For example, the Cash balance is up to date, so it receives no adjustment. Accounts Receivable's adjusted balance of $2,500 is computed by adding the trial balance amount of $2,250 to the $250 debit adjustment. Supplies' adjusted balance of $400 is determined by subtracting the $300 credit adjustment from the unadjusted debit balance of $700. An account may receive more than one adjustment, as does Service Revenue. The column totals should maintain the equality of debits and credits.

4. Extend the asset, liability, and owner's equity amounts from the Adjusted Trial Balance to the Balance Sheet columns. Extend the revenue and expense amounts to the Income Statement columns. Total the statement columns. Every account is either a balance sheet account or an income statement account. The asset, liability, and owner's equity accounts go to the balance sheet, and the revenues and expenses go to the income statement. Debits on the adjusted trial balance remain debits in the statement columns, and likewise for credits. Each account's adjusted balance should appear in only one statement column, as shown in Exhibit 4-5.

The income statement indicates total expenses in the debit column ($3,875) and total revenues ($7,400) in the credit column. The balance sheet shows total debits of $49,400 and total credits of $45,875. At this stage, the column totals should *not* necessarily be equal.

5. Compute net income or net loss as the difference between total revenues and total expenses on the income statement. Enter net income or net loss as a balancing amount on the income statement and on the balance sheet and compute the adjusted column totals. Exhibit 4-6 presents the completed work sheet, which shows net income of $3,525, computed as follows:

Revenue (total credits on the income statement)........	$7,400
Expenses (total debits on the income statement)........	3,875
Net income	$3,525

Net income of $3,525 is entered in the debit column of the income statement, and the income statement columns are totaled at $7,400. The net income amount is then extended to the credit column of the balance sheet. This is because an excess of revenues over expenses increases capital, and increases in capital are recorded by a credit. In the closing process, which we discuss later, net income will find its way into the capital account.

If expenses exceed revenue, the result is a net loss. In that event, the accountant writes the words *Net loss* on the work sheet. The loss amount should be entered in the credit column of the income statement and in the debit column of the balance

EXHIBIT 4-4

Gary Lyon, CPA
Work Sheet
For the Month Ended April 30, 19X1

Account Title	Trial Balance		Adjustments		Adjusted Trial Balance		Income Statement		Balance Sheet	
	Debit	Credit	Debit	Credit	Debit	Credit	Debit	Credit	Debit	Credit
Cash	24,800				24,800					
Accounts receivable	2,250		(a) 250		2,500					
Supplies	700			(b) 300	400					
Prepaid rent	3,000			(c) 1,000	2,000					
Furniture	16,500				16,500					
Accumulated depreciation				(d) 275		275				
Accounts payable		13,100				13,100				
Salary payable				(e) 950		950				
Unearned service revenue		450	(f) 150			300				
Gary Lyon, capital		31,250				31,250				
Gary Lyon, withdrawals	3,200				3,200					
Service revenue		7,000		(a) 250		7,400				
				(f) 150						
Rent expense			(c) 1,000		1,000					
Salary expense	950		(e) 950		1,900					
Supplies expense			(b) 300		300					
Depreciation expense			(d) 275		275					
Utilities expense	400				400					
	51,800	51,800	2,925	2,925	53,275	53,275				

EXHIBIT 4-5

Gary Lyon, CPA
Work Sheet
For the Month Ended April 30, 19X1

Account Title	Trial Balance Debit	Trial Balance Credit	Adjustments Debit	Adjustments Credit	Adjusted Trial Balance Debit	Adjusted Trial Balance Credit	Income Statement Debit	Income Statement Credit	Balance Sheet Debit	Balance Sheet Credit
Cash	24,800				24,800				24,800	
Accounts receivable	2,250		(a) 250		2,500				2,500	
Supplies	700			(b) 300	400				400	
Prepaid rent	3,000			(c) 1,000	2,000				2,000	
Furniture	16,500				16,500				16,500	
Accumulated depreciation				(d) 275		275				275
Accounts payable		13,100				13,100				13,100
Salary payable				(e) 950		950				950
Unearned service revenue		450	(f) 150			300				300
Gary Lyon, capital		31,250				31,250				31,250
Gary Lyon, withdrawals	3,200				3,200				3,200	
Service revenue		7,000		(a) 250 (f) 150		7,400		7,400		
Rent expense			(c) 1,000		1,000		1,000			
Salary expense	950		(e) 950		1,900		1,900			
Supplies expense			(b) 300		300		300			
Depreciation expense			(d) 275		275		275			
Utilities expense	400				400		400			
	51,800	51,800	2,925	2,925	53,275	53,275	3,875	7,400	49,400	45,875

EXHIBIT 4-6

Gary Lyon, CPA
Work Sheet
For the Month Ended April 30, 19X1

Account Title	Trial Balance Debit	Trial Balance Credit	Adjustments Debit	Adjustments Credit	Adjusted Trial Balance Debit	Adjusted Trial Balance Credit	Income Statement Debit	Income Statement Credit	Balance Sheet Debit	Balance Sheet Credit
Cash	24,800				24,800				24,800	
Accounts receivable	2,250		(a) 250		2,500				2,500	
Supplies	700			(b) 300	400				400	
Prepaid rent	3,000			(c) 1,000	2,000				2,000	
Furniture	16,500				16,500				16,500	
Accumulated depreciation				(d) 275		275				275
Accounts payable		13,100				13,100				13,100
Salary payable				(e) 950		950				950
Unearned service revenue		450	(f) 150			300				300
Gary Lyon, capital		31,250				31,250				31,250
Gary Lyon, withdrawals	3,200				3,200				3,200	
Service revenue		7,000		(a) 250		7,400		7,400		
				(f) 150						
Rent expense			(c) 1,000		1,000		1,000			
Salary expense	950		(e) 950		1,900		1,900			
Supplies expense			(b) 300		300		300			
Depreciation expense			(d) 275		275		275			
Utilities expense	400				400		400			
	51,800	51,800	2,925	2,925	53,275	53,275	3,875	7,400	49,400	45,875
Net income							3,525			3,525
							7,400	7,400	49,400	49,400

sheet. This is because an excess of expenses over revenue decreases capital, and decreases in capital are recorded by a debit.

The balance sheet columns are totaled at $49,400. An out-of-balance condition indicates an error in preparing the work sheet. Common mistakes include arithmetic errors and carrying an amount to the wrong column—to the incorrect statement column or extending a debit as a credit or vice versa. Columns that balance offer some, but not complete, assurance that the work sheet is correct. For example, it is possible to have offsetting errors. Fortunately, that is unlikely.

Summary Problem for Your Review

The trial balance of State Service Company at December 31, 19X1, the end of its fiscal year, is presented below:

State Service Company
Trial Balance
December 31, 19X1

Cash	$ 198,000	
Accounts receivable...............................	370,000	
Supplies	6,000	
Furniture and fixtures	100,000	
Accumulated depreciation–furniture and fixtures.........		$ 40,000
Building	250,000	
Accumulated depreciation–building		130,000
Accounts payable..................................		380,000
Salary payable		
Unearned service revenue..........................		45,000
Capital		293,000
Withdrawals.....................................	65,000	
Service revenues		286,000
Salary expense....................................	172,000	
Supplies expense		
Depreciation expense–furniture and fixtures.............		
Depreciation expense–building		
Miscellaneous expense.............................	13,000	
Total	$1,174,000	$1,174,000

Data needed for the adjusting entries include:

a. Supplies on hand at year end, $2,000.

b. Depreciation on furniture and fixtures, $20,000.

c. Depreciation on building, $10,000.

d. Salaries owed but not yet paid, $5,000.

e. Accrued service revenue, $12,000.

f. Of the $45,000 balance of Unearned Service Revenue, $32,000 was earned during 19X1.

Required

Prepare the work sheet of State Service Company for the year ended December 31, 19X1. Key each adjusting entry by the letter corresponding to the data given.

SOLUTION TO REVIEW PROBLEM

State Service Company
Work Sheet
For the Year Ended December 31, 19X1

Account Title	Trial Balance Debit	Trial Balance Credit	Adjustments Debit	Adjustments Credit	Adjusted Trial Balance Debit	Adjusted Trial Balance Credit	Income Statement Debit	Income Statement Credit	Balance Sheet Debit	Balance Sheet Credit
Cash	198,000				198,000				198,000	
Accounts receivable	370,000		(e) 12,000		382,000				382,000	
Supplies	6,000			(a) 4,000	2,000				2,000	
Furniture and fixtures	100,000				100,000				100,000	
Accumulated depreciation—furniture and fixtures		40,000		(b) 20,000		60,000				60,000
Building	250,000				250,000				250,000	
Accumulated depreciation—building		130,000		(c) 10,000		140,000				140,000
Accounts payable		380,000				380,000				380,000
Salary payable				(d) 5,000		5,000				5,000
Unearned service revenue		45,000	(f) 32,000			13,000				13,000
Capital		293,000				293,000				293,000
Withdrawals	65,000				65,000				65,000	
Service revenue		286,000		(e) 12,000 (f) 32,000		330,000		330,000		
Salary expense	172,000		(d) 5,000		177,000		177,000			
Supplies expense			(a) 4,000		4,000		4,000			
Depreciation expense—furniture and fixtures			(b) 20,000		20,000		20,000			
Depreciation expense—building			(c) 10,000		10,000		10,000			
Miscellaneous expense	13,000				13,000		13,000			
	1,174,000	1,174,000	83,000	83,000	1,221,000	1,221,000	224,000	330,000	997,000	891,000
Net income							106,000			106,000
							330,000	330,000	997,000	997,000

135

Using the Work Sheet

OBJECTIVE 3

Use the work sheet to complete the accounting cycle

As illustrated thus far, the work sheet helps to organize accounting data and to compute the net income or net loss for the period. It also aids in preparing the financial statements, recording the adjusting entries, and closing the accounts.

Preparing the Financial Statements

Even though the work sheet shows the amount of net income or net loss for the period, it is still necessary to prepare the financial statements. The sorting of accounts to the balance sheet and the income statement eases the preparation of the statements. The work sheet also provides the data for the statement of owner's equity. Exhibit 4-7 presents the April financial statements for the accounting practice of Gary Lyon, CPA (based on data from the work sheet in Exhibit 4-6).

The financial statements can be prepared directly from the adjusted trial balance as shown in Chapter 3. That is why completion of the work sheet is optional.

Recording the Adjusting Entries

The adjusting entries are a key element of accrual-basis accounting. The work sheet helps identify the accounts that need adjustments, which may be conveniently entered directly on the work sheet as shown in Exhibits 4-2 through 4-6. However, these work sheet procedures do *not* adjust the accounts in the ledger itself. Recall that the work sheet is neither a journal nor a ledger. Actual adjustment of the accounts requires journal entries that are posted to the ledger accounts. Therefore, the adjusting entries must be recorded in the journal as shown in Panel A of Exhibit 4-8. Panel B of the exhibit shows the postings to the accounts, with "Adj." denoting an amount posted from an adjusting entry. Only the revenue and expense accounts are presented here in order to focus on the closing process, which is discussed in the next section.

The adjusting entries could have been recorded in the journal as they were entered on the work sheet. However, it is not necessary to journalize them at that time. Most companies go ahead and prepare the financial statements immediately after completing the work sheet. They can wait to journalize and post the adjusting entries just before they make the closing entries.

Delaying the journalizing and posting of the adjusting entries illustrates another use of the work sheet. Many companies journalize and post the adjusting entries—as in Exhibit 4-8—only once annually, at the end of the year. The need for monthly and quarterly financial statements, however, requires a tool like the work sheet. The entity can use the work sheet to aid in preparing interim statements without entering the adjusting entries in the journal and posting them to the ledger.

Closing the Accounts

Accountants use the term **closing the accounts** to refer to the step at the end of the period that prepares the accounts for recording the transactions of the next period. Closing the accounts consists of journalizing and posting the closing entries. Closing sets the balances of the revenue and expense accounts back to zero in order to measure the net income of the next period. Closing is a clerical procedure devoid of any new accounting theory. Recall that the income statement reports only one period's income. For example, net income for McDonald's, Inc., for 1990

EXHIBIT 4-7 *April Financial Statements of Gary Lyon, CPA*

Gary Lyon, CPA
Income Statement
For the Month Ended April 30, 19X1

Revenues:		
Service revenue...		$7,400
Expenses:		
Salary expense.....................................	$1,900	
Rent expense..	1,000	
Utilities expense	400	
Supplies expense..................................	300	
Depreciation expense	275	
Total expenses		3,875
Net income		$3,525

Gary Lyon, CPA
Statement of Owner's Equity
For the Month Ended April 30, 19X1

Gary Lyon, capital, April 1, 19X1	$31,250
Add: Net income	3,525
	34,775
Less: Withdrawals	3,200
Gary Lyon, capital, April 30, 19X1	$31,575

Gary Lyon, CPA
Balance Sheet
April 30, 19X1

Assets			Liabilities		
Cash		$24,800	Accounts payable.....		$13,100
Accounts receivable		2,500	Salary payable		950
Supplies.....................		400	Unearned service		
Prepaid rent		2,000	revenue		300
Furniture............	$16,500		Total liabilities		14,350
Less Accumulated			**Owner's Equity**		
depreciation	275	16,225			
			Gary Lyon, capital		31,575
			Total liabilities and		
Total assets		$45,925	owner's equity		$45,925

relates exclusively to 1990. At December 31, 1990, McDonald's accountants close the company's revenue and expense accounts for that year. Because these accounts' balances relate to a particular accounting period and are therefore closed at the end of the period, the revenue and expense accounts are called **temporary (nominal) accounts.** The owner's withdrawal account—although not a revenue or an expense—is also a temporary account because it is important to measure withdrawals for a specific period. The closing process applies only to temporary accounts.

EXHIBIT 4-8 *Journalizing and Posting the Adjusting Entries*

Panel A—Journalizing: **Page 4**

Adjusting Entries

Apr. 30	Accounts Receivable	250	
	Service Revenue		250
30	Supplies Expense	300	
	Supplies		300
30	Rent Expense	1,000	
	Prepaid Rent		1,000
30	Depreciation Expense	275	
	Accumulated Depreciation		275
30	Salary Expense	950	
	Salary Payable		950
30	Unearned Service Revenue	150	
	Service Revenue		150

Panel B—Posting the Adjustments to the Revenue and Expense Accounts:

Revenue   **Expenses**

Service Revenue		Rent Expense		Salary Expense	
	7,000	Adj. 1,000			950
	Adj. 250			Adj. 950	
	Adj. 150	Bal. 1,000			
				Bal. 1,900	
	Bal. 7,400				

Supplies Expense		Depreciation Expense		Utilities Expense	
Adj. 300		Adj. 275			400
Bal. 300		Bal. 275		Bal. 400	

Adj. = Amount posted from an adjusting entry
Bal. = Balance

To better understand the closing process, contrast the nature of the temporary accounts with the nature of the **permanent (real) accounts**—the assets, liabilities, and capital. The permanent accounts are *not* closed at the end of the period because their balances are not used to measure income. Consider Cash, Accounts Receivable, Supplies, Buildings, Accounts Payable, Notes Payable, and Gary Lyon, Capital. These accounts are not increases and decreases like the revenues and expenses, which relate exclusively to only one accounting period. Instead, the permanent accounts represent assets, liabilities, and capital that are on hand at a specific time. This is why their balances at the end of one accounting period carry over to become the beginning balances of the next period. For example, the Cash balance at December 31, 19X1, is also the beginning balance for 19X2.

Briefly, **closing entries** transfer the revenue, expense, and owner withdrawal balances from their respective accounts to the capital account. As you know, revenues increase owner's equity, and expenses and owner withdrawals decrease it. It is when we post the closing entries that the capital account absorbs the impact of the balances in the temporary accounts. As an intermediate step, however, the revenues and the expenses are transferred first to an account entitled **Income Summary,** which is like a temporary "holding tank" that is used only in the closing process. Then the balance of Income Summary is transferred to capital. The steps in closing the accounts of a proprietorship like Gary Lyon, CPA, are as follows:

1. Debit each revenue account for the amount of its credit balance. Credit Income Summary for the sum of the revenues. This entry transfers the sum of the revenues to the credit side of Income Summary.

2. Credit each expense account for the amount of its debit balance. Debit Income Summary for the sum of the expenses. This entry transfers the sum of the expenses to the debit side of Income Summary.

3. Debit Income Summary for the amount of its credit balance (revenues minus expenses) and credit the Capital account. If Income Summary has a debit balance, then credit Income Summary for this amount, and debit Capital. This entry transfers the net income or loss from Income Summary to the Capital account.

4. Credit the Withdrawals account for the amount of its debit balance. Debit the Capital account of the proprietor. Withdrawals are not expenses and do not affect net income or net loss. Therefore, this account is *not* closed to the Income Summary. This entry transfers the withdrawal amount to the debit side of the Capital account.

To illustrate, suppose Gary Lyon closes the books at the end of April. Exhibit 4-9 presents the complete closing process for Lyon's business. Panel A gives the closing journal entries, and Panel B shows the accounts after the closing entries have been posted.

The amount in the debit side of each expense account is its adjusted balance. For example, Rent Expense has a $1,000 debit balance. Also note that Service Revenue has a credit balance of $7,400 before closing. These amounts come directly from the adjusted balances in Exhibit 4-8, Panel B.

EXHIBIT 4-9   *Journalizing and Posting the Closing Entries*

OBJECTIVE 4
Close the revenue, expense, and withdrawal accounts

Panel A—Journalizing:

		Closing Entries		Page 5
1.	Apr. 30	Service Revenue	7,400	
		Income Summary		7,400
2.	30	Income Summary	3,875	
		Rent Expense		1,000
		Salary Expense		1,900
		Supplies Expense		300
		Depreciation Expense		275
		Utilities Expense		400
3.	30	Income Summary ($7,400 − $3,875)	3,525	
		Gary Lyon, Capital		3,525
4.	30	Gary Lyon, Capital	3,200	
		Gary Lyon, Withdrawals		3,200

Exhibit 4-9 continues on the following page.

Panel B—Posting:

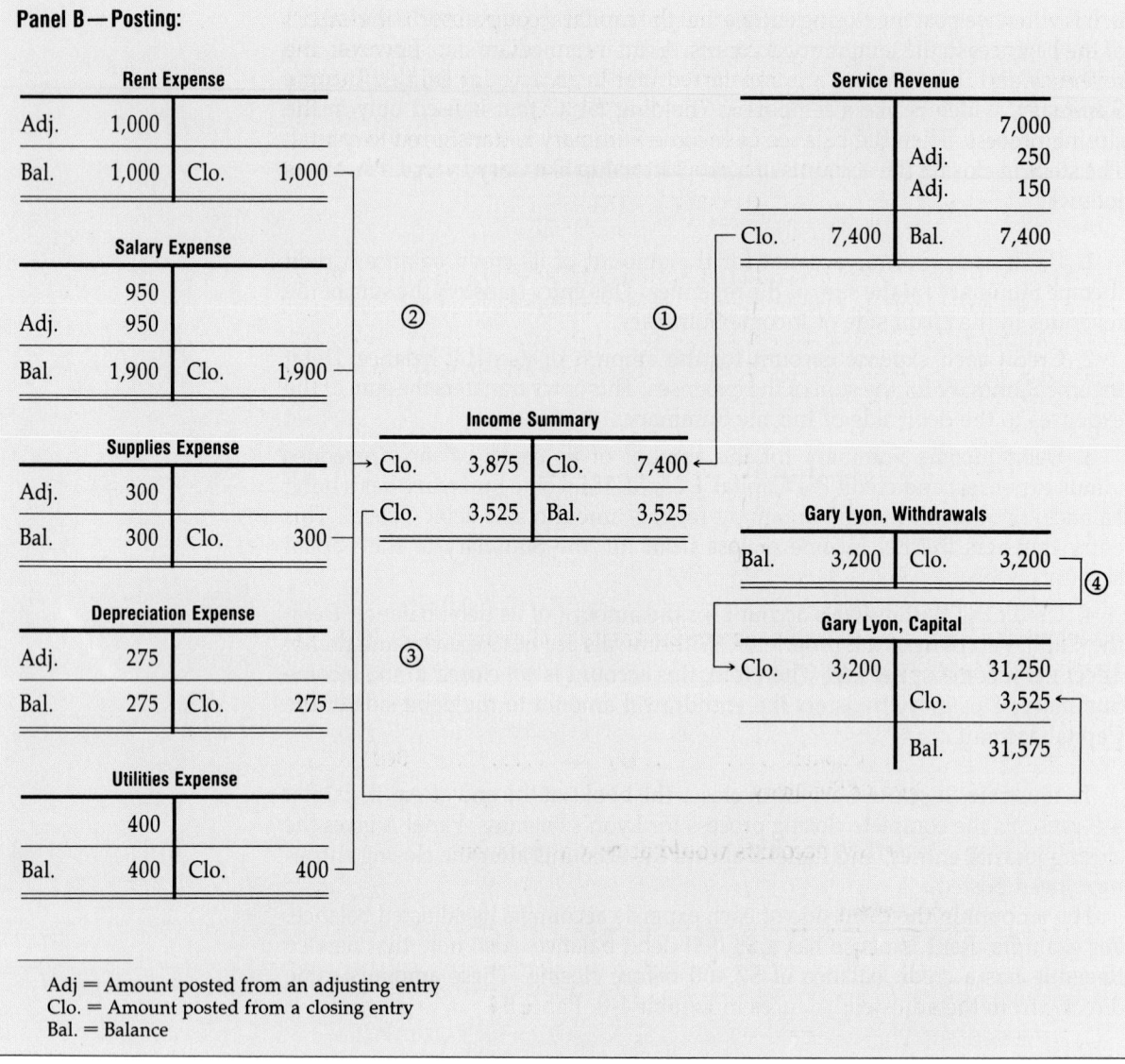

Rent Expense				
Adj.	1,000			
Bal.	1,000	Clo.	1,000	

Salary Expense				
	950			
Adj.	950			
Bal.	1,900	Clo.	1,900	

Supplies Expense				
Adj.	300			
Bal.	300	Clo.	300	

Depreciation Expense				
Adj.	275			
Bal.	275	Clo.	275	

Utilities Expense				
	400			
Bal.	400	Clo.	400	

Service Revenue

				7,000
		Adj.		250
		Adj.		150
Clo.	7,400	Bal.		7,400

Income Summary

Clo.	3,875	Clo.	7,400
Clo.	3,525	Bal.	3,525

Gary Lyon, Withdrawals

Bal.	3,200	Clo.	3,200

Gary Lyon, Capital

Clo.	3,200		31,250
		Clo.	3,525
		Bal.	31,575

Adj = Amount posted from an adjusting entry
Clo. = Amount posted from a closing entry
Bal. = Balance

Closing entry 1, denoted in the Service Revenue account by *Clo.,* transfers Service Revenue's balance to the Income Summary account. This entry zeroes out Service Revenue for April and places the revenue on the credit side of Income Summary. Closing entry 2 zeroes out the expenses and moves their total ($3,875) to the debit side of Income Summary. At this point, Income Summary contains the impact of April's revenues and expenses and hence Income Summary's balance is the month's net income ($3,525). Closing entry 3 closes the Income Summary account by transferring net income to the credit side of Gary Lyon, Capital.[1] The last closing entry (entry 4) moves the owner withdrawals to the debit side of Gary Lyon, Capital, leaving a zero balance in the Withdrawals account.

After all the closing entries, the revenues, the expenses, and the Withdrawals

---

[1] The Income Summary account is a convenience for combining the effects of the revenues and expenses prior to transferring their income effect to Capital. It is not necessary to use the Income Summary account in the closing process. Another way of closing the revenues and expenses makes no use of this account. In this alternative procedure, the revenues and expenses are closed directly to Capital.

account are set back to zero to make ready for the next period. The owner's Capital account includes the full effects of the April revenues, expenses, and withdrawals. These amounts, combined with the beginning Capital balance, give Capital an ending balance of $31,575. Note that this Capital balance agrees with the amount reported on the statement of owner's equity and on the balance sheet in Exhibit 4-7. Also note that the ending balance of Capital remains. We do not close it out—because it is a balance sheet account.

Closing a Net Loss.   What would the closing entries be if Lyon's business had suffered a net *loss* during April? Suppose April expenses totaled $7,700 and all other factors were unchanged. Only closing entries 2 and 3 would be altered. Closing entry 2 would transfer expenses of $7,700 to the debit side of Income Summary, which would appear as follows:

Income Summary

Clo.	7,700	Clo.	7,400
Bal.	300		

Closing entry 3 would then credit Income Summary to close its debit balance and to transfer the net loss to Capital:

3. Apr. 30   Gary Lyon, Capital............................... 300
                      Income Summary 300

After posting, these two accounts would appear as follows:

Income Summary

Clo.	7,700	Clo.	7,400
Bal.	300	Clo.	300

Gary Lyon, Capital

Clo.	300	31,250

Finally, the Withdrawals balance would be closed to Capital, as before.

Postclosing Trial Balance

The accounting cycle ends with the **postclosing trial balance** (see Exhibit 4-10). The postclosing trial balance is the final check on the accuracy of journalizing and posting the adjusting and closing entries. Like the trial balance that begins the work sheet, the postclosing trial balance is a list of the ledger's accounts and balances. This step ensures that the ledger is in balance for the start of the next accounting period. The postclosing trial balance is dated as of the end of the accounting period for which the statements have been prepared.

Note that the postclosing trial balance resembles the balance sheet. It contains the ending balances of the permanent accounts—the balance sheet accounts: the assets, liabilities, and capital. No temporary accounts—revenues, expenses, or withdrawal accounts—are included because their balances have been closed. The ledger is up-to-date and ready for the next period's transactions.

EXHIBIT 4-10   *Postclosing Trial Balance*

Gary Lyon, CPA
Postclosing Trial Balance
April 30, 19X1

Cash	$24,800	
Accounts receivable	2,500	
Supplies	400	
Prepaid rent	2,000	
Furniture	16,500	
Accumulated depreciation		$ 275
Accounts payable		13,100
Salary payable		950
Unearned service revenue		300
Gary Lyon, capital		31,575
Total	$46,200	$46,200

Classification of Assets and Liabilities

OBJECTIVE 5

Classify assets and liabilities as current or long-term

On the balance sheet, assets and liabilities are classified as either *current* or *long-term* to indicate their relative *liquidity*. **Liquidity** is a measure of how quickly an item may be converted to cash. Therefore, cash is the most liquid asset. Accounts receivable is a relatively liquid asset because the business expects to collect the amount in cash in the near future. Supplies are less liquid than accounts receivable, and furniture and buildings are even less so.

Users of financial statements are interested in liquidity because business difficulties often arise owing to a shortage of cash. How quickly can the business convert an asset to cash and pay a debt? How soon must a liability be paid? These are questions of liquidity. Balance sheets list assets and liabilities in the order of their relative liquidity.

Current Assets.   **Current assets** are assets that are expected to be converted to cash, sold, or consumed during the next 12 months or within the business's normal operating cycle if longer than a year. The *operating cycle* is the time span during which (1) cash is used to acquire goods and services, and (2) these goods and services are sold to customers, who in turn pay for their purchases with cash. For most businesses, the operating cycle is a few months. A few types of business have operating cycles longer than a year. Cash, Accounts Receivable, Notes Receivable due within a year or less, and Prepaid Expenses are current assets. Merchandising entities such as Sears, Penney's and K Mart have an additional current asset, Inventory. This account shows the cost of goods that are held for sale to customers.

Long-Term Assets.   **Long-term assets** are all assets other than current assets. They are not held for sale, but rather they are used to operate the business. One category of long-term assets is plant assets, or fixed assets. Land, Buildings, Furniture and Fixtures, and Equipment are examples of plant assets.

Financial statement users such as creditors are interested in the due dates of an entity's liabilities. The sooner a liability must be paid, the more current it is.

Liabilities that must be paid on the earliest future date create the greatest strain on cash. Therefore, the balance sheet lists liabilities in the order in which they are due. Knowing how many of a business's liabilities are current and how many are long-term helps creditors assess the likelihood of collecting from the entity. Balance sheets usually have at least two liability classifications, *current liabilities* and *long-term liabilities.*

Current Liabilities.   **Current liabilities** are debts that are due to be paid within one year or within the entity's operating cycles if the cycle is longer than a year. Accounts Payable, Notes Payable due within one year, Salary Payable, Unearned Revenue, and Interest Payable owed on notes payable are current liabilities.

Long-Term Liabilities.   All liabilities that are not current are classified as **long-term liabilities.** Many notes payable are long-term. Other notes payable are paid in installments, with the first installment due within one year, the second installment due the second year, and so on. In this case, the first installment would be a current liability and the remainder a long-term liability.

An Actual Classified Balance Sheet

Exhibit 4-11 is a classified balance sheet of Hawaiian Airlines, Inc. Hawaiian Airlines labels its plant assets Property and Equipment. (Another common title is Property, Plant, and Equipment.) It is also common to report the *book value,* or *net* amount, of property and equipment ($121,532,000), along with the amount of accumulated depreciation ($32,398,000). The original cost of the assets included in the property and equipment category is the sum of the two amounts, $153,930,000 ($121,532,000 + $32,398,000).

As you study the balance sheet, you will be delighted at how much of it you already understand. So far, you have been exposed to every type of asset and liability reported by this actual company. Other Assets and Other Liabilities are catchall categories for items that are difficult to classify. Stockholders' equity is the owners' equity of a corporation.

Formats of Balance Sheets

The balance sheet of Hawaiian Airlines shown in Exhibit 4-11 lists the assets at the top, with the liabilities and the owners' equity below. This is the **report format.** The balance sheet of Gary Lyon, CPA, presented in Exhibit 4-7 lists the assets at the left, with the liabilities and the owner's equity at the right. That is the **account format.**

Either format is acceptable. A recent survey of 600 companies indicated that 56 percent use the account format, and 44 percent use the report format.

Detecting and Correcting Accounting Errors

You have now learned all the steps that an accountant takes from opening the books and recording a transaction in the journal through closing the books and the postclosing trial balance. Along the way, errors may occur. Accounting errors

EXHIBIT 4-11 *Classified Balance Sheet*

<table>
<tr><td colspan="2" align="center">**Hawaiian Airlines, Inc.**
Balance Sheet
March 31, 19XX</td></tr>
<tr><td>**Assets**</td><td align="right">**(dollar amounts in thousands)**</td></tr>
<tr><td>Current assets:</td><td></td></tr>
<tr><td>Cash ....</td><td align="right">$ 25,116</td></tr>
<tr><td>Accounts receivable ....</td><td align="right">10,061</td></tr>
<tr><td>Inventories ....</td><td align="right">2,307</td></tr>
<tr><td>Prepaid expenses and other current assets ....</td><td align="right">2,864</td></tr>
<tr><td>Total current assets...............................</td><td align="right">40,348</td></tr>
<tr><td>Property and equipment</td><td></td></tr>
<tr><td>Less Accumulated depreciation of $32,398 ....</td><td align="right">121,532</td></tr>
<tr><td>Other assets ....</td><td align="right">5,285</td></tr>
<tr><td>Total ....</td><td align="right">$167,165</td></tr>
<tr><td>**Liabilities**</td><td></td></tr>
<tr><td>Current liabilities:</td><td></td></tr>
<tr><td>Current portion of long-term debt ....</td><td align="right">$ 6,258</td></tr>
<tr><td>Notes payable.....................................</td><td align="right">3,103</td></tr>
<tr><td>Accounts payable.................................</td><td align="right">12,243</td></tr>
<tr><td>Accrued liabilities.................................</td><td align="right">19,192</td></tr>
<tr><td>Other current liabilities ....</td><td align="right">1,696</td></tr>
<tr><td>Total current liabilities ....</td><td align="right">42,492</td></tr>
<tr><td>Long-term debt ....</td><td align="right">111,156</td></tr>
<tr><td>Other liabilities and deferred credits ....</td><td align="right">4,622</td></tr>
<tr><td>**Owners' Equity**</td><td></td></tr>
<tr><td>Stockholders' equity ....</td><td align="right">8,895</td></tr>
<tr><td>Total ....</td><td align="right">$167,165</td></tr>
</table>

include incorrect journal entries, mistakes in posting, and transpositions and slides. This section discusses their detection and correction.

OBJECTIVE 6

Correct typical accounting errors

Incorrect Journal Entries. When a journal entry contains an error, the entry can be erased and corrected — if the error is caught immediately. Other accountants prefer to draw a line through the incorrect entry to maintain a record of all entries to the journal. After the incorrect entry is crossed out, the accountant can make the correct entry.

If the error is detected later, the accountant makes a *correcting entry*. Suppose Gary Lyon paid $5,000 cash for furniture and erroneously debited Supplies as follows:

Incorrect Entry

May 13	Supplies	5,000	
	Cash		5,000
	Bought supplies.		

The debit to Supplies is incorrect, so it is necessary to make a correcting entry as follows:

Correcting Entry

May 15	Furniture	5,000	
	Supplies		5,000
	To correct May 13 entry.		

The credit to Supplies in the second entry offsets the incorrect debit of the first entry. The debit to Furniture in the correcting entry places the purchase amount in the correct account.

Incorrect posting.   Sometimes an accountant posts a debit as a credit or a credit as a debit. Such an error shows up in the trial balance — total debits do not equal total credits.

Suppose a $100 debit to Cash is posted as a $100 credit. The trial balance's total debits are $100 too low. Total credits are $100 too high. The difference is $200. Whenever a debit or credit has been misplaced, the resulting difference is evenly divisible by 2, as is the $200 figure in our example. Dividing that difference by 2 yields the amount of the incorrect posting, which in this case we know is $100. The accountant may then search the journal for the $100 entry and make the corrections.

Transpositions and slides.   A **transposition** occurs when digits are flip-flopped — for example, $85 is a transposition of $58. Transpositions cause errors that are evenly divisible by 9. In this particular case, the transposition causes a $27 error ($85 − $58), which is evenly divisible by 9 ($27/9 = $3).

A **slide** results from adding one or more zeroes to a number or from dropping off a zero, for example, writing $500 as $5,000 or vice versa. The difference of $4,500 ($5,000 − $500) is evenly divisible by 9 ($4,500/9 = $500). Transpositions and slides occur in the transfer of numbers, for example, from the journal to the ledger or from the ledger to the trial balance.

Incorrect postings, transpositions, and slides can be corrected by crossing out the incorrect amount and then inserting the correct amount in its appropriate place.

Microcomputer Spreadsheets _____

Companies offer a variety of specialized computer programs — known as *software* — that require almost no computer programming expertise. Some software programs create an electronically prepared work sheet, also called a **spreadsheet.** The spreadsheet can be programmed to complete the work sheet after the accountant has entered the trial balance and the adjustment amounts. This is a big time saver because once the spreadsheet program is set up, it can be used over and over again without having to rewrite the account titles and do the arithmetic by hand. The spreadsheet can also be programmed to journalize and post the adjusting and closing entries and prepare the financial statements directly from the data on the work sheet.

To illustrate how a spreadsheet can be programmed to complete the work sheet, let's focus on the Accounts Receivable account. Assume that the goal is to determine Accounts Receivable's balance sheet amount of $2,500. The Accounts Receivable line from Exhibit 4-5 follows:

OBJECTIVE 7
Explain how a microcomputer spreadsheet can be used in accounting

Account Title	Trial Balance		Adjustments		Adjusted Trial Balance		Income Statement		Balance Sheet	
	Debit	Credit	Debit	Credit	Debit	Credit	Debit	Credit	Debit	Credit
Cash										
Accounts receivable	2,250		250		2,500				2,500	
Supplies										

How can the accountant use a spreadsheet program to accomplish this task? The spreadsheet appears on a video screen as a matrix of columns and rows—with no amounts or labels. Assume the spreadsheet provides a work space of 500 columns and 500 rows, as follows:

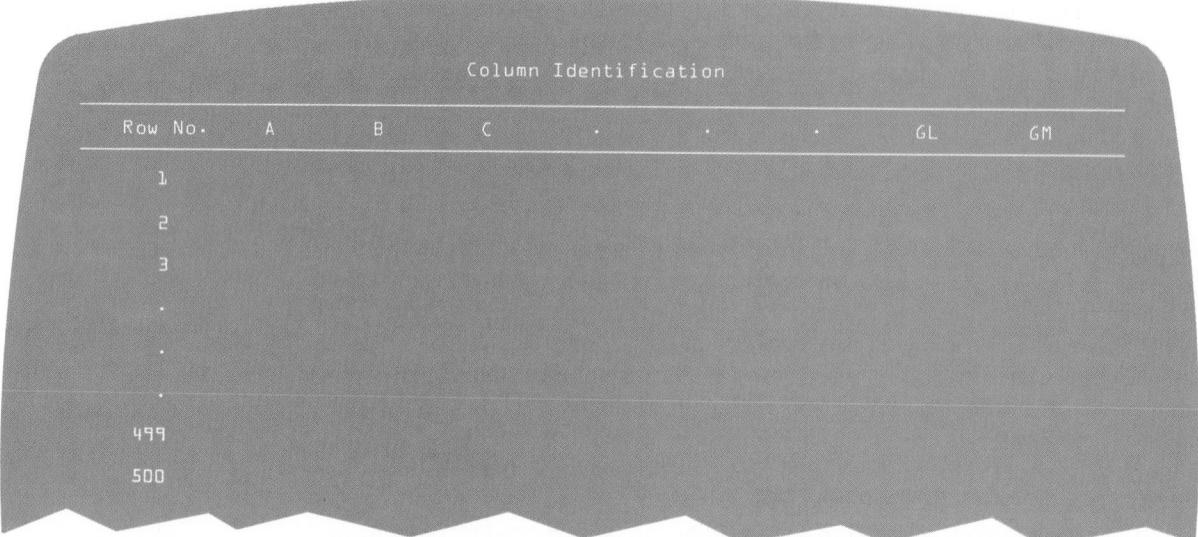

Using the keyboard of a microcomputer, the accountant can program the spreadsheet to resemble a work sheet. The columns are labeled to represent the work sheet columns, and the rows represent the accounts listed on the trial balance. It is also necessary to label the spaces where the dollar amounts go. The accountant may denote Accounts Receivable's unadjusted trial balance amount as W, a debit adjustment as X, a credit adjustment as Y, and Accounts Receivable's adjusted balance as Z. Thus labeled, the partial spreadsheet appears on the video screen as follows:

A fully computerized accounting system can transfer the account balances from the ledger to the trial balance. These amounts, plus or minus the adjustments, equal the adjusted balances. The accountant can program the computer to complete the work sheet as follows:

Account Title	Trial Balance		Adjustments		Adjusted Trial Balance		Income Statement		Balance Sheet	
	Debit	Credit	Debit	Credit	Debit	Credit	Debit	Credit	Debit	Credit
Cash										
Accounts Receivable	W		X	Y	W + X −Y = Z				Z	
Supplies										

Gary Lyon can use the keyboard to enter the following values into the computer: W = $2,250; X = $250; and Y = $0. The spreadsheet takes over and computes Z = $2,500 for the adjusted trial balance and the balance sheet. The accountant gives the computer a print command, and it prints the completed work sheet as shown for Accounts Receivable at the beginning of this section. The other account balances are generated similarly.

As in a manual system, the completed work sheet yields the amounts for the adjusting entries, the closing entries, and the financial statements. The beauty of the spreadsheet is that once the computer program is written, it can perform its task as often as desired with no arithmetic errors. As the business changes and new accounts are needed, the accountant can simply insert the new account titles and adapt the spreadsheet program accordingly.

Summary Problem for Your Review

Refer to the data in the earlier Summary Problem for Your Review, presented on page 134.

Required

1. Journalize and post the adjusting entries. (Before posting to the accounts, enter their balances as shown in the trial balance. For example, enter the $370,000 balance in the Accounts Receivable account before posting its adjusting entry.) Key adjusting entries by *letter*, as shown in the work sheet solution to the first review problem. You can take the adjusting entries straight from the work sheet on page 135.

2. Journalize and post the closing entries. (Each account should carry its balance as shown in the adjusted trial balance.) To distinguish closing entries from adjusting entries, key the closing entries by *number*. Draw the arrows to illustrate the flow of data, as shown in Exhibit 4-9, page 140. Indicate the balance of the Capital account after the closing entries are posted.

3. Prepare the income statement for the year ended December 31, 19X1. List Miscellaneous Expense last among the expenses, a common practice.
4. Prepare the statement of owner's equity for the year ended December 31, 19X1. Draw the arrow that links the income statement to the statement of owner's equity.
5. Prepare the classified balance sheet at December 31, 19X1. Use the report form. All liabilities are current. Draw the arrow that links the statement of owner's equity to the balance sheet.

SOLUTION TO REVIEW PROBLEM

Requirement 1

a.	Dec. 31	Supplies Expense	4,000	
		Supplies...............................		4,000
b.	31	Depreciation Expense–Furniture and Fixtures	20,000	
		Accumulated Depreciation–Furniture and Fixtures.........................		20,000
c.	31	Depreciation Expense–Building...............	10,000	
		Accumulated Depreciation–Building		10,000
d.	31	Salary Expense	5,000	
		Salary Payable		5,000
e.	31	Accounts Receivable........................	12,000	
		Service Revenue		12,000
f.	31	Unearned Service Revenue	32,000	
		Service Revenue		32,000

Accounts Receivable		Supplies		Accumulated Depreciation– Furniture and Fixtures
370,000		6,000 | (a) 4,000		40,000
(e) 12,000				(b) 20,000

Accumulated Depreciation– Building	Salary Payable	Unearned Service Revenue
130,000	(d) 5,000	(f) 32,000 | 45,000
(c) 10,000		

Service Revenue	Salary Expense	Supplies Expense
286,000	172,000	(a) 4,000
(e) 12,000	(d) 5,000	Bal. 4,000
(f) 32,000	Bal. 177,000	
Bal. 330,000		

Depreciation Expense– Building	Depreciation Expense– Furniture and Fixtures
(c) 10,000	(b) 20,000
Bal. 10,000	Bal. 20,000

Requirement 2

1.	Dec. 31	Service Revenue	330,000	
		Income Summary		330,000
2.	31	Income Summary	224,000	
		Salary Expense		177,000
		Supplies Expense		4,000
		Depreciation Expense–Furniture and Fixtures.		20,000
		Depreciation Expense–Building.		10,000
		Miscellaneous Expense.		13,000
3.	31	Income Summary ($330,000 − $224,000).	106,000	
		Capital.		106,000
4.	31	Capital.	65,000	
		Withdrawals		65,000

Salary Expense

	172,000		
(d)	5,000		
Bal.	177,000	(2)	177,000

Supplies Expense

(a)	4,000		
Bal.	4,000	(2)	4,000

Depreciation Expense– Furniture & Fixtures

(b)	20,000		
Bal.	20,000	(2)	20,000

Depreciation Expense– Building

(c)	10,000		
Bal.	10,000	(2)	10,000

Miscellaneous Expense

	13,000		
Bal.	13,000	(2)	13,000

Income Summary

(2)	224,000	(1)	330,000
(3)	106,000	Bal.	106,000

Service Revenue

			286,000
		(e)	12,000
		(f)	32,000
(1)	330,000	Bal.	330,000

Withdrawals

Bal.	65,000	(4)	65,000

Capital

(4)	65,000		293,000
		(3)	106,000
		Bal.	334,000

Requirement 3

State Service Company
Income Statement
For the Year Ended December 31, 19X1

Revenues:		
Service revenue		$330,000
Expenses:		
Salary expense	$177,000	
Depreciation expense–furniture and fixtures	20,000	
Depreciation expense–building	10,000	
Supplies expense	4,000	
Miscellaneous expense	13,000	
Total expenses		224,000
Net Income		$106,000

Requirement 4

State Service Company
Statement of Owner's Equity
For the Year Ended December 31, 19X1

Capital, January 1, 19X1	$293,000
Add: Net income	106,000
	399,000
Less: Withdrawals	65,000
Capital, December 31, 19X1	$334,000

Requirement 5

State Service Company
Balance Sheet
December 31, 19X1

Assets

Current assets:		
Cash		$198,000
Accounts receivable		382,000
Supplies		2,000
Total current assets		582,000
Plant assets:		
Furniture and fixtures	$100,000	
Less Accumulated depreciation	60,000	40,000
Building	250,000	
Less Accumulated depreciation	140,000	110,000
Total assets		$732,000

Liabilities

Current liabilities:	
Accounts payable	$380,000
Salary payable	5,000
Unearned service revenue	13,000
Total current liabilities	398,000

Owner's Equity

Capital	334,000
Total liabilities and owner's equity	$732,000

Summary

The *accounting cycle* is the process by which accountants produce the financial statements for a specific period of time. The cycle starts with the beginning account balances. During the period, the business journalizes transactions and posts them to the ledger accounts. At the end of the period, the trial balance is prepared, and the accounts are adjusted in order to measure the period's net income or net loss.

Completion of the accounting cycle is aided by use of a *work sheet*. This columnar document summarizes the effects of all the activity of the period. It is neither a journal nor a ledger but merely a convenient device for completing the accounting cycle.

The work sheet has columns for the trial balance, the adjustments, the adjusted trial balance, the income statement, and the balance sheet. It aids the adjusting process, and it is the place where the period's net income or net loss is first computed. The work sheet also provides the data for the financial statements and the closing entries. However, it is *not* necessary. The accounting cycle can be completed from the less elaborate adjusted trial balance.

Revenues, expenses, and withdrawals represent increases and decreases in owner's equity for a specific period. At the end of the period, their balances are closed out to zero, and, for this reason, they are called *temporary accounts*. Assets, liabilities, and owner's equity are not closed because they are the *permanent accounts*. Their balances at the end of one period become the beginning balances of the next period. The final accuracy check of the period is the *postclosing trial balance*.

Four common accounting errors are *incorrect journal entries, incorrect postings, transpositions,* and *slides*. Techniques exist for detecting and correcting these errors.

Microcomputer *spreadsheets* are extremely useful for tasks such as completing the accounting cycle. Their main advantage is that they can be programmed to print documents such as the work sheet and perform repetitious calculations without errors.

Self-Study Questions

Test your understanding of the chapter by marking the best answer to each of the following questions.

1. The focal point of the accounting cycle is the *(p. 125)*
    a. Financial statements
    b. Trial balance
    c. Adjusted trial balance
    d. Work sheet

2. Arrange the following accounting cycle steps in their proper order *(p. 126)*:
    a. Complete the work sheet
    b. Journalize and post adjusting entries
    c. Prepare the postclosing trial balance
    d. Journalize and post cash transactions
    e. Prepare the financial statements
    f. Journalize and post closing entries

3. The work sheet is a *(p. 126)*
    a. Journal
    b. Ledger
    c. Financial statement
    d. Convenient device for completing the accounting cycle

4. The usefulness of the work sheet is *(p. 126)*
    a. Identifying the accounts that need to be adjusted
    b. Summarizing the effects of all the transactions of the period
    c. Aiding the preparation of the financial statements
    d. All of the above

5. Which of the following accounts is not closed? *(pp. 137, 138)*
    a. Supplies Expense
    b. Prepaid Insurance
    c. Interest Revenue
    d. Owner Withdrawals

6. The closing entry for Salary Expense, with a balance of $322,000, is (p. 139)

    a. Salary Expense 322,000
        Income Summary   322,000
    b. Salary Expense 322,000
        Salary Payable...........................   322,000
    c. Income Summary 322,000
        Salary Expense   322,000
    d. Salary Payable............................... 322,000
        Salary Expense   322,000

7. The purpose of the postclosing trial balance is to (p. 141)
    a. Provide the account balances for preparation of the balance sheet
    b. Ensure that the ledger is in balance for the start of the next period
    c. Aid the journalizing and posting of the closing entries
    d. Ensure that the ledger is in balance for completion of the work sheet

8. Which of the following accounts will appear on the postclosing trial balance? (p. 141)
    a. Building
    b. Depreciation Expense–Building
    c. Service Revenue
    d. Owner Withdrawals

9. The classification of assets and liabilities as current or long-term depends on (p. 142)
    a. Their order of listing in the general ledger
    b. Whether they appear on the balance sheet or the income statement
    c. The relative liquidity of the item
    d. The format of the balance sheet—account format or report format

10. Posting a $300 debit as a credit causes an error (p. 145)
    a. That is evenly divisible by 9
    b. That is evenly divisible by 2
    c. In the journal
    d. Known as a transposition

Answers to the self-study questions are at the end of the chapter.

Accounting Vocabulary

account format of the balance sheet (p. 143), accounting cycle (p. 125), closing entry (p. 138), closing the accounts (p. 136), current assets (p. 142), current liabilities (p. 143), income summary (p. 139), liquidity (p. 142), long-term assets (p. 142), long-term liabilities (p. 143), nominal account (p. 137) permanent account (p. 138), postclosing trial balance (p. 141), real account (p. 138), report format of the balance sheet (p. 143), slide (p. 145), spreadsheet (p. 145), temporary account (p. 137), transposition (p. 145), work sheet (p. 126).

ASSIGNMENT MATERIAL

Questions

1. Identify the steps in the accounting cycle, distinguishing those that occur during the period from those that are performed at the end.
2. Why is the work sheet a valuable accounting tool?
3. Name two advantages the work sheet has over the adjusted trial balance.
4. Why must the adjusting entries be journalized and posted if they have already been entered on the work sheet?

5. Why should the adjusting entries be journalized and posted before making the closing entries?

6. Which types of accounts are closed?

7. What purpose is served by closing the accounts?

8. State how the work sheet helps with recording the closing entries.

9. Distinguish between permanent accounts and temporary accounts, indicating which type is closed at the end of the period. Give five examples of each type of account.

10. Is Income Summary a permanent account or a temporary account? When and how is it used?

11. Give the closing entries for the following accounts (balances in parentheses): Service Revenue ($4,700), Salary Expense ($1,100), Income Summary (credit balance of $2,000), Rhonda McGill, Withdrawals ($2,300).

12. Why are assets classified as current or long-term? On what basis are they classified? Where do the classified amounts appear?

13. Indicate which of the following accounts are *current assets* and which are *long-term assets:* Prepaid Rent, Building, Furniture, Accounts Receivable, Merchandise Inventory, Cash, Note Receivable (due within one year), Note Receivable (due after one year).

14. In what order are assets and liabilities listed on the balance sheet?

15. Name an outside party that is interested in whether a liability is current or long-term. Why is this party interested in this information?

16. A friend tells you that the difference between a current liability and a long-term liability is that they are payable to different types of creditors. Is your friend correct? Include in your answer the definitions of these two categories of liabilities.

17. Give the name of the following accounting errors:
    a. Posted a $300 debit from the journal as a $300 credit in the ledger.
    b. Posted a $300 debit from the journal as a $3,000 debit in the ledger.
    c. Recorded a transaction by debiting one account for $3,100 and crediting the other account for $1,300.

18. How would you detect each of the errors in the preceding question?

19. Capp Company purchased supplies of $120 on account. The accountant debited Supplies and credited Cash for $120. A week later, after this entry has been posted to the ledger, the accountant discovers the error. How should he correct the error?

20. Briefly explain how a microcomputer spreadsheet can be programmed to complete the work sheet.

Exercises

Exercise 4-1   *Preparing a work sheet*

The trial balance of Alban's TV Repair Service is on the next page.

Additional information at September 30, 19X6:

a. Accrued salary expense, $600.
b. Prepaid rent expired, $900.
c. Supplies used, $2,250.
d. Accrued service revenue, $210.
e. Depreciation, $70.

Required

Complete Alban's work sheet for September 19X6.

Alban's TV Repair Service
Trial Balance
September 30, 19X6

Cash..................................	$ 1,560	
Accounts receivable	2,840	
Prepaid rent..........................	1,200	
Supplies.............................	3,390	
Equipment...........................	12,600	
Accumulated depreciation		$ 2,240
Accounts payable		1,600
Salary payable........................		
Ned Alban, capital		16,030
Ned Alban, withdrawals.................	3,000	
Service revenue.......................		7,300
Depreciation expense		
Salary expense........................	1,800	
Rent expense.........................		
Utilities expense	780	
Supplies expense......................		
Total................................	$27,170	$27,170

Exercise 4-2   *Journalizing adjusting and closing entries*

Journalize the adjusting and closing entries in Exercise 4-1.

Exercise 4-3   *Posting adjusting and closing entries*

Set up T-accounts for those accounts affected by the adjusting and closing entries in Exercise 4-1. Post the adjusting and closing entries to the accounts, denoting adjustment amounts by Adj., closing amounts by Clo., and balances by Bal. Double rule the accounts with zero balances after closing and show the ending balance in each account.

Exercise 4-4   *Preparing a postclosing trial balance*

Prepare the postclosing trial balance in Exercise 4-1.

Exercise 4-5   *Identifying and journalizing closing entries*

From the following selected accounts that Rodriguez Sales Company reported in its June 30, 19X4, annual financial statements, prepare the entity's closing entries.

D. Rodriquez, capital	$45,600	Interest expense	$ 2,200
Service revenue	90,500	Accounts receivable	26,000
Unearned revenues	1,350	Salary payable	850
Salary expense	15,500	Depreciation expense	10,200
Accumulated depreciation	35,000	Rent expense	5,900
Supplies expense	1,400	D. Rodriguez, withdrawals	40,000
Interest revenue	700	Supplies	1,100

Exercise 4-6 *Identifying and journalizing closing entries*

The accountant for Trish Nunley, Attorney, has posted adjusting entries *a* through *e* to the accounts at December 31, 19X2. All the revenue, expense, and owner's equity accounts of the entity are listed here in T-account form.

Accounts Receivable		Supplies		Accumulated Depreciation – Furniture	
23,000		4,000	(a) 2,000		5,000
(e) 3,500					(b) 3,000

Accumulated Decpreciation – Building				Salary Payable	
	33,000				(d) 1,500
	(c) 6,000				

Trish Nunley, Capital		Trish Nunley, Withdrawals		Service Revenue	
	49,400	52,400			103,000
					(e) 3,500

Salary Expense		Supplies Expense		Depreciation Expense – Furniture		Depreciation Expense – Building	
28,000		(a) 2,000		(b) 3,000		(c) 6,000	
(d) 1,500							

Required

Journalize Nunley's closing entries at December 31, 19X2.

Exercise 4-7 *Preparing a statement of owner's equity*

From the following accounts of Kathryn Hopkins Realty Company, prepare the entity's statement of owner's equity for the year ended December 31, 19X5:

Kathryn Hopkins, Capital				Kathryn Hopkins, Withdrawals			
Dec. 31	34,000	Jan. 1	35,000	Mar. 31	8,000	Dec. 31	34,000
		Mar. 9	28,000	Jun. 30	8,000		
		Dec. 31	43,000	Sep. 30	8,000		
				Dec. 31	10,000		

Income Summary			
Dec. 31	85,000	Dec. 31	128,000
Dec. 31	43,000		

Exercise 4-8 *Identifying and recording adjusting and closing entries*

The trial balance and income statement amounts from the March work sheet of Tekell Service Company are presented on the next page.

Required

Journalize the adjusting and closing entries of Tekell Service Company at March 31.

Account Title	Trial Balance		Income Statement	
Cash	$ 3,100			
Supplies	2,400			
Prepaid rent	1,100			
Office equipment	36,800			
Accumulated depreciation.............		$ 6,900		
Accounts payable....................		10,600		
Salary payable				
Unearned service revenue.............		4,400		
Angela Tekell, capital		14,800		
Angela Tekell, withdrawals............	1,000			
Service revenue		12,700		$16,000
Salary expense......................	3,000		$ 3,800	
Rent expense	1,200		1,400	
Depreciation expense.................			400	
Supplies expense			1,700	
Utilities expense.....................	800		800	
	$49,400	$49,400	$ 8,100	$16,000
Net income.........................			7,900	
			$16,000	$16,000

Exercise 4-9   *Preparing a classified balance sheet*

Use the data in Exercise 4-8 to prepare Tekell Service Company's classified balance sheet at March 31 of the current year. Use the report format.

Exercise 4-10   *Correcting accounting errors*

Prepare a correcting entry for each of the following accounting errors:

a. Recorded a $400 cash purchase of supplies by debiting Supplies and crediting Accounts Payable.

b. Debited Office Furniture and credited Accounts Payable for a $2,300 credit purchase of office equipment.

c. Adjusted prepaid rent by debiting Prepaid Rent and crediting Rent Expense for $900. This adjusting entry should have debited Rent Expense and credited Prepaid Rent for $900.

d. Debited Salary Expense and credited Cash to accrue salary expense of $300.

e. Recorded the earning of $3,200 service revenue collected in advance by debiting Accounts Receivable and crediting Service Revenue.

f. Accrued interest revenue of $800 by a debit to Accounts Receivable and a credit to Interest Revenue.

(Group A)

Problem 4-1A   *Preparing financial statements from an adjusted trial balance; journalizing, adjusting, and closing entries*

The adjusted trial balance of Merced Service Company at June 30, 19X1, the end of the company's fiscal year, is on the next page.

Additional data at June 30, 19X1:

a. Supplies used during the year, $3,580.

b. Prepaid insurance expired during the year, $3,100.

Merced Service Company
Adjusted Trial Balance
June 30, 19X1

Cash.............................	$ 3,350	
Accounts receivable	11,470	
Supplies..........................	1,290	
Prepaid insurance...................	1,700	
Equipment.........................	55,800	
Accumulated depreciation–equipment ...		$ 16,480
Building..........................	144,900	
Accumulated depreciation–building		16,850
Accounts payable		36,900
Interest payable.....................		1,490
Wage payable		770
Unearned service revenue		2,300
Note payable, long-term...............		104,000
Ramon DeSoto, capital		37,390
Ramon DeSoto, withdrawals	52,300	
Service revenue.....................		108,360
Depreciation expense–equipment	6,300	
Depreciation expense–building	3,470	
Wage expense	18,800	
Insurance expense....................	3,100	
Interest expense.....................	11,510	
Utilities expense	4,300	
Property tax expense.................	2,670	
Supplies expense....................	3,580	
Total.............................	$324,540	$324,540

c. Accrued interest expense, $680.
d. Accrued service revenue, $940.
e. Depreciation for the year: equipment, $6,300; building, $3,470.
f. Accrued wage expense, $770.
g. Unearned service revenue earned during the year, $6,790.

Required

1. Prepare Merced's income statement and statement of owner's equity for the year ended June 30, 19X1, and the classified balance sheet on that date. Use the account format for the balance sheet.
2. Journalize the adjusting and closing entries.

Problem 4-2A *Preparing a work sheet*

The trial balance of Schoepplein Painting Contractors at July 31, 19X3 is on the next page.

Additional data at July 31, 19X3:

a. Accrued wage expense, $440.
b. Supplies on hand, $14,740.

Schoepplein Painting Contractors
Trial Balance
July 31, 19X3

Cash...............................	$ 4,200	
Accounts receivable	37,820	
Supplies............................	17,660	
Prepaid insurance	2,300	
Equipment..........................	32,690	
Accumulated depreciation–equipment ...		$ 26,240
Building............................	36,890	
Accumulated depreciation–building		10,500
Land...............................	28,300	
Accounts payable		22,690
Interest payable......................		
Wage payable		
Unearned service revenue		10,560
Note payable, long-term...............		22,000
Leslie Schoepplein, capital		62,130
Leslie Schoepplein, withdrawals	4,200	
Service revenue......................		17,190
Depreciation expense–equipment		
Depreciation expense–building		
Wage expense	5,800	
Insurance expense....................		
Interest expense......................		
Utilities expense	270	
Property tax expense..................	840	
Advertising expense	340	
Supplies expense.....................		
Total..............................	$171,310	$171,310

c. Prepaid insurance expired during July, $500.
d. Accrued interest expense, $180.
e. Unearned service revenue earned during July, $4,770.
f. Accrued advertising expense, $100 (credit Accounts Payable).
g. Accrued service revenue, $1,100.
h. Depreciation: equipment, $430; building, $270.

Required

Complete Schoepplein's work sheet for July.

Problem 4-3A   *Taking the accounting cycle through the closing entries*

The unadjusted T-accounts of Julie Warner, M.D., at December 31, 19X2, and the related year-end adjustment data follow:

Cash	**Accounts Receivable**	**Supplies**
Bal. 7,000	Bal. 38,000	Bal. 9,000

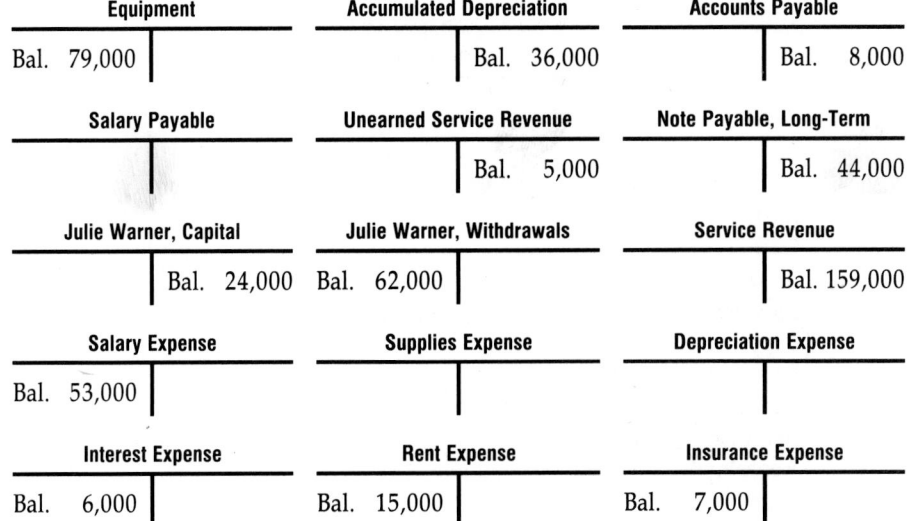

Equipment	Accumulated Depreciation	Accounts Payable
Bal. 79,000	Bal. 36,000	Bal. 8,000

Salary Payable	Unearned Service Revenue	Note Payable, Long-Term
	Bal. 5,000	Bal. 44,000

Julie Warner, Capital	Julie Warner, Withdrawals	Service Revenue
Bal. 24,000	Bal. 62,000	Bal. 159,000

Salary Expense	Supplies Expense	Depreciation Expense
Bal. 53,000		

Interest Expense	Rent Expense	Insurance Expense
Bal. 6,000	Bal. 15,000	Bal. 7,000

Adjustment data at December 31, 19X2, include:

a. Supplies on hand, $1,000.
b. Depreciation for the year, $9,000.
c. Accrued salary expense, $2,000.
d. Accrued service revenue, $1,000.
e. Unearned service revenue earned during the year, $5,000.

Required

1. Write the trial balance on a worksheet, and complete the worksheet. Key each adjusting entry by the letter corresponding to the data given.
2. Prepare the income statement, the statement of owner's equity, and the classified balance sheet in account format.
3. Journalize the adjusting and closing entries.

Problem 4-4A   *Completing the accounting cycle*

This problem should be used only in conjunction with Problem 4-3A. It completes the accounting cycle by posting to T-accounts and preparing the postclosing trial balance.

Required

1. Using the Problem 4-3A data, post the adjusting and closing entries to the T-accounts, denoting adjusting amounts by Adj., closing amounts by Clo., and account balances by Bal., as shown in Exhibit 4-9. Double underline all accounts with a zero ending balance.
2. Prepare the postclosing trial balance.

Problem 4-5A   *Completing the accounting cycle*

The trial balance of Moore Realty at August 31, 19X9, and the data needed for the month-end adjustments follow.

Adjustment data:

a. Prepaid insurance still in force at August 31, $1,190.
b. Supplies used during the month, $140.

Moore Realty
Trial Balance
August 31, 19X9

Account Number	Account Title	Debit	Credit
11	Cash......................................	$ 6,800	
12	Accounts receivable	17,560	
13	Prepaid insurance.........................	1,290	
14	Supplies..................................	900	
15	Furniture	15,350	
16	Accumulated depreciation–furniture		$ 12,800
17	Building..................................	89,900	
18	Accumulated depreciation–building..............		28,600
21	Accounts payable		6,240
22	Salary payable............................		
23	Unearned commission revenue		8,900
31	B. J. Moore, capital		74,920
32	B. J. Moore, withdrawals	4,800	
41	Commission revenue		7,800
51	Salary expense	1,600	
52	Insurance expense.........................		
53	Utilities expense	410	
54	Depreciation expense–furniture		
55	Depreciation expense–building.................		
56	Advertising expense	650	
57	Supplies expense..........................		
	Total....................................	$139,260	$139,260

c. Depreciation on building for the month, $130.
d. Depreciation on furniture for the month, $370.
e. Accrued salary expense at August 31, $460.
f. Unearned commission revenue still unearned at August 31, $7,750.

Required

1. Open the accounts listed in the trial balance, inserting their August 31 unadjusted balances. Also open the Income Summary account, number 33. Use four column accounts. Date the balances of the following accounts as of August 1: Prepaid Insurance, Supplies, Building, Accumulated Depreciation–Building, Furniture, Accumulated Depreciation–Furniture, Unearned Commission Revenue, and B. J. Moore, Capital.

2. Write the trial balance on a work sheet and complete the work sheet of Moore Realty for the month ended August 31 of the current year.

3. Prepare the income statement, the statement of owner's equity, and the classified balance sheet in report format.

4. Using the work sheet data, journalize and post the adjusting and closing entries. Use dates and posting references. Use page 7 as the number of the journal page.

5. Prepare a postclosing trial balance.

Problem 4-6A *Preparing a classified balance sheet in report format*

The accounts of Matusak Sales Agency at December 31, 19X6, are listed in alphabetical order. All adjustments have been journalized and posted, but the closing entries have not yet been made. Prepare the company's classified balance sheet in report format at December 31, 19X6. Use captions for total assets, total liabilities, and total liabilities and owner's equity.

Accounts payable	$ 3,100	Interest receivable	$ 200
Accounts receivable	4,600	Inventory	6,600
Accumulated depreciation– building	37,800	Lou Matusak, capital, December 31, 19X5	50,300
Accumulated depreciation– furniture	11,600	Lou Matusak, withdrawals	47,400
Advertising expense	2,200	Note payable, long-term	7,800
Building	84,400	Note receivable, long-term	4,000
Cash	4,500	Other assets	3,600
Commission revenue	93,500	Other current assets	1,700
Current portion of note payable	2,200	Other current liabilities	4,700
Current portion of note receivable	1,000	Prepaid insurance	1,100
Depreciation expense	1,300	Salary expense	22,600
Furniture	22,700	Salary payable	1,900
Insurance expense	800	Supplies	2,500
Interest payable	600	Supplies expense	5,700
		Unearned commission revenue	3,400

Problem 4-7A *Analyzing and journalizing corrections, adjustments, and closing entries*

Accountants for Mills Service Company, a proprietorship, encountered the following situations while adjusting and closing the books at December 31. Consider each situation independently.

a. The company bookkeeper made the following entry to record a $400 credit purchase of office supplies:

Nov. 12   Office Furniture 400
                Accounts Payable......................... 400

Prepare the correcting entry, dated December 31.

b. A $750 debit to Cash was posted as a credit.
(1) At what stage of the accounting cycle will this error be detected?
(2) Describe the technique for identifying the amount of the error.

c. The $35,000 balance of Equipment was entered as $3,500 on the trial balance.
(1) What is the name of this type of error?
(2) Assume this is the only error in the trial balance. Which will be greater, the total debits or the total credits, and by how much?
(3) How can this type of error be identified?

d. The accountant failed to make the following adjusting entries at December 31:
(1) Accrued property tax expense, $600.
(2) Supplies expense, $1,390.
(3) Accrued interest revenue on a note receivable, $950.
(4) Depreciation of equipment, $4,000.
(5) Earned service revenue that had been collected in advance, $5,300.
   Compute the overall net income effect of these omissions.

e. Record each of the adjusting entries identified in item *d*.

f. The revenue and expense accounts, after the adjusting entries had been posted were Service Revenue, $55,800; Salary Expense, $13,200; Rent Expense, $5,100; Advertising Expense, $3,550; Utilities Expense, $1,530; and Miscellaneous Expense, $1,190. Two balances prior to closing were J. E. Mills, Capital, $58,600; and J. E. Mills, Withdrawals, $30,000.
    Journalize the closing entries.

(Group B)

Problem 4-1B *Preparing financial statements from an adjusted trial balance; journalizing, adjusting, and closing entries*

The adjusted trial balance of Chun Consultants at April 30, 19X2, the end of the company's fiscal year, follows:

Chun Consultants		
Adjusted Trial Balance		
April 30, 19X2		
Cash..............................	$ 2,370	
Accounts receivable	25,740	
Supplies...........................	3,690	
Prepaid insurance	2,290	
Equipment.........................	63,930	
Accumulated depreciation–equipment ...		$ 28,430
Building...........................	74,330	
Accumulated depreciation–building		18,260
Accounts payable		19,550
Interest payable.....................		2,280
Wage payable		830
Unearned service revenue		3,660
Note payable, long-term..............		77,900
Vivian Chun, capital.................		46,200
Vivian Chun, withdrawals.............	55,500	
Service revenue.....................		99,550
Depreciation expense–equipment	6,700	
Depreciation expense–building	3,210	
Wage expense	29,800	
Insurance expense.	5,370	
Interest expense..	8,170	
Utilities expense	5,670	
Property tax expense..................	3,010	
Supplies expense.....................	6,880	
Total.............................	$296,660	$296,660

Additional data at April 30, 19X2:

a. Supplies used during the year, $6,880.
b. Prepaid insurance expired during the year, $5,370.
c. Accrued interest expense, $2,280.
d. Accrued service revenue, $2,200.
e. Depreciation for the year: equipment, $6,700; building, $3,210.
f. Accrued wage expense, $830.
g. Unearned service revenue earned during the year, $5,180.

Required

1. Prepare Chun's income statement and statement of owner's equity for the year ended April 30, 19X2, and the classified balance sheet on that date. Use the account format for the balance sheet.
2. Journalize the adjusting and closing entries.

Problem 4-2B   *Preparing a work sheet*

The trial balance of Broadmoor Realty Brokers at May 31, 19X2, follows:

Broadmoor Realty Brokers Trial Balance May 31, 19X2		
Cash	$ 1,670	
Notes receivable	10,340	
Interest receivable		
Supplies	560	
Prepaid insurance	1,790	
Furniture	27,410	
Accumulated depreciation–furniture		$ 1,480
Building	55,900	
Accumulated depreciation–building		33,560
Land	13,700	
Accounts payable		14,730
Interest payable		
Salary payable		
Unearned commission revenue		6,800
Note payable, long-term		18,700
Rex Jennings, capital		34,290
Rex Jennings, withdrawals	3,800	
Commission revenue		9,970
Interest revenue		
Depreciation expense–furniture		
Depreciation expense–building		
Salary expense	2,170	
Insurance expense		
Interest expense		
Utilities expense	490	
Property tax expense	640	
Advertising expense	1,060	
Supplies expense		
Total	$119,530	$119,530

Additional data at May 31, 19X2:

a. Accrued salary expense, $600.
b. Supplies on hand, $410.
c. Prepaid insurance expired during May, $390.
d. Accrued interest expense, $220.
e. Unearned commission revenue earned during May, $1,400.
f. Accrued advertising expense, $60 (credit Accounts Payable).

g. Accrued interest revenue, $170.

h. Depreciation: furniture, $380; building, $160.

Required

Complete Broadmoor's work sheet for May.

Problem 4-3B *Taking the accounting cycle through the closing entries*

The unadjusted T-accounts of Steve Deitmer, M.D., at December 31, 19X2, and the related year-end adjustment data follow:

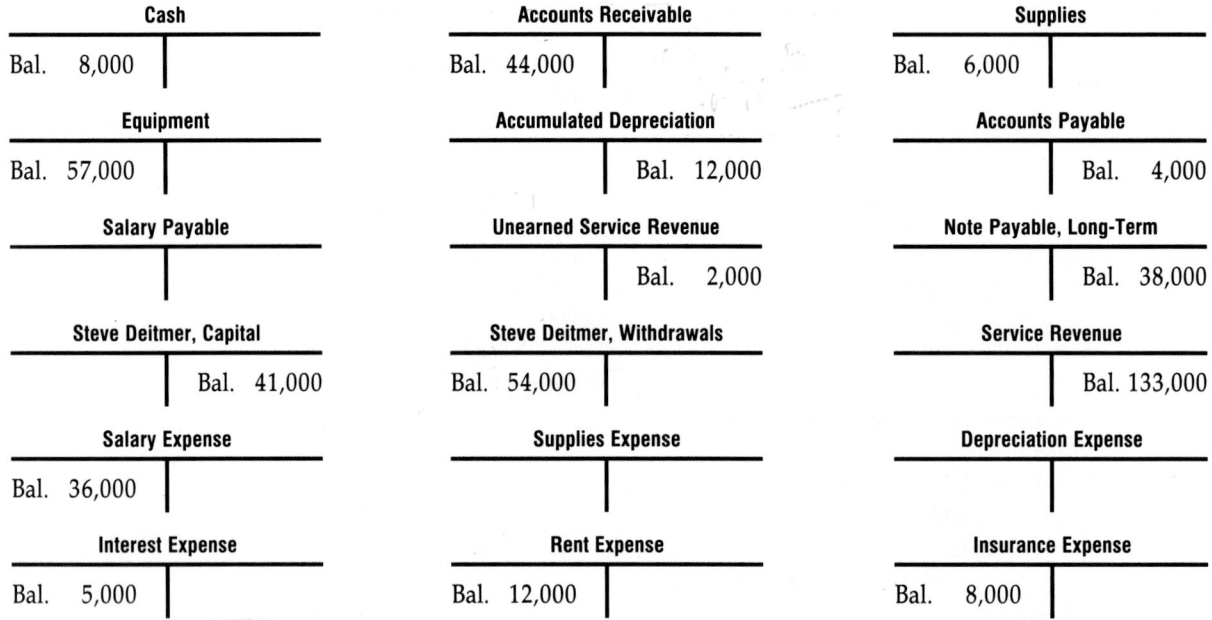

Cash			Accounts Receivable			Supplies		
Bal. 8,000			Bal. 44,000			Bal. 6,000		

Equipment			Accumulated Depreciation			Accounts Payable		
Bal. 57,000				Bal. 12,000			Bal. 4,000	

Salary Payable			Unearned Service Revenue			Note Payable, Long-Term		
				Bal. 2,000			Bal. 38,000	

Steve Deitmer, Capital			Steve Deitmer, Withdrawals			Service Revenue		
	Bal. 41,000		Bal. 54,000				Bal. 133,000	

Salary Expense			Supplies Expense			Depreciation Expense		
Bal. 36,000								

Interest Expense			Rent Expense			Insurance Expense		
Bal. 5,000			Bal. 12,000			Bal. 8,000		

Adjustment data at December 31, 19X2, include:

a. Supplies on hand, $2,000.

b. Depreciation for the year, $6,000.

c. Accrued salary expense, $3,000.

d. Accrued service revenue, $4,000.

e. Unearned service revenue earned during the year, $2,000.

Required

1. Write the trial balance on a work sheet and complete the work sheet. Key each adjusting entry by the letter corresponding to the data given.

2. Prepare the income statement, the statement of owner's equity, and the classified balance sheet in account format.

3. Journalize the adjusting and closing entries.

Problem 4-4B *Completing the accounting cycle*

This problem should be used only in conjunction with Problem 4-3B. It completes the accounting cycle by posting to T-accounts and preparing the postclosing trial balance.

Required

1. Using the Problem 4-3B data, post the adjusting and closing entries to the T-accounts, denoting adjusting amounts by *Adj.*, closing amounts by *Clo.*, and account balances by *Bal.*, as shown in Exhibit 4-9. Double underline all accounts with a zero ending balance.
2. Prepare the postclosing trial balance.

Problem 4-5B *Completing the accounting cycle*

The trial balance of James Realty at October 31, 19X0, and the data needed for the month-end adjustments are as follows:

James Realty
Trial Balance
October 31, 19X0

Account Number	Account Title	Debit	Credit
11	Cash	$ 1,900	
12	Accounts receivable	12,310	
13	Prepaid insurance.........................	2,200	
14	Supplies	840	
15	Furniture..................................	26,830	
16	Accumulated depreciation – furniture		$ 3,400
17	Building	68,300	
18	Accumulated depreciation – building		9,100
21	Accounts payable..........................		7,290
22	Salary payable		
23	Unearned commission revenue................		5,300
31	L. E. James, capital........................		85,490
32	L. E. James, withdrawals	3,900	
41	Commission revenue		8,560
51	Salary expense	1,840	
52	Insurance expense		
53	Utilities expense	530	
54	Depreciation expense – furniture		
55	Depreciation expense – building................		
56	Advertising expense........................	490	
57	Supplies expense		
	Total	$119,140	$119,140

Adjustment data:

a. Prepaid insurance still in force at October 31, $2,000.
b. Supplies used during the month, $570.
c. Depreciation on building for the month, $280.
d. Depreciation on furniture for the month, $250.
e. Accrued salary expense at October 31, $310.
f. Unearned commission revenue still unearned at October 31, $4,700.

Required

1. Open the accounts listed in the trial balance, inserting their October 31 unadjusted balances. Also open the Income Summary account, number 33. Use four-column accounts. Date the balances of the following accounts October 1: Prepaid Insurance, Supplies, Building, Accumulated Depreciation–Building, Furniture, Accumulated Depreciation–Furniture, Unearned Commission Revenue, and L. E. James, Capital.

2. Write the trial balance on a work sheet and complete the work sheet of James Realty for the month ended October 31 of the current year.

3. Prepare the income statement, the statement of owner's equity, and the classified balance sheet in report format.

4. Using the work sheet data, journalize and post the adjusting and closing entries. Use dates and posting references. Use 12 as the number of the journal page.

5. Prepare a postclosing trial balance.

Problem 4-6B   *Preparing a classified balance sheet in report format*

The accounts of Snyder Travel Agency at March 31, 19X3, are listed in alphabetical order. All adjustments have been journalized and posted, but the closing entries have not yet been made. Prepare the company's classified balance sheet in report format at March 31, 19X3. Use captions for total assets, total liabilities, and total liabilities and owner's equity.

Accounts payable	$ 2,700	Interest receivable	800
Accounts receivable	11,500	Inventory	$ 4,700
Accumulated depreciation–		Dot Snyder, capital,	
building	47,300	March 31, 19X2	32,800
Accumulated depreciation–		Dot Snyder, withdrawals	31,200
furniture	27,700	Note payable, long-term	3,200
Advertising expense	900	Note receivable, long-term	6,900
Building	55,900	Other assets	1,300
Cash	1,400	Other current assets	900
Commission revenue	71,100	Other current liabilities	1,100
Current portion of note payable	800	Prepaid insurance	600
Current portion of note		Salary expense	17,800
receivable	3,100	Salary payable	1,400
Depreciation expense	1,900	Supplies	3,800
Furniture	43,200	Supplies expense	4,600
Insurance expense	600	Unearned commission revenue	2,800
Interest payable	200		

Problem 4-7B   *Analyzing and journalizing corrections, adjustments, and closing entries*

The accountants of Lane Service Company, a proprietorship, encountered the following situations while adjusting and closing the books at February 28. Consider each situation independently.

a. The company bookkeeper made the following entry to record a $950 credit purchase of office supplies:

Feb. 26   Office Supplies.   950
           Cash.   950

Prepare the correcting entry, dated February 28.

b. A $390 credit to Accounts Receivable was posted as $930.
  (1) At what stage of the accounting cycle will this error be detected?
  (2) Describe the technique for identifying the amount of the error.

c. The $5,630 balance of Utilities Expense was entered as $56,300 on the trial balance.
   (1) What is the name of this type of error?
   (2) Assume this is the only error in the trial balance. Which will be greater, the total debits or the total credits, and by how much?
   (3) How can this type of error be identified?
d. The accountant failed to make the following adjusting entries at February 28:
   (1) Accrued service revenue, $700
   (2) Insurance expense, $1,460
   (3) Accrued interest expense on a note payable, $520
   (4) Depreciation of building, $3,300
   (5) Earned service revenue that had been collected in advance, $2,700
   Compute the overall net income effect of these omissions.
e. Record each of the adjusting entries identified in item *d*.
f. The revenue and expense accounts after the adjusting entries had been posted, were Service Revenue, $95,330; Wage Expense, $29,340; Rent Expense, $6,180; Interest Expense, $4,590; Utilities Expense, $1,620; and Supplies Expense, $740. Two balances prior to closing were W. T. Lane, Capital, $75,150; and W. T. Lane, Drawing, $48,000. Journalize the closing entries.

Decision Problem

Completing the accounting cycle to develop the information for a bank loan

One year ago, your friend John T. Williams founded Williams Computing Service. The business has prospered. Williams, who remembers that you took an accounting course while in college, comes to you for advice. He wishes to know how much net income his business earned during the past year. He also wants to know what the entity's total assets, liabilities, and capital are. His accounting records consist of the T-accounts of his ledger, which were prepared by an accountant who moved to another city. The ledger at December 31 of the current year is

Cash		Accounts Receivable	
Dec. 31 6,830		Dec. 31 12,360	

Prepaid Rent		Supplies	
Jan. 2 2,800		Jan. 2 2,600	

Equipment		Accumulated Depreciation	
Jan. 2 23,600			

Accounts Payable		Unearned Service Revenue	
	Dec. 31 15,540		Dec. 31 4,130

Salary Payable		J. T. Williams, Capital	
			Jan. 2 25,000

J. T. Williams, Drawing		Service Revenue	
Dec. 31 39,420			Dec. 31 61,740

Salary Expense		Depreciation Expense	
Dec. 31 18,000			

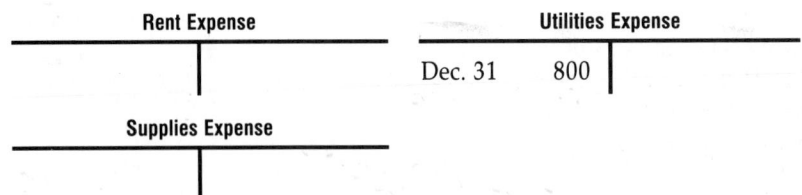

Williams indicates that at the year's end customers owe him $1,600 accrued service revenue, which he expects to collect early next year. These revenues have not been recorded. During the year he collected $4,130 service revenue in advance from customers, but he earned only $1,190 of that amount. Rent expense for the year was $2,400, and he used up $2,100 in supplies. Williams estimates that depreciation on his equipment was $5,900 for the year. At December 31 he owes his employee $1,200 accrued salary.

At the conclusion of your meeting, Williams expresses concern that his withdrawals during the year might have exceeded his net income. To get a loan to expand the business, Williams must show the bank that his capital account has grown from its original $25,000 balance. Has it? You and Williams agree that you will meet again in one week. You perform the analysis and prepare the financial statements to answer his questions.

Financial Statement Problem

Using An Actual Balance Sheet
This problem, based on Gulf+Western's balance sheet in Appendix C, will familiarize you with some of the assets and liabilities of this actual company. Answer these questions, using Gulf+Western's balance sheet.

1. Which balance sheet format does Gulf+Western use?
2. Name the company's largest current asset and largest current liability at October 31, 1987.
3. How much were total current assets and total current liabilities at October 31, 1987? Which increased by the greater percentage during the year ended October 31, 1987: total current assets or total current liabilities?
4. Under what category does Gulf+Western report land, buildings, and machinery and equipment?
5. What account title does Gulf+Western use in place of Accumulated Depreciation?
6. What was the cost of the company's plant assets at October 31, 1987? What was the book value of the plant assets?

Answers to Self-Study Questions

1. a	3. d	5. b	7. b	9. c
2. d, a, e, b, f, c	4. d	6. c	8. a	10. b

5

Merchandising and the Accounting Cycle

LEARNING OBJECTIVES

After studying this chapter, you should be able to

1 Explain the operating cycle of a merchandising business

2 Account for the purchase and sale of inventory

3 Compute cost of goods sold and gross margin

4 Prepare a merchandiser's financial statements

5 Adjust and close the accounts of a merchandising business

6 Recognize different formats of the income statement

In the first four chapters Gary Lyon, CPA, provided an illustration of a business that earns revenue by selling its services. Service enterprises include Holiday Inns, American Airlines, physicians, lawyers, CPAs, the Atlanta Braves baseball team, and the twelve-year-old who cuts lawns in your neighborhood. A *merchandising entity* earns its revenue by selling products, called *merchandise inventory* or simply *inventory.* A Goodyear tire store, a Safeway grocery, a Macy's department store, and an ice-cream shop are merchandising entities. Exhibit 5-1 shows the income statement for a merchandising business. You will notice that this income statement differs from those shown earlier.

The amount that a merchandiser earns from selling its inventory is called **net sales revenue,** often abbreviated as **net sales.** The income statement in Exhibit 5-1 reports net sales revenue of $680,000. The major revenue of a merchandising entity, sales revenue, represents the increase in owner's equity from delivering inventory to customers. The major expense of a merchandiser is *Cost of Goods Sold.* This expense's title is well chosen, because this account represents the entity's cost of the goods (inventory) it has sold to customers. As long as inventory is held, it is an asset. When the inventory is sold to the customer, the inventory's cost becomes an expense. The excess of Sales Revenue over Cost of Goods Sold is called **gross margin** or **gross profit.** This important business statistic is often mentioned in the business press because it helps measure a business's success. A sufficiently high gross margin is vital to success.

The following illustration will clarify the nature of gross margin. Consider a concession stand at a football game. Assume the business sells a soft drink for $1.00 and the vendor's cost is $.20. Gross margin per unit is $.80 ($1.00 − $.20), and the overall gross margin is $.80 multiplied by the number of drinks sold. If the concession stand sells 400 drinks on a Saturday afternoon, its gross margin on drink sales is $320 (400 × $.80). The gross margin on all sales, including hot dogs,

EXHIBIT 5-1   *A Merchandiser's Income Statement*

Midwest Supply Company		
Income Statement		
For the Year Ended December 31, 19X6		
Net sales revenue		$680,000
Cost of goods sold		370,000
Gross margin		310,000
Operating expenses:		
Salary expense.	$130,000	
Rent expense	60,000	
Insurance expense	18,000	
Depreciation expense	14,000	
Supplies expense	8,000	
Net income		$ 80,000

popcorn, and candy, is the sum of the gross margins on all the items sold. IBM's gross margin—and that of a Safeway store, a neighborhood drug store, and every other merchandiser—is computed in exactly the same way: Sales Revenue − Cost of Goods Sold = Gross Margin.

Margin in gross margin refers to the excess of revenue over expense. *Gross* indicates that the operating expenses (rent, depreciation, advertising, and so on) have not yet been subtracted. After subtracting all the expenses we have *net income.* Gross margin and net income are *not* accounts in the ledger, so we cannot make journal entries to them. Instead, we compute these amounts by subtracting one amount from another: Gross Margin − Operating Expenses = Net Income. Study Exhibit 5-1, focusing on the sales revenue, cost of goods sold, and gross margin. Note the separate category for operating expenses.

The Operating Cycle for a Merchandising Business

A merchandising entity buys inventory, sells the inventory to its customers, and uses the cash to purchase more inventory to repeat the cycle. Exhibit 5-2 diagrams the operating cycle for *cash sales* and for *sales on account.* For a cash sale—item *a* in the exhibit—the cycle is from cash to inventory, which is purchased for resale, and back to cash. For a sale on account—item *b*—the cycle is from cash to inventory to accounts receivable and back to cash.

Purchase of Merchandise Inventory

The cycle of a merchandising entity begins with cash, which is used to purchase inventory, as Exhibit 5-2 shows. **Purchases,** in the accounting sense, are only those items of merchandise inventory that a firm buys to resell to customers in the normal course of business. For example, a stereo center records in the Purchases account the price it pays for tape decks, turntables, and other items of inventory

EXHIBIT 5-2   *Operating Cycle of a Merchandiser*

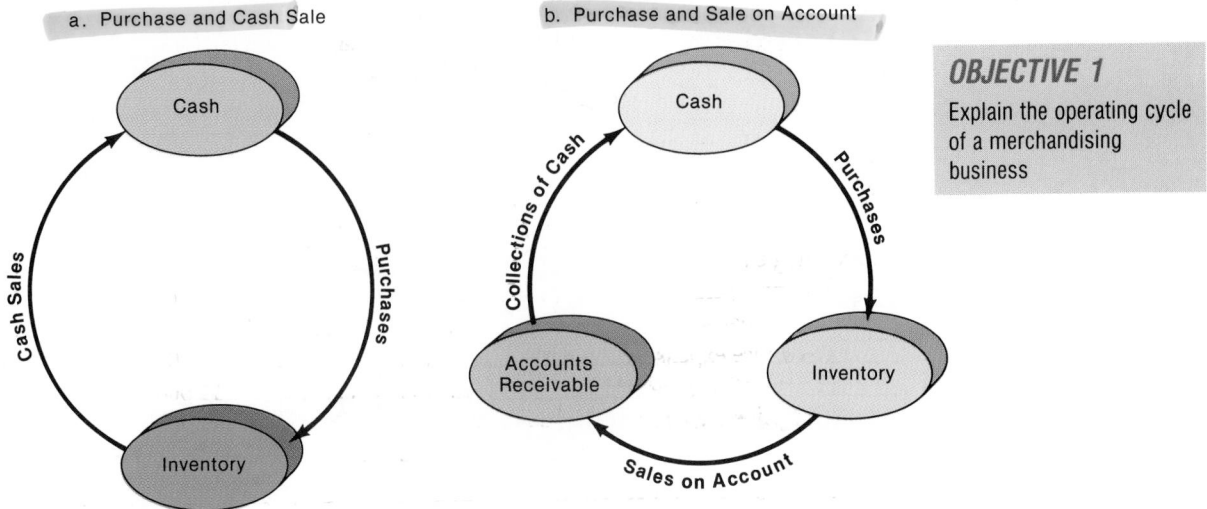

a. Purchase and Cash Sale

b. Purchase and Sale on Account

OBJECTIVE 1

Explain the operating cycle of a merchandising business

acquired for resale. A bicycle shop debits Purchases when it buys ten-speeds for its inventory. A grocery store debits Purchases when it buys canned goods, meat, frozen food, and other inventory. A $500 purchase on account is recorded as follows:

June 14	Purchases	500	
	Accounts Payable		500
	Purchased inventory on account.		

The Purchase Invoice: A Basic Business Document

Business documents are the tangible evidence of transactions. As we trace the steps that Austin Sound Stereo Center, an actual business, takes in ordering, receiving, and paying for inventory, we point out the roles that documents play in carrying on business.

1. Suppose Austin Sound wants to stock JVC brand turntables, cassette decks, and speakers. Austin Sound prepares a *purchase order* and mails it to JVC.
2. On receipt of the purchase order, JVC scans its warehouse for the inventory that Austin Sound ordered. JVC ships the equipment and mails the invoice to Austin on the same day. The **invoice** is the seller's request for payment from the purchaser. It is also called the *bill.*
3. Often the purchaser receives the invoice before the inventory arrives. Austin Sound does not pay immediately. Instead, Austin waits until the inventory arrives in order to ensure that it is (1) the correct type, (2) the quantity ordered, and (3) in good condition. After the inventory is inspected and approved, Austin Sound pays JVC the invoice amount.

Exhibit 5-3 is a copy of an actual invoice from JVC to Austin Sound Stereo Center. From Austin Sound's perspective, this document is a *purchase invoice,* whereas to JVC it is a *sales invoice.* The circled numbers that appear on the exhibit correspond to the following numbered explanations:

EXHIBIT 5-3 *Business Invoice*

			Invoice	
JVC® HIGH FIDELITY Division	②		Date	Number
US JVC CORP.			05/27/89	4104798-A

Page 1

Shipped To: AUSTIN SOUND
            STEREO CENTER
40191-00   305 WEST MLK BLVD. ③
            AUSTIN TX 78701

① JVC SOUTHWEST BRANCH
   P.O. BOX 100876
   HOUSTON, TX 77212
   TL (713) 694-0666

Invoice To:

④

AUSTIN SOUND
STEREO CENTER
305 WEST MLK BLVD. ③
AUSTIN TX 78701

PLEASE MAIL REMITTANCES TO THE ABOVE ADDRESS

Account No.	S/Mo	P.O. Date	P.O. Number		Shipped Via	Approval No.
40191-00	145	05/25/89	10542	1059004		

Terms of Sale		Special Instruction		Reference	Process Date
3% 15, NET 30DAYS ⑤					05/27/89

Quantity			Description	Set Name	Model No.	Quantity Shipped	Unit Price	Extension
Ordered	Prev. Ship.	B/O						
⑥ 1	0	0	TURNTABLE		LA100	⑦ 1	70.00	70.00
1	0	1	TURNTABLE		QLA200	0		
1	0	0	TURNTABLE		LL1	1	133.00	133.00
3	0	0	TURNTABLE		QLL2	3	168.00	504.00
1	0	1	CASSETTE DECK		KDV33J	0		
2	0	2	CASSETTE DECK		KDU40J	0		
2	0	2	SPEAKER		SKS11	0		

⑨ *Pd. 6-10-89*

	Sub Total	707.00
Due Date & Due Amount	Ship. or Handl. Chg.	-
06/11/89 06/27/89	Tax (%)	-
685 79 707 00	Total(s)	707.00

⑩   ⑧

1. The seller is JVC Southwest Branch.

2. The invoice date is 05/27/89. The date is needed for determining whether the purchaser gets a discount for prompt payment (see item 5 below).

3. The purchaser is Austin Sound Stereo Center. The inventory is invoiced (billed) and shipped to the same address, 305 West Martin Luther King Blvd., Austin, Texas.

4. Austin Sound's purchase order (P.O.) date was 05/25/89.

5. Credit terms of the transaction are 3% 15, NET 30 DAYS. This means that Austin Sound may deduct 3 percent of the total amount due if Austin pays within 15 days of the invoice date. Otherwise, the full amount—net—is due in 30 days. (A full discussion of discounts appears in the next section.)

6. Austin Sound ordered six turntables, three cassettes decks, and two speakers.

7. JVC shipped five turntables, no cassette decks, and no speakers.

8. Total invoice amount is $707.

9. Austin Sound paid on 6-10-89. How much did Austin pay? (See item 10.)

10. Payment occurred 14 days after the invoice date—within the discount period. Therefore, Austin Sound paid $685.79 ($707 minus the 3 percent discount).

Discounts from Purchase Prices

There are two major types of discounts from purchase prices; cash discounts (called purchase discounts) and trade discounts.

Purchase Discounts

Many businesses offer purchase discounts to their customers. A **purchase discount** is a reward for prompt payment. JVC's credit terms of 3% 15 NET 30 DAYS can also be expressed as 3/15 n/30. Terms of simply n/30 indicate that no discount is offered and that payment is due 30 days after the invoice date. Terms of eom mean that payment is due at the end of the month.

Let's use the Exhibit 5-3 transaction to illustrate accounting for a purchase discount. Austin Sound records this purchase on account as follows:

May 27	Purchases......................................	707.00	
	Accounts Payable		707.00
	Purchased inventory on account.		

> **OBJECTIVE 2**
> Account for the purchase and sale of inventory

Since Austin Sound paid within the discount period, its cash payment entry is

June 10	Accounts Payable	707.00	
	Cash ($707.00 × .97).....................		685.79
	Purchase Discounts ($707.00 × .03)..........		21.21
	Paid on account within discount period.		

Purchase Discounts, which has a credit balance, is a contra account to Purchases. We show how to report Purchase Discounts on the income statement later in the chapter.

Alternatively, if Austin Sound pays this invoice after the discount period, it must pay the full invoice amount. In this case, the payment entry is

June 29	Accounts Payable	707.00	
	Cash		707.00
	Paid on account after discount period.		

Trade Discounts

A second type of discount is the **trade discount,** which works this way: the larger the quantity purchased, the lower the price per item. For example, JVC may offer no trade discount for the purchase of only one or two cassette decks and charge the list price—the full price—of $200 per unit. However, JVC may offer the following trade discount terms in order to persuade customers to buy a larger number of cassette decks:

Quantity	Trade Discount	Net Price Per Unit
Buy minimum quantity, 3 cassette decks	5%	$190 [$200 − .05($200)]
Buy 4–9 decks	10%	$180 [$200 − .10($200)]
Buy more than 9 decks	20%	$160 [$200 − .20($200)]

Suppose Austin Sound purchases five cassette decks from this manufacturer. The cost of each cassette deck is, therefore, $180. Purchase of five units on account would be recorded by debiting Purchases and crediting Accounts Payable for the total price of $900 ($180 × 5).

There is no trade discount account, and there is no special accounting entry for a trade discount. Instead, all accounting entries are based on the net price of a purchase after subtracting the trade discount.

Purchase Returns and Allowances

Most businesses allow their customers to *return* merchandise that is defective, damaged in shipment, or otherwise unsuitable. Or if the buyer chooses to keep damaged goods, the seller may deduct an *allowance* from the amount the buyer owes. Because returns and allowances are closely related, they are usually recorded in a single account, **Purchase Returns and Allowances.** This account is a contra account to Purchases. Later in the chapter, we show how to report this account on the income statement.

Suppose the $70 turntable purchased by Austin Sound (in Exhibit 5-3) was not the turntable ordered. Austin returns the merchandise to the seller and records the purchase return as follows:

June 3	Accounts Payable	70.00	
	Purchase Returns and Allowances		70.00
	Returned inventory to seller.		

Now assume that one of the JVC turntables is damaged in shipment to Austin Sound. The damage is minor, and Austin decides to keep the turntable in exchange for a $10 allowance from JVC. To record this purchase allowance, Austin Sound makes this entry:

June 4	Accounts Payable	10.00	
	Purchase Returns and Allowances		10.00
	Received a purchase allowance.		

Observe that the return and the allowance had two effects. (1) They decreased Austin Sound's liability, which is why we debit Accounts Payable. (2) They decreased the net cost of the purchase, which is why we credit Purchase Returns and Allowances. It would be incorrect to credit Purchases because Austin Sound did in fact make the purchase. Changes because of returns and allowances are recorded in the contra account.

During the period, the business records the cost of all inventory bought in the Purchases account. The balance of Purchases is a *gross* amount because it does not include subtractions for purchase discounts, returns, or allowances. **Net purchases** is the remainder that is computed by subtracting the contra accounts as follows:

Purchases (*debit* balance account)
− **Purchase Discounts** (*credit* balance account)
− **Purchase Returns and Allowances** (*credit* balance account)
= **Net purchases** (a subtotal, not a separate account)

Transportation Costs

The transportation cost of moving inventory from seller to buyer can be significant. The purchase agreement specifies FOB terms to indicate who pays the shipping charges. The term *FOB* stands for *free on board* and governs when the legal title to the goods passes from seller to buyer. Under *FOB shipping point* terms, title passes when the inventory leaves the seller's place of business—the shipping point. The buyer owns the goods while they are in transit and therefore pays the transportation cost. Under *FOB destination* terms, title passes when the goods reach the destination, so the seller pays transportation cost.

	FOB Shipping Point	FOB Destination
When does title pass to buyer?	Shipping point	Destination
Who pays transportation cost?	Buyer	Seller

Generally, the buyer bears the shipping cost. The buyer debits Freight In (sometimes called Transportation In) and credits Cash or Accounts Payable for the amount. Suppose the buyer receives a shipping bill directly from the freight company. The payment entry is:

March 3	Freight In.	190	
	Cash		190
	Paid a freight bill.		

The seller sometimes prepays the transportation cost as a convenience and lists this cost on the invoice. The buyer would *not* debit Purchases for the combined cost of the inventory and the shipping cost. Rather, the buyer would debit Purchases for the cost of the goods and Freight In separately as follows:

March 12	Purchases	5,000	
	Freight In	400	
	Accounts Payable.		5,400
	Purchased inventory on account plus freight.		

Purchase discounts and trade discounts are computed only on the cost of the inventory, *not* on the freight charges. Suppose the $5,000 credit purchase allows a $100 discount for early payment. The cash payment within the discount period would be $5,300 [net payment of $4,900 on the inventory ($5,000, less the $100 purchase discount), plus the freight charges of $400].

Sale of Inventory

The sale of inventory may be for cash or on account, as Exhibit 5-2 shows.

Cash Sale. Sales of retailers like department stores, drug stores, gift shops, and restaurants are often for cash. A $3,000 cash sale is recorded by debiting Cash and crediting the revenue account, Sales Revenue, as follows:

Jan. 9	Cash.	3,000	
	Sales Revenue.		3,000
	Cash sale.		

Sale on Account. Most sales by wholesalers, manufacturers, and retailers are made on account (on credit). A $5,000 sale on account is recorded by a debit to Accounts Receivable and a credit to Sales Revenue, as follows:

Jan. 11	Accounts Receivable..............................	5,000	
	Sales Revenue................................		5,000
	Sale on account.		

The related cash receipt on account is journalized as follows:

Jan. 19	Cash...	5,000	
	Accounts Receivable.........................		5,000
	Collection on account.		

Sales Discounts, Sales Returns and Allowances

Sales Discounts and **Sales Returns and Allowances** are contra accounts to Sales Revenue, just as Purchase Discounts and Purchase Returns and Allowances are contra accounts to Purchases. Let's examine a sequence of the sale transactions of JVC.

On July 7, JVC sells stereo components for $7,200 on credit terms of 2/10 n/30. JVC's entry to record this credit sale follows:

July 7	Accounts Receivable	7,200	
	Sales Revenue		7,200
	Sale on account.		

Assume the buyer returns goods that cost $600. JVC records the sales return and the related decrease in Accounts Receivable as follows:

July 12	Sales Returns and Allowances.........................	600	
	Accounts Receivable...........................		600
	Received returned goods.		

JVC grants a $100 sales allowance for damaged goods. JVC journalizes this transaction by debiting Sales Returns and Allowances and crediting Accounts Receivable as follows:

July 15	Sales Returns and Allowances.........................	100	
	Accounts Receivable...........................		100
	Granted a sales allowance for damaged goods.		

After the preceding entries are posted, Accounts Receivable has a $6,500 debit balance, as follows:

Accounts Receivable			
July 7	7,200	July 12	600
		15	100
Bal.	6,500		

On July 17, the last day of the discount period, JVC collects half ($3,250) of this receivable ($6,500 × ½ = $3,250). The cash receipt is $3,185 [$3,250 − ($3,250 × .02)], and the collection entry is

July 17	Cash	3,185	
	Sales Discounts ($3,250 × .02)	65	
	Accounts Receivable.........................		3,250
	Cash collection within the discount period.		

Suppose JVC collects the remainder on July 28—after the discount period—so there is no sales discount. To record this collection on account, JVC debits Cash and credits Accounts Receivable for the same amount, as follows:

July 28   Cash   3,250
                Accounts Receivable.   3,250
                Cash collection after the discount period.

Net sales is computed in a manner similar to net purchases. We subtract the contra accounts as follows:

> **Sales Revenue** (*credit* balance account)
> − **Sales Discounts** (*debit* balance account)
> − **Sales Returns and Allowances** (*debit* balance account)
> _____
> = **Net sales (a subtotal, not a separate account)**

Cost of Goods Sold

Cost of goods sold is the largest single expense of most merchandising businesses. It is the cost of the inventory that the business has sold to customers. Another name for cost of goods sold is cost of sales. How is it computed?

Recall from Chapter 3 that supplies expense is computed as follows:

> **Beginning supplies**
> + **Supplies purchased during the period**
> _____
> = **Supplies available for use during the period**
> − **Supplies on hand at the end of the period**
> _____
> = **Supplies expense**

Cost of goods sold is computed this same way, as shown in Exhibit 5-4.

By studying the exhibit, you will see that the computation and the diagram tell the same story. That is, a company's goods available for sale during a period come from beginning inventory plus the period's net purchases and freight costs. Either the merchandise is sold during the period, or it remains on hand at the end. The merchandise that remains is an asset, Inventory, and the cost of the inventory that has been sold is an expense, Cost of Goods Sold.

Two main types of inventory accounting systems exist: the periodic system and the perpetual system. In this chapter, we illustrate the periodic inventory system because it highlights the relationship between inventory and cost of goods sold, as shown in Exhibit 5-4. This model for computing expense is used throughout accounting and is extremely useful for analytical purposes. Furthermore, the periodic system is used by many small businesses, such as the proprietorships we illustrated in the early chapters of this book. Chapter 9 discusses the perpetual system.

Under the periodic system, the business does not keep a running record of the cost of its inventory on hand. Instead, it counts the goods on hand at the end of each period to determine the inventory to be reported on the balance sheet. This ending inventory amount becomes the beginning inventory of the next period and is used to compute cost of goods sold for the income statement. *In the periodic inventory system, entries to the Inventory account are made only at the end of the period.*

EXHIBIT 5-4 *Measurement of Cost of Goods Sold*

Computation:

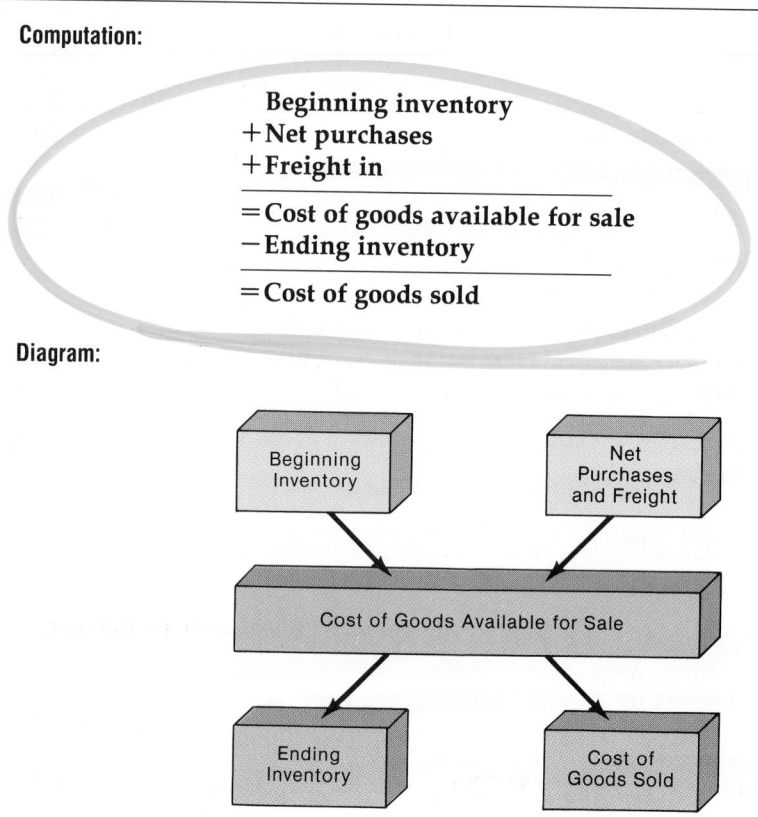

Beginning inventory
+ Net purchases
+ Freight in
= Cost of goods available for sale
− Ending inventory
= Cost of goods sold

Diagram:

Beginning Inventory		Net Purchases and Freight

Cost of Goods Available for Sale

Ending Inventory		Cost of Goods Sold

OBJECTIVE 3
Compute cost of goods
sold and gross margin

In this inventory system, cost of goods sold is *not* a ledger account like Salary Expense, Rent Expense, and the other operating expenses. Instead, it is the cost left over when we subtract the cost of ending inventory from the cost of goods available for sale. Computationally, cost of goods sold is more complex than the other expenses.

Exhibit 5-5 summarizes the first half of the chapter by showing Austin Sound's net sales revenue, cost of goods sold—including net purchases—and gross margin on the income statement.

Note that arithmetic operations—addition and subtraction—move across the columns from left to right. For example, the figures for Sales Discounts and for Sales Returns and Allowances appear in a separate column. Their sum—$3,400—appears to the right, where it is subtracted from Sales Revenue. The net sales amount of $135,900 appears in the right-most column.

Contra accounts—discounts, returns and allowances, and the like—are frequently netted against their related accounts parenthetically. Thus many accountants would report sales in our example as follows:

Net sales revenue (net of sales discounts, $1,400,
    and returns and allowances, $2,000). $135,900

EXHIBIT 5-5 *Partial Income Statement*

Austin Sound Income Statement For the Year Ended December 31, 19X6			
Sales revenue			$139,300
Less: Sales discounts		$ 1,400	
Sales returns and allowances		2,000	3,400
Net sales			$135,900
Cost of goods sold:			
Beginning inventory			$ 50,500
Purchases		$89,300	
Less: Purchase discounts	$3,000		
Purchase returns and allowances	1,200	4,200	
Net purchases			85,100
Freight in			5,200
Cost of goods available for sale			140,800
Less: Ending inventory			52,000
Cost of goods sold			88,800
Gross margin			$ 47,100

Purchases can also be reported at its net amount in the following manner:

Cost of goods sold:	
Beginning inventory	$ 50,500
Net purchases (net of purchase discounts, $3,000,	
and returns and allowances, $1,200)	85,100
Freight in	5,200
Cost of goods available for sale	$140,800
Less: Ending inventory	52,000
Cost of goods sold	$ 88,800

These presentations of *net* sales and *net* purchases underscore an important fact: published financial statements usually report only *net* amounts for these items because discounts and returns and allowances are relatively small in amount. For most businesses, these contra items are details of primary interest only to managers and therefore are not highlighted in the financial statements.

Summary Problem for Your Review

Brun Sales Company engaged in the following transactions during June of the current year:

June 3   Purchased inventory on credit terms of 1/10 net eom (end of month), $1,610.

9   Returned 40 percent of the inventory purchased on June 3. It was defective.

9	Sold goods for cash, $920.
15	Purchased merchandise of $5,100, less a $100 trade discount. Credit terms were 3/15 net 30.
16	Paid a $260 freight bill on goods purchased.
18	Sold inventory on credit terms of 2/10 n/30, $2,000.
22	Received damaged merchandise from the customer to whom the June 18 sale was made, $800.
24	Borrowed money from the bank to take advantage of the discount offered on the June 15 purchase. Signed a note payable to the bank for the net amount.
24	Paid supplier for goods purchased on June 15, less all discounts.
28	Received cash in full settlement of the account from the customer who purchased inventory on June 18.
29	Paid the amount owed on account from the purchase of June 3.
30	Purchased inventory for cash, $900, less a trade discount of $35.

Required

1. Journalize the above transactions. Explanations are not required.
2. Assume the note payable signed on June 24 requires the payment of $95 interest expense. Was the decision wise or unwise to borrow funds to take advantage of the cash discount? Support your answer by comparing the discount to the interest paid.

SOLUTION TO REVIEW PROBLEM

Requirement 1

June 3	Purchases	1,610	
	Accounts Payable		1,610
9	Accounts Payable ($1,610 × .40)	644	
	Purchase Returns and Allowances		644
9	Cash	920	
	Sales Revenue		920
15	Purchases ($5,100 − $100)	5,000	
	Accounts Payable		5,000
16	Freight In	260	
	Cash		260
18	Accounts Receivable	2,000	
	Sales Revenue		2,000
22	Sales Returns and Allowances	800	
	Accounts Receivable		800
24	Cash [$5,000 − .03($5,000)]	4,850	
	Note Payable		4,850
24	Accounts Payable	5,000	
	Purchase Discounts ($5,000 × .03)		150
	Cash ($5,000 × .97)		4,850
28	Cash [($2,000 − $800) × .98]	1,176	
	Sales Discounts [($2,000 − $800) × .02]	24	
	Accounts Receivable ($2,000 − $800)		1,200
29	Accounts Payable ($1,610 − $644)	966	
	Cash		966

```
30   Purchases ($900 − $35) . . . . . . . . . . . . . . . . . . . . .    865
         Cash. . . . . . . . . . . . . . . . . . . . . . . . . . . . . . . . .              865
```

Requirement 2.   The decision to borrow funds was wise because the discount ($150) exceeded the interest paid on the amount borrowed ($95). Thus the entity was $55 better off as a result of its decision.

The Adjusting and Closing Process
for a Merchandising Business

A merchandising business adjusts and closes the accounts much as a service entity does. The steps of this end-of-period process are the same: If a work sheet is used, enter the trial balance, and complete the work sheet to determine net income or net loss. The work sheet provides the data for preparing the financial statements and for journalizing the adjusting and closing entries. After these entries are posted to the ledger, a post-closing trial balance can be prepared.

The Inventory account affects the adjusting and closing entries of a merchandiser. At the end of the period, before any adjusting or closing entries, the Inventory account balance is still the cost of the inventory that was on hand at the beginning date. It is necessary to remove this beginning balance and replace it with the cost of the ending inventory. Various acceptable bookkeeping techniques might be used to bring the inventory records up to date. In this chapter we illustrate the closing-entry method. In Appendix D, which begins on page 1165, we present an alternative approach, the adjusting-entry method.

To illustrate a merchandiser's adjusting and closing process, let's use Austin Sound's December 31, 19X6, trial balance in Exhibit 5-6. All the new accounts — Inventory, Freight In, and the contra accounts — are highlighted for emphasis. However, Inventory is the only account that is affected by the new closing procedures. Note that additional-data item *g* gives the ending inventory of $52,000.

Work Sheet of a Merchandising Business

The Exhibit 5-7 work sheet is similar to the work sheets we have seen so far, but a few differences appear. Note that this work sheet does not include adjusted trial balance columns. In most accounting systems, a single operation combines trial balance amounts with the adjustments and extends the adjusted balances directly to the income statement and balance sheet columns. Therefore, to reduce clutter, the adjusted trial balance columns are omitted. A second difference is that the merchandiser's work sheet includes inventory and purchase amounts (which are highlighted). Let's examine the entire work sheet.

Account Title Columns.   The trial balance lists a number of accounts without balances. Ordinarily, these accounts are affected by the adjusting process. Examples include Interest Receivable, Interest Payable, and Depreciation Expense. The accounts are listed in the order they appear in the ledger. This eases the preparation of the work sheet. If additional accounts are needed, they can be written in at the bottom of the work sheet before net income is determined. Simply move net income down to make room for the additional accounts.

EXHIBIT 5-6 Trial Balance

**Austin Sound
Trial Balance
December 31, 19X6**

Cash	$ 4,850	
Accounts receivable	17,000	
Note receivable, current	10,000	
Interest receivable		
Inventory	**50,500**	
Supplies	650	
Prepaid insurance	1,200	
Furniture and fixtures	6,800	
Accumulated depreciation		$ 2,400
Accounts payable		7,000
Unearned sales revenue		2,000
Note payable, long-term		12,600
Interest payable		
C. Ernest, capital		65,900
C. Ernest, withdrawals	34,100	
Sales revenue		**138,000**
Sales discounts	**1,400**	
Sales returns and allowances	**2,000**	
Interest revenue		600
Purchases	**89,300**	
Purchase discounts		**3,000**
Purchase returns and allowances		**1,200**
Freight in	**5,200**	
Rent expense	8,400	
Depreciation expense		
Insurance expense		
Supplies expense		
Interest expense	1,300	
Total	$232,700	$232,700

Additional data at December 31, 19X6:

a. Interest revenue earned but not yet collected, $400.
b. Supplies on hand, $100.
c. Prepaid insurance expired during the year, $1,000.
d. Depreciation, $600.
e. Unearned sales revenue earned during the year, $1,300.
f. Interest expense incurred but not yet paid, $200.
g. Inventory on hand, $52,000.

Trial Balance columns. Examine the Inventory account, $50,500 in the trial balance. This $50,500 is the cost of the beginning inventory. The work sheet is designed to replace this outdated amount with the new ending balance, which in our example is $52,000 (additional-data item *g* in Exhibit 5-6). As we shall see, this task is accomplished later in the columns for the income statement and the balance sheet.

Adjustments Columns. The adjustments are similar to those discussed in Chapters 3 and 4. They may be entered in any order desired. The debit amount of

EXHIBIT 5-7   *Work Sheet*

Austin Sound
Work Sheet
For the Year Ended December 31, 19X6

Account Title	Trial Balance Debit	Trial Balance Credit	Adjustments Debit	Adjustments Credit	Income Statement Debit	Income Statement Credit	Balance Sheet Debit	Balance Sheet Credit
Cash	4,850						4,850	
Accounts receivable	17,000						17,000	
Note receivable, current	10,000						10,000	
Interest receivable			(a) 400				400	
Inventory	50,500				50,500	52,000	52,000	
Supplies	650			(b) 550			100	
Prepaid insurance	1,200			(c) 1,000			200	
Furniture and fixtures	6,800						6,800	
Accumulated depreciation		2,400		(d) 600				3,000
Accounts payable		7,000						7,000
Unearned sales revenue		2,000	(e) 1,300					700
Interest payable				(f) 200				200
Note payable, long-term		12,600						12,600
C. Ernest, capital		65,900						65,900
C. Ernest, withdrawals	34,100						34,100	
Sales revenue		138,000		(e) 1,300		139,300		
Sales discounts	1,400				1,400			
Sales returns and allowances	2,000				2,000			
Interest revenue		600		(a) 400		1,000		
Purchases	89,300				89,300			
Purchase discounts		3,000				3,000		
Purchase returns and allowances		1,200				1,200		
Freight in	5,200				5,200			
Rent expense	8,400				8,400			
Depreciation expense			(d) 600		600			
Insurance expense			(c) 1,000		1,000			
Supplies expense			(b) 550		550			
Interest expense	1,300		(f) 200		1,500			
	232,700	232,700	4,050	4,050	160,450	196,500	125,450	89,400
Net income					36,050			36,050
					196,500	196,500	125,450	125,450

each entry should equal the credit amount, and total debits should equal total credits.

Income Statement Columns.   The income statement columns contain adjusted amounts for the revenues and the expenses. Sales Revenue, for example, is $139,300, which includes the $1,300 adjustment.

You may be wondering why the two inventory amounts appear in the income statement columns. The reason is that beginning inventory and ending inventory enter the computation of cost of goods sold. Recall that beginning inventory is added to purchases and ending inventory is subtracted. Even though the resulting cost-of-goods-sold amount does not appear on the work sheet, all the components of cost of goods sold are evident there. Placement of beginning inventory ($50,500) in the work sheet's income statement debit column has the effect of adding beginning inventory in computing cost of goods sold. Placing ending inventory ($52,000) in the credit column has the opposite effect.

Purchases and Freight In appear in the debit column because they are added in computing cost of goods sold. Purchase Discounts and Purchase Returns and Allowances appear as credits because they are subtracted. Together, all these items are used to compute cost of goods sold—$88,800 on the income statement in Exhibit 5-5.

The income statement column subtotals on the work sheet indicate whether the business earned net income or incurred a net loss. If total credits are greater, the result is net income, as shown in the exhibit. Inserting the net income amount in the debit column brings total debits into agreement with total credits. If total debits are greater, a net loss has occurred. Inserting a net loss amount in the credit column would equalize total debits and total credits. Net income or net loss is then extended to the opposite column of the balance sheet.

Balance Sheet Columns.   The only new item on the balance sheet is inventory. The balance listed is the ending amount of $52,000, which is determined by a physical count of inventory on hand at the end of the period.

Financial Statements of a Merchandising Business

Exhibit 5-8 presents Austin Sound's financial statements. The *income statement* through gross margin repeats Exhibit 5-5. This information is followed by the **operating expenses,** which are those expenses other than cost of goods sold that are incurred in the entity's major line of business—merchandising. Rent is the cost of obtaining store space for Austin Sound's operations. Insurance is necessary to protect the inventory. The business's store furniture and fixtures wear out, and that expense is depreciation. Supplies expense is the cost of stationery, mailing, packages, and the like, used in operations.

Many companies report their operating expenses in two categories. *Selling expenses* are those expenses related to marketing the company's products—sales salaries; sales commissions; advertising; depreciation, rent, utilities, and property taxes on store buildings; depreciation on store furniture; delivery expense, and the like. *General expenses* include *office* expenses, such as the salaries of the company president and office employees, depreciation, rent, utilities, property taxes on the home office building, and office supplies.

Gross margin minus operating expenses equals **income from operations,** or **operating income,** as it is also called. Many businesspeople view operating income as the most reliable indicator of a business's success because it measures the entity's major ongoing activities.

The last section of Austin Sound's income statement is **other revenue and expense.** This category reports revenues and expenses that are outside the main operations of the business. Examples include gains and losses on the sale of plant assets (not inventory) and gains and losses on lawsuits. Accountants have traditionally viewed Interest Revenue and Interest Expense as "other" items because they arise from loaning money and borrowing money—activities that are outside the scope of selling merchandise or, for a service entity, rendering services.

The bottom line of the income statement is net income, which includes the effects of all the revenues and gains less all the expenses and losses. We often hear the term *bottom line* used to refer to a final result. The term originated in the position of net income on the income statement.

A merchandiser's *statement of owner's equity* looks exactly like that of a service business. In fact, you cannot determine whether the entity is merchandising or service oriented from looking at the statement of owner's equity.

If the business is a merchandiser, the *balance sheet* shows inventory as a major asset. In contrast, service businesses usually have minor amounts of inventory.

EXHIBIT 5-8 *Financial Statements of Austin Sound*

Austin Sound
Income Statement
For the Year Ended December 31, 19X6

Sales revenue			$139,300
Less: Sales discounts		$ 1,400	
Sales returns and allowances		2,000	3,400
Net sales			$135,900
Cost of goods sold:			
Beginning inventory			50,500
Purchases		89,300	
Less: Purchase discounts	$3,000		
Purchase returns and allowances	1,200	4,200	
Net purchases		85,100	
Freight in		5,200	
Cost of goods available for sale		140,800	
Less: Ending inventory		52,000	
Cost of goods sold			88,800
Gross margin			47,100
Operating expenses:			
Rent expense		8,400	
Insurance expense		1,000	
Depreciation expense		600	
Supplies expense		550	10,550
Income from operations			36,550
Other revenue and (expense):			
Interest revenue		1,000	
Interest expense		(1,500)	(500)
Net income			$ 36,050

Austin Sound
Statement of Owner's Equity
For the Year Ended December 31, 19X6

C. Ernest, capital, December 31, 19X5	$ 65,900
Add: Net income	36,050
	101,950
Less: Withdrawals	34,100
C. Ernest, capital, December 31, 19X6	$ 67,850

Austin Sound
Balance Sheet
December 31, 19X6

Assets

Current:		
Cash		$ 4,850
Accounts receivable		17,000
Note receivable		10,000
Interest receivable		400
Inventory		52,000
Prepaid insurance		200
Supplies		100
Total current assets		84,550
Plant:		
Furniture and fixtures	$6,800	
Less: Accumulated depreciation	3,000	3,800
Total assets		$88,350

Liabilities

Current:	
Accounts payable	$ 7,000
Unearned sales revenue	700
Interest payable	200
Total current liabilities	7,900
Long-term:	
Note payable	12,600
Total liabilities	20,500

Owner's Equity

C. Ernest, capital	67,850
Total liabilities and owner's equity	$88,350

Adjusting and Closing Entries for a Merchandising Business

Exhibit 5-9 presents Austin Sound's adjusting entries, which are similar to those you have seen previously.

The closing entries in the exhibit include two new effects. The first closing entry debits Inventory for the ending balance of $52,000 and also debits the revenue and expense accounts that have credit balances. For Austin Sound these accounts are Sales Revenue, Interest Revenue, Purchase Discounts, and Purchase Returns and Allowances. The offsetting credit of $196,500 transfers their sum to Income Summary. This amount comes directly from the credit column of the income statement on the work sheet (Exhibit 5-7).

The second closing entry includes a credit to Inventory for its beginning balance and credits to the revenue and expense accounts with debit balances. These

OBJECTIVE 5

Adjust and close the accounts of a merchandising business

EXHIBIT 5-9A   Journalizing and Posting the Adjusting and Closing Entries

Journal
Adjusting Entries

a.	Dec. 31	Interest Receivable............................	400	
		Interest Revenue		400
b.	31	Supplies Expense ($650 − $100).................	550	
		Supplies		550
c.	31	Insurance Expense	1,000	
		Prepaid Insurance		1,000
d.	31	Depreciation Expense.........................	600	
		Accumulated Depreciation		600
e.	31	Unearned Sales Revenue.......................	1,300	
		Sales Revenue		1,300
f.	31	Interest Expense..............................	200	
		Interest Payable		200

Closing Entries

	Dec. 31	Inventory (ending balance)	52,000	
		Sales Revenue	139,300	
		Interest Revenue	1,000	
		Purchase Discounts	3,000	
		Purchase Returns and Allowances	1,200	
		Income Summary..........................		196,500
	31	Income Summary.............................	160,450	
		Inventory (beginning balance)		50,500
		Sales Discounts		1,400
		Sales Returns and Allowances		2,000
		Purchases................................		89,300
		Freight In		5,200
		Rent Expense		8,400
		Depreciation Expense......................		600
		Insurance Expense		1,000
		Supplies Expense		550
		Interest Expense..........................		1,500
	31	Income Summary ($196,500 − $160,450)	36,050	
		C. Ernest, Capital.........................		36,050
	31	C. Ernest, Capital............................	34,100	
		C. Ernest, Withdrawals		34,100

EXHIBIT 5-9B *Ledger Accounts of Austin Sound*

Assets

Cash		Accounts Receivable		Note Receivable		Interest Receivable	
4,850		17,000		10,000		(A) 400	

Inventory		Supplies		Prepaid Insurance		Furniture and Fixtures	
50,500	(C) 50,500	650	(A) 550	1,200	(A) 1,000	6,800	
(C) 52,000		100		200			

Accumulated Depreciation	
	2,400
	(A) 600
	3,000

Liabilities

Accounts Payable		Unearned Sales Revenue		Interest Payable		Note Payable	
	7,000	(A) 1,300	2,000		(A) 200		12,600
			700				

Owner's Equity

C. Ernest, Capital		C. Ernest, Withdrawals		Income Summary	
(C) 34,100	65,900	34,100	(C) 34,100	(C) 160,450	(C) 196,500
	(C) 36,050			(C) 36,050	
	67,850				

Revenues

Sales Revenue		Sales Discounts		Sales Returns and Allowances		Interest Revenue	
	138,000	1,400	(C) 1,400	2,000	(C) 2,000		600
	(A) 1,300						(A) 400
(C) 139,300	139,300					(C) 1,000	1,000
							1,000

Expenses

Purchases		Purchase Discounts		Purchase Returns and Allowances		Freight In	
89,300	(C) 89,300	(C) 3,000	3,000	(C) 1,200	1,200	5,200	(C) 5,200

Rent Expense		Depreciation Expense		Insurance Expense		Supplies Expense	
8,400	(C) 8,400	(A) 600	(C) 600	(A) 1,000	(C) 1,000	(A) 550	(C) 550

Interest Expense	
1,300	
(A) 200	
1,500	(C) 1,500

A = Adjusting entry; C = Closing entry

are Sales Discounts, Sales Returns and Allowances, Purchases, Freight In, and the expense accounts. The offsetting $160,450 debit to Income Summary comes from the debit column of the income statement on the work sheet.

The last two closing entries close net income from Income Summary and also close owner Withdrawals into the Capital account.

The entries to the Inventory account deserve additional explanation. Recall that before the closing process Inventory still has the period's beginning balance. At the end of the period, this balance is one year old and must be replaced with the ending balance in order to prepare the financial statements at December 31, 19X6. The closing entries give Inventory its correct ending balance of $52,000, as shown here:

Inventory

Beginning balance (same as last period's ending balance)	50,500	Closing entry to eliminate beginning balance	50,500
Closing entry to set up ending balance	52,000		
Ending balance for the current balance sheet	52,000		

The inventory amounts for these closing entries are taken directly from the income statement columns of the work sheet. The offsetting debits and credits to Income Summary in these closing entries also serve to record the dollar amount of cost of goods sold in the accounts. Income Summary contains the cost of goods sold amount after Purchases and its related contra accounts and Freight In are closed.

Study Exhibits 5-7, 5-8, and 5-9 carefully because they illustrate the entire end-of-period process that leads to the financial statements. As you progress through this book, you may want to refer to these exhibits to refresh your understanding of the adjusting and closing process for a merchandising business.

Income Statement Format

We have seen that the balance sheet appears in two formats: the account format and the report format. There are also two basic formats for the income statement: *multiple step* and *single step.*

OBJECTIVE 6

Recognize different formats of the income statement

Multiple-Step Income Statement

The income statements presented thus far in this chapter have been multiple-step income statements. The **multiple-step format** contains subtotals to highlight significant relationships. In addition to net income, it also presents gross margin and income from operations. This format communicates a merchandiser's results of operations especially well because gross margin and income from operations are two key measures of operating performance.

Single-Step Income Statement

The **single-step format** groups all revenues together and then lists and deducts all expenses together without drawing any subtotals. The single-step format has the advantage of listing all revenues together and all expenses together, as shown in

EXHIBIT 5-10 *Single-Step Income Statement*

Austin Sound Income Statement For the Year Ended December 31, 19X6		
Revenues:		
Net sales (net of sales discounts, $1,400, and returns and allowances, $2,000)........		$135,900
Interest revenue.........................		1,000
Total revenues		136,900
Expenses:		
Cost of goods sold		$ 88,800
Rent expense		8,400
Interest expense.......................		1,500
Insurance expense		1,000
Depreciation expense...................		600
Supplies expense		550
Total expenses		100,850
Net income............................		$ 36,050

Exhibit 5-10. Thus it clearly distinguishes revenues from expenses. The income statements in Chapters 1 through 4 were single step. This format works well for service entities because they have no gross margin to report. A recent survey of 600 companies indicated that 56 percent use the single-step format and 44 percent use the multiple-step format.

Most published financial statements are highly condensed. Of course, condensed statements can be supplemented with desired details. For example, in Exhibit 5-10, the single-step income statement could be accompanied by a supporting schedule that gives the detailed computation of cost of goods sold.

Summary Problem for Your Review

The trial balance of Jan King Distributing Company is on the next page.

Required:

1. Make a single summary journal entry to record King's
   a. Unadjusted sales for the year, assuming all sales were made on credit.
   b. Sales returns and allowances for the year.
   c. Sales discounts for the year, assuming the cash collected on account was $329,000 and the credit to Accounts Receivable was $339,300.
   d. Purchases of inventory for the year, assuming all purchases were made on credit.
   e. Purchase returns and allowances for the year.
   f. Purchase discounts for the year, $6,000. Cash paid on account was $188,400 and the debit to Accounts Payable was $194,400.
   g. Transportation costs for the year, assuming a cash payment in a separate entry.

2. Enter the trial balance on a work sheet and complete the work sheet.

3. Journalize the adjusting and closing entries at December 31. Post to the Income Summary account as an accuracy check on the entries affecting that account. The credit balance closed out of Income Summary should equal net income computed on the work sheet.

4. Prepare the company's multiple-step income statement, statement of owner's equity, and balance sheet in account format.

Jan King Distributing Company
Trial Balance
December 31, 19X3

Cash...............................	$ 5,670	
Accounts receivable	37,100	
Inventory.........................	190,500	
Supplies..........................	3,930	
Prepaid rent.......................	6,000	
Furniture and fixtures..............	26,500	
Accumulated depreciation............		$ 21,200
Accounts payable...................		46,340
Salary payable.....................		
Interest payable....................		
Unearned sales revenue.............		3,500
Note payable, long-term.............		35,000
Jan King, capital		153,680
Jan King, withdrawals...............	48,000	
Sales revenue		346,700
Sales discounts	10,300	
Sales returns and allowances	8,200	
Purchases.........................	175,900	
Purchases discounts		6,000
Purchase returns and allowances........		7,430
Freight in.........................	9,300	
Salary expense.....................	82,750	
Rent expense......................	7,000	
Depreciation expense		
Utilities expense	5,800	
Supplies expense....................		
Interest expense....................	2,900	
Total.............................	$619,850	$619,850

Additional data at December 31, 19X3:

a. Supplies used during the year, $2,580.
b. Prepaid rent in force, $1,000.
c. Unearned sales revenue still not earned, $2,400. The company expects to earn this amount during the next few months.
d. Depreciation, $2,650.
e. Accrued salaries, $1,300.
f. Accrued interest expense, $600.
g. Inventory on hand, $195,800.

Note: If your instructor assigned Appendix D, which illustrates the adjusting-entry method, turn to page 1170 for the Alternate Solution to Review Problem. If you were not assigned Appendix D, then study the Solution to Review Problem that follows.

SOLUTION TO REVIEW PROBLEM

Requirement 1

Sales, purchases, and related discount and return and allowance entries:

19X3			
a.	Accounts Receivable	346,700	
	Sales Revenue		346,700
b.	Sales Returns and Allowances	8,200	
	Accounts Receivable		8,200
c.	Cash	329,000	
	Sales Discounts	10,300	
	Accounts Receivable		339,300
d.	Purchases	175,900	
	Accounts Payable		175,900
e.	Accounts Payable	7,430	
	Purchase Returns and Allowances		7,430
f.	Accounts Payable	194,400	
	Purchase Discounts		6,000
	Cash		188,400
g.	Freight In	9,300	
	Cash		9,300

Requirement 2

Jan King Distributing Company
Work Sheet
For the Year Ended December 31, 19X3

Account Title	Trial Balance Debit	Trial Balance Credit	Adjustments Debit	Adjustments Credit	Income Statement Debit	Income Statement Credit	Balance Sheet Debit	Balance Sheet Credit
Cash	5,670						5,670	
Accounts receivable	37,100						37,100	
Inventory	190,500				190,500	195,800	195,800	
Supplies	3,930			(a) 2,580			1,350	
Prepaid rent	6,000			(b) 5,000			1,000	
Furniture and fixtures	26,500						26,500	
Accumulated depreciation		21,200		(d) 2,650				23,850
Accounts payable		46,340						46,340
Salary payable				(e) 1,300				1,300
Interest payable				(f) 600				600
Unearned sales revenue		3,500	(c) 1,100					2,400
Note payable, long-term		35,000						35,000
Jan King, capital		153,680						153,680
Jan King, withdrawals	48,000						48,000	
Sales revenue		346,700		(c) 1,100		347,800		
Sales discounts	10,300				10,300			
Sales returns and allowances	8,200				8,200			
Purchases	175,900				175,900			
Purchase discounts		6,000				6,000		
Purchase returns and allowances		7,430				7,430		
Freight in	9,300				9,300			
Salary expense	82,750		(e) 1,300		84,050			
Rent expense	7,000		(b) 5,000		12,000			
Depreciation expense			(d) 2,650		2,650			
Utilities expense	5,800				5,800			
Supplies expense			(a) 2,580		2,580			
Interest expense	2,900		(f) 600		3,500			
	619,850	619,850	13,230	13,230	504,780	557,030	315,420	263,170
Net income					52,250			52,250
					557,030	557,030	315,420	315,420

Requirement 3
Adjusting entries:

19X3

Dec. 31	Supplies Expense		2,580	
	Supplies			2,580
31	Rent Expense		5,000	
	Prepaid Rent			5,000
31	Unearned Sales Revenue		1,100	
	Sales Revenue			1,100
31	Depreciation Expense		2,650	
	Accumulated Depreciation			2,650
31	Salary Expense		1,300	
	Salary Payable			1,300
31	Interest Expense		600	
	Interest Payable			600

Closing entries:

19X3

Dec. 31	Inventory (ending balance)	195,800	
	Sales Revenue	347,800	
	Purchase Discounts	6,000	
	Purchase Returns	7,430	
	Income Summary		557,030
31	Income Summary	504,780	
	Inventory (beginning balance)		190,500
	Sales Discounts		10,300
	Sales Returns and Allowances		8,200
	Purchases		175,900
	Freight In		9,300
	Salary Expense		84,050
	Rent Expense		12,000
	Depreciation Expense		2,650
	Utilities Expense		5,800
	Supplies Expense		2,580
	Interest Expense		3,500
31	Income Summary ($557,030 − $504,780)	52,250	
	Jan King, Capital		52,250
31	Jan King, Capital	48,000	
	Jan King, Withdrawals		48,000

Income Summary

Clo.	504,780	Clo.	557,030
Clo.	52,250	Bal.	52,250

Requirement 4

Jan King Distributing Company
Income Statement
For the Year Ended December 31, 19X3

Sales revenue........................			$347,800
Less: Sales discounts		$ 10,300	
Sales returns and allowances....		8,200	18,500
Net sales revenue..................			$329,300
Cost of goods sold:			
Beginning inventory...............			190,500
Purchases		175,900	
Less: Purchase discounts..........	$6,000		
Purchase returns and			
allowances	7,430	13,430	
Net purchases.....................		162,470	
Freight in		9,300	
Cost of goods available for sale		362,270	
Less: Ending inventory		195,800	
Cost of goods sold			166,470
Gross margin			162,830
Operating expenses:			
Salary expense		84,050	
Rent expense		12,000	
Utilities expense..................		5,800	
Depreciation expense..............		2,650	
Supplies expense		2,580	107,080
Income from operations			55,750
Other expense:			
Interest expense			3,500
Net income........................			$ 52,250

Jan King Distributing Company
Statement of Owner's Equity
For the Year Ended December 31, 19X3

Jan King, capital, December 31, 19X2................................	$153,680
Add: Net income	52,250
	205,930
Less: Withdrawals	48,000
Jan King, capital, December 31, 19X3..............................	$157,930

Requirement 4 (cont.)

Jan King Distributing Company
Balance Sheet
December 31, 19X3

Assets			Liabilities		
Current:			**Current:**		
Cash		$ 5,670	Accounts payable		$ 46,340
Accounts receivable		37,100	Salary payable		1,300
Inventory		195,800	Interest payable		600
Supplies		1,350	Unearned sales revenue		2,400
Prepaid rent		1,000	Total current liabilities		50,640
Total current assets		240,920	**Long-term:**		
Plant:			Note payable		35,000
Furniture and fixtures	$26,500		Total liabilities		85,640
Less: Accumulated depreciation . .	23,850	2,650	**Owner's Equity**		
			Jan King, capital		157,930
			Total liabilities and		
Total assets		$243,570	owner's equity		$243,570

SUMMARY

The major revenue of a merchandising business is *sales revenue,* or *sales.* The major expense is *cost of goods sold.* Net sales minus cost of goods sold is called *gross margin,* or *gross profit.* This amount measures the business's success or failure in selling its products at a higher price than it paid for them.

The merchandiser's major asset is *inventory.* In a merchandising entity the accounting cycle is from cash to inventory as the inventory is purchased for resale, and back to cash as the inventory is sold.

Cost of goods sold is unlike the other expenses in that it is not an account in the ledger. Instead, cost of goods sold is the remainder when beginning inventory and net purchases and freight in are added and ending inventory is subtracted from that sum.

The *invoice* is the business document generated by a purchase/sale transaction. Most merchandising entities offer *discounts* to their customers and allow them to *return* unsuitable merchandise. They also grant *allowances* for damaged goods that the buyer chooses to keep. Discounts and Returns and Allowances are *contra* accounts to both Purchases and Sales.

The end-of-period adjusting and closing process of a merchandising business is similar to that of a service business. In addition, a merchandiser makes inventory entries at the end of the period. These closing entries replace the period's beginning balance with the cost of inventory on hand at the end. A by-product of these closing entries is the computation of cost of goods sold for the income statement.

The income statement may appear in the *single-step format* or the *multiple-step format.* A single-step income statement has only two sections—one for revenues and the other for expenses—and a single income amount for net income. A multiple-step income statement has subtotals for gross margin and income from operations. Both formats are widely used in practice.

Self-Study Questions

Test your understanding of the chapter by marking the best answer for each of the following questions.

1. The major expense of a merchandising business is *(p. 169)*
   a. Cost of goods sold
   b. Depreciation
   c. Rent
   d. Interest

2. Sales total $440,000, cost of goods sold is $210,000, and operating expenses are $160,000. How much is gross margin? *(pp. 169, 170)*
   a. $440,000
   b. $230,000
   c. $210,000
   d. $70,000

3. A purchase discount results from *(p. 173)*
   a. Returning goods to the seller
   b. Receiving a purchase allowance from the seller
   c. Buying a large enough quantity of merchandise to get the discount
   d. Paying within the discount period

4. Which one of the following pairs includes items that are the most similar? *(p. 177)*
   a. Purchase discounts and purchase returns
   b. Cost of goods sold and inventory
   c. Net sales and sales discounts
   d. Sales returns and sales allowances

5. Which of the following is *not* an account? *(p. 177)*
   a. Sales revenue
   b. Net sales
   c. Inventory
   d. Supplies expense

6. Cost of goods sold is computed by adding beginning inventory and net purchases and subtracting X. What is X? *(p. 178)*
   a. Net sales
   b. Sales discounts
   c. Ending inventory
   d. Net purchases

7. Which account causes the main difference between a merchandiser's adjusting and closing process and that of a service business? *(p. 181)*
   a. Advertising Expense
   b. Interest Revenue
   c. Inventory
   d. Accounts Receivable

8. The major item on a merchandiser's income statement that a service business does not have is *(p. 185)*
   a. Cost of goods sold
   b. Inventory
   c. Net purchases
   d. Net sales

9. The closing entry for Sales Discounts is *(p. 186)*
   a. Sales Discounts
        Income Summary
   b. Sales Discounts
        Sales Revenue
   c. Income Summary
        Sales Discounts
   d. Not used because Sales Discounts is a permanent account, which is not closed.

10. Which income statement format reports income from operations? *(p. 188)*
    a. Account format
    b. Report format
    c. Single-step format
    d. Multiple-step format

Answers to the self-study questions are at the end of the chapter.

Accounting Vocabulary

cost of goods sold *(p. 177)*,   gross margin *(p. 169)*,   gross profit *(p. 169)*,   income from operations *(p. 184)*,   invoice *(p. 171)*,   multiple-step income statement *(p. 188)*,   net purchases *(p. 174)*,   net sales *(p. 177)*,   operating expenses *(p. 184)*,   operating income *(p. 184)*,   other expense *(p. 184)*, other revenue *(p. 184)*, purchases *(p. 170)*, purchase discount *(p. 173)*, purchase returns and allowances *(p. 174)*, sales *(p. 169)*, sales discount *(p. 176)*, sales returns and allowances *(p. 176)*, sales revenue *(p. 169)*, single-step income statement *(p. 188)*, trade discount *(p. 173)*.

ASSIGNMENT MATERIAL

Questions

1. Gross margin is often mentioned in the business press as an important measure of success. What does gross margin measure, and why is this important?

2. Describe the operating cycle for (a) the purchase and cash sale of inventory and (b) the purchase and sale of inventory on account.

3. Identify 10 items of information on an invoice.

4. What is the similarity and what is the difference between purchase discounts and trade discounts?

5. Indicate what accounts are debited and credited for (a) a credit purchase of inventory and the subsequent cash payment and (b) a credit sale of inventory and subsequent cash collection. Assume no discounts, returns, allowances, or freight.

6. Inventory costing $1,000 is purchased and invoiced on July 28 under terms of 3/10 n/30. Compute the payment amount on August 6. How much would the payment be on August 8? What explains the difference? What is the latest acceptable payment date under the terms of sale?

7. Inventory listed at $35,000 is sold subject to a trade discount of $3,000 and under payment terms of 2/15 n/45. What is the net sales revenue on this sale if the customer pays within 15 days?

8. Name four contra accounts introduced in this chapter.

9. Briefly discuss the similarity in computing supplies expense and computing cost of goods sold.

10. Why is the title of cost of goods sold especially descriptive? What type of item is cost of goods sold?

11. Beginning inventory is $5,000, net purchases total $30,000, and freight in is $1,000. If ending inventory is $8,000, what is cost of goods sold?

12. Identify two ways that cost of goods sold differs from operating expenses such as Salary Expense and Depreciation Expense.

13. Suppose you are evaluating two companies as possible investments. One entity sells its services, and the other entity is a merchandiser. How can you identify the merchandiser by examining the two entities' balance sheets and their income statements?

14. You are beginning the adjusting and closing process at the end of your company's fiscal year. Does the trial balance carry the beginning or the ending amount of inventory? Will the balance sheet that you prepare report the beginning or the ending inventory?

15. Give the two closing entries for inventory (using no specific amount).

16. After the closing entries have been journalized and posted, what account contains the amount of cost of goods sold for the period?

17. What is the identifying characteristic of the "other" category of revenues and expenses? Give an example of each.

18. Name and describe the two income statement formats and identify the type of business to which each format best applies.

19. List eight different operating expenses.

20. Which financial statement reports sales discounts, sales returns and allowances, purchase discounts, and purchase returns and allowances? Show how they are reported, using any reasonable amounts in your illustration.

Exercises

Exercise 5-1   *Computing the elements of a merchandiser's income statement*

Supply the missing income statement amounts in each of the following situations:

Sales	Sales Discounts	Net Sales	Beginning Inventory	Net Purchases	Ending Inventory	Cost of Goods Sold	Gross Margin
$96,000	(a)	$92,800	$32,500	$66,700	$39,400	(b)	$33,000
82,400	$2,100	(c)	27,450	43,000	(d)	$44,100	36,200
91,500	1,800	89,700	(e)	54,900	22,600	59,400	(f)
(g)	3,000	(h)	40,700	(i)	48,230	62,500	36,600

Exercise 5-2   *Journalizing transactions from a purchase invoice*

As the proprietor of Davidson Tire Company, you receive the following invoice from a supplier:

ABC TIRE WHOLESALE DISTRIBUTORS, INC.
2600 Commonwealth Avenue
Boston, Massachusetts 02215

Invoice date: May 14, 19X3   **Payment terms:** 2/10 n/30

Sold to: Davidson Tire Co.
4219 Crestwood Parkway
Lexington, Mass. 02173

Quantity Ordered	Description	Quantity Shipped	Price	Amount
6	P135-X4 Radials.........	6	$37.14	$ 222.84
8	L912 Belted-bias........	8	41.32	330.56
14	R39 Truck tires	10	50.02	500.20

Total...................................... $1,053.60

Due date: **Amount:**
May 24, 19X3 $1,032.53
May 25 through June 13, 19X3 $1,053.60

Paid:

Required

1. Record the May 15 purchase on account.
2. The R39 truck tires were ordered by mistake and therefore were returned to ABC. Journalize the return on May 19, assuming no refund of shipping charges.
3. Record the May 22 payment of the amount owed.

Exercise 5-3   *Journalizing purchase and sale transactions*

Journalize, without explanations, the following transactions of Mattox, Inc., during July:

July 3 Purchased $1,200 of inventory under terms of 2/10 n/eom (end of month) and fob shipping point.

7 Returned $300 of defective merchandise purchased on July 3.

9 Paid freight bill of $90 on July 3 purchase.

10 Sold inventory for $2,200, collecting cash of $400. Payment terms on the remainder were 2/15 n/30.

12 Paid amount owed on credit purchase of July 3, less the discount and the return.

16 Granted a sales allowance of $800 on the July 10 sale.

23 Received cash from July 10 customer in full settlement of her debt, less the allowance and the discount.

Exercise 5-4   *Journalizing purchase transactions*

On April 30 Reagan Jewelers purchased inventory of $3,800 on account from a wholesale jewelry supplier. Terms were 3/15 net 45. On receiving the goods May 3, Reagan checked the order and found $800 of items that were not ordered. Therefore, Reagan returned this amount of merchandise to the supplier on May 4.

To pay the remaining amount owed, Reagan had to borrow $2,910 from the bank because of a temporary cash shortage. On May 14 Reagan signed a short-term note payable to the bank and immediately paid the borrowed funds to the wholesale jewelry supplier. On May 31 Reagan paid the bank $2,940, which included $30 interest.

Required

Record the indicated transactions in the journal of Reagan Jewelers. Explanations are not required.

Exercise 5-5   *Journalizing sale transactions*

Refer to the business situation in Exercise 5-4. Journalize the transactions of the wholesale jewelry supplier. Explanations are not required.

Exercise 5-6   *Computing cost of goods sold for an actual company*

For the year ended December 31, 19X3, General Motors Corporation, the auto maker, reported net sales of $74.6 billion and cost of goods sold of $60.7 billion. The company's balance sheet at December 31, 19X2 and 19X3, reported inventories of $6.2 billion and $6.6 billion, respectively. What were General Motors' net purchases during 19X3?

Hint: Set up the computation of cost of goods sold and ignore freight.

Exercise 5-7   *Preparing a merchandiser's multiple-step income statement*

Selected accounts of Garcia Hardware Company are listed in alphabetical order.

Accounts receivable	$48,300	Purchase discounts	$ 3,000
Accumulated depreciation	18,700	Purchase returns	2,000
Freight in	2,200	Owner's equity, May 31	126,070
General expenses	23,800	Sales revenue	186,000
Interest revenue	1,500	Sales discounts	9,000
Inventory, May 31	39,450	Sales returns	4,600
Inventory, June 30	41,870	Selling expenses	37,840
Purchases	71,300	Unearned sales revenue	6,500

Required

Prepare the business's multiple-step income statement for June of the current year.

Exercise 5-8 *Preparing a single-step income statement for a merchandising business*

Prepare Garcia Hardware Company's single-step income statement for June, using the data from the preceding exercise. In a separate schedule, show the computation of cost of goods sold.

Exercise 5-9 *Using work sheet data to prepare a merchandiser's income statement*

The trial balance and adjustments columns of the work sheet of Brownlee Supply Company include the following accounts and balances at March 31, 19X2:

| | Trial Balance | | Adjustments | |
Account Title	Debit	Credit	Debit	Credit
Cash	2,000			
Accounts receivable	8,500		(a) 2,100	
Inventory	76,070			
Supplies	13,000			(b) 8,600
Store fixtures	22,500			
Accumulated depreciation		11,250		(c) 2,250
Accounts payable		9,300		
Salary payable				(d) 1,200
Note payable, long-term		27,500		
K. Brownlee, Capital		53,920		
K. Brownlee, Withdrawals	35,000			
Sales revenue		203,000		(a) 2,100
Sales discounts	2,000			
Purchases	94,200			
Purchase returns		2,600		
Selling expense	31,050		(b) 5,200	
			(d) 1,200	
General expense	20,500		(b) 3,400	
			(c) 2,250	
Interest expense	2,750			
Total	307,570	307,570	14,150	14,150

Ending inventory at March 31, 19X2, is $74,500.
Prepare the company's multiple-step income statement for the year ended March 31, 19X2.

Exercise 5-10 *Use work sheet data to prepare the closing entries of a merchandising business*

Use the data from Exercise 5-9 to journalize Brownlee Supply Company's closing entries at March 31, 19X2.

Problems *(Group A)*

Problem 5-1A *Journalizing purchase and sale transactions*

Jastrow Distributing Company engaged in the following transactions during May of the current year:

May 3 Purchased office supplies for cash, $300.
7 Purchased inventory on credit terms of 3/10 net eom (end of month), $2,000.

8 Returned half the inventory purchased on May 7. It was not the inventory ordered.

10 Sold goods for cash, $450.

13 Sold inventory on credit terms of 2/15 n/45, $3,900, less $600 trade discount offered to customers who purchased in large quantities.

16 Paid the amount owed on account from the purchase of May 7, less the discount and the return.

17 Received defective inventory returned from May 13 sale, $900, which is the net amount after the trade discount.

18 Purchased inventory of $4,000 on account. Payment terms were 2/10 net 30.

26 Borrowed $3,920 from the bank to take advantage of the discount offered on May 18 purchase. Signed a note payable to the bank for this amount.

26 Paid supplier for goods purchased on May 18, less the discount.

28 Received cash in full settlement of his account from the customer who purchased inventory on May 13, less the discount and the return.

29 Purchased inventory for cash, $2,000, less a trade discount of $400, plus freight charges of $160.

Required

1. Journalize the above transactions.
2. Assume the note payable signed on May 26 requires the payment of $30 interest expense. Was the decision wise or unwise to borrow funds to take advantage of the cash discount? Support your answer by comparing the discount to the interest paid.

Problem 5-2A *Preparing a merchandiser's financial statements*

The accounts of Yosemite Trading Company are listed in alphabetical order.

Accounts receivable	$ 43,700	Office equipment	$ 33,680
Accounts payable	16,950	Purchases	364,000
Accumulated depreciation– office equipment	22,450	Purchase discounts	1,990
Accumulated depreciation– store equipment	16,000	Purchase returns and allowances	3,400
		Salary payable	2,840
Capital, April 30	74,620	Sales revenue	706,000
Cash	7,890	Sales discounts	10,400
General expenses	116,700	Sales returns and allowances	18,030
Interest expense	5,400	Selling expenses	132,900
Interest payable	1,100	Store equipment	48,000
Inventory: April 30	69,350	Supplies	5,100
May 31	71,520	Unearned sales revenue	13,800
Note payable, long-term	45,000	Withdrawals	49,000

Required

1. Prepare the business's multiple-step income statement for May of the current year.
2. Prepare the income statement in single-step format.
3. Prepare the balance sheet in report format at May 31 of the current year. Show your computation of the May 31 balance of Capital.

Problem 5-3A *Using work sheet data to prepare financial statements*

The trial balance and adjustments columns of the work sheet of Schepps Auto Supply include the following accounts and balances at November 30, 19X4:

Account Title	Trial Balance		Adjustments	
	Debit	Credit	Debit	Credit
Cash	4,000			
Accounts receivable	14,500		(a) 6,000	
Inventory	67,340			
Supplies	2,800			(b) 1,900
Furniture......................	19,600			
Accumulated depreciation...........		4,900		(c) 2,450
Accounts payable.................		12,600		
Salary payable				(e) 1,000
Unearned sales revenue.............		13,570	(d) 6,700	
Note payable, long-term		15,000		
A. J. Schepps, capital		60,310		
A. J. Schepps, drawing.............	42,000			
Sales revenue		164,000		(a) 6,000
				(d) 6,700
Sales returns	6,300			
Purchases	73,200			
Purchase discounts................		2,040		
Selling expense...................	28,080		(e) 1,000	
General expense..................	13,100		(b) 1,900	
			(c) 2,450	
Interest expense	1,500			
Total	272,420	272,420	18,050	18,050

Required

Inventory on hand at November 30, 19X4, is $72,650. Without entering the preceding data on a formal work sheet, prepare the company's multiple-step income statement for the year ended November 30, 19X4, and its November 30, 19X4, balance sheet. Show your computation of the ending balance of A. J. Schepps, Capital. Drawing is another name for Withdrawals.

Problem 5-4A   *Preparing a merchandiser's work sheet*

Nicosia Shoe Store's trial balance at December 31 of the current year is on the next page.

Additional data at December 31, 19XX:

a. Rent expense for the year, $10,200.
b. Depreciation for the year, $3,130.
c. Accrued salaries at December 31, $900.
d. Accrued interest expense at December 31, $360.
e. Inventory on hand at December 31, $80,200.

Required

Complete Nicosia's work sheet for the year ended December 31 of the current year.

Nicosia Shoe Store
Trial Balance
December 31, 19XX

Cash...............................	$ 1,270	
Accounts receivable	4,430	
Inventory..........................	73,900	
Prepaid rent.......................	4,400	
Store fixtures	22,100	
Accumulated depreciation		$ 8,380
Accounts payable		6,290
Salary payable......................		
Interest payable.....................		
Note payable, long term..............		18,000
Angelina Nicosia, capital		55,920
Angelina Nicosia, withdrawals	39,550	
Sales revenue		170,150
Purchases..........................	67,870	
Salary expense......................	24,700	
Rent expense.......................	7,700	
Advertising expense	4,510	
Utilities expense	3,880	
Depreciation expense		
Insurance expense...................	2,770	
Interest expense....................	1,660	
Total............................	$258,740	$258,740

Problem 5-5A *Journalizing the adjusting and closing entries of a merchandising business*

Required

1. Journalize the adjusting and closing entries for the data in Problem 5-4A.
2. Determine the December 31 balance of Angelina Nicosia, Capital.

Problem 5-6A *Preparing a merchandiser's work sheet, financial statements, and adjusting and closing entries*

The year-end trial balance of McKee Sales Company at March 31 of the current year is on the next page.

Additional data at March 31, 19XX:

a. Accrued interest revenue $1,030.
b. Insurance expense for the year, $3,000.
c. Depreciation for the year, $1,000.
d. Unearned sales revenue still unearned, $8,200.
e. Accrued salaries, $1,200.
f. Accrued sales commissions, $1,700.
g. Inventory on hand, $133,200.

McKee Sales Company
Trial Balance
March 31, 19XX

Cash..............................	$ 7,880	
Notes receivable, current	12,400	
Interest receivable....................		
Inventory...........................	130,050	
Prepaid insurance	3,600	
Notes receivable, long-term	62,000	
Furniture	6,000	
Accumulated depreciation		$ 4,000
Accounts payable		12,220
Sales commission payable		
Salary payable......................		
Unearned sales revenue		9,610
J. R. McKee, capital..................		167,380
J. R. McKee, withdrawals	66,040	
Sales revenue		440,000
Interest revenue		8,600
Purchases..........................	233,000	
Freight in..........................	10,000	
Sales commission expense	78,300	
Salary expense......................	24,700	
Rent expense.......................	6,000	
Utilities expense	1,840	
Depreciation expense		
Insurance expense....................		
Total	$641,810	$641,810

Required

1. Enter the trial balance on a work sheet, and complete the work sheet for the year ended March 31 of the current year.
2. Prepare the company's multiple-step income statement and statement of owner's equity for the year ended March 31 of the current year. Also prepare its balance sheet at that date. Long-term notes receivable should be reported on the balance sheet between current assets and plant assets in a separate section labeled Investments.
3. Journalize the adjusting and closing entries at March 31.
4. Post to the J. R. McKee, Capital account and to the Income Summary account as an accuracy check on the adjusting and closing process.

Problem 5-7A *Completing a merchandiser's accounting cycle*

The end-of-month trial balance of Bucyk Trading Company at October 31 of the current year is on the next page.

Additional data at October 31, 19XX:

a. Supplies consumed during the month, $2,400. Two thirds is selling expense, and one third is general expense.
b. Depreciation for the month: building, $7,000; furniture, $1,700. Depreciation is evenly divided between selling expense and general expense.

Bucyk Trading Company
Trial Balance
October 31, 19XX

Account Number	Account Title	Balance Debit	Balance Credit
11	Cash.	$ 8,310	
12	Accounts receivable	14,390	
13	Inventory.	82,300	
14	Supplies.	4,100	
15	Building.	140,000	
16	Accumulated depreciation–building		$ 23,000
17	Furniture	17,500	
18	Accumulated depreciation–furniture		7,500
21	Accounts payable		16,380
22	Salary payable.		
23	Interest payable.		
24	Unearned sales revenue		5,300
25	Note payable, long-term.		79,000
31	Stu Bucyk, capital		105,860
32	Stu Bucyk, withdrawals	6,000	
41	Sales revenue		143,000
42	Sales discounts	4,290	
43	Sales returns and allowances	4,100	
51	Purchases.	81,000	
52	Purchase discounts		3,750
53	Purchase returns and allowances.		1,800
54	Selling expense	14,360	
55	General expense	9,240	
56	Interest expense		
	Total.	$385,590	$385,590

c. Of the unadjusted balance of Unearned Sales Revenue, $2,000 was earned during October.

d. Accrued salaries, a selling expense, $1,400.

e. Accrued interest expense, $900.

f. Inventory on hand, $86,000.

Required

1. Using four-column accounts, open the accounts listed on the trial balance, inserting their unadjusted balances. Date the balances of the following accounts October 1: Inventory; Supplies; Building; Accumulated Depreciation–Building; Furniture; Accumulated Depreciation–Furniture; Unearned Sales Revenue; and Stu Bucyk, Capital. Date all other unadjusted balances October 31.

2. Enter the trial balance on a work sheet, and complete the work sheet for the month ended October 31 of the current year. Bucyk Trading Company groups all operating expenses under two accounts, Selling Expense and General Expense. Leave three blank lines under Selling Expense and two blank lines under General Expense.

3. Prepare the company's multiple-step income statement and statement of owner's equity for the month ended October 31 of the current year. Also prepare the balance sheet at that date in report form.

4. Journalize the adjusting and closing entries, using page 6 of the journal.
5. Post the adjusting and closing entries, using dates and posting references.

(Group B)

Problem 5-1B   *Journalizing purchase and sale transactions*

Rogers Furniture Company engaged in the following transactions during July of the current year:

July 2 Purchased inventory for cash, $800, less a trade discount of $150.

5 Purchased store supplies on credit terms of net eom (end of month), $450.

8 Purchased inventory of $3,000 less a trade discount of 10 percent, plus freight charges of $230. Credit terms are 3/15 n/30.

9 Sold goods for cash, $1,200.

11 Returned $200 (net amount after the trade discount) of the inventory purchased on July 8. It was damaged in shipment.

12 Purchased inventory on credit terms of 3/10 n/30, $3,330.

14 Sold inventory on credit terms of 2/10 n/30, $9,600, less a $600 trade discount.

16 Paid the electricity and water bills, $275.

20 Received returned inventory from July 14 sale, $400 (net amount after the trade discount). Rogers shipped the wrong goods by mistake.

21 Borrowed the amount owed on the July 8 purchase. Signed a note payable to the bank for $2,655, which takes into account the return of inventory on July 11.

21 Paid supplier for goods purchased on July 8 less the discount and the return.

23 Received $6,860 cash in partial settlement of his account from the customer who purchased inventory on July 14. Granted the customer a 2 percent discount and credited his account receivable for $7,000.

30 Paid for the store supplies purchased on July 5.

Required

1. Journalize the above transactions.
2. Compute the amount of the receivable at July 31 from the customer to whom Rogers sold inventory on July 14. What amount of cash discount applies to this receivable at July 31?

Problem 5-2B   *Preparing a merchandiser's financial statements*

The accounts of Big Bend Trading Company are listed in alphabetical order.

Accounts receivable	$31,200	Office equipment	$ 49,000
Accounts payable	27,380	Purchases	273,100
Accumulated depreciation–		Purchase discounts	4,670
office equipment	9,500	Purchase returns	
Accumulated depreciation–		and allowances	10,190
store equipment	6,880	Salary payable	6,120
Capital, June 30	73,720	Sales revenue	501,580
Cash	12,320	Sales discounts	8,350
General expenses	75,830	Sales returns and allowances . .	17,900
Interest expense	7,200	Selling expenses	84,600
Interest payable	3,000	Store equipment	47,500
Inventory: June 30	60,060	Supplies	4,350
July 31	57,390	Unearned sales revenue	9,370
Note payable, long-term	30,000	Withdrawals	11,000

Required

1. Prepare the entity's multiple-step income statement for July of the current year.
2. Prepare the income statement in single-step format.
3. Prepare the balance sheet in report format at July 31 of the current year. Show your computation of the July 31 balance of Capital.

Problem 5-3B   *Using work sheet data to prepare financial statements*

The trial balance and adjustments columns of the work sheet of Francis Toy Company include the following accounts and balances at September 30, 19X5:

Account Title	Trial Balance		Adjustments	
	Debit	Credit	Debit	Credit
Cash	7,300			
Accounts receivable	4,360		(a) 1,800	
Inventory	51,530			
Supplies	10,700			(b) 7,640
Equipment	79,450			
Accumulated depreciation		29,800		(c) 9,900
Accounts payable.................		13,800		
Salary payable				(e) 800
Unearned sales revenue............		3,780	(d) 2,600	
Note payable, long-term		10,000		
M. Francis, capital		78,360		
M. Francis, drawing...............	35,000			
Sales revenue		182,000		(a) 1,800
				(d) 2,600
Sales returns....................	3,100			
Purchases	67,400			
Purchase discounts................		3,700		
Selling expense..................	40,600		(b) 7,640	
			(e) 800	
General expense..................	21,000		(c) 9,900	
Interest expense	1,000			
Total	321,440	321,440	22,740	22,740

Required

Inventory on hand at September 30, 19X5, is $52,580. Without entering the preceding data on a formal work sheet, prepare the company's multiple-step income statement for the year ended September 30, 19X5, and its September 30, 19X5, balance sheet. Show your computation of the ending balance of M. Francis, Capital. Drawing is another name for Withdrawals.

Problem 5-4B   *Preparing a merchandiser's work sheet*

Fairview Hardware's trial balance at December 31 of the current year is on the next page.

Additional data at December 31, 19XX:

a. Insurance expense for the year, $6,090.
b. Depreciation for the year, $7,240.
c. Accrued salaries at December 31, $1,260.
d. Accrued interest expense at December 31, $870.

Fairview Hardware
Trial Balance
December 31, 19XX

Cash.................................	$ 2,910	
Accounts receivable	6,560	
Inventory...........................	101,760	
Store supplies	1,990	
Prepaid insurance	3,200	
Store fixtures.......................	63,920	
Accumulated depreciation		$ 37,640
Accounts payable		29,770
Salary payable.......................		
Interest payable.....................		
Note payable, long-term..............		37,220
Ed Sanger, capital...................		63,120
Ed Sanger, withdrawals	36,300	
Sales revenue		286,370
Purchases...........................	161,090	
Salary expense.......................	46,580	
Rent expense........................	14,630	
Utilities expense	6,780	
Depreciation expense		
Insurance expense....................	5,300	
Store supplies expense		
Interest expense.....................	3,100	
Total...............................	$454,120	$454,120

e. Store supplies on hand at December 31, $760.
f. Inventory on hand at December 31, $99,350.

Required

Complete Fairview's work sheet for the year ended December 31 of the current year.

Problem 5-5B   *Journalizing the adjusting and closing entries of a merchandising business*

Required

1. Journalize the adjusting and closing entries for the data in Problem 5-4B.
2. Determine the December 31 balance of Ed Sanger, Capital.

Problem 5-6B   *Preparing a merchandiser's work sheet, financial statements, and adjusting and closing entries*

The year-end trial balance of Port Arthur Sales Company at July 31 of the current year is on the next page.

Additional data at July 31, 19XX:

a. Accrued interest revenue, $350.
b. Prepaid insurance still in force, $310.

Port Arthur Sales Company
Trial Balance
July 31, 19XX

Cash.	$ 3,120	
Notes receivable, current	6,900	
Interest receivable		
Inventory.	104,000	
Prepaid insurance	2,810	
Notes receivable, long-term	19,300	
Furniture	16,000	
Accumulated depreciation		$ 12,000
Accounts payable		14,360
Salary payable.		
Sales commission payable		
Unearned sales revenue		4,090
G. M. Blake, capital.		97,790
G. M. Blake, withdrawals.	59,000	
Sales revenue		337,940
Interest revenue		1,910
Purchases.	163,200	
Freight in	11,100	
Salary expense.	39,030	
Sales commission expense	31,500	
Rent expense	10,000	
Utilities expense	2,130	
Insurance expense.		
Depreciation expense		
Total.	$468,090	$468,090

c. Depreciation for the year, $2,000.
d. Unearned sales revenue still unearned, $1,900.
e. Accrued salaries, $1,640.
f. Accrued sales commissions, $1,430.
g. Inventory on hand, $102,600.

Required

1. Enter the trial balance on a work sheet, and complete the work sheet for the year ended July 31 of the current year.
2. Prepare the company's multiple-step income statement and statement of owner's equity for the year ended July 31 of the current year. Also prepare its balance sheet at that date. Long-term notes receivable should be reported on the balance sheet between current assets and plant assets in a separate section labeled Investments.
3. Journalize the adjusting and closing entries at July 31.
4. Post to the G. M. Blake, Capital account and to the Income Summary account as an accuracy check on the adjusting and closing process.

Problem 5-7B   *Completing a merchandiser's accounting cycle*

The end-of-month trial balance of Lansing Building Materials at January 31 of the current year is

Lansing Building Materials
Trial Balance
January 31, 19XX

Account Number	Account Title	Balance Debit	Balance Credit
11	Cash..	$ 6,430	
12	Accounts receivable	19,090	
13	Inventory....................................	65,400	
14	Supplies.....................................	2,700	
15	Building.....................................	195,000	
16	Accumulated depreciation–building..............		$ 36,000
17	Fixtures	45,600	
18	Accumulated depreciation–fixtures..............		5,800
21	Accounts payable		28,300
22	Salary payable...............................		
23	Interest payable..............................		
24	Unearned sales revenue		6,560
25	Note payable, long-term.......................		87,000
31	Ed Lansing, capital		144,980
32	Ed Lansing, withdrawals	9,200	
41	Sales revenue		177,970
42	Sales discounts	7,300	
43	Sales returns and allowances	8,140	
51	Purchases.	103,000	
52	Purchase discounts		4,230
53	Purchase returns and allowances...............		2,600
54	Selling expense	21,520	
55	General expense	10,060	
56	Interest expense		
	Total.......................................	$493,440	$493,440

Additional data at January 31, 19XX:

a. Supplies consumed during the month, $1,500. One half is selling expense, and the other half is general expense.

b. Depreciation for the month: building, $4,000; fixtures, $4,800. One fourth of depreciation is selling expense, and three fourths is general expense.

c. Unearned sales revenue still unearned, $1,200.

d. Accrued salaries, a general expense, $1,150.

e. Accrued interest expense, $780.

f. Inventory on hand, $60,720.

Required

1. Using four-column accounts, open the accounts listed on the trial balance, inserting their unadjusted balances. Date the balances of the following accounts January 1:

Inventory; Supplies; Building; Accumulated Depreciation–Building; Fixtures; Accumulated Depreciation–Fixtures; Unearned Sales Revenue; and Ed Lansing, Capital. Date the balance of Ed Lansing, Withdrawals, January 31.

2. Enter the trial balance on a work sheet, and complete the work sheet for the month ended January 31 of the current year. Lansing groups all operating expenses under two accounts, Selling Expense and General Expense. Leave two blank lines under Selling Expense and three blank lines under General Expense.

3. Prepare the company's multiple-step income statement and statement of owner's equity for the month ended January 31 of the current year. Also prepare the balance sheet at that date in report form.

4. Journalize the adjusting and closing entries at January 31, using page 3 of the journal.

5. Post the adjusting and closing entries, using dates and posting references.

Decision Problem

Using the Financial Statements to Decide on a Business Expansion

Lynn Kraft owns Westlake Pharmacy, which has prospered during its first year of operation. In deciding whether to open another pharmacy in the area, Lynn has prepared the current financial statements of the business.

Westlake Pharmacy
Income Statement
For the Year Ended December 31, 19X1

Sales revenue		$175,000
Interest revenue		24,600
Total revenue		199,600
Cost of goods sold		
Beginning inventory	$ 27,800	
Net purchases	87,500	
Cost of goods available for sale	115,300	
Less: Ending inventory	30,100	
Cost of goods sold		85,200
Gross margin		114,400
Operating expenses:		
Salary expense	18,690	
Rent expense	12,000	
Interest expense	6,000	
Depreciation expense	4,900	
Utilities expense	2,330	
Supplies expense	1,400	
Total operating expense		45,320
Income from operations		69,080
Other expense:		
Sales discounts ($3,600) and returns ($7,100)		10,700
Net income		$ 58,380

Westlake Pharmacy
Statement of Owner's Equity
For the Year Ended December 31, 19X1

L. Kraft, capital, January 1, 19X1	$20,000
Add increases in owner's equity:	
Net income	58,380
L. Kraft, capital, December 31, 19X1.	$78,380

Westlake Pharmacy
Balance Sheet
December 31, 19X1

Assets

Current:	
Cash	$ 5,320
Accounts receivable	9,710
Inventory	30,100
Supplies.	2,760
Store fixtures.	63,000
Total current assets.	110,890
Other:	
Withdrawals	45,000
Total assets	$155,890

Liabilities

Current:	
Accumulated depreciation–store fixtures . .	$ 6,300
Accounts payable	10,310
Salary payable	900
Total current liabilities	17,510
Other:	
Note payable due in 90 days	60,000
Total liabilities	77,510

Owner's Equity

L. Kraft, capital.	78,380
Total liabilities and owner's equity	$155,890

Lynn recently read in an industry trade magazine that a successful pharmacy meets these criteria:

(a)   Gross margin is at least one half of net sales
(b)   Current assets are at least two times current liabilities
(c)   Owner's equity is at least as great as total liabilities

Basing her opinion on the entity's financial statement data, Lynn believes the business meets all three criteria. She plans to go ahead with her expansion plan and asks your advice on preparing the pharmacy's financial statements in accordance with generally accepted accounting principles. She assures you that all amounts are correct.

Required

1. Prepare a correct multiple-step income statement, a statement of owner's equity, and a balance sheet in report format.
2. Based on the corrected financial statements, compute correct measures of the three criteria listed in the trade journal.
3. Assuming the criteria are valid, make a recommendation about whether to undertake the expansion at this time.

Financial Statement Problem

Closing entries for a merchandising corporation

This problem uses both the income statement (statement of earnings) and the balance sheet of Gulf+Western, Inc., in Appendix C. It will aid your understanding of the closing process of a merchandising business.

Assume that the inventory and closing procedures outlined in this chapter are appropriate for Gulf+Western. Further, from the balance sheet, use only the amounts of inventories listed among current assets. Ignore freight in, and assume net purchases for the year ended October 31, 1987, totaled $1,800.5 million.

Required

1. Show the computation of Gulf+Western's cost of goods sold ($1,753.5 million) for the year ended October 31, 1987, by this formula from the chapter:

> **Beginning inventory**
> **+ Net purchases**
> _____
> **= Cost of goods available for sale**
> **− Ending inventory**
> _____
> **= Cost of goods sold**

2. Using Net Purchases and Net Revenues from the income statement (ignore the items above Net Revenues), journalize Gulf+Western's closing entries for the year ended October 31, 1987. Close Interest Expense and Interest Income (another name for Interest Revenue) separately—their amounts are given in Note J. Provision for Income Taxes is an expense. Corporations like Gulf+Western close Income Summary into an account called Retained Earnings (instead of Capital). Also, corporations have no Withdrawals account to close.
3. What amount was closed to Retained Earnings? How is this net income amount labeled on Gulf+Western's income statement?

Answers to Self-Study Questions

1.	a	6.	c
2.	b ($440,000 − $210,000 = $230,000)	7.	c
3.	d	8.	a
4.	d	9.	c
5.	b	10.	d

6

Accounting Information Systems

LEARNING OBJECTIVES
After studying this chapter, you should be able to

1 Describe the features of an effective information system

2 Use the sales journal

3 Use control accounts and subsidiary ledgers

4 Use the cash receipts journal

5 Use the purchases journal

6 Use the cash disbursements journal

An **accounting information system**—often called simply an *information system* —is the combination of personnel, records, and procedures that a business uses to meet its routine needs for financial data. Because each business has different information demands, each uses a different accounting information system. For example, a jewelry store earns revenue by selling inventory, so the store's management usually wants an up-to-the-minute, accurate level of goods on hand for sale. A physician, however, earns revenue by providing service, and there is little or no inventory to control. The physician needs to keep track of the time spent on each patient. The jewelry store and the physician, then, need different information systems to answer the special sorts of questions that arise as they conduct their business. For maximum effectiveness, the information system is tailored to the business's specific needs.

A basic understanding of accounting systems is important for managing and evaluating a business. As a manager, you may be tempted to reply, "I can always hire an accountant to design the information system and do the accounting." Perhaps, but you will be better able to communicate with the members of your organization if you understand how the accounting system operates. The accounting system is the glue that holds the various parts of an organization together. It helps managers stay on top of their responsibilities. Indeed, a potential buyer of a business examines its accounting system to understand how the organization works.

Also, you do not want your employees to take advantage of you by manipulating your accounting system to cover theft. Business owners who are unfamiliar with accounting systems are victims of this practice to an alarming degree.

This chapter describes accounting information system designs and how they are implemented. It also provides a basic model of information processing and discusses what makes an information system effective. The chapter then discusses computer data processing and illustrates special journals and ledgers that accountants use to streamline information systems.

Accounting System Design and Installation

System Design. An accounting information system begins with a design. The manager and the designer study the business's goals and organizational structure. They also identify management's information needs, breaking down the required information-processing tasks. The designer must consider the personnel who will operate the system, the documents and reports to be produced, and the equipment to be used. Almost every information system uses a computer for at least some tasks. Some CPA firms specialize in system design and install accounting systems for their clients.

System Installation. Installation includes selecting and training employees to operate the system, testing the system, and modifying it as needed. For a large system, installation may take months or even years. Often installation is more difficult than planned. Even after careful consideration in the design phase, unforeseen difficulties may emerge. If the system is not debugged, it will not perform its intended tasks.

Basic Model of Information Processing

Processing information means collecting, organizing, and processing data, and communicating the information to statement users. In addition, accounting data are used by managers. For example, accounts receivable might be analyzed to identify the biggest customers, who will receive special privileges. Exhibit 6-1 shows how the *basic model of information processing* relates to an accounting system.

1. The *source data* for the accounting system are the *documents,* such as invoices and canceled checks, that business transactions generate.
2. *Organizing and processing* data requires transaction analysis, journalizing, posting, and preparation of the work sheet.
3. The output is *information*—the *financial statements.*

Notice that the system converts data to reports, fulfilling accounting's role of providing information.

An Effective Information System

Each business's accounting information system follows the basic model shown in Exhibit 6-1. Also, a well-designed information system offers control, compatibility, flexibility, and an acceptable cost/benefit relationship.

EXHIBIT 6-1 *Information-Processing Model and the Accounting System*

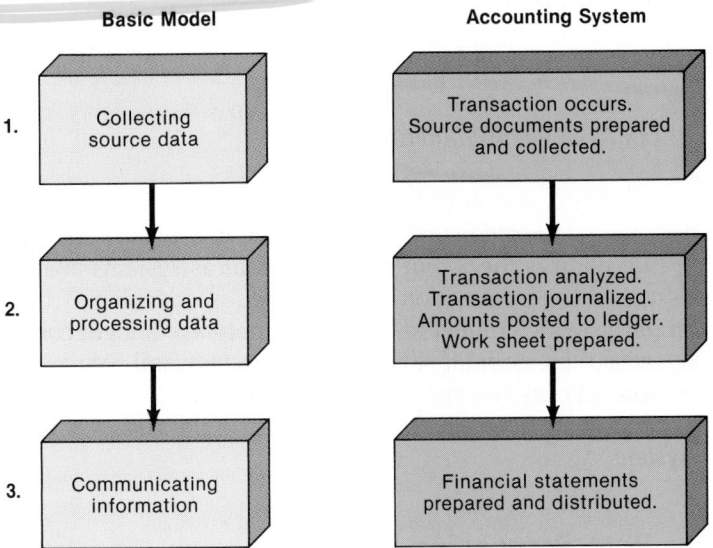

Control

A good accounting system gives management control over operations. *Internal controls* are the methods and procedures a business uses to authorize transactions, safeguard its assets, and ensure the accuracy of its accounting records. For example, most companies exert tight controls over cash disbursements to avoid theft through unauthorized payments. Also, keeping accurate records of accounts receivable is the only way to ensure that customers are billed and collections are received on time. The accounting system controls assets to different degrees. Usually control over cash is tighter than control over supplies and prepaid expenses because cash is more open to theft. Chapter 7 details internal control procedures.

OBJECTIVE 1
Describe the features of an effective information system

Compatibility

An information system meets the compatibility guideline when it works smoothly with the business's particular structure, personnel, and special features. For example, one company may be organized by geographical region, another company by product line. The accounting system for the first company would accumulate revenues and expenses by region. The second company's system would group revenues and expenses by product. Any combination of data accumulation by region and by product is possible — whatever best suits the business. The compatibility guideline means designing the information system with the human factor in mind.

Flexibility

Organizations evolve. They develop new products, sell off unprofitable operations, and adjust employee pay scales. Changes in the business often call for changes in the accounting system. A well-designed system meets the flexibility guideline if it can accommodate such changes without needing a complete overhaul. In most organizations, systems are rarely replaced in their entirety. For example, a system for control of cash might be installed one year and a system for controlling inventories a year later.

Acceptable Cost/Benefit Relationship

Control, compatibility, and flexibility can be achieved in an accounting system, but they cost money. At some point, the cost of the system outweighs its benefits. Identifying that point is the job of the accountant as systems analyst and the manager as user of the information.

Consider the growing number of businesses that have bought computers. For many companies, the computer saves time and money and results in improved decisions. The benefits usually far exceed the cost of a simple computer system. In other cases, the savings are not sufficient to justify the cost of an increasingly elaborate system.

Computer Data Processing

Much data processing in business is done by computer. Computers offer significant advantages in accuracy and in the volume of accounting work that can be performed.

EXHIBIT 6-2 *Mainframe Computer System*

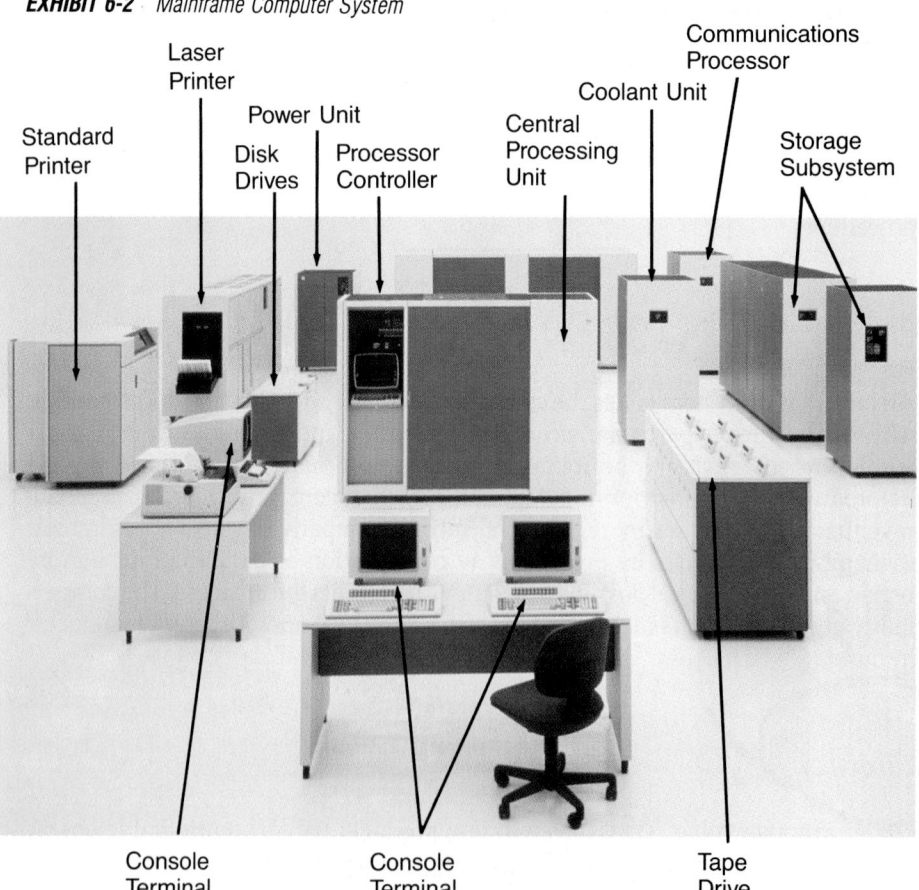

Standard Printer · Laser Printer · Disk Drives · Power Unit · Processor Controller · Central Processing Unit · Coolant Unit · Communications Processor · Storage Subsystem

Console Terminal · Console Terminal · Tape Drive

Components of a Computer System

The components of a computer data processing system are *hardware, software,* and *personnel.* This topic is covered in more detail in Chapter 28.

Hardware. Computer **hardware** is the equipment that makes up the system. Exhibit 6-2 shows the hardware components of a mainframe system. A **mainframe system** is characterized by a single computer that can handle a large volume of transactions very quickly. It can be used locally or by employees at various locations. Employees enter data into the mainframe through remote terminals. In large systems, the employees may be scattered all over the world yet have access to the same computer. Smaller computers, called **minicomputers,** operate like large systems but on a smaller scale.

Exhibit 6-3 shows a microcomputer system, which is based on a different concept. In a **microcomputer** system, each work station has its own computer, often called a personal computer (PC). These small computers can be connected so that employees can work on the same project together. A group of microcomputers connected for common use is called a *network,* which achieves many of the benefits of a mainframe system. Micro systems are popular because they are more flexible and less expensive than large mainframes.

Software. Computer **software** is the set of programs, or instructions, that cause the computer to perform the work desired. In a computer system, transactions are not entered into the accounting records by writing entries in a journal. They are entered by typing data on a keyboard similar to that of a typewriter. The keyboard is wired to the computer, which converts the typed data into instructions the computer uses to process the data. In some systems, the data are entered into the computer on punched cards.

EXHIBIT 6-3 *Microcomputer System*

Printer

Display Monitor
Atop Personal Computer (PC)

Mainframe software includes programs written in computer languages such as FORTRAN, COBOL, and PL/1. Microcomputers use software based on computer languages such as BASIC and PASCAL. Other micro software is designed to do specialized tasks. For example, LOTUS® 1-2-3 performs financial analysis, and dBASE III organizes, stores, and retrieves large quantities of data. BPI System's® General Accounting program processes data and prints the balance sheet, income statement, and subsidiary records of accounts receivable, accounts payable, and payroll, among many other accounting tasks. Microcomputer software is popular because much of it is menu driven. This means that by following instructions— the "menu"—you can do complex tasks with little or no computer training.

Personnel.   Computer personnel in a mainframe system include a systems analyst, a programmer, and a machine operator. The *systems analyst* designs the system, based on managers' information needs and the available accounting data. It is the analyst's job to design systems that convert data into useful information —at the lowest cost. The *programmer* writes the programs (instructions) that direct the computer's actions. The computer *operator* runs the machine.

In microcomputer systems, the distinction between the programmer and the operator becomes blurry because employees may handle both responsibilities. For example, a marketing manager may use a microcomputer to identify the territory needing an advertising campaign. The company treasurer may use a micro to analyze the effects of borrowing money at various interest rates. The controller may prepare the budget on a micro. These people may program the computer to meet their specific needs and also operate the machine.

Batch versus On-line Processing

Computers process data in two main ways, in batches and on-line. **Batch processing** handles similar transactions in a group, or batch. Payroll accounting systems use batch processing. Suppose each employee fills out a weekly time sheet showing the number of hours worked. Stored in the computer are the employee's hourly pay and payroll deductions. The machine operator enters the hours worked, and the computer multiplies hours by hourly pay to determine each employee's gross pay. The computer subtracts deductions to compute net pay and prints payroll checks for the net amount. It also prints the weekly payroll report and updates the ledger accounts—all in one batch operation.

On-line processing handles transaction data continuously, often from various locations, rather than in batches at a single location. In retail stores like Sears and Penney's, the cash register does more than make change. It also doubles as a computer terminal. When you charge merchandise at a Penney's store in the United States, the transaction is recorded at Penney's dataprocessing center in Dallas, Texas, directly from the store cash register. For any one transaction the computer in Dallas may perform the following steps:

1.   Accounts receivable—
     a. Compares your account number to the list of approved accounts.
        Assume your account is approved.
     b. Adds the amount of this transaction to your previous balance and determines whether the new balance, including this transaction amount, exceeds your credit limit.
        Assume it does not exceed your credit limit.
     c. Debits the Accounts Receivable account and updates your personal account balance to include the effect of this transaction.

2. Sales Revenue—Credits the Sales Revenue account.
3. Inventory—
   a. Updates inventory records for the decrease due to this transaction.
   b. Prepares an order for replacement merchandise if the updated quantity on hand is below the reorder point.

The interactive nature of on-line processing—accounting for accounts receivable, sales, and inventory simultaneously—requires a large share of the computer's capacity. On-line processing, therefore, is used more in mainframe systems than in micro systems.

Overview of an Accounting Information System _____

The purpose of an accounting information system is to produce the financial statements and other reports used by managers, creditors, and interested people to evaluate the business. Companies use computers to meet specific needs. One company's accounting system may use a computer for accounts receivable and cash receipts and a manual system for the rest of its business. Another business may computerize payroll, accounts payable, and cash disbursements, with the remainder accounted for manually. Many large companies have completely computerized systems, and many small businesses use mostly manual systems. Each entity designs its system to achieve the goals of control, compatibility, flexibility, and an acceptable cost/benefit relationship. Exhibit 6-4 diagrams a typical accounting system for a merchandising business.

Accounting procedures may be manual or computerized, mainframe or microcomputer, batch or on-line. The remainder of the chapter describes some of the more important aspects of the system described in Exhibit 6-4. Later chapters discuss the remaining system topics diagrammed in the exhibit.

EXHIBIT 6-4 *Overview of an Accounting System*

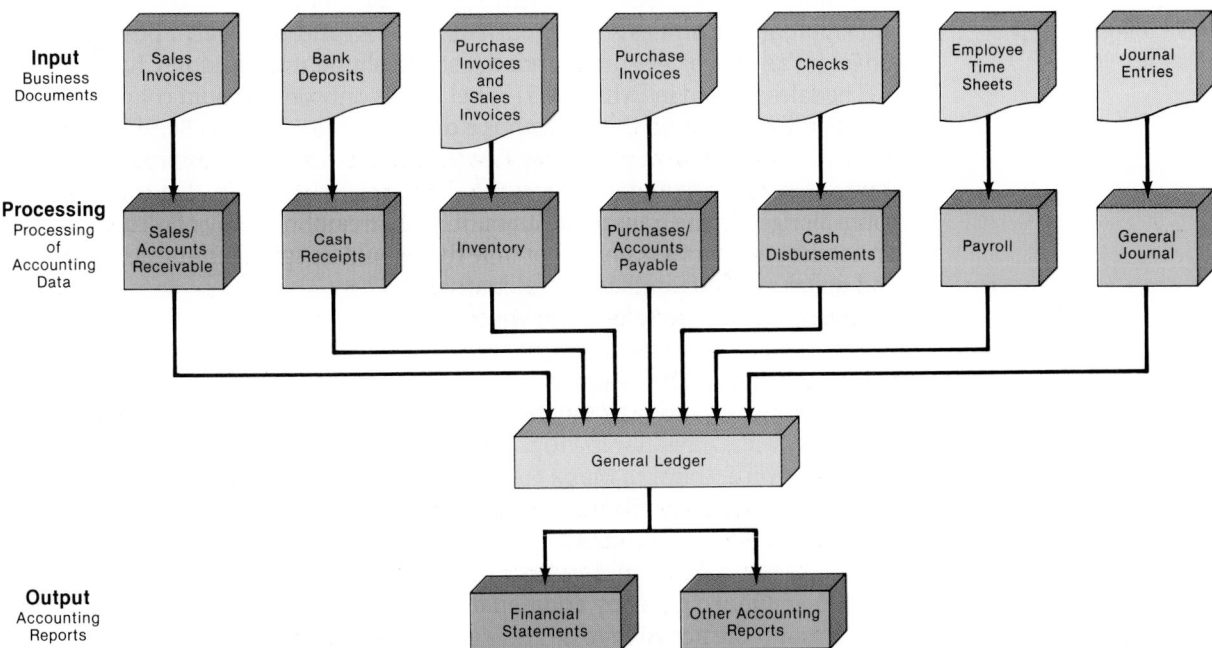

Special Accounting Journals

The journal entries illustrated so far in this book have been made in the *general journal.* In practice, however, it is inefficient to record all transactions there.

Think of using the general journal to debit Accounts Receivable and credit Sales Revenue for each credit sale made in a department store on a busy Saturday! Assuming you survived that, consider posting each journal entry to the ledger. Not only would the work be tedious, but it would be time consuming and expensive.

In fact, most of a business's transactions fall into one of four categories, so accountants use special journals to record these transactions. This system reduces the time and cost otherwise spent journalizing, as we will see. The four categories of transactions, the related special journal, and the posting abbreviations follow.

Transaction	Special Journal	Posting Abbreviation
1. Sale on account	Sales journal	S
2. Cash receipt	Cash receipts journal	CR
3. Purchase on account	Purchases journal	P
4. Cash disbursement	Cash disbursements journal	CD

Businesses use the **general journal** for transactions that do not fit one of the special journals. For example, adjusting and closing entries are entered in the general journal. Its posting abbreviation is J.

OBJECTIVE 2
Use the sales journal

Sales Journal

Most merchandisers sell at least some of their inventory on account. These *credit sales* are recorded in the **sales journal,** also called the *credit sales journal.* Credit sales of assets other than inventory—for example, buildings—occur infrequently and are recorded in the general journal.

Exhibit 6-5 illustrates a sales journal (Panel A) and the related posting to the ledgers (Panel B) of Austin Sound, the stereo shop introduced in Chapter 5.

The sales journal in Exhibit 6-5 (Panel A) has only one amount column, on the far right. Each entry in this column is a debit (Dr.) to Accounts Receivable and a credit (Cr.) to Sales Revenue, as the heading above this column indicates. For each transaction, the accountant enters the date, invoice number, and customer account along with the transaction amount. This streamlined way of recording sales on account saves a vast amount of time that would be spent writing account titles and dollar amounts in the general journal.

In recording credit sales in previous chapters, we did not keep a record of the names of credit sale customers. In practice the business must know the amount receivable from each customer. How else can the company keep track of who owes it money—and how much?

Consider the first transaction. On November 2 Austin Sound sold stereo equipment on account to Maria Galvez for $935. The invoice number is 422. All this information appears on a single line in the sales journal. Note that no explanation is necessary. The transaction's presence in the sales journal means that it is a credit sale—debited to Accounts Receivable—Maria Galvez and credited to Sales Revenue. To gain any additional information about the transaction, a person looks up the actual invoice.

EXHIBIT 6-5 *Sales Journal and Posting to Ledgers*

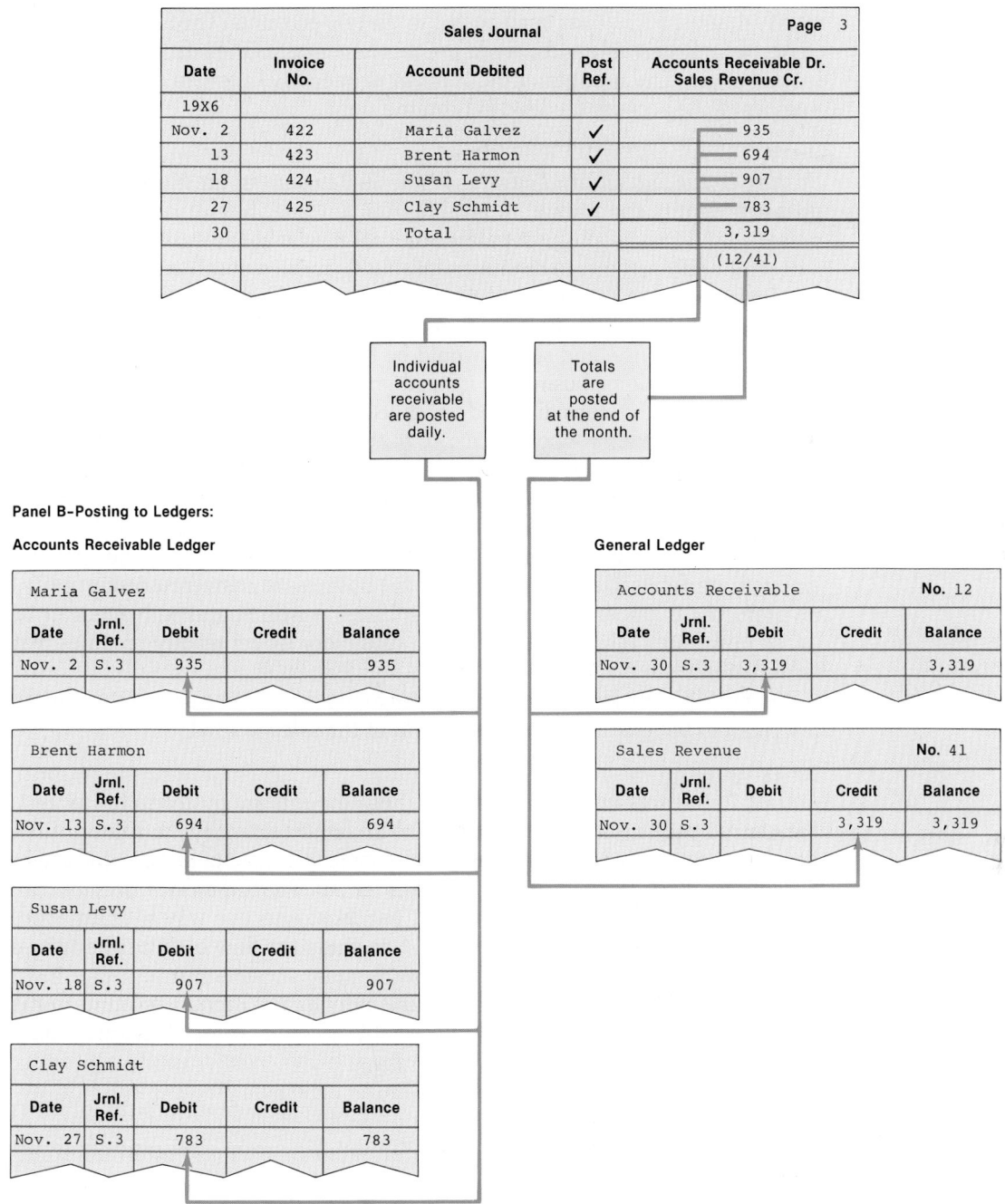

Panel A–Sales Journal:

Sales Journal				Page 3
Date	Invoice No.	Account Debited	Post Ref.	Accounts Receivable Dr. Sales Revenue Cr.
19X6				
Nov. 2	422	Maria Galvez	✓	935
13	423	Brent Harmon	✓	694
18	424	Susan Levy	✓	907
27	425	Clay Schmidt	✓	783
30		Total		3,319
				(12/41)

Individual accounts receivable are posted daily.

Totals are posted at the end of the month.

Panel B–Posting to Ledgers:

Accounts Receivable Ledger

Maria Galvez

Date	Jrnl. Ref.	Debit	Credit	Balance
Nov. 2	S.3	935		935

Brent Harmon

Date	Jrnl. Ref.	Debit	Credit	Balance
Nov. 13	S.3	694		694

Susan Levy

Date	Jrnl. Ref.	Debit	Credit	Balance
Nov. 18	S.3	907		907

Clay Schmidt

Date	Jrnl. Ref.	Debit	Credit	Balance
Nov. 27	S.3	783		783

General Ledger

Accounts Receivable   No. 12

Date	Jrnl. Ref.	Debit	Credit	Balance
Nov. 30	S.3	3,319		3,319

Sales Revenue   No. 41

Date	Jrnl. Ref.	Debit	Credit	Balance
Nov. 30	S.3		3,319	3,319

Posting to the General Ledger.   Note the term *general ledger.* The ledger we have used so far is the **general ledger,** which holds the accounts reported in the financial statements. However, we will soon introduce other ledgers.

Posting from the sales journal to the general ledger is done monthly. First, the amounts in the journal are summed. In Exhibit 6-5, the total credit sales for November are $3,319. Recall that this column has two headings, Accounts Receivable and Sales Revenue. When the $3,319 is posted to these accounts in the general ledger, the accountant enters their account numbers beneath the total in the sales journal. Note in Panel B of Exhibit 6-5 that the account number for Accounts Receivable is 12 and the account number for Sales Revenue is 41. These account numbers are written beneath the credit sales total in the sales journal to signify that the $3,319 has been posted to the two accounts. The $3,319 is a debit to Accounts Receivable and a credit to Sales Revenue, as the heading in the sales journal states. The number of the account debited (12) appears on the left, the number of the account credited (41) on the right.

Posting to the Subsidiary Ledger. The $3,319 sum of the November debits does not identify the amount receivable from any specific customer. Most businesses would find keeping a separate accounts receivable account in the general ledger for each customer to be unmanageable. A business may have thousands of customers. Imagine how many pages thick the general ledger for Sears would be. Locating a specific customer's account among the other accounts (Cash, Inventory, Salary Expense, and so on) would be frustrating and time consuming. To streamline operations, businesses instead place the accounts of their individual credit customers in a subsidiary ledger, called the Accounts Receivable ledger. A **subsidiary ledger** is a book of accounts that provides supporting details on individual balances, the total of which appears in a general ledger account. The customer accounts are filed alphabetically.

OBJECTIVE 3

Use control accounts and subsidiary ledgers.

Amounts in the sales journal are posted to the subsidiary ledger daily to keep a current record of the amount receivable from each customer. Note that the amounts are debits. Daily posting allows the business to answer customer inquiries promptly. Suppose Maria Galvez telephones Austin Sound on November 11 to ask how much money she owes. The subsidiary ledger readily provides that information.

When each transaction amount is posted to the subsidiary ledger, a check mark is written in the posting reference column of the sales journal.

Journal References in the Ledgers. When amounts are posted to the ledgers, the journal page number is written in the account to identify the source of the data. All transaction data in Exhibit 6-5 originated on page 3 of the sales journal so all journal references in the ledger accounts are S.3. The S. indicates sales journal.

Trace all the postings in Exhibit 6-5. The most effective way to learn about accounting systems and special journals is to study the flow of data. The arrows indicate the direction of the information.

The arrows show the links between the individual customer accounts in the subsidiary ledger and the Accounts Receivable account. These links are summarized as follows:

Accounts Receivable debit balance	$3,319
Balances of individual customer accounts in the subsidiary ledger:	
Maria Galvez	$935
Brent Harmon	694
Susan Levy	907
Clay Schmidt	783
Total	$3,319

Accounts Receivable in the general ledger is a **control account**, which is an account whose balance equals the sum of the balances of a group of related accounts in a subsidiary ledger. In this simple illustration, its balance is the total amount of credit sales. The individual customer accounts are subsidiary accounts. They are "controlled" by the Accounts Receivable account in the general ledger.

Let's look at the advantages the sales journal offers. Each transaction is entered on a single line, and the account titles do not have to be written. The accountant, then, does not have to write as much in the sales journal as in the general journal. Also, the sales journal streamlines posting. That is, fewer postings to the general ledger are necessary. Suppose that Austin Sound had 400 credit sales for the month. How many postings to the general ledger would be made from the sales journal? There are only two, one to Accounts Receivable and one to Sales Revenue. How many postings would there be from the general journal? The total would be 800 (400 debits to Accounts Receivable and 400 credits to Sales Revenue).

Additional data can be recorded in the sales journal. For example, a company may add a column to record sale terms, such as 2/10 n/30. The design of the journal depends on managers' needs for information.

Cash Receipts Journal

Cash transactions are common in most businesses because cash receipts from customers are the lifeblood of business. To streamline the recording of repetitive cash receipt transactions, accountants use the **cash receipts journal.**

OBJECTIVE 4
Use the cash receipts journal

Exhibit 6-6, Panel A, illustrates the cash receipts journal. The related posting to ledgers is shown in Panel B. The exhibit illustrates November transactions for Austin Sound.

Every transaction recorded in this journal is a cash receipt, so the first column is for debits to the Cash account. The next column is for debits to Sales Discounts on collections from customers. In a typical merchandising business, the main sources of cash are collections on account and cash sales. Thus the cash receipts journal has credit columns for Accounts Receivable and Sales Revenue. The journal also has a credit column for Other Accounts, which lists sources of cash other than cash sales and collections on account. This Other Accounts column is also used to record the names of customers from whom cash is received on account.

In Exhibit 6-6, cash sales occurred on November 6, 19, and 28. Observe the debits to Cash and the credits to Sales Revenue ($517, $853, and $1,802).

On November 11 Austin Sound borrowed $1,000 from First Bank. Cash is debited, and Note Payable to First Bank is credited in the Other Accounts column because no specific credit column is set up to account for borrowings. For this transaction, it is necessary to write the account title, Note Payable to First Bank, in the Other Accounts/Account Title column to record the source of cash.

On November 25 Austin Sound collected $762 of interest revenue. The account credited, Interest Revenue, must be written in the Other Accounts column. The November 11 and 25 transactions illustrate an important fact about business. Different entities have different types of transactions, and they design their special journals to meet their particular needs. In this case, the Other Accounts Credit column is the catchall that is used to record all nonroutine cash receipt transactions.

On November 14 Austin Sound collected $900 from Maria Galvez. Referring back to Exhibit 6-5, we see that on November 2 Austin Sound sold merchandise for $935 to Ms. Galvez. Assume that the terms of sale allowed a $35 discount for prompt payment and that she paid within the discount period. Austin's cash receipt is recorded by debiting Cash for $900 and Sales Discounts for $35 and by crediting Accounts Receivable for $935. Note that the customer's name appears in

EXHIBIT 6-6 *Cash Receipts Journal and Posting to Ledgers*

Panel A–Cash Receipts Journal:

	Debits		Credits				
					Other Accounts		
Date	**Cash**	**Sales Discounts**	**Accounts Receivable**	**Sales Revenue**	**Account Title**	**Post. Ref.**	**Amount**
19X6							
Nov. 6	517			517			
11	1,000				Note Payable to First Bank	22	1,000
14	900	35	935		Maria Galvez	✓	
19	853			853			
22	300		300		Brent Harmon	✓	
25	762				Interest Revenue	46	762
28	1,802			1,802			
30	6,134	35	1,235	3,172	Totals		1,762
	(11)	(42)	(12)	(41)			(✓)

Cash Receipts Journal — Page 5

Totals are posted at the end of the month.

Individual accounts receivable are posted daily.

Individual amounts are posted at the end of the month.

Total is not posted.

Panel B–Posting to Ledgers:

Accounts Receivable Ledger

Maria Galvez

Date	Jrnl. Ref.	Debit	Credit	Balance
Nov. 2	S.3	935		935
14	CR.5		935	-0-

Brent Harmon

Date	Jrnl. Ref.	Debit	Credit	Balance
Nov. 13	S.3	694		694
22	CR.5		300	394

Susan Levy

Date	Jrnl. Ref.	Debit	Credit	Balance
Nov. 18	S.3	907		907

Clay Schmidt

Date	Jrnl. Ref.	Debit	Credit	Balance
Nov. 27	S.3	783		783

General Ledger

Cash — No. 11

Date	Jrnl. Ref.	Debit	Credit	Balance
Nov. 30	CR.5	6,134		6,134

Accounts Receivable — No. 12

Date	Jrnl. Ref.	Debit	Credit	Balance
Nov. 30	S.3	3,319		3,319
30	CR.5		1,235	2,084

Note Payable to First Bank — No. 22

Date	Jrnl. Ref.	Debit	Credit	Balance
Nov. 11	CR.5		1,000	1,000

Sales Revenue — No. 41

Date	Jrnl. Ref.	Debit	Credit	Balance
Nov. 30	S.3		3,319	3,319
30	CR.5		3,172	6,491

Sales Discounts — No. 42

Date	Jrnl. Ref.	Debit	Credit	Balance
Nov. 30	CR.5	35		35

Interest Revenue — No. 46

Date	Jrnl. Ref.	Debit	Credit	Balance
Nov. 25	CR.5		762	762

the Other Accounts/Account Title column. This enables the business to keep exact track of each customer's account in the subsidiary ledger.

On November 22 the business collected $300 on account from Brent Harmon, who was paying for part of the November 13 purchase. Assume no discount applied to this collection.

Total debits should equal total credits in the cash receipts journal. This equality holds for each transaction and for the monthly totals. For example, the first transaction has a $517 debit and an equal credit. For the month, total debits ($6,134 + $35 = $6,169) equal total credits ($1,235 + $3,172 + $1,762 = $6,169).

Posting to the General Ledger. The column totals are posted monthly. To indicate their posting, the account number is written below the column total in the cash receipts journal. Note the account number for Cash (11) below the column total $6,134, and trace the posting to Cash in the general ledger. Likewise, the Sales Discounts, Accounts Receivable, and Sales Revenue column totals also are posted to the general ledger.

The column total for *Other Accounts* is not posted. Instead, these credits are posted individually. In Exhibit 6-6, the November 11 transaction reads "Note Payable to First Bank." This account's number (22) in the Post. Ref. column indicates that the transaction amount was posted individually. The check mark, instead of an account number, below the column total indicates that the column total was not posted. The November 25 collection of interest revenue is also posted individually. These amounts can be posted to the general ledger at the end of the month. However, they should be dated in the ledger accounts based on their actual date in the journal. This makes it easy to trace the amounts back to the journal.

Posting to the Subsidiary Ledger. Amounts from the cash receipts journal are posted to the subsidiary accounts receivable ledger daily to keep the individual balances up to date. The postings to the accounts receivable ledger are credits. Trace the $935 posting to Maria Galvez's account. It reduces her balance to zero. The $300 receipt from Brent Harmon reduces his accounts receivable balance to $394.

After posting, the sum of the individual balances that remain in the accounts receivable ledger equals the general ledger balance in Accounts Receivable ($2,084). Austin Sound may prepare a November 30 list of account balances from the subsidiary ledger as a check of the accuracy of journalizing and posting:

Customer Accounts Receivable

Customer	Balance
Brent Harmon.	$ 394
Susan Levy.	907
Clay Schmidt.	783
Total accounts receivable.	$2,084

Keeping good accounts receivable records reduces errors and helps customer relations.

The cash receipts journal offers the same advantages as the sales journal: streamlined journalizing of transactions and fewer postings to the ledgers.

Summary Problem for Your Review

A company completed the following selected transactions during March:

Mar. 4 Received $500 from a cash sale to a customer.

6 Received $60 on account from Brady Lee. The full invoice amount was $65, but Lee paid within the discount period to gain the $5 discount.

9 Received $1,080 on a note receivable from Beverly Mann. This amount includes the $1,000 note receivable plus $80 of interest revenue.

15 Received $800 from a cash sale to a customer.

24 Borrowed $2,200 by signing a note payable to Interstate Bank.

27 Received $1,200 on account from Lance Albert. Payment was received after the discount period lapsed.

The general ledger showed the following balances at February 28: Cash, debit balance of $1,117; Accounts Receivable, debit balance of $2,790; Note Receivable–Beverly Mann, debit balance of $1,000. The accounts receivable subsidiary ledger at February 28 contained debit balances as follows: Lance Albert, $1,840; Brady Lee, $65; Melinda Fultz, $885.

Required

1. Record the transactions in the cash receipts journal, page 7.
2. Compute column totals at March 31. Show that total debits equal total credits in the cash receipts journal.
3. Post to the general ledger and the accounts receivable subsidiary ledger. Use complete posting references, including the account numbers illustrated: Cash, 11; Accounts Receivable, 12; Note Receivable–Beverly Mann, 13; Note Payable–Interstate Bank, 22; Sales Revenue, 41; Sales Discounts, 42; Interest Revenue, 46. Insert a check mark (✓) in the posting reference column for each February 28 account balance.
4. Prove the accuracy of posting by showing that the total of the balances in the subsidiary ledger equals the general ledger balance in Accounts Receivable.

SOLUTION TO REVIEW PROBLEM

Requirements 1 and 2

Cash Receipts Journal   Page 7

	Debits		Credits				
					Other Accounts		
Date	Cash	Sales Discounts	Accounts Receivable	Sales Revenue	Account Title	Post. Ref.	Amount
Mar. 4	500			500			
6	60	5	65		Brady Lee	✓	
9	1,080				Note Receivable–		
					Beverly Mann	13	1,000
					Interest Revenue	46	80
15	800			800			
24	2,200				Note Payable–		
					Interstate Bank	22	2,200
27	1,200		1,200		Lance Albert	✓	
31	5,840	5	1,265	1,300	Total		3,280
	(11)	(42)	(12)	(41)			(✓)

5,845   5,845

Requirement 3

Accounts Receivable Ledger

Lance Albert

Date	Jrnl. Ref.	Debit	Credit	Balance
Feb. 28	✓			1,840
Mar. 27	CR. 7		1,200	640

Brady Lee

Date	Jrnl. Ref.	Debit	Credit	Balance
Feb. 28	✓			65
Mar. 6	CR. 7		65	—

Melinda Fultz

Date	Jrnl. Ref.	Debit	Credit	Balance
Feb. 28	✓			885

General Ledger

Cash No. 11

Date	Jrnl. Ref.	Debit	Credit	Balance
Feb. 28	✓			1,117
Mar. 31	CR.7	5,840		6,957

Accounts Receivable No. 12

Date	Jrnl. Ref.	Debit	Credit	Balance
Feb. 28	✓			2,790
Mar. 31	CR.7		1,265	1,525

Note Receivable – Beverly Mann No. 13

Date	Jrnl. Ref.	Debit	Credit	Balance
Feb. 28	✓			1,000
Mar. 9	CR.7		1,000	—

Note Payable – Interstate Bank No. 22

Date	Jrnl. Ref.	Debit	Credit	Balance
Mar. 24	CR.7		2,200	2,200

Sales Revenue No. 41

Date	Jrnl. Ref.	Debit	Credit	Balance
Mar. 31	CR. 7		1,300	1,300

Sales Discounts No. 42

Date	Jrnl. Ref.	Debit	Credit	Balance
Mar. 31	CR. 7	5		5

Interest Revenue No. 46

Date	Jrnl. Ref.	Debit	Credit	Balance
Mar. 9	CR. 7		80	80

Requirement 4

Lance Albert............................	$ 640
Melinda Fultz..........................	885
Total	$1,525

This total agrees with the balance in Accounts Receivable.

Purchases Journal

OBJECTIVE 5

Use the purchases journal

A merchandising business purchases inventory and supplies frequently. Such purchases are usually made on account. The **purchases journal** is designed to account for all purchases of inventory, supplies, and other assets *on account*. It can also be used to record expenses incurred on account. Cash purchases are recorded in the cash disbursements journal.

Exhibit 6-7 illustrates Austin Sound's purchases journal (Panel A) and posting to ledgers (Panel B).[1]

The purchases journal in Exhibit 6-7 has amount columns for credits to Accounts Payable and debits to Purchases, Supplies, and Other Accounts. The Other Accounts columns accommodate purchases of items other than inventory and supplies. These columns make the journal flexible enough to accommodate a wide variety of transactions. Each business designs its purchases journal to meet its own needs for information and efficiency. Accounts Payable is credited for all transactions recorded in the purchases journal. Inventory purchases are debited to Purchases. Purchases of supplies are debited to Supplies.

On November 2 Austin Sound purchased from JVC Corporation stereo inventory costing $700. The creditor's name (JVC Corporation) is entered in the Account Credited column. The purchase terms of 3/15 n/30 are also entered to help identify the due date and the discount available. Accounts Payable is credited and Purchases is debited for the transaction amount. On November 19 a credit purchase of supplies is entered as a debit to Supplies and a credit to Accounts Payable.

Note the November 9 purchase of fixtures from City Office Supply. Since the purchases journal contains no column for fixtures, the Other Accounts debit column is used. Because this was a credit purchase, the accountant enters the creditor name (City Office Supply) in the Account Credited column and writes "Fixtures" in the Other Accounts/Account Title column.

The total credits in the journal ($2,876) are compared to the total debits ($1,706 + $103 + $1,067 = $2,876) to prove the accuracy of the entries in the purchases journal.

To pay debts efficiently, a company must know how much it owes particular creditors. The Accounts Payable account in the general ledger shows only a single total, however, and therefore does not indicate the amount owed to each creditor. Companies keep an accounts payable subsidiary ledger. The accounts payable ledger lists the creditors in alphabetical order, along with the amounts owed to them. Exhibit 6-7, Panel B, shows Austin Sound's accounts payable subsidiary ledger, which includes accounts for Audio Electronics, City Office Supply, and

---

[1] This is the only special journal that we illustrate with the credit column placed to the left and the debit columns to the right. This arrangement of columns focuses on Accounts Payable, which is credited for each entry to this journal—and on the individual supplier to be paid.

EXHIBIT 6-7 *Purchases Journal and Posting to Ledgers*

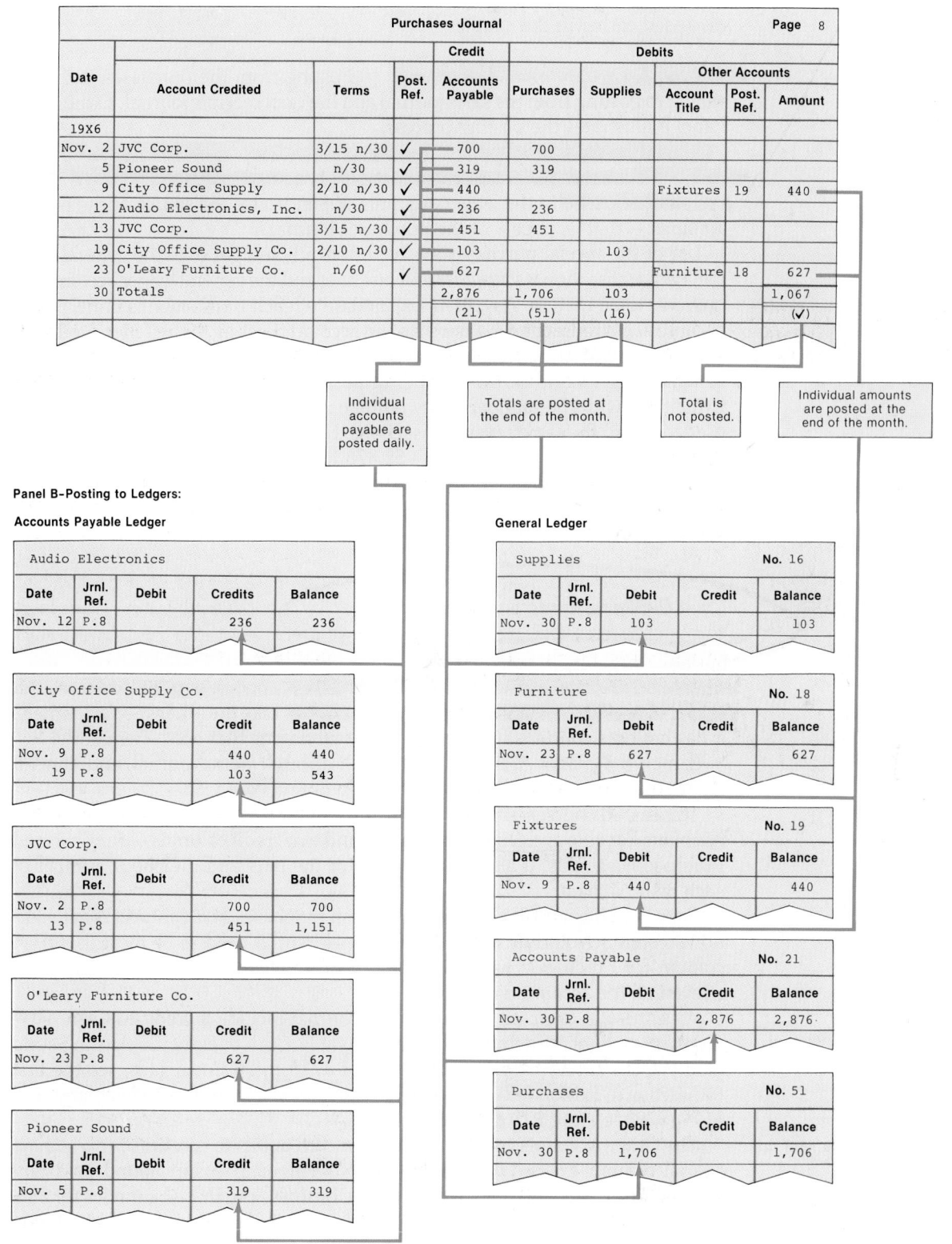

Panel A–Purchases Journal:

Purchases Journal									Page 8
				Credit	Debits				
							Other Accounts		
Date	Account Credited	Terms	Post. Ref.	Accounts Payable	Purchases	Supplies	Account Title	Post. Ref.	Amount
19X6									
Nov. 2	JVC Corp.	3/15 n/30	✓	700	700				
5	Pioneer Sound	n/30	✓	319	319				
9	City Office Supply	2/10 n/30	✓	440			Fixtures	19	440
12	Audio Electronics, Inc.	n/30	✓	236	236				
13	JVC Corp.	3/15 n/30	✓	451	451				
19	City Office Supply Co.	2/10 n/30	✓	103		103			
23	O'Leary Furniture Co.	n/60	✓	627			Furniture	18	627
30	Totals			2,876	1,706	103			1,067
				(21)	(51)	(16)			(✓)

| Individual accounts payable are posted daily. | Totals are posted at the end of the month. | Total is not posted. | Individual amounts are posted at the end of the month. |

Panel B–Posting to Ledgers:

Accounts Payable Ledger

Audio Electronics

Date	Jrnl. Ref.	Debit	Credits	Balance
Nov. 12	P.8		236	236

City Office Supply Co.

Date	Jrnl. Ref.	Debit	Credit	Balance
Nov. 9	P.8		440	440
19	P.8		103	543

JVC Corp.

Date	Jrnl. Ref.	Debit	Credit	Balance
Nov. 2	P.8		700	700
13	P.8		451	1,151

O'Leary Furniture Co.

Date	Jrnl. Ref.	Debit	Credit	Balance
Nov. 23	P.8		627	627

Pioneer Sound

Date	Jrnl. Ref.	Debit	Credit	Balance
Nov. 5	P.8		319	319

General Ledger

Supplies   No. 16

Date	Jrnl. Ref.	Debit	Credit	Balance
Nov. 30	P.8	103		103

Furniture   No. 18

Date	Jrnl. Ref.	Debit	Credit	Balance
Nov. 23	P.8	627		627

Fixtures   No. 19

Date	Jrnl. Ref.	Debit	Credit	Balance
Nov. 9	P.8	440		440

Accounts Payable   No. 21

Date	Jrnl. Ref.	Debit	Credit	Balance
Nov. 30	P.8		2,876	2,876

Purchases   No. 51

Date	Jrnl. Ref.	Debit	Credit	Balance
Nov. 30	P.8	1,706		1,706

others. After posting at the end of the period, the total of the individual balances in the subsidiary ledger equals the balance in the Accounts Payable control account in the general ledger. This system is like the accounts receivable system discussed earlier in the chapter.

Posting from the Purchases Journal.   Posting from the purchases journal is similar to posting from the sales journal and the cash receipts journal. Exhibit 6-7, Panel B illustrates the posting process.

Individual accounts payable in the *accounts payable subsidiary ledger* are posted daily, and column totals and other amounts are posted to the *general ledger* at the end of the month. In the ledger accounts, P.8 indicates the source of the posted amounts—that is, page 8 of the purchases journal.

Use of the special purchases journal offers advantages over the general journal. Each transaction is *journalized* on one line, and the general ledger accounts do not have to be written. A written explanation of each transaction is unnecessary because each transaction is a purchase on account. Posting to the general ledger is streamlined with the special journal because monthly totals can be posted to the general ledger. Contrast the number of postings from the purchases journal in Exhibit 6-7 with the number that would be required if the general journal were used to record the same seven transactions. Use of the purchases journal requires only five general ledger postings—$2,876 to Accounts Payable, $1,706 to Purchases, $103 to Supplies, $440 to Fixtures, and $627 to Furniture. Without the purchases journal, there would have been fourteen postings, two for each of the seven transactions.

OBJECTIVE 6
Use the cash
disbursements journal

Cash Disbursements Journal

Businesses make most cash disbursements by check. All payments by check are recorded in the **cash disbursements journal.** Other titles of this special journal are the *check register* and the *cash payments journal.* Like the other special journals, it has multiple columns for recording cash payments that occur frequently.

Exhibit 6-8, Panel A, illustrates the cash disbursements journal, and Panel B shows the postings to the ledgers of Austin Sound.

The cash disbursements journal in the exhibit has two debit columns—for Accounts Payable and Other Accounts—and two credit columns—for Cash and Purchase Discounts. It also has columns for the date and the check number of each cash payment.

Suppose a business makes numerous cash purchases of inventory. What additional column would its cash disbursements journal need to be most useful? A column for Purchases, which would appear under the Debits heading, would streamline the accounting.

All entries in the cash disbursements journal include a credit to Cash. Payments on account are debits to Accounts Payable. On November 15 Austin Sound paid JVC on account, with credit terms of 3/15 n/30 (for details, see the first transaction in Exhibit 6-7). Therefore, Austin took the 3 percent discount and paid $679 ($700 less the $21 discount).

The Other Accounts column is used to record debits to accounts for which no special column exists. For example, on November 3 Austin Sound paid rent expense of $1,200, and on November 8 the business purchased supplies for $61.

As with all other journals, the total debits ($3,161 + $819 = $3,980) should equal the total credits ($21 + $3,959 = $3,980).

Posting from the Cash Disbursements Journal.   Posting from the cash disbursements journal is similar to posting from the cash receipts journal. Individual

EXHIBIT 6-8 *Cash Disbursements Journal and Posting to Ledgers.*

Panel A–Cash Disbursements Journal:

				Debits		Credits	
Cash Disbursements Journal							**Page** 6
Date	**Ck. No.**	**Account Debited**	**Post. Ref.**	**Other Accounts**	**Accounts Payable**	**Purchase Discounts**	**Cash**
19X6							
Nov. 3	101	Rent Expense	54	1,200			1,200
8	102	Supplies	16	61			61
15	103	JVC Corp.	✓		700	21	679
20	104	Pioneer Sound	✓		119		119
26	105	Purchases	51	1,900			1,900
30		Totals		3,161	819	21	3,959
				(✓)	(21)	(52)	(11)

Total is not posted.

Totals are posted at the end of the month.

Individual accounts payable are posted daily

Individual amounts are posted at the end of the month.

Panel B–Posting to Ledgers:

Accounts Payable Ledger

Audio Electronics

Date	Jrnl. Ref.	Debit	Credit	Balance
Nov. 12	P.8		236	236

City Office Supply

Date	Jrnl. Ref.	Debit	Credit	Balance
Nov. 9	P.8		440	440
19	P.8		103	543

JVC Corp.

Date	Jrnl. Ref.	Debit	Credit	Balance
Nov. 2	P.8		700	700
13	P.8		451	1151
15	CD.6	700		451

O'Leary Furniture Co.

Date	Jrnl. Ref.	Debit	Credit	Balance
Nov. 23	P.8		627	627

Pioneer Sound

Date	Jrnl. Ref.	Debit	Credit	Balance
Nov. 5	P.8		319	319
20	CD.6	119		200

General Ledger

Cash No. 11

Date	Jrnl. Ref.	Debit	Credit	Balance
Nov. 30	CR.5	6,134		6,134
30	CD.6		3,959	2,175

Supplies No. 16

Date	Jrnl. Ref.	Debit	Credit	Balance
Nov. 30	P.8	103		103
8	CD.6	61		164

Accounts Payable No. 21

Date	Jrnl. Ref.	Debit	Credit	Balance
Nov. 30	P.8		2,876	2,876
30	CD.6	819		2,057

Purchases No. 51

Date	Jrnl. Ref.	Debit	Credit	Balance
Nov. 30	P.8	1,706		1,706
26	CD.6	1,900		3,606

Purchase Discounts No. 52

Date	Jrnl. Ref.	Debit	Credit	Balance
Nov. 30	CD.6		21	21

Rent Expense No. 54

Date	Jrnl. Ref.	Debit	Credit	Balance
Nov. 3	CD.6	1,200		1,200

creditor amounts are posted daily, and column totals and Other Accounts are posted at the end of the month. Exhibit 6-8, Panel B illustrates the posting process.

Observe the effect of posting to the Accounts Payable account in the general ledger. The first posted amount in the Accounts Payable account (credit $2,876) originated in the purchases journal, page 8 (P.8). The second posted amount (debit $819) came from the cash disbursements journal, page 6 (CD.6). The resulting credit balance in Accounts Payable is $2,057. Also, see the Cash account. After posting, its debit balance is $2,175.

Amounts in the Other Accounts column are posted individually (for example, Rent Expense—debit $1,200). When each Other Accounts amount is posted to the general ledger, the account number is written in the Post. Ref. column of the journal.

As a proof of accuracy, companies total the individual creditor balances in the accounts payable subsidiary ledger for comparison with the Accounts Payable balance in the general ledger:

Creditor Accounts Payable

Creditor	Balance
Audio Electronics	$ 236
City Office Supply	543
JVC Corp.	451
O'Leary Furniture	627
Pioneer Sound	200
Total accounts payable	$2,057

This total, computed at the end of the period, agrees with the Accounts Payable balance in Exhibit 6-8. Agreement of the two amounts indicates that journalizing and posting have been performed correctly and that the resulting account balances are correct.

Use of the cash disbursements journal streamlines journalizing and posting in the same way as for the other special journals.

The Credit Memorandum—A Basic Business Document

Customers sometimes bring merchandise back to the seller, and sellers grant sales allowances to customers because of product defects and for other reasons. The effect of sales returns and sales allowances is the same—both decrease net sales in the same way a sales discount does. The document issued by the seller to indicate having credited the customer's Account Receivable is called a **credit memorandum,** or **credit memo,** because the company gives the customer credit for the returned merchandise. When a company issues a credit memo, it records the transaction by debiting Sales Returns and Allowances and crediting Accounts Receivable.

Suppose Austin Sound sold two stereo speakers for $198 on account to Stephanie Baker. Later she discovered a defect and returned the speakers. Austin Sound would issue to Ms. Baker a credit memo like the one in Exhibit 6-9.

To record the *sale return,* Austin Sound would make the following entry in the general journal:

EXHIBIT 6-9   *Credit Memorandum*

Credit Memorandum			No. 27
Austin Sound 305 West Martin Luther King Blvd. Austin, Texas 78701		**Date** November 6, 19X6	

Customer Name   Stephanie Baker

538 Rio Grande, Apt. 236

Austin, Texas 78703

Reason for Credit   Defective merchandise returned

	Description	Amount
2	Trailblazer JU170456 Speakers	$198

General Journal   **Page 9**

Date	Accounts	Post Ref.	Debit	Credit
Nov. 6	Sales Returns and Allowances . . . . Accounts Receivable—Stephanie Baker . . . . . Credit memo no. 27	43 12/✓	198	 198

The debit side of the entry is posted to Sales Returns and Allowances. Its account number (43) is written in the posting reference column when $198 is posted. The credit side of the entry requires two $198 postings, one to Accounts Receivable, the control account in the general ledger (account number 12), and the other to Stephanie Baker's account in the accounts receivable subsidiary ledger. These credit postings explain why the document is called a *credit memo.*

Observe that the posting references of the credit include two notations. The account number (12) denotes the posting to Accounts Receivable in the general ledger. The check mark (✓) denotes the posting to Ms. Baker's account in the subsidiary ledger. Why are two postings needed? Because this is the general journal. Without specially designed columns, it is necessary to write both posting references on the same line. Posting to the general ledger usually occurs monthly; and posting to the subsidiary ledger, daily.

Suppose Ms. Baker had paid cash. Austin Sound would either give her a credit memo or refund her cash. Austin Sound would record the cash refund in the *cash disbursements journal* as follows:

Cash Disbursements Journal   **Page 8**

Date	Ck. No.	Account Debited	Post. Ref.	Debits		Credits	
				Other Accounts	Accounts Payable	Purchase Discounts	Cash
Nov. 6	106	Sales Returns and Allowances	43	198			198

A business with a high volume of sales returns, such as a department store chain, may find it efficient to use a special journal for sales returns and allowances.

The Debit Memorandum—A Basic Business Document

Purchase Returns occur when a business returns goods to the seller. The procedures for handling purchase returns are similar to those dealing with sales returns. The purchaser gives the merchandise back to the seller and receives either a cash refund or replacement goods.

When a business returns merchandise to the seller, it may also send a business document known as a **debit memorandum,** or **debit memo.** This document states that the buyer no longer owes the seller for the amount of the returned purchases. The buyer debits the Accounts Payable to the seller and credits Purchase Returns and Allowances. If the volume of purchase returns is high enough, the business may use a special journal for purchase returns.

Many businesses record their purchase returns in the general journal. Austin Sound would record its return of defective speakers to JVC as follows:

	General Journal			Page 9
Date	**Accounts**	**Post. Ref.**	**Debit**	**Credit**
Nov. 6	Accounts Payable—JVC Corp.	21/✓	244	
	Purchase Returns and Allowances.	53		244
	Debit memo no. 16			

Sales Tax

Most states and many cities levy tax on sales (sales tax). Sellers must add the tax to the sale amount, then pay the tax to the government. In most jurisdictions, sales tax is levied only on final consumers, so retail businesses usually do not pay sales tax on the goods they purchase for resale. For example, Austin Sound would not pay tax on a purchase of equipment from JVC, a wholesaler. However, when retailers like Austin Sound make sales, they must collect sales tax from the consumer. In effect, retailers serve as collecting agents for the taxing authorities. The amount of tax depends on the total sales.

Retailers set up procedures to collect the tax, account for it, and pay it on time. Invoices may be preprinted with a place for entering the sales tax amount, and the general ledger has an account entitled Sales Tax Payable. The sales journal may include a special column for sales tax, such as the one illustrated in Exhibit 6-10.

Note that the amount debited to Accounts Receivable ($3,484.95) is the sum of the credits to Sales Tax Payable ($165.95) and Sales Revenue ($3,319.00). This is so because the customers' payments—the Accounts Receivable figures—are partly for the purchase of merchandise (Sales Revenue) and partly for tax created by the sale. Individual customer accounts are posted daily to the accounts receiv-

EXHIBIT 6-10 *Sales Journal Designed to Account for Sales Tax*

				Sales Journal		**Page 4**
Date	Invoice No.	Account Debited	Post. Ref.	Accounts Receivable Dr.	Sales Tax Payable Cr.	Sales Revenue Cr.
19X6						
Nov. 2	422	Maria Galvez	✓	981.75	46.75	935.00
13	423	Brent Harmon	✓	728.70	34.70	694.00
18	424	Susan Levy	✓	952.35	45.35	907.00
27	425	Clay Schmidt	✓	822.15	39.15	783.00
30		Totals		3,484.95	165.95	3,319.00

able subsidiary ledger, and each column total is posted at the end of the month. The check marks in the Posting Reference column show that individual amounts have been posted to the customer accounts. The absence of account numbers under the column totals shows that the total amounts have not yet been posted.

Another way to account for sales tax is to enter a single amount—which is the sum of sales revenue and sales tax—in the Sales Revenue account. This amount is what the customer pays the retailer. At the end of the period, the business computes the tax collected and transfers that amount from Sales Revenue to Sales Tax Payable through a general journal entry. This procedure eliminates the need for a special multicolumn journal.

Suppose a retailer's Sales Revenue account shows a $10,500 balance at the end of the period. This retailer chooses to enter the full amount of each sale—the actual sales revenue and the sales tax—as Sales Revenue. How does the retailer divide the total amount into its two parts?

To compute the actual sales revenue, the Sales Revenue balance is divided by 1 plus the tax rate. Assume that sales tax is 5 percent. Thus the retailer divides $10,500 by 1.05 (1 + .05), which yields $10,000. Subtracting the actual sales revenue—the $10,000—from the $10,500 total yields $500, the sales tax. The retailer records sales tax with the following entry in the general journal:

Date	Accounts	Post. Ref.	Debit	Credit
	General Journal			**Page 9**
July 31	Sales Revenue.............................	41	500	
	Sales Tax Payable....................	28		500
	To transfer sales tax to the liability account.			

Balancing the Ledgers

At the end of the period, after all postings, equality should exist between:

1. Total debits and total credits in the general ledger. These amounts are used to prepare the trial balance that has been used throughout Chapters 3 through 5.

2. The balance of the Accounts Receivable control account in the general ledger and the sum of individual customer accounts in the accounts receivable subsidiary ledger.

3. The balance of the Accounts Payable control account in the general ledger and the sum of individual creditor accounts in the accounts payable subsidiary ledger.

This process is called **balancing the ledgers,** or proving the ledgers. It is an important control procedure because it helps assure the accuracy of the accounting records. Equality between Accounts Receivable control and the accounts receivable subsidiary ledger was proved as shown on page 227. A simpler and less costly procedure is to total the individual customer balances on a calculator tape for comparison to Accounts Receivable control. Balancing the accounts payable ledger follows the same pattern as illustrated on page 234.

Documents as Journals

Many small businesses streamline their accounting systems to save money by using the actual business documents as the journals. For example, Austin Sound could let its sales invoices serve as its sales journal and keep all invoices for credit sales in a looseleaf binder. At the end of the period, the accountant simply totals the sales on account and posts that amount to Accounts Receivable and Sales Revenue. Also, the accountant can post directly from invoices to customer accounts in the accounts receivable ledger. This "journal-less" system reduces accounting cost because the accountant does not have to write in journals the information already in the business documents.

Summary Problem for Your Review

Identify the journal in which each of the following transactions would be recorded. Use journal abbreviations: sales journal = S; cash receipts journal = CR; purchases journal = P; cash disbursements journal = CD; general journal = J.

Cash sale _____

Sale on account _____

Loaned cash on note receivable _____

Received cash on account _____

Purchase of building on long-term note payable _____

Paid cash on account _____

Cash purchase of inventory _____

Owner investment of cash in the business _____

Closing entries _____

Purchase of supplies on account _____

Receipt of cash on account _____

Adjusting entry for accrued salaries _____

Cash purchase of land _____

Credit purchase of inventory _____

Collection of interest revenue _____

Paid interest expense _____

Cash sale of equipment _____

Owner withdrawal of cash _____

Owner investment of land in the business _____

SOLUTION TO REVIEW PROBLEM

Cash sale	CR	Purchase of supplies on account	P
Sale on account	S	Receipt of cash on account	CR
Loaned cash on note receivable	CD	Adjusting entry for accrued salaries	J
Received cash on account	CR	Cash purchase of land	CD
Purchase of building on long-term note payable	J	Credit purchase of inventory	P
Paid cash on account	CD	Collection of interest revenue	CR
Cash purchase of inventory	CD	Paid interest expense	CD
Owner investment of cash in the business	CR	Cash sale of equipment	CR
Closing entries	J	Owner withdrawal of cash	CD
		Owner investment of land in the business	J

Summary

An efficient accounting system combines *personnel, records,* and *procedures* to meet a business's information needs. Processing accounting information means collecting data from source documents, organizing and recording the data, and communicating the information through the financial statements. Each business designs its accounting system to satisfy its particular information needs.

To be effective, the system must provide management with the information needed to *control* the organization. Also, the system must be *compatible* with the business's operations. As businesses change, the system must be *flexible* enough to handle new needs. Finally, the system must be *cost beneficial.*

Computer data processing systems include *hardware, software,* and *personnel.* Hardware may consist of a mainframe computer or microcomputers. Computer operators use software to process data *on-line* or in *batches.*

Many businesses use special journals to account for repetitive transactions such as credit sales, cash receipts, credit purchases and cash disbursements. Special journals reduce the amount of writing and posting required. Some businesses find it efficient to use source documents as journals.

Computer systems can be programmed to possess all the special journal features described in this chapter. The major goal of system design is efficient, routine handling of high volumes of transactions. Special journals were originally created to meet that objective. Similarly, computer systems can store records of sales, cash receipts, purchases, and cash disbursements and print special journals as desired.

Businesses use a subsidiary ledger to account for individual customer accounts receivable. The subsidiary ledger gives information on each customer's account. The total of the subsidiary ledger's individual account balances must match the balance in the Accounts Receivable control account in the general ledger. Companies may also keep a subsidiary ledger for accounts payable.

Self-Study Questions

Test your understanding of the chapter by marking the best answer for each of the following questions.

1. Why does a jewelry store need a different kind of accounting system than a physician uses? *(p. 215)*
   a. They have different kinds of employees.

   b. They have different kinds of journals and ledgers.
   c. They have different kinds of business transactions.
   d. They work different hours.

2. Which feature of an effective information system is most concerned with safeguarding assets? *(p. 217)*
   a. Control
   b. Compatibility
   c. Flexibility
   d. Acceptable cost/benefit relationship

3. Which of the following components of a computerized accounting system is more likely to be developed in-house rather than by outsiders? Why? *(pp. 218 through 220)*
   a. Hardware, because of the desire for control
   b. Hardware, because of the desire for compatibility
   c. Software, because of the desire for control
   d. Software, because of the desire for compatibility

4. Special journals help most by *(p. 222)*
   a. Limiting the number of transactions that have to be recorded
   b. Reducing the cost of operating the accounting system
   c. Improving accuracy in posting to subsidiary ledgers
   d. Easing the preparation of the financial statements

5. Galvan Company recorded 523 credit sale transactions in the sales journal. How many postings would be required if these transactions were recorded in the general journal? *(p. 225)*
   a. 523
   b. 1,046
   c. 1,569
   d. 2,092

6. Which two dollar-amount columns in the cash receipts journal will be used the most by a department store that makes half of its sales for cash and half on credit? *(p. 226)*
   a. Cash Debit and Sales Discounts Debit
   b. Cash Debit and Accounts Receivable Credit
   c. Cash Debit and Other Accounts Credit
   d. Accounts Receivable Debit and Sales Revenue Credit

7. Entries in the purchases journal are posted to the *(p. 231)*
   a. General ledger only
   b. General ledger and the Accounts payable ledger
   c. General ledger and the Accounts receivable ledger
   d. Accounts receivable ledger and the Accounts payable ledger

8. Every entry in the cash disbursements journal includes a *(p. 233)*
   a. Debit to Accounts Payable
   b. Debit to an Other Account
   c. Credit to Purchase Discounts
   d. Credit to Cash

9. Mazarotti Company has issued a debit memo. The related journal entry is *(p. 236)*

   a. Accounts Payable XXX
      Purchase Returns and Allowances.   XXX
   b. Purchase Returns and Allowances XXX
      Accounts Payable   XXX
   c. Accounts Receivable. XXX
      Sales Returns and Allowances   XXX
   d. Sales Returns and Allowances. XXX
      Accounts Receivable.   XXX

10. Balancing the ledgers at the end of the period is most closely related to *(p. 238)*
    a. Control
    b. Compatibility
    c. Flexibility
    d. Acceptable cost/benefit relationship

Answers to the self-study questions are at the end of the chapter.

Accounting Vocabulary

accounting information system *(p. 215)*,   balancing the ledgers *(p. 238)*,   batch processing *(p. 220)*,   cash disbursements journal *(p. 232)*,   cash receipts journal *(p. 225)*,   control account *(p. 224)*,   credit memo *(p. 234)*,   debit memo *(p. 236)*,   general journal *(p. 222)*,   general ledger *(p. 223)*, hardware *(p. 219)*, mainframe system *(p. 219)*, microcomputer *(p. 219)*, minicomputers *(p. 219)*, on-line processing *(p. 220)*, purchases journal *(p. 230)*, sales journal *(p. 222)*, software *(p. 219)*, subsidiary ledger *(p. 224)*.

ASSIGNMENT MATERIAL

Questions

1. Briefly describe the two phases of implementing an accounting system.
2. Describe the basic information processing model of an accounting system.
3. What are the attributes of an effective information system? Briefly describe each attribute.
4. How does a mainframe computer system differ from a microcomputer system?
5. Identify three computer languages used with mainframes. Identify four software programs used with microcomputers.
6. Distinguish batch computer processing from on-line processing.
7. Describe an on-line computer processing operation for accounts receivable, sales, and inventory by a large retailer, such as Sears or Penney's.
8. Name four special journals used in accounting systems. For what type of transaction is each designed?
9. Describe the two advantages that special journals have over recording all transactions in the general journal.
10. What is a control account, and how is it related to a subsidiary ledger? Name two common control accounts.
11. Graff Company's sales journal has one amount column headed Accounts Receivable Dr. and Sales Revenue Cr. In this journal, 86 transactions are recorded. How many posting references appear in the journal? State what each posting reference represents.
12. Use S = Sales; CR = Cash Receipts; P = Purchases; CD = Cash Disbursements; and SRA = Sales Returns and Allowances to identify the special journal in which the following column headings appear. Some headings may appear in more than one journal.

Sales Revenue Cr. _____   Invoice No. _____

Accounts Payable Dr. _____   Sales Discounts Dr. _____

Cash Dr. _____   Other Accounts Cr. _____

Purchase Discounts Cr. _____   Purchases Dr. _____

Accounts Receivable Cr. _____   Cash Cr. _____

Check No. _____   Credit Memo No. _____

Other Accounts Dr. _____   Accounts Payable Cr. _____

Post. Ref. _____   Accounts Receivable Dr. _____

13. Identify two ways a check mark (✓) is used as a posting reference in the cash receipts journal.
14. The accountant for Bannister Company posted all amounts correctly from the cash receipts journal to the general ledger. However, she failed to post three credits to customer accounts in the accounts receivable subsidiary ledger. How would this error be detected?
15. In posting from the cash receipts journal of Enfield Homebuilders, the accountant failed to post the amount of the sales revenue credit column. Identify two ways this error can be detected.
16. At what two times is posting done from a special journal? What items are posted at each time?
17. For what purposes are a credit memo and a debit memo issued? Who issues each document, the seller or the purchaser?

18. The following entry appears in the general journal:

Nov. 25   Sales Returns and Allowances . . . .   ?   539
                Accounts Receivable – B. Goodwin . . . .   ?   539

Prepare likely posting references.

19. Describe two ways to account for sales tax collected from customers.
20. What is the purpose of balancing the ledgers?
21. Posting from the journals of McKedrick Realty is complete. However, the total of the individual balances in the accounts payable subsidiary ledger does not equal the balance in the Accounts Payable control account in the general ledger. Does this necessarily indicate that the trial balance is out of balance? Give your reason.
22. Assume that posting is completed. The trial balance shows no errors, but the sum of the individual accounts payable does not equal the Accounts Payable control balance in the general ledger. What two errors could cause this problem?
23. Describe how some businesses use their documents as journals.

Exercises

Exercise 6-1   *Using the sales and cash receipts journals*

The sales and cash receipts journals of Advanced Design Company include the following entries:

Sales Journal

Date	Account Debited	Post Ref.	Amount
Oct. 7	C. Carlson	✓	730
10	T. Muecke	✓	1,960
10	E. Lovell	✓	190
12	B. Goebel	✓	5,470
31	Total		8,350

Cash Receipts Journal

	Debits		Credits		Other Accounts		
Date	Cash	Sales Discounts	Accounts Receivable	Sales Revenue	Account Title	Post Ref.	Amount
Oct. 16					C. Carlson	✓	
19					E. Lovell	✓	
24	100			100			
30					T. Muecke	✓	

Advanced Design makes all sales on credit terms of 2/10 n/30. Complete the cash receipts journal for those transactions indicated. Also, total the journal and show that total debits equal total credits. Assume that each cash receipt was for the full amount of the receivable.

Exercise 6-2 *Classifying postings from the cash receipts journal*

The cash receipts journal of Cranbrook, Inc., follows.

Cash Receipts Journal   **Page 26**

| | Debits | | Credits | | | | |
| | | | | | Other Accounts | | |
Date	Cash	Sales Discounts	Accounts Receivable	Sales Revenue	Account Title	Post. Ref.	Amount
Dec. 2	794	16	810		Johnson-McBee	(a)	
9	1,291		1,291		B. R. Blake Co.	(b)	
14	3,904			3,904		(c)	
19	4,480				Note Receivable	(d)	4,000
					Interest Revenue	(e)	480
30	314	7	321		L. M. Roose	(f)	
31	4,235			4,235		(g)	
31	15,018	23	2,422	8,139	Totals		4,480
	(h)	(i)	(j)	(k)			(l)

Required

Identify each posting reference (a) through (l) as (1) a posting to the general ledger as a column total, (2) a posting to the general ledger as an individual amount, (3) a posting to a subsidiary ledger account, or (4) an amount not posted.

Exercise 6-3 *Recording purchase transactions in the general journal and in the purchases journal*

During April, Monarch Tile Company completed the following credit purchase transactions:

April 4   Purchased inventory, $912, from McGraw Co.
     7   Purchased supplies, $107, from Paine Corp.
   19   Purchased equipment, $1,903, from Liston-Fry Co.
   27   Purchased inventory, $2,210, from Milan, Inc.

Record these transactions first in the general journal—with explanations—and then in the purchases journal. Omit credit terms and posting references. Which procedure for recording transactions is quicker?

Exercise 6-4 *Identifying transactions from postings to the accounts receivable ledger*

An account in the accounts receivable ledger of McCray Company follows.

William H. Crocker

| | | | | | Balance | |
Date		Jrnl. Ref.	Dr.	Cr.	Dr.	Cr.
May 1	....				703	
10	....	S.5	1,180		1,883	
15	....	J.8		191	1,692	
21	....	CR.9		703	989	

Required

Describe the three posted transactions.

Exercise 6-5   *Posting from the purchases journal; balancing the ledgers*

The purchases journal of Best Merchandise Company follows.

Purchases Journal   Page 7

Date	Account Credited	Terms	Post. Ref.	Account Payable Cr.	Purchases Dr.	Supplies Dr.	Other Accounts Dr.		
							Acct. Title	Post. Ref.	Amt. Dr.
Sep. 2	Audio-Video	n/30		600	600				
5	Green Stationers	n/30		175		175			
13	Audio-Video	2/10 n/30		347	347				
26	Marks Equipment Co.	n/30		916			Equipment		916
30	Totals			2,038	947	175			916

Required

1. Open general ledger accounts for Supplies, Equipment, Accounts Payable, and Purchases. Post to these accounts from the purchase journal. Use dates and posting references in the ledger accounts.
2. Open accounts in the accounts payable subsidiary ledger for Audio-Video, Green Stationers, and Marks Equipment Company. Post from the purchase journal. Use dates and journal references in the ledger accounts.
3. Balance the Accounts Payable control account in the general ledger with the total of the balances in the accounts payable subsidiary ledger.

Exercise 6-6   *Using business documents to record transactions*

The following documents describe two business transactions:

Invoice		
Date:	August 14, 19X0	
Sold to:	Zephyr Bicycle Shop	
Sold by:	Schwinn Company	
Terms:	2/10 n/30	
Items Purchased	Bicycles	
Quantity	Price	Total
3	$90	$270
2	70	140
5	60	300
Total		$710

Debit Memo		
Date:	August 20, 19X0	
Issued to:	Schwinn Company	
Issued by:	Zephyr Bicycle Shop	
Items Returned	Bicycles	
Quantity	Price	Total
1	$90	$ 90
1	$70	70
Total		$160
Reason:	Wrong sizes	

Use the general journal to record these transactions and Zephyr's cash payment on August 21. Record the transactions first on the books of Zephyr Bicycle Shop and, second, on the books of Schwinn Company, which makes and sells bicycles. Explanations are not required. Set up your answer in the following format:

Date	Zephyr Journal Entries	Schwinn Journal Entries

Exercise 6-7 *Using the cash disbursements journal*

During July Mancini Company had the following transactions:

July 3   Paid $392 on account to Miller, Inc., net of an $8 discount.
6   Purchased inventory for cash, $599.
11   Paid $375 for supplies.
13   Purchased inventory on credit from Monroe Corporation, $774.
16   Paid $8,062 on account to LaGrange Associates; there was no discount.
21   Purchased furniture for cash, $960.
26   Paid $3,910 on account to Graff Software. The discount was $90.
31   Made a semiannual interest payment of $800 on a long-term note payable. The entire payment was for interest.

Required

1. Draw a cash disbursements journal similar to the one illustrated in this chapter. Omit the check number (Ck. No.) and posting reference (Post. Ref.) columns.
2. Record the transactions in the journal. Note: One transaction should *not* be recorded in the cash disbursement journal. Which is it? In what journal does it belong?
3. Total the amount columns of the journal. Determine that the total debits equal the total credits.

Exercise 6-8 *Journalizing return and allowance transactions*

Greenberg Company records returns and allowances in its general journal. During April the company had the following transactions:

April 4	Issued credit memo to W. A. Wang for inventory that Wang returned to us	$ 369
10	Received debit memo from B. R. Inman, who purchased merchandise from us on April 6. We shipped the wrong items, and Inman returned them to us....................................	1,238
14	Issued debit memo for merchandise we purchased from Wyle Supply Company that was damaged in shipment. We returned the damaged inventory to Wyle	4,600
22	Received credit memo from Dietrich Distributing Co., from whom we purchased inventory on April 15. Dietrich discovered that they overcharged us..	900

Required

Journalize the transactions in the general journal. Explanations are not required.

Exercise 6-9 *Posting directly from sales invoices; balancing the ledgers*

Parson, Inc., uses its sales invoices as the sales journal and posts directly from them to the accounts receivable subsidiary ledger. During June the company made the following sales on account:

Date	Invoice No.	Customer Name	Amount
June 6	256	Anita Harris	$1,404
9	257	Forrest Ashworth	798
13	258	Paul Scott	550
16	259	Jan Childres	3,678
22	261	Anita Harris	1,915
30	262	Jan Childres	800
		Total	$9,145

Required

1. Open general ledger accounts for Accounts Receivable and Sales Revenue and post to those accounts. Use dates and use June Sales as the journal reference in the ledger accounts.
2. Open customer accounts in the accounts receivable subsidiary ledger and post to those accounts. Use dates and use invoice numbers as journal references.
3. Balance the ledgers.

Exercise 6-10   *Detecting errors in the special journals*

Monarch Sales Company uses special journals for credit sales, cash receipts, credit purchases, and cash disbursements, and the subsidiary ledgers illustrated in this chapter. During March the accountant made four errors. State the procedure that will detect each error described in the following:

(a) Posted a $40 debit to J. B. Carnes's account in the accounts receivable subsidiary ledger as a $400 credit.
(b) Added the Cash Credit column of the cash disbursements journal as $3,976 and posted this incorrect amount to the Cash account. The correct total was $3,796.
(c) Recorded receipt of $500 on account from Electrosystems, Inc., incorrectly as a credit to Sales Revenue in the cash receipts journal.
(d) Failed to post the total of the Accounts Receivable Dr./Sales Revenue Cr. column of the sales journal.

Problems   *(Group A)*

Problem 6-1A   *Using the sales, cash receipts, and general journals*

The general ledger of Sanchez Plaza, Inc., includes the following accounts, among others:

Cash	11	Sales Revenue...................	41
Accounts Receivable.............	12	Sales Discounts.................	42
Notes Receivable	15	Sales Returns and Allowances......	43
Supplies	16	Interest Revenue................	47
Land	18		

All credit sales are on the company's standard terms of 2/10 n/30. Transactions in May that affected sales and cash receipts were as follows:

May 2   Sold inventory on credit to Dockery Co., $550.
 4   As an accommodation to a competitor, sold supplies at cost, $85, receiving cash.
 7   Cash sales for the week totaled $1,890.

9 Sold merchandise on account to A. L. Prince, $7,320.

10 Sold land that cost $10,000 for cash of $10,000.

11 Sold goods on account to Sloan Electric, $5,104.

12 Received cash from Dockery Co. in full settlement of its account receivable, net of the discount, from May 2.

14 Cash sales for the week were $2,106.

15 Sold inventory on credit to the partnership of Wilkie & Blinn, $3,650.

18 Issued credit memo to A. L. Prince for $600 of merchandise returned to us by Prince. The goods shipped were unsatisfactory.

20 Sold merchandise on account to Sloan Electric, $629.

21 Cash sales for the week were $990.

22 Received $4,000 cash from A. L. Prince in partial settlement of his account receivable. There was no discount.

25 Received cash from Wilkie & Blinn for the discounted amount of their account receivable from May 15.

25 Sold goods on account to Olsen Co., $720.

27 Collected $5,125 on a note receivable, of which $125 was interest.

28 Cash sales for the week totaled $3,774.

29 Sold inventory on account to R. O. Bankston, $242.

30 Issued credit memo to Olsen Co. for $40 for inventory they returned to us because it was damaged in shipment.

31 Received $2,720 cash on account from A. L. Prince. There was no discount.

Required

1. Sanchez Plaza records sales returns and allowances in the general journal. Use the appropriate journal to record the above transactions in a single-column sales journal (omit the Invoice No. column), a cash receipts journal, and a general journal.

2. Total each column of the cash receipts journal. Show that the total debits equal the total credits.

3. Show how postings would be made from the journals by writing the account numbers and check marks in the appropriate places in the journals.

Problem 6-2A *Using the purchases, cash disbursements, and general journals*

The general ledger of Dreyfuss Company includes the following accounts:

Cash	11	Purchases	51
Prepaid Insurance	16	Purchase Discounts	52
Supplies	17	Purchase Returns and Allowances	53
Furniture	19	Rent Expense	56
Accounts Payable	21	Utilities Expense	58

Transactions in August that affected purchases and cash disbursements were as follows:

Aug. 1 Purchased inventory on credit from Wood Co., $3,900. Terms were 2/10 n/30.

1 Paid monthly rent, debiting Rent Expense for $2,000.

5 Purchased supplies on credit terms of 2/10 n/30 from Ross Supply, $450.

8 Paid electricity bill, $588. Debit Utilities Expense.

9 Purchased furniture on account from A-1 Office Supply, $4,100. Payment terms were net 30.

10 Returned the furniture to A-1 Office Supply. It was the wrong color. Issued a debit memo for $4,100, and mailed a copy to A-1 Office Supply.

11 Paid Wood Co. the discounted amount owed on the purchase of August 1.

12 Purchased inventory on account from Wynne, Inc., $4,400. Terms were 3/10 n/30.

13 Purchased inventory for cash, $655.

14 Paid a semiannual insurance premium, debiting Prepaid Insurance, $1,200.

15 Paid our account payable to Ross Supply, less the discount, from August 5.

18 Paid gas and water bills, $196. Debit Utilities Expense.

21 Purchased inventory on credit terms of 1/10 n/45 from Software, Inc., $5,200.

21 Paid account payable to Wynne, Inc., less discount, from August 12.

22 Purchased supplies on account from Office Sales, Inc., $274. Terms were net 30.

25 Returned part of the inventory purchased on August 21 to Software, Inc., issuing a debit memo for $1,200.

31 Paid Software, Inc., the net amount owed from August 21, less the return, on August 25.

Required

1. Dreyfuss Company records purchase returns in the general journal. Use the appropriate journal to record the above transactions in a purchase journal, a cash disbursements journal (omit the Check No. column), and a general journal.

2. Total each column of the special journals. Show that the total debits equal the total credits in each special journal.

3. Show how postings would be made from the journals by writing the account numbers and check marks in the appropriate places in the journals.

Problem 6-3A *Using the sales, cash receipts, and general journals, posting, and balancing the ledgers*

During April, North Bay Sales Company had these transactions:

Apr. 2 Issued invoice no. 436 for credit sale to Vail Co., $5,200. All credit sales are made on the company's standard terms of 2/10 n/30.

3 Collected cash of $3,038 from H. M. Burger in payment of his account receivable, $3,100, within the discount period.

5 Cash sales for the week totaled $2,057.

7 Collected note receivable, $2,000, plus interest of $210.

10 Issued invoice no. 437 for sale on account to Van Allen Co., $1,850.

11 Sold supplies to an employee for cash of $54, which was the cost.

12 Received $5,096 cash from Vail Co. in full settlement of their account receivable, net of the discount, from the sale of April 2.

12 Cash sales for the week were $1,698.

14 Sold inventory on account to Electro, Inc., issuing invoice no. 438 for $2,000.

16 Issued credit memo to Electro, Inc., for $610 of merchandise returned to us by Electro. Part of the shipped goods were damaged.

19 Cash sales for the week were $3,130.

20 Received $1,813 from Van Allen Co. in full settlement of its account receivable, $1,850, from April 10.

25 Received cash of $7,455 from Electro, Inc., on account. There was no discount.

26 Cash sales for the week totaled $2,744.

27 Issued invoice no. 439 to Clay Co. for credit sales of inventory, $3,640.

28 Sold goods on credit to H. M. Burger, issuing invoice no. 440 for $2,689.

30 Issued credit memo to H. M. Burger for $873 for inventory he returned to us because it was unsatisfactory.

The general ledger of North Bay Sales Company includes the following accounts and balances at April 1:

Account Number	Account Title	Balance	Account Number	Account Title	Balance
111	Cash	$ 3,579	411	Sales Revenue......	
112	Accounts Receivable.	10,555	412	Sales Discounts.....	
116	Supplies..........	1,756	413	Sales Returns	
141	Notes Receivable ...	5,000		and Allowances...	
			418	Interest Revenue....	

North Bay's accounts receivable subsidiary ledger includes the following accounts and balances at April 1: H. M. Burger, $3,100; Clay Company, -0-; Electro, Inc., $7,455; Vail Company, -0-; and Van Allen Co., -0-.

Required

1. Open the general ledger and the accounts receivable subsidiary ledger accounts given, inserting their balances at April 1.
2. Record the transactions on page 4 of a single-column sales journal, page 13 of a cash receipts journal, and page 7 of a general journal, as appropriate. North Bay records sales returns and allowances in the general journal.
3. Post daily to the accounts receivable subsidiary ledger, and on April 30 post to the general ledger.
4. Show that the total debits equal the total credits in each special journal.
5. Balance the total of the customer account balances in the accounts receivable subsidiary ledger against the Accounts Receivable balance in the general ledger.

Problem 6-4A *Using the purchases, cash disbursements, and general journals; posting and balancing the ledgers*

Windsor Company's November purchases and cash disbursement transaction are as follows:

Nov. 1 Issued check no. 346 for $2,058 to pay ENTEL Corp. on account. Windsor received a $42 discount for prompt payment.

  1 Issued check no. 347 to pay quarterly rent, debiting Prepaid Rent for $2,400.

  2 Issued check no. 348 to pay net amount owed to Arbor Machine Co., $637. Windsor took a $13 discount.

  5 Purchased supplies on credit terms of 1/10 n/30 from Chin Music Co., $264.

  7 Paid delivery expense, issuing check no. 349 for $388. Debit Delivery Expense.

  10 Purchased inventory on account from W. A. Mozart, Inc., $1,681. Payment terms were net 30.

  11 Returned the inventory to W. A. Mozart, Inc. It was defective. We issued a debit memo for $1,681 and mailed a copy to Mozart.

  15 Issued check no. 350 for a cash purchase of inventory, $2,889.

  15 Paid semimonthly payroll with check no. 351, debiting Salary Expense for $1,595.

  19 Issued check no. 352 to pay our account payable to Chin Music Co. from November 5. We did not earn the discount.

  21 Purchased inventory on credit terms of 2/10 n/30 from Arbor Machine Co., $3,250.

  24 Purchased machinery on credit terms of 2/10 n/30 from ENTEL Corp., $1,558.

  26 Purchased supplies on account from W. A. Mozart, Inc., $309. Terms were net 30.

29   Issued check no. 353 to Arbor Machine Co., paying the net amount owed from November 21.

30   Paid semimonthly payroll with check no. 354, debiting Salary Expense for $1,595.

The general ledger of Windsor Company includes the following accounts and balances at November 1:

Account Number	Account Title	Balance	Account Number	Account Title	Balance
111	Cash	$17,674	511	Purchases	
115	Prepaid Rent.	800	512	Purchase Discounts	
116	Supplies	884	513	Purchase Returns	
151	Machinery.	33,600		and Allowances .	
211	Accounts Payable. .	2,750	521	Salary Expense	
			551	Delivery Expense . .	

Windsor's accounts payable subsidiary ledger includes the following balances at November 1: Arbor Machine Co., $650; Chin Music Co., -0-; ENTEL Corp., $2,100; and W. A. Mozart, Inc., -0-.

Required

1. Open the general ledger and the accounts payable subsidiary ledger accounts given, inserting their balances at November 1.
2. Record the above transactions on page 3 of a purchases journal, page 8 of a cash disbursements journal, and page 12 of a general journal, as appropriate. Windsor records purchase returns in the general journal.
3. Post daily to the accounts payable subsidiary ledger. Post to the general ledger on November 30.
4. Total each column of the special journals. Show that the total debits equal the total credits in each special journal.
5. Balance the total of the creditor account balances in the accounts payable subsidiary ledger against the balance of the Accounts Payable control account in the general ledger.

Problem 6-5A   *Using all the journals, posting, and balancing the ledgers*

Kent Sales Company had these transactions during January:

Jan. 2   Issued invoice no. 191 for sale on account to L. E. Wooten, $2,350.

  3   Purchased inventory on credit terms of 3/10 n/60 from Delwood Plaza, $1,900.

  4   Sold inventory for cash, $808.

  5   Issued check no. 473 to purchase furniture for cash, $1,087.

  8   Collected interest revenue of $440.

  9   Issued invoice no. 192 for sale on account to Cortez Co., $6,250.

  10   Purchased inventory for cash, $776, issuing check no. 474.

  12   Received $2,303 cash from L. E. Wooten in full settlement of her account receivable, net of the discount, from the sale of January 2.

  13   Issued check no. 475 to pay Delwood Plaza net amount owed from January 3, $1,843. We received a $57 discount.

13 Purchased supplies on account from Havrilla Corp., $689. Terms were net end-of-month.

15 Sold inventory on account to J. R. Wakeland, issuing invoice no. 193 for $743.

17 Issued credit memo to J. R. Wakeland for $743 for defective merchandise returned to us by Wakeland.

18 Issued invoice no. 194 for credit sale to L. E. Wooten, $1,825.

19 Received $6,125 from Cortez Co. in full settlement of its account receivable, $6,250, from January 9.

20 Purchased inventory on credit terms of net 30 from Jasper Sales, $2,150.

22 Purchased furniture on credit terms of 3/10 n/60 from Delwood Plaza, $775.

22 Issued check no. 476 to pay for insurance coverage, debiting Prepaid Insurance for $1,345.

24 Sold supplies to an employee for cash of $86, which was their cost.

25 Issued check no. 477 to pay utilities. Debit Utilities Expense for $388.

28 Purchased inventory on credit terms of 2/10 n/30 from Havrilla Corp., $421.

29 Returned damaged inventory to Havrilla Corp., issuing a debit memo for $421.

29 Sold goods on account to Cortez Co., issuing invoice no. 195 for $567.

30 Issued check no. 478 to pay Havrilla Corp. $689 on account from January 13.

31 Received $1,825 on account from L. E. Wooten on credit sale of January 18. There was no discount.

31 Issued check no. 479 to pay monthly salaries, debiting Salary Expense for $2,600.

Required

1. Open the following general ledger accounts using the account numbers given:

Cash	111	Sales Returns and Allowances	413
Accounts Receivable	112	Interest Revenue	419
Supplies	116	Purchases	511
Prepaid Insurance	117	Purchase Discounts	512
Furniture	151	Purchase Returns	
Accounts Payable	211	and Allowances	513
Sales Revenue	411	Salary Expense	531
Sales Discounts	412	Utilities Expense	541

2. Open these accounts in the subsidiary ledgers. Accounts receivable subsidiary ledger: Cortez Co., J. R. Wakeland, and L. E. Wooten.
Accounts payable subsidiary ledger: Delwood Plaza, Havrilla Corp., and Jasper Sales.

3. Enter the transactions in a sales journal (page 8), a cash receipts journal (page 3), a purchases journal (page 6), a cash disbursements journal (page 9), and a general journal (page 4), as appropriate.

4. Post daily to the accounts receivable subsidiary ledger and to the accounts payable subsidiary ledger. On January 31 post to the general ledger.

5. Total each column of the special journals. Show that the total debits equal the total credits in each special journal.

6. Balance the total of the customer account balances in the accounts receivable subsidiary ledger against Accounts Receivable in the general ledger. Do the same for the accounts payable subsidiary ledger and Accounts Payable in the general ledger.

Problem 6-6A   *Correcting errors in the cash receipts journal*

The cash receipts journal below contains five entries. All five entries are for legitimate cash receipt transactions, but the journal contains some errors in recording the transactions. In fact, only one entry is correct, and each of the other four entries contains one error.

Cash Receipts Journal   **Page 13**

Date	Cash	Sales Discounts	Accounts Receivable	Sales Revenue	Account Title	P.R.	Amount
5/6		500		500			
7	429	22			Ron Bynum	✓	451
12	3170				Note Receivable	13	3000
					Interest Revenue	45	170
18				330			
24	1100		770				
	4699	522	770	830	Totals		3621
	(11)	(42)	(12)	(41)			(✓)

Total Dr. = $5,221   Total Cr. = $5221

Required

1. Identify the correct entry.
2. Identify the error in each of the other four entries.
3. Using the following format, prepare a corrected cash receipts journal.

Cash Receipts Journal   **Page 13**

Date	Cash	Sales Discounts	Accounts Receivable	Sales Revenue	Account Title	P.R.	Amount
5/6							
7					Ron Bynum	✓	
12					Note Receivable	13	
					Interest Revenue	45	
18							
24							
	5199	22	1221	830	Totals		3170
	(11)	(42)	(12)	(41)			(✓)

Total Dr. = $5,221   Total Cr. = $5,221

(Group B)

Problem 6-1B   *Using the sales, cash receipts, and general journals*

The general ledger of Carmel Trading Company includes the following accounts:

Cash	111	Sales Revenue	411
Accounts Receivable	112	Sales Discounts	412
Notes Receivable	115	Sales Returns and Allowances	413
Equipment	141	Interest Revenue	417
Land	142	Gain on Sale of Land	418

All credit sales are on the company's standard terms of 2/10 n/30. Transactions in February that affected sales and cash receipts were as follows:

Feb. 1 Sold inventory on credit to G. M. Titcher, $900.

5 As an accommodation to another company, sold new equipment for its cost of $770, receiving cash in this amount.

6 Cash sales for the week totaled $1,007.

8 Sold merchandise on account to McNair Co., $2,830.

9 Sold land that cost $22,000 for cash of $40,000, which includes a gain of $18,000.

11 Sold goods on account to Nickerson Builders, $6,099.

11 Received cash from G. M. Titcher in full settlement of her account receivable, net of the discount, from February 1.

13 Cash sales for the week were $1,995.

15 Sold inventory on credit to Montez and Montez, a partnership, $800.

18 Issued credit memo to McNair Co. for $120 of merchandise returned to us by McNair. The goods we shipped were unsatisfactory.

19 Sold merchandise on account to Nickerson Builders, $3,900.

20 Cash sales for the week were $2,330.

21 Received $1,200 cash from McNair Co. in partial settlement of their account receivable. There was no discount.

22 Received cash from Montez and Montez for the discounted amount of their account receivable from February 15.

22 Sold goods on account to Diamond Co., $2,022.

25 Collected $4,200 on a note receivable, of which $200 was interest.

27 Cash sales for the week totaled $2,970.

27 Sold inventory on account to Littleton Corporation, $2,290.

28 Issued credit memo to Diamond Co. for $680 for damaged goods they returned to us.

28 Received $1,510 cash on account from McNair Co. There was no discount.

Required

1. Use the appropriate journal to record the above transactions in a single-column sales journal (omit the Invoice No. column), a cash receipts journal, and a general journal. Carmel records sales returns and allowances in the general journal.

2. Total each column of the cash receipts journal. Determine that the total debits equal the total credits.

3. Show how postings would be made from the journals by writing the account numbers and check marks in the appropriate places in the journals.

Problem 6-2B *Using the purchases, cash disbursements, and general journals*

The general ledger of Enfield Corporation includes the following accounts:

Cash	111	Purchases	511
Prepaid Insurance	116	Purchase Discounts	512
Supplies	117	Purchase Returns and Allowances .	513
Equipment	149	Rent Expense	562
Accounts Payable..............	211	Utilities Expense...............	565

Transactions in March that affected purchases and cash disbursements were as follows:

Mar. 1 Paid monthly rent, debiting Rent Expense for $1,600.

3 Purchased inventory on credit from Broussard Co., $4,600. Terms were 2/15 n/45.

6   Purchased supplies on credit terms of 2/10 n/30 from Harmon Sales, $800.

7   Paid gas and water bills, $406. Debit Utilities Expenses.

10 Purchased equipment on account from Lancer Co., $1,050. Payment terms were 2/10 n/30.

11 Returned the equipment to Lancer Co. It was defective. We issued a debit memo for $1,050 and mailed a copy to Lancer.

12 Paid Broussard Co. the discounted amount owed on the purchase of March 3.

12 Purchased inventory on account from Lancer Co., $1,100. Terms were 2/10 n/30.

14 Purchased inventory for cash, $1,585.

15 Paid an insurance premium, debiting Prepaid Insurance, $2,416.

16 Paid our account payable to Harmon Sales, less the discount, from March 6.

17 Paid electricity bill, $165. Debit Utilities Expense.

20 Paid account payable to Lancer Co., less the discount, from March 12.

21 Purchased supplies on account from Master Supply, $754. Terms were net 30.

22 Purchased inventory on credit terms of 1/10 n/30 from Linz Brothers, $3,400.

26 Returned inventory purchased on March 22, to Linz Brothers, issuing a debit memo for $500.

31 Paid Linz Brothers the net amount owed from March 22, less the return on March 26.

Required

1. Use the appropriate journal to record the above transactions in a purchase journal, a cash disbursements journal (omit the Check No. column), and a general journal. Enfield Corporation records purchase returns in the general journal.

2. Total each column of the special journals. Show that the total debits equal the total credits in each special journal.

3. Show how postings would be made from the journals by writing the account numbers and check marks in the appropriate places in the journals.

Problem 6-3B   *Using the sales, cash receipts, and general journal, posting, and balancing the ledgers*

During June, Harwood Systems engaged in the following transactions:

June 1   Issued invoice no. 113 for credit sale to Aspen Co., $4,750. All credit sales are on the company's standard terms of 2/10 n/30.

3   Collected cash of $882 from Leah Burnet in payment of her account receivable, $900, within the discount period.

6   Cash sales for the week totaled $1,748.

7   Collected note receivable, $3,400, plus interest of $367.

9   Issued invoice no. 114 for sale on account to Wilder Co., $4,300.

11 Received $4,655 cash from Aspen Co. in full settlement of its account receivable, net of the discount, from the sale on June 1.

13 Cash sales for the week were $2,964.

14 Sold inventory on account to Goss Corp., issuing invoice no. 115 for $858.

15 Issued credit memo to Goss Corp. for $154 of merchandise returned to us by Goss. Part of the goods we shipped were defective.

19 Received $4,214 from Wilder Co. in full settlement of its account receivable, $4,300, from June 9.

20 Cash sales for the week were $2,175.

22 Received cash of $2,904 from Goss Corporation on account. There was no discount.

24 Sold supplies to an employee for cash of $106, which was their cost.

27 Cash Sales for the week totaled $1,650.

28 Issued invoice no. 116 to Thompson Co. for credit sale of inventory, $5,194.

29 Sold goods on credit to Leah Burnett, issuing invoice no. 117 for $3,819.

29 Issued credit memo to Leah Burnet for $1,397 of inventory she returned to us because it was unsatisfactory.

The general ledger of Harwood Systems includes the following accounts and balances at June 1:

Account Number	Account Title	Balance	Account Number	Account Title	Balance
111	Cash..............	$4,217	411	Sales Revenue......	
112	Accounts Receivable .	3,804	412	Sales Discounts.....	
116	Supplies...........	1,290	413	Sales Returns	
141	Notes Receivable....	7,100		and Allowances...	
			418	Interest Revenue....	

Harwood's accounts receivable subsidiary ledger includes the following accounts and balances at June 1: Aspen Company, -0-; Leah Burnet, $900; Goss Corporation, $2,904; Thompson Company, -0-; and Wilder Co., -0-.

Required

1. Open the general ledger and the accounts receivable subsidiary ledger accounts given, inserting their balances at June 1.

2. Record the above transactions on page 6 of a single-column sales journal, page 9 of a cash receipts journal, and page 5 of a general journal, as appropriate. Harwood Systems records sales returns and allowances in the general journal.

3. Post daily to the accounts receivable subsidiary ledger. On June 30 post to the general ledger.

4. Total each column of the special journals. Show that the total debits equal the total credits in each special journal.

5. Balance the total of the customer account balances in the accounts receivable subsidiary ledger against the Accounts Receivable balance in the general ledger.

Problem 6-4B *Using the purchases, cash disbursements, and general journals; posting and balancing the ledgers*

Montana Company's September transactions affecting purchases and cash disbursements were as follows:

Sep. 1 Issued check no. 406 for $1,176 to pay AmeriCorp. on account. Montana received a $24 discount for prompt payment.

1 Issued check no. 407 to pay quarterly rent, debiting Prepaid Rent for $1,800.

2 Issued check no. 408 to pay net amount owed to Lynn Co., $1,455. Montana took a $45 discount.

5 Purchased supplies on credit terms of 2/10 n/30 from Westside Supply, $121.

7 Paid delivery expense, issuing check no. 409 for $739. Debit Delivery Expense.

10 Purchased inventory on account from Hayden, Inc., $2,008. Payment terms were net 30.

11 Returned the inventory to Hayden, Inc., because it was defective. We issued a debit memo for $2,008 and mailed a copy to Hayden.

15 Issued check no. 410 for a cash purchase of inventory, $2,332.

15 Paid semimonthly payroll with check no. 411, debiting Salary Expense for $1,224.

19 Issued check no. 412 to pay our account payable to Westside Supply from September 5. We did not earn the discount.

21 Purchased inventory on credit terms of 2/10 n/30 from Lynn Co., $4,150.

24 Purchased machinery on credit terms of 2/10 n/30 from AmeriCorp., $3,195.

26 Purchased supplies on account from Hayden, Inc., $467. Terms were net 30.

29 Issued check no. 413 to Lynn Co., paying the net amount owed from September 21.

30 Paid semimonthly payroll with check no. 414, debiting Salary Expense for $1,224.

The general ledger of Montana Company includes the following accounts and balances at September 1:

Account Number	Account Title	Balance	Account Number	Account Title	Balance
111	Cash	$15,996	511	Purchases	
115	Prepaid Rent.	600	512	Purchase Discounts	
116	Supplies	703	513	Purchase Returns	
151	Machinery.	21,800		and Allowances .	
211	Accounts Payable. .	2,700	521	Salary Expense	
			551	Delivery Expense . .	

Montana's accounts payable subsidiary ledger includes the following balances at September 1: AmeriCorp., $1,200; Hayden, Inc., -0-; Lynn Company, $1,500; and Westside Supply, -0-.

Required

1. Open the general ledger and the accounts payable subsidiary ledger accounts, inserting their balances at September 1.

2. Record the above transactions on page 10 of a purchases journal, page 5 of a cash disbursements journal, and page 8 of a general journal, as appropriate. Montana records purchase returns in the general journal.

3. Post daily to the accounts payable subsidiary ledger. On September 30 post to the general ledger.

4. Total each column of the special journals. Determine that the total debits equal the total credits in each special journal.

5. Balance the total of the creditor account balances in the accounts payable subsidiary ledger against the balance of the Accounts Payable control account in the general ledger.

Problem 6-5B *Using all the journals, posting, and balancing the ledgers*

Lang Company completed the following transactions during July:

July 2 Issued invoice no. 913 for sale on account to N. J. Seiko, $4,100.

3 Purchased inventory on credit terms of 3/10 n/60 from Chicosky Co., $2,467.

5 Sold inventory for cash, $1,077.

5 Issued check no. 532 to purchase furniture for cash, $2,185.

8 Collected interest revenue of $1,775.

9 Issued invoice no. 914 for sale on account to Bell Co., $5,550.

10 Purchased inventory for cash, $1,143, issuing check no. 533.

12 Received $4,018 cash from N. J. Seiko in full settlement of her account receivable, net of the discount, from the sale on July 2.

13 Issued check no. 534 to pay Chicosky Co. the net amount owed from July 3, $2,393. We received a $74 discount.

13 Purchased supplies on account from Manley, Inc., $441. Terms were net end-of-month.

15 Sold inventory on account to M. O. Brown, issuing invoice no. 915 for $665.

17 Issued credit memo to M. O. Brown for $665 for defective merchandise returned to us by Brown.

18 Issued invoice no. 916 for credit sale to N. J. Seiko, $357.

19 Received $5,439 from Bell Co. in full settlement of its account receivable, $5,550, from July 9.

20 Purchased inventory on credit terms of net 30 from Sims Distributing, $2,047.

22 Purchased furniture on credit terms of 3/10 n/60 from Chicosky Co., $645.

22 Issued check no. 535 to pay for insurance coverage, debiting Prepaid Insurance for $1,000.

24 Sold supplies to an employee for cash of $54, which was their cost.

25 Issued check no. 536 to pay utilities, $453. Debit Utilities Expense.

28 Purchased inventory on credit terms of 2/10 n/30 from Manley, Inc., $675.

29 Returned damaged inventory to Manley, Inc., issuing a debit memo for $675.

29 Sold goods on account to Bell Co., issuing invoice no. 917 for $496.

30 Issued check no. 537 to pay Manley, Inc., $441 on account from July 13.

31 Received $357 on account from N. J. Seiko on credit sale of January 18. There was no discount.

31 Issued check no. 538 to pay monthly salaries, debiting Salary Expense for $2,347.

Required

1. Open the following general ledger accounts using the account numbers given:

Cash.	111	Sales Returns	
Accounts Receivable.	112	and Allowances.	413
Supplies.	116	Interest Revenue	419
Prepaid Insurance.	117	Purchases.	511
Furniture	151	Purchase Discounts.	512
Accounts Payable	211	Purchase Returns	
Sales Revenue.	411	and Allowances.	513
Sales Discounts	412	Salary Expense	531
		Utilities Expense	541

2. Open these accounts in the subsidiary ledgers:
   Accounts receivable subsidiary ledger: Bell Co., M. O. Brown, and N. J. Seiko.
   Accounts payable subsidiary ledger: Chicosky Co., Manley, Inc., and Sims Distributing.
3. Enter the transactions in a sales journal (page 7), a cash receipts journal (page 5), a purchases journal (page 10), a cash disbursements journal (page 8), and a general journal (page 6), as appropriate.
4. Post daily to the accounts receivable subsidiary ledger and the accounts payable subsidiary ledger. On July 31 post to the general ledger.
5. Total each column of the special journals. Show that the total debits equal the total credits in each special journal.
6. Balance the total of the customer account balances in the accounts receivable subsidiary ledger against Accounts Receivable in the general ledger. Do the same for the accounts payable subsidiary ledger and Accounts Payable in the general ledger.

Problem 6-6B *Correcting errors in the cash receipts journal*

The cash receipts journal below contains five entries. All five entries are for legitimate cash receipt transactions, but the journal contains some errors in recording the transactions. In fact, only one entry is correct, and each of the other four entries contains one error.

Cash Receipts Journal   **Page 5**

Date	Cash	Sales Discounts	Accounts Receivable	Sales Revenue	Account Title	P.R.	Amount
Debits			**Credits**				
					Other Accounts		
7/5	611	34	645		Meg Davis	✓	
9			229	229	Lou Metz	✓	
10	8000			8000	Land	19	
19	73						
31	1060			1133			
	9744	34	874	9362	Totals		
	(11)	(42)	(12)	(41)			(✓)

Total Dr. = $9,778   Total Cr. = $10,236

Required

1. Identify the correct entry.
2. Identify the error in each of the other four entries.
3. Using the following format, prepare a corrected cash receipts journal.

Cash Receipts Journal   **Page 5**

Date	Cash	Sales Discounts	Accounts Receivable	Sales Revenue	Account Title	P.R.	Amount
Debits			**Credits**				
					Other Accounts		
7/5					Meg Davis	✓	
9					Lou Metz	✓	
10					Land	19	
19							
31							
	9973	34	874	1133	Totals		8000
	(11)	(42)	(12)	(41)			(✓)

Total Dr. = $10,007   Total Cr. = $10,007

Decision Problem

Reconstructing transactions from amounts posted to the accounts receivable ledger

A fire destroyed some accounting records of Dimkoff Company. The owner, Greg Dimkoff, asks your help in reconstructing the records. *He needs to know the beginning and ending balances of Accounts Receivable and the credit sales and cash receipts on account from customers during March.* All Dimkoff Company's sales are on credit, with payment terms of 2/10 n/30. All cash receipts on account reached Dimkoff within the 10-day discount period, except as noted. The only accounting record preserved from the fire is the accounts receivable subsidiary ledger, which follows.

Grant Adams

Date	Item	Jrnl. Ref.	Debit	Credit	Balance
Mar. 8		S.6	2,178		2,178
16		S.6	903		3,081
18		CR.8		2,178	903
19		J.5		221	682
27		CR.8		682	-0-

Lou Gross

Date	Item	Jrnl. Ref.	Debit	Credit	Balance
Mar. 1	Balance				1,096
5		CR.8		1,096	-0-
11		S.6	396		396
21		CR.8		396	-0-
24		S.6	2,566		2,566

Norris Associates

Date	Item	Jrnl. Ref.	Debit	Credit	Balance
Mar. 1	Balance				883
15		S.6	2,635		3,518
29		CR.8		883*	2,635

* Cash receipt did not occur within the discount period.

Suzuki, Inc.

Date	Item	Jrnl. Ref.	Debit	Credit	Balance
Mar. 1	Balance				440
3		CR.8		440	-0-
25		S.6	3,655		3,655
29		S.6	1,123		4,778

Hint: Use the journal references to reconstruct the entries in the sales journal and the cash receipts journal. Then compute the amounts for total credit sales and total cash receipts on account. Round all sales discounts to the nearest dollar.

Answers to Self-Study Questions

1. c
2. a
3. d
4. b
5. c [523 × 3 (one debit, one credit, and one to the accounts receivable ledger) = 1,569]
6. b
7. b
8. d
9. a
10. a

Practice Set

DeHaviland Company closes its books and prepares financial statements at the end of each month. The company completed the following transactions during August:

Aug. 1 Issued check no. 682 for August office rent of $2,000. (Debit Rent Expense.)

2 Issued check no. 683 to pay salaries of $1,240, which includes salary payable of $930 from July 31.

2 Issued invoice no. 503 for sale on account to R. T. Loeb, $600.

3 Purchased inventory on credit terms of 1/15 n/60 from Grant Publishers, $1,400.

4 Received net amount of cash on account from Fullam Company, $2,156, within the discount period.

4 Sold inventory for cash, $330.

5 Issued credit memo no. 267 to Park-Hee, Inc., for merchandise returned to us, $550.

5 Issued check no. 684 to purchase supplies for cash, $780.

6 Collected interest revenue of $1,100.

7 Issued invoice no. 504 for sale on account to K. D. Skipper, $2,400.

8 Purchased inventory on credit terms of 3/15 n/30 from Beaver Corporation, $4,300.

8 Issued check no. 685 to pay Federal Company $2,600 of the amount owed at July 31. This payment occurred after the end of the discount period.

9 Issued invoice no. 505 for sale on account to Iba & Frazier, $5,100.

11 Issued check no. 686 to pay Grant Publishers the net amount owed from August 3.

12 Received cash from R. T. Loeb in full settlement of her account receivable from August 2.

15 Sold inventory on account to Fullam Company, issuing invoice no. 506 for $466.

16 Issued check no. 687 to pay salary expense of $1,240.

18 Received $4,998 from Iba & Frazier in full settlement of their account receivable from August 9.

19 Purchased inventory for cash, $850, issuing check no. 688.

20 Purchased inventory on credit terms of net 30 from McMinn Sales, $2,150.

22 Purchased furniture on credit terms of 3/15 n/60 from Beaver Corporation, $510.

22 Issued check no. 689 to pay Beaver Corporation the net amount owed from August 8.

24 Received half the July 31 amount receivable from K. D. Skipper—after the end of the discount period.

25 Issued check no. 690 to pay utilities, $432.

26 Purchased supplies on credit terms of 2/10 n/30 from Federal Company, $180.

27 Returned damaged inventory to company from whom we made the cash purchase on August 19, receiving cash of $850.

28 Paid the amount payable to McMinn Sales at July 31, issuing check no. 691. There was no discount.

29 Sold goods on account to Iba & Frazier, issuing invoice no. 507 for $3,970.

30 Granted a sales allowance of $175 to K. D. Skipper, issuing credit memo no. 268.

31 Received $7,000 on account from Park-Hee, Inc. There was no discount.

31 Purchased inventory on credit terms of 1/10 n/30 from Suncrest Supply, $1,330.

31 Issued check no. 692 to J. M. DeHaviland, owner of the business, for personal withdrawal, $1,700.

Required:

1. Open these accounts with their account numbers and July 31 balances in the various ledgers.

General Ledger:

101	Cash	$ 4,490
102	Accounts Receivable	22,560
104	Interest Receivable	
105	Inventory	41,800
109	Supplies	1,340
117	Prepaid Insurance	2,200
140	Note Receivable, Long-term	11,000
160	Furniture	37,270
161	Accumulated Depreciation	10,550
201	Accounts Payable	19,050
204	Salary Payable	930
207	Interest Payable	320
208	Unearned Sales Revenue	
220	Note Payable, Long-term	42,000
301	J. M. DeHaviland, Capital	47,810
302	J. M. DeHaviland, Withdrawals	
400	Income Summary	
401	Sales Revenue	
402	Sales Discounts	
403	Sales Returns and Allowances	
410	Interest Revenue	
501	Purchases	
502	Purchase Discounts	
503	Purchase Returns and Allowances	
510	Salary Expense	
513	Rent Expense	
514	Depreciation Expense	

516 Insurance Expense . . . .

517 Utilities Expense . . . .

519 Supplies Expense . . . .

523 Interest Expense . . . .

Accounts Receivable Subsidiary Ledger: Fullam Company, $2,200; Iba & Frazier; R. T. Loeb; Park-Hee, Inc., $11,590; K. D. Skipper, $8,770.

Accounts Payable Subsidiary Ledger: Beaver Corporation; Federal Company, $12,600; Grant Publishers; McMinn Sales, $6,450; Suncrest Supply.

2. Journalize the August transactions in a sales journal (page 4), a cash receipts journal (page 11), a purchases journal (page 8), a cash disbursements journal (page 5), and a general journal (page 9). Use the journals as illustrated in Chapter 6. DeHaviland makes all credit sales on terms of 2/10 n/30.

3. Post daily to the accounts receivable subsidiary ledger and the accounts payable subsidiary ledger. On August 31, post to the general ledger.

4. Prepare a trial balance in the Trial Balance columns of a work sheet, and use the following information to complete the work sheet for the month ended August 31:

   a. Accrued interest revenue, $100
   b. Supplies on hand, $990.
   c. Prepaid insurance expired, $550.
   d. Depreciation expense, $230.

   e. Accrued salary expense, $1,030.
   f. Accrued interest expense, $320.
   g. Unearned sales revenue, $450.*
   h. Inventory on hand, $47,700.

   * Sales Revenue was credited when collected in advance. At August 31, $450 of unearned sales revenue needs to be recorded.

5. Prepare DeHaviland's multiple-step income statement and statement of owner's equity for August. Prepare the balance sheet at August 31.

6. Journalize and post the adjusting and closing entries.

7. Prepare a post-closing trial balance at August 31. Also, balance the total of the customer accounts in the accounts receivable subsidiary ledger against the Accounts Receivable balance in the general ledger. Do the same for the accounts payable subsidiary ledger and Accounts Payable in the general ledger.

7

Internal Control and Cash Transactions

LEARNING OBJECTIVES
After studying this chapter, you should be able to

1 Define internal control

2 Identify the characteristics of an effective system of internal control

3 Prepare a bank reconciliation and related journal entries

4 Apply internal controls to cash receipts

5 Apply internal controls to cash disbursements

6 Account for petty cash transactions

7 Use the voucher system

You learned in Chapter 6 that a well-designed accounting system helps managers control the business. Chapter 7 looks in more detail at **internal control,** which is the organizational plan and all the related measures adopted by an entity to

OBJECTIVE 1
Define internal control

1. Safeguard assets
2. Ensure accurate and reliable accounting records
3. Promote operational efficiency
4. Encourage adherence to company policies

Internal controls include *administrative controls* and *accounting controls.*

Administrative controls include the plan of organization, the methods, and the procedures that help managers achieve operational efficiency and adherence to company policies. The goal of administrative controls is to eliminate waste.

Accounting controls include the methods and procedures that safeguard assets, authorize transactions, and ensure the accuracy of the financial records. Of these elements, safeguarding assets is most important. This chapter focuses on internal accounting controls, with emphasis on cash transactions.

The need for laws requiring internal control has received increased attention in the 1970s and 1980s. During this time many illegal payments, embezzlements, and other criminal business practices came to light. Concerned citizens wanted to know why the companies' internal controls had failed to alert management that these illegalities had occurred. To answer these growing worries, the U.S. Congress passed the Foreign Corrupt Practices Act. This act requires companies under SEC jurisdiction to maintain an appropriate system of internal control whether or not they have foreign operations.[1] Thus its title is a bit misleading.

---

[1] The Foreign Corrupt Practices Act contains specific prohibitions against bribery and other corrupt practices in addition to requiring the maintenance of accounting records in reasonable detail and accuracy.

EXHIBIT 7-1   *Management Statement about Internal Controls*
                    General Motors Corporation

Responsibilities for Financial Statements

The following financial statements of General Motors Corporation . . . were prepared by the management which is responsible for their integrity and objectivity.

Management is further responsible for maintaining a system of *internal accounting controls* designed to provide reasonable assurance that the books and records reflect the transactions of the companies and that the established policies and procedures are carefully followed. Perhaps the most important feature in the *system of control* is that it is continually reviewed for its effectiveness and is augmented by written policies and guidelines, the careful selection and training of qualified personnel, and a strong program of *internal audit.*

Deloitte Haskins & Sells, independent certified public accountants, are engaged to examine the financial statements of General Motors Corporation.

The Board of Directors, through the Audit Committee . . . is responsible for assuring that management fulfills its responsibilities in the preparation of the financial statements. . . . To assure complete independence, Deloitte Haskins & Sells have full and free access to meet with the Committee . . . to discuss . . . the adequacy of *internal controls.* . . .

Signed by the *Chairman of the Board of Directors* and the *Chief Financial Officer*

Wise management has always kept a system of strong internal control, so before the law was enacted many businesses had already met the requirements for internal control policies. However, the Foreign Corrupt Practices Act has affected companies' approaches to internal control. Formerly, internal control was viewed as an auditing consideration. The act shifted responsibility for internal control to company managers. Furthermore, boards of directors, to comply with the act and with other SEC requirements, compile written evidence of management's evaluations and ongoing reviews of the internal control system.

Exhibit 7-1 presents excerpts from General Motors Management's Statement, included in its annual report. Note the frequent references to internal controls and audits and observe that the chairman of the board of directors, who heads the entire organization, and the chief financial officer, who is one of the top five officers of the company, sign the statement. Likewise, management teams in other businesses state their responsibility for internal control in their annual reports.

Effective Systems of Internal Control _____

Whether the business is General Motors or a local department store, its system of internal controls, if effective, has the following noteworthy characteristics.

Competent and Reliable Personnel

OBJECTIVE 2

Identify the characteristics of an effective system of internal control

Employees should be *competent* and *reliable*. Paying top salaries to attract top-quality employees, training them to do their job well, and supervising their work all help to build a competent staff. A business adds flexibility to its staffing by rotating employees through various jobs. If one employee is sick or on vacation, a second employee is already trained to step in and do the job.

Rotating employees through various jobs also promotes reliability. An employee is less likely to handle her job improperly if she knows that her misconduct may come to light when a second employee takes over the job. This same reasoning leads businesses to require that employees take an annual vacation. A second employee, stepping in to handle the position, may uncover any wrongdoing.

Assignment of Responsibilities

In a business with an effective internal control system, no important duty is overlooked. A model of such assignment of responsibilities appears in the corporate organizational chart in Exhibit 7-2.

Notice that the corporation has a vice-president of finance and accounting.

EXHIBIT 7-2 *Organization Chart of a Corporation*

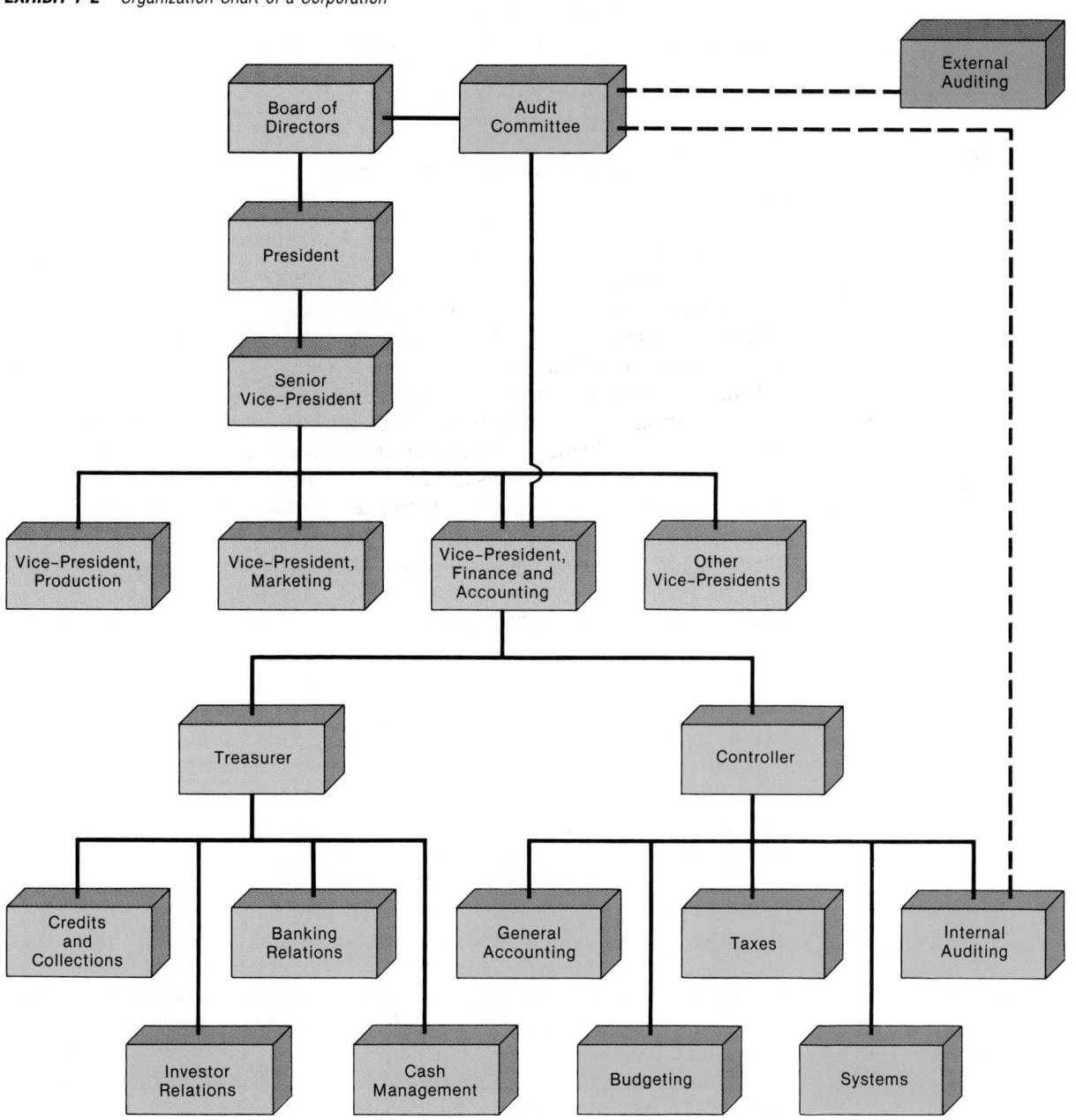

Two other officers, the treasurer and the controller, report to the vice-president. The treasurer is responsible for cash management. The controller performs accounting duties.

Within this organization, the controller may be responsible for approving invoices for payment, and the treasurer may actually sign the checks. Working under the controller, one accountant may be responsible for property taxes, another accountant for income taxes. In sum, all duties are clearly defined and assigned to individuals who bear responsibility for carrying them out.

Proper Authorization

An organization generally has a written set of rules that outlines approved procedures. Any deviation from standard policy requires *proper authorization*. For example, managers or assistant managers of retail stores must approve customer checks for amounts above the store's usual limit. Likewise, deans or department chairpersons of colleges and universities must give the authorization for a freshman, sophomore, or junior to enroll in courses otherwise restricted to seniors.

Separation of Duties

Smart management divides the responsibilities for transactions between two or more people or departments. Separation of duties limits the chances for fraud and also promotes the accuracy of the accounting records. This crucial and often neglected component of the internal control system may be subdivided into four parts.

1. Separation of operations from accounting. The entire accounting function should be completely separate from operating departments so that objective records may be kept. For example, product inspectors, not machine operators, should count units produced by a manufacturing process. Accountants, not salespersons, should keep inventory records. Observe the separation of accounting from production and marketing in Exhibit 7-2.

2. Separation of the custody of assets from accounting. To reduce temptation and fraud, the accountant should not handle cash, and the cashier should not have access to the accounting records. If one employee had both cash-handling and accounting duties, this person could steal cash and conceal the theft by making a bogus entry on the books. We see this component of internal control in the organization chart in Exhibit 7-2. Note that the treasurer has custody of the cash and the controller accounts for the cash. Neither person has both responsibilities.

Warehouse employees with no accounting duties should handle inventory. If they were allowed to account for the inventory, they could steal it and write it off as obsolete. In a computerized accounting system, a person with custody of assets should not have access to the computer programs. Similarly, the programmer should not have access to tempting assets like cash.

3. Separation of the authorization of transactions from the custody of related assets. If possible, persons who authorize transactions should not handle the related asset. For example, the same individual should not authorize the payment of a supplier's invoice and also sign the check to pay the bill. With both duties, the person can authorize payments to himself and then sign the checks. By separating these duties, only legitimate bills are paid.

For another example, an individual who handles cash receipts should not have the authority to write off accounts receivable. (Businesses that sell on credit declare certain of their accounts receivable as uncollectible, realizing that these receivables will never be collected. Chapter 8 looks at uncollectible accounts receivable in detail.) Suppose the company shown in Exhibit 7-2 employs V. Saucier. He works in Credits and Collections (under the treasurer) and handles cash receipts from customers.

Among the business's accounts receivable in the subsidiary ledger is Gina Kowalski's $500 balance. Saucier could label Kowalski's account as uncollectible, and the business might cease trying to collect from her. When Kowalski mails a $500 check to pay off her balance, Saucier forges the endorsement and pockets the money. Kowalski, of course, has no reason to notify anyone else at the business that she has mailed a check, so Saucier's crime goes undetected. This theft would have been avoided by denying Saucier either the access to cash receipts or the authority to declare accounts uncollectible.

4. Separation of duties within the accounting function. Independent performance of various phases of accounting helps to minimize errors and the opportunities for fraud. For example, different accountants in a manual system keep the cash receipts journal and the cash disbursements journal. In a computer system, the employees who enter data into the computer do not also operate the machines.

Internal and External Audits

It is not economically feasible for auditors to examine all the transactions during a period, so they must rely to some degree on the accounting system to produce accurate accounting records. To gauge the reliability of the company's accounting system, auditors evaluate its system of internal controls. Auditors also spot the weaknesses in the system and recommend corrections. Auditors offer *objectivity* in their reports, while managers immersed in operations may overlook weaknesses.

Audits are internal or external. Exhibit 7-2 shows *internal auditors* as employees of the business, under the controller. Some organizations have the internal auditors report directly to the audit committee. Throughout the year, they audit various segments of the organization. *External auditors* are entirely independent of the business. These people, employed by an accounting firm, are hired by an entity as outsiders to audit the entity as a whole. Both groups of auditors are independent of the operations they examine, and their reviews of internal controls often are similar.

An auditor may find that an employee has both cash-handling and cash-accounting duties or may learn that a cash shortage has resulted from lax efforts to collect accounts receivable. In such cases, the auditor suggests improvements. Auditors' recommendations assist the business in running smoothly and economically.

Documents and Records

Business *documents and records* vary considerably, from source documents like sales invoices and purchase orders to special journals and subsidiary ledgers. Specially designed records—for example, the special journals discussed in the last chapter—speed the flow of paper work and enhance efficiency.

Documents should be prenumbered. A gap in the numbered sequence calls attention to a missing document.

Prenumbering cash sale receipts discourages theft by the cashier because the copy retained by the cashier, which lists the amount of the sale, can be checked against the actual amount of cash received. If the receipts are not prenumbered, the cashier can destroy the copy and pocket the cash sale amount. However, if the receipts are prenumbered, the missing copy can easily be identified.

Limitations of Internal Control

Most internal control measures can be overcome. Systems designed to thwart an *individual* employee's fraud can be beaten by two or more employees working as a team—colluding—to defraud the firm. Consider a movie theater. The ticket seller takes in the cash, and the ticket taker tears the tickets in half so they cannot be reused, retaining the torn ticket stub. But suppose they put a scheme together in which the ticket seller pockets the cash for ten tickets and the ticket taker pockets ten stubs. Who would catch them? The manager could take the additional control measure of counting the people in the theater and matching that figure against the number of ticket stubs retained. But that takes time away from other duties. As you see, the stricter the internal control system, the more expensive it becomes.

A system of internal control that is too complex may strangle people in red tape. Efficiency and control are hurt rather than helped. The more complicated the system, the more time and money it takes to maintain. Just how tight should an internal control system be? Managers must make sensible judgments. Investments in internal control must be judged in the light of the costs and benefits.

The Bank Account as a Control Device

Keeping cash in a *bank account* is part of internal control because banks have established practices for safeguarding cash. Banks also provide depositors with detailed records of cash transactions. To take full advantage of these control features, the business should deposit all cash receipts in the bank account and make all cash payments through it (except petty cash disbursements, which we look at later). We now discuss banking records and documents.

For many businesses, cash is the most important asset. After all, cash is the most common means of exchange, and most transactions ultimately affect cash.

Cash is the most tempting asset for theft. Consequently, internal controls for cash are more elaborate than for most other assets. The rest of this chapter describes internal control over cash. We consider cash to be not just paper money and coins but also checks, money orders, and money kept in bank accounts. Cash includes neither stamps, because they are supplies, nor IOUs payable to the business, because these are receivables.

The documents used to control a bank account include the signature card, the deposit ticket, the check, and the bank reconciliation.

Signature Card.   Banks require each person authorized to transact business through an account in that bank to sign a *signature card.* The bank compares the signatures on documents against the signature card to protect the bank and the depositor against forgery.

Deposit Ticket.   Banks supply standard forms as *deposit tickets.* The customer fills in the dollar amount and the date of deposit. The customer retains either (1) a duplicate copy of the deposit ticket or (2) a deposit receipt, depending on the bank's practice, as proof of the transaction.

Check.   To draw money from an account, the depositor writes a **check,** which is the document that instructs the bank to pay the designated person or business the specified amount of money. There are three parties to a check: the *maker,* who signs the check; the *payee,* to whose order the check is drawn; and the *bank* on which the check is drawn.

Most checks are serially numbered and preprinted with the name and address of the depositor and the bank. The checks have places for the date, the name of the payee, the signature of the maker, and the amount. The bank name and bank identification number and the depositor account number are usually imprinted in magnetic ink for machine processing.

Exhibit 7-3 shows a check drawn on the bank account of Business Research, Inc. The check has two parts, the check itself and the remittance advice. The *remittance advice,* an optional attachment, tells the payee the reason for the payment. The maker (Business Research) retains a carbon copy of the check for its recording in the check register (cash disbursements journal). Note that internal controls at Business Research require two signatures on checks.

Bank Statement.   Most banks send monthly **bank statements** to their depositors. The statement shows the account's beginning and ending balance for the period and lists the month's transactions. Included with the statement are the maker's *canceled checks,* those checks that have been paid by the bank on behalf of the depositor. The bank statement also lists any other deposits and changes in the account. Deposits appear in chronological order, checks in a logical order, along with the date each check cleared the bank.

EXHIBIT 7-3   *Check with Remittance Advice*

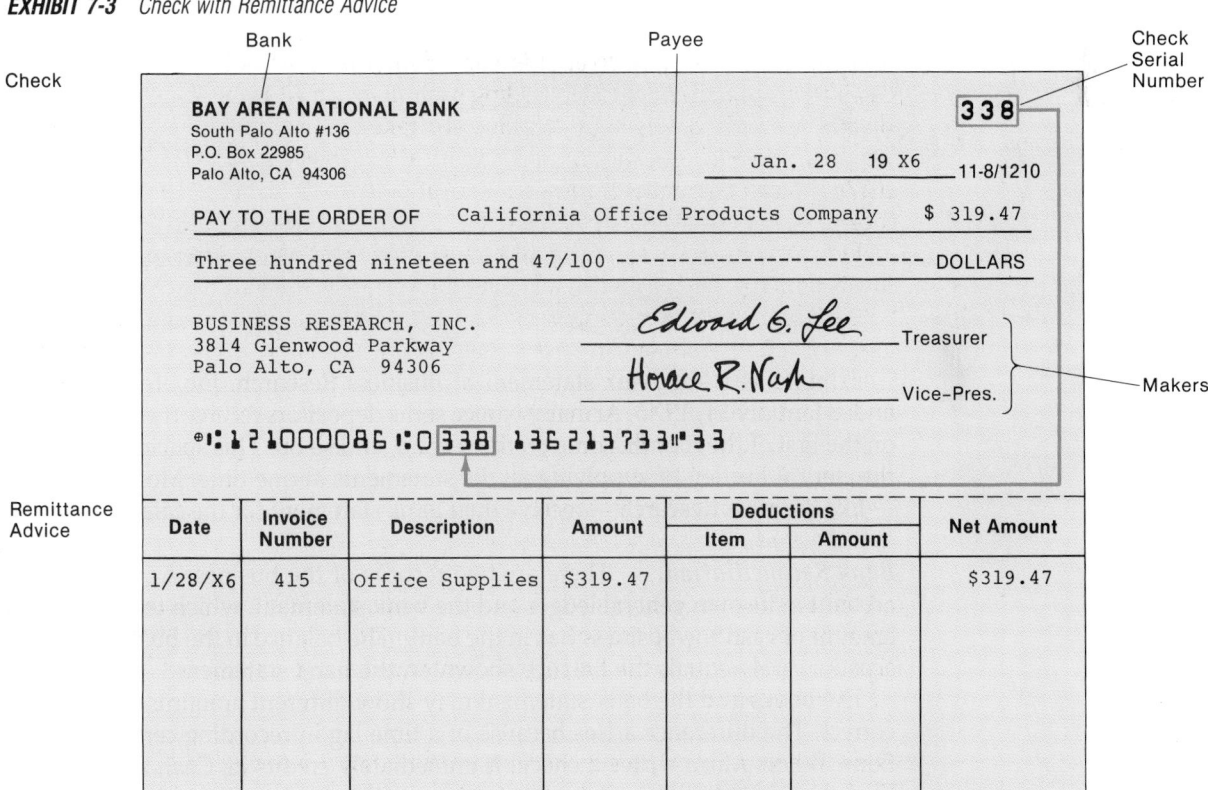

EXHIBIT 7-4   *Bank Statement*

BAY AREA NATIONAL BANK   **ACCOUNT STATEMENT**
South Palo Alto #136
P.O. Box 22985
Palo Alto, CA   94306

```
Business Research, Inc.                    CHECKING ACCOUNT   136-213733
3814 Glenwood Parkway
Palo Alto, CA  94306


                                      CHECKING ACCOUNT SUMMARY AS OF  01-31-X6
```

BEGINNING BALANCE	TOTAL DEPOSITS	TOTAL WITHDRAWALS	SERVICE CHARGES	ENDING BALANCE
6556.12	3448.61	4602.00	14.25	5388.48

```
───────────────────────CHECKING ACCOUNT TRANSACTIONS───────────────────────

DEPOSITS

DEPOSIT                                                  01-04    1000.00
DEPOSIT                                                  01-04     112.00
DEPOSIT                                                  01-08     194.60
BANK COLLECTION                                          01-26    2114.00
INTEREST                                                 01-31      28.01

CHARGES

SERVICE CHARGE                                           01-31      14.25
CHECKS:
```

	CHECKS			CHECKS			BALANCES
NUMBER	DATE	AMOUNT	NUMBER	DATE	AMOUNT	DATE	BALANCE
332	01-12	3000.00	334	01-12	100.00	12-31	6556.12
656	01-06	100.00	335	01-06	100.00	01-04	7616.12
333	01-12	150.00	336	01-31	1100.00	01-06	7416.12
						01-08	7610.72
						01-12	4360.72
						01-26	6474.72
						01-31	5388.48

```
OTHER CHARGES                                            DATE      AMOUNT
    NSF                                                  01-04      52.00


                            MONTHLY SUMMARY

    7 WITHDRAWALS              4360 MINIMUM BALANCE          5812 AVERAGE BALANCE
```

Exhibit 7-4 is the bank statement of Business Research, Inc., for the month ended January 31, 19X6. At many banks, some depositors receive their statements on the first of the month, some on the second, and so on. This spacing eliminates the clerical burden of supplying all the statements at one time. Most businesses —like Business Research—receive their bank statement for the calendar month.

Bank Reconciliation.   There are two records of the business's cash: its Cash account in its own general ledger and the bank statement, which tells the actual amount of cash the business has in the bank. The balance in the business's Cash account rarely equals the balance shown on the bank statement.

The books and the bank statement may show different amounts but both are correct. The difference arises because of a time lag in recording certain transactions. When a firm writes a check, it immediately credits its Cash account. The bank, however, will not subtract the amount of the check until the check reaches it for payment. This may take days, even weeks if the payee waits to cash the check. Likewise, the business debits Cash for all cash receipts, and it may take a day or so for the bank to add this amount to the business's bank balance.

Good internal control means knowing where a company's money comes from, how it is spent, and the current cash balance. How else can the accountant keep the accurate records management needs to make informed decisions? The accountant must explain the reasons for the difference between the firm's records and the bank statement figures and determine the actual amount of cash in the bank on a certain date. This process is called the **bank reconciliation.** Properly done, the bank reconciliation assures that all cash transactions have been accounted for and that the bank and book records of cash are correct.

Common items that cause differences between the bank balance and the book balance are

1. Items recorded by the *company* but not yet recorded by the *bank:*
    a. **Deposits in transit** (outstanding deposits). The company has recorded these deposits but the bank has not.
    b. **Outstanding checks.** These checks have been issued by the company and recorded on its books but have not yet been paid by its bank.
2. Items recorded by the *bank* but not yet recorded by the *company:*
    a. **Bank collections.** The bank sometimes collects money on behalf of depositors. Many businesses have their customers pay directly to the company bank account. This practice, called a lock-box system, reduces the possibility of theft and also places the business's cash in circulation faster than if the cash had to be collected and deposited by company personnel. An example is a bank's collecting cash on a note receivable and the related interest revenue for the depositor. The bank may notify the depositor of these bank collections on the bank statement.
    b. **Service charge.** This amount is the bank's fee for processing the depositor's transactions. Banks commonly base the service charge on the balance in the account. The depositor learns the amount of the service charge from the bank statement.
    c. *Interest revenue on checking account.* Many banks pay interest to depositors who keep a large enough balance of cash in the account. This is generally the case with business checking accounts. The bank notifies the depositor of this interest on the bank statement.
    d. **NSF (nonsufficient funds) checks** received from customers. To understand how to handle NSF checks, also called hot checks, you first need to know the route a check takes. The maker writes the check, credits Cash to record the payment on the books, and gives the check to the payee. On receiving the check, the payee debits Cash on his or her books and deposits the check in the bank. The payee's bank immediately adds the receipt amount to the payee's bank balance on the assumption that the check is good. The check is returned to the maker's bank, which then deducts the check amount from the maker's bank balance. If the maker's bank balance is insufficient to pay the check, the maker's bank refuses to pay the check, reverses this deduction, and sends an NSF notice back to the payee's bank. The payee bank subtracts the receipt amount from the payee's bank balance and notifies the payee of this action. This process may take from three to seven days. The company may learn of NSF checks through the bank statement, which lists the NSF check as a charge (subtraction), as shown near the bottom of Exhibit 7-4.
    e. *Checks collected, deposited, and returned to payee by the bank for reasons other than NSF.* Banks return checks to the payee if (1) the maker's account has closed, (2) the date is stale (some checks state "void after 30 days"), (3) the

signature is not authorized, (4) the check has been altered, or (5) the check form is improper. Accounting for all returned checks is the same as for NSF checks.

    f. *The cost of printed checks.* This charge against the company's bank account balance is handled like a service charge.

3. Errors by either the company or the bank. For example, a bank may improperly charge (decrease) the bank balance of Business Research, Inc., for a check drawn by another company, perhaps Business Research Associates. Or a company may miscompute its bank balance on its own books. Computational errors are becoming less frequent with widespread use of computers. Nevertheless, all errors must be corrected, and the corrections will be a part of the bank reconciliation.

Steps in Preparing the Bank Reconciliation

The steps in preparing the bank reconciliation are

1. Start with two figures, the balance shown on the bank statement *(balance per bank)* and the balance in the company's Cash account *(balance per books).* These two amounts will probably disagree because of the timing differences discussed earlier.

2. Add to, or subtract from, the *bank* balance those items that appear on the books but not on the bank statement:
   a. Add *deposits in transit* to the bank balance. Deposits in transit are identified by comparing the deposits listed on the bank statement to the company list of cash receipts. They show up as cash receipts on the books but not as deposits on the bank statement. As a control measure, the accountant should also ensure that deposits in transit from the preceding month appear on the current month's bank statement. If they do not, the deposits may be lost.
   b. Subtract *outstanding checks* from the bank balance. Outstanding checks are identified by comparing the canceled checks returned with the bank statement to the company list of checks in the cash disbursements journal. They show up as cash payments on the books but not as paid checks on the bank statement. This comparison also verifies that all checks paid by the bank were valid company checks and were correctly recorded by the bank and by the company. Outstanding checks are usually the most numerous items on a bank reconciliation.

3. Add to, or subtract from, the *book* balance those items that appear on the bank statement but not on the company books:
   a. Add to the book balance (a) *bank collections* and (b) any *interest revenue* earned on the money in the bank. These items are identified by comparing the deposits listed on the bank statement to the company list of cash receipts. They show up as cash receipts on the bank statement but not on the books.
   b. Subtract from the book balance (a) *service charges,* (b) *cost of printed checks,* and (c) *other bank charges* (for example, charges for NSF or stale date checks). These items are identified by comparing the other charges listed on the bank statement to the cash disbursements recorded on the company books. They show up as subtractions on the bank statement but not as cash payments on the books.

4. Compute the *adjusted bank balance* and the *adjusted book balance.* The two adjusted balances should be equal.

5. Journalize each item in 3, that is, each item listed on the book portion of the bank reconciliation. These items must be recorded on the company books because they affect cash.
6. Correct all book errors and notify the bank of any errors it has made.

Bank Reconciliation Illustrated

The bank statement in Exhibit 7-4 indicates that the January 31 bank balance of Business Research, Inc., is $5,388.48. However, the company's Cash account has a balance of $3,294.21. In following the steps outlined above, the accountant finds these reconciling items:

1. The January 30 deposit of $1,591.63 does not appear on the bank statement.
2. The bank erroneously charged a $100 check—number 656—written by Business Research Associates against the Business Research, Inc., account.
3. Five company checks issued late in January and recorded in the cash disbursements journal have not been paid by the bank:

Check No.	Date	Amount
337	Jan. 27	$286.00
338	28	319.47
339	28	83.00
340	29	203.14
341	30	458.53

4. The bank collected on behalf of the company a note receivable, $2,114 (including interest revenue of $214). This cash receipt has not been recorded in the cash receipts journal.
5. The bank statement shows interest revenue of $28.01 that the bank has paid the company on its cash balance.
6. Check number 333 for $150 paid to Brown Company on account was recorded in the cash disbursements journal as a $510 amount, creating a $360 understatement of the Cash balance per books.
7. The bank service charge for the month was $14.25.
8. The bank statement shows an NSF check for $52 that was received from customer L. Ross.

OBJECTIVE 3
Prepare a bank reconciliation and related journal entries

Exhibit 7-5 is the bank reconciliation based on the above data. Panel A lists the reconciling items, which are keyed by number to the actual reconciliation in Panel B. Note that after the reconciliation, the adjusted bank balance equals the adjusted book balance. This equality is the accuracy check for the reconciliation.

Recording Entries from the Reconciliation

The bank reconciliation does not directly affect the journals or the ledgers. Like the work sheet, the reconciliation is an accountant's tool, separate from the company's books.

The bank reconciliation acts as a control device by signaling the company to record the transactions listed as reconciling items in the Books section because the company has not yet done so. For example, the bank collected the note receivable on behalf of the company, but the company has not yet recorded this cash receipt. In fact, the company learned of the cash receipt only when it received the bank statement.

EXHIBIT 7-5 *Bank Reconciliation*

Panel A—Reconciling Items:

1. Deposit in transit, $1,591.63.
2. Bank error; add $100 to bank balance.
3. Outstanding checks: no. 337, $286; no. 338, $319.47; no. 339, $83; no. 340, $203.14; no. 341, $458.53.

4. Bank collection, $2,114, including interest revenue of $214.
5. Interest earned on bank balance, $28.01.
6. Book error; add $360 to book balance.
7. Bank service charge, $14.25.
8. NSF check from L. Ross, $52.

Panel B—Bank Reconciliation:

Business Research, Inc.
Bank Reconciliation
January 31, 19X6

Bank:			Books:		
Balance, January 31		$5,388.48	Balance, January 31		$3,294.21
Add:			Add:		
1. Deposit of January 30 in transit		1,591.63	4. Bank collection of note receivable, including interest revenue of $214		2,114.00
2. Correction of bank error—Business Research Associates check erroneously charged against company account		100.00	5. Interest revenue earned on bank balance		28.01
		7,080.11	6. Correction of book error—Overstated amount of check no. 333		360.00
3. Less outstanding checks:					5,796.22
No. 337	$286.00		Less:		
No. 338	319.47		7. Service charge	$14.25	
No. 339	83.00		8. NSF check	52.00	(66.25)
No. 340	203.14				
No. 341	458.53	(1,350.14)			
Adjusted bank balance		$5,729.97	Adjusted book balance		$5,729.97

Why does the company *not* need to record the reconciling items on the Bank side of the reconciliation? Those items have already been recorded on the company books.

Based on the reconciliation in Exhibit 7-5, Business Research, Inc., makes these entries. They are dated January 31 to bring the Cash account to the correct balance on that date:

Jan. 31	Cash		2,114.00	
	Notes Receivable			1,900.00
	Interest Revenue			214.00
	Note receivable collected by bank.			
31	Cash		28.01	
	Interest Revenue			28.01
	Interest earned on bank balance.			
31	Cash		360.00	
	Accounts Payable—Brown Co.			360.00
	Correction of check register, check no. 333.			
31	Miscellaneous Expense		14.25	
	Cash			14.25
	Bank service charge.			

Note: Miscellaneous Expense is debited for the bank
service charge because the service charge pertains to
no particular expense category.

31	Accounts Receivable – L. Ross	52.00	
	Cash		52.00
	NSF check returned by bank.		

These entries bring the business's books up to date.

The entry for the NSF check needs explanation. Upon learning that L. Ross's
$52 check was not good, Business Research credits Cash to bring the Cash account
up to date. Since Business Research still has a receivable from Ross, it debits
Accounts Receivable — L. Ross and pursues collection from him.

Summary Problem for Your Review

1. The Cash account of Bain Company at February 28, 19X3, follows.

Cash

Feb. 1	Balance	4,195	Feb. 3	400	
6		800	12	3,100	
15		1,800	19	1,100	
23		900	25	500	
28		2,400	27	900	
Feb. 28	Balance	4,095			

2. Bain Company receives this bank statement on February 28, 19X3 (negative
amounts appear in parentheses):

Bank Statement for February 19X3

Beginning balance.		$4,195
Deposits:		
Feb. 7.	$ 800	
15.	1,800	
24.	900	3,500
Checks (total per day):		
Feb. 8.	$ 400	
16.	3,100	
23.	1,100	(4,600)
Other items:		
Service charge		(10)
NSF check from M. E. Crown		(700)
Bank collection of note receivable for the company		1,000*
Interest on account balance		15
Ending balance		$3,400

_____

* Includes interest of $119.

Additional data:

Bain Company deposits all cash receipts in the bank and makes all cash disbursements by check.

Required:

1. Prepare the bank reconciliation of Bain Company at February 28, 19X3.
2. Record the entries based on the bank reconciliation.

SOLUTION TO REVIEW PROBLEM

Requirement 1

Bain Company
Bank Reconciliation
February 28, 19X3

Bank:

Balance, February 28, 19X3.............................		$3,400
Add: Deposit of February 28 in transit		2,400
		5,800
Less: Outstanding checks issued on Feb. 25 ($500) and Feb. 27 ($900)		(1,400)
Adjusted bank balance, February 28, 19X3		$4,400

Books:

Balance, February 28, 19X3.............................		$4,095
Add: Bank collection of note receivable, including interest of $119		1,000
Interest earned on bank balance....................		15
		5,110
Less: Service charge	$ 10	
NSF check.....................................	700	(710)
Adjusted book balance, February 28, 19X3		$4,400

Requirement 2

Feb. 28	Cash...	1,000	
	Note Receivable ($1,000 − $119)................		881
	Interest Revenue		119
	Note receivable collected by bank.		
28	Cash...	15	
	Interest Revenue		15
	Interest earned on bank balance.		
28	Miscellaneous Expense	10	
	Cash.......................................		10
	Bank service charge.		
28	Accounts receivable—M. E. Crown	700	
	Cash.......................................		700
	NSF check returned by bank.		

Reporting of Cash

Cash is the first current asset listed on the balance sheet of most companies. Even small businesses have several bank accounts and one or more petty cash funds that are kept on hand for making small disbursements. However, companies usually combine all cash amounts into a single total for reporting on the balance sheet. They also include liquid assets like time deposits and certificates of deposit. These are interest-bearing accounts that can be withdrawn with no penalty after a short period of time. Although they are slightly less liquid than cash, they are sufficiently similar to be reported along with cash. For example, the balance sheet of Kraft, Inc., maker of Miracle Whip, Philadelphia Cream Cheese, Duracell batteries, and other well-known products, recently reported (in millions of dollars):

Assets:

Cash, time deposits, and certificates of deposit	$ 194.1
Temporary investments	127.6
Accounts and notes receivable	941.7
Inventories	1,211.3
Total current assets	$2,474.7

It is important to perform the bank reconciliation on the balance sheet date in order to be assured of reporting the correct amount of cash.

Internal Control over Cash Receipts

Internal control over cash receipts ensures that all cash receipts are deposited in the bank and the company's accounting record is correct. Many businesses receive cash over the counter and through the mail. Each source of cash receipts calls for specific controls.

OBJECTIVE 4
Apply internal controls to cash receipts

The cash register offers management control over cash received in a store. First, the machine should be positioned so that customers can see the amounts the cashier enters into the register. No person willingly pays more than the marked price for an item, so the customer helps prevent the sales clerk from overcharging and pocketing the excess over actual prices. Also, company policy should require issuance of a receipt to make sure each sale is recorded in the register.

Second, the register's cash drawer opens only when the sales clerk enters an amount on the keys, and a roll of tape locked inside the machine records each amount. At the end of the day, a manager proves the cash by comparing the total amount in the cash drawer against the tape's total. This step helps prevent outright theft by the clerk. For security reasons, the clerk should not have access to the tape.

Third, pricing merchandise at "uneven" amounts—say, $3.95 instead of $4.00—means that the clerk generally must make change, which in turn means having to get into the cash drawer. This requires entering the amount of the sale on the keys and so onto the register tape.

At the end of the day, the cashier or other employee with cash-handling duties deposits the cash in the bank. The tape goes to the accounting department as the basis for an entry in the cash receipts journal. These security measures, coupled with periodic on-site inspection by a manager, discourage fraud.

All incoming mail should be opened by a mail-room employee. This person should compare the actual enclosed amount of cash or check with the attached remittance advice. If no advice was sent, the mail-room employee should prepare one and enter the amount of each receipt on a control tape. At the end of the day, this control tape is given to a responsible official, such as the controller, for verification. Cash receipts should be given to the cashier, who combines them with any cash received over the counter and prepares the bank deposit.

Having a mail-room employee be the first to handle postal cash receipts is just another application of a good internal control procedure—in this case, separation of duties. If the accountants opened postal cash receipts, they could easily hide a theft.

The mail-room employee forwards the remittance advices to the accounting department. They provide the data for entries in the cash receipts journal and postings to customers' accounts in the accounts receivable ledger. As a final step, the controller compares the three records of the day's cash receipts: (1) the control tape total from the mail room, (2) the bank deposit amount from the cashier, and (3) the debit to Cash from the accounting department.

An added measure used to control cash receipts is a *fidelity bond,* which is an insurance policy that the business buys to guard against theft. The fidelity bond helps in two ways. First, the insurance company that issues the policy investigates the backgrounds of the workers whose activities will be covered, such as the mail-room employees who handle incoming cash and the employees who handle inventory. Second, if the company suffers a loss due to the misconduct of a covered employee, the insurance company reimburses the business.

Cash Short and Over.   A difference often exists between actual cash receipts and the day's record of cash received. Usually the difference is small and results from honest errors. Suppose the cash register tapes of a large department store indicate sales revenue of $25,000, but the cash received is $24,980. To record the day's sales, the store would make this entry:

Cash... 24,980
Cash Short and Over 20
    Sales Revenue 25,000
Daily cash sales.

As the entry shows, Cash Short and Over is debited when sales revenue exceeds cash receipts. This account is credited when cash receipts exceed sales. A debit balance appears on the income statement as Miscellaneous Expense, a credit balance as Other Revenue.

This account's balance should be small. The debits and credits for cash over and short collected over an accounting period tend to cancel each other out. A large balance signals the accountant to investigate. For example, too large a debit balance may mean an employee is stealing. Cash Short and Over, then, acts as an internal control device.

Internal Control Over Cash Disbursements

Payment by *check* is an important control over cash disbursements. First, the check acts as a source document. Second, to be valid the check must be signed by an authorized official, so each payment by check draws the attention of management. Before signing the check, the manager should study the invoice, the receiving report, the purchase order, and other supporting documents. (A discussion of these documents follows.) As further security and control over cash disbursements, many firms require two signatures on a check, as we saw in Exhibit 7-3. To avoid document alteration, some firms also use machines that indelibly stamp the amount on the check.

In very small businesses, the proprietor or partners may control cash disbursements by reviewing the supporting documents themselves and personally writing all checks. However, in larger businesses this is impractical, so the duties of approving invoices for payment and writing checks are performed by authorized employees. Strong internal control is achieved through clear-cut assignment of responsibility, proper authorization, and separation of duties.

OBJECTIVE 5

Apply internal controls to cash disbursements

Controlling the Cost of Inventory

Cost of goods sold is the major expense of most merchandising businesses. Therefore, it is important to control the cost of inventory purchases. Overall control is achieved by the same measures used to control all other cash disbursements—assignment of responsibility, authorization for payment, separation of duties, and so on.

A measure that is designed specifically to control the cost of inventory concerns the manner of recording purchases. There are two ways to record purchases: (1) at the *gross* cost, as illustrated thus far; and (2) at the *net* cost, which takes into account any discount on the purchase. For example, a $2,000 invoice subject to credit terms of 2/10 n/30 could be recorded at gross ($2,000) or net ($1,960). The discount terms of 2/10 n/30 (that is, a 2 percent discount for payment within 10 days, or the full $2,000 within 30 days) indicate a very high rate of interest when expressed as an annual rate. Paying after the discount period costs 2 percent for the extra 20 days of credit, an annual rate of 36 percent (.02 $\times$ 360 days/20 days = .36). For this reason, companies adopt the policy of taking all such discounts.

Recording the purchase at its net amount has a control advantage because it highlights the inefficiency of paying late. Recorded at net cost, the purchase entry is

Purchases ($2,000 − $40)	1,960	
Accounts Payable		1,960
Purchase on account.		

The actual cost of the inventory is $1,960 because this is the cash cost of the goods if they are paid for immediately. The gross cost of $2,000 includes a $40 charge for payment beyond the discount period. Therefore, the net cost method is helpful. To see the control advantage of the net cost approach, suppose the invoice is *not* paid within the discount period. This inefficiency costs an extra $40, debited to Purchase Discounts Lost as follows:

Accounts Payable	1,960	
Purchase Discounts Lost	40	
Cash in Bank		2,000
Payment after discount period.		

Purchase Discounts Lost is an expense account reported as Other Expense on the income statement:

Grant Company
Income Statement
Year Ended December 31, 19X8

Sales revenue	$700,000
Cost of goods sold	380,000
Gross margin	320,000
Operating expenses	230,000
Income from operations	90,000
Other revenue (expense):	
Purchase discounts lost	**(2,000)**
Net income	$ 88,000

Reporting Purchase Discounts Lost on the income statement draws attention to the inefficiency of losing the discounts. The net method thus captures the information needed to evaluate employee performance. Managers can then correct those actions that led to payment of the full amount. Contrast this accounting treatment with recording the purchases at gross cost. If the invoice is paid late, there is no record of the discount because the purchase and the related payment are both recorded at $2,000. Managers lose the notification provided by the Purchase Discounts Lost account.

Petty Cash Disbursements

It would be uneconomical for a business to write a separate check for an executive's taxi fare, a box of pencils needed right away, or the delivery of a special message across town. Therefore, companies keep a small amount of cash on hand to pay for such minor amounts. This fund is called **petty cash.**

Even though the individual amounts paid through the petty cash fund may be small, such expenses occur so often that the total amount over an accounting period may grow quite large. Thus the business needs to set up these controls over petty cash: (1) designate an employee to administer the fund as its custodian, (2) keep a specific amount of cash on hand, (3) support all fund disbursements with a petty cash ticket, and (4) replenish the fund through normal cash disbursement procedures.

OBJECTIVE 6

Account for petty cash transactions

To open the petty cash fund, a payment is approved for a predetermined amount and a check for this amount is issued to Petty Cash. Assume that on February 28 the business decides to establish a petty cash fund of $200. The custodian cashes the check and places the currency and coin in the fund, which may be a cash box, safe, or other device. The petty cash custodian is assigned the responsibility for controlling the fund. Starting the fund is recorded as follows:

Feb. 28	Petty Cash	200	
	Cash in Bank		200
	To open the petty cash fund.		

For each petty cash disbursement, the custodian prepares a *petty cash ticket* like the one illustrated in Exhibit 7-6.

Observe the signatures (or initials, for the custodian) that identify the recipient of petty cash and the fund custodian. Requiring both signatures reduces unauthorized cash disbursements. The custodian keeps all the petty cash tickets in the

EXHIBIT 7-6 *Petty Cash Ticket*

Petty Cash
Ticket

PETTY CASH TICKET		
Date Mar. 25, 19X4		**No.** 45
Amount $23.00		
For Box of floppy diskettes		
Debit Office Supplies, Acct. No. 145		
Received by *Lewis Wright*	**Fund Custodian** WAR	

fund. The sum of the cash plus the total of the ticket amounts should equal the opening balance at all times—in this case, $200. Also, the Petty Cash account keeps its prescribed $200 balance at all times. Maintaining the Petty Cash account at this balance, supported by the fund (cash plus tickets totaling the same amount) is a characteristic of an *imprest system.* The control feature of an imprest system is that it clearly identifies the amount that the custodian is responsible for.

Disbursements reduce the amount of cash in the fund, so periodically the fund must be replenished. Suppose that on March 31 the fund has $118 in cash and $82 in tickets. A check for $82 is issued, made payable to Petty Cash. The fund custodian cashes this check for currency and coins and puts the money in the fund to return its actual cash to $200. The petty cash tickets identify the accounts to be debited: Office Supplies for $23, Delivery Expense for $17, and Miscellaneous Selling Expense for $42. The entry to record replenishment of the fund is

Mar. 31	Office Supplies......................................	23	
	Delivery Expense....................................	17	
	Miscellaneous Selling Expense	42	
	Cash in Bank		82
	To replenish the petty cash fund.		

If this cash payment exceeds the sum of the tickets—that is, if the fund comes up short, Cash Short and Over is debited for the missing amount. If the sum of the tickets exceeds the payment, Cash Short and Over is credited. Note that replenishing the fund does *not* affect the Petty Cash account. Petty Cash keeps its $200 balance at all times.

Whenever petty cash runs low, the fund is replenished. It *must* be replenished on the balance sheet date. Otherwise, the reported balance for Petty Cash will be overstated by the amount of the tickets in the fund. The income statement will understate the expenses listed on these tickets.

Petty Cash is debited only when starting the fund (see the February 28 entry) or changing its amount. In our illustration, suppose the business decides to raise the fund amount from $200 to $250 because of increased demand for petty cash. This step would require a $50 debit to Petty Cash.

The Voucher System

As we saw in Chapter 6, some businesses use the purchases journal and the cash disbursements journal to record cash payments. Other businesses use a voucher system. The **voucher system** for recording cash payments offers the business greater internal control by formalizing the process of approving and recording

OBJECTIVE 7

Use the voucher system

invoices for payment. We will examine the voucher system as it is used by a merchandising business.

The voucher system uses (1) vouchers, (2) a voucher register, (3) an unpaid voucher file, (4) a check register, and (5) a paid voucher file. The merchandising business we discuss has separate departments for purchasing goods, receiving goods, disbursing cash, and accounting.

Vouchers. A **voucher** is a document authorizing a cash disbursement. The accounting department prepares vouchers. Exhibit 7-7 illustrates the voucher of Bliss Wholesale Company. In addition to places for writing in the *payee, due date, terms, description,* and *invoice amount,* the voucher includes a section for designated officers to sign their *approval* for payment. The back of the voucher has places for recording the *account debited, date paid,* and *check number.* You should locate these nine items in Exhibit 7-7.

To better understand the voucher system, let's take an in-depth look at the purchasing process. Exhibit 7-8 lists the various business documents used to ensure that the company receives the goods it ordered and pays only for the goods it has actually received.

EXHIBIT 7-7 *Voucher*

Front of Voucher

			Voucher No. 326
	BLISS WHOLESALE COMPANY		

Payee / Address: Van Heusen, Inc.
4619 Shotwell Avenue
Brooklyn, NY 10564

Due Date: March 7
Terms: 2/10, n/30

Date	Invoice No.	Description	Amount
Mar. 1	6380	144 men's shirts stock no. X14	$1,800

Approved *Jane Trent* — Controller   Approved *Bob Kraft* — Treasurer

Back of Voucher

Voucher No. 326
Payee Van Heusen, Inc.

Invoice Amount $1,800

Discount 36

Net Amount $1,764

Due Date Mar. 7

Date Paid Mar. 6

Check No. 694

Account Distribution

Account Debited	Acct. No.	Amount
Purchases	501	$1,800
Store Supplies	145	
Salary Expense	538	
Advertising Expense	542	
Utilities Expense	548	
Delivery Expense	544	
Total		$1,800

EXHIBIT 7-8   *Purchasing Process*

Business Document	Prepared by	Sent to
Purchase request	Sales department	Purchasing department
Purchase order	Purchasing department	Outside company that sells the needed merchandise (supplier, or vendor)
Invoice	Outside company that sells the needed merchandise (supplier, or vendor)	Accounting department
Receiving report	Receiving department	Accounting department
Voucher	Accounting department	Officer who signs the check

The purchasing process starts when the sales department identifies the need for merchandise and prepares a *purchase request* (or requisition). A separate purchasing department specializes in locating the best buys and mails a *purchase order* to the supplier, the outside company that sells the needed goods. When the supplier ships the goods to the requesting business, the supplier also mails the *invoice* (or bill), which is a notification of the need to pay. As the goods arrive, the receiving department checks them for any damage and lists the merchandise received on a document called the *receiving report*. The accounting department prepares a *voucher* and attaches all the foregoing documents, checks them for accuracy and agreement, and forwards this voucher packet to designated officers for approval and payment. Exhibit 7-9 shows how a voucher packet looks.

Before approving the voucher, the controller and the treasurer should examine a sample of vouchers to determine that the following control steps have been performed by the accounting department:

1. The invoice is compared to a copy of the purchase order and purchase request to ensure that the business pays cash only for the goods that it ordered.
2. The invoice is compared to the receiving report to ensure that cash is paid only for the goods that are actually received.
3. The mathematical accuracy of the invoice is proved.

The voucher packet includes the voucher, invoice, receiving report, purchase order, and purchase request, as shown in Exhibit 7-9.

EXHIBIT 7-9   *Voucher Packet*

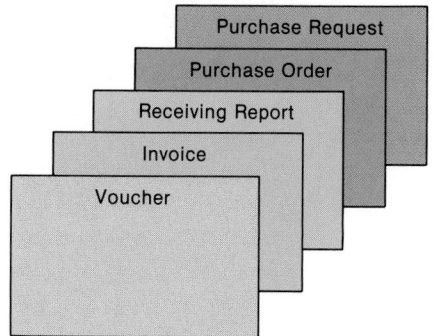

EXHIBIT 7-10   *Voucher Register*

Voucher Register   Page 16

Date	Voucher No.	Payee	Date	Check No.	Vouchers Payable	Purchases	Store Supplies	Salary Expense	Advertising Expense	Utilities Expense	Delivery Expense	Title	No.	Amount
			Payment		Credit	Debit						Other Accounts		
Mar. 1	326	Van Heusen, Inc.	3/6	694	1,800	1,800								
1	327	Howell Properties	3/2	693	1,500							Rent Expense	547	1,500
4	328	Bell Telephone	3/10	696	128					128				
5	329	Schick Supplies	3/11	697	85		85							
8	330	Daily Journal			369				369					
9	331	Ace Delivery Service	3/9	695	37						37			
26	348	Carr Products			1,638	1,638								
28	349	Petty Cash	3/31	717	82		23				17	Miscellaneous Selling Expense	563	42
29	350	Consumers Gas Co.			195					195				
30	351	City National Bank	3/31	718	360							Interest Expense	546	360
31	352	Ralph Grant	3/31	719	864			864						
31		Totals			12,580	6,209	137	1,781	753	602	185			2,913
					(201)	(501)	(145)	(538)	(542)	(548)	(544)			(✓)

Account numbers in parentheses indicate the accounts to which these amounts have been posted.

Voucher Register.   After approval by the designated officers, the voucher goes to the accounting department where it is recorded in the **voucher register.** This journal is similar to the purchases journal (discussed in Chapter 6), but the voucher register is more comprehensive. In a voucher system, *all* expenditures are recorded first in the voucher register. This is a fundamental control feature of the voucher system because it centralizes the initial recording of all expenditures in this one journal. That is, all cash payments must be vouchered and approved prior to payment. For each transaction, the debit is to the account for which payment is being made, and the credit is to Vouchers Payable, the account that replaces Accounts Payable if a voucher system is used. Exhibit 7-10 illustrates the voucher register of Bliss Wholesale Company.

The voucher register has columns to record payment date and check number, which are entered when the voucher is paid. The absence of a payment date and check number means that the voucher is unpaid. In Exhibit 7-10, for example, Bliss Wholesale has a $2,202 liability at March 31 for vouchers 330 ($369 payable to the *Daily Journal*), 348 ($1,638 payable to Carr Products), and 350 ($195 payable to Consumers Gas Company). If these were the company's only unpaid vouchers at March 31, the balance sheet would report:

Current liabilities:
    Vouchers payable* $2,202
* Usually reported as Accounts Payable, even by companies that use a voucher system.

Unpaid Voucher File.   After recording a voucher in the voucher register, the accountant places the voucher packet in the unpaid voucher file, where it stays until the voucher is paid. The unpaid voucher file acts as the accounts payable subsidiary ledger because each voucher serves as an individual account payable. There is no need for a separate accounts payable ledger.

The unpaid voucher file has 31 slots, one for each day of the month. Each voucher is filed according to its due date. For example, voucher no. 326, in Exhibit 7-7, was due March 7, so it was filed in the slot marked 7.

Check Register.   The **check register** is the journal in which are recorded all checks issued in a voucher system. It replaces the cash disbursements journal. All entries in the check register debit Vouchers Payable and credit Cash (and Purchase Discounts, as appropriate).

Exhibit 7-11 shows a check register. Notice that all the transactions include a credit to the Cash in Bank account.

On or before the due date, the accountant removes the voucher packet from the unpaid voucher file and sends it to the officers for signing. After the checks are signed, the check number and payment date are entered on the back of the voucher, in the check register, and in the voucher register.

Paid Voucher File.   After payment, the voucher packet is canceled to avoid paying the bill twice. Typically, a hole is punched through the voucher packet. It is then filed alphabetically by payee name. Most businesses also file a copy in numerical sequence by voucher number as a cross reference. With this dual filing system, a voucher can be located using either classification scheme.

In summary, the voucher system works as follows:

1.   The accounting department prepares a *voucher* for each invoice to be paid.
2.   Supporting documents (invoice, receiving report, purchase order, and purchase request) are compared in the accounting department for accuracy and attached to the voucher. These documents make up the *voucher packet.*

EXHIBIT 7-11 *Check Register*

Check Register   **Page 9**

Date	Check No.	Payee	Voucher No.	Debit Vouchers Payable	Credit Purchase Discounts	Credit Cash in Bank
Mar. 1	692	Trent Co.	322	600	18	582
2	693	Howell Properties	327	1,500		1,500
6	694	Van Heusen, Inc.	326	1,800	36	1,764
9	695	Ace Delivery Service	331	37		37
10	696	Bell Telephone	328	128		128
11	697	Schick Supplies	329	85		85
31	717	Petty Cash	349	82		82
31	718	City National Bank	351	360		360
31	719	Ralph Grant	352	864		864
31	720	Krasner Supply Co.	336	92		92
31		Totals		11,406	317	11,089
				(201)	(503)	(103)

Account numbers in parentheses indicate the accounts to which these amounts have been posted.

3. Designated officials examine the supporting documents and approve the voucher for payment.
4. The accounting department enters the voucher payable in the *voucher register.* The entry is a debit to the account of the item purchased (for example, Purchases) and a credit to Vouchers Payable. The voucher remains in the *unpaid voucher file* until payment.
5. Prior to the invoice due date, a check is issued to pay the voucher. The official reviews the supporting documents and signs the check.
6. The accounting department enters the check in the *check register* and updates the voucher and the voucher register to record payment. All checks are debits to Vouchers Payable and credits to Cash.
7. Paid vouchers are canceled and filed by payee name and by voucher number.

   To gain a complete understanding of the voucher system, trace voucher no. 326 from Exhibit 7-7 through the voucher register in Exhibit 7-10 to the check register in Exhibit 7-11. Also, trace the check register entries from Exhibit 7-11 back to Exhibit 7-10.

Computers and Internal Control

Computers have had both positive and negative effects on internal control. On the positive side, their speed of operation and high reliability increase efficiency. On the negative side, computer systems are less flexible than manual systems.

Computers can take data in only one programmed format, whereas humans can process data if it is merely legible.

Effective internal control is as important to computer systems as it is to manual systems. For example, consider the separation of duties. Programmers should not be allowed to physically operate the computers. A computer consultant commented that he had opportunities to steal when he ran computer operations for a large bank. "I alone designed the dividend-payment operation, wrote the program for it, and ran the job on the machine. The operation was so big that it had a mistake tolerance of nearly $100,000. I could have paid at least half that much to myself, in small checks, and the money wouldn't even have been missed." To avoid theft, no one person should have complete control over system design, programming, and machine operation.

The computer has brought about an important development in cash payments. **Electronic funds transfer (EFT)** is a system that relies on electronic impulses— not paper documents—to account for cash transactions. To manage payroll, an employer enters the employee's name, pay rate, and any other needed data on a magnetic tape, which is transferred to a bank. The bank runs the tape, which automatically decreases the business's cash account and increases the employee's cash account. Some retailers use EFT to handle sales. Customers pay with a card that activates a computer. The computer automatically decreases the customer's bank account balance and increases the store's account balance.

EFT systems reduce the cost of processing cash transactions. However, this savings is achieved by reducing the documentary evidence of transactions. Traditional approaches to internal control have relied on documents, so EFT and other computer systems pose a significant challenge to managers and accountants who design and enforce internal control systems. Computer systems also create problems in protecting private information. For example, a group of students in Milwaukee gained access to highly confidential national defense data by computer! Such situations point to the need for computer security measures.

Summary Problem for Your Review

Grudnitski Company established a $300 petty cash fund. James C. Brown is the fund custodian. At the end of the first week, the petty cash fund contains the following:

1. Cash: $171
2. Petty cash tickets:

No.	Amount	Issued to	Signed by	Account Debited
44	$14	B. Jarvis	B. Jarvis and JCB	Office Supplies
45	9	S. Bell	S. Bell	Miscellaneous Expense
47	43	R. Tate	R. Tate and JCB	—
48	33	L. Blair	L. Blair and JCB	Travel Expense

Required

1. Identify the four internal control weaknesses revealed in the above data.
2. Prepare the general journal entries to record:
   a. Establishment of the petty cash fund.

b. Replenishment of the fund. Assume petty cash ticket no. 47 was issued for the purchase of office supplies.

3. What is the balance in the Petty Cash account immediately before replenishment? Immediately after replenishment?

SOLUTION TO REVIEW PROBLEM

Requirement 1. The four internal control weaknesses are

a. Petty cash ticket no. 46 is missing. Coupled with weakness b, this omission raises questions about the administration of the petty cash fund and about how the petty cash funds were used.

b. The $171 cash balance means that $129 has been disbursed ($300 − $171 = $129). However, the total amount of the petty cash tickets is only $99 ($14 + $9 + $43 + $33). The fund, then, is $30 short of cash ($129 − $99 = $30). Was petty cash ticket no. 46 issued for $30? The data in the problem offer no hint that helps answer this question. In a real-world setting, management would investigate the problem.

c. The petty cash custodian (JCB) did not sign petty cash ticket no. 45. This omission may have been an oversight on his part. However, it raises the question of whether he authorized the disbursement. Both the fund custodian and the recipient of cash should sign the ticket.

d. Petty cash ticket no. 47 does not indicate which account to debit. This omission raises two internal control questions. What did Tate do with the money, and what account should be debited? At worst, the funds have been stolen. At best, asking the custodian to reconstruct the transaction from memory is a haphazard way to identify the account to debit.

Requirement 2. Petty cash journal entries:

a. Entry to establish the petty cash fund:

Petty Cash	300	
Cash in Bank		300

b. Entry to replenish the fund:

Office Supplies	14	
Miscellaneous Expense ($9 + $43)	52	
Travel Expense	33	
Cash Short and Over	30	
Cash in Bank		129

Requirement 3. The balance in Petty cash is *always* its specified balance, in this case $300, as shown by posting the above entries to the account:

Petty Cash

(a) 300	

Note that the entry to establish the fund (entry a) debits Petty Cash. The entry to replenish the fund (entry b) neither debits nor credits Petty Cash.

Summary

Internal controls should safeguard assets, ensure accurate accounting records, promote operational efficiency, and encourage adherence to company policies. An effective internal control system includes these features: *reliable personnel, clear-cut assignment of responsibility, proper authorization,* and *separation of duties,* which is the primary element of internal control. Many businesses use security devices, audits, and specially designed documents and records in their internal control systems.

The *bank account* helps to control and safeguard cash. Businesses use the *bank statement* and the *bank reconciliation* to account for banking transactions. An *imprest system* is used to control petty cash disbursements. Many companies record purchases at *net cost* in order to highlight the inefficiency of paying invoices late and thus losing purchase discounts.

Businesses often control cash disbursements by using a *voucher system,* which features the voucher, the unpaid voucher file, the voucher register, and the check register.

Businesses may handle their payroll by computer and through *electronic funds transfers.* Effective computerized internal control systems must meet the same basic standards that good manual systems do.

Self-Study Questions

Test your understanding of the chapter by marking the best answer for each of the following questions.

1. Which of the following is an element of internal control? *(p. 265)*
   a. Safeguarding assets
   b. Ensuring accurate and reliable accounting records
   c. Promoting operational efficiency
   d. Encouraging adherence to company policies
   e. All the above are elements of internal control

2. Which of the characteristics of an effective system of internal control is violated by allowing the employee who handles inventory to also account for inventory? *(p. 268)*
   a. Competent and reliable personnel   c. Proper authorization
   b. Assignment of responsibilities   d. Separation of duties

3. What control function is performed by auditors? *(p. 269)*
   a. Objective opinion of the effectiveness of the internal control system
   b. Assurance that all transactions are accounted for correctly
   c. Communication of the results of the audit to regulatory agencies
   d. Guarantee that a proper separation of duties exists within the business

4. The bank account serves as a control device over *(pp. 270, 279, 280, 281)*
   a. Cash receipts   c. Both of the above
   b. Cash disbursements   d. None of the above

5. Which of the following items appears on the bank side of a bank reconciliation? *(p. 276)*
   a. Book error   c. NSF check
   b. Outstanding check   d. Interest revenue earned on bank balance

6. Which of the following reconciling items requires a journal entry on the books of the company? *(pp. 276, 277)*
   a. Book error   d. Interest revenue earned on bank balance
   b. Outstanding check   e. All but b
   c. NSF check   f. None of the above

7. What is the major internal control measure over the cash receipts of a K-Mart store? *(p. 279)*
   a. Reporting the day's cash receipts to the controller
   b. Preparing a petty cash ticket for all disbursements from the fund
   c. Pricing merchandise at uneven amounts, coupled with use of a cash register

    d. Channeling all cash receipts through the mail room, whose employees have no cash-accounting responsibilities

8. What is the control advantage of the net method of accounting for inventory purchases? *(pp. 281, 282)*
    a. It highlights the inefficiency of losing purchase discounts
    b. It guarantees that all purchase discounts will be taken
    c. It automatically increases the business's cash balance
    d. It results in a higher quality of inventory on hand for customers

9. The internal control feature that is specific to petty cash is *(p. 283)*
    a. Separation of duties   c. Proper authorization
    b. Assignment of responsibility   d. The imprest system

10. The most fundamental control feature provided by a voucher system is *(p. 287)*
    a. Assuring that only approved invoices are paid
    b. Centralizing the recording of all expenditures in one place—the voucher register
    c. Using the check register along with the voucher register
    d. Placing all incoming invoices in the unpaid voucher file

Answers to the self-study questions are at the end of the chapter.

Accounting Vocabulary

accounting controls *(p. 265)*, administrative controls *(p. 265)*, bank collections *(p. 273)*, bank reconciliation *(p. 273)*, bank statement *(p. 271)*, check *(p. 271)*, check register *(p. 287)*, deposit in transit *(p. 273)*, electronic fund transfer *(p. 289)*, internal control *(p. 265)*, nonsufficient fund (NSF) check *(p. 273)*, outstanding check *(p. 273)*, petty cash *(p. 282)*, service charge *(p. 273)*, voucher *(p. 284)*, voucher register *(p. 287)*, voucher system *(p. 283)*.

ASSIGNMENT MATERIAL

Questions

1. Which of the features of effective internal control is the most fundamental? Why?
2. What is the title of the federal act that affects internal control? What requirement does it place on management?
3. Which company employees bear primary responsibility for a company's financial statements and for maintaining the company's system of internal control? How do these persons carry out this responsibility?
4. Identify features of an effective system of internal control.
5. Separation of duties may be divided into four parts. What are they?
6. How can internal control systems be circumvented?
7. Are internal control systems designed to be foolproof and perfect? What is a fundamental constraint in planning and maintaining systems?
8. Briefly state how each of the following serves as an internal control measure over cash: bank account, signature card, deposit ticket, and bank statement.
9. What is the remittance advice of a check? What use does it serve?
10. Each of the items in the following list must be accounted for in the bank reconciliation. Next to each item, enter the appropriate letter from the following possible treatments: (a) bank side of reconciliation—add the item; (b) bank side of reconciliation—subtract the item; (c) book side of reconciliation—add the item; (d) book side of reconciliation—subtract the item.
    _____ Outstanding check   _____ Deposit in transit
    _____ NSF check   _____ Bank collection

_____ Bank service charge
_____ Cost of printed checks
_____ Bank error that decreased bank balance

_____ Customer check returned because of unauthorized signature
_____ Book error that increased balance of Cash account

11. What purpose does a bank reconciliation serve?

12. Suppose a company has six bank accounts, two petty cash funds, and three certificates of deposit that can be withdrawn on demand. How many cash amounts would this company likely report on its balance sheet?

13. What role does a cash register play in an internal control system?

14. Describe internal control procedures for cash received by mail.

15. Large businesses often have elaborate internal control systems that may be uneconomical for small businesses. Where does the internal control rest in small proprietorships, and how do they control cash disbursements?

16. What is the internal control advantage of recording purchases at net cost?

17. What balance does the Petty Cash account have at all times? Does this balance always equal the amount of cash in the fund? When are the two amounts equal? When are they unequal?

18. List the five elements of a voucher system, and briefly describe the purpose of each.

19. Describe how a voucher system works.

20. What documents make up the voucher packet? Describe three procedures that use the voucher packet to ensure that each payment is appropriate.

21. Why should the same employee not write the computer programs for cash disbursements, sign checks, and mail the checks to payees?

Exercises

Exercise 7-1   *Identifying internal control strengths and weaknesses*

The following situations suggest either a strength or weakness in internal control. Identify each as *strength* or *weakness,* and give the reason for your answer.

a. Cash received over the counter is controlled by the sales clerk, who rings up the sale and places the cash in the register. The sales clerk has access to the control tape stored in the register.

b. Cash received by mail goes straight to the accountant, who debits Cash and credits Accounts Receivable from the customer.

c. The vice-president who signs checks assumes the accounting department has matched the invoice with other supporting documents and therefore does not examine the voucher packet.

d. Purchase invoices are recorded at net amount to highlight purchase discounts lost because of late payment.

e. The accounting department orders merchandise and approves vouchers for payment.

f. The operator of the computer has no other accounting or cash-handling duties.

Exercise 7-2   *Identifying internal controls*

Identify the missing internal control characteristic in the following situations:

1. Business is slow at Westwood Movie Theater on Tuesday, Wednesday, and Thursday nights. To reduce expenses the owner decides not to use a ticket taker on those nights. The ticket seller (cashier) is told to keep the tickets as a record of the number sold.

2. The manager of a discount store wants to speed the flow of customers through checkout. She decides to reduce the time spent by cashiers making change, so she prices merchandise at round dollar amounts—such as $8.00 and $15.00—instead of the customary amounts—$7.95 and $14.95.

3. Grocery stores such as Safeway and A&P purchase large quantities of their merchandise from a few suppliers. At another grocery store the manager decides to reduce

paper work. He eliminates the requirement that a receiving department employee prepare a receiving report, which lists the quantities of items received from the supplier.

4. When business is brisk, Seven-Eleven and many other retail stores deposit cash in the bank several times during the day. The manager at another convenience store wants to reduce the time spent by employees delivering cash to the bank, so he starts a new policy. Cash will build up over Saturdays and Sundays, and the total two-day amount will be deposited on Sunday evening.

5. In the course of auditing the records of a company, you find that the same employee orders merchandise and approves invoices for payment.

Exercise 7-3   *Classifying bank reconciliation items*

The following seven items may appear on a bank reconciliation:

1. Outstanding checks.
2. Bank error: the bank charged our account for a check written by another customer.
3. Service charge.
4. Deposits in transit.
5. NSF check.
6. Bank collection of a note receivable on our behalf.
7. Book error: we debited Cash for $1,000. The correct debit was $100.

Classify each item as (a) an addition to the bank balance, (b) a subtraction from the bank balance, (c) an addition to the book balance, or (d) a subtraction from the book balance.

Exercise 7-4   *Bank reconciliation*

Rachel Lazimy's checkbook lists the following:

Date	Check No.	Item	Check	Deposit	Balance
9/1					$525
4	622	Apple Tree Gift Shop	$19		506
9		Dividends		$ 116	622
13	623	Bell Telephone Co.	43		579
14	624	Gulf Oil Co.	58		521
18	625	Cash	50		471
26	626	St. Alban's Episcopal Church	25		446
28	627	Bent Tree Apartments	275		171
30		Paycheck		1,000	1,171

The September bank statement shows:

Balance		$525
Add: Deposits...............................		116
Deduct checks: No.	Amount	
622	$19	
623	43	
624	68*	
625	50	(180)
Other charges:		
Printed checks...........................	$8	
Service charge...........................	6	(14)
Balance		$447

* This is the correct amount of check number 624.

Required:

Prepare Rachel's bank reconcilation at September 30.

Exercise 7-5   *Bank reconciliation*

Gary Walters operates four EXXON stations. He has just received the monthly bank statement at October 31 from First National Bank, and the statement shows an ending balance of $3,968. Listed on the statement are a service charge of $12, two NSF checks totaling $46, and a $9 charge for printed checks. In reviewing his cash records, Walters identifies outstanding checks totaling $467 and an October 31 deposit of $788, which does not appear on the bank statement. During October he recorded a $190 check for the salary of a part-time employee by debiting Salary Expense and crediting Cash for $19. Walters's cash account shows an October 31 cash balance of $4,527. Prepare the bank reconciliation at October 31.

Exercise 7-6   *Journal entries from a bank reconciliation*

Using the data from Exercise 7-5, record the entries that Walters should make in the general journal on October 31. Include an explanation for each entry.

Exercise 7-7   *Income statements with purchases at gross and at net*

Motorex, Inc., began July with inventory of $470,000 and ended the month with inventory of $510,000. During July the company purchased $800,000 of inventory and took the 2 percent discount on $700,000 of the purchases. The remaining $100,000 in inventory cost was paid after the discount period. Sales during July were $1,600,000, and operating expenses (including income tax) were $490,000.

Required:

1. Prepare the company's income statement for July assuming Motorex records inventory purchases at gross cost.
2. Prepare the company's income statement for July assuming the company records inventory purchases at net cost.
3. Which method provides the internal control advantage? Describe how this internal control feature works.

Exercise 7-8   *Accounting for petty cash*

United Way of Altoona, Pennsylvania, created a $100 imprest petty cash fund. During the first month of use, the fund custodian authorized and signed petty cash tickets as follows:

Ticket No.	Item	Account Debited	Amount
1	Delivery of pledge cards to donors	Delivery Expense	$19.22
2	Mail package	Postage Expense	2.80
3	Newsletter	Supplies Expense	4.14
4	Key to closet	Miscellaneous Expense	.85
5	Waste basket	Miscellaneous Expense	3.78
6	Staples	Supplies Expense	5.37

Required:

1. Make general journal entries for creation of the petty cash fund and its replenishment. Include explanations.
2. Immediately prior to replenishment, describe the items in the fund.
3. Immediately after replenishment, describe the items in the fund.

Exercise 7-9   *Purchases at gross and at net*

McCabe Hardware Company uses a voucher system. Prepare its general journal entries for the following transactions under two assumptions (explanations are not required):

Assumption 1 — Inventory purchases recorded at gross cost
Assumption 2 — Inventory purchases recorded at net cost

May 3   Purchased inventory costing $3,600 on account, subject to terms of 2/10 n/30
     11   Paid the liability created on May 3.
     14   Purchased inventory costing $2,200 on account, subject to terms of 2/10 n/30.
     27   Paid the liability created on May 14.

Which method provides the hardware store with a measure of discounts lost? Describe how this internal control feature works.

Exercise 7-10   *Petty cash; cash short and over*

Record the following selected transactions in general journal format (explanations are not required):

April 1   Issued voucher no. 637 to establish a petty cash fund with a $250 balance.
       1   Issued check no. 344 to pay voucher no. 637.
       2   Journalized the day's cash sales. Cash register tapes show a $2,859 total, but the cash in the register is only $2,853.
      10   The petty cash fund has $119 in cash and $131 in petty cash tickets issued to pay for Office Supplies ($61), Delivery Expense ($23), and Entertainment Expense ($47). Issued voucher no. 669 to replenish the fund.
      10   Issued check no. 402 to pay voucher no. 669.

Problems   *(Group A)*

Problem 7-1A   *Identifying internal control weaknesses*

Each of the following situations has an internal control weakness:

   a. Myra Jones, a widow with no known sources of outside income, has been a trusted employee of Stone Products Company for 15 years. She performs all cash handling and accounting duties, including opening the mail, preparing the bank deposit, accounting for all aspects of cash and accounts receivable, and preparing the bank reconciliation. She has just purchased a new Cadillac and a new home in an expensive suburb. Lou Stone, the owner of the company, wonders how she can afford these luxuries on her salary.

   b. Linda Cyert employs three professional interior designers in her design studio. She is located in an area with a lot of new construction, and her business is booming. Ordinarily, Linda does all the purchasing of furniture, draperies, carpets, fabrics, sewing services, and other materials and labor needed to complete jobs. During the summer she takes a long vacation, and in her absence she allows each designer to purchase materials and labor. At her return, Cyert reviews operations and notes that expenses are much higher and net income much lower than in the past.

   c. Discount stores such as Target, Solo-Serve, and Medallion receive a large portion of their sales revenue in cash, with the remainder in credit card sales. To reduce expenses, a store manager ceases purchasing fidelity bonds on the cashiers.

   d. The office supply company from which Dysan Stereo Center purchases cash receipt forms recently notified Dysan that the last shipped receipts were not prenumbered. Stan

Dysan, the owner, replied that he did not use the receipt numbers, so the omission is not important.

   e. Lancer Computer Programs is a software company that specializes in computer programs with accounting applications. Their most popular program prepares the general journal, cash receipts journal, voucher register, check register, accounts receivable subsidiary ledger, and general ledger. In the company's early days, the owner and eight employees wrote the computer programs, lined up manufacturers to produce the diskettes, sold the products to stores such as ComputerLand and ComputerCraft, and performed the general management and accounting of the company. As the company has grown, the number of employees has increased dramatically. Recently, the development of a new software program stopped while the programmers redesigned Lancer's accounting system. Lancer's own accountants could have performed this task.

Required

1. Identify the missing internal control characteristic in each situation.
2. Identify the business's possible problem.
3. Propose a solution to the problem.

Problem 7-2A   *Bank reconciliation and related journal entries*

The May 31 bank statement of Malcolm & Fisk, a partnership, has just arrived from Lake Star Bank. To prepare the Malcolm & Fisk bank reconciliation, you gather the following data:

1. The May 31 bank balance is $4,119.82.
2. The bank statement includes two charges for returned checks from customers. One is an NSF check in the amount of $67.50 received from Harley Doherty, a customer, recorded on the books by a debit to Cash, and deposited on May 19. The other is a $195.03 check received from Maria Gucci and deposited on May 21. It was returned by Ms. Gucci's bank with the imprint "Unauthorized Signature."
3. The following Malcolm & Fisk checks are outstanding at May 31:

Check No.	Amount
616	$403.00
802	74.25
806	36.60
809	161.38
810	229.05
811	48.91

4. The bank statement includes two special deposits: $688.14, which is the amount of dividend revenue the bank collected from General Electric Company on behalf of Malcolm & Fisk; and $16.86, the interest revenue Malcolm & Fisk earned on its bank balance during May.
5. The bank statement lists a $6.25 subtraction for the bank service charge.
6. On May 31 the Malcolm & Fisk treasurer deposited $381.14, but this deposit does not appear on the bank statement.
7. The bank statement includes a $410.00 deduction for a check drawn by Marimont Freight Company. Malcolm & Fisk promptly notified the bank of its error.
8. Malcolm & Fisk's Cash account shows a balance of $3,521.55 on May 31.

Required

1. Prepare the bank reconciliation for Malcolm & Fisk at May 31.
2. Record in general journal form the entries necessary to bring the book balance of Cash into agreement with the adjusted book balance on the reconciliation. Include an explanation for each entry.

Problem 7-3A   *Bank reconciliation and related journal entries*

Assume selected columns of the cash receipts journal and the check register of Radio Shack Store No. 147 appear as follows at March 31, 19X5:

Cash Receipts Journal (Posting reference is CR)		*Check Register* (Posting reference is CD)	
Date	Cash Debit	Check No.	Cash Credit
Mar. 4	$2,716	1413	$ 1,465
9	544	1414	1,004
11	1,655	1415	450
14	896	1416	8
17	367	1417	775
25	890	1418	88
31	2,038	1419	4,126
Total	$9,106	1420	760
		1421	200
		1422	2,267
		Total	$11,143

Assume the Cash account of the Radio Shack store shows the following information on March 31, 19X5.

Cash

Date	Item	Jrnl. Ref.	Debit	Credit	Balance
Mar. 1	Balance				14,188
31		CR. 10	9,106		23,294
31		CD. 16		11,143	12,151

Radio Shack Store No. 147 received the following bank statement on March 31, 19X5.

Bank Statement for March 19X5

Beginning balance		$14,188
Deposits and other Credits:		
Mar. 5.	$2,716	
10.	544	
11.	1,655	
15.	896	
18.	367	
25.	890	
31.	1,000 BC	8,068
Checks and other Debits:		
Mar. 8.	441 NSF	
9.	1,465	
13.	1,004	
14.	450	
15.	8	
22.	775	
29.	88	
31.	4,216	
31.	25 SC	8,472
Ending balance		$13,784

Explanation: BC-Bank Collection   NSF-Nonsufficient Fund Check   SC-Service Charge

Additional data for the bank reconciliation include:

1. The NSF check was received late in February from L. M. Arnett.
2. The $1,000 bank collection of a note receivable on March 31 included $122 interest revenue.
3. The correct amount of check number 1419, a payment on account, is $4,216. (The Radio Shack accountant mistakenly recorded the check for $4,126.)

Required

1. Prepare the bank reconciliation of Radio Shack Store No. 147 at March 31, 19X5.
2. Record the entries based on the bank reconciliation. Include explanations.

Problem 7-4A   *Recording and reporting purchases at gross and at net*

Superior Products Company does not use a voucher system. On May 1 of the current year the company had inventory of $58,000. On May 31 the company had inventory of $53,700. Net sales for May were $212,800, and operating expenses were $65,100. During May Superior completed the following transactions:

May 3 Purchased inventory costing $38,500 under terms of 2/10 n/30.
  7 Returned $2,000 of the inventory purchased on May 3.
  10 Purchased inventory costing $28,500 on credit terms of 2/10 n/45.
  12 Paid the amount owed from the May 3 invoice, net of the return on May 7 and also net of the discount.
  18 Purchased inventory costing $31,900 on credit terms of 2/10 n/30.
  19 Paid for the inventory purchased on May 10, less the discount.
  29 Paid the gross amount of the purchase on May 18, missing the discount because payment occurred after the discount period.

Required

1. Assuming Superior records inventory purchases at gross cost:
   a. Record the transactions in a general journal. Explanations are not required.
   b. Prepare the company's income statement for May of the current year.
2. Assuming Superior records inventory purchases at net cost:
   a. Record the transactions in a general journal. Explanations are not required.
   b. Prepare the company's income statement for May of the current year.
3. Which method of recording purchases offers the internal control advantage? Give your reason.

Problem 7-5A   *Accounting for petty cash transactions*

Suppose that on April 1 Texaco opens a regional office in Oklahoma City and creates a petty cash fund with an imprest balance of $200. During April, Eleanor McGillicuddy, the fund custodian, signs the following petty cash tickets:

Ticket Number	Item	Amount
101	Pencils	$ 6.89
102	Cab fare for executive	14.50
103	Delivery of package across town	7.75
104	Dinner money for executives entertaining a customer	80.00
105	Postage for package received	10.00
106	Christmas decorations for office party	18.22
107	Two boxes of floppy disks	14.37

On April 30, prior to replenishment, the fund contains these tickets plus $45.27. The accounts affected by petty cash disbursements are Office Supplies Expense, Travel Expense, Delivery Expense, Entertainment Expense, and Postage Expense.

Required

1. Discuss the characteristics and the internal control features of an imprest fund.
2. Make the general journal entries to create the fund and to replenish it. Include explanations. Also, briefly describe what the custodian does on these dates.
3. Make the entry on May 1 to increase the fund balance to $300. Include an explanation, and briefly describe what the custodian does.

Problem 7-6A   *Voucher system entries*

Assume R. H. Macy & Company, Inc., the department-store chain, uses a voucher system and records purchases at *gross* cost. Assume further that a Macy store completed the following transactions during July:

July 2 Issued voucher no. 614 payable to Hathaway Shirt Company for the purchase of inventory costing $16,000, with payment terms of 2/10 n/30.

3 Issued voucher no. 615 payable to Edison Electric for electricity usage of $2,589.

5 Issued check no. 344 to pay voucher no. 614, less the discount.

6 Issued voucher no. 616 payable to Baylor Supply Company for inventory costing $850, with payment terms of 2/10 n/45.

7 Issued check no. 345 to pay voucher no. 615.

13 Issued voucher no. 617 payable to replenish the petty cash fund. The payee is Petty Cash, the amount is $203, and the petty cash tickets list store supplies ($119), delivery expense ($48), and miscellaneous expense ($36). Also issued check no. 346 to pay the voucher.

14 Issued check no. 347 to pay voucher no. 616, less the discount.

18 Issued voucher no. 618 payable to the *New York Times* for advertising, $2,800.

19 Issued voucher no. 619 payable to Levi Strauss & Company for inventory costing $65,800, with payment terms of 3/10 n/30.

28 Issued voucher no. 620 payable to city of New York for property tax of $9,165.

30 Issued check no. 348 to pay voucher no. 619. Because of a filing error, we failed to earn the discount.

31 Issued voucher no. 621 payable to Maine Bank for interest expense of $7,000.

31 Issued voucher no. 622 to pay executive salary of $4,644 to Sharon Kratzman. Also issued check no. 349 to pay the voucher.

Required

1. Record Macy's transactions in a voucher register and a check register like those illustrated in the chapter. Posting references are unnecessary.
2. Open the Vouchers Payable account with a zero beginning balance, and post amounts to that account.
3. Prepare the list of unpaid vouchers at July 31 and show that the total matches the balance of Vouchers Payable.

Problem 7-7A   *Voucher system; purchases at net*

Assume that the Macy store in Problem 7-6A records its purchases of inventory and supplies at *net* cost.

Required

1. Record the transactions of Problem 7-6A in a voucher register and a check register. To

account for purchase discounts lost, it is necessary to use a check register designed as follows:

Check Register

				Debit		Credit
Date	Check No.	Payee	Voucher No.	Vouchers Payable	Purchase Discounts Lost	Cash in Bank

2. Post to the Vouchers Payable account.
3. Prepare the list of unpaid vouchers at July 31 and show that the total matches the balance of Vouchers Payable.

(Group B)

Problem 7-1B   *Identifying internal control weaknesses*

Each of the following situations has an internal control weakness.

a. Most large companies have internal audit staffs that continuously evaluate the business's internal control. Part of the auditor's job is to evaluate how efficiently the company is running. For example, is the company purchasing inventory from the least expensive wholesaler? After a particularly bad year, Mason Tile Company eliminates its internal audit department to reduce expenses.

b. CPA firms, law firms, and other professional organizations use paraprofessional employees to do some of their routine tasks. For example, an accounting paraprofessional might examine documents to assist a CPA in conducting an audit. In the CPA firm of Grosso & Howe, Lou Grosso, the senior partner, turns over a significant portion of his high-level audit work to his paraprofessional staff.

c. In evaluating the internal control over cash disbursements, an auditor learns that the purchasing agent is responsible for purchasing diamonds for use in the company's manufacturing process, approving the invoices for payment, and signing the checks. No supervisor reviews the purchasing agent's work.

d. Grant Kowalzyak owns a firm that performs engineering services. His staff consists of twelve professional engineers, and he manages the office. Often his work requires him to travel to meet with clients. During the past six months he has observed that when he returns from a business trip, the engineering jobs in the office have not progressed satisfactorily. He learns that when he is away several of his senior employees take over office management and neglect their engineering duties. One employee could manage the office.

e. Lew Jackson has been an employee of Brazleton Lumber Company for many years. Because the business is relatively small, Lew performs all accounting duties, including opening the mail, preparing the bank deposit, and preparing the bank reconciliation.

Required

1. Identify the missing internal control characteristic in each situation.
2. Identify the business's possible problem.
3. Propose a solution to the problem.

Problem 7-2B   *Bank reconciliation and related journal entries*

The August 31 bank statement of Spinnaker Software has just arrived from United Bank. To prepare the Spinnaker bank reconciliation, you gather the following data:

1. Spinnaker's Cash account shows a balance of $5,503.77 on August 31.
2. The bank statement includes two charges for returned checks from customers. One is a $395.00 check received from Shoreline Express and deposited on August 20, returned by Shoreline's bank with the imprint "Unauthorized Signature." The other is an NSF check in the amount of $146.67 received from Lipsey, Inc. This check had been deposited on August 17.
3. The following Spinnaker checks are outstanding at August 31:

Check No.	Amount
237	$ 46.10
288	141.00
291	578.05
293	11.87
294	609.51
295	8.88
296	101.63

4. The bank statement includes a deposit of $1,191.17, collected by the bank on behalf of Spinnaker. Of the total, $1,011.81 is collection of a note receivable, and the remainder is interest revenue.
5. The bank statement shows that Spinnaker earned $38.19 on its bank balance during August. This amount was added to Spinnaker's account by the bank.
6. The bank statement lists a $10.50 subtraction for the bank service charge.
7. On August 31 the Spinnaker treasurer deposited $193.78, but this deposit does not appear on the bank statement.
8. The bank statement includes a $300.00 deposit that Spinnaker did not make. The bank erroneously had credited the Spinnaker account for another bank customer's deposit.
9. The August 31 bank balance is $7,784.22.

Required

1. Prepare the bank reconciliation for Spinnaker Software at August 31.
2. Record in general journal form the entries necessary to bring the book balance of Cash into agreement with the adjusted book balance on the reconciliation. Include an explanation for each entry.

Problem 7-3B *Bank reconciliation and related journal entries*

Assume selected columns of the cash receipts journal and the check register of Computer-Land Store No. 89 appear as follows at April 30, 19X4:

Cash Receipts Journal (Posting reference is CR)		Check Register (Posting reference is CD)	
Date	Cash Debit	Check No.	Cash Credit
Apr. 2	$ 4,174	3113	$ 991
8	407	3114	147
10	559	3115	1,930
16	2,187	3116	664
22	1,854	3117	1,472
29	1,060	3118	1,000
30	337	3119	632
		3120	1,675
Total	$10,578	3121	100
		3122	2,413
		Total	$11,024

Assume the Cash account of the ComputerLand store shows the following information at April 30, 19X4.

Cash

Date	Item	Jrnl. Ref.	Debit	Credit	Balance
Apr. 1	Balance				7,911
30		CR.6	10,578		18,489
30		CD.11		11,024	7,465

ComputerLand Store No. 89 received the following bank statement on April 30, 19X4.

Bank Statement for April 19X4

Beginning balance....................................		$ 7,911
Deposits and other Credits:		
Apr. 4.........................	$4,174	
9.........................	407	
12.........................	559	
17.........................	2,187	
22.........................	1,185 BC	
23.........................	1,854	10,366
Checks and other Debits:		
Apr. 7.........................	$ 991	
13.........................	1,390	
14.........................	903 US	
15.........................	147	
18.........................	664	
26.........................	1,472	
30.........................	1,000	
30.........................	20 SC	6,587
Ending Balance		$11,690

Explanation: BC-Bank Collection US-Unauthorized Signature SC-Service Charge

Additional data for the bank reconciliation include:

1. The unauthorized signature check was received from S. M. Holt.
2. The $1,185 bank collection of a note receivable on April 22 included $185 interest revenue.
3. The correct amount of check number 3115, a payment on account, is $1,390. (The ComputerLand accountant mistakenly recorded the check for $1,930.)

Required

1. Prepare the bank reconciliation of ComputerLand Store No. 89 at April 30, 19X4.
2. Record the entries based on the bank reconciliation. Include explanations.

Problem 7-4B *Recording and reporting purchases at gross and at net*

Randolph Distributing Company does not use a voucher system. On June 1 of the current year, the company had inventory of $71,300. On June 30 the company had inventory of $74,100. Net sales for June were $263,700, and operating expenses were $106,200. During June Randolph completed the following transactions:

June 2 Purchased inventory costing $41,800 under terms of 2/10 n/30.

   8 Returned $5,800 of the inventory purchased on June 2.

   11 Purchased inventory costing $39,000 on credit terms of 2/10 n/45.

   11 Paid the amount owed from the June 2 invoice, net of the return on June 8 and also net of the discount.

   17 Purchased inventory costing $52,300 on credit terms of 2/10 n/30.

   20 Paid for the inventory purchased on June 11, less the discount.

   30 Paid the gross amount of the purchase on June 17, missing the discount because payment occurred after the discount period.

Required

1. Assuming Randolph records inventory purchases at gross cost:
   a. Record the transactions in a general journal. Explanations are not required.
   b. Prepare the company's income statement for June of the current year.
2. Assuming Randolph records inventory purchases at net cost:
   a. Record the transactions in a general journal. Explanations are not required.
   b. Prepare the company's income statement for June of the current year.
3. Which method of recording purchases offers the internal control advantage? Give your reason.

Problem 7-5B   *Accounting for petty cash transactions*

Suppose that on June 1 Goodyear Tire and Rubber Company opens a district office in Salt Lake City and creates a petty cash fund with an imprest balance of $350. During June Mordecai Klever, the fund custodian, signs the following petty cash tickets:

Ticket Number	Item	Amount
1	Postage for package received	$26.20
2	Decorations and refreshments for office party	13.19
3	Two boxes of floppy disks	16.82
4	Typewriter ribbons	27.13
5	Dinner money for sales manager entertaining a customer	50.00
6	Plane ticket for executive business trip to Cody, Wyoming	69.00
7	Delivery of package across town	6.30

On June 30, prior to replenishment, the fund contains these tickets plus $155.51. The accounts affected by petty cash disbursements are Office Supplies Expense, Travel Expense, Delivery Expense, Entertainment Expense, and Postage Expense.

Required

1. Discuss the characteristics and the internal control features of an imprest fund.
2. Make the general journal entries to create the fund and to replenish it. Include explanations. Also, briefly describe what the custodian does on these dates.
3. Make the entry on July 1 to increase the fund balance to $500. Include an explanation, and briefly describe what the custodian does.

Problem 7-6B   *Voucher system entries*

Assume a ComputerLand store in Phoenix, Arizona, uses a voucher system and records purchases at *gross* cost. Assume further that the store completed the following transactions during January:

Jan 3 Issued voucher no. 135 payable to Western Telephone for telephone service of $1,007.

5 Issued voucher no. 136 payable to IBM for the purchase of inventory costing $21,500, with payment terms of 3/10 n/30.

6 Issued voucher no. 137 payable to City Supply Company for inventory costing $250, with payment terms of 2/10 n/45.

7 Issued check no. 404 to pay voucher no. 136, less the discount.

10 Issued check no. 405 to pay voucher no. 135.

14 Issued check no. 406 to pay voucher no. 137, less the discount.

15 Issued voucher no. 138 payable to the *Phoenix Sun* for advertising of $1,990.

17 Issued voucher no. 139 payable to replenish the petty cash fund. The payee is Petty Cash, the amount is $176, and the petty cash tickets list Store Supplies ($16), Delivery Expense ($96), and Miscellaneous Expense ($64). Also issued check no. 407 to pay the voucher.

18 Issued voucher no. 140 payable to Apple Computer Company for inventory costing $27,600, with payment terms of 2/10 n/30.

24 Issued voucher no. 141 payable to city of Phoenix for property tax of $4,235. Debit Property Tax Expenses.

27 Issued voucher no. 142 payable to First State Bank for payment of a note payable ($10,000) and interest expense ($1,200).

30 Issued check no. 408 to pay voucher no. 140. Because of a filing error, we paid after the discount period and failed to earn the discount.

31 Issued voucher no. 143 to pay salesperson salary of $2,309 to Lester Gibbs. Also issued check no. 409 to pay the voucher.

Required

1. Record ComputerLand's transactions in a voucher register and a check register like those illustrated in the chapter. Posting references are unnecessary.

2. Open the Vouchers Payable account and post amounts to that account.

3. Prepare the list of unpaid vouchers at January 31 and show that the total matches the balance of Vouchers Payable.

Problem 7-7B   *Voucher system; purchases at net*

Assume that the ComputerLand store in Problem 7-6B records its purchases of inventory and supplies at *net* cost.

Required

1. Record the transactions of Problem 7-6B in a voucher register and a check register. To account for purchase discounts lost, it is necessary to use a check register designed as follows:

				Debit		Credit
Date	Check No.	Payee	Voucher No.	Vouchers Payable	Purchase Discounts Lost	Cash in Bank

Check Register Page 4

2. Post to the Vouchers Payable account.

3. Prepare the list of unpaid vouchers at July 31, and show that the total matches the balance of Vouchers Payable.

Decision Problem

Using the Bank Reconciliation to Detect a Theft

Schaeffer Art Supply has poor internal control over its cash transactions. Recently G. M. Schaeffer, the owner, has suspected the cashier of stealing. Details of the business's cash position at September 30 follow.

1. The Cash account shows a balance of $19,502. This amount includes a September 30 deposit of $3,794 that does not appear on the September 30 bank statement.
2. The September 30 bank statement shows a balance of $15,924. The bank statement lists a $200 credit for a bank collection, an $8 debit for the service charge, and a $36 debit for an NSF check. The Schaeffer accountant has not recorded any of these items on the books.
3. At September 30 the following checks are outstanding:

Check No.	Amount
154	$116
256	150
278	253
291	190
292	206
293	145

4. The cashier handles all incoming cash and makes bank deposits. He also reconciles the monthly bank statement. His September 30 reconciliation follows.

Balance per books, September 30...............			$19,502
Add: Outstanding checks......................			60
Bank collection			200
			19,762
Less: Deposits in transit................		$3,794	
Service charge..................		8	
NSF check......................		36	3,838
Balance per bank, September 30			$15,924

Schaeffer has requested that you determine whether the cashier has stolen cash from the business and, if so, how much. Schaeffer also asks you to identify how the cashier has attempted to conceal the theft. To make this determination, you perform your own bank reconciliation using the format illustrated in the chapter. There are no bank or book errors. Schaeffer also asks you to evaluate the internal controls and to recommend any changes needed to improve them.

Financial Statement Problem

Internal Controls and Cash

Study the audit opinion of Gulf+Western's financial statements, given at the beginning of Appendix C. Answer the following questions about Gulf+Western's internal controls and cash position.

1. What is the name of Gulf+Western's outside auditing firm? What office of this firm signed the audit? How long after Gulf+Western's fiscal year end did the auditors issue their opinion?
2. Does it appear that Gulf+Western's internal controls are adequate? How can you tell?

3. What standard of auditing did the outside auditors use in examining the Gulf+Western financial statements? By what accounting standards were the Gulf+Western statements evaluated?

4. By how much did Gulf+Western's cash position increase during fiscal 1987? The statement of cash flows (discussed in detail in a later chapter) tells why this increase occurred. Which type of activity—operating, investment, or financing—contributed most to this increase?

Answers to Self-Study Questions

1. e	3. a	5. b	7. c	9. d
2. d	4. c	6. e	8. a	10. b

Accounts and Notes Receivable

From automobiles to houses to bicycles to dinners, people buy on credit every day. As high as annual credit sales for retailers are, credit sales are even higher for manufacturers and wholesalers. Clearly, credit sales lie at the heart of the United States economy, as they do in other developed countries.

Each credit transaction involves at least two parties—the **creditor,** who sells a service or merchandise and obtains a receivable, and the **debtor,** who makes the purchase and creates a payable. This chapter focuses on the creditor's accounting. The accounts that generally appear on a creditor's balance sheet are highlighted in Exhibit 8-1. We will discuss these accounts in our study of receivables.

Different Types of Receivables

A receivable arises when a business (or person) sells goods or services to a second business (or person) on credit. A receivable is the seller's claim against the buyer for the amount of the transaction.

Receivables are monetary claims against businesses and individuals. They are acquired mainly by selling goods and services and by lending money.

The two major types of receivables are accounts receivable and notes receivable. A business's *accounts receivable* are the amounts that its customers owe it. These accounts receivable are sometimes called *trade receivables.* They are *current assets.*

Accounts receivable should be distinguished from accruals, notes and other assets not arising from everyday sales because accounts receivable pertain to the main thrust of the business's operations. Moreover, amounts included as accounts receivable should be collectible according to the business's normal sale terms (such as net 30, or 2/10 n/30).

EXHIBIT 8-1 *Balance Sheet*

Example Company			
Balance Sheet			
Date			

Assets			**Liabilities**		
Current:			Current:		
Cash		$X,XXX	Accounts payable		$X,XXX
Accounts receivable	$X,XXX		Notes payable, short-term		X,XXX
Less Allowance for uncollectible			Accrued current liabilities		X,XXX
accounts	(XXX)	X,XXX	Total current liabilities		X,XXX
Notes receivable, short-term		X,XXX			
Inventories............................		X,XXX			
Prepaid expenses........................		X,XXX	Long-term:		
Total.............................		X,XXX	Notes payable, long-term........		X,XXX
			Total liabilities		X,XXX
Investments and long-term receivables:					
Investments in other companies		X,XXX			
Notes receivable, long-term		X,XXX			
Other receivables		X,XXX			
Total.............................		X,XXX	**Owner's Equity**		
Plant assets:					
Property, plant, and equipment............		X,XXX	Capital		X,XXX
Total assets		$X,XXX	Total liabilities and owner's equity....		$X,XXX

Notes receivable are more formal than accounts receivable. The debtor in a note receivable arrangement promises in writing to pay the creditor a definite sum at a definite future date. The terms of these notes usually extend for at least 60 days. A written document known as a *promissory note,* serves as evidence of the receivable. A note may require the debtor to pledge *security* for the loan. This means that the borrower promises that the lender may claim certain assets if the borrower fails to pay the amount due at maturity.

Notes receivable due within one year or less are *current assets.* Those notes due beyond one year are *long-term receivables.* Some notes receivable are collected in periodic installments. The portion due within one year is a current asset, with the remaining amount a long-term asset. GM may hold a $6,000 note receivable from you, but only the $1,500 you owe on it this year is a current asset to GM.

Other receivables is a miscellaneous category that includes loans to employees and branch companies. Usually these are long-term assets but they are current if receivable within one year or less. Long-term notes receivable, and other receivables are often reported on the balance sheet after current assets and before plant assets as shown in Exhibit 8-1.

Each type of receivable is a separate account in the general ledger and may be supported by a subsidiary ledger if needed.

The Credit Department

A customer who buys goods using a credit card is buying on account. This transaction creates a receivable for the store. Most companies with a high proportion of sales on account have a separate credit department. This department evaluates customers who apply for credit cards by using standard formulas—which include the applicant's income and credit history, among other factors—for deciding which customers the store will sell to on account. After approving a customer, the credit department monitors customer payment records. Customers with a history of paying on time may receive higher credit limits. Those who fail to pay on time have their limits reduced or eliminated. The credit department also assists the accounting department in measuring collection losses on customers who do not pay.

Uncollectible Accounts (Bad Debts) _____

Selling on credit creates both a benefit and a cost. Customers unwilling or unable to pay cash immediately may make a purchase on credit. Revenue and profit rise as sales increase. The cost to the seller of extending credit arises from the failure to collect from some credit customers. Accountants label this cost **uncollectible account expense, doubtful account expense,** or **bad debt expense.**

The extent of uncollectible account expense varies from company to company. It depends on the credit risks that managers are willing to accept. Many small retail businesses accept a higher level of risk than do large stores like Sears. Why? Small businesses often have personal ties to customers, which increases the likelihood that customers will pay their accounts.

Measuring Uncollectible Accounts

For a firm that sells on credit, uncollectible account expense is as much a part of doing business as salary expense and depreciation expense. Uncollectible Account Expense—an operating expense—must be measured, recorded, and reported. To do so, accountants use the direct write-off method or the allowance method.

Direct Write-off Method. Under the **direct write-off method** of accounting for bad debts, the company waits until the credit department decides that a customer's account receivable is uncollectible. Then the accountant debits Uncollectible Account Expense and credits the customer's account receivable to write off the account.

Assume it is 19X2 and most credit customers have paid for their 19X1 purchases. At this point, the credit department believes that two customers—Garcia and Smith—will never pay. The department directs the accountant to write off Garcia and Smith as bad debts.

The following entries show the business's accounting for 19X1 credit sales and 19X2 collections and uncollectible accounts.

19X1	Accounts Receivable–Garcia	800	
	Accounts Receivable–Smith	1,200	
	Accounts Receivable–Various Customers	98,000	
	Sales Revenue		100,000
	To record credit sales of $100,000.		
19X2	Cash	97,000	
	Accounts Receivable–Various Customers		97,000
	To record cash collections of $97,000.		

19X2	Uncollectible Account Expense.....................	2,000	
	Accounts Receivable – Garcia		800
	Accounts Receivable – Smith		1,200
	To write off uncollectible accounts and record bad debt expense of $2,000.		

Of course, this company would continue making credit sales as an important part of doing business. But what we want to know right now is how the direct write-off method affects financial statements. To see its impact most clearly, let's assume that the company stopped making credit sales altogether in 19X2. Consider the following partial financial statements for 19X1 and 19X2, based on the above journal entries.

Income Statement:	**19X1**	**19X2**
Revenue		
Sales revenue.....................................	$100,000	$ -0-
Expense		
Uncollectible account expense	-0-	2,000

	December 31,	
Balance Sheet:	**19X1**	**19X2**
Accounts receivable................................	$100,000	$1,000

Let's ask two important questions about this approach to accounting for bad debts.

1. How accurately does the direct write-off method measure income? As we have seen, following generally accepted accounting principles means matching an accounting period's expenses against its revenues. This provides the most accurate picture of operating income, which measures how well a business's operations are running. But the direct write-off method does not match a period's bad debt expense against the same period's sales revenues. In our example, the full amount of sales revenue appears for 19X1, but the expenses incurred to generate this revenue—the bad debts—appear in 19X2. This gives misleading income figures for both years, as would failing to report any other expense— salary, depreciation, and so on—in the correct period. The $2,000 bad debt expense should be matched against the $100,000 sales revenue.

2. How accurately does the direct write-off method value accounts receivable? The 19X1 balance sheet shows accounts receivable at the full $100,000 figure. But any businessperson knows that bad debts are unavoidable when selling on credit. No intelligent manager expects to collect the entire amount. Is the $100,000 figure, then, the expected realizable value of the account? No, showing the full $100,000 in the balance sheet falsely implies that these accounts receivable are worth their face value.

The direct write-off method is simple to use, and it causes no great error if collection losses are insignificant in amount. However, you see that the resulting accounting records are not as accurate as they could be. The allowance method is a better way to account for uncollectible account expense.

Allowance Method.   To present the most accurate financial statements possible, accountants in firms with large credit sales use the **allowance method** of measuring bad debts. This method records collection losses based on estimates prior to determining that the business will not collect from specific customers.

Smart managers know that not every customer will pay in full. But they should not simply credit Accounts Receivable for the amount they believe will not be collected. That would cause the balance of Accounts Receivable to be less than the total of the individual accounts, and managers do not simply write off a customer's account on a hunch.

Rather than try to guess which accounts will go bad, managers, based on collection experience, estimate the total bad debt expense for the period. The business debits Uncollectible Account Expense (or Doubtful Account Expense) for the estimated amount and credits **Allowance for Uncollectible Accounts** (or **Allowance for Doubtful Accounts**), a contra account related to Accounts Receivable. This account shows the estimated amount of collection losses.

To properly match expense against revenue, the uncollectible account expense is estimated — based on past collection experience — and recorded when the sales are made. This expense entry has two effects: (1) it decreases net income by debiting an expense account, and (2) it decreases *net* accounts receivable by crediting the allowance account. (Allowance for Uncollectible Accounts, the contra account, is subtracted from Accounts Receivable to measure *net* accounts receivable.)

Assume the company's sales for 19X1 are $240,000 and that past collection experience suggests estimated bad debts of $3,100. The 19X1 journal entries are as follows, with accounts receivable from customers Rolf and Anderson separated for emphasis:

19X1	Accounts Receivable – Rolf	1,300	
	Accounts Receivable – Anderson	1,700	
	Accounts Receivable – Various Customers	237,000	
	Sales Revenue		240,000
	To record credit sales.		
19X1	Uncollectible Account Expense	3,100	
	Allowance for Uncollectible Accounts		3,100
	To record estimated bad debt expense, based on past collection experience.		

OBJECTIVE 2
Use the allowance method of accounting for uncollectibles

The account balances at December 31, 19X1, are as follows:

Accounts Receivable	Allowance for Uncollectible Accounts	Sales Revenue	Uncollectible Account Expense
240,000	3,100	240,000	3,100

Net accounts receivable = $236,900

The 19X1 financial statements will report:

Income Statement:	**19X1**
Revenue:	
Sales revenue	$240,000
Expense:	
Uncollectible account expense	3,100

Balance Sheet:	December 31, 19X1
Current assets:	
Accounts receivable..	$240,000
Less: Allowance for uncollectible accounts....................	3,100
Net accounts receivable	$236,900

Writing off Uncollectible Accounts

During 19X2 the company collects on most of the accounts receivable. However, the credit department determines that customers Rolf and Anderson cannot pay the amounts they owe. The accountant writes off their receivables and makes the following entries:

19X2	Cash	235,000	
	Accounts Receivable—Various Customers		235,000
	To record collections on account.		
19X2	Allowance for Uncollectible Accounts	3,000	
	Accounts Receivable—Rolf		1,300
	Accounts Receivable—Anderson.............		1,700
	To write off uncollectible accounts.		

The write-off entry has no effect on net income because it includes no debit to an expense account. The entry also has no effect on *net* accounts receivable because both the Allowance account debited and the Accounts Receivable account credited are part of *net* accounts receivable. The account balances at December 31, 19X2, are as follows:

Accounts Receivable		Allowance for Uncollectible Accounts	
240,000	235,000		
	1,300	3,000	3,100
	1,700		100
2,000			

The financial statements for 19X1 and 19X2 will report the following. In order to highlight the matching of expense and revenue, we are assuming no sales are made in 19X2.

Income Statement:	19X1	19X2
Revenue:		
Sales revenue....................................	$240,000	$ 0
Expense:		
Uncollectible account expense	3,100	0

	December 31,	
Balance Sheet:	19X1	19X2
Current assets:		
Accounts receivable.............................	$240,000	$ 2,000
Less: Allowance for uncollectible accounts.........	3,100	100
Net accounts receivable	$236,900	$ 1,900

Compare these income statement and balance sheet effects with those for the direct write-off method on page 312. Which method, direct write-off or allowance, better matches bad debt expense with sales revenue? The allowance method ties this expense of 19X1 to 19X1 revenue and so provides a better matching of expense to revenue—a key objective of accounting. The allowance method also reports accounts receivable at their expected realizable value.

Bad Debt Write-Offs Rarely Equal the Allowance for Uncollectibles

Bad debt write-offs of customer accounts are actual amounts due from customers, but the allowance amount is based on estimates. Write-offs equal the allowance only if the estimate of bad debts is perfect—a rare occurrence. Usually the difference between write-offs and the allowance is small, as shown in the preceding example. If the allowance is too large for one period, the estimate of bad debts for the next period can be cut back. If the allowance is too low, an adjusting entry debiting Uncollectible Account Expense and crediting Allowance for Uncollectible Accounts can be made at the end of the period. This credit brings the Allowance account to a realistic balance. Estimating uncollectibles will be discussed shortly.

Recoveries of Uncollectible Accounts

When an account receivable is written off as uncollectible, the receivable does not die. The customer still has an obligation to pay. However, the likelihood of receiving cash is so low that the company ceases its collection effort and writes off the account. Such accounts are filed for use in future credit decisions. Some companies turn them over to an attorney for collection in the hope of recovering part of the receivable. To record a recovery, the accountant reverses the write-off and records the collection in the regular manner. The reversal of the write-off is needed to give the customer account receivable a debit balance.

Assume that the write-off of Rolf's account ($1,300) occurs in February 19X2. In August Rolf pays the account in full. The journal entries for this situation follow:

Feb. 19X2	To write off Rolf's account as uncollectible (same as above):		
	Allowance for Uncollectible Accounts..............	1,300	
	Accounts Receivable—Rolf.................		1,300
Aug. 19X2	To reinstate Rolf's account:		
	Accounts Receivable—Rolf......................	1,300	
	Allowance for Uncollectible Accounts.........		1,300
	To record collection from Rolf:		
	Cash...	1,300	
	Accounts Receivable—Rolf.................		1,300

Estimating Uncollectibles

We have seen that the allowance method results in more realistic financial statements. The more accurate the estimate, the more reliable the information in the statements. How are bad debt estimates made?

The most logical way to estimate bad debts is to look at the business's past records. Both the *percentage of sales* method and the *aging of accounts receivable* method use the company's collection experience.

Percentage of Sales. A business may compute uncollectible account expense as a percentage of total credit sales (or total sales). Uncollectible account expense is recorded as an adjusting entry at the end of the period.

Basing its decision on figures from the last four periods, a business estimates that bad debt expense will be 2.5 percent of credit sales. If credit sales for 19X3 total $500,000, the adjusting entry to record bad debt expense for the year is

Adjusting Entries

Dec. 31	Uncollectible Account Expense ($500,000 × .025) 12,500	
	Allowance for Uncollectible Accounts	12,500

Under the percentage of sales method, the amount of this entry ignores the prior balance in Allowance for Uncollectible Accounts.

A business may change the percentage rate from year to year, depending on its collection experience. Suppose collections of accounts receivable in 19X4 are greater, and write-offs are less, than expected. The credit balance in Allowance for Doubtful Accounts would be too large in relation to the debit balance of Accounts Receivable. How would the business change its bad debt percentage rate in this case? *Decreasing* the percentage rate would reduce the credit entry to the allowance account, and the allowance account balance would not grow too large.

New businesses, with no credit history on which to base their rates, may obtain estimated bad debt percentages from industry trade journals, government publications, and other sources of collection data.

Aging the Accounts. The second popular method of estimating bad debts is called **aging the accounts.** In this approach, individual accounts receivable are analyzed according to the length of time that they have been due. Performed manually, this is time consuming. Computers greatly ease the burden. Schmidt Home Builders groups its accounts receivable into 30-day periods, as the following table shows.

	Age of Account				
Customer Name	1–30 Days	31–60 Days	61–90 Days	Over 90 Days	Total Balance
Oxwall Tools Co.	$20,000				$ 20,000
Chicago Pneumatic Parts	10,000				10,000
Sarasota Pipe Corp.		$13,000	$10,000		23,000
Seal Coatings, Inc.			3,000	$1,000	4,000
Other accounts*	39,000	12,000	2,000	2,000	55,000
Totals	$69,000	$25,000	$15,000	$3,000	$112,000
Estimated percentage uncollectible	0.1%	1%	5%	90%	
Allowance for Uncollectible Accounts	$69	$250	$750	$2,700	$3,769

* Each of the "Other accounts" would appear individually.

Schmidt bases the percentage figures on the company's collection experience. In the past, the business has collected all but 0.1 percent of accounts aged from 1 to 30 days, all but 1 percent of accounts aged 31 to 60 days, and so on.

The total amount receivable in each age group is multiplied by the appropriate percentage figure. For example, the $69,000 in accounts aged 1 to 30 days is multiplied by 0.1 percent (.001), which comes to $69. The total balance needed in the Allowance for Uncollectible Accounts—$3,769—is the sum of the amounts computed for the various groups ($69 + $250 + $750 + $2,700).

Suppose the Allowance account has a $2,100 *credit* balance from the previous period:

Allowance for Uncollectible Accounts

	Unadjusted balance 2,100

Under the aging method, the adjusting entry is designed to adjust this account balance from $2,100 to $3,769, the needed amount determined by the aging schedule. To bring the Allowance balance up to date, Schmidt makes this entry:

Adjusting Entries

Dec. 31	Uncollectible Account Expense......................	1,669	
	Allowance for Uncollectible Accounts		
	($3,769 − $2,100)		1,669

Observe that under the aging method, the adjusting entry takes into account the prior balance in Allowance for Uncollectibles. Now the Allowance account has the correct balance:

Allowance for Uncollectible Accounts

	Unadjusted balance	2,100
	Adjustment amount	1,669
	Adjusted balance	3,769

It is possible that the allowance account might have a *debit* balance at year end prior to the adjusting entry. How can this occur? Bad debt write-offs during the year could have exceeded the allowance amount. Suppose the unadjusted Allowance for Uncollectible Accounts balance is a *debit* amount of $1,500:

Allowance for Uncollectible Accounts

Unadjusted balance 1,500	

In this situation, the adjusting entry is

Adjusting Entries

Dec. 31	Uncollectible Account Expense ($3,769 + $1,500)	5,269	
	Allowance for Uncollectible Accounts		5,269

After posting, the allowance account is up to date:

Allowance for Uncollectible Accounts

Unadjusted balance	1,500	Adjustment amount	5,269
		Adjusted balance	3,769

On the balance sheet, the $3,769 is subtracted from the Accounts Receivable figure—which the table at the bottom of page 316 shows is $112,000—to report the expected realizable value of the accounts receivable—$108,231 ($112,000 − $3,769).

In addition to supplying the information needed for sound financial reporting, the aging method directs management's attention to the accounts that need to be pursued for payment.

Comparing the Two Methods.   In practice, many companies use both the percentage of sales and the aging of accounts methods. For interim statements (monthly or quarterly), companies use the percent of sales method because it is easier to apply. At the end of the year, these companies use the aging method to ensure that they report Accounts Receivable at their expected realizable value. For this reason auditors usually require an aging of the accounts on the year-end date. The two methods work well together because the percent of sales approach focuses on measuring bad debt expense on the income statement whereas the aging approach is designed to measure net accounts receivable on the balance sheet.

Credit Balances in Accounts Receivable

Occasionally, customers overpay their accounts or return merchandise for which they have already paid. The result is a credit balance in the customer's account receivable. Assume the company's subsidiary ledger contains 213 accounts, with balances as shown:

210 accounts with *debit* balances totaling............................	$185,000
3 accounts with *credit* balances totaling	2,800
Net total of debit balances...	$182,200

The company should not report the asset Accounts Receivable at the net amount—$182,200. Why not? The credit balance—the $2,800—is a liability. Like any other liability, customer credit balances are debts of the business. A balance sheet that did not indicate to management or to other financial statement users that the company had this liability amount would be misleading if the $2,800 is material in relation to net income or total current assets. Therefore, the company would report on its balance sheet:

Assets		**Liabilities**	
Current:		Current:	
Accounts receivable.....	$185,000	Credit balances in cus-	
		tomer accounts.......	$ 2,800

Credit Card Sales

Credit card sales are common in the retail industry. American Express, Diners Club, Carte Blanche, VISA, and MasterCard are popular.

The customer presents the credit card as payment for a purchase. The seller prepares a sales invoice in triplicate. The customer and the seller keep copies as receipts. The third copy goes to the credit card company, which then pays the seller the transaction amount and bills the customer.

Credit cards offer consumers the convenience of buying without having to pay the cash immediately. Also, consumers receive a monthly statement from the credit card company, detailing each credit card transaction. They can write a single check to cover the entire month's credit card purchases.

Retailers also benefit from credit card sales. They do not have to check a customer's credit rating. The company that issues the card has already done so. Retailers do not have to keep an accounts receivable subsidiary ledger account for each customer, and they do not have to collect cash from customers. The copy of the sale invoice that retailers send to the credit card company signals the card issuer to pursue payment. Further, retailers receive cash more quickly from the credit card companies than they would from the customers themselves. Of course, these services to the seller do not come free.

The seller receives less than 100 percent of the face value of the invoice. The credit card company takes a 5 percent[1] discount on the sale to cover its services. The seller's entry to record a $100 Diners Club sale is

Accounts Receivable – Diners Club.............................	100	
Sales Revenue		100

On collection of the discounted value, the seller records:

Cash..	95	
Credit Card Discount Expense	5	
Accounts Receivable – Diners Club.........................		100

Internal Control over Collections of Accounts Receivable

Businesses that sell on credit receive most of their cash receipts by mail. Internal control over collections on account is an important part of the overall internal control system. Chapter 7 detailed control procedures over cash receipts, but a critical element of internal control deserves emphasis here: the separation of cash-handling and cash-accounting duties. Consider the following case.

Butler Supply Co. is a small, family-owned business that takes pride in the loyalty of its workers. Most company employees have been with the Butlers for at least five years. The company makes 90 percent of its sales on account.

The office staff consists of a bookkeeper and a supervisor. The bookkeeper maintains the general ledger and the accounts receivable subsidiary ledger. He

---

[1] The rate varies among companies and over time.

also makes the daily bank deposit. The supervisor prepares monthly financial statements and any special reports the Butlers require. She also takes sales orders from customers and serves as office manager.

OBJECTIVE 4

Identify internal control weaknesses in accounts receivable

Can you identify the internal control weakness? The bookkeeper has access to the general ledger, the accounts receivable subsidiary ledger, and the cash. The bookkeeper could take a customer check and write off the customer's account as uncollectible.[2] Unless the supervisor or some other manager reviews the book-keeper's work regularly, the theft may go undetected. In small businesses like Butler Supply Co., such a review may not be routinely performed.

How can this control weakness be corrected? The supervisor could open in-coming mail and make the daily bank deposit. The bookkeeper should not be allowed to handle cash. Only the remittance slips would be forwarded to the bookkeeper to indicate which customer accounts to credit. Removing cash-handling duties from the bookkeeper, and keeping the accounts receivable sub-sidiary ledger away from the supervisor, separates duties and strengthens internal control. It reduces an employee's opportunity to steal cash and then cover it up with a false credit to a customer account. Also, the owner should prepare the bank reconciliation.

---

[2] The bookkeeper would need to forge the endorsements of the checks and deposit them in a bank account he controls. This is easier to do than you might imagine.

Summary Problem for Your Review

CPC International, Inc., is the food-products company that produces Skippy peanut butter, Hellman's mayonnaise, and Mazola corn oil. The company bal-ance sheet at December 31, 19X7, reported:

	Millions
Notes and accounts receivable [total].	$549.9
Allowances for doubtful accounts	(12.5)

Required

a. How much of the December 31, 19X7, balance of notes and accounts receivable did CPC expect to collect? Stated differently, what was the expected realizable value of these receivables?
b. Journalize, without explanations, 19X8 entries for CPC International, assuming:
    1) Estimated Doubtful Account Expense of $19.2 million, based on the percentage of sales method.
    2) Write-offs of accounts receivable totaling $23.6 million.
    3) December 31, 19X8, aging of receivables, which indicates that $15.3 million of the total receivables of $582.7 million is uncollectible.
c. Show how CPC International's receivables and related allowance will appear on the December 31, 19X8, balance sheet.
d. What is the expected realizable value of receivables at December 31, 19X8? How much is doubtful account expense for 19X8?

SOLUTION TO REVIEW PROBLEM

		Millions
a.	Expected realizable value of receivables ($549.9 − $12.5)	$537.4

		Millions	
b.	1) Doubtful Account Expense	19.2	
	Allowance for Doubtful Accounts...................		19.2
	2) Allowance for Doubtful Accounts.......................	23.6	
	Accounts Receivable............................		23.6

Allowance for Doubtful Accounts

19X8	23.6	Dec. 31, 19X7	12.5
		19X8	19.2
		19X8 balance prior to December 31, 19X8	8.1

	3) Doubtful Account Expense ($15.3 − $8.1)	7.2	
	Allowance for Doubtful Accounts...................		7.2

		Millions
c.	Notes and accounts receivable	$582.7
	Allowance for doubtful accounts	(15.3)

		Millions
d.	Expected realizable value of receivables at December 31, 19X8 ($582.7 − $15.3)	$567.4
	Doubtful Account Expense for 19X8 ($19.2 + $7.2)............	26.4

Notes Receivable

As we pointed out earlier in this chapter, notes receivable are more formal arrangements than accounts receivable. Often the debtor signs a promissory note, which serves as evidence of the debt. Let's take a moment to define the special terms used to discuss notes receivable.

Promissory note. A written promise to pay a specified amount of money at a particular future date.

Maker of a note. The person or business that signs the note and promises to pay the amount required by the note agreement. The maker is the debtor.

Payee of the note. The person or business to whom the maker promises future payment. The payee is the creditor.

Principal amount, or **principal.** The amount loaned out by the payee and borrowed by the maker of the note.

OBJECTIVE 5

Use notes receivable terminology

EXHIBIT 8-2 *A Promissory Note*

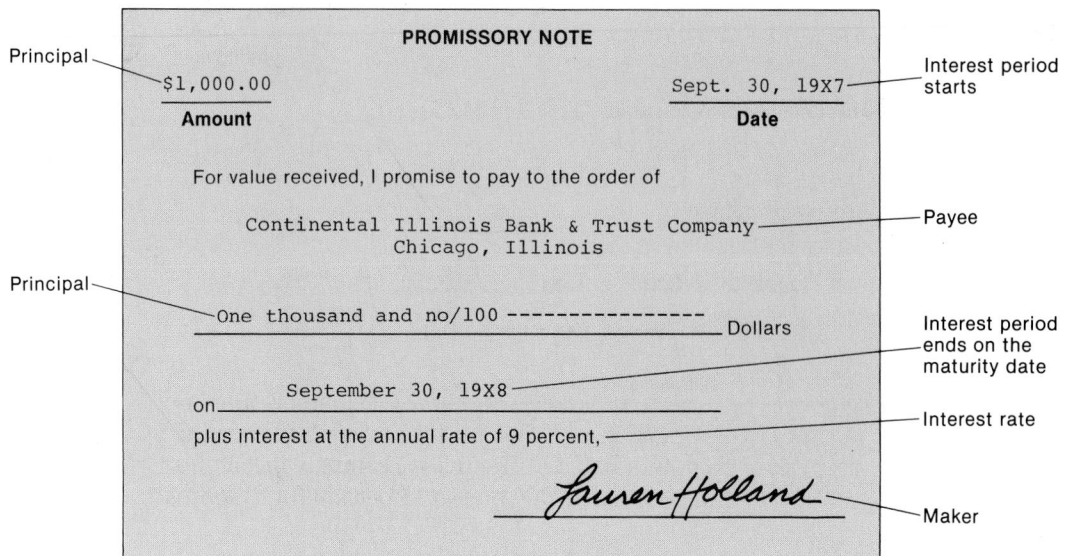

Interest. The revenue to the payee for loaning out the principal and the expense to the maker for borrowing the principal.

Interest period. The period of time during which interest is to be computed. It extends from the original date of the note to the maturity date.

Interest rate. The percentage rate that is multiplied by the principal amount to compute the amount of interest on the note.

Maturity date, or **due date.** The date on which final payment of the note is due.

Maturity value. The sum of principal and interest due at the maturity date of a note.

Note period or **note term.** Synonyms for the interest period.

Exhibit 8-2 illustrates a promissory note. Study it carefully, and identify each of the above items for the note agreement.

Identifying the Maturity Date of a Note

Some notes specify the maturity date of a note, as shown in Exhibit 8-2. Other notes state the period of the note, in days or months. When the period is given in months, the note's maturity date falls on the same day of the month as the date the note was issued. For example, a 6-month note dated February 16 matures on August 16.

When the period is given in days, the maturity date is determined by counting the days from date of issue. A 120-day note dated September 14, 19X2, matures on January 12, 19X3, as shown below:

Month	Number of Days	Cumulative Total
Sept. 19X2	16*	16
Oct. 19X2	31	47
Nov. 19X2	30	77
Dec. 19X2	31	108
Jan. 19X3	12	120

* 30 − 14 = 16.

Computing Interest on a Note

The formula for computing interest is

$$\textbf{Principal} \times \textbf{Rate} \times \textbf{Time} = \textbf{Amount of Interest}$$

Using the data in Exhibit 8-2, Continental Bank computes its interest revenue for one year on its note receivable as:

Principal	Rate	Time	Interest
$1,000	× .09	× 1 (yr.) =	$90

The *maturity value* of the note is $1,090 ($1,000 principal + $90 interest). Note that the time element is one (1) because interest is computed over a 1-year period.

When the interest period of a note is stated in months, we compute the interest based on the 12-month year. Interest on a $2,000 note at 15 percent for 3 months is computed as:

Principal	Rate	Time	Interest
$2,000	× .15	× 3/12 =	$75

(handwritten above 3/12: .25)

When the interest period of a note is stated in days, we sometimes compute interest based on a 360-day year rather than a 365-day year. The interest on a $5,000 note at 12 percent for 60 days is computed as:

Principal	Rate	Time	Interest
$5,000	× .12	× 60/360 =	$100

Recording Notes Receivable

Consider the loan agreement shown in Exhibit 8-2. After Holland signs the note and presents it to the bank, Continental Bank gives her $1,000 cash. At maturity, Holland pays the bank $1,090 ($1,000 principal plus $90 interest). The bank's entries are

Sept. 30, 19X7	Note Receivable–L. Holland.................	1,000	
	Cash		1,000
	To record the loan.		
Sept. 30, 19X8	Cash	1,090	
	Note Receivable–L. Holland.............		1,000
	Interest Revenue ($1,000 × .09 × 1).......		90
	To record collection at maturity.		

OBJECTIVE 6
Account for notes receivable

Some companies sell merchandise in exchange for notes receivable. This arrangement occurs often when the payment term extends beyond the customary accounts receivable period, which generally ranges from 30 to 60 days.

Suppose that on October 20, 19X3, General Electric sells equipment for $15,000 to Dorman Builders. Dorman signs a 90-day promissory note at 10 percent annual interest. General Electric's entries to record the sale and collection from Dorman are

Oct. 20, 19X3	Note Receivable–Dorman Builders	15,000	
	Sales Revenue		15,000
	To record sale.		
Jan. 18, 19X4	Cash	15,375	
	Note Receivable–Dorman Builders		15,000
	Interest Revenue ($15,000 × .10 × 90/360)		375
	To record collection at maturity.		

A company may accept a note receivable from a trade customer who fails to pay an account receivable within the customary 30 to 60 days. The customer signs a promissory note — that is, becomes the maker of the note — and gives it to the creditor, who becomes the payee.

Suppose Casa de Sanchez, Inc., sees that it will not be able to pay off its account payable to Hoffman Supply that is due in 15 days. Hoffman may accept a note receivable from Casa de Sanchez. Hoffman's entry is

May 3	Note Receivable–Casa de Sanchez, Inc.	2,400	
	Accounts Receivable–Casa de Sanchez, Inc.		2,400
	To receive a note on account from a customer.		

Hoffman later records interest and collection as illustrated in the preceding examples.

Why does a company accept a note receivable instead of pressing its demand for payment of the account receivable? The company may pursue receipt but learn that its customer does not have the money. A note receivable gives the company written evidence of the maker's debt, which may aid any legal action for collection. Also, the note receivable may carry a pledge by the maker that gives the payee certain assets if cash is not received by the due date. The company's reward for its patience is the interest revenue that it earns on the note receivable.

Discounting a Note Receivable

A note receivable is a *negotiable instrument,* which means it is readily transferrable from one business or person to another and may be sold for cash. To get cash quickly, payees sometimes sell a note receivable to another party before the note matures. The payee endorses the note and hands it over to the note purchaser — often a bank — who collects the maturity value of the note at the maturity date.

Selling a note receivable before maturity is called **discounting a note receivable** because the payee of the note receives less than its maturity value. This lower price decreases the amount of interest revenue the payee earns on the note. Giving up some of this interest is the price the payee is willing to pay for the convenience of receiving cash early.

Return to the preceding example with General Electric and Dorman Builders. Recall that the maturity date of the Dorman note is January 18, 19X4. Let's assume General Electric discounts the Dorman note at First City National Bank on December 9, 19X3. The discount period — which is the number of days from the date of discounting to the date of maturity (this is the period the bank will hold the note) — is 40 days; 22 days in December, and 18 days in January. Assume the bank applies a 12 percent annual interest rate in computing the discounted value of the note. The bank will want to use a discount rate that is higher than the interest rate on the note in order to increase its earnings. GE may be willing to accept this higher rate in order to get cash quickly. The discounted value, called the *proceeds,* is the amount that GE receives from the bank. The proceeds are computed as follows:

Principal amount................... $15,000
+ Interest ($15,000 × .10 × 90/360).... 375
= Maturity value.................... $15,375 $170 $170
− Discount ($15,375 × .12 × 40/360)... (205)
= Proceeds........................ $15,170

At maturity the bank collects $15,375 from the maker of the note, earning $205 of interest revenue.

Observe two points in the above computation: (1) The discount is computed on the *maturity value* of the note (principal plus interest) rather than on the original principal amount, and (2) the discount period extends *backward* from the maturity date (January 18, 19X4) to the date of discounting (December 9, 19X3). Follow this diagram:

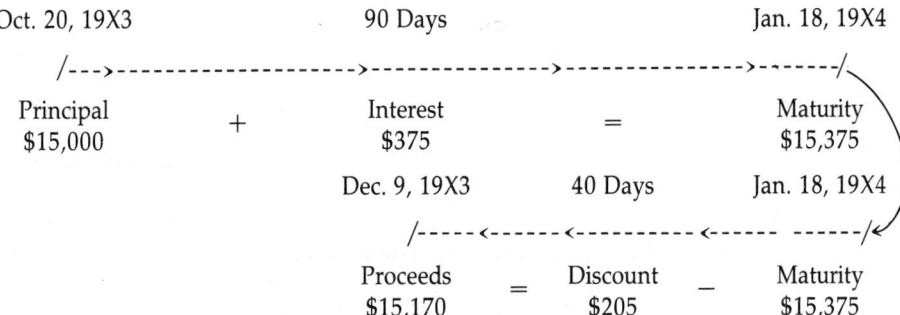

Oct. 20, 19X3   90 Days   Jan. 18, 19X4

| Principal $15,000 | + | Interest $375 | = | Maturity $15,375 |

Dec. 9, 19X3   40 Days   Jan. 18, 19X4

| Proceeds $15,170 | = | Discount $205 | − | Maturity $15,375 |

General Electric's entry to record discounting the note is

Dec. 9, 19X3   Cash...................................... 15,170
           Note Receivable—Dorman Builders   15,000
           Interest Revenue ($15,170 − $15,000).....   170
         To record discounting a note receivable.

When the proceeds from discounting a note receivable are less than the principal amount of the note, the payee records a debit to Interest Expense for the amount of the difference. The term *discount* has been used here to distinguish the interest earned by the payee of the note from the interest to be earned by the purchaser of the note. Fundamentally, the discount is interest.

Contingent Liabilities on Discounted Notes Receivable

Discounting a note receivable creates a **contingent**—that is, a potential—**liability** for the endorser. The contingent liability is this: If the maker of the note (Dorman, in our example) fails to pay the maturity value to the new payee (the bank), then the original payee (General Electric, the note's endorser) legally must pay the bank the amount due.[3] Now we see why the liability is "potential." If

---

[3] The discounting agreement between the endorser and the purchaser may specify that the endorser has no liability if the note is dishonored at maturity.

Dorman pays the bank, then General Electric can forget the note. But if Dorman dishonors the note—fails to pay it—General Electric has an actual liability.

This contingent liability of General Electric exists from the time of endorsement to the maturity date of the note. In our example, the contingent liability exists from December 9, 19X3—when General Electric endorsed the note—to the January 18, 19X4, maturity date.

Contingent liabilities are not reported with actual liabilities on the balance sheet. After all, they are not real debts. However, financial-statement users should be alerted that the business has *potential* debts. Many businesses report contingent liabilities in a footnote to the financial statements. General Electric's end-of-period balance sheet might carry this note:

> As of December 31, 19X3, the Company is contingently liable on notes receivable discounted in the amount of $15,000.

Dishonored Notes Receivable

If the maker of a note does not pay a note receivable at maturity, the maker is said to **dishonor,** or **default on,** the note. Because the term of the note has expired, the note agreement is no longer in force, nor is it negotiable. However, the payee still has a claim against the maker of the note and usually transfers the claim from the note receivable account to Accounts Receivable. The payee records interest revenue earned on the note and debits Accounts Receivable for the full maturity value of the note.

Suppose Rubinstein Jewelers has a six-month, 10 percent note receivable for $1,200 from D. Hatachi. On the February 3 maturity date, Hatachi defaults. Rubinstein Jewelers would record the default as follows:

Feb. 3	Accounts Receivable–D. Hatachi [$1,200 + ($1,200 × .10 × 6/12)]	1,260	
	Note Receivable–D. Hatachi.		1,200
	Interest Revenue ($1,200 × .10 × 6/12).		60
	To record dishonor of note receivable.		

Rubinstein would pursue collection from Hatachi as a promissory note default. The company may treat accounts receivable such as this as a special category to highlight them for added collection efforts. If the account receivable later proves uncollectible, the account is written off against Allowance for Uncollectible Accounts in the manner previously discussed.

The maker may dishonor a note after it has been discounted by the original payee. For example, suppose Dorman Builders dishonors its note (maturity value, $15,375) to General Electric (GE) after GE has discounted the note to the bank. On dishonor, the bank adds a *protest fee* to cover the cost of a statement about the facts of the dishonor and requests payment from General Electric, which then becomes the holder of the dishonored note. Assume GE pays the maturity value of the note, plus the $25 protest fee, to the bank. This creates an obligation for Dorman to pay GE. GE then presents the statement to Dorman and makes the following entry on the maturity date of the note:

Jan. 18, 19X4	Accounts Receivable–Dorman Builders ($15,375 + $25)	15,400	
	Cash		15,400
	To record payment of dishonored note receivable that has been discounted.		

GE's collection of cash, or write off of the uncollectible account receivable, would be recorded in the normal manner, depending on the ultimate outcome. If GE charges Dorman additional interest, GE's collection entry debits Cash and credits Accounts Receivable and Interest Revenue.

Accruing Interest Revenue

Notes receivable may be outstanding at the end of the accounting period. The interest revenue that was accrued on the note up to that point should be recorded as part of that period's earnings. Recall that interest revenue is earned over time, not just when cash is received.

Suppose First City Bank receives a one-year $1,000 note receivable, with 9 percent interest, on October 1, 19X7. The bank's accounting period ends December 31. How much of the total interest revenue does First City Bank earn in 19X7? How much in 19X8?

The bank will earn three months' interest in 19X7—for October, November, and December. In 19X8, the bank will earn nine months' interest—for January through September. Therefore, at December 31, 19X7, First City will make the following adjusting entry to accrue interest revenue:

Dec. 31, 19X7	Interest Receivable ($1,000 × .09 × 3/12)	22.50	
	Interest Revenue		22.50
	To accrue interest revenue earned in 19X7 but not yet received.		

Then, on the maturity date First City Bank may record collection of principal and interest as follows:

Sept. 30, 19X8	Cash [$1,000 + ($1,000 × .09)]	1,090.00	
	Note Receivable.....................		1,000.00
	Interest Receivable ($1,000 × .09 × 3/12).		22.50
	Interest Revenue ($1,000 × .09 × 9/12) ..		67.50
	To record collection of note receivable on which interest has been previously accrued.		

The entries to accrue interest revenue earned in 19X7 and to record collection in 19X8 assign the correct amount of interest to each year.

Reporting Receivables and Allowances: Actual Reports _____

Let's take a look at how some well-known companies report their receivables and related allowances for uncollectibles on the balance sheet. The terminology and setup vary, but you can understand these actual presentations based on what you have learned in this chapter.

Bobbie Brooks, a manufacturer of women's clothing, reports under Current Assets (in thousands):

Accounts receivable, less allowance
for doubtful accounts of $602 .... $35,873

OBJECTIVE 7

Report receivables on the balance sheet

To figure the total accounts receivable amount, add the allowance to the net accounts receivable amount: $602 + $35,873 = $36,475.

Premark International, Inc., which makes Tupperware plastic food-storage containers, combines accounts and notes receivable (amounts in millions):

> Accounts and notes receivable, less
>   allowances of $19.5 . . . . $309.9

General Electric Company reports a single amount for its current receivables in the body of the balance sheet and supplements it with a detailed note (amounts in millions):

Current receivables (note 8)		$4,872
Note 8:	Current Receivables	
	Customers' accounts and notes.	$3,989
	Associated companies	49
	Nonconsolidated affiliates	21
	Other	927
		4,986
	Less allowance for losses.	(114)
		$4,872

Deere & Company, maker of farm machinery, lists more detail in the body of the balance sheet (amounts in thousands of dollars):

Trade receivables:	
Dealer accounts and notes	$2,373,018
Retail notes	40,558
Total	2,413,576
Less allowances	39,183
Trade receivables, net	$2,374,393

Nashua Corporation, manufacturer of copying machines and paper products, reported approximately $70,000,000 in net accounts and notes receivable. In addition, the company disclosed a contingent liability for discounted accounts and notes receivable in its Notes to Financial Statements:

ACCOUNTS RECEIVABLE:

At December 31, 19X1 and 19X0, the company was contingently liable to third parties as a result of the sale of certain accounts and notes receivable of approximately $19,000,000 and $16,000,000, respectively.

The companies we have featured so far list receivables as *current assets.* National Can Corporation, however, had some long-term receivables that it reported as other assets (amounts in thousands of dollars).

OTHER ASSETS:

Notes and accounts receivable, less allowances . . . $36,970

National Can also disclosed in a note entitled Notes and Accounts Receivable that:

> Notes and accounts receivable included in other assets are net of allowances for doubtful accounts of $16,772.

Using Computers to Account for Receivables _____

A computer greatly eases accounting for receivables. Painstaking work—like posting credit sales and collections, aging accounts receivable, and computing interest—can be performed with a computer in far less time than it takes to do them manually, and with fewer errors. Once the program is written and the data are entered, the machine can perform the calculations again and again. Commercial software is available to perform these tasks on a microcomputer, so even small businesses use them.

Suppose a homebuilder uses an Apple micro and commercial software to handle routine accounting work. Assume the business accepts notes receivable for its work and, rather than hold the notes for several years, sells them to a local bank. The owner can use a program to compute a range of cash proceeds amounts that depend on different discount rates the bank is likely to propose. With this knowledge, the business person can probably strike a better deal with the bank. Instead of having to perform a half dozen such calculations by hand, the business owner or accountant can program the micro to do the arithmetic.

Suppose the homebuilder's accountant "roughs out" the calculations for discounting prior to writing the program in BASIC programming language. In computer programming, symbols are less cumbersome to work with than full terms because each term may be lengthy and may have to be written several times. For each note receivable,

Let: M = Maturity value
      P = Principal value
      R = Interest rate
      T = Time period
      D = Dollar amount of the discount
      BR = Bank's interest rate used to discount the note (the discount rate)
      BT = Time period the bank will hold the note (the discount period)
      C = Cash proceeds from discounting the note

Then the cash proceeds (C) can be computed as follows:

$$M = P + (P \times R \times T)$$
$$D = M \times BR \times BT$$
$$C = M - D$$

Prior to discounting a note, the builder or his accountant can simply enter the value of each variable into the computer, and it will determine the cash proceeds. The program and all the data on notes receivable can be stored on a floppy disk for future use. The information can be retrieved when needed—for example, for preparation of the financial statements, including the note for contingent liabilities.

Summary Problem for Your Review

Suppose Exxon, Inc., engaged in the following transactions:

19X4

Apr. 1 Loaned $8,000 to Bland Co., a service station. Received a one-year, 10 percent note.

June 1 Discounted the Bland note at the bank at a discount rate of 12 percent.

Nov.30 Loaned $6,000 to Flores, Inc., a regional distributor of Exxon products, on a three-month, 11 percent note.

19X5

Feb. 28 Collected the Flores note at maturity.

Exxon's accounting period ends on December 31.

Required

Explanations are not needed.

1. Record the 19X4 transactions on April 1, June 1, and November 30 on Exxon's books.
2. Make any adjusting entries needed on December 31, 19X4.
3. Record the February 28, 19X5, collection of the Flores note.
4. Which transaction creates a contingent liability for Exxon? When does the contingency begin? When does it end?
5. Write a footnote that Exxon could use in its 19X4 financial statements to report the contingent liability.

SOLUTION TO REVIEW PROBLEM

1.
19X4

Apr. 1 Note Receivable–Bland Co. 8,000
    Cash 8,000

June 1 Cash 7,920*
    Interest Expense 80
      Note Receivable–Bland Co. 8,000

    * Computation of proceeds:
     Principal $8,000
     + Interest ($8,000 × .10 × 12/12) 800
     = Maturity value 8,800
     − Discount ($8,800 × .12 × 10/12) 880
     = Proceeds $7,920

Nov.30 Note Receivable–Flores, Inc. 6,000
    Cash 6,000

2.   Adjusting Entry
19X4
Dec. 31 Interest Receivable ($6,000 × .11 × 1/12) 55
    Interest Revenue 55

19X5

3. Feb. 28 Cash [$6,000 + ($6,000 × .11 × 3/12)] 6,165

Note Receivable–Flores, Inc. 6,000

Interest Receivable. 55

Interest Revenue ($6,000 × .11 × 2/12) . . 110

4. Discounting the Bland note receivable creates a contingent liability for Exxon. The contingency exists from the date of discounting the note receivable (June 1) to the maturity date of the note (April 1, 19X5).

5. Note XX—Contingent liabilities: At December 31, 19X4, the Company is contingently liable on notes receivable discounted in the amount of $8,000.

Summary

Credit sales create receivables. Accounts receivable are usually current assets, and notes receivable may be current or long term.

Uncollectible receivables are accounted for by the direct write-off method or the allowance method. The *direct write-off method* is easy to apply, but it fails to match the uncollectible account expense to the corresponding sales revenue. Also, Accounts Receivable are reported at their full amount, which misleadingly suggests that the company expects to collect all its accounts receivable. The *allowance method* matches expenses to sales revenue and also results in a more realistic measure of net accounts receivable. The *percent of sales method* and the *aging of accounts receivable method* are the two main approaches to estimating bad debts under the allowance method.

In *credit card* sales, the seller receives cash from the credit card company (American Express, for example), which bills the customer. For the convenience of receiving cash immediately, the seller pays a fee, which is a percentage of the sale.

Companies that sell on credit receive most customer collections in the mail. Good *internal control* over mailed-in cash receipts means separating cash-handling duties from cash-accounting duties.

Notes receivable are formal credit agreements. Interest earned by the creditor is computed by multiplying the note's principal amount by the interest rate times the length of the interest period.

Because notes receivable are negotiable, they may be sold. Selling a note receivable—called *discounting a note*—creates a *contingent (possible) liability* for the note's payee.

All accounts receivable, notes receivable, and allowance accounts appear in the balance sheet. However, companies use various formats and terms to report these assets.

Self-Study Questions

Test your understanding of the chapter by marking the best answer for each of the following questions.

1. The party that holds a receivable is called the *(p. 309)*
   a. Creditor
   b. Debtor
   c. Maker
   d. Security holder
2. The function of the credit department is to *(p. 311)*
   a. Collect accounts receivable from customers
   b. Report bad credit risks to other companies
   c. Evaluate customers who apply for credit
   d. Write off uncollectible accounts receivable

3. Longview, Inc., made the following entry related to uncollectibles:

    Uncollectible Account Expense   1,900
       Allowance for Uncollectible Accounts   1,900

    The purpose of this entry is to *(p. 313)*
    a. Write off uncollectibles   c. Age the accounts receivable
    b. Close the expense account   d. Record bad debt expense

4. Longview, Inc., also made this entry:

    Allowance for Uncollectible Accounts   2,110
       Accounts Receivable (detailed)   2,110

    The purpose of this entry is to *(p. 314)*
    a. Write off uncollectibles   c. Age the accounts receivable
    b. Close the expense account   d. Record bad debt expense

5. The credit balance in Allowance for Uncollectibles is $14,300 prior to the adjusting entries at the end of the period. The aging of accounts indicates that an allowance of $78,900 is needed. The amount of expense to record is *(p. 317)*
    a. $14,300   c. $78,900
    b. $64,600   d. $93,200

6. The most important internal control over cash receipts is *(p. 319)*
    a. Assigning an honest employee the responsibility for handling cash
    b. Separating the cash-handling and cash-accounting duties
    c. Ensuring that cash is deposited in the bank daily
    d. Centralizing the opening of incoming mail in a single location

7. A six-month, $30,000 note specifies interest of 9 percent. The full amount of interest on this note will be *(p. 323)*
    a. $450   c. $1,350
    b. $900   d. $2,700

8. The note in the preceding question was issued on August 31, and the company's accounting year ends on December 31. The year-end balance sheet will report interest receivable of *(p. 327)*
    a. $450   c. $1,350
    b. $900   d. $2,700

9. Discounting a note receivable is a way to *(p. 324)*
    a. Collect on a note   c. Both of the above
    b. Increase interest revenue   d. None of the above

10. Discounting a note receivable creates a (an) *(p. 325)*
    a. Cash disbursement   c. Protest fee
    b. Interest expense   d. Contingent liability

Answers to the self-study questions are at the end of the chapter.

Accounting Vocabulary

aging of accounts receivable *(p. 316)*,   allowance for doubtful accounts *(p. 313)*,   allowance for uncollectible accounts *(p. 313)*,   allowance method *(p. 312)*,   bad debt expense *(p. 311)*, contingent liability *(p. 325)*,   creditor *(p. 309)*,   debtor *(p. 309)*,   default on a note *(p. 326)*, direct write-off method *(p. 311)*,   discounting a note receivable *(p. 324)*,   dishonor of a note *(p. 326)*,   doubtful account expense *(p. 311)*,   interest *(p. 322)*,   interest period *(p. 322)*, interest rate *(p. 322)*,   maker of a note *(p. 321)*,   maturity date *(p. 322)*,   maturity value *(p. 322)*,   other receivables *(p. 310)*,   payee of a note *(p. 321)*,   principal amount *(p. 321)*, promissory note *(p. 321)*,   receivable *(309)*,   uncollectible account expense *(p. 311)*.

ASSIGNMENT MATERIAL _____

Questions

1. Name the two parties to a receivable/payable transaction. Which party has the receivable? Which party has the payable? Which party has the asset? Which party has the liability?

2. List three categories of receivables. State how each category is classified for reporting on the balance sheet.

3. Name the two methods of accounting for uncollectible receivables. Which method is easier to apply? Which method is consistent with generally accepted accounting principles?

4. Which of the two methods of accounting for uncollectible accounts is preferable? Why?

5. Identify the accounts debited and credited to account for uncollectibles under (a) the direct write-off method and (b) the allowance method.

6. What is another term for Allowance for Uncollectible Accounts? What are two other terms for Uncollectible Account Expense?

7. Which entry decreases net income under the allowance method of accounting for uncollectibles: the entry to record uncollectible account expense or the entry to write off an uncollectible account receivable?

8. May a customer pay his or her account receivable after it has been written off? If not, why not? If so, what entries are made to account for reinstating the customer's account and collecting cash from the customer?

9. Identify and briefly describe the two ways to estimate bad debt expense and uncollectible accounts.

10. Briefly describe how a company may use both the percentage of sales method and the aging method to estimate uncollectibles.

11. How does a credit balance arise in a customer's account receivable? How does the company report this credit balance on its balance sheet?

12. Many businesses receive most of their cash on credit sales through the mail. Suppose you own a business so large that you must hire employees to handle cash receipts and perform the related accounting duties. What internal control feature should you use to ensure that the cash received from customers is not taken by a dishonest employee?

13. Use the terms *maker, payee, principal amount, maturity date, promissory note,* and *interest* in an appropriate sentence or two.

14. For each of the following notes receivable, compute the amount of interest revenue earned during 19X6:

	Principal	Interest Rate	Interest Period	Maturity Date
a. Note 1	$ 10,000	9%	90 days	11/30/19X6
b. Note 2	$ 50,000	10%	6 months	9/30/19X6
c. Note 3	$100,000	8%	5 years	12/31/19X7
d. Note 4	$ 15,000	12%	60 days	1/15/19X7

15. Name three situations in which a company might receive a note receivable. For each situation, show the account debited and the account credited to record receipt of the note.

16. Suppose you hold a 180-day, $5,000 note receivable that specifies 10 percent interest. After 60 days you discount the note at 12 percent. How much cash do you receive?

17. How does a contingent liability differ from an ordinary liability? How does discounting a note receivable create a contingent liability? When does the contingency cease to exist?

18. When the maker of a note dishonors the note at maturity, what accounts does the payee debit and credit?

19. Why does the payee of a note receivable usually need to make adjusting entries for interest at the end of the accounting period?

20. Recall the real-world disclosures of receivables the chapter presents. Show three ways to report Accounts Receivable of $100,000 and Allowance for Uncollectible Accounts of $2,800 on the balance sheet or in the related notes.

Exercises

Exercise 8-1   *Using the direct write-off method for bad debts*

On September 30, Maxwell Co. had a $32,000 debit balance in Accounts Receivable. During October the company had sales revenue of $135,000, which included $88,000 in credit sales. Other data for October include:

Collections on accounts receivable, $91,000
Write-offs of uncollectible receivables, $1,520

Required

1. Record uncollectible account expense for October by the *direct write-off* method.

2. What amount of *net* accounts receivable would Maxwell report on its October 31 balance sheet under the direct write-off method? Does Maxwell expect to collect this much of the receivable? Give your reason.

Exercise 8-2   *Using the allowance method for bad debts*

Refer to the situation in Exercise 8-1, and add these facts:

September 30 credit balance in Allowance for Uncollectible Accounts, $2,100
Uncollectible account expense, estimated as 2 percent of credit sales

Required

1. Prepare journal entries to record sales, collections, uncollectible account expense by the allowance method, and write-offs of uncollectibles during October.

2. Show the ending balances in Accounts Receivable, Allowance for Uncollectible Accounts, and *net* accounts receivable at October 31. Does Maxwell expect to collect the net amount of the receivable?

Exercise 8-3   *Recording bad debts by the allowance method*

Prepare general journal entries to record the following transactions under the allowance method of accounting for uncollectibles:

Apr. 2 Sold merchandise for $4,650 on credit terms of 2/10 n/30 to McBee Sales Company.

May 28 Received legal notification that McBee Sales Company was bankrupt. Wrote off McBee's accounts receivable balance.

Aug. 11 Received $2,000 from McBee Sales Company, together with a letter indicating that the company intended to pay its account within the next month.

30 Received the remaining amount due from McBee.

Exercise 8-4   *Recording bad debts by the allowance method*

At December 31, 19X5, Knudsen Company has an accounts receivable balance of $129,000. Sales revenue for 19X5 is $950,000, including credit sales of $600,000. For each of the following situations, prepare the year-end adjusting entry to record doubtful account expense. Show how the accounts receivable and the allowance for doubtful accounts are reported on the balance sheet.

a. Allowance for Doubtful Accounts has a credit balance before adjustment of $1,600. Knudsen Company estimates that doubtful account expense for the year is 3/4 of 1 percent of credit sales.

b. Allowance for Doubtful Accounts has a debit balance before adjustment of $1,100. Knudsen Company estimates that $6,100 of the accounts receivable will prove uncollectible.

Exercise 8-5   *Using the aging approach to estimate bad debts*

At December 31, 19X7, the accounts receivable balance of Granite Shoals Co. is $266,000. The allowance for doubtful accounts has a $3,910 credit balance. Accountants for Granite Shoals Company prepare the following aging schedule for its accounts receivable:

Total Balance	Age of Accounts			
	1-30 Days	31-60 Days	61-90 Days	Over 90 Days
$266,000	$104,000	$78,000	$69,000	$15,000
Estimated percentage uncollectible	.3%	1.2%	4.0%	50%

Journalize the adjusting entry for doubtful accounts based on the aging schedule. Show the T-account for the allowance.

Exercise 8-6   *Reporting receivables with credit balances*

The accounts receivable subsidiary ledger includes the following summarized data:

83 accounts with debit balances totaling	$63,240
9 accounts with credit balances totaling	2,690
Net total of balances	$60,550

Show how these data should be reported on the balance sheet.

Exercise 8-7   *Recording a note receivable and accruing interest revenue*

Record the following transactions in the general journal.

Nov. 1   Loaned $10,000 cash to E. Gomez on a 1-year, 9% note.
Dec. 3   Sold goods to Lofland, Inc., receiving a 90-day, 12% note for $3,750.
     16   Received a $2,000, 6-month, 12% note on account from J. Baker.
     31   Accrued interest revenue on all notes receivable.

Exercise 8-8   *Recording notes receivable, discounting a note, and reporting the contingent liability in a note*

Prepare general journal entries to record the following transactions:

Aug. 14   Sold goods on account to Bert Lewis, $4,000.
Dec. 2   Received a $4,000, 90-day, 10% note from Bert Lewis in satisfaction of his past-due account receivable.
     30   Sold the Lewis note by discounting it to a bank at 15%. (Use a 360-day year, and round amounts to the nearest dollar.)

Write the note to disclose the contingent liability at December 31.

Exercise 8-9   *Accounting for a dishonored note receivable*

Record the following transactions in the general journal, assuming the company uses the allowance method to account for uncollectibles:

May 18   Sold goods to Computer Specialties, receiving a 120-day, 10% note for $2,700.
Sep. 15   The note is dishonored.
Nov. 30   After pursuing collection from Computer Specialties, wrote off their account as uncollectible.

Exercise 8-10   *Recording a note receivable and accruing interest revenue*

Record the following transactions in the general journal:

Apr. 1, 19X2   Loaned $4,800 to Linda Rutishauser on a 1-year, 9% note.
Dec. 31, 19X2   Accrued interest revenue on the Rutishauser note.
Dec. 31, 19X2   Closed the interest revenue account.
Apr. 1, 19X3   Received the maturity value of the note from Linda Rutishauser.

Problems   *(Group A)*

Problem 8-1A   *Accounting for uncollectibles by the direct write-off and allowance methods*

On February 28 Contessa Gallery had a $61,800 debit balance in Accounts Receivable. During March the company had sales revenue of $509,000, which includes $443,000 in credit sales. Other data for March include:

Collections on accounts receivable, $451,600
Write-offs of uncollectible receivables, $4,990
February 28 unadjusted balance in Allowance for Uncollectible Accounts, $800 (debit)
Uncollectible account expense, estimated as 2 percent of credit sales

Required

1. Record uncollectible account expense for March by the *direct write-off* method. Show all March activity in Accounts Receivable and Uncollectible Account Expense.
2. Record uncollectible account expense and write-offs of customer accounts for March by the *allowance* method. Show all March activity in Accounts Receivable, Allowance for Uncollectible Accounts, and Uncollectible Account Expense.
3. What amount of uncollectible account expense would Contessa Gallery report on its March income statement under the two methods? Which amount better matches expense with revenue? Give your reason.
4. What amount of *net* accounts receivable would Contessa Gallery report on its March 31 balance sheet under the two methods? Which amount is more realistic? Give your reason.

Problem 8-2A   *Using the percent of sales and aging approaches for uncollectibles*

Masters Company completed the following transactions during 19X1 and 19X2:

19X1
Dec. 31   Estimated that uncollectible account expense for the year was 3/4 of 1 percent on credit sales of $300,000, and recorded that amount as expense.
        31   Made the appropriate closing entry.
19X2
Jan. 17   Sold inventory to Mary Lee, $652, on credit terms of 2/10 n/30.

June 29 Wrote off the Mary Lee account as uncollectible after repeated efforts to collect from her.

Aug. 6 Received $250 from Mary Lee, along with a letter stating her intention to pay her debt in full within 30 days. Reinstated her account in full.

Sept. 4 Received the balance due from Mary Lee.

Dec. 31 Made a compound entry to write off the following accounts as uncollectible: Bernard Klaus, $737, Louis Mann, $348, and Millie Burnett, $622.

31 Estimated that uncollectible account expense for the year was 2/3 of 1 percent on credit sales of $420,000, and recorded that amount as expense.

31 Made the appropriate closing entry.

Required

1. Open general ledger accounts for Allowance for Uncollectible Accounts and Uncollectible Account Expense. Keep running balances.
2. Record the transactions in the general journal, and post to the two ledger accounts.
3. The December 31, 19X2, balance of Accounts Receivable is $139,000. Show how Accounts Receivable would be reported at that date.
4. Assume that Masters Company begins aging accounts receivable on December 31, 19X2. The balance in Accounts Receivable is $139,000, the credit balance in Allowance for Uncollectible Accounts is $543, and the company estimates that $2,600 of its accounts receivable will prove uncollectible.
   a. Make the adjusting entry for uncollectibles.
   b. Show how Accounts Receivable will be reported on the December 31, 19X2, balance sheet.

Problem 8-3A *Using the percent of sales and aging approaches for uncollectibles*

The December 31, 19X6, balance sheet of Marlin Products Co. reports the following:

Accounts Receivable $256,000
Allowance for Doubtful Accounts (credit balance) 7,100

At the end of each quarter, Marlin Products Company estimates doubtful account expense to be 2 percent of credit sales. At the end of the year, the company ages its accounts receivable and adjusts the balance in Allowance for Doubtful Accounts to correspond to the aging schedule. During 19X7 Marlin completes the following selected transactions:

Jan. 31 Wrote off as uncollectible the $855 account receivable from Spinelli Company and the $3,287 account receivable from J. M. Bartlett.

Mar. 31 Recorded doubtful account expense based on credit sales of $120,000.

May 2 Received $1,000 from J. M. Bartlett after prolonged negotiations with Bartlett's attorney. Marlin has no hope of collecting the remainder.

June 15 Wrote off as uncollectible the $1,120 account receivable from Lisa Brown.

June 30 Recorded doubtful account expense based on credit sales of $166,000.

July 14 Made a compound entry to write off the following uncollectible accounts: C. H. Harris, $766; Graphics Unlimited, $2,413; and Ben McQueen, $134.

Sept. 30 Recorded doubtful account expense based on credit sales of $141,400.

Nov. 22 Wrote off the following accounts receivable as uncollectible: Monet Corp., $1,345; Blocker, Inc., $2,109; and Main Street Plaza, $755.

Dec. 31 Recorded doubtful account expense based on the following summary of the aging of accounts receivable:

	Total Balance	Age of Accounts			
		1–30 Days	31–60 Days	61–90 Days	Over 90 Days
	$287,600	$154,500	$86,000	$32,000	$15,100
Estimated percentage uncollectible		0.2%	0.5%	3.0%	40.0%

Dec. 31   Made the closing entry for Doubtful Account Expense for the entire year.

Required

1. Record the transactions in the general journal.
2. Open the Allowance for Doubtful Accounts, and post entries affecting that account. Keep a running balance.
3. Most companies report two-year comparative financial statements. If Marlin's Accounts Receivable balance is $287,600 at December 31, 19X7, show how the company would report its accounts receivable in a comparative balance sheet for 19X7 and 19X6, as follows:

	19X7	19X6
Accounts receivable............................	_____	_____
Less: Allowance for doubtful accounts.............	_____	_____
Net accounts receivable.........................	_____	_____

Problem 8-4A   *Accounting for notes receivable, including discounting notes and accruing interest revenue*

A company received the following notes during 19X3. Notes (1), (2), and (3) were discounted on the dates and at the rates indicated.

Note	Date	Principal Amount	Interest Rate	Term	Date Discounted	Discount Rate
(1)	July 12	$10,000	10%	3 months	Aug. 12	15%
(2)	Aug. 4	6,000	11%	90 days	Aug. 30	13%
(3)	Oct. 21	8,000	15%	60 days	Nov. 3	18%
(4)	Nov. 30	12,000	12%	6 months	—	—
(5)	Dec. 7	9,000	10%	30 days	—	—
(6)	Dec. 23	15,000	9%	1 year	—	—

Required

As necessary in requirements 1 through 5, identify each note by number, compute interest using a 360-day year for those notes with terms specified in days or years, round all interest amounts to the nearest dollar, and present entries in general journal form. Explanations are not required.

1. Determine the due date and maturity value of each note.
2. For each discounted note, determine the discount and proceeds from sale of the note.
3. Journalize the discounting of notes (1) and (2).
4. Journalize a single adjusting entry at December 31, 19X3, to record accrued interest revenue on notes (4), (5), and (6).
5. Journalize the collection of principal and interest on note (5).

Problem 8-5A   *Notes receivable, discounted notes, dishonored notes, and accrued interest revenue*

Record the following selected transactions in the general journal. Explanations are not required.

19X6

Dec. 19 Received a $2,000, 60-day, 12 percent note on account from Claude Bernard.

31 Made an adjusting entry to accrue interest on the Bernard note.

31 Made an adjusting entry to record doubtful account expense in the amount of 1 percent of credit sales of $474,500.

31 Made a compound closing entry for interest revenue and doubtful account expense.

19X7

Feb. 17 Collected the maturity value of the Bernard note.

Mar. 22 Sold merchandise to Idaho Power Co., receiving $1,400 cash and a 90-day, 10 percent note for $6,000.

May 3 Discounted the Idaho Power Co. note to First National Bank at 15 percent.

June 1 Loaned $10,000 cash to Linz Brothers, receiving a 6-month, 11 percent note.

Oct. 31 Received a $1,500, 60-day, 12 percent note from Ned Pierce on his past-due account receivable.

Dec. 1 Collected the maturity value of the Linz Brothers note.

30 Ned Pierce dishonored his note at maturity; wrote off the note receivable as uncollectible, debiting Allowance for Doubtful Accounts.

31 Wrote off as uncollectible the accounts receivable of Al Bynum, $435, and Ray Sharp, $276.

Problem 8-6A   *Uncollectibles, notes receivable, discounting notes, dishonored notes, and accrued interest revenue*

Assume Chesapeake Corp. of Virginia, a major manufacturer of paper products, completed the following selected transactions:

19X4

Dec. 1 Sold goods to McNamara Company, receiving a $24,000, 3-month, 10 percent note.

31 Made an adjusting entry to accrue interest on the McNamara note.

31 Made an adjusting entry to record doubtful account expense based on an aging of accounts receivable. The aging analysis indicates that $355,800 of accounts receivable will not be collected. Prior to this adjustment, the credit balance in Allowance for Uncollectible Accounts is $341,900.

19X5

Feb. 18 Received a 90-day, 10 percent, $5,000 note from Dilley, Inc., on account. (This year February has 28 days.)

Mar. 1 Collected the maturity value of the McNamara Company note.

8 Discounted the Dilley note to First State Bank at 16 percent.

Apr. 21 Sold merchandise to Brown Group, receiving a 60-day, 9 percent note for $4,000.

June 20 Brown Group dishonored its note at maturity and converted the maturity value of the note to an account receivable.

July 12 Loaned $60,000 cash to Consolidated Investments, receiving a 90-day, 13 percent note.

13 Sold merchandise to Scott Corp., receiving a 4-month, 12 percent, $2,500 note.

Aug. 2 Collected $4,060 on account from Brown Group.

Sept. 13 Discounted the Scott Corp. note to First State Bank at 18 percent.

Oct. 10 Collected the maturity value of the Consolidated Investments note.

Nov. 13 Scott Corp. dishonored its note at maturity; paid First State Bank the maturity value of the note plus a protest fee of $35 and debited an account receivable from Scott Corp.

Dec. 31 Wrote off as uncollectible the account receivable from Scott Corp.

Required

Record the transactions in the general journal. Explanations are not required.

(Group B)

Problem 8-1B   *Accounting for uncollectibles by the direct write-off and allowance methods*

On May 31, Krakow Tool Company had a $104,300 debit balance in Accounts Receivable. During June the company had sales revenue of $788,000, which includes $640,000 in credit sales. Other data for June include:

Collections on accounts receivable, $599,400

Write-offs of uncollectible receivables, $6,100

May 31 unadjusted balance in Allowance for Uncollectible Accounts, $2,200 (credit)

Uncollectible account expense, estimated as 2 percent of credit sales

Required

1. Record uncollectible account expense for June by the *direct write-off* method. Show all June activity in Accounts Receivable and Uncollectible Account Expense.
2. Record uncollectible account expense and write-offs of customer accounts for June by the *allowance* method. Show all June activity in Accounts Receivable, Allowance for Uncollectible Accounts, and Uncollectible Account Expense.
3. What amount of uncollectible account expense would Krakow Tool Company report on its June income statement under the two methods? Which amount better matches expense with revenue? Give your reason.
4. What amount of *net* accounts receivable would Krakow Tool Company report on its June 30 balance sheet under the two methods? Which amount is more realistic? Give your reason.

Problem 8-2B   *Using the percent of sales and aging approaches for uncollectibles*

Reynaldo Company completed the following selected transactions during 19X1 and 19X2:

19X1

Dec. 31   Estimated that uncollectible account expense for the year was 2/3 of 1 percent on credit sales of $450,000 and recorded that amount as expense.

   31   Made the appropriate closing entry.

19X2

Feb. 4   Sold inventory to Gary Carter, $1,521, on credit terms of 2/10 n/30.

July 1   Wrote off Gary Carter's account as uncollectible after repeated efforts to collect from him.

Oct. 19   Received $521 from Gary Carter, along with a letter stating his intention to pay his debt in full within 30 days. Reinstated his account in full.

Nov.15   Received the balance due from Gary Carter.

Dec. 31   Made a compound entry to write off the following accounts as uncollectible: Kris Moore, $899; Marie Mandue, $530; and Grant Frycer, $1,272.

   31   Estimated that uncollectible account expense for the year was 2/3 of 1 percent on credit sales of $540,000 and recorded the expense.

   31   Made the appropriate closing entry.

Required

1. Open general ledger accounts for Allowance for Uncollectible Accounts and Uncollectible Account Expense. Keep running balances.
2. Record the transactions in the general journal, and post to the two ledger accounts.
3. The December 31, 19X2, balance of Accounts Receivable is $164,500. Show how Accounts Receivable would be reported at that date.

4. Assume that Reynaldo Company begins aging its accounts receivable on December 31, 19X2. The balance in Accounts Receivable is $164,500, the credit balance in Allowance for Uncollectible Accounts is $299, and the company estimates that $3,545 of its accounts receivable will prove uncollectible.
   a. Make the adjusting entry for uncollectibles.
   b. Show how Accounts Receivable will be reported on the December 31, 19X2, balance sheet.

Problem 8-3B *Using the percent of sales and aging approaches for uncollectibles*

The December 31, 19X4, balance sheet of Bonini Corporation reports the following:

Accounts Receivable $141,000
Allowance for Doubtful Accounts (credit balance) 3,200

At the end of each quarter, Bonini estimates doubtful account expense to be 1½ percent of credit sales. At the end of the year, the company ages its accounts receivable and adjusts the balance in Allowance for Doubtful Accounts to correspond to the aging schedule. During 19X5 Bonini completes the following selected transactions:

Jan. 16 Wrote off as uncollectible the $403 account receivable from Platt Co. and the $1,719 account receivable from Wise Corp.

Mar. 31 Recorded doubtful account expense based on credit sales of $100,000.

Apr. 15 Received $300 from Wise Corp. after prolonged negotiations with Wise's attorney. Bonini has no hope of collecting the remainder.

May 13 Wrote off as uncollectible the $2,980 account receivable from M. E. Cate.

June 30 Recorded doubtful account expense based on credit sales of $114,000.

Aug. 9 Made a compound entry to write off the following uncollectible accounts: Clifford, Inc., $235; Matz Co., $188; and Lew Norris, $1,006.

Sept. 30 Recorded doubtful account expense based on credit sales of $130,000.

Oct. 18 Wrote off as uncollectible the $767 account receivable from Bliss Co. and the $430 account receivable from Micro Data.

Dec. 31 Recorded doubtful account expense based on the following summary of the aging of accounts receivable.

Total Balance	Age of Accounts			
	1–30 Days	31–60 Days	61–90 Days	Over 90 Days
$167,400	$114,600	$31,100	$12,000	$9,700
Estimated percentage uncollectible	0.1%	.4%	5.0%	30.0%

Dec. 31 Made the closing entry for Doubtful Account Expense for the entire year.

Required

1. Record the transactions in the general journal.
2. Open the Allowance for Doubtful Accounts and post entries affecting that account. Keep a running balance.
3. Most companies report two-year comparative financial statements. If Bonini's Accounts Receivable balance is $167,400 at December 31, 19X5, show how the company would report its accounts receivable on a comparative balance sheet for 19X5 and 19X4, as follows:

	19X5	19X4
Accounts receivable..................................	————	————
Less: Allowance for doubtful accounts..............	————	————
Net accounts receivable............................	————	————

Problem 8-4B *Accounting for notes receivable, including discounting notes and accruing interest revenue*

A company received the following notes during 19X5. Notes (1), (2), and (3) were discounted on the dates and at the rates indicated.

Note	Date	Principal Amount	Interest Rate	Term	Date Discounted	Discount Rate
(1)	July 15	$ 6,000	10%	6 months	Oct. 15	12%
(2)	Aug. 19	9,000	12%	90 days	Aug. 30	15%
(3)	Sept. 1	8,000	15%	120 days	Nov. 2	20%
(4)	Oct. 30	7,000	12%	3 months	—	—
(5)	Nov. 19	15,000	10%	60 days	—	—
(6)	Dec. 1	12,000	9%	1 year	—	—

Required

As necessary in requirements 1 through 5, identify each note by number, compute interest using a 360-day year for those notes with terms specified in days or years, round all interest amounts to the nearest dollar, and present entries in general journal form. Explanations are not required.

1. Determine the due date and maturity value of each note.
2. For each discounted note, determine the discount and proceeds from sale of the note.
3. Journalize the discounting of notes (1) and (2).
4. Journalize a single adjusting entry at December 31, 19X5, to record accrued interest revenue on notes (4), (5), and (6).
5. Journalize the collection of principal and interest on note (4).

Problem 8-5B *Notes receivable, discounted notes, dishonored notes, and accrued interest revenue*

Record the following selected transactions in the general journal. Explanations are not required.

19X2

Dec. 21 Received a $3,600, 30-day, 10 percent note on account from Myron Blake.

31 Made an adjusting entry to accrue interest on the Blake note.

31 Made an adjusting entry to record doubtful account expense in the amount of ¾ of 1 percent on credit sales of $604,800.

31 Made a compound closing entry for interest revenue and doubtful account expense.

19X3

Jan. 20 Collected the maturity value of the Blake note.

Apr. 19 Sold merchandise to city of Akron, receiving $500 cash and a 120-day, 12 percent note for $5,000.

May 1 Discounted the city of Akron note to First National Bank at 15 percent.

Sept. 14 Loaned $6,000 cash to Allstate Investors, receiving a 3-month, 13 percent note.

30 Received a $1,675, 60-day, 16 percent note from Matt Kurtz on his past-due account receivable.

Nov. 29 Matt Kurtz dishonored his note at maturity; wrote off the note as uncollectible, debiting Allowance for Doubtful Accounts.

Dec. 14 Collected the maturity value of the Allstate Investors note.

     31 Wrote off as uncollectible the accounts receivable of Ty Larson, $1,005; and Terry Gee, $140.

Problem 8-6B *Uncollectibles, notes receivable, discounting notes, dishonored notes, and accrued interest revenue*

Assume Chesebrough-Ponds, manufacturer of cosmetic and other products, completed the following selected transactions:

19X5

Nov. 1 Sold goods to Eckerd Drug Co., receiving a $15,000, 3-month, 12 percent note.

Dec. 31 Made an adjusting entry to accrue interest on the Eckerd Drug note.

     31 Made an adjusting entry to record doubtful account expense based on an aging of accounts receivable. The aging analysis indicates that $202,670 of accounts receivable will not be collected. Prior to this adjustment, the credit balance in Allowance for Uncollectible Accounts is $189,900.

19X6

Feb. 1 Collected the maturity value of the Eckerd Drug note.

     23 Received a 90-day, 15 percent, $4,000 note from Bliss Company on account. (This year February has 28 days.)

Mar. 31 Discounted the Bliss Co. note to Lakewood Bank at 20 percent.

Apr. 23 Sold merchandise to K Lynn Corporation, receiving a 60-day, 10 percent note for $9,000.

June 22 K Lynn Corp. dishonored its note at maturity; converted the maturity value of the note to an account receivable.

July 15 Loaned $8,500 cash to McNeil, Inc., receiving a 30-day, 12 percent note.

     17 Sold merchandise to Grant Corp., receiving a 3-month, 10 percent, $8,000 note.

Aug. 5 Collected $9,150 on account from K Lynn Corporation.

     14 Collected the maturity value of the McNeil, Inc., note.

     17 Discounted the Grant Corp. note to Lakewood Bank at 15 percent.

Oct. 17 Grant Corp. dishonored its note at maturity; paid Lakewood Bank the maturity value of the note plus a protest fee of $50 and debited an account receivable from Grant Corp.

Dec. 15 Wrote off as uncollectible the account receivable from Grant Corp.

Required

Record the transactions in the general journal. Explanations are not required.

Decision Problem

Uncollectible Accounts and Evaluating a Business

Bentwood Appliances sells its products either for cash or on notes receivable that earn interest. The business uses the direct write-off method to account for bad debts. Mark Moore, the owner, has prepared the financial statements of the store. The most recent comparative income statements, for 19X3 and 19X2, are as follows:

	19X3	19X2
Total revenue	$210,000	$195,000
Total expenses	157,000	153,000
Net income	$ 53,000	$ 42,000

Based on the increase in net income, Moore seeks to expand his operations. He asks you to invest $50,000 in the business. You and Moore have several meetings, at which you learn that notes receivable from customers were $100,000 at the end of 19X1 and $300,000 at the end of 19X2. Also, total revenues for 19X3 and 19X2 include interest at 15 percent on the year's beginning notes receivable balance. Total expenses include doubtful account expense of $5,000 each year, based on the direct write-off basis. Moore estimates that doubtful account expense would be 4 percent of sales revenue if the allowance method were used.

Required

1. Prepare for the Bentwood Appliances a comparative single-step income statement that identifies sales revenue, interest revenue, doubtful account expense, and other expenses.
2. Is Bentwood's future as promising as Moore's income statement makes it appear? Give the reason for your answer.

Financial Statement Problem

Accounts Receivable and Related Uncollectibles

Use data from the Gulf+Western balance sheet, in Appendix C, to answer these questions. Show all amounts in millions, rounded to the nearest $100,000. For example, show $8,600,000 as $8.6 million.

1. How much did Gulf+Western's customers owe the company at October 31, 1987? Of this amount, how much did Gulf+Western expect to collect?
2. Journalize the following for the fiscal year ended October 31, 1988, using Gulf+Western account titles. Explanations are not required.
   a. Net revenues of $3,117.1 million. Give one entry for the year's total, assuming all net revenues are earned on account.
   b. Cash collections on account, $3,040.5 million.
   c. Doubtful account expense, estimated to equal 1½ percent of net revenues.
   d. Write-offs of uncollectibles totaling $44.9 million.
3. Post to Trade Receivable and Allowance for Doubtful Accounts, inserting these accounts' October 31, 1987, balances.
4. Show trade receivables as Gulf+Western would report this asset on the October 31, 1988, balance sheet.

Answers to Self-Study Questions

1. a	6. b
2. c	7. c ($30,000 × .09 × 6/12 = $1,350)
3. d	8. b ($30,000 × .09 × 4/12 = $ 900)
4. a	9. a
5. b ($78,900 − $14,300 = $64,600)	10. d

9

Merchandise Inventory

LEARNING OBJECTIVES

After studying this chapter, you should be able to

1 Apply four inventory costing methods

2 Distinguish between the income effects and the tax effects of the inventory costing methods

3 Read and understand actual company inventory disclosures

4 Apply the lower-of-cost-or-market rule to inventory

5 Explain why inventory errors counterbalance

6 Estimate inventory by two methods

7 Account for inventory by the periodic and perpetual systems

Merchandise inventory is the largest *current asset* on the balance sheet of most businesses that manufacture or buy inventory for resale. Polaroid Corporation reported inventories of $412.7 million, compared to receivables of $289.5 million and cash of $187.0 million. Inventories are important to merchandisers of all sizes. Buying and selling inventory is the heart of wholesaling and retailing, whether the business is Sears, Safeway, or the corner hardware store.

Inventory is the major current asset of most merchandisers. What is their major expense? It is *cost of sales,* or *cost of goods sold.* For example, Westinghouse Electric Corporation reported its cost of sales at $7.1 billion compared to distribution, administrative, and general expenses of $1.5 billion. For Westinghouse and many other companies, cost of goods sold is greater than all other expenses combined.

Exhibit 9-1 traces the flow of inventory costs during the accounting period. The model presented in Exhibit 9-1 is fundamental to accounting for inventory.

The business starts each period with **beginning inventory,** the goods that are left over from the preceding period. During the period, the business purchases additional goods for resale. Together, beginning inventory and net purchases make up **goods available for sale.** Over the course of the period, the business sells some of the available goods. The cost of the inventory sold to customers is called the **cost of goods sold.** This cost is an expense because the inventory is no longer of use to the company. The goods still on hand at the end of the period are called **ending inventory.** Its cost is an asset because these goods are still available for sale.

Exhibit 9-2 uses data from the financial statements of Revco D. S., Inc., a chain of discount drug stores concentrated in Ohio, Texas, and the Southeast, to present

EXHIBIT 9-1 *Flow of Inventory Costs*

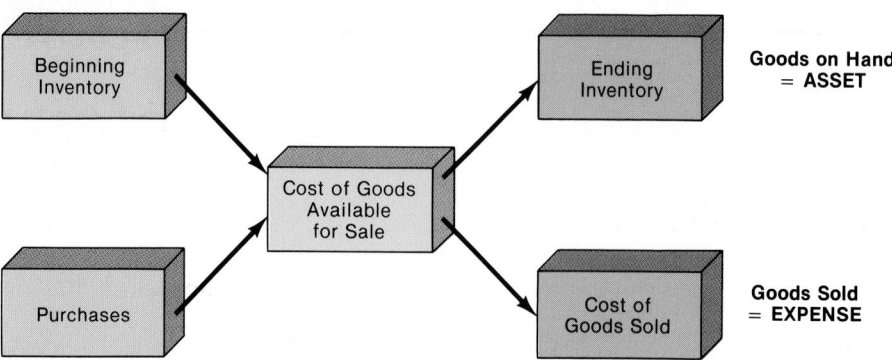

the flow of inventory costs in a different format from that shown in Exhibit 9-1. Notice that ending inventory is subtracted from cost of goods available for sale to figure the cost of goods sold. Throughout this chapter we ignore freight-in to avoid clutter.

The rest of this chapter fills in the details of our inventory cost flow model.

Figuring the Cost of Inventory

A necessary step in accounting for inventory is determining the cost of *ending inventory.* At the end of each period the *quantity* of inventory is multiplied by the *unit cost* of inventory to compute the cost of ending inventory.

Determining the Quantity of Inventory. Most businesses physically count their inventory at least once each year, often on the last day of the fiscal year. Inventory, an asset, must be reported accurately on the balance sheet.

You may have worked at a grocery store or some other type of retail business. If so, you will recall the process of "taking the inventory." Some entities shut the business down to get a good count of inventory on hand. Others count the goods on a weekend. Still others inventory the merchandise while business is being conducted. How is it done in a large organization?

Assume Revco Drug takes a complete physical inventory on its year-end date. Teams of counters in the company's approximately 1,700 stores record the quantities of each inventory item on hand. Each store forwards its total count to corporate headquarters, where home office employees determine the inventory grand total.

Complications may arise in determining the inventory quantity. Suppose the

EXHIBIT 9-2 *Inventory and Cost of Goods Sold for Revco D.S., Inc.*

	(amounts in millions)
Beginning inventory	$ 276
+ Net purchases	1,348
= Cost of goods available for sale	1,624
− Ending inventory..................................	317
= Cost of goods sold.................................	$1,307

business has purchased some goods that are in transit when the inventory is counted. Even though these items are not physically present, they should be included in the inventory count if title to the goods has passed to the purchaser. When title passes from seller to purchaser, the purchaser becomes the legal owner of the goods.

The FOB—free on board—terms of the transaction govern when title passes from the seller to the purchaser. **FOB shipping point** indicates that title passes when the goods leave the seller's place of business. **FOB destination** means that title passes when the goods arrive at the purchaser's location. Therefore, goods in transit that are purchased FOB shipping point should be included in the purchaser's inventory. Goods in transit that are bought FOB destination should not be included.

Usually, the business has a purchase invoice, which lists the quantity of goods in transit and shows the FOB terms. Similarly, the business may have sold inventory that has not yet been shipped to the customer. If title has passed, these goods should be excluded from the seller's inventory, even though they may still be at the seller's place of business.

Another complication in counting inventory arises from consigned goods. In a **consignment** arrangement, the owner of the inventory (the consignor) transfers the goods to another business (the consignee). For a fee, the consignee sells the inventory on the owner's behalf. The consignee does *not* take title to the consigned goods and, therefore, should not include them in its own inventory. Consignments are common in retailing. Suppose Revco Drug is the consignee for some L'Eggs hosiery in its stores. Should Revco include this consigned merchandise in its inventory count? No, because Revco does not own the goods. Instead, the L'Eggs wholesaler—the consignor—includes the consigned goods in his or her inventory. A rule of thumb is to include in inventory only what the business owns.

Determining the Unit Cost of Inventory.   Inventories are normally accounted for at historical cost, as the *cost principle* requires. **Inventory cost** is the price the business pays to acquire the inventory—not the selling price of the goods. Suppose a business purchases inventory for $10 and offers it for sale at $15. The inventory cost is reported at $10, not $15. Inventory cost includes its invoice price, less any purchase discount, plus sales tax, tariffs, transportation charges, insurance while in transit, and all other costs incurred to make the goods ready for sale.

The inventory quantity multiplied by the unit cost equals the cost of inventory. Thirty tape recorders at a cost of $100 each results in an inventory cost of $3,000.

Inventory Costing Methods

Determining the unit cost of inventory is easy when the unit cost remains constant during the period. However, the unit cost often changes. For example, during times of inflation, prices rise. The tape recorder model that cost the retailer $100 in January may cost $115 in June and $122 in October. Suppose the retailer sells 15 tape recorders in November. How many of them cost $100, how many cost $115, and how many cost $122? To compute the cost of goods sold and ending inventory amounts, the accountant must have some means of assigning the business's cost to each item sold. The four costing methods that GAAP allows are

OBJECTIVE 1
Apply four inventory costing methods

1. Specific unit cost
2. Average cost

3.   First-in, first-out (FIFO) cost

4.   Last-in, first-out (LIFO) cost

A company can use any of these methods.

Specific Unit Cost

Some businesses deal in inventory items that may be identified individually, like automobiles, jewels, and real estate. These businesses usually cost their inventory at the **specific cost** of the particular unit. For instance, a Chevrolet dealer may have two vehicles in the showroom—a "stripped-down" model that cost $12,000 and a "loaded" model that cost $15,000. If the dealer sells the loaded model for $16,700, cost of goods sold is $15,000, the cost of the specific unit. The gross margin on this sale is $1,700 ($16,700 − $15,000). If the stripped-down auto is the only unit left in inventory at the end of the period, ending inventory is $12,000, the cost to the retailer of the specific unit on hand.

   The specific unit cost method is also called the *specific identification* or *specific invoice cost* method. This method is not practical for inventory items that have common characteristics, such as bushels of wheat, gallons of paint, or boxes of laundry detergent.

Average Cost, FIFO Cost, and LIFO Cost

The average cost, first-in, first-out (FIFO), and last-in, first-out (LIFO) methods are fundamentally different from the specific unit cost method. These methods do not assign to inventory the specific cost of particular units. Instead, they assume different flows of costs into and out of inventory.

Average Cost.   The **average cost method** is based on the average cost of inventory during the period. Average cost is determined by dividing the cost of goods available for sale (beginning inventory plus purchases) by the number of units available. Ending inventory and cost of goods sold are computed by multiplying the number of units by average cost per unit. Assume that cost of goods available for sale is $90, and 60 units are available. Average cost is $1.50 per unit ($90/60 = $1.50). Ending inventory of 20 units has an average cost of $30 (20 × $1.50 = $30). Cost of goods sold (40 units) is $60 (40 × $1.50). Panel A of Exhibit 9-3 gives the data in more detail. Panel B of the exhibit shows the average cost computations.

First-in, First-out (FIFO) Cost.   Under the **first-in, first-out (FIFO) method,** the company must keep a record of the cost of each inventory unit purchased. The unit costs used in computing the ending inventory may be different from the unit costs used in computing the cost of goods sold. Under FIFO, the first costs into inventory are the first costs out to cost of goods sold—hence the name *first-in, first-out.* Ending inventory is based on the costs of the most recent purchases. In our example, the FIFO cost of ending inventory is $36. Cost of goods sold is $54. Panel A of Exhibit 9-3 gives the data, and Panel B shows the FIFO computations.

Last-in, First-out (LIFO) Cost.   The **last-in, first-out (LIFO) method** also depends on the costs of particular inventory purchases. LIFO is the opposite of

EXHIBIT 9-3 *Inventory and Cost of Goods Sold under Average, FIFO, and LIFO Inventory Costing Methods*

Panel A—Illustrative Data:

Beginning inventory (10 units @ $1 per unit)........		$ 10
Purchases:		
No. 1 (25 units @ $1.40 per unit)	$ 35	
No. 2 (25 units @ $1.80 per unit)	45	
Total..		80
Cost of goods available for sale (60 units)...........		$ 90
Ending inventory (20 units @ $? per unit)		?
Cost of goods sold (40 units @ $? per unit		$?

Panel B—Ending Inventory and Cost of Goods Sold:

Average Cost Method:

Cost of goods available for sale—see Panel A (60 units @ average cost of $1.50* per unit)	$ 90
Ending inventory (20 units @ $1.50 per unit)	30
Cost of goods sold (40 units @ $1.50 per unit)	$ 60

* Cost of goods available for sale..............	$ 90
Number of units available for sale	÷ 60
Average cost per unit	$1.50

FIFO Cost Method:

Cost of goods available for sale (60 units—see Panel A)..............		$ 90
Ending inventory (cost of the *last* 20 units available):		
20 units @ $1.80 per unit		36
Cost of goods sold (cost of the *first* 40 units available):		
10 units @ $1.00 per unit	$ 10	
25 units @ $1.40 per unit	35	
5 units @ $1.80 per unit	9	
Total		$ 54

LIFO Cost Method:

Cost of goods available for sale (60 units—see Panel A)..............		$ 90
Ending inventory (cost of the *first* 20 units available):		
10 units @ $1.00 per unit	$ 10	
10 units @ $1.40 per unit	14	
Total		24
Cost of goods sold (cost of the *last* 40 units available):		
25 units @ $1.80 per unit	45	
15 units @ $1.40 per unit	21	
Total		$ 66

FIFO. Under LIFO, the last costs into inventory are the first costs out to cost of goods sold. This leaves the oldest costs—those of beginning inventory and the earliest purchases of the period—in ending inventory. In our example, the LIFO cost of ending inventory is $24. Cost of goods sold is $66. Panel A of Exhibit 9-3 gives the data, and Panel B shows the LIFO computations.

Income Effects of FIFO, LIFO, and Average Cost _____

In our discussion and examples, the cost of inventory rose during the accounting period. When prices change, different costing methods produce different cost of goods sold and ending inventory figures, as Exhibit 9-3 shows. When inventory costs are increasing, FIFO ending inventory is *highest* because it is priced at the most recent costs, which are the highest. LIFO ending inventory is *lowest* because it is priced at the oldest costs, which are the lowest. *Average* cost avoids the extremes of FIFO and LIFO. When inventory costs are decreasing, FIFO ending inventory is lowest, and LIFO is highest.

Exhibit 9-4 summarizes the income effects of the three inventory methods. Study the exhibit carefully, focusing on ending inventory, cost of goods sold, and gross margin.

The Income Tax Advantage of LIFO _____

OBJECTIVE 2

Distinguish between the income effects and the tax effects of the inventory costing methods

When prices are rising, applying the LIFO method results in the *lowest taxable income* and thus the *lowest income taxes*. Let's use the gross margin data of Exhibit 9-4.

	FIFO	LIFO	Average
Gross margin	$46,000	$34,000	$40,000
Operating expenses (assumed)	26,000	26,000	26,000
Income before income tax	$20,000	$ 8,000	$14,000
Income tax expense (40%).	$ 8,000	$ 3,200	$ 5,600

Income tax expense is lowest under LIFO ($3,200) and highest under FIFO ($8,000). The most attractive feature of LIFO is reduced income tax payments.

The Internal Revenue Service allows companies to use LIFO for tax purposes only if they use LIFO for financial reporting purposes. Therefore, businesses that use LIFO for tax purposes must report inventory and income on the LIFO basis for

EXHIBIT 9-4   *Income Effects of FIFO, LIFO, and Average Cost Inventory Methods*

	FIFO		LIFO		Average	
Sales revenue (assumed).		$100,000		$100,000		$100,000
Cost of goods sold:						
Goods available for sale (assumed) .	$ 90,000		$ 90,000		$ 90,000	
Ending inventory.	**36,000**		**24,000**		**30,000**	
Cost of goods sold		54,000		66,000		60,000
Gross margin		$ 46,000		$ 34,000		$ 40,000

Summary of Income Effects — When Inventory Costs Are Increasing:

FIFO—Highest ending inventory	LIFO—Lowest ending inventory	Average—Results fall between
Lowest cost of goods sold	Highest cost of goods sold	the extremes of FIFO
Highest gross margin	Lowest gross margin	and LIFO

their financial statements. However, they may also report an alternative inventory amount in the notes to their financial statements. Federal-Mogul Corporation, a maker of industrial products, reported inventories at LIFO cost but also disclosed the FIFO cost of inventory in Note D, as follows. Observe that FIFO cost is higher than LIFO cost (amounts in millions).

	19X6	19X5
Inventories—Note D	$189	$148

Note D: *Inventories*
Inventories are stated at . . . last-in, first-out (LIFO) cost. . . . Use of the first-in, first-out (FIFO) cost method would have increased inventories by $95 million in 19X6 and $89 million in 19X5. . . .

Of what use is Federal-Mogul's disclosure of the alternate amounts under FIFO? An investor may be comparing Federal-Mogul with another retail company that uses FIFO. Federal-Mogul's inventory and cost of goods sold amounts under LIFO are not comparable to the other company's FIFO figures. To compare the two companies, the investor can convert Federal-Mogul's LIFO amounts to the FIFO basis. Simply substitute the FIFO amounts in place of those reported under LIFO. Here are the cost of goods figures (amounts in millions):

	LIFO Amounts as Reported in the Income Statement	FIFO Amounts Based on Information in the Notes
Beginning inventory	$ 148	$ 237
Net purchases	765	765
Cost of goods available for sale	913	1,002
Less: Ending inventory	189	284
Cost of goods sold	$ 724	$ 718

Cost of goods sold under FIFO ($718 million) can now be used to compare the two companies. In the computation, notice that purchases is the same under FIFO and LIFO. Beginning FIFO inventory is the LIFO amount ($148 million) plus the increase to FIFO ($89 million), a total of $237 million. Ending FIFO inventory is the LIFO amount ($189 million) plus the increase ($95 million), a total of $284 million. These changes cause FIFO cost of goods sold to be less than the LIFO amount, which would cause income to be higher under FIFO. This is valuable information for an investor.

The 1970s were marked by high inflation, so many companies changed to LIFO for its tax advantage. Figure 9-1, based on an American Institute of Certified Public Accountants (AICPA) survey of 600 companies, indicates that LIFO is the most popular inventory costing method.

Comparison of the Inventory Methods _____

We may ask three questions to judge the inventory costing methods. (1) How well does each method match inventory expense—the cost of goods sold—to sales revenue on the income statement? (2) Which method reports the most up-to-date

Figure 9-1   *Use of the Various Inventory Methods*

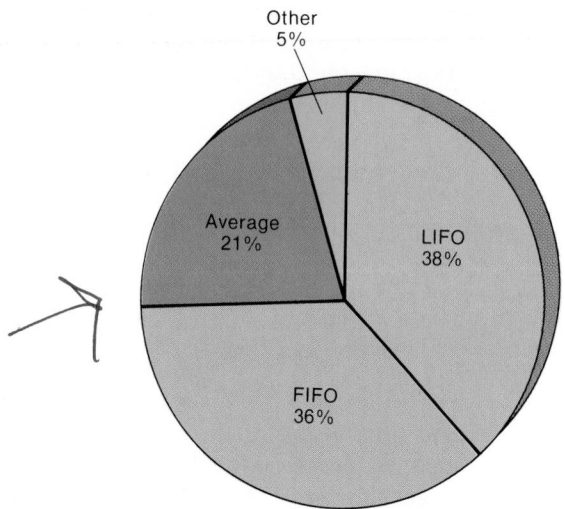

inventory amount on the balance sheet? (3) What effect do the methods have on income taxes? The average cost method produces amounts between the extremes of LIFO and FIFO. The specific unit cost method is used only for inventory made up of individually identifiable units. Therefore, we focus these questions on the differences between LIFO and FIFO.

LIFO better matches the current value of cost of goods sold with current revenue by assigning to this expense the most recent inventory costs. By contrast, FIFO matches the oldest inventory costs against the period's revenue — a poor matching of current expense with current revenue.

FIFO reports the most current inventory costs on the balance sheet. LIFO can result in absurd balance sheet valuations of inventories because the oldest prices are left in ending inventory.

As shown in the preceding section, LIFO results in the lowest income tax payments when prices are rising. Tax payments are highest under FIFO. When inventory prices are decreasing, tax payments are highest under LIFO and lowest under FIFO.

FIFO is criticized because it overstates income by so-called inventory profit during periods of inflation. Briefly, **inventory profit** is the difference between gross margin figured on the FIFO basis and gross margin figured on the LIFO basis. Exhibit 9-4 illustrates inventory profit. The $12,000 difference between FIFO and LIFO gross margins ($46,000 − $34,000 = $12,000) results from the difference in cost of goods sold and in ending inventory. This $12,000 amount is called FIFO inventory profit, phantom profit, or illusory profit. Why? Because to stay in business the company must replace the inventory it has sold. The replacement cost of the merchandise is essentially the same as the cost of goods sold under LIFO ($66,000) not the FIFO amount ($54,000).

LIFO is criticized because it allows managers to manipulate net income. Assume inventory prices are rising rapidly, and a company wants to show less income for the year (in order to pay less taxes). Managers can buy a large amount of inventory near the end of the year. Under LIFO these high inventory costs immediately become expense — as cost of goods sold. As a result, the income statement reports a lower net income. Conversely, if the business is having a bad year, management may wish to increase reported income. To do so, managers can delay a large purchase of high-cost inventory until the next period. This inventory is not expensed as cost of good sold in the current year. Thus management avoids decreasing the current year's reported income.

A company may want to report the highest income, and FIFO meets this need when prices are rising. But the company must pay the highest income taxes under FIFO. When prices are falling, LIFO reports the highest income.

Which inventory method is best? There is no single answer to this question. Different companies have different motives for the inventory method they choose. Polaroid Corporation uses FIFO, J. C. Penny uses LIFO, and Motorola, Inc., uses average cost. Still other companies use more than one method. The Black and Decker Manufacturing Company uses both LIFO and FIFO, as they stated in an annual report (amounts in millions):

> **OBJECTIVE 3**
> Read and understand actual company inventory disclosures

Inventories $390

NOTES TO CONSOLIDATED FINANCIAL STATEMENTS
Note 1: Summary of Accounting Policies
Inventories: The cost of United States inventories is based on the last-in, first-out (LIFO) method; all other inventories are based on the first-in, first-out (FIFO) method. The cost of . . . inventories stated under the LIFO method represents approximately 40% of the value of total inventories.

Consistency Principle

The **consistency principle** states that businesses should use the same accounting methods and procedures from period to period. Consistency makes it possible to compare a company's financial statements from one period to the next.

Suppose you are analyzing a company's net income pattern. The company has switched from LIFO to FIFO. Its net income has increased dramatically but only as a result of the change in inventory method. If you did not know of the change, you might believe that the company's increased income arose from improved operations, which is not the case.

The consistency principle does not require that all companies within an industry use the same accounting method. Nor does it mean that a company may *never* change its own accounting method. However, a company making an accounting change must disclose the effect of the change on net income, as shown below for Midland-Ross Corporation, a large company that makes electrical products, mechanical controls, foundry products, and thermal systems:

EXCERPT FROM NOTE A OF THE MIDLAND-ROSS FINANCIAL STATEMENT
Inventories: The LIFO method of valuing inventories was extended to substantially all of the electrical and mechanical controls inventories. . . . The effect of the change was to reduce net income . . . by $4,638,000. . . .

Summary Problem for Your Review

Suppose an IBM division that handles computer components has these inventory records for January 19X6:

Date	Item	Quantity	Unit Cost	Sale Price
Jan. 1	Beginning inventory	100 units	$ 8	$ —
6	Purchase	60 units	9	—
13	Sale	70 units	—	20
21	Purchase	150 units	9	—
24	Sale	210 units	—	22
27	Purchase	90 units	10	—
30	Sale	30 units	—	25

Company accounting records reveal that related operating expense for January was $1,900.

Required

1. Prepare the January income statement, using the following format. (Round figures to whole dollar amounts.)

IBM Corporation
Income Statement
Month Ended January 31, 19X6

	LIFO	FIFO	Average
Sales revenue...........................	—	—	—
Cost of goods sold:			
Beginning inventory	—	—	—
Net purchases	—	—	—
Cost of goods available for sale	—	—	—
Ending inventory......................	—	—	—
Cost of goods sold....................	—	—	—
Gross margin..........................	—	—	—
Operating expenses.....................	—	—	—
Operating income	—	—	—

2. Suppose you are the financial vice-president of IBM Corporation. Which inventory method would you use if your motive is to
   a. Minimize income taxes?
   b. Report the highest operating income?
   c. Report operating income between the extremes of FIFO and LIFO?
   d. Report inventory at the most current cost?
   e. Attain the best matching of current expense with current revenue?

State the reason for each of your answers.

SOLUTION TO REVIEW PROBLEM

Requirement 1

IBM Corporation
Income Statement for Component
Month Ended January 31, 19X6

	LIFO		FIFO		Average	
Sales revenue.............		$6,770		$6,770		$6,770
Cost of goods sold:						
Beginning inventory	$ 800		$ 800		$ 800	
Net purchases	2,790		2,790		2,790	
Cost of goods available for sale	3,590		3,590		3,590	
Ending inventory........	720		900		808	
Cost of goods sold		2,870		2,690		2,782
Gross margin		3,900		4,080		3,988
Operating expenses........		1,900		1,900		1,900
Operating income		$2,000		$2,180		$2,088

Computations:

Sales revenue: $(70 \times \$20) + (210 \times \$22) + (30 \times \$25) = \$6,770$

Beginning inventory: $100 \times \$8 = \$800$

Purchases: $(60 \times \$9) + (150 \times \$9) + (90 \times \$10) = \$2,790$

Ending inventory – LIFO: $90^* \times \$8 = \$720$

FIFO: $90 \times \$10 = \$900$

Average: $90 \times \$8.975^{**} = \$808$ (rounded from $807.75)

* Number of units in ending inventory $= 100 + 60 - 70 + 150 - 210 + 90 - 30 = 90$

** $3,590/400 units $= \$8.975$ per unit
 Number of units available $= 100 + 60 + 150 + 90 = 400$

Requirement 2

a. Use LIFO to minimize income taxes. Operating income under LIFO is lowest when inventory unit costs are increasing, as they are in this case (from $8 to $10). (If inventory costs were decreasing, income under FIFO would be lowest.)

b. Use FIFO to report the highest operating income. Income under FIFO is highest when inventory unit costs are increasing, as in this situation.

c. Use *average cost* to report an operating income amount between the FIFO and LIFO extremes. This is true in this problem situation and in others whether inventory unit costs are increasing or decreasing.

d. Use FIFO to report inventory at the most current cost. The oldest inventory costs are expensed as cost of goods sold, leaving in ending inventory the most recent (most current) costs of the period.

e. Use LIFO to attain the best matching of current expense with current revenue. The most recent (most current) inventory costs are expensed as cost of goods sold.

Accounting Conservatism _____

Conservatism in accounting means to present the gloomiest possible figures in the financial statements. What advantage does conservatism give a business? Management often looks on the brighter side of operations and may overstate a company's income and asset values. Many accountants regard conservatism as a counterbalance to management's optimistic tendencies. The goal is for financial statements to present realistic figures.

Conservatism appears in accounting guidelines like "anticipate no gains, but provide for all probable losses" and "if in doubt, record an asset at the lowest reasonable amount and a liability at the highest reasonable amount."

Accountants generally regard the historical cost of acquiring an asset as its maximum value. Even if the current market value of the asset increases above its cost, businesses do *not* write up (that is, increase) the asset's accounting value. Assume that a company purchased land for $100,000, and its value increased to $300,000. Accounting conservatism dictates that the historical cost $100,000 be maintained as the accounting value of the land.

Conservatism also directs accountants to decrease the accounting value of an asset if it appears unrealistically high—even if no transaction occurs. Assume that a company paid $35,000 for inventory that has become obsolete, and its current value is only $12,000. Conservatism dictates that the inventory be written down (that is, decreased) to $12,000.

Lower-of-Cost-or-Market Rule

The **lower-of-cost-or-market rule** (abbreviated as *LCM*) shows accounting conservatism in action. LCM requires that an asset be reported in the financial statements at the lower of its historical cost or its market value. Applied to inventories, *market value* means *current replacement cost* (that is, how much the business would have to pay in the market on that day to purchase the same amount of inventory that it has on hand). If the replacement cost of inventory falls below its historical cost, the business must write down the value of its goods. The business reports ending inventory at its LCM value on the balance sheet.

Suppose a business paid $3,000 for inventory on September 26. By December 31, its value has fallen. The inventory can now be replaced for $2,200. Market value is below cost, and the December 31 balance sheet reports this inventory at its LCM value of $2,200. Usually, the market value of inventory is higher than historical cost, so inventory's LCM value is cost for most companies. Exhibit 9-5 presents the effects of LCM on the income statement and the balance sheet. The point of the exhibit is to show that the lower of (a) cost or (b) market value—replacement cost—is the relevant amount for valuing inventory on the income statement and the balance sheet. Companies are not required to show both cost and market value amounts. However, they may report the higher amount in parentheses, as shown on the balance sheet in the exhibit.

LCM states that of the $3,000 cost of ending inventory in Exhibit 9-5, $800 is considered to have expired even though the inventory was not sold during the period. Its replacement cost is only $2,200, and that amount is carried forward to the next period as the cost of beginning inventory. Suppose during the next period the replacement cost of this inventory increases to $2,500. Accounting conservatism states that it would not be appropriate to write up the book value of inven-

EXHIBIT 9-5 *Lower-of-Cost-or-Market (LCM) Effects*

Income Statement:

Sales revenue.		$20,000
Cost of goods sold:		
Beginning inventory (LCM = Cost).	$ 2,800	
Net purchases	11,000	
Cost of goods available for sale	13,800	
Ending inventory-		
Cost = $3,000		
Replacement cost (market value) = $2,200		
LCM = Market	2,200	
Cost of goods sold.		11,600
Gross margin		$ 8,400

Balance Sheet:

Current assets:		
Cash	$ XXX	
Short-term investments.	XXX	
Accounts receivable.	XXX	
Inventories, at LCM (Cost, $3,000)	2,200	
Prepaid investments	XXX	
Total current assets	$ X,XXX	

OBJECTIVE 4
Apply the lower-of-cost-or-market rule to inventory

tory. The LCM value of inventory ($2,200 in this case) is used as its cost in future LCM determinations.

Examine the following income statement effect of LCM summarized from Exhibit 9-5. What expense absorbs the impact of the $800 inventory write down? *Cost of goods sold* is increased by $800 because ending inventory is $800 less at LCM ($2,200) than it would have been at cost ($3,000).

	Ending Inventory at		
	Cost	LCM	
Cost of goods available for sale	$13,800	$13,800	
Ending inventory:			
Cost	3,000		$800 Lower
Replacement cost (market value)		2,200	at LCM
Cost of goods sold.	$10,800	$11,600	$800 Higher
			at LCM

Exhibit 9-5 also reports the application of LCM for inventories in the body of the balance sheet. Companies often disclose LCM in notes to their financial statements, as shown below for CBS, Inc.:

NOTE 1: STATEMENT OF SIGNIFICANT ACCOUNTING POLICIES

Inventories. Inventories are stated at the *lower of cost* (principally based on average cost) *or market value.* [emphasis added]

Effect of Inventory Errors _____

OBJECTIVE 5

Explain why inventory errors counterbalance

Businesses determine inventory amounts at the end of the period. In the process of counting the items, applying unit costs, and computing amounts, errors may arise. As the period 1 segment of Exhibit 9-6 shows, an error in the ending inventory amount creates errors in the cost of goods sold and gross margin amounts. Compare periods 1 and 3.

Recall that one period's ending inventory is the next period's beginning inventory. Thus the error in ending inventory carries over into the next period: note the highlighted amounts in Exhibit 9-6.

Because the same ending inventory figure that is *subtracted* in computing cost of goods sold in one period is *added* to compute cost of goods sold in the next period, the error's effect cancels out. The overstatement of cost of goods sold in period 2 counterbalances the understatement in cost of goods sold in period 1. Thus the total gross margin amount for the two periods is the correct $100,000 figure whether or not an error entered into the computation.

However, inventory errors should not be dismissed lightly. Suppose you are analyzing trends in the business's operations. Exhibit 9-6 reports a drop in gross margin from period 1 to period 2, followed by an increase in period 3. But that picture of operations is untrue because of the inventory error. Correct gross margin is $50,000 each period. To provide accurate information for decision making, all inventory errors should be corrected.

Methods of Estimating Inventory _____

OBJECTIVE 6

Estimate inventory by two methods

Often a business must *estimate* the value of its inventory. Because of cost and inconvenience, few companies physically count their inventories at the end of each month, yet they may need monthly financial statements. A fire or a flood may destroy inventory, and to file an insurance claim, the business must estimate the value of its loss. In both cases, the business needs to know the value of ending inventory without being able to count it. Two methods for estimating ending

EXHIBIT 9-6   *Effects of Inventory Errors*

	Period 1 Ending Inventory Overstated By $5,000		Period 2 Beginning Inventory Overstated By $5,000		Period 3 Correct
Sales revenue		$100,000		$100,000	$100,000
Cost of goods sold:					
Beginning inventory	$10,000		**$15,000**		$10,000
Net purchases	50,000		50,000		50,000
Cost of goods available for sale	60,000		65,000		60,000
Ending inventory	**15,000**		10,000		10,000
Cost of goods sold		45,000		55,000	50,000
Gross margin		$55,000		$45,000	$50,000
			$100,000		

The authors thank Carl High for this example.

inventory are the *gross margin method* (or *gross profit method*) and the *retail method.* These methods are widely used in actual practice.

Gross Margin (Gross Profit) Method

The **gross margin method** is a way of estimating inventory based on the familiar cost of goods sold model:

> **Beginning inventory**
> **+ Net purchases**
> **= Cost of goods available for sale**
> **− Ending inventory**
> **= Cost of goods sold**

Rearranging *ending inventory* and *cost of goods sold,* the model becomes useful for estimating ending inventory:

> **Beginning inventory**
> **+ Net purchases**
> **= Cost of goods available for sale**
> **− Cost of goods sold**
> **= Ending inventory**

Suppose a fire destroys your business's inventory. To collect insurance, you must estimate the cost of the ending inventory. If the fire did not also destroy your accounting records, beginning inventory and net purchases amounts may be taken directly from the accounting records. The Sales Revenue, Sales Returns, and Sales Discounts accounts indicate net sales up to the date of the fire. Using the entity's normal *gross margin rate* (that is, gross margin divided by net sales revenue), you can estimate cost of goods sold. The last step is to subtract cost of goods sold from goods available to estimate ending inventory. Exhibit 9-7 illustrates the gross margin method.

Accountants, managers, and auditors use the gross margin method to test the overall reasonableness of an ending inventory amount that has been determined by a physical count for all types of businesses. This method helps to detect large errors.

Retail Method

Retail establishments (department stores, drug stores, hardware stores, and so on) use the **retail method** to estimate their inventory cost. The retail method, like the gross margin method, is based on the cost of goods sold model. However, the

EXHIBIT 9-7   *Gross Margin Method of Estimating Inventory (amounts assumed)*

Beginning inventory		$14,000
Net purchases		66,000
Cost of goods available for sale		80,000
Cost of goods sold:		
Net sales revenue	$100,000	
Less estimated gross margin of 40%	40,000	
Estimated cost of goods sold		60,000
Estimated cost of *ending inventory*		$20,000

EXHIBIT 9-8   *Retail Method of Estimating Inventory (amounts assumed)*

	Cost	Retail
Beginning inventory.............................	$ 24,000	$ 40,000
Net purchases....................................	144,000	240,000
Goods available for sale..........................	$168,000	280,000
Cost ratio: $168,000/$280,000 = .60		
Less: Net sales revenue (which is stated at retail)		(230,000)
Ending inventory, at retail.........................		$ 50,000
Ending inventory, at cost ($50,000 × .60)	$ 30,000	

retail method requires that the business record inventory purchases both at *cost* — as shown in the purchase records — and at *retail* (selling) price — as shown on the price tags. This is not a burden because price tags show the retail price of inventory, and most retailers set their retail prices by adding standard markups to their cost. For example, a department store may pay $6 for a man's belt, mark it up $4, and price the belt at $10 retail. In the retail method, the seller's inventory cost is determined by working backward from its retail value. Exhibit 9-8 illustrates the process.

In Exhibit 9-8 the accounting records show the goods available for sale at cost ($168,000) and at retail ($280,000). The cost ratio is .60 ($168,000/$280,000). For simplicity, we round all such percentages to two decimal places in this chapter. Subtracting *net sales revenue* (a retail amount) from *goods available for sale at retail* yields *ending inventory at retail* ($50,000). The business multiplies *ending inventory at retail* by the cost ratio to figure *ending inventory at cost* ($30,000).

Suppose the retailer has four categories of inventory, each with a different cost ratio. How would the business use the retail method to estimate the overall cost of the ending inventory? Apply the retail method separately to each category of inventory, using its specific cost ratio, then add the costs of the four categories to determine the overall cost of inventory.

Even though the retail method is an estimation technique, some retailers use it to compute the inventory value for their financial statements. They make physical counts of inventory throughout the year to validate the retail-method amounts. For example, Marshall Field & Company, a department store chain headquartered in Chicago, uses the retail method, as disclosed in its annual report:

Merchandise inventories (note 1C) $179,007,250

Note 1C: Inventory Pricing
      Substantially all merchandise inventories are valued by use of the *retail method.* [emphasis added]

Periodic and Perpetual Inventory Systems _____

Different businesses have different inventory information needs. We now look at the two main inventory systems: the *periodic system* and the *perpetual system.*

Periodic Inventory System.   In the **periodic inventory system,** the business does not keep a continuous record of the inventory on hand. Instead, at the end of the period, the business makes a physical count of the on-hand inventory and applies the appropriate unit costs to determine the cost of ending inventory. The business makes the standard end-of-period inventory entries, as discussed in Chapter 5 and shown in the example that follows. This system is also called the *physical system* because it relies on the actual physical count of inventory. The periodic system is used to account for inventory items that have a low unit cost. Low-cost items may not be valuable enough to warrant the cost of keeping a running record of the inventory on hand.

Entries Under the Periodic System.   In the periodic system, the business records purchases of inventory in the Purchases account (an expense account). At the end of the period, the business removes the beginning balance from the Inventory account and enters the ending balance, as determined by the physical count. Assume the following data for a K-Mart store's April transactions.

Beginning inventory	$ 80,000
Ending inventory	102,000
Credit purchases (net of discounts and returns)	600,000
Credit sales (net of discounts and returns)	900,000

OBJECTIVE 7
Account for inventory by the periodic and perpetual systems

Summary entries for April:

To record credit purchases:

Purchases	600,000	
Accounts Payable		600,000

To record credit sales:

Accounts Receivable	900,000	
Sales Revenue		900,000

Inventory entries at the end of the period:

Income Summary	80,000	
Inventory (beginning balance)		80,000
Inventory (ending balance)	102,000	
Income Summary		102,000

Reporting on the financial statements:

Balance sheet at April 30:

Inventory	$102,000

Income statement for April:

Sales revenue		$900,000
Cost of goods sold:		
Beginning inventory	$ 80,000	
Net purchases	600,000	
Cost of goods available	680,000	
Ending inventory	102,000	
Cost of goods sold		578,000
Gross margin		$322,000

Perpetual Inventory System.   In the **perpetual inventory system,** the business keeps a continuous record for each inventory item. The records thus show the inventory on hand at all times. Perpetual records are useful in preparing monthly, quarterly, or other interim financial statements. The business can determine the cost of ending inventory and the cost of goods sold directly from the accounts without having to physically count the merchandise.

The perpetual system offers a higher degree of control than the periodic system

EXHIBIT 9-9 *Perpetual Inventory Record*

Item   Home Computer Model RK-42

Date	Received Qty.	Received Unit Cost	Received Total	Sold Qty.	Sold Unit Cost	Sold Total	Balance Qty.	Balance Unit Cost	Balance Total
Nov. 1							14	$300	$4,200
5				4	$300	$1,200	10	300	3,000
7				9	300	2,700	1	300	300
12	5	$320	$1,600				1	300	300
							5	320	1,600
26	7	330	2,310				1	300	300
							5	320	1,600
							7	330	2,310
30				1	300	300	1	320	320
				4	320	1,280	7	330	2,310
Totals	12	—	$3,910	18	—	$5,480	8	—	$2,630

does because the inventory information is always up to date. Consequently businesses use the perpetual system for high-unit-cost inventories, such as gemstones and automobiles. Nevertheless, companies physically count their inventory at least once each year to check the accuracy of their perpetual records.

Perpetual inventory records can be computer listings of inventory items or inventory cards like the Computerworld record shown in Exhibit 9-9. The accountant adds information to the computer list or the card on a daily basis. A running balance conveniently shows the latest inventory value. The perpetual record serves as a subsidiary record to the inventory account in the general ledger.

The perpetual inventory record indicates that the business uses the FIFO basis, as shown by the November 30 sale. The cost of the first unit sold is the oldest unit cost on hand. Perpetual records may also be kept on the LIFO basis or the average basis. Perpetual inventory records provide information such as the following:

1. When customers inquire about how soon they can get a home computer, the salesperson can answer the question after referring to the perpetual inventory record. On November 7 the salesperson would reply that the company's stock is low, and the customer may have to wait a few days. On November 26 the salesperson could offer immediate delivery.

2. The perpetual records alert the business to reorder when inventory becomes low. On November 7 the company would be wise to purchase inventory. Sales may be lost if the business cannot promise immediate delivery.

3. At November 30 the company prepares monthly financial statements. The perpetual inventory records show the company's ending inventory of home computers at $2,630, and its cost of goods sold for this product at $5,480. No physical count is necessary at this time. However, a physical inventory is needed once a year to verify the accuracy of the records.

Entries under the Perpetual System. In the perpetual system, the business records purchases of inventory by debiting the Inventory account. When the business makes a sale, two entries are necessary. The company records the sale in the usual manner—debits Cash or Accounts Receivable and credits Sales Revenue for the sale price of the goods. The company also debits Cost of Goods Sold and credits Inventory for cost. The debit to Inventory (for purchases) and the credit to Inventory (for sales) serve to keep an up-to-date record of inventory on hand. Therefore, no end-of-period adjusting entries are needed. The Inventory account already carries the correct ending balance.

In the perpetual system, Cost of Goods Sold is an account in the general ledger. By contrast, in the periodic system, cost of goods sold is simply a total on the income statement.

To illustrate the entries under the perpetual system, let's use the same data we used in discussing the periodic system, which follow.

Ending inventory	$102,000
Credit purchases (net of discounts and returns)	600,000
Credit sales (net of discounts and returns)	900,000
Cost of goods sold	578,000

Summary entries for April:

To record credit purchases:

Inventory	600,000	
Accounts Payable		600,000

To record credit sales:

Accounts Receivable	900,000	
Sales Revenue		900,000
Cost of Goods Sold	578,000	
Inventory		578,000

Reporting on the financial statements:

Balance sheet at April 30:

Inventory	$102,000

Income statement for April:

Sales revenue	$900,000
Cost of goods sold	578,000
Gross margin	$322,000

You should compare the entries and financial statement presentations under the *periodic* and the *perpetual* systems. Note that the entries to record purchases and sales differ under the two systems but that the financial statement amounts are the same.

Internal Control over Inventory

Internal control over inventory is important because inventory is the lifeblood of a merchandiser. Successful companies take great care to protect their inventory. Elements of good internal control over inventory include:

1. Physically counting inventory at least once each year no matter which system is used
2. Maintaining efficient purchasing, receiving, and shipping procedures
3. Storing inventory to protect it against theft, damage, and decay

4. Limiting access to inventory to personnel who do *not* have access to the accounting records
5. Keeping perpetual inventory records for high-unit-cost merchandise
6. Purchasing inventory in economical quantities
7. Keeping enough inventory on hand to prevent shortage situations, which lead to lost sales
8. Not keeping too large an inventory stockpiled, thus avoiding the expense of tying up money in unneeded items

The annual physical count of inventory (item 1) is necessary because the only way to be certain of the amount of inventory on hand is to count it. Errors arise in the best accounting systems, and the count is needed to establish the correct value of the inventory. When an error is detected, the records are brought into agreement with the physical count.

Keeping inventory handlers away from the accounting records (item 4) is an essential separation of duties, discussed in Chapter 7. An employee with access to inventory and the accounting records can steal the goods and make an entry to conceal the theft. For example, he could increase the amount of an inventory write-down to make it appear that goods decreased in value when in fact they were stolen.

Computerized Inventory Records

Computer systems have revolutionized accounting for inventory. They can provide up-to-the-minute inventory data useful for managing the business. They help cut accounting cost by processing large numbers of transactions without computational error. Computer systems also enhance internal control. They increase efficiency because managers always know the quantity and cost of inventory on hand. Managers can make better decisions about quantities to buy, prices to pay for the inventory, prices to charge customers, and sale terms to offer. Knowing the quantity on hand helps to safeguard the inventory.

Computer inventory systems vary considerably. At one extreme are complex systems used by huge retailers like Sears, Penney's, and K-Mart. Purchases of inventory are recorded in perpetual records stored in a central computer. The inventory tags are coded electronically for updating the perpetual records when a sale is recorded on the cash register. Have you noticed sales clerks passing the inventory ticket over a particular area of the checkout counter? A sensing device in the counter reads the stock number, quantity, cost, and sale price of the item sold. In other systems, the sales clerk passes an electronic device over the inventory tag. The computer records the sale and updates the inventory records. In effect, a journal entry is recorded for each sale, a procedure that is not economical without a computer.

Small companies also use minicomputers and microcomputers to keep perpetual inventory records. These systems may be similar to the systems used by large companies. In less sophisticated systems, a company may have sales clerks write inventory stock numbers on sales slips. The stock number identifies the particular item of inventory, such as men's shirts or children's shoes. The business may accumulate all sales slips for the week. If the company has its own computer system, an employee may type the sales information into the computer and store the perpetual records on a magnetic disk. To learn the quantity, cost, or other characteristic of a particular item of inventory, a manager can view the inventory record on the computer monitor. For broader-based decisions affecting the entire inventory, managers use printouts of all items in stock. Many small businesses hire outside computer service centers to do much of the accounting for inventory. Regardless of the arrangement, managers get periodic printouts showing inventory data needed for managing the business. Manual reporting of this information is more time consuming and expensive.

Summary Problems for Your Review

Problem 1

Centronics Data Computer Corporation reported a net loss for the year. In its financial statements, the company noted:

Balance Sheet:

Current assets:
Inventories (notes 1C and 2)............................. $48,051,000

> Note 1C: Inventories are stated at the lower of cost or market. Cost is determined on a first-in, first-out (FIFO) basis.
> Note 2: Declining . . . market conditions during [the] fiscal [year] adversely affected anticipated sales of the Company's older printer products; . . . Accordingly, the statement of loss . . . includes a [debit] of $9,600,000.

Required

1. At which amount did Centronics report its inventory, cost or market value? How can you tell?
2. If the reported inventory of $48,051,000 represents market value, what was the cost of the inventory?

Problem 2

American Hospital Supply Corporation reported using the LIFO inventory method. Its inventory amount was $490.5 million.

Required

1. Suppose that during the period covered by this report, the company made an error that understated its inventory by $15 million. What effect would this error have on *cost of goods sold* and *gross margin* of the period? On *cost of goods sold* and *gross margin* of the following period? On *total gross margin* of both periods combined?
2. When American Hospital Supply reported the above amount for inventory, prices were rising. Would FIFO or LIFO have shown a higher gross margin? Why?

SOLUTIONS TO REVIEW PROBLEMS

Problem 1

1. Centronics reported its inventory at *market value,* as indicated by (a) their valuing inventories at LCM and (b) the declining market conditions that caused the company to "include a [debit] of $9,600,000" in "the statement of

loss." The company debited the $9,600,000 to a loss account or to cost of goods sold. The credit side of the entry was to Inventory—for a write-down to market value.

2. The cost of inventory before the write-down was $57,651,000 ($48,051,000 + $9,600,000). The $48,051,000 market value is what is left of the original cost. Thus the amount to be carried forward to future periods is $48,051,000.

Problem 2

1. Understating ending inventory by $15 million has the following effects on *cost of goods sold* and *gross margin*:

	Cost of Goods Sold	Gross Margin
Period during which error was made	OVERSTATED by $15 million	UNDERSTATED by $15 million
Following period	UNDERSTATED by $15 million	OVERSTATED by $15 million
Combined total	CORRECTLY STATED	CORRECTLY STATED

2. When prices are rising, FIFO results in higher gross margin than LIFO. FIFO matches against sales revenue the lower inventory costs of beginning inventory and purchases made during the early part of the period.

Summary

Accounting for inventory plays an important part in merchandisers' accounting systems because selling inventory is the heart of their business. Inventory is generally the largest current asset on their balance sheet, and inventory expense—called cost of goods sold—is usually the largest expense on the income statement.

Businesses multiply the quantity of inventory items by their unit cost to determine inventory cost. Inventory costing methods are *specific unit cost; average cost; first-in, first-out (FIFO) cost; and last-in, first-out (LIFO)* cost. Businesses that sell individually identifiable items, like automobiles and jewels, use the specific unit cost method. Most other companies use the other methods.

FIFO reports ending inventory at the most current cost. LIFO reports cost of goods sold at the most current cost. When inventory costs increase, LIFO produces the highest cost of goods sold and the lowest income, thus minimizing income taxes. FIFO results in the highest income. The average cost method avoids the extremes of FIFO and LIFO.

The *consistency principle* demands that a business stick with the inventory method it chooses. If a change in inventory method is warranted, the company must report the effect of the change on income. The *lower-of-cost-or-market rule*—an example of accounting *conservatism*—requires that businesses report inventory on the balance sheet at the lower of its cost or current replacement value.

The *gross profit method* and the *retail method* are two techniques for estimating the cost of inventory. These methods come in handy for preparing interim financial statements and for estimating the cost of inventory destroyed by fire and other casualties.

Merchandisers with high-price-tag items generally use the *perpetual inventory system,* which features a running inventory balance. Merchandisers handling low-price-tag items usually use the *periodic system.* A physical count of inventory is needed in both systems for control purposes.

Self-Study Questions

Test your understanding of the chapter by marking the best answer to each of the following questions.

1. Which of the following items is the greatest in dollar amount? *(p. 346)*
   a. Beginning inventory
   b. Purchases
   c. Cost of goods available for sale
   d. Ending inventory
   e. Cost of goods sold

2. Sound Warehouse counts 15,000 stereo albums, including 1,000 albums held on consignment, in its Waco, Texas, store. The business has purchased an additional 2,000 units on FOB destination terms. These goods are still in transit. Each album cost $3.40. The cost of the inventory to report on the balance sheet is *(p. 347)*
   a. $47,600
   b. $51,000
   c. $54,400
   d. $57,800

3. The inventory costing method that best matches current expense with current revenue is *(p. 352)*
   a. Specific unit cost
   b. Average cost
   c. FIFO
   d. LIFO
   e. FIFO or LIFO, depending on whether inventory costs are increasing or decreasing

4. The consistency principle has the most direct impact on *(p. 353)*
   a. Whether to include or exclude an item in inventory
   b. Whether to change from one inventory method to another
   c. Whether to write inventory down to a market value below cost
   d. Whether to use the periodic or the perpetual inventory system

5. Application of the lower-of-cost-or-market rule often results in *(p. 357)*
   a. Higher ending inventory
   b. Lower ending inventory
   c. A counterbalancing error
   d. A change from one inventory method to another

6. An error understated ending inventory of 19X7. This error will *(p. 358)*
   a. Overstate 19X7 cost of sales
   b. Understate 19X8 cost of sales
   c. Not affect owner's equity at the end of 19X8
   d. All of the above

7. Beginning inventory was $35,000, purchases were $146,000, and sales totaled $240,000. With a normal gross margin rate of 35 percent, how much is ending inventory? *(p. 359)*
   a. $25,000
   b. $35,000
   c. $97,000
   d. $181,000

8. Beginning inventory was $20,000 at cost and $40,000 at retail. Purchases were $120,000 at cost and $210,000 at retail. Sales were $200,000. How much is ending inventory at cost? *(p. 360)*
   a. $22,000
   b. $26,000
   c. $28,000
   d. $50,000

9. The year-end entry to close beginning inventory in a perpetual inventory system is *(p. 363)*

   a. Income Summary XXX
          Inventory.   XXX
   b. Inventory. XXX
          Income Summary   XXX
   c. Either of the above, depending on whether inventory increased or decreased during the period
   d. Not needed

10. Which of the following statements is true? *(pp. 363, 364)*
    a. Separation of duties is not an important element of internal control for inventories.

b. The perpetual system is used primarily for low-unit-cost inventory.
c. An annual physical count of inventory is needed regardless of the type of inventory system used.
d. All the above are true.

Answers to the self-study questions are at the end of the chapter.

Accounting Vocabulary

average cost method *(p. 348)*, beginning inventory *(p. 345)*, conservatism *(p. 356)*, consignment *(p. 347)*, consistency principle *(p. 353)*, ending inventory *(p. 345)*, first-in, first-out (FIFO) method *(p. 348)*, FOB destination *(p. 347)*, FOB shipping point *(p. 347)*, goods available for sale *(p. 345)*, gross margin (gross profit) method *(p. 359)*, inventory cost *(p. 347)*, inventory profit *(p. 352)*, last-in, first-out (LIFO) method *(p. 348)*, lower-of-cost-or-market (LCM) rule *(p. 356)*, periodic inventory system *(p. 360)*, perpetual inventory system *(p. 361)*, retail method *(p. 359)*, specific cost method *(p. 348)*.

ASSIGNMENT MATERIAL

Questions

1. Why is merchandise inventory so important to a retailer or wholesaler?
2. If beginning inventory is $10,000, purchases total $85,000, and ending inventory is $12,700, how much is cost of goods sold?
3. If beginning inventory is $32,000, purchases total $119,000, and cost of goods sold is $127,000, how much is ending inventory?
4. What role does the cost principle play in accounting for inventory?
5. What two items determine the cost of ending inventory?
6. Briefly describe the four generally accepted inventory cost methods. During a period of rising prices, which method produces the highest reported income? Which produces the lowest reported income?
7. Which inventory costing method produces the ending inventory valued at the most current cost? Which method produces the cost-of-goods-sold amount valued at the most current cost?
8. What is the most attractive feature of LIFO? Does LIFO have this advantage during periods of increasing prices or during periods of decreasing prices? Why has LIFO had this advantage recently?
9. Which inventory costing method is used the most in practice? Which method is used second most? third most?
10. What is inventory profit? Which method produces it?
11. Identify the chief criticism of LIFO.
12. How does the consistency principle affect accounting for inventory?
13. Briefly describe the influence that the concept of conservatism has on accounting for inventory.
14. Manley Company's inventory has a cost of $48,000 at the end of the year, and the current replacement cost of the inventory is $51,000. At which amount should the company report the inventory on its balance sheet? Suppose the current replacement cost of the inventory is $45,000 instead of $51,000. At which amount should Manley report the inventory? What rule governs your answers to these questions?
15. Gabriel Company accidentally overstated its ending inventory by $10,000 at the end of period 1. Is gross margin of period 1 overstated or understated? Is gross margin of period 2 overstated, understated, or unaffected by the period 1 error? Is total gross

margin for the two periods overstated, understated, or correct? Give the reason for your answer.

16. Identify two methods of estimating inventory amounts. What familiar model underlies both estimation methods?

17. A fire destroyed the inventory of Olivera Company, but the accounting records were saved. The beginning inventory was $22,000, purchases for the period were $71,000, and sales were $140,000. Olivera's customary gross margin is 45 percent of sales. Use the gross margin method to estimate the cost of the inventory destroyed by the fire.

18. Suppose your company deals in expensive jewelry. Which inventory system should you use to achieve good internal control over the inventory? If your business is a hardware store that sells low-cost goods, what inventory system would you be likely to use? Why would you choose this system?

19. Identify the accounts debited and credited in the standard purchase and sale entries under (a) the periodic inventory system and (b) the perpetual inventory system.

20. What is the role of the physical count of inventory in (a) the periodic inventory system and (b) the perpetual inventory system?

21. True or false? A company that sells inventory of low unit cost needs no internal controls over the goods. Any inventory loss would probably be small.

Exercises

Exercise 9-1 *Computing ending inventory by four methods*

The inventory records for stereo tuner/amplifiers indicate the following at October 31:

Oct.	1	Beginning inventory	10 units @ $130
	8	Purchase	4 units @ 140
	15	Purchase	11 units @ 150
	26	Purchase	5 units @ 156

The physical count of inventory at October 31 indicates that seven units are on hand, and the company owns them. Compute ending inventory and cost of goods sold using each of the following methods:

1. Specific unit cost, assuming five $150 units and two $130 units are on hand
2. Average cost
3. First in, first out
4. Last in, first out

Exercise 9-2 *Recording periodic inventory transactions*

Assume the data in Exercise 9-1 pertain to Ching Company. Prepare the general journal entries under the periodic inventory system to record:

1. Total October purchases in one summary entry. All purchases were on credit.
2. Total October sales in one summary entry. Assume the selling price was $300 per unit, and all sales were on credit.
3. October 31 entries for inventory. Ching uses FIFO.

Exercise 9-3 *Computing the tax advantage of LIFO over FIFO*

Use the data in Exercise 9-1 to illustrate the income tax advantage of LIFO over FIFO, assuming sales revenue is $6,500, operating expenses are $1,100, and the income tax rate is 40 percent.

Exercise 9-4 *Converting LIFO financial statements to the FIFO basis*

Maxus Corporation reported:

Balance sheet:	19X5	19X4
Inventories—note 4	$ 65,800	$ 59,300
Income statement:		
Net purchases	404,100	372,700
Cost of sales	397,600	381,400

Note 4. The company determines inventory cost by the last-in, first-out method. If the first-in, first-out method were used, inventories would be $8,200 higher at year end 19X5 and $7,500 higher at year end 19X4.

Required

Show the cost of goods sold computations for 19X5 under LIFO and FIFO. Which method would result in higher reported income? Show the amount of the difference.

Exercise 9-5 *Note disclosure of a change in inventory method*

A company has used the first-in, first-out inventory method for many years. At the start of the current year the company switched to the last-in, first-out method. This change decreased net income by $263,000. Write the note to disclose this accounting change in the company's financial statements.

Exercise 9-6 *The effect of lower-of-cost-or-market on the income statement*

From the following inventory records of Barnet, Inc., for 19X7, prepare the company's income statement through gross margin. Apply the lower-of-cost-or-market rule.

Beginning inventory (average cost)	300 @	$41.33	=	$ 12,399
(replacement cost)	300 @	41.91	=	12,573
Purchases during the year	2,600 @	45.50	=	118,300
Ending inventory (average cost)	400 @	45.07	=	18,028
(replacement cost)	400 @	42.10	=	16,840
Sales during the year	2,500 @	91.00*	=	227,500

* Selling price per unit.

Exercise 9-7 *Applying the lower-of-cost-or-market rule*

Danos Company's income statement for March reported the following data:

Income Statement:

Sales revenue		$83,000
Cost of goods sold:		
Beginning inventory	$17,200	
Net purchases	51,700	
Cost of goods available for sale	68,900	
Ending inventory	22,800	
Cost of goods sold		46,100
Gross margin		$36,900

Prior to releasing the financial statements, it was discovered that the current replacement cost of ending inventory was $19,600. Correct the above data to include the lower-of-cost-or-market value of ending inventory. Also, show how inventory would be reported on the balance sheet.

Exercise 9-8   *Correcting an inventory error*

Lee Corporation reported the following comparative income statement for the years ended September 30, 19X5 and 19X4:

Lee Corporation
Income Statements
For the Years Ended September 30,

	19X5		19X4	
Sales revenue		$132,300		$121,700
Cost of goods sold:				
Beginning inventory	$14,000		$12,800	
Net purchases	72,000		66,000	
Cost of goods available	86,000		78,800	
Ending inventory	16,600		14,000	
Cost of goods sold		69,400		64,800
Gross margin		62,900		56,900
Operating expenses		30,300		26,100
Net income		$ 32,600		$ 30,800

During 19X5 accountants for the company discovered that ending 19X4 inventory was overstated by $1,500. Prepare the corrected comparative income statement for the two-year period. What was the effect of the error on net income for the two years combined? Explain your answer.

Exercise 9-9   *Estimating inventory by the gross margin method*

McIntosh Company began April with inventory of $41,000. The business made net purchases of $37,600 and had net sales of $51,000 before a fire destroyed the company's inventory. For the past several years, McIntosh's gross margin on sales has been 30 percent. Estimate the cost of the inventory destroyed by the fire.

Exercise 9-10   *Estimating inventory by the retail method*

Assume the inventory records of a small department of Macy's, a large chain of department stores, revealed the following:

	At Cost	At Retail
Beginning inventory	$ 26,000	$ 48,000
Net purchases	103,000	191,000
Net sales.		201,000

Use the retail inventory method to estimate the ending inventory of the department. Round the cost ratio to two decimal places.

Exercise 9-11   *Recording perpetual inventory transactions*

King Chevrolet Company keeps perpetual inventory records for its automobile inventory. During May the company made credit purchases of inventory costing $111,300. Cash sales came to $26,800, credit sales totaled $130,400, and cost of goods sold reached $119,550. Record these summary transactions in the general journal.

Problems

(Group A)

Problem 9-1A   *Computing inventory by three methods*

Hernandez Imports began the year with 230 units of inventory that cost $80 each. During the year Hernandez made the following purchases:

Feb. 3	217 @ $81
Apr. 12	95 @ 82
Aug. 8	210 @ 84
Oct. 24	248 @ 88

The company uses the periodic inventory system, and the physical count at December 31 indicates that ending inventory consists of 319 units.

Required

Compute the ending inventory and cost of goods sold amounts under (1) average cost, (2) FIFO cost, and (3) LIFO cost. Round average cost per unit to the nearest cent, and round all other amounts to the nearest dollar.

Problem 9-2A   *Computing inventory, cost of goods sold, and FIFO inventory profits*

Campus Sportswear specializes in men's shirts. The store began operations on January 1, 19X1, with an inventory of 200 shirts that cost $13 each, a $2,600 total. During the year the store purchased inventory as follows:

Purchase no. 1	110 @ $14
Purchase no. 2	80 @ 15
Purchase no. 3	320 @ 15
Purchase no. 4	100 @ 18

The ending inventory consists of 250 shirts.

Required

1. Complete the following tabulation, rounding average cost to the nearest cent and all other amounts to the nearest dollar:

	Ending Inventory	Cost of Goods Sold
a. Average cost	_____	_____
b. FIFO cost	_____	_____
c. LIFO cost	_____	_____

2. Compute the amount of inventory profit under FIFO.
3. Which method produces the most current ending inventory cost? Which method produces the most current cost-of-goods-sold amount? Give the reason for your answers.

Problem 9-3A   *Preparing an income statement directly from the accounts*

The records of Janeway Retailers include the following accounts for one of its products at December 31 of the current year:

Inventory

Jan. 1	Balance	{ 300 units @ $3.00 } { 100 units @ 3.10 }	1,210	

Purchases

Feb. 6	800 units @ $3.15	2,520	
May 19	600 units @ 3.35	2,010	
Aug. 12	460 units @ 3.50	1,610	
Oct. 4	800 units @ 3.75	3,000	
Dec. 31	Balance	9,140	

Sales Revenue

	Mar. 12	500 units @ $4.00	2,000
	June 9	1,100 units @ 4.20	4,620
	Aug. 21	300 units @ 4.50	1,350
	Nov. 2	400 units @ 4.50	1,800
	Dec. 18	100 units @ 4.75	475
	Dec. 31	Balance	10,245

Required

1. Compute the quantities of goods in (a) ending inventory and (b) cost of goods sold during the year.
2. Prepare the following partial income statement under the average cost, FIFO cost, and LIFO cost methods. Round average cost to the nearest cent and all other amounts to the nearest dollar.

Janeway Retailers
Income Statement
For the year ended December 31, 19XX

	Average Cost	FIFO Cost	LIFO Cost
Sales revenue	$ 10,245	$ 10,245	$ 10,245
Cost of goods sold:			
Beginning inventory	$ 1,210	$ 1,210	$ 1,210
Purchases	9,140	9,140	9,140
Cost of goods available	10,350	10,350	10,350
Ending inventory	2,231	2,475	2,029
Cost of goods sold	8,119	7,875	8,321
Gross margin	$ 2,126	$ 2,370	$ 1,924

Problem 9-4A *Recording periodic and perpetual inventory transactions*

Using the data in Problem 9-3A, make summary entries in the general journal to record:

1. Purchases, sales, and end-of-period inventory entries, assuming Janeway Retailers uses the periodic inventory system and the average cost method. All purchases are on credit. Cash sales are $4,000, with the remaining sales on account.
2. Purchases, sales, and cost of goods sold, assuming Janeway Retailers uses the perpetual inventory system and the average cost method. All purchases are on credit. Cash sales total $4,000, with the remainder on account.

Problem 9-5A *Applying the lower-of-cost-or-market rule*

Assume that accountants prepared the financial statements of Dysan Company on the cost basis without considering whether the replacement value of ending inventory was less than cost. Following are selected data from those statements:

From the income statement:

Sales revenue..........................		$832,000
Cost of goods sold:		
Beginning inventory	$104,000	
Net purchases	587,000	
Cost of goods available for sale	691,000	
Ending inventory.................	143,000	
Cost of goods sold		548,000
Gross margin		$284,000

From the balance sheet:

Current assets:	
Inventory	$143,000

The replacement costs were $122,000 for beginning inventory and $138,000 for ending inventory.

Required

1. Revise the data to include the appropriate lower-of-cost-or-market value of inventory.
2. How is the lower-of-cost-or-market rule conservative?

Problem 9-6A *Correcting inventory errors over a three-year period*

The Power & Masters Company books show these data (in millions):

	19X3		19X2		19X1	
Net sales revenue..................		$200		$160		$175
Cost of goods sold:						
Beginning inventory.............	$ 15		$ 25		$ 40	
Net purchases..................	135		100		90	
Cost of goods available	150		125		130	
Less ending inventory	30		15		25	
Cost of goods sold		120		110		105
Gross margin		80		50		70
Operating expenses................		74		38		46
Net income......................		$ 6		$ 12		$ 24

In early 19X4, a team of internal auditors discovered that the ending inventory of 19X1 had been overstated by $20 million. Also, the ending inventory for 19X3 had been understated by $5 million. The ending inventory at December 31, 19X2, was correct.

Required

1. Prepare corrected income statements for the three years.
2. State whether each year's net income and owner's equity amounts are understated or overstated. For each incorrect figure, indicate the amount of the understatement or overstatement.

Problem 9-7A *Estimating inventory by the gross margin method; preparing a multiple-step income statement*

Assume Kentucky Fried Chicken, Inc., estimates its inventory by the gross margin method when preparing monthly financial statements. For the past two years, gross margin has averaged 35 percent of net sales. Assume further that the company's inventory records for stores in the southeastern region reveal the following data:

Inventory, March 1	$ 398,000
Transactions during March:	
Purchases	5,685,000
Purchase discounts.	49,000
Purchase returns.	8,000
Sales	8,667,000
Sales returns	17,000

Required

1. Estimate the March 31 inventory using the gross margin method.
2. Prepare the March income statement through gross margin, for the Kentucky Fried Chicken, Inc., stores in the southeastern region. Use the multiple-step format.

Problem 9-8A *Estimating inventory by the retail method; recording periodic inventory transactions*

The fiscal year of J. C. Penney Company, Inc., (and many other retailers) ends on January 31. Assume the following inventory data for the women's sportswear department of a J. C. Penney store:

	Cost	Retail
Inventory, Jan. 31, 19X5	$ 84,500	$153,636
Transactions during the year ended January 31, 19X6:		
Purchases	419,220	762,500
Purchase returns.	18,090	33,172
Sales		783,740
Sales returns		9,676

Required

1. Use the retail method to estimate the cost of the store's ending inventory of women's sportswear at January 31, 19X6. Round off the ratio to two decimal places.
2. Assuming J. C. Penney uses the periodic inventory system, prepare general journal entries to record:
   a. Inventory purchases and sales during fiscal year 19X6. Assume all purchases and one-half of company sales were on credit. All other sales were for cash.
   b. Inventory entries at January 31, 19X6. Closing entries for Purchases and Purchase Returns are not required.

Problem 9-9A *Using the perpetual inventory system; applying the lower-of-cost-or-market rule*

Rockwell International Corporation manufactures high-technology products used in the aviation and automotive industries. Perhaps its most famous product is the United States space shuttle. Assume the following data for Rockwell's product TU477:

	Purchased	Sold	Balance
Dec. 31, 19X1			110 @ $5 = $550
Feb. 10, 19X2	80 @ $6 = $480		
Apr. 7		60	
May 29	110 @ 7 = 770		
July 13		120	
Oct. 4	100 @ 8 = 800		
Nov. 22		80	

Required

1. Prepare a perpetual inventory record for product TU477, using the FIFO method.
2. Assume Rockwell sold the 60 units on April 7 on account for $13 each. Record the sale and related cost of goods sold in the general journal under the FIFO method.
3. Suppose the current replacement cost of the ending inventory of product TU477 is $970 at December 31, 19X2. Use the answer to Requirement 1 to compute the lower-of-cost-or-market (LCM) value of the ending inventory.

(Group B)

Problem 9-1B   *Computing inventory by three methods*

Microdot Software began the year with 73 units of inventory that cost $26 each. During the year Microdot made the following purchases:

Mar. 11	113 @ $27
May 2	81 @ 29
July 19	167 @ 32
Nov. 18	44 @ 36

The company uses the periodic inventory system, and the physical count at December 31 indicates that ending inventory consists of 131 units.

Required

Compute the ending inventory and cost of goods sold amounts under (1) average cost, (2) FIFO cost, and (3) LIFO cost. Round average cost per unit to the nearest cent, and round all other amounts to the nearest dollar.

Problem 9-2B   *Computing inventory, cost of goods sold, and FIFO inventory profit*

University Paperbacks specializes in softcover books. The store began operations on January 1, 19X1, with an inventory of 500 books that cost $2.01 each, a $1,005 total. During the first month of operations the store purchased inventory as follows:

Purchase no. 1	60 @ $2.10
Purchase no. 2	120 @ 2.35
Purchase no. 3	600 @ 2.50
Purchase no. 4	40 @ 2.75

The ending inventory consists of 600 books.

Required

1. Complete the following tabulation, rounding average cost to the nearest cent and all other amounts to the nearest dollar.

	Ending Inventory	Cost of Goods Sold
a. Average cost	———	———
b. FIFO cost	———	———
c. LIFO cost	———	———

2. Compute the amount of inventory profit under FIFO.
3. Which method produces the most current ending inventory cost? Which method produces the most current cost-of-goods-sold amount? Give the reason for your answers.

Problem 9-3B *Preparing an income statement directly from the accounts*

The records of Blaine Wholesale Company include the following accounts for one of its products at December 31 of the current year:

Inventory

Jan. 1	Balance	700 units @ $7.00	4,900	

Purchases

Jan. 6	300 units @ $7.05	2,115	
Mar. 19	1,100 units @ 7.35	8,085	
June 22	8,400 units @ 7.50	63,000	
Oct. 4	500 units @ 8.80	4,400	
Dec. 31	Balance	77,600	

Sales Revenue

		Feb. 5	1,000 units @ $12.00	12,000
		Apr. 10	700 units @ 12.10	8,470
		July 31	1,800 units @ 13.25	23,850
		Sept. 4	2,200 units @ 13.50	29,700
		Nov. 27	3,100 units @ 15.00	46,500
		Dec. 31	Balance	120,520

Required

1. Compute the quantities of goods in (a) ending inventory and (b) cost of goods sold during the year.
2. Prepare the following partial income statement under the average cost, FIFO cost, and LIFO cost methods.

Blaine Wholesale Company
Income Statement
For the year ended December 31, 19XX

	Average Cost	FIFO Cost	LIFO Cost
Sales revenue	$ ———	$ ———	$ ———
Cost of goods sold:			
Beginning inventory	$ ———	$ ———	$ ———
Purchases	———	———	———
Cost of goods available	———	———	———
Ending inventory	———	———	———
Cost of goods sold	$ ———	$ ———	$ ———
Gross margin			

Problem 9-4B   *Recording periodic and perpetual inventory transactions*

Using the data in Problem 9-3B, make summary journal entries in the general journal to record:

1. Purchases, sales, and end-of-period inventory entries, assuming Blaine Wholesale Company uses the periodic inventory system and the FIFO cost method. All purchases are on credit. Cash sales are $50,000, with the remaining sales on account.
2. Purchases, sales, and cost of goods sold, assuming Blaine Wholesale Company uses the perpetual inventory system and the FIFO cost method. All purchases are on credit. Cash sales are $50,000, with the remaining sales on account.

Problem 9-5B   *Applying the lower-of-cost-or-market rule*

The financial statements of LaValle Company were prepared on the cost basis without considering whether the replacement value of ending inventory was less than cost. Following are selected data from those statements:

From the income statement:

Sales revenue.....................		$278,000
Cost of goods sold:		
Beginning inventory	$ 54,000	
Net purchases	119,000	
Cost of goods available for sale	173,000	
Ending inventory................	53,000	
Cost of goods sold		120,000
Gross margin		$158,000

From the balance sheet:

Current assets:	
Inventory	$ 53,000

The replacement costs were $57,000 for beginning inventory and $49,000 for ending inventory.

Required

1. Revise the data to include the appropriate lower-of-cost-or-market value of inventory.
2. How is the lower-of-cost-or-market rule conservative? How is conservatism shown in LaValle's situation?

Problem 9-6B   *Correcting inventory errors over a three-year period*

The Balcones Company books show these data (in millions):

	19X6		19X5		19X4	
Net sales revenue..................		$350		$280		$240
Cost of goods sold:						
Beginning inventory.............	$ 65		$ 55		$ 70	
Net purchases..................	195		135		130	
Cost of goods available	260		190		200	
Less Ending inventory	70		65		55	
Cost of goods sold		190		125		145
Gross margin		160		155		95
Operating expenses		113		109		76
Net income.......................		$ 47		$ 46		$ 19

In early 19X7, a team of internal auditors discovered that the ending inventory of 19X4 had been understated by $12 million. Also, the ending inventory for 19X6 had been overstated by $8 million. The ending inventory at December 31, 19X5, was correct.

Required

1. Prepare corrected income statements for the three years.
2. State whether each year's net income and owner's equity amount are understated or overstated. For each incorrect figure, indicate the amount of the understatement or overstatement.

Problem 9-7B   *Estimating inventory by the gross margin method; preparing a multiple-step income statement*

Assume Burger King, Inc., estimates its inventory by the gross margin method when preparing monthly financial statements. For the past two years, the gross margin has averaged 40 percent of net sales. Assume further that the company's inventory records for stores in the southwestern region reveal the following data:

Inventory, July 1	$ 267,000
Transactions during July:	
Purchases	3,589,000
Purchase discounts..................	26,000
Purchase returns....................	12,000
Sales	5,773,000
Sales returns......................	22,000

Required

1. Estimate the July 31 inventory using the gross margin method.
2. Prepare the July income statement through gross margin for the Burger King, Inc., stores in the southwestern region. Use the multiple-step format.

Problem 9-8B   *Estimating inventory by the retail method; recording periodic inventory transactions*

The fiscal year of K-Mart Corporation ends on January 31. Assume the following inventory data for the hardware department of a K-Mart Store:

	Cost	Retail
Inventory, Jan. 31, 19X3	$ 31,200	$ 63,300
Transactions during the year ended January 31, 19X4:		
Purchases	154,732	301,190
Purchase returns.................................	5,800	11,290
Sales		283,420
Sales returns....................................		3,320

Required

1. Use the retail method to estimate the cost of the store's ending inventory of hardware at January 31, 19X4.
2. Assuming K-Mart uses the periodic inventory system, prepare general journal entries to record:
   - a. Inventory purchases and sales during fiscal year 19X4. Assume all purchases and one-half of company sales were on credit. All other sales were for cash.
   - b. Inventory entries at January 31, 19X4. Closing entries for Purchases and Purchase Returns are not required.

Problem 9-9B *Using the perpetual inventory system; applying the lower-of-cost-or-market rule*

Coachman Industries, Inc., manufactures recreational vehicles and products. Assume the following data for Coachman's product EK-133:

	Purchased	Sold	Balance
Dec. 31, 19X3			120 @ $6 = $720
Mar. 15, 19X4	50 @ $7 = $350		
Apr. 10		80	
May 29	100 @ 8 = 800		
Aug. 3		110	
Nov. 16	90 @ 9 = 810		
Dec. 12		70	

Required

1. Prepare a perpetual inventory card for product EK-133, using the FIFO method.
2. Assume Coachman sold the 110 units on August 3 on account for $16 each. Record the sale and related cost of goods sold in the general journal under the FIFO method.
3. Suppose the current replacement cost of the ending inventory of product EK-133 is $750 at December 31, 19X4. Use the answer to requirement 1 to compute the lower-of-cost-or-market (LCM) value of the ending inventory.

Decision Problem

Assessing the impact of a year-end purchase of inventory

Yakima Paper Corporation is nearing the end of its first year of operations. The company made the following inventory purchases:

January	1,000	$10	$10,000
March	1,000	10	10,000
May	1,000	11	11,000
July	1,000	13	13,000
September	1,000	14	14,000
November	1,000	15	15,000
Totals	6,000		$73,000

Sales for the year will be 5,000 units for $120,000 revenue. Expenses other than cost of goods sold and income taxes will be $20,000. The president of the company is undecided about whether to adopt FIFO or LIFO.

The company has storage capacity for 5,000 additional units of inventory. Inventory prices are expected to stay at $15 per unit for the next few months. The president is considering purchasing 4,000 additional units of inventory at $15 each before the end of the year. He wishes to know how the purchase would affect net income under both FIFO and LIFO. The income tax rate is 40 percent, and income tax is an expense.

Required

1. To aid company decision making, prepare income statements under FIFO and under LIFO, both without and with the year-end purchase of 4,000 units of inventory at $15 per unit.
2. Compare net income under FIFO without and with the year-end purchase. Make the same comparison under LIFO. Under which method does the year-end purchase have the greater effect on net income?

3. Under which method can a year-end purchase be made in order to manipulate net income?

Financial Statement Problem

Inventories

The notes are an important part of a company's financial statements, giving valuable details that would clutter the tabular data presented in the statements. This problem will help you learn to use a company's inventory notes. Refer to the Gulf+Western statements and related notes in Appendix C. Answer the following questions.

1. How much were Gulf+Western's total inventories at October 31, 1987? Of this amount, how much were current assets? How much were long-term assets? Describe the difference between these current assets and long-term assets?
2. How does Gulf+Western value its inventories? Which cost method does the company use?
3. Note D lists four categories of inventories that are classified as current assets. Name these, and briefly explain what you think each category means.
4. The financial statement problem in Chapter 5 required the computation of cost of goods sold. By rearranging the cost-of-goods-sold formula, you can solve for purchases, which are not disclosed in Gulf+Western's statements. Using only the inventories classified as current assets, show how to compute Gulf+Western's purchases during fiscal 1987.

Answers to the Self-Study Questions

1. c
2. a $(15,000 - 1,000) \times \$3.40 = \$47,600$
3. d
4. b
5. b
6. d
7. a $\$35,000 + \$146,000 = \$181,000$
   $\$240,000 - (.35 \times \$240,000) = \$156,000$
   $\$181,000 - \$156,000 = \$25,000$

		Cost	Retail	
8. c	Beginning inventory	$ 20,000	$ 40,000	
	Purchases	120,000	210,000	**Cost Ratio**
	Goods available.	140,000 ÷	250,000	= .56
	Sales.		200,000	
	Ending inventory–at retail		$ 50,000	
	at cost ($50,000 × .56)	$ 28,000		

9. d
10. c

10

Plant Assets, Intangible Assets, and Related Expenses

LEARNING OBJECTIVES
After studying this chapter, you should be able to

1 Identify the elements of a plant asset's cost

2 Explain the concept of depreciation

3 Account for depreciation by four methods

4 Identify the best depreciation method for income tax purposes

5 Account for disposal of plant assets

6 Account for natural resource assets and depletion

7 Account for intangible assets and amortization

8 Distinguish capital expenditures from revenue expenditures

Business assets are separated into current assets—those useful for one year or less—and long-lived assets—those useful for longer than a year. Long-lived assets used in the operation of the business and not held for sale as investments are further divided into plant assets and intangible assets.

Plant assets are those long-lived assets that are tangible. Their physical form provides their usefulness, for instance, land, buildings, equipment, and coal and other minerals. Of the plant assets, land is unique. Its cost is *not* depreciated—expensed over time—because its usefulness does not decrease like that of other assets. Most companies report plant assets under the heading Property, Plant, and Equipment.

Intangible assets are useful not because of their physical characteristics but because of the special rights they carry. Patents, copyrights, and trademarks are intangible assets. Examples of famous patents are the recipe for Coca-Cola and the Dolby noise-reduction process. Accounting for intangibles is similar to accounting for plant assets.

This area has its own terminology. Different names apply to the expense for the cost of the various assets, as shown in Exhibit 10-1.

The first half of the chapter discusses and illustrates how to identify the cost of a plant asset and how to expense its cost. The second half considers disposing of plant assets and how to account for natural resources and intangible assets. Unless stated otherwise, we describe accounting in accordance with generally accepted accounting principles, as distinguished from reporting to the IRS for income tax purposes.

EXHIBIT 10-1   *Terminology Used in Accounting for Plant Assets and Intangible Assets*

Asset Account on the Balance Sheet	Related Expense Account on the Income Statement
Land	None

Buildings, Machinery and Equipment,
   Furniture and Fixtures, and Land
   Improvements
	Depreciation

Natural Resources	Depletion
Intangibles	Amortization

The Cost of a Plant Asset

The cost principle directs a business to carry an asset on the balance sheet at the amount paid for it. The **cost of a plant asset** is the purchase price, applicable taxes, purchase commissions, and all other amounts paid to acquire the asset and to ready it for its intended use. Because the types of cost differ for various categories of plant assets, we discuss the major groups individually.

Land

The cost of land includes its purchase price (cash plus any note payable given), brokerage commission, survey fees, legal fees, and any back property taxes that the purchaser pays. Land cost also includes any expenditures for grading and clearing the land and for demolishing or removing any unwanted buildings.

The cost of land does *not* include the cost of fencing, paving, sprinkler systems, and lighting. These separate plant assets—called land improvements—are subject to depreciation.

Suppose you are a real estate developer, and you sign a $300,000 note payable to purchase 100 acres of land for subdivision into 5-acre lots. You also pay $10,000 in back property tax, $8,000 in transfer taxes, $5,000 for removal of an old building, a $1,000 survey fee, and $260,000 for the construction of roads, all in cash. What is the cost of this land?

Purchase price of land		$300,000
Add related costs:		
Back property tax	$10,000	
Transfer taxes	8,000	
Removal of building	5,000	
Survey fee	1,000	
Total incidental costs.		24,000
Total cost of land		$324,000

The entry to record purchase of the land is

Land	324,000	
Note Payable		300,000
Cash		24,000

Buildings

The cost of constructing a building includes architectural fees, building permits, contractors' charges, and payments for materials, labor, and overhead. When an existing building (new or old) is purchased, its cost includes the purchase price, brokerage commission, sales and other taxes, and expenditures for repairing and renovating the building for its intended purpose.

Machinery and Equipment

The cost of machinery and equipment includes its purchase price (less any discounts), transportation charges, insurance while in transit, sales and other taxes, purchase commission, installation costs, and any expenditures to test the asset before placing it in service.

Land Improvements

In the land example, the cost of the roads ($260,000) is not part of the cost of the land. Instead, the $260,000 would be recorded in a separate account entitled Land Improvements. This account includes costs for such other items as fences, driveways, parking lots, and sprinkler systems. Although these assets are located on the land, they are subject to decay, and therefore their cost should be depreciated, as we discuss later in this chapter. Also, the cost of a new building constructed on the land is a debit to the asset account Building.

Group (or Basket) Purchases of Assets

Businesses often purchase several assets (as a group, or in a "basket") for a single amount. For example, a company may pay one price for land and an office building. The company must identify the cost of each asset. The total cost is divided between the assets according to their relative sales (or market) values. This allocation technique is called the **relative-sales-value method.**

Suppose Xerox Corporation purchases land and a building in Kansas City for a midwestern sales office. The building sits on two acres of land, and the combined purchase price of land and building is $2,800,000. An appraisal indicates that the land's market (sales) value is $300,000 and the building's market (sales) value is $2,700,000.

An accountant first figures the ratio of each asset's market price to the total market price. Total appraised value is $3,000,000. Thus land, valued at $300,000, is 10 percent of the total market value. Building's appraised value is 90 percent of the total.

Asset	Market (Sales) Value		Total Market Value		Percentage
Land	$ 300,000	÷	$3,000,000	=	10%
Building	2,700,000	÷	$3,000,000	=	90%
Total	$3,000,000				100%

The percentage for each asset is multiplied by the total purchase price to give its cost in the purchase.

Asset	Total Purchase Price		Percentage		Allocated Cost
Land	$2,800,000	×	.10	=	$ 280,000
Building	$2,800,000	×	.90	=	2,520,000
Total			1.00		$2,800,000

Assuming Xerox pays cash, the entry to record the purchase of the land and building is

Land	280,000	
Building	2,520,000	
Cash		2,800,000

Depreciation of Plant Assets

OBJECTIVE 2

Explain the concept of depreciation

The process of allocating a plant asset's cost to expense over the period the asset is used is called *depreciation*. It is designed to match this expense against revenue over the asset's life, as the matching principle directs.

Suppose a company buys a computer. The business believes the computer offers four years of service after which obsolescence will make it worthless. Using straight-line depreciation (which we discuss later in this chapter), the business expenses one quarter of the asset's cost in each of its four years of use.

Let's contrast what depreciation accounting is with what it is *not*. (1) *Depreciation is not a process of valuation*. Businesses do not record depreciation based on appraisals of their plant assets made at the end of each period. Instead, businesses allocate the asset's cost to the periods of its useful life based on a specific depreciation method. (We discuss these methods in this chapter.) (2) *Depreciation does not mean that the business sets aside cash to replace assets as they become fully depreciated*. Establishing such a cash fund is a decision entirely separate from depreciation. *Accumulated depreciation* is that portion of the plant asset's cost that has already been recorded as expense. Accumulated depreciation does not represent a growing amount of cash.

Determining the Useful Life of a Plant Asset

No asset (other than land) offers an unlimited useful life. For some plant assets physical *wear and tear* from operations and the elements may be the important cause of depreciation. For example, physical deterioration takes its toll on the usefulness of trucks and furniture.

Assets like computers, other electronic equipment, and airplanes may become *obsolete* before they physically deteriorate. An asset is obsolete when another asset can do the job better or more efficiently. Thus an asset's useful life may be much shorter than its physical life. Accountants usually depreciate computers over a short period of time—perhaps four years—even though they know the computers will remain in working condition much longer. Whether wear and tear or obsolescence causes depreciation, the asset's cost is depreciated over its expected useful life.

Measuring Depreciation

To measure depreciation for a plant asset, we must know its *cost*, its *estimated useful life*, and its *estimated residual value.*

Cost is the purchase price of the asset. We discussed cost under the heading The Cost of a Plant Asset, beginning on page 384.

Estimated useful life is the length of the service the business expects to get from the asset. Useful life may be expressed in years (as we have seen so far), units of output, miles, or other measures. For example, the useful life of a building is stated in years. The useful life of a bookbinding machine may be stated as the number of books the machine is expected to bind—that is, its expected units of output. A reasonable measure of a delivery truck's useful life is the total number of miles the truck is expected to travel. Companies base such estimates on past experience and information from industry trade magazines and government publications.

Estimated residual value—also called *scrap value* and *salvage value*—is the expected cash value of the asset at the end of its useful life. For example, a business may believe that a machine's useful life will be seven years. After that time, the company expects to sell the machine as scrap metal. The amount the business believes it can get for the machine is the estimated residual value. In computing depreciation, estimated residual value is *not* depreciated because the business expects to receive this amount from disposing of the asset. The full cost of a plant asset is depreciated if the asset is expected to have no residual value. The plant asset's cost minus its estimated residual value is called the *depreciable cost.*

Of the factors entering the computation of depreciation, only one factor is known—cost. The other two factors—residual value and useful life—must be estimated. Depreciation, then, is an estimated amount.

The basic equation for computing depreciation is

$$\text{Depreciation} = \frac{\text{cost} - \text{estimated residual value}}{\text{expected useful life}} = \frac{\text{depreciable cost}}{\text{expected useful life}}$$

The equation shows that depreciable cost is depreciated over the useful life of the asset.

Depreciation Methods

OBJECTIVE 3

Account for depreciation by four methods

Four basic methods exist for computing depreciation: straight-line, units-of-production, declining-balance, and sum-of-years-digits. These four methods allocate different amounts of depreciation expense to different periods. However, they all result in the same total amount of depreciation, the asset's depreciable cost over the life of the asset. Exhibit 10-2 presents the data used to illustrate depreciation computations by the four methods.

Straight-Line (SL) Method

In the **straight-line (SL)** method, an equal amount of depreciation expense is assigned to each year (or period) of asset use. Depreciable cost is divided by useful life in years to determine the annual depreciation expense. The equation for SL

EXHIBIT 10-2 *Data for Depreciation Computations*

Data Item	Amount
Cost of limousine..............	$41,000
Estimated residual value..........	1,000
Depreciable cost...............	$40,000
Estimated useful life:	
Years......................	5 years
Units of production...........	400,000 units

depreciation, applied to the limo data from Exhibit 10-2, is

$$\frac{\text{Straight-line depreciation}}{\text{per year}} = \frac{\text{cost} - \text{residual value}}{\text{useful life in years}}$$

$$= \frac{\$41,000 - \$1,000}{5}$$

$$= \$8,000$$

The entry to record this depreciation is

Depreciation Expense 8,000
    Accumulated Depreciation   8,000

Assume that the limo was purchased on January 1, 19X1, and the business's fiscal year ends on December 31. A *straight-line depreciation schedule* is presented in Exhibit 10-3.

The final column of Exhibit 10-3 shows the asset's *book value*, which is its cost less accumulated depreciation. Book value is also called carrying value.

As an asset is used, accumulated depreciation increases, and the book value decreases. (Note the Accumulated Depreciation column and the Book Value column.) An asset's final book value is its *residual value* ($1,000 in the exhibit). At the end of its useful life, the asset is said to be fully depreciated.

EXHIBIT 10-3 *Straight-Line Depreciation Schedule*

		Depreciation for the Year				Asset
Date	Asset Cost	Depreciation Rate	Depreciable Cost	Depreciation Amount	Accumulated Depreciation	Book Value
1- 1-X1	$41,000					$41,000
12-31-X1		.20 ×	$40,000 =	$8,000	$ 8,000	33,000
12-31-X2		.20 ×	40,000 =	8,000	16,000	25,000
12-31-X3		.20 ×	40,000 =	8,000	24,000	17,000
12-31-X4		.20 ×	40,000 =	8,000	32,000	9,000
12-31-X5		.20 ×	40,000 =	8,000	40,000	1,000

EXHIBIT 10-4   *Units-of-Production Depreciation Schedule*

| Date | Asset Cost | Depreciation for the Year | | | Accumulated Depreciation | Asset Book Value |
		Depreciation Per Unit	Number of Units	Depreciation Amount		
1-1-19X1	$41,000					$41,000
12-31-19X1		$.10	× 90,000 =	$ 9,000	$ 9,000	32,000
12-31-19X2		.10	× 120,000 =	12,000	21,000	20,000
12-31-19X3		.10	× 100,000 =	10,000	31,000	10,000
12-31-19X4		.10	× 60,000 =	6,000	37,000	4,000
12-31-19X5		.10	× 30,000 =	3,000	40,000	1,000

Units-of-Production (UOP) Method

In the **units-of-production (UOP)** method, a fixed amount of depreciation is assigned to each unit of output produced by the plant asset. Depreciable cost is divided by useful life in units to determine this amount. This per-unit depreciation expense is multiplied by the number of units produced each period to compute depreciation for the period. The UOP depreciation equation for the limo data in Exhibit 10-2 is

$$\frac{\text{Units-of-production depreciation}}{\text{per unit of output}} = \frac{\text{cost} - \text{residual value}}{\text{useful life in units}}$$

$$= \frac{\$41,000 - \$1,000}{400,000 \text{ miles}}$$

$$= \$.10$$

Assume the limo is expected to be driven 90,000 miles (*miles* are the *units* in our example) during the first year, 120,000 during the second, 100,000 during the third, 60,000 during the fourth, and 30,000 during the fifth. The UOP depreciation schedule for this asset is shown in Exhibit 10-4.

The amount of UOP depreciation per period varies with the number of units the asset produces. Note that the total number of units produced is 400,000, the measure of this asset's useful life. Therefore, UOP depreciation does not depend directly on time as the other methods do.

Double-Declining-Balance (DDB) Method

Double-declining-balance (DDB) is one of the accelerated-depreciation methods. An **accelerated-depreciation** method writes off a relatively larger amount of the asset's cost nearer the start of its useful life than does straight-line. **DDB depreciation** computes annual depreciation by multiplying the asset's book value by a constant percentage, which is two times the straight-line depreciation rate. DDB amounts are computed as follows:

First, the straight-line depreciation rate per year is computed. For example, a 5-year limousine has a straight-line depreciation rate of 1/5, or 20 percent. A 10-year asset has a straight-line rate of 1/10, or 10 percent, and so on.

Second, the straight-line rate is multiplied by 2 to compute the DDB rate. The DDB rate for a 5-year asset is 40 percent (20% × 2 = 40%). For a 10-year asset the DDB rate is 20 percent (10% × 2 = 20%).

Third, The DDB rate is multiplied by the period's beginning asset book value (cost less accumulated depreciation). Residual value of the asset is ignored in computing depreciation by the DDB method, except during the last year.

The DDB rate for the limousine in Exhibit 10-2 is

$$\text{DDB rate per year} = \left(\frac{1}{\text{useful life in years}} \times 2\right) = \left(\frac{1}{5 \text{ years}} \times 2\right) = (20\% \times 2) = 40\%$$

Fourth, the final year's depreciation amount is the amount needed to reduce the asset's book value to its residual value. In the following schedule, the fifth and final year's depreciation is $4,314—the $5,314 book value less the $1,000 residual value. The DDB depreciation schedule for the asset is illustrated in Exhibit 10-5.

The DDB method differs from the other methods in two ways. (1) The asset's residual value is ignored initially. Depreciation is computed on the asset's full cost. (2) The final year's calculation is changed in order to bring the asset's book value to the residual value.

Sum-of-Years-Digits (SYD) Method

In the **sum-of-years-digits** (SYD) method—another accelerated method—depreciation is figured by multiplying the depreciable cost of the asset by a fraction. The *denominator* of the SYD fraction is the sum of the years' digits. For a 5-year asset, the years' digits are 1, 2, 3, 4, and 5, and their sum is 15 (1 + 2 + 3 + 4 + 5 = 15). For a 10-year asset, the denominator is 55. Adding the years for a very long-lived asset is tedious. Chances arise for error in the mathematics. Thus we have an easy formula for computing the sum of the years' digits:

Sum of the years' digits = N(N + 1)/2

where N is the useful life of the asset expressed in years. For example, when N equals 5, we have:

$$\frac{5(5 + 1)}{2} = \frac{30}{2} = 15$$

EXHIBIT 10-5 *Double-Declining-Balance Depreciation Schedule*

			Depreciation for the Year			
Date	Asset Cost	DDB Rate	Asset Book Value	Depreciation Amount	Accumulated Depreciation	Asset Book Value
1-1-19X1	$41,000					$41,000
12-31-19X1		.40 ×	$41,000 =	$16,400	$16,400	24,600
12-31-19X2		.40 ×	24,600 =	9,840	26,240	14,760
12-31-19X3		.40 ×	14,760 =	5,904	32,144	8,856
12-31-19X4		.40 ×	8,856 =	3,542	35,686	5,314
12-31-19X5				4,314*	40,000	1,000

* Last-year depreciation is the amount needed to reduce asset book value to the residual value ($5,314 − $1,000 = $4,314).

The *numerator* of the SYD fraction for the first year of a 5-year asset is 5. The numerator is 4 for the second year, 3 for the third year, 2 for the fourth year, and 1 for the fifth year.

The SYD depreciation equation for the limo in Exhibit 10-2 is

$$\text{SYD depreciation per year} = (\text{cost} - \text{residual value}) \times \frac{\text{years' digits, largest first}}{\text{sum of years' digits}}$$

$$= (\$41,000 - \$1,000) \times \frac{5^*}{1+2+3+4+5}$$

$$= \$40,000 \times \frac{5}{15} = \$13,333$$

Exhibit 10-6 is the SYD depreciation schedule based on our example data. Note that each year's fraction is multiplied by the depreciable cost ($40,000).

Comparison of the Depreciation Methods

Compare the four methods in terms of the yearly amount of depreciation:

Amount of Depreciation Per Year

			Accelerated Methods	
Year	Straight-Line	Units-of-Production	Double-Declining-Balance	Sum-of-Years-Digits
1	$ 8,000	$ 9,000	$16,400	$13,333
2	8,000	12,000	9,840	10,667
3	8,000	10,000	5,904	8,000
4	8,000	6,000	3,542	5,333
5	8,000	3,000	4,314	2,667
Total	$40,000	$40,000	$40,000	$40,000

EXHIBIT 10-6 *Sum-of-Years-Digits Depreciation Schedule*

			Depreciation for the Year			Asset
Date	Asset Cost	SYD Fraction	Depreciable Cost	Depreciation Amount	Accumulated Depreciation	Book Value
1-1-19X1	$41,000					$41,000
12-31-19X1		5/15 ×	$40,000 =	$13,333	$13,333	27,667
12-31-19X2		4/15 ×	40,000 =	10,667	24,000	17,000
12-31-19X3		3/15 ×	40,000 =	8,000	32,000	9,000
12-31-19X4		2/15 ×	40,000 =	5,333	37,333	3,667
12-31-19X5		1/15 ×	40,000 =	2,667	40,000	1,000

* 5 for first year; 4 for second year; 3 for third year; 2 for fourth year; 1 for fifth year.

EXHIBIT 10-7 *Depreciation Patterns*

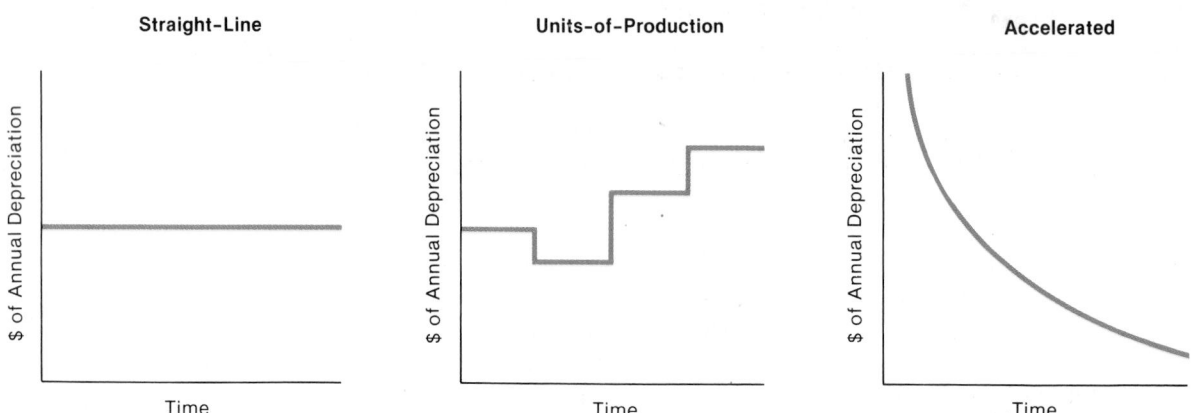

The yearly amount of depreciation varies by method, but the total $40,000 depreciable cost systematically becomes expense under all four methods.

Generally accepted accounting principles (GAAP) direct a business to match the expense of an asset against the revenue that the asset produces. For a plant asset that generates revenue evenly over time, the straight-line method best meets the matching principle. During each period the asset is used, an equal amount of depreciation is recorded.

The units-of-production method best fits those assets that wear out because of physical use, not obsolescence. Depreciation is recorded only when the asset is used, and the more units the asset generates in a given year, the greater the depreciation expense.

The accelerated methods (DDB and SYD) apply best to those assets that generate greater revenue earlier in their useful lives. The greater expense recorded under the accelerated methods in the early periods is matched against those periods' greater revenue.

Exhibit 10-7 graphs the relationship between annual depreciation amounts for straight-line, units-of-production, and the accelerated depreciation methods.

The graph of straight-line depreciation is flat because annual depreciation is the same amount in each period. Units-of-production depreciation follows no particular pattern because annual depreciation depends on the use of the asset. The greater the use, the greater is the amount of depreciation. Accelerated depreciation is greatest in the asset's first year and less in the later years.

A recent survey indicated that over 70 percent of companies use the straight-line method, approximately 20 percent use an accelerated method, and the remainder use the units-of-production method. For example, Sears uses straight-line, Motorola uses double-declining-balance, Eastman Kodak uses sum-of-years-digits, and Gulf Oil uses units-of-production.

Summary Problem for Your Review

Hubbard Company purchased equipment on January 1, 19X5, for $44,000. The expected life of the equipment is 10 years, and its residual value is $4,000. Under three depreciation methods, the annual depreciation expense and the balance of accumulated depreciation at the end of 19X5 and 19X6 are

Year	Method A Annual Depreciation Expense	Method A Accumulated Depreciation	Method B Annual Depreciation Expense	Method B Accumulated Depreciation	Method C Annual Depreciation Expense	Method C Accumulated Depreciation
19X5	$4,000	$4,000	$7,273	$ 7,273	$8,800	$ 8,800
19X6	4,000	8,000	6,545	13,818	7,040	15,840

Required

1. Identify the depreciation method used in each instance, and show the equation and computation for each. (Round off to the nearest dollar.)
2. Assume continued use of the same method through year 19X7. Determine the annual depreciation expense, accumulated depreciation, and book value of the equipment for 19X5 through 19X7 under each method.

SOLUTION TO REVIEW PROBLEM

Requirement 1

Method A: Straight-line

$$\textbf{Depreciable cost} = \textbf{\$40,000 (\$44,000} - \textbf{\$4,000)}$$

$$\textbf{Each year: \$40,000/10 years} = \textbf{\$4,000}$$

Method B: Sum-of-years-digits

$$\textbf{SYD} = \textbf{N(N} + \textbf{1)/2} = \textbf{10(10} + \textbf{1)/2} = \textbf{55}$$

$$\textbf{Depreciable cost} = \textbf{\$40,000 (\$44,000} - \textbf{\$4,000)}$$

$$\textbf{19X5: 10/55} \times \textbf{\$40,000} = \textbf{\$7,273}$$

$$\textbf{19X6: 9/55} \times \textbf{\$40,000} = \textbf{\$6,545}$$

Method C: Double-declining-balance

$$\textbf{Rate} = \left(\frac{1}{\textbf{10 years}} \times \textbf{2} \right) = \textbf{(10\%} \times \textbf{2)} = \textbf{20\%}$$

$$\textbf{19X5: } \textbf{.20} \times \textbf{\$44,000} = \textbf{\$8,800}$$

$$\textbf{19X6: } \textbf{.20} \times \textbf{(\$44,000} - \textbf{\$8,800)} = \textbf{\$7,040}$$

Requirement 2

Year	Method A Straight-Line Annual Depreciation Expense	Method A Accumulated Depreciation	Method A Book Value	Method B Sum-of-Years-Digits Annual Depreciation Expense	Method B Accumulated Depreciation	Method B Book Value	Method C Double-Declining-Balance Annual Depreciation Expense	Method C Accumulated Depreciation	Method C Book Value
Start			$44,000			$44,000			$44,000
19X5	$4,000	$4,000	40,000	$7,273	$ 7,273	36,727	$8,800	$ 8,800	35,200
19X6	4,000	8,000	36,000	6,545	13,818	30,182	7,040	15,840	28,160
19X7	4,000	12,000	32,000	5,818	19,636	24,364	5,632	21,472	22,528

Computations for 19X7:

Straight-line: $40,000/10 years = $4,000

Sum-of-years-digits: 8/55 × $40,000 = $5,818

Double-declining-balance: .20 × $28,160 = $5,632

Depreciation and Income Taxes

The majority of companies use the straight-line depreciation method for reporting to their stockholders and creditors on their financial statements. Companies keep a separate set of depreciation records for computing their income taxes. For income tax purposes, most companies use an accelerated depreciation method.

Suppose you are a business manager. The IRS allows an accelerated depreciation method, which most managers choose in preference to straight-line depreciation. Why? Because it provides the most depreciation expense as quickly as possible, thus decreasing your immediate tax payments. The cash you save may be applied to best fit your business needs. This is the strategy most businesses follow.

To understand the relationships among cash flow (cash provided by operations), depreciation, and income tax, recall our earlier depreciation example: First-year depreciation under straight-line is $8,000, and under double-declining-balance it is $16,400. For illustrative purposes here, assume that DDB is permitted for reporting to the income tax authorities. Assume that the business has $400,000 in cash sales and $300,000 in cash operating expenses during the asset's first year, and the income tax rate is 40 percent. The cash flow analysis appears in Exhibit 10-8.

OBJECTIVE 4

Identify the best depreciation method for income tax purposes

Exhibit 10-8 highlights several important business relationships. Compare the amount of cash provided by operations before income tax. Both columns show $100,000. If there were no income taxes, the total cash provided by operations would be the same regardless of the depreciation method used. Depreciation is a noncash expense and so does not affect cash from operations.

However, depreciation is a tax-deductible expense. The higher the depreciation expense, the lower the income before tax and thus the lower the income tax payment. Therefore, accelerated depreciation helps conserve cash for use in the business. Exhibit 10-8 indicates that the business will have $3,360 more cash at the end of the first year if it uses accelerated depreciation instead of SL ($66,560 against $63,200). Suppose the company invests this money to earn a return of 10 percent during the second year. Then the company will be better off by $336 ($3,360 × 10% = $336). The cash advantage of using the accelerated method is the $336 of additional revenue.

The Tax Reform Act of 1986 created a special depreciation method—used only for income tax purposes—called the Modified Accelerated Cost Recovery System (MACRS). Under this method, assets are grouped into one of eight classes: 3-year, 5-year, 7-year, 10-year, 15-year, and 20-year assets. Real estate assets, such as buildings, are depreciated over 27½ years or 31½ years. Cars and light trucks belong in the 5-year class. Many types of equipment are classified as 7-year assets or 10-year assets. Depreciation for the first four classes is computed by the double-declining-balance method. Depreciation for 15-year assets and 20-year

EXHIBIT 10-8 *Cash Flow Advantage of Accelerated Depreciation over Straight-Line (SL) Depreciation for Income Tax Purposes*

	Income Tax Rate 40 Percent	
	SL	Accelerated
Revenues	$400,000	$400,000
Cash operating expenses...........................	300,000	300,000
Cash provided by operations before income tax	100,000	100,000
Depreciation expense (a noncash expense)	8,000	16,400
Income before income tax..........................	92,000	83,600
Income tax expense (40%).........................	36,800	33,440
Net income.....................................	$ 55,200	$ 50,160
Supplementary cash flow analysis:		
Cash provided by operations before income tax	$100,000	$100,000
Income tax expense	36,800	33,440
Cash provided by operations...................	$ 63,200	$ 66,560
Extra cash available for investment if DDB is used ($66,560 − $63,200)........................		$3,360
Assumed earnings rate on investment of extra cash .		× .10
Cash advantage of using DDB over SL...........		$ 336

assets is computed by the 150-percent-declining-balance method. Under this method, the annual depreciation rate is computed by multiplying the straight-line rate by 1.50. For a 20-year asset, the straight-line rate is .05 ($1/20 = .05$), so the annual depreciation rate is .075 (.05 × 1.50 = .075). Real estate is depreciated by the straight-line method.

Special Issues in Depreciation Accounting

Two special issues in depreciation accounting are (1) depreciation for partial periods and (2) change in the useful life of a depreciable asset.

Depreciation for Partial Years

Companies purchase plant assets as needed. They do not wait until the beginning of a year or a month. Therefore, companies must develop policies to compute *depreciation for partial years*. Suppose a company purchases a building on April 1 for $500,000. The building's estimated life is 20 years, and its estimated residual value is $20,000. The company's fiscal year ends on December 31. Consider how the company computes depreciation for the year ended December 31.

    Many companies compute partial-year depreciation by first computing a full year's depreciation. They then multiply this amount by the fraction of the year they held the asset. Assuming the straight-line method, the year's depreciation is $18,000, computed as follows:

$$\frac{(\$500,000 - \$20,000)}{20} = \$24,000 \text{ per year} \times \frac{9}{12} = \$18,000$$

What if the company bought the asset on April 18? A widely used policy directs businesses to record no depreciation on assets purchased after the fifteenth of the month and to record a full month's depreciation on an asset bought on or before the fifteenth. Thus the company would record no depreciation for April on an April 18 purchase. In this case, the year's depreciation would be $16,000 ($24,000 × 8/12).

How is partial-year depreciation computed under the other depreciation methods? Suppose this building is acquired on October 4 and the company uses the double-declining-balance method. For a 20-year asset, the DDB rate is 10 percent (1/20 = 5% × 2 = 10%). First-year depreciation is $50,000 ($500,000 × .10), and the DDB amount for October, November, and December is $12,500 ($50,000 × 3/12). For the second calendar year, DDB depreciation is $48,750 [($500,000 – $12,500) × .10]. For year three, DDB depreciation is $43,875 [($500,000 – $12,500 – $48,750) × .10], and so on.

Partial-year depreciation under the sum-of-years-digits method is computed similarly, by taking the appropriate fraction of a full year's amount. No special computation is needed for partial-year depreciation under the units-of-production method. Simply use the number of units produced, regardless of the time period the asset is held.

Change in the Useful Life of a Depreciable Asset

As previously discussed, a business must estimate the useful life of a plant asset to compute depreciation. This prediction is the most difficult part of accounting for depreciation. After the asset is put into use, the business is able to refine its estimate based on experience and new information. Such a change is called a *change in accounting estimate.* In an actual example, Walt Disney Productions included the following note in its financial statements:

Note 5

. . . the Company extended the estimated useful lives of certain theme park ride and attraction assets based upon historical data and engineering studies. The effect of this change was to decrease depreciation by approximately $8 million (an increase in net income of approximately $4.2 million . . .).

Such accounting changes are common because no business has perfect foresight. Generally accepted accounting principles require the business to report the nature, reason, and effect of the change on net income, as the Disney example shows. To *record* a change in accounting estimate, the remaining book value of the asset is spread over its adjusted remaining useful life. The adjusted useful life may be longer or shorter than the original useful life.

Assume that a Disney hot dog stand cost $40,000 and the company originally believed the asset had an 8-year useful life with no residual value. Using the straight-line method, the company would record $5,000 depreciation each year ($40,000/8 years = $5,000). Suppose Disney used the asset for 2 years. Accumulated depreciation reached $10,000, leaving a book value of $30,000 ($40,000 – $10,000). From its experience with the asset during the first 2 years, management believes the asset will remain useful for an additional 10 years. The company would compute a revised annual depreciation amount and record it as follows:

Asset's Remaining Book Value		(New) Estimated Useful Life Remaining		(New) Annual Depreciation Amount
$30,000	÷	10 years	=	$3,000

Yearly depreciation entry based on new estimated useful life:

Depreciation Expense—Hot Dog Stand	3,000	
Accumulated Depreciation—Hot Dog Stand		3,000

Using Fully Depreciated Assets

A fully depreciated asset is one that has reached the end of its *estimated* useful life. No more depreciation is recorded for the asset. If the asset is no longer suitable for its purpose, the asset is disposed of, as discussed in the next section. However, the company may be in a cash bind and unable to replace the asset. Or the asset's useful life may have been underestimated at the outset. Foresight is not perfect. In any event, companies sometimes continue using fully depreciated assets. The asset account and its related accumulated depreciation account remain in the ledger even though no additional depreciation is recorded for the asset.

Disposal of Plant Assets

Eventually, a plant asset ceases to serve a company's needs. The asset may have become worn out, obsolete, or for some other reason no longer useful to the business. Generally, a company disposes of a plant asset by selling or exchanging it. If the asset cannot be sold or exchanged, then disposal takes the form of junking the asset. Whatever the method of disposal, the business should bring depreciation up to date to measure the asset's final book value properly.

To account for disposal, credit the asset account and debit its related accumulated depreciation account. Suppose the final year's depreciation expense has just been recorded for a machine that cost $6,000 and was estimated to have zero residual value. The machine's accumulated depreciation thus totals $6,000. Assuming this asset cannot be sold or exchanged, the entry to record its disposal is

Accumulated Depreciation–Machinery.	6,000	
Machinery		6,000
To dispose of fully depreciated machine.		

OBJECTIVE 5
Account for disposal of plant assets

If assets are junked prior to being fully depreciated, the company records a loss equal to the asset's book value. Suppose store fixtures that cost $4,000 are disposed of in this manner. Accumulated depreciation is $3,000, and book value is therefore $1,000. Disposal of these store fixtures is recorded as follows:

Accumulated Depreciation–Store Fixtures	3,000	
Loss on Disposal of Store Fixtures	1,000	
Store Fixtures.		4,000
To dispose of store fixtures.		

Loss accounts such as Loss on Disposal of Store Fixtures decrease net income. Losses are reported on the income statement and closed to Income Summary along with expenses.

Selling a Plant Asset

Suppose the business sells furniture on September 30, 19X4, for $5,000 cash. The furniture cost $10,000 when purchased on January 1, 19X1, and has been depreciated on a straight-line basis. Managers estimated a 10-year useful life and no residual value. Prior to recording the sale of the furniture, accountants must update depreciation. Since the business uses the calendar year as its accounting period, partial depreciation must be recorded for the asset's expense from January 1, 19X4, to the sale date. The straight-line depreciation entry at September 30, 19X4, is

Sep. 30   Depreciation Expense ($10,000/10 years × %/12) 750
        Accumulated Depreciation–Furniture 750
    To update depreciation.

After this entry is posted, the Furniture account and the Accumulated Depreciation–Furniture account appear as follows. The furniture book value is $6,250 ($10,000 − $3,750).

Furniture		Accumulated Depreciation–Furniture	
Jan. 1, 19X1 10,000		Dec. 31, 19X1	1,000
		Dec. 31, 19X2	1,000
		Dec. 31, 19X3	1,000
		Sept. 30, 19X4	750
		Balance	3,750

The entry to record sale of the furniture for $5,000 cash is

Sep. 30   Cash 5,000
    Accumulated Depreciation–Furniture. 3,750
    Loss on Sale of Furniture 1,250
        Furniture 10,000
    To sell furniture.

When recording the sale of a plant asset the business must remove the balances in the asset account (Furniture, in this case) and its related accumulated depreciation account and also record a gain or a loss if the amount of cash received differs from the asset's book value. In our example, cash of $5,000 is less than the book value of the furniture, $6,250. The result is a loss of $1,250.

Suppose the sale price had been $7,000. The business would have had a gain of $750 (Cash, $7,000 − asset book value, $6,250).

The entry to record this transaction would be

Sep. 30   Cash 7,000
    Accumulated Depreciation–Furniture. 3,750
        Furniture 10,000
        Gain on Sale of Furniture. 750
    To sell furniture.

A gain is recorded when an asset is sold for a price greater than the asset's book value. A loss is recorded when the sale price is less than book value. Gains increase net income. Gains are reported on the income statement and closed to Income Summary along with the revenues.

Exchanging Plant Assets

Businesses often exchange (trade in) their old plant assets for similar assets that are newer and more efficient. For example, a pizzeria may decide to trade in its five-year-old Nissan delivery car for a newer model. To record the exchange, the business must remove from the books the balances for the asset being exchanged and its related accumulated depreciation account.

Assume that the pizzeria's old delivery car cost $7,000 and has accumulated depreciation totaling $6,000. The book value, then, is $1,000. The cash price for a new delivery car is $9,000, and the auto dealer offers a $1,000 trade-in allowance. The pizzeria pays cash for the remaining $8,000. The trade-in is recorded with this entry:

Delivery Auto (new)	9,000	
Accumulated Depreciation (old)	6,000	
Delivery Auto (old)		7,000
Cash ($9,000 − $1,000)		8,000

In this example, the book value and the trade-in allowance are both $1,000, and so no gain or loss occurs on the exchange. Usually, however, an exchange results in a gain or a loss. If the trade-in allowance received is greater than the book value of the asset being given, the business has a gain. If the trade-in allowance received is less than the book value of the asset given, the business has a loss. Generally accepted accounting principles allow losses, but not gains, to be recognized on the exchange of similar assets. We now turn to the entries for gains and losses on exchanges, continuing our delivery-car example and its data.[1]

Situation 1.   Loss recognized on asset exchange:

Assume that the new Nissan has a cash price of $9,000 and the dealer gives a trade-in allowance of $600 on the old vehicle. The pizzeria pays the balance, $8,400, in cash. The loss on the exchange is $400 (book value of old asset given, $1,000, minus trade-in allowance received, $600). The account Loss on Exchange of Delivery Auto is debited for $400. The entry to record this exchange is

Delivery Auto (new)	9,000	
Accumulated Depreciation–Delivery Auto (old)	6,000	
Loss on Exchange of Delivery Auto	400	
Delivery Auto (old)		7,000
Cash ($9,000 − $600)		8,400

Situation 2.   Gain *not* recognized on asset exchange:

Assume that the new Nissan's cash price is $9,000 and the dealer gives a $1,300 trade-in allowance. The pizzeria pays the balance, $7,700, in cash. The gain is $300 (trade-in allowance received, $1,300, minus book value of old asset given, $1,000). However, the pizzeria does not recognize the gain. Instead, it reduces the cost of the new asset by the amount of the unrecognized gain.

Delivery Auto (new) ($9,000 − gain of $300)	8,700	
Accumulated Depreciation–Delivery Auto (old)	6,000	
Delivery Auto (old)		7,000
Cash ($9,000 − $1,300)		7,700

---

[1] GAAP rules for exchanges may differ from income tax rules. In this discussion, we are concerned with the accounting rules.

Why are losses, and not gains, recognized? The Accounting Principles Board reasons a company should not record a gain merely because it has substituted one plant asset for a similar plant asset. However, losses are recorded because conservatism favors the recognition of losses rather than gains.

Control of Plant Assets

Control of plant assets includes safeguarding them and having an adequate accounting system. To see the need for controlling plant assets, consider the following actual situation. The home office and top managers of the company are in New Jersey. The company manufactures gas pumps in Canada, which are sold in Europe. Top managers and owners of the company rarely see the manufacturing plant and therefore cannot control plant assets by on-the-spot management. What features does their internal control system need?

Safeguarding plant assets includes:

1. Assigning responsibility for custody of the assets.
2. Separating custody of assets from accounting for the assets. (This is a cornerstone of internal control in almost every area.)
3. Setting up security measures, for instance, armed guards and restricted access to plant assets, to prevent theft.
4. Protecting assets from the elements (rain, snow, and so on).
5. Having adequate insurance against fire, storm, and other casualty losses.
6. Training operating personnel in the proper use of the asset.
7. Keeping a regular maintenance schedule.

Plant assets are controlled in much the same way that high-priced inventory is controlled—with subsidiary records. For plant assets, companies use a plant asset ledger. Each plant asset is represented by a card describing the asset and listing its location and the employee responsible for it. These details aid in safeguarding the asset. The ledger card also shows the asset's cost, useful life, and other accounting data. Exhibit 10-9 is an example.

EXHIBIT 10-9 *Plant Asset Ledger Card*

Asset	Clothing racks		Location	Ladies better dresses	
Employee responsible for the asset	Department manager				

Cost	$190,000	Purchased From	Boone Supply Co.
Depreciation Method	SL		
Useful Life	10 years	Residual Value	$10,000
General Ledger Account	Store fixtures		

Date	Explanation	Asset			Accumulated Depreciation		
		Dr	Cr	Bal	Dr	Cr	Bal
Jul. 3, 19X4	Purchase	190,000		190,000			
Dec. 31, 19X4	Deprec.					9,000	9,000
Dec. 31, 19X5	Deprec.					18,000	27,000
Dec. 31, 19X6	Deprec.					18,000	45,000

The ledger card provides the data for computing depreciation on the asset. It serves as a subsidiary record of accumulated depreciation. The asset balance ($190,000) and accumulated depreciation amount ($45,000) agree with the balances in the respective general ledger accounts (Store Fixtures and Accumulated Depreciation–Store Fixtures).

Accounting for Natural Resources and Depletion

Natural resources such as iron ore, coal, oil, gas, and timber are plant assets of a special type. An investment in natural resources could be described as an investment in inventories in the ground (coal) or on top of the ground (timber). As plant assets (such as machines) are expensed through depreciation, so natural resource assets are expensed through depletion. **Depletion expense** is that portion of the cost of natural resources that is used up in a particular period. Depletion expense is computed in the same way as *units-of-production* depreciation.

An oil well may cost $100,000 and contain an estimated 10,000 barrels of oil. The depletion rate would be $10 per barrel ($100,000/10,000 barrels). If 3,000 barrels are extracted during the first year, depletion expense is $30,000 (3,000 barrels × $10 per barrel). If 4,500 barrels are removed the second year, that period's depletion is $45,000 (4,500 barrels × $10 per barrel). The depletion entry for the first year is

Depletion Expense (3,000 barrels × $10)	30,000	
Accumulated Depletion–Oil		30,000

Accumulated Depletion is a contra account similar to Accumulated Depreciation. Natural resource assets can be reported as follows:

Property, Plant, and Equipment:		
Land		$120,000
Buildings	$800,000	
Equipment	160,000	
	960,000	
Less: Accumulated depreciation	410,000	550,000
Coal	$340,000	
Less: Accumulated depletion	90,000	250,000
Total property, plant, and equipment		$920,000

Accounting for Intangible Assets and Amortization _____

Intangible assets are a class of long-lived assets that are not physical in nature. Instead, these assets are special rights to current and expected future benefits from patents, copyrights, trademarks, franchises, leaseholds, and goodwill.

The acquisition cost of an intangible asset is debited to an asset account. The intangible is expensed through **amortization,** which applies to intangible assets in the same way depreciation applies to plant assets and depletion applies to natural resources. All three methods of expensing assets are conceptually the same.

Amortization is generally computed on a straight-line basis over the asset's estimated useful life—up to a maximum of 40 years, according to GAAP. However, obsolescence often cuts an intangible asset's useful life shorter than its legal life. Amortization expense is written off directly against the asset account rather than held in an accumulated amortization account. The residual value of most intangible assets is zero.

Assume that a business purchases a patent on a special manufacturing process. Legally, the patent may run for 17 years. However, the business realizes that new technologies will limit the patented process's life to 4 years. If the patent cost $80,000, each year's amortization expense is $20,000 ($80,000/4). The balance sheet reports the patent at its acquisition cost less amortization expense to date. After 1 year, the patent has a $60,000 balance ($80,000 − $20,000), after 2 years a $40,000 balance, and so on.

Patents are federal government grants giving a holder the exclusive right for 17 years to produce and sell an invention. Patented products include IBM computers and the recipe for Coca-Cola. Like any other asset, a patent may be purchased. Suppose a company pays $170,000 to acquire a patent and the business believes the expected useful life of the patent is only 5 years. Amortization expense is $34,000 per year ($170,000/5 years). The company's acquisition and amortization entries for this patent are

OBJECTIVE 7

Account for intangible assets and amortization

Jan. 1	Patents	170,000	
	Cash		170,000
	To acquire a patent.		
Dec. 31	Amortization Expense–Patents ($170,000/5)	34,000	
	Patents		34,000
	To amortize the cost of a patent.		

Copyrights are exclusive rights to reproduce and sell a book, musical composition, film, or other work of art. Issued by the federal government, copyrights extend 50 years beyond the author's (composer's, artist's) life. The cost of obtaining a copyright from the government is low, but a company may pay a large sum to purchase an existing copyright from the owner. For example, a publisher may pay the author of a popular novel $1 million or more for the book's copyright. The useful life of a copyright is usually no longer than 2 or 3 years, so each period's amortization amount is a high proportion of the copyright's cost.

Trademarks and **trade names** are distinctive identifications of products or services. The "eye" symbol that flashes across the television screen is a trademark that identifies the CBS television network. NBC uses the peacock as its trademark. Seven-Up, Pepsi, Egg McMuffin, and Rice-a-Roni are everyday trade names. Advertising slogans that are legally protected include United Airlines' "Fly the friendly skies" and Avis Rental Car's "We try harder."

The cost of a trademark or trade name is amortized over its useful life, not to exceed 40 years. The cost of advertising and promotions that use the trademark or trade name is not a part of the asset's cost but a debit to the advertising expense account.

Franchises and **licenses** are privileges granted by a private business or a government to sell a product or service in accordance with specified conditions. The Dallas Cowboys football organization is a franchise granted to its owner by the National Football League. McDonald's restaurants and Holiday Inns are popular franchises. Consolidated Edison Company (ConEd) holds a New York City franchise right to provide electricity to residents. The acquisition costs of franchises and licenses are amortized over their useful lives rather than over legal lives, subject to the 40-year maximum.

A **leasehold** is a prepayment that a lessee (renter) makes to secure the use of an asset from a lessor (landlord). Often leases require the lessee to make this prepayment in addition to monthly rental payments. The lessee debits the monthly lease payments to the Rent Expense account. The prepayment, however, is a debit to an intangible asset account entitled Leaseholds. This amount is amortized over the life of the lease by debiting Rent Expense and crediting Leaseholds. Some leases stipulate that the last year's rent must be paid in advance when the lease is signed. This prepayment is debited to Leaseholds and transferred to Rent Expense during the last year of the lease.

Sometimes lessees modify or improve the leased asset. For example, a lessee may construct a fence on leased land. The lessee debits the cost of the fence to a separate intangible asset account, Leasehold Improvements, and amortizes its cost over the term of the lease or the life of the asset, if shorter.

Goodwill in accounting is a more limited term than in everyday use, as in "goodwill among men." In accounting, *goodwill* is defined as the excess of the cost of an acquired company over the sum of the market values of its net assets (assets minus liabilities). Suppose Company A acquires Company B at a cost of $10 million. The market value of Company B's assets is $9 million, and its liabilities total $1 million. In this case, Company A paid $2 million for goodwill, computed as follows:

Purchase price paid for Company B		$10 million
Market value of Company B's assets	$9 million	
Less: Company B's liabilities	1 million	
Market value of Company B's net assets		8 million
Excess is called *goodwill*		$ 2 million

Company A's entry to record the acquisition of Company B, including its goodwill, would be

Assets (Cash, Receivables, Inventories, Plant Assets, all at market value)	9,000,000	
Goodwill	2,000,000	
Liabilities		1,000,000
Cash		10,000,000

Goodwill has special features, which include the following points:

1. Goodwill is recorded, at its cost, only when it is purchased in the acquisition of another company. Even though a favorable location, a superior product, or an outstanding reputation may create goodwill for a company, it is never recorded by that entity. Instead, goodwill is recorded only by another company that purchases the entity with goodwill. A purchase transaction provides objective evidence of the value of the goodwill.

2. According to generally accepted accounting principles, goodwill is amortized over a period not to exceed 40 years. In reality, the goodwill of many entities increases in value. Nevertheless, the Accounting Principles Board specified in *Opinion No. 17* that the cost of all intangible assets must be amortized as expense. The *Opinion* prohibits a lump-sum write-off of the cost of goodwill upon acquisition.

Capital Expenditures versus Revenue Expenditures (Expenses)

When a company makes a plant asset expenditure, it must decide whether to debit an asset account or an expense account. In this context, *expenditure* refers to either a cash or credit purchase of goods or services related to the asset. Examples of these expenditures range from replacing the windshield wipers on an automobile to adding a wing to a building.

Expenditures that increase the capacity or efficiency of the asset or extend its useful life are called **capital expenditures.** For example, the cost of a major overhaul that extends a taxi's useful life is a capital expenditure. Repair work that generates a capital expenditure is called an **extraordinary repair.** The amount of the capital expenditure, said to be capitalized, is a debit to an asset account. For an extraordinary repair on a taxi, we would debit the asset account Automobile.

Other expenditures do not extend the asset's capacity or efficiency. Expenditures that merely maintain the asset in its existing condition or restore the asset to good working order are called **revenue expenditures** because these costs are matched against revenue. Examples include the costs of repainting a taxi, repairing a dented fender, and replacing tires. The work that creates the revenue expenditure, said to be expensed, is a debit to an expense account. For the **ordinary repairs** on the taxi, we would debit Repair Expense.

The distinction between capital and revenue expenditures is often a matter of opinion. Does the work extend the life of the asset, or does it only maintain the asset in good order? When doubt exists as to whether to debit an asset or an expense, companies tend to debit an expense for two reasons. First, many expenditures are minor in amount, and most companies have a policy of debiting expense for all expenditures below a specified minimum, such as $1,000. Second, the income tax motive favors debiting all borderline expenditures to expense in order to create an immediate tax deduction. Capital expenditures are not immediate tax deductions.

Exhibit 10-10 illustrates the distinction between capital expenditures and revenue expenditures (expense) for several delivery truck expenditures. Note also the difference between extraordinary and ordinary repairs.

Treating a capital expenditure as a revenue expenditure, or vice versa, creates errors in the financial statements. Suppose a company makes an extraordinary repair to equipment and erroneously expenses this cost. It is a capital expenditure that should have been debited to an asset account. This accounting error overstates expenses and understates net income on the income statement. On the balance sheet, the equipment account is understated, and so is owner's equity. Capitalizing the cost of an ordinary repair creates the opposite error. Expenses are understated and net income is overstated on the income statement. The balance sheet reports overstated amounts for assets and owners' equity.

EXHIBIT 10-10 *Delivery Truck Expenditures*

Debit an Asset Account for Capital Expenditures	Debit Repair and Maintenance Expense for Revenue Expenditures
Extraordinary repairs:	Ordinary repairs:
Major engine overhaul	Repair of transmission or other mechanism
Modification of body for new use of truck	Oil change, lubrication, and so on
Addition to storage capacity of truck	Replacement tires, windshield, and the like
	Paint job

Summary Problems for Your Review

Problem 1. The figures that follow appear in the Solution to the Summary Problem, Requirement 2, on page 393.

	Method A Straight-Line			Method C Double-Declining-Balance		
Year	Annual Depreciation Expense	Accumulated Depreciation	Book Value	Annual Depreciation Expense	Accumulated Depreciation	Book Value
Start			$44,000			$44,000
19X5	$4,000	$4,000	40,000	$8,800	$ 8,800	35,200
19X6	4,000	8,000	36,000	7,040	15,840	28,160
19X7	4,000	12,000	32,000	5,632	21,472	22,528

Required

Suppose the income tax authorities permitted a choice between these two depreciation methods. Which method would you select for income tax purposes? Why?

Problem 2. A corporation purchased a building at a cost of $500,000 on January 1, 19X3. Management has depreciated the building by using the straight-line method, a 35-year life, and a residual value of $150,000. On July 1, 19X7, the company sold the building for $575,000 cash. The fiscal year of the corporation ends on December 31.

Required

Record depreciation for 19X7 and record the sale of the building on July 1, 19X7.

SOLUTIONS TO REVIEW PROBLEMS

1. For tax purposes, most companies select the accelerated method because it results in the most depreciation in the earliest years of the equipment's life. Accelerated depreciation minimizes taxable income and income tax payments in the early years of the asset's life, thereby maximizing the business's cash at the earliest possible time.

2. To record depreciation to date of sale and related sale of building:

19X7

July 1	Depreciation Expense–Building		
	[($500,000 − $150,000)/35 years × ½ year]	5,000	
	Accumulated Depreciation–Building		5,000
	To update depreciation.		
July 1	Cash	575,000	
	Accumulated Depreciation–Building		
	[($500,000 − $150,000)/35 years × 4½ years] . . .	45,000	
	Building		500,000
	Gain on Sale of Building		120,000
	To record sale of building.		

Summary

Plant assets are long-lived assets that the business uses in its operation. These assets are not held for sale as inventory. The cost of all plant assets but land is expensed through *depreciation*. The cost of natural resources, a special category of long-lived assets, is expensed through *depletion*. Long-lived assets called *intangibles* are rights that have no physical form. The cost of intangibles is expensed through *amortization*. Depreciation, depletion, and amortization are identical in concept.

Businesses may compute the depreciation of plant assets by four methods: *straight-line*, *units-of-production*, and the *accelerated* methods: *double-declining-balance* and *sum-of-years-digits*. To measure depreciation, the accountant subtracts the asset's estimated residual value from its cost and divides that amount by the asset's estimated useful life. Most companies use the straight-line method for financial reporting purposes, and almost all companies use an accelerated method for income tax purposes. Accelerated depreciation results in greater tax deductions early in the asset's life. These deductions decrease income tax payments and conserve cash that the company can use in its business.

Before disposing of a plant asset, the business updates the asset's depreciation. Disposal is recorded by removing the book balances from both the asset account and its related accumulated depreciation account. Disposal often results in recognition of a gain or a loss.

Depletion of natural resources is computed on a units-of-production basis. *Amortization* of intangibles is computed on a straight-line basis over a maximum of 40 years. However, the useful lives of most intangibles are shorter than their legal lives.

Capital expenditures increase the capacity or the efficiency of an asset or extend its useful life. Accordingly, they are debited to an asset account. *Revenue expenditures*, on the other hand, merely maintain the asset's usefulness and are debited to an expense account.

Self-Study Questions

Test your understanding of the chapter by marking the best answer for each of the following questions.

1. Which of the following payments is *not* included in the cost of land? *(p. 384)*
   a. Removal of old building
   b. Legal fees
   c. Back property taxes paid at acquisition
   d. Cost of fencing and lighting

2. A business paid $120,000 for two machines valued at $90,000 and $60,000. The business will record these machines at *(p. 385)*
   a. $90,000 and $60,000
   b. $60,000 each
   c. $72,000 and $48,000
   d. $70,000 and $50,000

3. Which of the following definitions fits depreciation? *(pp. 385, 386)*
   a. Allocation of the asset's market value to expense over its useful life
   b. Allocation of the asset's cost to expense over its useful life
   c. Decreases in the asset's market value over its useful life
   d. Increases in the fund set aside to replace the asset when it is worn out

4. Which depreciation method's amounts are not computed based on time? *(p. 389)*
   a. Straight-line
   b. Units-of-production
   c. Double-declining-balance
   d. Sum-of-years-digits

5. Which depreciation method gives the largest amount of expense in the early years of using the asset and therefore is best for income tax purposes? *(p. 394)*
   a. Straight-line
   b. Units-of-production
   c. Accelerated
   d. All are equal.

6. A company paid $450,000 for a building and was depreciating it by the straight-line method over a 40-year life with estimated residual value of $50,000. After 10 years, it became evident that the building's remaining useful life would be 40 years. Depreciation for the eleventh year is *(p. 396)*
   a. $7,500
   b. $8,750
   c. $10,000
   d. $12,500

7. Labrador, Inc., scrapped an automobile that cost $14,000 and had book value of $1,100. The entry to record this disposal is *(p. 397)*

   a. Loss on Disposal of Automobile.................... 1,100
      Automobile   1,100

   b. Accumulated Depreciation 14,000
      Automobile   14,000

   c. Accumulated Depreciation 12,900
      Automobile   12,900

   d. Accumulated Depreciation 12,900
      Loss of Disposal of Automobile 1,100
      Automobile   14,000

8. Depletion is computed in the same manner as which depreciation method? *(p. 401)*

   a. Straight-line
   b. Units-of-production
   c. Double-declining-balance
   d. Sum-of-years-digits

9. Lacy Corporation paid $550,000 to acquire Gentsch, Inc. Gentsch's assets had a market value of $900,000, and its liabilities were $400,000. In recording the acquisition, Lacy will record goodwill of *(p. 403)*

   a. $50,000
   b. $100,000
   c. $550,000
   d. $0

10. Which of the following items is a revenue expenditure? *(p. 404)*

    a. Property tax paid on land one year after it is acquired
    b. Survey fee paid during the acquisition of land
    c. Legal fee paid to acquire land
    d. Building permit paid to construct a warehouse on the land

Answers to the self-study questions are at the end of the chapter.

Accounting Vocabulary

accelerated depreciation *(p. 389)*,   amortization *(p. 401)*,   capital expenditure *(p. 404)*, copyright *(p. 402)*,   cost of a plant asset *(p. 384)*,   double-declining-balance (DDB) method *(p. 389)*,   depletion *(p. 401)*,   estimated residual value *(p. 387)*,   estimated useful life *(p. 387)*, extraordinary repair *(p. 404)*,   franchises and licenses *(p. 402)*,   goodwill *(p. 403)*,   intangible assets *(p. 383)*,   leasehold *(p. 402)*,   ordinary repair *(p. 404)*,   patent *(p. 402)*,   plant asset *(p. 383)*,   relative-sales-value method *(p. 385)*,   revenue expenditure *(p. 404)*,   straight-line (SL) method *(p. 387)*,   sum-of-years-digits (SYD) method *(p. 390)*,   trademarks and trade names *(p. 402)*,   units-of-production (UOP) method *(p. 389)*.

ASSIGNMENT MATERIAL _____

Questions

1. To what types of long-lived assets do the following expenses apply: depreciation, depletion, and amortization?

2. Describe how to measure the cost of a plant asset. Would an ordinary cost of repairing the asset after it is placed in service be included in the asset's cost?

3. Suppose land is purchased for $100,000. How do you account for the $8,000 cost of removing an unwanted building?

4. When assets are purchased as a group for a single price and no individual asset cost is given, how is each asset's cost determined?

5. Define depreciation. Present the common misconceptions about depreciation.

6. Which depreciation method does each of the graphs on the next page characterize — straight-line, units-of-production, or accelerated?

7. Which of the four depreciation methods results in the most depreciation in the first year of the asset's life?

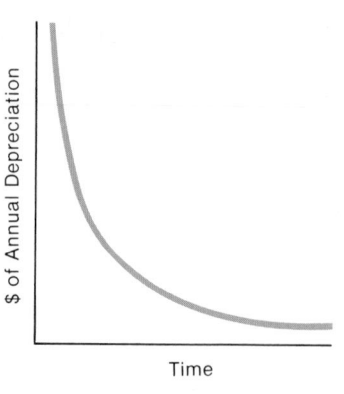
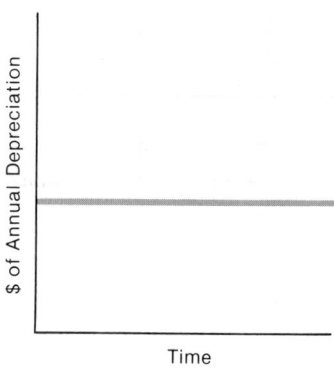

8. Explain the concept of accelerated depreciation. Which other depreciation method is used in the definition of accelerated depreciation?

9. The level of business activity fluctuates widely for Harwood Delivery Service, reaching its peak around Christmas each year. At other times, business is slow. What depreciation method is most appropriate for the company's fleet of Chevy Luv trucks?

10. Oswalt Computer Service Center uses the most advanced computers available to keep a competitive edge over other service centers. To maintain this advantage, Oswalt usually replaces its computers before they are worn out. Describe the major factors affecting the useful life of a plant asset and indicate which seems more relevant to Oswalt's computers.

11. Estimated residual value is not considered in computing depreciation during the early years of the asset's life by one of the methods. Which method is it?

12. Which type of depreciation method is best from an income tax standpoint? Why?

13. How does depreciation affect income taxes? How does depreciation affect cash provided by operations?

14. Describe how to compute depreciation for less than a full year and how to account for depreciation for less than a full month.

15. Ragland Company paid $10,000 for office furniture. The company expected it to remain in service for 6 years and to have a $1,000 residual value. After 2 years' use, company accountants believe the furniture will last an additional 6 years. How much depreciation will Ragland record for each of these 6 years, assuming straight-line depreciation and no change in the estimated residual value?

16. What three pieces of information should a company disclose about a change in accounting estimate, such as extending the useful life of a depreciable asset?

17. When a company sells a plant asset before the year's end, what must it record before accounting for the sale?

18. Describe how to determine whether a company experiences a gain or a loss when an old plant asset is exchanged for a new one. Does generally accepted accounting favor the recognition of gains or losses? Which accounting concept underlies your answer?

19. Identify seven elements of internal control designed to safeguard plant assets.

20. What expense applies to natural resources? By which depreciation method is this expense computed?

21. How do intangible assets differ from most other assets? Why are they assets at all? What expense applies to intangible assets?

22. Why is the cost of patents and other intangible assets often expensed over a shorter period than the legal life of the asset?

23. Your company has just purchased another company for $400,000. The market value of the other company's net assets is $325,000. What is the $75,000 excess called? What type of asset is it? What is the maximum period over which its cost is amortized under generally accepted accounting principles?

24. IBM Corporation is recognized as a world leader in the manufacture and sale of computers. The company's success has created vast amounts of business goodwill.

Would you expect to see *this* goodwill reported on IBM's financial statements? Why or why not?

25. Distinguish a capital expenditure from a revenue expenditure. The title "revenue expenditure" is curious in that a revenue expenditure is a debit to an expense account. Explain why revenue expenditures are so named.

26. Are ordinary repairs capital expenditures or revenue expenditures? Which type of expenditures are extraordinary repairs?

Exercises

Exercise 10-1 *Identifying the elements of a plant asset's cost*

A company purchased land, paying $30,000 cash as a down payment and signing a $120,000 note payable for the balance. In addition, the company paid back property tax of $6,000, a title fee of $500, and a $3,100 charge for leveling the land and removing an unwanted building. The company constructed an office building on the land at a cost of $640,000. It also paid $12,000 for a fence around the boundary of the property, $2,400 for the company sign near the entrance to the property, and $6,000 for special lighting of the grounds. Determine the cost of the company's land, land improvements, and building.

Exercise 10-2 *Allocating cost to assets acquired in a basket purchase*

Balcones Research Center bought three used machines in a $21,000 purchase. An independent appraisal of the machines produced the following figures:

Machine No.	Appraised Value
1	$ 4,000
2	12,000
3	8,000

Assuming Balcones paid cash for the machines, record the purchase in the general journal, identifying each machine's individual cost in a separate Machine account.

Exercise 10-3 *Computing depreciation by four methods*

A company delivery truck was acquired on January 2, 19X1, for $12,000. The truck was expected to remain in service for 4 years and last 88,000 miles. At the end of its useful life, company officials estimated that the truck's residual value would be $1,000. The truck traveled 24,000 miles in the first year, 28,000 in the second year, 21,000 in the third year, and 15,000 in the fourth year. Prepare a schedule of *depreciation expense* per year for the truck under the four depreciation methods. Show your computations.

			Depreciation Expense per Year		
Year	Straight-line	Units-of-Production	Double-Declining-Balance	Sum-of-Years-Digits
19X1				
19X2				
19X3				
19X4				

Exercise 10-4 *Identifying depreciation methods for income tax and financial reporting purposes*

Using the data in Exercise 10-3, identify the depreciation method that would be most advantageous from an income tax perspective. Which depreciation method do most companies use for reporting to their stockholders and creditors on their financial statements?

Exercise 10-5 *Recording partial-year depreciation computed by two methods*

Situation 1. Hunt Corporation purchased office furniture on March 3, 19X4, for $2,600 cash. Donna Hunt expects it to remain useful for 8 years and to have a residual value of $200. Hunt uses the straight-line depreciation method. Record Hunt's depreciation on the furniture for the year ended December 31, 19X4.

Situation 2. Chen Company purchased equipment on May 19, 19X2, for $19,500, signing a note payable for that amount. Chen estimated that this equipment will be useful for 3 years and have a residual value of $1,500. Assuming Chen uses sum-of-years-digits depreciation, record Chen's depreciation on the machine for the year ended December 31, 19X2.

Exercise 10-6 *Journalizing a change in a plant asset's useful life*

A company purchased a building for $680,000 and depreciated it on a straight-line basis over a 30-year period. The estimated residual value was $80,000. After using the building for 10 years, the company realized that wear and tear on the building would force the company to replace it before 30 years. Starting with the 11th year, the company began depreciating the building over a revised total life of 20 years, retaining the $80,000 estimate of residual value. Record depreciation expense on the building for years 10 and 11.

Exercise 10-7 *Recording the sale of a plant asset*

On January 2, 19X1, Oakwood Sales Company purchased store fixtures for $7,700 cash, expecting the fixtures to remain in service for 10 years. Oakwood has depreciated the fixtures on a sum-of-years-digits basis, assuming no estimated residual value. On June 30, 19X8, Oakwood sold the fixtures for $1,600 cash. Record depreciation expense on the fixtures for the 6 months ended June 30, 19X8, and also record the sale of the fixtures.

Exercise 10-8 *Exchanging plant assets*

A machine cost $10,000. At the end of 4 years, its accumulated depreciation was $4,500. For each of the following situations, record the trade-in of this old machine for a new, similar machine.

Situation 1. The new machine had a cash price of $12,400; the dealer allowed a trade-in allowance of $5,200 on the old machine, and you paid the $7,200 balance in cash.

Situation 2. The new machine had a cash price of $13,000; the dealer allowed a trade-in allowance of $6,300 on the old machine; and you signed a note payable for the $6,700 balance.

Exercise 10-9 *Preparing a plant ledger card*

McBee Delivery Service uses a plant ledger card to account for its delivery vehicles, which are located at the company's service garage. The fleet of vehicles cost $96,000 when purchased from Ericksen Ford Company on September 1, 19X2. This cost is the debit balance in the Delivery Vehicles account in the general ledger. McBee uses the straight-line depreciation method and estimates a four-year useful life and a $6,000 residual value for the trucks. The garage foreman is responsible for the vehicles. The company's fiscal year ends on December 31. Complete a plant ledger card for these vehicles through December 31, 19X4, using a format similar to Exhibit 10-9.

Exercise 10-10 *Recording natural resource assets and depletion*

Sasquatch Mining Company paid $178,500 for the right to extract ore from a 200,000-ton mineral deposit. In addition to the purchase price, Sasquatch also paid a $500 filing fee and a $1,000 license fee to the state of Wyoming. Because Sasquatch purchased the rights to the minerals only, the company expected the asset to have zero residual value when fully depleted. During the first year of production, Sasquatch removed 35,000 tons of ore. Make general journal entries to record (a) purchase of the mineral rights (debit Mineral Asset), (b) payment of fees, and (c) depletion for first-year production.

Exercise 10-11 *Recording intangibles, amortization, and a change in the asset's useful life*

Part 1.   Lutz Corporation manufactures high-speed printers and has recently purchased for $4 million a patent for the design for a new laser printer. Although it gives legal protection for 17 years, the patent is expected to provide Lutz with a competitive advantage for only 8 years. Assuming the straight-line method of amortization, use general journal entries to record (a) the purchase of the patent and (b) amortization for 1 year.

Part 2.   After using the patent for 3 years, Lutz learns at an industry trade show that another company is designing a more efficient printer. Based on this new information, Lutz decides, starting with year 4, to amortize the remaining cost of the patent over 2 additional years, giving the patent a total useful life of 5 years. Record amortization for year 4.

Exercise 10-12 *Computing and recording goodwill*

Company P purchased Company S, paying $1 million cash. The market value of Company S assets was $1.7 million, and Company S had liabilities of $.9 million.

(a) Compute the cost of the goodwill purchased by Company P.
(b) Record the purchase by Company P.
(c) Record amortization of goodwill for year 1, assuming the straight-line method and a useful life of 20 years.

Exercise 10-13 *Distinguishing capital expenditures from revenue expenditures*

Classify each of the following expenditures as a capital expenditure or a revenue expenditure (expense) related to machinery: (a) purchase price, (b) sales tax paid on the purchase price, (c) transportation and insurance while machinery is in transport from seller to buyer, (d) installation, (e) training of personnel for initial operation of the machinery, (f) special reinforcement to the machinery platform, (g) income tax paid on income earned from the sale of products manufactured by the machinery, (h) major overhaul to extend useful life by three years, (i) ordinary recurring repairs to keep the machinery in good working order, (j) lubrication of the machinery before it is placed in service, (k) periodic lubrication after the machinery is placed in service.

Problems   *(Group A)*

Problem 10-1A *Identifying the elements of a plant asset's cost*

Mazzoti Company incurred the following costs in acquiring land and a garage, making land improvements, and constructing and furnishing a home office building.

(a) Purchase price of 3½ acres of land, including an old building that will be used as a garage for company vehicles (land market value is $600,000; building market value is $60,000) $605,000
(b) Delinquent real estate taxes on the land to be paid by Mazzoti 14,600
(c) Landscaping (additional dirt and earth moving)................... 3,550
(d) Title insurance on the land acquisition 1,000
(e) Fence around the boundary of the land 12,500
(f) Building permit for the home office building 200
(g) Architect fee for the design of the home office building 25,000

(h)	Company signs near front and rear approaches to the company property.. 23,550
(i)	Renovation of the garage....................................... 23,800
(j)	Concrete, wood, steel girders, and other materials used in the construction of the home office building.............................. 385,000
(k)	Masonry, carpentry, roofing, and other labor to construct home office building... 734,000
(l)	Repair of vandalism damage to home office building during construction.. 4,100
(m)	Parking lots and concrete walks on the property................. 17,450
(n)	Lights for the parking lot, walkways, and company signs........... 8,900
(o)	Supervisory salary of construction supervisor (90 percent to home office building, 6 percent to fencing, parking lot, and concrete walks, and 4 percent to garage renovation) 55,000
(p)	Office furniture for the home office building 267,500
(q)	Transportation of furniture from seller to the home office building ... 700
(r)	Landscaping (trees and shrubs) 9,100

Mazotti depreciates buildings over 40 years, land improvements over 20 years, and furniture over 8 years, all on a straight-line basis with zero residual value.

Required

1. Using the following format, account for each cost by listing it as a debit to Land, Land Improvements, Home Office Building, Garage, or Furniture:

Item	Land	Land Improvements	Home Office Building	Garage	Furniture
(a)	$	$	$	$	$
⋮					
(r)					
Totals	$	$	$	$	$

2. Assuming that all construction was complete and the assets were placed in service on March 19, record depreciation for the year ended December 31. Round figures to the nearest dollar.

Problem 10-2A *Computing depreciation by four methods and the cash flow advantage of accelerated depreciation for tax purposes*

On January 2, 19X1, Morse, Inc., purchased 3 used delivery trucks at a total cost of $41,000. Before placing the trucks in service, the company spent $1,200 painting them, $1,800 replacing their tires, and $4,000 overhauling their engines and reconditioning their bodies. Morse management estimates that the trucks will remain in service for 6 years and have a residual value of $6,000. The trucks' combined annual mileage is expected to be 16,000 miles in each of the first 4 years and 18,000 miles in each of the next 2 years. In trying to decide which depreciation method to use, Ted Morse requests a depreciation schedule for each of the four generally accepted depreciation methods (straight-line, units-of-production, double-declining-balance, and sum-of-years-digits).

Required

1. Assuming Morse depreciates its delivery trucks as a unit, prepare a depreciation schedule for each of the four generally accepted depreciation methods, showing asset cost, depreciation expense, accumulated depreciation, and asset book value. Use the formats of Exhibits 10-3 through 10-6. (Note: Double-declining-balance depreciation for

year 6 is the amount needed to reduce asset book value to the residual value.)

2. Morse reports to stockholders and creditors in the financial statements using the depreciation method that maximizes reported income in the early years of asset use. For income tax purposes, however, the company uses the depreciation method that minimizes income tax payments in those early years. Consider the first year that Morse uses the delivery trucks. Identify the depreciation methods that meet Morse's objectives, assuming the income tax authorities would permit the use of any of the methods.

3. Assume cash provided by operations before income tax is $80,000 for the delivery trucks' first year. The income tax rate is 40 percent. For the two depreciation methods identified in Requirement 2, compare the net income and cash provided by operations (cash flow). Use the following outline for your answer.

| | Depreciation Method That in the Early Years | |
	A Maximizes Reported Income	B Minimizes Income Tax Payments
Comparison of net income for first year:		
Cash provided by operations before income tax	$	$
Depreciation expense		
Income before income tax		
Income tax expense (40%)		
Net income	$	$
Advantage of Method A over Method B.	$	
Cash flow analysis for first year:		
Cash provided by operations before income tax	$	$
Income tax expense		
Cash provided by operations (called cash flow).	$	$
Advantage of Method B over Method A.	$	

Problem 10-3A *Journalizing and posting plant asset transactions; capital expenditures versus revenue expenditures*

Pennsylvania Power & Light Company provides electrical power to part of eastern Pennsylvania. Assume that the company completed the following transactions:

19X4

Jan. 3 Paid $16,000 cash for a used service truck.
  5 Paid $1,200 to have the truck engine overhauled.
  7 Paid $300 to have the truck modified for business use.
Oct. 3 Paid $855 for transmission repair and oil change.
Dec. 31 Used the double-declining-balance method to record depreciation on the truck. (Assume a 4-year life.)
  31 Closed the appropriate accounts.
19X5
Mar. 13 Replaced the truck's broken windshield for $275 cash.
June 26 Traded in the service truck for a new truck costing $22,000. The dealer granted a $6,000 allowance on the old truck, and Pennsylvania Power paid the balance in cash. Recorded 19X5 depreciation for the year to date and then recorded the exchange of trucks.

Dec. 31   Used the double-declining-balance method to record depreciation on the new truck. (Assume a 4-year life.)

31   Closed the appropriate accounts.

Required

1. Open the following accounts in the general ledger: Service Trucks; Accumulated Depreciation – Service Trucks; Truck Repair Expense; Depreciation Expense – Service Trucks; and Loss on Exchange of Service Trucks.
2. Record the transactions in the general journal and post to the ledger accounts opened.

Problem 10-4A   *Recording plant asset transactions; exchanges; changes in useful life.*

A. C. Nielsen Company surveys American viewing trends. Nielsen's balance sheet reports the following assets under Property and Equipment: Land, Buildings, Office Furniture, Communication Equipment, Televideo Equipment, and Leasehold Improvements. The company has a separate accumulated depreciation account for each of these assets except land and leasehold improvements. Amortization on leasehold improvements is credited directly to the Leasehold Improvements account rather than to Accumulated Depreciation – Leasehold Improvements.

Assume that Nielsen completed the following transactions:

Jan. 4   Traded in communication equipment with book value of $22,000 (cost of $51,000) for similar new equipment with a cash cost of $78,000. The seller gave Nielsen a trade-in allowance of $15,000 on the old equipment, and Nielsen paid the remainder in cash.

19   Purchased office furniture for $45,000 plus 6 percent sales tax and $300 shipping charge. The company gave a 90-day, 10 percent note in payment.

Apr. 19   Paid the furniture note and related interest.

Aug. 29   Sold a building that had cost $475,000 and had accumulated depreciation of $353,500 through December 31 of the preceding year. Depreciation is computed on a straight-line basis. The building has a 30-year useful life and a residual value of $47,500. Nielsen received $250,000 cash and a $750,000 note receivable.

Sep. 6   Paid cash to improve leased assets at a cost of $39,000.

Nov. 10   Purchased used communication and televideo equipment from the Gallup polling organization. Total cost was $90,000 paid in cash. An independent appraisal valued the communication equipment at $65,000 and the televideo equipment at $35,000.

Dec. 31   Recorded depreciation as follows:

Equipment is depreciated by the double-declining-balance method over a 6-year life with zero residual value. Record depreciation on the equipment purchased on January 4 and on November 10 separately.

Office furniture has an expected useful life of 8 years with an estimated residual value of $5,000. Depreciation is computed by the sum-of-years-digits method.

Amortization on leasehold improvements is computed on a straight-line basis over the life of the lease, which is 6 years, with zero residual value.

Depreciation on buildings is computed by the straight-line method. The company had assigned buildings an estimated useful life of 30 years and a residual value that is 10 percent of cost. After using the buildings for 20 years, the company has come to believe that their total useful life will be 35 years. Residual value remains unchanged. The buildings cost $96,000,000.

Required

Record the transactions in the general journal.

Problem 10-5A *Distinguishing capital expenditures from revenue expenditures; preparing a plant ledger card*

Suppose Public Service Company of Colorado uses plant ledger cards to control its service trucks, purchased from Wallen Motor Company. The supervisor is responsible for the trucks, which are located at the company's service garage. The following transactions were completed during 19X6 and 19X7:

19X6

Jan. 10   Paid $14,000 cash for a used service truck (truck no. 214).

     11   Paid $1,500 to have the truck engine overhauled.

     12   Paid $250 to have the truck modified for business use.

Aug. 3   Paid $603 for transmission repair and oil change.

Dec. 31   Recorded depreciation on the truck by the double-declining-balance method, based on a 4-year life and a $1,500 residual value.

19X7

Mar. 13   Replaced a damaged bumper on truck no. 214 at a cash cost of $295.

Aug. 12   Traded in service truck no. 214 for a new one (truck no. 267) with a cash cost of $20,000. The dealer granted a $7,000 allowance on the old truck, and Public Service Company paid the balance in cash. Recorded 19X7 depreciation for year to date and then recorded exchange of the trucks.

Dec. 31   Recorded depreciation on truck no. 267 by the double-declining-balance method, based on a 4-year life and a $2,000 residual value.

Required

1. Identify the capital expenditures and the revenue expenditures in the transactions. Which expenditures are debited to an asset account? Which expenditures are debited to an expense account?
2. Prepare a separate plant ledger card for each of the trucks.

Problem 10-6A *Recording intangibles, natural resources, and the related expenses*

Part 1.   United Telecommunications, Inc., (United Telecom) provides communication services in Florida, North Carolina, New Jersey, Texas, and other states. The company's balance sheet reports the asset Cost of Acquisitions in Excess of the Fair Market Value of the Net Assets of Subsidiaries. Assume that United Telecom purchased this asset as part of the acquisition of another company, which carried these figures:

Book value of assets.....................	$215,000
Market value of assets	300,000
Liabilities..............................	135,000

Required

1. What is another title for the asset Cost of Acquisitions in Excess of the Fair Market Value of the Net Assets of Subsidiaries?
2. Make the general journal entry to record United Telecom's purchase of the other company for $220,000 cash.
3. Assuming United Telecom amortizes Cost of Acquisitions in Excess of the Fair Market Value of the Net Assets of Subsidiaries over 20 years, record the straight-line amortization for 1 year.

Part 2.   Suppose United Telecom purchased a patent for $455,000. Before using the patent, United incurred an additional cost of $25,000 for a lawsuit to defend the company's right to purchase it. Even though the patent gives United legal protection for 17 years, company management has decided to amortize its cost over an 8-year period because of the industry's fast-changing technologies.

Required

Make general journal entries to record the patent transactions, including straight-line amortization for 1 year.

Part 3.   Transco Energy Company operates a pipeline that provides natural gas to Atlanta, Washington, D.C., Philadelphia, and New York City. The company's balance sheet includes the asset Oil Properties.

Suppose Transco paid $2,800,000 cash for an oil lease that contained an estimated reserve of 300,000 barrels of oil. Assume that the company paid $350,000 for additional geological tests of the property and $50,000 to prepare the surface for drilling. Prior to production, the company signed a $40,000 note payable to have a building constructed on the property. Because the building provides on-site headquarters for the drilling effort and will be abandoned when the oil is depleted, its cost is debited to the Oil properties account and included in depletion charges. During the first year of production, Transco removed 26,000 barrels of oil, which it sold on credit for $19 per barrel.

Required

Make general journal entries to record all transactions related to the oil and gas property, including depletion and sale of the first-year production.

(Group B)

Problem 10-1B   *Identifying the elements of a plant asset's cost*

Anotelli Company incurred the following costs in acquiring land, making land improvements, and constructing and furnishing an office building.

(a)	Purchase price of four acres of land, including an old building that will be used for storage (land market value is $380,000; building market value is $20,000)......	$350,000
(b)	Landscaping (additional dirt and earth moving)............	8,100
(c)	Fence around the boundary of the land	23,650
(d)	Attorney fee for title search on the land	600
(e)	Delinquent real estate taxes on the land to be paid by Anotelli.......	5,900
(f)	Company signs at front of the company property	7,600
(g)	Building permit for the office building............	350
(h)	Architect fee for the design of the office building............	19,800
(i)	Masonry, carpentry, roofing, and other labor to construct office building............	509,000
(j)	Concrete, wood, steel girders, and other materials used in the construction of the office building............	453,000
(k)	Renovation of the storage building	41,800
(l)	Repair of storm damage to storage building during construction	2,200
(m)	Landscaping (trees and shrubs)	6,400
(n)	Parking lot and concrete walks on the property............	19,750
(o)	Lights for the parking lot, walkways, and company signs............	7,300
(p)	Supervisory salary of construction supervisor (85 percent to office building, 9 percent to fencing, parking lot, and concrete walks, and 6 percent to storage building renovation)............	40,000
(q)	Office furniture for the office building............	174,400
(r)	Transportation and installation of furniture	1,100

Anotelli depreciates buildings over 40 years, land improvements over 20 years, and furniture over 8 years, all on a straight-line basis with zero residual value.

Required

1. Using the following format, account for each cost by listing it as a debit to Land, Land Improvements, Office Building, Storage Building, or Furniture:

Item	Land	Land Improvements	Office Building	Storage Building	Furniture
(a)	$	$	$	$	$
⋮					
(r)					
Totals	$	$	$	$	$

2. Assuming that all construction was complete and the assets were placed in service on May 4, record depreciation for the year ended December 31. Round off figures to the nearest dollar.

Problem 10-2B *Computing depreciation by four methods and the cash flow advantage of accelerated depreciation for tax purposes*

On January 9, 19X1, Lynch, Inc., paid $82,000 for equipment that manufactures stereo cassette tapes. In addition to the basic purchase price, the company paid $700 transportation charges, $100 insurance for the goods in transit, $4,100 sales tax, and $3,100 for a special platform on which to place the equipment in the plant. Lynch management estimates that the equipment will remain in service for 5 years and have a residual value of $11,250. The equipment will produce 45,000 units in the first year, with annual production decreasing by 5,000 units during each of the next 4 years (that is, 40,000 units in year 2, 35,000 units in year 3, and so on). In trying to decide which depreciation method to use, Charlene Lynch has requested a depreciation schedule for each of the four generally accepted depreciation methods (straight-line, units-of-production, double-declining-balance and sum-of-years-digits).

Required

1. For each of the four generally accepted depreciation methods, prepare a depreciation schedule showing asset cost, depreciation expense, accumulated depreciation, and asset book value. Use the format of Exhibits 10-3 through 10-6.
2. Lynch reports to stockholders and creditors in the financial statements using the depreciation method that maximizes reported income in the early years of asset use. For income tax purposes, however, the company uses the depreciation method that minimizes income tax payments in those early years. Consider the first year Lynch uses the equipment. Identify the depreciation methods that meet Lynch's objectives, assuming the income tax authorities would permit the use of any of the methods.
3. Assume cash provided by operations before income tax is $110,000 for the equipment's first year. The income tax rate is 40 percent. For the two depreciation methods identified in Requirement 2, compare the net income and cash provided by operations (cash flow). Use the following outline for your answer.

Comparison of net income for first year:	**Depreciation Method That in the Early Years**	
	A Maximizes Reported Income	**B** Minimizes Income Tax Payments
Cash provided by operations before income tax	$	$
Depreciation expense............................		
Income before income tax		
Income tax expense (40%)........................		
Net income.....................................	$	$
Advantage of Method A over Method B............	$	

	Depreciation Method That in the Early Years	
	A	B
Cash flow analysis for first year:	**Maximizes Reported Income**	**Minimizes Income Tax Payments**
Cash provided by operations before income tax	$	$
Income tax expense		
Cash provided by operations (called cash flow)......	$	$
Advantage of Method B over Method A............	$	

Problem 10-3B   *Journalizing and posting plant asset transactions; capital expenditures versus revenue expenditures*

Assume that a Revco drugstore completed the following transactions:

19X2

Jan.   6   Paid $6,000 cash for a used delivery truck.
      7   Paid $800 to have the truck engine overhauled.
      8   Paid $200 to have the truck modified for business use.
Aug. 21   Paid $127 for a minor tuneup.
Dec. 31   Recorded depreciation on the truck by the sum-of-years-digits method (assume a 4-year life and a $1,500 residual value).
     31   Closed the appropriate accounts.

19X3

May 8   Traded in the delivery truck for a new truck costing $10,000. The dealer granted a $4,000 allowance on the old truck, and the store paid the balance in cash. Recorded 19X3 depreciation for the year to date and then recorded the exchange of trucks.
July 8   Repaired the new truck's damaged fender for $625 cash.
Dec. 31   Recorded depreciation on the new truck by the sum-of-years-digits method. (Assume a 4-year life and a residual value of $2,000).
     31   Closed the appropriate accounts.

Required

1. Open the following accounts in the general ledger: Delivery Trucks; Accumulated Depreciation – Delivery Trucks; Truck Repair Expense; Depreciation Expense – Delivery Trucks; and Loss on Exchange of Delivery Trucks.
2. Record the transactions in the general journal, and post to the ledger accounts opened.

Problem 10-4B   *Recording plant asset transactions; exchanges; changes in useful life*

Consolidated Freightways, Inc., provides nationwide general freight service. The company's balance sheet includes the following assets under Property, Plant, and Equipment: Land, Buildings, Motor Carrier Equipment, and Leasehold Improvements. Assume the company has a separate accumulated depreciation account for each of these assets except land and leasehold improvements. Amortization on leasehold improvements is credited directly to the Leasehold Improvements account rather than to Accumulated Amortization – Leasehold Improvements.

Assume that Consolidated Freightways completed the following transactions:

Jan. 5   Traded in motor-carrier equipment with book value of $34,000 (cost of $90,000) for similar new equipment with a cash cost of $128,000. Consolidated received a trade-in allowance of $40,000 on the old equipment and paid the remainder in cash.

Feb. 22 Purchased motor-carrier equipment for $136,000 plus 5 percent sales tax and $200 title fee. The company gave a 60-day, 12 percent note in payment.

Apr. 23 Paid the equipment note and related interest.

July 9 Sold a building that had cost $550,000 and had accumulated depreciation of $247,500 through December 31 of the preceding year. Depreciation is computed on a straight-line basis. The building has a 30-year useful life and a residual value of $55,000. Consolidated received $100,000 cash and a $600,000 note receivable.

Aug. 16 Paid cash to improve leased assets at a cost of $21,600.

Oct. 26 Purchased land and a building for a single price of $300,000. An independent appraisal valued the land at $115,000 and the building at $230,000.

Dec. 31 Recorded depreciation as follows:

Motor-carrier equipment has an expected useful life of 6 years and an estimated residual value of 5 percent of cost. Depreciation is computed on the sum-of-years-digits method. Make separate depreciation entries for equipment acquired on January 5 and February 22.

Amortization on leasehold improvements is computed on a straight-line basis over the life of the lease, which is 5 years, with zero residual value.

Depreciation on buildings is computed by the straight-line method. The company had assigned to its older buildings, which cost $200,000,000, an estimated useful life of 30 years with a residual value equal to 10 percent of the asset cost. However, management has come to believe that the buildings will remain useful for a total of 40 years. Residual value remains unchanged. The company has used all its buildings, except for the one purchased on October 26, for 10 years. The new building carries a 40-year useful life and a residual value equal to 10 percent of its cost. Make separate entries for depreciation on the building acquired on October 26 and the other buildings purchased in earlier years.

Required

Record the transactions in the general journal.

Problem 10-5B *Distinguishing capital expenditures from revenue expenditures; preparing a plant ledger card*

Suppose Pacific Power & Light Company uses plant ledger cards to control its service trucks, purchased from Grant Motor Co. The supervisor is responsible for the trucks, which are located at the company's service garage. The following transactions were completed during 19X3 and 19X4:

19X3

Jan. 6 Paid $13,800 cash for a used service truck (truck no. 501).

7 Paid $2,500 to have the truck engine overhauled.

8 Paid $180 to have the truck modified for business use.

Nov. 5 Paid $107 for replacement of one tire.

Dec. 31 Recorded depreciation on the truck by the double-declining-balance method, based on a 4-year useful life and a $2,000 residual value.

19X4

Apr. 19 Repaired a damaged fender on truck no. 501 at a cash cost of $877.

Nov. 6 Traded in service truck no. 501 for a new one (truck no. 633) with a cash cost of $18,000. The dealer granted a $6,000 allowance on the old truck, and Pacific Power paid the balance in cash. Recorded 19X4 depreciation for year to date and then recorded exchange of the trucks.

Dec. 31 Recorded depreciation on truck no. 633 by the double-declining-balance method, on a 4-year life and a $2,500 residual value.

Required

1. Identify the capital expenditures and the revenue expenditures in the transactions. Which expenditures are debited to an asset account? Which expenditures are debited to an expense account?

2. Prepare a separate plant ledger card for each of the trucks.

Problem 10-6B *Recording intangibles, natural resources, and the related expenses*

Part 1. Collins Foods International, Inc., is the largest of the companies that operate Kentucky Fried Chicken franchised restaurants and is also the majority owner of Sizzler Restaurants. The company's balance sheet reports the asset Cost in Excess of Net Assets of Purchased Businesses. Assume that Collins purchased this asset as part of the acquisition of another company, which carried these figures:

Book value of assets..................... $275,000
Market value of assets 420,000
Liabilities............................. 167,500

Required

1. What is another title for the asset Cost in Excess of Net Assets of Purchased Businesses?

2. Make the general journal entry to record Collins's purchase of the other company for $292,500 cash.

3. Assuming Collins amortizes Cost in Excess of Net Assets of Purchased Businesses over 10 years, record the straight-line amortization for 1 year.

Part 2. Suppose Collins purchased a Kentucky Fried Chicken franchise license for $162,000. In addition to the basic purchase price, Collins also paid a lawyer $8,000 for assistance with the negotiations. Collins management believes the appropriate amortization period for its cost of the franchise license is 8 years.

Required

Make general journal entries to record the franchise transactions, including straight-line amortization for one year.

Part 3. Georgia-Pacific Corporation is one of the world's largest forest products companies. The company's balance sheet includes the assets Natural Gas, Oil, and Coal.

Suppose Georgia-Pacific paid $800,000 cash for a lease giving the firm the right to work a mine that contained an estimated 80,000 tons of coal. Assume that the company paid $5,000 to remove unwanted buildings from the land and $15,000 to prepare the surface for mining. Further assume that Georgia-Pacific signed a $20,000 note payable for a landscaping company to return the land surface to its original condition after the lease ends. During the first year, Georgia-Pacific removed 15,000 tons of coal, which it sold on account for $17 per ton.

Required

Make general journal entries to record all transactions related to the coal, including depletion and sale of the first-year production.

Decision Problem

Measuring Profitability Based on Different Inventory and Depreciation Methods

Suppose you are considering investing in two businesses, Frycer Company and Bergdahl Company. The two companies are virtually identical, and both began operations at the beginning of the current year. During the year, each company purchased inventory as follows:

Jan.	4	12,000 units at $4 =	$ 48,000
Apr.	6	5,000 units at 5 =	25,000
Aug.	9	7,000 units at 6 =	42,000
Nov.	27	10,000 units at 7 =	70,000
Totals		34,000	$185,000

Over the first year, both companies sold 25,000 units of inventory.

In early January both companies purchased equipment costing $100,000 that had a 10-year estimated useful life and a $10,000 residual value. Frycer Company uses the first-in, first-out (FIFO) method for its inventory and straight-line depreciation for its equipment. Bergdahl Company uses last-in, first-out (LIFO) and double-declining-balance depreciation. Both companies' trial balances at December 31 included the following:

Sales revenue	$250,000
Purchases	185,000
Operating expenses	80,000

Required

1. Prepare both companies' income statements.
2. Prepare a schedule that shows why one company appears to be more profitable than the other. Explain the schedule and amounts in your own words. What accounts for the different amounts?
3. Is one company more profitable than the other? Give your reason.

Financial Statement Problem

Plant Assets and Intangible Assets

Refer to the Gulf+Western financial statements in Appendix C, and answer the following questions.

1. Which depreciation method does Gulf+Western use for the purpose of reporting to stockholders and creditors in the financial statements? Although Gulf+Western does not disclose it in the statements, what type of depreciation method does the company probably use for income tax purposes?
2. Depreciation and amortization expenses are embedded in the expense amounts listed on the income statement (statement of earnings). The statement of cash flows gives the amounts of depreciation and amortization. What were their amounts for fiscal 1987?
3. The statement of cash flows also reports purchases of plant assets and the proceeds (sale prices) on disposal of plant assets. How much were Gulf+Western's plant asset expenditures during fiscal 1987? Were these capital expenditures or revenue expenditures? How much did Gulf+Western receive on the sale of plant assets this year?
4. In what category on the income statement are revenue expenditures most likely included?
5. What is Gulf+Western's major intangible asset? As of October 31, 1987, what was the company's cost of intangible assets? Identify the nature of the transactions in which Gulf+Western acquired this asset. What is the maximum period over which the cost of an intangible asset can be expensed under GAAP?

Answers to Self-Study Questions

1. d
2. c $90,000/($90,000 + $60,000) × $120,000 = $72,000;
   $60,000/($90,000 + $60,000) × $120,000 = $48,000
3. b
4. b
5. c
6. a Depreciable cost = $450,000 − $50,000 = $400,000
   $400,000/40 years = $10,000 per year
   $400,000 − ($10,000 × 10 years) = $300,000/40 years = $7,500 per year
7. d
8. b
9. a $550,000 − ($900,000 − $400,000) = $50,000
10. a

11

Current Liabilities and Payroll Accounting

A *liability* is an obligation to transfer assets or to provide services in the future. The obligation may arise from a transaction with an outside party. For example, a business incurs a liability when it issues a note payable to buy equipment or to borrow money. Also, the obligation may arise in the absence of individual transactions. For example, interest expense accrues with the passage of time. Until this interest is paid it is a liability. Income tax, a liability of corporations, accrues as income is earned. Proper accounting for liabilities is as important as proper accounting for assets. The failure to record an accrued liability causes the balance sheet to understate the related expense and thus overstates owner's equity. An overly positive view of the business is the result.

All liabilities are classified as current—those due within one year or the company's operating cycle if longer than a year, or long-term—those liabilities not classified as current. We discuss long-term liabilities in Chapter 16. We now turn to accounting for current liabilities, including those arising from payroll expenses.

OBJECTIVE 1
Classify liabilities as current or long-term

Current Liabilities of Known Amount

Current liabilities fall into one of two categories: those of a known amount and those whose amount must be estimated. We look first at current liabilities of known amount.

Trade Accounts Payable

Amounts owed to suppliers for products or services that are purchased on open account are accounts payable. We have seen many accounts payable examples in previous chapters. For example, a business may purchase inventories and office supplies on an account payable.

Short-Term Notes Payable

Short-term notes payable, a common form of financing, are notes payable that are due within one year. Companies often issue short-term notes payable to borrow cash or to purchase inventory or plant assets. In addition to recording the note payable and its eventual payment, the business must also accrue interest expense and interest payable at the end of the period. The following entries are typical of this liability:

19X1				
Sep. 30	Purchases...................................	8,000	
	Note Payable, Short-Term		8,000
	Purchase of inventory by issuing a one-year 10 percent note payable.		

OBJECTIVE 2
Account for current liabilities

Dec. 31	Interest Expense ($8,000 × .10 × 3/12)..............	200	
	Interest Payable............................		200
	Adjusting entry to accrue interest expense at year end.		

The balance sheet at December 31, 19X1, will report the Note Payable of $8,000 and the related Interest Payable of $200 as current liabilities. The 19X1 income statement will report interest expense of $200.

The following entry records the note's payment:

19X2			
Sep. 30	Note Payable, Short-Term........................	8,000	
	Interest Payable.................................	200	
	Interest Expense ($8,000 × .10 × 9/12)..............	600	
	Cash [$8,000 + ($8,000 × .10)]................		8,800
	Payment of a note payable and interest at maturity.		

The cash payment entry must split the total interest on the note between the portion accrued at the end of the previous period ($200) and the current period's expense ($600).

Short-Term Notes Payable Issued at a Discount

In another common borrowing arrangement, a company may **discount a note payable** at the bank. Discounting means that the bank subtracts the interest amount from the note's face value. The borrower receives the net amount. In effect, the borrower prepays the interest, which is computed on the principal of the note.

Suppose Procter & Gamble discounts a $100,000, 60-day note payable to their bank at 12 percent. The company will receive $98,000 — that is, the $100,000 face value less interest of $2,000 ($100,000 × .12 × 60/360). Assume this transaction occurs on November 25, 19X1. Procter & Gamble's entries to record discounting the note would be

19X1			
Nov. 25	Cash ($100,000 − $2,000)	98,000	
	Discount on Note Payable ($100,000 × .12 × 60/360)................................	2,000	
	Note Payable, Short-Term		100,000
	Discounted a $100,000, 60-day, 12-percent note payable to borrow cash.		

Discount on Note Payable is a contra account to the liability Note Payable, Short-Term. A balance sheet prepared immediately after this transaction would report the note payable at its net amount of $98,000, as follows:

Current liabilities:
Note payable, short-term. $100,000
Less: Discount on note payable . . . . (2,000)
Note payable, short-term, net . . . . $ 98,000

The accrued interest at year end must still be recorded, as it would for any note payable. The adjusting entry at December 31 records interest for 36 days as follows:

19X1

Dec. 31 Interest Expense ($100,000 × .12 × 36/360). 1,200
        Discount on Note Payable 1,200
        Adjusting entry to accrue interest expense at year end.

This entry credits the Discount account instead of Interest Payable. Why? Because the Discount balance is like prepaid interest, and the accrual of interest uses up part of the prepayment. Furthermore, crediting the Discount reduces this contra account's balance and increases the net amount of the Note Payable. After the adjusting entry, only $800 of the Discount remains, and the carrying value of the Note Payable increases to $99,200, as follows:

Current liabilities:
Note payable, short-term $100,000
Less: Discount on note payable ($2,000 − $1,200) . . . . (800)
Note payable, short-term, net . . . . $ 99,200

Finally, the business records the note's payment:

19X2

Jan. 24 Interest Expense ($100,000 × .12 × 24/360) 800
        Discount on Note Payable 800
        To record interest expense.

        Note Payable, Short-Term 100,000
        Cash 100,000
        To pay note payable at maturity.

After these entries, the balances in the note payable account and the discount account are zero. Each period's income statement reports the appropriate amount of interest expense.

Sales Tax Payable

Most states levy a sales tax on retail sales. Retailers charge their customers the sales tax in addition to the price of the item sold. Because the retailers owe the state the sales tax collected, the account Sales Tax Payable is a current liability. For example, Pizza Time Theatre, Inc., (home of Chuck E. Cheese) reported sales tax payable of $737,712 as a current liability. States do not levy sales tax on the sales of manufacturers like Procter & Gamble and General Motors. Such companies sell their products to wholesalers and retailers rather than to final consumers. Therefore, they have no sales tax liability.

Suppose one Saturday's sales at a Pizza Time Theatre totaled $2,000. The business would have collected an additional 5 percent in sales tax, which would equal $100 ($2,000 × .05). The business would record that day's sales as follows:

Cash ($2,000 × 1.05)	2,100	
Sales Revenue		2,000
Sales Tax Payable ($2,000 × .05)		100

To record cash sales of $2,000 subject to 5 percent sales tax.

Companies forward the collected sales tax to the taxing authority at regular intervals, at which time they debit Sales Tax Payable and credit Cash. Observe that Sales Tax Payable does *not* correspond to any sales tax expense that the business is incurring. Nor does this liability arise from the purchase of any asset. Rather, it is the cash that the business is collecting for the government.

Many companies consider it inefficient to credit Sales Tax Payable when recording sales. They record the sale in an amount that includes the tax. Then prior to paying tax to the state, they make a single entry for the entire period's transactions to bring Sales Revenue and Sales Tax Payable to their correct balances.

Suppose a company made July sales of $100,000, subject to a tax of 6 percent. Its summary entry to record the month's sales could be

July 31	Cash ($100,000 × 1.06)	106,000	
	Sales Revenue		106,000
	To record sales for the month.		

The entry to adjust Sales Revenue and Sales Tax Payable to their correct balances is

July 31	Sales Revenue [$106,000 − ($106,000 ÷ 1.06)]	6,000	
	Sales Tax Payable		6,000
	To record sales tax.		

Companies that follow this procedure need to make an adjusting entry at the end of the period in order to report the correct amounts of revenue and sales tax liability on their financial statements.

Current Portion of Long-Term Debt

Some long-term notes payable and long-term bonds payable must be paid in installments. The **current portion of long-term debt,** or *current maturity,* is the amount of the principal that is payable within one year. This amount does not include the interest due. Of course, any liability for accrued interest payable must also be reported, but a separate account, Interest Payable, is used for that purpose.

H. J. Heinz Company, probably best known for its ketchup, owed almost $200 million on long-term debt at April 30, the end of its fiscal year. Nearly $14 million was a current liability because it was due within one year. The remaining $186 million was a long-term liability. Suppose the interest rate on the debt was 6 percent and that interest was last paid the preceding November 30. Heinz Company's April 30 balance sheet would report:

Current Liabilities (in part)	Millions
Portion of long-term debt due within one year	$ 14
Interest payable ($200 × .06 × 5/12)	5

Long-Term Debt and Other Liabilities (in part)	
Long-term debt	$186

Accrued Expenses

As shown in the Heinz Company presentation, *accrued expenses,* such as interest expense, create current liabilities because the interest is due within the year. Therefore, the interest payable (accrued interest) is reported as a current liability. Other important liabilities for accrued expenses are payroll and the related payroll taxes, which we discuss in the second part of this chapter.

Unearned Revenues

Unearned revenues are also called *deferred revenues, revenues collected in advance,* and *customer prepayments.* Each account title indicates that the business has received cash from its customers before earning the revenue. The company has an obligation to provide goods or services to the customer.

The Dun & Bradstreet (D&B) Corporation provides credit evaluation services on a subscription basis. When finance companies pay in advance to have D&B investigate the credit histories of potential customers, D&B incurs a liability to provide future service. The liability account is called Unearned Subscription Revenue (which could also be titled Unearned Subscription Income).

Assume that Dun & Bradstreet charges $150 for a finance company's three-year subscription. Dun & Bradstreet's entries would be

```
19X1
Jan. 1  Cash . . . . . . . . . . . . . . . . . . . . . . . . . . . . . . . . . . .   150
             Unearned Subscription Revenue. . . . . . . . . . . . . . . . .        150
        To record receipt of cash at start of the three-year
        subscription agreement.


19X1, 19X2, 19X3
Dec. 31  Unearned Subscription Revenue. . . . . . . . . . . . . . . . . . . . .    50
             Subscription Revenue ($150/3) . . . . . . . . . . . . . . . . .        50
         To record subscription revenue earned at the
         end of each of three years.
```

Dun & Bradstreet's financial statements would report this sequence:

	December 31		
Balance Sheet	**Year 1**	**Year 2**	**Year 3**
Current liabilities			
Unearned subscription revenue	$100	$50	$-0-
Income Statement	**Year 1**	**Year 2**	**Year 3**
Revenues			
Subscription revenue	$50	$50	$50

Customer Deposits Payable

Some companies require cash deposits from customers as security on borrowed assets. These amounts are called Customer Deposits Payable because the company must refund the cash to the customer under certain conditions.

For example, telephone companies demand a cash deposit from a customer before installing a telephone. Utility companies and businesses that lend tools and appliances commonly demand a deposit as protection against damage and theft. When the customer ends service or returns the borrowed asset, the company refunds the cash deposit—if the customer has paid all the bills and has not damaged the company's property. Because the company generally must return the deposit, that obligation is a liability. The uncertainty of when the deposits will be refunded and their relatively small amounts cause many companies to classify Customer Deposits Payable as current liabilities. This is consistent with the concept of conservatism.

Certain manufacturers demand security deposits from the merchandisers who sell their products. Stanley Home Products, Inc., for example, demands a deposit from its dealers. The security deposits, called Dealers' Security Deposits, recently came to $4 million on Stanley's balance sheet, a small amount compared to its total current liabilities of over $62 million.

Current Liabilities That Must Be Estimated

A business may know that a liability exists but not know the exact amount. The liability may not simply be ignored. The unknown amount of a liability must be estimated for reporting on the balance sheet.

Estimated current liabilities vary among companies. As an example, let's look at Estimated Warranty Payable, a liability account common among merchandisers.

Estimated Warranty Payable

Many merchandising companies guarantee their products against defects under *warranty* agreements. The warranty period may extend for any length of time. Ninety-day warranties and one-year warranties are common.

Whatever the warranty's lifetime, the matching principle demands that the company record the *warranty expense* in the same period that the business recognizes sales revenue. After all, offering the warranty—and incurring any possible expense through the warranty agreement—is a part of generating revenue through sales. At the time of the sale, however, the company does not know which products are defective. The exact amount of warranty expense cannot be known with certainty, so the business must estimate its warranty expense and open the related liability account—Estimated Warranty Payable (also called Accrued Warranty Costs and Product Warranty Liability). Even though the warranty liability is a contingency, it is accounted for as an actual liability because it is probable that warranty expense has occurred and its amount can be estimated.

Companies may make a reliable estimate of their warranty expense based on their experience. Assume a company made sales of $200,000, subject to product warranties. Company management, noting that in past years between 2 percent and 4 percent of products proved defective, estimates that 3 percent of the products will require repair or replacement during the one-year warranty period.

The company records warranty expense of $6,000 ($200,000 × .03) for the period:

Warranty Expense..	6,000	
Estimated Warranty Payable		6,000

To accrue warranty expense.

Assume that defective merchandise totals $5,800. The company may either repair or replace it. Corresponding entries follow.

Estimated Warranty Payable	5,800	
Cash...		5,800

To repair defective products sold under warranty.

Estimated Warranty Payable	5,800	
Inventory.......................................		5,800

To replace defective products sold under warranty.

Note that the expense is $6,000 on the income statement no matter what the cash payment or the cost of the replacement inventory. In future periods, the company may come to debit the liability Estimated Warranty Payable for the remaining $200. However, *when* the company repairs or replaces defective merchandise has no bearing on when the company records warranty expense. The business records warranty expense in the same period as the sale.

Contingent Liabilities

A *contingent liability* is not an actual liability. Instead, it is a potential liability that depends on a *future* event arising out of a past transaction. For example, a town government may sue the company that installed new street lights, claiming that the electrical wiring is faulty. The past transaction is the street-light installation. The future event is the court case that will decide the suit. The lighting company thus faces a contingent liability, which may or may not become an actual obligation.

Sometimes the contingent liability has a definite amount. From Chapter 8 recall that the payee of a discounted note has a contingent liability. If the maker of the note pays at maturity, the contingent liability ceases to exist. However, if the maker defaults, the payee, who sold the note, must pay its maturity value to the purchaser. In this case, the payee knows the note's maturity value, which is the amount of the contingent liability.

Another contingent liability of known amount arises from guaranteeing that another company will pay a note payable that the other company owes a third party. This practice, called cosigning a note, obligates the guarantor to pay the note and interest if, and only if, the primary debtor fails to pay. Thus the guarantor has a contingent liability until the note becomes due. If the primary debtor pays off, the contingent liability ceases to exist. If the primary debtor fails to pay, the guarantor's liability becomes actual.

The amount of a contingent liability may be hard to determine. For example, companies face lawsuits, which may cause possible obligations of amounts to be determined by the courts.

Contingent liabilities may be reported in two ways. In what is called a **short**

presentation, the contingent liability appears in the body of the balance sheet, after total liabilities, but with no amount given. Generally an explanatory note accompanies a short presentation. Sears, Roebuck and Company reported contingent liabilities this way:

	Millions
Total liabilities	$27,830.7
Contingent liabilities (note 10)	—

Note 10: Various legal actions and governmental proceedings are pending against Sears, Roebuck and Co. and its subsidiaries. . . . The consequences of these matters are not presently determinable but, in the opinion of management, the ultimate liability resulting, if any, will not have a material effect on the company.

OBJECTIVE 3
Account for contingent liabilities

Contingent liabilities do not have to be mentioned in the body of the balance sheet. Many companies use a second method of reporting, presenting the footnote only. International Business Machines Corporation (IBM) mentions its contingent liabilities in a half-page supplementary note labeled *litigation.*

The line between a contingent liability and a real liability may be hard to draw. As a practical guide, the FASB says to record an actual liability if (1) it is probable that the business has suffered a loss and (2) its amount can be reasonably estimated. If both of these conditions are met, the FASB reasons that the obligation has passed from contingent to real, even if its amount must be estimated. Suppose that at the balance sheet date, a hospital expects to lose a court case for uninsured malpractice but the amount of damages is uncertain. The hospital estimates that the liability will fall between $1.0 and $2.5 million. In this case, the hospital must record a loss or expense and a liability for $1.0 million. The income statement will report the loss and the balance sheet the liability. Also, the hospital must disclose in a note the possibility of an additional $1.5 million loss.

Summary Problem for Your Review

This problem consists of three independent parts.

1. A Wendy's hamburger restaurant made cash sales of $4,000 subject to a 5 percent sales tax. Record the sales and the related sales tax. Also record Wendy's payment of the tax to the state government.

2. At April 30, 19X2, H. J. Heinz Company reported its 6 percent long-term debt:

Current Liabilities (in part)	Millions
Portion of long-term debt due within one year. . . .	$ 14
Interest payable ($200 × .06 × 5/12)	5
Long-Term Debt and Other Liabilities (in part)	
Long-term debt	$186

The company pays interest on its long-term debt on November 30 each year.

Show how Heinz Company would report its liabilities on the year-end balance sheet at April 30, 19X3. Assume the current maturity of its long-term debt is $16 million, and the long-term portion is $170 million.

3. What distinguishes a contingent liability from an actual liability?

SOLUTION TO REVIEW PROBLEM

1.

Cash ($4,000 × 1.05)	4,200	
Sales Revenue.......................................		4,000
Sales Tax Payable ($4,000 × .05).....................		200
To record cash sales and related sales tax.		
Sales Tax Payable.......................................	200	
Cash		200
To pay sales tax to the state government.		

2.   H. J. Heinz Company balance sheet at April 30, 19X3:

Current Liabilities (in part)	Millions
Portion of long-term debt due within one year ...	$ 16.00
Interest payable ($186 × .06 × 5/12)...........	4.65
Long-Term Debt and Other Liabilities (in part)	
Long-term debt............................	$170.00

3. A contingent liability is a *potential* liability, which may or may not become an actual liability.

Accounting for Payroll _____

Payroll, also called *employee compensation,* is a major expense of many businesses. For service organizations, such as CPA firms, real estate brokers, and travel agents, payroll is *the* major expense of conducting business. Service organizations sell their employees' service, so employee compensation is their primary cost of doing business, just as cost of goods sold is the largest expense in merchandising.

Employee compensation takes different forms. Some employees collect a **salary,** which is income stated at a yearly, monthly, or weekly rate. Other employees work for **wages,** which is employee pay stated at an hourly figure. Sales employees often receive a **commission,** which is a percentage of the sales the employee has made. Some companies reward excellent performance with a **bonus,** an amount over and above regular compensation.

Businesses often pay employees at a base rate for a set number of hours—called straight time. For working any additional hours—called overtime—the employee receives a higher rate.

Assume that Lucy Childres is an accountant for an electronics company. Lucy earns $600 per week straight time. The company work week runs 40 hours, so Lucy's hourly straight-time pay is $15 ($600/40). Her company pays her **time and a half** for overtime. That rate is 150 percent (1.5 times) the straight-time rate. Thus Lucy earns $22.50 for each hour of overtime she works ($15.00 × 1.5 = $22.50). For working 42 hours during a week, she earns $645, computed as follows:

Straight-time pay for 40 hours	$600
Overtime pay for 2 overtime hours:	
2 × $22.50	45
Total pay	$645

Gross Pay and Net Pay

Many years ago, employees brought home all that they had earned. For example, Lucy Childres would have taken home the full $645 total that she made. Payroll accounting was straightforward. Those days are long past.

The federal government, most state governments, and even some city governments demand that employers act as collection agents for employee taxes, which are deducted from employee checks. Insurance companies, labor unions, and other organizations may also receive pieces of employees' pay. Amounts withheld from an employee's check are called deductions.

Gross pay is the total amount of salary, wages, commissions, or any other employee compensation before taxes and other deductions are taken out. **Net pay** —the gross pay minus all deductions—is the amount that the employee actually takes home.

Many companies also pay employee **fringe benefits,** which are a form of employee compensation like health and life insurance and retirement pay, which the employee does not receive immediately in cash. Payroll accounting has become quite complex. Let's turn now to a discussion of payroll deductions.

Payroll Deductions

Payroll deductions that are *withheld* from employees' pay fall into two categories: (1) *required deductions,* which include employee income tax and social security tax; and (2) *optional deductions,* which include union dues, insurance premiums, charitable contributions, and other amounts that are withheld at the employee's request. After they are withheld, payroll deductions become the liability of the employer who assumes responsibility for paying the outside party. For example, the employer pays the government the employee income tax withheld and pays the union the employee union dues withheld.

Required Payroll Deductions

Employee Income Tax. The law requires most employers to withhold income tax from their employees' salaries and wages. The amount of income tax deducted from gross pay is called **withheld income tax.** For many employees, this deduc-

EXHIBIT 11-1 *W-4 Form*

```
- - - - - - - - - - - - Cut here and give the certificate to your employer. Keep the top portion for your records. - - - - - - - - - - - -

Form  W-4        Employee's Withholding Allowance Certificate              OMB No. 1545-0010
Department of the Treasury    ▶ For Privacy Act and Paperwork Reduction Act Notice, see reverse.    1988
Internal Revenue Service
1 Type or print your first name and middle initial    Last name              2 Your social security number
  R.C.                                                  Dean                    344-86-4529
Home address (number and street or rural route)                    □ Single  [X] Married
  4376 Palm Drive                                    3 Marital  □ Married, but withhold at higher Single rate.
City or town, state, and ZIP code                      Status   Note: If married, but legally separated, or spouse is a
  Fort Lauderdale, FL 33317                                     nonresident alien, check the Single box.

4 Total number of allowances you are claiming (from line G above or from the Worksheets on back if they apply) . . . 4 | 4
5 Additional amount, if any, you want deducted from each pay  . . . . . . . . . . . . . . . . . . 5 | $
6 I claim exemption from withholding because (check boxes below that apply):
  a  □ Last year I did not owe any Federal income tax and had a right to a full refund of ALL income tax withheld, AND
  b  □ This year I do not expect to owe any Federal income tax and expect to have a right to a full refund of
        ALL income tax withheld.
  c  If both a and b apply and you satisfy the additional conditions outlined above under "Exemption From     Year
     Withholding," enter the year effective and "EXEMPT" here. Do not complete lines 4 and 5 above . . . ▶ 19

7 Are you a full-time student? ( Note: Full-time students are not automatically exempt.)                     □ Yes [X] No
Under penalties of perjury, I certify that I am entitled to the number of withholding allowances claimed on this certificate or, if claiming exemption from withholding, that I am
entitled to claim the exempt status.
Employee's signature ▶  R.C. Dean                                  Date ▶ 7-22          , 1988
8 Employer's name and address (Employer: Complete 8, 9, and 10 only if sending to IRS)  9 Office  10 Employer identification number
  Blumenthal's                                                                             code
  Crescent Square Shopping Center                                                           14        83-19475
  Fort Lauderdale, FL 33310
```

tion is the largest. The amount withheld depends on the employee's gross pay and on the number of withholding allowances the employee claims.

Each employee may claim himself or herself, his or her spouse, and each dependent as a withholding allowance. An unmarried taxpayer has one allowance, a married couple two allowances, a married couple with one child three allowances, and so on. Each allowance lowers the amount of tax withheld from the employee's paycheck. The employee files a Form W-4 with the employer to indicate the number of allowances claimed for withholding purposes. Exhibit 11-1 shows a W-4 for R. C. Dean, who claims four.

The employer sends its employees' withheld income tax to the government. The amount of the income tax withheld determines how often the employer submits tax payments. The employer must remit the taxes to the government at least quarterly. Every business must account for payroll taxes on a calendar-year basis regardless of its fiscal year.

The employer accumulates taxes in the Employee Income Tax Payable account. The word *payable* indicates that the account is the employer's liability to the government, even though the employees are the people taxed.

Employee Social Security (FICA) Tax. The *Federal Insurance Contributions Act (FICA)*, also known as the *Social Security Act*, created the Social Security Tax. The Social Security program provides retirement, disability, and medical benefits. The law requires employers to withhold Social Security (FICA) tax from employees' pay.

The amount of tax withheld from employees' pay varies from year to year as Congress adjusts tax rates and the level of employee pay subject to the tax. In recent years, both of these factors have risen dramatically, as shown in Exhibit 11-2.

Because the FICA tax rate has hovered near 7 percent for the first $40,000 that the employee earns in a year, we use these figures in our examples and in the assignment materials at the end of the chapter. For each employee who earns $40,000 or more, the employer withholds $2,800 ($40,000 × .07) from the employee's pay and sends that amount to the federal government. The employer records this employee tax in the account, FICA Tax Payable.

Assume that Rex Jennings, an employee, earned $38,500 prior to December.

EXHIBIT 11-2   *Social Security Taxes*

Year	Employee Earnings Subject to the Tax	Social Security (FICA) Tax Rate	Maximum Amount of Social Security (FICA) Tax Withheld from Employee Pay during the Year
1980	$25,900	.0613	$1,588
1985	39,600	.0705	2,792
1987	43,800	.0715	3,132
1989	48,000	.0751	3,605
1990 and beyond	*	.0765	?

* Adjusted for the increase in the cost of living.

Jennings's salary for December is $3,500. How much FICA tax will be withheld from his December paycheck? The computation follows.

Employee earnings subject to the tax in one year	$40,000
Employee earnings prior to the current pay period	38,500
Current pay subject to FICA tax	$ 1,500
FICA tax rate	× .07
FICA tax to be withheld from current pay	$105.00

Optional Payroll Deductions

As a convenience to its employees, many companies make payroll deductions and disburse cash according to employee instructions. Union dues, insurance payments, payroll savings plans, and gifts to charities are examples. The account Employees' Union Dues Payable holds employee deductions for union membership.

Employer Payroll Taxes

Employers must bear the expense of at least three payroll taxes: (1) Social Security (FICA) tax, (2) state unemployment compensation tax, and (3) federal unemployment compensation tax.

Employer FICA Tax.   In addition to the responsibility of handling the employee contribution to Social Security, the employer also must pay into the program. The employer's Social Security tax is the same as the amount withheld from employee pay. Thus the Social Security system is funded by equal contributions from employees and employers. Using our 7 percent and $40,000 annual pay figures, the maximum annual employer tax on each employee is $2,800 ($40,000 × .07). The liability account the employer uses for this payroll tax is the same FICA Tax Payable account used for the amount withheld from employee pay. The tax rate and the amount of earnings subject to the tax both change as Congress passes new legislation.

State and Federal Unemployment Compensation Taxes. These two payroll taxes are products of the Federal Unemployment Tax Act (FUTA). In recent years, employers have paid a combined tax of 6.2 percent on the first $7,000 of each employee's annual earnings. The proportion paid to the state is 5.4 percent, and .8 percent is paid to the federal government. The government then uses the money to pay unemployment benefits to people who are out of work. The employer uses the accounts Federal Unemployment Tax Payable and State Unemployment Tax Payable.

Payroll Entries

Exhibit 11-3 summarizes an employer's entries to record a monthly payroll of $10,000 (all amounts are assumed for illustration only).

Entry A in Exhibit 11-3 records the employer's *salary expense.* The *gross salary* of all employees, $10,000, is their monthly pay before any deductions. The federal government imposes the two taxes. Most states and some cities also levy income taxes, which are accounted for in like manner. The union dues are optional. Employees' take-home (net) pay is $7,960. The important point about this payroll transaction is that the employees pay their own income and FICA taxes and union dues. The employer serves merely as a collecting agent and sends these amounts to the government and the union.

Entry B records the employer's *payroll taxes.* In addition to the employees' FICA tax ($700 in entry A), the employer must also pay the $700 FICA tax shown in entry B. The other two employer payroll taxes are state and federal unemployment taxes. *Employees* make no payments for unemployment taxes.

Entry C records employee *fringe benefits* paid by the employer. The company in

EXHIBIT 11-3 *Payroll Accounting by the Employer*

OBJECTIVE 4
Make basic payroll entries

A.	Salary Expense (or Wage Expense or Commission Expense)	10,000	
	Employee Income Tax Payable		1,200
	FICA Tax Payable ($10,000 × .07)		700
	Employee Union Dues Payable................		140
	Salary Payable to Employees (take-home pay) ...		7,960
	To record *salary expense.*		
B.	Payroll Tax Expense.............................	1,320	
	FICA Tax Payable ($10,000 × .07)		700
	State Unemployment Tax Payable ($10,000 × .054)...........................		540
	Federal Unemployment Tax Payable ($10,000 × .008)............................		80
	To record employer's *payroll taxes.*		
C.	Health Insurance Expense for Employees	800	
	Life Insurance Expense for Employees...............	200	
	Pension Expense	500	
	Employee Benefits Payable		1,500
	To record employee *fringe benefits* payable by employer.		

the exhibit pays health and life insurance for its employees, a common practice. Also, the employer funds pensions (that is, pays cash into a pension plan) for the benefit of employees when they retire. In the exhibit, the employer's pension expense for the month is $500, and the total employer expense for fringe benefits is $1,500. The total payroll expense of the employer in Exhibit 11-3 is $12,820 (gross salary of $10,000 + employer payroll taxes of $1,320 + fringe benefits of $1,500).

A company's payments to people who are not employees—outsiders called independent contractors—are *not* company payroll expenses. Consider two CPAs, Fermi and Scott. Fermi is a corporation's chief financial officer. Scott is the corporation's outside auditor. Fermi is an employee of the corporation and his compensation is a debit to Salary Expense. Scott, on the other hand, performs auditing service for many clients, and the corporation debits Auditing Expense when it pays her. Any payment for services performed by a person outside the company is a debit to an expense account other than payroll.

The Payroll System

Good business means paying employees all that they have earned—and paying them on time. Also, companies face the legal responsibility of handling employees' and their own payroll taxes, as we have seen. These demands require companies to process a great deal of payroll data. Efficient accounting is important. To make payroll accounting accurate and effective, accountants have developed the payroll system.

The components of the payroll system are a *payroll register*, a special *payroll bank account*, *payroll checks*, and an *earnings record* for each employee.

Payroll Register

OBJECTIVE 5

Use a payroll-accounting system

Each pay period, the company organizes the payroll data in a special journal called the *payroll register*, or *payroll journal*. This register lists each employee and the figures the business needs to record payroll amounts. The payroll register, which resembles the cash disbursement register, or check register, also serves as a check register by providing a column for recording each payroll check number.

The payroll register in Exhibit 11-4 includes sections for recording Gross Pay, Deductions, Net Pay, and Account Debited. *Gross Pay* has columns for straight-time pay, overtime pay, and total gross pay for each employee. Columns under the *Deductions* heading vary from company to company. Of course the employer must deduct federal income tax and FICA tax. (State tax is left out for convenience.) Additional column headings depend on which optional deductions the business handles. In the exhibit, the employer deducts employee payroll taxes, union dues, and gifts to United Way and then sends the amounts to the proper parties. The business may add deduction columns as needed. The *Net Pay* section lists each employee's net (take-home) pay and the number of the check issued to him or her. The last two columns indicate the *Account Debited* for the employee's gross pay. (The company has office workers and sales people.)

In the exhibit, W. L. Chen earned gross pay of $500. His net pay was $386.45, paid with check number 1621. Chen is an office worker, so his salary is debited to Office Salary Expense.

Note that the business deducted no FICA tax from E. A. Trimble. She has

EXHIBIT 11-4 *Payroll Register*

Week ended December 27, 19X3

Employee Name	Hours	Gross Pay			Deductions						Net Pay		Account Debited	
		a Straight-time	b Overtime	c Total	d Federal Income Tax	e FICA Tax	f Union Dues	g United Way Charities	h Total	(c – h) Amount	Check No.	Office Salary Expense	k Sales Salary Expense
Chen, W. L.	40	500.00		500.00	71.05	35.00	5.00	2.50	113.55	386.45	1621	500.00	
Dean, R. C.	46	400.00	90.00	490.00	59.94	34.30	5.00	2.00	96.24	393.76	1622		490.00
Ellis, M.	41	560.00	21.00	581.00	86.14	40.67			131.81	449.19	1623	581.00	
Trimble, E. A.	40	1,360.00		1,360.00	463.22		85.00	15.00	478.22	881.78	1641		1,360.00
Total		12,940.00	714.00	13,654.00	3,167.76	801.36		155.00	4,209.12	9,444.88		4,464.00	9,190.00

already earned more than $40,000. Any employee whose earnings exceed this annual maximum pays no additional FICA tax during that year.

The payroll register in Exhibit 11-4 gives the employer the information needed to record salary expense for the pay period. Using the total amounts for columns d through l, the employer records total salary expense as follows:

Dec. 27	Office Salary Expense	4,464.00	
	Sales Salary Expense	9,190.00	
	Employee Income Tax Payable		3,167.76
	FICA Tax Payable		801.36
	Employee Union Dues Payable		85.00
	Employee United Way Payable		155.00
	Salary Payable to Employees		9,444.88

Payroll Bank Account

After recording the payroll, the company books include a credit balance in Salary Payable to Employees for net pay of $9,444.88. (See Column i in Exhibit 11-4.) How the business pays this liability depends on its payroll system. Many companies disburse paychecks to employees from a special payroll bank account. The employer draws a check for net pay ($9,444.88 in our illustration) on its regular bank account and deposits this check in the special payroll bank account. Then the company writes paychecks to employees out of the payroll account. When the paychecks clear the bank, the payroll account has a zero balance, ready for the activity of the next pay period. Disbursing paychecks from a separate bank account isolates net pay for analysis and control, as discussed later in the chapter.

Other payroll disbursements—for withheld taxes, union dues, and so on—are neither as numerous nor as frequent as weekly or monthly paychecks. The employer pays taxes, union dues, and charities from its regular bank account.

Payroll Checks

Most companies pay employees by check. A *payroll check* is like any other check except that its perforated attachment lists the employee's gross pay, payroll deductions, and net pay. These amounts are taken from the payroll register. Exhibit 11-5 shows payroll check number 1622, issued to R. C. Dean for net pay of $393.76 earned during the week ended December 27, 19X3. To enhance your ability to use payroll data, trace all amounts on the check attachment to the payroll register in Exhibit 11-4.

Recording Cash Disbursements for Payroll _____

Most employers must make at least three entries to record payroll cash disbursements: net pay to employees, payroll taxes to the government and payroll deductions, and employee fringe benefits.

Net Pay to Employees.   When the employer issues payroll checks to employees, the company debits Salary Payable to Employees and credits Cash.

EXHIBIT 11-5   *Payroll Check*

| Blumenthal's Payroll Account Fort Lauderdale, FL | | | | | | | | | 1622 |

Blumenthal's
Payroll Account
Fort Lauderdale, FL

12-27 19 X3

Pay to the Order of   R. C. Dean $ 393.76

Three hundred ninety-three & 76/100 ---------------------------- Dollars

Republic Bank
Fort Lauderdale,
Florida 33310

Anna Figaro
Treasurer

⊙ ⑈:𝟣𝟣𝟣𝟫𝟢𝟢𝟢𝟥𝟣⑈: 𝟢𝟩𝟪𝟩⑈" 𝟧𝟢𝟢𝟢𝟢𝟦𝟧𝟦⑈"

Pay			Deductions					Net Pay	Check No.
Straight-time	Over-time	Gross	Income Tax	FICA	Union Dues	United Way	Total		
400.00	90.00	490.00	59.94	34.30		2.00	96.24	393.76	1622

Using the data in Exhibit 11-4, the company would make the following entry to record the cash payment (column i) for the December 27 weekly payroll:

Dec. 27   Salary Payable to Employees 9,444.88
          Cash 9,444.88

Payroll Taxes to the Government and Payroll Deductions.   The employer must send to the government two sets of payroll taxes: those withheld from employees' pay and those paid by the employer. Based on Exhibit 11-4, columns d through g, the business would record a series of cash payment entries summarized as follows (employer tax amounts are assumed):

Dec. 27   Employee Income Tax Payable 3,167.76
          FICA Tax Payable ($801.36 × 2) 1,602.72
          Employee Union Dues Payable 85.00
          Employee United Way Payable 155.00
          State Unemployment Tax Payable 104.62
          Federal Unemployment Tax Payable 15.50
          Cash 5,130.60

Fringe Benefits.   The employer might pay for employees' insurance coverage and pension plan. Assuming the total cash payment for these benefits is $1,927.14, this entry for payments to third parties would be

Dec. 27   Employee Benefits Payable 1,927.14
          Cash 1,927.14

Earnings Record

The employer must file payroll tax returns with the federal and state governments and must provide the employee with a wage and tax statement, Form W-2, at the end of the year. Therefore, employers maintain an earnings record for each

EXHIBIT 11-6 *Employee Earnings Record for 19X3*

Employee Name and Address:

Dean, R. C.
4376 Palm Drive
Fort Lauderdale, FL 33317

Social Security No.: 344-86-4529
Marital Status: Married
Withholding Exemptions: 4
Pay Rate: $400 per week
Job Title: Salesperson

Week Ended	Gross Pay				Deductions					Net Pay	
	Hours	Straight-time	Overtime	Total	To Date	Federal Income Tax	FICA Tax	Union Dues	United Way Charities	Total	Amount	Check No.
Nov. 29	40	400.00		400.00	21,340.00	42.19	28.00		2.00	72.19	327.81	1525
Dec. 6	40	400.00		400.00	21,740.00	42.19	28.00		2.00	72.19	327.81	1548
Dec. 13	44	400.00	60.00	460.00	22,200.00	54.76	32.20		2.00	88.96	371.04	1574
Dec. 20	48	400.00	120.00	520.00	22,720.00	66.75	36.40		2.00	105.15	414.85	1598
Dec. 27	46	400.00	90.00	490.00	23,210.00	59.94	34.30		2.00	96.24	393.76	1622
Total		20,800.00	2,410.00	23,210.00		2,346.72	1,555.07		104.00	4,005.79	19,204.21	

employee. Exhibit 11-6 is a five-week excerpt from the earnings record of employee R. C. Dean.

The employee earnings record is not a journal or a ledger, and it is not required by law. It is an accounting tool — like the worksheet — that the employer uses to prepare payroll tax reports. Year-to-date earnings also indicate when an employee has earned $40,000, the point at which the employer can stop deducting FICA tax.

Exhibit 11-7 is the Wage and Tax Statement, Form W-2, for employee R. C. Dean. The employer prepares this statement and gives copies to the employee and to the Internal Revenue Service (IRS). Dean uses the W-2 to prepare his personal income tax return. The IRS uses the W-2 to ensure that Dean is paying income tax on all his income from that job. The IRS matches Dean's income as reported on his tax return with his earnings as reported on the W-2.

Internal Control over Payrolls _____

The internal controls over cash disbursements discussed in Chapter 7 apply to payroll. In addition, companies adopt special controls in payroll accounting. The large number of transactions and the many different parties involved increase the risk of a control failure. Accounting systems feature two types of special controls over payroll: controls for efficiency and controls for safeguarding cash.

Controls for Efficiency

For companies with many employees, reconciling the bank account can be time consuming because of the large number of outstanding payroll checks. For example, a March 30 payroll check would probably not have time to clear the bank before a bank statement on March 31. This check and others in a March 30 payroll would be outstanding. Identifying a large number of outstanding checks for the bank reconciliation increases accounting expense. To limit the number of outstanding checks, many companies use two payroll bank accounts. They make payroll disbursements from one payroll account one month and from the other

EXHIBIT 11-7 *Employee Wage and Tax Statement, Form W-2*

1 Control number 22222	For Paperwork Reduction Act Notice, see back of Copy D. OMB No. 1545-0008	For Official Use Only ▶		
2 Employer's name, address, and ZIP code	3 Employer's identification number 83-19475	4 Employer's state I.D. number		
Blumenthal's Crescent Square Shopping Ctr. Fort Lauderdale, FL 33310	5 Statutory employee ☒ Deceased ☐ Pension plan ☐ Legal rep. ☐ 942 emp. ☐ Subtotal ☐ Deferred compensation ☐ Void ☐			
	6 Allocated tips	7 Advance EIC payment		
8 Employee's social security number 344-86-4529	9 Federal income tax withheld 2,346.72	10 Wages, tips, other compensation 23,210.00	11 Social security tax withheld 1,624.70	
12 Employee's name (first, middle, last) R.C. Dean	13 Social security wages 23,210.00	14 Social security tips		
4376 Palm Drive Fort Lauderdale, FL 33317	16 (See Instr. for Forms W-2/W-2P)	16a Fringe benefits incl. in Box 10		
	17 State income tax	18 State wages, tips, etc.	19 Name of state	
15 Employee's address and ZIP code	20 Local income tax	21 Local wages, tips, etc.	22 Name of locality	
Form **W-2** Wage and Tax Statement **1988**	Copy A For Social Security Administration	Dept. of the Treasury—IRS		

payroll account the next month. By reconciling each account every other month, a March 30 paycheck has until April 30 to clear the bank before the account is reconciled. This essentially eliminates outstanding checks, cuts down the time it takes to prepare the bank reconciliation, and decreases accounting expense. Also, many companies' checks become void if not cashed within a certain period of time. This too limits the number of outstanding checks.

Other payroll controls for efficiency include following established policies for hiring and firing employees and complying with government regulations. Hiring and firing policies provide guidelines for keeping a qualified, diligent work force dedicated to achieving the business's goals. Complying with government regulations avoids paying fines and penalties.

Controls for Safeguarding of Cash

Owners and managers of small businesses can monitor their payroll disbursements by personal contact with their employees. Large corporations cannot do so. These businesses must establish controls to assure that payroll disbursements are made only to legitimate employees and for the correct amounts. A particular danger is that payroll checks may be written to a fictitious employee and cashed by a dishonest employee. To guard against this crime and other possible breakdowns in internal control, large businesses adopt strict internal control policies.

The duties of hiring and firing employees should be separated from the duties of distributing paychecks. Otherwise, a dishonest supervisor, for example, could add a fictitious employee to the payroll. When paychecks are issued, the supervisor could simply pocket the nonexistent person's paycheck for his or her own use.

Requiring an identification badge bearing an employee's photograph helps internal control. Issuing pay checks only to employees with badges ensures that only actual employees receive pay.

On occasion management should instruct an employee from the home office, perhaps an internal auditor, to distribute checks in the branch office personally rather than have the payroll department mail the checks. No one will claim a paycheck that has been issued to a fictitious employee. Any check left over after the distribution signals that payroll fraud has been attempted. Management would pursue an investigation.

A time-keeping system helps ensure that employees have actually worked the number of hours claimed. Having employees punch time cards at the start and end of the work day proves their attendance—as long as management makes sure that no employee punches in and out for others too. Some companies have their workers fill in weekly or monthly time sheets.

Again we see that the key to good internal control is separation of duties. The responsibilities of the personnel department, the payroll department, the accounting department, time-card management, and paycheck distribution should be kept separate.

Reporting Payroll Expense and Liabilities _____

At the end of its fiscal year, the company reports the amount of *payroll liability* owed to all parties—employees, state and federal governments, unions, and so forth. Payroll liability is *not* the payroll expense for the year. The liability at year end is the amount of the expense that is still unpaid. Payroll expense appears on the income statement, payroll liability on the balance sheet.

Exhibit 11-8 *Partial Burroughs Corporation Balance Sheet*

OBJECTIVE 6
Report current liabilities

Current Liabilities	Millions
Notes payable within one year	$ 397
Current maturities of long-term debt	31
Accounts payable	397
Accrued payrolls and commissions	**164**
Accrued taxes other than income taxes	69
Customers' deposits and prepayments	155
Dividends payable to shareholders	28
Estimated income taxes	111
Total current liabilities	$1,352

Burroughs Corporation reported accrued payrolls and commissions of approximately $164 million as a current liability on its year-end balance sheet (see Exhibit 11-8). However, Burroughs's payroll expense for the year far exceeded $164 million. (Exhibit 11-8 also presents the other current liabilities that we have discussed in this chapter.)

Exhibit 11-9 summarizes all the current liabilities that we have discussed in this chapter.

Computer Accounting Systems for Current Liabilities

Current liabilities arising from a high volume of similar transactions are well suited for computerized accounting. One of the most common transactions of a merchandiser is the credit purchase of inventory. It is efficient to integrate the

EXHIBIT 11-9 *Categories of Current Liabilities*

Amount of Liability Known When Recorded	Amount of Liability Must Be Estimated When Recorded
Trade accounts payable	Warranty payable
Short-term notes payable	Income tax payable
Sales tax payable	
Current portion of long-term debt	
Accrued expenses payable:	
Interest payable	
Payroll liabilities (salary payable, wages payable, and commissions payable)	
Payroll taxes payable (employee and employer)	
Unearned revenues (revenues collected in advance of being earned)	
Customer deposits payable	

accounts payable and perpetual inventory systems. When merchandise dips below a predetermined level, the system automatically prepares a purchase request. After the order is placed and the goods are received, inventory and accounts payable data are entered on magnetic tape. The computer reads the tape, then debits Inventory and credits Accounts Payable to account for the purchase. For payments, the computer debits Accounts Payable and credits Cash. The program may also update account balances and print journals, ledger accounts, and the financial statements.

The face amount of notes payable and their interest rates and payment dates can be stored for electronic data processing. Computer programs calculate interest, print the interest checks, journalize the transactions, and update account balances.

Payroll transactions are also ideally suited for computer processing. Employee pay rates and withholding data are stored on magnetic tape. Each payroll period, computer operators enter the number of hours worked by each employee. The machine performs the calculations, prints the payroll register and pay checks, and updates the employee earnings records. The program also computes payroll taxes and prepares quarterly reports to government agencies. Expense and liability accounts are automatically updated for the payroll transactions.

The estimated amounts of current liabilities for warranties and income taxes may require personal attention. However, once accountants estimate these liabilities, their amounts can be entered into accounts that are maintained in computerized form.

Summary Problem for Your Review

Beth Denius, Limited, a clothing store, employs one salesperson, Alan Kingsley. His straight-time pay is $360 per week. He earns time and a half for hours worked in excess of 40 per week. Denius withholds income tax (11.0 percent) and FICA tax (7.0 percent) from Kingsley's pay. She also pays the following employer payroll taxes: FICA (7.0 percent) and state and federal unemployment (5.4 percent and 0.8 percent, respectively). In addition, Denius contributes to a pension plan an amount equal to 10 percent of Kingsley's gross pay.

During the week ended December 26, 19X4, Kingsley worked 48 hours. Prior to this week Kingsley has earned $5,470.

Required

1. Compute Kingsley's gross pay and net pay for the week.
2. Record the following payroll entries that Denius would make:
   a. Expense for Kingsley's salary, including overtime pay
   b. Employer payroll taxes
   c. Expense for fringe benefits
   d. Payment of cash to Kingsley
   e. Payment of all payroll taxes
   f. Payment for fringe benefits
3. How much total payroll expense did Denius incur for the week? How much cash did the business spend on its payroll?

SOLUTION TO REVIEW PROBLEM

Requirement 1

Gross Pay: Straight-time pay for 40 hours................. $360.00

Overtime pay:

Rate per hour ($360/40 × 1.5)........ $13.50

Hours (48 − 40)................... X 8   108.00

Total gross pay $468.00

Net Pay: Gross pay..................................... $468.00

Less: Withheld income tax ($468 × .11) .... $ 51.48

Withheld FICA tax ($468 × .07)........... 32.76   84.24

Net pay $383.76

Requirement 2

a. Sales Salary Expense 468.00

Employee Income Tax Payable 51.48

FICA Tax Payable................................. 32.76

Salary Payable to Employee......................... 383.76

b. Payroll Tax Expense............................... 61.77

FICA Tax Payable ($468 × .07)...................... 32.76

State Unemployment Tax Payable ($468 × .054)........... 25.27

Federal Unemployment Tax Payable ($468 × .008)......... 3.74

c. Pension Expense ($468 × .10)........................... 46.80

Employee Benefits Payable 46.80

d. Salary Payable to Employee 383.76

Cash 383.76

e. Employee Income Tax Payable 51.48

FICA Tax Payable ($32.76 × 2)...................... 65.52

State Unemployment Tax Payable 25.27

Federal Unemployment Tax Payable 3.74

Cash 146.01

f. Employee Benefits Payable 46.80

Cash 46.80

Requirement 3

Denius incurred *total payroll expense* of $576.57 (gross salary of $468.00 + payroll taxes of $61.77 + fringe benefits of $46.80). See entries a–c.

Denius *paid cash* of $576.57 on payroll (Kingsley's net pay of $383.76 + payroll taxes of $146.01 + fringe benefits of $46.80). See entries d–f.

Summary

Current liabilities may be divided into those of *known amount* and those that must be *estimated.* Trade accounts payable, short-term notes payable, and the related liability for accrued expenses are among current liabilities of known amount. Current liabilities that must be estimated are warranties payable and corporations' income tax payable.

Contingent liabilities are not actual liabilities but potential liabilities that may arise in the future. Contingent liabilities, like current libilities, may be of known amount or an indefinite amount. A business that faces a lawsuit not yet decided in court has a contingent liability of indefinite amount.

Payroll accounting handles the expenses and liabilities arising from compensating employees. Employers must withhold income and FICA taxes from employees' pay and send these *employee payroll taxes* to the government. In addition, many employers allow their employees to pay for insurance and union dues and to make gifts to charities through payroll deductions. An employee's net pay is the gross pay less all payroll taxes and optional deductions.

An *employer's* payroll expenses include FICA and unemployment taxes, which are separate from the payroll taxes borne by the employees. Also, most employers provide their employees with fringe benefits, like insurance coverage and retirement pensions.

A *payroll system* consists of a payroll register, a payroll bank account, payroll checks, and an earnings record for each employee. Good *internal controls* over payroll disbursements help the business to conduct payroll accounting efficiently and to safeguard the company's cash. The cornerstone of internal controls is the separation of duties.

Current liabilities arising from a high volume of repetitive transactions are well suited for computer processing. Trade accounts payable, notes payable and the related interest, and payrolls are three examples.

Self-Study Questions

Test your understanding of the chapter by marking the best answer for each of the following questions.

1. A $10,000, 9 percent, one-year note payable was issued on July 31. The balance sheet at December 31 will report interest payable of *(p. 424)*
   a. $0 because the interest is not due yet
   b. $300
   c. $375
   d. $900

2. If the note payable in the preceding question had been discounted, the cash proceeds from issuance would have been *(p. 424)*
   a. $9,100
   b. $9,625
   c. $9,700
   d. $10,000

3. Which of the following liabilities creates *no* expense for the company? *(p. 426)*
   a. Interest
   b. Sales tax
   c. FICA tax
   d. Warranty

4. Suppose Unitex Tire Company estimates that warranty costs will equal 1 percent of tire sales. Assume that November sales totaled $900,000, and the company's outlay in tires and cash to satisfy warranty claims was $7,400. How much warranty expense should the November income statement report? *(p. 428, 429)*
   a. $1,600
   b. $7,400
   c. $9,000
   d. $16,400

5. XYZ Company is a defendant in a lawsuit that claims damages of $55,000. On the balance sheet date, it appears likely that the court will render a judgment against the company. How should XYZ report this event in its financial statements? *(p. 430)*
   a. Omit mention because no judgment has been rendered
   b. Disclose the contingent liability in a note
   c. Use a short presentation only
   d. Report the loss on the income statement and the liability on the balance sheet

6. Emilie Frontenac's weekly pay is $320, plus time and half for overtime. The tax rates applicable to her earnings are 8 percent for income tax and 7 percent for FICA. What is Emilie's take-home pay for a week in which she works 50 hours? *(pp. 432, 435)*
   a. $374.00
   b. $392.00
   c. $404.80
   d. $440.00

7. Which payroll tax applies (or taxes apply) only to the employer? *(pp. 434, 435)*
   a. Withheld income tax
   b. FICA tax
   c. Unemployment compensation tax
   d. Both b and c

8. The main reason for using a separate payroll bank account is to *(p. 438)*
   a. Safegurd cash by avoiding writing payroll checks to fictitious employees
   b. Safeguard cash by limiting paychecks to amounts based on time cards
   c. Increase efficiency by isolating payroll disbursements for analysis and control
   d. All of the above

9. The key to good internal controls in the payroll area is *(p. 442)*
   a. Using a payroll bank account
   b. Separating payroll duties
   c. Using a payroll register
   d. Using time cards

10. Which of the following items is reported as a current liability on the balance sheet? *(p. 443)*
    a. Short-term notes payable
    b. Estimated warranties
    c. Accrued payroll taxes
    d. All of the above

Answers to the self-study questions are at the end of the chapter.

Accounting Vocabulary

bonus *(p. 431)*, commission *(p. 431)*, current portion of long-term debt *(p. 426)*, discounting a note payable *(p. 424)*, FICA tax *(p. 433)*, fringe benefits *(p. 432)*, gross pay *(p. 432)*, net pay *(p. 432)*, payroll *(p. 431)*, salary *(p. 431)*, short presentation *(pp. 429, 430)*, short-term note payable *(p. 424)*, Social Security tax *(p. 433)*, time and a half *(p. 432)*, unemployment compensation tax *(p. 435)*, wages *(p. 431)*, withheld income tax *(p. 432)*.

ASSIGNMENT MATERIAL _____

Questions

1. Give a more descriptive account title for each of the following current liabilities: Accrued Interest, Accrued Salaries, Accrued Income Tax.

2. What distinguishes a current liability from a long-term liability? What distinguishes a contingent liability from an actual liability?

3. A company purchases a machine by signing a $21,000, 10 percent, one-year note payable on July 31. Interest is to be paid at maturity. What two current liabilities related to this purchase does the company report on its December 31 balance sheet? What is the amount of each liability?

4. A company borrowed cash by discounting a $15,000, 8 percent, six-month note payable to the bank, receiving cash of $14,400. (a) Show how the amount of cash was computed. Also, identify (b) the total amount of interest expense to be recognized on this note and (c) the amount of the borrower's cash payment at maturity.

5. Explain how sales tax that is paid by consumers is a liability of the store that sold the merchandise.

6. What is meant by the term *current portion of long-term debt,* and how is this item reported in the financial statements?

7. At the beginning of the school term, what type of account is the tuition that your college or university collects from students? What type of account is the tuition at the end of the school term?

8. Why is a customer deposit a liability? Give an example.

9. Patton Company warrants its products against defects for three years from date of sale. During the current year, the company made sales of $300,000. Store manage-

ment estimates warranty costs on those sales will total $18,000 over the three-year warranty period. Ultimately, the company paid $22,000 cash on warranties. What is the company's warranty expense for the year? What accounting principle governs this answer?

10. Identify two contingent liabilities of a definite amount and two contingent liabilities of an indefinite amount.

11. Describe two ways to report contingent liabilities.

12. Why is payroll expense relatively more important to a service business such as a CPA firm, than it is to a merchandising company?

13. Two persons are studying Allen Company's manufacturing process. One person is Allen's factory supervisor, and the other person is an outside consultant who is an expert in the industry. Which person's salary is the payroll expense of Allen Company? Identify the expense account that Allen would debit to record the pay of each person.

14. What are two elements of an employer's payroll expense in addition to salaries, wages, commissions, and overtime pay?

15. What determines the amount of income tax that is withheld from employee paychecks?

16. What are FICA taxes? Who pays them? What are the funds used for?

17. Identify two required deductions and four optional deductions from employee paychecks.

18. Identify three employer payroll taxes.

19. Who pays state and federal unemployment taxes? What are these funds used for?

20. Briefly describe a payroll accounting system's components and their functions.

21. How much Social Security tax has been withheld from the pay of an employee who has earned $42,000 during the current year? How much Social Security tax must the employer pay for this employee?

22. Briefly describe the two principal categories of internal controls over payroll.

23. Why do some companies use two special payroll bank accounts?

24. Identify three internal controls designed to safeguard payroll cash.

Exercises

Exercise 11-1 *Recording note payable transactions*

Record the following note payable transactions of McBee Company in the company's general journal. Explanations are not required.

19X2

May 1 Purchased equipment costing $4,500 by issuing a one-year, 10 percent note payable.

Dec. 31 Accrued interest on the note payable.

19X3

May 1 Paid the note payable at maturity.

Exercise 11-2 *Discounting a note payable*

On November 1, 19X4, Maxwell Company discounted a six-month, $8,000 note payable to the bank at 12 percent.

Required

1. Prepare general journal entries to record (a) issuance of the note, (b) accrual of interest at December 31, and (c) payment of the note at maturity in 19X5. Explanations are not required.

2. Show how Maxwell would report the note on the December 31, 19X4, balance sheet.

Exercise 11-3   *Recording sales tax two ways*

Make general journal entries to record the following transactions of Ransom Distributors, Inc., for a two-month period. Explanations are not required.

March 31   Recorded cash sales of $68,100 for the month, plus sales tax of 7 percent collected on behalf of the state of California. Record sales tax in a separate account.

April   6   Sent March sales tax to the state.

Journalize these transactions a second time. Record the sales tax initially in the Sales Revenue account.

Exercise 11-4   *Reporting current and long-term liabilities*

Suppose Taco Bell borrowed $400,000 on December 31, 19X0, by issuing 9 percent long-term debt that must be paid in annual installments of $100,000 plus interest each January 2. By inserting appropriate amounts in the following excerpts from the company's partial balance sheet, show how Taco Bell would report its long-term debt.

	December 31,			
	19X1	**19X2**	**19X3**	**19X4**
Current liabilities:				
Current portion of long-term debt	$100K	$100K	$100K	$100K
Interest payable	36K	27K	18K	9K
Long-term liabilities:				
Long-term debt	300K	200K	100K	—

Exercise 11-5   *Accounting for warranty expense and the related liability*

The accounting records of Shotwell, Inc., included the following balances at the end of the period:

Estimated Warranty Payable	Sales Revenue	Warranty Expense
Beg. bal 3,800	141,000	

In the past, Shotwell's warranty expense has been 8 percent of sales. During the current period, Shotwell paid $11,790 to satisfy the warranty claims of customers.

Required

1. Record Shotwell's warranty expense for the period and the company's cash payments during the period to satisfy warranty claims. Explanations are not required.
2. What ending balance of Estimated Warranty Payable will Shotwell report on its balance sheet?

Exercise 11-6   *Reporting a contingent liability*

Falcon Lamp Company is a defendant in lawsuits brought against the marketing and distribution of its products. Damages of $2 million are claimed against Falcon, but the company denies the charges and is vigorously defending itself. In a recent talk-show interview, the president of the company stated that he could not predict the outcome of the lawsuits. Nevertheless, he said, management does not believe that any actual liabilities resulting from the lawsuits will significantly affect the company's financial position.

Required

Prepare a partial balance sheet to show how Falcon Lamp Company would report this contingent liability in a short presentation. Total actual liabilities are $3 million. Also, write the disclosure note to describe the contingency.

Exercise 11-7 *Accruing a contingency*

Refer to the Falcon Lamp Company situation in the preceding exercise. Suppose that Falcon Lamp's attorneys believe it is probable that a judgment of $350,000 will be rendered against the company.

Required

Describe how to report this situation in the Falcon Lamp Company financial statements. Journalize any entry required under GAAP. Explanations are not required.

Exercise 11-8 *Computing net pay*

Chil Pilsbury is a salesman in the men's department of Rich's Department Store in Atlanta. He earns a base monthly salary of $550 plus an 8 percent commission on his sales. Through payroll deductions, Chil donates $5 per month to a charitable organization, and he authorizes Rich's to deduct $16.25 monthly for health insurance on his family. Tax rates on Chil's earnings are 9 percent for income tax and 7 percent for FICA, subject to the maximum. During the first 11 months of the year, he earned $37,140. Compute Chil's gross pay and net pay for December, assuming his sales for the month are $61,300.

Exercise 11-9 *Computing and recording gross pay and net pay*

Melanie Baker works for a Seven-Eleven store for straight-time earnings of $6 per hour, with time-and-a-half compensation for hours in excess of 40 per week. Melanie's payroll deductions include withheld income tax of 12 percent of total earnings, FICA tax of 7 percent of total earnings, and a weekly deduction of $5 for a charitable contribution to United Fund. Assuming Melanie worked 43 hours during the week, (a) compute her gross pay and net pay for the week, and (b) make a general journal entry to record the store's wage expense for Melanie's work, including her payroll deductions. Explanations are not required. Round all amounts to the nearest cent.

Exercise 11-10 *Recording a payroll*

Filene's Department Store incurred salary expense of $42,000 for December. The store's payroll expense includes employer FICA tax of 7 percent in addition to state unemployment tax of 5.4 percent and federal unemployment tax of .8 percent. Of the total salaries, $38,400 is subject to FICA tax, and $9,100 is subject to unemployment tax. Also, the store provides the following fringe benefits for employees: health insurance (cost to the store, $1,134.68); life insurance (cost to the store, $351.07); and pension benefits (cost to the store, $707.60). Record Filene's payroll taxes and its expenses for employee fringe benefits. Explanations are not required.

Problems   *(Group A)*

Problem 11-1A *Reporting current liabilities*

Following are six pertinent facts about events during the current year at Woodhaven Sales.

1. On September 30, Woodhaven signed a six-month, 9 percent note payable to purchase inventory costing $22,000. The note requires payment of principal and interest at maturity.

2. On October 31, Woodhaven discounted a $50,000 note payable to Lake Air National Bank and received cash of $44,000. The interest rate on the one-year note is 12 percent.

3. On November 30, Woodhaven received rent of $4,200 in advance for a lease on a building. This rent will be earned evenly over three months.

4. December sales totaled $38,000 and Woodhaven collected an additional state sales tax of 7 percent. This amount will be sent to the State of Arizona early in January.

5. Woodhaven owes $100,000 on a long-term note payable. At December 31, $20,000 of this principal plus $2,100 of accrued interest are payable within one year.

6. Sales of $430,000 were covered by Woodhaven's product warranty. At December 31 estimated warranty payable is $8,100.

Required

For each item, indicate the account and the related amount to be reported as a current liability on Woodhaven's December 31 balance sheet.

Problem 11-2A   *Journalizing liability-related transactions*

The following transactions of Ortega, Inc., occurred during 19X4 and 19X5. Record the transactions in the company's general journal. Explanations are not required.

19X4

Jan. 9 Purchased inventory for $3,100, signing a six-month, 8 percent note payable.

    29 Recorded the week's sales of $10,240, three fourths on credit, and one fourth for cash. Sales amounts are subject to an additional 5 percent state sales tax.

Feb. 5 Sent the last week's sales tax to the state.

    28 Borrowed $300,000 on a 10 percent, long-term note payable that calls for annual installment payments of $50,000 principal plus interest.

Apr. 8 Received $778 in deposits from distributors of company products. Ortega refunds the deposits after six months.

July 9 Paid the six-month, 8 percent note at maturity.

Oct. 8 Refunded security deposits of $778 to distributors.

    22 Discounted a $5,000, 10 percent, 90-day note payable to the bank, receiving cash for the net amount after interest was deducted from the note's maturity value.

Nov. 30 Purchased a machine at a cost of $3,000, signing a 12 percent, six-month note payable for that amount.

Dec. 31 Accrued warranty expense, which is estimated at 2 1/2 percent of sales of $650,000.

    31 Accrued interest on all outstanding notes payable. Make a separate interest accrual entry for each note payable.

19X5

Jan. 20 Paid off the 10 percent discounted note payable. Made a separate entry for the interest.

Feb. 28 Paid the first installment and interest for one year on the long-term note payable.

May 31 Paid off the 12 percent machine note plus interest at maturity.

Problem 11-3A   *Journalizing, posting, and reporting liabilities*

The general ledger of Mayes Company at June 30, 19X3, end of the company's fiscal year, includes the following account balances before adjusting entries. Parentheses indicate a debit balance.

Notes Payable, Short-Term ..	$ 21,000	Employer Payroll	
Discount on Notes Payable ..	(900)	Taxes Payable	$ —
Accounts Payable	105,520	Employee Benefits Payable ..	—
Current Portion of Long-		Sales Tax Payable	738
Term Debt Payable	—	Customer Deposits Payable ..	6,950
Interest Payable	—	Estimated Warranty Payable .	—
Salary Payable	—	Unearned Rent Revenue	4,800
Employee Payroll		Long-Term Debt Payable. . . .	120,000
Taxes Payable	—	Contingent Liabilities	—

The additional data needed to develop the adjusting entries at June 30 are as follows:

a. The $21,000 balance in Notes Payable, Short-Term consists of two notes. The first note, with a principal amount of $15,000, was issued on January 31. It matures six months from date of issuance and was discounted at 12 percent. The second note, with a principal amount of $6,000, was issued on April 22 for a term of 90 days. It bears interest at 10 percent. It was not discounted. Interest on this note will be paid at maturity.

b. The long-term debt is payable in annual installments of $20,000 with the next installment due on July 31. On that date, Mayes will also pay one year's interest at 9 percent. Interest was last paid on July 31 of the preceding year. To shift the current installment of the long-term debt to a current liability, debit Long-Term Debt Payable and credit Current Portion of Long-Term Debt Payable.

c. Gross salaries for the last payroll of the fiscal year were $5,044. Of this amount, employee payroll taxes payable were $1,088, and salary payable was $3,956.

d. Employer payroll taxes payable were $876, and Mayes's liability for employee health insurance was $1,253.

e. Mayes estimates that warranty expense is 2 percent of sales, which were $494,000. The company has not yet recorded warranty expense for the year.

f. On February 1 the company collected one year's rent of $4,800 in advance.

g. At June 30 Mayes is the defendant in a $200,000 lawsuit, which the company expects to win. However, the outcome is uncertain. Mayes reports contingent liabilities short, with an explanatory note.

Required

1. Open the listed accounts, inserting their unadjusted June 30 balances.
2. Journalize and post the June 30 adjusting entries to the accounts opened. Key adjusting entries by letter.
3. Prepare the liability section of the balance sheet at June 30.

Problem 11-4A   *Computing and recording payroll amounts*

The partial monthly records of Wilcox Company show the following figures:

Employee Earnings:

(1) Straight-time employee		(7) Medical insurance	$ 668
earnings	$16,246	(8) Total deductions	3,884
(2) Overtime pay	?	(9) Net pay	15,936
(3) Total employee earnings. . .	?		

Accounts Debited:

Deductions and Net Pay:

		(10) Salary Expense	?
(4) Withheld income tax.	1,903	(11) Wage Expense	4,573
(5) FICA tax	?	(12) Sales Commission	
(6) Charitable contributions. . .	340	Expense	5,077

Required

1. Determine the missing amounts on lines (2), (3), (5), and (10).
2. Prepare the general journal entry to record Wilcox's payroll for the month. Credit Payrolls Payable for net pay. No explanation is required.

Problem 11-5A *Computing and recording payroll amounts*

Assume that Joyce Stankov is a vice-president of Bank of America's leasing operations in San Francisco. During 19X6 she worked for the company all year at a $3,625 monthly salary. She also earned a year-end bonus equal to 10 percent of her salary.

Stankov's federal income tax withheld during 19X6 was $537 per month. Also, she paid a one-time federal withholding tax of $1,007 on her bonus check. State income tax withheld came to $43 per month, and she paid a one-time state withholding tax of $27 on the bonus. The FICA tax withheld was 7.0 percent of the first $40,000 in annual earnings. Stankov authorized the following payroll deductions: United Fund contribution of 1 percent of total earnings, and life insurance of $19 per month.

Bank of America incurred payroll tax expense on Stankov for FICA tax of 7 percent of the first $40,000 in annual earnings. The bank also paid state unemployment tax of 5.4 percent and federal unemployment tax of .8 percent on the first $7,000 in annual earnings. In addition, the bank provides Stankov with health insurance at a cost of $35 per month and pension benefits. During 19X6 Bank of America paid $7,178 into Stankov's pension program.

Required

1. Compute Stankov's gross pay, payroll deductions, and net pay for the full year 19X6. Round all amounts to the nearest dollar.
2. Compute Bank of America's total 19X6 payroll cost for Stankov.
3. Prepare Bank of America's summary general journal entries to record its expense for
   a. Stankov's total earnings for the year, her payroll deductions, and her net pay. Debit Salary Expense and Executive Bonus Compensation as appropriate. Credit liability accounts for the payroll deductions and Cash for net pay.
   b. Employer payroll taxes on Stankov. Credit liability accounts.
   c. Fringe benefit provided to Stankov. Credit a liability account.
   Explanations are not required.

Problem 11-6A *Selecting the correct data to record a payroll*

Assume that the payroll information on the following page appeared in the records of the *Bristol Globe* newspaper.

Required

1. Prepare the general journal entries to record the payroll for the week ended March 31, including payroll taxes and fringe benefits.
2. Prepare the general journal entry to record the payment of the week's salaries to employees on March 31.
3. Assume that the *Globe* pays all its liabilities to the federal government in a single monthly amount. Prepare the general journal entry to record the April 1, 19X9, payment of federal taxes. (Liabilities to the federal government include FICA taxes and those items with *federal* and *U.S.* in the account title.)
4. Assume that the *Globe* pays all other payroll liabilities shortly after the end of the month. Prepare a single general journal entry to record the April 4 payment for these March liabilities.

Explanations are not required for journal entries.

	Payroll for Week Ended Friday, March 31, 19X9	Payroll for Month of March 19X9
Salaries:		
Editorial salaries.........................	$6,455	$27,178
Warehousing salaries.....................	3,118	13,128
Deductions:		
Employee federal income tax	1,415	5,958
FICA tax...............................	641	2,699
Employee health insurance	481	2,025
Employee contributions to United Fund.......	367	1,545
Employee U.S. savings bonds	288	1,213
Net pay..................................	6,381	26,866
Employer payroll taxes:		
FICA tax...............................	641	2,699
State unemployment tax	520	2,160
Federal unemployment tax	77	320
Employer cost of fringe benefits for employees:		
Health insurance	663	2,791
Life insurance...........................	324	1,368
Pensions	451	1,899

Note: One challenge of this problem is to use only the relevant data. Not all the information given is necessary for making the required journal entries.

Problem 11-7A *Using payroll register; recording a payroll*

Assume that the payroll records of a district sales office of Carolina Freight Corporation provided the following information for the weekly pay period ended December 21, 19X5:

Employee	Hours Worked	Hourly Earnings Rate	Federal Income Tax	Union Dues	United Way Contributions	Earnings through Previous Week
Maria Burnett	42	$18	$153	$6	$5	$42,474
James English	47	8	56	4	4	23,154
Louise French	40	11	72	-	4	4,880
Roberto Garza	41	16	137	6	8	39,600

James English and Louise French work in the office, and Maria Burnett and Roberto Garza work in sales. All employees are paid time and a half for hours worked in excess of 40 per week. For convenience, round all amounts to the nearest dollar. Show computations. Explanations are not required for journal entries.

Required

1. Enter the appropriate information in a payroll register similar to Exhibit 11-4. In addition to the deductions listed, the employer also takes out FICA tax: 7 percent of the first $40,000 of each employee's annual earnings.
2. Record the payroll information in the general journal.
3. Assume that the first payroll check is number 319, paid to Maria Burnett. Record the check numbers in the payroll register. Also, prepare the general journal entry to record payment of net pay to the employees.
4. The employer's payroll taxes include FICA tax of 7 percent of the first $40,000 of each employee's earnings. The employer also pays unemployment taxes of 6.2 percent (5.4

percent for the state and .8 percent for the federal government on the first $7,000 of each employee's annual earnings). Record the employer's payroll taxes in the general journal.

(Group B)

Problem 11-1B *Reporting current liabilities*

Following are six pertinent facts about events during the current year at Brookview Products.

1. On August 31, Brookview signed a six-month, 12 percent note payable to purchase a machine costing $14,000. The note requires payment of principal and interest at maturity.
2. On September 30, Brookview discounted a $10,000 note payable to InterBank Savings and received cash of $9,000. The interest rate on the one-year note is 10 percent.
3. On October 31, Brookview received rent of $2,000 in advance for a lease on a building. This rent will be earned evenly over four months.
4. December sales totaled $63,000 and Brookview collected sales tax of 9 percent. This amount will be sent to the State of Tennessee early in January.
5. Brookview owes $75,000 on a long-term note payable. At December 31, $25,000 of this principal plus $900 of accrued interest are payable within one year.
6. Sales of $509,000 were covered by Brookview's product warranty. At December 31 estimated warranty payable is $11,300.

Required

For each item, indicate the account and the related amount to be reported as a current liability on Brookview's December 31 balance sheet.

Problem 11-2B *Journalizing liability-related transactions*

The following transactions of Lancaster Company occurred during 19X2 and 19X3. Record the transactions in the company's general journal. Explanations are not required.

19X2

Feb. 3 Purchased a machine for $2,200, signing a six-month, 11 percent note payable.

28 Recorded the week's sales of $9,000, one third for cash, and two thirds on credit. All sales amounts are subject to a 5 percent state sales tax.

Mar. 7 Sent the last week's sales tax to the state.

Apr. 30 Borrowed $500,000 on a 9 percent, long-term note payable that calls for annual installment payments of $100,000 principal plus interest.

May 10 Received $1,125 in security deposits from customers. Lancaster refunds most deposits within three months.

Aug. 3 Paid the six-month, 11 percent note at maturity.

10 Refunded security deposits of $1,125 to customers.

Sep. 14 Discounted a $6,000, 12 percent, 60-day note payable to the bank, receiving cash for the net amount after interest was deducted from the note's maturity value.

Nov. 13 Recognized interest on the 12 percent discounted note and paid off the note at maturity.

30 Purchased inventory at a cost of $7,200, signing a 10 percent, three-month note payable for that amount.

Dec. 31 Accrued warranty expense, which is estimated at 3 percent of sales of $145,000.

31 Accrued interest on all outstanding notes payable. Make a separate interest accrual entry for each note payable.

19X3

Feb. 28   Paid off the 10 percent inventory note, plus interest, at maturity.

Apr. 30   Paid the first installment and interest for one year on the long-term note payable.

Problem 11-3B   *Journalizing, posting, and reporting liabilities*

The Loflin Company general ledger at September 30, 19X7, the end of the company's fiscal year, includes the following account balances before adjusting entries. Parentheses indicate a debit balance.

Notes Payable, Short-Term	$ 32,000	Employer Payroll	
Discount on Notes Payable	(2,100)	Taxes Payable	$ —
Accounts Payable	88,240	Employee Benefits Payable	—
Current Portion of Long-		Sales Tax Payable	372
Term Debt Payable	—	Property Tax Payable	1,433
Interest Payable	—	Estimated Warranty Payable	—
Salary Payable	—	Unearned Rent Revenue	3,900
Employee Payroll		Long-Term Debt Payable	165,000
Taxes Payable	—	Contingent Liabilities	—

The additional data needed to develop the adjusting entries at September 30 are as follows:

a.   The $32,000 balance in Notes Payable, Short-Term consists of two notes. The first note, with a principal amount of $21,000, was issued on August 31, matures one year from data of issuance, and was discounted at 10 percent. The second note, with a principal amount of $11,000, was issued on September 2 for a term of 90 days and bears interest at 9 percent. It was not discounted.

b.   The long-term debt is payable in annual installments of $55,000, with the next installment due on January 31, 19X8. On that date, Loflin will also pay one year's interest at 10.5 percent. Interest was last paid on January 31. To shift the current installment of the long-term debt to a current liability, debit Long-Term Debt Payable and credit Current Portion of Long-Term Debt Payable.

c.   Gross salaries for the last payroll of the fiscal year were $4,319. Of this amount, employee payroll taxes payable were $958, and salary payable was $3,361.

d.   Employer payroll taxes payable were $755, and Loflin's liability for employee life insurance was $1,004.

e.   Loflin estimates that warranty expense is 3 percent of sales, which were $387,000. The company has not yet recorded warranty expense for the year.

f.   On August 1 the company collected six months' rent of $3,900 in advance.

g.   At June 30 Loflin is the defendant in a $50,000 lawsuit, which the company expects to win. However, the outcome is uncertain. Loflin reports contingent liabilities "short," with an explanatory note.

Required

1.   Open the listed accounts, inserting their unadjusted September 30 balances.
2.   Journalize and post the September 30 adjusting entries to the accounts opened. Key adjusting entries by letter.
3.   Prepare the liability section of Loflin's balance sheet at September 30.

Problem 11-4B   *Computing and recording payroll amounts*

The partial monthly records of Friedrich Company show the following figures.

Employee Earnings:

(1) Straight-time earnings .... $?   (7) Medical insurance....... $ 1,373
(2) Overtime pay 5,109   (8) Total deductions .... ?
(3) Total employee earnings...   ?   (9) Net pay 58,813

Deductions and Net Pay: **Accounts Debited:**

(4) Withheld income tax...... 8,993   (10) Salary Expense 31,278
(5) FICA tax 4,784   (11) Wage Expense.......... ?
(6) Charitable contributions... 885   (12) Sales Commission
                                       Expense 27,931

Required

1. Determine the missing amounts on lines (1), (3), (8), and (11).
2. Prepare the general journal entry to record Friedrich's payroll for the month. Credit Payrolls Payable for net pay. No explanation is required.

Problem 11-5B   *Computing and recording payroll amounts*

Assume that Leslie Walker is a commercial lender in Chase Manhattan Bank's mortgage banking department in New York City. During 19X2 she worked for the bank all year at a $4,195 monthly salary. She also earned a year-end bonus equal to 12 percent of her salary.

Walker's federal income tax withheld during 19X2 was $822 per month. Also, she paid a one-time withholding of $2,487 on her bonus check. State income tax withheld came to $61 per month, and the city of New York withheld income tax of $21 per month. In addition, Walker paid one-time withholdings of $64 (state) and $19 (city) on the bonus. The FICA tax withheld was 7 percent of the first $40,000 in annual earnings. Walker authorized the following payroll deductions: United Fund contribution of 1 percent of total earnings, and life insurance of $17 per month.

Chase Manhattan Bank incurred payroll tax expense on Walker for FICA tax of 7 percent of the first $40,000 in annual earnings. The bank also paid state unemployment tax of 5.4 percent, and federal unemployment tax of .8 percent on the first $7,000 in annual earnings. The bank also provided Walker with the following fringe benefits: health insurance at a cost of $48 per month, and pension benefits to be paid to Walker during her retirement. During 19X2 Chase Manhattan's cost of Walker's pension program was $8,083.

Required

1. Compute Walker's gross pay, payroll deductions, and net pay for the full year of 19X2. Round all amounts to the nearest dollar.
2. Compute Chase Manhattan Bank's total 19X2 payroll cost for Walker.
3. Prepare Chase Manhattan Bank's summary general journal entries to record its expense for
   a. Walker's total earnings for the year, her payroll deductions, and her net pay. Debit Salary Expense and Executive Bonus Compensation as appropriate. Credit liability accounts for the payroll deductions and Cash for net pay.
   b. Employer payroll taxes for Walker. Credit liability accounts.
   c. Fringe benefits provided to Walker. Credit a liability account.
   Explanations are not required.

Problem 11-6B   *Selecting the correct data to record a payroll*

Assume the following payroll information appeared in the records of a small plant operated by Ford Motor Company:

	Payroll for Week Ended Friday July 31, 19X4	Payroll for Month of July 19X4
Salaries:		
Supervisor salaries	$39,668	$162,639
Office salaries	9,088	37,261
Deductions:		
Employee federal income tax	5,960	24,435
FICA tax	3,266	13,392
Employee health insurance	922	3,780
Employee union dues	708	2,903
Employee U.S. savings bonds	665	2,727
Net Pay.	37,235	152,663
Employer payroll taxes:		
FICA tax	3,266	13,392
State unemployment tax	2,633	10,793
Federal unemployment tax	390	1,599
Employer cost of fringe benefits for employees:		
Health insurance	2,034	8,339
Life insurance.	1,857	7,614
Pension.	1,667	6,835

Note: One challenge of this problem is to use only the relevant data. Not all the information given is necessary for making the required journal entries.

Required

1. Prepare the general journal entry to record the payroll for the week ended July 31, including payroll taxes and fringe benefits.
2. Prepare the general journal entry to record the payment of the week's salaries to employees on July 31.
3. Assume that Ford pays all its liabilities to the federal government in a single monthly amount. Prepare the general journal entry to record the August 1, 19X4, payment of federal taxes. (Liabilities to the federal government include FICA taxes and those items with *federal* and *U.S.* in the account title.)
4. Assume that Ford pays all other payroll liabilities shortly after the end of the month. Prepare a single general journal entry to record the August 3 payment for these July liabilities.

Explanations are not required for journal entries.

Problem 11-7B *Using a payroll register; recording a payroll*

Assume that payroll records of a district sales office of Emery Air Freight Corporation provided the following information for the weekly pay period ended December 18, 19X3:

Employee	Hours Worked	Weekly Earnings Rate	Federal Income Tax	Health Insurance	United Way Contribution	Earnings through Previous Week
Tina Cruz	43	$400	$ 94	$9	$7	$17,060
Leroy Dixon	46	480	121	5	5	22,365
Karol Stastny	41	800	196	6	—	39,247
David Trent	40	240	32	4	2	3,413

Tina Cruz and David Trent work in the office, and Leroy Dixon and Karol Stastny work in sales. All employees are paid time and a half for hours worked in excess of 40 per week. For convenience, round all amounts to the nearest dollar. Show computations. Explanations are not required for journal entries.

Required

1. Enter the appropriate information in a payroll register similar to Exhibit 11-4. In addition to the deductions listed, the employer also takes out FICA tax: 7 percent of the first $40,000 of each employee's annual earnings.
2. Record the payroll information in the general journal.
3. Assume that the first payroll check is number 178, paid to Tina Cruz. Record the check numbers in the payroll register. Also, prepare the general journal entry to record payment of net pay to the employees.
4. The employer's payroll taxes include FICA of 7 percent of the first $40,000 of each employee's annual earnings. The employer also pays unemployment taxes of 6.2 percent (5.4 percent for the state and .8 percent for the federal government) on the first $7,000 of each employee's annual earnings. Record the employer's payroll taxes in the general journal.

Decision Problem

Identifying Internal Control Weaknesses and their Solution

Hall Custom Homes is a large home-building business in Phoenix, Arizona. The owner and manager is Lawrence Hall, who oversees all company operations. He employs 15 work crews, each made up of 6 to 10 members. Construction supervisors, who report directly to Hall, lead the crews. Most supervisors are long-time employees, so Hall trusts them greatly. Hall's office staff consists of an accountant and an office manager.

Because employee turnover is rapid in the construction industry, supervisors hire and terminate their own crew members. Supervisors notify the office of all personnel changes. Also, supervisors forward to the office the employee W-4 forms, which the crew members fill out to claim tax-withholding exemptions. Each Thursday the supervisors submit weekly time sheets for their crews, and the accountant prepares the payroll. At noon on Friday the supervisors come to the office to get paychecks for distribution to the workers at 5 P.M.

Hall's accountant prepares the payroll, including the payroll checks, which are written on a single payroll bank account. Hall signs all payroll checks after matching the employee name to the time sheets submitted by the foremen. Often the construction workers wait several days to cash their pay checks. To verify that each construction worker is a bona fide employee, the accountant matches the employee's endorsement signature on the back of the canceled payroll check with the signature on that employee's W-4 form.

Required

1. List one *efficiency* weakness in Hall's payroll accounting system. How can Hall correct this weakness?
2. Identify one way that a supervisor can defraud Hall under the present system.
3. Discuss a control feature Hall can use to *safeguard* against the fraud you identified in Requirement 2.

Financial Statement Problem

Current and Contingent Liabilities and Payroll

Details about a company's current and contingent liabilities and payroll costs appear in a number of places in the annual report. Use the Gulf+Western financial statements to answer these questions.

1. How much were the current maturities of Gulf+Western's long-term debt at October 31, 1987? In Note F, what interest rates applied to the current maturities payable in 1988?

2. Give the breakdown of accrued expenses and other liabilities. Identify the two un-earned revenues in this group. Give the fiscal 1988 entries to record the earning of these revenues.

3. Does Gulf+Western use a short presentation for contingent liabilities? Where does the company report contingencies? What is the attorney's opinion as to the ultimate effect of lawsuits pending against the company?

4. What employee fringe benefit is mentioned in Note I? How much expense did Gulf+Western incur for this item during fiscal 1987? Which liability in Note J includes any year-end accrual for this item?

5. Note J lists a $77.7 million liability for "Accrued compensation and other employee benefit related items." Was compensation expense for the year equal to, less than, or greater than this amount? Give your reason.

Answers to Self-Study Questions

1. c $10,000 \times .09 \times 5/12 = $375

2. a $10,000 - ($10,000 \times .09) = $9,100

3. b

4. c $900,000 \times .01 = $9,000

5. d

6. a Overtime pay: $320/40 = $8 \times 1.5 = $12 per hour $\times$ 10 hours = $120
   Gross pay = $320 + $120 = $440
   Deductions = $440 \times (.08 + .07) = $66
   Take-home pay = $440 - $66 = $374

7. c

8. c

9. b

10. d

12

The Foundation
for Generally Accepted
Accounting Principles

LEARNING OBJECTIVES
After studying this chapter, you should be able to

1 Identify the basic objective of financial reporting

2 Identify and apply the underlying concepts of accounting

3 Identify and apply the principles of accounting

4 Allocate revenue to the appropriate period by four methods

5 Report information that satisfies the disclosure principle

6 Apply two constraints to accounting

7 Name and define the elements of financial statements

Every technical area seems to have professional associations and regulatory bodies that govern the practice of the profession. Accounting is no exception. During the 1970s and 1980s generally accepted accounting principles in the United States have been influenced most by the Financial Accounting Standards Board (FASB) and its predecessor, the Accounting Principles Board (APB). The FASB consists of seven full-time members. A large staff and an annual budget of $10 million support the FASB. Its financial support comes from various professional associations, such as the American Institute of Certified Public Accountants.

From 1962 to 1973 the APB issued accounting pronouncements called *Opinions*, many of which are still part of generally accepted accounting principles (GAAP). In 1973 the FASB was established to replace the APB. The FASB is an independent organization with no government or professional affiliation. The FASB's pronouncements, called *Statements of Financial Accounting Standards*, currently specify how to account for certain business transactions. Each new *Standard* becomes part of GAAP, the "accounting law of the land." In the same way that our laws draw authority from their acceptance by the people, GAAP depends upon the general acceptance by the business community. Throughout this book, we refer to GAAP as the proper way to do accounting.

The United States Congress has given the Securities and Exchange Commission (SEC) ultimate responsibility for establishing accounting rules for companies that are owned by the general investing public. However, the SEC has delegated much of its rule-making power to the FASB. Exhibit 12-1 outlines the flow of authority for developing GAAP.

EXHIBIT 12-1 *Flow of Authority for Developing GAAP*

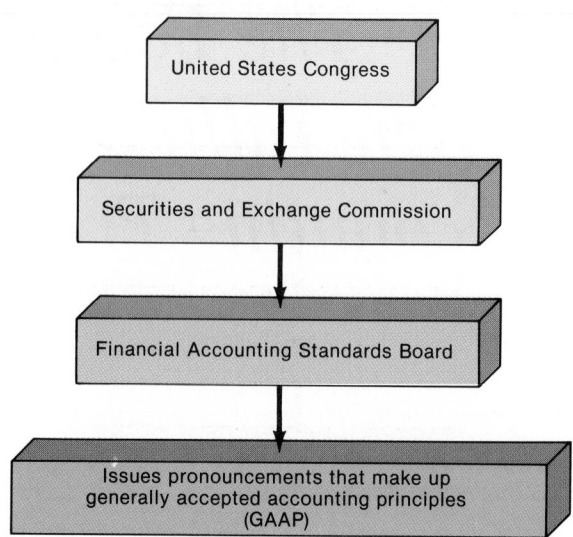

Setting accounting standards is a complex process involving the FASB, the SEC, and occasionally Congress. Also, individuals and companies often exert pressure on all three bodies in their efforts to shape accounting decisions to their advantage. Accountants also try to influence accounting decisions. Although any overruling is rare, the SEC has the authority to override an FASB decision, and Congress itself can override an SEC or an FASB decision, as the authority structure in Exhibit 12-1 shows. In most cases, however, the FASB plays the key role.

We have seen that GAAP guides companies in their financial statement preparation. Independent auditing firms of certified public accountants (CPAs) hold the responsibility for making sure companies do indeed follow GAAP.

The Conceptual Framework

Throughout the first 11 chapters, we have introduced key concepts and principles as they have applied to the topics under discussion. For example, Chapter 1 introduced the entity concept so that we could account for the transactions of a particular business. In Chapter 2, we discussed the revenue and matching principles as the guidelines for measuring income. Now that you have an overview of the accounting process, we consider the full range of accounting concepts and principles. Collectively, they form the foundation for accounting practice—GAAP.

Shortly after its formation in 1973, the Financial Accounting Standards Board (FASB) began the Conceptual Framework Project. The FASB's goal is to develop a constitution that will define the nature and function of financial accounting. This project provides a framework for the various accounting concepts and principles that are used to prepare the financial statements.

Accounting principles differ from natural laws like the law of gravity. Accounting principles draw their authority from their acceptance in the business community rather than from their ability to explain physical phenomena. Thus they really are *generally accepted* by those people and organizations who need guidelines in accounting for their financial undertakings. Exhibit 12-2 diagrams how we move from the conceptual framework to the financial statements.

EXHIBIT 12-2 *Overview of Generally Accepted Accounting Principles*

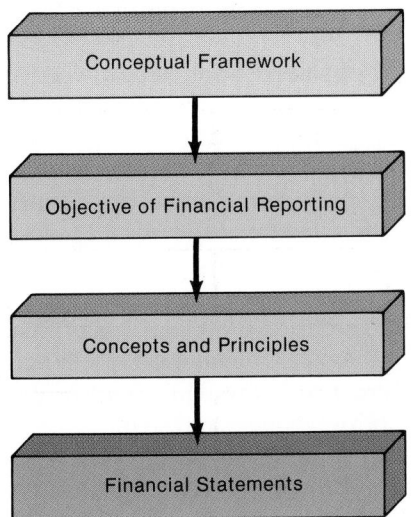

We now look at the objective of financial reporting. This objective tells what financial accounting is intended to accomplish. Thus it provides the goal for accounting information. Next, we examine particular accounting concepts and principles used to implement the objective. What is the difference between a concept and a principle? The concepts are broader in their application, and the principles are more specific. Last, we discuss the financial statements—the end product of financial accounting—and their elements—assets, liabilities, owner's equity, revenues, expenses, and so on.

Objective of Financial Reporting

The basic *objective of financial reporting* is to provide information that is useful in making investment and lending decisions. To be useful in decision making, the FASB believes accounting information should be *relevant, reliable,* and *comparable.*

Relevant information is useful for making predictions and for evaluating past performance. *Reliable* information is free from significant error and free from the bias of a particular viewpoint. *Comparable* information can be compared from period to period to help investors and creditors track the business's progress through time. These characteristics combine to shape the concepts and principles that make up GAAP.

OBJECTIVE 1

Identify the basic objective of financial reporting

Underlying Concepts

Entity Concept

The **entity concept** is the most basic concept in accounting because it draws a boundary around the organization being accounted for. That is, the transactions of each entity are accounted for separately from transactions of all other organiza-

OBJECTIVE 2

Identify and apply the underlying concepts of accounting

tions and persons, including the owners of the entity. This separation allows us to measure the performance and the financial position of each entity independent of all other entities.

A business entity may be a sole proprietorship (owned and operated by a single individual), a partnership of two or more persons, or a large corporation like EXXON. The entity concept applies with equal force to all types and sizes of organizations. The proprietor of a travel agency, for example, accounts for her personal transactions separately from those of her business. This division allows her to evaluate the success or failure of the travel agency. If she were to mix her personal and business accounting records, she would lose sight of the information needed to evaluate the business alone.

At the other end of the spectrum, EXXON is a giant company with oil-refining, retail gasoline sales, and chemical operations. EXXON accounts for each of these divisions separately in order to know which part of the business is earning a profit, which needs to borrow money, and so on.

The entity concept also applies to nonprofit organizations such as churches, synagogues, and government agencies. A hospital, for example, may be organized as a nonprofit entity, and it may have an emergency room, a pediatrics unit, and a surgery unit. The accounting system of the hospital should account for each separately to allow the managers to evaluate the progress of each unit.

The entity concept also provides the basis for consolidating subentities into a single set of financial statements. For example, the directors want to know the overall result of operating the entire hospital. Accountants, therefore, summarize the results of the various subentities into a consolidated set of financial statements. This is also done for profit-oriented businesses like EXXON, which has a single set of consolidated financial statements.

Going-Concern Concept

Under the **going-concern concept,** accountants assume the business will continue operating for the foreseeable future. The logic behind the going-concern concept is best illustrated by considering the alternative assumption: going out of business.

When a business stops, it sells its assets, converting them to cash. This process is called liquidation. With the cash, the business pays off its liabilities, and the owners keep any remaining cash. In liquidation, the amount of cash for which the assets are sold measures their current value. Likewise, the liabilities are paid off at their current value. However, if the business does not halt operations—if it remains a going concern—how are its assets and liabilities reported on the balance sheet?

For a going concern, the balance sheet reports assets and liabilities based on historical cost. For example, in a normal buyer-seller transaction, cost is an objective measure of the asset's worth. To consider what the asset may be worth on the current market requires making an estimate. This may or may not be objective. Under the going-concern concept, it is assumed that the entity will continue long enough for it to recover the cost of its assets.

The going-concern concept allows for the reporting of assets and liabilities as current or long-term, a distinction that investors and creditors find useful in evaluating a company. For example, a creditor wants to know the portion of a company's liabilities that are scheduled to come due within the next year and the portion payable beyond the year. The assumption is that the entity will continue in business and honor its commitments.

Time-Period Concept

The **time-period concept** ensures that accounting information is reported at regular intervals. This timely presentation of accounting data aids the comparison of business operations over time; from year to year, quarter to quarter, and so on. Managers, owners, lenders, and other people and businesses need regular reports to assess the business's success—or failure. These persons are making decisions daily. Although the ultimate success of a company cannot be known for sure until the business liquidates, decision makers cannot wait until liquidation to learn whether operations yielded a profit.

Nearly all companies use the year as their basic time period. *Annual* reports are common in business. Companies also prepare quarterly and monthly reports—called interim reports—to meet managers', investors', and creditors' need for timely information.

The time-period concept underlies the use of accruals. Suppose the business's accounting year ends at December 31 and the business has accrued—but will not pay until the next accounting period—$900 in salary expense. To tie this expense to the appropriate period, the accountant enters this adjusting entry, as we have seen:

Dec. 31	Salary Expense.............	900	
	Salary Payable........		900

Accrual entries assign revenue and expense amounts to the correct accounting period and thus help produce meaningful financial statements.

Approximately 70 percent of all companies report their financial statements on a calendar-year basis, January through December. The remaining 30 percent use a fiscal year that ends at the business's annual low point in operations. For example, K-Mart and most large retailers use a fiscal year ending January 31. Their operations reach their most active point during December and then taper off at the end of January when the after-Christmas sales have finished.

Stable-Monetary-Unit Concept

Accounting information is expressed primarily in monetary terms. The monetary unit is the prime means of measuring assets. This measure is not surprising given that money is the common denominator in business transactions. In the United States, the monetary unit is the dollar; in Great Britain, the pound sterling; in Japan, the yen. The stable-monetary-unit concept provides an orderly basis for handling account balances to produce the financial statements.

Unlike a liter, a foot, and many other measurements, the value of the monetary unit may change over time. Most of us are familiar with inflation. Groceries that cost $50 three years ago may cost $60 today. The value of the dollar changes. In view of the fact that the dollar does not maintain a constant value, how does a business measure the worth of assets and liabilities acquired over a long span of time? The business records all assets and liabilities at cost. Each asset and each liability on the balance sheet is the sum of all the individual dollar amounts added over time. For example, if a company bought 100 acres of land in 1975 for $60,000 and another 100 acres of land in 1990 for $300,000, the asset Land on the balance sheet carries a $360,000 balance, and the change in the purchasing power of the dollar is ignored. The **stable-monetary-unit concept** is the accountant's basis for ignoring the effect of inflation and making no adjustments for the changing value of the dollar. Let's look at the shortcomings of this concept.

The December 26, 1987, balance sheet of Kraft, Inc., reported Land at $47.6 million. Assume that Kraft purchased land in 1971 for $4 million and land in 1987 for $43.6 million. The period from 1971 to 1987 witnessed high inflation. We know, therefore, that the dollar had significantly higher value in 1971. Kraft may have bought more land in 1971 for $4 million than it did in 1987 for so much more money. Now suppose that a second company spent a full $47.6 million on land in 1987. The acreage would be far less than the acreage purchased with mixed 1971 and 1987 dollars. How do we compare the two companies' balance sheets? The comparison based on the stable monetary unit concept may not be valid because mixing dollar values at different times is like mixing apples and oranges.

Many businesspeople believe that accounting information must be adjusted for changes in the dollar's purchasing power. The FASB encourages large companies to present supplementary inflation-adjusted information in their financial reports, a topic we examine in Chapter 17. Generally, however, accounting is based on historical costs.

Accounting Principles

Reliability (Objectivity) Principle

OBJECTIVE 3

Identify and apply the principles of accounting

The **reliability principle** requires that accounting information be dependable. Reliable information is free from significant error and bias. Users of this accounting information may rely on its truthfulness. To be reliable, information must be verifiable by people outside the business. Financial statement users may consider information reliable if independent experts would agree that the information is based on objective and honest measurement.

Consider the error in a company's failure to accrue interest revenue at the end of an accounting period. This error results in understated interest revenue and understated net income. Clearly, this company's accounting information is unreliable.

Biased information — data prepared from a particular viewpoint and not based on objective facts — is also unreliable. Suppose a company purchased inventory for $25,000. At the end of the accounting period, the inventory has declined in value and can be replaced for $20,000. Under the lower-of-cost-or-market rule, the company must record a $5,000 loss for the decrease in the inventory's value. Company management may believe that the appropriate value for the inventory is $22,000, but that amount is only an opinion. If management reports the $22,000 figure, total assets and owner's equity will be overstated on the balance sheet. Income will be overstated on the income statement.

To establish a *reliable* figure for the inventory's value, management could get a current price list from the inventory supplier or call in an outside professional appraiser to revalue the inventory. Evidence obtained from outside the company leads to reliable, verifiable information. The reliability principle applies to all financial accounting information — from assets to owner's equity on the balance sheet and from revenue to net income on the income statement.

Comparability Principle

The **comparability principle** has two requirements. First, accounting information must be comparable from business to business. Second, a single business's financial statements must be comparable from one period to the next. The FASB encourages comparability in order to make possible useful analysis from business to business, from period to period.

Standard formats for financial statements promote comparability among different companies. Using the same terms to describe the statement elements—assets, liabilities, revenues, and so on—also aids the comparison process.

Even among companies that adhere to standard formats and standard terms, comparability may be less than perfect. Comparisons of companies that use different inventory methods—LIFO and FIFO, for example—are difficult. Likewise, comparisons of companies that use different depreciation methods—straight-line and double-declining-balance, for example—are also quite complex. When GAAP allows a choice among acceptable accounting methods—in inventory, depreciation, and other areas—comparability may be harder to achieve.

Recall that the comparability principle directs each individual company to produce accounting information that is comparable over time. To achieve this quality—which accountants call *consistency*—companies must follow the same accounting practices from period to period. The business that uses FIFO for inventory and straight-line for depreciation in one period ought to use those same methods in the next period. Otherwise, a financial statement user could not tell whether changes in income and asset values result from operations or from the way the business accounts for operations.

Companies may change accounting methods in response to a change in business operations. A company may open up a new product line that calls for a different inventory method. GAAP allows the company to make a change in accounting method, but the business must disclose the change, the reason for making the change, and the effect of the change on net income. This disclosure is made in a note to the financial statements.

Cost Principle

The **cost principle** states that assets and services are recorded at their purchase cost and that the accounting record of the asset continues to be based on cost rather than current market value. By specifying that assets be recorded at cost, this principle also governs the recording of liabilities and owner's equity. Suppose that a land developer purchased 20 acres of land for $50,000. Additional costs included fees paid to the county ($1,500), removal of an unwanted building ($10,000), and landscaping ($20,000), a total cost of $81,500. The Land account carries this balance because it is the cost of bringing the land to its intended use. Assume that the developer holds the land for one year, then offers it for sale at a price of $200,000. The cost principle requires the accounting value of the land to remain at $81,500.

The developer may wish to lure buyers by showing them a balance sheet that reports the land at $200,000. However, this would be inappropriate under GAAP because $200,000 is merely the developer's opinion of what the land is worth.

The underlying basis for the cost principle is the reliability principle. Cost is a reliable value for assets and services because cost is supported by completed transactions between parties with opposing interests. Buyers try to pay the lowest price possible, and sellers try to sell for the highest price. The actual cost of an asset or service is objective evidence of its value.

Revenue Principle

The **revenue principle** provides guidance on the *timing* of the recording of revenue and the *amount* of revenue to record. The general rule is that revenue should be recorded when it is earned and not before.

Some revenues, such as interest and rent, accrue with the passage of time. Their timing and amount are easy to figure. The accountant records the amount of revenue earned over each period of time.

Other revenues are earned by selling goods or rendering services. Identifying *when* these revenues are earned depends on more factors than the passage of time. Under the revenue principle, three conditions must be met before revenue is recorded: (1) the seller has done everything necessary to expect to collect from the buyer; (2) the amount of revenue can be objectively measured; and (3) collectibility is reasonably assured. In most cases, these conditions are met at the point of sale or when services are performed.

The *amount* of revenue to record is the value of the assets received—usually cash or a receivable. However, situations may arise in which the amount of revenue or the timing of earning the revenue is not easily determined. We turn now to four methods that guide the accountant in applying the revenue principle in different circumstances.

OBJECTIVE 4

Allocate revenue to the appropriate period by four methods

Sales Method.   Under the **sales method,** revenue is recorded at the point of sale. Consider a retail sale in a hardware store. At the point of sale, the customer pays the store and takes the merchandise. The store records the sale by debiting Cash and crediting Sales Revenue. In other situations, the point of sale occurs when the seller ships the goods to the buyer. Suppose a mining company sells iron ore to Bethlehem Steel Corporation. By shipping the ore to Bethlehem Steel, the mining company has completed its duty and may expect to collect revenue. If the amount of revenue can be objectively measured and collection is reasonably certain, the mining company can then record revenue. The sale entry is a debit to Accounts Receivable and a credit to Sales Revenue. The sales method is used for most sales of goods and services.

Collection Method.   The **collection method** is used only if the receipt of cash is uncertain. Under this method, the seller waits until cash is received to record the sale. Professionals such as physicians and attorneys use the collection method because they often find it difficult to collect their receivables. They may not reasonably assume that they can collect the revenue, so they wait until actual receipt of the cash before recording it. The collection method is conservative in that revenue is not recorded in advance of its receipt.

Installment Method.   The **installment method** is a type of collection method that is used for installment sales. In a typical installment sale, the buyer makes a down payment when the contract is signed and pays the remainder in installments. Department stores, such as Sears and J. C. Penney, auto dealers, and real estate companies sell on the installment plan. Under the installment method, gross profit (sales revenue minus cost of goods sold) is recorded as cash is collected.

Suppose a real estate developer sells land for a down payment of $80,000 plus three annual installments of $120,000, $140,000, and $160,000 (a total of $500,000). The developer's cost of the land is $300,000, so the gross profit is $200,000, computed as follows:

Installment sale	$500,000
Cost of the land sold	300,000
Gross profit.	$200,000

To determine the gross profit associated with each collection under the installment method, we must compute the gross profit percentage, as follows:

$$\text{Gross profit percentage} = \frac{\text{Gross profit}}{\text{Installment sale}} = \frac{\$200,000}{\$500,000} = 40\%$$

We next apply the gross profit percentage to each collection. The result is the amount of gross profit recorded as revenue at the time of cash receipt.

Year	Collections	×	Gross Profit Percentage	=	Gross Profit
1	$ 80,000	×	40%	=	$ 32,000
2	120,000	×	40%	=	48,000
3	140,000	×	40%	=	56,000
4	160,000	×	40%	=	64,000
Total	$500,000	×	40%	=	$200,000

Accountants would record gross profit of $32,000 in year 1, $48,000 in year 2, and so on. The total gross profit ($200,000) is the same as under the sales method. However, under the sales method, the full $200,000 of gross profit would be recorded at the beginning of the contract.

Of course, companies make installment sales year after year. Each year's sales may have a different gross profit percentage. In the preceding example, year 1 installment sales earned gross profit of 40 percent. Suppose year 2 sales earn gross profit of 45 percent, year 3 sales earn 42 percent, and year 4 sales earn 35 percent. The total gross profit for a year is the sum of all the gross profit amounts recorded on cash collections made that year.

Using assumed cash receipts on installment sales made in years 2, 3, and 4, the gross profit computations for years 1 through 4 follow. All year 1 amounts are taken from our computations above.

	Year 1 Sales	Year 2 Sales	Year 3 Sales	Year 4 Sales
Gross profit percentage	40%	45%	42%	35%

Gross profit by year:

	Year 1	Year 2	Year 3	Year 4
Year 1 sales:	$80,000 × .40 = $32,000	$120,000 × .40 = $48,000	$140,000 × .40 = $56,000	$160,000 × .40 = $64,000
Year 2 sales:		90,000 × .45 = 40,500	100,000 × .45 = 45,000	20,000 × .45 = 9,000
Year 3 sales:			75,000 × .42 = 31,500	65,000 × .42 = 27,300
Year 4 sales:				30,000 × .35 = 10,500
Total gross profit	$32,000	$88,500	$132,500	$110,800

The installment method is attractive for income tax purposes because it postpones the recording of revenue and thus the payment of taxes. However, it can be used only under limited circumstances. Under generally accepted accounting principles, this method is permissible only when no reasonable basis exists for estimating collections.

Percentage-of-Completion Method. Construction of office buildings, bridges, dams, and other large assets often extends over several years. The accounting issue for the construction company is *when* to record the revenue. The most conservative approach is to record all the revenue earned on the project in the period when the project is completed. This procedure, called the **completed-contract method,** is acceptable under limited circumstances.

Under the preferred method, called the **percentage-of-completion method,** the construction company recognizes revenue as work is performed. Each year the company estimates the percentage of project completion as construction progresses. One way to make this estimate is to compare the cost incurred for the year to the total estimated project cost. This percentage is then multiplied by the total project revenue to compute the construction revenue for the year. Construction income for the year is revenue minus cost.

Assume Combustion Engineering Company receives a contract to build a power plant for a price of $42 million. Combustion estimates total costs of $36 million over the three-year construction period: $6 million in year 1, $18 million in year 2, and $12 million in year 3. Construction revenue and income during the three years are as follows (amounts in millions):

Year	Cost for Year	Total Project Cost	Percentage of Project Completion for Year	Total Project Revenue	Construction Revenue for Year	Construction Income for Year
1	$ 6	$36	$ 6/$36 = ⅙	$42	$42 × ⅙ = $ 7	$ 7 − $ 6 = $1
2	18	36	18/ 36 = ½	42	42 × ½ = 21	21 − 18 = 3
3	12	36	12/ 36 = ⅓	42	42 × ⅓ = 14	14 − 12 = 2
	$36	$36		$42	$42	$42 $36 $6

The percentage-of-completion method is appropriate when the company can estimate the degree of completion during the construction period, which most construction companies can do. When estimates are not possible, the completed-contract method is required. If Combustion Engineering had used the completed-contract method, its income statement for year 3 would report total project revenue of $42 million, total project expenses of $36 million, and income of $6 million. The income statements of years 1 and 2 would report nothing concerning this project. Most accountants believe the results under the percentage-of-completion method are more realistic.

Matching Principle

The **matching principle** governs the recording and reporting of expenses. This principle goes hand in hand with the revenue principle to govern income recognition in accounting. Recall that income is revenue minus expense. During any period, the company first measures its revenues by the revenue principle. The company then identifies and measures all the expenses it incurred during the period to earn the revenues. To *match* the expenses against the revenues means to subtract the expenses from the revenues. The result is the income for the period.

Some expenses are easy to match against particular revenues. For example, cost of goods sold relates directly to sales revenue, because without the sales, there would be no cost of goods sold. Commissions and fees paid for selling the goods, delivery expense, and sales supplies expense relate to sales revenue for the same reason.

Other expenses are not so easily linked to particular sales because they occur whether or not any revenues arise. Depreciation, salaries, and all types of home-office expense are in this category. Accountants usually match these expenses against revenue on a time basis. For example, the company's home-office building may be used for general management, manufacturing, and marketing. Straight-line depreciation of a 40-year building assigns one fortieth of the building's cost to expense each year, whatever the level of revenue. The annual salary expense for an employee is the person's total salary for the year, regardless of revenue.

Losses, like expenses, are matched against revenue on a time basis. For example, if an asset like inventory loses value, the loss is recorded when it occurs, without regard for the revenues earned during the period.

Disclosure Principle

The **disclosure principle** holds that a company's financial statements should report enough information for outsiders to make knowledgeable decisions about the company. In short, the company should report *relevant, reliable,* and *comparable* information about its economic affairs. This section of the chapter discusses and illustrates different types of disclosures.

Summary of Significant Accounting Policies. To evaluate a company, investors and creditors need to know how its financial statements were prepared. This consideration is especially important when the company can choose from several acceptable methods. Companies summarize their accounting policies in the first note to their financial statements. The note may include both monetary amounts and written descriptions. Companies commonly disclose revenue-recognition method, inventory method, and depreciation method.

Dresser Industries, Inc., reported the following:

OBJECTIVE 5
Report information that satisfies the disclosure principle

NOTE A—SUMMARY OF SIGNIFICANT ACCOUNTING POLICIES (IN PART)

Long-Term Contracts

Revenues and earnings related to products requiring long-term construction periods, principally draglines and electrostatic precipitators, are recognized for financial reporting purposes on the percentage of completion basis.

Inventories

Substantially all the U.S. inventories of the Company are recorded on a last-in, first-out (LIFO) cost basis. Inventories not on LIFO cost valuation, principally foreign inventories, are recorded at the "lower of cost (principally average cost) or market."

Fixed Assets

Fixed assets are depreciated over the estimated service life. Accelerated depreciation methods are used for financial statement purposes, except for U.S. fixed assets with a service life of 10 years or less which are depreciated on a straight-line basis. Accelerated depreciation methods are also used for tax purposes wherever permitted.

Probable Losses. The disclosure principle directs a business to record and report a probable loss *before* it occurs if the loss is likely and its amount can be estimated. Phillips Petroleum Company reported such a loss in its 1985 financial statements. Observe that the disposal of assets has not occurred yet, but the company does *expect* the disposal to result in a loss.

NOTE 1—DISCONTINUED OPERATION [IN PART]
During 1985, the company announced plans to discontinue its minerals operation. Assets associated with these operations were sold, abandoned, or written down . . . in anticipation of their future sale or abandonment, resulting in an estimated net loss on disposal in 1985 of $171 million, net of income tax. . . .

The $171 million loss on disposal appeared on Phillips's 1985 income statement as follows:

	Millions
Income from Continuing Operations	$ 596
Discontinued operations (net of income taxes)	
Loss from operations	(7)
Loss on disposal.	**(171)**
Net Income	$ 418

Accounting Changes.   Consistent use of accounting methods and procedures is important, as we saw in discussing comparability. When a company does change from one accounting method or procedure to another, it must disclose the change, the reason for making the change, and the effect of the change on net income. Two common accounting changes are *changes in accounting principles* and *changes in accounting estimates.*

A **change in accounting principle** is a change in accounting method. A switch from the LIFO method to the FIFO method for inventories and a switch from the sum-of-years-digits depreciation method to the straight-line method are examples of accounting changes. Special rules that apply to changes in accounting principles are discussed in later accounting courses. Whatever the change in principle, the notes to the financial statements must inform the reader that the change has occurred.

A **change in accounting estimate** occurs in the normal course of business as the company alters earlier expectations. A company may record uncollectible account expense based on the estimate that bad debts will equal 2 percent of sales. If actual collections exceed this estimate, the company may lower its estimated expense to 1½ percent of sales in the future.

A company may originally estimate that a new delivery truck will provide four years' service. After two years of using the truck, the company sees that the truck's full useful life will stretch to six years. The company must recompute depreciation based on this new information at the start of the truck's third year of service. Assume that this truck cost $14,000, has an estimated residual value of $2,000, and is depreciated by the straight-line method.

Annual depreciation for each of the first two years of the asset's life is $3,000, computed as follows:

$$\text{Depreciation per year} = \frac{\$14,000 - \$2,000}{4 \text{ years}} = \$3,000$$

Changes in estimate are accounted for by spreading the asset's remaining depreciable cost over its remaining life. Annual depreciation after the accounting change is $1,500, computed in the following manner:

$$\text{Depreciation per year} = \frac{\text{Asset depreciable cost}}{\text{Remaining life}} = \frac{\$14,000 - \$2,000 - (\$3,000 \times 2)}{6 \text{ total years} - 2 \text{ years used}}$$

$$= \frac{\$6,000}{4 \text{ years}} = \$1,500$$

This revised amount of depreciation is recorded in the usual manner.

Walt Disney Productions disclosed a similar change in accounting estimate. Observe that Disney reported the nature of the change, the reason for making the change, and its effect on income.

NOTE 5 [IN PART]:

Effective [at the beginning of the year], the Company extended the estimated useful lives of certain theme park ride and attraction assets based upon historical data and engineering studies. The effect of this change was to decrease depreciation by approximately $8 million (an increase in net income of approximately $4.2 million . . .).

Subsequent Events.   A company usually takes several weeks after the end of the year to close its books and to publish its financial statements. Occasionally, events occur during this period that affect the interpretation of the information in those financial statements. Such an occurrence is called a **subsequent event** and should be disclosed in the prior period's statements. The most common examples of subsequent events are borrowing money, paying debts, making investments, selling assets, and becoming a defendant in a lawsuit.

United Merchants and Manufacturers, Inc., operates principally in the apparel, textiles, and home furnishings industries. The company reported the following subsequent event in its financial statements for the year ended June 30, 19X6:

NOTE 17—SUBSEQUENT EVENTS

On September 11, 19X6, the Company sold 17 percent of [its investment in] Victoria Creations, Inc., which is in the costume jewelry business. The sale resulted in cash proceeds to the Company of $13,910,000, which has been used to reduce indebtedness. The sale also resulted in a gain . . . of approximately $6,400,000, which will be reflected in the Company's results of operations for . . . 19X7.

Business Segments.   Most large companies operate in more than one area. Each area is called a *business segment.* Sears, Roebuck, and Company, best known for its retail stores, also has real estate, investment banking, and other financial service operations. Union Pacific Corporation, the railroad company, is also active in the oil and gas business. The Coca-Cola Company not only sells soft drinks and food, but it also operates in the entertainment business. Diversification like this is not limited to large international companies. A realtor may also own a restaurant. A farmer may sell farm implements. An automobile dealer may also own a furniture store.

Suppose you are considering investing in a company that is active in the steel industry but also owns a meat packer and several leisure resorts. Assume the American steel industry is in retreat because of intense foreign competition. With income and asset data broken down by business segments, you can determine how much of the company's assets are committed to each segment and which lines of business are most (and least) profitable. Companies disclose segment data in notes to their financial statements.

The Scott Paper Company data at the top of the next page meet the GAAP requirement for adequate disclosure.

To satisfy the disclosure principle, Scott Paper breaks down sales, income before taxes, and assets two ways: by business segments and by geographic area. GAAP also requires companies to disclose capital expenditures and depreciation by business segment, as shown in the last two columns.

Disclosure Techniques.   Companies use parenthetical notes in the financial statements. An example is the allowance for uncollectibles, reported as follows by

Year 19X6	(Millions)	Sales	Income before Taxes	Identifiable Assets	Capital Expenditures	Depreciation and Cost of Timber Harvested
Business Segment	Personal Care and Cleaning	$2,349.5	$252.7	$2,105.4	$220.0	$124.1
	Printing and Publishing Papers	921.2	149.2	1,217.4	178.3	62.4
	Pulp, Forest Products and Minerals	166.3	17.6	188.4	16.7	11.6
	Total business segments	3,437.0	419.5	3,511.2	415.0	198.1
	Corporate	—	(51.1)	428.2	5.7	4.7
	Interest expense	—	(122.0)	—	—	—
	Other income and (expense)	—	28.7	—	—	—
	Consolidated total	$3,437.0	$275.1	$3,939.4	$420.7	$202.8
Geographic Area	United States	$2,786.6	$342.4	$2,870.4		
	Europe	580.1	66.4	575.5		
	Pacific	73.6	10.7	65.2		
		3,440.3	419.5	3,511.1		
	Intergeographic sales	(3.3)	—	—		
	Corporate	—	(51.1)	428.3		
	Interest expense	—	(122.0)	—		
	Other income and (expense)	—	28.7	—		
	Consolidated total	$3,437.0	$275.1	$3,939.4		

RJR Nabisco, Inc. (in millions):

	December 31, 19X7	19X6
Accounts and notes receivable (less allowances of $61 and $67, respectively)	$1,745	$1,675

Other companies, including CPC International, Inc., list the allowance on a separate line of the balance sheet, as follows (in millions):

	December 31, 19X7	19X6
Notes and accounts receivable [summarized]	$549.9	$592.5
Allowances for doubtful accounts	(12.5)	(14.2)

Both disclosure techniques provide adequate information on the total amount receivable and the net amount expected to be collected.

Constraints on Accounting

Do financial statements report every detail, no matter how small, to meet the need for relevant, reliable, and comparable information? The result would be an avalanche of data. To address this problem, accountants use the *materiality concept.* Also, a company's top managers are responsible for its financial statements. To add balance to managers' optimism—which could bias the statements and so present too favorable a picture of company operations — accountants follow the *conservatism concept*. This section discusses these constraints on accounting information.

Materiality Concept

[handwritten annotations: "1 paragraph what is it? why is it used?"]

The **materiality concept** states that a company must perform strictly proper accounting only for items and transactions that are significant to the business's financial statements. Information is significant — what accountants call *material* — when its inclusion and correct presentation in the financial statement would cause a statement user to change a decision because of that information. Immaterial — insignificant — items justify less than perfect accounting. The inclusion and proper presentation of *immaterial* items would not affect a statement user's decision. The materiality concept frees accountants from having to compute and report every last item in strict accordance with GAAP. Thus the materiality concept reduces the cost of recording accounting information.

> **OBJECTIVE 6**
> Apply two constraints to accounting

How does a business decide where to draw the line between what is material and what is immaterial? This decision rests to a great degree on how large the business is. Wendy's, for example, has close to $500 million in assets. Management would likely treat as immaterial a $100 purchase of wastebaskets. These wastebaskets may well remain useful for ten years, and strictly speaking, Wendy's should capitalize their cost and depreciate the wastebaskets. However, this treatment is not practical. The accounting cost of computing, recording, and properly reporting this asset outweighs the information provided. No statement user — a potential investor or lender, for example — would change a decision based on so insignificant (immaterial) an amount. The cost of accounting in this case outweighs the benefit of the resulting information.

Large companies may draw the materiality line at as high a figure as $10,000 and expense any smaller amount. Smaller firms may choose to expense only those items less than $50. Materiality varies from company to company. An amount that is material to the local service station may not be material to General Motors.

The materiality concept does not free a business from having to account for every item. Wendy's, for example, must still account for the wastebaskets. Wendy's would credit Cash (or Accounts Payable) to record their purchase, of course, but what account would the company debit? Because the amount is immaterial, management may decide to debit Supplies, which is an asset account, or Supplies Expense. No matter what account receives the debit, no statement user's decision would be changed by the information.

Conservatism Concept

Business managers are often optimists. Asked how well the company is doing, its president will likely answer, "Great, we're having our best year ever." Without constraints this optimism could find its way into the company's reported assets and profits. Managers may try to present too favorable a view of the company. For example, they may pressure accountants to capitalize costs associated with fixed assets that should be expensed. This would result in less immediate expense and higher current income on the income statement. The balance sheet would report unduly high fixed asset values and owner's equity. The overall result would be that the managers' performance would appear to be better than it actually was. Traditionally, accountants have been conservative, to counter management's optimism.

Conservatism has been interpreted as "Anticipate no profits, but anticipate all losses." A clear-cut example is the lower-of-cost-or-market (LCM) method for inventories. Under LCM, inventory is reported at the *lower* of its cost or market value, which results in higher cost of goods sold and lower net income. Thus profits and assets are reported at their lowest reasonable amount. Other conservative accounting practices include the LIFO method for inventories when inventory costs are increasing, accelerated depreciation, and the completed-contract method for construction revenues. These methods result in earlier recording of expenses or later recording of revenues. Both effects postpone the reporting of net income and therefore are conservative.

In recent years, conservatism's effect on accounting has decreased. The FASB has stated that conservatism should not mean deliberate understatement of assets, profits, and owner's equity. However, if two different values can be used for an asset or a liability, the concept suggests using the less optimistic value. Conservatism is a secondary consideration in accounting. Relevant, reliable, and comparable information is the goal, and conservatism is a factor only after these primary goals are met.

Financial Statements and Their Elements

We have examined the concepts and principles that shape accounting practice. The FASB aims for financial statements that best meet user needs for business information.

This accounting information appears in four statements: the balance sheet, the income statement, the statement of owner's equity, and the statement of cash flows (which we cover in Chapter 18). The FASB provides definitions for the elements that make up these statements. Financial information presentation, to be most useful to the greatest number of statements users, must be presented in a standard format with well-defined terms, as we learned in our discussion of the comparability concept.

FASB Concepts Statement No. 3 provides authoritative definitions of the elements of financial statements.[1]

Balance Sheet Elements

Assets are future economic benefits obtained or controlled by a particular entity as a result of past transactions.

Liabilities are the obligations of an entity to transfer assets or provide services to other entities as a result of past transactions.

OBJECTIVE 7

Name and define the elements of financial statements

Equity (Owner's Equity) is the interest in the assets of an entity that remains after subtracting its liabilities. It is the ownership interest in the entity.

Income Statement Elements

Revenues are inflows of assets that arise from delivering or producing goods, rendering services, or performing other activities that constitute the entity's ongoing central operations.

Expenses are outflows of assets or the incurrences of liabilities that arise from delivering or producing goods, rendering services, or carrying out activities that constitute the entity's ongoing central operations.

Gains are increases in owner's equity that do not result from revenues or investments by owners.

---

[1] The definitions here are paraphrased from FASB, *Concepts Statement No. 3,* "Elements of Financial Statements of Business Enterprises" (Stamford, CT: December 1980), highlights.

EXHIBIT 12-3 *Reporting Revenues, Expenses, Gains, and Losses*

Multiple-Step Income Statement			Single-Step Income Statement		
Sales revenue		$XXX	Revenues and gains:		
Cost of goods sold.................		XXX	Sales revenue...................		$XXX
Gross profit		XXX	Gain on sale of land		XXX
Operating expenses...............		XXX	Total revenues and gains.......		XXX
Income from operations		XXX	Expenses and losses:		
Other items:			Cost of goods sold..............	$XXX	
Gain on sale of land	$XXX		Operating expenses.............	XXX	
Loss due to fire.................	XXX	XXX	Loss due to fire.................	XXX	
			Total expenses and losses......		XXX
Net income....................		$XXX	Net income		$XXX

Losses are decreases in owner's equity that do not result from expenses or distributions to owners.

Note that *revenues* and *expenses* arise from the business's ongoing central operations, but *gains* and *losses* do not. Sales are revenues because most companies make sales and earn interest as part of their central operations. Selling cars and trucks lies at the heart of an automobile dealership. To this business, a gain on the sale of a truck is revenue, and a loss on the sale is expense. However, a gain on the sale of a truck is not revenue for a trucking company because that entity buys trucks for use rather than for sale. Selling a truck is not a part of central operations. Exhibit 12-3 shows how to report revenues, expenses, gains, and losses on a multiple-step and a single-step income statement.

Statement of Owner's Equity Elements

Investments by owners are increases in owner's equity that result from the owner's transferring to the entity something of value. The most common investment is cash, but owners sometimes invest land, buildings, legal services, or other assets. In some cases, an owner's investment in the business may consist of paying off its liabilities.

Distributions to owners are decreases in owner's equity that result from the owner's transferring assets or services from the business to himself or herself, or from the business taking on the owner's liabilities. When the business is a corporation, owner withdrawals are called dividends. The most commonly distributed asset is cash, but businesses sometimes distribute other assets, such as stock investments they hold in other companies, to their owners.

Summary Problem for Your Review

This chapter has discussed the following principles and concepts:

Entity concept	Cost principle
Going-concern concept	Revenue principle
Time-period concept	Matching principle
Reliability principle	Disclosure principle
Comparability principle	Materiality concept

Indicate which of these concepts is being violated in each of the following situations:

1. A construction company signs a two-year contract to build a bridge for the state of Montana. The president of the company immediately records the full contract price as revenue.

2. Competition has taken away much of the business of a small airline. The airline is unwilling to report its plans to sell half its fleet of planes.

3. After starting the business in February 19X2, a coal-mining company keeps no accounting records for 19X2, 19X3, and 19X4. The owner is waiting until the mine is exhausted to determine the success or failure of the business.

4. Assets recorded at cost by a drug store chain are written up to their fair market value at the end of each year.

5. The accountant for a manufacturing company keeps detailed depreciation records on every asset no matter how small its value.

6. A physician mixes her personal accounting records with those of the medical practice.

7. Expenses are reported whenever the bookkeeper records them rather than when related revenues are earned.

8. The damaged inventory of a discount store is being written down. The store manager bases the write-down entry on his own subjective opinion in order to minimize income taxes.

9. A quick-copy center changes accounting methods every year in order to report the maximum amount of net income possible under generally accepted accounting principles.

10. The owners of a private hospital base its accounting records on the assumption that the hospital might have to close at any time. The hospital has a long record of service to the community.

SOLUTION TO REVIEW PROBLEM

1. Revenue principle
2. Disclosure principle
3. Time-period concept
4. Cost principle
5. Materiality concept
6. Entity concept
7. Matching principle
8. Reliability principle
9. Comparability principle
10. Going-concern concept

Summary

The Financial Accounting Standards Board (FASB) formulates generally accepted accounting principles (GAAP) to provide relevant, reliable, and comparable accounting information. *Relevant* information allows users to make business predictions and to evaluate past decisions. *Reliable* data are free from material error and bias. Accounting information is also intended to be *comparable* from company to company and from period to period.

Four concepts underlie accounting. The most basic, the *entity concept,* draws clear boundaries around the accounting entity. The entity, based on the *going-concern concept* is assumed to remain in business for the foreseeable future. The *time-period concept* is the basis for reporting accounting information for particular time periods such as months, quarters, and years. Under the *stable-monetary-unit concept,* no adjustment is made for the changing value of the dollar.

Accounting principles provide detailed guidelines for recording transactions and preparing the financial statements. The *reliability* and *comparability principles* require that accounting information be based on objective data and be useful for comparing companies across different time periods. The *cost principle* governs accounting for assets and liabilities, and the *revenue principle* governs accounting for revenues. *Matching* is the basis for recording expenses. The *disclosure* principle requires companies to report their accounting policies, probable future losses, accounting changes, subsequent events, and business-segment data. They use different disclosure techniques.

Two constraints on accounting are materiality and conservatism. The *materiality concept* allows companies to avoid excessive cost in accounting for immaterial items. *Conservatism* constrains the optimism of managers by anticipating no profits, but anticipating all losses.

Financial statements and their elements include:

Balance sheet: assets, liabilities, and *equity (owner's equity)*

Income statement: revenues, expenses, gains, and *losses*

Statement of owner's equity: investments by owners and *distributions to owners.*

Self-Study Questions

Test your understanding of the chapter by marking the best answer for each of the following questions.

1. The organization that issues accounting pronouncements that make up GAAP is the *(p. 461, 462)*
    a. U.S. Congress
    b. Accounting Principles Board
    c. Financial Accounting Standards Board
    d. Securities and Exchange Commission

2. Which of the following characteristics of accounting information does the objective of financial reporting omit? *(p. 463)*
    a. Timeliness
    b. Relevance
    c. Reliability
    d. Comparability

3. A new business is starting. The president wishes to wait until significant contracts have been fulfilled before reporting the results of the business's operations. Which underlying concept serves as the basis for preparing financial statements at regular intervals? *(p. 465)*
    a. Entity
    b. Going concern
    c. Time period
    d. Stable monetary unit

4. Which of these revenue methods is the most conservative? *(pp. 468, 475, 476)*
    a. Sales method
    b. Collection method
    c. Percentage-of-completion method
    d. All the above are equally conservative

5. Suppose a Montgomery Ward store sells $10,000 worth of kitchen appliances on the installment plan and collects a down payment of $1,500. Ward's cost of the appliances is $7,000. How much gross profit will the company report this period under the installment revenue method *(pp. 468, 469)*
    a. $450
    b. $1,500
    c. $3,000
    d. $10,000

6. A construction company spent $180,000 during the current year on a building with a contract price of $900,000. The company estimated total construction cost at $720,000. How much construction *income* will the company report under the percentage-of-completion method? *(p. 470)*
    a. $45,000
    b. $144,000
    c. $180,000
    d. $225,000

7. Which of the following items should be disclosed to satisfy the disclosure principle? *(pp. 471, 472, 473)*
   a. Business segment data
   b. Probable losses
   c. Accounting changes
   d. All of the above

8. Important subsequent events should be disclosed because they *(p. 473)*
   a. Occur immediately after the current period
   b. Describe changes in accounting methods
   c. Reveal losses that have a high probability of occuring in the future
   d. May affect the interpretation of the current-period financial statements

9. Which of the following statements is most in keeping with the materiality concept? *(p. 475)*
   a. Accountants record material losses but are reluctant to record material gains
   b. Different companies have different materiality limits, depending on their size
   c. Business-segment data are disclosed to fulfill the materiality concept
   d. Companies report all the information needed to communicate a material view of the entity

10. Gains and losses are most similar to *(pp. 476, 477)*
    a. Assets and liabilities
    b. Revenues and expenses
    c. Investments by owners and distributions to owners

Answers to the self-study questions are at the end of the chapter.

Accounting Vocabulary

change in accounting estimate *(p. 472)*,   change in accounting principle *(p. 472)*,   collection method *(p. 468)*,   comparability principle *(p. 466)*,   completed-contract method *(p. 470)*,   cost principle *(p. 467)*,   disclosure principle *(p. 471)*,   gains *(p. 476)*,   going-concern concept *(p. 464)*,   installment method *(p. 468)*,   losses *(p. 477)*,   materiality concept *(p. 475)*, percentage-of-completion method *(p. 470)*,   reliability principle *(p. 466)*,   sales method *(p. 468)*,   stable-monetary-unit concept *(p. 465)*,   subsequent event (p. 473),   time-period concept *(p. 465)*.

ASSIGNMENT MATERIAL _____

Questions

1. How do accounting principles differ from natural laws?
2. State the basic objective of financial reporting.
3. What three characteristics make accounting information useful for decision making? Briefly discuss each characteristic.
4. What is the entity concept?
5. How does the going-concern concept affect accounting? What is liquidation?
6. Identify two practical results of the time-period concept.
7. What is the shortcoming of the stable-monetary-unit concept?
8. What are the two requirements of the comparability principle?
9. Why is consistency important in accounting?
10. Discuss the relationship between the cost principle and the reliability principle.
11. What three conditions must be met before revenue is recorded? What determines the amount of the revenue?
12. Which revenue recognition method is more conservative, the sales method or the collection method? Give your reason.
13. Suppose Montgomery Ward sold a lawn mower on an installment basis, receiving a down payment of $50 to be followed by 12 monthly installments of $12.50 each. If

Ward's cost of the mower was $120, how much gross profit would Ward record under the installment method (a) when the down payment is received and (b) when each installment is received?

14. Briefly discuss two methods of recognizing revenue on long-term construction contracts.

15. Give two examples of expenses that are easy to relate to sales revenue and two examples of expenses that are not so easy to relate to particular sales. On what basis are the latter expenses matched against revenue?

16. ABC Company agreed on November 22, 19X7, to sell an unprofitable manufacturing plant. ABC estimates on December 31 that the company is likely to incur a $4 million loss on the sale when it is finalized in 19X8. In which year should ABC report the loss? What accounting principle governs this situation?

17. Identify three items commonly disclosed in a company's summary of significant accounting policies.

18. What is a subsequent event? Why should companies disclose important subsequent events in their financial statements?

19. How does information on business segments help an investor?

20. Classify each of the following as a change in accounting principle or a change in accounting estimate:
    a. Change from straight-line to sum-of-years-digits depreciation.
    b. Change in the uncollectibility of accounts receivable.
    c. Change from LIFO to FIFO for inventory.
    d. Change from the percentage-of-completion method to the completed-contract method for revenue on long-term construction contracts.
    e. Change from an 8-year life to a 10-year life for a machine.
    f. Change in estimated warranty expense rate stated as a percent of sales.

21. Sloan Sales Company expenses the cost of plant assets below $500 at the time of purchase. What accounting concept allows this departure from strictly proper accounting? Why would Sloan Sales follow such a policy?

22. Give three examples of conservative accounting methods, stating why the methods are conservative.

23. Identify two balance sheet elements that are defined independently and give the definition of the third balance sheet element.

24. The four income statement elements may be divided into two pairs of similar elements. What elements make up these two pairs?

Exercises

Exercise 12-1 *Reporting assets under GAAP*

Identify the amount at which each of the following assets should be reported in the financial statements of Monroe Company. Cite the principle or concept that is most applicable to each answer.

a. Monroe purchased land for $100,000 and paid $2,500 to have the land surveyed, $15,400 to have old buildings removed, and $40,300 for landscaping. Monroe is offering the land for sale at $225,000 and has received a $200,000 offer.

b. Inventory has a cost of $45,000, but its current market value is $39,600.

c. Monroe purchased a machine for $25,000 less a $2,100 cash discount. To ship the machine to the office, Monroe paid transportation charges of $500 and insurance of $200 while in transit. After using the machine for one month, Monroe purchases lubricating oil costing $150 for use in operating the machine.

Exercise 12-2 *Reporting assets as a going concern and as a liquidating entity*

Lincoln Company has the following assets:

Cash, $15,000

Accounts Receivable, $25,600; allowance for uncollectible accounts, $4,300

Office supplies, cost $280; scrap value $70

Office machinery, cost $72,000; accumulated depreciation, $54,000; current sales value, $8,400

Land, cost $85,000; current sales value, $135,000

Required

1. Assume Lincoln continues as a going concern. Compute the amount of its assets for reporting on the balance sheet.
2. Assume Lincoln is going out of business by liquidating its assets. Compute the amount of its assets at liquidation value.

Use the following format for your answers.

	Assets of a Going Concern	Assets at Liquidation Value
Cash............................	$_____	$_____
Accounts receivable	$_____	
Less: Allowance for uncollectible accounts.........................	_____	_____
Office supplies.....................	_____	_____
Office machinery...................	_____	
Less: Accumulated depreciation.......	_____	
Land.............................	_____	_____
Total............................	$_____	$_____

Exercise 12-3 *Reporting revenues under GAAP*

For each of the following situations, indicate the amount of revenue to report for the current year ended December 31 and for the following year:

a. On July 1 collected one year's rent of $12,000 in advance on a building leased to another company.
b. Sold gift certificates, collecting $4,000 in advance. At December 31, $2,200 of the gifts have been claimed. The remainder were claimed during the next year.
c. Sold merchandise for $5,900, receiving a down payment of $1,100 and the customer's receivable for the balance. The company accounts for these sales by the sales method.
d. On April 1 loaned $25,000 at 12 percent on a three-year note.
e. Performed $900 of services for a high-risk customer on August 18, accounting for the revenue by the collection method. At December 31 the company had received $200 of the total; $550 was received the following year.

Exercise 12-4 *Reporting income under GAAP*

Lotus Management Company failed to record the following items at December 31, 19X4, the end of its fiscal year:

Accrued salary expense, $2,800	Prepaid insurance, $400
Accrued interest expense, $600	Depreciation expense, $500

Instead of recording the accrued expenses at December 31, 19X4, Lotus recorded the expenses when it paid them in 19X5. The company recorded the insurance as expense when it was prepaid for one year, late in 19X4. Depreciation expense for 19X5 was correctly recorded.

Lotus incorrectly reported net income of $9,000 in 19X4 and $5,300 in 19X5 because of the above errors.

Required

Compute Lotus's correct net income for 19X4 and 19X5.

Exercise 12-5 *Computing gross profit under the sales method and the installment method*

Allied Appliance Store sells on the installment plan. The store's installment sales figures for 19X7 follow.

Sales	$420,000
Down payments received on the sales	80,000
Collections on installments	170,000
Inventory at beginning of 19X7............	60,000
Inventory at end of 19X7................	45,000
Purchases	216,000

Required

Compute the store's gross profit if it uses (a) the sales method of revenue recognition and (b) the installment method.

Exercise 12-6 *Computing construction revenue under the completed-contract method and the percentage-of-completion method*

McMinn Construction Company builds bridges for the state of Florida. The construction period typically extends for several years. During 19X5 McMinn completed a small bridge with a contract price of $400,000. McMinn's $320,000 cost of the bridge was incurred as follows: $20,000 in 19X3, $180,000 in 19X4, and $120,000 in 19X5. Compute McMinn's revenue for each year 19X3 through 19X5 if the company uses (a) the completed-contract method and (b) the percentage-of-completion method.

Exercise 12-7 *Changing the useful life of a depreciable asset*

McMinn Construction Company uses a crane on its construction projects. The company purchased the crane early in January 19X3 for $500,000. For 19X3 and 19X4 depreciation was taken by the straight-line method based on a six-year life and an estimated residual value of $80,000. In early 19X5 it became evident that the crane would be useful beyond the original life of six years. Therefore, beginning in 19X5, McMinn changed the depreciable life of the crane to a total life of nine years. The company retained the straight-line method and did not alter the residual value.

Required

Prepare McMinn's depreciation entries for 19X4 and 19X5.

Exercise 12-8 *Identifying subsequent events for the financial statements*

Bush, Inc., experienced the following events after May 31, 19X8, the end of the company's fiscal year, but before publication of its financial statements on July 12:

a. Bush collected $126,000 of the $480,000 accounts receivable reported on the May 31 balance sheet. Bush expects to collect the remainder in the course of business during the next fiscal year.

b. A major customer, who owed Bush $220,000 at May 31, declared bankruptcy on June 21.

c. Bush sales personnel received a contract to supply Bronson Company with laser equipment.

d. Increased demand for Bush products suggests that the next fiscal year will be the best in the company's history.

e. On July 6 Bush is sued for $3 million. Loss of the lawsuit could lead to Bush's bankruptcy.

Required

Identify the subsequent events that Bush should disclose in its May 31, 19X8, financial statements.

Exercise 12-9 *Using accounting concepts and principles*

Identify the accounting concept or principle, if any, that is violated in each of the following situations. You may choose from among *disclosure, conservatism, cost, entity,* and *matching.*

a. The owner of a travel agency used the business bank account to pay her family's household expenses, making no note that the expenses were personal.

b. A manufacturing company changed from the FIFO inventory method to the LIFO method and failed to report the accounting change in the financial statements.

c. A paper company that purchased 5,000 acres of timberland at $150 per acre in 1953 reports the land at its current market value of $3,000 per acre.

d. A railroad records depreciation during years when net income is high but fails to record depreciation when net income is low. Revenues are relatively constant.

e. The inventory of a clothing store has a current market value of $80,000. The store reports the inventory at its cost of $124,000.

Exercise 12-10 *Using accounting concepts and principles*

Indicate the accounting concept or principle that applies to the following situations. Choose from among *comparability, materiality, reliability, revenue,* and *time period.*

a. New Wave Distributors expenses the cost of plant assets that cost less than $300.

b. Although Bracken Company could increase its reported income by changing depreciation methods, Bracken management has decided not to make the change.

c. Lim Ting Restaurant was recently sued for $200,000, but the plaintiff has indicated a willingness to settle for less than that amount. Lim Ting hopes to settle for $50,000, but their attorneys believe the settlement will be between $90,000 and $100,000. Lim Ting's auditor reports it as a real liability on the balance sheet. The only remaining issue is whether to report the liability at $50,000 or at $95,000.

d. Northern Union Company is considering publishing quarterly financial statements to provide more current information about its affairs.

e. POA, Inc., is negotiating the sale of $500,000 of inventory. POA has been in financial difficulty and desperately needs to report this sale on its income statement of the current year. At December 31, the end of the company's accounting year, the sale has not been closed.

Problems   (Group A)

Problem 12-1A *Identifying the basis for good accounting practices*

The following accounting practices are in accord with generally accepted accounting principles. Identify all the accounting concepts and principles that form the basis for each accounting practice. More than one concept or principle may apply.

a. The personal residence of the owner of a freight company is not disclosed in the financial statements of the business.

b. A manufacturing company's plant assets are carried on the books at cost under the assumption that the company will remain in operation for the foreseeable future.

c. A clothing store discloses in notes to its financial statements that it uses the FIFO inventory method.

d. A real estate developer paid $450,000 for land and held it for three years before selling it for $800,000. There was significant inflation during this period, but the developer reports the $350,000 gain on sale with no adjustment for the change in the value of the dollar.

e. Liabilities are reported in two categories, current and long-term.

f. A travel agent's payments for fire insurance are so small that the company expenses them and makes no year-end adjustment for prepaid insurance.

g. The inventory of a personal computer store declined substantially in value because of changing technology, and the store wrote its computer inventory down to the lower of cost or market.

h. A construction company changed from the completed-contract method to the percentage-of-completion method of recording revenue on its long-term construction contracts. The company disclosed this accounting change in the notes to its financial statements.

i. A mining company recorded an intangible asset at the cost of the mineral lease and all other cost necessary to bring the mine to the point of production. After the mine was in operation, the company amortized the asset's cost as expense in proportion to the revenues from sale of the minerals.

j. Because of a downturn in the economy, a jeweler increased his business's allowance for doubtful accounts.

Problem 12-2A   *Identifying the concepts and principles violated by bad accounting practices*

The following accounting practices are *not* in accord with generally accepted accounting principles. Identify the single accounting concept or principle that is most clearly violated by each accounting practice.

a. Royal Iron Works regularly changes accounting methods in order to report a target amount of net income each year.

b. Texas Land Company reports land at its market value of $820,000, which is greater than the cost of $400,000.

c. A flood on July 2 caused $150,000 in damage to Tyler Construction property. The company did not report the flood as a subsequent event in the June 30 financial statements.

d. Hernandez, Inc., overstates depreciation expense in order to report low amounts of net income.

e. The balance sheet of Rhonda Green's medical practice includes receivables that she will probably never collect. Nevertheless, Green's accountant refuses to use the collection method to account for revenue.

f. The current market value of Miska Electronics's inventory is $65,000, but the company reports its inventory at cost of $91,000. The decline in value is permanent.

g. The liabilities of Waco Jet Company exceed the company's assets. In order to get a loan from the bank, Waco Jet's owner, Slade McQueen, includes his personal investments as assets on the balance sheet of the business.

h. Lancer Corporation increases the carrying value of its land based on recent sales of adjacent property.

i. Mission Ford Sales records expenses on an irregular basis without regard to the pattern of the company's revenues.

j. Frisco Software Company omits the significant accounting policies note from its financial statements because the company uses the same accounting methods that its competitors use.

Problem 12-3A   *Recording and reporting transactions according to GAAP*

The accounting records of San Felipe Wholesale Distributors reveal the following information prior to closing the books at September 30, the end of the current fiscal year:

a. Accounts receivable include $42,000 from Glenwood Drug Company, which has declared bankruptcy. San Felipe, which uses the allowance method to account for bad debts, expects to receive one third of the amount receivable from Glenwood.

b. No interest has been accrued on a $50,000, 12 percent, six-month note receivable that was received on May 31.

c. The merchandise inventory, with a cost of $69,000, has a current market value of only $31,000. San Felipe uses a periodic inventory system and has not made the September 30 entry to record ending inventory.

d. Accrued salaries of $21,800 have been earned by San Felipe employees but have not been recorded at September 30 because the company plans to record the salaries when it pays them in October.

e. The company's office building has been valued recently by independent appraisers at $400,000. This valuation is $180,000 more than San Felipe paid for the building and is $270,000 more than its cost less accumulated depreciation.

f. Two years ago on October 1, San Felipe paid $120,000 for its delivery trucks. During the prior year the company has depreciated the trucks by the straight-line method over an expected useful life of 4 years, using a residual value of $20,000. After using the trucks for the first year, San Felipe decided at the beginning of the current year that the trucks will remain in service for a total of 5 years. The company will continue to use the straight-line method and the $20,000 residual value for accounting purposes.

g. On October 19, before San Felipe issued its financial statements for the year ended September 30, a competitor sued the company for damages of $500,000. Attorneys for San Felipe believe San Felipe will win the case. However, a $500,000 loss would make it difficult for the company to continue in business.

Required

Make all journal entries needed at September 30 to record this information. Explanations are not required. Identify those items *not* requiring a journal entry, giving the reason why an entry is not needed. If a note to the financial statements is needed, write the note.

Problem 12-4A   *Using the installment-revenue method*

Fountain City Appliances sells on the installment plan. Collections of installment receivables have deteriorated. The store's accountants are considering the different methods of recording revenues. Revenue, expense, and collection data for the current year are as follows:

	19X6
Installment sales.	$90,000
Cost of goods sold	54,000
Collections of installment receivables from sales of 19X5.	20,000
19X6.	24,000

The gross profit percentage on 19X5 installment sales was 42 percent.

Required

1. Which method should be used to account for revenues if collections are reasonably assured? If collections are extremely doubtful? Which method is more advantageous for income tax purposes? Why?

2. Compute gross profit for 19X6 under the sales method, the collection method, and the installment method.

Problem 12-5A *Using the installment-revenue method*

Pine Valley Appliance Store makes all sales on the installment basis but uses the sales method to record revenue. The company's income statements for the most recent three years follow.

	Year 1	Year 2	Year 3
Sales	$240,000	$210,000	$290,000
Cost of goods sold	144,000	121,800	179,800
Gross profit	96,000	88,200	110,200
Operating expenses	51,400	49,300	61,300
Net income	$ 44,600	$ 38,900	$ 48,900
Collections from sales of year 1	$ 80,000	$105,000	$ 40,000
Collections from sales of year 2		68,000	120,000
Collections from sales of year 3			145,000

Required

Compute the amount of net income Pine Valley would have reported if the company had used the installment method for revenue. Ignore the effect of uncollectible accounts and present your answer in the following format:

Installment-method net income:	Year 1	Year 2	Year 3
Gross profit	$	$	$
Operating expenses	51,400	49,300	61,300
Net income	$	$	$

Problem 12-6A *Accounting for construction income*

Newport Shipbuilding Company participates in the construction of small ships under long-term contracts. During 19X7 Newport began three projects that progressed according to the following schedule during 19X7, 19X8, and 19X9:

Project	Contract Price	Total Project Cost	19X7		19X8		19X9	
			Cost for Year	% Completed During Year	Cost for Year	% Completed During Year	Cost for Year	% Completed During Year
1	$3,500,000	$2,800,000	$ 924,000	33%	$1,876,000	67%	—	—
2	1,200,000	880,000	880,000	100	—	—	—	—
3	7,400,000	6,300,000	1,260,000	20	2,205,000	35	$2,835,000	45%

Required

1. Assume Newport uses the completed-contract method for construction revenue. Compute the company's construction revenue and income to be reported in 19X7, 19X8, and 19X9.
2. Compute Newport's construction revenue and income to be reported in the three years if the company uses the percentage-of-completion method.

Problem 12-7A *Accounting for revenues and expenses according to GAAP*

Nathan Nielsen established Nielsen Furniture Importers in January 19X4 to import furniture from Denmark. During 19X4 and 19X5 Nielsen kept the company's books and prepared the financial statements, although he had no training or experience in accounting. As a result, the accounts contain numerous errors. Nielsen recorded revenue from sales on the collection method, which is not appropriate for the company. Nielsen should have been using the sales method for revenues. He also recorded inventory purchases as the cost of goods sold.

When the value of the company warehouse increased by $35,000 in 19X6, Nielsen recorded an increase in the Warehouse Building account and credited Revenue. On January 2, 19X4, he borrowed $100,000 on a 9 percent, three-year note. He intended to wait until 19X7, when the note was due, to record the full amount of interest expense for three years. The company's records reveal the following amounts:

	19X4	19X5	19X6
Reported net income (net loss)...............	$ (24,200)	$ 41,600	$ 44,100
Sales	256,700	303,500	366,800
Cash collections from customers	210,400	309,000	317,800
Purchases of inventory......................	141,000	187,400	202,300
Ending inventory	35,800	59,900	73,400
Accrued expenses not recorded at year end; these expenses were recorded during the next year, when paid	13,500	22,600	30,100
Interest expense recorded....................	-0-	-0-	-0-
Revenue recorded for increase in the value of the warehouse building			35,000

Required

In early 19X7 Nielsen employed you as an accountant. Apply the concepts and principles of GAAP to compute the correct net income of Nielsen Furniture Importers for 19X4, 19X5, and 19X6.

(Group B)

Problem 12-1B   *Identifying the basis for good accounting practices*

The following accounting practices are in accord with generally accepted accounting principles. Identify all the accounting concepts and principles that form the basis for each accounting practice. More than one concept or principle may apply.

a. The cost of office equipment such as staplers and wastebaskets is not capitalized and depreciated because of their relative insignificance.

b. A fire destroyed the company warehouse after December 31, 19X7, and before the financial statements were published in early February 19X8. Although the fire loss is insured, reconstruction of the warehouse will disrupt the company's operations. This subsequent event will be reported in the 19X7 financial statements.

c. A chemical company accounts for its operations by dividing the business into four separate units. This division enables the company to evaluate each unit apart from the others.

d. A building-materials company accrues employee salaries at year end even though the salaries will be paid during the first few days of the new year.

e. Assets are reported at liquidation value on the financial statements of a company that is going out of business.

f. The cost of machinery is being depreciated over a 5-year life because independent engineers believe the machinery will become obsolete after that time. (The company had hoped to depreciate the machinery over 10 years to report lower depreciation and higher net income in the early years of the asset's life.)

g. A manufacturing firm built some specialized equipment for its own use. The equipment would have cost $75,000 if purchased from an outside company, but the cost of constructing the equipment was only $48,000. The firm recorded the equipment at cost of $48,000.

h. Depreciation of the home-office building is difficult to relate to particular sales. Therefore, the company records depreciation expense on a time basis.

i. A company wishes to change its method of accounting for revenue. However, the company does not switch because it wants to use the same accounting method that other companies in the industry use.

j. Because it is often difficult to collect installment receivables, a retailer uses the installment method of revenue recognition rather than the sales method.

Problem 12-2B *Identifying the concepts and principles violated by bad accounting practices*

The following accounting practices are *not* in accord with generally accepted accounting principles. A few of the practices violate more than one concept or principle. Identify all the accounting concepts and principles not followed in each situation.

a. Butler Manufacturing does not report a lawsuit in which it is the defendant. Alvin Butler, the president, argues that the outcome of the case is uncertain and that to report the lawsuit would introduce subjective data into the financial statements.

b. Todd Department Store records cost of goods sold in a predetermined amount each month regardless of the level of sales.

c. Tim Ihnacek is having difficulty evaluating the success of his advertising firm because he fails to separate business assets from personal assets.

d. Tapes Unlimited is continuing in business, but its owner accounts for assets as though the store were liquidating.

e. Major Construction Company recognizes all revenue on long-term construction projects at the start of construction.

f. All amounts on the balance sheet and income statement of Business Products Company have been adjusted for changes in the value of the dollar during the period.

g. Rizzuto Grain Company records one half of the depreciation of its grain silos when it purchases them and the other half over their estimated useful lives.

h. Day's Boutique sells high-fashion clothing to customers on credit. Thus far, collection losses on receivables have been very small. Nevertheless, Bonnie Day, the owner, uses the collection method to recognize revenue. The entity's revenue is understated because credit sales are not accounted for properly.

i. Alvarez Importers changed from the FIFO method to the LIFO method for inventory but did not report the accounting change in the financial statements.

j. Martin Supply Company applied the lower-of-cost-or-market method to account for its inventory. Martin used an estimate of the inventory value developed by its management. This estimate differed widely from estimates supplied by two independent appraisers. The estimates of the two appraisers were close together.

Problem 12-3B *Recording and reporting transactions according to GAAP*

The accounting records of Mortensen Publishing Company reveal the following information prior to closing the books at April 30, the end of the current fiscal year:

a. Accounts receivable include $29,800 from Miller Bookstore, which has declared bankruptcy. Mortensen, which uses the allowance method to account for bad debts, expects to receive only one fourth of the amount receivable from Miller.

b. No interest has been accrued on a $60,000, 11 percent, 90-day note payable issued on March 31.

c. The merchandise inventory, with a cost of $54,000, has a current market value of only $40,700. Mortensen uses a periodic inventory system and has not made the April 30 entry to record ending inventory.

d. Property tax is due each April 30, and Mortensen has received the city/county property tax bill of $3,650. However, the company has not recorded property tax at April 30 because Mortensen plans to record the tax when it is paid in May.

e. The company's office building was recently valued by independent appraisers at

$640,000. This valuation is $290,000 more than Mortensen paid for the building and is $410,000 more than its cost less accumulated depreciation.

f. Three years ago on May 1, Mortensen paid $440,000 for its printing equipment. The company has depreciated the equipment by the straight-line method over an expected useful life of 10 years using a residual value of $40,000. Having used the equipment for 2 years, Mortensen determined at the beginning of the current year that it will remain in service for a total of only 8 years. The company will continue to use the straight-line method and $40,000 residual value for accounting purposes.

g. On May 13, before Mortensen issued its financial statements for the year ended April 30, the company's principal customer, Mears, Rareback and Co., declared its intention to cease doing business with Mortensen. This event is significant because for the past 10 years Mears has accounted for approximately 65 percent of Mortensen's sales. Consequently, Mortensen's ability to sustain its recent level of sales in future years is seriously in doubt.

Required

Make all journal entries needed at April 30 to record this information. Explanations are not required. Identify those items *not* requiring a journal entry, giving the reason why an entry is not needed. If a note to the financial statements is needed, write the note.

Problem 12-4B   *Using the installment-revenue method*

Bayview Resorts sells land on the installment plan. Collections of installment receivables have deteriorated. The company's accountants are considering the different methods of recording revenues. Revenue, expense, and collection data for the current year are as follows:

	19X3
Installment sales	$1,200,000
Cost of land sold	660,000
Collections of installment receivables from sales of 19X2	240,000
19X3	210,000

The gross profit percentage on 19X2 installment sales was 46 percent.

Required

1. Which method should be used to account for revenues if collections are extremely doubtful? If collections are reasonably assured? Which method is more advantageous for income tax purposes? Why?
2. Compute gross profit for 19X3 under the sales method, the collection method, and the installment method.

Problem 12-5B   *Using the installment-revenue method*

Meridian Electrical makes all sales on the installment basis but uses the sales method to record revenue. The company's income statements for the most recent three years are as follows:

	Year 1	Year 2	Year 3
Sales	$380,000	$404,000	$370,000
Cost of goods sold	190,000	181,800	199,800
Gross profit	190,000	222,200	170,200
Operating expenses	110,600	130,700	125,100
Net income	$ 79,400	$ 91,500	$ 45,100
Collections from sales of year 1	$108,000	$181,000	$ 82,000
Collections from sales of year 2		143,000	209,000
Collections from sales of year 3			163,000

Required

Compute the amount of net income Meridian would have reported if the company had used the installment method for revenue. Ignore the effect of uncollectible accounts and present your answer in the following format:

Installment-method net income:	Year 1	Year 2	Year 3
Gross profit	$	$	$
Operating expenses.........	110,600	130,700	125,100
Net income	$	$	$

Problem 12-6B   *Accounting for construction income*

Diamond Bridge Company constructs bridges under long-term contracts. During 19X5, Diamond began three projects that progressed according to the following schedule during 19X5, 19X6, and 19X7:

			19X5		19X6		19X7	
Project	Contract Price	Total Project Cost	Cost for Year	% Completed During Year	Cost for Year	% Completed During Year	Cost for Year	% Completed During Year
1	$2,100,000	$1,600,000	$1,600,000	100%	—	—	—	—
2	3,100,000	2,200,000	484,000	22	$1,716,000	78%	—	—
3	1,800,000	1,400,000	140,000	10	840,000	60	$420,000	30%

Required

1. Assume Diamond uses the completed-contract method for construction revenue. Compute the company's construction revenue and income to be reported in 19X5, 19X6, and 19X7.

2. Compute Diamond's construction revenue and income to be reported in the three years if the company uses the percentage-of-completion method.

Problem 12-7B   *Accounting for revenues and expenses according to GAAP*

Roberta Katz established Katz Home Furnishings in January 19X7. During 19X7, 19X8, and most of 19X9 Katz kept the company's books and prepared its financial statements, although she had no training or experience in accounting. As a result, the accounts and statements contain numerous errors. For example, Katz recorded only cash receipts from customers as revenue. The sales method is appropriate for the business. She recorded inventory purchases as the cost of goods sold. When the current market value of her company's inventory increased by $15,600 in 19X7 and by $3,900 in 19X9, Katz debited the Inventory account and credited Revenue. She recorded no depreciation during 19X7, 19X8, and 19X9.

Late in 19X9 Katz employed an accountant, who determined that depreciable assets of the firm cost $170,000 on June 30, 19X7, had an expected residual value of $10,000, and a total useful life of eight years. The accountant believes the straight-line depreciation method is appropriate for Katz's plant assets. The company's fiscal year ends December 31. At the end of 19X9 the company's records reveal the amounts on the following page.

Required

Apply the concepts and principles of GAAP to compute the correct net income of Katz Home Furnishings for 19X7, 19X8, and 19X9.

	19X7	19X8	19X9
Reported net income (net loss)..................	$ 9,300	$ (11,200)	$ 52,900
Sales	131,800	164,700	226,100
Cash collections from customers	106,500	151,300	239,600
Purchases of inventory.......................	100,600	136,000	191,700
Ending inventory	20,800	47,400	83,700
Accrued expenses not recorded at year end; these expenses were recorded during the next year, when paid............	3,800	2,700	6,800
Depreciation expense recorded	-0-	-0-	-0-
Revenue recorded for increase in the value of inventory	15,600		3,900

Decision Problem

Measuring Income According to GAAP

O'Hara Furniture Company was founded in January 19X5 by Bernard and Virginia O'Hara, who share the management of the business. Virginia does the purchasing and manages the sales staff. Bernard keeps the books and handles financial matters. The O'Haras believe the store has prospered, but they are uncertain about precisely how well it has done. It is now December 31, 19X5, and they are trying to decide whether to borrow a substantial sum in order to expand the business.

They have asked your help because of your accounting knowledge. You learn that the O'Haras opened the store with an initial investment of $45,000 cash and a building valued at $100,000. The cash receipts totaled $180,000, which included collections, $15,000 invested by the O'Haras, $50,000 borrowed from the bank in the name of the furniture store, and $7,500 of earnings from a family inheritance. The store made credit sales of $95,000 that have not been collected at December 31. The O'Haras purchased furniture inventory on credit for $160,000, and inventory at December 31, 19X5, was $75,000. The store paid $90,000 on account.

The 19X5 cash expenses were $92,000. Additional miscellaneous expenses totaled $2,700 at year's end. These expenses included the O'Haras' household costs of $10,000 and interest on the business debt. The $5,000 of depreciation on the store building was omitted.

Bernard and Virginia have decided to proceed with the expansion plan only if net income for the first year was $40,000 or more. Bernard's analysis of the cash account leads him to believe that net income was $43,000, so he is ready to expand. You are less certain than Bernard of the wisdom of this decision primarily because the O'Haras have mixed personal and business assets.

Required

1. Use a Cash T-account to show how Bernard arrived at the $43,000 amount for net income.
2. Prepare the income statement of the furniture store for 19X5.
3. Should the O'Haras borrow to expand their business?
4. Which accounting concept or principle is most fundamental to this problem situation?

Financial Statement Problem

Disclosure in action
The most fundamental note in a company's financial statement is the summary of significant policies. Examine Gulf+Western's statements in Appendix C, and answer these questions.

1. The section headed "Theatrical and Television Inventories, Revenues and Costs" in Note A—Significant Accounting Policies tells how Gulf+Western accounts for its theatrical and television revenues. When does the company record theatrical revenues? Revenues from television license agreements? Revenues from the sale of videocassettes?
2. The last paragraph in the "theatrical" section in Note A refers to *unamortized film costs.* What does this term mean? What was this item's remaining life at October 31, 1987?
3. Do the notes indicate any important subsequent events? If so, describe them.
4. Page 26—immediately after the income statement—reports revenues and operating income by business segment. Which segment produced the most revenue in fiscal 1987? Which segment generated the highest operating income?
5. Explain how the concept of materiality is clearly evident in the financial statements.

Answers to Self-Study Questions

1. c
2. a
3. c
4. b
5. a ($10,000 − $7,000)/$10,000 = .30 × $1,500 = $450
6. a $180,000/$720,000 = .25 × $900,000 = $225,000; $225,000 − $180,000 = $45,000
7. d
8. d
9. b
10. b

13

Accounting for Partnerships

LEARNING OBJECTIVES
After studying this chapter, you should be able to

1 Identify the characteristics, including advantages and disadvantages, of a partnership

2 Account for partners' initial investments in a partnership

3 Use different methods to allocate profits and losses to the partners

4 Account for the admission of a new partner to the business

5 Account for the withdrawal of a partner from the business

6 Account for the liquidation of a partnership

Forming a partnership is easy. It requires no permission from government authorities and involves no legal procedures. When two persons decide to go into business together, a partnership is automatically formed.

A **partnership** is an association of two or more persons who co-own a business for profit. This definition stems from the Uniform Partnership Act, which nearly every state has adopted to regulate partnership practice.

A partnership brings together the capital, talents, and experience of the partners. Business opportunities closed to an individual may open up to a partnership. Suppose neither Pedigo nor Lee has enough capital individually to buy a $300,000 parcel of land. They may be able to afford it together in a partnership. Or VanAllen, a tax accountant, and Kahn, an investment counselor, may pool their talents and know-how. Their partnership may offer a fuller range of money management services than either person could offer alone. Combining their experience may increase income for each of them.

Partnerships come in all sizes. Many partnerships have fewer then 10 partners. Some physician and law firms may have 20 or more partners. The largest CPA firms have 1,000 or more partners.

Characteristics of a Partnership _____

Starting a partnership is voluntary. A person cannot be forced to join a partnership, and partners cannot be forced to accept another person as a partner. Although the partnership agreement may be oral, a written agreement between the partners reduces the chance of a misunderstanding. Several features are unique to the partnership form of business. The following characteristics distinguish partnerships from sole proprietorships and corporations, which we examine in later chapters.

The Written Partnership Agreement

OBJECTIVE 1

Identify the characteristics, including advantages and disadvantages, of a partnership

A business partnership is like a marriage. To be successful, the partners must cooperate. However, business partners do not vow to remain together for life. Business partnerships come and go. To make certain that each partner fully understands how a particular partnership operates, and to cut down on the chances that any partner might misunderstand how the business is run, partners may draw up a **partnership agreement,** also called the **articles of partnership.** This agreement is a contract between the partners, so transactions involving the agreement are governed by contract law. The articles of partnership should make the following points clear:

1. Name, location, and nature of the business
2. Name, capital investment, and duties of each partner
3. Method of sharing profits and losses by the partners
4. Withdrawals allowed to the partners
5. Procedures for settling disputes between the partners
6. Procedures for admitting new partners
7. Procedures for settling up with a partner who withdraws from the business
8. Procedures for liquidating the partnership—selling the assets, paying the liabilities, and disbursing any remaining cash to the partners

As partners enter and leave the business, the old partnership is dissolved and a new partnership is formed. Drawing up a separate agreement for each new partnership may be expensive and time consuming.

Limited Life

A partnership has a life limited by the length of time that all partners continue to own the business. When a partner withdraws from the business, that partnership ceases to exist. A new partnership may emerge to continue the same business, but the old partnership has been *dissolved.* **Dissolution** is the ending of a partnership. Likewise, the addition of a new partner dissolves the old partnership and creates a new partnership. Partnerships are sometimes formed for a particular business venture, like a mining operation or a real estate investment. When the mine is depleted or the real estate is sold, the partnership may be dissolved.

Mutual Agency

Mutual agency in a partnership means that every partner can bind the business to a contract within the scope of the partnership's regular business operations. If an individual partner in a CPA firm enters into a contract with a person or another business to provide accounting service, then the firm—not the individual who signs the contract—is bound to provide that service. However, if that same CPA signs a contract to purchase home lawn services for the summer months, the partnership would not be bound to pay. Contracting for lawn services does not fall within the partnership's regular business operations.

Unlimited Liability

Each partner has an **unlimited personal liability** for the debts of the partnership. When a partnership cannot pay its debts with business assets, the partners must use their personal assets to meet the debt.

Avilla and Davis are the two partners in AD Company. The business has had an unsuccessful year, and the partnership's liabilities exceed its assets by $120,000. Davis and Avilla must pay this amount with their personal assets.

Recall that each partner has *unlimited* liability. If a partner is unable to pay his or her part of the debt, the other partner (or partners) must make payment. If Davis can pay only $50,000 of the liability, Avilla must pay $70,000 ($120,000 − $50,000).

Unlimited liability and mutual agency are closely related. A dishonest partner or a partner with poor judgment may commit the partnership to a contract under which the business loses money. In turn, creditors may force *all* the partners to pay the debt from their personal assets. Hence, a business partner should be chosen with great care.

Co-ownership of Property

Any asset — cash, inventory, machinery, and so on — that a partner invests in the partnership becomes the joint property of all the partners. Also, each partner has a claim to the business's profits.

No Partnership Income Taxes

A partnership pays no income tax on its business income. Instead, the net income of the partnership is divided and becomes the taxable income of the partners. Suppose AD Company earned net income of $80,000, shared equally by partners Avilla and Davis. AD Company would pay no income tax *as a business entity*. However, Avilla and Davis would pay income tax as individuals on their $40,000 shares of partnership income.

Accounting for a partnership is much like accounting for a proprietorship. We record buying and selling, collecting and paying in a partnership just as we do for a business with only one owner. However, because a partnership has more than one owner, the partnership must have more than one owner's equity account. Every partner in the business — whether the firm has two or two thousand partners — has an individual owner's equity account. Often these accounts carry the name of the particular partner and the word *capital*. For example, the owner's equity account for Larry Insdorf would read "Insdorf, Capital." Similarly, each partner has a withdrawal account. If the number of partners is large, the general ledger may contain the single account Partners' Capital, or Owners' Equity. A subsidiary ledger can be used for individual partner accounts.

Let's see how to account for the multiple owner's equity accounts — and learn how they appear on the balance sheet — by taking a look at how to account for starting up a partnership.

Initial Investments by Partners _____

Partners in a new partnership may invest assets and liabilities in the business. These contributions are entered in the books in the same way that a proprietor's assets and liabilities are recorded. Subtracting each person's liabilities from his or her assets yields the amount to be credited to the capital account for that person. Often the partners hire an independent firm to appraise their assets and liabilities at current market value at the time a partnership is formed. This outside evaluation assures an objective accounting for what each partner brings into the business.

Assume Benz and Hanna form a partnership to manufacture and sell computer software. Benz brings to the partnership cash of $10,000, accounts receivable of $30,000, inventory of $70,000, computer equipment with a cost of $400,000, and accounts payable of $85,000. Hanna contributes cash of $5,000 and a software program. The development of this program cost Hanna $18,000, but its current market value is much greater. Suppose the partners agree on the following values based on an independent appraisal:

Benz's contributions:

Cash, $10,000; inventory, $70,000; and accounts payable, $85,000 (the appraiser believes the current market values for these items equal Benz's values)
Accounts receivable, $30,000, less allowance for doubtful accounts of $5,000
Computer equipment, $500,000, less accumulated depreciation of $50,000

Hanna's contributions:

Cash, $5,000
Computer software, $100,000

Note that current market value differs only slightly from book value for Benz's computer equipment. However, the appraiser valued Hanna's $18,000 computer software at the much higher $100,000 figure. The partners record their initial investments at the current market values. The title of each owner's equity account includes the owner's name and *Capital* — exactly as for a proprietorship.

Benz's investment:

OBJECTIVE 2

Account for partners' initial investments in a partnership

June 1	Cash	10,000	
	Accounts Receivable	30,000	
	Inventory	70,000	
	Computer Equipment	500,000	
	Allowance for Doubtful Accounts		5,000
	Accumulated Depreciation		50,000
	Accounts Payable		85,000
	Benz, Capital		470,000
	To record Benz's investment in the partnership.		

Hanna's investment:

June 1	Cash	5,000	
	Computer Software	100,000	
	Hanna, Capital.		105,000
	To record Hanna's investment in the partnership.		

The initial partnership balance sheet reports these amounts as follows:

Benz and Hanna				
Balance Sheet				
June 1, 19X5				

Assets			Liabilities	
Cash.		$ 15,000	Accounts payable . . .	$ 85,000
Accounts receivable .	$ 30,000			
Less allowance for				
doubtful accounts	(5,000)	25,000		
Inventory.		70,000	**Capital**	
Computer equipment	500,000			
Less accumulated			Benz, capital	470,000
depreciation.	50,000	450,000	Hanna, capital.	105,000
Computer software. .		100,000	Total liabilities and	
Total assets		$660,000	capital	$660,000

Each owner's capital account appears under the heading Capital. Having more than one capital account distinguishes a partnership balance sheet from a proprietorship balance sheet.

Sharing Partnership Profits and Losses _____

How to distribute profits and losses among partners is one of the most challenging aspects of managing a partnership. If the partners have not drawn up an agreement, or if the agreement does not state how the partners will divide profits and losses, then, according to law, the partners must share profits and losses equally. If the agreement specifies a method for sharing profits but not losses, then losses are shared in the same proportion as profits. For example, a partner receiving 75 percent of the profits would likewise absorb 75 percent of any losses.

In some cases, an equal division is not fair. One partner may perform more work for the business than the other partner, or one partner may make a larger capital contribution. In the preceding example, Hanna might agree to work longer hours for the partnership than Benz in order to earn a greater share of profits. Benz could argue that he should receive more of the profits because he contributed more net assets ($470,000) than Hanna did ($105,000). Hanna might contend that her computer software program is the partnership's most important asset and that her share of the profits should be greater than Benz's share. Arriving at fair sharing of profits and losses in a partnership may be difficult. We now discuss the options available in determining partners' shares.

Sharing Based on a Stated Fraction

Partners may agree to any profit-and-loss-sharing method they desire. Suppose the partnership agreement of Cagle and Dean allocates two thirds of the business profits and losses to Cagle and one third to Dean. If net income for the year is $90,000 and all revenue and expense accounts have been closed, the Income Summary account has a credit balance of $90,000, as follows:

Income Summary

	Bal.　90,000

The entry to close this account and allocate the profit to the partners' capital accounts is

Dec. 31	Income Summary............................	90,000	
	Cagle, Capital ($90,000 × ⅔)		60,000
	Dean, Capital ($90,000 × ⅓)		30,000
	To allocate net income to partners.		

Consider the effect of this entry. Does Cagle get cash of $60,000 and Dean cash of $30,000? No. The increase in the capital accounts of the partners cannot be linked to any particular asset, including cash. Instead, the entry indicates that Cagle's ownership in *all* the assets of the business increased by $60,000 and Dean's by $30,000.

If the year's operations resulted in a net loss of $66,000, the Income Summary account would have a debit balance of $66,000. In that case, the closing entry to allocate the loss to the partners' capital accounts would be

Dec. 31	Cagle, Capital ($66,000 × ⅔)	44,000	
	Dean, Capital ($66,000 × ⅓)	22,000	
	Income Summary........................		66,000
	To allocate net loss to partners.		

Sharing Based on Partners' Capital Contributions

Profits and losses are often allocated in proportion to the partners' capital contributions in the business. Suppose Antoine, Barber, and Cabañas are partners in ABC Company. Their capital accounts have the following balances at the end of the year, before the closing entries:

Antoine, Capital........................	$ 40,000
Barber, Capital	60,000
Cabañas, Capital	50,000
Total capital balances..................	$150,000

Assume that the partnership earned a profit of $120,000 for the year. To allocate this amount based on capital contributions, each partner's percentage share of the partnership's total capital balance must be computed. We simply divide each partner's contribution by the total capital amount. These figures, multiplied by the $120,000 profit amount, yield each partner's share of the year's profits:

Antoine:	$40,000/$150,000 × $120,000	= $ 32,000
Barber:	$60,000/$150,000 × $120,000	= 48,000
Cabañas:	$50,000/$150,000 × $120,000	= 40,000
	Net income allocated to partners =	**$120,000**

The closing entry to allocate the profit to the partners' capital accounts is

Dec. 31 Income Summary.   120,000

           Antoine, Capital.   32,000

           Barber, Capital.   48,000

           Cabañas, Capital   40,000

    To allocate net income to partners.

After this closing entry, the partners' capital balances are

Antoine, Capital ($40,000 + $32,000)	$ 72,000
Barber, Capital ($60,000 + $48,000).	108,000
Cabañas, Capital ($50,000 + $40,000).	90,000
Total capital balances after allocation of net income. . . .	$270,000

Sharing Based on Capital Contributions and Service to the Partnership

One partner, regardless of his or her capital contribution, may put more work into the business than the other partners. Even among partners who log equal service time, one person's superior experience and knowledge may command a greater share of income. To reward the harder-working or more valuable person, the profit-and-loss-sharing method may be based on a combination of contributed capital *and* service to the business.

Assume Randolph and Scott formed a partnership in which Randolph invested $60,000 and Scott invested $40,000, a total of $100,000. Scott devotes more time to the partnership and earns the larger salary. Accordingly, the two partners have agreed to share profits as follows:

1. The first $50,000 of partnership profits is to be allocated based on partners' capital contributions to the business.
2. The next $60,000 of profits is to be allocated based on service, with Randolph receiving $24,000 and Scott receiving $36,000.
3. Any remaining amount is allocated equally.

If net income for the first year is $125,000, the partners' shares of this profit are computed as follows:

	Randolph	Scott	Total
Total net income.			$125,000
Sharing of first $50,000 of net income, based on capital contributions:			
Randolph ($60,000/$100,000 × $50,000).	$30,000		
Scott ($40,000/$100,000 × $50,000).		$20,000	
Total.			50,000
Net income remaining for allocation.			75,000
Sharing of next $60,000, based on service:			
Randolph.	24,000		
Scott.		36,000	
Total.			60,000
Net income remaining for allocation.			15,000
Remainder shared equally:			
Randolph ($15,000 × ½)	7,500		
Scott ($15,000 × ½)		7,500	
Total.			15,000
Net income remaining for allocation.			$ -0-
Net income allocated to the partners.	$61,500	$63,500	$125,000

Based on this allocation, the closing entry is

Dec. 31	Income Summary.............................	125,000	
	Randolph, Capital		61,500
	Scott, Capital		63,500
	To allocate net income to partners.		

Sharing Based on Salaries and Interest

Partners may be rewarded for their service and their capital contributions to the business in other ways. In one sharing plan, the partners are allocated salaries plus interest on their capital balances. Assume Lewis and Clark form an oil-exploration partnership. At the beginning of the year, their capital balances are $80,000 and $100,000, respectively. The partnership agreement allocates annual salary of $43,000 to Lewis and $35,000 to Clark. After salaries are allocated, each partner earns 8 percent interest on his beginning capital balance. Any remaining net income is divided equally. Partnership profit of $96,000 would be allocated as follows:

	Lewis	Clark	Total
Total net income................................			$96,000
First, salaries:			
Lewis......................................	$43,000		
Clark		$35,000	
Total......................................			78,000
Net income remaining for allocation..............			18,000
Second, interest on beginning capital balances:			
Lewis ($80,000 × .08)........................	6,400		
Clark ($100,000 × .08).......................		8,000	
Total......................................			14,400
Net income remaining for allocation..............			3,600
Third, remainder shared equally:			
Lewis ($3,600 × ½).........................	1,800		
Clark ($3,600 × ½).........................		1,800	
Total......................................			3,600
Net income remaining for allocation..............			$ -0-
Net income allocated to the partners	$51,200	$44,800	$96,000

Based on this allocation, the closing entry is

Dec. 31	Income Summary.............................	96,000	
	Lewis, Capital		51,200
	Clark, Capital............................		44,800
	To allocate net income to partners.		

These salaries and interest amounts are *not* business expenses in the usual sense. Partners do not work for their own business to earn a salary, as an employee does. They do not loan money to their own business to earn interest. Their goal is for the partnership to earn a profit. Therefore, salaries and interest in partnership agreements are simply ways of expressing the allocation of profits and losses to the partners. For example, the salary component of partner income rewards service to the partnership. The interest component rewards a partner's investment of cash or other assets in the business.

In the preceding illustration, net income exceeded the sum of salary and interest. If the partnership profit is less than the allocated sum of salary and interest, a negative remainder will occur at some stage in the allocation process. Even so, the partners use the same method for allocation purposes. For example, assume that Lewis and Clark Partnership earned only $82,000.

	Lewis	Clark	Total
Total net income			$ 82,000
First, salaries:			
Lewis	$43,000		
Clark.		$35,000	
Total			78,000
Net income remaining for allocation			4,000
Second, interest on beginning capital balances:			
Lewis ($80,000 × .08)	6,400		
Clark ($100,000 × .08)		8,000	
Total			14,400
Net income remaining for allocation			(10,400)
Third, remainder shared equally:			
Lewis ($10,400 × ½)	(5,200)		
Clark ($10,400 × ½)		(5,200)	
Total			(10,400)
Net income remaining for allocation			$ -0-
Net income allocated to the partners	$44,200	$37,800	$ 82,000

A net loss would be allocated to Lewis and Clark in the same manner outlined for net income. The sharing procedure would begin with the net loss and then allocate salary, interest, and any other specified amounts to the partners.

We see that partners may allocate profits and losses based on a stated fraction, contributed capital, service, interest on capital, or any combination of these factors. Each partnership shapes its profit-and-loss-sharing ratio to fit its own needs.

Partner Drawings ────────────────────────────────

Partners, like anyone else, need cash for personal living expenses. Partnership agreements usually allow partners to withdraw cash or other assets from the business. Drawings from a partnership are recorded exactly as illustrated in previous chapters for drawings from a proprietorship. Assume Lewis and Clark are each allowed a monthly withdrawal of $3,500. The partnership records the March withdrawal with this entry:

Mar. 31	Lewis, Drawing.	3,500	
	Clark, Drawing	3,500	
	Cash.		7,000
	Monthly partner withdrawals.		

During the year, each partner drawing account accumulates 12 such amounts, a total of $42,000 ($3,500 × 12). At the end of the period, the general ledger shows the following account balances immediately after net income has been closed to the partners' capital accounts. Assume these beginning balances for Lewis and Clark at the start of the year and that $82,000 of profit has been allocated based on the preceding illustration.

Lewis, Capital		
	Jan. 1 Bal.	80,000
	Dec. 31 Net inc.	44,200

Clark, Capital		
	Jan. 1 Bal.	100,000
	Dec. 31 Net inc.	37,800

Lewis, Drawing	
Dec. 31 Bal. 42,000	

Clark, Drawing	
Dec. 31 Bal. 42,000	

The withdrawal accounts must be closed at the end of the period. The final closing entries transfer their balances to the partner's capital account as follows:

Dec. 31	Lewis, Capital	42,000	
	Lewis, Drawing		42,000
	Clark, Capital	42,000	
	Clark, Drawing		42,000
	To close partner drawing accounts.		

After closing, the accounts appear as follows:

Lewis, Capital				
Dec. 31 Clo.	42,000	Jan. 1 Bal.	80,000	
		Dec. 31 Net inc.	44,200	
		Dec. 31 Bal.	82,200	

Clark, Capital				
Dec. 31 Clo.	42,000	Jan. 1 Bal.	100,000	
		Dec. 31 Net inc.	37,800	
		Dec. 31 Bal.	95,800	

Lewis, Drawing			
Dec. 31 Bal.	42,000	Dec. 31 Clo.	42,000

Clark, Drawing			
Dec. 31 Bal.	42,000	Dec. 31 Clo.	42,000

In this case, Lewis withdrew less than his share of the partnership net income. Consequently, his capital account grew during the period. Clark, however, withdrew more than his share of net income. His capital account decreased.

Partnerships, as we have mentioned, do not last forever. We turn now to a discussion of how partnerships dissolve—and how new partnerships arise.

Dissolution of a Partnership

A partnership lasts only as long as its partners remain in the business. The addition of a new member or the withdrawal of an existing member dissolves the partnership.

Often a new partnership is formed to carry on the former partnership's business. In fact, the new partnership may choose to retain the dissolved partnership's name. Price Waterhouse & Company, for example, is an accounting firm that retires and hires partners during the year. Thus the former partnership dissolves and a new partnership begins many times. The business, however, retains the name and continues operations. Other partnerships may dissolve and then re-form under a new name. Let's look now at the ways that a new member may gain admission into an existing partnership.

Admission by Purchasing a Partner's Interest

A person may become a member of a partnership by gaining the approval of the other partner (or partners) for entrance into the firm *and* by purchasing a present partner's interest in the business. Let's assume that Fisher and Garcia have a partnership that carries these figures:

Cash....................	$ 40,000	Total liabilities............	$120,000
Other assets..............	360,000	Fisher, capital	110,000
		Garcia, capital............	170,000
Total assets	$400,000	Total liabilities and capital ...	$400,000

Business is going so well that Fisher receives an offer from Dynak, an outside party, to buy her $110,000 interest in the business for $150,000. Fisher agrees to sell out to Dynak, and Garcia approves Dynak as a new partner. The firm records the transfer of capital interest in the business with this entry:

Apr. 16	Fisher, Capital	110,000	
	Dynak, Capital.........................		110,000
	To transfer Fisher's equity in the business to Dynak.		

OBJECTIVE 4

Account for the admission of a new partner to the business

The debit side of the entry closes Fisher's capital account because she is no longer a partner in the firm. The credit side opens Dynak's capital account because Fisher's equity has been transferred to Dynak. Notice that the entry amount is Fisher's capital balance ($110,000) and not the $150,000 price that Dynak paid Fisher to buy into the business. The full $150,000 goes to Fisher, including the $40,000 difference between her capital balance and the price received from Dynak. In this example, the partnership receives no cash because the transaction was between Dynak and Fisher, not between Dynak and the partnership. Suppose Dynak pays Fisher less than Fisher's capital balance. That does not affect the entry on the partnership books. Fisher's equity is transferred to Dynak at book value ($110,000).

The old partnership has dissolved. Garcia and Dynak draw up a new partnership agreement, with a new profit-and-loss-sharing ratio, and continue business operations. If Garcia does not accept Dynak as a partner, Dynak gets no voice in management of the firm. However, under the Uniform Partnership Act, the purchaser shares in the profits and losses of the firm and in its assets at liquidation.

Admission by Investing in the Partnership

A person may also be admitted as a partner by investing directly in the partnership rather than by purchasing an existing partner's interest. The new partner contributes assets—for example, cash, inventory, or equipment—to the business. Assume that the partnership of Ingel and Jay has the following assets, liabilities, and capital:

Cash..................	$ 20,000	Total liabilities.............	$100,000
Other assets..............	240,000	Ingel, capital	70,000
		Jay, capital...............	90,000
Total assets	$260,000	Total liabilities and capital ...	$260,000

Kahn offers to invest equipment and land (Other assets) with a market value of $80,000 to persuade the existing partners to take her into the business. Ingel and Jay agree to dissolve the existing partnership and to start up a new business, giving Kahn one-third interest in exchange for the contributed assets. The entry to record Kahn's investment is

July 18	Other Assets................................	80,000	
	Kahn, Capital		80,000
	To admit L. Kahn as a partner with a one-third interest in the business.		

After this entry, the partnership books show:

Cash....................	$ 20,000	Total liabilities.............	$100,000
Other assets ($240,000 +		Ingel, capital	70,000
$80,000)...............	320,000	Jay, capital...............	90,000
		Kahn, capital	80,000
Total assets	$340,000	Total liabilities and capital ...	$340,000

Kahn's one-third interest in the partnership [$80,000/($70,000 + $90,000 + $80,000) = 1/3] does not necessarily entitle her to one third of the profits. The sharing of profits and losses is a separate consideration in the partnership agreement.

In the previous example, Dynak paid an individual member (Fisher), not the partnership. Note that Kahn's payment (the other assets) goes into the partnership.

Admission by Investing in the Partnership — Bonus to the Old Partners.

The more successful a partnership, the higher the payment the partners may demand from a person entering the business. Partners in a business that is doing quite well might require an incoming person to pay them a bonus. The bonus increases the current partners' capital accounts.

Suppose that Nagasawa and Osburn's partnership has earned above-average profits for 10 years. The two partners share profits and losses equally. The balance sheet carries these figures:

Cash....................	$ 40,000	Total liabilities.............	$100,000
Other assets..............	210,000	Nagasawa, capital..........	70,000
		Osburn, capital	80,000
Total assets	$250,000	Total liabilities and capital ...	$250,000

The partners agree to admit Parker to a one-fourth interest with his cash investment of $90,000. Parker's capital balance on the partnership books is $60,000, computed as follows:

Partnership capital before Parker is admitted ($70,000 + $80,000)	$150,000
Parker's investment in the partnership.	90,000
Partnership capital after Parker is admitted	$240,000
Parker's capital in the partnership ($240,000 × ¼)	$ 60,000

The entry on the partnership books to record Parker's investment is

Mar. 11	Cash.	90,000	
	Parker, Capital.		60,000
	Nagasawa, Capital ($30,000 × ½)		15,000
	Osburn, Capital ($30,000 × ½)		15,000

To admit G. Parker as a partner with a one-fourth interest in the business.

Parker's capital account is credited for his one-fourth interest in the partnership. The other partners share the $30,000 difference between Parker's investment ($90,000) and his equity in the business ($60,000). This difference is accounted for as income to the old partners and is, therefore, allocated to them based on their profit-and-loss ratio.

The new partnership's balance sheet reports these amounts:

Cash ($40,000 + $90,000) . . .	$130,000	Total liabilities	$100,000
Other assets.	210,000	Nagasawa, capital ($70,000 + $15,000)	85,000
		Osburn, capital ($80,000 + $15,000)	95,000
		Parker, capital	60,000
Total assets	$340,000	Total liabilities and capital . . .	$340,000

Admission by Investing in the Partnership — Bonus to the New Partner. A potential new partner may be so important that the existing partners offer him or her a partnership share that includes a bonus. A law firm may strongly desire a former governor or other official as a partner because of the person's reputation. A restaurant owner may want to go into partnership with a famous sports personality like Jack Nicklaus or Magic Johnson.

Suppose Page and Osuka is a law partnership. The firm's balance sheet appears as follows:

Cash.	$140,000	Total liabilities	$120,000
Other assets.	360,000	Page, capital	230,000
		Osuka, capital	150,000
Total assets	$500,000	Total liabilities and capital . . .	$500,000

The partners admit Schiller, a former attorney general, as a partner with a one-third interest in exchange for his cash investment of $100,000. At the time of Schiller's admission, the firm's capital is $380,000 — Page, $230,000, and Osuka, $150,000. Page and Osuka share profits and losses in the ratio of two thirds to Page and one third to Osuka. The computation of Schiller's equity in the partnership is

Partnership capital before Schiller is admitted ($230,000 + $150,000)	$380,000
Schiller's investment in the partnership	100,000
Partnership capital after Schiller is admitted	$480,000
Schiller's capital in the partnership ($480,000 × ⅓)	$160,000

The capital accounts of Page and Osuka are debited for the $60,000 difference between the new partner's equity ($160,000) and his investment ($100,000). The existing partners share this decrease in capital, which is accounted for as though it were a loss, based on their profit-and-loss ratio.

The entry to record Schiller's investment is

Aug. 24	Cash.....................................	100,000	
	Page, Capital ($60,000 × ⅔)	40,000	
	Osuka, Capital ($60,000 × ⅓)	20,000	
	Schiller, Capital........................		160,000
	To admit M. Schiller as a partner with a one-third interest in the business.		

The new partnership's balance sheet reports these amounts:

Cash ($140,000 + $100,000)..............	$240,000	Total liabilities.............	$120,000
Other assets..............	360,000	Page, capital ($230,000 − $40,000)................	190,000
		Osuka, capital ($150,000 − $20,000)................	130,000
		Schiller, capital	160,000
Total assets	$600,000	Total liabilities and capital ...	$600,000

Summary Problem for Your Review

The partnership of Taylor and Uvalde is considering admitting Vaughn as a partner on January 1, 19X8. The partnership general ledger includes the following balances on that date:

Cash.....................	$ 9,000	Total liabilities.............	$ 50,000
Other assets..............	110,000	Taylor, capital	45,000
		Uvalde, capital.............	24,000
Total assets	$119,000	Total liabilities and capital ...	$119,000

Taylor's share of profits and losses is 60 percent, and Uvalde's share is 40 percent.

Required

1. Suppose Vaughn pays Uvalde $31,000 to acquire Uvalde's interest in the business. Taylor approves Vaughn as a partner.
    a. Record the transfer of owner's equity on the partnership books.
    b. Prepare the partnership balance sheet immediately after Vaughn is admitted as a partner.
2. Suppose Vaughn becomes a partner by investing $31,000 cash to acquire a one-fourth interest in the business.
    a. Compute Vaughn's capital balance, and record Vaughn's investment in the business.

b. Prepare the partnership balance sheet immediately after Vaughn is admitted as a partner. Include the heading.

3. Which way of admitting Vaughn to the partnership increases its total assets? Give your reason.

SOLUTION TO REVIEW PROBLEM

Requirement 1

a. Jan. 1   Uvalde, Capital   24,000

                Vaughn, Capital   24,000

              To transfer Uvalde's equity in the partnership to Vaughn.

b. The balance sheet for the partnership of Taylor and Vaughn is identical to the balance sheet given for Taylor and Uvalde in the problem, except that Vaughn's name replaces Uvalde's name in the title and in the listing of capital accounts.

Requirement 2

a. Computation of Vaughn's capital balance:

Partnership capital before Vaughn is admitted ($45,000 + $24,000) .	$ 69,000
Vaughn's investment in the partnership	31,000
Partnership capital after Vaughn is admitted	$100,000
Vaughn's capital in the partnership ($100,000 × ¼)	$ 25,000

Jan. 1.   Cash   31,000

              Vaughn, Capital   25,000

              Taylor, Capital [($31,000 − $25,000) × .60] . .   3,600

              Uvalde, Capital [($31,000 − $25,000) × .40] .   2,400

              To admit Vaughn as a partner with a one-fourth interest in the business.

b.

Taylor, Uvalde, and Vaughn
Balance Sheet
January 1, 19X8

Cash ($9,000 + $31,000)	$ 40,000	Total liabilities		$ 50,000
Other assets	110,000	Taylor, capital ($45,000 + $3,600)		48,600
		Uvalde, capital ($24,000 + $2,400)		26,400
		Vaughn, capital		25,000
Total assets.	$150,000	Total liabilities and capital		$150,000

Requirement 3

Vaughn's investment in the partnership increases its total assets by the amount of his contribution. Total assets of the business are $150,000 after his investment, compared to $119,000 before. By contrast, Vaughn's purchase of Uvalde's interest in the business is a personal transaction between the two individuals. It does not affect the assets of the partnership regardless of the amount Vaughn pays Uvalde.

Withdrawal of a Partner

OBJECTIVE 5

Account for the withdrawal of a partner from the business

A partner may withdraw from the business for many reasons, including retirement or a dispute with the other partners. The partnership agreement should contain a provision to govern how to settle with a withdrawing partner. In the simplest case, as illustrated on page 505, a partner may withdraw and sell his or her interest to another partner in a personal transaction. The only entry needed to record this transfer of equity debits the withdrawing partner's capital account and credits the purchaser's capital account. The dollar amount of the entry is the capital balance of the withdrawing partner, regardless of the price paid by the purchaser. The accounting when one current partner buys a second partner's interest is the same as when an outside party buys a current partner's interest.

If the partner withdraws in the middle of the accounting period, it is necessary to update the partnership books to determine the withdrawing partner's capital balance. The business must measure net income or net loss for the fraction of the year up to the withdrawal date and allocate profit or loss according to the existing ratio. After closing the books, the business then accounts for the change in partnership capital.

The withdrawing partner may receive his or her share of the business in partnership assets other than cash. The question arises as to what value to assign the partnership assets: book value or current market value. The settlement procedure may specify an independent appraisal of assets to determine their current market value. If market values have changed, the appraisal will result in revaluing the partnership assets. This way the partners share in any market value changes that their efforts caused.

Suppose Isaac is retiring in midyear from the partnership of Green, Henry, and Isaac. After the books have been adjusted for partial-period income but before the asset appraisal, revaluation, and closing entries, the balance sheet reports:

Cash	$ 39,000	Total liabilities	$ 80,000
Inventory	44,000	Green, capital	54,000
Land	55,000	Henry, capital	43,000
Building	$95,000	Issac, capital	21,000
Less accum. depr.	35,000	60,000	Total liabilities and
Total assets		$198,000	capital	$198,000

Assume an independent appraiser revalues the inventory at $38,000 (down from $44,000) and the land at $101,000 (up from $55,000). The partners share the differences between these assets' market values and their prior book values based on their profit-and-loss ratio. The partnership agreement has allocated one fourth of the profits to Green, one half to Henry, and one fourth to Isaac. (This ratio may be written 1 : 2 : 1 for one part to Green, two parts to Henry, and one part to Isaac.) For each share that Green or Isaac has, Henry has two. The entries to record the revaluation of the inventory and land are

July 31	Green, Capital ($6,000 × ¼)	1,500	
	Henry, Capital ($6,000 × ½)	3,000	
	Isaac, Capital ($6,000 × ¼)	1,500	
	Inventory ($44,000 − $38,000)		6,000
	To revalue the inventory and allocate the loss in value to the partners.		

31   Land ($101,000 − $55,000).......................... 46,000

         Green, Capital ($46,000 × ¼)................   11,500

         Henry, Capital ($46,000 × ½)................   23,000

         Isaac, Capital ($46,000 × ¼)................   11,500

       To revalue the land and allocate the gain in value to the partners.

After the revaluations, the partnership balance sheet reports:

Cash	$ 39,000	Total liabilities	$ 80,000
Inventory	38,000	Green, capital	
Land	101,000	($54,000 − $1,500 +	
Building $95,000		$11,500)	64,000
Less accum. depr..... 35,000	60,000	Henry, capital	
		($43,000 − $3,000 +	
		$23,000)	63,000
		Isaac, capital ($21,000 −	
		$1,500 + $11,500) ...	31,000
		Total liabilities and	
Total assets	$238,000	capital	$238,000

The books now carry the assets at current market value, which becomes the new book value, and the capital accounts have been adjusted accordingly. Isaac has a claim to $31,000 in partnership assets. How is his withdrawal from the business accounted for?

Withdrawal at Book Value

If Isaac withdraws by taking cash equal to the book value of his owner's equity, the entry would be

July 31   Isaac, Capital.................................. 31,000

         Cash   31,000

       To record withdrawal of K. Isaac from the partnership.

This entry records the payment of partnership cash to Isaac and the closing of his capital account upon withdrawal from the business.

Withdrawal at Less Than Book Value

The withdrawing partner may be so eager to leave the business that he is willing to take less than his equity. This situation has occurred in real estate and oil-drilling partnerships. Assume Isaac withdraws from the business and agrees to take partnership cash of $10,000 and the new partnership's note for $15,000. This $25,000 settlement is $6,000 less than Isaac's $31,000 equity in the business. The remaining partners share this $6,000 difference—which is a gain to them—according to their profit-and-loss ratio. However, since Isaac has withdrawn from the partnership, a new agreement—and a new profit-and-loss ratio—must be drawn up. Henry and Green, in forming a new partnership, may decide on any ratio that they see fit. Let's assume they agree that Henry will earn two thirds of partnership profits and losses and Green one third. The entry to record Isaac's withdrawal at less than book value is

July 31	Isaac, Capital.................................	31,000	
	Cash		10,000
	Note Payable to K. Isaac		15,000
	Green, Capital ($6,000 × ⅓).................		2,000
	Henry, Capital ($6,000 × ⅔).................		4,000
	To record withdrawal of K. Isaac from the partnership.		

Isaac's account is closed, and Henry and Green may or may not continue the business.

Withdrawal at More Than Book Value

The settlement with a withdrawing partner may allow him to take assets of greater value than the book value of his capital. Also, the remaining partners may be so eager for the withdrawing partner to leave the firm that they pay him a bonus to withdraw from the business. In either case, the partner's withdrawal causes a decrease in the book equity of the remaining partners. This decrease is allocated to the partners based on their profit-and-loss ratio.

Assume Chang, Daley, and Evans share profits in a ratio of 3:2:1. Their partnership accounts include the following balances:

Cash.....................	$ 50,000	Total liabilities.............	$110,000
Other assets..............	220,000	Chang, capital.............	80,000
		Daley, capital.............	50,000
		Evans, capital.............	30,000
Total assets	$270,000	Total liabilities and capital ...	$270,000

Assume Evans withdraws, taking cash of $15,000 and the new partnership's note for $25,000. This $40,000 settlement exceeds Evans's capital balance by $10,000. Chang and Daley share this loss in equity based on their profit-and-loss ratio (3:2). The withdrawal entry is

Nov. 30	Evans, Capital...............................	30,000	
	Chang, Capital ($10,000 × ⅗)...................	6,000	
	Daley, Capital ($10,000 × ⅖)	4,000	
	Cash......................................		15,000
	Note Payable to R. Evans..................		25,000
	To record withdrawal of R. Evans from the partnership.		

The withdrawal entry closes Evans's capital account and updates those of Chang and Daley.

Death of a Partner

Death of a partner, like any other form of partnership withdrawal, dissolves a partnership. The partnership accounts are adjusted to measure net income or loss for the fraction of the year up to the date of death, then closed to determine the partners' capital balances on that date. Settlement with the deceased partner's estate is based on the partnership agreement, with the estate commonly receiving partnership assets equal to the partner's capital balance. The partnership closes the deceased partner's capital account with a debit. This entry credits a payable to the estate.

Alternatively, a remaining partner may purchase the deceased partner's equity. The deceased partner's equity is debited and the purchaser's equity is credited. The amount of this entry is the ending credit balance in the deceased partner's capital account.

Liquidation of a Partnership

Admission of a new partner or withdrawal or death of an existing partner dissolves the partnership. However, the business may continue operating with no apparent change to outsiders such as customers and creditors.

Business **liquidation,** however, is the process of going out of business by selling the entity's assets and paying its liabilities. The final step in liquidation of a business is the *distribution of the remaining cash to the owners.* Before liquidating the business, the books should be adjusted and closed. After closing, only asset, liability, and partners' capital accounts remain open.

Liquidation of a partnership includes three basic steps:

1. Sell the assets. Allocate the gain or loss to the partners' capital accounts based on the profit-and-loss ratio.
2. Pay the partnership liabilities.
3. Disburse the remaining cash to the partners based on their capital balances.

In actual practice, the liquidation of a business can stretch over weeks or months. Selling every asset and paying every liability of the entity may take a long time. To avoid excessive detail in our illustrations, we include only two asset categories—Cash and Noncash Assets—and a single liability category—Liabilities. Our examples also assume that the business sells the noncash assets in a single transaction and pays the liabilities in a single transaction.

Assume that Aviron, Bloch, and Crane have shared profits and losses in the ratio of 3:1:1. (This ratio is equal to ⅗, ⅕, ⅕, or a 60-percent, 20-percent, 20-percent sharing ratio.) They decide to liquidate their partnership. After the books are adjusted and closed, the general ledger contains the following balances:

Cash	$ 10,000	Liabilities	$ 30,000
Noncash assets	90,000	Aviron, capital	40,000
		Bloch, capital	20,000
		Crane, capital	10,000
Total assets	$100,000	Total liabilities and capital	$100,000

We will use the Aviron, Bloch, and Crane partnership data to illustrate accounting for liquidation in three different situations.

Sale of Noncash Assets at a Gain

Assume the partnership sells its noncash assets (shown on the balance sheet at $90,000) for cash of $150,000. The partnership realizes a gain of $60,000, which is allocated to the partners based on their profit-and-loss-sharing ratio. The entry to record this sale and allocation of the gain is

OBJECTIVE 6

Account for the liquidation of a partnership

Oct. 31	Cash	150,000	
	Noncash Assets		90,000
	Aviron, Capital ($60,000 × .60)		36,000
	Bloch, Capital ($60,000 × .20)		12,000
	Crane, Capital ($60,000 × .20)		12,000
	To sell noncash assets in liquidation and allocate gain to partners.		

The partnership must next pay off its liabilities:

Oct. 31	Liabilities	30,000	
	Cash		30,000
	To pay liabilities in liquidation.		

In the final liquidation transaction, the remaining cash is disbursed to the partners. *The partners share in the cash according to their capital balances.* (By contrast, *gains and losses* on the sale of assets are shared by the partners based on their profit-and-loss-sharing ratio.) The amount of cash left in the partnership is $130,000—the $10,000 beginning balance plus the $150,000 cash sale of assets minus the $30,000 cash payment of liabilities. The partners divide the remaining cash according to their capital balances:

Oct. 31	Aviron, Capital ($40,000 + $36,000)	76,000	
	Bloch, Capital ($20,000 + $12,000)	32,000	
	Crane, Capital ($10,000 + $12,000)	22,000	
	Cash		130,000
	To disburse cash to partners in liquidation.		

A convenient way to summarize the transactions in a partnership liquidation is given in Exhibit 13-1.

After the disbursement of cash to the partners, the business has no assets, liabilities, or owners' equity. The balances are all zero. At all times, partnership

EXHIBIT 13-1 *Partnership Liquidation—Sale of Assets at a Gain*

				Capital		
	Cash	+ Noncash Assets = Liabilities +		Aviron (60%) +	Bloch (20%) +	Crane (20%)
Balances before sale of assets .	$ 10,000	$ 90,000	$ 30,000	$ 40,000	$ 20,000	$ 10,000
Sale of assets and sharing of gain	150,000	(90,000)		36,000	12,000	12,000
Balances	160,000	-0-	30,000	76,000	32,000	22,000
Payment of liabilities	(30,000)		(30,000)			
Balances	130,000	-0-	-0-	76,000	32,000	22,000
Disbursement of cash to partners	(130,000)			(76,000)	(32,000)	(22,000)
Balances	$ -0-	$ -0-	$ -0-	$ -0-	$ -0-	$ -0-

assets must equal partnership liabilities plus partnership capital, by the accounting equation:

Total assets = Total liabilities + Total capital

Before liquidation	$100,000 =	$30,000 +	$ 70,000
After sale of assets	160,000 =	30,000 +	130,000
After payment of liabilities............	130,000 =	0 +	130,000
After final disbursement to the partners	0 =	0 +	0

Sale of Noncash Assets at a Loss

Assume that Aviron, Bloch, and Crane sell the noncash assets for $75,000, realizing a loss of $15,000. The summary of transactions appears in Exhibit 13-2. The journal entries to record the liquidation transactions are

Oct. 31	Cash	75,000	
	Aviron, Capital ($15,000 × .60)	9,000	
	Bloch, Capital ($15,000 × .20)	3,000	
	Crane, Capital ($15,000 × .20)	3,000	
	Noncash Assets		90,000
	To sell noncash assets in liquidation and allocate loss to partners.		
31	Liabilities	30,000	
	Cash		30,000
	To pay liabilities in liquidation.		
31	Aviron, Capital ($40,000 − $9,000)	31,000	
	Bloch, Capital ($20,000 − $3,000)	17,000	
	Crane, Capital ($10,000 − $3,000)	7,000	
	Cash		55,000
	To disburse cash to partners in liquidation.		

EXHIBIT 13-2 *Partnership Liquidation—Sale of Assets at a Loss*

				Capital		
	Cash	+ Noncash Assets = Liabilities +		Aviron (60%) +	Bloch (20%) +	Crane (20%)
Balances before sale of assets...	$ 10,000	$ 90,000	$ 30,000	$ 40,000	$ 20,000	$ 10,000
Sale of assets and sharing of loss.....................	75,000	(90,000)		(9,000)	(3,000)	(3,000)
Balances	85,000	-0-	30,000	31,000	17,000	7,000
Payment of liabilities	(30,000)		(30,000)			
Balances	55,000	-0-	-0-	31,000	17,000	7,000
Disbursement of cash to partners.................	(55,000)			(31,000)	(17,000)	(7,000)
Balances	$ -0-	$ -0-	$ -0-	$ -0-	$ -0-	$ -0-

Sale of Noncash Assets at a Loss—Deficiency in a Partner's Capital Account. The sale of noncash assets at a loss may result in a debit balance in a partner's capital account. This situation is called a *capital deficiency* because the partner's capital balance is insufficient to cover his share of the partnership's loss. The unlimited liability of partners forces the other partners to absorb this deficiency through debits to their own capital accounts if the deficient partner does not erase his deficiency. The deficiency is a loss to the other partners, and they share it based on their profit-and-loss ratio.

DEFICIENT PARTNER UNABLE TO ERASE DEFICIENCY. Assume that Aviron, Bloch, and Crane's partnership has had losses for several years. The market value of the noncash assets of the business is far less than book value ($90,000). In liquidation, the partnership sells these assets for $30,000, realizing a loss of $60,000. Crane's 20 percent share of this loss is $12,000. Because the loss exceeds his $10,000 capital balance, Crane's account has a $2,000 deficit. Crane is obligated to contribute personal funds to the business in order to meet this debt. Assume that Crane cannot erase the deficiency by contributing personal assets. Because of mutual agency, the other partners must absorb the deficiency before the final distribution of cash.

Because Aviron and Bloch share losses in the ratio of 3:1, Aviron absorbs three fourths of the deficiency [3/(3 + 1) = 3/4] and Bloch absorbs one fourth [1/(3 + 1) = 1/4]. Aviron's share of Crane's $2,000 deficiency is $1,500 ($2,000 × 3/4), and Bloch's share is $500 ($2,000 × 1/4).

The journal entries to record the foregoing liquidation transactions are

Oct. 31	Cash	30,000	
	Aviron, Capital ($60,000 × .60)	36,000	
	Bloch, Capital ($60,000 × .20)	12,000	
	Crane, Capital ($60,000 × .20)	12,000	
	Noncash Assets		90,000
	To sell noncash assets in liquidation and allocate loss to partners.		
31	Liabilities	30,000	
	Cash		30,000
	To pay liabilities in liquidation.		
31	Aviron, Capital ($2,000 × 3/4)	1,500	
	Bloch, Capital ($2,000 × 1/4)	500	
	Crane, Capital		2,000
	To allocate Crane's capital deficiency to the other partners.		
31	Aviron, Capital ($40,000 − $36,000 − $1,500)	2,500	
	Bloch, Capital ($20,000 − $12,000 − $500)	7,500	
	Cash		10,000
	To disburse cash to partners in liquidation.		

The summary of transactions in Exhibit 13-3 includes a separate transaction (highlighted) to allocate Crane's deficiency to Aviron and Bloch.

DEFICIENT PARTNER ERASES DEFICIENCY. A partner may erase his or her deficiency by contributing cash or other assets to the partnership. Such contributions are credited to the deficient partner's account and then distributed to the other

EXHIBIT 13-3 *Partnership Liquidation—Deficient Partner Unable to Erase a Capital Deficiency*

				Capital		
	Cash	+ Noncash Assets =	Liabilities +	Aviron (60%) +	Bloch (20%) +	Crane (20%)
Balances before sale of assets...	$ 10,000	$ 90,000	$ 30,000	$ 40,000	$ 20,000	$ 10,000
Sale of assets and sharing of loss......................	30,000	(90,000)		(36,000)	(12,000)	(12,000)
Balances	40,000	-0-	30,000	4,000	8,000	(2,000)
Payment of liabilities.........:	(30,000)		(30,000)			
Balances	10,000	-0-	-0-	4,000	8,000	(2,000)
Sharing of Crane's deficiency by Aviron and Bloch.......				**(1,500)**	**(500)**	**2,000**
Balances	10,000	-0-	-0-	2,500	7,500	-0-
Disbursement of cash to partners..................	(10,000)			(2,500)	(7,500)	-0-
Balances	$ -0-	$ -0-	$ -0-	$ -0-	$ -0-	$ -0-

partners. Suppose Crane erases his deficiency by investing $2,000 cash in the partnership.

The journal entries to record Crane's contribution and the disbursement of cash to the partners are

Oct. 31	Cash	2,000	
	Crane, Capital		2,000
	Crane's contribution to erase his capital deficiency in liquidation.		
31	Aviron, Capital.................................	4,000	
	Bloch, Capital.................................	8,000	
	Cash		12,000
	To disburse cash to partners in liquidation.		

In this case, the summary of transactions, beginning with the balances after payment of the liabilities, appears in Exhibit 13-4.

EXHIBIT 13-4 *Partnership Liquidation—Partner Erases Capital Deficiency*

				Capital		
	Cash	+ Noncash Assets =	Liabilities +	Aviron (60%) +	Bloch (20%) +	Crane (20%)
Balances after payment of liabilities	$ 10,000	$ -0-	$ -0-	$ 4,000	$ 8,000	$(2,000)
Crane's contribution to erase his deficiency	2,000					2,000
Balances	12,000	-0-	-0-	4,000	8,000	-0-
Disbursement of cash to partners ..	(12,000)			(4,000)	(8,000)	
Balances	$ -0-	$ -0-	$ -0-	$ -0-	$ -0-	$ -0-

Partnership Financial Statements

Partnership financial statements are much like those of a proprietorship. However, a partnership income statement includes a section showing the division of net income to the partners. For example, the partnership of Gray and Hayward might report its income statement for the year ended June 30, 19X6, as follows:

Gray and Hayward **Income Statement** **For the Year Ended June 30, 19X6**	
Sales revenue	$381,000
Net income	$ 79,000
Allocation of net income:	
M. Gray.............................	$ 36,600
L. Hayward..........................	42,400
Total	$ 79,000

Large partnerships may not find it feasible to report the net income of every partner. Instead, the firm may report the allocation of net income to active and retired partners and average earnings per partner. For example, the CPA firm of Arthur Andersen & Company reported the following:

The Arthur Andersen Worldwide Organization **Combined Statement of Earnings** **For the Year Ended August 31, 19X0**	
Dollar amounts in thousands	
Fees for Professional Services	$805,492
Earnings for the year	$181,880
Allocation of earnings:	
To partners active during the year—	
Resigned, retired, and deceased partners......................	$ 9,901
Partners active at year end	160,270
To retired and deceased partners—retirement and death benefits ...	4,310
Not allocated to partners—retained for specific partnership	
purposes...	7,399
	$181,880
Average earnings per partner active at year end	
(1,170 partners)...	$137

Exhibit 13-5 summarizes the financial statements of a proprietorship and a partnership.

EXHIBIT 13-5 *Financial Statements of a Proprietorship and a Partnership*

Income Statements
For the Year Ended December 31, 19X1

Proprietorship		Partnership		
Revenues...............	$460	Revenues....................		$460
Expenses...............	(270)	Expenses....................		(270)
Net income............	$190	Net income..................		$190
		Allocation of net income:		
		To Smith.............	$114	
		To Jones.............	76	$190

Statements of Owner Equity
For the Year Ended December 31, 19X1

Proprietorship		Partnership	Smith	Jones
Capital, December 31, 19X0................	$ 90	Capital, December 31, 19X0................	$ 50	$ 40
Additional investments ...	10	Additional investments ...	10	—
Net income.............	190	Net income.............	114	76
Subtotal................	290	Subtotal................	174	116
Drawings	(120)	Drawings	(72)	(48)
Capital, December 31, 19X1................	$170	Capital, December 31, 19X1................	$102	$ 68

Balance Sheets
December 31, 19X1

Proprietorship		Partnership	
Assets			
Cash and other assets	$170	Cash and other assets............	$170
		Equities	
		Smith, capital	$102
		Jones, capital	68
Smith, capital	$170	Total capital	$170

Summary Problem for Your Review

The partnership of Prolux, Roberts, and Satulsky is liquidating. Its accounts have the following balances after closing:

Cash.....................	$ 22,000	Liabilities.................	$ 77,000
Noncash assets	104,000	Prolux, capital.............	23,000
		Roberts, capital	10,000
		Satulsky, capital	16,000
		Total liabilities	
Total assets	$126,000	and capital..............	$126,000

The partnership agreement allocates profits to Prolux, Roberts, and Satulsky in the ratio of 3 : 4 : 3. In liquidation, the noncash assets were sold in a single transaction for $64,000 on May 31, 19X7. The partnership paid the liabilities the same day.

Required

1. Journalize the liquidation transactions. The partnership books remain open until June 7 to allow Roberts to make an additional $4,000 contribution to the business in view of her capital deficiency. This cash is immediately disbursed to the other partners. Use T-accounts if necessary.

2. Prepare a summary of the liquidation transactions, as illustrated in the chapter. Roberts invests cash of $4,000 in the partnership in partial settlement of her capital deficiency. The other partners absorb the remainder of Roberts's capital deficiency.

SOLUTION TO REVIEW PROBLEM

Requirement 1
(Liquidation journal entries)

May 31	Cash......................................	64,000	
	Prolux, Capital [($104,000 − $64,000) × .30]	12,000	
	Roberts, Capital [($104,000 − $64,000) × .40]	16,000	
	Satulsky, Capital [($104,000 − $64,000) × .30]......	12,000	
	Noncash Assets		104,000
	To sell noncash assets in liquidation and distribute loss to partners.		
31	Liabilities	77,000	
	Cash.....................................		77,000
	To pay liabilities in liquidation.		
June 7	Cash......................................	4,000	
	Roberts, Capital		4,000
	Roberts's contribution to erase part of her capital deficiency in liquidation.		

After posting the entries, Roberts's capital account still has a $2,000 deficiency, indicated by its debit balance:

Roberts, Capital

Loss on sale	16,000	Bal.	10,000
		Investment	4,000
Bal.	2,000		

Prolux and Satulsky must make up Roberts's remaining $2,000 deficiency. Since Prolux and Satulsky had equal shares in the partnership profit-and-loss ratio (30 percent each), they divide Roberts's deficiency equally.

June 7   Prolux, Capital ($2,000 × ½)   1,000

         Satulsky, Capital ($2,000 × ½)......................   1,000

            Roberts, Capital............................   2,000

         To allocate Roberts's capital deficiency to the other partners.

At this point, the capital accounts of Prolux and Satulsky appear as follows:

Prolux, Capital					Satulsky, Capital			
Loss on sale	12,000	Bal.	23,000		Loss on sale	12,000	Bal.	16,000
Loss on Roberts	1,000				Loss on Roberts	1,000		
		Bal.	10,000				Bal.	3,000

The final disbursement entry is

June 7   Prolux, Capital...............................   10,000

         Satulsky, Capital   3,000

            Cash   13,000

         To disburse cash to partners in liquidation.

Activity in the Cash account appears as follows:

Cash			
Bal.	22,000	Payment of liabilities	77,000
Sale of assets	64,000		
Roberts's contribution	4,000		
Bal.	13,000	Final distribution	13,000

Requirement 2.   (Summary of liquidation transactions)

	Cash	+	Noncash Assets	=	Liabilities +	Prolux (30%)	+	Roberts (40%)	+	Satulsky (30%)
Balances before sale of assets......	$ 22,000		$ 104,000		$ 77,000	$ 23,000		$ 10,000		$ 16,000
Sale of assets and sharing of loss...	64,000		(104,000)			(12,000)		(16,000)		(12,000)
Balances......................	86,000		-0-		77,000	11,000		(6,000)		4,000
Payment of liabilities	(77,000)				(77,000)					
Balances......................	9,000		-0-		-0-	11,000		(6,000)		4,000
Roberts's investment of cash to erase part of her deficiency......	4,000							4,000		
Balances......................	13,000		-0-		-0-	11,000		(2,000)		4,000
Sharing of Roberts's deficiency by Prolux and Satulsky						(1,000)		2,000		(1,000)
Balances......................	13,000		-0-		-0-	10,000		-0-		3,000
Disbursement of cash to partners ..	(13,000)					(10,000)				(3,000)
Balances......................	$ -0-		$ -0-		$ -0-	$ -0-		$ -0-		$ -0-

Summary

A *partnership* is a business co-owned by two or more persons for profit. The characteristics of this form of business organization are its *ease of formation, limited life, mutual agency, unlimited liability,* and *no partnership income taxes.*

A written *partnership agreement,* or *articles of partnership,* establishes procedure for admission of a new partner, withdrawals of a partner, and the sharing of profits and losses among the partners.

When a new partner is admitted to the firm or an existing partner withdraws, the old partnership is *dissolved,* or ceases to exist. A new partnership may or may not emerge to continue the business.

Accounting for a partnership is similar to accounting for a proprietorship. However, a partnership has more than one owner. Each partner has an individual capital account and a withdrawal account.

Partners share net income or loss in any manner they choose. Common sharing agreements base the *profit-and-loss ratio* on a stated fraction, partners' capital contributions, and/or their service to the partnership. Some partnerships call the cash withdrawals of partners *salaries* and *interest,* but these amounts are not expenses of the business. Instead, they are merely ways of allocating partnership net income to the partners.

An outside person may become a partner by purchasing a current partner's interest or by investing in the partnership. In some cases the new partner must pay the current partners a bonus to join. In other situations the new partner may receive a bonus to join.

When a partner withdraws, partnership assets may be reappraised. Partners share any gain or loss on the asset revaluation based on their profit-and-loss ratio. The withdrawing partner may receive payment equal to, greater than, or less than, his or her capital book value, depending on the agreement with the other partners.

In *liquidation,* a partnership goes out of business by selling the assets, paying the liabilities, and disbursing any remaining cash to the partners. Any partner's capital deficiency, which may result from sale of assets at a loss, must be absorbed before remaining cash is distributed.

Partnership *financial statements* are similar to those of a proprietorship. However, the partnership income statement commonly reports the allocation of net income to the partners.

Self-Study Questions

Test your understanding of the chapter by marking the best answer for each of the following questions.

1. Which of these characteristics does *not* apply to a partnership? *(p. 496)*
   a. Unlimited life   c. Unlimited liability
   b. Mutual agency   d. No business income tax
2. A partnership records a partner's investment of assets in the business at *(p. 498)*
   a. The partner's book value of the assets invested
   b. The market value of the assets invested
   c. A special value set by the partners
   d. Any of the above, depending upon the partnership agreement
3. The partnership of Lane, Murdock, and Nu divides profits in the ratio of 4:5:3. During 19X6 the business earned $40,000. Nu's share of this income is *(p. 499)*
   a. $10,000   b. $13,333   c. $16,000   d. $16,667
4. Suppose the partnership of Lane, Murdock, and Nu in the preceding question lost $40,000 during 19X6. Murdock's share of this loss is *(p. 499)*
   a. Not determinable because the ratio applies only to profits
   b. $13,333
   c. $16,000
   d. $16,667

5. Placido, Quinn, and Rolfe share profits and losses $\frac{1}{5}$, $\frac{1}{6}$, and $\frac{19}{30}$. During 19X3 the first year of their partnership, the business earned $120,000, and each partner withdrew $50,000 for personal use. What is the balance in Rolfe's capital account after all closing entries? *(p. 504)*
   a. Not determinable because Rolfe's beginning capital balance is not given
   b. Minus $10,000
   c. $26,000
   d. $70,000

6. Fuller buys into the partnership of Graff and Harrell by purchasing a one-third interest for $55,000. Prior to Fuller's entry, Graff's capital balance was $46,000, and Harrell's balance was $52,000. The entry to record Fuller's buying into the business is *(p. 507)*

   a. Cash 55,000
         Fuller, Capital   55,000

   b. Graff, Capital. 27,500
      Harrell, Capital 27,500
         Fuller, Capital   55,000

   c. Cash 55,000
         Fuller, Capital   51,000
         Graff, Capital.   2,000
         Harrell, Capital . . .   2,000

   d. Cash 51,000
      Graff, Capital.   2,000
      Harrell, Capital   2,000
         Fuller, Capital   55,000

7. Thomas, Valik, and Wollenberg share profits and losses equally. Their capital balances are $40,000, $50,000, and $60,000, respectively, when Wollenberg sells her interest in the partnership to Valik for $90,000. Thomas and Valik continue the business. Immediately after Wollenberg's retirement, the total assets of the partnership are *(p. 510)*
   a. Increased by $30,000
   b. Increased by $90,000
   c. Decreased by $60,000
   d. The same as before Wollenberg sold her interest to Valik

8. Prior to Hogg's withdrawal from the partnership of Hogg, Hamm, and Bacon, the partners' capital balances were $140,000, $110,000, and $250,000, respectively. The partners share profits and losses $\frac{1}{3}$, $\frac{1}{4}$, and $\frac{5}{12}$. The appraisal indicates that assets should be written down by $36,000. Hamm's share of the write-down is *(p. 510)*
   a. $7,920   b. $9,000   c. $12,000   d. $18,000

9. Closing the business, selling the assets, paying the liabilities, and disbursing remaining cash to the owners is called *(p. 513)*
   a. Dissolution   c. Withdrawal
   b. Forming a new partnership   d. Liquidation

10. A and B have shared profits and losses equally. Immediately prior to the final cash disbursement in a liquidation of their partnership, the books show:

Cash	= Liabilities	+ A, Capital	+ B, Capital
$100,000	$ -0-	$60,000	$40,000

   How much cash should A receive? *(p. 514)*
   a. $40,000   b. $50,000   c. $60,000   d. None of the above

Answers to the self-study questions are at the end of the chapter.

Accounting Vocabulary

articles of partnership *(p. 496)*,   capital deficiency *(p. 516)*,   dissolution *(p. 496)*,   liquidation *(p. 513)*,   mutual agency *(p. 496)*,   partnership agreement *(p. 496)*,   unlimited personal liability *(p. 497)*.

ASSIGNMENT MATERIAL _____

Questions

1. What is another name for a partnership agreement? List eight items that the agreement should specify.

2. Montgomery, who is a partner in M&N Associates, commits the firm to a contract for a job within the scope of its regular business operations. What term describes Montgomery's ability to obligate the partnership?

3. If a partnership cannot pay a debt, who must make payment? What term describes this obligation of the partners?

4. How is partnership income taxed?

5. Identify the advantages and disadvantages of the partnership form of business organization.

6. Randall and Smith's partnership agreement states that Randall gets 60 percent of profits and Smith gets 40 percent. If the agreement does not discuss the treatment of losses, how are losses shared? How do the partners share profits and losses if the agreement specifies no profit-and-loss-sharing ratio?

7. Are salary and interest allocated to partners expenses of the business? Why or why not?

8. What determines the amount of the credit to a partner's capital account when the partner contributes assets other than cash to the business?

9. Do partner withdrawals of cash for personal use affect the sharing of profits and losses by the partner? If so, explain how. If not, explain why not.

10. Name two events that can cause the dissolution of a partnership.

11. Briefly describe how to account for the purchase of an existing partner's interest in the business.

12. Malcolm purchases Brown's interest in the Brown & Kareem partnership. What right does Malcolm obtain from the purchase? What is required for Malcolm to become Kareem's partner?

13. Assissi and Carter each have capital of $75,000 in their business and share profits in the ratio of 55:45. Denman acquires a one-fifth share in the partnership by investing cash of $50,000. What are the capital balances of the three partners immediately after Denman is admitted?

14. When a partner resigns from the partnership and receives assets greater than her capital balance, how is the excess shared by the other partners?

15. Why are the assets of a partnership often revalued when a partner is about to withdraw from the firm?

16. Distinguish between dissolution and liquidation of a partnership.

17. Name the three steps in liquidating a partnership.

18. Why does the cash of a partnership equal the sum of its partner capital balances after the business sells its noncash assets and pays its liabilities?

19. The partnership of Ralls and Sauls is in the process of liquidation. How do the partners share (a) gains and losses on the sale of noncash assets and (b) the final cash disbursement?

20. Fernandez, Garcia, and Estrada are partners, sharing profits and losses in the ratio of 3:2:1. In liquidation, Estrada's share of losses on the sale of assets exceeds his capital balance. What becomes of Estrada's capital deficiency if Estrada cannot make it up?

21. Compare and contrast the financial statements of a proprietorship and a partnership.

22. Summarize the situations in which partnership allocations are based on (a) the profit-and-loss ratio and (b) the partners' capital balances.

Exercises

Exercise 13-1   *Recording a partner's investment*

Ann Clinton has operated an apartment-locater service as a proprietorship. She and Amanda Doss have decided to reorganize the business as a partnership. Ann's investment in the partnership consists of cash, $8,100; accounts receivable, $13,600 less allowance for uncollectibles, $800; office furniture, $2,700 less accumulated depreciation, $1,100; a small building, $55,000 less accumulated depreciation, $27,500; accounts payable, $3,300; and a note payable to the bank, $10,000.

To determine Ann's equity in the partnership, she and Amanda hire an independent appraiser. This outside party provides the following market values of the assets and liabilities that Ann is contributing to the business: cash, accounts receivable, office furniture and related accumulated depreciation, accounts payable, and note payable—the same as Ann's book value; allowance for uncollectible accounts, $2,900; building, $70,000 less accumulated depreciation, $35,000; and accrued expenses payable (including interest on the note payable), $1,200.

Required

Make the entry on the partnership books to record Ann's investment.

Exercise 13-2   *Preparing a partnership balance sheet*

On October 31, 19X9, Alpha and Beta agree to combine their proprietorships as a partnership. Their balance sheets on October 31 are as follows:

Assets	Alpha's Business Book Value	Alpha's Business Current Market Value	Beta's Business Book Value	Beta's Business Current Market Value
Cash	$ 8,000	$ 8,000	$ 3,700	$ 3,700
Accounts receivable (net)	13,000	11,800	22,000	20,200
Inventory	34,000	35,100	51,000	46,000
Plant assets (net)	53,500	57,400	121,800	123,500
Total assets	$108,500	$112,300	$198,500	$193,400

Liabilities and Capital				
Accounts payable	$ 9,100	$ 9,100	$ 23,600	$ 23,600
Accrued expenses payable	800	800	2,200	2,200
Notes payable	—	—	75,000	75,000
Alpha, capital	98,600	102,400		
Beta, capital			97,700	92,600
Total liabilities and capital	$108,500	$112,300	$198,500	$193,400

Required

Prepare the partnership balance sheet at October 31, 19X9.

Exercise 13-3   *Computing partners' shares of net income*

Roy Dean and Joe Edwards form a partnership, investing $30,000 and $60,000, respectively. Determine their shares of net income or net loss for each of the following situations:

a. Net loss is $69,000, and the partners have no written partnership agreement.
b. Net income is $84,000, and the partnership agreement states that the partners share profits and losses based on their capital contributions.

c. Net loss is $63,000, and the partnership agreement states that the partners share profits based on their capital contributions.

d. Net income is $105,000. The first $40,000 is shared based on the partner capital contributions. The next $30,000 is based on partner service, with Dean receiving 30 percent and Edwards receiving 70 percent. The remainder is shared equally.

Exercise 13-4   *Computing partners' capital balances*

Roy Dean withdrew cash of $52,000 for personal use, and Joe Edwards withdrew cash of $60,000 during the year. Using the data from situation d in Exercise 13-3, journalize the entries to close the (a) income summary account and (b) the partners' drawing accounts. Explanations are not required.

Indicate the amount of increase or decrease in each partner's capital balance. What was the overall effect on partnership capital?

Exercise 13-5   *Admitting a new partner*

Jack Phillips is admitted to a partnership. Prior to the admission of Phillips, the partnership books show Susan Reckers's capital balance at $80,000 and Lewis Schmitz's capital balance at $40,000. Compute the amount of each partner's equity on the books of the new partnership under each of the following plans:

a. Phillips pays $30,000 for Schmitz's equity. Phillips's payment is not an investment in the partnership but instead goes directly to Schmitz.

b. Phillips invests $30,000 to acquire a one-fifth interest in the partnership.

c. Phillips invests $60,000 to acquire a one-fourth interest in the partnership.

Exercise 13-6   *Recording the admission of a new partner*

Make the partnership journal entry to record the admission of Phillips under plans a, b, and c in Exercise 13-5. Explanations are not required.

Exercise 13-7   *Withdrawal of a partner*

After closing the books, T&W's partnership balance sheet reports capital of $50,000 for T and $70,000 for W. T is withdrawing from the firm. The partners agree to write down partnership assets by $30,000. They have shared profits and losses in the ratio of one third to T and two thirds to W. If the partnership agreement states that a withdrawing partner will receive assets equal to the book value of his owner's equity, how much will T receive?

W will continue to operate the business as a proprietorship. What is W's beginning capital on the proprietorship books?

Exercise 13-8   *Withdrawal of a partner*

Lana Brown is retiring from the partnership of Brown, Green, and White on May 31. After the books are closed on that date, the partner capital balances are Brown, $36,000; Green, $51,000; and White, $22,000. The partners agree to have the partnership assets revalued to current market values. The independent appraiser reports that the book value of the inventory should be decreased by $8,000, and the book value of the building should be increased by $32,000. The partners agree to these revaluations. The profit-and-loss ratio has been 5:3:2 for Brown, Green, and White, respectively. In retiring from the firm, Brown receives $25,000 cash and a $25,000 note from the partnership. Journalize (a) the asset revaluations and (b) Brown's withdrawal from the firm.

Exercise 13-9   *Liquidation of a partnership*

Marsh, Ng, and Orsulak are liquidating their partnership. Before selling the noncash assets and paying the liabilities, the capital balances are Marsh, $23,000; Ng, $14,000; and Orsulak, $11,000. The partnership agreement divides profits and losses equally.

a. After selling the noncash assets and paying the liabilities, the partnership has cash of $48,000. How much cash will each partner receive in final liquidation?

b. After selling the noncash assets and paying the liabilities, the partnership has cash of $45,000. How much cash will each partner receive in final liquidation?

Exercise 13-10   *Liquidation of a partnership*

Prior to liquidation, the accounting records of Pratt, Qualls, and Ramirez included the following balances and profit-and-loss-sharing percentages:

				Capital		
	Cash +	Noncash Assets	= Liabilities +	Pratt (40%)	Qualls (30%)	Ramirez (30%)
Balances before sale of assets...	$8,000	$57,000	$19,000	$20,000	$15,000	$11,000

73,000   — 19,000

The partnership sold the noncash assets for $73,000, paid the liabilities, and disbursed the remaining cash to the partners. Complete the summary of transactions in the liquidation of the partnership. Use the format illustrated in the chapter.

(Group A)

Problems

Problem 13-1A   *Investments by partners*

Geraci and Hutton formed a partnership on March 15. The partners agreed to invest equal amounts of capital. Hutton invested her proprietorship's assets and liabilities (credit balances in parentheses):

	Hutton's Book Value	Current Market Value
Accounts receivable...............	$ 12,000	$ 12,000
Allowance for doubtful accounts	(740)	(1,360)
Inventory	43,850	51,220
Prepaid expenses................	2,400	2,400
Store equipment..................	36,700	31,000
Accumulated depreciation..........	(9,200)	(7,800)
Accounts payable................	(22,300)	(22,300)

On March 15 Geraci invested cash in an amount equal to the current market value of Hutton's partnership capital, which was $65,160. The partners decided that Hutton would earn 70 percent of partnership profits because she would manage the business. Geraci agreed to accept 30 percent of profits. During the period ended December 31, the partnership earned $55,000. Geraci's drawings were $12,000, and Hutton's drawings were $36,000.

Required

1. Journalize the partners' initial investments.
2. Prepare the partnership balance sheet immediately after its formation on March 15.
3. Journalize the December 31 entries to close the income summary account and the partner drawing accounts.

Problem 13-2A *Computing partners' shares of net income and net loss*

J. Warner, S. Deitmer, and R. Mullaney have formed a partnership. Warner invested $20,000, Deitmer $40,000, and Mullaney $60,000. Warner will manage the store, Deitmer will work in the store three quarters of the time, and Mullaney will not work in the business.

Required

1. Compute the partners' shares of profits and losses under each of the following plans. Use this format for your answer:

	Warner	Deitmer	Mullaney	Total
Total net income (net loss)...............				
Allocation to the partners:				
Warner............................				
Deitmer...........................				
Mullaney..........................				
Total...........................				
Net income (loss) left for allocation........				

Add a line for "Net income allocated to partners" as necessary.

   a. Net income is $27,000, and the articles of partnership do not specify how profits and losses are shared.

   b. Net loss is $47,000, and the partnership agreement allocates 45 percent of profits to Warner, 35 percent to Deitmer, and 20 percent to Mullaney. The agreement does not discuss the sharing of losses.

   c. Net income is $104,000. The first $50,000 is allocated based on salaries of $34,000 for Warner and $16,000 for Deitmer. The remainder is allocated based on partner capital contributions.

   d. Net income for the year ended September 30, 19X4, is $81,000. The first $42,000 is allocated based on partner capital contributions. The next $30,000 is based on service, with $20,000 going to Warner and $10,000 going to Deitmer. Any remainder is shared equally.

2. Revenues for the year ended September 30, 19X4, were $621,000, and expenses were $540,000. Under plan d, prepare the partnership income statement for the year.

Problem 13-3A *Recording changes in partnership capital*

Red River Resort is a partnership, and its owners are considering admitting Greg Lake as a new partner. On July 31 of the current year the capital accounts of the three existing partners and their shares of profits and losses are as follows:

	Capital	Profit-and-Loss Ratio
Ellen Urlang	$48,000	1/6
Amy Sharp	64,000	1/3
Bob Hayes..................	88,000	1/2

Required

Journalize the admission of Lake as a partner on July 31 for each of the following independent situations:

1. Urlang gives her partnership share to Lake, who is her nephew.
2. Lake pays Hayes $50,000 cash to purchase one half of Hayes's interest.
3. Lake invests $50,000 in the partnership, acquiring a one-fifth interest in the business.

4. Lake invests $40,000 in the partnership, acquiring a one-eighth interest in the business.

5. Lake invests $30,000 in the partnership, acquiring a 15 percent interest in the business.

Problem 13-4A *Recording changes in partnership capital*

Boat Town is a partnership owned by three individuals. The partners share profits and losses in the ratio of 30 percent to Golden, 40 percent to Miller, and 30 percent to Ramos. At December 31, 19X6, the firm has the following balance sheet:

Cash...............		$ 25,000	Total liabilities........	$103,000
Accounts receivable ...	$ 16,000			
Less allowance for uncollectibles.....	1,000	15,000		
Inventory...........		51,000	Golden, Capital.......	23,000
Equipment..........	130,000		Miller, Capital	41,000
Less accumulated depreciation......	30,000	100,000	Ramos, Capital	24,000
			Total liabilities and	
Total assets		$191,000	capital	$191,000

Golden withdraws from the partnership on this date.

Required

Record Golden's withdrawal from the partnership under the following plans:

1. Golden gives his interest in the business to Wilson, his son-in-law.
2. In personal transactions, Golden sells his equity in the partnership to Meyers and Sloan, who each pay Golden $15,000 for one half of his interest. Miller and Ramos agree to accept Meyers and Sloan as partners.
3. The partnership pays Golden cash of $5,000 and gives him a note payable for the remainder of his book equity in settlement of his partnership interest.
4. Golden receives cash of $10,000 and a note for $20,000 from the partnership.
5. The partners agree that the equipment is worth $150,000 and that accumulated depreciation should remain at $30,000. After the revaluation, the partnership settles with Golden by giving him cash of $10,000 and inventory for the remainder of his book equity.

Problem 13-5A *Liquidation of a partnership*

The partnership of Yagoda, Kelly, and Dobbs has experienced operating losses for three consecutive years. The partners, who have shared profits and losses in the ratio of Yagoda 15 percent, Kelly 60 percent, and Dobbs 25 percent, are considering the liquidation of the business. They ask you to analyze the effects of liquidation under various possibilities about the sale of the noncash assets. They present the following condensed partnership balance sheet at December 31, end of the current year:

Cash....................	$ 18,000	Liabilities	$ 74,000
Noncash assets	163,000	Yagoda, Capital............	19,000
		Kelly, Capital..............	66,000
		Dobbs, Capital.............	22,000
Total assets	$181,000	Total liabilities and capital ...	$181,000

Required

1. Prepare a summary of liquidation transactions (as illustrated in the chapter) for each of the following situations:

a. The noncash assets are sold for $175,000.

b. The noncash assets are sold for $133,000.

c. The noncash assets are sold for $63,000, and the partner with a capital deficiency is personally bankrupt.

d. The noncash assets are sold for $60,000, and the partner with a capital deficiency pays cash of $1,500 to the partnership to erase part of the deficiency.

2. Make the journal entries to record the liquidation transactions in requirement 1d.

Problem 13-6A *Liquidation of a partnership*

RMG & Company is a partnership owned by Ryan, Morales, and Goldberg, who share profits and losses in the ratio of 1:3:4. The adjusted trial balance of the partnership (in condensed form) at June 30, end of the current fiscal year, follows.

RMG & Company
Adjusted Trial Balance
June 30, 19XX

Cash...............................	$ 14,000	
Noncash assets	116,000	
Liabilities..........................		$100,000
Ryan, capital		22,000
Morales, capital.....................		41,000
Goldberg, capital....................		62,000
Ryan, drawing.......................	24,000	
Morales, drawing....................	35,000	
Goldberg, drawing	54,000	
Revenues...........................		108,000
Expenses	90,000	
Totals.............................	$333,000	$333,000

Required

1. Prepare the June 30 entries to close the revenue, expense, income summary, and drawing accounts.

2. Insert the opening capital balances in the partner capital accounts, post the closing entries to the capital accounts, and determine each partner's ending capital balance.

3. The partnership liquidates on June 30 by selling the noncash assets for $100,000. Using the ending balances of the partner capital accounts, prepare a summary of liquidation transactions (as illustrated in the chapter). Any partner with a capital deficiency is unable to contribute assets to erase the deficiency.

(Group B)

Problem 13-1B *Investments by partners*

On June 30 McMinn and Carrico formed a partnership. The partners agreed to invest equal amounts of capital. McMinn invested her proprietorship's assets and liabilities (credit balances in parentheses).

On June 30 Carrico invested cash in an amount equal to the current market value of McMinn's partnership capital, which was $46,250. The partners decided that McMinn would earn two thirds of partnership profits because she would manage the business. Carrico agreed to accept one third of profits. During the remainder of the year, the partnership earned $48,000. McMinn's drawings were $35,200, and Carrico's drawings were $14,000.

	McMinn's Book Value	Current Market Value
Accounts receivable..................	$ 8,100	$ 8,100
Allowance for doubtful accounts........	(-0-)	(1,050)
Inventory.........................	22,340	29,000
Prepaid expenses....................	1,700	1,700
Office equipment....................	45,900	41,400
Accumulated depreciation	(15,300)	(13,800)
Accounts payable	(19,100)	(19,100)

Required

1. Journalize the partners' initial investments.
2. Prepare the partnership balance sheet immediately after its formation on June 30.
3. Journalize the December 31 entries to close the income summary account and the partner drawing accounts.

Problem 13-2B   *Computing partners' shares of net income and net loss*

D. Hogan, E. Stanford, and S. Reichlin have formed a partnership. Hogan invested $6,000, Stanford $18,000, and Reichlin $36,000. Hogan will manage the store, Stanford will work in the store half time, and Reichlin will not work in the business.

Required

1. Compute the partners' shares of profits and losses under each of the following plans. Use this format for your answer:

	Hogan	Stanford	Reichlin	Total
Total net income (net loss).............				
Allocation to the partners:				
Hogan				
Stanford......................				
Reichlin				
Total......................				
Net income (loss) left for allocation........				

Add a line for "Net income allocated to partners" as necessary.

   a. Net loss is $51,600, and the articles of partnership do not specify how profits and losses are shared.
   b. Net loss is $70,000, and the partnership agreement allocates 40 percent of profits to Hogan, 25 percent to Stanford, and 35 percent to Reichlin. The agreement does not discuss the sharing of losses.
   c. Net income is $88,000. The first $40,000 is allocated based on salaries, with Hogan receiving $28,000 and Stanford receiving $12,000. The remainder is allocated based on partner capital contributions.
   d. Net income for the year ended January 31, 19X8, is $132,000. The first $75,000 is allocated based on partner capital contributions, and the next $36,000 is based on service, with Hogan receiving $28,000 and Stanford receiving $8,000. Any remainder is shared equally.
2. Revenues for the year ended January 31, 19X8, were $872,000, and expenses were $740,000. Under plan d, prepare the partnership income statement for the year.

Problem 13-3B   *Recording changes in partnership capital*

Englewood Consulting Associates is a partnership, and its owners are considering admitting Hilda Newton as a new partner. On March 31 of the current year the capital accounts of the three existing partners and their shares of profits and losses are as follows:

	Capital	Profit-and-Loss Percent
Jim Zook.	$ 40,000	15%
Richard Land	100,000	30
Jennifer Lim	160,000	55

Required

Journalize the admission of Newton as a partner on March 31 for each of the following independent situations:

1. Land gives his partnership share to H. Newton, who is his daughter.
2. Newton pays Lim $145,000 cash to purchase Lim's interest in the partnership.
3. Newton invests $60,000 in the partnership, acquiring a one-sixth interest in the business.
4. Newton invests $60,000 in the partnership, acquiring a one-fifth interest in the business.
5. Newton invests $40,000 in the partnership, acquiring a 10 percent interest in the business.

Problem 13-4B   *Recording changes in partnership capital*

Pediatric Associates is a partnership owned by three individuals. The partners share profits and losses in the ratio of 31 percent to Turman, 38 percent to Herron, and 31 percent to Tyler. At December 31, 19X7, the firm has the following balance sheet.

Cash.		$ 31,000	Total liabilities	$ 94,000
Accounts receivable . . .	$ 22,000			
Less allowance for				
uncollectibles	4,000	18,000	Turman, capital	61,000
Office equipment.	$310,000		Herron, capital.	72,000
Less accumulated			Tyler, capital	62,000
depreciation	70,000	240,000	Total liabilities and	
Total assets		$289,000	capital	$289,000

Herron withdraws from the partnership on December 31, 19X7, to establish her own medical practice.

Required

Record Herron's withdrawal from the partnership under the following plans:

1. Herron gives her interest in the business to Zagat, her niece.
2. In personal transactions, Herron sells her equity in the partnership to Grimes and Hirsh, who each pay Herron $50,000 for one half of her interest. Turman and Tyler agree to accept Grimes and Hirsh as partners.
3. The partnership pays Herron cash of $15,000 and gives her a note payable for the remainder of her book equity in settlement of her partnership interest.
4. Herron receives cash of $10,000 and a note for $70,000 from the partnership.
5. The partners agree that the office equipment is worth only $280,000 and that its accumulated depreciation should remain at $70,000. After the revaluation, the partnership settles with Herron by giving her cash of $10,600 and a note payable for the remainder of her book equity.

Problem 13-5B   *Liquidation of a partnership*

The partnership of Monet, Dixon, and Palma has experienced operating losses for three consecutive years. The partners, who have shared profits and losses in the ratio of Monet 20 percent, Dixon 30 percent, and Palma 50 percent, are considering the liquidation of the business. They ask you to analyze the effects of liquidation under various possibilities about the sale of the noncash assets. They present the following condensed partnership balance sheet at December 31, end of the current year:

Cash....................	$ 27,000	Liabilities	$131,000
Noncash assets	202,000	Monet, capital	13,000
		Dixon, capital	39,000
		Palma, capital	46,000
Total assets	$229,000	Total liabilities and capital ...	$229,000

Required

1. Prepare a summary of liquidation transactions (as illustrated in the chapter) for each of the following situations:
   a. The noncash assets are sold for $212,000.
   b. The noncash assets are sold for $194,000.
   c. The noncash assets are sold for $122,000, and the partner with a capital deficiency pays cash to the partnership to erase the deficiency.
   d. The noncash assets are sold for $124,000, and the partner with a capital deficiency is personally bankrupt.
2. Make the journal entries to record the liquidation transactions in requirement 1d.

Problem 13-6B   *Liquidation of a partnership*

BP&O is a partnership owned by Bell, Pastena, and O'Donnell, who share profits and losses in the ratio of 5:3:2. The adjusted trial balance of the partnership (in condensed form) at September 30, end of the current fiscal year, follows.

BP&O **Adjusted Trial Balance** **September 30, 19XX**		
Cash..............................	$ 7,000	
Noncash assets	177,000	
Liabilities		$135,000
Bell, capital		57,000
Pastena, capital		44,000
O'Donnell, capital...................		18,000
Bell, drawing	45,000	
Pastena, drawing....................	37,000	
O'Donnell, drawing..................	18,000	
Revenues		211,000
Expenses	181,000	
Totals.............................	$465,000	$465,000

Required

1. Prepare the September 30 entries to close the revenue, expense, income summary, and drawing accounts.
2. Insert the opening capital balances in the partner capital accounts, post the closing entries to the capital accounts, and determine each partner's ending capital balance.
3. The partnership liquidates on September 30 by selling the noncash assets for $132,000. Using the ending balances of the partner capital accounts, prepare a summary of liquidation transactions (as illustrated in the chapter). Any partner with a capital deficiency is unable to contribute assets to erase the deficiency.

Decision Problem — Disagreements Among Partners

Clay Grant invested $20,000 and Elaine Marsh invested $10,000 in a public relations firm that has operated for 10 years. Neither partner has made an additional investment. They have shared profits and losses in the ratio of 2:1, which is the ratio of their investments in the business. Grant manages the office, supervises the 16 employees, and does the accounting. Marsh, the moderator of a television talk show, is responsible for marketing. Her high profile generates important revenue for the business. During the year ended December 19X4 the partnership earned net income of $87,000, shared in the 2:1 ratio. On December 31, 19X4, Grant's capital balance was $120,000, and Marsh's capital balance was $80,000.

Required

Respond to each of the following situations:

1. What explains the difference between the ratio of partner capital balances at December 31, 19X4, and the 2:1 ratio of partner investments and profit sharing?
2. Marsh believes the profit-and-loss-sharing ratio is unfair. She proposes a change, but Grant insists on keeping the 2:1 ratio. What two factors may underlie Marsh's unhappiness?
3. During January 19X5 Grant learned that revenues of $18,000 were omitted from the reported 19X4 income. He brings this to Marsh's attention, pointing out that his share of this added income is two thirds, or $12,000, and Marsh's share is one third, or $6,000. Marsh believes they should share this added income based on their capital balances—60 percent, or $10,800, to Grant and 40 percent, or $7,200, to Marsh. Which partner is correct? Why?
4. Assume the 19X4 $18,000 omission was an account payable for an operating expense. How would the partners share this amount?

Answers to Self-Study Questions

1. a
2. b
3. a ($40,000 × 3/12 = $10,000)
4. d ($40,000 × 5/12 = $16,667)
5. a
6. c [($46,000 + $52,000 + $55,000) × 1/3 = $51,000; $55,000 − $51,000 = $4,000; $4,000 ÷ 2 = $2,000 each to Graff and Harrell]
7. d
8. b ($36,000 × 1/4 = $9,000)
9. d
10. c

14

Corporations: Organization, Paid-In Capital, and the Balance Sheet

LEARNING OBJECTIVES
After studying this chapter, you should be able to

1 Identify the characteristics of a corporation

2 Record the issuance of stock

3 Prepare the stockholders' equity section of a corporation balance sheet

4 Account for the incorporation of a going business

5 Allocate dividends to preferred and common stock

6 Distinguish among various stock "values"

The corporation is the dominant form of business organization in the United States. Although proprietorships and partnerships are more numerous, corporations transact more business and are larger in terms of total assets, sales revenue, and number of employees. Most well-known companies, such as CBS, General Motors, IBM, and Pillsbury, are corporations. Their full names include *Corporation* or *Incorporated* (abbreviated *Corp.* and *Inc.*) to indicate that they are corporations, for example, CBS, Inc. and General Motors Corporation. This chapter and the next three discuss corporations and how to account for them.

Characteristics of a Corporation

Why is the corporation form of business so attractive? We now look at the features that distinguish corporations from proprietorships and partnerships.

Separate Legal Entity

A **corporation** is a business entity formed under state law. The state grants a **charter,** which is the document that gives the state's permission to form a corporation.

A corporation is a distinct entity from a legal perspective. We may consider the corporation as an artificial person that exists apart from its owners, who are called **stockholders** or **shareholders.** The corporation has many of the rights that a person has. For example, a corporation may buy, own, and sell property. Assets

> **OBJECTIVE 1**
> Identify the characteristics of a corporation

and liabilities in the business belong to the corporation. The corporation may enter into contracts, sue, and be sued.

The owners' equity of a corporation is divided into shares of **stock.** A person becomes a stockholder by purchasing the stock of the corporation. The corporate charter specifies how much stock the corporation can issue (sell) and lists the other details of its relationship with the state.

Continuous Life and Transferability of Ownership

Most corporations have continuous lives regardless of changes in the ownership of their stock. Stockholders may transfer stock as they wish. They may sell or trade the stock to another person, give it away, bequeath it in a will, or dispose of it in any other way they desire. The transfer of the stock does not affect the continuity of the corporation. Proprietorships and partnerships, on the other hand, terminate when their ownership changes.

No Mutual Agency

Mutual agency of the owners is *not* present in a corporation. The stockholder of a corporation cannot commit the corporation to a contract (unless he or she is also an officer in the business). For this reason, a stockholder need not exercise the care that partners must in selecting co-owners of the business.

Limited Liability of Stockholders

A stockholder has **limited liability** for corporation debts. He or she has no personal obligation for corporation liabilities. The most that a stockholder can lose on an investment in a corporation's stock is the cost of the investment. Recall that proprietors and partners are personally liable for the debts of their businesses.

The combination of limited liability and no mutual agency means that persons can invest limited amounts in a corporation without fear of losing all their personal wealth because of a business failure. This feature enables a corporation to raise more capital from a wider group of investors than proprietorships and partnerships.

Separation of Ownership and Management

Stockholders own the business, but a board of directors—elected by the stockholders—appoints corporate officers to manage the business. Thus stockholders may invest $1,000 or $1 million in the corporation without having to manage the business or disrupt their personal affairs.

However, this separation between owners—stockholders—and management may create problems. Corporate officers may decide to run the business for their own benefit and not to the stockholders' advantage. Stockholders may find it difficult to lodge an effective protest against management policy because of the distance between them and management.

Corporate Taxation

Corporations are separate taxable entities. They pay a variety of taxes not borne by proprietorships or partnerships. These taxes include an annual franchise tax levied by the state. The franchise tax is paid to keep the corporation charter in force and enables the corporation to continue in business. Corporations also pay federal and state income taxes. Corporate earnings are subject to **double taxation.** First, corporations pay their own income taxes on corporate income. Then, the stockholders pay personal income tax on the cash dividends that they receive from corporations. This is different from proprietorships and partnerships, which pay no business income tax. Instead, the tax falls solely on the owners.

Government Regulation

Strong government regulation is an important disadvantage to the corporation. Because stockholders have only limited liability for corporation debts, outsiders doing business with the corporation can look no further than the corporation itself for any claims that may arise against the business. To protect persons who loan money to a corporation or who invest in its stock, states monitor the affairs of corporations. This government regulation consists mainly of ensuring that corporations disclose the business information that investors and creditors need to make informed decisions. For many corporations, this government regulation is expensive.

Organization of a Corporation

Creation of a corporation begins when its organizers, called the **incorporators,** obtain a charter from the state. The **charter** includes the authorization for the corporation to issue a certain number of shares of stock, which are shares of ownership in the corporation. The incorporators pay fees, sign the charter, and file the required documents with the state. Then the corporation comes into existence. The incorporators agree to a set of **bylaws,** which act as the constitution for governing the corporation.

The ultimate control of the corporation rests with the stockholders, who receive one vote for each share of stock they own. The stockholders elect the members of the **board of directors,** which sets policy for the corporation and appoints the officers. The board elects a **chairperson,** who usually is the most powerful person in the corporation. The board also designates the **president,** who is the chief operating officer in charge of managing day-to-day operations. Most corporations also have vice-presidents in charge of sales, manufacturing, accounting and finance, and other key areas. Often the president and one or more vice-presidents are also elected to the board of directors. Exhibit 14-1 shows the authority structure in a corporation.

Most corporations have an annual meeting at which the stockholders elect directors and make other stockholder decisions. Stockholders unable to attend this annual meeting may vote on corporation matters by use of a **proxy,** which is a legal document that expresses the stockholder's preference and appoints another person to cast the vote.

The structure of proprietorships, partnerships, and corporations is similar in that all three types of business have owners, managers, and employees. In proprietorships and partnerships, policy decisions are usually made by the owners — the proprietor and the partners. In a corporation, however, the managers who set policy — the board of directors — may or may not be owners (stockholders).

A corporation keeps a subsidiary record of its stockholders. The business must notify the stockholders of the annual stockholder meeting and mail them dividend payments (which we discuss later in this chapter). Large companies use a

EXHIBIT 14-1 *Authority Structure in a Corporation*

```
                    ┌──────────────────┐
                    │   Stockholders   │
                    └──────────────────┘
                             │
                             ▼
                    ┌──────────────────┐
                    │ Board of Directors │
                    └──────────────────┘
                             │
                             ▼
                    ┌──────────────────┐
                    │ Chairperson of the Board │
                    └──────────────────┘
                             │
                             ▼
                    ┌──────────────────┐
                    │    President     │
                    └──────────────────┘
                             │
                             ▼
                    ┌──────────────────┐
                    │  Vice-Presidents │
                    └──────────────────┘
                             │
                             ▼
                    ┌──────────────────┐
                    │ All Other Employees │
                    └──────────────────┘
```

registrar to maintain the stockholder list and a transfer agent to issue stock certificates. Banks provide these registration and transfer services. The transfer agent handles the change in stock ownership from one shareholder to another.

Capital Stock

A corporation issues stock certificates to its owners in exchange for their investments in the business. The basic unit of capital stock is called a *share*. A corporation may issue a stock certificate for any number of shares it wishes — one share, one hundred shares, or any other number. Exhibit 14-2 depicts an actual stock certificate for one share of IBM stock. The certificate shows the company name, the stockholder name, the number of shares, and the par value of the stock (which we discuss later).

Stock in the hands of a stockholder is said to be **outstanding.** The total number of shares of stock outstanding at any time represents 100 percent ownership of the corporation. Because stock represents the corporation's capital, it is often called capital stock.

Stockholders' Equity

The balance sheet of a corporation reports assets and liabilities in the same way as a proprietorship or a partnership. However, owners' equity of a corporation — called **stockholders' equity** — is reported differently. State laws require corpora-

EXHIBIT 14-2 *Stock Certificate*

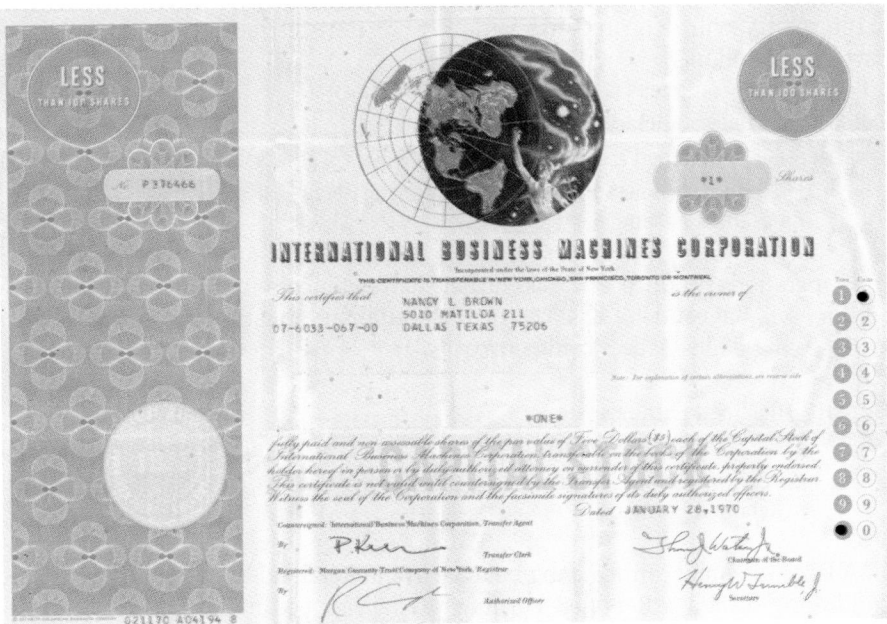

tions to report the sources of their capital. The two most basic sources of capital are investments by the stockholders, called **paid-in capital** or **contributed capital,** and capital earned through profitable operation of the business, called **retained earnings.** Exhibit 14-3 outlines a simplified corporation balance sheet to show how to report these categories of stockholders' equity.

An investment of cash or any other asset in a corporation increases its assets and stockholders' equity. The corporation's entry for receipt of a $20,000 stockholder investment in the business is

Oct. 20	Cash	20,000
	Capital Stock	20,000
	Investment by stockholders.	

Capital stock is paid-in capital. It is regarded as the permanent capital of the business because it is *not* subject to withdrawal by the stockholders.

Profitable operations produce income, which increases stockholders' equity through an account called Retained Earnings. At the end of the year, the balance

EXHIBIT 14-3 *Simplified Corporation Balance Sheet*

Assets..................	$600,000	Liabilities	$240,000
		Stockholders' Equity	
		Paid-in capital:	
		Capital stock	200,000
		Retained earnings......	160,000
		Total stockholders'	
		equity	360,000
		Total liabilities and	
Total assets..............	$600,000	stockholders' equity.....	$600,000

of the Income Summary account is closed to Retained Earnings. For example, if net income is $95,000, Income Summary will have a $95,000 credit balance. The closing entry will debit Income Summary to transfer net income to Retained Earnings as follows:

Dec. 31   Income Summary.............................   95,000
                  Retained Earnings   95,000
           To close Income Summary by transferring net *income* to
           Retained Earnings.

If operations produce a net *loss* rather than net income, the Income Summary account will have a debit balance. Income Summary must be credited to close it. With a $60,000 loss, the closing entry is:

Dec. 31   Retained Earnings   60,000
                  Income Summary.........................   60,000
           To close Income Summary by transferring net *loss* to
           Retained Earnings.

A large loss may cause a debit balance in the Retained Earnings account. This condition—called a Retained Earnings **deficit,** or accumulated deficit—is reported on the balance sheet as a negative amount in stockholders' equity. Assume a $50,000 deficit:

Stockholders' Equity

Paid-in capital:	
Capital stock	$200,000
Deficit............................	(50,000)
Total stockholders' equity.............	$150,000

If the corporation has been profitable and has sufficient cash, a distribution of cash may be made to the stockholders. Such distributions—called **dividends**—decrease both the assets and the retained earnings of the business. The balance of the Retained Earnings account at any time is the sum of earnings accumulated since incorporation, minus any losses, and minus all dividends distributed to stockholders. Retained Earnings is entirely separate from the paid-in capital invested in the business by the stockholders.

Some people think of Retained Earnings as a fund of cash. It is not, because Retained Earnings is an element of stockholders' equity, representing a claim against all assets resulting from earnings that have not been distributed to the owners.

Stockholder Rights

The ownership of stock entitles stockholders to four basic rights, unless specific rights are withheld by agreement with the stockholders.

1. The right to participate in management by voting on matters that come before the stockholders. This is the stockholder's sole right to a voice in the management of the corporation. Each share of stock entitles the owner to one vote.

2. The right to receive a proportionate part of any dividend. Each share of stock in a particular class receives an equal dividend.

3. The right to receive a proportionate share (based on number of shares held) of any assets remaining after the corporation pays its liabilities in liquidation.

4. The right to maintain one's proportionate ownership in the corporation. Suppose you own 5 percent of a corporation's stock. If the corporation issues 100,000 new shares of stock, it must offer you the opportunity to buy 5 percent (5,000) of the new shares. This right, called the **preemptive right,** is usually withheld from the stockholders.

Classes of Stock

Corporations issue different types of stock to appeal to a wide variety of investors. The stock of a corporation may be either common or preferred and either par or no-par.

Common and Preferred Stock

Every corporation issues **common stock,** the most basic form of capital stock. Unless designated otherwise, the word *stock* is understood to mean "common stock." Common stockholders have the four basic rights of stock ownership, unless a right is specifically withheld. For example, some companies issue Class A common stock, which usually carries the right to vote, and Class B common stock, which may be nonvoting. (Classes of common stock may also be designated Series A, Series B, and so on.) The general ledger has a separate account for each class of common stock. In describing a corporation, we would say the common stockholders are the owners of the business.

Owners of **preferred stock** also have the four basic stockholder rights, unless a right is specifically denied. Often the right to vote is withheld from preferred stockholders. Preferred stock gives its owners certain advantages over common stockholders. These benefits include the priority to receive dividends before the common stockholders and the priority to receive assets before the common stockholders if the corporation liquidates. Because of the priorities that preferred stockholders have, we see that common stock represents the residual ownership in the corporation's assets after subtracting the liabilities and the claims of preferred stockholders. Companies may issue different classes of preferred stock. (Class A and Class B or Series A and Series B, for example). Each class is recorded in a separate account.

Par Value and No-Par Stock

Stock may be par value stock or no-par stock. **Par value** is an arbitrary amount assigned to a share of stock. Most companies set the par value of their common stock quite low. J.C. Penney's common stock par value is 50¢ per share, Bethlehem Steel's common stock par value is $8 per share, and Ralston Purina's common stock par value is $41\frac{2}{3}$¢ per share. Par value of preferred stock is often higher; $100 per share is typical, but some preferred stocks have par value of $25 and $10. Par value is used to compute dividends, as we shall see. **No-par** stock does not have par value, but some no-par stock has a *stated value*, which makes it similar to par value stock.

Issuing Stock

The charter that the incorporators receive from the state includes an **authorization** for the business to issue—that is, to sell—a certain number of shares of stock. Corporations may sell the stock directly to the stockholders or they may use the service of an *underwriter,* such as the brokerage firms Merrill Lynch and Dean Witter. An underwriter agrees to buy all the stock it cannot sell to its clients.

The corporation need not issue all the stock that the state allows. Management may hold some stock back and issue it later if the need for additional capital arises. The stock that the corporation does issue to stockholders is called issued stock. Only by issuing stock—not by receiving authorization—does the corporation increase the asset and equity amounts on its balance sheet.

The price that the stockholder pays to acquire stock from the corporation is called the issue price. Often the issue price bears no relation to the stock's par value because the par value was intentionally set quite low. A combination of market factors, including the company's comparative earnings record, financial position, prospects for success, and general business conditions, determines issue price. Investors will not pay more than market value for the stock. The following sections show how to account for the issuance of stock.

Issuing Common Stock

Issuing Common Stock at Par.   Suppose Medina Corporation issues 500 shares of its $10 par common stock for cash equal to its par value. The stock issuance entry is

OBJECTIVE 2

Record the issuance of stock

Jan. 8	Cash (500 × $10)	5,000	
	Common Stock		5,000
	To issue common stock at par.		

The amount invested in the corporation, $5,000 in this case, is called paid-in capital or contributed capital. The credit to Common Stock records an increase in the paid-in capital of the corporation.

Issuing Common Stock at a Premium.   A corporation usually issues its common stock for a price above par value. The excess amount above par is called a **premium.** Assume Medina issues $10 par common stock for a price of $25. The $15 difference is a premium. This sale of stock increases the corporation's paid-in capital by $25, the total issue price of the stock. Both the par value of the stock and the premium are part of paid-in capital. A premium on the sale of stock is not gain, income, or profit to the corporation, because the entity is dealing with its own stockholders. This illustrates one of the fundamentals of accounting: a company cannot earn a profit, nor can it incur a loss, when it sells its stock to, or buys its stock from, its own stockholders.

Suppose Medina Corporation issues 4,000 shares of its $10 par common stock for $25 per share—a total of $100,000 (4,000 × $25). The premium per share is $15 ($25 − $10), and the entry to record the issuance of the stock is

Jan. 23	Cash (4,000 × $25).............................	100,000	
	Common Stock (4,000 × $10)		40,000
	Paid-in Capital in Excess of Par—Common		
	(4,000 × $15)...........................		60,000
	To issue common stock at a premium.		

Account titles that could be used in place of Paid-in Capital in Excess of Par—Common are Additional Paid-In Capital—Common and Premium on Common Stock. Since both par value and premium amounts increase the corporation's capital, they appear in the stockholders' equity section of the balance sheet.

At the end of the first year, Medina Corporation would report stockholders' equity on its balance sheet as follows, assuming the corporate charter authorizes 20,000 shares of common stock and retained earnings is $85,000:

Stockholders' Equity	
Paid-in capital:	
Common stock, $10 par, 20,000 shares authorized, 4,500 shares issued.................................	$ 45,000
Paid-in capital in excess of par	60,000
Total paid-in capital	105,000
Retained earnings..	85,000
Total stockholders' equity	$190,000

We determine the dollar amount reported for common stock by multiplying the total number of shares *issued* (500 + 4,000) by the par value per share. The *authorization* reports the maximum number of shares the company may issue under its charter.

Issuing Common Stock at a Discount. Stock issued at a price below par is said to be issued at a **discount.** For example, the issuance of $5 par common stock for $3 creates a $2 discount per share. The entry to record 1,000 shares of $5 par common stock issued for $3 per share is

Feb. 18	Cash (1,000 × $3)	3,000	
	Discount on Common Stock (1,000 × $2)	2,000	
	Common Stock (1,000 × $5).................		5,000
	To issue common stock at a discount.		

What is the paid-in capital in this case? It is $3,000, the amount invested by the stockholders. The discount is reported in the stockholders' equity section of the balance sheet immediately after the stock account (as just shown for reporting a premium). However, the discount account—because it has a debit balance—is subtracted from the credit-balance par value of the stock issued to figure the capital amount.

The issuance of stock at a discount is rare. In fact, it is illegal in most states. When stock is sold at a discount, the stockholder has a *contingent liability* for the discount amount. If the corporation later liquidates, its creditors can require the original stockholder to pay the discount amount. Many companies set the par value of their common stock very low to avoid this contingent liability. A company is not likely to issue its stock at a price below an already low par value.

Issuing No-Par Common Stock. The contingent liability on common stock issued at a discount may explain why some state laws allow companies to issue no-par stock. If the stock has no par value, there can be no discount and thus no contingent liability. A recent survey of 600 companies revealed that they had 108 issues of no-par stock.

When no-par stock is issued, the asset received is debited and the stock account is credited. Glenwood Corporation issues 300 shares of no-par common stock for $20 per share. The stock issuance entry is

Aug. 14   Cash (300 × $20)   6,000
                   Common Stock   6,000
             To issue no-par common stock.

Regardless of the stock's price, Cash is debited and Common Stock is credited for the amount of cash received. There is no Paid-in Capital in Excess of Par for true no-par stock.

Assume that the charter authorizes Glenwood to issue 5,000 shares of no-par stock and the company has $3,000 in retained earnings. The corporation would report stockholders' equity as follows:

Stockholders' Equity

Paid-in capital:	
Common stock, no-par, 5,000 shares authorized, 300 shares issued	$6,000
Retained earnings...	3,000
Total stockholders' equity	$9,000

Issuing No-par Common Stock with a Stated Value.   Accounting for no-par stock with a stated value is identical to accounting for par value stock. The premium account for no-par common is entitled Paid-in Capital in Excess of *Stated* Value — Common.

Issuing Common Stock for Assets Other Than Cash.   When a corporation issues stock in exchange for assets other than cash, it debits the assets received for their current market value and credits the capital accounts accordingly. The assets' prior book value does not matter because the stockholder will demand stock equal to the market value of the asset given. Assume Kahn Corporation issues 15,000 shares of its $1 par common stock for equipment worth $4,000 and a building worth $120,000. The entry is

Nov. 12   Equipment.................................   4,000
             Building...................................   120,000
                   Common Stock (15,000 × $1)   15,000
                   Paid-in Capital in Excess of Par — Common
                       ($124,000 − $15,000).................   109,000
             To issue common stock in exchange for equipment
             and a building.

Paid-in capital increases by the amount of the assets' current market value, $124,000 in this case.

Issuing Common Stock through Subscriptions.   Established companies usually issue stock and receive the full price in a single transaction. New corporations, to gauge their ability to raise capital, often take subscriptions for their stock. A **stock subscription** is a contract that obligates an investor to purchase the corporation's stock at a later date. Because a contract exists between the two parties, the corporation acquires an asset, Subscription Receivable, when it receives the subscription. The investor gains an equity in the corporation by promising to pay the subscription amount. Depending on the subscription agreement, the subscriber may pay the subscription in a lump sum or in installments.

Assume Medina Corporation receives a subscription on May 31 for 1,000 shares of $10 par common stock. The subscription price is $22 per share. The subscriber makes a down payment of $6,000 and agrees to pay the $16,000 balance in two monthly installments of $8,000 each. Medina Corporation will issue the stock when the subscriber pays in full. The entry to record receipt of the subscription is

May 31	Cash...	6,000	
	Subscription Receivable—Common		
	($22,000 − $6,000)	16,000	
	Common Stock Subscribed (1,000 × $10)......		10,000
	Paid-in Capital in Excess of Par—Common		
	(1,000 × $12)..........................		12,000
	To receive common stock subscription at $22 per share.		

Subscription Receivable—Common, is a current asset if collection is expected within one year. Otherwise it is long-term and is reported in the Other Assets category on the balance sheet. Common Stock Subscribed is an element of stockholders' equity, reported immediately beneath Common Stock (and above Paid-in Capital in Excess of Par—Common) on the balance sheet. The "Subscribed" label will be dropped when the subscription is paid off and the stock is issued. Paid-in Capital in Excess of Par—Common is the same premium account that is credited when stock is sold for cash at a price in excess of par. The entries to record receipt of the two installments and issuance of the stock are

June 30	Cash ($16,000 × ½)............................	8,000	
	Subscription Receivable—Common		8,000
	To collect first installment on common stock subscription.		
July 31	Cash ($16,000 × ½)............................	8,000	
	Subscription Receivable—Common		8,000
	To collect second installment on common stock subscription.		
31	Common Stock Subscribed......................	10,000	
	Common Stock		10,000
	To issue common stock under subscription agreement.		

The last entry is needed to transfer the par value of the stock from the Subscribed account to Common Stock.

Because the subscription is a legally binding contract, subscribers must pay their subscriptions in full. If they fail to do so, state laws govern the settlement between the corporation and the defaulting subscriber.

Issuing Preferred Stock

Not all corporations issue preferred stock. A recent survey of 600 companies indicated that only 213 had preferred stock outstanding. Accounting for preferred stock follows the pattern illustrated for common stock. Assume the Medina Corporation charter authorizes issuance of 5,000 shares of 5 percent, $100 par preferred stock. On July 31 the company issues 400 shares at a price of $110.

(Preferred stock often sells at its par value or at a premium but seldom at a discount.) The issuance entry is

July 31	Cash (400 × $110)	44,000	
	Preferred Stock (400 × $100).		40,000
	Paid-in Capital in Excess of Par—Preferred (400 × $10)		4,000
	To issue preferred stock at a premium.		

Observe that the Paid-in Capital in Excess of Par account title includes the word Preferred. A corporation lists separate accounts for Paid-in Capital in Excess of Par on Preferred Stock and on Common Stock to differentiate the two classes of equity.

Accounting for *no-par preferred stock* follows the pattern illustrated for no-par common stock.

Let's review the first half of this chapter by showing the stockholder's equity section of Medina Corporation's balance sheet. (Assume that all figures, which are arbitrary, are correct.) Note the two sections of stockholders' equity: paid-in capital and retained earnings. Also observe the order of the equity accounts: preferred stock at par value, paid in capital in excess of par on preferred stock, common stock at par value, common stock subscribed, and paid in capital in excess of par on common stock. If Medina had a Preferred Stock Subscribed account, it would appear after Preferred Stock and before Paid-in Capital in Excess of Par—Preferred (corresponding to the order illustrated for the common stock accounts).

Stockholders' Equity

Paid-in capital:	
Preferred stock, 5% $100 par, 5,000 shares authorized, 400 shares issued	$ 40,000
Paid-in capital in excess of par—preferred	4,000
Common stock, $10 par, 20,000 shares authorized,	
4,500 shares issued	45,000
Common stock subscribed, 1,000 shares	10,000
Paid-in capital in excess of par—common	72,000
Total paid-in capital	171,000
Retained earnings	85,000
Total stockholders' equity	$256,000

OBJECTIVE 3

Prepare the stockholders' equity section of a corporation balance sheet

Summary Problems for Your Review

1. Test your understanding of the first half of this chapter by answering whether each of the following statements is true or false.

_____ a. A stockholder may bind the corporation to a contract.

_____ b. The policy-making body in a corporation is called the board of directors.

_____ c. The owner of 100 shares of preferred stock has greater voting rights than the owner of 100 shares of common stock.

_____ d. Par value stock is worth more than no-par stock.

_____ e. Issuance of 1,000 shares of $5 par value stock at $12 increases contributed capital by $12,000.

_____ f. The issuance of stock at a discount occurs less frequently than issuance of stock at a premium.

_____ g. The issuance of no-par stock with a stated value is fundamentally different from issuing par value stock.

_____ h. A corporation issues its preferred stock in exchange for land and a building with a combined market value of $200,000. This transaction increases the corporation's owner equity by $200,000 regardless of the assets' prior book value.

_____ i. Receipt of a subscription contract does not increase the stockholders' equity of the corporation unless the subscriber makes a down payment.

_____ j. Common Stock Subscribed is a part of stockholders' equity.

2. Adolph Coors Company is a leading brewery. The company has two classes of common stock. Note that only the Class A common stockholders are entitled to vote. The company's balance sheet included the following presentation:

Shareholders' Equity

Capital stock
Class A common stock, voting, $1 par value, authorized and issued
1,260,000 shares .... $ 1,260,000
Class B common stock, non-voting, no-par value, authorized and
issued 46,200,000 shares............................... 11,000,000
12,260,000
Additional paid-in capital.................................. 2,011,000
Retained earnings 872,403,000
$886,674,000

Required

a. Record the issuance of the Class A common stock. Assume the additional paid-in capital amount relates to the Class A common stock. Use the Coors account titles.

b. Record the issuance of the Class B common stock. Use the Coors account titles.

c. Rearrange the Coors stockholders' equity section to correspond to the following format:

Shareholders' Equity

Paid-in Capital:
Class A common stock..................................... $ 1,260,000
Paid-in capital in excess of par—Class A common stock 2,011,000
Class B common stock 11,000,000
Total paid-in capital 14,271,000
Retained earnings....................................... 872,403,000
Total shareholders' equity $886,674,000

d. What is the total paid-in capital of the company?

e. How did Coors withhold the voting privilege from their Class B common stockholders?

SOLUTIONS TO SUMMARY PROBLEMS

1. Answers to true-false statements:
   a. False   b. True   c. False   d. False   e. True
   f. True   g. False   h. True   i. False   j. True

2.

a.

Cash	3,271,000	
Class A Common Stock		1,260,000
Additional Paid-in Capital.		2,011,000

To record issuance of Class A common stock
at a premium.

b.

Cash	11,000,000	
Class B Common Stock		11,000,000

To record issuance of Class B common stock.

c. Shareholders' Equity
   Paid-in Capital:

Class A common stock, voting, $1 par value, authorized and issued 1,260,000 shares	$ 1,260,000
Paid-in capital in excess of par—Class A common stock .	2,011,000
Class B common stock, non-voting, no par value, authorized and issued 46,200,000 shares	11,000,000
Total paid-in capital	14,271,000
Retained earnings	872,403,000
Total shareholders equity.	$886,674,000

d. Total paid-in capital is $14,271,000, as shown in the answer to c.

e. The voting privilege was withheld from stockholders by specific agreement with them.

Donated Capital

Corporations occasionally receive gifts, or donations. For example, city council members may offer a company free land to encourage it to locate in their city. Cities in the southern United States have lured some companies away from the North using this offer. The free land is called a donation. Also, a stockholder may make a donation to the corporation in the form of cash, land, or other assets or stock that the corporation can resell.

A donation is a gift that increases the assets of the corporation. However, the donor (giver) receives no ownership interest in the company in return. A transaction to receive a donation does not increase the corporation's revenue, and thus it does not affect income. Instead, the donation creates a special category of stockholders' equity called **donated capital.** The corporation records a donation by debiting the asset received at its current market value, and by crediting Donated Capital, a stockholders' equity account.

Suppose Burlington Industries receives 100 acres of land as a donation from the city of Raleigh, North Carolina. The current market value of the land is $150,000. Burlington records receipt of the donation as follows:

Apr. 18	Land	150,000	
	Donated Capital.		150,000
	To receive land as a donation from the city.		

Donated capital is reported on the balance sheet after the stock accounts in the paid-in capital section of stockholders' equity.

Incorporation of a Going Business _____

You may dream of having your own business someday, or you may currently be a business proprietor or partner. Businesses that begin as a proprietorship or a partnership often incorporate at a later date. By incorporating a going business, the proprietor or partners avoid the unlimited liability for business debts. And as we discussed earlier, incorporating also makes it easier to raise capital.

To account for the incorporation of a going business, we close the owner equity accounts of the prior entity and set up the stockholder equity accounts of the corporation. Suppose Santa Fe Travel Associates is a partnership owned by Joe Brown and Monica Lee. The partnership balance sheet, after all adjustments and closing entries, reports Joe Brown, Capital, of $50,000, and Monica Lee, Capital, of $70,000. They incorporate the travel agency as Santa Fe Travel Company, Inc., with an authorization to issue 200,000 shares of $1 par common stock. Joe and Monica agree to receive common stock equal in par value to their partnership owner equity balances. The entry to record the incorporation of the business is

Feb. 1	Joe Brown, Capital............................	50,000	
	Monica Lee, Capital...........................	70,000	
	Common Stock..........................		120,000
	To incorporate the business, close the capital accounts of the partnership, and issue common stock to the incorporators.		

OBJECTIVE 4

Account for the incorporation of a going business

Organization Cost _____

The costs of organizing a corporation include legal fees, taxes and fees paid to the state, and charges by promoters for selling the stock. These costs are grouped in an account titled Organization Cost, which is an asset because these costs contribute to a business's start-up. Suppose Mary Kay Cosmetics, Inc., pays legal fees of $15,000 and the state of Texas incorporation fee of $500 to organize the corporation. In addition, a promoter charges a fee of $24,000 for selling the stock and receives the corporation's no-par stock as payment. Mary Kay's journal entries to record these organization costs are

Mar. 31	Organization Cost ($15,000 + $500).............	15,500	
	Cash..................................		15,500
	Legal fees and state incorporation fee to organize the corporation.		
Apr. 3	Organization Cost............................	24,000	
	Common Stock		24,000
	Promoter fee for selling stock in organization.		

Organization Cost is an *intangible asset,* reported on the balance sheet along with patents, trademarks, goodwill, and any other intangibles. We know that an intangible asset should be amortized over its useful life, and organization costs will benefit the corporation for as long as the corporation operates. But how long will that be? We cannot know in advance, but we still must expense these costs over some period of time. The Internal Revenue Service tax laws allow corporations to use a minimum 5-year useful life for amortization. GAAP allows a maximum 40-year useful life. Companies therefore amortize organization costs over a period between 5 and 40 years. Assume a 10-year life, and the preceding organization cost of $39,500 ($15,500 + $24,000) would be amortized by a debit to Amortization Expense and a credit to Organization Cost for $3,950 ($39,500/10) each year.

Dividends on Preferred and Common Stock

A corporation must declare a dividend before paying it. The board of directors alone has the authority to declare a dividend. The corporation has no obligation to pay a dividend until the board declares one, but once declared, the dividend becomes a legal liability of the corporation. Declaration of a cash dividend is recorded by debiting Retained Earnings and crediting Dividends Payable as follows:

June 19	Retained Earnings	XXX	
	Dividends Payable............................		XXX
	To declare a cash dividend.		

Payment of the dividend, which usually follows declaration by a few weeks, is recorded by debiting Dividends Payable and crediting Cash:

July 2	Dividends Payable	XXX	
	Cash.......................................		XXX
	To pay a cash dividend.		

Dividends Payable is a current liability. When a company has issued both preferred and common stock, the preferred stockholders receive their dividends first. The common stockholders receive dividends only if the total declared dividend is large enough to pay the preferred shareholders first.

Pine Industries, Inc., in addition to its common stock, has approximately 9,000 shares of preferred stock outstanding. Preferred dividends are paid at the annual rate of $1.75 per share. Assume Pine declares an annual dividend of $150,000. The allocation to preferred and common stockholders is

OBJECTIVE 5

Allocate dividends to preferred and common stock

	Total Dividend of $150,000
Preferred dividend (9,000 shares × $1.75 per share)	$ 15,750
Common dividend (remainder: $150,000 − $15,750)...............	134,250
Total dividend	$150,000

If Pine declares only a $20,000 dividend, preferred stockholders receive $15,750, and the common stockholders receive $4,250 ($20,000 − $15,750).

This example illustrates an important relationship between preferred stock and common stock. To an investor, the preferred stock is safer because it receives dividends first. For example, if Pine Industries earns only enough net income to pay the preferred stockholders' dividends, the owners of common stock receive no dividends at all. However, the earnings potential from an investment in common stock is much greater than from an investment in preferred stock. Preferred dividends are usually limited to the specified amount, but there is no upper limit on the amount of common dividends.

We noted that preferred stockholders enjoy the advantage of priority over common stockholders in receiving dividends. The dividend preference is stated as a percentage rate or a dollar amount. For example, preferred stock may be "6 percent preferred," which means that owners of the preferred stock receive an annual dividend of 6 percent of the par value of the stock. If par value is $100 per share, preferred stockholders receive an annual cash dividend of $6 per share (6 percent of $100). The preferred stock may be "$3 preferred," which means that stockholders receive an annual dividend of $3 per share regardless of the preferred stock's par value. The dividend rate on no-par preferred stock is stated in a dollar amount per share.

Cumulative and Noncumulative Preferred Stock

The allocation of dividends may be complex if the preferred stock is *cumulative.* Corporations sometimes fail to pay a dividend to their preferred stockholders. This occurrence is called *passing the dividend,* and the passed dividends are said to be **in arrears.** The owners of **cumulative preferred stock** must receive all dividends in arrears before the corporation pays dividends to the common stockholders.

The preferred stock of Pine Industries is cumulative. Suppose the company passed the 19X4 preferred dividend of $15,750. Before paying dividends to its common stockholders in 19X5, the company must first pay preferred dividends of $15,750 for both 19X4 and 19X5, a total of $31,500. *Preferred stock is cumulative in the eyes of the law unless it is specifically labeled as noncumulative.*

Assume that Pine Industries passes its 19X4 preferred dividend. In 19X5 the company declares a $50,000 dividend. The entry to record the declaration is

Sep. 6	Retained Earnings	50,000	
	Dividends Payable, Preferred ($15,750 × 2)		31,500
	Dividends Payable, Common		
	($50,000 − $31,500)......................		18,500
	To declare a cash dividend.		

If the preferred stock is **noncumulative,** the corporation is not obligated to pay dividends in arrears. Suppose that the Pine Industries preferred stock was noncumulative, and the company passed the 19X4 preferred dividend of $15,750. The preferred stockholders would lose the 19X4 dividend forever. Of course, the common stockholders would not receive a 19X4 dividend either. Before paying any common dividends in 19X5, the company would have to pay the 19X5 preferred dividend of $15,750.

Having dividends in arrears on cumulative preferred stock is *not* a liability to the corporation. (A liability for dividends arises only after the board of directors declares the dividend.) Nevertheless, a corporation must report cumulative preferred dividends in arrears. This information alerts common stockholders as to how much in cumulative preferred dividends must be paid before any dividends will be paid on the common stock. This gives the common stockholders an idea about the likelihood of receiving dividends and satisfies the disclosure principle.

Dividends in arrears are often disclosed in notes, as follows (all dates and amounts assumed). Observe the two references to Note 3 in this section of the balance sheet. The "6 percent" after "Preferred stock" is the dividend rate.

Preferred stock, 6 percent, par $50, 2,000 shares issued (Note 3). $100,000
Retained earnings (Note 3)   414,000

Note 3—Cumulative preferred dividends in arrears. At December 31, 19X2, dividends on the company's 6 percent preferred stock were in arrears for 19X1 and 19X2, in the amount of $12,000 (6% × $100,000 × 2 years).

Participating and Nonparticipating Preferred Stock

The owners of **participating preferred stock** may receive—that is *participate in*—dividends beyond the stated amount or stated percentage. Assume that the corporation declares a dividend. First, the preferred stockholders receive their dividends. If the corporation has declared a large enough dividend, then the common stockholders receive their dividends. If an additional dividend amount remains to be distributed, common stockholders and participating preferred stockholders share it. For example, the owners of a $4 preferred stock must receive the specified annual dividend of $4 per share before the common stockholders receive any dividends. Then a $4 dividend is paid on each common share. The participation feature takes effect only after the preferred and common stockholders have received the specified $4 rate. Payment of an extra *common* dividend of, say, $1.50 is accompanied by a $1.50 dividend on each preferred share.

Participating preferred stock is rare. In fact, preferred stock is nonparticipating unless it is specifically described as participating on the stock certificate and in the financial statements. Therefore, if the preferred stock in our example is nonparticipating (the usual case), the largest annual dividend that a preferred stockholder will receive is $4.

Convertible Preferred Stock

Convertible preferred stock may be exchanged by the preferred stockholders, if they choose, for another class of stock in the corporation. For example, the Pine Industries preferred stock may be converted into the company's common stock. A note to Pine's balance sheet describes the conversion terms as follows:

The . . . preferred stock is convertible at the rate of 6.51 shares of common stock for each share of preferred stock outstanding.

If you owned 100 shares of Pine's convertible preferred stock, you could convert it into 651 (100 × 6.51) shares of Pine common stock. Under what condition would you exercise the conversion privilege? You would do so if the market value of the common stock that you could receive from conversion exceeded the market value of the preferred stock that you presently held. This way, you as an investor could increase your personal wealth.

Pine Industries preferred stock has par value of $100 per share, and the par value of the common stock is $1. The company would record conversion of 100 shares of preferred stock, issued previously at par, into 651 shares of common stock as follows:

Mar 7	Preferred Stock (100 × $100)	10,000	
	Common Stock (651 × $1)		651
	Paid-in Capital in Excess of Par—Common		9,349
	Conversion of preferred stock into common.		

If the preferred stock was issued at a premium, Paid-in Capital in Excess of Par—Preferred must also be debited to remove its balance from the books.

Preferred stock, we see, offers alternative features not available to common stock. Preferred stock is cumulative or noncumulative, participating or nonparticipating, and convertible or not convertible.

Different Values of Stock

The business community refers to several different *stock values* in addition to par value. These values include market value, redemption value, liquidation value, and book value.

OBJECTIVE 6
Distinguish among various stock "values"

Market Value

A stock's **market value** is the price for which a person could buy or sell a share of the stock. The issuing corporation's net income, financial position, its future prospects, and the general economic conditions determine market value (also called market price). Daily newspapers report the market price of many stocks. In almost all cases, stockholders are more concerned about the market value of a stock than any of the other values discussed below. A stock listed at (an alternative term is *quoted at*) 29¼ sells for, or may be bought for, $29.25 per share. The purchase of 100 shares of this stock would cost $2,925 ($29.25 × 100), plus a commission. If you were selling 100 shares of this stock, you would receive cash of $2,925 less a commission. The commission is the fee an investor pays to a stockbroker for buying or selling the stock.

Redemption Value

Preferred stock's fixed dividend rate makes it somewhat like debt. However, companies do not get a tax deduction for preferred dividend payments. Thus they may wish to buy back, or redeem, their preferred stock to avoid paying the dividends. Preferred stock that provides for redemption at a set price is called redeemable preferred stock. In some cases, the company has the *option* of redeeming its preferred stock at a set price. In other cases, the company is *obligated* to redeem the preferred stock. The price the corporation agrees to pay for the stock, which is set when the stock is issued, is called **redemption value.**

The preferred stock of Pine Industries, Inc., is "redeemable at the option of the Company at $25 per share." Beginning in 1992, Pine is "required to redeem annually 6,765 shares of the preferred stock ($169,125 annually)." Pine's annual redemption payment to the preferred stockholders will include this redemption value plus any dividends in arrears.

Liquidation Value

Liquidation value, which applies only to preferred stock, is the amount the corporation agrees to pay the preferred stockholder per share if the company liquidates. Great Northern Nekoosa Corporation, a large paper company, has preferred stock with "a preference of $50 in liquidation." Dividends in arrears are added to liquidation value in determining the payment to the preferred stockholders if the company liquidates.

Book Value

The **book value** of a stock is the amount of owners' equity on the company's books for each share of its stock. Corporations often report this amount in their annual reports. If the company has only common stock outstanding, its book value is computed by dividing total stockholders' equity by the number of shares outstanding. A company with stockholders' equity of $180,000 and 5,000 shares of common stock outstanding has book value of $36 per share ($180,000/5,000 shares).

If the company has both preferred and common stock outstanding, the preferred stockholders have the first claim to owners' equity. Ordinarily, preferred stock has a specified liquidation or redemption value. The book value of preferred is its redemption value plus any cumulative dividends in arrears on the stock. Its book value *per share* equals the sum of redemption value and any cumulative dividends in arrears divided by the number of preferred shares outstanding. After the corporation figures the preferred shares' book value, it computes the common stock book value per share. The corporation divides the common equity (total stockholders' equity minus preferred equity) by the number of common shares outstanding.

Assume that the company balance sheet reports the following amounts:

Stockholders' Equity

Paid-in capital:	
Preferred stock, 6%, $100 par, 5,000 shares authorized, 400 shares issued	$ 40,000
Paid-in capital in excess of par—preferred	4,000
Common stock, $10 par, 20,000 shares authorized, 4,500 shares issued	45,000
Common stock subscribed, 1000 shares	10,000
Paid-in capital in excess of par—common	72,000
Total paid-in capital	171,000
Retained earnings	85,000
Total stockholders' equity	$256,000

Suppose that four years (including the current year) of cumulative preferred dividends are in arrears and preferred stock has a redemption value of $130 per share.

Book value computations treat subscribed stock as though it were issued stock. The book value per share computations for this corporation follow.

Preferred:	
Redemption value (400 shares × $130)	$ 52,000
Cumulative dividends ($40,000 × .06 × 4)	9,600
Stockholders' equity allocated to preferred	$ 61,600
Book value per share ($61,600/400 shares)	$ 154.00

Common:

Total stockholders' equity	$256,000
Less stockholders' equity allocated to preferred......................	61,600
Stockholders' equity allocated to common	$194,400
Book value per share [$194,400/(4,500 shares + 1,000 shares)]........	$35.35

How is book value per share used in decision making? Companies may agree to buy a corporation based on the book value of its stock. Corporations may settle up with a stockholder, agreeing to pay the book value of the person's stock in the company. In general, however, book value is not directly related to the market value of stock.

Summary Problems for Your Review

1. Use the following accounts and related balances to prepare the classified balance sheet of Whitehall, Inc., at September 30, 19X4. Use the account format of the balance sheet.

Common stock, $1 par,		Long-term note payable	$ 74,000
50,000 shares authorized,		Inventory	85,000
20,000 shares issued	$ 20,000	Property, plant, and	
Dividends payable	4,000	equipment, net...........	225,000
Cash	9,000	Donated capital...........	18,000
Accounts payable	28,000	Accounts receivable, net.....	23,000
Stock subscription receivable		Preferred stock, $3.75,	
—common	2,000	no-par, 10,000 shares,	
Retained earnings	56,000	authorized, 2,000 shares	
Paid-in capital in excess of par		issued	24,000
—common	115,000	Common stock subscribed	
Organization cost, net	1,000	3,000 shares.............	3,000
		Accrued liabilities	3,000

2. The balance sheet of Trendline Corporation reported the following at March 31, 19X6, end of its fiscal year. Note that Trendline reports paid-in capital in excess of par or stated value after the stock accounts.

Stockholders' Equity

Preferred stock, 4%, $10 par, 11,000 shares authorized	
(redemption value, $110,000)	$110,000
Common stock, no-par, $5 stated value, 100,000 shares authorized	250,000
Common stock subscribed	17,500
Paid-in capital in excess of par or stated value:	
Common stock	214,000
Donated capital	55,000
Retained earnings	330,000
Total stockholders' equity	$976,500

Required

a. Is the preferred stock cumulative or noncumulative? Is it participating or nonpartici-pating? How can you tell?

b. What is the total amount of the annual preferred dividend?

c. How many shares of preferred stock and common stock has the company issued?

d. How many shares of common stock are subscribed?

e. What was the market value of the assets donated to the corporation?

f. Compute the book value per share of the preferred stock and the common stock. No prior year preferred dividends are in arrears, but Trendline has not declared the current-year dividend.

SOLUTIONS TO REVIEW PROBLEMS

1.

Whitehall, Inc.
Balance Sheet
September 30, 19X4

Assets		Liabilities		
Current:		Current:		
Cash........................	$ 9,000	Accounts payable		$ 28,000
Accounts receivable, net..........	23,000	Dividends payable		4,000
Stock subscription receivable–		Accrued liabilities		3,000
common....................	2,000	Total current liabilities		35,000
Inventory.....................	85,000	Long-term note payable............		74,000
Total current assets	119,000	Total liabilities...............		109,000
Property, plant, and equipment, net ..	225,000			
Intangible assets:		**Stockholders' Equity**		
Organization cost, net............	1,000	Paid-in capital:		
		Preferred stock, $3.75, no-par, 10,000 shares authorized, 2,000 shares issued	$ 24,000	
		Common stock, $1 par, 50,000 shares authorized, 20,000 shares issued......................	20,000	
		Common stock subscribed, 3,000 shares......................	3,000	
		Paid-in capital in excess of par— common....................	115,000	
		Donated capital.................	18,000	
		Total paid-in capital	180,000	
		Retained earnings.................	56,000	
		Total stockholders' equity.......		236,000
		Total liabilities and		
Total assets	$345,000	stockholders' equity............		$345,000

2.   Answers to Trendline Corporation questions:

a.   The preferred stock is *cumulative* and *nonparticipating* because it is not specifically labeled otherwise.

b. Total annual preferred dividend: $4,000 ($100,000 × .04)

c. Preferred stock issued: 10,000 shares ($100,000/$10 par)
  Common stock issued: 50,000 shares ($250,000/$5 stated value)

d. Common stock subscribed: 3,500 shares ($17,500/$5 stated value)

e. Market value of donated assets: $55,000

f. Book values per share of preferred and common stock:

Preferred:

Redemption value	$110,000
Cumulative dividend for current year ($100,000 × .04)	4,000
Stockholders' equity allocated to preferred	$114,000
Book value per share ($114,000/10,000 shares)	$11.40

Common:

Total stockholders' equity	$976,500
Less stockholders' equity allocated to preferred	114,000
Stockholders' equity allocated to common	$862,500
Book value per share [$862,500/(53,500 shares = 50,000 shares issued + 3,500 shares subscribed)]	$16.12

Summary

A corporation is a separate legal and business entity. *Continuous life,* the ease of raising large amounts of capital and transferring ownership, and *limited liability* are among the advantages of the corporate form of organization. An important disadvantage is *double taxation.* Corporations pay *income taxes,* and stockholders pay tax on dividends. *Stockholders* are the owners of corporations. They elect a *board of directors,* which elects a chairperson and appoints the officers to manage the business.

Corporations may issue different classes of stock: *par value, no-par value, common,* and *preferred.* Stock is usually issued at a *premium*—an amount above par value. Also, corporations may issue stock under a *subscription* agreement. The balance sheet carries the capital raised through stock issuance under the heading Paid-in Capital or Contributed Capital in the stockholders' equity section.

Corporations may receive *donations* from outsiders or from stockholders. Donated Capital is a stockholders' equity account.

Only when the board of directors declares a *dividend* does the corporation incur the liability to pay dividends. Preferred stock has priority over common stock as to dividends, which may be stated as a percentage of par value or as a dollar amount per share. In addition, preferred stock has a claim to dividends in arrears if it is *cumulative* and a claim to further dividends if it is *participating. Convertible* preferred stock may be exchanged for the corporation's common stock.

A stock's *market value* is the price for which a share may be bought or sold. *Redemption value, liquidation value, and book value*—the amount of owners' equity per share of company stock—are other values that may apply to stock.

Self-Study Questions

Test your understanding of the chapter by marking the best answer for each of the following questions.

1. Which of the following is a *disadvantage* of the corporate form of business organization? *(p. 537)*
   a. Limited liability of stockholders
   b. Government regulation
   c. No mutual agency
   d. Transferability of ownership

2. The person with the most power in a corporation is the *(p. 537)*
   a. Incorporator
   b. Chairman of the board
   c. President
   d. Vice-president

3. The dollar amount of the stockholder investments in a corporation is called *(p. 539)*
   a. Outstanding stock
   b. Total stockholders' equity
   c. Paid-in capital
   d. Retained earnings

4. The arbitrary value assigned to a share of stock is called *(p. 541)*
   a. Market value
   b. Liquidation value
   c. Book value
   d. Par value

5. Which is the most widely held class of stock? *(p. 541)*
   a. Par value common stock
   b. No-par common stock
   c. Par value preferred stock
   d. No-par preferred stock

6. Mangum Corporation receives a subscription for 1,000 shares of $100 par preferred stock at $104 per share. This transaction increases Mangum's paid-in capital by *(pp. 545, 546)*
   a. $0 because the corporation received no cash
   b. $4,000
   c. $100,000
   d. $104,000

7. Organization cost is classified as a (an) *(p. 549)*
   a. Operating expense
   b. Current asset
   c. Contra item in stockholders' equity
   d. None of the above

8. Trade Days, Inc., has 10,000 shares of $3.50, $50 par preferred stock, and 100,000 of $4 par common stock outstanding. Two years' preferred dividends are in arrears. Trade Days declares a cash dividend large enough to pay the preferred dividends in arrears, the preferred dividend for the current period, and a $1.50 dividend to common. What is the total amount of the dividend? *(p. 550)*
   a. $255,000   b. $220,000   c. $150,000   d. $105,000

9. The preferred stock of Trade Days, Inc., in the preceding question was issued at $55 per share. Each preferred share can be converted into 10 common shares. The entry to record the conversion of this preferred stock into common is *(pp. 552, 553)*

   a. Cash 550,000
         Preferred Stock.................................. 500,000
         Paid-in Capital in Excess of Par—Preferred Stock 50,000
   b. Preferred Stock.................................. 500,000
         Paid-in Capital in Excess of Par—Preferred Stock 50,000
         Common Stock.................................. 550,000
   c. Preferred Stock.................................. 500,000
         Paid-in Capital in Excess of Par—Preferred Stock 50,000
         Common Stock.................................. 400,000
         Paid-in Capital in Excess of Par—Common Stock 150,000
   d. Preferred Stock.................................. 550,000
         Common Stock.................................. 400,000
         Paid-in Capital in Excess of Par—Common Stock 150,000

10. When an investor is buying stock as an investment, the value of most direct concern is *(p. 553)*
    a. Par value   b. Market value   c. Liquidation value   d. Book value

Answers to the self-study questions are at the end of the chapter.

Accounting Vocabulary

additional paid-in capital *(p. 543)*, authorization of stock *(p. 542)*, board of directors *(p. 537)*, book value of stock *(p. 554)*, bylaws *(p. 537)*, chairperson of the board *(p. 537)*, charter *(pp. 535, 537)*, common stock *(p. 541)*, contributed capital *(p. 539)*, convertible preferred stock *(p. 542)*, cumulative preferred stock *(p. 551)*, deficit *(p. 540)*, discount on stock *(p. 543)*, dividends *(p. 540)*, dividends in arrears *(p. 551)*, donated capital *(p. 548)*, double taxation *(p. 537)*, incorporator *(p. 537)*, limited liability *(p. 536)*, liquidation value of stock *(p. 554)*, market value of stock *(p. 553)*, organization cost *(p. 549)*, outstanding stock *(p. 538)*, paid-in capital *(p. 539)*, par value *(p. 541)*, participating preferred stock *(p. 552)*, preemptive right *(p. 541)*, preferred stock *(p. 541)*, premium on stock *(p. 542)*, president *(p. 537)*, proxy *(p. 537)*, redemption value of stock *(p. 553)*, retained earnings *(p. 539)*, shareholder *(p. 535)*, stock *(p. 536)*, stockholders' equity *(p. 538)*, stock subscription *(p. 544)*.

ASSIGNMENT MATERIAL _____

Questions

1. Why is a corporation called a creature of the state?
2. Identify the characteristics of a corporation.
3. Explain why corporations face a tax disadvantage.
4. Briefly outline the steps in the organization of a corporation.
5. How are the structures of a partnership and a corporation similar and different?
6. Name the four rights of a stockholder. Is preferred stock automatically nonvoting? Explain how a right may be withheld from a stockholder.
7. Dividends on preferred stock may be stated as a percentage rate or a dollar amount. What is the annual dividend on these preferred stocks: 4 percent, $100 par; $3.50, $20 par; and 6 percent, no-par with $50 stated value?
8. Which event increases the assets of the corporation: authorization of stock or issuance of stock? Explain.
9. Suppose H. J. Heinz Company issued 1,000 shares of its 3.65 percent, $100 par preferred stock for $120. How much would this transaction increase the company's paid-in capital? How much would it increase Heinz's retained earnings? How much would it increase Heinz's annual cash dividend payments?
10. Give two alternative account titles for Paid-in Capital in Excess of Par—Common Stock.
11. Explain the contingent liability created by issuance of stock at a discount.
12. How does issuance of 1,000 shares of no-par stock for land and a building, together worth $150,000, affect paid-in capital?
13. Why does receipt of a stock subscription increase the corporation's assets and owners' equity?
14. Give an example of a transaction that creates donated capital for a corporation.
15. Journalize the incorporation of the Barnes & Connally partnership. The partners' capital account balances exceed the par value of the new corporation's common stock. (Omit amounts.)
16. Rank the following accounts in the order they would appear on the balance sheet: Common Stock, Organization Cost, Donated Capital, Preferred Stock, Common Stock Subscribed, Stock Subscription Receivable (due within six months), Retained Earnings, Dividends Payable. Also, give each account's balance sheet classification.
17. What type of account is Organization Cost? Briefly describe how to account for organization cost.

18. Mancini Inc. has 3,000 shares of its $2.50, $10 par preferred stock outstanding. Dividends for 19X1 and 19X2 are in arrears, and the company has declared no dividends on preferred stock for the current year, 19X3. Assume that Mancini declares total dividends of $35,000 at the end of 19X3. Show how to allocate the dividends to preferred and common (a) if preferred is cumulative and (b) if preferred is noncumulative.

19. As a preferred stockholder, would you rather own cumulative or noncumulative preferred? If all other factors are the same, would the corporation rather the preferred stock be cumulative or noncumulative? Give your reason.

20. How are cumulative preferred dividends in arrears reported in the financial statements? When do dividends become a liability of the corporation?

21. Distinguish between the market value of stock and the book value of stock.

22. How is book value per share of common stock computed when the company has both preferred stock and common stock outstanding?

Exercises

Exercise 14-1   *Issuing Stock*

Journalize the following stock issuance transactions of Washington Corporation. Explanations are not required.

Feb. 19   Issued 4,000 shares of $10 par common stock for cash of $12.50 per share

Mar. 3   Sold 300 shares of $2.25, no-par Class A preferred stock for $6,000 cash.

Mar. 11   Received inventory valued at $25,000 and equipment with market value of $16,000 for 3,300 shares of the $10 par common stock.

Mar. 15   Issued 1,000 shares of 5 percent, no-par Class B preferred stock with stated value of $50 per share. The issue price was cash of $55 per share.

Exercise 14-2   *Stockholders' equity section of a balance sheet*

The charter of Washington Corporation authorizes the issuance of 5,000 shares of Class A preferred stock, 1,000 shares of Class B preferred stock, and 10,000 shares of common stock. Prepare the stockholders' equity section of the Washington balance sheet for the transactions given in the preceding exercise. Retained Earnings has a balance of $63,000.

Exercise 14-3   *Stock subscriptions*

Betsy Ross Corporation has just been organized and is selling its stock through stock subscriptions. Record the following selected transactions that occurred during June 19X6.

June 3   Received a subscription to 200 shares of $1 par common stock at the subscription price of $20 per share. The subscriber paid one fourth of the subscription amount as a down payment. The corporation will issue the stock when it is fully paid.

June 18   Collected one half of the amount receivable from the subscriber.

July 3   Collected the remainder from the subscriber and issued the stock.

Exercise 14-4   *Paid-in capital for a corporation*

Errico Inc. has recently organized. The company issued common stock to an attorney who gave Errico legal services of $2,400 to help her in organizing the corporation. It issued common stock to another person in exchange for his patent with a market value of $40,000. In addition, Errico received cash both for 2,000 shares of its preferred stock at $110 per share and for 32,000 shares of its common stock at $15 per share. The city of Arlington donated 50 acres of land to the company as a plant site. The market value of the land was $180,000. Without making journal entries, determine the total paid-in capital created by these transactions.

Exercise 14-5   *Recording issuance of stock*

The actual balance sheet of Gulf Resources & Chemical Corporation reported the following stockholders' equity. Note that Gulf has two separate classes of preferred stock, labeled as Series A and Series B.

Stockholders' Investment
(same as stockholders' equity)

Preferred stock, $1 par, authorized 4,000,000 shares (Note 7)	
Series A	$ 58,451
Series B..	375,765
Common stock, $.10 par, authorized 20,000,000, [issued and]	
outstanding 9,125,390 shares.................................	912,539
Capital in excess of par......................................	75,542,382

Note 7. Preferred Stock:	Shares [Issued and] Outstanding
Series A	58,451
Series B..................................	375,765

Required

Assume that the Series A preferred stock was issued for $3 cash per share, the Series B preferred was issued for $20 cash per share, and the common was issued for cash of $69,198,484. Make the summary journal entries to record issuance of all the Gulf Resources stock. Explanations are not required.

Exercise 14-6   *Incorporating a partnership*

The Podunk Jaybirds are a semiprofessional baseball team that has been operated as a partnership by D. Robertson and G. Childres. In addition to their management responsibilities, Robertson also plays second base and Childres sells hot dogs. Journalize the following transactions in the first month of operation as a corporation:

May 14   The incorporators paid legal fees of $1,440 and state taxes and fees of $600 to obtain a corporate charter.

May 14   Issued 2,500 shares of $10 par common stock to Robertson and 1,000 shares to Childres. Robertson's capital balance on the partnership books was $30,000, and Childres's capital balance was $12,000.

May 18   The city of Podunk donated 20 acres of land to the corporation for a stadium site. The land value was $20,000.

Exercise 14-7   *Recording issuance of no-par stock*

Fanous, Inc., is an importer of European furniture and Oriental rugs. The corporation issues 10,000 shares of no-par common stock for $75 per share. Record issuance of the stock (a) if the stock is true no-par stock and (b) if the stock has stated value of $5 per share.

Exercise 14-8   *Computing dividends on preferred and common stock*

The following elements of stockholders' equity are excerpted from the balance sheet of Gulf Resources & Chemical Corporation.

Stockholders' Equity

Preferred stock, cumulative and nonparticipating, $1 par (Note 7)
Series A, 58,451 shares issued.................................... $ 58,451
Series B, 375,765 shares issued 375,765
Common stock, $.10 par, 9,125,390 shares issued................... 912,539

Note 7. Preferred Stock: **Designated Annual
Cash Dividend**

Series A .... $ .20
Series B.................................... 1.30

Assume that the Series A preferred has preference over the Series B preferred and the company has paid all preferred dividends through 19X4.

Required

Compute the dividends to both series of preferred and to common for 19X5 and 19X6 if total dividends are $0 in 19X5 and $1,500,000 in 19X6. Round to the nearest dollar.

Exercise 14-9   *Stockholders' equity section of a balance sheet*

China Palace Corporation has the following selected account balances at June 30, 19X7. Prepare the stockholders' equity section of the company's balance sheet. (Not all accounts listed are part of stockholders' equity).

Common stock, no-par with $5 stated value, 500,000 shares authorized, 120,000 shares issued	$600,000	Preferred stock subscribed 1,000 shares.............	$ 20,000
Donated capital............	34,000	Inventory.................	112,000
Accumulated depreciation– machinery and equipment .	62,000	Machinery and equipment ...	109,000
Retained earnings..........	119,000	Preferred stock subscription receivable...............	8,000
Paid-in capital in excess of par—preferred stock	60,000	Preferred stock, 5%, $20 par, 20,000 shares authorized, 10,000 shares issued	200,000
		Organization cost, net.......	3,000

Exercise 14-10   *Book value per share of preferred and common stock*

The balance sheet of International Graphics Corporation reported the following:

Redeemable preferred stock; redemption value $5,103,000........... $ 4,860,000
Common stockholders' equity 8,120,375 shares issued
and outstanding....................................... 216,788,000
Total stockholders' equity.................................. $221,648,000

Assume that International has paid preferred dividends for the current year and all prior years (no dividends in arrears), and the company has 100,000 shares of preferred stock outstanding. Compute the book value per share of the preferred stock and the common stock.

Exercise 14-11   *Book value per share of preferred and common stock; preferred dividends in arrears*

Refer to Exercise 14-10. Compute the book value per share of the preferred stock and the common stock, assuming that three years' preferred dividends (including dividends for the current year) are in arrears. Assume the preferred stock is cumulative and its dividend rate is 6 percent.

Problems

Problem 14-1A *Journalizing corporation transactions and preparing the stockholders' equity section of the balance sheet*

Greenlawn, Inc., was organized under the laws of the state of Delaware. The charter authorizes Greenlawn to issue 100,000 shares of $3, no-par preferred stock and 500,000 shares of common stock with $1 par value. During its start-up phase, the company completed the following transactions:

July	5	Paid fees and incorporation taxes of $1,500 to the state of Delaware to obtain the charter and file the required documents for incorporation.
	6	Issued 500 shares of common stock to the promoters who organized the corporation. Their fee was $15,000.
	7	Accepted subscriptions for 1,000 shares of common stock at $30 per share and received a down payment of one third of the subscription amount.
	12	Issued 300 shares of preferred stock for cash of $18,000.
	14	Issued 800 shares of common stock in exchange for land valued at $24,000.
	31	Collected one half of the stock subscription receivable.
	31	Earned a small profit for July and closed the $4,000 credit balance of Income Summary into the Retained Earnings account.

Required

1. Record the transactions in the general journal.
2. Prepare the stockholders' equity section of the Greenlawn balance sheet at July 31.

Problem 14-2A *Stockholders' equity section of the balance sheet*

The following summaries for Lopez, Inc., and Monroe Corporation provide the information needed to prepare the stockholders' equity section of the company balance sheet. The two companies are independent.

Lopez, Inc. Lopez, Inc., is authorized to issue 25,000 shares of $1 par common stock. All the stock was issued at $6 per share. The company incurred net losses of $30,000 in 19X1 and $14,000 in 19X2. It earned net incomes of $8,000 in 19X3 and $41,000 in 19X4. The company declared no dividends during the four-year period.

Monroe Corporation. Monroe's charter authorizes the company to issue 5,000 shares of 5 percent, $100 par preferred stock and 500,000 shares of no-par common stock. Monroe issued 1,000 shares of the preferred stock at $105 per share. It issued 200,000 shares of the common stock for $300,000. The company's retained earnings balance at the beginning of 19X4 was $120,000. Net income for 19X4 was $65,000, and the company correctly subtracted the 5 percent preferred dividend for 19X4 from retained earnings. No preferred dividends are in arrears.

Required

For each company, prepare the stockholders' equity section of its balance sheet at December 31, 19X4. Show the computation of all amounts. Entries are not required.

Problem 14-3A *Journalizing corporation transactions and preparing the stockholders' equity section of the balance sheet*

The partnership of Starr & Wagner needed additional capital to expand into new markets, so the business incorporated as Micro Devices, Inc. The charter from the state of Ohio authorizes Micro Devices to issue 50,000 shares of 5 percent, $20 par preferred stock and 100,000 shares of no-par common stock with a stated value of $5 per share. In its first month, Micro Devices completed the following transactions:

Dec. 1   Paid a charter fee of $500 and incorporation taxes of $2,100 to the state of Ohio and paid legal fees of $1,000 to organize as a corporation.

     2   Issued 500 shares of common stock to the promoter for assistance with issuance of the common stock. The promotional fee was $3,000.

     2   Issued 9,000 shares of common stock to Starr and 12,000 shares to Wagner in return for the net assets of the partnership. Starr's capital balance on the partnership books was $54,000, and Wagner's capital balance was $72,000.

     4   Accepted subscriptions for 4,000 shares of common stock at $6 per share and received a down payment of 20 percent of the subscription amount.

     8   Received a small parcel of land valued at $35,000 as a donation from the city of Akron.

    10   Issued 400 shares of preferred stock to acquire a patent with a market value of $10,000.

    16   Issued 600 shares of common stock for cash of $3,600.

    30   Collected one third of the stock subscription receivable.

Required

1. Record the transactions in the general journal.
2. Prepare the stockholders' equity section of the Micro Devices balance sheet at December 31. Retained Earnings' balance is $19,970.

Problem 14-4A   *Analyzing the stockholders' equity of an actual corporation*

The purpose of this problem is to familiarize you with the financial statement information of a real company. Bethlehem Steel Corporation is one of the nation's largest steel companies. Bethlehem included the following stockholders' equity on its balance sheet:

Stockholders' Equity	($ Millions)
Preferred stock—	
Authorized 20,000,000 shares in each class; issued:	
$5.00 Cumulative Convertible Preferred Stock, at $50.00 stated value,	
2,500,000 shares......................................	$ 125
$2.50 Cumulative Convertible Preferred Stock, at $25.00 stated value,	
4,000,000 shares......................................	100
Common stock—$8 par value—	
Authorized 80,000,000 shares; issued 48,308,516 shares	621
Retained earnings...	529
	$1,375

Observe that Bethlehem reports no Paid-in Capital in Excess of Par or Stated Value. Instead, the company reports these items in the stock accounts.

Required

1. Identify the different issues of stock Bethlehem has outstanding.
2. Is the preferred stock participating or nonparticipating? How can you tell?
3. Which class of stock did Bethlehem issue at par or stated value, and which class did it issue above par or stated value?
4. Rearrange the Bethlehem Steel stockholders' equity section to correspond, as appropriate, to the terminology and format illustrated on page 554. Assume Bethlehem is authorized to issue 20,000,000 shares of the $5 preferred stock and an additional 20,000,000 shares of the $2.50 preferred. Assume the total stockholders' equity of $1,375 million is correct. Report dollar amounts in millions, as Bethlehem does.
5. Suppose Bethlehem passed its preferred dividends for one year. Would the company have to pay these dividends in arrears before paying dividends to the common stockholders? Give your reason.

6. What amount of preferred dividends must Bethlehem declare and pay each year to avoid having preferred dividends in arrears?
7. Assume preferred dividends are in arrears for 19X5.
    a. Write Note 6 of the December 31, 19X5, financial statements to disclose the dividends in arrears.
    b. Journalize the declaration of a $60 million dividend for 19X6. An explanation is not required.

Problem 14-5A *Computing dividends on preferred and common stock*

Heinz Company has 5,000 shares of 4 percent, $10 par value preferred stock and 100,000 shares of $1.50 par common stock outstanding. During a three-year period Heinz declared and paid cash dividends as follows: 19X1, $0; 19X2, $5,000; and 19X3, $34,000.

Required

1. Compute the total dividends to preferred stock and common stock for each of the three years if
    a. Preferred is noncumulative and nonparticipating.
    b. Preferred is cumulative and nonparticipating.
2. For case *1b*, record the declaration of the 19X3 dividends on December 22, 19X3, and the payment of the dividends on January 14, 19X4.

Problem 14-6A *Analyzing the stockholders' equity of an actual corporation*

The balance sheet of Oak Manufacturing, Inc., reported the following:

Stockholders' Investment (same as stockholders' equity)	($ Thousands)
Cumulative convertible preferred stock	$ 45
Common stock, $1 par value, authorized 40,000,000 shares; issued 16,000,000 shares.	16,000
[Additional] paid-in capital	176,000
Retained earnings	(77,165)
Total stockholders' investment	$114,880

Notes to the financial statements indicate that 9,000 shares of $1.60 preferred stock with a stated value of $5 per share were issued and outstanding. The preferred stock has a redemption value of $25 per share, and preferred dividends are in arrears for two years, including the current year. The additional paid-in capital was contributed by the common stockholders. On the balance sheet date, the market value of the Oak Manufacturing common stock was $7.50 per share.

Required

1. Is the preferred stock cumulative or noncumulative, participating or nonparticipating? How can you tell?
2. What is the amount of the annual preferred dividend?
3. What is the total paid-in capital of the company?
4. What was the total market value of the common stock?
5. Compute the book value per share of the preferred stock and the common stock.

Problem 14-7A *Preparing a corporation balance sheet*

The following accounts and related balances of Texas Mesa Corporation are arranged in no particular order. Use them to prepare the company's classified balance sheet in the account format at November 30, 19X7.

Accounts payable	$ 47,000	Accounts receivable, net	$ 87,000
Stock subscription receivable, preferred	1,000	Preferred stock, 4%, $10 par, 25,000 shares authorized, 3,000 shares issued	30,000
Retained earnings	101,000	Cash	41,000
Common stock, $5 par, 100,000 shares authorized, 42,000 shares issued	210,000	Inventory . . . . Property, plant, and equipment, net	176,000 328,000
Dividends payable	3,000	Organization cost, net	6,000
Donated capital	109,000	Prepaid expenses	13,000
Additional paid-in capital — common	73,000	Preferred stock subscribed 700 shares	7,000
Accrued liabilities	17,000		
Long-term note payable	86,000	Patent, net	31,000

(Group B)

Problem 14-1B   *Journalizing corporation transactions and preparing the stockholders' equity section of the balance sheet*

Multipurpose Corporation received a charter from the state of Colorado. The company is authorized to issue 50,000 shares of 5 percent, $40 par preferred stock and 300,000 shares of no-par common stock. During its start-up phase, the company completed the following transactions:

Oct. 2   Paid fees of $800 and incorporation taxes of $2,000 to the state of Colorado to obtain the charter and file the required documents for incorporation.

   4   Issued 900 shares of common stock to the promoters who organized the corporation. Their fee was $45,000.

   5   Accepted subscriptions for 1,000 shares of common stock at $50 per share and received a down payment of one fourth of the subscription amount.

   9   Issued 1,000 shares of common stock in exchange for equipment valued at $50,000.

   14   Issued 600 shares of preferred stock for cash of $44 per share.

   30   Collected one third of the stock subscription receivable.

   31   Earned a small profit for October and closed the $6,100 credit balance of Income Summary into Retained Earnings.

Required

1. Record the transactions in the general journal.
2. Prepare the stockholders' equity section of the Multipurpose balance sheet at October 31.

Problem 14-2B   *Stockholders' equity section of the balance sheet*

Stockholders' equity information is given for Baker Corporation and Wang, Inc. The two companies are independent.

Baker Corporation.   Baker Corporation is authorized to issue 10,000 shares of $5 par common stock. All the stock was issued at $8 per share. The company incurred a net loss of $12,000 in 19X1. It earned net incomes of $5,000 in 19X2 and $21,000 in 19X3. The company declared no dividends during the three-year period.

Wang, Inc.   Wang's charter authorizes the company to issue 7,500 shares of $2.50 preferred stock with par value of $50 and 120,000 shares of no-par common stock. Wang issued 800 shares of the preferred stock at $60 per share. It issued 20,000 shares of the common stock for a total of $240,000. The company's retained earnings balance at the beginning of 19X3 was $72,000, and net income for the year was $49,000. During 19X3 the company correctly subtracted the specified dividend on preferred and a $.50 per share dividend on common from retained earnings. No preferred dividends are in arrears.

Required

For each company, prepare the stockholders' equity section of its balance sheet at December 31, 19X3. Show the computation of all amounts. Entries are not required.

Problem 14-3B *Journalizing corporation transactions and preparing the stockholders' equity section of the balance sheet*

The partners who owned Wolfson & Stauffer wished to avoid the unlimited personal liability of the partnership form of business, so they incorporated the partnership as Financial Consultants, Inc. The charter from the state of Arizona authorizes the corporation to issue 10,000 shares of 6 percent, $100 par preferred stock and 250,000 shares of no-par common stock with a stated value of $2 per share. In its first month, Financial Consultants completed the following transactions:

Dec. 1   Paid incorporation taxes of $900 and a charter fee of $1,100 to the state of Arizona and paid legal fees of $1,900 to organize as a corporation.

3   Issued 750 shares of common stock to the promoter for assistance with issuance of the common stock. The promotion fee was $7,500.

3   Issued 4,100 shares of common stock to Wolfson and 3,800 shares to Stauffer in return for the net assets of the partnership. Wolfson's capital balance on the partnership books was $41,000, and Stauffer's capital balance was $38,000.

5   Accepted subscriptions for 5,000 shares of common stock at $10 per share and received a down payment of 25 percent of the subscription amount.

7   Received a small parcel of land valued at $42,000 as a donation from the city of Phoenix.

12   Issued 1,000 shares of preferred stock to acquire a patent with a market value of $110,000.

22   Issued 1,500 shares of common stock for $10 cash per share.

28   Collected 20 percent of the stock subscription receivable.

Required

1. Record the transactions in the general journal.
2. Prepare the stockholders' equity section of the Financial Consultants balance sheet at December 31. Retained Earnings balance is $20,820.

Problem 14-4B *Analyzing the stockholders' equity of an actual corporation*

The purpose of this problem is to familiarize you with the financial statement information of a real company, U and I, Inc. U and I included the following stockholders' equity on its year-end balance sheet at February 28:

Stockholders' Equity	($ Thousands)
Voting Preferred Stock, 5.5% cumulative—par value $23 per share; authorized 100,000 shares in each class:	
Class A—issued 75,473 shares	$ 1,736
Class B—issued 92,172 shares	2,120
Common stock—par value $5 per share; authorized 5,000,000 shares;	
issued 2,870,950 shares	14,355
[Additional] Paid-in Capital.	5,548
Retained earnings.	8,336
	$32,095

Required

1. Identify the different issues of stock U and I has outstanding.
2. Is the preferred stock participating or nonparticipating? How can you tell?
3. Give the summary entries to record issuance of all the U and I stock. Assume that all the stock was issued for cash and that the additional paid-in capital applies to the common stock. Explanations are not required.
4. Rearrange the U and I stockholders' equity section to correspond, as appropriate, to the format and terminology illustrated on page 554. Assume the total stockholders' equity of $32,095,000 is correct.
5. Suppose U and I passed its preferred dividends for one year. Would the company have to pay these dividends in arrears before paying dividends to the common stockholders? Give your reason.
6. What amount of preferred dividends must U and I declare and pay each year to avoid having preferred dividends in arrears?
7. Assume preferred dividends are in arrears for 19X8.
   a. Write Note 5 of the February 28, 19X8, financial statements to disclose the dividends in arrears.
   b. Record the declaration of a $500,000 dividend in the year ended February 28, 19X9. An explanation is not required.

Problem 14-5B *Computing dividends on preferred and common stock*

Continental Corporation has 10,000 shares of $4.25, no-par preferred stock and 40,000 shares of no-par common stock outstanding. Continental declared and paid the following dividends during a three-year period: 19X1, $10,000; 19X2, $80,000; and 19X3, $265,000.

Required

1. Compute the total dividends to preferred stock and common stock for each of the three years if
   a. Preferred is noncumulative and nonparticipating.
   b. Preferred is cumulative and nonparticipating.
2. For case 1b, record the declaration of the 19X3 dividends on December 28, 19X3, and the payment of the dividends on January 17, 19X4.

Problem 14-6B *Analyzing the stockholders' equity of an actual corporation*

The balance sheet of St. Louis Drilling Company reported the following:

Shareholders' Investment
(same as stockholders' equity)

Redeemable non-voting preferred stock, no-par (Redemption value $358,000)	$320,000
Common stock, $1 par value, authorized 60,000 shares; issued 28,000 shares	28,000
[Additional] paid-in capital	231,000
Retained earnings.	7,000
Total shareholders' investment	$586,000

Notes to the financial statements indicate that 8,000 shares of $3.90 preferred stock with a stated value of $40 per share were issued and outstanding. Preferred dividends are in arrears for three years, including the current year. The additional paid-in capital was contributed by the common stockholders. On the balance sheet date, the market value of the St. Louis common stock was $4.50 per share.

Required

1. Which class of stockholders controls the company? Give your reason.
2. Is the preferred stock cumulative or noncumulative, participating or nonparticipating? How can you tell?
3. What is the amount of the annual preferred dividend?
4. What is the total paid-in capital of the company?
5. What was the total market value of the common stock?
6. Compute the book value per share of the preferred stock and the common stock.

Problem 14-7B *Preparing a corporation balance sheet*

The following accounts and related balances of Kentucky Coal and Iron, Inc., are arranged in no particular order. Use them to prepare the company's classified balance sheet in the account format at June 30, 19X2.

Trademark, net	$ 9,000	Inventory	$122,000
Organization cost, net	14,000	Dividends payable	9,000
Preferred stock, $.65, no-par,		Retained earnings	48,000
10,000 shares authorized,		Accounts payable	53,000
2,700 shares issued	27,000	Property, plant, and	
Stock subscription receivable		equipment, net	167,000
—common	3,000	Common stock, $.50 par,	
Cash	19,000	500,000 shares authorized,	
Accounts receivable, net	34,000	214,000 shares issued	107,000
Paid-in capital in excess of		Prepaid expenses	10,000
par—common	19,000	Common stock subscribed	
Accrued liabilities	26,000	22,000 shares	11,000
Long-term note payable	72,000	Donated capital	6,000

Decision Problem

Evaluating Alternative Ways Of Raising Capital

J. McDade and M. Fineberg have written a computer program for a video game that they believe will rival Nintendo. They need additional capital to market the product, and they plan to incorporate their partnership. They are considering alternative capital structures for the corporation. Their primary goal is to raise as much capital as possible without giving up control of the business. The partners plan to receive 120,000 shares of the corporation's common stock in return for the net assets of the partnership. After the partnership books are closed and the assets adjusted to current market value, McDade's capital balance is $65,000 and Fineberg's balance is $55,000.

The corporation's plans for a charter include an authorization to issue 5,000 shares of preferred stock and 500,000 shares of $1 par common stock. McDade and Fineberg are uncertain about the most desirable features for the preferred stock. Prior to incorporating, the partners have discussed their plans with two investment groups. The corporation can obtain capital from outside investors under either of the following plans:

Plan 1.   Group 1 will invest $75,000 to acquire 600 shares of $5, no-par preferred stock and $100,000 to acquire 100,000 shares of common stock. Each preferred share receives 50 votes on matters that come before the stockholders. The investors in Group 1 would attempt to control the corporation if they have the majority of the corporate votes.

Plan 2.   Group 2 will invest $150,000 to acquire 1,000 shares of 6 percent, $100 par nonvoting, noncumulative, participating preferred stock.

Required

Assume the corporation is chartered.

1. Journalize the issuance of common stock to McDade and Fineberg.
2. Journalize the issuance of stock to the outsiders under both plans.
3. Assume net income for the first year is $130,000 and total dividends of $19,800 are properly subtracted from retained earnings. Prepare the stockholders' equity section of the corporation balance sheet under both plans.
4. Recommend one of the plans to McDade and Fineberg. Give your reasons.

Financial Statement Problem

Stockholder's equity

The Gulf+Western balance sheet appears in Appendix C. Answer these questions about the company's common stock.

1. What class of stock does the balance sheet report? What is its par value? How many shares are authorized? How many shares were outstanding at October 31, 1987?
2. Under what title does Gulf+Western report paid-in capital in excess of par? Give another title for this account.
3. Total stockholders' equity is not labeled. What is its amount at October 31, 1987?
4. Journalize the issuance of 50,000 shares of Gulf+Western common stock for cash of $68 per share. Use Gulf+Western terminology. No explanation is required.
5. The Selected Financial Data on page 24 show book value per common share of $35.05 at October 31, 1987. Show this book value computation. (Note G mentions preferred stock that is not reported on the balance sheet. You may ignore the preferred stock.)

Answers to Self-Study Questions

1. b
2. b
3. c
4. d
5. a
6. d (1,000 shares $\times$ $104 = $104,000)
7. d Intangible asset
8. a [(10,000 $\times$ $3.50 $\times$ 3 = $105,000) + (100,000 $\times$ $1.50 = $150,000) = $255,000]
9. c
10. b

15

Corporations: Retained Earnings, Dividends, Treasury Stock, and the Income Statement

LEARNING OBJECTIVES
After studying this chapter, you should be able to

1 Account for stock dividends

2 Distinguish stock splits from stock dividends

3 Account for treasury stock

4 Report restrictions of retained earnings

5 Identify the elements of a corporation income statement

6 Account for prior period adjustments

Chapter 14 introduced the corporate form of business. Chapter 15 continues our discussion of corporation retained earnings and cash dividends and also considers stock dividends, treasury stock, and the corporate income statement.

Retained Earnings and Dividends

We have seen that the equity section on the corporation balance sheet is called stockholders' equity or shareholders' equity. The paid-in capital accounts and retained earnings make up the stockholders' equity section.

Retained Earnings is the corporation account that carries the balance of the business's net income from operations accumulated over the corporation's lifetime less its net losses and any declared dividends. *Retained* means "held on to." Retained Earnings is accumulated income to cover dividends and any future losses. Because Retained Earnings is an owners' equity account, it normally has a credit balance. Corporations may use other labels for Retained Earnings, among them Earnings Reinvested in the Business and Retained Income.

A debit balance in Retained Earnings, which arises when a corporation's expenses exceed its revenues, is called a *deficit.* This amount is subtracted from the sum of the credit balances in the other equity accounts on the balance sheet to determine total stockholders' equity. In a recent survey, 37 of 600 companies (6.2 percent) had a retained earnings deficit.

At the end of each accounting period, the Income Summary account—which carries the balance of net income for the period—is closed to the Retained Earnings account. Assume the following amounts are drawn from a corporation's temporary accounts.

Income Summary

Dec. 31, 19X1	Expenses	750,000	Dec. 31, 19X1	Revenues	850,000
			Dec. 31, 19X1	Bal.	100,000

This final closing entry transfers net income from Income Summary to Retained Earnings:

19X1
Dec. 31   Income Summary 100,000
                Retained Earnings 100,000
             To close net income to Retained Earnings.

If 19X1 was the corporation's first year of operations, the Retained Earnings account now has an ending balance of $100,000:

Retained Earnings

	Jan. 1, 19X1	Bal.		-0-
	Dec. 31, 19X1	Net income		100,000
	Dec. 31, 19X1	Bal.		100,000

A $60,000 net loss for the year would produce this debit balance in Income Summary:

Income Summary

Dec. 31, 19X3	Expenses	470,000	Dec. 31, 19X3	Revenues	410,000
Dec. 31, 19X3	Bal.	60,000			

To close a $60,000 loss, we would credit Income Summary and debit Retained Earnings, as follows:

19X3
Dec. 31   Retained Earnings 60,000
                Income Summary......................... 60,000
             To close net loss to Retained Earnings.

After posting, Income Summary's balance is zero, and the Retained Earnings balance is decreased by $60,000.

Remember that the account title includes the word *earnings. Credits to the Retained Earnings account arise only from net income.* When we examine a corporation income statement and want to learn how much net income has the corporation earned and retained in the business, we turn to Retained Earnings.

After the corporation has earned net income, its board of directors may declare and pay a cash dividend to the stockholders. The entry on January 15, 19X2, to record the declaration of a $35,000 dividend is

19X2
Jan. 15   Retained Earnings.............................. 35,000
                Dividends Payable 35,000
             To declare a cash dividend.

After the dividend declaration is posted, the Retained Earnings account has a $65,000 credit balance:

Retained Earnings

Jan. 15, 19X2	Dividend	35,000	Jan. 1, 19X2	Bal.	100,000
			Jan. 15, 19X2	Bal.	65,000

The Retained Earnings account is not a reservoir of cash waiting for the board of directors to pay dividends to the stockholders. Instead, Retained Earnings is an owners' equity account representing a claim on all assets in general and not on any asset in particular. Its balance is the cumulative, lifetime earnings of the company less its cumulative losses and dividends. In fact, the corporation may have a large balance in Retained Earnings but not have the cash to pay a dividend because the company purchased a building or the company may have abundant cash from borrowing but very little retained earnings. To *declare* a dividend, the company must have an adequate balance in Retained Earnings. To *pay* the dividend, it must have the cash. Cash and Retained Earnings are two entirely separate accounts sharing no necessary relationship.

Dividend Dates

Three relevant dates for dividends are

1. **Declaration date.** On the declaration date, the board of directors announces the intention to pay the dividend. The declaration creates a liability for the corporation. Declaration is recorded by debiting Retained Earnings and crediting Dividends Payable.
2. **Date of record.** The people who own the stock on the date of record receive the dividend. The corporation announces the record date, which follows the declaration date by a few weeks, as part of the declaration. The corporation makes no journal entry on the date of record because no transaction occurs. Nevertheless, much work takes place behind the scenes to properly identify the stockholders of record on this date because the stock is being traded continuously.
3. **Payment date.** Payment of the dividend usually follows the record date by two to four weeks. Payment is recorded by debiting Dividends Payable and crediting Cash.

Stock Dividends

A **stock dividend** is a proportional distribution by a corporation of its own stock to its stockholders. Stock dividends are fundamentally different from cash dividends because stock dividends do not transfer the assets of the corporation to the stockholders. Cash dividends are distributions of the asset cash, but stock dividends cause changes *only* in the stockholders' equity of the corporation. The effect of a stock dividend is an increase in the stock account and a decrease in Retained Earnings. Because both of these accounts are elements of stockholders' equity, total stockholders' equity is unchanged. There is merely a transfer from one stockholders' equity account to another, and no asset or liability is affected by a stock dividend.

The corporation distributes stock dividends to stockholders in proportion to the number of shares they already own. For example, suppose you owned 300 shares of Xerox Corporation common stock. If Xerox distributed a 10 percent common stock dividend, you would receive 30 ($300 \times .10$) additional shares. You would now own 330 shares of the stock. All other Xerox stockholders would receive additional shares equal to 10 percent of their prior holdings. You would all be in the same relative position after the dividend as you were before.

In distributing a stock dividend, the corporation gives up no assets. Why, then, do companies issue stock dividends?

Reasons for Stock Dividends

A corporation may choose to distribute stock dividends for the following reasons:

1. To continue dividends but conserve cash. A company may want to keep cash in the business in order to expand, buy inventory, pay off debts, and so on. Yet the company may wish to continue dividends in some form. To do so, the corporation may distribute a stock dividend. The debit to Retained Earnings also conserves cash by decreasing the Retained Earnings available for the declaration of future cash dividends. Stockholders pay tax on cash dividends but not on stock dividends.

2. To reduce the market price per share of its stock. Many companies pay low cash dividends and grow by reinvesting their earnings in operations. As they grow, the company's stock price increases. If the price gets high enough, eventually some potential investors may be prevented from purchasing the stock. Distribution of a stock dividend may cause the market price of a share of the company's stock to decrease because of the increased supply of the stock.

Suppose the market price of a share of stock is $50. If the corporation doubles the number of shares of its stock outstanding by issuing a stock dividend, the market price of the stock would drop by approximately one half, to $25 per share. The objective is to make the stock less expensive and thus attractive to a wider range of investors.

Entries for Stock Dividends

The board of directors announces stock dividends on the declaration date. The date of record and the distribution date follow. (This is the same sequence of dates used for a cash dividend.) The declaration of a stock dividend does *not* create a liability because the corporation is not obligated to pay assets. (Recall that a liability is a claim on *assets.*) Instead, the corporation has declared its intention to distribute its stock. Assume General Lumber Corporation has the following stockholders' equity prior to the dividend:

Stockholders' Equity

Paid-in capital:	
Common stock, $10 par, 50,000 shares authorized,	
20,000 shares issued...	$200,000
Paid-in capital in excess of par—common.........................	70,000
Total paid-in capital	270,000
Retained earnings...	85,000
Total stockholders' equity	$355,000

The entry to record a stock dividend depends on the size of the dividend. Generally accepted accounting principles (GAAP) distinguish between **small stock dividends** (less than 25 percent of the corporation's issued stock) and **large stock dividends** (25 percent or more of issued stock).

Assume General Lumber Corporation declares a 10 percent (small) common stock dividend on November 17. The company will distribute 2,000 (20,000 × .10) shares in the dividend. On November 17 the market value of its common stock is $16 per share. GAAP requires small stock dividends to be accounted for at market value. Therefore, Retained Earnings is debited for the market value of the 2,000 dividend shares. Common Stock Dividend Distributable is credited for par value, and Paid-in Capital in Excess of Par is credited for the remainder. General Lumber makes the following entry on the declaration date:[1]

Nov. 17 Retained Earnings (20,000 × .10 × $16)............	32,000	
Common Stock Dividend Distributable		
(20,000 × .10 × $10)...................		20,000
Paid-in Capital in Excess of Par—Common ...		12,000
To declare a 10 percent common stock dividend.		

> **OBJECTIVE 1**
> Account for stock dividends

On the distribution (payment) date, the company records issuance of the dividend shares as follows:

Dec. 12 Common Stock Dividend Distributable.............	20,000	
Common Stock		20,000
To issue common stock in a stock dividend.		

Common Stock Dividend Distributable is an owner's equity account. (It is *not* a liability because the corporation has no obligation to pay assets.) If the company prepares financial statements after the declaration of the stock dividend but before issuing it, Common Stock Dividend Distributable is reported in the stockholders' equity section of the balance sheet immediately after Common Stock and Common Stock Subscribed and before Paid-in Capital in Excess of Par—Common. However, this account holds the par value of the dividend shares only from the declaration date to the date of distribution.

The following tabulation shows the changes in stockholders' equity caused by the stock dividend:

Stockholders' Equity	Before the Dividend	After the Dividend	Change
Paid-in capital:			
Common stock, $10 par, 50,000 shares			
authorized, 20,000 shares issued	$200,000		
22,000 shares issued		$220,000	**up by $20,000**
Paid-in capital in excess of			
par—common...................	70,000	82,000	**up by $12,000**
Total paid-in capital..............	270,000	302,000	**up by $32,000**
Retained earnings	85,000	53,000	**down by $32,000**
Total stockholders' equity	$355,000	$355,000	**Unchanged**

---

[1] Committee on Accounting Procedure, "Accounting Research Bulletin No. 43," *Restatement and Revision of Accounting Research Bulletins* (New York: AICPA, 1961,) chap. 7, sec. B, pars. 10–14.

Compare stockholders' equity before and after the stock dividend. Observe the increase in the balances of Common Stock and Paid-in Capital in Excess of Par—Common and the decrease in Retained Earnings. Also observe that total stockholders' equity is unchanged from $355,000.

Amount of Retained Earnings Transferred in a Stock Dividend.   Stock dividends are said to be *capitalized retained earnings* because they transfer an amount from retained earnings to paid-in capital. The paid-in capital accounts are more permanent than retained earnings because they are not subject to owner withdrawals through dividends. As we saw in the preceding illustration, the amount transferred from Retained Earnings in a *small* stock dividend is the market value of the dividend shares because the effect on the market price of each share of the company's stock is likely to be small. Therefore, many stockholders view small stock dividends as distributions of earnings.

A *large* stock dividend, though, significantly increases the number of shares available in the market and so is likely to decrease the stock price significantly. Because of the drop in market price per share, a large stock dividend is not likely to be perceived as a distribution of earnings. GAAP does not require that large stock dividends be accounted for at a specific amount. A common practice is to use the par value of the dividend shares.

Suppose General Lumber declared a 50 percent common stock dividend. The declaration entry is

Dec. 7	Retained Earnings (20,000 × .50 × $10)	100,000	
	Common Stock Dividend Distributable		100,000
	To declare a 50 percent common stock dividend.		

Issuance of the dividend shares on the payment date is recorded by this entry:

Dec. 22	Common Stock Dividend Distributable	100,000	
	Common Stock		100,000
	To issue common stock in a stock dividend.		

Once again, total stockholders' equity is unchanged. For a large stock dividend, the increase in Common Stock is exactly offset by the decrease in Retained Earnings.

Stock Splits

A large stock dividend may decrease the market price of the stock. The stock then becomes attractive to more people. A stock split also decreases the market price of stock—with the intention of making the stock more attractive. A **stock split** is an increase in the number of outstanding shares of stock coupled with a proportionate reduction in the par value of the stock. For example, if the company splits its stock 2 for 1, the number of outstanding shares is doubled and each share's par value is halved. Most leading companies in the United States—IBM, Ford Motor Company, Borg-Warner Corporation, Giant Food, Inc., and others—have split their stock.

Assume that the market price of a share of IBM common stock is $120 and that the company wishes to decrease the market price to approximately $30. IBM decides to split the common stock 4 for 1 in order to reduce the stock's market price from $120 to $30. A 4-for-1 stock split means that the company would have four times as many shares of stock outstanding after the split as it had before and that each share's par value would be quartered. Assume IBM had 150 million shares of $5 par common stock issued and outstanding before the split.

Stockholders' Equity	($ Millions)
Paid-in capital:	
Common stock, **$5 par,** 900 million shares authorized,	
150 million shares issued	$ 750
Paid-in capital in excess of par—common	5,200
Total paid-in capital	5,950
Retained earnings	20,000
Total stockholders' equity	$25,950

After the 4-for-1 stock split, IBM would have 600 million shares (150 million shares × 4) of $1.25 par ($5/4) common stock outstanding. Total stockholders' equity would be exactly as before the stock split. Indeed, the balance in the Common Stock account does not even change. Only the par value of the stock and the number of shares authorized and issued change. Compare the highlighted figures in the two stockholders' equity presentations.

Stockholders' Equity	($ Millions)
Paid-in capital:	
Common stock, $1.25 par, 3.6 billion shares authorized,	
600 million shares issued	$ 750
Paid-in capital in excess of par—common	5,200
Total paid-in capital	5,950
Retained earnings	20,000
Total stockholders' equity	$25,950

Because the stock split affects no account balances, no formal journal entry is necessary. Instead, the split is recorded in a memorandum entry such as the following:

Aug. 19   Called in the outstanding $5 par common stock and distributed four shares of $1.25 par common stock for each old share previously outstanding.

Stock Dividends and Stock Splits

A stock dividend and a stock split both increase the number of shares of stock owned per stockholder. Also, neither a stock dividend nor a stock split changes the investor's total cost of the stock owned. For example, assume you paid $3,000 to acquire 150 shares of Avon Products common stock. If Avon distributes a 100 percent stock dividend, your 150 shares increase to 300, but your total cost is still $3,000. Likewise, if Avon distributes a 2-for-1 stock split, your shares increase in number to 300, but your total cost is unchanged. Neither type of stock action is taxable income to the investor.

OBJECTIVE 2
Distinguish stock splits from stock dividends

Both a stock dividend and a stock split increase the corporation's number of shares outstanding. For example, a 100 percent stock dividend and a 2-for-1 stock split both double the outstanding shares and cut the stock's market price per share in half. They differ in that a stock *dividend* shifts an amount from retained earnings to paid-in capital, leaving par value per share unchanged. A stock *split*

EXHIBIT 15-1   *Effects on Total Stockholders' Equity*

	Declaration	Payment of Cash or Distribution of Stock
Cash dividend	Decrease	None
Stock dividend	None	None
Stock split	None	None

Source: Adapted from Beverly Terry.

affects no account balances whatsoever but instead changes the par value of the stock.

Exhibit 15-1 summarizes the effects of dividends and stock splits on total stockholders' equity.

Treasury Stock[2]

Corporations may purchase their own stock from their shareholders for several reasons. (1) The company may have issued all its authorized stock and need the stock for distributions to officers and employees under bonus plans or stock purchase plans. (2) The purchase may help support the stock's current market price by decreasing the supply of stock available to the public. (3) The business may be trying to increase net assets by buying its shares low and hoping to sell them for a higher price later. (4) Management may gather in the stock to avoid a takeover by an outside party.

A corporation's own stock that it has issued and later reacquired is called **treasury stock.** (In effect, the corporation holds the stock in its treasury.) For practical purposes, treasury stock is like unissued stock: neither category of stock is outstanding in the hands of shareholders. The company does not receive cash dividends on its treasury stock, and treasury stock does not entitle the company to vote or to receive assets in liquidation. The difference between unissued stock and treasury stock is that treasury stock has been issued and bought back.

The purchase of treasury stock decreases the company's assets and its stockholders' equity. The size of the company literally decreases, as shown on the balance sheet. The Treasury Stock account has a debit balance, which is the opposite of the other owners' equity accounts. Therefore, Treasury Stock is a contra stockholders' equity account.

Purchase of Treasury Stock

We record the purchase of treasury stock by debiting Treasury Stock and crediting the asset given in exchange—usually Cash. Suppose that Southwest Drilling Company had the following stockholders' equity before purchasing treasury stock:

---

[2] In this book we illustrate the *cost* method of accounting for treasury stock because it is used most widely. Alternative methods are presented in intermediate accounting courses.

Stockholders' Equity

Paid-in capital:
Common stock, $1 par, 10,000 shares authorized, 8,000 shares issued . . . . $ 8,000
     Paid-in capital in excess of par—common.   12,000
       Total paid-in capital   20,000
Retained earnings.   14,600
     Total stockholders' equity $34,600

On November 22 Southwest purchases 1,000 shares of its $1 par common as treasury stock, paying cash of $7.50 per share. Southwest records the purchase as follows:

Nov. 22   Treasury Stock, Common (1,000 × $7.50)   7,500
             Cash.   7,500
         Purchased 1,000 shares of treasury stock at $7.50 per
         share.

Treasury stock is recorded at cost, without reference to the par value of the stock. The Treasury Stock account appears beneath retained earnings on the balance sheet, and its balance is subtracted from the sum of total paid-in capital and retained earnings, as follows:

OBJECTIVE 3
Account for treasury stock

Stockholders' Equity

Paid-in capital:
Common stock, $1 par, 10,000 shares authorized, 8,000 shares issued . . . $ 8,000
     Paid-in capital in excess of par—common   12,000
       Total paid-in capital   20,000
Retained earnings   14,600
     Subtotal   34,600
Less Treasury stock (1,000 shares at cost) . . . .   (7,500)
     Total stockholders' equity $27,100

Observe that the purchase of treasury stock does not decrease the number of shares issued. The Common Stock, Paid in Capital in Excess of Par, and Retained Earnings accounts remain unchanged. However, total stockholders' equity decreases by the cost of the treasury stock. Also, shares of stock *outstanding* decrease from 8,000 to 7,000. To compute the number of outstanding shares, subtract the treasury shares (1,000) from the shares issued (8,000). Although the number of outstanding shares is not required to be reported on the balance sheet, this figure is important. Only outstanding shares have a vote, receive cash dividends, and share in assets if the corporation liquidates.

Sale of Treasury Stock

Sale of Treasury Stock at Cost. Treasury stock may be sold at any price agreeable to the corporation and the purchaser. If the stock is sold for the same price that the corporation paid to reacquire it, the entry is a debit to Cash and a credit to Treasury Stock for the same amount.

Sale of Treasury Stock above Cost. If the sale price is greater than reacquisition cost, the difference is credited to the account Paid-in Capital from Treasury

Stock Transactions. Suppose Southwest Drilling Company resold 200 of its treasury shares for $9 per share. The entry is

Dec. 7	Cash (200 × $9).................................	1,800	
	Treasury Stock, Common (200 × $7.50 — the		
	purchase cost per share)		1,500
	Paid-in Capital from Treasury Stock Transactions ..		300
	To sell 200 shares of treasury stock at $9 per share.		

Paid-in Capital from Treasury Stock Transactions is reported with the other paid-in capital accounts on the balance sheet, beneath the Common Stock and Capital in Excess of Par accounts.

Sale of Treasury Stock below Cost. At times the resale price is less than cost. The difference between these two amounts is debited to Paid-in Capital from Treasury Stock Transactions. If the difference between resale price and cost is greater than the credit balance in Paid-in Capital from Treasury Stock Transactions, then the company debits Retained Earnings for the remaining amount. For example, Southwest Drilling records the sale of 400 shares of treasury stock at $5 per share in the following entry:

Dec. 23	Cash (400 × $5).................................	2,000	
	Paid-in Capital from Treasury Stock Transactions	300	
	Retained Earnings	700	
	Treasury Stock, Common (400 × $7.50 — the		
	purchase cost per share)		3,000
	To sell 400 shares of treasury stock at $5 per share.		

Paid-in Capital from Treasury Stock Transactions receives only a $300 debit because that is the extent of this account's credit balance. (See the preceding example illustrating the sale of treasury stock above cost.) The remaining $700 is debited to Retained Earnings.

No Gain or Loss from Treasury Stock Transactions

The purchase and sale of treasury stock do not affect net income. Sale of treasury stock above cost is an increase in paid-in capital, not income. Likewise, sale of treasury stock below cost is a decrease in paid-in capital or Retained Earnings, not a loss. Treasury stock transactions take place between the business and its owner's, the stockholders. Because a company cannot earn a profit in dealing in its own stock with its owners, we credit Paid-in Capital from Treasury Stock Transactions for sale above cost and debit that account (and, if necessary, Retained Earnings) for a sale below cost. These accounts appear on the balance sheet, not on the income statement.

Does this mean that a company cannot increase its net assets by buying treasury stock low and selling it high? Not at all. Management often buys treasury stock because it believes the market price of its stock is too low. For example, a company may buy 500 shares of its stock at $10 per share. Suppose it holds the stock as the market price rises and resells the stock at $14 per share. The net assets of the company increase by $2,000 [500 shares × ($14 − $10 = $4 difference per share)]. This increase is reported as paid-in capital and not as income.

Summary Problem for Your Review

Simplicity Pattern Co., Inc., reported the following stockholders' equity:

Shareholders' Equity	($ Thousands)
Preferred stock, $1.00 par value	
Authorized—10,000,000 shares	
Issued—None	$ —
Common stock, 8 ⅓ cents par value	
Authorized, 30,000,000 shares	
Issued 13,733,229 shares	1,144
Capital in excess of par value	48,122
Earnings retained in business	89,320
	138,586
Less treasury stock, at cost (1,919,000 common shares)	14,742
	$123,844

Required

1. What was the average issue price per share of the common stock?
2. Journalize the issuance of 1,200 shares of common stock at $4 per share. Use Simplicity's account titles.
3. How many shares of Simplicity's common stock are outstanding?
4. How many shares of common stock would be outstanding after Simplicity split its common stock 3 for 1?
5. Using Simplicity account titles, journalize the declaration of a stock dividend when the market price of Simplicity common stock is $3 per share. Consider each of the following stock dividends independently:
   a. Simplicity declares a 10 percent common stock dividend on the shares outstanding, computed in 3.
   b. Simplicity declares a 100 percent common stock dividend on the shares outstanding, computed in 3.
6. Journalize the following treasury stock transactions, assuming they occur in the order given:
   a. Simplicity purchases 500 shares of treasury stock at $8 per share.
   b. Simplicity sells 100 shares of treasury stock for $9 per share. Credit Paid-in Capital from Treasury Stock Transactions.
   c. Simplicity sells 100 shares of treasury stock for $5 per share.

SOLUTION TO SUMMARY PROBLEM

1. Average issue price of the common stock was $3.59 per share [($1,144,000 + $48,122,000)/13,733,229 shares = $3.59].

2.

Cash (1,200 × $4)	4,800	
Common Stock (1,200 × $.08⅓)		100
Capital in Excess of Par Value		4,700
To issue common stock at a premium.		

3. Shares outstanding = 11,814,229 (13,733,229 shares issued minus 1,919,000 shares of treasury stock)

4. Shares outstanding after a 3-for-1 stock split = 35,442,687 (11,814,229 shares outstanding × 3)

5a. Earnings Retained in Business
   (11,814,229 × .10 × $3)...................... 3,544,269
       Common Stock Dividend Distributable
       (11,814,229 × .10 × $.08⅓)...............   98,452
       Capital in Excess of Par Value..............   3,445,817
   To declare a 10 percent common stock dividend.

b. Earnings Retained in Business
   (11,814,229 × $.08⅓)...................... 984,519
       Common Stock Dividend Distributable   984,519
   To declare a 100 percent common stock dividend.

6a. Treasury Stock (500 × $8)..................... 4,000
       Cash   4,000
   To purchase 500 shares of treasury stock at $8 per share.

b. Cash (100 × $9).............................. 900
       Treasury Stock (100 × $8).................   800
       Paid-in Capital from Treasury Stock
       Transactions   100
   To sell 100 shares of treasury stock at $9 per share.

c. Cash (100 × $5).............................. 500
   Paid-in Capital from Treasury Stock Transactions
       (balance from answer 6b) 100
   Earnings Retained in Business.................... 200
       Treasury Stock (100 × $8).................   800
   To sell 100 shares of treasury stock at $5 per share.

Retirement of Stock

A corporation may purchase its own common stock or preferred stock and retire it by canceling the stock certificates. The retired stock cannot be reissued. Companies usually retire their stock in order to replace it with another issue of stock or to liquidate shares when they go out of business. Retiring stock, like purchasing treasury stock, decreases the outstanding stock of the corporation. Unlike a treasury stock purchase, stock retirement decreases the number of shares issued. Assets are decreased by the amount paid to buy the shares being retired. In retiring stock, the corporation removes the balances from all paid-in capital amounts related to the retired shares, like Capital in Excess of Par.

A corporation may repurchase shares for retirement for a price that is below the stock's issue price (par value plus any capital in excess of par). This difference between purchase price and issue price is a credit to Paid-in Capital from Retirement of Common Stock (or Preferred Stock).

Assume that a corporation issued its $10 par common stock for $14, a $4 premium per share. If the company later purchases 500 shares of the stock for retirement at $13 per share, the retirement entry is

May 22	Common Stock (500 × $10)	5,000	
	Paid-in Capital in Excess of Par—Common (500 × $4). .	2,000	
	Cash (500 × $13).		6,500
	Paid-in Capital from Retirement of		
	Common Stock.		500
	To purchase and retire common stock.		

Paid-in Capital from Retirement of Common Stock is reported after Capital in Excess of Par—Common Stock, along with any other paid-in capital accounts related to the common.

If the corporation must pay more for the stock than its issue price, the excess is debited to Retained Earnings. Assume the corporation paid $16 per share to purchase the stock for retirement. The entry is

May 22	Common Stock (500 × $10)	5,000	
	Paid-in Capital in Excess of Par—Common (500 × $4). .	2,000	
	Retained Earnings	1,000	
	Cash (500 × $16).		8,000
	To purchase and retire common stock.		

Retiring stock, like purchasing stock, is a transaction that does not affect net income. No gain or loss arises from stock retirement because the company is doing business with its owners. The entries we presented in illustrating stock retirement affect *balance sheet accounts*, not income statement accounts.

Restrictions on Retained Earnings

Dividends, purchases of treasury stock, and retirements of stock require payments by the corporation to its stockholders. In fact, treasury stock purchases and stock retirements are returns of paid-in capital to the stockholders. These outlays decrease the corporation's assets, so fewer assets are available to pay liabilities. Therefore, its creditors seek to restrict a corporation's dividend payments and treasury stock purchases. For example, a bank may agree to loan $500,000 only if the borrowing corporation limits dividend payments and purchases of its stock.

To ensure that corporations maintain a minimum level of stockholders' equity for the protection of creditors, state laws restrict the amount of its own stock that a corporation may purchase. The maximum amount a corporation can pay its stockholders without decreasing paid-in capital is its balance of retained earnings. Therefore, restrictions on dividends and stock purchases focus on the balance of retained earnings.

Companies usually report their retained earnings restrictions in notes to the financial statements. The following actual disclosure by RTE Corporation, a manufacturer of electronic transformers, is typical:

NOTES TO CONSOLIDATED FINANCIAL STATEMENTS
NOTE F—LONG-TERM DEBT

The . . . loan agreements . . . restrict cash dividends and similar payments to shareholders. Under the most restrictive of these provisions, retained earnings of $4,300,000 were unrestricted as of December 31, 19X3.

OBJECTIVE 4
Report restrictions of retained earnings

In another actual example, Chromalloy American Corporation could not declare dividends, purchase treasury stock, or purchase stock for retirement, as indicated by its Note 8:

> **NOTES TO CONSOLIDATED FINANCIAL STATEMENTS 8:**
> **LONG-TERM DEBT**
>
> The Company's loan agreements contain covenants which restrict the declaration or payment of cash dividends and the purchase . . . or retirement of capital stock. At December 31, 19X3, . . . all of the Company's [retained] earnings were restricted due to these convenants.

Appropriations of Retained Earnings

Appropriations are restrictions of Retained Earnings that are recorded by formal journal entries. A corporation may appropriate—segregate in a separate account—a portion of Retained Earnings for a specific use. For example, the board of directors may appropriate part of Retained Earnings for building a new manufacturing plant, for meeting possible future liabilities, or for other reasons. A debit to Retained Earnings and a credit to a separate account—Retained Earnings Appropriated for Plant Expansion—records the appropriation. This appropriated retained earnings account appears directly above the regular Retained Earnings account on the balance sheet.

An appropriation does *not* decrease total retained earnings. Any appropriated amount is simply a portion of retained earnings that is earmarked for a particular purpose. When the need for the appropriation no longer exists, an entry debits the Retained Earnings Appropriated account and credits Retained Earnings. This entry closes the Appropriation account and returns its amount back to the regular Retained Earnings account.

Retained earnings appropriations are rare. Corporations generally disclose any retained earnings restrictions in the notes to the financial statements. The notes give the corporation more room to describe the nature and amounts of any restrictions. Thus corporations satisfy the requirement for adequate disclosure.

Disclosing any restriction on retained earnings is important to stockholders and possible investors because the restricted amounts may not be used for dividends. A corporation with a $100,000 balance in Retained Earnings and a $60,000 restriction may declare a maximum dividend of $40,000—if the cash is available and the board of directors so decides.

Variations in Reporting Stockholders' Equity _____

Real-world accounting and business practices may use terminology and formats in reporting stockholders' equity that differ from our general examples. We use a more detailed format in this book to help you learn the components of the stockholders' equity section. Companies assume that readers of their statements already understand the omitted details.

One of the most important skills you will learn in this course is the ability to understand the financial statements of actual companies. Thus we present in Exhibit 15-2 a side-by-side comparison of our general teaching format and the format that you are more likely to encounter in real-world balance sheets. Note the following points in the real-world format:

1. The heading Paid-in Capital does not appear. It is commonly understood that Preferred Stock, Common Stock, and Additional Paid-in Capital are elements of paid-in capital.

EXHIBIT 15-2 *Stockholders' Equity*

General Teaching Format		Real-World Format	
Stockholders' Equity		**Stockholders' Equity**	
Paid-in capital:		Preferred stock, 8%, $10 par, 30,000 shares authorized and issued	$ 310,000
Preferred stock, 8%, $10 par, 30,000 shares authorized and issued	$ 300,000	Common stock, $1 par, 100,000 shares authorized, 60,000 shares issued	60,000
Paid-in capital in excess of par— preferred	10,000	Additional paid-in capital.	2,160,000
		Retained earnings (Note 7).	1,565,000
Common stock, $1 par, 100,000 shares authorized, 60,000 shares issued	60,000	Less treasury stock, common (1,400 shares at cost)	(42,000)
			$4,053,000
Paid-in capital in excess of par— common	1,940,000		
Paid-in capital from treasury stock transactions, common	9,000		
Paid-in capital from retirement of preferred stock.	11,000		
Donated capital–plant site	200,000		
Total paid-in capital	2,530,000		
Retained earnings appropriated for contingencies.	400,000		
Retained earnings–unappropriated. . .	1,165,000		
Total retained earnings	1,565,000		
Total.	4,095,000		
Less treasury stock, common (1,400 shares at cost)	(42,000)		
Total stockholders' equity	$4,053,000		

Note 7—Restriction on retained earnings.
At December 31, 19XX, $400,000 of retained earnings is restricted by the company's board of directors to absorb the effect of any contingencies that may arise. Accordingly, possible dividend declarations are restricted to a maximum of $1,165,000 ($1,565,000 – $400,000).

2. Preferred stock is often reported in a single amount that combines its par value and premium.

3. For presentation in the financial statements, all additional paid-in capital— from capital in excess of par on common stock, treasury stock transactions, stock retirement, and donated capital—appears as a single amount labeled Additional Paid-in Capital. Additional Paid-in Capital belongs to the common stockholders, and so it follows Common Stock in the real-world format.

4. Often, total stockholders' equity ($4,053,000 in the exhibit) is not specifically labeled.

Corporation Income Statement

A corporation's net income receives more attention than any other item in the financial statements. Net income measures the business's ability to earn a profit and answers the question of how successfully the company has managed its operations. To stockholders, the larger the corporation's profit, the greater the likelihood of dividends. To creditors, the larger the corporation's profit, the better able it is to pay its debts. Net income builds up a company's assets and owners' equity. It also helps to attract capital from new investors who hope to receive dividends from future successful operations.

Suppose you are considering investing in the stock of two manufacturing companies. In reading their annual reports and examining their past records, you learn that the companies showed the same net income figure for last year and that each company has increased its net income by 15 percent annually over the last five years. You observe, however, that the two companies have generated income in different ways.

Company A's income has resulted from the successful management of its central operations (manufacturing). Company B's manufacturing operations have been flat for two years. Its growth in net income has resulted from selling off segments of its business at a profit. Which company would you invest in?

Company A holds the promise of better future earnings. This corporation earns profits from continuing operations. We may reasonably expect the business to match its past earnings in the future. Company B shows no growth from operations. Its net income results from one-time transactions, the selling off of its operating assets. Sooner or later, Company B will have sold off the last of its assets used in operations. When that occurs, the business will have no means of generating income. Based on this reasoning, your decision is to invest in the stock of Company A.

This example points to two important investment considerations: the *trend* of a company's earnings and the *makeup* of its net income. The probability of making intelligent investment decisions is improved if the income statement separates the results of central, continuing operations from special, one-time gains and losses. We now discuss the components of the corporation income statement. We will see how the income statement reports the results of operations in a manner that allows statement users to get a good look at the business's operations. Exhibit 15-3 will be used throughout these discussions. The items of primary interest are highlighted for emphasis.

Continuing Operations

We have seen that income from a business's continuing operations helps financial statement users make predictions about the business's future earnings. In the income statement of Exhibit 15-3, the top-most section reports income from continuing operations. This part of the business is expected to continue from period to period. We may use this information to predict that Electronics Corporation will earn income of approximately $54,000 next year.

Note that income tax expense has been deducted in arriving at income from continuing operations. The tax that corporations pay on their income is a significant expense. The federal income tax rate for corporations varies from time to time, and the current maximum rate is 34 percent. For computational ease, let's use an income tax rate of 40 percent in our illustrations. This is a reasonable estimate of combined federal and state income taxes. The $36,000 income tax expense in Exhibit 15-3 equals the pretax income from continuing operations multiplied by the tax rate ($90,000 $\times$ .40 = $36,000).

Discontinued Operations

Most large corporations engage in several lines of business. For example, General Mills, Inc., best known for its food products, also has retailing and restaurant operations. Sears, Roebuck & Co., in addition to its retail stores, has a real estate

EXHIBIT 15-3   *Corporation Income Statement*

Electronics Corporation Income Statement For the Year Ended December 31, 19X5		
Sales revenue		$500,000
Cost of goods sold		240,000
Gross margin		260,000
Operating expenses (detailed)		181,000
Operating income		79,000
Other gains (losses)		
Gain on sale of machinery		11,000
Income from continuing operations before income tax		90,000
Income tax expense		36,000
Income from continuing operations		54,000
Discontinued operations:		
Operating income, $30,000, less income tax of $12,000	$18,000	
Gain on disposal, $5,000, less income tax of $2,000	3,000	21,000
Income before extraordinary items		75,000
Extraordinary flood loss	(10,000)	
Less income tax saving	4,000	(6,000)
Net income		$ 69,000
Earnings per share of common stock (30,000 shares outstanding):		
Income from continuing operations		$1.80
Income from discontinued operations		.70
Income before extraordinary items		2.50
Extraordinary loss		(.20)
Net income		$2.30

subsidiary, an insurance company, and a savings and loan enterprise. We call each significant part of a company a **segment of the business.**

   A company may sell a segment of its business. Such a sale is not a regular source of income because a company cannot keep on selling its segments indefinitely. The sale of a business segment is viewed as a one-time transaction. The income statement carries information on the segment that has been disposed of under the heading Discontinued Operations. This section of the income statement is divided into two components: (1) operating income or (loss) on the segment that is disposed of and (2) any gain (or loss) on the disposal. Income and gain are taxed at the 40 percent rate and reported as follows:

> Discontinued operations:
> Operating income, $30,000, less income tax, $12,000 . . . . $18,000
> Gain on disposal, $5,000, less income tax, $2,000   3,000
> $21,000

Trace this presentation to Exhibit 15-3.

   It is necessary to separate discontinued operations into these two components because the company may operate the discontinued segment for part of the year.

This is the operating income (or loss) component. Then, usually a gain (or loss) on the disposal of the segment occurs.

Discontinued operations are common in business. The Black and Decker Manufacturing Company disposed of its gasoline chain saw business. Purolator, Inc., sold its armored-car segment, and RJR Nabisco disposed of its fast-food business, including Kentucky Fried Chicken. Each of these items was disclosed as discontinued operations in the company's income statement.

Extraordinary Gains and Losses

Extraordinary gains and losses, also called extraordinary items, are both unusual for the company and infrequent. Losses from natural disasters (like earthquakes, floods, and tornadoes) and the taking of company assets by a foreign government (expropriation), are extraordinary.

Extraordinary items are reported along with their income tax effect. Assume Electronics Corporation lost $10,000 of inventory in a flood. This flood loss, which reduces income, also reduces the company's income tax. The tax effect of the loss is computed by multiplying the amount of the loss by the tax rate. The tax effect decreases the net amount of the loss in the same way that the tax effect of income reduces the amount of net income. An extraordinary loss is reported along with its tax effect as follows:

Extraordinary flood loss................	$(10,000)	
Less income tax saving..............	4,000	$(6,000)

Trace this item to the income statement in Exhibit 15-3. An extraordinary gain is reported the same way, net of the income tax on the gain.

Gains and losses due to employee strikes, the settlement of lawsuits, discontinued operations, and the sale of plant assets are *not* extraordinary items. They are considered normal business occurrences. However, because they are outside the business's central operations, they are reported on the income statement as other gains and losses. An example is the gain on sale of machinery in Exhibit 15-3.

Earnings Per Share (EPS)

The final segment of a corporation income statement presents the company's earnings per share, abbreviated as EPS. In fact, GAAP requires that corporations disclose EPS figures on the income statement.

Earnings per share is the amount of a company's net income per share of its outstanding common stock. EPS is a key measure of a business's success. Consider a corporation with net income of $200,000 and 100,000 shares of common stock outstanding. Its EPS is $2 ($200,000/100,000). A second corporation may also have net income of $200,000 but only 50,000 shares of common stock outstanding. Its EPS is $4 ($200,000/50,000).

Just as the corporation lists separately its different sources of income—from continuing operations, discontinued operations, and so on—it lists separately the EPS figure based on different income sources. Consider that Electronics Corporation had $54,000 in income from continuing operations, $21,000 in income from discontinued operations, and an extraordinary loss of $6,000. Net income was $69,000 ($54,000 + $21,000 − $6,000). Electronics had 30,000 common shares outstanding for the entire accounting period. The company's EPS is reported on the income statement as follows:

Earnings per share of common stock (30,000 shares outstanding):

Income from continuing operations ($54,000/30,000)	$1.80
Income from discontinued operations ($21,000/30,000)	.70
Income before extraordinary items ($75,000/30,000)	2.50
Extraordinary loss ($6,000/30,000)	(.20)
Net income ($69,000/30,000)	$2.30

The income statement user can understand the sources of the business's EPS amounts when presented in this detail.

Exhibit 15-3 presents the detailed income statement of Electronics Corporation for the year ended December 31, 19X5. The income statement is in multiple-step format.

Weighted Average Number of Shares of Common Stock Outstanding.   Computing EPS is straightforward if the number of common shares outstanding does not change over the entire accounting period. For many corporations, however, this figure varies over the course of the year. Consider a corporation that had 100,000 shares outstanding from January through November, then purchased 60,000 shares as treasury stock. This company's EPS would be misleadingly high if computed using 40,000 (100,000 − 60,000) shares. To make EPS as meaningful as possible, corporations use the weighted average number of common shares outstanding during the period.

Let's assume the following figures for Diskette Demo Corporation. From January through May the company had 240,000 shares of common stock outstanding; from June through August, 200,000 shares; and from September through December, 210,000 shares. We compute the weighted average by considering the outstanding shares per month as a fraction of the year:

Number of Common Shares Outstanding		Fraction of Year		Weighted Average Number of Common Shares Outstanding
240,000	×	5/12	(January through May)	= 100,000
200,000	×	3/12	(June through August)	= 50,000
210,000	×	4/12	(September through December)	= 70,000
			Weighted average number of common shares outstanding during the year	220,000

The 220,000 weighted average would be divided into net income to compute the corporation's EPS.

Preferred Dividends.   Throughout the EPS discussion we have used only the number of shares of common stock outstanding. Holders of preferred stock have no claim to the business's income beyond the stated preferred dividend. However, preferred dividends do affect the EPS figure. Recall that EPS is earnings per share of *common* stock. Also recall that dividends on preferred stock are paid first. Therefore, preferred dividends must be subtracted from income subtotals (income from continuing operations, income before extraordinary items, and net income) in the computation of EPS. Preferred dividends are not subtracted from income or loss from discontinued operations, and they are not subtracted from extraordinary gains and losses.

If Electronics Corporation had 10,000 shares of preferred stock outstanding, each with a $1.50 dividend, the annual preferred dividend would be $15,000 (10,000 × $1.50). The $15,000 would be subtracted from each of the different income subtotals, resulting in the following EPS computations for the company:

Earnings per share of common stock (30,000 shares outstanding):

Income from continuing operations ($54,000 − $15,000)/30,000...........	$1.30
Income from discontinued operations ($21,000/30,000)....................	.70
Income before extraordinary items ($75,000 − $15,000)/30,000	2.00
Extraordinary loss ($6,000/30,000)....................................	(.20)
Net income ($69,000 − $15,000)/30,000	$1.80

Dilution. Some corporations make their preferred stock more attractive to investors by offering convertible preferred stock. Holders of convertible preferred may exchange the preferred stock for common stock. If in fact the preferred stock is converted to common stock, then the EPS will be *diluted*—reduced—because more common stock shares are divided into net income. Because convertible preferred can be traded in for common stock, the common stockholders want to know the amount of the decrease in EPS if the preferred stock is converted into common. To provide this information, corporations present two sets of EPS amounts: EPS based on outstanding common shares (primary EPS), and EPS based on outstanding common shares plus the number of additional common shares that would arise from conversion of the preferred stock into common (diluted EPS).

EPS is the most widely used accounting figure. Many income statement users place top priority on EPS. Also, a stock's market price is related to the company's EPS. By dividing the market price of a company's stock by its EPS, we compute a statistic called the price-to-earnings ratio. *The Wall Street Journal* reports the price-to-earnings ratios (listed as P/E) daily for more than 3,000 companies.

Statement of Retained Earnings

Retained earnings may be a significant portion of a corporation's owner's equity. The year's income increases the retained earnings balance, and dividends decrease it. Retained earnings are so important that corporations draw up a financial statement outlining the major changes in this equity account, much as the statement of owner's equity presents information on changes in the equity of a proprietorship. The statement of retained earnings for Electronics Corporation appears in Exhibit 15-4.

Some companies report income and retained earnings on a single statement. Exhibit 15-5 illustrates how Electronics would combine its income statement and its statement of retained earnings.

EXHIBIT 15-4   *Statement of Retained Earnings*

Electronics Corporation **Statement of Retained Earnings** **For the Year Ended December 31, 19X5**	
Retained earnings balance, December 31, 19X4..................	$130,000
Net income for 19X5	69,000
	199,000
Dividends for 19X5...	(21,000)
Retained earnings balance, December 31, 19X5.................	$178,000

EXHIBIT 15-5 *Statement of Income and Retained Earnings*

Electronics Corporation Statement of Income and Retained Earnings For the Year Ended December 31, 19X5	
Sales revenue.	$500,000
Cost of goods sold.	240,000
Net income for 19X5.	69,000
Retained earnings, December 31, 19X4	130,000
	199,000
Dividends for 19X5	(21,000)
Retained earnings, December 31, 19X5	$178,000
Earnings per share of common stock (30,000 shares outstanding):	
Income from continuing operations	$1.80
Income from discontinued operations	.70
Income before extraordinary items.	2.50
Extraordinary loss	(.20)
Net income.	$2.30

Prior Period Adjustments

OBJECTIVE 6
Account for prior period adjustments

What happens when a company makes an error in recording revenues or expenses? Detecting the error in the period in which it occurs allows the company to make a correction before preparing that period's financial statements. But failure to detect the error until a later period means that the business will have reported an incorrect amount of income on its income statement. After closing the revenue and expense accounts, the Retained Earnings account will absorb the effect of the error, and its balance will be wrong until the error is corrected.

Corrections to the beginning balance of Retained Earnings for errors of an earlier period are called **prior period adjustments.** The correcting entry includes a debit or credit to Retained Earnings for the error amount and a debit or credit to the asset or liability account that was misstated. The prior period adjustment appears on the corporation's statement of retained earnings to indicate to readers the amount and the nature of the change in the Retained Earnings balance.

Assume that McDonald Corporation recorded income tax expense for 19X4 as $30,000. The correct amount was $40,000. This error resulted in understating 19X4 expenses by $10,000 and overstating net income by $10,000. A bill from the government in 19X5 for the additional $10,000 in taxes alerts the McDonald management to the mistake. The entry to record this prior period adjustment in 19X5 is

19X5			
June 19	Retained Earnings	10,000	
	Income Tax Payable		10,000
	Prior period adjustment to correct error in recording		
	income tax expense of 19X4.		

The debit to Retained Earnings excludes the error correction from the income statement of 19X5. Recall the matching principle. If Income Tax Expense is debited when the prior period adjustment is recorded in 19X5, then this $10,000 in taxes would appear on the 19X5 income statement. This would not be proper since the expense arose from 19X4 operations.

This prior period adjustment would appear on the statement of retained earnings, as follows:

McDonald Corporation Statement of Retained Earnings For the Year Ended December 31, 19X5	
Retained earnings balance, December 31, 19X4, **as originally reported**	$390,000
Prior period adjustment–debit to correct error in recording income tax expense of 19X4	(10,000)
Retained earnings balance, December 31, 19X4, **as adjusted**.........	380,000
Net income for 19X5.......................................	114,000
	494,000
Dividends for 19X5..	(41,000)
Retained earnings balance, December 31, 19X5	$453,000

Our example shows a prior period adjustment for additional expense. To make a prior period adjustment for additional income, retained earnings is credited and the misstated asset or liability is debited.

Summary Problem for Your Review

The following information was taken from the ledger of Kraft Corporation:

Loss on sale of discontinued operations	$ 20,000	Selling expenses	$ 78,000

Prior period adjustment—
   credit to Retained Earnings
	5,000	Common stock, no-par,
		   45,000 shares issued......
			180,000

Gain on sale of plant assets ..	21,000	Sales revenue	620,000
Cost of goods sold	380,000	Interest expense	30,000
Income tax expense (saving)		Extraordinary gain	26,000
Continuing operations	32,000	Operating income,	
Discontinued operations:		discontinued operations ...	30,000
Operating income	12,000	Loss due to lawsuit.........	11,000
Loss on sale	(8,000)	General expenses	62,000
Extraordinary gain	10,000	Preferred stock, 8%, $100	
Treasury stock, common		par, 500 shares issued.....	50,000
(5,000 shares at cost)	25,000	Paid-in capital in excess of	
Dividends	16,000	par—preferred	7,000
		Retained earnings, beginning, as originally reported	103,000

Required

Prepare a single-step income statement and a statement of retained earnings for Kraft Corporation for the current year ended December 31. Include the earnings per share presentation and show computations. Assume no changes in the stock accounts during the year.

SOLUTION TO SUMMARY PROBLEM

Kraft Corporation
Income Statement
For the Year Ended December 31, 19—

Revenue and gains:			
Sales revenue..........................			$620,000
Gain on sale of plant assets			21,000
Total revenues and gains			641,000
Expenses and losses:			
Cost of goods sold		$380,000	
Selling expenses		78,000	
General expenses		62,000	
Interest expense		30,000	
Loss due to lawsuit.......................		11,000	
Income tax expense.......................		32,000	
Total expenses and losses.................			593,000
Income from continuing operations..............			48,000
Discontinued operations:			
Operating income........................	$30,000		
Less income tax.........................	12,000	18,000	
Loss on sale of discontinued operations	20,000		
Less income tax saving	8,000	(12,000)	6,000
Income before extraordinary items			54,000
Extraordinary gain		26,000	
Less income tax............................		10,000	16,000
Net income			$ 70,000

Earnings per share:
Income from continuing operations [($48,000 − $4,000)/40,000 shares]..... $1.10
Income from discontinued operations ($6,000/40,000 shares) 15
Income before extraordinary items ($54,000 − $4,000)/40,000 shares]......   1.25
Extraordinary gain ($16,000/40,000 shares)...........................   .40
Net income [($70,000 − $4,000)/40,000 shares] $1.65

Computations:

$$EPS = \frac{Income - Preferred\ dividends}{Common\ shares\ outstanding}$$

Preferred dividends: $50,000 × .08 = $4,000
Common shares outstanding: 45,000 shares issued − 5,000 treasury shares = 40,000 shares outstanding

Kraft Corporation
Statement of Retained Earnings
For the Year Ended December 31, 19—

Retained earnings balance, beginning, as originally reported	$103,000
Prior period adjustment–credit	5,000
Retained earnings balance, beginning, as adjusted.....................	108,000
Net income for current year.......................................	70,000
	178,000
Dividends for current year..	(16,000)
Retained earnings balance, ending	$162,000

Summary

Retained Earnings carries the balance of the business's net income accumulated over its lifetime, less its declared dividends and any net losses. *Cash dividends* are distributions of corporate assets made possible by earnings. *Stock dividends* are distributions of the corporation's own stock to its stockholders. Stock dividends and *stock splits* increase the number of shares outstanding and lower the market price per share of stock.

Treasury stock is the corporation's own stock that has been issued and reacquired and is currently held by the company. The corporation may sell treasury stock for its cost or for more or less than cost. *Retirement* of stock cancels the designated shares, which cannot then be reissued.

Retained earnings may be *restricted* by law or contract or by the corporation itself. An *appropriation* is a restriction of retained earnings that is recorded by formal journal entries.

The corporate *income statement* lists separately the various sources of income—*continuing operations*, which include other gains and losses, *discontinued operations*, and *extraordinary gains and losses*. The bottom line of the income statement reports *net income* or *net loss* for the period. *Income tax expense* and *earnings-per-share* figures also appear on the income statement, likewise divided into different categories based on the nature of income. The *statement of retained earnings* reports the causes for changes in the Retained Earnings account. This statement may be combined with the income statement.

Self-Study Questions

Test your understanding of the chapter by marking the best answer for each of the following questions.

1. A corporation has total stockholders' equity of $100,000, including retained earnings of $19,000. The cash balance is $35,000. The maximum cash dividend the company can declare and pay is *(p. 573)*
    a. $19,000   c. $65,000
    b. $35,000   d. $100,000

2. An entry debiting Dividends Payable and crediting Cash is recorded on the *(p. 573)*
    a. Declaration date   c. Payment date
    b. Date of record   d. None of the above

3. Meyer's Thrifty Acres has 100,000 shares of $20 par common stock outstanding. The stock's market value is $37 per share. Meyer's board of directors declares and distributes a 1 percent common stock dividend. Which of the following entries shows the full effect of declaring and distributing the dividend? *(p. 575)*

    a. Retained Earnings 37,000
          Common Stock Dividend Distributable   20,000
          Paid-in Capital in Excess of Par—Common   17,000

    b. Retained Earnings 20,000
          Common Stock......................................   20,000

    c. Retained Earnings 17,000
          Paid-in Capital in Excess of Par—Common   17,000

    d. Retained Earnings 37,000
          Common Stock......................................   20,000
          Paid-in Capital in Excess of Par—Common   17,000

4. Lang Real Estate Investment Corporation declared and distributed a 50 percent stock dividend. Which of the following stock splits would have the same effect on the number of Lang shares outstanding? *(pp. 577, 578)*
    a. 2 for 1   c. 4 for 3
    b. 3 for 2   d. 5 for 4

5. A company purchased 10,000 of its $1.50 par common stock as treasury stock, paying $6 per share. This transaction *(p. 579)*
   a. Has no effect on company assets
   b. Has no effect on owners' equity
   c. Decreases owners' equity by $15,000
   d. Decreases owners' equity by $60,000

6. A restriction of retained earnings *(pp. 583, 584)*
   a. Has no effect on total retained earnings
   b. Reduces retained earnings available for the declaration of dividends
   c. Can be reported by a note or by appropriation of retained earnings, or both
   d. All of the above

7. Which of the following items is *not* reported on the income statement? *(p. 587)*
   a. Premium on stock
   b. Extraordinary gains and losses
   c. Income tax expense
   d. Earnings per share

8. The income statement item that is likely to be most useful for predicting income from year to year is *(p. 586)*
   a. Extraordinary items
   b. Discontinued operations
   c. Income from continuing operations
   d. Net income

9. In computing earnings per share (EPS), dividends on preferred stock are *(p. 589)*
   a. Added because they represent earnings to the preferred stockholders
   b. Subtracted because they represent earnings to the preferred stockholders
   c. Ignored because they do not pertain to the common stock
   d. Reported separately on the income statement

10. A corporation accidentally overlooked an accrual of property tax expense at December 31, 19X4. Accountants for the company detect the error early in 19X5 before the expense is paid. The entry to record this prior period adjustment is *(p. 591)*

    a. Retained Earnings   XXX
          Property Tax Expense.   XXX

    b. Property Tax Expense . .   XXX
          Property Tax Payable.   XXX

    c. Retained Earnings.   XXX
          Property Tax Payable.   XXX

    d. Property Tax Payable. . .   XXX
          Property Tax Expense.   XXX

Answers to the self-study questions are at the end of the chapter.

Accounting Vocabulary

appropriation of retained earnings *(p. 584)*,   date of record *(p. 573)*,   declaration date *(p. 573)*,
earnings per share (EPS) *(p. 588)*,   extraordinary item *(p. 588)*,   large stock dividend *(p. 575)*,
payment date *(p. 573)*,   prior period adjustment *(p. 591)*,   segment of a business *(p. 587)*,
small stock dividend *(p. 575)*,   stock dividend *(p. 573)*,   stock split *(p. 576)*,   treasury stock
(p. 578).

ASSIGNMENT MATERIAL ───────────────

Questions

1. Identify the two main parts of stockholders' equity.
2. Identify the account debited and the account credited from the last closing entry a corporation makes each year. What is the purpose of this entry?
3. Ametek, Inc., reported a cash balance of $73 million and a retained earnings balance of $162.5 million. Explain how Ametek can have so much more retained earnings than cash. In your answer, identify the nature of retained earnings and state how it ties to cash.
4. Briefly discuss the three important dates for a dividend.
5. A friend of yours receives a stock dividend on an investment. He believes stock dividends are the same as cash dividends. Explain why this is not true.

6. Give two reasons for a corporation to distribute a stock dividend.

7. A corporation declares a stock dividend on December 21 and reports Stock Dividend Payable as a liability on the December 31 balance sheet. Is this correct? Give your reason.

8. What percentage distinguishes a small stock dividend from a large stock dividend? What is the main difference in accounting for small and large stock dividends?

9. To an investor, a stock split and a stock dividend have essentially the same effect. Explain the similarity and difference to the corporation between a 100 percent stock dividend and a 2-for-1 stock split.

10. Give four reasons why a corporation may purchase treasury stock.

11. What effect does the purchase of treasury stock have on the (a) assets, (b) issued stock, and (c) outstanding stock of the corporation?

12. What is the normal balance of the Treasury Stock account? What type of account is Treasury Stock? Where is Treasury Stock reported on the balance sheet?

13. Revell Inc. purchased treasury stock for $25,000. If Revell sells half the treasury stock for $15,000, what account should it credit for the $2,500 difference? If Revell sells half the treasury stock for $9,000, what accounts should be debited for the $3,500 difference?

14. What effect does the purchase and retirement of common stock have on the (a) assets, (b) issued stock, and (c) outstanding stock of the corporation?

15. Why do creditors wish to restrict a corporation's payment of cash dividends and purchases of treasury stock?

16. What are two ways to report a retained earnings restriction? Which way is more common?

17. Identify three items on the income statement that generate income tax expense. What is an income tax saving, and how does it arise?

18. Why is it important for a corporation to report income from continuing operations separately from discontinued operations and extraordinary items?

19. Give two examples of extraordinary gains and losses and four examples of gains and losses that are *not* extraordinary.

20. What is the most widely used of all accounting statistics? What is the price-to-earnings ratio? Compute the price-to-earnings ratio for a company with EPS of $2 and market price of $12 per share of common stock.

21. What is the earnings per share of a company with net income of $5,500, issued common stock of 12,000 shares, and treasury common stock of 1,000 shares.

22. What account do all prior period adjustments affect? On what financial statement are prior period adjustments reported?

Exercises

Exercise 15-1 *Journalizing dividends and reporting stockholders' equity*

Eatmore Hamburger System, Inc., is authorized to issue 300,000 shares of $1 par common stock. The company issued 100,000 shares at $6 per share, and all 100,000 shares are outstanding. When the retained earnings balance was $300,000, Eatmore declared and distributed a 50 percent stock dividend. Later, Eatmore declared and paid a $.20 per share cash dividend.

Required

1. Journalize the declaration and distribution of the stock dividend.
2. Journalize the declaration and payment of the cash dividend.
3. Prepare the stockholders' equity section of the balance sheet after both dividends.

Exercise 15-2 *Journalizing a stock dividend and reporting stockholders' equity*

The stockholders' equity for Tick Tock Jewelry Corporation on September 30, 19X4—end of the company's fiscal year—follows.

Stockholders' Equity

Common stock, $10 par, 100,000 shares authorized, 50,000 shares issued..........	$500,000
Paid-in capital in excess of par—common...	50,000
Retained earnings......................	280,000
Total stockholders' equity	$830,000

On November 16 the market price of Tick Tock's common stock was $15 per share and the company declared a 10 percent stock dividend. Tick Tock issued the dividend shares on November 30.

Required

1. Journalize the declaration and distribution of the stock dividend.
2. Prepare the stockholders' equity section of the balance sheet after the stock dividend.

Exercise 15-3 *Journalizing treasury stock transactions*

Journalize the following transactions of Shoe Renewry, Inc., a national chain of shoe repair shops:

May 19 Issued 3,000 shares of no-par common stock at $12 per share.
Aug. 22 Purchased 600 shares of treasury stock at $14 per share.
Nov. 11 Sold 200 shares of treasury stock at $15 per share.
Dec. 28 Sold 100 shares of treasury stock at $11 per share.

Exercise 15-4 *Journalizing treasury stock transactions and reporting stockholders' equity*

Northwest Distributing Company had the following stockholders' equity on November 30:

Stockholders' Equity

Common stock, $5 par, 500,000 shares authorized, 50,000 shares issued.............	$250,000
Paid-in capital in excess of par	150,000
Retained earnings......................	220,000
Total stockholders' equity	$620,000

On December 19 the company purchased 1,000 shares of treasury stock at $6 per share. Journalize the purchase of the treasury stock and prepare the stockholders' equity section of the balance sheet at December 31.

Exercise 15-5 *Reporting stockholders' equity after a stock split*

Assume Northwest Distributing Company (the business in the preceding exercise) split its $5 par common stock 4 for 1 on December 10. Make the memorandum entry to record the stock split, and prepare the stockholder's equity section of the balance sheet immediately after the split. Assume the number of authorized shares increases to 2,000,000.

Exercise 15-6 *Reporting a retained earnings restriction*

The agreement under which Brookview Sales, Inc., issued its long-term debt requires the restriction of $351,000 of the company's retained earnings balance. Total retained earnings is $609,000, and total paid-in capital is $822,000.

Required

Show how to report stockholders' equity (including retained earnings) on Brookview's balance sheet, assuming:

a. Brookview discloses the restriction in a note. Write the note.
b. Brookview appropriates retained earnings in the amount of the restriction and includes no note in its statements.

Exercise 15-7   *Preparing a multiple-step income statement*

The ledger of a corporation contains the following information for 19X7 operations:

Cost of goods sold	$45,000	Income tax saving—loss on	
Loss on discontinued		discontinued operations....	$ 20,000
operations	50,000	Extraordinary gain	12,000
Income tax expense—		Sales revenue	130,000
extraordinary gain	4,800	Operating expenses (including	
		income tax)	60,000

Required

Prepare a multiple-step income statement for 19X7. Omit earnings per share.

Exercise 15-8   *Computing earnings per share*

Benavides Inc. earned net income of $56,000 for the second quarter of 19X6. The ledger reveals the following figures:

Preferred stock, $2.50 per year, no-par, 1,400 shares issued and outstanding	$ 50,000
Common stock, $10 par, 32,000 shares issued	320,000
Treasury stock, common, 2,000 shares at cost	36,000

Required

Compute EPS for the quarter, assuming no changes in the stock accounts during the quarter.

Exercise 15-9   *Preparing a statement of retained earnings with a prior period adjustment*

Posen Inc., a soft-drink company, reported a prior period adjustment in 19X9. An accounting error caused net income of prior years to be overstated by $3.8 million. Retained earnings at January 1, 19X9, as previously reported, stood at $395.3 million. Net income for 19X9 was $78.1 million, and dividends were $39.8 million. Prepare the company's statement of retained earnings for the year ended December 31, 19X9.

Exercise 15-10   *Preparing a combined statement of income and retained earnings*

The Kroger Company, a large grocery company, had retained earnings of $792.6 million at the beginning of 19X3. The company showed these figures at December 31, 19X3:

	($ Millions)
Increases in retained earnings:	
Net income	$127.1
Decreases in retained earnings:	
Cash dividends—preferred	2.3
common	85.2
Debit to retained earnings due to purchase of preferred stock	11.3

Required

Beginning with net income, prepare a combined statement of income and retained earnings for the Kroger Company for 19X3. The debit to Retained Earnings was caused by

Kroger's paying $11.3 more to retire its preferred stock than the original issue price of the stock.

Exercise 15-11 *Computing earnings per share*

Greenlawn Supply had 40,000 shares of common stock and 10,000 shares of $10 par, 5 percent preferred stock outstanding on December 31, 19X8. On April 30, 19X9, the company issued 9,000 additional common shares and ended 19X9 with 49,000 shares of common stock outstanding. Income from continuing operations of 19X9 was $106,200, and loss on discontinued operations was $8,280. The company had an extraordinary gain of $50,600.

Required

Compute Greenlawn's EPS amounts for 19X9, starting with income from continuing operations.

Problems

(Group A)

Problem 15-1A *Journalizing dividend and treasury stock transactions*

Pecos Corporation completed the following selected transactions during the current year:

Jan. 9 Discovered that income tax expense of the preceding year was overstated by $8,000. Recorded a prior period adjustment to correct the error.

Feb. 10 Split common stock 2 for 1 by calling in the 20,000 shares of $10 par common and issuing 40,000 shares of $5 par common.

Mar. 18 Declared a cash dividend on the 5 percent, $100 par preferred stock (1,000 shares outstanding). Declared a $.20 per share dividend on the 40,000 shares of common stock outstanding. The date of record was April 2, and the payment date was April 23.

Apr. 23 Paid the cash dividends.

July 30 Declared a 10 percent stock dividend on the common stock to holders of record August 21, with distribution set for September 11. The market value of the common stock was $21 per share.

Sep. 11 Issued the stock dividend shares.

Sep. 26 Purchased 3,000 shares of the company's own common stock at $18 per share.

Nov. 8 Sold 1,000 shares of treasury common stock for $20 per share.

Dec. 13 Sold 500 shares of treasury common stock for $17 per share.

Required

Record the transactions in the general journal.

Problem 15-2A *Journalizing prior period adjustments and dividend and treasury stock transactions; reporting retained earnings and stockholders' equity*

The balance sheet of Abilene, Inc., at December 31, 19X1, reported the following stockholders' equity:

Paid-in capital:	
Common stock, $10 par, 100,000 shares authorized, 20,000 shares issued...........	$200,000
Paid-in capital in excess of par—common...	300,000
Total paid-in capital	500,000
Retained earnings......................	240,000
Total stockholders' equity.............	$740,000

During 19X2 Abilene completed the following selected transactions:

Jan. 11 Discovered that income tax expense of 19X1 was understated by $14,000. Recorded a prior period adjustment to correct the error.

Apr. 30 Declared a 10 percent stock dividend on the common stock. The market value of Abilene common stock was $24 per share. The record date was May 21, with distribution set for June 5.

June 5 Issued the stock dividend shares.

July 29 Purchased 2,000 shares of the company's own common stock at $19 per share.

Nov. 13 Sold 1,000 shares of treasury common stock for $24 per share.

Nov. 27 Declared a $.30 per share dividend on the 21,000 shares of common stock outstanding. The date of record was Dec. 17, and the payment date was January 7, 19X3.

Dec. 31 Closed the $103,000 credit balance of Income Summary to Retained Earnings.

Required

1. Record the transactions in the general journal.
2. Prepare a retained earnings statement at December 31, 19X2.
3. Prepare the stockholders' equity section of the balance sheet at December 31, 19X2.

Problem 15-3A *Journalizing dividend and treasury stock transactions and reporting stockholders' equity*

The balance sheet of Sausalito Sales Company at December 31, 19X5, reported 100,000 shares of no-par common stock authorized, with 30,000 shares issued and a Common Stock balance of $180,000. Sausalito Sales also had 5,000 shares of 5 percent, $10 par preferred stock authorized and outstanding. The preferred stock was issued in 19X1 at par. Retained Earnings had a credit balance of $65,000. During the two-year period ended December 31, 19X7, the company completed the following selected transactions:

19X6

Mar. 15 Purchased 2,000 shares of the company's own common stock for the treasury at $5 per share.

July 2 Declared the annual 5 percent cash dividend on the preferred stock and a $.75-per-share cash dividend on the common stock. The date of record was July 16, and the payment date was July 31.

July 31 Paid the cash dividends.

Nov. 30 Declared a 20 percent stock dividend on the *outstanding* common stock to holders of record December 21, with distribution set for January 11, 19X7. The market value of Sausalito common stock was $10 per share.

Dec. 31 Earned net income of $60,000 for the year.

19X7

Jan. 11 Issued the stock dividend shares.

June 30 Declared the annual 5 percent cash dividend on the preferred stock. The date of record was July 14, and the payment date was July 29.

July 29 Paid the cash dividends.

Aug. 2 Purchased and retired all the preferred stock at $14 per share.

Oct. 8 Sold 800 shares of treasury common stock for $12 per share.

Dec. 19 Split the no-par common stock 2 for 1 by issuing two new no-par shares for each old no-par share previously issued. The corporation had issued 35,600 shares, so after the split it had 71,200 shares issued. (Stock splits affect all issued stock, including treasury stock as well as stock that is outstanding.)

31 Earned net income of $81,000 during the year.

Required

1. Record the transactions in the general journal. Explanations are not required.
2. Prepare the stockholders' equity section of the balance sheet at two dates: December 31, 19X6, and December 31, 19X7.

Problem 15-4A *Preparing a single-step income statement and a statement of retained earnings; reporting stockholders' equity on the balance sheet*

The following information was taken from the ledger and other records of Rivera Corporation at September 30, 19X6.

Loss on sale of plant assets	$ 8,000	Interest revenue	$ 4,000
Sales returns	9,000	Extraordinary loss	30,000
Income tax expense (saving):		Operating loss, discontinued segment	15,000
Continuing operations	72,000	Loss on insurance settlement	12,000
Discontinued segment:		General expenses	113,000
Operating loss	(6,000)	Preferred stock, $3, no-par 10,000 shares	
Gain on sale	8,000	authorized, 5,000 shares issued	200,000
Extraordinary loss	(12,000)	Paid-in capital in excess of par—common	20,000
Sales revenue	903,000	Retained earnings, beginning, as originally	
Treasury stock, common (1,000 shares at		reported	88,000
cost)	11,000	Selling expenses	136,000
Dividends	35,000	Common stock, $10 par, 25,000 shares	
Gain on sale of discontinued segment	20,000	authorized and issued	250,000
Prior period adjustment—credit to Retained		Sales discounts	18,000
Earnings	6,000	Interest expense	11,000
Contributed capital from treasury stock		Cost of goods sold	420,000
transactions	7,000		

Required

Prepare a single-step income statement and a statement of retained earnings for Rivera Corporation for the fiscal year ended September 30, 19X6. Also prepare the stockholders' equity section of the balance sheet at that date. Include the earnings-per-share presentation, and show computations.

Problem 15-5A *Preparing a corrected combined statement of income and retained earnings*

Monica Hearn, accountant for International Food Incorporated, was injured in a skiing accident. Another employee prepared the income statement on the following page for the fiscal year ended December 31, 19X3.

The individual amounts listed on the income statement are correct. However, some accounts are reported incorrectly, and others do not belong on the income statement at all. Also, income tax (40 percent) has not been applied to all appropriate figures. International issued 52,000 shares of common stock in 19X1 and held 2,000 shares as treasury stock during 19X3. The retained earnings balance, as originally reported at December 31, 19X2, was $92,000.

Required

Prepare a corrected combined statement of income and retained earnings for 19X3. Prepare the income statement in single-step format.

International Foods Incorporated
Income Statement
19X3

Revenue and gains:		
Sales		$349,000
Prior period adjustment–credit.		14,000
Gain on retirement of preferred stock (issued for		
$100,000; purchased for $93,000).		7,000
Paid-in capital in excess of par—common		80,000
Total revenues and gains.		450,000
Expenses and losses:		
Cost of goods sold	$145,000	
Selling expenses.	76,000	
General expenses	61,000	
Sales returns.	11,000	
Dividends	7,000	
Sales discounts	6,000	
Income tax expense	20,000	
Total expenses and losses		326,000
Income from operations		124,000
Other gains and losses:		
Gain on sale of discontinued operations	10,000	
Flood loss	(20,000)	
Operating loss on discontinued segment	(15,000)	
Total other losses		(25,000)
Net income.		$149,000
Earnings per share		$2.98

Problem 15-6A   *Using actual-company data to record transactions and report earnings per share*

The following items were taken from the financial statements of actual companies that showed amounts in millions and rounded to the nearest $100,000.

The General Tire & Rubber Company declared and paid cash dividends of $35.2 million to its common stockholders and also declared and issued a 2 percent stock dividend on its 23.6 million common shares outstanding. The par value of General's common stock was $.30 per share, and the market value of the stock at the time of the stock dividend was $60 per share.

Required

1. Journalize the declaration and payment of the cash dividend.
2. Journalize declaration and issuance of the stock dividend.

At the beginning of the year, IU International Corporation had a treasury stock balance of $288.3 million. During the year, IU paid $2.2 million to purchase treasury stock. The company also sold treasury stock for $79.9 million. The cost of the treasury stock sold was $68.3 million. In addition, IU paid $19.6 million to purchase and retire preferred stock with par value of $18.8 million. The preferred stock had been issued at par in previous years.

Required

3. Journalize the purchase and the sale of treasury stock.

4. Compute the ending balance of the Treasury Stock account.
5. Journalize the purchase and retirement of preferred stock.

Chesapeake Corporation of Virginia, a paper company, reported a $4.0 million extraordinary gain that resulted from issuing 200,000 shares of its $5 par common stock and giving $4.5 million in cash to pay off long-term debt of $16.5 million. Chesapeake's income before the extraordinary item was $8.5 million, and the company had 6.4 million shares of common stock outstanding.

Note: An extraordinary gain or loss is recorded exactly as any other gain or loss, but with "Extraordinary" in its account title.

Required

6. Journalize the transaction.
7. Show how Chesapeake reported earnings per share for the year.

Problem 15-7A *Computing earnings per share and reporting a retained earnings restriction*

The capital structure of Montpelier Gardens at December 31, 19X6, included 20,000 shares of $1.25 preferred stock and 44,000 shares of common stock. Common shares outstanding during 19X7 were 44,000 January through May, 50,000 June through August, and 60,500 September through December. Income from continuing operations during 19X7 was $47,440. The company discontinued a segment of the business at a loss of $6,630, and an extraordinary item generated a gain of $33,660. Montpelier's board of directors restricts $60,000 of retained earnings for contingencies.

Required

1. Compute Montpelier's earnings per share. Start with income from continuing operations.
2. Show two ways of reporting Montpelier's retained earnings restriction. Assume total retained earnings is $190,000 and total paid-in capital is $230,000.

(Group B)

Problem 15-1B *Journalizing dividend and treasury stock transactions*

El Paso Corporation completed the following selected transactions during 19X6:

Jan. 13 Discovered that income tax expense of 19X5 was understated by $11,000. Recorded a prior period adjustment to correct the error.

Jan. 21 Split common stock 3 for 1 by calling in the 10,000 shares of $15 par common and issuing 30,000 shares of $5 par common.

Feb. 6 Declared a cash dividend on the 4,000 shares of $2.25, no-par preferred stock. Declared a $.50 per share dividend on the 30,000 shares of common stock outstanding. The date of record was February 27, and the payment date was March 20.

Mar. 20 Paid the cash dividends.

Apr. 18 Declared a 50 percent stock dividend on the common stock to holders of record April 30, with distribution set for May 30. The market value of the common stock was $11 per share.

May 30 Issued the stock dividend shares.

June 18 Purchased 2,000 shares of the company's own common stock at $12 per share.

Nov. 14 Sold 800 shares of treasury common stock for $10 per share. Debited Retained Earnings for the difference between sale price and cost because there was no Paid-in Capital from Treasury Stock Transactions.

Dec. 22 Sold 1,000 shares of treasury common stock for $16 per share.

Required
Record the transactions in the general journal.

Problem 15-2B *Journalizing prior period adjustments and dividend and treasury stock transactions; reporting retained earnings and stockholders' equity*

The balance sheet of Odessa Corporation at December 31, 19X3, presented the following stockholders' equity:

Paid-in capital:

Common stock, $1 par, 250,000 shares authorized, 50,000 shares issued	$ 50,000
Paid-in capital in excess of par—common	350,000
Total paid-in capital	400,000
Retained earnings	110,000
Total stockholders' equity	$510,000

During 19X4, Odessa completed the following selected transactions:

Jan. 7 Discovered that income tax expense of 19X3 was overstated by $7,000. Recorded a prior period adjustment to correct the error.

Mar. 29 Declared a 50 percent stock dividend on the common stock. The market value of Odessa common stock was $9 per share. The record date was April 19, with distribution set for May 19.

May 19 Issued the stock dividend shares.

July 13 Purchased 5,000 shares of the company's own common stock at $6 per share.

Oct. 4 Sold 3,000 shares of treasury common stock for $9 per share.

Dec. 27 Declared a $.20 per share dividend on the 73,000 shares of common stock outstanding. The date of record was January 17, 19X5, and the payment date was January 31.

       31 Closed the $62,000 credit balance of Income Summary to Retained Earnings.

Required

1. Record the transactions in the general journal.
2. Prepare the retained earnings statement at December 31, 19X4.
3. Prepare the stockholders' equity section of the balance sheet at December 31, 19X4.

Problem 15-3B *Journalizing dividend and treasury stock transactions and reporting stockholders' equity*

The balance sheet of Carmel Service Company at December 31, 19X7, reported 10,000 shares of $.50, no-par preferred stock authorized and outstanding. The preferred was issued in 19X1 at $8 per share. Carmel also had 500,000 shares of $1 par common stock authorized with 100,000 shares issued. Paid-in Capital in Excess of Par—Common had a balance of $300,000. Retained Earnings had a balance of $18,000, and the preferred dividend for 19X7 was in arrears. During the two-year period ended December 31, 19X9, the company completed the following selected transactions:

19X8

Feb. 15 Purchased 5,000 shares of the company's own common stock for the treasury at $3 per share.

Apr. 2 Declared the cash dividend on the preferred stock in arrears for 19X7 and the current cash dividend on preferred. The date of record was April 16, and the payment date was May 1.

May 1 Paid the cash dividends.

May 2 Purchased and retired all the preferred stock at $7.50 per share.

Dec. 31   Earned net income of $45,000 for the year.
19X9

Mar. 8   Sold 2,000 shares of treasury common stock for $4 per share.

Sep. 28   Declared a 5 percent stock dividend on the *outstanding* common stock to holders of record October 15, with distribution set for October 31. The market value of Carmel Common stock was $5 per share.

Oct. 31   Issued the stock dividend shares.

Nov. 5   Split the common stock 2 for 1 by calling in the 104,850 shares of old $1 par common stock and issuing 209,700 shares of $.50 par common. (Stock splits affect all issued stock, including treasury stock and stock that is outstanding.)

Dec. 31   Earned net income of $62,000 during the year.

Required

1. Record the transactions in the general journal. Explanations are not required.
2. Prepare the stockholders' equity section of the balance sheet at two dates: December 31, 19X8, and December 31, 19X9.

Problem 15-4B   *Preparing a single-step income statement and a statement of retained earnings and reporting stockholders' equity on the balance sheet*

The following information was taken from the ledger and other records of Mancini Corporation at June 30, 19X5:

Treasury stock, common (2,000 shares at cost)	$ 28,000	Sales revenue	$559,000
General expenses	71,000	Retained earnings, beginning, as originally reported	63,000
Loss on sale of discontinued segment	8,000	Selling expenses	87,000
Prior period adjustment – debit to Retained Earnings	4,000	Common stock, no-par, 22,000 shares authorized and issued	350,000
Cost of goods sold	319,000	Sales discounts	7,000
Interest expense	23,000	Paid-in capital from retirement of preferred	
Gain on settlement of lawsuit	8,000	stock	16,000
Sales returns	15,000	Interest revenue	5,000
Income tax expense (saving):		Extraordinary gain	27,000
Continuing operations	16,000	Operating loss, discontinued segment	9,000
Discontinued segment:		Loss on sale of plant assets	10,000
Operating loss	(3,600)	Dividends on preferred stock	?
Loss on sale	(3,200)	Preferred stock, 6%, $25 par, 20,000	
Extraordinary gain	10,800	shares authorized, 4,000 shares issued	100,000
Dividends on common stock	12,000		

Required

Prepare a single-step income statement and a statement of retained earnings for Mancini Corporation for the fiscal year ended June 30, 19X5. Also prepare the stockholders' equity section of the balance sheet at that date. Include the earnings-per-share presentation and show computations.

Problem 15-5B   *Preparing a corrected combined statement of income and retained earnings*

Leslie Gose, accountant for Stinnett Catering Company, was injured in a sailing accident. Another employee prepared the following income statement for the fiscal year ended June 30, 19X4:

Stinnett Catering Company
Income Statement
June 30, 19X4

Revenues and gains:		
Sales.......		$522,000
Gain on retirement of preferred stock (issued for $50,000; purchased for $48,000)		2,000
Paid-in capital in excess of par—common		100,000
Total revenues and gains		624,000
Expenses and losses:		
Cost of goods sold.......	$233,000	
Selling expenses	103,000	
General expenses	74,000	
Sales returns	22,000	
Prior period adjustment–debit.......	4,000	
Dividends	15,000	
Sales discounts	10,000	
Income tax expense.......	32,000	
Total expenses and losses		493,000
Income from operations		131,000
Other gains and losses:		
Extraordinary gain.......	30,000	
Operating income on discontinued segment.......	25,000	
Loss on sale of discontinued operations	(40,000)	
Total other gains		15,000
Net income		$146,000
Earnings per share		$7.30

The individual amounts listed on the income statement are correct. However, some accounts are reported incorrectly, and others do not belong on the income statement at all. Also, income tax (40 percent) has not been applied to all appropriate figures. Stinnett issued 24,000 shares of common stock in 19X1 and held 4,000 shares as treasury stock during the fiscal year 19X4. The retained earnings balance, as originally reported at June 30, 19X3, was $56,000.

Required

Prepare a corrected combined statement of income and retained earnings for fiscal year 19X4. Prepare the income statement in single-step format.

Problem 15-6B *Using actual-company data to record transactions and report earnings per share*

The following items were taken from actual financial statements that reported amounts in millions, rounded to the nearest $100,000.

Hampton Industries, Inc., declared and paid cash dividends of $.1 million to preferred stockholders and also declared and issued a 10 percent stock dividend on its 2.0 million common shares outstanding. The par value of Hampton's common stock was $1.00 per share, and the market value of the stock at the time of the stock dividend was $6.50 per share.

Required

1. Journalize the declaration and payment of the cash dividend.
2. Journalize the declaration and issuance of the stock dividend.

At the beginning of the period, the Louisiana Land and Exploration Company had a treasury stock balance of $1.2 million. During the period, Louisiana paid $212.8 million to purchase treasury stock, and the company also sold treasury stock for $.6 million. The cost of the treasury stock was $.5 million.

Required

3. Journalize the purchase and the sale of treasury stock.
4. Compute the ending balance of the Treasury Stock account.

Crown Cork & Seal Company, Inc., purchased and retired 800,000 shares of its common stock at a cost of $40 per share. Assume that par value was $1 per share and that the common stock was issued for $9 per share.

Required

5. Journalize the purchase and retirement of the common stock.

G. C. Murphy Company reported a $1.3 million extraordinary gain on the issuance of treasury stock, which cost $3.4 million, to pay off long-term debt of $4.7 million. Murphy's income before extraordinary item was $17.0 million, and the company had 4.1 million shares of common stock outstanding.
Note: An extraordinary gain or loss is recorded exactly as any other gain or loss, but with ''Extraordinary'' in its account title.

Required

6. Journalize the transaction.
7. Show how Murphy reported earnings per share for the year.

Problem 15-7B   *Computing earnings per share and reporting a retained earnings restriction*

Tradewinds Travel's capital structure at December 31, 19X2, included 5,000 shares of $2.50 preferred stock and 130,000 shares of common stock. Common shares outstanding during 19X3 were 130,000 January through February; 119,000 during March; 121,000 April through October; and 128,000 during November and December. Income from continuing operations during 19X7 was $349,655. The company discontinued a segment of the business at a gain of $69,160, and an extraordinary item generated a loss of $49,510. The board of directors of Tradewinds has restricted $240,000 of retained earnings for expansion of the company's office facilities.

Required

1. Compute Tradewinds's earnings per share. Start with income from continuing operations.
2. Show two ways of reporting Tradewinds's retained earnings restriction. Assume total retained earnings is $739,800 and total paid-in capital is $947,610.

Decision Problem

Analyzing Cash Dividends and Stock Dividends

Pacific Union Corporation had the following stockholders' equity on June 30 of the current year:

Common stock, no-par, 100,000 shares issued	$ 750,000
Retained earnings	830,000
Total stockholders' equity	$1,580,000

In the past, Pacific Union has paid an annual cash dividend of $1.50 per share. Despite the large retained earnings balance, the board of directors wished to conserve cash for expansion. The board delayed the payment of cash dividends by one month and in the meantime distributed a 20 percent stock dividend. During the following year, the company's cash position improved. The board declared and paid a cash dividend of $1.25 per share.

Suppose you own 1,000 shares of Pacific Union common stock, acquired three years ago. The market price of the stock was $24 per share before any of the above dividends.

Required

1. How does the stock dividend affect your proportionate ownership in the company? Explain.
2. What amount of cash dividends did you receive last year? What amount of cash dividends will you receive after the above dividend action?
3. Immediately after the stock dividend was distributed, the market value of Pacific Union stock decreased from $24 per share to $20 per share. Does this represent a loss to you? Explain.
4. Suppose Pacific Union announces at the time of the stock dividend that the company will continue to pay the annual $1.50 cash dividend per share, even after the stock dividend. Would you expect the market price of the stock to decrease to $20 per share as in 3 above? Explain.

Financial Statement Problem

Treasury Stock, Retained Earnings, and the Corporation Income Statement
Use the Gulf+Western financial statements in Appendix C to answer these questions.

1. How many shares of common stock did Gulf+Western have outstanding at October 31, 1987? How many shares were in the treasury? How many shares had Gulf+Western issued through October 31, 1987?
2. Gulf+Western uses a method of accounting for treasury stock that is different from the method discussed in this chapter. Nevertheless, you can determine from the Statement of Changes in Stockholders' Equity the company's cost of treasury stock acquired during fiscal 1987. It is the total reduction in stockholders' equity for the acquisition of treasury stock. What was this amount?
3. What was the retained earnings balance at October 31, 1987? In Note F, how much of retained earnings was unrestricted as to the payment of cash dividends? How much was restricted?
4. What transactions caused the extraordinary items during fiscal 1986? Identify each individual item as a gain or a loss and give its net amount. Show the total amount reported on the income statement.
5. What transaction caused the earnings from discontinued operations during fiscal 1985? Show all the components of this item, including the related income tax amounts.
6. Income taxes for fiscal 1985 include the $83.6 million reported on the income statement plus the income tax effects of discontinued operations given in Note B. What was Gulf+Western's total income tax expense for fiscal 1985? Gulf+Western refers to income tax expense as "Provision for income taxes," a common title.

Answers to Self-Study Questions

1. a 3. d 5. d 7. a 9. b
2. c 4. b 6. d 8. c 10. c

16

Corporations: Long-Term Liabilities and Bond Investments

LEARNING OBJECTIVES

After studying this chapter, you should be able to

1 Amortize bond discount and premium by the straight-line method

2 Amortize bond discount and premium by the effective interest method

3 Account for retirement of bonds payable

4 Account for conversion of bonds payable

5 Account for operating leases and capital leases

6 Explain the advantages and disadvantages of borrowing

7 Account for investments in bonds

Corporations may finance—that is, raise money for—their operations in different ways. They may issue stock to their owners, and they may reinvest assets earned by profitable operations, as we have seen. This chapter discusses the third way of financing operations, **long-term liabilities.**

Two common long-term liabilities are notes payable and bonds payable. A note payable, which we studied in Chapter 11, is a promissory note issued by the company to borrow money from a single lender, like a bank or an insurance company. **Bonds payable** are groups of notes payable issued to multiple lenders, called bondholders. This chapter focuses on bonds and bond investments and also discusses accounting for lease liabilities.

The Nature of Bonds

A company needing millions of dollars may be unable to borrow so large an amount from a single lender. To gain access to more investors, the company may issue bonds. Each bond is, in effect, a long-term note payable that bears interest. Bonds are debts to the company for the amounts borrowed from the investors.

Purchasers of bonds receive a bond certificate, which carries the issuing company's name. The certificate also states the *principal*, which is the amount that the company has borrowed from the bondholder. This figure, typically stated in units of $1,000, is also called the bond's face value, maturity value, or par value. The bond obligates the issuing company to pay the holder the principal amount at a specific future date, called the maturity date, which also appears on the certificate.

EXHIBIT 16-1 *Bond (Note) Certificate*

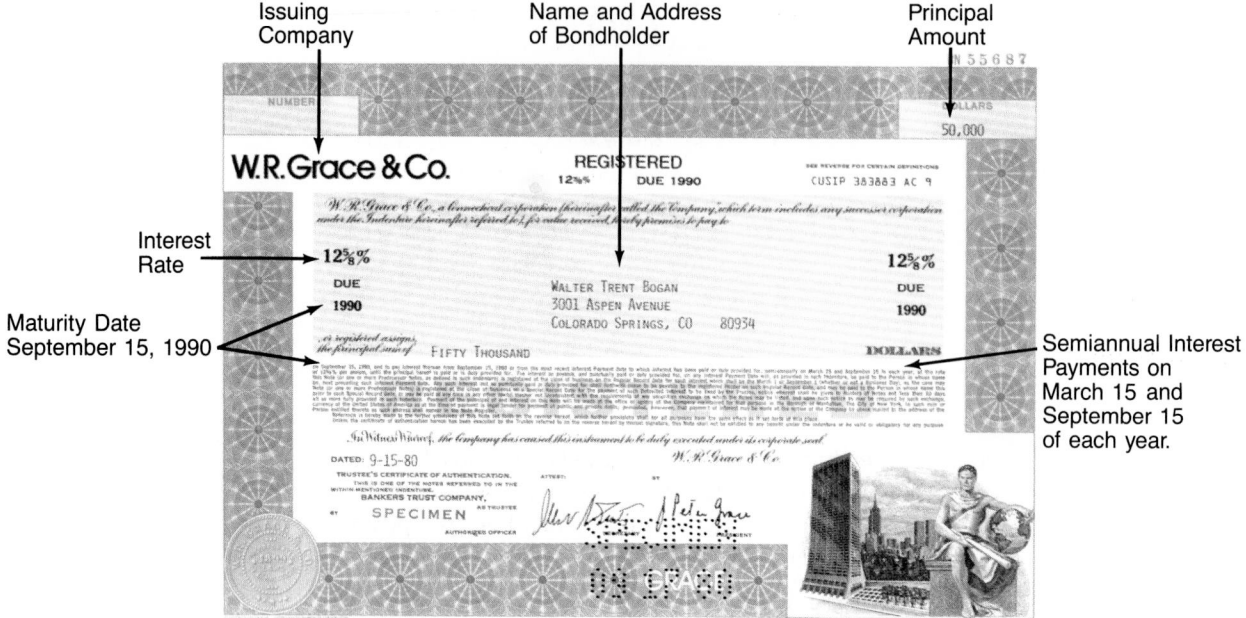

Bondholders loan their money to companies for a price: interest on the principal. The bond certificate states the interest rate that the issuer will pay the holder and the dates that the interest payments are due (generally twice a year). Some bond certificates name the bondholder (the investor). When the company pays back the principal, the holder returns the certificate, which the company retires (or cancels). Exhibit 16-1 shows an actual bond certificate, with the various features highlighted.

The board of directors may authorize a bond issue. In some companies the stockholders—as owners—may also have to vote their approval.

Issuing bonds usually requires the services of a securities firm, like Merrill Lynch, to act as the *underwriter* of the bond issue. The **underwriter** purchases the bonds from the issuing company and resells them to its clients, or it may sell the bonds for a commission from the issuer, agreeing to buy all unsold bonds.

Types of Bonds

Bonds may be *registered* bonds or *coupon* bonds. The owner of a **registered bond** receives interest checks from the issuing company, which keeps a listing of the names and addresses of the bondholders. Owners of **coupon bonds** receive interest by detaching a perforated coupon—which states the interest due and the date of payment—from the bond and depositing it in a bank for collection. A company with coupon bonds needs no registry of bondholders. The responsibility for cashing coupons rests with the bondholders. All bonds issued today are registered.

All the bonds in a particular issue may mature at the same time **(term bonds),** or they may mature in installments over a period of time **(serial bonds).** By issuing serial bonds, the company spreads its principal payments over time and avoids paying the entire principal at one time. Serial bonds are like installment notes payable.

Secured, or *mortgage,* bonds give the bondholder the right to take specified assets of the issuer if the company *defaults,* that is, fails to pay interest or principal. Unsecured bonds, called **debentures,** are backed only by the good faith of the borrower.

A secured bond is not necessarily more attractive to an investor than is a debenture. The primary motive of a person investing in bonds is to receive the interest amounts and the bonds' maturity value on time. Thus a debenture from a business with an excellent record in meeting obligations may be more attractive to an investor than is a secured bond from a business that has just been started or that has a bad credit record.

Bond Prices

Investors may transfer bond ownership through bond markets. The most famous bond market is the New York Exchange, which lists several thousand bonds. Bond prices are quoted at a percentage of their maturity value. For example, a $1,000 bond quoted at 100 is bought or sold for $1,000, which is 100 percent of its par value. The same bond quoted at 101½ has a market price of $1,015 (101.5 percent of par value, or $1,000 × 1.015). Prices are quoted to the 8th of 1 percent. A $1,000 bond quoted at 88⅜ is priced at $883.75 ($1,000 × .88375).

Exhibit 16-2 contains actual price information for the bonds of Ohio Edison Company, taken from *The Wall Street Journal.*

On this particular day, 12 of Ohio Edison's 9½ percent, $1,000 par value bonds maturing in the year 2006 (indicated by *06*) were traded. The bonds' highest price on this day was $795 ($1,000 × .795). The lowest price of the day was $785 ($1,000 × .785). The closing price (last sale of the day) was $795. This price was 2 points higher than the closing price of the preceding day. What was the bonds' closing price the preceding day? It was 77½ (79½ − 2).

The factors that affect the market price of a bond include the length of time until the bond matures. The sooner the maturity date, the more attractive the bond, and the more an investor is willing to pay for it. Also, the bonds issued by a company with a proven ability to meet all payments commands a higher price than an issue from a company with a poor record. Bond price hinges too on the rates of other available investment plans. Is a 12 percent bond the best way to invest $1,000, or does another investment strategy pay a higher rate? Of course, the higher the percentage rate, the higher the market price. Buying a 13 percent bond will cost you more than buying an 8 percent bond, given that both issues have the same maturity date and have been issued by equally sound businesses.

A bond issued at a price above its maturity (par) value is said to be issued at a **premium,** and a bond issued at a price below maturity (par) value has a **discount.** As a bond nears maturity, its market price moves toward par value. On the maturity date the market value of a bond exactly equals its par value because the company that issued the bond pays that amount to retire the bond.

EXHIBIT 16-2 *Bond Price Information*

Bonds	Volume	High	Low	Close	Net Change
OhEd 9½ 06	12	79½	78½	79½	+2

Present Value

A dollar received today is worth more than a dollar received in the future. You may invest today's dollar and earn income from it. Likewise, deferring any payment gives your money a longer period to grow. Money earns income over time, a fact called the *time value of money.* Let's examine how the time value of money affects the pricing of bonds.

Assume a bond with a face value of $1,000 reaches maturity three years from today and carries no interest. Would you pay $1,000 to purchase the bond? No, because the payment of $1,000 today to receive the same amount in the future provides you with no income on the investment. You would not be taking advantage of the time value of money. Just how much would you pay today in order to receive $1,000 at the end of three years? The answer is some amount *less* than $1,000. Let's suppose that you feel $750 is a good price. By investing $750 now to receive $1,000 later, you earn $250 interest revenue over the three years. The issuing company sees the transaction this way: It pays you $250 interest expense for the use of your $750 for three years.

The amount that a person would invest *at the present time* to receive a greater amount at a future date is called the **present value** of a future amount. In our example, $750 is the present value of the $1,000 amount to be received three years later.

Our $750 bond price is a reasonable estimate. The exact present value of any future amount depends on (1) the amount of the future payment (or receipt) (2) the length of time from the investment to the date when the future amount is to be received (or paid), and (3) the interest rate during the period. Present value is always less than the future amount. We discuss the method of computing present value in the appendix that follows this chapter. We need to be aware of the present-value concept, however, in the discussion of bond prices that follows.

Bond Interest Rates

Bonds are sold at market price, which is the amount that investors are willing to pay. Market price is the bond's present value, which equals the present value of the principal payment plus the present value of the cash interest payments (which are made semiannually, annually, or quarterly over the term of the bond).

Two interest rates work to set the price of a bond. The **contract interest rate,** or **stated rate,** is the interest rate that determines the amount of cash interest the borrower pays—and the investor receives—each year. For example, Chrysler's 8 percent bonds have a contract interest rate of 8 percent. Thus Chrysler pays $8,000 of interest annually on each $100,000 bond. Each semiannual interest payment is $4,000 ($100,000 × .08 × ½).

The **market interest rate,** or **effective rate,** is the rate that investors demand in order to loan their money. The market rate varies, sometimes daily. A company may issue bonds with a contract interest rate that differs from the prevailing market interest rate. Chrysler may issue its 8 percent bonds when the market rate has risen to 9 percent. Will the Chrysler bonds attract investors in this market? No, because investors can earn 9 percent on other bonds. Therefore, investors will purchase Chrysler bonds only at a price less than par value. The difference between the lower price and face value is a *discount.* Conversely, if the market interest rate is 7 percent, Chrysler's 8 percent bonds will be so attractive that investors will pay more than face value for them. The difference between the higher price and face value is a *premium.*

Issuing Bonds Payable

Suppose Chrysler Corporation has $50 million in 8 percent bonds that mature in 10 years. Assume that Chrysler issues these bonds at par on January 1, 1989. The issuance entry is

1989
Jan. 1   Cash   50,000,000
             Bonds Payable   50,000,000
             To issue 8%, 10-year bonds at par.

The corporation that is borrowing money makes a one-time entry similar to this to record the receipt of cash and the issuance of bonds. Afterward, investors buy and sell the bonds through the bond markets. The buy-and-sell transactions between investors do not involve the corporation that issued the bonds. It keeps no records of these transactions, except for the names and addresses of the bondholders. This information is needed for mailing the interest and principal payments.

Interest payments occur each January 1 and July 1. Chrysler's entry to record the first semiannual interest payment is

1989
July 1   Interest Expense ($50,000,000 × .08 × 6/12)   2,000,000
             Cash   2,000,000
             To pay semiannual interest on bonds payable.

At maturity, Chrysler will record payment of the bonds as follows:

1999
Jan. 1   Bonds Payable   50,000,000
             Cash   50,000,000
             To pay bonds payable at maturity.

Issuing Bonds Payable between Interest Dates

The foregoing entries to record Chrysler's bond transactions are straightforward because the company issued the bonds on an interest payment date (January 1). However, corporations often issue bonds between interest dates.

Suppose Cincinnati Milacron, Inc., issues $75 million of 12 percent debentures due June 15, 2009. These bonds are dated June 15, 1989, and carry the price "100 plus accrued interest from date of original issue." An investor purchasing the bonds after the bond date must pay market value *plus accrued interest.* The issuing company will pay the full semiannual interest amount to the bondholder at the next interest payment date. Companies do not split semiannual interest payments.

Assume that Cincinnati Milacron sells $100,000 of its bonds on July 15, 1989, one month after the date of original issue on June 15. Also assume that the market price of the bonds on July 15 is the face value. The company receives one month's accrued interest in addition to the bond's face value. Cincinnati's entry to record issuance of the bonds payable is

1989

July 15 Cash 101,000

Bonds Payable 100,000

Interest Payable ($100,000 × .12 × 1/12) 1,000

To issue 12%, 20-year bonds at par, one month after the original issue date.

Cincinnati's entry to record the first semiannual interest payment is

1989

Dec. 15 Interest Expense ($100,000 × .12 × 5/12)............... 5,000

Interest Payable................................. 1,000

Cash ($100,000 × .12 × 6/12).................. 6,000

To pay semiannual interest on bonds payable.

The debit to Interest Payable eliminates the credit balance in that account (from July 15). Cincinnati has now paid off that liability.

Note that Cincinnati Milacron pays a full six months' interest on December 15. After subtracting the one month's accrued interest received at the time of issuing the bond, Cincinnati has recorded interest expense for five months ($5,000). This interest expense is the correct amount for the five months that the bonds have been outstanding.

Selling bonds between interest dates at market value plus accrued interest simplifies the borrower's bookkeeping. The business pays the same amount of interest on each bond regardless of the length of time the person has held the bond. The business need not compute each bondholder's interest payment on an individual basis. Imagine the paperwork necessary to keep track of the interest due hundreds of bondholders who each bought bonds on a different date.

When an investor sells bonds to another investor, the price is always "plus accrued interest." Suppose you hold bonds as an investment for two months of a semiannual interest period and sell the bonds to another investor before receiving your interest. The person who buys the bonds will receive your two months of interest on the next specified interest date. Business practice dictates that you must collect your share of the interest when you sell the bonds. For this reason, all bond transactions are "plus accrued interest."

Issuing Bonds Payable at a Discount

We know that market conditions may force the issuing corporation to accept a discount price for its bonds. Suppose Chrysler issues $100,000 of its 8 percent, 10-year bonds when the market interest rate is slightly above 8 percent. The market price of the bonds drops to 98, which means 98 percent of par value. Chrysler receives $98,000 ($100,000 × .98) at issuance. The entry is

1989

Jan. 1 Cash ($100,000 × .98) 98,000

Discount on Bonds Payable...................... 2,000

Bonds Payable 100,000

To issue 8%, 10-year bonds at a discount.

After posting, the bond accounts have the following balances:

Bonds Payable	Discount on Bonds Payable
100,000	2,000

Chrysler's balance sheet immediately after issuance of the bonds reports:

Long-term liabilities:
Bonds payable, 8%, due 1999 . . . . $100,000
Less: Discount on bonds payable 2,000 $98,000

Discount on Bonds Payable is a contra account to Bonds Payable. Subtracting its balance from Bonds Payable yields the book value, or carrying value, of the bonds. The relationship between Bonds Payable and the Discount account is similar to the relationships between Equipment and Accumulated Depreciation and between Accounts Receivable and Allowance for Uncollectible Accounts. Thus Chrysler's liability is $98,000, which is the amount the company borrowed. If Chrysler were to pay off the bonds immediately (an unlikely occurrence), Chrysler's required outlay would be $98,000 because the market price of the bonds is $98,000.

Interest Expense on Bonds Issued at a Discount.   We earlier discussed the difference between the contract interest rate and the market interest rate. Suppose the market rate is $8\frac{1}{4}$ percent when Chrysler issues its 8 percent bonds. The $\frac{1}{4}$ percent interest rate difference creates the $2,000 discount on the bonds. Chrysler borrows $98,000 cash but must pay $100,000 cash when the bonds mature, 10 years later. What happens to the $2,000 balance of the discount account over the life of the bond issue?

The $2,000 is in reality an additional interest expense to the issuing company. That amount is a cost—beyond the stated interest rate—that the business pays for borrowing the investors' money.

The discount amount is an interest expense not paid until the bond matures. However, the borrower—the bond issuer—benefits from the use of the investors' money each accounting period over the full term of the bond issue. The matching principle directs the business to match expense against its revenues on a period-by-period basis. The discount is allocated to interest expense through amortization each accounting period over the life of the bonds.

> **OBJECTIVE 1**
> Amortize bond discount and premium by the straight-line method

Straight-Line Amortization of Discount.   We may amortize bond discount by dividing it into equal amounts for each interest period. This method is called straight-line amortization. In our example, the beginning discount is $2,000, and there are 20 semiannual interest periods during the bonds' 10-year life. Therefore, $\frac{1}{20}$ of the $2,000 ($100) of bond discount is amortized each interest period. Chrysler's semiannual interest entry on July 1, 1989, is

1989
July 1   Interest Expense 4,100
              Cash ($100,000 × .08 × $\frac{6}{12}$)   4,000
              Discount on Bonds Payable ($2,000/20).   100
         To pay semiannual interest and amortize discount on bonds
         payable.

Interest expense of $4,100 is the sum of the contract interest ($4,000, which is paid in cash) plus the amount of discount amortized ($100). Discount on Bonds Payable is credited to amortize (reduce) the account's debit balance. Because Discount on Bonds Payable is a contra account, each reduction in its balance increases the book value of Bonds Payable. Twenty amortization entries will decrease the discount balance to zero, which means that Bonds Payable will have increased by $2,000 up to its face value of $100,000. The entry to pay off the bonds at maturity is

1999
Jan. 1 Bonds Payable 100,000
                Cash   100,000
            To pay bonds payable at maturity.

Issuing Bonds Payable at a Premium

To illustrate issuing bonds at a premium, let's change the Chrysler example. Assume that the market interest rate is 7½ percent when the company issues its 8 percent, 10-year bonds. Because 8 percent bonds are attractive in this market, investors pay a premium price to acquire them. If the bonds are priced at 103½ (103.5 percent of par value) Chrysler receives $103,500 cash upon issuance. The entry is

1989
Jan. 1 Cash ($100,000 × 1.035) 103,500
                Bonds Payable   100,000
                Premium on Bonds Payable.................   3,500
            To issue 8%, 10-year bonds at a premium.

After posting, the bond accounts have the following balances:

Bonds Payable	Premium on Bonds Payable
100,000	3,500

Chrysler's balance sheet immediately after issuance of the bonds reports:

Long-term liabilities:
    Bonds payable, 8%, due 1999 .... $100,000
    Premium on bonds payable 3,500 $103,500

Premium on Bonds Payable is added to Bonds Payable to show the book value, or carrying value, of the bonds. Chrysler's liability is $103,500, which is the amount that the company borrowed. Immediate payment of the bonds would require an outlay of $103,500 because the market price of the bonds at issuance is $103,500. The investors would be unwilling to give up the bonds for less than their market value.

Interest Expense on Bonds Issued at a Premium.   The ½ percent difference between the 8 percent contract rate on the bonds and the 7½ percent market interest rate creates the $3,500 premium. Chrysler borrows $103,500 cash but must pay only $100,000 cash at maturity. We treat the premium as a savings of interest expense to Chrysler. The premium cuts Chrysler's cost of borrowing the money. We account for the premium much as we handled the discount. We amortize the bond premium as a decrease in interest expense over the life of the bonds.

STRAIGHT-LINE AMORTIZATION OF PREMIUM.   In our example, the beginning premium is $3,500, and there are 20 semiannual interest periods during the bonds'

10-year life. Therefore, $\frac{1}{20}$ of the $3,500 ($175) of bond premium is amortized each interest period. Chrysler's semiannual interest entry on July 1, 1989 is

1989

July 1	Interest Expense................................	3,825	
	Premium on Bonds Payable ($3,500/20)	175	
	Cash ($100,000 × .08 × $^{6}/_{12}$)		4,000
	To pay semiannual interest and amortize premium on bonds payable.		

Interest expense of $3,825 is the remainder of the contract cash interest ($4,000) less the amount of premium amortized ($175). The debit to Premium on Bonds Payable reduces its credit balance. Twenty amortization entries will decrease the premium balance to zero. The payment at maturity will debit Bonds Payable and credit Cash for $100,000.

Adjusting Entries for Interest Expense

Companies issue bonds when they need cash. The interest payments seldom occur on December 31 (or the end of the fiscal year). Nevertheless, interest expense must be accrued at the end of the period to properly measure income. The accrual entry may often be complicated by the need to amortize a discount or a premium for only a partial interest period.

Suppose Xenon issues $100,000 of its 8 percent, 10-year bonds at a $2,000 discount on October 1, 1989. Assume that interest payments occur on March 31 and September 30 each year. On December 31 Xenon records interest for the three-month period (October, November, and December) as follows:

1989

Dec. 31	Interest Expense................................	2,050	
	Interest Payable ($100,000 × .08 × $^{3}/_{12}$)..........		2,000
	Discount on Bonds Payable ($2,000/10 × $^{3}/_{12}$)		50
	To accrue three months' interest and amortize discount on bonds payable for three months.		

Interest Payable is credited for the three months of cash interest that have accrued since September 30. Discount on Bonds Payable is credited for three months of amortization.

The balance sheet at December 31, 1989, reports Interest Payable of $2,000 as a current liability. Bonds Payable appears as a long-term liability, presented as follows:

Long-term liabilities:		
Bonds payable, 8%, due 1999.........................	$100,000	
Less: Discount on bonds payable ($2,000 − $50)...........	1,950	$98,050

Observe that the balance of Discount on Bonds Payable decreases by $50. The bonds' carrying value increases by the same amount. The bonds' carrying value continues to increase over its 10-year life, reaching $100,000 at maturity, when the discount will be fully amortized.

The next semiannual interest payment occurs on March 31, 1990:

```
1990
Mar. 31   Interest Expense ...............................  2,050
          Interest Payable...............................  2,000
                Cash ($100,000 × .08 × 6/12)..................       4,000
                Discount on Bonds Payable ($2,000/10 × 3/12) ....       50
          To pay semiannual interest, part of which was accrued,
          and amortize three months' discount on bonds payable.
```

Amortization of a premium over a partial interest period is similar except that Premium on Bonds Payable is debited.

Summary Problem for Your Review

Assume that Alabama Power Company has outstanding an issue of 9 percent bonds that mature on May 1, 2010. Further, assume that the bonds are dated May 1, 1990 and Alabama Power pays interest each April 30 and October 31.

Required

1. Will the bonds be issued at par, at a premium, or at a discount if the market interest rate is 8 percent at date of issuance? if the market interest rate is 10 percent?
2. Assume Alabama Power issued $1,000,000 of the bonds at 104 on May 1, 1990.
   a. Record issuance of the bonds.
   b. Record the interest payment and amortization of premium or discount on October 31, 1990.
   c. Accrue interest and amortize premium or discount on December 31, 1990.
   d. Show how the company would report the bonds on the balance sheet at December 31, 1990.
   e. Record the interest payment on April 30, 1991.

SOLUTION TO REVIEW PROBLEM

Requirement 1. If the market interest rate is 8 percent, 9 percent bonds will be issued at a *premium*. If the market rate is 10 percent, the 9 percent bonds will be issued at a *discount*.

Requirement 2

```
      1990
a. May  1   Cash ($1,000,000 × 1.04) ...............  1,040,000
                Bonds Payable .................            1,000,000
                Premium on Bonds Payable ........               40,000
            To issue 9%, 20-year bonds at a premium.
```

b. Oct. 31   Interest Expense.   44,000

            Premium on Bonds Payable ($40,000/40).   1,000

                 Cash ($1,000,000 × .09 × $^6/_{12}$)   45,000

            To pay semiannual interest and amortize
premium on bonds payable.

c. Dec. 31   Interest Expense.   14,667

            Premium on Bonds Payable

                 ($40,000/40 × $^2/_6$)   333

                 Interest Payable ($1,000,000 ×

                   .09 × $^2/_{12}$)   15,000

            To accrue interest and amortize bond premium for two months.

d. Long-term liabilities:

            Bonds payable, 9%, due 2010. . . . . $1,000,000

            Premium on bonds payable ($40,000 −

                 $1,000 − $333).   38,667 $1,038,667

1991

e. Apr. 30   Interest Expense.   29,333

            Interest Payable   15,000

            Premium on Bonds Payable

                 ($40,000/40 × $^4/_6$)   667

                 Cash ($1,000,000 × .09 × $^6/_{12}$)   45,000

            To pay semiannual interest, part of which
was accrued, and amortize four months'
premium on bonds payable.

SUPPLEMENT TO SUMMARY PROBLEM SOLUTION

Bond problems include many details. You may find it helpful to check your work. We verify the answers to the Summary Problem in this supplement.

On April 30, 1991, the bonds have been outstanding for one year. After the entries have been recorded, the account balances should show the results of one year's cash interest payments and one year's bond premium amortization.

Fact 1:   Cash interest payments should be $90,000 ($1,000,000 × .09).

Accuracy check: Two credits to Cash of $45,000 each = $90,000. Cash payments are correct.

Fact 2:   Premium amortization should be $2,000 ($40,000/40 semiannual periods × 2 semiannual periods in 1 year).

Accuracy check: Three debits to Premium on Bonds Payable ($1,000 + $333 + $667) = $2,000. Premium amortization is correct.

Fact 3:   Also we can check the accuracy of interest expense recorded during the year ended December 31,1990.

                     The bonds in this problem will be outstanding for a total of 20 years, or 240 (that is, 20 × 12) months. During 1990 the bonds are outstanding for 8 months (May through December).

                     Interest expense for 8 months *equals* payment of cash interest for 8 months *minus* premium amortization for 8 months.

Interest expense should therefore be ($1,000,000 $\times$ .09 $\times$ $8/12$ = \$60,000) minus [(\$40,000/240) $\times$ 8 = \$1,333] or (\$60,000 − \$1,333 = \$58,667).

Accuracy check: Two debits to Interest Expense (\$44,000 + \$14,667) = \$58,667. Interest expense for 1990 is correct.

Effective Interest Method of Amortization

The straight-line amortization method has a theoretical weakness. Each period's amortization amount for a premium or discount is the same dollar amount over the life of the bonds. However, over that time the bonds' carrying value continues to increase (with a discount) or decrease (with a premium). Thus the fixed dollar amount of amortization changes as a percentage of the bonds' carrying value, making it appear that the bond issuer's interest rate changes over time. This appearance is misleading because in fact the issuer locked in a fixed interest rate when the bonds were issued. The interest rate on the bonds does not change.

GAAP specifies that discounts and premiums be amortized using the effective interest method unless the difference between the straight-line method and the effective interest method is immaterial. In that case, either method is permitted.[1] We will see how the effective interest method keeps each interest expense amount at the same percentage of the bonds' carrying value for every interest payment over the bonds' life. The total amount amortized over the life of the bonds is the same under both methods.

Effective Interest Method of Amortizing Discount

Assume that Bethlehem Steel Corporation issues \$100,000 of its 9 percent bonds at a time when the market rate of interest is 10 percent. Also assume that these bonds mature in five years and pay interest semiannually, so there are 10 semiannual interest payments. The issue price of the bonds is \$96,149.[2] The discount on these bonds is \$3,851 (\$100,000 − \$96,149).

Exhibit 16-3 illustrates amortization of the discount by the effective interest method.

The exhibit reveals the following important facts about effective interest method amortization of bond discount:

Column A. The semiannual interest payments are constant because they are governed by the contract interest rate and the bonds' maturity value.

Column B. The interest expense each period is computed by multiplying the preceding bond carrying value by the market interest rate (5 percent semiannually). This rate is the **effective interest rate** because its effect determines the interest expense each period. The amount of interest each period increases as the effective interest rate, a constant, is applied to the increasing bond carrying value (column E).

---

[1] Accounting Principles Board, *Opinion No. 21,* "Interest on Receivables and Payables" (New York: AICPA, 1971), par. 15.

[2] We compute this present value using the tables that appear in the appendix to this chapter.

EXHIBIT 16-3 *Effective Interest Method of Amortizing Bond Discount*

Panel A—Bond Data

Maturity value—$100,000

Contract interest rate—9%

Interest paid—4½% semiannually, $4,500 ($100,000 × .045)

Market interest rate at time of issue—10% annually, 5% semiannually

Issue price—$96,149

Panel B—Amortization Table

Semiannual Interest Period	A Interest Payment (4½% of Maturity Value)	B Interest Expense (5% of Preceding Bond Carrying Value)	C Discount Amortization (B − A)	D Discount Account Balance (D − C)	E Bond Carrying Value ($100,000 − D)
Issue Date				$3,851	$ 96,149
1	$4,500	$4,807	$307	3,544	96,456
2	4,500	4,823	323	3,221	96,779
3	4,500	4,839	339	2,882	97,118
4	4,500	4,856	356	2,526	97,474
5	4,500	4,874	374	2,152	97,848
6	4,500	4,892	392	1,760	98,240
7	4,500	4,912	412	1,348	98,652
8	4,500	4,933	433	915	99,085
9	4,500	4,954	454	461	99,539
10	4,500	4,961*	461	-0-	100,000

* Adjusted for effect of rounding.

Column C. The excess of each interest expense amount (column B) over each interest payment amount (column A) is the discount amortization for the period.

Column D. The discount balance decreases by the amount of amortization for the period (column C). The discount decreases from $3,851 at the bonds' issue date to zero at their maturity. The balance of the discount plus the bonds' carrying value equal the bonds' maturity value.

Column E. The bonds' carrying value increases from $96,149 at issuance to $100,000 at maturity.

Recall that we want to present interest expense amounts over the full life of the bonds at a fixed percentage of the bonds' carrying value. The 5 percent rate—the effective interest rate—*is* that percentage. We have figured the cost of the money borrowed by the bond issuer—the interest expense—as a constant percentage of the carrying value of the bonds. The dollar *amount* of interest expense varies from period to period but not the interest percentage *rate*.

The accounts debited and credited under the effective interest amortization method and the straight-line method are the same. Only the amounts differ. We may take the amortization amounts directly from the table in the exhibit. We assume that the first interest payment occurs on July 1 and use the appropriate amounts from Exhibit 16-3, reading across the line for the first interest payment date:

July 1	Interest Expense (column B).........................	4,807	
	Discount on Bonds Payable (column C)		307
	Cash (column A)...............................		4,500
	To pay semiannual interest and amortize discount on bonds payable.		

OBJECTIVE 2

Amortize bond discount and premium by the effective interest method

Effective Interest Method of Amortizing Premium

Let's modify the Bethlehem Steel example to illustrate the interest method of amortizing bond premium. Assume that Bethlehem Steel issues $100,000 of five-year, 9 percent bonds that pay interest semiannually. If the bonds are issued when the market interest rate is 8 percent, their issue price is $104,100.[3] The premium on these bonds is $4,100, and Exhibit 16-4 illustrates amortization of the premium by the interest method.

Exhibit 16-4 reveals the following important facts about the effective interest method of amortizing bond premium:

Column A. The semiannual interest payments are a constant amount fixed by the contract interest rate and the bonds' maturity value.

Column B. The interest expense each period is computed by multiplying the preceding bond carrying value by the effective interest rate (4 percent semiannually). Observe that the amount of interest decreases each period as the bond carrying value decreases.

Column C. The excess of each interest payment (Column A) over the period's interest expense (Column B) is the premium amortization for the period.

Column D. The premium balance decreases by the amount of amortization for the period (Column C) from $4,100 at issuance to zero at maturity. The bonds' carrying value plus the premium balance equal the bonds' maturity value.

Column E. The bonds' carrying value decreases from $104,100 at issuance to $100,000 at maturity.

Assuming that the first interest payment occurs on October 31, we read across the line for the first interest payment date and pick up the appropriate amounts.

Oct. 31	Interest Expense (Column B)........................	4,164	
	Premium on Bonds Payable (Column C)	336	
	Cash (Column A)............................		4,500
	To pay semiannual interest and amortize discount on bonds payable.		

At year end it is necessary to make an adjusting entry for accrued interest and amortization of the bond premium for a partial period. In our example, the last interest payment occurred on October 31. The adjustment for November and

---

[3] Again, we compute the present value of the bonds using the tables in this chapter's appendix.

EXHIBIT 16-4 *Interest Method of Amortizing Bond Premium*

Panel A—Bond Data

Maturity value—$100,000

Contract interest rate—9%

Interest paid—4½% semiannually, $4,500 ($100,000 × .045)

Market interest rate at time of issue—8% annually, 4% semiannually

Issue price—$104,100

Panel B—Amortization Table

Semiannual Interest Period	A Interest Payment (4½% of Maturity Value)	B Interest Expense (4% of Preceding Bond Carrying Value)	C Premium Amortization (A − B)	D Premium Account Balance (D − C)	E Bond Carrying Value ($100,000 + D)
Issue Date				$4,100	$104,100
1	$4,500	$4,164	$336	3,764	103,764
2	4,500	4,151	349	3,415	103,415
3	4,500	4,137	363	3,052	103,052
4	4,500	4,122	378	2,674	102,674
5	4,500	4,107	393	2,281	102,281
6	4,500	4,091	409	1,872	101,872
7	4,500	4,075	425	1,447	101,447
8	4,500	4,058	442	1,005	101,005
9	4,500	4,040	460	545	100,545
10	4,500	3,955*	545	-0-	100,000

* Adjusted for effect of rounding.

December must cover two months, or one third of a semiannual period. The entry, with amounts drawn from Exhibit 16-4, line 2, is

Dec. 31	Interest Expense ($4,151 × ⅓)	1,384	
	Premium on Bonds Payable ($349 × ⅓)	116	
	Interest Payable ($4,500 × ⅓)		1,500

To accrue two months' interest and amortize premium on bonds payable for two months.

The second interest payment occurs on April 30 of the following year. The payment of $4,500 includes interest expense for four months (January through April), the interest payable at December 31, and premium amortization for four months. The payment entry is

Apr. 30	Interest Expense ($4,151 × ⅔)	2,767	
	Interest Payable	1,500	
	Premium on Bonds Payable ($349 × ⅔)	233	
	Cash		4,500

To pay semiannual interest, some of which was accrued, and amortize premium on bonds payable for four months.

If these bonds had been issued at a discount, procedures for these interest entries would be the same, except that Discount on Bonds Payable would be credited.

Bond Sinking Fund

Bond indentures—the contracts under which bonds are issued—often require the borrower to make regular periodic payments to a *bond sinking fund.* A fund is a group of assets that are segregated for a particular purpose. A **bond sinking fund** is used to retire bonds payable at maturity. A trustee manages this fund for the issuer, investing the company's payments in income-earning assets. The company's payments into the fund and the interest revenue—which the trustee reinvests in the fund—accumulate. The target amount of the sinking fund is the face value of the bond issue at maturity. When the bonds come due, the trustee sells the sinking-fund assets and uses the cash proceeds to pay off the bonds. The bond sinking fund provides security of payment to investors in unsecured bonds.

Most companies report sinking funds under the heading Investments, a separate asset category between current assets and plant assets on the balance sheet. A bond sinking fund is not a current asset because it may not be used to pay current liabilities. Accounting for the interest, dividends, and other earnings on the bond sinking fund requires use of the accounts Sinking Fund and Sinking Fund Revenue.

Sperry Corporation has outstanding $40 million of 8.2 percent sinking fund debentures. The company must make annual sinking-fund payments. The entry to deposit $2 million with the trustee is

Jan. 5	Sinking Fund.	2,000,000	
	Cash		2,000,000
	To make annual sinking fund deposit.		

If the trustee invests the cash and reports annual sinking fund revenue of $150,000, the fund grows by this amount, and Sperry makes the following entry at year end:

Dec. 31	Sinking Fund	150,000	
	Sinking Fund Revenue		150,000
	To record sinking fund earnings.		

Assume that Sperry has made the required sinking fund payments over a period of years and that these payments plus the fund earnings have accumulated a cash balance of $40.2 million at maturity. The trustee pays off the bonds and returns the excess cash to Sperry, which makes the following entry:

Jan. 4	Cash	200,000	
	Bonds Payable	40,000,000	
	Sinking Fund		40,200,000
	To record payment of bonds payable and receipt of excess sinking fund cash at maturity.		

If the fund balance is less than the bonds' maturity value, the entry is similar to the foregoing entry. However, the company pays the extra amount and credits Cash.

Retirement of Bonds Payable

Normally companies wait until maturity to pay off, or retire, their bonds payable. All bond discount or premium has been amortized, and the retirement entry debits Bonds Payable and credits Cash for the bonds' maturity value.

OBJECTIVE 3
Account for retirement of bonds payable

Companies sometimes retire their bonds payable prior to maturity. The main reason for retiring bonds early is to relieve the pressure of making interest payments. Interest rates fluctuate. The company may be able to borrow at a lower interest rate and use the proceeds from new bonds to pay off the old bonds, which bear a higher rate.

Some bonds are **callable,** which means that the issuer may *call,* or pay off, the bonds at a specified price whenever the issuer wants. The call price is usually a few percent above par, perhaps 104 or 105. Callable bonds give the issuer the benefit of being able to take advantage of low interest rates by paying off the bonds at the most favorable time. An alternative to calling the bonds is to purchase them in the open market at their current market price.

Air Products and Chemicals, Inc., has $70,000,000 of debentures outstanding with unamortized discount of $350,000. Lower interest rates in the market may convince management to pay off these bonds now. Assume that the bonds are callable at 103. If the market price of the bonds is 99¼, will Air Products call the bonds or purchase them in the open market? The market price is lower than the call price, so market price is the better choice. Retiring the bonds at 99¼ results in a gain of $175,000, computed as follows:

Par value of bonds being retired	$70,000,000
Unamortized discount	350,000
Book value	69,650,000
Market price ($70,000,000 × .9925)	69,475,000
Gain on retirement	$ 175,000

The entry to record retirement of the bonds, immediately after an interest date, is

June 30	Bonds Payable	70,000,000	
	Discount on Bonds Payable		350,000
	Cash ($70,000,000 × .9925)		69,475,000
	Extraordinary Gain on Retirement of Bonds Payable		175,000
	To retire bonds payable before maturity.		

The entry removes the bonds payable and the related discount from the accounts and records a gain on retirement. Of course, any existing premium would be removed with a debit. If Air Products and Chemicals had retired only half of these bonds, the accountant would remove half of the discount or premium. Likewise, if the price paid to retire the bonds exceeds their carrying value, the retirement entry would record a loss with a debit to the account Extraordinary Loss on Retirement of Bonds. GAAP identifies gains and losses on early retirement of debt as *extraordinary,* and they are reported separately on the income statement.

Convertible Bonds and Notes

Many corporate bonds and notes payable may be converted into the common stock of the issuing company at the option of the investor. These bonds and notes, called **convertible bonds** (or **notes**), combine the safety of assured interest receipts and receipt of principal on the bonds with the opportunity for large gains on the stock. The conversion feature is so attractive that investors usually accept a lower interest rate than they would on nonconvertible bonds. The lower interest rate benefits the issuer. Convertible bonds are recorded like any other debt at issuance.

If the market price of the issuing company's stock gets high enough, the bondholders will convert the bonds into stock. The corporation records conversion by debiting the bond accounts and crediting the stockholders' equity accounts. The carrying value of the bonds becomes the book value of the newly issued stock. No gain or loss is recorded.

Gulf+ Western, Inc., had convertible *notes* outstanding with a carrying value of $12.5 million. Assume that the maturity value of the notes was $13 million. Also assume that Gulf+Western's stock rose significantly so that noteholders converted the notes into 400,000 shares of the company's $1 par common stock. Gulf+Western's entry to record conversion is

OBJECTIVE 4

Account for conversion of bonds payable

May 14	Notes Payable	13,000,000	
	Discount on Notes Payable..........		500,000
	Common Stock (400,000 × $1)		400,000
	Paid-in Capital in Excess of Par—Common		12,100,000
	To record conversion of notes payable.		

Observe that the carrying value of the notes ($13,000,000 − $500,000) becomes the amount of increase in stockholders' equity ($400,000 + $12,100,000). The entry closes the notes (or bonds) payable account and the related discount or premium account.

Current Portion of Long-Term Debt

Serial bonds and serial notes are payable in serials, or installments. The portion payable within one year is a current liability, and the remaining debt is long-term. At December 31, 1988, Mapco, Inc., had $70 million of 8.7 percent notes payable. The notes are due in $8 million annual installments through 1996 with a final installment of $6 million due in 1997. Therefore, $8 million is a current liability at December 31, 1988, and $62 million is a long-term liability. Mapco reported this installment note payable among its liabilities as follows:

	$ Millions
Current liabilities:	
Current portion of long-term debt................................	$ 8
Long-term debt, excluding amounts payable within one year	62

Mortgage Notes Payable _____

You have probably heard of mortgage payments. Many notes payable are mortgage notes, which actually contain two agreements. The *note* is the borrower's promise to pay the lender the amount of the debt. The **mortgage** is the borrower's promise to transfer the legal title to certain assets to the lender if the debt is not paid on schedule. The borrower is said to pledge these assets as security for the note. Often the asset that is pledged was acquired with the borrowed money. For example, most homeowners sign mortgage notes to purchase their residence, pledging that property as security for the loan. Businesses sign mortgage notes to acquire buildings, equipment, and other long-term assets. Mortgage notes are usually serial notes that require monthly or quarterly payments.

Lease Liabilities _____

A **lease** is a rental agreement in which the tenant **(lessee)** agrees to make rent payments to the property owner **(lessor)** in exchange for the use of the asset. Leasing allows the lessee to acquire the use of a needed asset without having to make the large initial cash down payment that purchase agreements require. Accountants divide leases into two types: operating and capital.

Operating Leases

You are already familiar with **operating leases,** which are usually short-term or cancelable. Many apartment leases and most car-rental agreements extend a year or less. These operating leases give the lessee the right to use the asset but provide the lessee with no continuing rights to the asset. The lessor retains the usual risks and rewards of owning the leased asset. To account for an operating lease, the lessee debits Rent Expense (or Lease Expense) and credits Cash for the amount of the lease payment. The lessee's books do not report the leased asset or any lease liability (except perhaps a prepaid rent amount or a rent accrual at the end of the period).

> **OBJECTIVE 5**
> Account for operating leases and capital leases

Capital Leases

More and more businesses nationwide are turning to capital leasing to finance the acquisition of assets. A *capital lease* is long-term and noncancelable. Accounting for a capital lease is much like accounting for a purchase. The lessor removes the asset from her books. The lessee enters the asset into his accounts and records a lease liability at the beginning of the lease term.

Most companies lease some of their plant assets rather than buy them. A recent survey of 600 companies indicates that they have more leases than any other type of long-term debt.

Southland Corporation owns 7-Eleven convenience stores. Suppose the company leases a building, agreeing to pay $10,000 annually for a 20-year period, with the first payment due immediately. This arrangement is similar to purchasing the building on an installment plan. In an installment purchase, Southland would debit Building and credit Cash and Installment Note Payable. The company would then pay interest and principal on the note payable and record depreciation on the building. Accounting for a capital lease follows this pattern.

Southland records the building at cost, which is the sum of the $10,000 initial payment plus the present value of the 19 future lease payments of $10,000 each. The company credits Cash for the initial payment and credits Lease Liability for the present value of the future lease payments. Assume the interest rate on Southland's lease is 10 percent and the present value (PV) of the future lease payments is $83,650.[4] At the beginning of the lease term, Southland makes the following entry:

Jan. 2	Building ($10,000 + $83,650)	93,650	
	Cash......................................		10,000
	Lease Liability (PV of future lease payments).....		83,650
	To acquire a building and make the first annual lease payment on a capital lease.		

Because Southland has capitalized the building, the company records depreciation. Assume the building has an expected life of 25 years. It is depreciated over the lease term of 20 years because the lessee has the use of the building only for that period. No residual value enters into the depreciation computation because the lessee will have no residual asset when the building is returned to the lessor at the expiration of the lease. Therefore, the annual depreciation entry is

19X1

Dec. 31	Depreciation Expense ($93,650/20).................	4,683	
	Accumulated Depreciation–Building............		4,683
	To record depreciation on leased building.		

At year end Southland must also accrue interest on the lease liability. Interest expense is computed by multiplying the lease liability by the interest rate on the lease. The following entry credits Lease Liability (not Interest Payable) for this interest accrual:

19X1

Dec. 31	Interest Expense ($83,650 × .10)	8,365	
	Lease Liability		8,365
	To accrue interest on the lease liability.		

The balance sheet at December 31, 19X1 reports:

Assets

Plant assets:		
Building..	$93,650	
Less Accumulated depreciation..........................	4,683	$88,967

Liabilities

Current liabilities:	
Lease liability (next payment due on Jan. 2, 19X2)	$10,000
Long-term liabilities:	
Lease liability [beginning balance ($83,650) + interest accrual ($8,365) − current portion ($10,000)]	82,015

---

[4] This computation appears in the chapter appendix.

The lease liability is split into current and long-term portions because the next payment ($10,000) is a current liability and the remainder is long-term.

The January 2, 19X2, lease payment is recorded as follows:

Jan. 2	Lease Liability	10,000	
	Cash		10,000
	To make second annual lease payment on building.		

Distinguishing a Capital Lease from an Operating Lease. How would you distinguish a capital lease from an operating lease? *FASB Statement No. 13* provides the guidelines. To be classified as a **capital lease,** a particular lease agreement must meet any *one* of the following criteria:

1. The lease transfers title of the leased asset to the lessee at the end of the lease term. Thus the lessee becomes the legal owner of the leased asset.
2. The lease contains a *bargain purchase option.* The lessee can be expected to purchase the leased asset and become its legal owner.
3. The lease term is 75 percent or more of the estimated useful life of the leased asset. The lessee uses up most of the leased asset's service potential.
4. The present value of the lease payments is 90 percent or more of the market value of the leased asset. In effect, the lease payments operate as installment payments for the leased asset.

Only those leases that fail to meet *all* of these criteria may be accounted for as operating leases.

Off-Balance-Sheet Financing

An important part of business is obtaining the funds needed to acquire assets. To finance operations a company may issue stock, borrow money, or retain earnings in the business. Notice that all three of these financing plans affect the right-hand side of the balance sheet. Issuing stock affects preferred or common stock. Borrowing creates notes or bonds payable. Internal funds come from retained earnings.

Off-balance-sheet financing is the acquisition of assets or services, with debt that is not reported on the balance sheet. A prime example is an operating lease. The lessee has the use of the leased asset, but neither the asset nor any lease liability is reported on the balance sheet. In the past, most leases were accounted for by the operating method. However, *FASB Statement No. 13* has required businesses to account for an increasing number of leases by the capital lease method. Also, *FASB Statement No. 13* has brought about detailed reporting of operating lease payments in the notes to the financial statements. The inclusion of more lease information—be they capital or operating leases—makes the accounting information for decision making more complete.

Pension Liabilities

Most companies have a pension plan for their employees. A **pension** is employee compensation that will be received during retirement. Employees earn the pensions by their service, so the company records pension expense as employees work for the company. *FASB Statement No. 87* gives the rules for measuring pension expense. To record the company's payment into a pension plan, the company debits Pension Expense and credits Cash. Insurance companies and pension trusts manage pension plans. They receive the employer payments and any employee contributions, then invest these amounts for the future benefit of the employees. The goal is to have the funds available to meet any obligations to retirees, much as a bond sinking fund is designed to retire bonds payable at maturity.

Pensions are perhaps the most complex area of accounting. As employees earn their pensions and the company pays into the pension plan, the assets of the plan grow. The obligation for future pension payments to employees also accumulates. At the end of each period, the company compares the fair market value of the assets in the pension plan — cash and investments — to the accumulated benefit obligation of the pension plan. The *accumulated benefit obligation* is the present value of promised future pension payments to retirees. If the plan assets exceed the accumulated benefit obligation, the plan is said to be overfunded. In this case, the asset and obligation amounts need be reported only in the notes to the financial statements. However, if the accumulated benefit obligation exceeds plan assets, the company must report the excess liability amount as a long-term pension liability in the balance sheet.

The pension plan of Mainstream Manufacturing & Sales, Inc., has assets with a fair market value of $3 million on December 31, 19X0. On this date the accumulated pension benefit obligation to employees is $4 million. Mainstream's balance sheet will report Long-Term Pension Liability of $1 million. This liability will be listed, in no particular order, along with Bonds Payable, Long-Term Notes Payable, Lease Liabilities, and other long-term liabilities.

FASB Statement No. 87 started requiring companies to report pension liabilities in this manner in 1987. Before that date, pensions were another example of off-balance-sheet financing. Companies received the benefit of their employees' service but could avoid reporting pension liabilities on the balance sheet.

Advantage of Financing Operations with Debt versus Stock

OBJECTIVE 6

Explain the advantages and disadvantages of borrowing

Businesses have different ways to acquire assets. Management may decide to purchase or to lease equipment. The money to finance the asset may come from the business's retained earnings, a note payable, a stock issue, or a bond issue. Each financing strategy has its advantages and disadvantages. Let's examine how issuing stock compares to issuing bonds.

Bonds differ from stocks in important ways. Stock shares give the holder part ownership of the corporation and a voice in management. Bonds merely give the holder a creditor's claim to the debtor's assets. Bond certificates carry dates for maturity and interest payments, unlike stock, which does not come due at any specific time. Companies are not obligated to declare dividends on stock.

Issuing stock raises capital without incurring the liabilities and interest expense that accompany bonds. However, by issuing stock the business spreads the ownership, control and income of the corporation among more shares. Management may wish to avoid this dilution of its ownership. Borrowing money through bonds raises liabilities and interest expense, which the corporation must pay whether or not it earns a profit. But borrowing does not affect stockholder control:

EXHIBIT 16-5 *Earnings-per-Share Advantage of Borrowing*

	Plan 1 Borrow $500,000 at 10%	Plan 2 Issue $500,000 of Common Stock
Income before interest and income tax	$200,000	$200,000
Less interest expense ($500,000 X .10)	50,000	-0-
Income before income tax...............	150,000	200,000
Less income tax expense (40%)	60,000	80,000
Net income..........................	$ 90,000	$120,000
Earnings per share on new project:		
Plan 1 ($90,000/100,000 shares)	$ .90	
Plan 2 ($120,000/150,000 shares)		$ .80

bondholders are creditors with no voice in management. Borrowing also provides a tax advantage in that interest expense is tax deductible. Dividends paid to stockholders are not tax deductible because they are not an expense.

Exhibit 16-5 illustrates the earnings-per-share (EPS) advantage of borrowing. Suppose a corporation with 100,000 shares of common stock outstanding needs $500,000 for expansion. Management is considering two financing plans. Plan 1 is to issue $500,000 of 10 percent bonds payable, and plan 2 is to issue 50,000 shares of common stock for $500,000. Management believes the new cash can be invested in operations to earn income of $200,000 before interest and taxes.

The earnings-per-share amount is higher if the company borrows. The business earns more on the investment ($90,000) than the interest it pays on the bonds ($50,000). Earning more income than the borrowed amount increases the earnings for common stockholders and is called **trading on the equity.** It is widely used in business to increase earnings per share of common stock.

Dividend payments to the new stockholders under plan 2 would also make borrowing more attractive than issuing stock. Assume that net income is entirely an increase in cash. If under plan 2 the company were to pay dividends of $50,000—the same as the interest expense under plan 1—its net cash inflow would be $70,000 ($120,000–$50,000), compared to $90,000 under plan 1.

Borrowing has its disadvantages. If the interest rate is high enough, the advantage of borrowing disappears as the interest expense reduces net income. Also, borrowing creates liabilities that accrue during bad years as well as during good years. In contrast, a company that issues stock can omit its dividends during a bad year.

Investments in Bonds and Notes

For every issuer of bonds payable, at least one investor owns the bonds. The relationship between the issuer and the investor may be diagrammed as follows:

Issuing Corporation		*Investor (Bondholder)*
Bonds payable	←——————→	Investment in bonds
Interest expense	←——————→	Interest revenue

OBJECTIVE 7

Account for investments in bonds

The dollar amount of a bond transaction is the same for issuer and investor, but the accounts debited and credited differ. However, the accounts are parallel. For example, the issuer's interest expense is the investor's interest revenue.

An investment in bonds is classified either as short-term (a current asset) or as long-term. An investment is a current asset if (1) the investment is liquid (can readily be sold for cash) and (2) the owner intends to convert it to cash within one year or to use it to pay a current liability. An investment that is intended to be held longer than a year is classified as long-term. **Long-term investments** is a separate asset category reported on the balance sheet between current assets and plant assets.

Bond investments are recorded at cost, which includes the purchase price and any brokerage fees. Amortization of bond premium or discount is *not* recorded on short-term investments because the investor plans to hold the bonds for so short a period that any amortization would be immaterial. Investors hold long-term investments for a significant period and therefore amortize any premium or discount on the bonds.

Let's look at accounting for a *short-term* bond investment. Suppose that an investor purchases $10,000 of bonds on August 1, 19X2, paying 93 plus accrued interest and a brokerage commission of $250. The annual contract interest rate is 12 percent, paid semiannually on April 1 and October 1. The cost of the bonds is $9,550 [($10,000 × .93) + $250]. In addition, the investor pays accrued interest for the four months (April through July) since the last interest payment. The investor records the purchase on August 1 as follows:

Aug. 1	Short-Term Investment in Bonds		
	[($10,000 × .93) + $250]........................	9,550	
	Interest Receivable ($10,000 × .12 × 4/12)	400	
	Cash......................................		9,950
	To purchase short-term bond investment.		

Accrued interest is *not* included in the cost of the investment but is debited to Interest Receivable.

The investor's entry for receipt of the first semiannual interest amount on October 1 is

Oct. 1	Cash ($10,000 × .12 × 6/12)	600	
	Interest Receivable...............................		400
	Interest Revenue ($10,000 × .12 × 2/12)		200
	To receive semiannual interest, part of which was accrued.		

At October 1 the investor has held the bonds for two months. The entry correctly credits Interest Revenue for two months' interest. This entry does not include discount amortization on the bonds because the investment is short-term.

At December 31 the investor accrues interest revenue for three months (October, November, and December), debiting Interest Receivable and crediting Interest Revenue for $300 ($10,000 × .12 × 3/12). The investor's December 31 balance sheet reports the following information (we assume that the market price of the bonds is 96):

Current assets:	
Short-term investment in bonds (Note 4)............................	$9,550
Interest receivable...	300

Note 4: Short-term investments:
At December 31 the current market value of short-term investments in bonds was $9,600.

Observe that the investment is reported at cost, with the current market value disclosed in a note. The market value may also be reported parenthetically.

Current assets:
Short-term investment in bonds (Current market value, $9,600) $9,550
Interest receivable.   300

The investor measures any gain or loss on sale as the difference between the sale price and the cost of the investment. For example, sale of the bonds for $9,700 will result in a gain of $150. This gain is reported as Other Revenue on a multiple-step income statement or beneath Sales Revenue among the revenues and gains on a single-step statement. A loss would be reported as Other Expense on a multiple-step statement or among the expenses on a single-step statement.

Accounting for *long-term* investments in bonds follows the general pattern illustrated for short-term investments. For long-term investments, however, discount or premium is amortized to account more precisely for interest revenue. This additional step is needed because the bond investment will be held for longer than a year and, therefore, the amortization amount is likely to be material. The amortization of discount or premium on a bond investment affects Interest Revenue in the same way that the amortization affects Interest Expense for the company that issued the bonds.

The accountant records amortization on the cash interest dates and at year end, along with the accrual of interest receivable. Accountants rarely use separate discount and premium accounts for investments. Amortization of a discount is recorded by directly debiting the Long-Term Investment in Bonds account and crediting Interest Revenue. Amortization of a premium is credited directly to the Long-Term Investment account. This entry debits Interest Revenue. These entries bring the investment balance to the bonds' face value on the maturity date and record the correct amount of interest revenue each period.

Suppose the $10,000 of 12 percent bonds in the preceding illustration were purchased on August 1, 19X2, as a long-term investment. Interest dates are April 1 and October 1. These bonds mature on October 1, 19X6, so they will be outstanding for 50 months. Assume amortization of the discount by the straight-line method. The following entries for a long-term investment highlight the differences between accounting for a short-term bond investment and for a long-term bond investment:

Aug. 1	**Long-Term** Investment in Bonds		
	[($10,000 × .93) + $250].	9,550	
	Interest Receivable ($10,000 × .12 × 4/12).	400	
	Cash		9,950
	To purchase long-term bond investment.		
Oct. 1	Cash ($10,000 × .12 × 6/12)	600	
	Interest Receivable.		400
	Interest Revenue ($10,000 × .12 × 2/12)		200
	To receive semiannual interest, part of which was accrued.		
Oct. 1	**Long-Term Investment in Bonds**		
	[($10,000 − $9,550)/50 × 2].	**18**	
	Interest Revenue.		**18**
	To amortize discount on bond investment for two months.		
Dec. 31	Interest Receivable ($10,000 × .12 × 3/12).	300	
	Interest Revenue		300
	To accrue interest revenue for three months.		

Dec. 31 **Long-term Investment in Bonds**
      [($10,000 − $9,550)/50 × 3]...................... 27
           Interest Revenue............................ 27
      To amortize discount on bond investment for three months.

The financial statements at December 31, 19X2, report the following effects of this long-term investment in bonds (assume the bonds' market price is 102):

Balance sheet at December 31, 19X2:
  Current assets:
    Interest receivable .... $ 300
    Total current assets .... X,XXX
  Long-term investments in bonds ($9,550 + $18 + $27)—Note 6.......... 9,595
  Property, plant, and equipment...................................... X,XXX

Note 6: Long-term investments:
  At December 31, 19X1, the current market value of long-term investments in bonds was $10,200.

Income statement (multiple-step) for the year ended December 31, 19X2:
  Other revenues:
    Interest revenue ($200 + $18 + $300 + $27) .... $ 545

The amortization entry for a premium debits Interest Revenue and credits Long-Term Investment in Bonds. Where discount or premium is amortized by the effective interest method, accounting for long-term investments follows the pattern illustrated here. Effective interest amortization amounts are computed as shown for bonds payable in Exhibits 16-3 and 16-4.

Summary Problem for Your Review

The Cessna Aircraft Company has outstanding an issue of 8 percent convertible bonds that mature in 2008. Suppose the bonds were dated October 1, 1988, and pay interest each April 1 and October 1.

Required

1. Complete the following effective amortization table through October 1, 1990.

    Bond data:

    Maturity value—$100,000
    Contract interest rate—8%
    Interest paid—4% semiannually, $4,000 ($100,000 × .04)
    Market interest rate at time of issue—9% annually, 4½% semiannually
    Issue price—90¾

    Amortization Table:

Semiannual Interest Date	A Interest Payment (4% of Maturity Value)	B Interest Expense (4½% of Preceding Bond Carrying Value)	C Discount Amortization (B − A)	D Discount Account Balance (D − C)	E Bond Carrying Value ($100,000 − D)
10-1-88	*4000*				*96,000*
4-1-89	*4,000*				
10-1-89					
4-1-90					
10-1-90					

2. Using the amortization table, record the following transactions:
   a. Issuance of the bonds on October 1, 1988.
   b. Accrual of interest and amortization of discount on December 31, 1988.
   c. Payment of interest and amortization of discount on April 1, 1989.
   d. Conversion of one third of the bonds payable into no-par stock on October 2, 1990.
   e. Retirement of two thirds of the bonds payable on October 2, 1990. Purchase price of the bonds was 102.

SOLUTION TO REVIEW PROBLEM

Requirement 1   (Amortization Table)

Semiannual Interest Date	A Interest Payment (4% of Maturity Value)	B Interest Expense (4½% of Preceding Bond Carrying Value)	C Discount Amortization (B − A)	D Discount Account Balance (D − C)	E Bond Carrying Value ($100,000 − D)
10-1-88				$9,250	$ 90,750
4-1-89	$4,000	$4,084	$ 84	9,166	90,834
10-1-89	4,000	4,088	88	9,078	90,922
4-1-90	4,000	4,091	91	8,987	91,013
10-1-90	4,000	4,096	96	8,891	91,109

Requirement 2

1988

a. Oct. 1
Cash ($100,000 × .9075)...................	90,750	
Discount on Bonds Payable..................	9,250	
Bonds Payable		100,000

To issue 8%, 20-year bonds at a discount.

b. Dec. 31
Interest Expense ($4,084 × ⅜)	2,042	
Discount on Bonds Payable ($84 × ⅜).....		42
Interest Payable ($4,000 × ⅜)..........		2,000

To accrue interest and amortize bond discount for three months.

1989

c. Apr. 1
Interest Expense.........................	2,042	
Interest Payable	2,000	
Discount on Bonds Payable ($84 × ⅜).....		42
Cash		4,000

To pay semiannual interest, part of which was accrued, and amortize three months' discount on bonds payable.

1990

d. Oct. 2	Bonds Payable ($100,000 × ⅓)................		33,333	
	Discount on Bonds Payable ($8,891 × ⅓) ..			2,964
	Common Stock ($91,109 × ⅓)			30,369
	To record conversion of bonds payable.			
e. Oct. 2	Bonds Payable ($100,000 × ⅔)................		66,667	
	Extraordinary Loss on Retirement of Bonds......		7,260	
	Discount on Bonds Payable ($8,891 × ⅔) ..			5,927
	Cash ($100,000 × ⅔ × 1.02).............			68,000
	To retire bonds payable before maturity.			

Summary

A corporation may borrow money by issuing bonds and long-term notes payable. A bond contract, called an *indenture,* specifies the maturity value of the bonds, the contact interest rate, and the dates for paying interest and principal. The owner of *registered* bonds receives an interest check from the company. The owner of *coupon* bonds deposits an interest coupon in the bank. Bonds may be secured (*mortgage* bonds) or unsecured (*debenture* bonds).

Bonds are traded through organized markets, like the New York Exchange. Bonds are typically divided into $1,000 units. Their prices are quoted at a percentage of face value.

Market interest rates fluctuate and may differ from the contract rate on a bond. If a bond's contract rate exceeds the market rate, the bond sells at a *premium.* A bond with a contract rate below the market rate sells at a *discount.*

Money earns income over time, a fact that gives rise to the present value concept. An investor will pay a price for a bond equal to the present value of the bond principal plus the present value of the bond interest.

Straight-line amortization allocates an equal amount of premium or discount to each interest period. In the *effective interest method* of amortization, the market rate at the time of issuance is multiplied by the bonds' carrying value to determine the interest expense each period and to compute the amount of discount or premium amortization.

A *bond sinking fund* accumulates the money to pay the bonds' face value at maturity. Companies may retire their bonds payable before maturity. *Callable* bonds give the borrower the right to pay off the bonds at a specified call price, or the company may purchase the bonds in the open market. Any gain or loss on early extinguishment of debt is classified as *extraordinary.*

Convertible bonds and notes give the investor the privilege of trading the bonds in for stock of the issuing corporation. The carrying value of the bonds becomes the book value of the newly issued stock.

A lease is a rental agreement between the *lessee* and the *lessor.* In an *operating lease* the lessor retains the usual risks and rights of owning the asset. The lessee debits Rent Expense and credits Cash when making lease payments. A *capital lease* is long-term, noncancelable, and similar to an installment purchase of the leased asset. In a capital lease, the lessee capitalizes the leased asset and reports a lease liability. Companies also report a *pension liability* on the balance sheet if the accumulated benefit obligation exceeds the market value of pension plan assets.

Bonds and notes are assets to the investor. These assets are short-term or long-term depending on how long the investor plans to hold them and whether they can be readily sold for cash.

Self-Study Questions

Test your understanding of the chapter by marking the best answer for each of the following questions.

1. An unsecured bond is called a *(p. 611)*
   a. Serial bond
   b. Registered bond
   c. Debenture bond
   d. Mortgage bond

2. How much will an investor pay for a $100,000 bond priced at 101⅞, plus a brokerage commission of $1,100? *(p. 611)*
   a. $100,000
   b. $101,100
   c. $101,875
   d. $102,975

3. A bond with a stated interest rate of 9½ percent is issued when the market interest rate is 9¾ percent. This bond will sell at *(p. 612)*
   a. Par value
   b. A discount
   c. A premium
   d. A price minus accrued interest

4. Ten-year, 11 percent bonds payable of $500,000 were issued for $532,000. Assume the straight-line amortization method is appropriate. The total annual interest expense on these bonds is *(pp. 616, 619)*
   a. $51,800
   b. $55,000
   c. $58,200
   d. A different amount each year because the bonds' book value decreases as the premium is amortized

5. Use the facts in the preceding question but assume the effective interest method of amortization is used. Total annual interest expense on the bonds is *(p. 623)*
   a. $51,800
   b. $55,000
   c. $58,200
   d. A decreasing amount each year because the bonds' book value decreases as the premium is amortized

6. Bonds payable with face value of $300,000 and carrying value of $288,000 are retired before their scheduled maturity with a cash outlay of $292,000. Which of the following entries correctly records this bond retirement? *(p. 625)*

   a. Bonds Payable 300,000
      Discount on Bonds Payable....................... 12,000
         Cash 292,000
         Extraordinary Gain on Retirement of Bonds Payable. . . 20,000

   b. Bonds Payable 300,000
      Extraordinary Loss on Retirement of Bonds Payable..... 4,000
         Discount on Bonds Payable..................... 12,000
         Cash 292,000

   c. Bonds Payable 300,000
         Discount on Bonds Payable..................... 6,000
         Cash 292,000
         Extraordinary Gain on Retirement of Bonds Payable. . . 2,000

   d. Bonds Payable 288,000
      Discount on Bonds Payable....................... 12,000
         Extraordinary Gain on Retirement of Bonds Payable. . . 8,000
         Cash 292,000

7. In a capital lease, the lessee records *(pp. 627–629)*
   a. A leased asset and a lease liability
   b. Depreciation on the leased asset
   c. Interest on the lease liability
   d. All of the above

8. Which of the following is an example of off-balance-sheet financing? *(p. 629)*
   a. Operating lease   c. Debenture bonds
   b. Current portion of long-term debt   d. Convertible bonds

9. An advantage of financing operations with debt versus stock is *(pp. 630–631)*
   a. The tax deductibility of interest expense on debt
   b. The legal requirement to pay interest and principal
   c. Lower interest payments compared to dividend payments
   d. All of the above

10. The main difference between accounting for long-term investments in bonds and accounting for short-term investments in bonds is *(p. 633)*
   a. Lower cost of short-term investments
   b. Higher cost of short-term investments
   c. No amortization of premium or discount on short-term investments in bonds
   d. No amortization of premium or discount on long-term investments in bonds

Answers to the self-study questions are at the end of the chapter.

Accounting Vocabulary

bond discount *(p. 611)*,   bond indenture *(p. 624)*,   bond premium *(p. 611)*,   bond sinking fund *(p. 624)*,   bonds payable *(p. 609)*,   callable bonds *(p. 625)*,   capital lease *(p. 629)*,   contract interest rate *(p. 612)*,   convertible bonds *(p. 626)*,   coupon bonds *(p. 610)*,   debentures *(p. 611)*,   effective interest rate *(p. 612)*,   lease *(p. 627)*,   lessee *(p. 627)*,   lessor *(p. 627)*, long-term investment *(p. 632)*,   market interest rate *(p. 612)*,   mortgage *(p. 627)*,   off-balance-sheet financing *(p. 629)*,   operating lease *(p. 627)*,   pension *(p. 629)*,   present value *(p. 612)*, registered bonds *(p. 610)*,   serial bonds *(p. 610)*,   stated interest rate *(p. 612)*,   term bonds *(p. 610)*,   trading on the equity *(p. 631)*,   underwriter *(p. 610)*.

ASSIGNMENT MATERIAL _____

Questions

1. Identify three ways to finance the operations of a corporation.
2. How do bonds payable differ from a note payable?
3. How does an underwriter assist with the issuance of bonds?
4. Why would an investor require the borrower to set up a sinking fund?
5. Compute the price to the nearest dollar for the following bonds with a face value of $10,000:

   a. 93   b. 88¾   c. 101⅜   d. 122½   e. 100

6. In which of the following situations will bonds sell at par? at a premium? at a discount?

   a. 9% bonds sold when the market rate is 9%.
   b. 9% bonds sold when the market rate is 10%.
   c. 9% bonds sold when the market rate is 8%.

7. Identify the accounts to debit and credit for transactions (a) to issue bonds at *par*, (b) to pay interest, (c) to accrue interest at year end, and (d) to pay off bonds at maturity.

8. Identify the account to debit and credit for transactions (a) to issue bonds at a *discount*, (b) to pay interest, (c) to accrue interest at year end, and (d) to pay off bonds at maturity.

9. Identify the accounts to debit and credit for transactions (a) to issue bonds at a *premium*, (b) to pay interest, (c) to accrue interest at year end, and (d) to pay off bonds at maturity.

10. Why are bonds sold for a price "plus accrued interest"? What happens to accrued interest when bonds are sold by an individual?
11. How does the straight-line method of amortizing bond discount (or premium) differ from the effective interest method?
12. A company retires ten-year bonds payable of $100,000 after five years. The business issued the bonds at 104 and called them at 103. Compute the amount of gain or loss on retirement. How is this gain or loss reported on the income statement?
13. Bonds payable with a maturity value of $100,000 are callable at 102½. Their market price is 101¼. If you are the issuer of these bonds, how much will you pay to retire them before maturity?
14. Why are convertible bonds attractive to investors? Why are they popular with borrowers?
15. Describe how to report serial bonds payable on the balance sheet.
16. Identify the accounts a lessee debits and credits when making operating lease payments.
17. What characteristics distinguish a capital lease from an operating lease?
18. A business signs a capital lease for the use of a building. What accounts are debited and credited (a) to begin the lease term and make the first lease payment, (b) to record depreciation, (c) to accrue interest on the lease liability, and (d) to make the second lease payment?
19. Show how a lessee reports on the balance sheet any leased equipment and the related lease liability under a capital lease.
20. What is off-balance-sheet financing? Give two examples.
21. Distinguish an overfunded pension plan from an underfunded plan. Which situation requires the company to report a pension liability on the balance sheet? How is this liability computed?
22. Contrast the effects on a company of issuing bonds versus issuing stock.
23. What is the same in accounting for bonds payable and accounting for a long-term investment in bonds? What is different?
24. What distinguishes a short-term investment (current asset) from a long-term investment? Describe premium and discount amortization for a short-term bond investment.

Exercises

Exercise 16-1   *Issuing bonds payable and paying interest*

Electronix, Inc., issues $500,000 of 10 percent, 20-year bonds payable that are dated April 30. Record (a) issuance of bonds at par on May 31 and (b) the next semiannual interest payment on October 31.

Exercise 16-2   *Issuing bonds payable, paying and accruing interest, and amortizing discount by the straight-line method.*

On February 1 MiniCalc issues 20-year, 10 percent bonds payable with a face value of $1,000,000. The bonds sell at 96½ and pay interest on January 31 and July 31. MiniCalc amortizes bond discount by the straight-line method. Record (a) issuance of the bonds on February 1, (b) the semiannual interest payment on July 31, and (c) the interest accrual on December 31.

Exercise 16-3   *Issuing bonds payable, paying and accruing interest, and amortizing premium by the straight-line method*

XIT Transportation Company issues 30-year, 8 percent bonds payable with a face value of $5,000,000 on March 31. The bonds sell at 103 and pay interest on March 31 and September 30. Assume XIT amortizes bond premium by the straight-line method. Record (a) issuance of the bonds on March 31, (b) payment of interest on September 30, and (c) accrual of interest on December 31.

Exercise 16-4 *Preparing an effective interest amortization table; recording interest payments and the related discount amortization*

Optic Devices Incorporated is authorized to issue $1,000,000 of 11 percent, 10-year bonds payable. On January 2, when the market interest rate is 12 percent, the company issues $500,000 of the bonds and receives cash of $471,325. Optic Devices amortizes bond discount by the effective interest method.

Required

1. Prepare an amortization table for the first four semiannual interest periods. Follow the format of Exhibit 16-3, Panel B.
2. Record the first semiannual interest payment on June 30 and the second payment on December 31.

Exercise 16-5 *Preparing an effective interest amortization table; recording interest accrual and payment and the related premium amortization*

On August 31, 1990, the market interest rate is 11 percent. Lancer Corporation issues $300,000 of 12 percent, 20-year sinking-fund bonds payable at 108. The bonds pay interest on February 28 and August 31. Lancer amortizes bond premium by the effective interest method.

Required

1. Prepare an amortization table for the first four semiannual interest periods. Follow the format of Exhibit 16-4, Panel B.
2. Record issuance of the bonds on August 31, 1990, the accrual of interest at December 31, 1990, and the semiannual interest payment on February 28, 1991.

Exercise 16-6 *Journalizing sinking fund transactions*

Lancer established a sinking fund for the bond issue in Exercise 16-5. Record payment of $6,000 into the sinking fund on February 28, 1991. Also record sinking-fund revenue of $900 on December 31, 1991, and the payment of the bonds at maturity on August 31, 2010. At maturity date the sinking-fund balance was $291,500.

Exercise 16-7 *Recording early retirement and conversion of bonds payable*

High Value Hardware Company reported the following at September 30:

Long-term liabilities:
Convertible bonds payable, 9%, 8 years to maturity........	$200,000	
Discount on bonds payable............................	6,000	$194,000

Required

1. Record retirement of one fourth of the bonds on October 1 at the call price of 101.
2. Record conversion of one half of the bonds into 8,000 shares of High Value's $5 par common stock on October 1.

Exercise 16-8 *Reporting long-term debt and pension liability on the balance sheet*

a. A note to the financial statements of Mapco, Inc., reports:

Note 5: Long-Term Debt
Total	$537,888,000
Less—Current portion.................................	22,085,000
Unamortized discount	1,391,000
Long-term debt.......................................	$514,412,000

Assume that none of the unamortized discount relates to the current portion of long-term debt. Show how Mapco's balance sheet would report these liabilities.

b. El Campo Incorporated's pension plan has assets with a market value of $720,000. The plan's accumulated benefit obligation is $840,000. What amount of long-term pension liability, if any, will El Campo report on its balance sheet?

Exercise 16-9   *Journalizing capital lease and operating lease transactions*

A capital lease agreement for equipment requires 10 annual payments of $8,000, with the first payment due on January 2, 19X5. The present value of the 9 future lease payments at 10 percent is $46,072.

a. *Journalize the following lessee transactions:*

19X5
Jan. 2   Beginning of lease term and first annual payment.
Dec. 31   Depreciation of equipment.
      31   Interest expense on lease liability.
19X6
Jan. 2   Second annual lease payment.

b. *Journalize the January 2, 19X5, lease payment if this is an operating lease.*

Exercise 16-10   *Analyzing alternative plans for raising money*

ABC Corporation is considering two plans for raising $1,000,000 to expand operations. Plan A is to borrow at 9 percent, and Plan B is to issue 200,000 shares of common stock. Before any new financing, ABC has 300,000 shares of common stock outstanding. Management believes the company can use the new funds to earn income of $420,000 before interest and taxes. The income tax rate is 40 percent.

Required

Prepare an analysis like Exhibit 16-5 to determine which plan will result in higher earnings per share.

Exercise 16-11   *Recording short-term bond investment transactions*

On June 30 Cartwright Corporation paid 92¼ for 8 percent bonds of Klein, Inc., as a short-term investment. The maturity value of the bonds is $50,000, and they pay interest on March 31 and September 30. Record Cartwright's purchase of the bond investment, the receipt of semiannual interest on September 30, and the accrual of interest revenue on December 31.

Exercise 16-12   *Recording long-term bond investment transactions*

Assume the Cartwright Corporation bonds in the preceding exercise are purchased as a long-term investment on June 30, 19X3. The bonds mature on September 30, 19X7.

Required

a. Using the straight-line method of amortizing the discount, journalize all transactions on the bonds for 19X3.
b. How much more interest revenue would the investor record in 19X3 for a long-term investment than for a short-term investment in these bonds? What accounts for this difference?

Problems   *(Group A)*

Problem 16-1A   *Journalizing bond transactions (at par) and reporting bonds payable on the balance sheet*

The board of directors of Tennessee Volunteer Co. authorizes the issue of $3 million of 9 percent, 10-year bonds payable. The semiannual interest dates are May 31 and November 30. The bonds are issued through an underwriter on July 31, 19X5, at par plus accrued interest.

Required

1. Journalize the following transactions:
    a. Issuance of the bonds on July 31, 19X5.
    b. Payment of interest on November 30, 19X5.
    c. Accrual of interest on December 31, 19X5.
    d. Payment of interest on May 31, 19X6.
2. Check your recorded interest expense for 19X5, using as a model the supplement to the summary problem on page 619.
3. Report interest payable and bonds payable as they would appear on the Tennessee Volunteer Co. balance sheet at December 31, 19X5.

Problem 16-2A   *Issuing bonds at a discount, amortizing by the straight-line method, and reporting bonds payable on the balance sheet*

On March 1, 19X4, Valdez, Inc., issues 10½ percent, 20-year bonds payable with a face value of $500,000. The bonds pay interest on February 28 and August 31. Valdez amortizes premium and discount by the straight-line method.

Required

1. If the market interest rate is 9 percent when Valdez issues its bonds, will the bonds be priced at par, at a premium, or at a discount? Explain.
2. If the market interest rate is 11¼ percent when Valdez issues its bonds, will the bonds be priced at par, at a premium, or at a discount? Explain.
3. Assume the issue price of the bonds is 92. Journalize the following bond transactions:
    a. Issuance of the bonds on March 1, 19X4.
    b. Payment of interest and amortization of discount on August 31, 19X4.
    c. Accrual of interest and amortization of discount on December 31, 19X4.
    d. Payment of interest and amortization of discount on February 28, 19X5.
4. Check your recorded interest expense for the year ended February 28, 19X5, using as a model the supplement to the summary problem on page 619.
5. Report interest payable and bonds payable as they would appear on the Valdez balance sheet at December 31, 19X4.

Problem 16-3A   *Issuing convertible bonds at a premium, amortizing by the effective interest method, retiring bonds early, converting bonds, and reporting the bonds payable on the balance sheet*

On December 31, 19X1, Southwest Distributing Company issues 12 percent, 10-year convertible bonds with a maturity value of $500,000. The semiannual interest dates are June 30 and December 31. The market interest rate is 11 percent, and the issue price of the bonds is 106. Southwest amortizes bond premium and discount by the effective interest method.

Required

1. Prepare an effective interest method amortization table like Exhibit 16-4 for the first four semiannual interest periods.

2. Journalize the following transactions:
   a. Issuance of the bonds on December 31, 19X1. Credit Convertible Bonds Payable.
   b. Payment of interest on June 30, 19X2.
   c. Payment of interest on December 31, 19X2.
   d. Retirement of bonds with face value of $100,000 on July 1, 19X3. Southwest pays the call price of 102.
   e. Conversion by the bondholders on July 1, 19X3, of bonds with face value of $300,000 into 10,000 shares of Southwest's $10 par common stock.
3. Prepare the balance sheet presentation of the bonds payable that are outstanding at December 31, 19X3.

Problem 16-4A *Analyzing an actual company's long-term debt, journalizing its transactions, and reporting the long-term debt on the balance sheet*

The notes to Baker International's financial statements recently reported the following data on September 30, Year 1 (the end of the fiscal year):

NOTE 4. INDEBTEDNESS

Long-Term debt at September 30, Year 1, included the following:

6.00% debentures due Year 20 with an effective interest rate of 14.66%, net of unamortized discount of $123,152,000	$101,848,000
Other indebtedness with an interest rate of 10.30%, due $12,108,000 in Year 6 and $19,257,000 in Year 7	31,365,000

Assume Baker amortizes discount by the effective interest method.

Required

1. Answer the following questions about Baker's long-term liabilities:
   a. What is the maturity value of the 6.00% debenture bonds?
   b. What are Baker's annual cash interest payments on the 6.00% debenture bonds?
   c. What is the carrying value of the 6.00% debenture bonds at September 30, Year 1?
2. Prepare an amortization table through September 30, Year 5, for the 6.00% debenture bonds. Round all amounts to the nearest thousand dollars, and assume Baker pays interest annually on September 30. Use the following format for the amortization table:

End of Annual Interest Period	A Interest Payment (6% of Maturity Value)	B Interest Expense (14.66% of Preceding Bond Carrying Value)	C Discount Amortization (B − A)	D Discount Balance (D − C)	E Bond Carrying Value ($225,000 − D)
Sep. 30, Yr. 1					
Sep. 30, Yr. 2					
Sep. 30, Yr. 3					
Sep. 30, Yr. 4					
Sep. 30, Yr. 5					

3. Record the September 30, Year 2 and Year 3, interest payments on the 6.00% debenture bonds.
4. There is no premium or discount on the other indebtedness. Assuming annual interest is paid on September 30 each year, record Baker's September 30, Year 2, interest payment on the other indebtedness. Round interest to the nearest thousand dollars.
5. Show how Baker would report the debenture bonds payable and other indebtedness of September 30, Year 5.

Problem 16-5A *Journalizing bonds payable, bond investment, and capital lease transactions*

Journalize the following transactions of Beltway United Corporation:

19X1

Jan. 1   Issued $1,000,000 of 8 percent, 10-year bonds payable at 93.

1   Signed a 5-year capital lease on equipment. The agreement requires annual lease payments of $20,000, with the first payment due immediately. At 12 percent, the present value of the four future lease payments is $60,750.

Mar. 31   Purchased a short-term investment in the 9 percent bonds of another company, paying 95½ plus interest accrued since January 31. Maturity value of the bonds is $50,000.

July 1   Paid semiannual interest and amortized discount by the straight-line method on our 8 percent bonds payable.

1   Made the $50,000 sinking-fund payment required by the indenture on our 8 percent bonds payable.

July 31   Received semiannual interest on the bond investment purchased March 31.

Dec. 31   Accrued semiannual interest expense, and amortized discount by the straight-line method on our 8 percent bonds payable.

31   Recorded depreciation on leased equipment.

31   Accrued interest expense on the lease liability.

31   Accrued interest revenue on the bond investment.

31   Recorded bond sinking-fund earnings of $2,000.

19X11

Jan. 1   Paid the 8 percent bonds at maturity from the sinking fund and received excess cash of $22,400.

Problem 16-6A *Reporting bond investments and liabilities on the balance sheet*

The accounting records of Musberger, Inc., include the following items:

Bond sinking fund..........	$130,000	Interest receivable..........	$ 1,100
Accumulated pension benefit obligation...............	260,000	Mortgage note payable, long-term...............	67,000
Bonds payable, long-term....	300,000	Building acquired under capital lease.............	190,000
Short-term investment in bonds.................	49,000	Interest expense............	47,000
Premium on bonds payable.................	22,000	Pension plan assets (market value).................	205,000
Interest payable............	9,200	Bonds payable, current portion................	60,000
Interest revenue............	5,300		
Capital lease liability, long-term...............	111,000	Accumulated depreciation, building	108,000

Required

Show how these items would be reported on the Musberger balance sheet, including headings for current assets, current liabilities, and so on. Note disclosures are not required. Not all the items are reported on the balance sheet.

Problem 16-7A *Accounting for a long-term bond investment purchased at a discount*

Financial institutions such as insurance companies and pension plans hold large quantities of bond investments. Suppose Mutual Life Insurance Company of New York (MONY) purchases $500,000 of 9 percent bonds of Ford Motor Company for 97 on March 31, 19X0. These bonds pay interest on January 31 and July 31 each year. They mature on July 31, 19X8.

Required

1. Journalize MONY's purchase of the bonds as a long-term investment on March 31, 19X0, receipt of cash interest and amortization of discount on July 31, 19X0, and accrual of interest revenue and amortization of discount at December 31, 19X0. Assume the amortization amounts are immaterial, so the straight-line method is appropriate for amortizing discount.
2. Show all financial statement effects of this long-term bond investment at December 31, 19X0. Assume a multiple-step income statement.
3. Repeat requirement 2 under the assumption that MONY purchased these bonds as a short-term investment.

(Group B)

Problem 16-1B *Journalizing bond transactions (at par) and reporting bonds payable on the balance sheet*

The board of directors of Kentucky Thoroughbred Company authorizes the issue of $2 million of 8 percent, 20-year bonds payable. The semiannual interest dates are February 28 and August 31. The bonds are issued through an underwriter on June 30, 19X7, at par plus accrued interest.

Required

1. Journalize the following transactions:
   a. Issuance of the bonds on June 30, 19X7.
   b. Payment of interest on August 31, 19X7.
   c. Accrual of interest on December 31, 19X7.
   d. Payment of interest on February 28, 19X8.
2. Check your recorded interest expense for 19X7, using as a model the supplement to the summary problem on page 619.
3. Report interest payable and bonds payable as they would appear on the Kentucky Thoroughbred Company balance sheet at December 31, 19X7.

Problem 16-2B *Issuing notes at a premium, amortizing by the straight-line method, and reporting notes payable on the balance sheet*

On March 1, 19X6, Crown Center Corporation issues $9\frac{1}{4}$ percent, 10-year notes payable with a face value of $300,000. The notes pay interest on February 28 and August 31, and Crown Center amortizes premium and discount by the straight-line method.

Required

1. If the market interest rate is 10 percent when Crown Center issues its notes, will the notes be priced at par, at a premium, or at a discount? Explain.
2. If the market interest rate is $8\frac{1}{2}$ percent when Crown Center issues its notes, will the notes be priced at par, at a premium, or at a discount? Explain.
3. Assume the issue price of the notes is 106. Journalize the following note payable transactions:
   a. Issuance of the notes on March 1, 19X6.
   b. Payment of interest and amortization of premium on August 31, 19X6.
   c. Accrual of interest and amortization of premium on December 31, 19X6.
   d. Payment of interest and amortization of premium on February 28, 19X7.
4. Check your recorded interest expense for the year ended February 28, 19X7, using as a model the supplement to the summary problem on page 619.
5. Report interest payable and notes payable as they would appear on the Crown Center balance sheet at December 31, 19X6.

Problem 16-3B   *Issuing convertible bonds at a discount, amortizing by the effective interest method, retiring bonds early, converting bonds, and reporting the bonds payable on the balance sheet*

On December 31, 19X1, Youth Development Institute issues 11 percent, 10-year convertible bonds with a maturity value of $400,000. The semiannual interest dates are June 30 and December 31. The market interest rate is 13 percent, and the issue price of the bonds is 89. The Institute amortizes bond premium and discount by the effective interest method.

Required

1. Prepare an effective interest method amortization table like Exhibit 16-3 for the first four semiannual interest periods.
2. Journalize the following transactions:
   a. Issuance of the bonds on December 31, 19X1. Credit Convertible Bonds Payable.
   b. Payment of interest on June 30, 19X2.
   c. Payment of interest on December 31, 19X2.
   d. Retirement of bonds with face value of $100,000 on July 1, 19X3. The Institute purchases the bonds at 94 in the open market.
   e. Conversion by the bondholders on July 1, 19X3, of bonds with face value of $250,000 into 50,000 shares of Youth Development $1 par common stock.
3. Prepare the balance sheet presentation of the bonds payable that are outstanding at December 31, 19X3.

Problem 16-4B   *Analyzing a company's long-term debt, journalizing its transactions, and reporting the long-term debt on the balance sheet*

The notes to Allof's Towers' financial statements reported the following data on July 31, Year 1 (the end of the fiscal year):

NOTE E—LONG-TERM DEBT

7% debentures due Year 20, net of unamortized discount of $71,645,000 (effective interest rate of 11%)	$159,855,000
Notes payable, interest of 8.67%, due in annual amounts of $22,840,000 in Years 6 through 17	274,080,000

Assume Allof's amortizes discount by the effective interest method.

Required

1. Answer the following questions about Allof's long-term liabilities:
   a. What is the maturity value of the 7% debenture bonds?
   b. What are Allof's annual cash interest payments on the 7% debenture bonds?
   c. What is the carrying value of the 7% debenture bonds at July 31, Year 1?
2. Prepare an amortization table through July 31, Year 5, for the 7% debenture bonds. Round all amounts to the nearest thousand dollars and assume Allof's pays interest annually on July 31. Use the following format for the amortization table:

End of Annual Interest Period	A Interest Payment (7% of Maturity Value)	B Interest Expense (11% of Preceding Bond Carrying Value)	C Discount Amortization (B − A)	D Discount Balance (D − C)	E Bond Carrying Value ($231,500 − D)
July 31, Yr. 1					
July 31, Yr. 2					
July 31, Yr. 3					
July 31, Yr. 4					
July 31, Yr. 5					

3. Record the July 31, Year 2 and Year 3, interest payments on the 7% debenture bonds.
4. There is no premium or discount on the notes payable. Assuming annual interest is paid on July 31 each year, record Allof's July 31, Year 2, interest payment on the notes payable. Round interest to the nearest thousand dollars.
5. Show how Allof's would report the debenture bonds payable and notes payable at July 31, Year 5.

Problem 16-5B *Journalizing bonds payable, bond investment, and capital lease transactions*

Journalize the following transactions of Oriental Rug Corporation:

19X1

Jan. 1 Issued $2,000,000 of 9 percent, 10-year bonds payable at 97.

   1 Signed a 10-year capital lease on machinery. The agreement requires annual lease payments of $16,000, with the first payment due immediately. At 12 percent, the present value of the nine future lease payments is $85,250.

Mar. 31 Purchased a short-term investment in the 7 percent bonds of another company, paying 88¼ plus interest accrued since January 31. Maturity value of the bonds is $60,000.

July 1 Paid semiannual interest and amortized discount by the straight-line method on our 9 percent bonds payable.

   1 Made the $100,000 sinking-fund payment required by the indenture on our 9 percent bonds payable.

July 31 Received semiannual interest on the bond investment purchased March 31.

Dec. 31 Accrued semiannual interest expense and amortized discount by the straight-line method on our 9 percent bonds payable.

   31 Recorded depreciation on leased machinery.

   31 Accrued interest expense on the lease liability.

   31 Accrued interest revenue on the bond investment.

   31 Recorded bond sinking-fund earnings of $5,500.

19X11

Jan 1 Paid the 9 percent bonds at maturity from the sinking fund ($1,981,000) and the remainder from company cash.

Problem 16-6B *Reporting bond investments and liabilities on the balance sheet*

The Silverstein Corporation accounting records include the following items:

Pension plan assets (market value)	$ 93,000	Mortgage note payable, long-term	$ 82,000
Interest payable	13,000	Accumulated depreciation, equipment	97,000
Interest expense	57,000	Bond sinking fund	119,000
Bonds payable, current portion	75,000	Capital lease liability, current	18,000
Capital lease liability, long-term	81,000	Mortgage note payable, current	19,000
Discount on bonds payable	7,000	Accumulated pension benefit obligation	89,000
Interest receivable	2,000	Bonds payable, long-term	400,000
Interest revenue	5,000	Equipment acquired under capital lease	208,000
Short-term investment in bonds	38,000		

Required

Show how these items would be reported on the Silverstein balance sheet, including headings for current assets, current liabilities, and so on. Note disclosures are not required. Not all the items are reported on the balance sheet.

Problem 16-7B *Accounting for a long-term bond investment purchased at a premium*

Financial institutions such as insurance companies and pension plans hold large quantities of bond investments. Suppose Variable Life Insurance Company (VALIC) purchases $600,000 of 8 percent bonds of Texell Corporation for 102 on July 1, 19X1. These bonds pay interest on March 1 and September 1 each year. They mature on March 1, 19X8.

Required

1. Journalize VALIC's purchase of the bonds as a long-term investment on July 1, 19X1, receipt of cash interest and amortization of premium on September 1, 19X1, and accrual of interest revenue and amortization of premium at December 31, 19X1. Assume the amortization amounts are immaterial, so the straight-line method is appropriate for amortizing premium.
2. Show all financial statement effects of this long-term bond investment at December 31, 19X1. Assume a multiple-step income statement.
3. Repeat requirement 2 under the assumption that VALIC purchased these bonds as a short-term investment.

Decision Problem

Analyzing Alternative Ways of Raising $5 Million

Business is going well for BPI Systems, Inc. The board of directors of this family-owned company believes that BPI could earn an additional $1,500,000 in income before interest and taxes by expanding into new markets. However, the $5,000,000 that the business needs for growth cannot be raised within the family. The directors, who strongly wish to retain family control of BPI, must consider issuing securities to outsiders. They are considering three financing plans.

Plan A is to borrow at 9 percent. Plan B is to issue 200,000 shares of common stock. Plan C is to issue 100,000 shares of nonvoting, $3.75 preferred stock. BPI presently has 500,000 shares of common stock outstanding. The income tax rate is 40 percent.

Required

1. Prepare an analysis similar to Exhibit 16-5 to determine which plan will result in the highest earnings per share of common stock.
2. Recommend one plan to the board of directors. Give your reasons.

Financial Statement Problem

Gulf+Western Inc.'s balance sheet and related notes A and F, all given in Appendix C, provide details about the company's long-term debt. Use those data to answer the following questions.

1. By which method does Gulf+Western amortize debt discount (same as discount on bonds payable)?
2. Examine Note F. How much long-term debt did Gulf+Western pay off during fiscal 1987? How much new long-term debt did the company create during fiscal 1987? Hint: Use a T-account for Long-Term Debt, as follows (amounts in millions):

Long-Term Debt (including Current Maturities)

	Oct. 31, 1986	Bal.	1,290.6
Fiscal 1987 Payments?	Fiscal 1987	New debt	?
	Oct. 31, 1987	Bal.	1,399.8

Journalize the payment entry and the entry for the issuance of new debt.

3. How much of the October 31, 1987, balance in the T-account did Gulf+Western expect to pay during fiscal 1988? Journalize the payment during fiscal 1988.
4. Examine the Note F description of the "7% subordinated debentures due 2003." Answer these questions:
   a. What collateral do holders of these bonds have? Give your reason.
   b. Compute the bonds' maturity value.
   c. Compute the amount of cash (contract) interest that Gulf+Western paid on these bonds during fiscal 1988.
   d. Compute the amount of interest expense that Gulf+Western recorded on these bonds during fiscal 1988.
5. Journalize, in a single summary entry, Gulf+Western's interest expense, cash interest payment, and amortization of Debt Discount for fiscal 1988. Use Gulf+Western account titles. Hint: Use the answers from requirement 4.

Appendix: Present Value _____

After studying this appendix, you should be able to

1. Compute the market value of a note or a bond.
2. Determine the cost of an asset acquired through a capital lease.

Present value (PV) has many applications in accounting. For example, a company may issue 10 percent bonds payable when the market interest rate is 11 percent. The company needs to know how much cash it will receive from issuing the bonds. The investors must determine how much to pay for the bonds. Both parties must compute the present value of the bonds. Another example is the acquisition of an asset through a capital lease. The lessee (tenant) must know the cost of the asset. The time value of money leads us to evaluate bonds, leases, and investments in terms of present value.

Suppose an investment promises to pay you $5,000 at the *end* of one year. How much would you pay *now* to acquire this investment? You would be willing to pay the present value of the $5,000, which is a future amount.

Present value depends on three factors: (1) the amount of payment (or receipt), (2) the length of time between investment and future receipt (or payment), and (3) the interest rate. The process of computing a present value is called **discounting** because the present value is *less* than the future value.

In our investment example, the future receipt is $5,000. The investment period is one year. Assume that you demand an annual interest rate of 10 percent on your investment. With all three factors specified, you can compute the present value of $5,000 at 10 percent for one year. The computation is

$$\frac{\textbf{Future value}}{(1 + \textbf{Interest rate})} = \frac{\$5,000}{1.10} = \$4,545$$

(Throughout this discussion we round off to the nearest dollar.) By turning the problem around, we verify the present value computation:

Amount invested (present value) $4,545
Expected earnings ($4,545 × .10)   455
Amount to be received one year from now (future value) $5,000

The $455 income amount is interest revenue, also called the return on the investment.

If the $5,000 is to be received two years from now, you would pay only $4,132 for the investment, computed as follows:

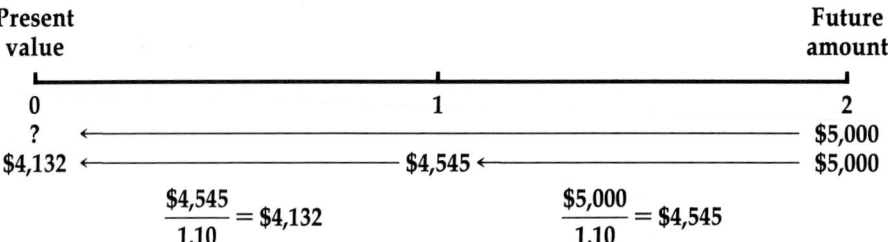

By turning the problem around, we verify that $4,132 accumulates to $5,000 at 10 percent for two years.

Amount invested (present value)	$4,132
Expected earnings for first year ($4,132 × .10)	413
Amount invested after one year	4,545
Expected earnings for second year ($4,545 × .10)	455
Amount to be received two years from now (future value)	$5,000

You would pay $4,132—the present value of $5,000—to receive the $5,000 future amount at the end of two years at 10 percent per year. The $868 difference between the amount invested ($4,132) and the amount to be received ($5,000) is the return on the investment, the sum of the two interest receipts: $413 + $455 = $868.

Present-Value Tables

We can compute present value by using the formula

$$\frac{\textbf{Future value}}{(1 + \textbf{interest rate})}$$

as we have shown. However, figuring present value "by hand" for investments spanning many years becomes drawn out. The "number crunching" presents too many opportunities for arithmetical errors. Present-value tables ease our work. Let's reexamine our examples of present value by using Table 16-1: Present Value of $1.

For the 10 percent investment for one year, we find the junction under 10% and across from 1 in the period column. The table figure of 0.909 is computed as follows: $1/1.10 = .909$. This work has been done for us, and only the present values are given in the table. Note that the table heading states $1. To figure present value for $5,000, we multiply 0.909 by $5,000. The result is $4,545, which matches the result we obtained by hand.

For the two-year investment, we read down from 10 percent and across from period 2. We multiply 0.826 (which is computed as follows: $.909/1.10 = .826$) by $5,000 and get $4,130, which confirms our earlier computation of $4,132 (the difference is due to rounding in the present-value table). We can compute the present value of any single future amount using the table.

Present Value of an Annuity

The investment in the preceding example provided the investor with only a single future receipt ($5,000 at the end of two years). Some investments, called annuities, provide multiple receipts of an equal amount at fixed intervals over the investment's duration.

Consider an investment that promises *annual* cash receipts of $10,000 to be received at

Table 16-1 *Present Value of $1*

	Present Value								
Periods	**4%**	**5%**	**6%**	**7%**	**8%**	**10%**	**12%**	**14%**	**16%**
1	0.962	0.952	0.943	0.935	0.926	0.909	0.893	0.877	0.862
2	0.925	0.907	0.890	0.873	0.857	0.826	0.797	0.769	0.743
3	0.889	0.864	0.840	0.816	0.794	0.751	0.712	0.675	0.641
4	0.855	0.823	0.792	0.763	0.735	0.683	0.636	0.592	0.552
5	0.822	0.784	0.747	0.713	0.681	0.621	0.567	0.519	0.476
6	0.790	0.746	0.705	0.666	0.630	0.564	0.507	0.456	0.410
7	0.760	0.711	0.665	0.623	0.583	0.513	0.452	0.400	0.354
8	0.731	0.677	0.627	0.582	0.540	0.467	0.404	0.351	0.305
9	0.703	0.645	0.592	0.544	0.500	0.424	0.361	0.308	0.263
10	0.676	0.614	0.558	0.508	0.463	0.386	0.322	0.270	0.227
11	0.650	0.585	0.527	0.475	0.429	0.350	0.287	0.237	0.195
12	0.625	0.557	0.497	0.444	0.397	0.319	0.257	0.208	0.168
13	0.601	0.530	0.469	0.415	0.368	0.290	0.229	0.182	0.145
14	0.577	0.505	0.442	0.388	0.340	0.263	0.205	0.160	0.125
15	0.555	0.481	0.417	0.362	0.315	0.239	0.183	0.140	0.108
16	0.534	0.458	0.394	0.339	0.292	0.218	0.163	0.123	0.093
17	0.513	0.436	0.371	0.317	0.270	0.198	0.146	0.108	0.080
18	0.494	0.416	0.350	0.296	0.250	0.180	0.130	0.095	0.069
19	0.475	0.396	0.331	0.277	0.232	0.164	0.116	0.083	0.060
20	0.456	0.377	0.312	0.258	0.215	0.149	0.104	0.073	0.051

the end of each of three years. Assume that you demand a 12 percent return on your investment. What is the investment's present value? What would you pay today to acquire the investment? The investment spans three periods, and you would pay the sum of three present values. The computation is

Year	**Annual Cash Receipt**	**Present Value of $1 at 12% (Table 1)**	**Present Value of Annual Cash Receipt**
1	$10,000	.893	$ 8,930
2	10,000	.797	7,970
3	10,000	.712	7,120
Total present value of investment . . .			$24,020

The present value of this annuity is $24,020. By paying this amount today, you would receive $10,000 at the end of each of three years while earning 12 percent on your investment.

The example illustrates repetitive computations of the three future amounts, a time-consuming process. One way to ease the computational burden is to add the three present values of $1 (.893 + .797 + .712) and multiply their sum (2.402) by the annual cash receipt ($10,000) to obtain the present value of the annuity ($10,000 × 2.402 = $24,020).

An easier approach is to use a present value of an annuity table. Table 16-2 shows the present value of $1 to be received periodically for a given number of periods. The present value of a three-period annuity at 12 percent is 2.402. Thus $10,000 received annually at the end of each of three years, discounted at 12 percent, is $24,020 ($10,000 × 2.402), which is the present value.

Table 16-2 *Present Value of Annuity of $1*

Periods	4%	5%	6%	Present Value 7%	8%	10%	12%	14%	16%
1	0.962	0.952	0.943	0.935	0.926	0.909	0.893	0.877	0.862
2	1.886	1.859	1.833	1.808	1.783	1.736	1.690	1.647	1.605
3	2.775	2.723	2.673	2.624	2.577	2.487	2.402	2.322	2.246
4	3.630	3.546	3.465	3.387	3.312	3.170	3.037	2.914	2.798
5	4.452	4.329	4.212	4.100	3.993	3.791	3.605	3.433	3.274
6	5.242	5.076	4.917	4.767	4.623	4.355	4.111	3.889	3.685
7	6.002	5.786	5.582	5.389	5.206	4.868	4.564	4.288	4.039
8	6.733	6.463	6.210	5.971	5.747	5.335	4.968	4.639	4.344
9	7.435	7.108	6.802	6.515	6.247	5.759	5.328	4.946	4.607
10	8.111	7.722	7.360	7.024	6.710	6.145	5.650	5.216	4.833
11	8.760	8.306	7.887	7.499	7.139	6.495	5.938	5.453	5.029
12	9.385	8.863	8.384	7.943	7.536	6.814	6.194	5.660	5.197
13	9.986	9.394	8.853	8.358	7.904	7.103	6.424	5.842	5.342
14	10.563	9.899	9.295	8.745	8.244	7.367	6.628	6.002	5.468
15	11.118	10.380	9.712	9.108	8.559	7.606	6.811	6.142	5.575
16	11.652	10.838	10.106	9.447	8.851	7.824	6.974	6.265	5.669
17	12.166	11.274	10.477	9.763	9.122	8.022	7.120	6.373	5.749
18	12.659	11.690	10.828	10.059	9.372	8.201	7.250	6.467	5.818
19	13.134	12.085	11.158	10.336	9.604	8.365	7.366	6.550	5.877
20	13.590	12.462	11.470	10.594	9.818	8.514	7.469	6.623	5.929

Present Value of Bonds Payable

The present value of a bond—its market price—is the present value of the future principal amount at maturity plus the present value of the future contract interest payments. The principal is a single amount to be paid at maturity. The interest is an annuity because it occurs periodically.

Let's compute the present value of the 9 percent, five-year bonds of Bethlehem Steel. The face value of the bonds is $100,000, and they pay 4½ percent contract (cash) interest semiannually. At issuance the market interest rate is 10 percent, and so the effective interest rate for each of the 10 semiannual periods is 5 percent. We use 5 percent in computing the present value of the maturity and of the interest. The market price of these bonds is $96,149, as follows:

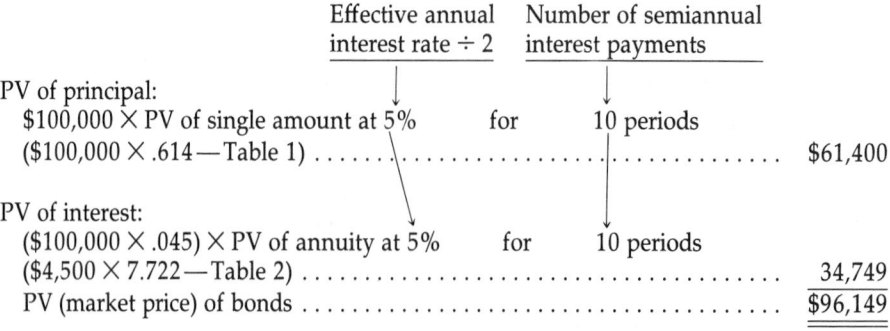

```
                                   Effective annual   Number of semiannual
                                   interest rate ÷ 2  interest payments

PV of principal:
  $100,000 × PV of single amount at 5%      for      10 periods
  ($100,000 × .614—Table 1) ...........................................  $61,400

PV of interest:
  ($100,000 × .045) × PV of annuity at 5%   for      10 periods
  ($4,500 × 7.722—Table 2) ..........................................     34,749
  PV (market price) of bonds ........................................    $96,149
```

The market price of the Bethlehem Steel bonds shows a discount because the contract interest rate on the bonds (9 percent) is less than the market interest rate (10 percent). We discuss these bonds in more detail on pages 620–622.

Let's consider a premium price for the Bethlehem Steel bonds. Assume that the market interest rate is 8 percent at issuance. The effective interest rate is 4 percent for each of the 10 semiannual periods.

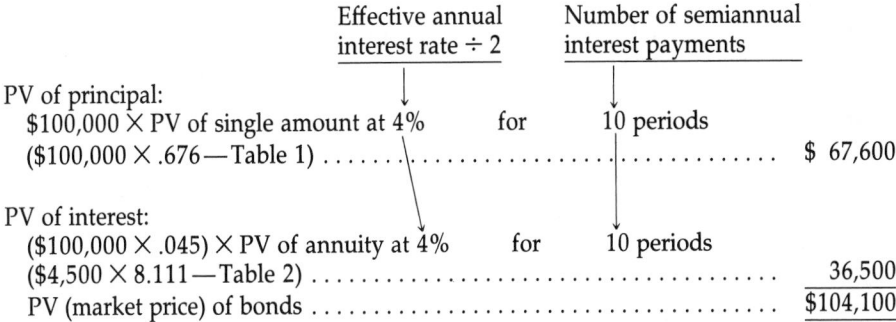

	Effective annual interest rate ÷ 2	Number of semiannual interest payments	
PV of principal:			
$100,000 × PV of single amount at 4%	for	10 periods	
($100,000 × .676—Table 1)			$ 67,600
PV of interest:			
($100,000 × .045) × PV of annuity at 4%	for	10 periods	
($4,500 × 8.111—Table 2)			36,500
PV (market price) of bonds			$104,100

We discuss accounting for these bonds on pages 622 and 623.

Capital Leases

How does a lessee compute the cost of an asset acquired through a capital lease? Consider that the lessee gets the use of the asset but does *not* pay for the leased asset in full at the beginning of the lease. Therefore, the lessee must record the leased asset at the present value of the lease liability. The time value of money must be weighed.

The cost of the asset to the lessee is the sum of any payment made at the beginning of the lease period plus the present value of the future lease payments. The lease payments are equal amounts occurring at regular intervals—that is, they are annuity payments.

Consider the 20-year building lease of the Southland Corporation, which owns 7-Eleven stores. The lease requires 20 annual payments of $10,000 each, with the first payment due immediately. The interest rate in the lease is 10 percent, and the present value of the 19 future payments is $83,650 ($10,000 × PV of annuity at 10 percent for 19 periods, or 8.365 from Table 16-2). Southland's cost of the building is $93,650 (the sum of the initial payment, $10,000, plus the present value of the future payments, $83,650). The entries for a capital lease are illustrated on pages 628 and 629.

Problems

Problem PV-1   *Computing the present values of notes and bonds*

Determine the present value of the following notes and bonds:

1. $20,000, five-year note payable with contract interest rate of 11 percent, paid annually. The market interest rate at issuance is 12 percent.
2. Ten-year bonds payable with maturity value of $100,000 and contract interest rate of 12 percent, paid semiannually. The market rate of interest is 12 percent at issuance.
3. Same bonds payable as in 2, but the market interest rate is 10 percent.
4. Same bonds payable as in 2, but the market interest rate is 14 percent.

Problem PV-2   *Computing a bond's present value; recording its issuance at a discount and interest payments*

On December 31, 19X1, when the market interest rate is 8 percent, Unitrode Corporation issues $500,000 of 10-year, 7.25 percent bonds payable. The bonds pay interest semiannually.

Required

1. Determine the present value of the bonds at issuance.
2. Assume that the bonds are issued at the price computed in 1. Prepare an effective interest method amortization table for the first two semiannual interest periods.
3. Using the amortization table prepared in 2, journalize issuance of the bonds and the first two interest payments.

Problem PV-3 *Computing a bond's present value; recording its issuance at a premium and interest payments*

On December 31, 19X1, when the market interest rate is 10 percent, RTE Corporation issues $4,000,000 of 10-year, 12.5 percent bonds payable. The bonds pay interest semiannually.

Required

1. Determine the present value of the bonds at issuance.
2. Assuming the bonds were issued at the price computed in 1, prepare an effective interest method amortization table for the first two semiannual interest periods.
3. Using the amortization table in 2, journalize issuance of the bonds on December 31, 19X1, and the first two interest payments on June 30 and December 31, 19X2.

Problem PV-4 *Computing the cost of equipment acquired under a capital lease and recording the lease transactions*

Montgomery Corporation acquired equipment under a capital lease that requires six annual lease payments of $5,000. The first payment is due when the lease begins, on January 1, 19X6. Future payments are due on January 1 of each year of the lease term. The interest rate in the lease is 16 percent.

Required

1. Compute Montgomery's cost of the equipment.
2. Journalize the (a) acquisition of the equipment, (b) depreciation for 19X6, (c) accrued interest at December 31, 19X6, and (d) second lease payment on January 1, 19X7.

Problem PV-5 *Computing the cost of a bond investment and journalizing its transactions*

An investor purchases $400,000 of the RTE bonds (Problem PV-3) at issuance. Determine the cost (present value) of the bond investment. Assume that the investment is short-term. Journalize the purchase on December 31, 19X1, the first semiannual interest receipt on June 30, 19X2, and the year-end interest receipt on December 31, 19X2.

Answers to Self-Study Questions

1. c		6. b	
2. d [($100,000 × 1.01875) + $1,100 = $102,975]		7. d	
3. b		8. a	
4. a [($500,000 × .11) − ($32,000/10) = $51,800]		9. a	
5. d		10. c	

Corporations: Investments in Stock and Accounting for the Effects of Changing Prices

In the preceding chapter, we discussed accounting for bond investments. In this chapter, we discuss how to account for investments in stock. We also consider the challenging area of accounting for the effects of inflation.

Accounting for Investments in Stock

Stock Prices

Investors buy more stocks in transactions among themselves than in purchases directly from the issuing company. Each share of stock is issued only once, but it may be traded among investors many times thereafter. People and businesses buy and sell stocks from each other in markets, such as the New York Stock Exchange and the American Stock Exchange. Recall that stock ownership is transferable. Investors trade millions of stock shares each day. Brokers like Merrill Lynch and Prudential Bache handle stock transactions for a commission.

A broker may "quote you a stock price," which means to state the current market price per share. The financial community quotes stock prices in dollars and one-eighth fractions. A stock selling at 32⅛ costs $32.125 per share. A stock listed at 55¾ sells at $55.75. Financial publications and many newspapers carry daily information on the stock issues of thousands of corporations. These one-line summaries carry information as of the close of trading the previous day.

EXHIBIT 17-1   Stock Price Information

| 52 Weeks | | | | | | | | |
High	Low	Stock	Dividend	Sales 100s	High	Low	Close	Net Change
64⅞	43¾	Boeing	1.40	6788	46½	45½	46⅛	+⅝

Exhibit 17-1 presents information for the common stock of the Boeing Company, a large aircraft manufacturer, just as this information appears in the newspaper listings.

During the previous 52 weeks, Boeing common stock reached a high of $64.875 and a low of $43.75. The annual cash dividend is $1.40 per share. During the previous day 678,800 (6,788 × 100) shares of Boeing common stock were traded. The prices of these transactions ranged from a high of $46.50 to a low of $45.50 per share. The day's closing price of $46.125 was $.625 (⅝ of one dollar) higher than the closing price of the preceding day.

What causes a change in a stock's price? The company's net income trend, the development of new products, court rulings, new legislation, business success, and upward market trends drive a stock's price up, and business failures and bad economic news pull it down. The market sets the price at which a stock changes hands.

Stock Investments

As we begin the discussion of investments in stock, let's define two key terms. The person or company that owns stock in a corporation is the *investor*. The corporation that issued the stock is the *investee*. If you own shares of Boeing common stock, you are an investor and Boeing is the investee.

A business may purchase another corporation's stock simply to put extra cash to work in the hope of earning dividends and gains on the sale of the stock. Alternatively, the business may make the investment to gain a degree of control over the investee's operation. After all, stock is ownership. An investor holding 25 percent of the outstanding stock of the investee owns one fourth of the business. This one-quarter voice in electing the directors of the corporation is likely to give the investor a lot of say in how the investee conducts its business. An investor holding more than 50 percent of the outstanding shares controls the investee.

Let's consider why one corporation might want to gain a say in another corporation's business. The investor may want to exert some control over the level of dividends paid by the investee. Or perhaps the investee has a line of products closely linked to the investor's own sales items. By influencing the investee's business, the investor may be able to exert some control on product distribution, product-line improvements, pricing strategies, and other important business considerations. A swimming-pool manufacturer might want to purchase stock in a diving-board company, a swimsuit maker, or some other corporation with related business.

Why doesn't the investor simply diversify its own operations, expanding into diving boards, swimsuits, and other related products? The cost may be too great. Also, the investor may not have experience with these other products. Why challenge a successful business in the marketplace when the investor can "buy into" a successful corporation's existing operations? The reasons for investing in a

EXHIBIT 17-2 *Reporting Investments on the Balance Sheet*

Current Assets	
Cash.	$X
Short-term investments	X
Accounts receivable	X
Inventories	X
Prepaid expenses	X
Total current assets	$X
Long-term investments (or simply Investments)	X
Property, plant, and equipment	X
Intangible assets	X
Other assets	X

corporation in order to affect its operations to some degree make corporate investments attractive to many businesses.

Investments are not without risk. To offset the ill effects of a sudden downturn in the operations of any one investee, smart investors hold a portfolio of stocks. The portfolio holds investments in different companies. By diversifying its holdings, the investor gains protection from losing too much if any one investee runs into problems and its stock price plummets.

Classifying Stock Investments

Investments in stock are assets to the investor. The investments may be short-term or long-term. Short-term investments are current assets. Because short-term investments may be sold any time the investor wishes, they are also called **marketable securities.** To be listed on the balance sheet as short-term, investments must be liquid (readily convertible to cash). Also, the investor must intend either to convert the investments to cash within one year or to use them to pay a current liability. Investments not meeting these two requirements are classified on the balance sheet as long-term.

Short-term investments include interest-bearing bank accounts, certificates of deposit, and stocks and bonds of other companies. *Long-term investments* include bond sinking funds and stocks and bonds that the investor expects to hold longer than one year or that are not readily marketable, for instance, real estate not used in the operations of the business. Exhibit 17-2 shows the positions of short-term and long-term investments on the balance sheet.

Observe that we report assets in the order of their liquidity. Cash is the most liquid asset, followed by Short-Term Investments, Accounts Receivable, and so on. Long-Term Investments are less liquid than Current Assets but more liquid than Property, Plant, and Equipment.

Accounting for Stock Investments

Accounting for stock investments varies with the nature and extent of the investment. The specific accounting method that GAAP directs us to follow depends first on whether the investment is short-term or long-term and second on the percentage of the investee's voting stock that the investor holds.

Short-term Investments—The Cost Method (with LCM)

The **cost method** (with lower of cost or market) is used to account for short-term investments in stock. *Cost* is used as the initial amount for recording investments and as the basis for measuring gains and losses on their sale. These investments are reported on the balance sheet at the *lower of their cost or market* value. Therefore, we refer to the overall method as cost (with lower of cost or market).

All investments, including short-term investments, are recorded initially at cost. Cost is the price paid for the stock plus the brokerage commission. Suppose that Dade, Inc., purchases 1,000 shares of Hewlett-Packard Company common stock at the market price of 36¼ and pays a $500 commission. Dade intends to sell this investment within one year or less and, therefore, classifies it as short-term. Dade's entry to record the investment is

July 23	Short-term Investment in Hewlett-Packard Common		
	Stock [(1,000 × $36.25) + $500]	36,750	
	Cash		36,750
	Purchased 1,000 shares of Hewlett-Packard common		
	stock at $36.25 plus commission of $500.		

OBJECTIVE 1

Account for investments by the cost (LCM) method

Assume Dade receives a $.22 per share cash dividend on the Hewlett-Packard stock. Dade's entry to record receipt of the dividends is

Oct. 14	Cash (1,000 × $.22)	220	
	Dividend Revenue		220
	Received $.22 per share cash dividend on Hewlett-Packard		
	common stock.		

Dividends do not accrue with the passage of time (as interest does). The investee has no liability for dividends until the dividends are declared. An investor makes no accrual entry for dividend revenue at year end in anticipation of a dividend declaration.

However, if a dividend declaration *does* occur before year end—say, on December 28—the investor debits Dividend Receivable and credits Dividend Revenue on that date. The investor reports this receivable and the revenue in the December 31 financial statements. Receipt of the cash dividend in January is recorded by a debit to Cash and a credit to Dividend Receivable.

Receipt of a *stock* dividend is *not* income to the investor, and no formal journal entry is needed. As we have seen, a stock dividend increases the number of shares held by the investor but does not affect the total cost of the investment. The cost per share of the stock investment therefore decreases. The investor usually makes a memorandum entry of the number of dividend shares received and the new cost per share. Assume that Dade, Inc., receives a 10 percent stock dividend on its 1,000-share investment in Hewlett-Packard Company, which cost $36,750. Dade would make a memorandum entry along this line:

Nov. 22   Received 100 shares of Hewlett-Packard common stock in 10 percent stock dividend. New cost per share is $33.41 ($36,750/1,100 shares).

Any gain or loss on the sale of the investment is the difference between the sale proceeds and the cost of the investment. Assume that Dade sells 400 shares of Hewlett-Packard stock for $35 per share, less a $280 commission. The entry to record the sale is

Dec. 18	Cash [(400 × $35) − $280]	13,720
	Short-Term Investment in Hewlett-Packard Common Stock (400 × $33.41).	13,364
	Gain on Sale of Investment	356
	Sold 400 shares of investment in Hewlett-Packard common stock.	

Observe that the cost per share of the investment ($33.41) is based on the total number of shares held, including those received as a dividend.

Reporting Short-Term Investments at Lower of Cost or Market (LCM)

Because of accounting conservatism, short-term investments in stock are reported at the lower of their cost or market (LCM) value. LCM is applied to the *entire* short-term investment portfolio, not to individual stocks in the portfolio. On the balance sheet date, the investor computes the total cost and the total market value of the short-term investment portfolio and reports the investments at the lower amount. Assume a company owns three short-term investments with the following costs and market values:

Short-term Investment Portfolio

Stock	Cost	Current Market Value
Ford Motor Co.	$122,000	$128,000
K mart.	79,000	74,000
Kellogg	160,000	142,000
Total	$361,000	$344,000

Because the total market value of the investment portfolio ($344,000) is less than cost ($361,000), the investor's balance sheet will report short-term investments at market value as follows:

Current Assets

Cash	$	XXX
Short-term investments, at market value (Note 4).		344,000
Accounts receivable, net of allowance of $XXX.		XXX

NOTE 4—SHORT-TERM INVESTMENTS:

Short-term investments are reported at the lower of their cost or market value. At December 31, 19XX, cost was $361,000.

If the portfolio cost is lower than market value, the investor reports short-term investments at cost and discloses market value in the note.

Long-Term Investments Accounted for by the Cost Method (with LCM)

An investor may own numerous investments, some short-term and others long-term. For accounting purposes, the two investment portfolios are *not* mixed. They are reported separately on the balance sheet, as shown in Exhibit 17-2. *Long-term* is not often used in the account title. An investment is understood to be long-term unless specifically labeled as short-term.

Accounting for long-term investments in which the investor holds less than 20 percent of the investee's voting stock follows the procedures outlined for short-term investments. The beginning accounting value is cost, which is debited to an Investments account at the date of purchase. Gains and losses are recorded on sales. Long-term investments are reported on the balance sheet at the lower of total portfolio cost or market value. Slight differences in accounting for long-term investments are covered in later accounting courses.

Long-Term Investments Accounted for by the Equity Method

The *cost* method (with LCM) of accounting for long-term investments applies when an investor holds less than 20 percent of the investee's voting stock. Such an investor usually plays no important role in the investee's operations. However, an investee with a larger stock holding—between 20 percent and 50 percent of the investee's voting stock—may *significantly influence* how the investee operates the business. Such an investor can likely affect the investee's decisions on dividend policy, product lines, sources of supply, and other important matters. Since the investor has a voice in shaping business policy and operations, accountants believe that some measure of the business's success and failure should be included in accounting for the investment. We use the **equity method** to account for investments in which the investor can significantly influence the decision of the investee.

Investments accounted for by the equity method are recorded initially at cost. Suppose Phillips Petroleum Company pays $400,000 for 30 percent of the common stock of White Rock Corporation. Phillips's entry to record the purchase of this investment is

Jan. 6	Investment in White Rock Common Stock..........	400,000	
	Cash		400,000
	To purchase 30% investment in White Rock common stock.		

Under the equity method, Phillips, as the investor, applies its percentage of ownership—30 percent, in our example—in recording its share of the investee's net income and dividends. If White Rock reports net income of $250,000 for the year, Phillips records 30 percent of this amount as an increase in the investment account and as equity-method investment revenue, as follows:

OBJECTIVE 2

Use the equity method for investments

Dec. 31	Investment in White Rock Common Stock		
	($250,000 × .30)	75,000	
	Equity-Method Investment Revenue		75,000
	To record 30% of White Rock net income.		

The Investment Revenue account carries the Equity-Method label to identify its source. This labeling is similar to distinguishing Sales Revenue from Service Revenue.

The investor increases the Investment account and records Investment Revenue when the investee reports income because of the close relationship between the two companies. As the investee's owner equity increases, so does the Investment account on the books of the investor.

Phillips records its proportionate part of cash dividends received from White Rock. Assuming White Rock declares and pays a cash dividend of $100,000, Phillips receives 30 percent of this dividend, recording it as follows:

Jan. 17 Cash ($100,000 × .30) 30,000
          Investment in White Rock Common Stock   30,000
         To record receipt of 30% of White Rock cash dividend.

Observe that the Investment account is credited for the receipt of a dividend on an equity-method investment. Why? Because the dividend decreases the investee's owner equity and so it also reduces the investor's investment. In effect, the investor received cash for this portion of the investment.

After the above entries are posted, Phillips's investment account reflects its equity in the net assets of White Rock:

Investment in White Rock Common Stock

19X1			19X2		
Jan. 6	Purchase	400,000	Jan. 17	Dividends	30,000
Dec. 31	Net income	75,000			
19X2					
Jan. 17	Balance	445,000			

Gain or loss on the sale of an equity-method investment is measured as the difference between the sale proceeds and the carrying value of the investment. For example, sale of one tenth of the White Rock common stock for $41,000 would be recorded as follows:

Feb. 13 Cash 41,000
        Loss on Sale of Investment 3,500
          Investment in White Rock Common Stock
             ($445,000 × 1/10)   44,500
         Sold one-tenth of investment in White Rock common
         stock.

Companies with investments accounted for by the equity method often refer to the investee as an *affiliated company.* The account title Investments in Affiliated Companies refers to investments that are accounted for by the equity method.

Consolidation Method

Most large corporations own controlling interests in other corporations. A **controlling** (or **majority**) **interest** is the ownership of more than 50 percent of the investee's voting stock. Such an investment enables the investor to elect a majority of the investee's board of directors and so control the investee. The investor is called the **parent company,** and the investee company is called the **subsidiary.** For example, Libbey-Owens-Ford, a glass manufacturer, is a subsidiary of General Motors Corporation, the parent. The stockholders of General Motors control GM, and because GM owns Libbey-Owens-Ford, the stockholders also control Libbey-Owens-Ford.

Consolidation accounting is a method of combining the financial statements of two or more companies that are controlled by the same owners. This method implements the entity concept by reporting a single set of financial statements for the consolidated entity, which carries the name of the parent company. The assets, liabilities, revenues, and expenses of each subsidiary are added to the parent's accounts. The consolidated financial statements—balance sheet, income statement, and so on—present the combined account balances. For example, the balance in the Cash account of Libbey-Owens-Ford is added to the balance in the GM Cash account, and the sum of the two amounts is presented as a single amount in the consolidated balance sheet of General Motors. Each account balance of a subsidiary loses its identity in the consolidated statements. GM's financial statements are entitled "General Motors Corporation and Consolidated Subsidiaries." Libby-Owens-Ford and the names of all other GM subsidiaries do not appear in the statement titles. But the names of the subsidiary companies are listed in the parent company's annual report.

No separate set of books exists for the consolidated entity. The parent company and the subsidiary company prepare their own financial statements separately. Accountants for the parent company then combine the two companies' statements into a single set of consolidated statements.

Combining balances in consolidation accounting requires special eliminating journal entries on a work sheet, which we examine later in the chapter. For example, the parent's books contain an Investment in Subsidiary account.[1] The subsidiary's books include its own owners' equity accounts. At least a part of its owners' equity balance is represented in the parent's investment account. That is, the same amount appears in the Investment in Subsidiary account of the parent and in the Common Stock account of the subsidiary. If these two accounts are combined in the consolidated statements, the *same resources* would be counted twice, which is clearly improper. In fact, intercompany accounts—those that appear in both the parent's books and the subsidiary's books—should *not* be included in consolidated statements at all.

Consider also an account receivable that the parent has from the subsidiary, or vice versa. The receivable and the payable represent the *same resources.* Because the receivable and the payable are entirely within the consolidated entity, they must be eliminated from the consolidated financial statements. Another way to state this is that the consolidated entity can have neither a receivable from, nor a payable to, itself. All intercompany accounts must be eliminated in the consolidated statements. Accountants accomplish this by making special eliminating journal entries, which we look at later in the chapter.

Consolidated Balance Sheet—Parent Company Owns All of Subsidiary's Stock.   Companies usually prepare a consolidated balance sheet immediately after the parent acquires a controlling interest in the subsidiary. This balance sheet provides the basis for evaluating the future progress of the consolidated entity.

Exhibit 17-3 shows the work sheet used to prepare a consolidated balance sheet immediately after Parent Company purchases Subsidiary Corporation. The amounts in the Parent and Subsidiary columns are taken directly from those companies' separate financial statements. The column labeled Eliminations summarizes the journal entries needed to eliminate amounts arising from intercompany transactions. The Consolidated Amounts column lists the balances that appear on the consolidated balance sheet.

We assume in this illustration that Parent Company has purchased all the outstanding common stock of Subsidiary Corporation at its book value of $150,000. Also, Subsidiary Corporation owes an $80,000 note payable to Parent Company. Let's look now at the elimination entries.

---

[1] The parent company may use either the cost method or the equity method for journal entries to the Investment account. Regardless of the method used, the consolidated statements are the same. Advanced accounting courses deal with this topic.

EXHIBIT 17-3   *Work Sheet for Consolidated Balance Sheet — Parent Company Owns All of Subsidiary's Stock*

Assets	Parent Company	Subsidiary Corporation	Eliminations Debit	Eliminations Credit	Consolidated Amounts
Cash	12,000	18,000			30,000
Notes receivable from Subsidiary	80,000	—		(a) 80,000	—
Inventory	104,000	91,000			195,000
Investment in Subsidiary.	150,000	—		(b) 150,000	—
Other assets	218,000	138,000			356,000
Total	564,000	247,000			581,000
Liabilities and Stockholders' Equity					
Accounts payable.	43,000	17,000			60,000
Notes payable	190,000	80,000	(a) 80,000		190,000
Common stock.	176,000	100,000	(b) 100,000		176,000
Retained earnings	155,000	50,000	(b) 50,000		155,000
Total	564,000	247,000	230,000	230,000	581,000

Explanation of Elimination Entries.   *Entry (a).* Parent Company loaned $80,000 to Subsidiary Corporation, and Subsidiary signed a note payable to Parent. Therefore, Parent's balance sheet includes an $80,000 note receivable and Subsidiary's balance sheet reports a note payable for this amount. This loan was entirely within the consolidated entity and so must be eliminated. Entry (*a*) accomplishes this. The $80,000 credit in the elimination column of the work sheet offsets Parent's debit balance in Notes Receivable from Subsidiary. After this work sheet entry, the consolidated amount for notes receivable is zero. The $80,000 debit in the elimination column offsets the credit balance of Subsidiary's notes payable, and the resulting consolidated amount for notes payable is the amount owed to businesses and people outside the consolidated entity.

> **OBJECTIVE 3**
> Consolidate parent and subsidiary balance sheets

> **OBJECTIVE 4**
> Eliminate intercompany items from a consolidated balance sheet

Entry (b). In Exhibit 17-3, the Parent Company balance sheet reports Investment in Subsidiary with a $150,000 debit balance. The balance sheet of Subsidiary Corporation includes Common Stock and Retained Earnings with combined balances totaling $150,000. Parent's investment is Subsidiary's owner equity. It would not be correct to include the same resources twice in the consolidated balance sheet. Therefore, the stock, additional paid-in capital, and retained earnings balances of the subsidiary should be eliminated from the consolidated statement because they are entirely intercompany accounts. Entry (b) credits the Investment account to eliminate its debit balance. It also eliminates the Subsidiary owners' equity by debiting its Common Stock for $100,000 and Retained Earnings for $50,000. The resulting consolidated balance sheet reports no Investment in Subsidiary account, and the Common Stock and Retained Earnings balances are those of Parent Company only. The consolidated balance sheet can be taken directly from the final column of the consolidation work sheet.

Parent Company Buys Subsidiary's Stock at a Price above Book Value.   A company may acquire a controlling interest in a subsidiary by paying a price above the book value of the subsidiary's owner equity. The excess of the price paid by the parent — the market value — over the subsidiary's book value is *goodwill.* What drives a company's market value up? The company may create goodwill through its superior products, service, or location. Goodwill is discussed in Chapter 10.

The subsidiary does not record goodwill. Doing so would violate the reliability principle. Goodwill is recorded only when a company purchases it as part of the acquisition of another company, that is, when a parent company purchases a subsidiary. The goodwill is recorded in the process of consolidating the parent and subsidiary financial statements.

Suppose Parent Company paid $450,000 to acquire 100 percent of the common stock of Subsidiary Corporation, which had Common Stock of $200,000 and Retained Earnings of $180,000. Parent's payment included $70,000 for goodwill ($450,000 − $200,000 − $180,000 = $70,000). The entry to eliminate Parent's Investment account against Subsidiary's equity accounts is

write off by straight line amortization

Dec. 31	Common Stock, Subsidiary....................	200,000	
	Retained Earnings, Subsidiary	180,000	
	Goodwill	70,000	
	Investment in Subsidiary		450,000
	To eliminate cost of investment in subsidiary against Subsidiary's equity balances and to recognize Subsidiary's unrecorded goodwill.		

In actual practice, this entry would be made only on the consolidation work sheet. Here we show it in general journal form for instructional purposes.

The asset goodwill is reported on the consolidated balance sheet among the intangible assets, after plant assets. Goodwill is amortized to expense over its useful life.

Consolidated Balance Sheet — Parent Company Owns Less Than 100 Percent of Subsidiary's Stock. When a parent company owns more than 50 percent (a majority) of the subsidiary's stock but less than 100 percent of it, a new category of owners' equity, called *minority interest*, must appear on the balance sheet. Sup-

EXHIBIT 17-4 *Work Sheet for Consolidated Balance Sheet — Parent Company Owns Less Than 100 Percent of Subsidiary's Stock*

Assets	P Company	S Company	Eliminations Debit	Eliminations Credit	Consolidated Amounts
Cash................................	33,000	18,000			51,000
Note receivable from P................	—	50,000		(a) 50,000	—
Accounts receivable, net...............	54,000	39,000			93,000
Inventory...........................	92,000	66,000			158,000
Investment in S......................	120,000	—		(b) 120,000	—
Plant and equipment, net..............	230,000	123,000			353,000
Total.............................	529,000	296,000			655,000
Liabilities and Stockholders' Equity					
Accounts payable	141,000	94,000			235,000
Notes payable	50,000	42,000	(a) 50,000		42,000
Common stock.......................	170,000	100,000	(b) 100,000		170,000
Retained earnings	168,000	60,000	(b) 60,000		168,000
Minority interest	—	—		(b) 40,000	40,000
Total.............................	529,000	296,000	210,000	210,000	655,000

pose Parent buys 75 percent of Subsidiary's common stock. The minority interest is the remaining 25 percent of Subsidiary's equity. Thus **minority interest** is the subsidiary's equity that is held by stockholders other than the parent company. Some companies report minority interest as a liability, while others show it as a separate element of stockholders' equity. In this book, we list minority interest as part of stockholders' equity on the consolidated balance sheet.

Assume P Company buys 75 percent of S Company's common stock. Also, P Company owes S Company $50,000 on a note payable. Exhibit 17-4 is the consolidation work sheet. Again, focus on the Eliminations columns and the Consolidation Amounts.

Entry (a) in Exhibit 17-4 eliminates S Company's $50,000 note receivable against P's note payable of the same amount. The consolidated amount of notes payable ($42,000) is the amount that S Company owes to outsiders.

Entry (b) eliminates P Company's Investment balance of $120,000 against the $160,000 owners' equity of S Company. Observe that all of S's equity is eliminated even though P holds only 75 percent of S's stock. The outside 25 percent interest in S's equity is credited to Minority Interest ($160,000 × .25 = $40,000). Thus entry (b) reclassifies 25 percent of S Company's equity as minority interest.

The consolidated balance sheet of P Company, based on the work sheet of Exhibit 17-4, is

P Company and Consolidated Subsidiary
Consolidated Balance Sheet
December 31, 19XX

Assets

Cash	$ 51,000
Accounts receivable, net	93,000
Inventory	158,000
Plant and equipment, net	353,000
Total assets	$655,000

Liabilities and Stockholders' Equity

Accounts payable	$235,000
Notes payable	42,000
Common stock	170,000
Retained earnings	168,000
Minority interest	40,000
Total liabilities and stockholders' equity	$655,000

The consolidated balance sheet reveals that ownership of P Company and its consolidated subsidiary is divided between P's stockholders (common stock and retained earnings totaling $338,000) and the minority stockholders of S Company ($40,000).

Income of a Consolidated Entity. The income of a consolidated entity is the net income of the parent plus the parent's proportion of the subsidiaries' net income. Suppose Parent Company owns all the stock of Subsidiary S-1 and 60 percent of the stock of Subsidiary S-2. During the year just ended, Parent earned net income of $330,000, S-1 earned $150,000, and S-2 had a net loss of $100,000. Parent Company would report net income of $420,000, computed as follows:

	Net Income (Net Loss)	Parent Stockholders' Ownership	Parent Net Income (Net Loss)
Parent Company	$330,000	100%	$330,000
Subsidiary S-1	150,000	100	150,000
Subsidiary S-2	(100,000)	60	(60,000)
Consolidated net income. . .			$420,000

The parent's net income is the same amount that would be recorded under the equity method. However, the equity method stops short of reporting the investees' assets and liabilities on the parent balance sheet because with an investment in the range of 20–50 percent, the investor owns less than a controlling interest in the investee company.

The procedures for preparation of a consolidated income statement parallel those outlined above for the balance sheet. The consolidated income statement is discussed in an advanced course. Exhibit 17-5 summarizes the accounting methods for investments.

EXHIBIT 17-5 *Accounting Methods for Investments*

Type of Investments	Accounting Method
Short-term investment	Cost (lower of cost or market)
Long-term investment:	
Investor owns less than 20 percent of investee stock	Cost (lower of cost or market)
Investor owns between 20 and 50 percent of investee stock	Equity
Investor owns greater than 50 percent of investee stock	Consolidation

Summary Problem for Your Review

This problem consists of four independent items.

1. Identify the appropriate accounting method for each of the following situations:
   (a) Investment in 25 percent of investee's stock
   (b) Short-term investment
   (c) Investment in more than 50 percent of investee's stock
2. At what amount should the following long-term investment portfolio be reported? All the investments are less than 5 percent of the investee's stock.

Stock	Investment Cost	Current Market Value
Eastman Kodak	$ 5,000	$12,500
Exxon	61,200	53,000
General Motors	3,680	6,230

3. Investor paid $67,900 to acquire a 40 percent equity-method investment in the common stock of Investee. At the end of the first year, Investee's net income was $80,000, and Investee declared and paid cash dividends of $55,000. Journalize Investor's (a) purchase of the investment, (b) share of Investee's net income, (c) receipt of dividends from Investee, and (d) sale of Investee stock for $80,100.

4. Parent Company paid $100,000 for all the common stock of Subsidiary Company, and Parent owes Subsidiary $20,000 on a note payable. Complete the following consolidation work sheet:

Assets	Parent Company	Subsidiary Company	Eliminations Debit	Eliminations Credit	Consolidated Amounts
Cash	7,000	4,000			
Note receivable from Parent	—	20,000			
Investment in Subsidiary........................	100,000	—			
Goodwill..	—	—			
Other assets	108,000	99,000			_____
Total	215,000	123,000			════════
Liabilities and Stockholders' Equity					
Accounts payable...............................	15,000	8,000			
Notes payable..................................	20,000	30,000			
Common stock	135,000	60,000			
Retained earnings..............................	45,000	25,000	_____	_____	_____
Total	215,000	123,000	════════	════════	════════

SOLUTION TO SUMMARY PROBLEM

1. (a) Equity   (b) Cost (LCM)   (c) Consolidation

2. Report the investments at cost, $69,880, because cost is less than market.

Stock	Investment Cost	Current Market Value
Eastman Kodak..............................	$ 5,000	$12,500
Exxon......................................	61,200	53,000
General Motors.............................	3,680	6,230
Totals.....................................	$69,880	$71,730

3.

a. Investment in Investee Common Stock............... 67,900
       Cash......................................   67,900
       To purchase 40% investment in Investee common stock.

b. Investment in Investee Common Stock
       ($80,000 × .40) 32,000
           Equity-Method Investment Revenue............   32,000
       To record 40% of Investee net income.

c. Cash ($55,000 × .40) 22,000
           Investment in Investee Common Stock..........   22,000
       To record receipt of 40% of Investee cash dividend.

d. Cash.. 80,100

    Investment in Investee Common Stock
        ($67,900 + $32,000 − $22,000)   77,900

    Gain on Sale of Investment   2,200

    Sold investment in Investee common stock.

4. Consolidation work sheet:

Assets	Parent Company	Subsidiary Company	Eliminations Debit	Eliminations Credit	Consolidated Amounts
Cash....................................	7,000	4,000			11,000
Note receivable from Parent...............	—	20,000		(a) 20,000	—
Investment in Subsidiary	100,000	—		(b) 100,000	—
Goodwill	—	—	(b) 15,000		15,000
Other assets...........................	108,000	99,000			207,000
Total.................................	215,000	123,000			233,000
Liabilities and Stockholders' Equity					
Accounts payable	15,000	8,000			23,000
Notes payable	20,000	30,000	(a) 20,000		30,000
Common stock	135,000	60,000	(b) 60,000		135,000
Retained earnings	45,000	25,000	(b) 25,000		45,000
Total.................................	215,000	123,000	120,000	120,000	233,000

Accounting for the Effects of Changing Prices (Inflation)

We use accounting information for making economic decisions. Of course, these decisions can only be as good as the information that we weigh in making them. Critics charge that accounting fails to provide the most accurate information possible because it fails to measure the effects of price changes. How intelligent, then, can our economic decisions be?

Assume that Brehme Company bought a building 20 years ago for $500,000. Management recorded straight-line depreciation using a 30-year estimated useful life and residual value of $50,000. Annual depreciation is $15,000 [($500,000 − $50,000)/30]. At the end of 20 years, the balance sheet lists the building carrying value at $200,000 [$500,000 − ($15,000 × 20)]. However, over the last 50 years or so, prices in general have risen, an increase we call inflation. During inflation historical costs on the balance sheet may bear little resemblance to current values. Assume that rising prices have pushed the current cost—what Brehme would pay for the building today—up to $1 million.

The difference between what the balance sheet lists as the carrying value of the building—$200,000—and its current cost—$1 million—is large. Also, since the value of the building has increased over time, a year's current-cost depreciation is greater than the $15,000 computed at the start of the building's life. If we raise depreciation expense to take into account the effect of rising prices, then we lower each year's net income figure. Suppose you were using the Brehme Company balance sheet and income statement for decision making. Would you feel confident making an economic decision based solely on the historical-cost information?

We know that GAAP directs companies to assume the stable-monetary-unit concept when preparing financial statements. For accounting purposes, companies use the historical cost of the building throughout the building's lifetime. However, critics maintain that historical-cost accounting does not provide the necessary information to allow statement users to make intelligent decisions. Is it valid to assume a stable monetary unit when prices—and the dollar's value itself—change over time?

An increase in the general price level is called **inflation.** The general price level is the weighted average of the prices of all goods and services in the economy. Changes in the general price level are measured by a general price index that assigns a value of 100 to a base year. The price index tracks the movement of prices in the economy over time. A 6 percent price increase during year 1 would cause the price index to rise to a value of 106 (100 × 1.06) at the end of the year. A 50 percent increase in prices over a six-year period would result in a price index of 150 (100 × 1.50) at the end of six years.

The most widely used general price index in the United States is the Consumer Price Index (CPI), published monthly by the U.S. Department of Labor. The CPI is based on a representative sample of food, clothing, shelter, transportation, and other items purchased by an average consumer. The base period for the CPI is 1967. Each month the average of these items' prices is compared to their prices the preceding month, and a new price index is computed. This price index reached the 300 mark in 1983, indicating that the general level of prices tripled over 16 years.

Another way to describe inflation is in terms of the purchasing power of the dollar. A dollar will buy less meat, less gasoline, less laundering for shirts and blouses, and less of most other goods and services than a dollar would buy in 1967. Inflation, therefore, can also be defined as a decrease in the purchasing power of the dollar.

How does inflation affect accounting? This question does not have a simple answer. Two approaches have received considerable attention from the FASB.

1. *Constant-dollar accounting* presents the financial statements adjusted to reflect dollars of equal purchasing power. The adjustment, based on the economywide movement of prices, uses the Consumer Price Index. Assume that a building cost $100,000 when the CPI was 100. In the current period, the CPI is 130. This building would be adjusted into a constant-dollar equivalent of $130,000 (historical cost of $100,000 multiplied by the increased general price level, 130/100). Another way to describe the $130,000 constant-dollar measure of the building: it would take 130,000 current-period dollars to equal the 100,000 dollars that were actually paid to acquire the building.

2. *Current-cost accounting* ignores historical cost altogether. The **current cost** of an asset is the present cost of replacing its particular service potential, or usefulness. Suppose it would cost $180,000 currently to replace the building in the preceding illustration. A current-cost balance sheet reports the building at $180,000. A current-cost income statement bases depreciation expense on the building's current cost. For example, if the building has a 30-year life with no residual value, current-cost depreciation is $6,000 ($180,000/30) per year.

FASB Pronouncements on the Effects of Changing Prices

Until 1979 financial statements prepared under GAAP were based solely on historical costs. That year the FASB began requiring large public corporations to report in the notes of their financial statements supplemental information on the effects of changing prices. The supplemental data consisted of a note that showed three income statements in parallel columns: historical cost, constant dollar, and current cost. The note also reported the current cost of selected assets. In 1984 the FASB ceased requiring the constant-dollar income statement, and in 1986 the supplemental disclosures became voluntary. At that time many companies ceased their disclosures of the effects of changing prices. The changing price data that companies have disclosed combine elements of constant-dollar accounting and current-cost accounting. Therefore, we refer to the supplemental data as current-cost/constant-dollar information. The discussion that follows is based on the current-cost/constant-dollar information that companies have reported most recently. For brevity we often refer to this simply as current-cost information.

Overview of Current-Cost/Constant-Dollar Accounting

As we have discussed, **current-cost accounting** uses the current cost of the company's assets and expenses in place of their historical cost. For many assets—such as cash, receivables, investments, and prepaid expenses—either current cost is not materially different from historical cost or the asset is not sufficiently material to warrant special changing-price disclosures. For these assets, the historical-cost basis is used with no adjustment for current cost.

Inventory and plant assets are usually two of a company's most valuable assets. These items' current costs often differ greatly from their historical cost. Therefore, current-cost accounting focuses on inventory and plant assets and the related expenses, which are cost of goods sold and depreciation. A current-cost balance sheet looks exactly like one prepared on the historical-cost basis, except that the current costs of the company's inventory and plant assets are substituted for their historical cost amounts, and stockholders' equity is adjusted accordingly. A current-cost income statement is the same as a historical-cost income statement but with the current-cost amounts of cost of goods sold and depreciation substituted in place of historical cost. The current-cost income statement also includes additional information that we explain later.

Actual Example of Current-Cost/Constant-Dollar Information

Exhibit 17-6 presents data that are adapted from the actual financial statements of AMF Incorporated, best known for its bowling products. Statement of Operations in the heading is a synonym for income statement. The items to be explained in more detail are highlighted for emphasis.

Current-Cost/Constant-Dollar Income Statement

Exhibit 17-6's heading indicates that the information on changing prices is supplemental to the historical-cost financial statements. The statement of operations, or income statement, includes two columns. The first column repeats the historical-cost income statement reported in the primary financial statements. The second column is a current-cost income statement. Total revenue; selling, general,

EXHIBIT 17-6 *Supplemental Statement of Operations Adjusted for Inflation*

AMF Incorporated		
Supplemental Statement of Operations Adjusted for Inflation		
Year Ended December 31, 19X4		
(millions of dollars)		

	Historical Cost	Current-Cost/ Constant-Dollar
Total revenue	$1,095	$1,095
Cost of sales	$ 703	$ 709
Selling, general, and administrative expenses ...	294	294
Depreciation................................	60	78
Interest expense, net.........................	9	9
Income taxes................................	14	14
Total expenses	1,080	1,104
Income (loss) from continuing operations	$ 15	$ (9)
Gain from decline in purchasing power of net amounts owed		$ 5
Increase in the current cost of the company's inventories and property...................		$ 43
Effect of general inflation		24
Excess of the increase in the current cost of the company's inventories and property over the effect of general inflation		$ 19

Additional current-cost information:

At December 31, 19X4, the current cost of inventories was $203 million (compared to $151 million historical cost), and the net current cost of property, plant, and equipment was $501 million (compared to $365 million historical cost).

OBJECTIVE 5

Report current-cost/ constant-dollar income statement information

and administrative expenses; interest expense; and income taxes are the same at historical cost and at current cost, so these items need no adjustment.

Cost of sales (cost of goods sold) and depreciation have current-cost amounts that differ from historical cost. AMF's historical cost of sales is $703 million, compared to $709 million at current cost. The higher current-cost amount means that AMF's cost of replacing its inventory increased between the time it was acquired and the time it was sold. Cost of goods sold at current cost is computed by totaling the replacement cost of the inventory at the time it is sold. For example, suppose AMF sold bowling inventory that the company manufactured at a cost of $100. The company's historical cost of goods sold is $100. Assume the current replacement cost of the inventory is $108 at the time it is sold. The current-cost measure for cost of goods sold is therefore $108. AMF's overall cost of goods sold at current cost ($709 million) is the sum of the current costs of all the goods sold.

Depreciation expense, at historical cost, is $60 million, compared to $78 million at current cost. Computing current-cost depreciation is similar to computing historical-cost depreciation. AMF's financial statements indicate the company depreciates its assets over approximately 12 years on a straight-line basis. The current cost of AMF's depreciable assets, before accumulated depreciation, is approximately $940 million. Assuming zero residual value, current-cost depreciation for the year is $78 million ($940 million/12 years = $78 million). This current-cost depreciation amount means that AMF could expect to pay $78 million *currently* to replace the portion of its depreciable assets that the company used in operations during the year. Because AMF purchased its assets when prices were lower, the company's historical-cost depreciation was lower ($60 million).

Income from continuing operations for the year is $15 million at historical cost. At current cost, the result is a loss of $9 million. This comparison suggests that inflation has turned AMF's operating profit into a loss. Supporters of current-cost accounting point out that a company must replace the inventory it has sold and its worn-out plant assets to remain in business. They believe the current-cost measure of income is more informative than historical cost.

You may have been wondering where constant-dollar accounting enters the income statement. The revenues and the expenses are all stated in constant dollars of the current year. The items immediately beneath income from continuing operations in Exhibit 17-6 also reflect constant-dollar accounting. We turn our attention to their explanation now.

Purchasing-Power Gain or Loss

Exhibit 17-6 reports "Gain from decline in the purchasing power of net amounts owed." The gain is $5 million. This gain is also called the **purchasing-power gain.** It occurs during inflation because the company is able to pay its liabilities with dollars that are cheaper than the dollars borrowed.

What does the purchasing-power gain mean? Suppose you borrow $5,000 to purchase a sailboat. You repay the loan after two years, during which time prices have risen 20 percent. If you are obligated to pay only $5,000 (ignoring interest for the moment), you experience a purchasing-power gain of $1,000 ($5,000 multiplied by the inflation rate of 20 percent). The creditor who loaned you the money incurs the corresponding **purchasing-power loss** of $1,000 because the dollars the creditor receives when you repay the loan are worth less than the dollars lent. Interest rates are intended to compensate for this purchasing-power gain or loss, but interest is accounted for separately. In Exhibit 17-6, AMF reports interest expense apart from the change in purchasing power.

The purchasing-power gain or loss depends on the company's monetary assets and monetary liabilities. **Monetary assets** are assets whose values are stated in a fixed number of dollars. This amount does *not* change, regardless of inflation. Examples include cash and receivables. Cash of $1,000 remains cash of $1,000 whether inflation occurs or not. If you hold $1,000 cash during a period of inflation, your $1,000 will buy fewer goods and services at the end of the period. The result is a purchasing-power loss. Likewise, if you sell $1,500 of merchandise on account and you receive the cash after a period of inflation, you receive only $1,500. Holding the receivable results in a purchasing-power loss.

Nonmonetary assets are those assets whose prices do change during inflation. Examples include inventory, land, buildings, and equipment. Holding nonmonetary assets does not result in a purchasing-power gain or loss.

Monetary liabilities are liabilities that are stated in a fixed number of dollars. Most liabilities are monetary. As discussed above in the sailboat example, you have a purchasing-power gain if you have a monetary liability during inflation.

The computation of the purchasing-power gain or loss is based on the company's **net monetary position** (monetary assets minus monetary liabilities). If the company has more monetary assets than monetary liabilities, it has **net monetary assets.** If its monetary liabilities exceed its monetary assets, it has **net monetary liabilities.** Most industrial corporations have net-monetary-liability positions and experience purchasing-power gains. Most financial institutions, such as banks, savings and loans, and insurance companies, have net-monetary-asset positions. They usually incur purchasing-power losses during inflation. A company's monetary assets and liabilities can be taken from its historical-cost balance sheet. Exhibit 17-7 shows the computation of AMF's purchasing power gain of $5 million.

EXHIBIT 17-7   *Purchasing-Power Gain*

AMF Incorporated
Gain from Decline in Purchasing Power of Net Amounts Owed (Purchasing-Power Gain)
Year Ended December 31, 19X4
(millions of dollars)

	Historical Cost	Constant-Dollar Adjustments for Inflation
Net monetary liabilities, beginning (Dec. 31, 19X3)...	\$126	$\times \dfrac{311.1}{303.5} = \$129$
Increase in net monetary liabilities during 19X4	27	27
Subtotal.....................................		156
Net monetary liabilities, ending (Dec. 31, 19X4)	\$153	$\times \dfrac{311.1}{315.5} =$ 151
Purchasing-power gain		\$ 5

The computation of the purchasing-power gain in Exhibit 17-7 follows the FASB approach. At December 31, 19X3 (the beginning of 19X4), AMF had a net-monetary-liability position of \$126 million. During 19X4 the company increased its net monetary liabilities by \$27 million and ended 19X4 with a net-monetary-liability position of \$153 million. These amounts are in the Historical Cost column. The historical 19X3 and 19X4 net-monetary-liability positions are not comparable because they are stated in dollars of different purchasing power. The beginning position is stated in December 19X3 dollars, which are not comparable to the December 19X4 dollars used in the ending balance. The reason is that the general price level in the United States increased during 19X4—that is, general inflation occurred. To compute AMF's overall purchasing-power gain or loss, it is necessary to make the beginning and ending monetary positions comparable.

The inflation adjustments of AMF's net monetary liabilities are in Exhibit 17-7 under the column Constant-Dollar Adjustments for Inflation. The data in that column restate the beginning and ending net-monetary-liability positions to dollars of constant purchasing power. The Consumer Price Index (CPI) is used for this adjustment. At the beginning of 19X4, when AMF had net monetary liabilities of \$126 million, the Consumer Price Index was 303.5. For 19X4 the average CPI was 311.1.

The beginning historical-cost balance is restated into average constant dollars of 19X4 by multiplying it by the ratio of the current-year average index (311.1) to the beginning price index (303.5). The numerator of the price-index ratio is the current-year average index, and the denominator is the price index that was in effect on the date of the balance. The adjustment of the beginning balance is (amounts rounded to the nearest million dollars)

$$\begin{array}{ccc} \textbf{Beginning} \\ \textbf{Net Monetary} \\ \textbf{Liabilities} \end{array} \times \dfrac{\textbf{Current-Year Average}}{\begin{array}{c}\textbf{Consumer Price Index}\\ \hline \textbf{Beginning-of-Year}\\ \textbf{Consumer Price Index}\end{array}} = \begin{array}{c}\textbf{Beginning Net Monetary}\\ \textbf{Liabilities Stated in Average Constant}\\ \textbf{Dollars of the Current Year}\end{array}$$

$$\$126 \quad \times \quad \dfrac{311.1}{303.5} \quad = \quad \$129$$

The change in net monetary liabilities during 19X4 ($27 million) is *not* adjusted because it occurred as the company transacted business all during the year. The average price index (311.1) is both the numerator and the denominator of the index ratio, resulting in a ratio of 1.

The subtotal in Exhibit 17-7 ($156 million) is the sum of the adjusted beginning net monetary liabilities plus the increase (or minus the decrease) in net monetary liabilities that arose from the transactions of the year. During 19X4 AMF *increased* its net monetary liabilities by $27 million. The subtotal of $156 million is the amount of net monetary liabilities that AMF would owe if the company's monetary assets and liabilities had just kept pace with inflation during the year.

The ending historical-cost balance ($153 million) is restated into average constant dollars of 19X4 by multiplying it by the ratio of the current-year average index (311.1) to the ending price index (315.5). The adjustment of the ending balance is (amounts rounded to the nearest million dollars)

$$\text{Ending Net Monetary Liabilities} \times \frac{\text{Current-Year Average Consumer Price Index}}{\text{End-of-Year Consumer Price Index}} = \text{Ending Net Monetary Liabilities Stated in Average Constant Dollars of the Current Year}$$

$$\$153 \times \frac{311.1}{315.5} = \$151$$

The purchasing-power gain can now be computed. Its amount is determined by subtracting the ending adjusted net monetary liability balance ($151 million) from the subtotal ($156 million). If AMF had just kept pace with general inflation during 19X4, its net-monetary-liability position would have been $156 million. But at year end, the company's net monetary liabilities are only $151 million. The result is a purchasing-power gain of $5 million. AMF's gain resulted primarily from (a) inflation during 19X4 and (b) the company's net-monetary-liability position during the year. If the company had had more monetary assets than liabilities during inflation, it would have experienced a purchasing-power loss.

The purchasing-power gain computation is useful for determining how well the entity is managing its monetary position during inflation. Purchasing-power gain (or loss) can be applied to individual persons as well as to businesses of all sizes.

Increase in the Current Cost of Inventories and Property, Plant, and Equipment

Exhibit 17-6 indicates that the current cost of AMF's inventories and property (plant assets) increased by $43 million during 19X4. Historical-cost accounting ignores such increases in assets because they are not the result of completed transactions.

The effect of *general inflation* on the current cost of the company's inventories and property during 19X4 was an increase of $24 million. Thus if the current costs of these assets had just kept pace with general inflation in the United States economy during 19X4, their current costs would have increased by $24 million.

The excess of the current-cost increase ($43 million) over the effect of general inflation ($24 million) is a measure of the *net* increase in the market value of the company's assets during the year. This excess of $19 million indicates that the current cost of AMF's assets increased faster during 19X4 than the rate of general inflation. According to the FASB, this net increase reflects favorably on the company. To better understand its meaning, let's consider an alternative.

Suppose that AMF's inventories and property had increased in value by only $24 million and that this entire increase resulted from economy wide inflation.

Would the increase suggest that the company's real value had grown during the year? No. It would mean that the company had just kept up with the average increase in the price of all commodities that make up the Consumer Price Index. However, the excess increase of $19 million, net of the effect of general inflation, indicates that the company's assets are increasing in value faster than economy-wide inflation.

Current-Cost/Constant-Dollar Balance Sheet

The bottom section of Exhibit 17-6 reports that AMF's inventory had a current cost of $203 million at December 31, 19X4, compared to historical cost of $151 million. The current cost of the company's property, plant, and equipment, net of accumulated depreciation, was $501 million, compared to $365 million at historical cost. These current-cost amounts reveal the current values of AMF's assets, and these amounts may be of interest to investors and creditors. An investor can substitute these current costs in place of historical costs to prepare a current-cost balance sheet. Exhibit 17-8 presents a condensed current-cost/constant-dollar balance sheet for AMF with items of special interest highlighted.

Exhibit 17-8 reports AMF's current costs of inventories and plant assets next to the historical costs. The current costs are higher than historical costs. Liabilities do not change significantly on a current-cost balance sheet, so the current-cost measure of stockholders' equity increases by the amount of the increase in asset value. AMF's stockholders' equity at current cost is $644 million. It is computed as total assets of $1,127 million minus total liabilities of $483 million. Stockholders' equity at current cost far exceeds the historical-cost measure of $456 million. The company's investors and creditors may take comfort in these higher values of assets and owners' equity.

Summary of Current-Cost Information

The current-cost disclosures of AMF Incorporated provide the following information about the company.

1. Exhibit 17-6 — Current-Cost/Constant-Dollar Income Statement:
   a. Current cost of goods sold and depreciation exceed the historical measures

EXHIBIT 17-8 *Condensed Balance Sheets*

AMF Incorporated Condensed Balance Sheets — Historical Cost and Current-Cost/Constant Dollar December 31, 19X4 (millions of dollars)		
	Historical Cost	**Current-Cost/ Constant-Dollar**
Cash, short-term investments, receivables, prepaid expenses, and other current assets	$364	$ 364
Inventories	151	203
Property, plant, and equipment, net	365	501
Intangible and other assets	59	59
Total assets	$939	$1,127
Total liabilities	$483	$ 483
Stockholders' equity	456	644
Total liabilities and stockholders' equity............	$939	$1,127

OBJECTIVE 7

Prepare a current-cost/constant-dollar balance sheet

of these expenses. The result of continuing operations at current cost was a $9 million *loss,* compared to *income* of $15 million at historical cost.

b. The gain from decline in purchasing power of net amounts owed (purchasing-power gain on net monetary liabilities) for the year was $5 million. Exhibit 17-7 shows the computation of this gain.

c. The current cost of the company's inventories and property (plant assets) increased during the year by $19 million *more* than the effect of general inflation.

2. Exhibit 17-8 — Current-Cost/Constant-Dollar Balance Sheet:

a. The current costs of AMF's inventories and plant assets are substantially higher than their historical cost.

b. The company's stockholder equity is greater than stockholders' equity at historical cost.

What is the overall interpretation of the current-cost/constant-dollar data? There is no single correct answer to this question. Evidence to date suggests that the current-cost data have not been considered very useful. However, experience with accounting for the effects of changing prices in the United States is too limited for a final evaluation.

Summary Problem for Your Review

McLaughlin, Inc., reported the following historical-cost financial statements at December 31, 19X5:

McLaughlin, Inc.
Income Statement
Year Ended December 31, 19X5

Sales revenue	$300,000
Cost of goods sold	$144,000
Operating expenses (excluding depreciation)	65,000
Depreciation	11,000
Income taxes	32,000
Total expenses	252,000
Net income	$ 48,000

McLaughlin, Inc.
Balance Sheet
December 31, 19X5

Current assets other than inventory	$ 53,000
Inventory	122,000
Plant assets, net	273,000
Goodwill and other assets	14,000
Total assets	$462,000
Total liabilities	$219,000
Stockholders' equity	243,000
Total liabilities and stockholders' equity	$462,000

McLaughlin's current cost of goods sold for 19X5 was $162,000, and current-cost depreciation was $18,000. Net monetary liabilities were $133,000 at December 31, 19X4, when the price index was 100. At December 31, 19X5, net monetary liabilities were $148,000, and the price index was 112. The average price index for 19X5 was 106. During 19X5 the current cost of the company's inventory and plant assets increased by $44,000, but the effect of general inflation was an increase of $51,000. At December 31, 19X5, the current cost of inventory was $145,000, and the current cost of plant assets, net of depreciation, was $343,000.

Required

Prepare a comparative historical-cost and current-cost/constant-dollar income statement and balance sheet patterned after Exhibits 17-6 and 17-8. Include computation of the purchasing-power gain or loss similar to Exhibit 17-7. Round all amounts to the nearest thousand dollars.

SOLUTION TO REVIEW PROBLEM

McLaughlin, Inc.
Income Statement
Year Ended December 31, 19X5

	Historical Cost	Current-Cost/ Constant-Dollar
Sales revenue	$300,000	$300,000
Cost of goods sold	$144,000	$162,000
Operating expenses (excluding depreciation)	65,000	65,000
Depreciation	11,000	18,000
Income taxes	32,000	32,000
Total expenses	252,000	277,000
Net income	$ 48,000	$ 23,000
Purchasing-power gain on net monetary liabilities (computed on the following page)		$ 16,000
Increase in the current cost of inventory and plant assets		$ 44,000
Effect of general inflation		51,000
Excess of the effect of general inflation over the increase in the current cost of inventory and plant assets		$ 7,000

McLaughlin, Inc.
Balance Sheet
December 31, 19X5

	Historical Cost	Current-Cost/ Constant-Dollar
Current assets other than inventory	$ 53,000	$ 53,000
Inventory	122,000	145,000
Plant assets, net	273,000	343,000
Goodwill and other assets	14,000	14,000
Total assets	$462,000	$555,000
Total liabilities	$219,000	$219,000
Stockholders' equity	243,000	336,000
Total liabilities and stockholders' equity	$462,000	$555,000

McLaughlin, Inc.
Purchasing Power Gain
Year Ended December 31, 19X5

	Historical Cost	Adjusted for Inflation
Net monetary liabilities, beginning (Dec. 31, 19X4)	$133,000 $\times \dfrac{106}{100}$ =	$141,000
Change in net monetary liabilities during 19X5	15,000	15,000
Subtotal......................................		156,000
Net monetary liabilities, ending (Dec. 31, 19X5).......	$148,000 $\times \dfrac{106}{112}$ =	140,000
Purchasing power gain...........................		$ 16,000

Summary

Investments are classified as short term or long term. *Short-term investments* are liquid, and the investor intends to convert them to cash within one year or less or to use them to pay a current liability. All other investments are *long term.*

Different methods are used to account for stock investments, depending on the investor's degree of influence over the investee. All investments are recorded initially at *cost.* Short-term investments and long-term investments of less than 20 percent of the investee's stock are accounted for by the cost method (with lower-of-cost-or-market). These investments are reported on the balance sheet at the lower of their cost or current market (LCM) value. Separate LCM determinations apply to the short-term investment portfolio and the long-term portfolio.

The *equity* method is used to account for investments of between 20 and 50 percent of the investee company's stock. Such an investment enables the investor to significantly influence the investee's activities. Investee income is recorded by the investor by debiting the Investment account and crediting an account entitled Equity-Method Investment Revenue. The investor records receipt of dividends from the investee by crediting the Investment account.

Ownership of more than 50 percent of the voting stock creates a parent-subsidiary relationship, and the *consolidation* method must be used. Because the parent has control over the subsidiary, the subsidiary's financial statements are included in the consolidated statements of the parent company. Two features of consolidation accounting are (1) addition of the parent and subsidiary accounts to prepare the parent's consolidated statements and (2) elimination of intercompany items. When a parent owns less than 100 percent of the subsidiary's stock, the portion owned by outside investors is called *minority interest.* Purchase of a controlling interest at a cost greater than the book value of the subsidiary creates an intangible asset called *goodwill.* A consolidation work sheet is used to prepare the consolidated financial statements.

Accounting for the effects of changing prices includes preparation of a supplemental income statement on a *current-cost/constant-dollar* basis. Current cost is the cost of replacing the company's assets with assets of equal service potential. The constant-dollar element means presenting the financial statements in dollars of equal purchasing power.

Additional changing price disclosures include the company's *purchasing-power gain or loss* on its net monetary items and *changes in the current cost* of the company's inventory and plant assets, net of the effect of general inflation. Companies also disclose the current cost of their *inventories* and *plant assets.* These data can be used to prepare a current-cost balance sheet. The current-cost/constant-dollar disclosures became voluntary in 1986.

Self-Study Questions

Test your understanding of the chapter by marking the best answer for each of the following questions.

1. Short-term investments are reported on the balance sheet *(p. 657)*
   a. Immediately after cash
   b. Immediately after accounts receivable
   c. Immediately after inventory
   d. Immediately after current assets

2. Byforth, Inc., distributes a 10 percent stock dividend. An investor who owns Byforth stock should *(p. 658)*
   a. Debit Investment and credit Dividend Revenue for the par value of the stock received in the dividend distribution
   b. Debit Investment and credit Dividend Revenue for the market value of the stock received in the dividend distribution
   c. Debit Cash and credit Investment for the market value of the stock received in the dividend distribution
   d. Make a memorandum entry to record the new cost per share of Byforth stock held

3. Short-term investments are reported at the *(p. 659)*
   a. Total cost of the portfolio
   b. Total market value of the portfolio
   c. Lower of total cost or total market value of the portfolio
   d. Total equity value of the portfolio

4. Putsch Corporation owns 30 percent of the voting stock of Mazelli, Inc. Mazelli reports net income of $100,000 and declares and pays cash dividends of $40,000. Which method should Putsch use to account for this investment? *(p. 660)*
   a. Cost (with LCM)
   b. Market value
   c. Equity
   d. Consolidation

5. Refer to the facts of the preceding question. What effect do Mazelli's income and dividends have on Putsch's net income? *(pp. 660, 661)*
   a. Increase of $12,000
   b. Increase of $18,000
   c. Increase of $30,000
   d. Increase of $42,000

6. In applying the consolidation method, elimination entries are *(p. 662)*
   a. Necessary
   b. Required only when the parent has a receivable from, or a payable to, the subsidiary
   c. Required only when there is a minority interest
   d. Required only for the preparation of the consolidated balance sheet

7. Parent Company has separate net income of $155,000. Subsidiary A, which Parent owns 90 percent of, reports net income of $60,000, and Subsidiary B, which Parent owns 60 percent of, reports net income of $80,000. What is Parent Company's consolidated net income? *(pp. 665, 666)*
   a. $155,000
   b. $257,000
   c. $263,000
   d. $295,000

8. The main differences between historical-cost and current-cost measures of income from continuing operations result from *(p. 671)*
   a. Inventory and plant assets
   b. Cost of goods sold and depreciation
   c. Purchasing-power gain or loss
   d. Changes in the general price level

9. Holding a net-monetary-asset position during a period of inflation results in a *(p. 672)*
   a. Purchasing-power gain
   b. Purchasing-power loss
   c. Neither a purchasing-power gain nor a loss
   d. Lower income from continuing operations

10. The historical-cost balance sheet reports total assets of $400,000 (including inventory of $100,000 and net plant assets of $120,000), total liabilities of $150,000, and stockholders' equity of $250,000. The current cost of inventory is $110,000, and the

current cost of net plant assets is $180,000. What is the current-cost measure of this company's stockholders' equity? *(p. 675)*

a. $250,000   c. $310,000

b. $260,000   d. $320,000

Answers to the self-study questions are at the end of the chapter.

Accounting Vocabulary

consolidation method for investments *(p. 661)*, controlling (majority) interest *(p. 661)*, cost method for investments *(p. 658)*, current cost *(p. 669)*, current-cost accounting *(p. 670)*, equity method for investments *(p. 660)*, inflation *(p. 669)*, marketable security *(p. 657)*, minority interest *(p. 665)*, monetary asset *(p. 672)*, monetary liability *(p. 672)*, net monetary assets *(p. 672)*, net monetary liabilities *(p. 672)*, nonmonetary asset *(p. 672)*, parent company *(p. 661)*, purchasing-power gain (or loss) *(p. 672)*, subsidiary company *(p. 661)*.

ASSIGNMENT MATERIAL _____

Questions

1. How are stock prices quoted in the securities market? What is the investor's cost of 1,000 shares of Ford Motor Company stock at 55¾, with a brokerage commission of $1,350?
2. What distinguishes a short-term investment from a long-term investment?
3. Show the positions of short-term investments and long-term investments on the balance sheet.
4. Outline the accounting methods for the different types of investment.
5. How does an investor record the receipt of a cash dividend on an investment accounted for by the cost method? How does this investor record receipt of a stock dividend?
6. An investor paid $11,000 for 1,000 shares of stock and later received a 10 percent stock dividend. Compute the gain or loss on sale of 300 shares of the stock for $2,600.
7. At what amount are short-term investments reported on the balance sheet? Are the short-term and long-term investment portfolios mixed, or are they kept separate?
8. When is an investment accounted for by the equity method? Outline how to apply the equity method. Include in your answer how to record the purchase of the investment, the investor's proportion of the investee's net income, and receipt of a cash dividend from the investee. Describe how to measure gain or loss on sale of this investment.
9. Identify three transactions that cause debits or credits to an equity-method investment account.
10. What are two special features of the consolidation method for investments?
11. Why are intercompany items eliminated from consolidated financial statements? Name two intercompany items that are eliminated.
12. Name the account that expresses the excess of cost of an investment over the book value of the subsidiary's owner equity. What type of account is this, and where in the financial statements is it reported?
13. When a parent company buys less than 100 percent of a subsidiary's stock, a certain type of equity is created. What is it called?
14. How would you measure the net income of a parent company with three subsidiaries? Assume that two subsidiaries are wholly (100 percent) owned and that the parent owns 60 percent of the third subsidiary.

15. Identify one problem with the historical-cost balance sheet and one problem with the historical-cost income statement that arise because of inflation.

16. Suppose you were preparing the current-cost financial statements of a company. What two assets and what two expenses are most likely to have different values in the historical-cost and the current-cost statements?

17. How do monetary assets differ from nonmonetary assets? Give examples of each.

18. If a company holds net monetary *assets* during inflation, does it experience a purchasing-power gain or a loss? If the company holds net monetary *liabilities,* does it experience a purchasing-power gain or a loss?

19. General Motors Corporation had net monetary liabilities of $9,948 million at the beginning of a recent year, when the price index was 303.5. The average price index for the year was 311.1. What is the inflation-adjusted beginning net-monetary-liability position?

20. For a recent year, Revco D. S. [Drug Stores], Inc., reported higher net earnings at historical cost than at current cost. What is the most likely explanation for the lower current-cost income?

21. How can a company have higher stockholders' equity measured at current cost but also report lower current-cost income than historical-cost income?

Exercises

Exercises 17-1 *Journalizing transactions under the cost method*

Journalize the following investment transactions of Chateau Rose, Inc.:

1. Purchased 300 shares (2 percent) of Madison Corporation common stock at $44 per share, with brokerage commission of $300.
2. Received cash dividend of $1 per share on the Madison investment.
3. Received 150 shares of Madison common stock in a 50 percent stock dividend.
4. Sold 200 shares of Madison stock for $29 per shares, less brokerage commission of $270.

Exercise 17-2 *Reporting investments at the lower of cost or market*

IBM recently reported the following information (not including the question mark) on its balance sheet:

Current Assets	(Dollars in millions)
Cash..	$ 616
Marketable securities [short-term investments], at lower of cost or market	?

NOTES TO CONSOLIDATED FINANCIAL STATEMENTS
Marketable Securities

(Dollars in millions)	
U. S. Government securities	$1,745
Other.....................................	3,175
Total.....................................	$4,920
Market value...............................	$4,929

Required

Apply the lower-of-cost-or-market method to IBM's short-term investments by inserting the appropriate amount in place of the question mark.

Exercise 17-3   *Journalizing transactions under the equity method*

Sears, Roebuck and Co. owns equity-method investments in several companies. Suppose Sears paid $180,000 to acquire a 25 percent investment in XYZ Company. Further, assume XYZ Company reported net income of $120,000 for the first year and declared and paid cash dividends of $70,000. Record the following in Sears's general journal: (a) purchase of the investment, (b) Sears's proportion of XYZ's net income, and (c) receipt of the cash dividends.

Exercise 17-4   *Recording equity-method transactions directly in the accounts*

Without making journal entries, record the transactions of Exercise 17-3 directly in the Investment in XYZ Common Stock account. Assume that after all the above transactions took place, Sears sold its entire investment in XYZ common stock for cash of $240,000. Journalize the sale of the investment.

Exercise 17-5   *Comparing the cost and equity methods*

Sonar Devices Corporation paid $100,000 for a 25 percent investment in the common stock of El Marko, Inc. For the first year, El Marko reported net income of $84,000 and at year end declared and paid cash dividends of $16,000. On the balance sheet date the market value of Sonar's investment in El Marko stock was $91,000.

Required

1. On Sonar Device's books, journalize the purchase of the investment, recognition of Sonar's portion of El Marko's net income, and receipt of dividends from El Marko under the equity method, which is appropriate for these circumstances.
2. Repeat Requirement 1 but follow the cost method for comparison purposes only.
3. Show the amount that Sonar Devices would report for the investment on Sonar's year-end balance sheet under the two methods.

Arrange the answer as follows:

Transaction	Equity Method	Cost Method (With LCM)
Investment............................		
El Marko net income.....................		
Receipt of El Marko dividend..............		
Investment amount to report on the balance sheet (show work)........		

Exercise 17-6   *Elimination entries under the consolidation method*

Assume on December 31 that Shearson Financial Consultants, a 100 percent-owned subsidiary of American Express Company, had the following owners' equity:

Common Stock.........................	$200,000
Retained Earnings	160,000

Assume further that American Express's cost of its investment in Shearson was $360,000 and that Shearson owed American Express $45,000 on a note.

Required

Give the work-sheet entry to eliminate (a) the investment of American Express and the stockholders' equity of Shearson and (b) the note receivable of American Express and note payable of Shearson.

Exercise 17-7 *Completing a consolidation work sheet with minority interest*

Maxim, Inc., owns an 85 percent interest in Ultra Corporation. Complete the following consolidation work sheet.

Assets	Maxim, Inc.	Ultra Corporation
Cash...........................	19,000	14,000
Accounts receivable, net............	82,000	53,000
Note receivable from Maxim........	—	12,000
Inventory......................	114,000	77,000
Investment in Ultra...............	85,000	—
Plant assets, net..................	186,000	129,000
Other assets....................	22,000	8,000
Total.........................	508,000	293,000

Liabilities and Equities		
Accounts payable.................	39,000	26,000
Notes payable...................	47,000 35	36,000
Other liabilities.................	52,000	131,000
Common stock...................	200,000	80,000
Retained earnings................	170,000	20,000
Minority interest.................	—	— 15
Total.........................	508,000	293,000

Exercise 17-8 *Preparing a current-cost income statement*

Short Incorporated reported the following historical cost income statement for the year ended September 30, 19X7:

Short Incorporated
Income Statement
Year Ended September 30, 19X7

Sales revenue...	$440,000
Cost of goods sold..	$206,000
Operating expenses.......................................	131,000
Depreciation...	43,000
Income taxes...	24,000
Total expenses...	404,000
Net income..	$ 36,000

Additional current-cost information includes:

a.	Current cost of goods sold...	$237,000
b.	Current cost depreciation..	47,000
c.	Purchasing power gain..	7,000
d.	Increase in the current cost of inventory and plant assets	31,000
e.	Effect of general inflation on the cost of inventory and plant assets..........	19,000

Required

Prepare Short's comparative historical cost and current-cost/constant-dollar income statement to conform to FASB guidelines. Use Exhibit 17-6 as a guide.

Exercise 17-9 *Computing a purchasing-power gain or loss*

Raytheon Company is a leading maker of electronic radar equipment. At the beginning of a recent year, when the price index was 292.4, Raytheon had a net-monetary-liability position of $1,161 million. The company's net-monetary-liability position at the end of the year was $1,203 million, and the price index was 303.5. The average price index for the year was 298.4.

Required

Compute Raytheon's purchasing-power gain for the year, rounding all amounts to the nearest million dollars.

Exercise 17-10 *Preparing a current-cost balance sheet*

Well-known brand names of Chesebrough-Pond's, Inc. include Bass shoes, Healthtex clothing, and Vaseline and Pond's health and beauty products. The company's condensed historical cost balance sheet at December 31, the end of a recent year, was

Chesebrough-Pond's, Inc.
Balance Sheet
December 31, 19XX

	(Thousands of dollars)
Current assets other than inventory.	$ 454,100
Inventories.	396,500
Property, plant, and equipment, net	241,800
Investments, goodwill, trademarks, and other assets	79,500
Total assets	$1,171,900
Total liabilities.	$ 522,000
Shareholders' equity	649,900
Total liabilities and shareholders' equity	$1,171,900

On the balance sheet date, the current cost of inventories was $402.4 million, and the current cost of net property, plant, and equipment was $374.7 million.

Required

Prepare a current-cost/constant-dollar balance sheet for Chesebrough-Pond's, Inc. It is not necessary to repeat the historical cost balance sheet.

Problems   *(Group A)*

Problem 17-1A *Journalizing transactions under the cost and equity methods*

General Motors Corporation (GM) owns numerous investments in the stock of other companies. Assume GM completed the following investment transactions:

19X4

Mar. 19   Purchased 500 shares of ROX Corporation common stock as a short-term investment, paying 22½ per share plus brokerage commission of $700.

Apr. 1   Purchased 8,000 shares, which exceeds 20 percent, of the common stock of MIC Company at total cost of $720,000.

July 1 Purchased 1,600 additional shares of MIC Company common stock at cost of $140,000.

Aug. 14 Received semiannual cash dividend of $.75 per share on the ROX investment.

Sep. 15 Received semiannual cash dividend of $1.40 per share (total of $13,440) on the MIC investment.

Oct. 12 Received 50 shares of ROX common stock in a 10 percent stock dividend. Round the new cost per share to the nearest cent.

Nov. 9 Sold 200 shares of ROX stock for 28¼ per share, less brokerage commission of $175.

Dec. 31 Received annual report from MIC Company. Net income for the year was $350,000. Of this amount, GM's proportion is 21.25 percent

19X5

Feb. 6 Sold 1,920 shares of MIC stock for net cash of $189,700.

Required

Record the transactions in the general journal of General Motors.

Problem 17-2A *Applying the cost method (with LCM) and the equity method*

The beginning balance sheet of Fairchild Industries, Inc., recently included:

Investments in Affiliates $84,057,000

Investments in Affiliates refers to investments accounted for by the equity method. Fairchild included its short-term investments among the current assets. Assume the company completed the following investment transactions during the year:

Jan. 3 Purchased 5,000 shares of common stock as a short-term investment, paying 9¼ per share plus brokerage commission of $1,350. Debit Short-Term Investments.

4 Purchased new long-term investment in affiliate at cost of $408,000. Debit Investments in Affiliates.

May 14 Received semiannual cash dividend of $.40 per share on the short-term investment purchased January 3.

June 15 Received cash dividend of $21,000 from affiliated company.

Aug. 28 Sold 1,000 shares of the short-term investment (purchased on January 3) for 11¼ per share, less brokerage commission of $750.

Oct. 24 Sold other short-term investments for $226,000, less brokerage commission of $11,400. Cost of these investments was $231,800.

Dec. 15 Received cash dividend of $23,000 from affiliated company.

31 Received annual reports from affiliated companies. Their total net income for the year was $740,000. Of this amount, Fairchild's proportion is 30 percent.

Required

1. Record the transactions in the general journal of Fairchild Industries.
2. Post entries to the Investments in Affiliates T-account, and determine its balance at December 31.
3. Assume the beginning balance of Short-Term Investments was cost of $356,400. Post entries to the Short-Term Investments T-account and determine its balance at December 31.
4. Assuming the market value of the short-term investment portfolio is $149,000 at December 31, show how Fairchild Industries would report short-term investments and investments in affiliates on the ending balance sheet. Use the following format:

	$XXX
Cash...	$XXX
Short-term investments, at lower of cost or market (cost, $___)...........	
Accounts receivable...	XXX
≈	≈
Total current assets..	XXX
Investments in affiliates...	___

Problem 17-3A *Preparing a consolidated balance sheet; no minority interest*

Prent Company paid $179,000 to acquire all the common stock of Stratford Corporation, and Stratford owes Prent $55,000 on a note payable. Immediately after the purchase on May 31, 19X7, the two companies' balance sheets were as follows:

Assets	Prent Company	Stratford Corporation
Cash	$ 18,000	$ 14,000
Accounts receivable, net	64,000	43,000
Note receivable from Stratford	55,000	—
Inventory	171,000	103,000
Investment in Stratford	179,000	—
Plant assets, net	205,000	138,000
Total	$692,000	$298,000

Liabilities and Stockholders' Equity		
Accounts payable...................	$ 76,000	$ 37,000
Notes payable.....................	196,000	55,000
Other liabilities...................	44,000	27,000
Common stock....................	282,000	90,000
Retained earnings..................	94,000	89,000
Total	$692,000	$298,000

Required

1. Prepare a consolidation work sheet.
2. Prepare the consolidated balance sheet on May 31, 19X7. Show total assets, total liabilities, and total stockholders' equity. It is not necessary to classify assets and liabilities as current and long-term.

Problem 17-4A *Preparing a consolidated balance sheet with goodwill*

On August 17,19X8, Marble Corporation paid $229,000 to purchase all the common stock of Granite Company, and Granite owes Marble $42,000 on a note payable. Immediately after the purchase, the two companies' balance sheets were as follows:

Assets	Marble Corporation	Granite Company
Cash	$ 23,000	$ 37,000
Accounts receivable, net	104,000	54,000
Note receivable from Granite	42,000	—
Inventory	213,000	141,000
Investment in Granite	229,000	—
Plant assets, net	197,000	175,000
Goodwill.........................	—	—
Total	$808,000	$407,000

Liabilities and Stockholders' Equity

Accounts payable....................	$119,000	$ 77,000
Notes payable......................	223,000	42,000
Other liabilities....................	33,000	88,000
Common stock	219,000	113,000
Retained earnings..................	214,000	87,000
Total	$808,000	$407,000

Required

1. Prepare a consolidation work sheet.
2. Prepare the consolidated balance sheet on August 17, 19X8. Show total assets, total liabilities, and total stockholders' equity. It is not necessary to classify assets and liabilities as current and long-term.

Problem 17-5A *Preparing current cost financial statements*

Emerson Minerals, Inc., reported the following historical cost financial statements at September 30, 19X9:

Emerson Minerals, Inc.
Income Statement
Year Ended September 30, 19X9

Total revenues................................	$623,000
Cost of goods sold............................	$305,000
Operating expenses (excluding depreciation)	76,000
Depreciation	42,000
Income taxes	80,000
Total expenses...............................	503,000
Net income	$120,000

Emerson Minerals, Inc.
Balance Sheet
September 30, 19X9

Current assets other than inventory................	$ 37,000
Inventory....................................	239,000
Plant assets, net..............................	533,000
Other assets..................................	22,000
Total assets	$831,000
Total liabilities...............................	$348,000
Stockholders' equity	483,000
Total liabilities and stockholders' equity	$831,000

Emerson's current cost of goods sold for fiscal year 19X9 was $337,000, and current-cost depreciation was $52,000. During fiscal year 19X9, the purchasing power gain on net monetary liabilities was $37,000. Also during the year, the current cost of the company's inventory and plant assets increased by $56,000, but the effect of general inflation was a $62,000 increase. At September 30, 19X9, the current cost of inventory was $278,000, and the current cost of plant assets, net of depreciation, was $563,000.

Required

Prepare a comparative historical cost and current-cost/constant-dollar income statement and balance sheet patterned after Exhibits 17-6 and 17-8.

Problem 17-6A   *Preparing current cost financial statements; computing a purchasing power gain or loss*

The historical cost financial statements of MajorCalc, Inc., at December 31, 19X6 were

MajorCalc, Inc.
Income Statement
Year Ended December 31, 19X6

Sales revenue.	$713,000
Cost of goods sold.	$308,000
Operating expenses (excluding depreciation)	149,000
Depreciation	126,000
Income taxes	52,000
Total expenses	635,000
Net income	$ 78,000

MajorCalc, Inc.
Balance Sheet
December 31, 19X6

Current assets other than inventory.	$ 95,000
Inventory	145,000
Plant assets, net.	612,000
Goodwill and other assets	62,000
Total assets	$914,000
Total liabilities	$389,000
Stockholders' equity	525,000
Total liabilities and stockholders' equity	$914,000

MajorCalc's current cost of goods sold for 19X6 was $323,000, and current-cost depreciation was $133,000. Net monetary liabilities were $263,000 at December 31, 19X5, when the price index was 100. At December 31, 19X6, net monetary liabilities were $304,000, and the price index was 110. The average price index for 19X6 was 104. During 19X6 the current cost of the company's inventory and plant assets increased by $19,000, but the effect of general inflation was a $27,000 increase. At December 31, 19X6, the current cost of inventory was $161,000, and the current cost of plant assets, net of depreciation, was $673,000.

Required

1. Prepare a comparative historical cost and current-cost income statement and balance sheet patterned after Exhibits 17-6 and 17-8.
2. Prepare a computation of the purchasing power gain or loss similar to Exhibit 17-7. Round all amounts to the nearest thousand dollars.

(Group B)

Problem 17-1B   *Journalizing transactions under the cost and equity methods*

ConAgra, Inc., owns numerous investments in the stock of other companies. Assume ConAgra completed the following investment transactions:

19X6

Jan. 2   Purchased 24,000 shares, which exceeds 20 percent, of the common stock of Agribusiness, Inc., at total cost of $640,000.

Mar. 16   Purchased 800 shares of Apex Company common stock as a short-term investment, paying 41½ per share plus brokerage commission of $800.

July 1   Purchased 8,000 additional shares of Agribusiness common stock at cost of $200,000.

Aug. 9   Received annual cash dividend of $.90 per share (total of $28,800) on the Agribusiness investment.

    30   Received semiannual cash dividend of $.60 per share on the Apex investment.

Sep. 14   Received 200 shares of Apex common stock in a 25 percent stock dividend.

Oct. 22   Sold 400 shares of Apex stock for 30¼ per share less brokerage commission of $450.

Dec. 31   Received annual report from Agribusiness, Inc. Net income for the year was $440,000. Of this amount, ConAgra's proportion is 35 percent.

19X7

Jan. 14   Sold 4,000 shares of Agribusiness stock for net cash of $141,000.

Required

Record the transactions in the general journal of ConAgra, Inc.

Problem 17-2B   *Applying the cost method (with LCM) and the equity method*

The beginning balance sheet of Ranco Incorporated recently included:

> Investments in Affiliates $10,984,000

Investments in Affiliates refers to investments accounted for by the equity method. Ranco included its short-term investments among the current assets. Assume the company completed the following investment transactions during the year:

Jan. 2   Purchased 4,000 shares of common stock as a short-term investment, paying 12¼ per share plus brokerage commission of $1,000. Debit Short-Term Investments.

    5   Purchased new long-term investment in affiliate at cost of $820,000. Debit Investments in Affiliates.

Apr. 21   Received semiannual cash dividend of $.35 per share on the short-term investment purchased January 2.

May 17   Received cash dividend of $47,000 from affiliated company.

July 16   Sold 1,600 shares of the short-term investment (purchased on January 2) for 10⅛ per share less brokerage commission of $720.

Sep. 8   Sold other short-term investments for $136,000 less brokerage commission of $5,100. Cost of these investments was $120,600.

Nov. 17   Received cash dividend of $49,000 from affiliated company.

Dec. 31   Received annual reports from affiliated companies. Their total net income for the year was $550,000. Of this amount, Ranco's proportion is 22 percent.

Required

1. Record the transactions in the general journal of Ranco Incorporated.
2. Post entries to the Investments in Affiliates T-account and determine its balance at December 31.
3. Assume the beginning balance of Short-Term Investments was cost of $293,600. Post entries to the Short-Term Investments T-account and determine its balance at December 31.
4. Assuming the market value of the short-term investment portfolio is $215,000 at

December 31, show how Ranco would report short-term investments and investments in affiliates on the ending balance sheet. Use the following format:

Cash	$XXX
Short-term investments, at lower of cost or market (market, $___)............	
Accounts receivable	XXX
⌇	⌇
Total current assets...	XXX
Investments in affiliates	

Problem 17-3B *Preparing a consolidated balance sheet; no minority interest*

Pittsburgh Company paid $166,000 to acquire all the common stock of Scranton Corporation, and Scranton owes Pittsburgh $81,000 on a note payable. Immediately after the purchase on June 30, 19X3, the two companies' balance sheets were as follows:

Assets	Pittsburgh Company	Scranton Corporation
Cash	$ 21,000	$ 20,000
Accounts receivable, net	91,000	42,000
Note receivable from Scranton	81,000	—
Inventory	145,000	114,000
Investment in Scranton	166,000	—
Plant assets, net	178,000	151,000
Total	$682,000	$327,000

Liabilities and Stockholders' Equity		
Accounts payable...................	$ 54,000	$ 49,000
Notes payable	177,000	81,000
Other liabilities....................	29,000	31,000
Common stock.....................	274,000	118,000
Retained earnings	148,000	48,000
Total	$682,000	$327,000

Required

1. Prepare a consolidation work sheet.
2. Prepare the consolidated balance sheet on June 30, 19X3. Show total assets, total liabilities, and total stockholders' equity. It is not necessary to classify assets and liabilities as current and long-term.

Problem 17-4B *Preparing a consolidated balance sheet with minority interest*

On March 22, 19X4, Abbott Corporation paid $180,000 to purchase 80 percent of the common stock of Zeta Company, and Zeta owes Abbott $67,000 on a note payable. Immediately after the purchase, the two companies' balance sheets were as follows:

Assets	Abbott Corporation	Zeta Company
Cash	$ 41,000	$ 43,000
Accounts receivable, net	86,000	75,000
Note receivable from Zeta	67,000	—
Inventory	128,000	107,000
Investment in Zeta	180,000	—
Plant assets, net	277,000	168,000
Goodwill.........................	—	—
Total	$779,000	$393,000

Liabilities and Stockholders' Equity

Accounts payable..................	$ 72,000	$ 65,000
Notes payable.....................	301,000	67,000
Other liabilities...................	11,000	36,000
Common stock....................	141,000	160,000
Retained earnings..................	254,000	65,000
Minority interest..................	—	—
Total	$779,000	$393,000

Required

1. Prepare a consolidation work sheet.
2. Prepare the consolidated balance sheet on March 22, 19X4. Show total assets, total liabilities, and total stockholders' equity. It is not necessary to classify assets and liabilities as current and long-term.

Problem 17-5B *Preparing current-cost financial statements*

Vargas Express Company reported the following historical cost financial statements at March 31, 19X6:

Vargas Express Company
Income Statement
Year Ended March 31, 19X6

Total revenues..................................	$451,000
Cost of goods sold.............................	$183,000
Operating expenses (excluding depreciation)	136,000
Depreciation	62,000
Income taxes	28,000
Total expenses.................................	409,000
Net income	$ 42,000

Vargas Express Company
Balance Sheet
March 31, 19X6

Current assets other than inventory...............	$ 24,000
Inventory.....................................	185,000
Plant assets, net...............................	320,000
Other assets...................................	17,000
Total assets	$546,000
Total liabilities................................	$249,000
Stockholders' equity	297,000
Total liabilities and stockholders' equity	$546,000

Vargas's current cost of goods sold for fiscal year 19X6 was $196,000, and current-cost depreciation was $69,000. During fiscal year 19X6, the purchasing-power gain on net monetary liabilities was $9,000. Also during the year, the current cost of the company's inventory and plant assets increased by $16,000, and the effect of general inflation was a $15,000 increase. At March 31, 19X6, the current cost of inventory was $194,000, and the current cost of plant assets, net of depreciation, was $362,000.

Required

Prepare a comparative historical cost and current-cost/constant-dollar income statement and balance sheet patterned after Exhibits 17-6 and 17-8.

Problem 17-6B *Preparing current-cost financial statements; computing a purchasing power gain or loss*

The historical-cost financial statements of Perry Photographic Laboratories at December 31, 19X2 were

---

Perry Photographic Laboratories
Income Statement
Year Ended December 31, 19X2

Sales revenue.	$503,000
Cost of goods sold.	$220,000
Operating expenses (excluding depreciation)	161,000
Depreciation	62,000
Income taxes	24,000
Total expenses.	467,000
Net income	$ 36,000

Perry Photographic Laboratories
Balance Sheet
December 31, 19X2

Current assets other than inventory.	$ 76,000
Inventory.	253,000
Plant assets, net.	505,000
Goodwill and other assets	38,000
Total assets	$872,000
Total liabilities.	$361,000
Stockholders' equity	511,000
Total liabilities and stockholders' equity	$872,000

Perry's current cost of goods sold for 19X2 was $254,000, and current-cost depreciation was $71,000. Net monetary liabilities were $384,000 at December 31, 19X1, when the price index was 100. At December 31, 19X2, net monetary liabilities were $309,000, and the price index was 110. The average price index for 19X2 was 105. During 19X2 the current cost of the company's inventory and plant assets increased by $52,000, and the effect of general inflation was a $28,000 increase. At December 31, 19X2, the current cost of inventory was $294,000, and the current cost of plant assets, net of depreciation, was $591,000.

Required

1. Prepare a comparative historical cost and current-cost/constant-dollar income statement and balance sheet patterned after Exhibits 17-6 and 17-8.
2. Prepare a computation of the purchasing-power gain or loss similar to Exhibit 17-7. Round all amounts to the nearest thousand dollars.

Decision Problem

Understanding the consolidation method for investments and current-cost accounting

Susan Bryan inherited some investments, and she has received the annual reports of the companies in which the funds are invested. The financial statements of the companies are puzzling to Susan, and she asks you the following questions:

1. The companies label their financial statements as *consolidated* balance sheet, *consolidated* income statement, and so on. What are consolidated financial statements?

2. Notes to the statements indicate that "certain intercompany transactions, loans, and other accounts have been eliminated in preparing the consolidated financial statements." Why does a company eliminate transactions, loans, and accounts? Susan states that she thought a transaction was a transaction and that a loan obligated a company to pay real money. She wonders if the company is juggling the books to defraud the IRS.

3. The balance sheet lists the asset Goodwill. What is Goodwill? Does this mean that the company's stock has increased in value?

4. The last note to the financial statements shows two income statements. One is labeled "Historical Cost," and the other is labeled "Current-Cost/Constant-Dollar." Because the two statements show different amounts of net income, Susan wonders which one is correct. Why do companies show two income statements? Which statement is required?

5. The current-cost/constant-dollar income statement reports net income, but it also includes "purchasing-power gain" and "excess of increase in the current cost of inventory and plant assets over the effect of general inflation." What do these items mean?

Required

Respond to each of Susan's questions.

Financial Statement Problem

Investments in Stock

The Gulf+Western Inc. financial statements and related notes in Appendix C describe some of the company's investment activity. The balance sheet reveals that Gulf+Western's equity-method investment account is titled Investment in Affiliated Companies. The statement of cash flows reports that Gulf+Western increased its investment in affiliated companies.

Required

1. Journalize the following transactions of fiscal 1987. Use Gulf+Western account titles, and show amounts in millions rounded to the nearest $100,000.
   a. Increase in investment in affiliated companies.
   b. Equity-method investment revenue of $510.6 million. Label this account Equity in Earnings of Affiliated Companies.
   c. Receipt of cash dividends of $84.0 million from affiliated companies.
      Insert the October 31, 1986, balance in Investment in Affiliated Companies, and post the foregoing entries to this account. Compare its balance to the amount shown on the balance sheet at October 31, 1987.

2. What was Gulf+Western's balance of short-term investments in stock at October 31, 1987? Give your reason.

3. What is the only word appearing in the title of all the Gulf+Western financial statements? What does this word indicate? Name the companies—listed in Note B—that Gulf+Western acquired during fiscal 1985, 1986, and 1987.

Answers to Self-Study Questions

1. a
2. d
3. c
4. c
5. c ($100,000 × .30 = $30,000; dividends have *no* effect on investor net income under the equity method)
6. a
7. b [$155,000 + ($60,000 × .90) + ($80,000 × .60) = $257,000]
8. b
9. b
10. d [$250,000 + ($110,000 − $100,000) + ($180,000 − $120,000) = $320,000]

Statement of Cash Flows

Income statements and balance sheets are anchored to the accrual basis of accounting for measuring performance and financial position. Another major statement, the statement of cash flows, is required to provide a more complete picture of performance and position.

Consider some common questions asked by managers, investors, and creditors. What were the company's sources of cash during the period? Did operations —buying and selling the company's major products—generate the bulk of its cash receipts, or did the business have to sell off plant assets to keep the cash balance at an acceptable level? Did the company have to borrow heavily during the period? How did the entity spend its cash? Was it busy paying off debts, or were cash disbursements devoted to expanding the business? This chapter discusses the statement of cash flows. As its title implies, the statement of cash flows helps explain a company's performance in generating cash.

Cash flows are cash receipts and cash payments (disbursements). The **statement of cash flows** reports cash receipts and cash disbursements classified according to the entity's major activities: operating, investing, and financing. The statement reports a net cash inflow or a net cash outflow for each activity and for the business overall. In 1988 the FASB started requiring this statement as a replacement for the statement of changes in financial position.

Purposes of the Statement of Cash Flows

The statement of cash flows is designed to fulfill the following purposes:

   1. *To predict future cash flows.* Cash, not reported accounting income, pays the bills. In many cases, a business's sources and uses of cash do not change dramati-

OBJECTIVE 1
Identify the purposes of the statement of cash flows

cally from year to year. Therefore, past cash receipts and disbursements are a reasonably good predictor of future cash receipts and disbursements.

2. To evaluate management decisions. If managers make wise investment decisions, their businesses prosper. If they make unwise decisions, the businesses suffer. The statement of cash flows reports the company's investment in plant and equipment and thus gives investors and creditors cash-flow information for evaluating managers' decisions. A classic example is Montgomery Ward's decision shortly after World War II *not* to expand the business. Ward's top management expected a recession and decided to play it safe until the United States economy settled down after the war. Sears, Roebuck, on the other hand, predicted a strong economy and went full speed ahead. Sears's decision proved better, and Montgomery Ward has fallen significantly behind Sears.

3. To determine the ability to pay dividends to stockholders and interest and principal to creditors. Stockholders are interested in receiving dividends on their investments in the company's stock. Creditors want to receive their interest and principal amounts on time. The statement of cash flows helps investors and creditors predict whether the business can make these payments.

4. To show the relationship of net income to changes in the business's cash. Usually, cash and net income move together. High levels of income tend to lead to increases in cash, and vice versa. However, a company's cash balance can decrease when net income is high, and cash can increase when income is low. The failures of companies such as W. T. Grant, which was earning net income but had insufficient cash, have pointed to the need for cash flow information.

Basic Concept of the Statement of Cash Flows

The balance sheet reports the cash balance at the end of the period. By examining two consecutive balance sheets, you can tell whether cash increased or decreased during the period. However, the balance sheet does not indicate *why* the cash balance changed. The income statement reports revenues, expenses, and net income—clues about the sources and uses of cash—but it still does not tell *why* cash increased or decreased.

The statement of cash flows reports the entity's cash receipts and cash payments during the period—where cash came from and how it was spent. It explains the *causes* for the change in the cash balance. This information cannot be learned solely from the other financial statements.

The balance sheet is the only financial statement that is dated as of the end of the period. The income statement and the statement of retained earnings cover the period from beginning to end. The statement of cash flows also covers the entire period and therefore is dated "For the Year Ended *XXX*" or "For the Month Ended *XXX*." Its timing and its position among the statements is shown in this diagram:

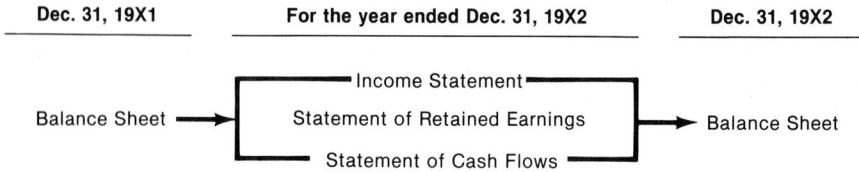

Operating, Investing, and Financing Activities _____

Fundamentally, businesses undertake three distinctly different types of activities. First, they must *finance* their operations. That is, they must acquire the money necessary to launch and sustain the business. Think back to Chapter 1. What was the first transaction that we accounted for? It was receipt of cash from the owner to start the business. Those investors who finance the business expect a return on their money, so financing activities also include paying dividends to the stockholders.

What was the business's second transaction in Chapter 1? It was an *investment.* Companies invest in land, buildings, office furniture, equipment, and other long-lived assets for use in the business. They pay close attention to their investing activities because the long-term assets they buy determine the future course of the business. Headlines such as "General Motors Investing in New Automobile Technology" and "Japanese Company Opening New Plant in South Carolina" are seen regularly in *The Wall Street Journal* and other business periodicals.

Why do businesses exist? The main purpose is to generate revenues in order to earn a profit. The way a company earns revenues is called its *operations.* For a grocery store, operations include buying and selling food and other grocery products. For a law firm, operations consist of providing legal services for clients. The operations of a company define the type of business it is. For example, IBM operates in the business-machines industry, McDonald's in the fast-food business, and Levi Strauss manufactures and sells clothing.

A good way to evaluate a business is based on these three types of business activities. After the business is up and running, operations are the most important activity, followed by investing activities and financing activities. The statement of cash flows therefore divides cash receipts and disbursements into operating activities, investing activities, and financing activities.

Operating activities create revenues and expenses in the entity's major line of business. Therefore, operating activities affect the income statement, which reports the accrual-basis effects of operating activities. The statement of cash flows reports their impact on cash.

Investing activities increase and decrease the assets that the business has to work with. A purchase or sale of a plant asset like land, a building, or equipment is an investing activity, as is the purchase or sale of an investment in stock or bonds of another company. On the statement of cash flows, investing activities include more than the buying and selling of assets that are classified as investments on the balance sheet. Making a loan—an investing activity because the loan creates a receivable for the lender—and collecting on the loan are also reported as investing activities on the statement of cash flows.

Financing activities obtain the funds from investors and creditors needed to launch and sustain the business. Financing activities include issuing stock, borrowing money by issuing notes and bonds payable, selling treasury stock, and making payments to the stockholders—dividends and purchases of treasury stock. Payments to the creditors include principal payments only. The payment of interest is an operating activity.

Each of these categories of activities includes both cash receipts and cash disbursements.

OBJECTIVE 2
Distinguish among operating, investing, and financing activities

Cash and Cash Equivalents

On a statement of cash flows, *Cash* has a broader meaning than just cash on hand and cash in the bank. It includes **cash equivalents,** which are highly liquid short-term investments that can be converted into cash with little delay. Examples include money market investments and investments in U.S. Government Treasury bills. Businesses invest their extra cash in these types of liquid assets rather than let it remain idle. Throughout this chapter, the term *cash* refers to cash and cash equivalents.

Format of the Statement of Cash Flows

Exhibit 18-1 displays the 19X2 statement of cash flows for Anchor Corporation.

As the exhibit illustrates, each set of activities (operating, investing, and financing) includes both cash inflows—receipts—and cash outflows—payments. Outflows are shown in parentheses to indicate that payments must be subtracted. Each section of the statement reports a net cash inflow or a net cash outflow.

The largest cash inflow from operations is the collection of cash from customers. Less important inflows are receipts of interest on loans and dividends on stock investments. The operating cash outflows include payments to suppliers and to employees and payments for interest and taxes. Anchor's net cash inflow from operating activities is $68,000.

The acquisition of plant assets dominates the company's investing activities, which produce a net cash outflow of $255,000. Financing activities brought in net cash of $167,000. Overall, cash decreased by $20,000 during 19X2. The company began the year with cash of $42,000 and ended with $22,000.

You may be puzzled by the listing of receipts of interest and dividends as operating activities. After all, these cash receipts result from investing activities. Interest comes from investments in loans, and dividends come from investments in stock. Equally puzzling is listing the payment of interest as part of operations. Interest expense results from borrowing money—a financing activity. After much debate, the FASB decided to include these items as part of operations. Why? Mainly because they affect the computation of net income. Interest revenue and dividend revenue increase net income, and interest expense decreases income. Therefore, cash receipts of interest and dividends and cash payments of interest are reported as operating activities on the cash flow statement.

In contrast, notice that dividend payments are not listed among the operating activities of Exhibit 18-1. Why? Because they do not enter the computation of income. Dividend payments are reported in the financing activities section of the cash flow statement because they go to the entity's owners, who finance the business by holding its stock.

Preparing the Statement of Cash Flows: The Direct Method

There are two basic ways to present the statement of cash flows. Both methods arrive at the same subtotals for operating activities, investing activities, financing activities, and the net change in cash for the period. They differ only in the manner of showing the cash flows from operating activities. The **direct method,** which the FASB prefers, lists the major categories of operating cash receipts and cash disbursements as shown in Exhibit 18-1. We discuss the indirect method later in the chapter.

EXHIBIT 18-1 *Statement of Cash Flows*

Anchor Corporation
Statement of Cash Flows
For the Year Ended December 31, 19X2
Increase (Decrease) in Cash and Cash Equivalents
(amounts in thousands)

Cash flows from operating activities:		
Receipts:		
Collections from customers		$ 271
Interest received on notes receivable		10
Dividends received on investments in stock		9
Total cash receipts		290
Payments:		
To suppliers	$(133)	
To employees	(58)	
For interest	(16)	
For income tax	(15)	
Total cash payments		(222)
Net cash inflow from operating activities		68
Cash flows from investing activities:		
Acquisition of plant assets	$(306)	
Loan to another company	(11)	
Proceeds from sale of plant assets	62	
Net cash outflow from investing activities		(255)
Cash flows from financing activities:		
Proceeds from issuance of common stock	$ 101	
Proceeds from issuance of long-term debt	94	
Payment of long-term debt	(11)	
Payment of dividends	(17)	
Net cash inflow from financing activities		167
Net decrease in cash		$ (20)
Cash balance, December 31, 19X1		42
Cash balance, December 31, 19X2		$ 22

OBJECTIVE 3
Prepare a statement of cash flows using the direct method

Illustrative Problem

Let's see how to prepare the statement of cash flows by the direct method in Exhibit 18-1. Suppose Anchor Corporation accountants have assembled the following summary of 19X2 transactions. Those transactions with cash effects are denoted by an asterisk.

Summary of 19X2 Transactions

Operating Activities:

1. Sales on credit, $284,000
*2. Collections from customers, $271,000
3. Interest revenue on notes receivable, $12,000
*4. Collection of interest receivable, $10,000
*5. Cash receipt of dividend revenue on investments in stock, $9,000
6. Cost of goods sold, $150,000

   7. Purchases of inventory on credit, $147,000

 *8. Payments to suppliers, $133,000

   9. Salary and wage expense, $56,000

*10. Payments of salaries and wages, $58,000

 11. Depreciation expense, $18,000

 12. Other operating expense, $17,000

*13. Interest expense and payments, $16,000

*14. Income tax expense and payments, $15,000

Investing Activities:

*15. Cash payments to acquire plant assets, $306,000

*16. Loan to another company, $11,000

*17. Proceeds from sale of plant assets, $62,000, including $8,000 gain

Financing Activities:

*18. Proceeds from issuance of common stock, $101,000

*19. Proceeds from issuance of long-term debt, $94,000

*20. Payment of long-term debt, $11,000

*21. Declaration and payment of cash dividends, $17,000

These summary transactions give the data for both the income statement and the statement of cash flows. Some transactions affect one statement, some the other. Sales, for example, are reported on the income statement, but cash collections appear on the cash flow statement. Other transactions, such as the cash receipt of dividend revenue, affect both statements. *The statement of cash flows reports only those transactions with cash effects.*

    Preparation of the statement of cash flows follows these steps: (1) identify the activities that increased cash and decreased cash—those items with asterisks in the Summary of 19X2 Transactions on page 699; (2) classify each cash increase and each cash decrease as an operating activity, an investing activity, or a financing activity; and (3) identify the cash effect of each transaction. Preparing the statement is discussed in the next section.

Cash Flows from Operating Activities.   Operating cash flows are listed first because they are the largest and most important source of cash for most businesses. The failure of a company's operations to generate the bulk of its cash inflows for an extended period may signal trouble. This is not true of Anchor Corporation in Exhibit 18-1. Its operating activities were the largest source of cash receipts, $290,000.

CASH COLLECTIONS FROM CUSTOMERS.   Cash sales bring in cash immediately. Credit sales, however, increase Accounts Receivable but not Cash. Receipts of cash on account are a separate transaction, and only cash receipts are reported on the statement of cash flows. "Collections from customers" on the statement include both cash sales and collections of accounts receivable from credit sales. Collections from customers are Anchor's major operating source of cash—$271,000—in Exhibit 18-1.

CASH RECEIPTS OF INTEREST.   Interest revenue is earned on notes receivable. The income statement reports interest revenue. As the clock ticks, interest accrues, but cash interest is received only on specified dates. Only the cash receipts of interest appear on the statement of cash flows—$10,000 in Exhibit 18-1.

CASH RECEIPTS OF DIVIDENDS.   Dividends are earned on investments in stock. Unlike interest, dividends do not accrue with the passage of time. Therefore, dividend revenue is recorded when cash is received. This cash receipt is reported on the statement of cash flows—$9,000 in Exhibit 18-1. (Note that dividends *received* are part of operating activities, but dividends *paid* are a financing activity.)

PAYMENTS TO SUPPLIERS.   Payments to suppliers include all cash disbursements for inventory and operating expenses except employee compensation, interest, and income taxes. Suppliers are those entities that provide the business with its inventory and essential services. For example, a clothing store's payments to Levi Strauss, Liz Claiborne, and Reebok are listed as payments to suppliers. A grocery store makes payments to suppliers like Nabisco, Campbell's, and Coca-Cola. Suppliers also provide advertising, utility, and other services that are classified as operating expenses. This category *excludes* payments to employees, payments for interest, and payments for income taxes because these are separate categories of operating cash payments. In Exhibit 18-1, Anchor Corporation reports payments to suppliers of $133,000.

PAYMENTS TO EMPLOYEES.   This category includes disbursements for salaries, wages, commissions, and other forms of employee compensation. Accrued amounts are excluded because they have not yet been paid. The income statement reports the expense, including accrued amounts. The statement of cash flows reports only the payments ($58,000) in Exhibit 18-1.

PAYMENTS FOR INTEREST EXPENSE AND INCOME TAX EXPENSE.   These cash payments are reported separately from the other expenses. Interest payments show the cash cost of borrowing money. Because excessive borrowing can lead to financial trouble, a large amount of interest payments may signal managers to examine this aspect of operations. Income tax payments also deserve emphasis because of their significant amount. In the Anchor Corporation illustration, these expenses equal the cash payments. Therefore, the same amount appears on the income statement and the statement of cash flows. In actual practice, this is rarely the case. Year-end accruals and other transactions usually cause the expense and cash payment amounts to differ. The cash flow statement reports the cash payments for interest ($16,000) and income tax ($15,000).

DEPRECIATION, DEPLETION, AND AMORTIZATION EXPENSES.   These expenses are *not* listed on the statement of cash flows in Exhibit 18-1 because they do not affect cash. For example, depreciation is recorded by debiting the expense and crediting Accumulated Depreciation. No debit or credit to the Cash account occurs.

Cash Flows from Investing Activities.   Many analysts regard investing as a critical activity because a company's investments determine its future course. Large purchases of plant assets signal expansion, which is usually a good sign about the company. Low levels of investing activities over a lengthy period mean the business is not replenishing its capital assets. Knowing these cash flows helps investors and creditors evaluate the direction that managers are charting for the business.

CASH PAYMENTS TO ACQUIRE PLANT ASSETS AND INVESTMENTS, AND LOANS TO OTHER COMPANIES.   These cash payments are similar because they acquire a noncash asset. The first transaction purchases plant assets, such as land, buildings, and equipment ($306,000) in Exhibit 18-1. In the second transaction, Anchor Corporation makes an $11,000 loan and obtains a note receivable. These are investing activities because the company is investing in assets for use in the business rather than for resale. These transactions have no effect on revenues or expenses and thus are not reported on the income statement. Another transaction in this category—not shown in Exhibit 18-1—is a purchase of an investment in stocks or bonds.

PROCEEDS FROM THE SALE OF PLANT ASSETS AND INVESTMENTS, AND COLLECTIONS OF LOANS.   These transactions are the opposites of acquisitions of plant assets and investments, and making loans. They are cash receipts from investment transactions.

The sale of the plant assets needs explanation. The statement of cash flows reports that Anchor Corporation received $62,000 cash on the sale of plant assets. The income statement shows an $8,000 gain on this transaction. What is the appropriate amount to show on the cash flow statement? It is $62,000, the cash proceeds from the sale. Assuming Anchor sold equipment that cost $64,000 and had accumulated depreciation of $10,000, the journal entry to record this sale is

Cash...	62,000	
Accumulated Depreciation...............................	10,000	
Equipment.......................................		64,000
Gain on Sale of Plant Assets (from income statement).....		8,000

The analysis indicates that the book value of the equipment was $54,000 ($64,000 − $10,000). However, the book value of the asset sold is not reported on the statement of cash flows. Only the cash proceeds of $62,000 are reported on the statement. For the income statement, only the gain is reported. Since a gain occurred, you may wonder why this cash receipt is not reported as part of operations. Operations consist of buying and selling merchandise or rendering services to earn revenue. Investing activities are the acquisition and disposition of assets used in operations. Therefore, the FASB views the sale of plant assets and the sale of investments as cash inflows from investing activities.

Investors and creditors are often critical of a company that sells large amounts of its plant assets. Such sales may signal an emergency. In other situations, selling off fixed assets may be good news about the company if it is getting rid of an unprofitable division. Whether sales of plant assets are good news or bad news should be evaluated in light of a company's operating and financing characteristics.

Cash Flows from Financing Activities.   These cash flows include the following:

PROCEEDS FROM ISSUANCE OF STOCK AND DEBT.   Readers of the financial statements want to know how the entity obtains its financing. Issuing stock (preferred and common) and debt are two common ways to finance operations. In Exhibit 18-1, Anchor Corporation issued common stock of $101,000 and long-term debt of $94,000.

PAYMENT OF DEBT AND PURCHASES OF THE COMPANY'S OWN STOCK.   The payment of debt decreases Cash, which is the opposite of borrowing money. Anchor Corporation reports debt payments of $11,000. Other transactions in this category are purchases of treasury stock and payments to retire the company's stock.

PAYMENT OF CASH DIVIDENDS.   The payment of cash dividends decreases Cash and is therefore reported as a cash payment, as illustrated by Anchor's $17,000 payment in Exhibit 18-1. A dividend in another form—a stock dividend, for example—has no effect on Cash and is *not* reported on the cash flow statement.

EXHIBIT 18-2 *Cash Receipts and Disbursements Reported on the Statement of Cash Flows*

Operating Activities	
Cash Receipts	**Cash Disbursements**
Collections from customers	Payments to suppliers
Receipts of interest and dividends on investments	Payments to employees
	Payments of interest and income tax
Other operating receipts	Other operating disbursements
Investing Activities	
Cash Receipts	**Cash Disbursements**
Sale of plant assets	Acquisition of plant assets
Sale of investments that are not cash equivalents	Acquisition of investments that are not cash equivalents
Cash receipts on loans receivable	Making loans
Financing Activities	
Cash Receipts	**Cash Disbursements**
Issuing stock	Purchase of treasury stock
Selling treasury stock	Payment of dividends
Borrowing money	Paying principal amounts of debts

Exhibit 18-2 summarizes the more common cash receipts and cash disbursements that appear on the statement of cash flows.

Focus of the Statement of Cash Flows

The statement of cash flows focuses on the increase or decrease in cash during the period (highlighted in Exhibit 18-1 for emphasis). This check figure is taken from the comparative balance sheet that shows the beginning and ending balances. The cash flow statement, which adds up to the change in cash, shows the reasons why cash changed.

Exhibit 18-1 illustrates how the cash-balance information may be shown at the bottom of a statement of cash flows, a common format. Another common practice places the beginning cash balance at the top of the statement and the ending balance at the bottom. However, the FASB does not require that the beginning and ending cash balances appear on the statement. Because the balance sheet reports these amounts, it is sufficient to show on the statement of cash flows only the change that occurred during the period.

In our example, cash decreased by $20,000. Readers of the annual report might wonder why cash decreased during a good year. After all, Exhibit 18-3, Anchor's income statement, reports net income of $41,000. When a business is expanding, its cash often declines. Why? Because cash is invested in plant assets, such as land, buildings, and equipment, as reported in the cash flow statement. Conversely, cash may increase in a year when income is low—if the company borrows heavily. The statement of cash flows gives its readers a direct picture of where cash came from (cash inflows) and how cash was spent (cash outflows).

EXHIBIT 18-3 *Income Statement*

Anchor Corporation
Income Statement
For the Year Ended December 31, 19X2
(amounts in thousands)

Revenues and gains:		
Sales revenue		$284
Interest revenue		12
Dividend revenue		9
Gain on sale of plant assets		8
Total revenues and gains		313
Expenses:		
Cost of goods sold	$150	
Salary and wage expense	56	
Depreciation expense	18	
Other operating expense	17	
Interest expense	16	
Income tax expense	15	
Total expenses		272
Net income		$ 41

Summary Problem for Your Review

Drexel Corporation accounting records include the following information for the year ended June 30, 19X8:

1. Salary expense, $104,000
2. Interest revenue, $8,000
3. Proceeds from issuance of common stock, $31,000
4. Declaration and payment of cash dividends, $22,000
5. Collection of interest receivable, $7,000
6. Payments of salaries, $110,000
7. Credit sales, $358,000
8. Loan to another company, $42,000
9. Proceeds from sale of plant assets, $18,000, including $1,000 loss
10. Collections from customers, $369,000
11. Cash receipt of dividend revenue on stock investments, $3,000
12. Payments to suppliers, $319,000
13. Cash sales, $92,000
14. Depreciation expense, $32,000
15. Proceeds from issuance of short-term debt, $38,000
16. Payments of long-term debt, $57,000
17. Interest expense and payments, $11,000
18. Loan collections, $51,000

19. Proceeds from sale of investments, $22,000, including $13,000 gain
20. Amortization expense, $5,000
21. Purchases of inventory on credit, $297,000
22. Income tax expense and payments, $16,000
23. Cash payments to acquire plant assets, $83,000
24. Cost of goods sold, $284,000
25. Cash balance: June 30, 19X7 — $83,000
    June 30, 19X8 — $54,000

Required

Prepare Drexel Corporation's statement of cash flows and income statement for the year ended June 30, 19X8. Follow the formats of Exhibits 18-1 and 18-3.

SOLUTION TO REVIEW PROBLEM

Drexel Corporation
Statement of Cash Flows
For the Year Ended June 30, 19X8
Increase (Decrease) in Cash and Cash Equivalents
(amounts in thousands)

Item No. (Reference Only)			
	Cash flows from operating activities:		
	Receipts:		
10, 13	Collections from customers ($369 + $92)		$ 461
5	Interest received on notes receivable........		7
11	Dividends received on investments in stock.............................		3
	Total cash receipts....................		471
	Payments:		
12	To suppliers..........................	$(319)	
6	To employees	(110)	
17	For interest..........................	(11)	
22	For income tax........................	(16)	
	Total cash payments..................		(456)
	Net cash inflow from operating activities ..		15
	Cash flows from investing activities:		
23	Acquisition of plant assets	$ (83)	
8	Loan to another company	(42)	
19	Proceeds from sale of investments...........	22	
9	Proceeds from sale of plant assets	18	
18	Collection of loans	51	
	Net cash outflow from investing activities....		(34)
	Cash flows from financing activities:		
15	Proceeds from issuance of short-term debt.....	$ 38	
3	Proceeds from issuance of common stock......	31	
16	Payments of long-term debt.................	(57)	
4	Dividends declared and paid	(22)	
	Net cash outflow from financing activities		(10)
	Net decrease in cash........................		$ (29)
25	Cash balance, June 30, 19X7		83
25	Cash balance, June 30, 19X8		$ 54

Drexel Corporation
Income Statement
For the Year Ended June 30, 19X8
(amounts in thousands)

Revenue and gains:		
Sales revenue ($358 + $92).....................................		$450
Gain on sale of investments..................................		13
Interest revenue		8
Dividend revenue.......................................		3
Total revenues and gains		474
Expenses and losses:		
Cost of goods sold	$284	
Salary expense	104	
Depreciation expense.....................................	32	
Income tax expense	16	
Interest expense	11	
Amortization expense.....................................	5	
Loss on sale of plant assets	1	
Total expenses..		453
Net income..		$ 21

Computing Individual Amounts for the Statement of Cash Flows

OBJECTIVE 4

Use the financial statements to compute the cash effects of a wide variety of business transactions

How do accountants compute the amounts for the statement of cash flows? Many accountants prepare the statement of cash flows using the income statement amounts and *changes* in the related balance sheet accounts. Learning to analyze accounts in this manner is one of the most useful skills you will acquire from accounting. It will enable you to identify the cash effects of a wide variety of transactions. The following discussions use Anchor Corporation's comparative balance sheet in Exhibit 18-4 and income statement in Exhibit 18-3. For continuity, trace the cash amounts on the balance sheet in Exhibit 18-4 to the bottom part of the cash flow statement in Exhibit 18-1.

Computing the Cash Amounts of Operating Activities

Computing Cash Collections from Customers. Collections can be computed by converting sales revenue (an accrual-basis amount) to the cash basis. A decrease in the balance of Accounts Receivable during the period indicates that cash collections exceeded sales revenue. Therefore, we add the decrease to sales revenue to compute collections. An increase in Accounts Receivable means that sales exceeded cash receipts. This amount is subtracted to compute collections. These relationships suggest the following computation for collections from customers:

$$\begin{matrix} \text{Collections} \\ \text{from} \\ \text{customers} \end{matrix} = \text{Sales Revenue} \begin{cases} + \text{ Decrease in Accounts Receivable} \\ \text{or} \\ - \text{ Increase in Accounts Receivable} \end{cases}$$

EXHIBIT 18-4 *Comparative Balance Sheet*

Anchor Corporation
Comparative Balance Sheet
December 31, 19X2 and 19X1
(amounts in thousands)

Assets	19X2	19X1	Increase (Decrease)
Current:			
Cash......	$ 22	$ 42	$(20)
Accounts receivable........	93	80	13
Interest receivable........	3	1	2
Inventory........	135	138	(3)
Prepaid expenses........	8	7	1
Long-term receivable from another company........	11	—	11
Plant assets, net........	453	219	234
Total........	$725	$487	$238
Liabilities			
Current:			
Accounts payable........	$ 91	$ 57	$ 34
Salary and wage payable........	4	6	(2)
Accrued liabilities........	1	3	(2)
Long-term debt........	160	77	83
Stockholders' Equity			
Common stock........	359	258	101
Retained earnings........	110	86	24
Total........	$725	$487	$238

Anchor Corporation's income statement (Exhibit 18-3) reports sales of $284,000. Exhibit 18-4 shows that Accounts Receivable increased from $80,000 at the beginning of the year to $93,000 at year end, a $13,000 increase. Based on these amounts, Collections equal $271,000: Sales Revenue, $284,000 minus the $13,000 increase in Accounts Receivable. Posting these amounts directly to Accounts Receivable highlights the Collections amount, $271,000.

Accounts Receivable

Beginning balance	80,000		
Sales	284,000	**Collections**	**271,000**
Ending balance..............	93,000		

We see that this computation required the income statement account Sales Revenue and the *change* in the related balance sheet account, Accounts Receivable. The amount of cash collections from customers is derived from these accounts. Cash collections — and the other amounts reported on the cash flow statement — are *not* the balances of separate ledger accounts. Instead, the cash flow amounts must be computed by analysis of related income statement and balance sheet accounts, as illustrated in this section.

All collections of receivables can be computed in the same way. For example, the illustrative problem indicates that Anchor Corporation received cash interest.

To compute this operating cash receipt, note that the income statement reports interest revenue of $12,000. Interest Receivable's balance in Exhibit 18-4 increased by $2,000. Cash receipts of interest must be $10,000 ($12,000 − $2,000).

Computing Payments to Suppliers.   This computation includes two parts, payments for inventory and payments for expenses other than interest and income tax.

Payments for inventory are computed by converting cost of goods sold to the cash basis. We accomplish this by analyzing Cost of Goods Sold and Accounts Payable. The computation of cash payments for inventory is

$$\begin{matrix} \text{Payments} \\ \text{for} \\ \text{inventory} \end{matrix} = \text{Cost of goods sold} \begin{cases} + \textbf{Increase in} \\ \textbf{Inventory} \\ \textit{or} \\ - \textbf{Decrease in} \\ \textbf{Inventory} \end{cases} \text{and} \begin{cases} + \textbf{Decrease in} \\ \textbf{Accounts Payable*} \\ \textit{or} \\ - \textbf{Increase in} \\ \textbf{Accounts Payable*} \end{cases}$$

* +Decrease (or −Increase) in Short-term Notes Payable for Inventory Purchases

The logic behind this computation is that an increase in inventory leads to an increase in accounts payable that finds its way into a cash payment. A decrease in accounts payable can occur only if cash was paid. By contrast, an increase in accounts payable indicates that cash was *not* paid. A detailed analysis will show the validity of this computation.

Anchor Corporation reports cost of goods sold of $150,000. The balance sheet shows that Inventory decreased by $3,000. Accounts Payable increased by $34,000. These amounts combine to compute payments for inventory of $113,000: Cost of Goods Sold, $150,000, minus the decrease in Inventory, $3,000, minus the increase in Accounts Payable, $34,000 — a total of $113,000.

The T-account analysis also indicates payments of $113,000 (with Purchases inserted for completeness):

Cost of Goods Sold

Beginning inventory	138,000	Ending inventory	135,000
Purchases	147,000		
Cost of goods sold	150,000		

Accounts Payable

		Beginning balance	57,000
Payments for inventory	113,000	Purchases	147,000
		Ending balance	91,000

Payments to suppliers ($133,000) equal the sum of payments for inventory ($113,000) plus payments for operating expenses ($20,000), as explained next.

Computing Payments for Operating Expenses.   Payments for operating expenses other than interest and income tax can be computed by analyzing Prepaid Expenses and Other Accrued Liabilities, as follows:

$$\begin{matrix} \text{Payments} \\ \text{for operating} \\ \text{expenses} \end{matrix} = \begin{matrix} \text{Operating} \\ \text{expenses other} \\ \text{than salaries,} \\ \text{wages, and} \\ \text{depreciation} \end{matrix} \begin{cases} + \textbf{Increase in} \\ \textbf{Prepaid Expenses} \\ \textit{or} \\ - \textbf{Decrease in} \\ \textbf{Prepaid Expenses} \end{cases} \text{and} \begin{cases} + \textbf{Decrease in} \\ \textbf{Accrued Liabilities} \\ \textit{or} \\ - \textbf{Increase in} \\ \textbf{Accrued Liabilities} \end{cases}$$

Increases in prepaid expenses require cash payments, and decreases indicate that payments were less than expenses. Decreases in accrued liabilities can occur only from cash payments, and increases mean that cash was *not* paid.

Anchor's income statement reports operating expenses—other than salaries, wages, and depreciation—of $17,000. The balance sheet shows that prepaid expenses increased by $1,000, and accrued liabilities decreased by $2,000. Based on these data, payments for operating expenses total $20,000 ($17,000 + $1,000 + $2,000).

This result is confirmed by the T-account analysis, as follows:

Prepaid Expenses

Beginning balance..........	7,000	Expiration of prepaid expense	7,000
Payments.................	**8,000**		
Ending balance	8,000		

Accrued Liabilities

Payment of beginning		Beginning balance.........	3,000
balance.................	**3,000**	Accrual of expense at year end....................	1,000
		Ending balance	1,000

Operating Expenses (other than Salaries, Wages, and Depreciation)

Expiration of prepaid expense	7,000	
Accrual of expense at year end....................	1,000	
Payments.................	**9,000**	
Ending balance	17,000	

Total payments = $20,000 ($8,000 + $3,000 + $9,000)

Computing Payments to Employees.   The company may have separate accounts for salaries, wages, and other forms of cash compensation to employees. To compute payments to employees, it is convenient to combine them into one account. Anchor's calculation begins with Salary and Wage Expense (an income statement account) and adjusts for the change in Salary and Wage Payable (a balance sheet account). The computation follows:

$$\begin{matrix} \text{Payments} \\ \text{to} \\ \text{employees} \end{matrix} = \begin{matrix} \text{Salary} \\ \text{and Wage} \\ \text{Expense} \end{matrix} \begin{cases} \textbf{+ Decrease in Salary and Wage Payable} \\ \textbf{or} \\ \textbf{- Increase in Salary and Wage Payable} \end{cases}$$

A decrease in the liability is added because it requires a cash payment. An increase in the liability indicates that the expense exceeds cash payments, so the increase is subtracted. Anchor's salary and wage expense is $56,000. The balance sheet in Exhibit 18-4 reports a $2,000 decrease in the liability. Thus cash payments to employees are $58,000 ($56,000 + $2,000). This is confirmed by analysis of the Salary and Wage Payable account:

Salary and Wage Payable

		Beginning balance	6,000
Payments	58,000	Salary and wage expense.	56,000
		Ending balance.	4,000

Computing Payments of Interest and Income Taxes.   In our illustrative problem, the expense and payment amount is the same for each of these expenses. Therefore, no analysis is required to determine the payment amount. If the expense and the payment differ, the payment can be computed by analyzing the related liability account. The payment computation follows the pattern illustrated for payments to employees.

Computing the Cash Amounts of Investing Activities

Investing activities affect asset accounts, such as Plant Assets, Investments, and Notes Receivable. The cash amounts of investing activities can be identified by analyzing these accounts.

Computing Acquisitions and Sales of Plant Assets.   Most companies have separate accounts for Land, Buildings, Equipment, and other plant assets. It is helpful to combine these accounts into a single summary for computing the cash flows from acquisitions and sales of these assets. Also, we subtract accumulated depreciation from the assets' cost and work with a net figure for plant assets. This allows us to work with a single plant asset account as opposed to a large number of plant asset and related accumulated depreciation accounts.

   To illustrate, observe that Anchor Corporation's balance sheet (Exhibit 18-4) reports beginning plant assets, net of depreciation, of $219,000 and an ending net amount of $453,000. The income statement shows depreciation of $18,000 and an $8,000 gain on sale of plant assets. Further, the acquisitions total $306,000. How much are the proceeds from the sale of plant assets? First, we must determine their book value, computed as follows:

$$\begin{array}{c}\text{Beginning} \\ \text{Plant Asset} \\ \text{balance (net)}\end{array} + \text{Acquisitions} - \text{Depreciation} - \begin{array}{c}\text{Book value} \\ \text{of plant} \\ \text{assets sold}\end{array} = \begin{array}{c}\text{Ending} \\ \text{Plant Asset} \\ \text{balance (net)}\end{array}$$

$$\$219{,}000 \quad + \quad \$306{,}000 \quad - \quad \$18{,}000 \quad - \quad \begin{array}{c}\textbf{Book} \\ \textbf{value} \\ \textbf{sold}\end{array} = \quad \$453{,}000$$

Isolating book value sold on the left-hand side rearranges the equation as follows:

$$-\textbf{Book value sold} = \$453{,}000 - \$219{,}000 - \$306{,}000 + \$18{,}000$$

$$\textbf{Book value sold} = \$54{,}000$$

Now we can compute the sale proceeds as follows:

$$\textbf{Sale proceeds} = \textbf{Book value sold, \$54{,}000} + \textbf{Gain, \$8{,}000} - \textbf{Loss, \$0}$$

$$= \$62{,}000$$

Trace the sale proceeds of $62,000 to the statement of cash flows in Exhibit 18-1. If the sale resulted in a loss of $3,000, the sale proceeds would be $51,000 ($54,000 − $3,000), and the statement would report $51,000 as a cash receipt from this investing activity.

The book value of plant assets sold can also be computed by analysis of the Plant Assets T-account:

Plant Assets (net)

Beginning balance	219,000	Depreciation.	18,000
Acquisitions	306,000	**Book value of assets sold. . . . . .**	**54,000**
Ending balance.	453,000		

Computing Acquisitions and Sales of Assets Classified as Investments, and Loans and Their Collections. Accountants use a separate category of assets for investments in stocks, bonds, and other types of assets. The cash amounts of transactions involving these assets can be computed in the manner illustrated for plant assets. Investments are easier to analyze, however, because there is no depreciation to account for.

Loan transactions follow the pattern illustrated on pages 706 and 707 for collections from customers. New loans cause an outflow of cash, and collections increase cash.

Computing the Cash Amounts of Financing Activities

Financing activities affect liability and stockholders' equity accounts, such as Notes Payable, Bonds Payable, Long-Term Debt, Common Stock, Paid-in Capital in Excess of Par, and Retained Earnings. The cash amounts of financing activities can be computed by analyzing these accounts.

Computing Issuances and Payments of Long-Term Debt. The beginning and ending balances of Long-Term Debt, Notes Payable, or Bonds Payable are taken from the balance sheet. If either the amount of new issuances or the amount of the payments is known, the other amount can be computed. New debt issuances total $94,000. The computation of debt payments follows, using balances from Exhibit 18-4:

Beginning Long-Term Debt balance	+ Issuance of new debt	− Payments =	Ending Long-Term Debt balance
$77,000	+ $94,000	− Payments =	$160,000

Rearranging this equation results in the following:

$$-\text{Payments} = \$160,000 - \$77,000 - \$94,000$$

$$\text{Payments} = \$11,000$$

Computing Issuances and Retirements of Stock and Purchases and Sales of Treasury Stock. The cash effects of these financing activities can be determined by analyzing the various stock accounts. For example, the amount of a new issuance of common stock is determined by combining the Common Stock and any related Capital in Excess of Par account. It is convenient to work with a single summary account for stock as we do for plant assets. Using Exhibit 18-4 data, we have:

Beginning stock balance	+ Issuance of new stock	− Retirements =	Ending stock balance
$258,000	+ New Stock	− $0	= $359,000

Isolating new stock gives the final equation:

$$\text{Issuance of new stock} = \$359,000 - \$258,000$$

$$\text{Issuance of new stock} = \$101,000$$

Cash flows affecting Treasury Stock, a debit balance account, can be analyzed using the following equation:

Beginning Treasury Stock balance	+ Purchases	− Cost of treasury stock sold	=	Ending Treasury Stock balance

If either the purchase amount or the cost of treasury stock sold is known, the other amount can be computed. For a sale of treasury stock, the amount to report on the cash flow statement is the sale proceeds. Suppose a sale brought in cash that was $2,000 less than the $14,000 cost of the treasury stock. In this case, the statement of cash flows would report a cash receipt of $12,000 ($14,000 − $2,000).

Computing Dividend Payments.   If the amount of the dividends is not given elsewhere (for example, in a statement of retained earnings), it can be computed by analyzing the Retained Earnings account. Beginning and ending amounts come from the balance sheet, and the income statement reports net income. Dividend declarations can be computed as shown here, using net income from Exhibit 18-3 and Retained Earnings balances from Exhibit 18-4. We assume Anchor Corporation had no stock dividends or other transactions that affected Retained Earnings during the year. If, for example, a stock dividend and a cash dividend occurred during the year, total dividends must be separated into stock dividends and cash dividends.

Beginning Retained Earnings balance	+ Net income	− Dividend declarations	=	Ending Retained Earnings balance
$86,000	+ $41,000	− Dividends	=	$110,000

Keeping dividends on the left-hand side produces the following equation:

$$-\text{Dividends} = \$110,000 - \$86,000 - \$41,000$$

$$\text{Dividends} = -\$110,000 + \$86,000 + \$41,000$$

$$\text{Dividends} = \$17,000$$

A change in the Dividends Payable account means that dividend payments differ from the amount declared. In this case, dividend payments are determined by first computing dividends declared as shown here. Then add the amount of any decrease in Dividends Payable or subtract the amount of any increase in that account. The result is the dividend payments figure.

Noncash Investing and Financing Activities _____

Companies make investments that do not require cash. They also obtain financing other than cash. Our illustrative problem included none of these transactions.
    Suppose Anchor Corporation issued no-par common stock valued at $320,000

EXHIBIT 18-5 *Noncash Investing and Financing Activities (amounts in thousands)*

Acquisition of building by issuing common stock	$320
Acquisition of land by issuing note payable	72
Payment of long-term debt by transferring investment assets to the creditor	
. . . .	104
Acquisition of equipment by issuing short-term note payable	37
Total noncash investing and financing activities	$533

to acquire a warehouse. Anchor would journalize this transaction as follows:

Warehouse Building	320,000	
Common Stock		320,000

This transaction would not be reported on the cash flow statement because Anchor paid no cash. But the importance of the investment in the warehouse and the financing aspect of issuing stock require that the transaction be reported. Noncash investing and financing activities like this transaction are reported in a separate schedule that accompanies the statement of cash flows. Exhibit 18-5 illustrates how to report noncash investing and financing activities. This information can be included in a schedule immediately following the cash flow statement or in a note.

> **OBJECTIVE 5**
> Name some typical noncash investing and financing activities

Preparing the Statement of Cash Flows: The Indirect Method

An alternative way to compute cash flows from *operating* activities is the **indirect method.** This method, also called the **reconciliation method,** starts with net income and shows the reconciliation from net income to operating cash flows. It shows the link between net income and cash flow from operations better than the direct method. The main drawback of the indirect method is that it does not report the detailed operating cash flows—collections from customers and other cash receipts, payments to suppliers, payments to employees, and payments for interest and taxes.

The indirect method and the direct method are both permitted by the FASB. These methods of preparing the cash flow statement affect only the operating activities section of the statement. No difference exists in the reporting of investing activities and financing activities.

Exhibit 18-6 is Anchor Corporation's statement prepared by the indirect method. You will see that only the operating section of the statement differs from the direct method format in Exhibit 18-1.

Logic behind the Indirect Method

The operating section of the statement begins with net income, taken directly from the income statement. A series of additions and subtractions follows. These are labeled "Add (subtract) items that affect net income and cash flow differently." In this section, we discuss those items.

Depreciation, Depletion, and Amortization Expenses.   These expenses are added back in going from net income to cash flow from operations. Let's see why.

EXHIBIT 18-6 *Statement of Cash Flows*

OBJECTIVE 6

Prepare a statement of cash flows using the indirect method

Anchor Corporation **Statement of Cash Flows — Indirect Method for Operating Activities** **For the Year Ended December 31, 19X2** **Increase (Decrease) in Cash and Cash Equivalents** **(amounts in thousands)**		
Cash flows from operating activities:		
Net income		$ 41
Add (subtract) items that affect net income and cash flow differently:		
Depreciation	$ 18	
Gain on sale of plant assets	(8)	
Increase in accounts receivable	(13)	
Increase in interest receivable	(2)	
Decrease in inventory	3	
Increase in prepaid expenses	(1)	
Increase in accounts payable	34	
Decrease in salary and wage payable	(2)	
Decrease in accrued liabilities	(2)	27
Net cash inflow from operating activities		68
Cash flows from investing activities:		
Acquisition of plant assets	$(306)	
Loan to another company	(11)	
Proceeds from sale of plant assets	62	
Net cash outflow from investing activities		(255)
Cash flows from financing activities:		
Proceeds from issuance of common stock	$ 101	
Proceeds from issuance of long-term debt	94	
Payment of long-term debt	(11)	
Payment of dividends	(17)	
Net cash inflow from financing activities		167
Net decrease in cash		$ (20)
Cash balance, December 31, 19X1		42
Cash balance, December 31, 19X2		$ 22

Depreciation is recorded as follows:

Depreciation Expense	18,000	
Accumulated Depreciation		18,000

This entry contains no debit or credit to Cash, so depreciation expense has no cash effect. However, depreciation is deducted from revenues in the computation of income. Therefore, in going from net income to cash flow from operations, we add depreciation back to net income. The addback simply cancels the earlier deduction. The following example should help: Suppose a company had two transactions during the period, a $1,000 cash sale and depreciation expense of $300. Net income is $700 ($1,000 − $300). Cash flow from operations is $1,000. To go from net income ($700) to cash flow ($1,000), we must add the depreciation amount of $300.

All expenses with no cash effects are added back to net income on the cash flow statement. Depletion and amortization are two other examples.

Gains and Losses on the Sale of Assets. Sales of plant assets are investing activities on the cash flow statement. A gain or loss on the sale is an adjustment to income. Exhibit 18-6 includes an adjustment for a gain. Recall that equipment with a book value of $54,000 was sold for $62,000, producing a gain of $8,000. The way to learn how to treat an item on the cash flow statement is to examine the journal entry that recorded it, as discussed on page 702.

The $8,000 gain is reported on the income statement and, therefore, is included in net income. However, the cash receipt from the sale is $62,000, which includes the gain. To avoid counting the gain twice, we need to remove its effect from income and report the cash receipt of $62,000 in the investing-activities section of the statement. Starting with net income, we subtract the gain. This deduction removes the gain's earlier effect on income. The sale of plant assets is reported as a $62,000 cash receipt from an investing activity, as shown in Exhibits 18-1 and 18-6.

A loss on the sale of plant assets is also an adjustment to net income on the statement of cash flows. However, a loss is added back to income to compute cash flow from operations. The sale proceeds are reported under investing activities.

Changes in the Current Asset and Current Liability Accounts. Most current assets and current liabilities result from operating activities. Accounts receivable result from sales, inventory generates revenues, and prepaid expenses are used up in operations. On the liability side, accounts payable are incurred to buy inventory, and accrued liabilities relate to salaries, utilities, and other expenses. Changes in these current accounts are reported as adjustments to net income on the cash flow statement. The following rules apply:

1. An *increase* in a current asset other than cash is subtracted from net income to compute cash flow from operations. Suppose a company makes a sale. Income is increased by the sale amount. However, collection of less than the full amount leaves Accounts Receivable with an increase. To compute the impact of revenue on the cash flow amount, it is necessary to subtract the $13,000 increase in Accounts Receivable from net income in Exhibit 18-6. The same logic applies to the other current assets. If they increase during the period, subtract the increase from net income.

2. A *decrease* in a current asset other than cash is added to net income. For example, suppose Accounts Receivable's balance decreased by $4,000 during the period. Cash receipts cause the Accounts Receivable balance to decrease, so decreases in Accounts Receivable and the other current assets are added to net income.

3. A *decrease* in a current liability is subtracted from net income. The payment of a current liability causes it to decrease, so decreases in current liabilities are subtracted from net income. For example, in Exhibit 18-6, the $2,000 decrease in Accrued Liabilities is subtracted from net income to compute net cash inflow from operating activities.

4. An *increase* in a current liability is added to net income. Suppose Accrued Liabilities increased during the year. This can occur only if cash is not spent to pay this liability, which means that cash payments are less than the related expense. Thus increases in current liabilities are added to net income.

The computation of net cash inflow or net cash outflow from *operating* activities by the indirect method takes a path that is very different from the computation by the direct method. However, the two methods arrive at the same amount of net cash flow. This is shown in Exhibits 18-1 and 18-6, which report a net cash inflow of $68,000.

Supplementary Disclosures

The company that uses the direct method for reporting operating activities on the cash flow statement must, according to *FASB Statement No. 95,* also report the reconciliation of net income to cash flow from operations. A format similar to the operating section under the indirect method (Exhibit 18-6) is suitable. The company that uses the indirect method may report the components of operating cash flows similar to that in the direct method. These supplementary disclosures can appear in notes to the statement or immediately beneath the statement near the

Exhibit 18-7   *Statement of Cash Flows*

Nike, Inc. Statement of Cash Flows For the Year Ended May 31, 1987 (in thousands)	
Cash provided (used) by operations:	
Net income...	$ 35,879
Income charges (credits) not affecting cash:	
Depreciation.......................................	12,078
Deferred income taxes....................................	8,486
Other	2,494
Changes in certain working capital components:	
Decrease in inventory	59,542
Decrease in accounts receivable	1,174
Decrease in other current assets	4,331
Increase in accounts payable, accrued liabilities, and income taxes payable	8,462
Cash provided by operations	132,446
Cash provided (used) by investing activities:	
Additions to property, plant and equipment	(11,874)
Disposals of property, plant and equipment	1,728
Additions to other assets.....................................	(930)
Cash used by investing activities	(11,076)
Cash provided (used) by financing activities:	
Additions to long-term debt	30,332
Reductions in long-term debt including current portion...........	(10,678)
Decrease in notes payable to banks	(18,489)
Proceeds from exercise of options	1,911
Dividends—common and preferred	(15,188)
Cash used by financing activities	(12,112)
Effect of exchange rate changes on cash	(529)
Net increase (decrease) in cash..................................	108,729
Cash and equivalents, beginning of year.........................	18,138
Cash and equivalents, end of year.............................	$126,867

noncash investing and financing activities. The goal is to give readers of the financial statements the information they need to make informed decisions about the company.

Exhibit 18-7 is the cash flow statement of Nike, Inc., maker of athletic shoes and clothing. Notice that Nike uses the indirect method to report cash flows from operating activities. Many companies use this format. Most of the items in Exhibit 18-7 have been discussed earlier, but three are new. First, deferred income taxes are added back to net income in the operating section. These taxes do not require current cash payments and are, therefore, similar to depreciation. Second, financing activities include proceeds from exercise of options. This is the amount of cash received from issuance of stock to executives. Third, changes in exchange rates show the cash effect of fluctuations in foreign currencies, a topic that is beyond the scope of this course. Nike's reporting of this item agrees with GAAP.

Summary Problem for Your Review

Prepare the 19X3 statement of cash flows for Robins Corporation, using the indirect method to report cash flows from operating activities. In a separate schedule, report Robins's noncash investing and financing activities.

	December 31,	
	19X3	**19X2**
Current assets:		
Cash and cash equivalents.	$19,000	$ 3,000
Accounts receivable	22,000	23,000
Inventories	34,000	31,000
Prepaid expenses	1,000	3,000
Current liabilities:		
Notes payable for inventory purchases.	$11,000	$ 7,000
Accounts payable.	24,000	19,000
Accrued liabilities.	7,000	9,000
Income tax payable	10,000	10,000

Transaction data for 19X3:

Purchase of equipment.	$98,000	Depreciation expense	$ 7,000
Payment of cash dividends. . . .	18,000	Issuance of long-term note	
Net income	26,000	payable to borrow cash.	7,000
Issuance of common stock to		Issuance of common stock for	
retire bonds payable	13,000	cash	19,000
Purchase of long-term		Sale of building.	74,000
investment.	8,000	Amortization expense	3,000
Issuance of long-term note		Purchase of treasury stock	5,000
payable to purchase patent. .	37,000	Loss on sale of building	2,000

SOLUTION TO REVIEW PROBLEM

Robins Corporation
Statement of Cash Flows
Year Ended December 31, 19X3
Increase (Decrease) in Cash and Cash Equivalents

Cash flows from operating activities:		
Net income..		$26,000
Add (subtract) items that affect net income and cash flow differently:		
Depreciation.....................................	$ 7,000	
Amortization	3,000	
Loss on sale of building........................	2,000	
Decrease in accounts receivable	1,000	
Increase in inventories.........................	(3,000)	
Decrease in prepaid expenses	2,000	
Increase in notes payable, short-term...........	4,000	
Increase in accounts payable....................	5,000	
Decrease in accrued liabilities	(2,000)	19,000
Net cash inflow from operating activities.............		45,000
Cash flows from investing activities:		
Purchase of equipment	$(98,000)	
Sale of building	74,000	
Purchase of long-term investment	(8,000)	
Net cash outflow from investing activities		(32,000)
Cash flows from financing activities:		
Issuance of common stock	$ 19,000	
Payment of cash dividends........................	(18,000)	
Issuance of long-term note payable	7,000	
Purchase of treasury stock	(5,000)	
Net cash inflow from financing activities		3,000
Net increase in cash and cash equivalents..................		$16,000
Noncash investing and financing activities:		
Issuance of long-term note payable to purchase patent		$37,000
Issuance of common stock to retire bonds payable		13,000
Total noncash investing and financing activities		$ 50,000

Summary

The *statement of cash flows* reports a business's cash receipts, cash disbursements, and net change in cash for the accounting period. It shows *why* cash increased or decreased during the period. A required financial statement, it gives a different view of the business from the accrual-basis statements. The cash flow statement helps financial statement users predict the future cash flows of the entity. Cash includes cash on hand, cash in bank, and *cash equivalents* such as liquid, short-term investments.

The statement is divided into *operating activities, investing activities,* and *financing activities.* Operating activities create revenues and expenses; investing activities affect long-term assets; and financing activities obtain the funds needed to launch and sustain the business. Each section of the statement includes cash receipts and cash payments and concludes with a net cash increase or decrease. In addition, *noncash investing and financing activities* are reported in an accompanying schedule.

Two formats are used to report operating activities. The *direct method* lists the major sources of cash receipts and disbursements—for example, cash collections from customers and cash payments to suppliers and to employees. The *indirect method* shows the reconciliation from net income to cash flow from operations. The FASB permits both methods but prefers the direct method.

Self-Study Questions

Test your understanding of the chapter by marking the best answer for each of the following questions.

1. The income statement and the balance sheet *(p. 695)*
   a. Report the cash effects of transactions
   b. Fail to report why cash changed during the period
   c. Report the sources and uses of cash during the period
   d. Are divided into operating, investing, and financing activities
2. A new business's first activity is to *(p. 697)*
   a. Obtain financing
   b. Make an investment
   c. Earn revenues
   d. Incur expenses
3. A successful company's major source of cash should be *(pp. 697, 700)*
   a. Operating activities
   b. Investing activities
   c. Financing activities
   d. A combination of the above
4. Dividends paid to stockholders are reported on the statement of cash flows as a (an) *(pp. 699, 702)*
   a. Operating activity
   b. Investing activity
   c. Financing activity
   d. Combination of the above
5. Which of the following items appears on a cash flow statement prepared by the direct method? *(p. 699)*
   a. Depreciation expense
   b. Decrease in accounts receivable
   c. Loss on sale of plant assets
   d. Cash payments to suppliers
6. Interest Receivable's beginning balance is $18,000, and its ending amount is $14,000. Interest revenue earned during the year is $43,000. How much cash interest was received? *(pp. 706, 707, 708)*
   a. $39,000
   b. $43,000
   c. $45,000
   d. $47,000
7. McGrath Company sold an investment at a gain of $22,000. The Investment account reports a beginning balance of $104,000 and an ending balance of $91,000. During the year, McGrath purchased new investments costing $31,000. What were the proceeds from the sale of investments? *(pp. 710, 711).*
   a. $22,000
   b. $44,000
   c. $66,000
   d. $186,000
8. Noncash investing and financing activities *(p. 713)*
   a. Are reported in the main body of the cash flow statement
   b. Are reported in a separate schedule that accompanies the cash flow statement
   c. Are reported on the income statement
   d. Are not reported in the financial statements
9. The indirect method does a better job than the direct method at *(p. 713)*
   a. Reporting the cash effects of financing activities
   b. Reporting why the cash balance changed
   c. Showing the link between net income and cash flow from operations
   d. Reporting the separate components of operating cash flows such as collections from customers and payments to suppliers and employees

10. Net income is $17,000, depreciation is $9,000, and amortization is $3,000. In addition, the sale of a plant asset generated a $4,000 gain. Current assets other than cash increased by $6,000, and current liabilities increased by $8,000. What was the amount of cash flow from operations? *(p. 714)*

a. $23,000   c. $31,000
b. $27,000   d. $35,000

Answers to the self-study questions are at the end of the chapter.

Accounting Vocabulary

cash equivalents *(p. 698)*,   cash flows *(p. 695)*,   direct method *(p. 698)*,   financing activities *(p. 697)*,   indirect method *(p. 713)*,   investing activities *(p. 697)*,   operating activities *(p. 697)*, reconciliation method *(p. 713)*,   statement of cash flows *(p. 695)*.

ASSIGNMENT MATERIAL _____

Questions

1. What information does the statement of cash flows report that is not shown on the balance sheet, the income statement, or the statement of retained earnings?
2. Identify four purposes of the statement of cash flows.
3. Identify and briefly describe the three types of activities that are reported on the statement of cash flows.
4. How is the statement of cash flows dated and why?
5. What is the check figure for the statement of cash flows, where is it obtained, and how is it used?
6. What is the most important source of cash for most successful companies?
7. How can cash decrease during a year when income is high? How can cash increase during a year when income is low? How can investors and creditors learn these facts about the company?
8. DeBerg, Inc., prepares its statement of cash flows using the *direct* method for operating activities. Identify the section of DeBerg's statement of cash flows where each of the following transactions will appear. If the transaction does not appear on the cash flow statement, give the reason.

a.	Cash..	14,000	
	Note Payable, Long-Term.....................		14,000
b.	Salary Expense.................................	7,300	
	Cash......................................		7,300
c.	Cash...	28,400	
	Sales Revenue		28,400
d.	Amortization Expense...........................	6,500	
	Goodwill		6,500
e.	Accounts Payable	1,400	
	Cash......................................		1,400

9. Why are depreciation, depletion, and amortization expenses *not* reported on a cash flow statement that reports operating activities by the direct method? Why and how are these expenses reported on a statement prepared by the indirect method?
10. Mainline Distributing Company collected cash of $92,000 from customers and $6,000 interest on notes receivable. Cash payments included $24,000 to employees, $13,000 to suppliers, $6,000 as dividends to stockholders, and $5,000 as a loan to

another company. How much was Mainline's net cash inflow from operating activities?

11. Summarize the major cash receipts and cash disbursements in the three categories of activities that appear on the cash flow statement.

12. Kirchner, Inc., recorded salary expense of $51,000 during a year when the balance of Salary Payable decreased from $10,000 to $2,000. How much cash did Kirchner pay to employees during the year? Where on the statement of cash flows should Kirchner report this item?

13. Marshall Corporation's beginning plant asset balance, net of accumulated depreciation, was $193,000, and the ending amount was $176,000. Marshall recorded depreciation of $37,000 and sold plant assets with a book value of $9,000. How much cash did Marshall pay to purchase plant assets during the period? Where on the statement of cash flows should Marshall report this item?

14. How should issuance of a note payable to purchase land be reported in the financial statements? Identify three other transactions that fall in this same category.

15. Which format of the cash flow statement gives a clearer description of the individual cash flows from operating activities? Which format better shows the relationship between net income and operating cash flow?

16. An investment that cost $65,000 was sold for $80,000, resulting in a $15,000 gain. Show how to report this transaction on a statement of cash flows prepared by the indirect method.

17. Identify the cash effects of increases and decreases in current assets other than cash. What are the cash effects of increases and decreases in current liabilities?

18. Milano Corporation earned net income of $38,000 and had depreciation expense of $22,000. Also, noncash current assets decreased $13,000, and current liabilities decreased $9,000. What was Milano's net cash flow from operating activities?

19. What is the difference between the direct method and the indirect method of reporting investing activities and financing activities?

20. Milgrom Company reports operating activities by the direct method. Does this method show the relationship between net income and cash flow from operations? If so, state how. If not, how can Milgrom satisfy this purpose of the cash flow statement?

Exercises

Exercise 18-1   *Identifying activities for the statement of cash flows*

Identify each of the following transactions as an operating activity (0), an investing activity (I), a financing activity (F), a noncash investing and financing activity (NFI), or a transaction that is not reported on the statement of cash flows (N). Assume the direct method is used to report cash flows from operating activities.

_____ a. Cash sale of land

_____ b. Payment of stock dividend

_____ c. Acquisition of equipment by issuance of note payable

_____ d. Payment of long-term debt

_____ e. Acquisition of building by issuance of common stock

_____ f. Accrual of salary expense

_____ g. Purchase of long-term investment

_____ h. Payment of wages to employees

_____ i. Collection of cash interest

_____ j. Amortization of bond discount

_____ k. Collection of account receivable

_____ l. Issuance of long-term note payable to borrow cash

_____ m. Depreciation of equipment

_____ n. Purchase of treasury stock

_____ o. Issuance of common stock for cash

_____ p. Payment of account payable

_____ q. Issuance of preferred stock for cash

_____ r. Payment of cash dividend

_____ s. Sale of long-term investment

Exercise 18-2   *Classifying transactions for the statement of cash flows*

Indicate where, if at all, each of the following transactions would be reported on a statement of cash flows prepared by the *direct* method and the accompanying schedule of noncash investing and financing activities.

a. Equipment	18,000	
Cash		18,000
b. Cash	7,200	
Long-Term Investment		7,200
c. Bonds Payable	45,000	
Cash		45,000
d. Building	164,000	
Note Payable, Long-Term		164,000
e. Cash	1,400	
Accounts Receivable		1,400
f. Dividends Payable	16,500	
Cash		16,500
g. Furniture and Fixtures	22,100	
Note Payable, Short-Term		22,100
h. Accounts Payable	8,300	
Cash		8,300
i. Cash	81,000	
Common Stock		12,000
Paid-in Capital in Excess of Par—Common		69,000
j. Treasury Stock	13,000	
Cash		13,000
k. Retained Earnings	36,000	
Common Stock		36,000
l. Cash	2,000	
Interest Revenue		2,000
m. Land	87,700	
Cash		87,700
n. Salary Expense	4,300	
Cash		4,300

Exercise 18-3   *Computing cash flows from operating activities—direct method*

Analysis of the accounting records of Gibson Transfer Company reveals the following:

Acquisition of land	$37,000	Payment of dividends	$ 7,000
Payment of accounts payable	45,000	Collection of accounts receivable	89,000
Net income	24,000	Payment of salaries and wages	34,000
Payment of income tax	13,000	Depreciation	8,000
Collection of dividend revenue	7,000	Decrease in current liabilities	20,000
Payment of interest	16,000	Increase in current assets other than cash	17,000
Cash sales	9,000		
Loss on sale of land	2,000		

Compute cash flows from operating activities by the direct method. Use the format of the operating section of Exhibit 18-1. Not all items are used.

Exercise 18-4   *Computing cash flows from operating activities—indirect method*

Use the data of Exercise 18-3 to compute cash flows from operating activities by the indirect method. Use the format of the operating section of Exhibit 18-6. Not all items are used.

Exercise 18-5   *Identifying items for the statement of cash flows—direct method*

Selected accounts of Bismark, Inc., show the following activity:

Interest Receivable

Beginning balance...........	11,000	Cash receipts of interest......	40,000
Interest revenue	37,000		
Ending balance	8,000		

Investments in Stock

Beginning balance...........	0	Cost of investments sold	4,000
Acquisitions................	27,000		
Ending balance	23,000		

Long-Term Debt

Payments..................	69,000	Beginning balance...........	134,000
		Issuance of debt for cash	17,000
		Ending balance	82,000

For each account, identify the item or items that should appear on a statement of cash flows prepared by the direct method. State where to report the item.

Exercise 18-6   *Computing amounts for the statement of cash flows*

Compute the following items for the statement of cash flows:

a. Beginning and ending Accounts Receivable are $14,000 and $19,000, respectively. Credit sales for the period total $81,000. How much are cash collections?
b. Cost of goods sold is $62,000. Beginning Inventory balance is $25,000, and ending Inventory balance is $21,000. Beginning and ending Accounts Payable are $11,000 and $8,000, respectively. How much are cash payments for inventory?

Exercise 18-7   *Computing amounts for the statement of cash flows*

Compute the following items for the statement of cash flows:

a. Beginning and ending Plant Assets, net, are $79,000 and $83,000, respectively. Depreciation for the period is $16,000, and acquisitions of new plant assets are $27,000. Plant assets were sold at a $4,000 loss. What were the cash proceeds of the sale?
b. Beginning and ending Retained Earnings are $45,000 and $73,000, respectively. Net income for the period is $62,000, and stock dividends are $19,000. How much are cash dividend payments?

Exercise 18-8 *Classifying transactions for the statement of cash flows*

Two transactions of Ferrari's Restaurant are recorded as follows:

a. Cash.. 17,000
   Accumulated Depreciation............................ 51,000
   Loss on Sale of Equipment............................ 67,000
        Equipment...................................... 135,000
b. Land... 110,000
        Cash.. 10,000
        Note Payable.................................. 100,000

Required

1. Indicate where, how, and in what amount to report these transactions on the statement of cash flows and accompanying schedule of noncash investing and financing activities. Ferrari reports cash flows from operating activities by the *direct* method.
2. Repeat Requirement 1, assuming Ferrari reports cash flows from operating activities by the *indirect* method.

Exercise 18-9 *Preparing the statement of cash flows—direct method*

The income statement and additional data of Hillcrest Electric Company follow.

Hillcrest Electric Company
Income Statement
Year Ended September 30, 19X2

Revenues:		
Sales revenue	$336,000	
Dividend revenue	22,000	$358,000
Expenses:		
Cost of goods sold	163,000	
Salary expense	85,000	
Depreciation expense	29,000	
Advertising expense	19,000	
Interest expense	2,000	
Income tax expense	9,000	307,000
Net income		$ 51,000

Additional data:

a. Collections from customers are $3,000 more than sales.
b. Payments to suppliers are $9,000 less than the sum of cost of goods sold plus advertising expense.
c. Payments to employees are $1,000 more than salary expense.
d. Dividend revenue, interest expense, and income tax expense equal their cash amounts.
e. Acquisition of plant assets are $141,000. Of this amount, $91,000 is paid in cash, $50,000 by signing a note payable.
f. Proceeds from sale of land, $19,000.
g. Proceeds from issuance of common stock, $30,000.
h. Payment of long-term note payable, $15,000.
i. Payment of dividends, $11,000.
j. Increase in cash balance, $23,000.

Prepare Hillcrest Electric Company's statement of cash flows and accompanying schedule of noncash investing and financing activities. Report operating activities by the *direct* method.

Exercise 18-10   *Reporting cash flows from operating activities—indirect method*

Use the information of Exercise 18-9 and the following changes in the current accounts to report Hillcrest Electric Company's cash flows from operating activities by the *indirect* method. All changes in the current accounts affected operations.

	September 30,	
	19X2	**19X1**
Current Assets:		
Accounts receivable	$51,000	$58,000
Inventory...........................	83,000	77,000
Prepaid expenses	9,000	8,000
Current Liabilities:		
Notes payable.......................	$20,000	$20,000
Accounts payable	35,000	22,000
Accrued liabilities	19,000	21,000

Problems   *(Group A)*

Problem 18-1A   *Preparing the statement of cash flows—direct method*

Randolph-Macon Corporation accountants have developed the following data from the company's accounting records for the year ended July 31, 19X9:

1. Collection of interest revenue, $11,700
2. Acquisition of equipment by issuing short-term note payable, $35,500
3. Payments of salaries, $104,000
4. Credit sales, $608,100
5. Loan to another company, $35,000
6. Income tax expense and payments, $56,400
7. Depreciation expense, $27,700
8. Collections on accounts receivable, $673,100
9. Loan collections, $74,400
10. Proceeds from sale of investments, $34,700, including $3,800 loss
11. Payment of long-term debt by issuing preferred stock, $107,300
12. Amortization expense, $23,900
13. Cash sales, $222,000
14. Proceeds from issuance of short-term debt, $44,100
15. Payments of long-term debt, $78,800
16. Proceeds from sale of plant assets, $49,700, including $10,600 gain
17. Interest revenue, $12,100
18. Cash receipt of dividend revenue on stock investments, $5,700
19. Payments to suppliers, $683,300
20. Interest expense and payments, $37,800
21. Salary expense, $105,300
22. Cash payments to purchase plant assets, $181,000
23. Cost of goods sold, $481,100

24. Proceeds from issuance of common stock, $116,900
25. Payment of cash dividends, $50,500
26. Cash balance: July 31, 19X8 — $53,800
                July 31, 19X9 — $59,300

Required

Prepare Randolph-Macon Corporation's statement of cash flows for the year ended July 31, 19X9. Follow the format of Exhibit 18-1, but do *not* show amounts in thousands. Include an accompanying schedule of noncash investing and financing activities. Warning: Some listed items are *not* used.

Problem 18-2A *Preparing the statement of cash flows — indirect method*

Accountants for LaDue Fashions have assembled the following data for the year ended December 31, 19X4:

Transaction data for 19X4:

Collection of loan	$10,300	Issuance of long-term debt to borrow cash	$21,000
Depreciation expense	19,200	Net income	83,600
Acquisition of equipment	69,000		
Payment of long-term debt by issuing common stock	89,400	Issuance of preferred stock for cash	36,200
Acquisition of long-term investment	44,800	Sale of long-term investment	12,200
		Amortization expense	1,100
Acquisition of building by issuing long-term note payable	94,000	Payment of long-term debt	47,800
		Gain on sale of investment	3,500
Stock dividends	12,600	Payment of cash dividends	48,300

	December 31,	
	19X4	**19X3**
Current accounts (all result from operations):		
Current assets:		
Cash and cash equivalents	$21,700	$34,800
Accounts receivable	70,100	73,700
Inventories	90,600	96,500
Prepaid expenses	3,200	2,100
Current liabilities:		
Notes payable for inventory purchases	$36,300	$36,800
Accounts payable	72,100	67,500
Income tax payable	5,900	6,800
Accrued liabilities	28,300	23,200

Required

Prepare LaDue Fashions's statement of cash flows, using the *indirect* method to report operating activities. Include an accompanying schedule of noncash investing and financing activities.

Problem 18-3A *Computing amounts for the statement of cash flows — direct method*

The 19X3 income statement and comparative balance sheet of Custom Trailers, Inc., follow:

Income Statement

Revenues:

Sales revenue......................		$436,800
Interest revenue....................		11,700
Total revenues...................		448,500

Expenses:

Cost of goods sold.................	$205,200	
Salary expense.....................	76,400	
Depreciation expense	15,300	
Other operating expense.............	49,700	
Interest expense....................	24,600	
Income tax expense.................	16,900	
Total expenses		388,100
Net income		$ 60,400

Comparative Balance Sheet

	19X3	19X2	Increase (Decrease)
Current assets:			
Cash and cash equivalents..................	$ 12,500	$ 15,600	$ (3,100)
Accounts receivable	41,500	43,100	(1,600)
Interest receivable.......................	600	900	(300)
Inventories	94,300	89,900	4,400
Prepaid expenses	1,700	2,200	(500)
Plant assets:			
Land	35,100	10,000	25,100
Equipment, net...........................	100,900	93,700	7,200
Total assets	$286,600	$255,400	$ 31,200
Current liabilities:			
Accounts payable	$ 16,400	$ 17,900	$ (1,500)
Interest payable	6,300	6,700	(400)
Salary payable	2,100	1,400	700
Other accrued liabilities	18,100	18,700	(600)
Income tax payable.......................	6,300	3,800	2,500
Long-term liabilities:			
Notes payable...........................	55,000	65,000	(10,000)
Stockholders' equity:			
Common stock, no-par....................	131,100	122,300	8,800
Retained earnings........................	51,300	19,600	31,700
Total liabilities and stockholders' equity.........	$286,600	$255,400	$ 31,200

Custom Trailers had no noncash investing and financing transactions during 19X3.

Required

Compute the following items for the 19X3 statement of cash flows:

Cash flows from operating activities:
  Cash receipts:
    Collections from customers .... $
    Receipts of interest ....

Cash payments:
    To suppliers:
        Inventory..
        Operating expenses..
    To employees ....
    For interest ....
    For income tax ....
        Net cash inflow from operating activities .... $ _____

Cash flows from investing activities:
    Acquisition of land (there were no sales of land)...................... $ _____
    Acquisition of equipment (there were no sales of equipment) ....
        Net cash outflow from investing activities .... $ _____

Cash flows from financing activities:
    Payment of dividends .... $ _____
    Payment of note payable (there were no issuances of notes payable) ......
    Issuance of common stock (there were no retirements of stock or
        purchases of treasury stock)..................................
        Net cash outflow from financing activities .... $ _____
Net decrease in cash... $3,100

Problem 18-4A *Preparing the statement of cash flows—indirect method*

The comparative balance sheet of Highland Recreation, Inc., at December 31, 19X5 reported the following:

	December 31,	
	19X5	19X4
Current assets:		
Cash and cash equivalents..............	$ 6,000	$ 2,500
Accounts receivable	28,600	29,300
Inventories	51,600	53,000
Prepaid expenses	4,200	3,700
Current liabilities:		
Notes payable for inventory purchases....	$ 9,200	$ -0-
Accounts payable	21,900	28,000
Accrued liabilities....................	14,300	16,800
Income tax payable...................	11,000	14,300

Highland's transactions during 19X5 included the following:

Retirement of bonds payable by issuing common stock......	$40,000	Sale of long-term investment...............	$ 6,000
Amortization expense........	5,000	Depreciation expense	15,000
Payment of cash dividends....	17,000	Cash acquisition of building...	84,000
Cash acquisition of equipment	55,000	Net income	42,000
		Issuance of common stock for	
Issuance of long-term note payable to borrow cash........	32,000	cash	60,600
		Stock dividend..............	13,000

Required

Prepare Highland Recreation's statement of cash flows for the year ended December 31, 19X5. Use the *indirect* method to report cash flows from operating activities. Report non-cash investing and financing activities in an accompanying schedule. All current account balances result from operating transactions.

Problem 18-5A   *Preparing the statement of cash flows—direct and indirect methods*

To prepare the statement of cash flows, accountants for Columbus Corporation have summarized 19X8 activity in two accounts as follows:

Cash

Beginning balance..............	37,100	Payments of operating expenses ...	46,100
Issuance of common stock	34,600	Payment of long-term debt........	78,900
Receipts of dividends	1,900	Purchase of treasury stock	10,400
Collection of loan	18,500	Payment of income tax...........	8,000
Sale of investments.............	9,900	Payments on accounts payable.....	101,600
Receipts of interest	7,700	Payments of dividends	1,800
Collections from customers........	268,100	Payments of salaries and wages....	67,500
Sale of treasury stock	26,200	Payments of interest	21,800
		Purchase of equipment...........	29,900
Ending balance	38,000		

Common Stock

		Beginning balance..............	103,500
		Issuance for cash...............	34,600
		Issuance to acquire land	62,100
		Issuance to retire long-term debt ...	21,100
		Ending balance	221,300

Required

1. Prepare Columbus Corporation's statement of cash flows for the year ended December 31, 19X8, using the *direct* method to report operating activities. Also prepare the accompanying schedule of noncash investing and financing activities.

Columbus's 19X8 income statement and selected balance sheet data follow.

Columbus Corporation
Income Statement
For the Year Ended December 31, 19X8

Revenues and gains:		
Sales revenue.....................		$251,800
Interest revenue...................		7,700
Dividend revenue		1,900
Gain on sale of investments..........		700
Total revenues and gains		262,100
Expenses:		
Cost of goods sold.................	$103,600	
Salary and wage expense	66,800	
Depreciation expense	10,900	
Other operating expense.............	44,700	
Interest expense....................	24,100	
Income tax expense.................	2,600	
Total expenses		252,700
Net income		$ 9,400

Columbus Corporation
Balance Sheet Data

	Increase (Decrease)
Current assets:	
Cash and cash equivalents	$ 900
Accounts receivable.........................	(16,300)
Inventories	5,700
Prepaid expenses	(1,900)
Current liabilities:	
Accounts payable............................	$ 7,700
Interest payable	2,300
Salary payable	(700)
Other accrued liabilities.....................	(3,300)
Income tax payable	(5,400)

Required

2. Use these data to prepare a supplementary schedule showing cash flows from operating activities by the *indirect* method. All activity in the current accounts results from operations.

Problem 18-6A   *Preparing the statement of cash flows—indirect and direct methods*

Henke-Parsons Corporation's comparative balance sheet at September 30, 19X4, included the following balances:

Henke-Parsons Corporation
Partial Balance Sheet
September 30, 19X4 and 19X3

	19X4	19X3	Increase (Decrease)
Current assets:			
Cash	$ 27,700	$ 17,600	$ 10,100
Accounts receivable	41,900	44,000	(2,100)
Interest receivable........................	4,100	2,800	1,300
Inventories	121,700	116,900	4,800
Prepaid expenses	8,600	9,300	(700)
Current liabilities:			
Notes payable, short-term..................	$ 22,000	$ -0-	$ 22,000
Accounts payable.........................	61,800	70,300	(8,500)
Income tax payable........................	21,800	24,600	(2,800)
Accrued liabilities........................	17,900	29,100	(11,200)
Interest payable	4,500	3,200	1,300
Salary payable	1,500	1,100	400

Transaction data for the year ended September 30, 19X4:

a. Net income, $72,900.

b. Depreciation expense on equipment, $8,500.

c. Acquired long-term investments, $37,300.

d. Sold land for $38,100, including $10,900 gain.

e. Acquired equipment by issuing long-term note payable, $26,300.

f. Paid long-term note payable, $24,700.

g. Received cash of $51,900 for issuance of common stock.

h. Paid cash dividends, $64,300.

i. Acquired equipment by issuing short-term note payable, $22,000.

Required

1. Prepare Henke-Parsons's statement of cash flows for the year ended September 30, 19X4, using the *indirect* method to report operating activities. Also prepare the accompanying schedule of noncash investing and financing activities. All current accounts except short-term notes payable result from operating transactions.

2. Prepare a supplementary schedule showing cash flows from operations by the *direct* method. The income statement reports the following: sales, $349,600; gain on sale of land, $10,900; interest revenue $7,300; cost of goods sold, $161,500; salary expense, $63,400; other operating expenses, $29,600; income tax expense, $18,400; interest expense, $13,500; depreciation expense, $8,500.

(Group B)

Problem 18-1B   *Preparing the statement of cash flows—direct method*

Pittsburgh Corporation accountants have developed the following data from the company's accounting records for the year ended April 30, 19X5:

1. Cash receipt of dividend revenue on stock investments, $4,100
2. Payments to suppliers, $478,500
3. Cash sales, $171,900
4. Depreciation expense, $59,900
5. Proceeds from issuance of short-term debt, $19,600
6. Payments of long-term debt, $50,000
7. Interest expense and payments, $13,300
8. Salary expense, $95,300
9. Loan collections, $12,800
10. Proceeds from sale of investments, $6,800, including $300 gain
11. Payment of short-term note payable by issuing common stock, $14,000
12. Amortization expense, $2,900
13. Income tax expense and payments, $37,900
14. Cash payments to acquire plant assets, $59,400
15. Cost of goods sold, $382,600
16. Proceeds from issuance of common stock, $8,000
17. Payment of cash dividends, $48,400
18. Collection of interest, $4,400
19. Acquisition of equipment by issuing short-term note payable, $16,400
20. Payments of salaries, $93,600
21. Credit sales, $533,900
22. Loan to another company, $12,500
23. Proceeds from sale of plant assets, $22,400, including $6,800 loss
24. Collections on accounts receivable, $521,100
25. Interest revenue, $3,800
26. Cash balance: April 30, 19X4—$39,300
    April 30, 19X5—$16,800

Required

Prepare Pittsburgh Corporation's statement of cash flows for the year ended April 30, 19X5. Follow the format of Exhibit 18-1, but do *not* show amounts in thousands. Include an accompanying schedule of noncash investing and financing activities. Warning: Some listed items are *not* used.

Problem 18-2B   *Preparing the statement of cash flows—indirect method*

McAlister Overhead Door Systems, Inc., accountants have assembled the following data for the year ended December 31, 19X7:

Transaction data for 19X7:

Collection of loan	$ 8,700	Issuance of long-term note	
Depreciation expense	26,800	payable to borrow cash. . . .	$ 34,400
Acquisition of building	125,300	Net income	55,100
Retirement of bonds payable		Issuance of common stock for	
by issuing common stock . .	65,000	cash	41,200
Acquisition of long-term		Sale of equipment	19,500
investment	31,600	Amortization expense	5,300
Acquisition of land by issuing		Purchase of treasury stock . . .	14,300
long-term note payable. . . .	83,000	Loss on sale of equipment . . .	11,700
Stock dividends.	31,800	Payment of cash dividends. . .	18,300

	December 31,	
	19X7	**19X6**
Current accounts (all result from operations):		
Current assets:		
Cash and cash equivalents.	$35,200	$22,700
Accounts receivable	59,700	64,200
Inventories.	88,600	83,000
Prepaid expenses	5,300	4,100
Current liabilities:		
Notes payable for inventory purchases . .	$22,600	$18,300
Accounts payable	52,900	55,800
Income tax payable.	18,600	16,700
Accrued liabilities	25,500	27,200

Required

Prepare McAlister's statement of cash flows, using the *indirect* method to report operating activities. Include an accompanying schedule of noncash investing and financing activities.

Problem 18-3B   *Computing amounts for the statement of cash flows—direct method*

The 19X5 income statement and comparative balance sheet of Loma Alto, Inc., follow.

Income Statement

Revenues:		
Sales revenue.		$194,000
Interest revenue.		8,600
Total revenues		202,600
Expenses:		
Cost of goods sold.	$92,400	
Salary expense.	27,800	
Depreciation expense	4,000	
Other operating expense.	10,500	
Interest expense.	11,600	
Income tax expense.	9,100	
Total expenses		155,400
Net income		$ 47,200

Comparative Balance Sheet

	19X5	19X4	Increase (Decrease)
Current assets:			
Cash and cash equivalents..................	$ 6,400	$ 5,300	$ 1,100
Accounts receivable	28,600	26,900	1,700
Interest receivable.........................	1,900	700	1,200
Inventories	83,600	87,200	(3,600)
Prepaid expenses	2,500	1,900	600
Plant assets:			
Land	69,000	60,000	9,000
Equipment, net...........................	53,500	49,400	4,100
Total assets	$245,500	$231,400	$ 14,100
Current liabilities:			
Accounts payable	$ 31,400	$ 28,800	$ 2,600
Interest payable	4,400	4,900	(500)
Salary payable	3,100	6,600	(3,500)
Other accrued liabilities	13,700	16,000	(2,300)
Income tax payable........................	8,900	7,700	1,200
Long-term liabilities:			
Notes payable.............................	75,000	100,000	(25,000)
Stockholders' equity:			
Common stock, no-par.....................	88,300	64,700	23,600
Retained earnings.........................	20,700	2,700	18,000
Total liabilities and stockholders' equity.........	$245,500	$231,400	$ 14,100

Loma Alto had no noncash investing and financing transactions during 19X5.

Required

Compute the following items for the 19X5 statement of cash flows:

Cash flows from operating activities:
  Cash receipts:
    Collections from customers .... $
    Receipts of interest ....
  Cash payments:
    To suppliers:
      Inventory...
      Operating expenses......................................
    To employees ....
    For interest ....
    For income tax ....
      Net cash inflow from operating activities .... $____

Cash flows from investing activities:
  Acquisition of land (there were no sales of land)..................... $
  Acquisition of equipment (there were no sales of equipment) ....
    Net cash outflow from investing activities .... $____

Cash flows from financing activities:
  Payment of dividends .... $
  Payment of note payable (there were no issuances of notes payable) ......
  Issuance of common stock (there were no retirements of stock or
    purchases of treasury stock)...................................
    Net cash outflow from financing activities .... $____
Net increase in cash... $1,100

Problem 18-4B   *Preparing the statement of cash flows—indirect method*

The comparative balance sheet of Westwood Sales, Inc., at March 31, 19X7, reported the following:

	March 31,	
	19X7	**19X6**
Current assets:		
Cash and cash equivalents	$ 2,800	$ 4,000
Accounts receivable.	19,400	21,700
Inventories.	63,200	60,600
Prepaid expenses.	1,900	1,700
Current liabilities:		
Notes payable for inventory purchases . . .	$ 4,000	$ 4,000
Accounts payable	30,300	27,600
Accrued liabilities	10,700	11,100
Income tax payable.	8,000	4,700

Westwood's transactions during the year ended March 31, 19X7, included the following:

Acquisition of land by issuing note payable	$36,000	Sale of long-term investment	$13,700
Amortization expense.	2,000	Depreciation expense	9,000
Payment of cash dividend	30,000	Cash acquisition of building. . .	47,000
Cash acquisition of equipment	78,000	Net income	63,000
		Issuance of common stock for	
Issuance of long-term note payable to borrow cash.	50,000	cash	11,000
		Stock dividend.	18,000

Required

Prepare Westwood Sales's statement of cash flows for the year ended March 31, 19X7, using the *indirect* method to report cash flows from operating activities. Report noncash investing and financing activities in an accompanying schedule. All current account balances resulted from operating transactions.

Problem 18-5B   *Preparing the statement of cash flows—direct and indirect methods*

To prepare the statement of cash flows, accountants for Akron Corporation have summarized 19X3 activity in two accounts as follows:

Cash			
Beginning balance.	53,600	Payments of operating expenses . . .	34,300
Issuance of common stock	19,300	Payment of long-term debt.	41,300
Receipts of dividends	4,500	Purchase of treasury stock	26,400
Collection of loan	13,000	Payment of income tax	18,900
Sale of treasury stock	8,200	Payments on accounts payable.	399,100
Receipts of interest	12,600	Payments of dividends	27,200
Collections from customers.	676,700	Payments of salaries and wages. . . .	143,800
		Payments of interest	26,900
		Purchase of equipment	31,400
Ending balance	38,600		

Common Stock

	Beginning balance...............	84,400
	Issuance for cash................	19,300
	Issuance to acquire land..........	41,100
	Issuance to retire long-term debt ...	19,000
	Ending balance	163,800

Required

1. Prepare Akron Corporation's statement of cash flows for the year ended December 31, 19X3, using the *direct* method to report operating activities. Also prepare the accompanying schedule of noncash investing and financing activities.

Akron's 19X3 income statement and selected balance sheet data follow.

Akron Corporation
Income Statement
For the Year Ended December 31, 19X3

Revenues:		
Sales revenue.......................		$704,300
Interest revenue....................		12,600
Dividend revenue		4,500
Total revenues		721,400
Expenses and losses:		
Cost of goods sold..................	$402,600	
Salary and wage expense	150,800	
Depreciation expense	24,300	
Other operating expense.............	44,100	
Interest expense....................	28,800	
Income tax expense.................	16,200	
Loss on sale of investments	1,100	
Total expenses		667,900
Net income		$ 53,500

Akron Corporation **Balance Sheet Data**	**Increase** **(Decrease)**
Current assets:	
Cash and cash equivalents	$(15,000)
Accounts receivable..........................	27,600
Inventories	(11,800)
Prepaid expenses	600
Current liabilities:	
Accounts payable............................	$ (8,300)
Interest payable	1,900
Salary payable	7,000
Other accrued liabilities......................	10,400
Income tax payable	(2,700)

Required

2. Use these data to prepare a supplementary schedule showing cash flows from operating activities by the *indirect* method. All activity in the current accounts results from operations.

Problem 18-6B *Preparing the statement of cash flows — indirect and direct methods*

Holmes-Thomas Corporation's comparative balance sheet at June 30, 19X7, included the following balances:

Holmes-Thomas Corporation
Partial Balance Sheet
June 30, 19X7 and 19X6

	19X7	19X6	Increase (Decrease)
Current assets:			
Cash	$17,600	$ 8,600	$ 9,000
Accounts receivable	45,900	48,300	(2,400)
Interest receivable	2,900	3,600	(700)
Inventories	68,600	60,200	8,400
Prepaid expenses	3,700	2,800	900
Current liabilities:			
Notes payable, short-term	$13,400	$18,100	$(4,700)
Accounts payable	42,400	40,300	2,100
Income tax payable	13,800	14,500	(700)
Accrued liabilities	8,200	9,700	(1,500)
Interest payable	3,700	2,900	800
Salary payable	900	2,600	(1,700)

Transaction data for the year ended June 30, 19X7:

a. Net income, $52,500.
b. Depreciation expense on equipment, $10,200.
c. Purchased long-term investment, $4,900.
d. Sold land for $46,900, including $6,700 loss.
e. Acquired equipment by issuing long-term note payable, $14,300.
f. Paid long-term note payable, $61,000.
g. Received cash for issuance of common stock, $3,900.
h. Paid cash dividends, $38,100.
i. Paid short-term note payable by issuing common stock, $42,000.

Required

1. Prepare Holmes-Thomas's statement of cash flows for the year ended June 30, 19X7, using the *indirect* method to report operating activities. Also prepare the accompanying schedule of noncash investing and financing activities. All current accounts except short-term notes payable result from operating transactions.
2. Prepare a supplementary schedule showing cash flows from operations by the *direct* method. The income statement reports the following: sales, $233,600; interest revenue, $10,600; cost of goods sold, $82,800; salary expense, $38,800; other operating expenses, $37,200; depreciation expense, $10,200; income tax expense, $9,900; loss on sale of land, $6,700; interest expense, $6,100.

Decision Problem

Preparing and Using the Statement of Cash Flows to Evaluate Operations

The 19X6 comparative income statement and the 19X6 comparative balance sheet of Adler, Inc., have just been distributed at a meeting of the company's board of directors.

Adler, Inc.
Comparative Income Statement
Years Ended December 31, 19X6 and 19X5
(amounts in thousands)

	19X6	19X5
Revenues and gains:		
Sales revenue.	$474	$310
Gain on sale of equipment (sale price, $33).	—	18
Totals	$474	$328
Expenses and losses:		
Cost of goods sold.	$221	$162
Salary expense.	48	28
Depreciation expense	46	22
Interest expense.	13	20
Amortization expense on patent.	11	11
Loss on sale of land (sale price, $61)	—	35
Totals	339	278
Net income	$135	$ 50

Adler, Inc.
Comparative Balance Sheet
December 31, 19X6 and 19X5
(amounts in thousands)

Assets	19X6	19X5
Cash	$ 13	$ 63
Accounts receivable, net	72	61
Inventories	194	181
Long-term investments	31	-0-
Property, plant, and equipment.	401	259
Accumulated depreciation	(244)	(198)
Patents	177	188
Totals.	$ 644	$ 554

Liabilities and Owners' Equity	19X6	19X5
Notes payable, short-term, general borrowing . .	$ 32	$ 101
Accounts payable	63	56
Accrued liabilities	12	17
Notes payable, long-term.	147	163
Common stock, no-par	139	61
Retained earnings.	251	156
Totals.	$ 644	$ 554

In discussing the company's results of operations and year-end financial position, the members of the board of directors raise a fundamental question: Why is the cash balance so low? This question is especially troublesome to the board members because 19X6 showed record profits. As the controller of the company, you must answer the question.

Required

1. Prepare a statement of cash flows for 19X6 in the format that best shows the relationship between net income and operating cash flow. The company sold no plant assets or long-term investments and issued no notes payable during 19X6. The changes in all current accounts except short-term notes payable arose from operations. There were *no* noncash investing and financing transactions during the year. Show all amounts in thousands.

2. Answer the board members' question: Why *is* the cash balance so low? In explaining the business's cash flows, identify two significant cash receipts that occurred during 19X5 but not in 19X6 (see the comparative income statement). Also point out the two largest cash disbursements during 19X6.

3. Considering net income and the company's cash flows during 19X6, was it a good year or a bad year? Give your reasons.

Financial Statement Problem

Using the Statement of Cash Flows
Gulf+Western's statement of cash flows appears in Appendix C. Use this statement along with the company's other financial statements to answer the following questions.

1. By which method does Gulf+Western report net cash flows from *operating* activities? How can you tell?

2. This question shows how to compute the expenditures for property, plant and equipment ($57.1 million) reported on the statement of cash flows for fiscal 1987. Show all amounts in millions, rounded to the nearest $100,000.
   a. Compute the debit to Accumulated Depreciation (Gulf+Western labels this account "Allowance for Depreciation") on plant assets disposed of (sold) during fiscal 1987. Hint: Set up a T-account for Allowance for Depreciation, and take Depreciation Expense from the statement of cash flows.
   b. Analysis of the Property, Plant and Equipment account indicates that the cost of plant assets disposed of (sold) during fiscal 1987 was $50.9 million. Take this figure, the answer to 2a., and the proceeds on disposal of property, plant and equipment (from the statement of cash flows). Journalize the sale of property, plant and equipment during the year.
   c. Prepare a T-account for Property, Plant and Equipment—Net to show all activity in this account during fiscal 1987.

3. Compute the cost of intangible assets disposed of during fiscal 1987. Acquisitions during the year were immaterial. Hint: Set up a T-account for Intangible Assets—Net.

Answers to Self-Study Questions

1. b
2. a
3. a
4. c
5. d
6. d ($43,000 + $4,000 decrease in Interest Receivable = $47,000)
7. c ($104,000 + $31,000 − Cost of investment sold = $91,000; Cost = $44,000; Proceeds = Cost, $44,000 + Gain, $22,000 = $66,000)
8. b
9. c
10. b ($17,000 + $9,000 + $3,000 − $4,000 − $6,000 + $8,000 = $27,000)

19

Using Accounting Information to Make Business Decisions

LEARNING OBJECTIVES
After studying this chapter, you should be able to

1 Perform a horizontal analysis of comparative financial statements

2 Perform a vertical analysis of financial statements

3 Prepare common-size financial statements

4 Use the statement of cash flows in decision making

5 Compute the standard financial ratios used for decision making

6 Explain how to use ratios in decision making

Investors, creditors, and other business people rely on accounting information to make intelligent, informed decisions. Should the bank officer lend money to the Joneses? Should the investor buy more stock in Xerox or sell those shares presently owned? People need information to make these decisions. The balance sheet, the income statement, and the statement of cash flows provide a large part of the information that is used for making decisions such as these. In Chapters 1 through 18, we have described the process of accounting and the preparation of the financial statements. We have tried to relate each topic to the real world of business by showing the relevance of the accounting data. In this chapter, we discuss in more detail how to use the information that appears in these statements. (Appendix C features the financial statements of Gulf+Western. You may apply the analytical skills you learn in this chapter to those real-world data.)

Financial Statement Analysis _____

We divide the tools and techniques that the business community uses in evaluating financial statement information into three broad categories: horizontal analysis, vertical analysis, and ratio analysis. These three categories make up the broad area of financial statement analysis.

Horizontal Analysis _____

Many business decisions hinge on whether the numbers—in sales, income, expenses, and so on—are increasing or decreasing over time. Has the sales figure risen from last year? From two years ago? By how many dollars? We may find that the net sales figure has risen by $20,000. This may be interesting, but considered alone it is not very useful for decision making. An analysis of the *percentage change* in the net sales figure over time improves our ability to use the dollar amounts. It is more useful to know that sales have increased by 20 percent than to know that the increase in sales is $20,000.

The study of percentage changes in comparative statements is called **horizontal analysis.** Computing a percentage change in comparative statements requires two steps: (1) Compute the dollar amount of the change from the earlier (base) period to the later period, and (2) divide the dollar amount of change by the base period amount. Horizontal analysis is illustrated as follows:

| | | | | Increase (Decrease) | | | |
| | | | | During Year 3 | | During Year 2 | |
	Year 3	Year 2	Year 1	Amount	%	Amount	%
Sales........	$120,000	$100,000	$ 80,000	$20,000	20%	$20,000	25%
Net income ..	12,000	8,000	10,000	4,000	50%	(2,000)	(20%)

The increase in sales is $20,000 in both year 3 and year 2. However, the percentage increase in sales differs from year to year because of the change in the base amount. To compute the percentage change for year 2, we divide the amount of increase ($20,000) by the base period amount ($80,000), an increase of 25 percent. For year 3 the dollar amount increases again by $20,000. However, the base period amount for figuring this percentage change is $100,000. Dividing $20,000 by $100,000 computes a percentage increase of only 20 percent during year 3. Observe that net income *decreases* by 20 percent during year 2 and *increases* by 50 percent during year 3.

Detailed horizontal analyses of a comparative income statement and a comparative balance sheet are shown in the two right-hand columns of Exhibits 19-1 and 19-2.

EXHIBIT 19-1 *Comparative Income Statement — Horizontal Analysis*

McColpin, Inc. Comparative Income Statement Years Ended December 31, 19X7 and 19X6				
			Increase (Decrease)	
	19X7	19X6	Amount	Percent
Net sales.....................	$858,000	$803,000	$55,000	6.8%
Cost of goods sold............	513,000	509,000	4,000	0.8
Gross profit	345,000	294,000	51,000	17.3
Operating expenses:				
Selling expenses............	126,000	114,000	12,000	10.5
General expenses...........	118,000	123,000	(5,000)	(4.1)
Total operating expenses.......	244,000	237,000	7,000	3.0
Income from operations	101,000	57,000	44,000	77.2
Interest revenue..............	4,000	—	4,000	—
Interest expense..............	24,000	14,000	10,000	71.4
Income before income taxes	81,000	43,000	38,000	88.4
Income tax expense...........	33,000	17,000	16,000	94.1
Net income	$ 48,000	$ 26,000	$22,000	84.6

OBJECTIVE 1

Perform a horizontal analysis of comparative financial statements

EXHIBIT 19-2 *Comparative Balance Sheet—Horizontal Analysis*

			Increase (Decrease)	
Assets	**19X7**	**19X6**	**Amount**	**Percent**
Current assets:				
Cash....................	$ 29,000	$ 32,000	$ (3,000)	(9.4%)
Accounts receivable, net.....	114,000	85,000	29,000	34.1
Inventories...............	113,000	111,000	2,000	1.8
Prepaid expenses...........	6,000	8,000	(2,000)	(25.0)
Total current assets.......	262,000	236,000	26,000	11.0
Long-term investments........	18,000	9,000	9,000	100.0
Property, plant, and equipment,				
net......................	507,000	399,000	108,000	27.1
Total assets.............	$787,000	$644,000	$143,000	22.2
Liabilities				
Current liabilities:				
Notes payable	$ 42,000	$ 27,000	$ 15,000	55.6
Accounts payable...........	73,000	68,000	5,000	7.4
Accrued liabilities	27,000	31,000	(4,000)	(12.9)
Total current liabilities.....	142,000	126,000	16,000	12.7
Long-term debt	289,000	198,000	91,000	46.0
Total liabilities	431,000	324,000	107,000	33.0
Stockholders' Equity				
Common stock, no-par........	186,000	186,000	—	0.0
Retained earnings	170,000	134,000	36,000	26.9
Total stockholders' equity ..	356,000	320,000	36,000	11.3
Total liabilities and stock-				
holders' equity	$787,000	$644,000	$143,000	22.2

McColpin, Inc.
Comparative Balance Sheet
December 31, 19X7 and 19X6

The comparative income statement in Exhibit 19-1 reveals that net sales increased by 6.8 percent during 19X7 and that the cost of goods sold grew by much less. As a result, gross profit rose by 17.3 percent. Note that general expenses actually decreased, and so the company significantly increased income from operations and net income during 19X7. Our analysis shows that 19X7 was a much better year than 19X6. We see that the growth in income resulted more from slowing the increase in expenses than from boosting sales revenue.

No percentage increase is computed for interest revenue because dividing the $4,000 increase by a zero amount would produce a meaningless percentage. Also, we compute no percentage change when a base-year amount is negative. For example, when a company goes from a net loss one year to a profit the next year, we would be dividing a positive number by a negative amount.

(Throughout this chapter, we discuss only some of the elements of the various statements that we present. For example, we mention McColpin's cost of goods sold but not its selling expenses. Understand, however, that the manager of the sales staff—and likely top management also—would examine the selling expenses in conducting a full analysis of the company's operations.)

The comparative balance sheet in Exhibit 19-2 shows that 19X7 was a year of expansion for the company. Property, plant, and equipment increased from $399,000 to $507,000, a growth rate of 27.1 percent. Total assets increased by 22.2 percent. To help finance this expansion, McColpin borrowed heavily, increasing short-term notes payable by 55.6 percent and long-term debt by 46 percent. The increase in assets was also financed in part by profitable operations, as shown by the 26.9 percent increase in retained earnings.

The sharpest percentage increase on the balance sheet is in long-term investments (100 percent). However, the dollar amounts are small compared to the other balance sheet figures. Note this key point of financial analysis: percentage changes must be evaluated in terms of the item's relative importance to the company as a whole. In this instance, the large percentage increase in long-term investments means little because the company holds such a small amount. The 27.1 percent increase in property, plant, and equipment is more important because their cost represents the largest asset and their use is intended to generate profits for years to come.

Trend Percentages

Trend percentages are a form of horizontal analysis. Trends are important indicators of the direction a business is taking. How have sales changed over a five-year period? What trend does gross profit show? These questions can be answered by an analysis of trend percentages over a representative period, such as the most recent five years or the most recent 10 years. To gain a realistic view of the company, it is often necessary to examine more than just a two- or three-year period.

Trend percentages are computed by selecting a base year, with each amount during that year set equal to 100 percent. The amounts of each following year are expressed as a percent of the base amount. To compute trend percentages, divide each item for years after the base year by the corresponding amount during the base year. Suppose McColpin, Inc., showed sales, cost of goods sold, and gross profit for the past six years as follows:

| | (amounts in thousands) | | | | | |
	19X7	19X6	19X5	19X4	19X3	19X2
Net sales..........................	$858	$803	$781	$744	$719	$737
Cost of goods sold.................	513	509	490	464	450	471
Gross profit......................	$345	$294	$291	$280	$269	$266

Assume we want trend percentages for a five-year period starting with 19X3. We use 19X2 as the base year. Trend percentages for net sales are computed by dividing each net sales amount by the 19X2 amount of $737,000. Likewise, dividing each year's cost-of-goods-sold amount by the base-year amount ($471,000) yields the trend percentages for cost of goods sold. Gross-profit trend percentages are computed similarly. The resulting trend percentages follow (19X2, the base year = 100%):

	19X7	19X6	19X5	19X4	19X3	19X2
Net sales	116%	109%	106%	101%	98%	100%
Cost of goods sold..............	109	108	104	99	96	100
Gross profit	130	111	109	105	101	100

McColpin's sales and cost of goods sold have trended upward since a downturn in 19X3. Gross profit has increased steadily, with the most dramatic growth coming during 19X7. What signal about the company does this information provide? It suggests that operations are becoming increasingly more successful. A similar analysis can be performed for any related set of items in the financial statements. For example, an increase in inventory and accounts receivable, coupled with a decrease in sales, may reveal difficulty in making sales and collecting receivables.

Vertical Analysis

Horizontal analysis highlights changes in an item over time. However, no single technique provides a complete picture of a business. Another way to analyze a company is called vertical analysis.

Vertical analysis of a financial statement reveals the relationship of each statement item to the total, which is the 100 percent figure. For example, suppose under normal conditions a company's gross profit is 50 percent of net sales. A drop in gross profit to 40 percent may cause the company to report a net loss on the income statement. Management, investors, and creditors view a large decline in gross profit with alarm.

The percentages in Exhibits 19-3 and 19-4 show vertical analyses of McColpin, Inc.'s income statement and balance sheet. Percentages on the income statement are computed by dividing all amounts by net sales. The vertical analysis, therefore, presents each amount as a percentage of net sales. The vertical analysis of the balance sheet shows all amounts as a percentage of total assets or the sum of liabilities and stockholders' equity (recall that total assets equal total liabilities and stockholders' equity).

EXHIBIT 19-3   *Comparative Income Statement — Vertical Analysis*

OBJECTIVE 2

Perform a vertical analysis of financial statements

	19X7		19X6	
McColpin, Inc. **Comparative Income Statement** **Years Ended December 31, 19X7 and 19X6**				
	Amount	**Percent**	**Amount**	**Percent**
Net sales	$858,000	100.0%	$803,000	100.0%
Cost of goods sold.	513,000	59.8	509,000	63.4
Gross profit	345,000	40.2	294,000	36.6
Selling expenses	126,000	14.7	114,000	14.2
General expenses.	118,000	13.7	123,000	15.3
Total operating expenses	244,000	28.4	237,000	29.5
Income from operations	101,000	11.8	57,000	7.1
Interest revenue	4,000	0.4	—	—
Interest expense.	24,000	2.8	14,000	1.8
Income before income tax	81,000	9.4	43,000	5.3
Income tax expense.	33,000	3.8	17,000	2.1
Net income	$ 48,000	5.6%	$ 26,000	3.2%

EXHIBIT 19-4 *Comparative Balance Sheet — Vertical Analysis*

McColpin, Inc.
Comparative Balance Sheet
December 31, 19X7 and 19X6

	19X7		19X6	
Assets	**Amount**	**Percent**	**Amount**	**Percent**
Current assets:				
Cash.........................	$ 29,000	3.7%	$ 32,000	5.0%
Accounts receivable, net	114,000	14.5	85,000	13.2
Inventories....................	113,000	14.3	111,000	17.2
Prepaid expenses..............	6,000	.8	8,000	1.2
Total current assets	262,000	33.3	236,000	36.6
Long-term investments............	18,000	2.3	9,000	1.4
Property, plant, and equipment,				
net.........................	507,000	64.4	399,000	62.0
Total assets.................	$787,000	100.0%	$644,000	100.0%
Liabilities				
Current liabilities:				
Notes payable	$ 42,000	5.3%	$ 27,000	4.2%
Accounts payable..............	73,000	9.3	68,000	10.6
Accrued liabilities	27,000	3.4	31,000	4.8
Total current liabilities.........	142,000	18.0	126,000	19.6
Long-term debt	289,000	36.7	198,000	30.7
Total liabilities	431,000	54.7	324,000	50.3
Stockholders' Equity				
Common stock, no-par	186,000	23.7	186,000	28.9
Retained earnings	170,000	21.6	134,000	20.8
Total stockholders' equity	356,000	45.3	320,000	49.7
Total liabilities and stockholders'				
equity	$787,000	100.0%	$644,000	100.0%

The 19X7 comparative income statement (Exhibit 19-3) reports that cost of goods sold dropped to 59.8 percent of net sales from 63.4 percent in 19X6. This explains why the gross profit percentage rose in 19X7. The gross profit percentage is one of the most important pieces of information in financial analysis because it shows the relationship between net sales and cost of goods sold. A company that can steadily increase its gross profit percentage over a long period is more likely to succeed than a business whose gross profit percentage is steadily declining. The net income percentage almost doubled in 19X7, mostly because of the decrease in the cost-of-goods-sold percentage.

Vertical analysis gives a view of the income statement that is different from the view provided by horizontal analysis. Decision makers use these two forms of analysis together. For example, Exhibit 19-1 reports that gross profit increased by 17.3 percent, and net income increased by 84.6 percent from 19X6 to 19X7. Exhibit 19-3 indicates that gross profit grew from 36.6 percent of sales in 19X6 to 40.2 percent of sales in 19X7 and that net income has increased from 3.2 percent of sales to 5.6 percent of sales. Together, vertical analysis and horizontal analysis paint a favorable picture of McColpin's operations.

We can apply trend analysis to the balance sheet of McColpin, Inc., as Exhibit 19-4 shows. For example, among the changes that occurred in the one-year period from 19X6 to 19X7, we note that current assets have become a smaller percentage of total assets. A decrease in current assets may make it difficult for the company to pay its bills. However, this does not present a problem for McColpin, Inc., because current liabilities also decreased as a percentage of total assets during 19X7. This kind of comparison is used in vertical analysis.

Common-Size Statements

The percentages in Exhibits 19-3 and 19-4 can be presented as a separate statement that reports only percentages (no dollar amounts). Such a statement, called a **common-size statement,** is a type of vertical analysis.

On a common-size income statement, each item is expressed as a percentage of the net sales amount. Net sales is the "common size" to which we relate the statement's other amounts. In the balance sheet, the "common size" is the total on each side of the accounting equation (total assets *or* the sum of total liabilities and stockholders' equity). A common-size statement eases the comparison of different companies because their amounts are stated in percentages.

Common-size statements may identify the need for corrective action. Exhibit 19-5 is the common-size analysis of current assets taken from Exhibit 19-4.

Exhibit 19-5 shows cash as a smaller percentage of total assets at December 31, 19X7, than at the previous year end. Accounts receivable, on the other hand, is a larger percentage of total assets. What could cause a decrease in cash and an increase in accounts receivable as percentages of total assets? McColpin may have been lax in collecting accounts receivable, which may explain a cash shortage and reveal that the company needs to pursue collection more vigorously. Or the company may have sold to less creditworthy customers. In any event, the company should monitor its cash position and collection of accounts receivable to avoid a cash shortage. Common-size statements provide information useful for this purpose.

EXHIBIT 19-5 *Common-Size Analysis of Current Assets*

McColpin, Inc. Common-Size Analysis of Current Assets December 31, 19X7 and 19X6	Percent of Total Assets	
	19X7	**19X6**
Current assets:		
Cash	3.7%	5.0%
Accounts receivable, net	14.5	13.2
Inventories	14.3	17.2
Prepaid expenses	.8	1.2
Total current assets............................	33.3%	36.6%

Industry Comparisons

We study the records of a company in order to understand past results and predict future performance. Still, the knowledge that we can develop from a single company's records is limited to that one company. We may learn that gross profit has decreased and net income has increased steadily for the last ten years. While this information is helpful, it does not consider how businesses in the same industry have fared over this time. Have other companies in the same line of business increased their sales? Is there an industrywide decline in gross profit? Has cost of goods sold risen steeply for other businesses that sell the same products? Managers, investors, creditors, and other interested parties need to know how one company compares to other companies in the same line of business.

Exhibit 19-6 gives the common-size income statement of McColpin, Inc., compared to the average for its industry. This analysis compares McColpin to all other companies in its line of business. Analysts specialize in a particular industry and make such comparisons in deciding which companies' stocks to buy or sell. For example, financial-service companies like Merrill Lynch have airline-industry specialists, health-care-industry specialists, and so on. Boards of directors evaluate top managers based on how well the company compares with other companies in the industry. Exhibit 19-6 shows that McColpin compares favorably with competing firms in its line of business. Its gross profit percentage, percentage of income from operations, and net income percentage are higher than the industry average.

Another use of common-size statements is to aid the comparison of different-sized companies. Suppose you are considering an investment in the stock of an automobile manufacturer, and you are choosing between General Motors (GM) and Chrysler. GM is so much larger than Chrysler that a direct comparison of their financial statements in dollar amounts is not meaningful. However, you can convert the two companies' income statements to common size and compare the percentages. You may find that one company has a higher percentage of its assets

OBJECTIVE 3
Prepare common-size financial statements

EXHIBIT 19-6   *Common-Size Income Statement Compared to the Industry Average*

McColpin, Inc. Common-Size Income Statement for Comparison with Industry Average Year Ended December 31, 19X7		
	McColpin, Inc.	**Industry Average**
Net sales	100.0%	100.0%
Cost of goods sold.......................	59.8	61.8
Gross Profit...........................	40.2	38.2
Operating expenses:		
Selling expenses	14.7	15.7
General expenses......................	13.7	12.9
Total operating expenses	28.4	28.6
Income from operations	11.8	9.6
Other revenue (expense).................	(2.4)	(3.5)
Income before income tax................	9.4	6.1
Income tax expense......................	3.8	2.4
Net income	5.6%	3.7%

in inventory and the other company has a higher percentage of its liabilities in long-term debt.

Information Sources

Financial analysts draw their information from various sources. Annual and quarterly reports offer readers a good look at an individual business's operations. Publicly held companies must, in addition, submit more detailed annual reports, called 10-Ks, to the Securities and Exchange Commission. Business publications — *The Wall Street Journal, Business Week, Forbes,* and others — carry industry analysis figures. Credit agencies — Dunn and Bradstreet, for example — and investment companies — Moody's, Standard & Poor's, and others — offer industry averages as a part of their financial service. Robert Morris Associates publishes *Annual Statement Studies,* which presents ratios and other facts for 223 different industries.

The Statement of Cash Flows in Decision Making

The chapter so far has centered on the income statement and balance sheet. We may also perform horizontal and vertical analysis on the statement of cash flows. In the preceding chapter, we discussed how to prepare the statement. To discuss its role in decision making, let's use Exhibit 19-7.

Some analysts use cash flow analysis to identify danger signals about a company's financial situation. For example, the statement in Exhibit 19-7 reveals what may be a weakness in DeMaris Corporation.

First, operations provided a net cash inflow of $52,000, which is much less than the $91,000 generated by the sale of fixed assets. An important question

OBJECTIVE 4

Use the statement of cash flows in decision making

EXHIBIT 19-7   *Statement of Cash Flows*

DeMaris Corporation Statement of Cash Flows For the Current Year		
Operating activities:		
Income from operations.		$ 35,000
Add (subtract) noncash items:		
Depreciation	$ 14,000	
Net increase in current assets other than cash . . .	(5,000)	
Net increase in current liabilities	8,000	17,000
Net cash inflow from operating activities		52,000
Investing activities:		
Sale of property, plant, and equipment	$ 91,000	
Net cash inflow from investing activities		91,000
Financing activities:		
Issuance of bond payable	$ 72,000	
Payment of long term debt	(170,000)	
Payment of interest expense	(9,000)	
Payment of dividends	(33,000)	
Net cash outflow from financing activities		(140,000)
Increase in cash		$ 3,000

arises: Can the company remain in business by generating the majority of its cash by selling its property, plant, and equipment? No, because these assets will be needed to manufacture the company's products in the future. Note also that borrowing by issuing bonds payable brought in $72,000. No company can long survive living on borrowed funds. DeMaris must eventually pay off the bonds. Indeed, the company paid $170,000 on older debt. Also, interest expense must be incurred as the price of borrowing. Successful companies like IBM, Coca-Cola, and Procter & Gamble generate the greatest percentage of their cash from operations, not from selling their fixed assets or from borrowing money. These conditions may be only temporary for DeMaris Corporation, but they are worth investigating.

The most important information that the statement of cash flows provides is a summary of the company's use of cash. How a company spends its cash today determines its sources of cash in the future. The company may wisely use its cash to purchase assets that will generate income in the years ahead. However, if a company invests unwisely, cash will eventually run short. DeMaris's statement of cash flows reveals problems. The exhibit information indicates that DeMaris invested in no fixed assets to replace those that it sold. The company may in fact be going out of business. Also, DeMaris paid dividends of $33,000, an amount that is very close to its net income. Is the company retaining enough of its income to finance future operations without excessive borrowing? Analysts seek answers to questions such as this. They analyze the information from the statement of cash flows along with the information from the balance sheet and the income statement to form a well-rounded complete picture of the business.

Summary Problem for Your Review

Perform a horizontal analysis and a vertical analysis of the comparative income statement of TRE Corporation. State whether 19X3 was a good year or a bad year and give your reasons.

TRE Corporation
Comparative Income Statement
Years Ended December 31, 19X3 and 19X2

	19X3	19X2
Total revenues	$275,000	$225,000
Expenses:		
Cost of products sold	$194,000	$165,000
Engineering, selling, and administrative expenses	54,000	48,000
Interest expense	5,000	5,000
Income tax expense	9,000	3,000
Other expense (income)	1,000	(1,000)
Total expenses	263,000	220,000
Net earnings	$ 12,000	$ 5,000

SOLUTION TO REVIEW PROBLEM

TRE Corporation
Horizontal Analysis of Comparative Income Statement
Years Ended December 31, 19X3 and 19X2

	19X3	19X2	Increase (Decrease) Amount	Increase (Decrease) Percent
Total revenues....................	$275,000	$225,000	$50,000	22.2%
Expenses:				
Cost of products sold	$194,000	$165,000	$29,000	17.6
Engineering, selling, and administrative expenses	54,000	48,000	6,000	12.5
Interest expense.................	5,000	5,000	—	—
Income tax expense..............	9,000	3,000	6,000	200.0
Other expense (income)	1,000	(1,000)	2,000	—
Total expenses................	263,000	220,000	43,000	19.5
Net earnings	$ 12,000	$ 5,000	$ 7,000	140.0

TRE Corporation
Vertical Analysis of Comparative Income Statement
Years Ended December 31, 19X3 and 19X2

	19X3 Amount	19X3 Percent	19X2 Amount	19X2 Percent
Total revenue	$275,000	100.0%	$225,000	100.0%
Expenses:				
Cost of products sold	$194,000	70.5	$165,000	73.3
Engineering, selling, and administrative expenses	54,000	19.6	48,000	21.3
Interest expense	5,000	1.8	5,000	2.2
Income tax expense...............	9,000	3.3	3,000	1.4
Other expense (income)	1,000	0.4	(1,000)	(0.4)
Total expenses..................	263,000	95.6	220,000	97.8
Net earnings	$ 12,000	4.4	$ 5,000	2.2

The horizontal analysis shows that total revenues increased 22.2 percent. This percentage increase was greater than the 19.5 percent increase in total expenses, resulting in a 140 percent increase in net earnings.

The vertical analysis shows decreases in the percentages of net sales consumed by the cost of products sold (from 73.3 percent to 70.5 percent) and the engineering, selling, and administrative expenses (from 21.3 percent to 19.6 percent). These two items are TRE's largest dollar expenses, so their percentage decreases are quite important. The relative reduction in expenses raised 19X3 net earnings to 4.4 percent of sales, compared to 2.2 percent the preceding year. The overall analysis indicates that 19X3 was significantly better than 19X2.

Using Ratios to Make Business Decisions _____

The preceding analyses were based on each financial statement considered alone. Another set of decision tools develops relationships among items taken from throughout the statements.

Ratios are important tools for financial analysis. A ratio expresses the relationship of one number to another number. For example, if the balance sheet shows current assets of $100,000 and current liabilities of $25,000, the ratio of current assets to current liabilities is $100,000 to $25,000. We simplify this numerical expression to the ratio of 4 to 1, which may also be written $4:1$ and $\frac{4}{1}$. Other acceptable ways of expressing this ratio include (1) "current assets are 400 percent of current liabilities" and (2) "the business has four dollars in current assets for every one dollar in current liabilities."

We often reduce the ratio fraction by writing the ratio as one figure over the other, for example, $\frac{4}{1}$, and then dividing the numerator by the denominator. In this way, the ratio $\frac{4}{1}$ may be expressed simply as 4. The 1 that represents the denominator of the fraction is understood, not written. Consider the ratio $175,000:$165,000. After dividing the first figure by the second, we come to $1.06:1$, which we state as 1.06. The second part of the ratio, the 1, again is understood. Ratios provide a convenient and useful way of expressing a relationship between numbers. For example, the ratio of current assets to current liabilities gives information about a company's ability to pay its current debts with existing current assets.

A manager, lender, or financial analyst may use any ratio that is relevant to a particular decision. We discuss the more important ratios used in credit and investment analysis and in managing a business. Many companies include these ratios in a special section of their annual financial reports. Investment services— Moody's, Standard & Poor's, Robert Morris Associates, and others—report these ratios for companies and industries. They are widely used in all aspects of business—finance, management, and marketing as well as accounting.

Measuring the Ability to Pay Current Liabilities _____

Working capital is defined as current assets minus current liabilities. Working capital is widely used to measure a business's ability to meet its short-term obligations with its current assets. The larger the working capital, the better able the business is to pay its debts. Recall that capital, or owners' equity, is total assets minus total liabilities. Working capital is like a "current" version of total capital. The working capital amount considered alone does not give a complete picture of the entity's working capital position, however. Consider two companies with equal working capital:

	Company A	Company B
Current assets	$100,000	$200,000
Current liabilities	50,000	150,000
Working capital	$ 50,000	$ 50,000

Both companies have working capital of $50,000, but Company A's working capital is as large as its current liabilities. Company B's working capital, on the other hand, is only one-third as large as its current liabilities. Which business has a better working capital position? Company A, because its working capital is a higher percentage of current assets and current liabilities. To use working capital data in decision making, it is helpful to develop ratios. Two decision tools based on working capital data are the *current ratio* and the *acid-test ratio.*

Current Ratio

The most common ratio using current asset and current liability data is the **current ratio,** which is current assets divided by current liabilities. Recall the makeup of current assets and current liabilities. Inventory is converted to receivables through sales, the receivables are collected in cash, and the cash is used to buy inventory and pay current liabilities. A company's current assets and current liabilities represent the core of its day-to-day operations.

OBJECTIVE 5

Compute the standard financial ratios used for decision making

The current ratios of McColpin, Inc. at December 31, 19X7 and 19X6, follow (data from Exhibit 19-2).

Current Ratio of McColpin, Inc.

Formula	19X7	19X6
$\text{Current ratio} = \dfrac{\text{Current assets}}{\text{Current liabilities}}$	$\dfrac{\$262,000}{\$142,000} = 1.85$	$\dfrac{\$236,000}{\$126,000} = 1.87$

The current ratio decreased slightly during 19X7. Lenders, stockholders, and managers closely monitor changes in a company's current ratio. In general, a higher current ratio indicates a stronger financial position. A high current ratio suggests that the business has sufficient liquid assets to maintain normal business operations. Compare McColpin's current ratio of 1.85 to the current ratios of some actual companies:

Company	Current Ratio
Chesebrough-Pond's, Inc.	2.50
General Motors Corporation (GM)	1.36
International Business Machines Corporation (IBM)	1.52
General Mills, Inc.	1.05
The Superior Oil Company	1.46

What is an acceptable current ratio? The answer to this question depends on the nature of the business. The norm for companies in most industries is between 1.60 and 1.90, as reported by Robert Morris Associates. McColpin's current ratio of 1.85 is within the range of these actual values.

Acid-Test Ratio

The **acid-test** (or **quick**) **ratio** tells us whether the entity could pay all its current liabilities if they came due immediately. That is, could the company pass this *acid test*? The company would convert its most liquid assets to cash. To compute the acid-test ratio, we add cash, short-term investments, and net current receivables (accounts and notes receivable, net of allowances) and divide by current liabilities. Inventory and prepaid expenses are the two current assets not included in the acid-test computations. These accounts are omitted because they are the least liquid of the current assets. A business may not be able to convert them to cash immediately to pay current liabilities. The acid-test ratio measures liquidity using a narrower asset base than the current ratio does.

McColpin's acid-test ratios for 19X7 and 19X6 follow (data from Exhibit 19-2).

Formula	Acid-Test Ratio of McColpin, Inc.	
	19X7	**19X6**
Acid-test ratio = $\dfrac{\text{Cash} + \text{short-term investments} + \text{net current receivables}}{\text{Current liabilities}}$	$\dfrac{\$29,000 + \$0 + \$114,000}{\$142,000} = 1.01$	$\dfrac{\$32,000 + \$0 + \$85,000}{\$126,000} = .93$

The company's acid-test ratio improved considerably during 19X7. Its ratio of 1.01 is within range of those of Chesebrough-Pond's (1.25), General Motors (.91), and IBM (1.07). McColpin's 19X6 ratio of .93 is also typical of many companies. The norm ranges from .20 for shoe retailers to 1.00 for manufacturers of paperboard containers and certain other equipment, as reported by Robert Morris Associates. An acid-test ratio of .90 to 1.00 is acceptable in most industries.

Measuring the Ability to Sell Inventory and Collect Receivables

The ability to sell inventory and collect receivables is fundamental to business success. Recall the operating cycle of a merchandiser: cash to inventory to receivables and back to cash. This section discusses three ratios that measure the ability to sell inventory and collect receivables.

Inventory Turnover

Companies generally seek to achieve the quickest possible return on their investments. A return on an investment in inventory—usually a substantial amount—is no exception. The faster inventory sells, the sooner the business creates accounts receivable, and the sooner it collects cash.

Inventory turnover is a measure of the number of times a company sells its average level of inventory during a year. A high rate of turnover indicates relative ease in selling inventory, whereas a low turnover indicates difficulty in selling. Generally, companies prefer a high inventory turnover. A value of 6 means that the company's average level of inventory has been sold 6 times during the year. In most cases this is better than a turnover of 3 or 4. However, a high value can mean that the business is not keeping enough inventory on hand, and this can result in lost sales if the company cannot fill a customer's order. Therefore, a business strives for the most profitable rate of inventory turnover, not necessarily the highest.

To compute the inventory turnover ratio we divide cost of goods sold by the average inventory for the period. We use the cost of goods sold—not sales—in the computation because both cost of goods sold and inventory are stated *at cost*. Sales is stated at the sales value of inventory and therefore is not comparable to inventory cost.

McColpin's inventory turnover for 19X7 is

Formula	Inventory Turnover of McColpin, Inc.
Inventory turnover $= \dfrac{\text{Cost of goods sold}}{\text{Average inventory}}$	$\dfrac{\$513,000}{\$112,000} = 4.58$

Cost of goods sold appears in the income statement (Exhibit 19-1). Average inventory is figured by averaging the beginning inventory ($111,000) and ending inventory ($113,000). (See the balance sheet, Exhibit 19-2.) If inventory levels vary greatly from month to month, compute the average by adding the 12 monthly balances and dividing this sum by 12.

Inventory turnover varies widely with the nature of the business. For example, most manufacturers of farm machinery have an inventory turnover close to 3 times a year. By contrast, companies that remove natural gas from the ground hold their inventory for a very short period of time and have an average turnover of 30. McColpin's turnover of 4.58 times a year is similar to retailers of building materials (4.9) and to department stores (3.5).

To evaluate fully a company's inventory turnover, compare the ratio over time. A sudden sharp decline or a steady decline over a long period suggests the need for corrective action. Analysts also compare a company's inventory turnover to other companies in the same industry and to the industry average.

Accounts Receivable Turnover

Accounts receivable turnover measures a company's ability to collect cash from credit customers. Generally, the higher the ratio, the more successfully the business collects cash, and the better off its operations are. However, too high a receivable turnover may indicate that credit is too tight, causing the loss of sales to good customers. To compute the accounts receivable turnover we divide net credit sales by average net accounts receivable. The resulting ratio indicates how many times during the year the average level of receivables was turned into cash.

McColpin's accounts receivable turnover ratio for 19X7 is computed as follows. (We assume that all sales were on credit.)

Formula	Accounts Receivable Turnover of McColpin, Inc.
Accounts receivable turnover $= \dfrac{\text{Net credit sales}}{\text{Average net accounts receivable}}$	$\dfrac{\$858,000}{\$99,500} = 8.62$

The sales figure comes from the income statement (Exhibit 19-1). McColpin makes all sales on credit. If the company makes both cash and credit sales, this ratio is best computed using only net credit sales. Average net accounts receivable is figured using the beginning accounts receivable balance ($85,000) and the ending balance ($114,000). (See the balance sheet, Exhibit 19-2.) If accounts receivable balances exhibit a seasonal pattern, compute the average using the 12 monthly balances.

Receivable turnover ratios vary little from company to company. Most companies' ratios range between 7.0 and 10.0. McColpin's receivable turnover of 8.62 falls within this range.

Days' Sales in Receivables

Businesses must convert accounts receivable to cash. The lower the Accounts Receivable balance, the more successful the business has been in converting receivables into cash, and the better off the business.

The **days'-sales-in-receivables** ratio tells us how many days' sales remain in Accounts Receivable. We express the money amount in terms of an average day's sales. This relation becomes clearer as we compute the ratio, a two-step process. First, divide net sales by 365 days to figure the average sales amount for one day. Second, divide this average day's sales amount into the average net accounts receivable.

The data to compute this ratio for McColpin, Inc., for 19X7 are taken from the income statement and the balance sheet.

Formula	Days' Sales in Accounts Receivable of McColpin, Inc.

Days' Sales in AVERAGE Accounts Receivable:

1. One day's sales $= \dfrac{\text{Net sales}}{365 \text{ days}}$ $\dfrac{\$858,000}{365 \text{ days}} = \$2,351$

2. Days' sales in average accounts receivable $= \dfrac{\text{Average net accounts receivable}}{\text{One day's sales}}$ $\dfrac{\$99,500}{\$2,351} = 42 \text{ days}$

The computation in two steps is designed to increase your understanding of the meaning of the ratio. We may compute days' sales in average receivables in one step: $\$99,500/(\$858,000/365 \text{ days}) = 42 \text{ days}$.

McColpin's ratio tell us that 42 average days' sales remain in accounts receivable and need to be collected. The company will increase its cash inflow if it can decrease this ratio. To detect any changes over time in McColpin's ability to collect its receivables, let's compute the days' sales in receivables ratio at the beginning and the end of 19X7.

Days' Sales in ENDING 19X6 Accounts Receivable:

$$\text{One day's sales} = \frac{\$803,000}{365 \text{ days}} = \$2,200$$

$$\text{Days' sales in ending 19X6 accounts receivable} = \frac{\$85,000}{\$2,200} = 39 \text{ days at beginning of 19X7}$$

Days' Sales in ENDING 19X7 Accounts Receivable:

$$\text{One day's sales} = \frac{\$858,000}{365 \text{ days}} = \$2,351$$

$$\text{Days' sales in ending 19X7 accounts receivable} = \frac{\$114,000}{\$2,351} = 48 \text{ days at end of 19X7}$$

This analysis shows a drop in McColpin's collection of receivables: days' sales in accounts receivable has increased from 39 at the beginning of the year to 48 at year end. The credit and collection department should strengthen its collection efforts. Otherwise, the company may experience a cash shortage in 19X8 and beyond.

Measuring the Ability to Pay Long-Term Debt ──────────

The ratios discussed so far give us insight into current assets and current liabilities. They help us measure a business's ability to sell inventory, to collect receivables, and to pay current liabilities. Most businesses also have long-term debts. Bondholders and banks that loan money on long-term notes payable and bonds payable take special interest in a business's ability to meet long-term obligations. Two key indicators of a business's ability to pay long-term liabilities are the *debt ratio* and the *times-interest-earned ratio*.

Debt Ratio

Suppose you are a loan officer at a bank and you are evaluating loan applications from two companies with equal sales revenue and total assets. Sales and total assets are the two most common measures of firm size. Both companies have asked to borrow $500,000, and each has agreed to repay the loan over a ten-year period. The first customer already owes $600,000 to another bank. The second owes only $250,000. Other things equal, which company is likely to get the loan at the lower interest rate? Why?

Company Two is more likely to get the loan. The bank faces less risk by loaning to Company Two because that company owes less to creditors than Company One owes.

This relationship between total liabilities and total assets—called the **debt ratio**—tells us the proportion of the company's assets that it has financed with debt. If the debt ratio is 1, then debt has been used to finance all the assets. A debt ratio of .50 means that the company has used debt to finance half its assets. The owners of the business have financed the other half. The higher the debt ratio, the higher the strain of paying interest each year and the principal amount at maturity. The lower the ratio, the less the business's future obligations. Creditors view a high debt ratio with caution. If a business seeking financing already has many liabilities, then additional debt payments may be too much for the business to handle. Creditors, to help protect themselves, generally charge higher interest rates on new borrowing to companies with an already high debt ratio.

McColpin's debt ratio at the end of 19X7 and 19X6 follow (data from Exhibit 19-2).

Debt Ratio of McColpin, Inc.

Formula	19X7	19X6
Debt ratio $= \dfrac{\text{Total liabilities}}{\text{Total assets}}$	$\dfrac{\$431,000}{\$787,000} = .55$	$\dfrac{\$324,000}{\$644,000} = .50$

Recall from our vertical and horizontal analyses that McColpin, Inc., expanded operations by financing the purchase of property, plant, and equipment through borrowing, which is common.

Even after the increase in 19X7, McColpin's debt is not very high. Robert Morris Associates reports that the average debt ratio for most companies ranges around .57 to .67, with relatively little variation from company to company. McColpin's .55 debt ratio indicates a fairly low-risk debt position.

Times-Interest-Earned Ratio

The debt ratio measures the effect of debt on the company's *financial position* (balance sheet) but says nothing about its ability to pay interest expense. Analysts use a second ratio—the **times-interest-earned ratio**—to relate income to interest expense. To compute this ratio, we divide income from operations by interest expense. This ratio measures the number of times that operating income can *cover* interest expense. For this reason, the ratio is also called the **interest-coverage ratio.** A high ratio indicates ease in paying interest expense; a low value suggests difficulty.

McColpin's times-interest-earned ratios follow (data from Exhibit 19-1).

Formula	Times-Interest-Earned Ratio of McColpin, Inc.	
	19X7	19X6
Times-interest-earned ratio $= \dfrac{\text{Income from operations}}{\text{Interest expense}}$	$\dfrac{\$101,000}{\$24,000} = 4.21$	$\dfrac{\$57,000}{\$14,000} = 4.07$

McColpin's interest-coverage ratio increased in 19X7. This is a favorable sign about the company, especially since the company's short-term notes payable and long-term debt rose substantially during the year. (See the horizontal analysis in Exhibit 19-2.) McColpin's new plant assets, we conclude, have earned more in operating income than they have cost the business in interest expense. The company's coverage ratio of around 4 is somewhat better than the norm for American business, which Robert Morris Associates reports in the range of 2.0 to 3.0 for most companies.

Based on its debt ratio and times-interest-earned ratio, McColpin appears to have little difficulty paying its liabilities, also called *servicing its debt.*

Measuring Profitability _____

The fundamental goal of business is to earn a profit. Ratios that measure profitability play a large role in decision making. These ratios are reported in the business press, by investment services, and in the annual financial reports of companies.

Rate of Return on Net Sales

In business, the term *return* is used broadly and loosely as an evaluation of profitability. For example, consider a percentage called the **rate of return on net sales,** or simply **return on sales.** (The word *net* is usually omitted for convenience, even though the net sales figure is used to compute the ratio.) McColpin's rate of return on sales ratios follow:

**Rate of Return on
Sales of McColpin, Inc.**

Formula	19X7	19X6
Rate of return on sales = $\dfrac{\text{Net income}}{\text{Net sales}}$	$\dfrac{\$48,000}{\$858,000} = .056$	$\dfrac{\$26,000}{\$803,000} = .032$

You will recognize this ratio from the vertical analysis of the income statement in Exhibit 19-3. The increase in McColpin's return on sales is significant. Companies strive for a high rate of return. The higher the rate of return, the more net sales dollars are providing income to the business and the fewer net sales dollars are absorbed by expenses. The 5.6 percent rate compares favorably with General Motors (5.4 percent) and Kraft [Foods], Inc. (4.7 percent) but is less than IBM (13.6 percent) and Chesebrough-Ponds's (7.6 percent). As these rates of return on sales indicate, this ratio varies widely from industry to industry.

One strategy for increasing the rate of return on sales is to develop a product that commands a premium price, such as IBM computers, Maytag appliances, and certain brands of clothing. Another strategy is to control costs. If successful, either strategy converts a higher proportion of sales into net income and increases the rate of return on net sales.

A return measure can be computed on any revenue and sales amount. Return on net sales, as we have seen, is net income divided by net sales. Return on total revenues is net income divided by total revenues. A company can compute a return on other specific portions of revenue as its information needs dictate.

Rate of Return on Total Assets

The **rate of return on total assets,** or simply **return on assets,** measures the success a company has in using its assets to earn a profit. Creditors have loaned money to the company, and the interest they receive is the return on their investment. Shareholders have invested in the company's stock, and net income is their return. The sum of interest expense and net income is the return to the two groups that have financed the company's operations, and this amount is the numerator of the return on assets ratio. Average total assets is the denominator.

McColpin's return on assets ratio follows.

**Rate of Return on
Total Assets of McColpin, Inc.**

Formula	19X7
Rate of return on assets = $\dfrac{\text{Net income} + \text{interest expense}}{\text{Average total assets}}$	$\dfrac{\$48,000 + \$24,000}{\$715,500} = .101$

Net income and interest expense are taken from the income statement. To compute average total assets, we use beginning and ending total assets from the comparative balance sheet. McColpin's 10.1 percent return on assets is higher than the 4.7 percent average return on assets in most industries and compares favorably with Superior Oil (8.0 percent) and General Motors (10.4 percent). General Mills, Inc. (12.4 percent) and IBM (15.0 percent) earn somewhat higher returns.

Rate of Return on Common Stockholders' Equity

One of the most important measures of profitability is **rate of return on common stockholders' equity.** This ratio shows the relationship between net income and common stockholders' investment in the company. To compute this ratio, we first subtract preferred dividends from net income. This leaves only net income available to the common stockholders, which is needed to compute the ratio. We then divide net income available to common stockholders by the average stockholders' equity during the year. Common stockholders' equity is total stockholders' equity minus preferred equity. McColpin's rate of return on common stockholders' equity follows. (Data from Exhibits 19-1 and 19-2.)

Formula	Rate of Return on Common Stockholders' Equity of McColpin, Inc.
	19X7
$$\text{Rate of return on common stockholders' equity} = \frac{\text{Net income} - \text{preferred dividends}}{\text{Average common stockholders' equity}}$$	$$\frac{\$48,000 - \$0}{\$338,000} = .142$$

We compute average equity using the beginning and ending balances [($356,000 + $320,000)/2 = $338,000]. Observe that common stockholders' equity includes Retained Earnings and any Paid-in Capital in Excess of Par on Common Stock.

McColpin's 14.2 percent return on common equity compares favorably with returns of companies in most industries, which average around 10 percent. However, some leading companies show higher ratios: IBM (22 percent), Chesebrough-Pond's (20 percent), and General Motors (20 percent).

Observe that return on equity (14.2 percent) is higher than return on assets (10.1 percent). This 4.1 percent difference results from borrowing at one rate, say 8 percent, and investing the funds to earn a higher rate, such as McColpin's 14.2 percent return on stockholders' equity. This practice is called **trading on the equity,** or the use of **leverage.** It is directly related to the debt ratio. The higher the debt ratio, the higher the leverage. Companies that finance operations with debt are said to *lever* their positions. Leverage increases the risk to common stockholders. For McColpin, Inc., and for many other companies leverage increases profitability. That is not always the case, however. Leverage can also have a negative impact on profitability. If revenues drop, debt and interest expense still must be paid. Therefore, leverage is a double-edged sword, increasing profits during good times but compounding losses during bad times.

Earnings per Share of Common Stock

Earnings per share of common stock, or simply **earnings per share (EPS),** is perhaps the most widely quoted of all financial statistics. EPS is the only ratio that must appear on the face of the income statement. EPS is the amount of net income per share of the company's *common* stock. Earnings per share is computed by dividing net income available to common stockholders by the number of common shares outstanding during the year. Preferred dividends are subtracted from net income because the preferred stockholders have a prior claim to their dividends. McColpin has no preferred stock outstanding and so has no preferred dividends.

McColpin's EPS for 19X7 and 19X6 follow. (Data are from Exhibits 19-1 and 19-2, and the company had 10,000 shares of common stock outstanding throughout 19X6 and 19X7.)

		Earnings Per Share of McColpin, Inc.	
Formula		**19X7**	**19X6**
Earnings per share of common stock (EPS)	$= \dfrac{\text{Net income} - \text{preferred dividends}}{\text{Number of shares of common stock outstanding}}$	$\dfrac{\$48,000 - \$0}{10,000} = \$4.80$	$\dfrac{\$26,000 - \$0}{10,000} = \$2.60$

McColpin's EPS rose from $2.60 to $4.80, an increase of 85 percent. McColpin's stockholders should not expect such a significant boost in EPS every year. However, most companies strive to increase EPS by 10 to 15 percent annually, and the more successful companies do so. However, even the most dramatic upward trends include an occasional bad year.

Analyzing Stock as an Investment

Investors purchase stock to earn a return on their investment. This return consists of two parts: (1) gains (or losses) from selling the stock at a price that is different from the investors' purchase price, and (2) dividends, the periodic distributions to stockholders. The ratios we examine in this section help analysts evaluate stock in terms of market price or dividend payments.

Price/Earnings Ratio

The **price/earnings ratio** is the ratio of the market price of a share of common stock to the company's earnings per share. This ratio, abbreviated P/E, appears in *The Wall Street Journal* stock listings. P/E plays an important part in evaluating decisions to buy, hold, and sell stocks.

The price/earnings ratios of McColpin, Inc., follow. The market price of its common stock was $50 at the end of 19X7 and $35 at the end of 19X6. These prices can be obtained from a financial publication, a stockbroker, or some other source outside the accounting records.

		Price/Earnings Ratio of McColpin, Inc.	
Formula		**19X7**	**19X6**
Price/ earnings ratio	$= \dfrac{\text{Market price per share of common stock}}{\text{Earnings per share}}$	$\dfrac{\$50.00}{\$4.80} = 10.4$	$\dfrac{\$35.00}{\$2.60} = 13.5$

Given McColpin's 19X7 price/earnings ratio of 10.4, we would say that the company's stock is selling at 10.4 times earnings. The decline from the 19X6 P/E ratio of 13.5 is not a cause for alarm because the numerator—market price of the stock—is not under McColpin's control. The denominator—net income—is more controllable, and it increased during 19X7. Like most other ratios, P/E ratios vary from industry to industry, ranging from 5 to 7 for auto makers (Ford and GM, for example) to 50 to 100 for glamour stocks such as Tenneco and United Telephone.

Dividend Yield

Dividend yield is the ratio of dividends per share of stock to the stock's market price per share. This ratio measures the percentage of a stock's market value that is returned annually as dividends, an important concern of stockholders. *Preferred* stockholders, who invest primarily to receive dividends, pay special attention to this ratio.

McColpin paid annual cash dividends of $1.20 per share in 19X7 and $1.00 in 19X6 and market prices of the company's common stock were $50 in 19X7 and $35.00 in 19X6. McColpin's dividend yields follow:

Formula		Dividend Yield on Common Stock of McColpin, Inc.	
		19X7	**19X6**
Dividend yield on common stock	$= \dfrac{\text{Dividend per share of common stock}}{\text{Market price per share of common stock}}$	$\dfrac{\$1.20}{\$50.00} = .024$	$\dfrac{\$1.00}{\$35.00} = .029$

An investor who buys McColpin common stock for $50 can expect to receive almost 2½ percent of her investment annually in the form of cash dividends. Dividend yields vary widely, from 5 to 8 percent for older established firms (like Procter & Gamble and General Motors) down to the range of 0 to 3 percent for young, growth-oriented companies (like Apple Computer). McColpin's dividend yield places the company in the second group.

Book Value per Share of Common Stock

Book value per share of common stock is simply common stockholders' equity divided by the number of shares of common stock outstanding. Common shareholders' equity equals total stockholders' equity less preferred equity. McColpin has no preferred stock outstanding. Its book value per share of common stock ratios follow. Recall that 10,000 shares of common stock were outstanding at the ends of years 19X7 and 19X6.

Formula		Book Value per Share of the Common Stock of McColpin, Inc.	
		19X7	**19X6**
Book value per share of common stock	$= \dfrac{\text{Total stockholders' equity} - \text{preferred equity}}{\text{Number of shares of common stock outstanding}}$	$\dfrac{\$356,000 - \$0}{10,000} = \$35.60$	$\dfrac{\$320,000 - \$0}{10,000} = \$32.00$

The market price of a company's stock usually exceeds its book value. Some investors buy a stock when its market value approaches book value. Suppose you decided to buy McColpin stock at the end of 19X6, when its market price of $35 was close to book value of $32. That investment would have proved wise. The stock's price increased to $50 in 19X7. Of course, when you bought the stock in 19X6, there was no guarantee the stock price would increase.

The Complexity of Business Decisions

Business decisions are made in a world of uncertainty. Legislation, international affairs, competition, scandals, and many other factors can turn profits into losses, and vice versa. To be most useful, ratios should be analyzed over a period of years to take into account a representative group of these factors. Any one year, or even any two years, may not be representative of the company's performance over the long term.

OBJECTIVE 6
Explain how to use ratios in decision making

For example, a business's acid-test ratio may show a substantial increase over a ten-year period. However, a two-year period during the early part of that decade might show a slight downturn. An evaluation based on the two-year analysis might lead to an unwise decision. To make the best use of ratios, we must consider them within a broad time frame.

As useful as ratios may be, they do have limitations. We may liken their use in decision making to a physician's use of a thermometer. A reading of 101.6 degrees Fahrenheit indicates that something is wrong with the patient, but the temperature alone does not indicate what the problem is or how to cure it.

In financial analysis, a sudden drop in a company's current ratio signals that *something* is wrong, but this change does not identify the problem or show how to correct it. The business manager must analyze the figures that go into the ratio to determine whether current assets have decreased, current liabilities have increased, or both. If current assets have dropped, is the problem a cash shortage? Are accounts receivable down? Are inventories too low? Only by analyzing the individual items that make up the ratio can the manager determine how to solve the problem. The manager must evaluate data on all ratios in the light of other information about the company and about its particular line of business, such as increased competition or a slowdown in the economy.

Uncertainty clouds business decisions. A decision maker can never be sure how a course of action will turn out. For example, a careful analysis of ratios and other accounting information may suggest to management that the business should invest its excess cash in the stock of a microcomputer company. This industry may hold the prospect for the fastest return on an investment. A competing microcomputer company may come out with a new computer that sweeps the market, leaving the first company's stock worthless and the investing company in financial trouble. Ratio analysis cannot predict the future, but knowledge gained by a study of ratios and related information can help the analyst to make informed decisions.

Summary Problem for Your Review

This problem is based on the following financial data adapted from the financial statements of Pizza Inn, Inc., which operates approximately 1,000 pizza restaurants.

Pizza Inn, Inc.
Balance Sheets
19X3 and 19X2

	19X3	19X2
	(Thousands of Dollars)	

Assets

Current assets:

Cash	$ 4,123	$ 6,453
Marketable securities (same as short-term investments)	4,236	—
Receivables, net	6,331	7,739
Inventories	5,840	4,069
Prepaid expenses and others	3,830	2,708
Total current assets	24,360	20,969
Net property, plant, and equipment	35,330	28,821
Net property under capital leases	23,346	20,886
Intangibles and other assets	10,493	11,349
	$93,529	$82,025

Liabilities and Stockholders' Equity

Current liabilities:

Notes payable	$ 1,244	$ 785
Current installments of long-term debt and capital lease obligations	5,220	6,654
Accounts payable–trade	8,631	8,791
Accrued liabilities	5,822	5,983
Total current liabilities	20,917	22,213
Long-term debt, less current installments	22,195	15,549
Capital lease obligations, less current portion	24,296	22,350
Deferred income and deferred income taxes	2,211	1,522
Total common stockholders' equity (shares outstanding 3,017,381 at year end 19X3 and 2,729,274 at year end 19X2)	23,910	20,391
	$93,529	$82,025

Pizza Inn, Inc.
Statements of Earnings
Years 19X3 and 19X2

	19X3	19X2
	(Thousands of Dollars)	

Total revenue	$148,889	$140,539
Costs and expenses:		
Cost of products sold	$114,335	$111,188
Selling, administrative, and general expenses	23,475	20,816
	137,810	132,004
Earnings from operations	11,079	8,535
Interest expense	5,771	5,902
Earnings before income taxes	5,308	2,633
Income taxes	1,713	932
Net earnings	$ 3,595	$ 1,701

Required

Compute the following ratios for Pizza Inn for 19X3:

a. Current ratio
b. Acid-test ratio
c. Inventory turnover
d. Days' sales (total revenue) in average receivables
e. Debt ratio
f. Times-interest-earned ratio
g. Rate of return on sales (total revenue)

h. Rate of return on total assets
i. Rate of return on common stockholders' equity
j. Price/earnings ratio, assuming the market price of common stock is $15.50 and earnings per share is $1.16.
k. Book value per share of common stock

SOLUTION TO REVIEW PROBLEM

a. Current Ratio $= \dfrac{\text{Current Assets}}{\text{Current Liabilities}} = \dfrac{\$24,360}{\$20,917} = 1.16$

b. Acid-Test Ratio $= \dfrac{\text{Cash} + \text{Short-Term Investments} + \text{Net Current Receivables}}{\text{Current Liabilities}} = \dfrac{\$4,123 + \$4,236 + \$6,331}{\$20,917} = .70$

c. Inventory Turnover $= \dfrac{\text{Cost of Goods Sold}}{\text{Average Inventory}} = \dfrac{\$114,335}{(\$5,840 + \$4,069)/2} = 23.08$

d. Days' Sales (Total Revenue) in Average Receivables:

1. One day's sales $= \dfrac{\text{Net Sales}}{365 \text{ Days}} = \dfrac{\$148,889}{365} = \$407.92$

2. Days' sales in average accounts receivable $= \dfrac{\text{Average Accounts Receivable}}{\text{One Day's Sales}} = \dfrac{(\$6,331 + \$7,739)/2}{\$407.92} = 17 \text{ days}$

e. Debt Ratio $= \dfrac{\text{Total Liabilities}}{\text{Total Assets}} = \dfrac{\$20,917 + \$22,195 + \$24,296 + \$2,211}{\$93,529} = .74$

f. Times-Interest-Earned Ratio $= \dfrac{\text{Income from Operations}}{\text{Interest Expense}} = \dfrac{\$11,079}{\$5,771} = 1.92$

g. Rate of Return on Sales (Total Revenue) $= \dfrac{\text{Net Income}}{\text{Total Revenue}} = \dfrac{\$3,595}{\$148,889} = .024$

h. Rate of Return on Total Assets $= \dfrac{\text{Net Income} + \text{Interest Expense}}{\text{Average Total Assets}} = \dfrac{\$3,595 + \$5,771}{(\$93,529 + \$82,025)/2} = .107$

i. Rate of Return on Common Stockholders' Equity $= \dfrac{\text{Net Income} - \text{Preferred Dividends}}{\text{Average Common Stockholders' Equity}} = \dfrac{\$3,595 - \$0}{(\$23,910 + \$20,391)/2} = .162$

j. $\dfrac{\text{Price}/}{\text{Earnings}}$ Ratio $= \dfrac{\text{Market Price per Share of Common Stock}}{\text{Earnings per Share}} = \dfrac{\$15.50^*}{\$1.16^*} = 13.4$

k. $\dfrac{\text{Book Value}}{\text{per Share of}}$ Common Stock $= \dfrac{\begin{array}{c}\text{Total Stockholders' Equity}\\ -\text{ Preferred Equity}\end{array}}{\begin{array}{c}\text{Number of Shares of}\\ \text{Common Stock Outstanding}\end{array}} = \dfrac{\$23,910,000^* - \$0^*}{3,017,381^*} = \$7.92$

* All dollar amounts are expressed in thousands except those denoted by *.

Summary

Accounting provides information for decision making. Banks loan money, investors buy stocks, and managers run businesses based on the analysis of accounting information.

Horizontal analysis shows the dollar amount and the percentage change in each financial statement item from one period to the next. *Vertical analysis* shows the relationship of each item in a financial statement to its total: total assets on the balance sheet and net sales on the income statement.

Common-size statements—a form of vertical analysis—show the component percentages of the items in a statement. Investment advisory services report common-size statements for various industries, and analysts use them to compare a company to its competitors and to the industry averages.

The *statement of cash flows* shows the net cash inflow or outflow caused by a company's operating, investing, and financing activities. By analyzing the inflows and outflows of cash listed on this statement, an analyst can see where a business's cash comes from and how it is being spent.

Ratios play an important part in business decision making because they show relationships between financial statement items. Analysis of ratios over a period of time is an important way to track a company's progress. The accompanying list presents the ratios discussed in this chapter:

Ratio	Computation	Information Provided
Measuring the ability to pay current liabilities:		
1. Current ratio	$\dfrac{\text{Current assets}}{\text{Current liabilities}}$	Measures ability to pay current liabilities from current assets.
2. Acid-test (quick) ratio	$\dfrac{\begin{array}{c}\text{Cash + short-term investments}\\ +\text{ net current receivables}\end{array}}{\text{Current liabilities}}$	Shows ability to pay current liabilities from the most liquid assets.
Measuring the ability to sell inventory and collect receivables:		
3. Inventory turnover	$\dfrac{\text{Cost of goods sold}}{\text{Average inventory}}$	Indicates saleability of inventory.
4. Accounts receivable turnover	$\dfrac{\text{Net credit sales}}{\begin{array}{c}\text{Average net}\\ \text{accounts receivable}\end{array}}$	Measures collectibility of receivables.

5. Days' sales in receivables	$\dfrac{\text{Average net accounts receivable}}{\text{One day's sales}}$	Shows how many days it takes to collect average receivables.

Measuring the ability to pay long-term debts:

6. Debt ratio	$\dfrac{\text{Total liabilities}}{\text{Total assets}}$	Indicates percentage of assets financed through borrowing.
7. Times-interest-earned ratio	$\dfrac{\text{Income from operations}}{\text{Interest expense}}$	Measures coverage of interest expense by operating income.

Measuring profitability:

8. Rate of return on net sales	$\dfrac{\text{Net income}}{\text{Net sales}}$	Shows the percentage of each sales dollar earned as net income.
9. Rate of return on total assets	$\dfrac{\text{Net income} + \text{interest expense}}{\text{Average total assets}}$	Gauges how profitably assets are used.
10. Rate of return on common stock-holders' equity	$\dfrac{\text{Net income} - \text{preferred dividends}}{\text{Average common stockholders' equity}}$	Gauges how profitably the assets financed by the common stockholders are used.
11. Earnings per share of common stock	$\dfrac{\text{Net income} - \text{preferred dividends}}{\text{Number of shares of common stock outstanding}}$	Gives the amount of earnings per one share of common stock.

Analyzing stock as an investment:

12. Price/earnings ratio	$\dfrac{\text{Market price per share of common stock}}{\text{Earnings per share}}$	Indicates the market price of one dollar of earnings.
13. Dividend yield	$\dfrac{\text{Dividend per share of common stock}}{\text{Market price per share of common stock}}$	Shows the proportion of the market price of each share of stock returned as dividends to stockholders each period.
14. Book value per share of common stock	$\dfrac{\text{Total stockholders' equity} - \text{preferred equity}}{\text{Number of shares of common stock outstanding}}$	Indicates the recorded accounting value of each share of common stock outstanding.

Self-Study Questions

Test your understanding of the chapter by marking the best answer for each of the following questions.

1. Net income was $240,000 in 19X4, $210,000 in 19X5, and $252,000 in 19X6. The change from 19X5 to 19X6 is a (an) *(p. 740)*
   a. Increase of 5 percent   c. Decrease of 10 percent
   b. Increase of 20 percent   d. Decrease of 12.5 percent
2. Vertical analysis of a financial statement shows *(p. 743)*
   a. Trend percentages

b. The percentage change in an item from period to period

c. The relationship of an item to its total on the statement

d. Net income expressed as a percentage of stockholders' equity

3. Common-size statements are useful for comparing *(pp. 745, 746)*
   a. Changes in the makeup of assets from period to period
   b. Different companies
   c. A company to its industry
   d. All of the above

4. The statement of cash flows is used for decision making by *(pp. 747, 748)*
   a. Reporting where cash came from and how it was spent
   b. Indicating how net income was earned
   c. Giving the ratio relationships between selected items
   d. Showing a horizontal analysis of cash flows

5. Cash is $10,000, net accounts receivable amount to $22,000, inventory is $55,000, prepaid expenses total $3,000, and current liabilities are $40,000. What is the acid-test ratio? *(p. 752)*
   a. .25   c. 2.18
   b. .80   d. 2.25

6. Inventory turnover is computed by dividing *(p. 752)*
   a. Sales revenue by average inventory
   b. Cost of goods sold by average inventory
   c. Credit sales by average inventory
   d. Average inventory by cost of goods sold

7. Capp Corporation is experiencing a severe cash shortage due to inability to collect accounts receivable. The decision tool most likely to help identify the appropriate corrective action is the *(p. 754)*
   a. Acid-test ratio   c. Times-interest-earned ratio
   b. Inventory turnover   d. Days' sales in receivables

8. Analysis of the Mendoza Company financial statements over five years reveals that sales are growing steadily, the debt ratio is higher than the industry average and is increasing, interest coverage is decreasing, return on total assets is declining, and earnings per share of common stock is decreasing. Considered together, these ratios suggest that *(pp. 755, 756, 757)*
   a. Mendoza should pursue collections of receivables more vigorously
   b. Competition is taking sales away from Mendoza
   c. Mendoza is in a declining industry
   d. The company's debt burden is hurting profitability

9. Which of the following is most likely to be true? *(p. 758)*
   a. Return on common equity exceeds return on total assets.
   b. Return on total assets exceeds return on common equity.
   c. Return on total assets equals return on common equity.
   d. None of the above.

10. How are financial ratios used in decision making? *(p. 761)*
    a. They remove the uncertainty of the business environment.
    b. They give clear signals about the appropriate action to take.
    c. They can help identify the reasons for success and failure in business, but decision making requires information beyond the ratios.
    d. They aren't useful because decision making is too complex.

Answers to the self-study questions are at the end of the chapter.

Accounting Vocabulary

accounts receivable turnover *(p. 753)*, acid-test ratio *(p. 751)*, book value per share of common stock *(p. 760)*, common-size statements *(p. 745)*, current ratio *(p. 751)*, days' sales in receivables *(p. 754)*, debt ratio *(p. 755)*, dividend yield *(p. 760)*,   horizontal analysis *(p. 740)*, interest-coverage ratio *(p. 756)*, inventory turnover *(p. 752)*, leverage *(p. 758)*, price/earnings ratio *(p. 759)*, quick ratio *(p. 751)*, rate of return on total assets *(p. 757)*, rate of return on common stockholders' equity *(p. 758)*, rate of return on net sales *(p. 756)*, return on assets *(p. 757)*, return on common stockholders' equity, *(p. 758)*, return on sales *(p. 756)*, times-interest-earned ratio *(p. 756)*, vertical analysis *(p. 743)*, working capital *(p. 750)*.

ASSIGNMENT MATERIAL _____

Questions

1. Identify two groups of users of accounting information and the decisions they base on accounting data.
2. What are three analytical tools that are based on accounting information?
3. Briefly describe horizontal analysis. How do decision makers use this tool of analysis?
4. What is vertical analysis, and what is its purpose?
5. What use is made of common-size statements?
6. State how an investor might analyze the statement of cash flows. How might the investor analyze investing activities data?
7. Why are ratios an important tool of financial analysis? Give an example.
8. Identify two ratios used to measure a company's ability to pay current liabilities. Show how they are computed.
9. Why is the acid-test ratio called by this name?
10. What does the inventory-turnover ratio measure?
11. Suppose the days' sales in receivables ratio of Gomez, Inc., increased from 36 at January 1 to 43 at December 31. Is this a good sign or a bad sign about the company? What would Gomez management do in response to this change?
12. Company A's debt ratio has increased from .50 to .70. Identify a decision maker to whom this increase is important, and state how the increase affects this party's decisions about the company.
13. Which ratio measures the *effect of debt* on (a) financial position (the balance sheet) and (b) the company's ability to pay interest expense (the income statement)?
14. Company A is a chain of grocery stores, and Company B is a computer manufacturer. Which company is likely to have the higher (a) current ratio, (b) inventory turnover, and (c) rate of return on sales? Give your reasons.
15. Identify four ratios used to measure a company's profitability. Show how to compute these ratios and state what information each ratio provides.
16. The price/earnings ratio of General Motors was 6, and the price/earnings ratio of American Express was 45. Which company did the stock market favor? Explain.
17. McDonald's Corporation, the hamburger company, paid cash dividends of $.78-⅔ (78 and ⅔ cents) per share when the market price of the company's stock was $58. What was the dividend yield on McDonald's stock. What does dividend yield measure?
18. Hold all other factors constant and indicate whether each of the following situations generally signals good or bad news about a company:
    - a. Increase in current ratio
    - b. Decrease in inventory turnover
    - c. Increase in debt ratio
    - d. Decrease in interest-coverage ratio
    - e. Increase in return on sales
    - f. Decrease in earnings per share
    - g. Increase in price/earnings ratio
    - h. Increase in book value per share
19. Explain how an investor might use book value per share of stock in making an investment decision.
20. Describe how decision makers use ratio data. What are the limitations of ratios?

Exercises

Exercise 19-1   *Computing year-to-year changes in current assets and total assets*

Using the following financial statement data of Chin Corporation, compute the dollar amount of change and the percentage change in total current assets and total assets during years 5 and 4:

				Increase (Decrease)			
				During Year 5		During Year 4	
	Year 5	Year 4	Year 3	Amount	%	Amount	%
Total current assets	$312,000	$260,000	$280,000				
Total assets	850,000	867,000	840,000				

Exercise 19-2   *Horizontal analysis of an income statement*

Prepare a horizontal analysis of the following comparative income statement of LaPaz Incorporated. Round percentage changes to the nearest one-tenth percent (three decimal places):

LaPaz Incorporated Comparative Income Statement Years Ended December 31, 19X9 and 19X8		
	19X9	19X8
Total Revenue	$431,000	$373,000
Expenses:		
Cost of goods sold..................	$202,000	$188,000
Selling and general expenses	118,000	93,000
Interest expense....................	7,000	4,000
Income tax expense.................	42,000	37,000
Total expenses.....................	369,000	322,000
Net Income	$ 62,000	$ 51,000

Why did net income increase by a higher percentage than total revenues increased during 19X9?

Exercise 19-3   *Computing trend percentages*

Compute trend percentages for net sales and net income for the following five-year period, using year 1 as the base year:

	Year 5	Year 4	Year 3	Year 2	Year 1
			(amounts in thousands)		
Net sales	$1,448	$1,287	$1,106	$944	$1,043
Net income	127	114	93	71	85

Which grew more during the period, net sales or net income?

Exercise 19-4   *Vertical analysis of a balance sheet*

Quattlebaum Company has requested that you perform a vertical analysis of its balance sheet to determine the component percentages of its assets, liabilities, and stockholders' equity.

Quattlebaum Company
Balance Sheet
December 31, 19X3

Assets

Total current assets	$ 74,000
Long-term investments	23,000
Property, plant, and equipment, net	227,000
Total assets....................................	$324,000

Liabilities

Total current liabilities	$ 48,000
Long-term debt	118,000
Total liabilities	166,000

Stockholders' Equity

Total stockholders' equity.......................	158,000
Total liabilities and stockholders' equity	$324,000

Exercise 19-5 *Preparing a common-size income statement*

Prepare a comparative common-size income statement for LaPaz Incorporated, using the
19X9 and 19X8 data of Exercise 19-2 and rounding percentages to one-tenth percent (three
decimal places).

Exercise 19-6 *Analyzing the statement of cash flows*

Identify any weaknesses revealed by the statement of cash flows of Tanglewood Home
Centers, Inc.

Tanglewood Home Centers, Inc.
Statement of Cash Flows
For the Current Year

Operating activities:		
Income from operations		$ 8,000
Add (subtract) noncash items:		
Depreciation....................................	$ 23,000	
Net increase in current assets other than cash.........	(15,000)	
Net increase in current liabilities exclusive of		
short-term debt	11,000	19,000
Net cash inflow from operating activities.............		27,000
Investing activities:		
Sale of property, plant, and equipment		76,000
Financing activities:		
Issuance of bonds payable	$ 81,000	
Payment of short-term debt	(101,000)	
Payment of long-term debt.........................	(79,000)	
Payment of dividends..............................	(8,000)	
Net cash outflow from financing activities............		(107,000)
Decrease in cash		$ (4,000)

Exercise 19-7 *Computing five ratios*

The financial statements of Snyder Company include the following items:

	Current Year	Preceding Year
Balance sheet:		
Cash......................................	$ 17,000	$ 22,000
Short-term investments......................	21,000	26,000
Net receivables	64,000	73,000
Inventory.................................	87,000	71,000
Prepaid expenses..........................	6,000	8,000
Total current assets	195,000	200,000
Total current liabilities.....................	107,000	91,000
Income statement:		
Net credit sales	$444,000	
Cost of goods sold.........................	237,000	

Required

Compute the following ratios for the current year: (a) current ratio, (b) acid-test ratio, (c) inventory turnover, (d) accounts receivable turnover, and (e) days' sales in average receivables.

Exercise 19-8 *Analyzing the ability to pay current liabilities*

Holmes, Inc., has requested that you determine whether the company's ability to pay its current liabilities and long-term debts has improved or deteriorated during 19X5. To answer this question, compute the following ratios for 19X5 and 19X4: (a) current ratio, (b) acid-test ratio, (c) debt ratio, and (d) times-interest-earned ratio. Summarize the results of your analysis.

	19X5	19X4
Cash...............................	$ 31,000	$ 37,000
Short-term investments................	28,000	—
Net receivables	132,000	116,000
Inventory..........................	226,000	263,000
Prepaid expenses....................	11,000	9,000
Total assets.........................	553,000	519,000
Total current liabilities	205,000	241,000
Total liabilities......................	261,000	273,000
Income from operations	165,000	158,000
Interest expense.....................	26,000	31,000

Exercise 19-9 *Analyzing profitability*

Compute four ratios that measure ability to earn profits for Mission Viejo, Inc. whose comparative income statement appears at the top of the next page. Additional data follow:

Additional data:		
1. Average total assets...................................	$204,000	$191,000
2. Average common stockholders' equity	$ 96,000	$ 89,000
3. Preferred dividends....................................	$ 3,000	$ 3,000
4. Shares of common stock outstanding	18,000	18,000

Did the company's operating performance improve or deteriorate during 19X1?

Mission Viejo, Inc.
Comparative Income Statement
Years Ended December 31, 19X1 and 19X0

	19X1	19X0
Net sales	$166,000	$158,000
Cost of goods sold	93,000	86,000
Gross profit	73,000	72,000
Selling and general expenses	48,000	41,000
Income from operations	25,000	31,000
Interest expense	9,000	10,000
Income before income tax	16,000	21,000
Income tax expense	6,000	8,000
Net income	$ 10,000	$ 13,000

Exercise 19-10 *Evaluating a stock as an investment*

Evaluate the common stock of Tidewater Virginia, Inc., as an investment. Specifically, use the three stock ratios to determine whether the stock has increased or decreased in attractiveness during the past year.

	Current Year	Preceding Year
Net income	$ 58,000	$ 55,000
Dividends (half on preferred stock)	28,000	28,000
Common stockholders' equity at year end (100,000 shares)	530,000	500,000
Preferred stockholders' equity at year end	200,000	200,000
Market price per share of common stock at year end	$6.63	$5.75

Problems   (Group A)

Problem 19-1A *Trend percentages, return on common equity, and comparison to the industry*

Net sales, net income, and common stockholders' equity for Nasdac Computing, Inc., for a six-year period follow.

	19X9	19X8	19X7	19X6	19X5	19X4
	(amounts in thousands)					
Net sales	$762	$714	$621	$532	$596	$634
Net income	49	45	42	38	37	40
Ending common stockholders' equity	386	354	330	296	272	252

Required

1. Compute trend percentages for 19X5 through 19X9, using 19X4 as the base year.
2. Compute the rate of return on average common stockholders' equity for 19X5 through 19X9, rounding to three decimal places. In this industry, rates of 13 percent are

average, rates above 16 percent are considered good, and rates above 20 percent are viewed as outstanding.

3.   How does Nasdac's return on common stockholders' equity compare to the industry?

Problem 19-2A   *Common-size statements, analysis of profitability, and comparison to the industry*

Middlebrook Sporting Goods has asked your help in comparing the company's profit performance and financial position with the average for the sporting goods retail industry. The proprietor has given you the company's income statement and balance sheet and also the industry average data for retailers of sporting goods.

Middlebrook Sporting Goods Income Statement Compared to Industry Average Year Ended December 31, 19X6			Middlebrook Sporting Goods Balance Sheet Compared to Industry Average December 31, 19X6		
	Middlebrook	**Industry Average**		**Middlebrook**	**Industry Average**
Net sales	$781,000	100.0%	Current assets	$350,000	80.9%
Cost of goods sold	476,000	65.8	Fixed assets, net	74,000	13.6
Gross profit	305,000	34.2	Intangible assets, net	4,000	.8
Operating expenses	243,000	29.7	Other assets	22,000	4.7
Operating income	62,000	4.5	Total	$450,000	100.0%
Other expenses	5,000	.4			
Net income	$ 57,000	4.1%	Current liabilities	$230,000	48.1%
			Long-term liabilities	72,000	16.6
			Stockholders' equity	148,000	35.3
			Total	$450,000	100.0%

Required

1.   Prepare a two-column common-size income statement and a two-column common-size balance sheet for Middlebrook. The first column of each statement should present Middlebrook's common-size statement, and the second column should show the industry averages.

2.   For the profitability analysis, compute Middlebrook's (a) ratio of gross profit to net sales, (b) ratio of operating income to net sales, and (c) ratio of net income to net sales. Compare these figures to the industry averages. Is Middlebrook's profit performance better or worse than the industry average?

3.   For the analysis of financial position, compute Middlebrook's (a) ratio of current assets to total assets and (b) ratio of stockholders' equity to total assets. Compare these ratios to the industry averages. Is Middlebrook's financial position better or worse than the industry averages?

Problem 19-3A   *Using the statement of cash flows for decision making*

You have been asked to evaluate two companies as possible investments. The two companies, similar in size, buy computers, airplanes, and other high-cost assets to lease to other businesses. Assume that all other available information has been analyzed, and the decision on which company's stock to purchase depends on the information given in their statements of cash flows.

Required

Discuss the relative strengths and weaknesses of each company. Conclude your discussion by recommending one company's stock as an investment.

LeaseAmerica, Inc.
Statements of Cash Flows
For the Years Ended September 30, 19X5 and 19X4

	19X5	19X4
Operating activities:		
Income from operations	$ 37,000	$ 74,000
Add (subtract) noncash items:		
Total	14,000	(4,000)
Net cash inflow from operating activities	51,000	70,000
Investing activities:		
Purchase of property, plant, and equipment	$ (13,000)	$ (3,000)
Sale of property, plant, and equipment	86,000	79,000
Sale of long-term investments	13,000	—
Net cash inflow from investing activities	86,000	76,000
Financing activities:		
Issuance of short-term notes payable	$ 73,000	$19,000
Issuance of long-term notes payable	31,000	42,000
Payment of short-term notes payable	(181,000)	(148,000)
Payment of long-term notes payable	(55,000)	(32,000)
Net cash outflow from financing activities	(132,000)	(119,000)
Increase in cash	$ 5,000	$ 27,000
Cash summary from balance sheet:		
Cash balance at beginning of year	$ 31,000	$ 4,000
Increase in cash during the year	5,000	27,000
Cash balance at end of year	$ 36,000	$ 31,000

TransPacific Leasing Corporation
Statements of Cash Flows
For the Years Ended September 30, 19X5 and 19X4

	19X5	19X4
Operating activities:		
Income from operations	$ 79,000	$ 71,000
Add (subtract) noncash items:		
Total	19,000	—
Net cash inflow from operating activities	98,000	71,000
Investing activities:		
Purchase of property, plant, and equipment	$(121,000)	$(91,000)
Sale of long-term investments	13,000	18,000
Net cash outflow from investing activities	(108,000)	(73,000)
Financing activities:		
Issuance of long-term notes payable	$ 46,000	$ 43,000
Payment of long-term notes payable	(15,000)	(40,000)
Payment of cash dividends	(12,000)	(9,000)
Net cash inflow (outflow) from financing activities	19,000	(6,000)
Increase (decrease) in cash	$ 9,000	$ (8,000)
Cash summary from balance sheet:		
Cash balance at beginning of year	$ 72,000	$ 80,000
Increase (decrease) in cash during the year	9,000	(8,000)
Cash balance at end of year	$ 81,000	$ 72,000

Problem 19-4A *Effects of business transactions on selected ratios*

Financial statement data of Bylinski Company include the following items.

Cash	$ 22,000
Short-term investments	19,000
Accounts receivable, net	83,000
Inventories	141,000
Prepaid expenses	8,000
Total assets	657,000
Short-term notes payable	49,000
Accounts payable	103,000
Accrued liabilities	38,000
Long-term notes payable	160,000
Other long-term liabilities	31,000
Net income	71,000
Number of common shares outstanding	40,000

Required

1. Compute Bylinski's current ratio, debt ratio, and earnings per share.
2. Compute each of the three ratios after evaluating the effect of each transaction that follows. Consider each transaction *separately*.
   a. Purchased merchandise of $26,000 on account, debiting Inventory.
   b. Paid off long-term liabilities, $31,000.
   c. Declared, but did not pay, a $22,000 cash dividend on the common stock.
   d. Borrowed $85,000 on a long-term note payable.
   e. Sold short-term investments for $18,000 (cost, $11,000); assume no income tax on the gain.
   f. Issued 5,000 shares of common stock, receiving cash of $120,000.
   g. Received cash on account $19,000.
   h. Paid short-term notes payable, $32,000.

Use the following format for your answer:

Requirement 1.		**Current Ratio**	**Debt Ratio**	**Earnings per Share**
		_____	_____	_____

Requirement 2.	**Transaction (letter)**	**Current Ratio**	**Debt Ratio**	**Earnings per Share**
	_____	_____	_____	_____

Problem 19-5A *Using ratios to evaluate a stock investment*

Comparative financial statement data of Oaktree Realty Company appear on the following page.

Required

1. Compute the following ratios for 19X7 and 19X6:
   a. Current ratio
   b. Inventory turnover
   c. Accounts receivable turnover
   d. Times-interest-earned ratio
   e. Return on assets
   f. Return on common stockholders' equity
   g. Earnings per share of common stock
   h. Price/earnings ratio
   i. Book value per share of common stock
2. Decide (a) whether Oaktree's financial position improved or deteriorated during 19X7 and (b) whether the investment attractiveness of its common stock appears to have increased or decreased.

Oaktree Realty Company
Comparative Income Statement
Years Ended December 31, 19X7 and 19X6

	19X7	19X6
Net sales	$462,000	$427,000
Cost of goods sold	229,000	218,000
Gross profit	233,000	209,000
Operating expenses	136,000	134,000
Income from operations	97,000	75,000
Interest expense	21,000	12,000
Income before income tax	76,000	63,000
Income tax expense	30,000	27,000
Net income	$ 46,000	$ 36,000

Oaktree Realty Company
Comparative Balance Sheet
December 31, 19X7 and 19X6
(selected 19X5 amounts given for computation of ratios)

	19X7	19X6	19X5
Current assets:			
Cash	$ 71,000	$ 77,000	
Current receivables, net	137,000	146,000	$153,000
Inventories	202,000	182,000	237,000
Prepaid expenses	16,000	7,000	
Total current assets	426,000	412,000	
Property, plant, and equipment, net	159,000	148,000	
Total assets	$585,000	$560,000	598,000
Total current liabilities	$206,000	$223,000	
Long-term liabilities	119,000	117,000	
Total liabilities	325,000	340,000	
Preferred stockholders' equity, 6%, $100 par	100,000	100,000	
Common stockholders' equity, no-par	160,000	120,000	90,000
Total liabilities and stockholders' equity	$585,000	$560,000	

Other information:

a. Market price of Oaktree common stock: $31 at December 31, 19X7, and $25.50 at December 31, 19X6.

b. Common shares outstanding: 10,000 during 19X7 and 9,000 during 19X6.

c. All sales on credit.

Problem 19-6A *Using ratios to decide between two stock investments*

Assume you are purchasing an investment and have decided to invest in a company in the air-conditioning and heating business. Suppose you have narrowed the choice to Linz Corp. and Hutton, Inc. You have assembled the following selected data:

Selected income statement data for current year:

	Linz Corp.	Hutton, Inc.
Net sales (all on credit)	$371,000	$497,000
Cost of goods sold	209,000	258,000
Income from operations	79,000	138,000
Interest expense	—	19,000
Net income	48,000	72,000

Selected balance sheet and market price data at end of current year:

	Linz Corp.	Hutton, Inc.
Current assets:		
Cash	$ 22,000	$ 19,000
Short-term investments	—	18,000
Current receivables, net	42,000	46,000
Inventories	87,000	100,000
Prepaid expenses	2,000	3,000
Total current assets	153,000	186,000
Total assets	265,000	328,000
Total current liabilities	108,000	98,000
Total liabilities	108,000	131,000
Preferred stock: 5%, $100 par		20,000
Common stock, $1 par (10,000 shares)	10,000	
$2.50 par (5,000 shares)		12,500
Total stockholders' equity	157,000	197,000
Market price per share of common stock	$48	$108

Selected balance sheet data at beginning of current year:

	Linz Corp.	Hutton, Inc.
Current receivables, net	$ 40,000	$ 48,000
Inventories	93,000	88,000
Total assets	259,000	270,000
Preferred stockholders' equity 5%, $100 par	—	20,000
Common stock, $1 par (10,000 shares)	10,000	
$2.50 par (5,000 shares)		12,500
Total stockholders' equity	118,000	126,000

Your investment strategy is to purchase the stocks of companies that have low price/ earnings ratios but appear to be in good shape financially. Assume you have analyzed all other factors, and your decision depends on the results of the ratio analysis to be performed.

Required

Compute the following ratios for both companies for the current year and decide which company's stock better fits your investment strategy.

1. Current ratio
2. Acid-test ratio
3. Inventory turnover

4. Days' sales in average receivables
5. Debt ratio
6. Times-interest-earned ratio

7. Return on net sales
8. Return on total assets
9. Return on common stockholders' equity
10. Earnings per share of common stock
11. Book value per share of common stock
12. Price/earnings ratio

(Group B)

Problem 19-1B *Trend percentages, return on common equity, and comparison to the industry*

Net sales, net income, and total assets for LeClerc Manufacturing, Inc., for a six-year period follow.

	19X6	19X5	19X4	19X3	19X2	19X1
			(amounts in thousands)			
Net sales..........................	$337	$303	$266	$271	$253	$241
Net income........................	24	21	12	17	14	13
Total assets.......................	286	244	209	197	181	166

Required

1. Compute trend percentages for 19X2 through 19X6, using 19X1 as the base year.
2. Compute the rate of return on net sales for 19X2 through 19X6, rounding to three decimal places. In this industry, rates above 5 percent are considered good, and rates above 7 percent are viewed as outstanding.
3. How does LeClerc's return on net sales compare to the industry?

Problem 19-2B *Common-size statements, analysis of profitability, and comparison to the industry*

The partners of Blanton & Bornhauser, a department store, have asked your help in comparing the company's profit performance and financial position with the average for the department-store industry. The accountant has given you the company's income statement and balance sheet and also the following actual data for the department-store industry.

Blanton & Bornhauser **Income Statement** **Compared to Industry Average** **Year Ended December 31, 19X3**			**Blanton & Bornhauser** **Balance Sheet** **Compared to Industry Average** **December 31, 19X3**		
	Blanton & Bornhauser	**Industry Average**		**Blanton & Bornhauser**	**Industry Average**
Net sales...................	$957,000	100.0%	Current assets..............	$440,000	74.4%
Cost of goods sold..........	653,000	65.9	Fixed assets, net............	135,000	20.0
Gross profit	304,000	34.1	Intangibles assets, net	42,000	.6
Operating expenses..........	306,000	31.1	Other assets	13,000	5.0
Operating income (loss).......	(2,000)	3.0	Total	$630,000	100.0%
Other expenses	2,000	.4	Current liabilities............	$246,000	35.6
Net income (loss)............	$ (4,000)	2.6%	Long-term liabilities..........	124,000	19.0
			Stockholders' equity	260,000	45.4
			Total	$630,000	100.0%

Required

1. Prepare a two-column common-size income statement and a two-column common-size balance sheet for Blanton & Bornhauser. The first column of each statement should present Blanton & Bornhauser's common-size statement, and the second column should show the industry averages.

2. For the profitability analysis, compute Blanton & Bornhauser's (a) ratio of gross profit to net sales, (b) ratio of operating income (loss) to net sales, and (c) ratio of net income (loss) to net sales. Compare these figures to the industry averages. Is Blanton & Bornhauser's profit performance better or worse than average for department stores?

3. For the analysis of financial position, compare Blanton & Bornhauser's (a) ratio of current assets to total assets and (b) ratio of stockholders' equity to total assets. Compare these ratios to the industry averages. Is Blanton & Bornhauser's financial position better or worse than the average for the industry?

Problem 19-3B   *Using the statement of cash flows for decision making*

You are evaluating two companies as possible investments. The two companies, similar in size, are in the commuter airline business. They fly passengers from St. Louis and Kansas City to smaller cities in the Midwest. Assume that all other available information has been analyzed, and the decision on which company's stock to purchase depends on the information given in their statements of cash flows shown on the next page.

Required

Discuss the relative strengths and weaknesses of MidAmerica and Mokan. Conclude your discussion by recommending one of the company's stocks as an investment.

Problem 19-4B   *Effects of business transactions on selected ratios*

Financial statement data of Goliad Corporation include the following items:

Cash..	$ 47,000
Short-term investments..........................	21,000
Accounts receivable, net.........................	102,000
Inventories....................................	274,000
Prepaid expenses..............................	15,000
Total assets..................................	933,000
Short-term notes payable	72,000
Accounts payable	96,000
Accrued liabilities	50,000
Long-term notes payable	146,000
Other long-term liabilities.......................	78,000
Net income	119,000
Number of common shares outstanding	32,000

Required

1. Compute Goliad's current ratio, debt ratio, and earnings per share.
2. Compute each of the three ratios after evaluating the effect of each transaction that follows. Consider each transaction *separately.*
   a. Purchased merchandise of $48,000 on account, debiting Inventory.
   b. Paid off long-term liabilities, $78,000.
   c. Declared, but did not pay, a $31,000 cash dividend on the common stock.
   d. Borrowed $56,000 on a long-term note payable.
   e. Sold short-term investments for $34,000 (cost, $46,000); assume no tax effect of the loss.
   f. Issued 14,000 shares of common stock, receiving cash of $168,000.
   g. Received cash on account, $6,000.
   h. Paid short-term notes payable, $51,000.

(continued on page 780)

Statements of Cash Flows for Problem 19-3B

Mid America Airline, Inc.
Statements of Cash Flows
For the Years Ended November 30, 19X9 and 19X8

	19X9	19X8
Operating activities:		
Income from operations		$ 131,000
Add (subtract) noncash items:		
Total		62,000
Net cash inflow from operating activities		193,000
Investing activities:		
Purchase of property, plant, and equipment	$(303,000)	$(453,000)
Sale of property, plant and equipment	46,000	39,000
Sale of long-term investments	—	33,000
Net cash outflow from investing activities	(257,000)	(381,000)
Financing activities:		
Issuance of long-term notes payable	$ 131,000	$ 83,000
Issuance of short-term notes payable	43,000	35,000
Payment of short-term notes payable	(66,000)	(18,000)
Net cash inflow from financing activities	108,000	100,000
Increase (decrease) in cash	$ 99,000	$ (88,000)
Cash summary from balance sheet:		
Cash balance at beginning of year	$116,000	$204,000
Increase (decrease) in cash during the year	99,000	(88,000)
Cash balance at end of year. . .	$ 215,000	$ 116,000

MoKan Flight Corporation
Statements of Cash Flow
For the Years Ended November 30, 19X9 and 19X8

	19X9	19X8
Operating activities:		
Income (loss) from operations	$ (67,000)	$154,000
Add (subtract) noncash items:		
Total	84,000	(23,000)
Net cash inflow from operating activities	17,000	131,000
Investing activities:		
Purchase of property, plant, and equipment	$(120,000)	$ (91,000)
Sale of property, plant, and equipment	118,000	39,000
Sale of long-term investments.	52,000	4,000
Net cash inflow (outflow) from investing activities . . .	50,000	(48,000)
Financing activities:		
Issuance of short-term notes payable	$ 122,000	$ 143,000
Payment of short-term notes payable	(179,000)	(134,000)
Payment of cash dividends	(45,000)	(64,000)
Net cash outflow from financing activities	(102,000)	
Increase (decrease) in cash.	$ (35,000)	(55,000)
Cash summary from balance sheet:		$ 28,000
Cash balance at beginning of year	$ 131,000	$ 103,000
Increase (decrease) in cash during the year	(35,000)	28,000
Cash balance at end of year. . .	$ 96,000	$ 131,000

779

Use the following format for your answer to Problem 19-4B:

Requirement 1.		Current Ratio	Debt Ratio	Earnings Per Share

Requirement 2.	Transaction (letter)	Current Ratio	Debt Ratio	Earnings Per Share

Problem 19-5B   *Using ratios to evaluate a stock investment*

Comparative financial statement data of Manatee Furniture Co. are as follows:

Manatee Furniture Co.
Comparative Income Statement
Years Ended December 31, 19X4 and 19X3

	19X4	19X3
Net sales	$667,000	$599,000
Cost of goods sold	378,000	283,000
Gross profit	289,000	316,000
Operating expenses	129,000	147,000
Income from operations	160,000	169,000
Interest expense	47,000	41,000
Income before income tax	113,000	128,000
Income tax expense	44,000	53,000
Net income	$ 69,000	$ 75,000

Manatee Furniture Co.
Comparative Balance Sheet
December 31, 19X4 and 19X3
(selected 19X2 amounts given for computation of ratios)

	19X4	19X3	19X2
Current assets:			
Cash	$ 37,000	$ 30,000	
Current receivables, net	188,000	151,000	$138,000
Inventories	372,000	306,000	184,000
Prepaid expenses	5,000	10,000	
Total current assets	602,000	497,000	
Property, plant, and equipment, net	287,000	276,000	
Total assets	$889,000	$773,000	707,000
Total current liabilities	$286,000	$267,000	
Long-term liabilities	245,000	235,000	
Total liabilities	531,000	502,000	
Preferred stockholders' equity, 4%, $20 par	50,000	50,000	
Common stockholders' equity, no-par	308,000	221,000	148,000
Total liabilities and stockholders' equity	$889,000	$773,000	

Other information:

a. Market price of Manatee common stock: $42 at December 31, 19X4, and $51.00 at December 31, 19X3.

b. Common shares outstanding: 20,000 during 19X4 and 19,000 during 19X3.

c. All sales on credit.

Required

1. Compute the following ratios for 19X4 and 19X3:

a. Current ratio   f. Return on common stockholders' equity

b. Inventory turnover   g. Earnings per share of common stock

c. Accounts receivable turnover   h. Price/earnings ratio

d. Times-interest-earned ratio   i. Book value per share of common stock

e. Return on assets

2. Decide (a) whether Manatee's financial position improved or deteriorated during 19X4 and (b) whether the investment attractiveness of its common stock appears to have increased or decreased.

Problem 19-6B   *Using ratios to decide between two stock investments*

Assume you are purchasing stock in a company in the grain business. Suppose you have narrowed the choice to AgriCorp and MultiGrains, Inc., and have assembled the following data:

Selected income statement data for current year:

	AgriCorp	MultiGrains, Inc.
Net sales (all on credit)	$603,000	$519,000
Cost of goods sold	454,000	387,000
Income from operations	93,000	72,000
Interest expense	—	8,000
Net income	56,000	38,000

Selected balance sheet and market price data at end of current year:

	AgriCorp	Multigrains, Inc.
Current assets:		
Cash	$ 35,000	$ 39,000
Short-term investments	16,000	13,000
Current receivables, net	189,000	164,000
Inventories	191,000	183,000
Prepaid expenses	5,000	15,000
Total current assets	436,000	414,000
Total assets	974,000	938,000
Total current liabilities	366,000	338,000
Total liabilities	667,000	691,000
Preferred stock, 4%, $100 par		25,000
Common stock, $1 par (150,000 shares)	150,000	
$5 par (20,000 shares)		100,000
Total stockholders' equity	307,000	247,000
Market price per share of common stock	$6	$47.50

Selected balance sheet data at beginning of current year:

	AgriCorp	MultiGrains, Inc.
Current receivables, net.	$142,000	$193,000
Inventories	209,000	197,000
Total assets.	842,000	909,000
Preferred stockholders' equity, 4%, $100 par		25,000
Common stock, $1 par (150,000 shares)	150,000	
$5 par (20,000 shares)		100,000
Total stockholders' equity	152,000	145,000

Your investment strategy is to purchase the stocks of companies that have low price/earnings ratios but appear to be in good shape financially. Assume you have analyzed all other factors, and your decision depends on the results of the ratio analysis to be performed.

Required

Compute the following ratios for both companies for the current year and decide which company's stock better fits your investment strategy.

1. Current ratio
2. Acid-test ratio
3. Inventory turnover
4. Days' sales in average receivables
5. Debt ratio
6. Times-interest-earned ratio
7. Return on net sales

8. Return on total assets
9. Return on common stockholders' equity
10. Earnings per share of common stock
11. Book value per share of common stock
12. Price/earnings ratio

Decision Problem

Identifying action to cut losses and establish profitability

Suppose you manage BiSports, a sporting goods and bicycle shop, which lost money during the past year. Before you can set the business on a successful course, you must first analyze the company and industry data for the current year in an effort to learn what is wrong. The data appear on the following page.

Required

Based on your analysis of these figures, suggest four courses of action BiSports should take to reduce its losses and establish profitable operations. Give your reasons for each suggestion.

BiSports Balance Sheet Data

	BiSports	Industry Average
Cash and short-term investments..........	2.5%	6.8%
Trade receivables, net	14.3	8.0
Inventory	64.6	63.5
Prepaid expenses	2.0	0.0
Total current assets	83.4	78.3
Fixed assets, net.......................	12.6	15.2
Other assets	4.0	6.5
Total assets...........................	100.0%	100.0%
Notes payable, short-term, 12%	19.6%	14.0%
Accounts payable......................	18.6	25.1
Accrued liabilities......................	7.8	7.9
Total current liabilities..................	46.0	47.0
Long-term debt, 11%...................	19.7	16.4
Total liabilities	65.7	63.4
Common stockholders' equity.............	34.3	36.6
Total liabilities and stockholders' equity.....	100.0%	100.0%

BiSports Income Statement Data

	BiSports	Industry Average
Net sales	100.0%	100.0%
Cost of sales	(69.7)	(64.8)
Gross profit	30.3	35.2
Operating expense	(35.6)	(32.3)
Operating income (loss)	(5.3)	2.9
Interest expense.......................	(6.8)	(1.3)
Other revenue........................	1.1	.3
Income (loss) before income tax...........	(11.0)	1.9
Income tax (expense) saving..............	4.4	(.8)
Net income (loss)......................	(6.6)%	1.1%

Financial Statement Problem

Measuring profitability and analyzing stock as an investment

Use the Selected Financial Data that appear in the Gulf+Western financial statements (Appendix C) to chart the company's progress during fiscal years 1984 through 1987. Compute the ratios that measure profitability and ratios that are used to analyze stock as an investment.

PROFITABILITY MEASURES

a. Return on net revenues
b. Return on common stockholders' equity (Ignore preferred stock and the related dividends because the amounts are immaterial.)

STOCK ANALYSIS MEASURES

c. Price/earnings ratio (Representative market prices of Gulf+Western common stock during fiscal years 1987, 1986, 1985, and 1984 were $93.50, $72.50, $45.25, and $32.25, respectively.)
d. Dividend yield

Is the trend in the profitability measures consistent with the trend in the stock analysis measures?

Answers to Self-Study Questions

1. b $252,000 − $210,000 = $42,000; $42,000/$210,000 = .20
2. c
3. d
4. a
5. b   ($10,000 + $22,000)/$40,000 = .80
6. b
7. d
8. d
9. a
10. c

20

Introduction to Management Accounting: The Master Budget

LEARNING OBJECTIVES
After studying this chapter, you should be able to

1 Identify the benefits of a budgeting system

2 Budget the components of the income statement

3 Prepare a budgeted income statement

4 Budget cash receipts and disbursements

5 Prepare a cash budget

6 Prepare a budgeted balance sheet

7 Use a continuous budget

Our study of accounting has focused on gathering, processing, and reporting information for decision makers outside the business. Some of these outside parties are investors, creditors, and government agencies. Thus far we have looked through their eyes at a businesses's past performance and financial position. The income statement tells users the results of the company's operations. The statement of cash flows reports where cash came from and how it was spent. The balance sheet shows the company's current financial position. Accounting designed to report to parties outside the business is called financial accounting.

We now shift our focus. We turn to a discussion of how accounting information helps shape the business's future, and we do this through the eyes of the people who run the business. The decision makers inside the company are called managers, and accounting designed to meet their information needs is called **management accounting.** Exhibit 20-1 summarizes the distinctions between management accounting and financial accounting.

Chapter 20 begins our study of management accounting by showing how budgets are prepared. We deal with the familiar financial statements: income statements and balance sheets. However, our statements will compile planned figures, not past figures, and we will evaluate performance by comparing actual results with budgeted amounts.

Chapter 21 introduces a model of cost-volume-profit relationships, a favorite planning tool of managers. Our first two chapters on management accounting are confined to nonmanufacturing organizations. In this way, we can explore two major tools (budgets and the cost-volume-profit model) without contending with the many new terms associated with manufacturing organizations. The latter appear in Chapters 22 and 23, which describe manufacturing accounting systems. Then Chapters 24, 25, and 26 pursue management accounting tools in more

785

EXHIBIT 20-1 *Distinctions Between Management Accounting and Financial Accounting*

	Management Accounting	Financial Accounting
1. Primary users	Managers of the business	Outside parties (investors and creditors) and managers of the business
2. Decision criterion	Comparison of costs and benefits of proposed action	Comparison of accounts with generally accepted accounting principles (GAAP)
3. Behavioral implications	Concern about how reports will affect employee behavior	Concern about adequacy of disclosure. Behavioral implications are secondary
4. Time focus	Future orientation: Example: 19X3 **budget** versus 19X3 **actual** performance	Past orientation: Example: 19X3 **actual** versus 19X2 **actual** performance
5. Reports	Detailed reports on parts of the entity: products, departments, territories	Summary reports primarily on the entity as a whole

depth. Above all, recognize that management accounting applies to all kinds of organizations, not just manufacturing companies.

Two Themes in Management Accounting

Two themes of management accounting are (1) the cost-benefit criterion and (2) behavioral implications. The *cost-benefit criterion* is a means for choosing among alternative accounting systems or methods—how well they help achieve management goals in relation to their costs. We use this common sense technique every day. For example, suppose you are asked whether you want cheese on your hamburger for an extra 25 cents. You weigh the benefit of adding the cheese against the cost. If the benefit exceeds the cost, you order cheese. If the benefit is less than 25 cents, you forgo the cheese.

A business application of the cost-benefit criterion is the installation of a budgeting system. A major benefit is to compel managers to plan and thus make different decisions than would have occurred from using only a historical system. Is an accounting system a good buy? The answer depends on managers' weighing perceived benefits against additional costs.

The *behavioral implications* of a course of action are also critical. Managers consider the effect of the action on people's behavior. Suppose the company in our example tries to increase sales by pressuring its sales staff to meet quotas. If a salesperson fails to meet quota for three consecutive months, he is fired. Depending on the personalities of the people involved, such a policy may lead to increased sales. But it may also create fear and cause a decline in sales. Effective management accounting systems apply the cost-benefit criterion in light of the behavioral implications of proposed action.

The Role of Management _____

How do managers use accounting information? Managers determine the company's goals and then plan and control its operations to reach those goals. They set long-range targets by asking questions such as: What will the company's total assets be in 5 years? By how much can the business increase sales over the next 10 years? Should the company spend $5 million on research to develop a new product line? Will it be profitable to enter the California-Oregon-Washington market? The most successful executives are able to consider a wide range of possible courses of action for their company. They answer these types of long-range questions by developing concrete plans of action.

Business must operate day by day also. Managers set short-range targets and communicate these goals to subordinates. To increase profits, suppose a business must increase production to 35,000 units next month. Similarly, cash inflow from operations must be $600,000 during December. Short-range goals like these must fit within the company's long-range strategy.

What features must an accounting system have to best meet management's information needs? What data help managers to plan and control business operations? How are decisions made by managers? This chapter and the next several answer these questions. We begin our discussion of management accounting by studying a manager's most valuable accounting tool: the budget.

The Budgeting System _____

A well-designed budgeting system includes the budget, the budget committee, and the budget period.

The Budget

The **budget** is management's tool for forecasting the company's future. Budgets include quantities of products to be sold and their expected selling prices, numbers of employees and their pay, and a host of other amounts that are ultimately expressed in dollars. The budget summarizes the planning decisions of the business. A company may use a single budget to control all its operations or a separate budget for each subunit. This choice depends on the plans of the particular company's management. Our discussion will center on a company that uses an overall master budget to guide its operations. The **master budget** includes the major financial statements and supporting schedules.

The Budget Committee

In many small businesses, the budgeting process is rather informal, with the owner and the employees deciding on goals for the future. In most medium-size-to-large organizations the **budget committee** oversees the preparation of the master budget. Because the master budget is the overall financial plan for the entire company, the budget committee includes representatives from all departments. Working together, they develop budget estimates "from the bottom up." Employees at the lowest level provide budget estimates to their supervisors, who make adjustments and forward the budget to middle managers, and so on up the line. For example, the vice-president of sales has each salesperson set a goal for the next period. The vice-president considers the goals of each salesperson and prepares an overall budget for the sales department. With sales personnel at all levels participating in the budget process, they are likely to work harder to achieve the budget than if it is handed down by top management. All other departments likewise collect budget information and forward it to the budget committee.

The committee coordinates the budget for the company as a whole. Without this coordination, the cost of goods sold budget or the operating expense budget may be out of line with the sales budget, and vice versa.

Although top management has the final say in establishing the budget, it is best when many employees contribute to the overall process. An ideal budget results in all employees striving for excellence by trying to meet a clear-cut, coordinated set of goals.

The Budget Period

Budgets may cover any time period. Many companies use monthly, weekly, and daily cash budgets to ensure that they have enough cash on hand to meet immediate needs. Sales and expense budgets usually cover the accounting period, which may be a month, a quarter, or a year. Aligning the budget period with the accounting period makes the comparison of budgeted amounts and actual amounts easy. Most long-range budgets cover a five-year period. However, spans of 2, 3, or even 10 years are used.

Benefits of a Budget _____

OBJECTIVE 1

Identify the benefits of a budgeting system

The budgeting process offers these advantages:

1. Provides direction. The budgeting system forces managers to set realistic goals for the future. Without a formal plan, managers lack direction. This lack of planning filters throughout the company. The budget guides managers and department employees toward the achievement of specific goals. We all work better with a goal in mind.

2. Motivates employees. The budget motivates employees at all levels to meet the business's goals. Their work in preparing the budget makes it their personal target. This motivational aspect of budgeting underscores how budgeting affects employee behavior. Budgets can have negative effects on employee morale if used improperly. For example, some top managers simply impose the budget on their employees and hold employees responsible for its achievement. In this case, the budgeting system may demoralize workers and actually result in lower, rather than higher, profits.

3. Coordinates activities. The budget coordinates the activities of the entire organization. Coordination is crucial because the budget for one department affects other departments. For example, the company may need to sell 50,000 units to earn its target net income. But the manufacturing plant may be able to

EXHIBIT 20-2 *Management Use of Budgeting and Accounting*

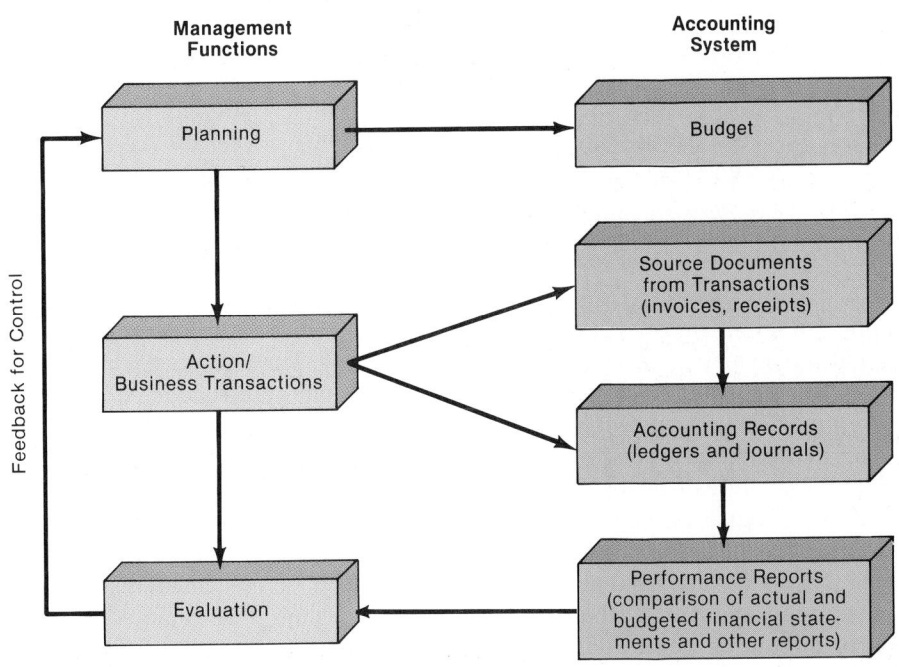

produce only 40,000 units. The budget thus helps top managers identify the need to expand the plant by purchasing additional equipment. In turn managers may identify the need for additional sales personnel, office workers, delivery vehicles, and so on.

4. *Helps performance evaluation.* A budgeting system aids performance evaluation. The comparison of budgeted and actual amounts highlights areas that are performing according to plan and areas that need improvement. Actual cost of goods sold in excess of the budgeted amount may lead the business to start buying from a new supplier, or it may lead top management to fire the purchasing manager responsible for paying too high a price for inventory. Without the budget, the top management may not even know the company is spending too much on inventory.

Exhibit 20-2 diagrams how managers use budgeting. Management planning (see the upper left corner of the exhibit) results in the budget. During the period, the business takes action by engaging in transactions—buying and selling. These transactions produce source documents, accounting records, and in turn performance reports. The performance reports are evaluated by managers whose feedback helps to control the organization. Managers then make new plans. Thus begins a new cycle of management planning and control.

The Performance Report

The comparison of budgeted goals to actual results is a key element in evaluating operations, identifying the need for corrective action, and preparing next period's budget. This point deserves a closer look. The performance report in Exhibit 20-3 serves as the basis for our discussion.

EXHIBIT 20-3 *Summarized Income Statement Performance Report for 19X7—Used for Control by Management*

	Actual	Budget	Actual – Budget
Sales revenue......	$550,000	$600,000	($50,000)
Total expenses.....	510,000	520,000	(10,000)
Net income........	$ 40,000	$ 80,000	($40,000)

Actual 19X7 sales in Exhibit 20-3 were $550,000, which is $50,000 less than budgeted sales. The low sales level reduced actual net income to half the budgeted amount. Top managers would ask what went wrong. The vice-president of sales would have to explain why sales revenue was so far below the budgeted goal. The vice-president, in turn, would meet with the sales staff to learn why they failed to meet the budget. At least one of two problems exists in this example: (1) the budget was unrealistic, or (2) the business did a poor job of selling during the period. Of course, both of these factors may have contributed to the poor results.

Managers also use performance reports like this one to identify corrective action. The sales department did not perform well, and management must decide what to do about it. Perhaps the sales manager should be replaced. Or the problem may be due to our selling an inferior product. In any event, should budgeted sales be lowered for the next period? The answers to these questions will affect next period's budget. This example illustrates how managers use a budget to plan operations and to control the company in its drive for success.

Components of the Master Budget

The master budget includes the operating budget, the capital expenditures budget, and the financial budget. The **operating budget** sets the target revenues and expenses—and thus net income—for the period. The **capital expenditures budget** presents the company's plan for purchases of property, plant, and equipment and other assets that management uses to produce revenues over a long time. The **financial budget** projects the means of raising money from stockholders and creditors and plans cash management. This chapter discusses components of the operating budget and the financial budget. Chapter 26 covers budgeting for capital expenditures.

We summarize the components of the master budget as follows:

A. Operating budget
  1. Sales or revenue budget
  2. Purchases budget
  3. Cost of goods sold budget
  4. Operating-expense budget
  5. Budgeted income statement
B. Capital expenditures budget
C. Financial budget
  1. Cash budget: Statement of budgeted cash receipts and disbursements
  2. Budgeted balance sheet

The capstone of the operating budget is the budgeted income statement, which shows target revenues, expenses, and net income for the period. The financial budget results in the budgeted balance sheet, which gives budgeted amounts for each asset, liability, and owner equity. The budgeted financial statements look exactly like ordinary statements. The only difference is that they list budgeted rather than actual figures.

Exhibit 20-4 diagrams the various sections of the master budget for a nonmanufacturing company, like K Mart, Safeway, or a wholesaler of auto parts. In addition to the components of the master budget in the preceding list, the diagram includes ending inventory, which is directly related to sales, purchases, and cost of goods sold. Without a budget for inventory, the company could accidentally end the period with too much or too little inventory, and either event would be unwelcome. Too much inventory is expensive to keep in stock, and too little inventory risks losing a customer who needs the goods immediately.

Sales is usually budgeted first because inventory levels, purchases, cost of goods sold and operating expenses depend on sales activity. Sales revenue is the major measure of business activity. After sales and expenses are projected, the budgeted income statement can be prepared.

EXHIBIT 20-4 *Master Budget for a Nonmanufacturing Company*

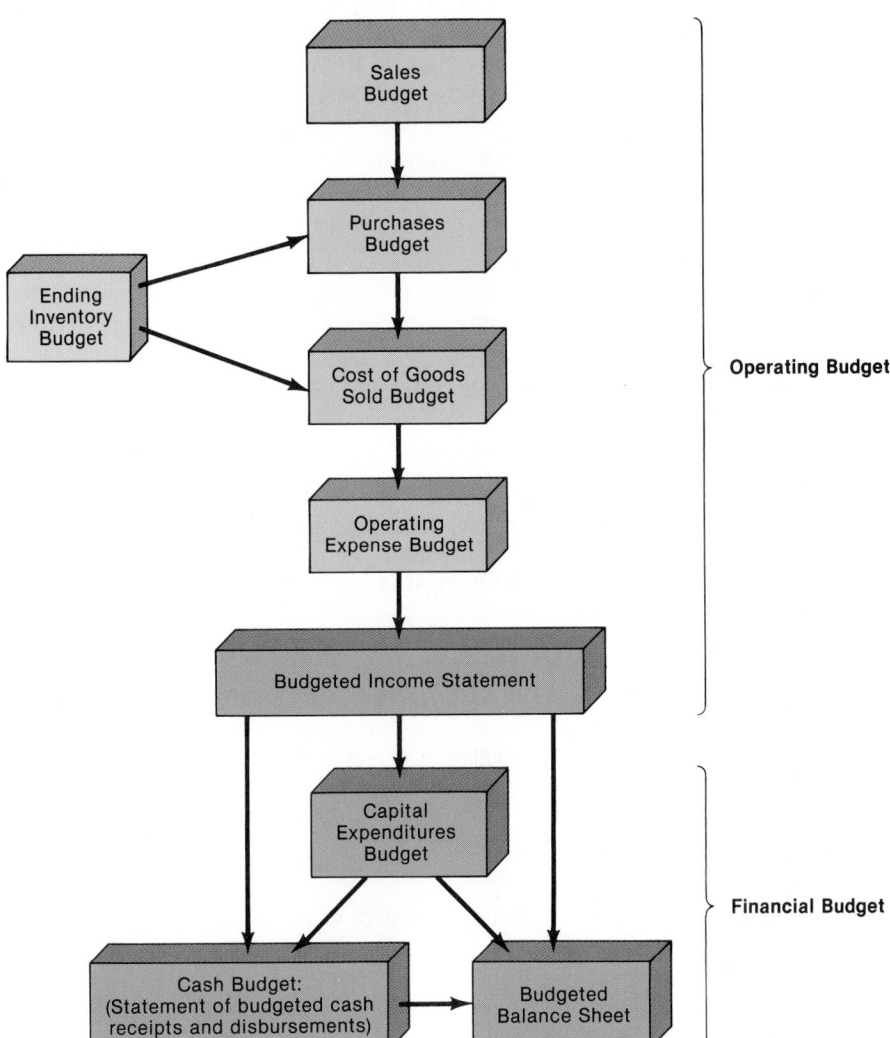

The sales budget is the cornerstone of the master budget. However, other parts of the master budget are often prepared simultaneously. Examples include budgeted amounts for executive salaries and for acquisitions of equipment.

The capital expenditures budget, the income statement, and the plans for raising cash and paying debts provide information for the cash budget, which feeds into the budgeted balance sheet. Preparing the budgeted balance sheet is usually the last step in the process. We use Exhibit 20-4 as the framework for the remainder of the chapter.

Preparing the Master Budget

To learn how to apply the concepts and methods of budgeting, you should prepare a master budget. The following problem and solutions provide an illustration of the budgeting process.

Facts for Illustration

1. Suppose you manage Whitewater Sporting Goods store number 18, which carries a complete line of canoeing, hiking, and other outdoor recreation gear. You know the merchandising end of the business but little about accounting and finance. Top management wants your input in the budgeting process. You are to prepare the master budget for your store for April, May, June, and July, the main selling season for these sporting goods. The division manager and the assistant controller (head of the accounting department) of the company will be here from headquarters tomorrow to review the budget with you.

2. Cash collections follow sales because the company sells on account. When extra cash is needed, the company borrows on six-month installment notes payable.

3. The balance sheet of your store at March 31, 19X5, beginning of the budget period, follows.

Whitewater Sporting Goods Store No. 18
Balance Sheet
March 31, 19X5

Assets		Liabilities	
Current assets:		Current liabilities:	
Cash..................	$ 15,000	Accounts payable	$ 16,800
Accounts receivable, net.	16,000	Wages and commissions	
Inventory.............	48,000	payable.............	4,250
Prepaid insurance	1,800	Total liabilities...........	21,050
	80,800	**Owners' Equity**	
Plant assets:			
Equipment and fixtures..	32,000	Owners' equity	78,950
Accumulated			
depreciation.........	(12,800)		
	19,200	Total liabilities	
Total assets	$100,000	and owners' equity	$100,000

4. Sales in March were $40,000. Monthly sales are projected by salespersons as follows:

April	$50,000
May	80,000
June	60,000
July	50,000

    Sales are 60 percent cash and 40 percent on credit. All accounts receivable amounts are collected in the month following sale. The $16,000 of accounts receivable at March 31 arose from credit sales made in March (40 percent of $40,000). Uncollectible accounts are insignificant, so you can ignore them.

5. Whitewater wishes to maintain inventory equal to $20,000 plus 80 percent of the budgeted cost of goods sold for the following month. (All these percentages are drawn from the business's past experience.) Cost of goods sold averages 70 percent of sales. These data explain why the inventory on March 31 is $48,000, computed as follows:

$$\frac{\text{March 31}}{\text{inventory}} = \$20{,}000 + .80 \times (.70 \times \textbf{April sales of } \$50{,}000)$$

$$= \$20{,}000 + (.80 \times \$35{,}000)$$

$$= \$20{,}000 + \$28{,}000$$

$$= \$48{,}000$$

    Whitewater pays for inventory as follows: 50 percent during the month of purchase and 50 percent during the next month.

6. Monthly payroll consists of two parts: fixed wages of $2,500 plus sales commissions equal to 15 percent of sales. The company pays half of this amount during the month and half early in the following month. Therefore, at the end of each month Whitewater reports wages and commissions payable equal to half the month's payroll. This is why the $4,250 liability appears on the March 31 balance sheet—half the March payroll of $8,500:

$$\frac{\text{March}}{\text{payroll}} = \frac{\text{Fixed wages}}{\text{of } \$2{,}500} + \frac{\text{Sales commissions}}{\text{of } \$6{,}000 \ (.15 \times \$40{,}000)}$$

$$= \$8{,}500$$

$$\frac{\text{March 31 wages and}}{\text{commissions payable}} = .50 \times \$8{,}500$$

$$= \$4{,}250$$

7. Other monthly expenses are

Rent expense	$2,000, paid as incurred
Depreciation expense, including truck	500
Insurance expense	200 expiration of prepaid amount
Miscellaneous expense	5% of sales, paid as incurred

8. A used delivery truck will be purchased in April for $3,000 cash.

9. The company wishes to maintain a minimum cash balance of $10,000 at the end of each month. If necessary, the business can borrow the money on notes payable of $1,000 each at an annual interest rate of 12 percent. Management borrows no more money than the amount needed to maintain the $10,000 minimum cash balance. Notes payable require six equal monthly payments consisting of principal plus monthly interest on the entire unpaid

principal. Borrowing and all principal and interest payments occur at the end of the month.

10.   Income taxes are the responsibility of corporate headquarters, so you can ignore them for budgeting purposes.

Assume you have studied the company guidelines on how to prepare a budget. The directions instruct you to prepare the following detailed schedules:

Schedule

A	Sales budget
B	Purchases, cost of goods sold, and inventory budget
C	Operating expense budget
D	Budgeted cash collections from customers
E	Budgeted cash disbursements for purchases
F	Budgeted cash disbursements for operating expenses

After compiling the schedules, you must prepare the following statements:

Exhibit

20-5	Budgeted income statement for the four months ended July 31, 19X5
20-6	Statement of budgeted cash receipts and disbursements by month for the four months ended July 31, 19X5
20-7	Budgeted balance sheet at July 31, 19X5

Preparing the Operating Budget

As you work through the preparation of this budget, keep in mind that you are developing the company's operating and financial plan for the next four months. The steps in this process may seem mechanical, but remember that budgeting stimulates thoughts about pricing, product lines, job assignments, needs for additional equipment, and negotiations of loans with banks. Preparation of the budget leads to decisions that affect the future course of the business. The operating budget—consisting of the sales budget, the purchases, cost of goods sold, and inventory budget, and the operating expense budget—results in the budgeted income statement.

Preparing the Budgeted Income Statement.   *Step 1.* Sales—Schedule A—is the start of the budget effort. The budgeted sales amount for each product is determined by multiplying its sale price by the predicted unit sales. The overall sales budget is the sum of the budgets for individual products.

OBJECTIVE 2

Budget the components of the income statement

Schedule A—Sales Budget
(Fact 4, page 793)

	April	May	June	July	April–July Total
Cash sales, 60%	$30,000	$48,000	$36,000	$30,000	
Credit sales, 40%	20,000	32,000	24,000	20,000	
Total sales, 100%	$50,000	$80,000	$60,000	$50,000	$240,000

Trace the April–July total sales—$240,000—to the budgeted income statement in Exhibit 20-5.

EXHIBIT 20-5 Budgeted Income Statement

	Amount	Source
Whitewater Sporting Goods Store No. 18		
Budgeted Income Statement		
Four Months Ending July 31, 19X5		
Sales...........................	$240,000	Schedule A
Cost of goods sold..................	168,000	Schedule B
Gross margin......................	72,000	
Operating expenses:		
Wages and commissions $46,000		Schedule C
Rent 8,000		
Depreciation.................. 2,000		
Insurance 800		
Miscellaneous................. 12,000	68,800	
Income from operations	3,200	
Interest expense...................	225	Exhibit 20-6
Net income	$ 2,975	

Step 2. After budgeting sales, prepare the purchases, cost of goods sold, and inventory budget, which is Schedule B. This schedule determines cost of goods sold for the budgeted income statement, ending inventory for the budgeted balance sheet, and purchases for the cash budget. The relationship among these items is given by the cost of goods sold computation:

Beginning Inventory + Purchases − Ending Inventory = Cost of Goods Sold

Beginning inventory is known, budgeted cost of goods is a fixed percentage of sales, and budgeted ending inventory is a specified amount. Therefore, you must solve for the budgeted purchases figure. By moving beginning inventory and ending inventory to the right side of the equation, isolate Purchases on the left side:

Purchases = Cost of Goods Sold + Ending Inventory − Beginning Inventory

Since Schedule B is a forecast, you cannot know the *actual* ending inventory amount. You must include the desired ending inventory figure in the computation of projected purchases.

Schedule B—Purchases, Cost of Goods Sold, and Inventory Budget
(Fact 5, page 793)

	April	May	June	July	April–July Total
Cost of goods sold (.70 × sales, from Schedule A)....	$35,000	$56,000	$42,000	$35,000	$168,000
+ Desired ending inventory ($20,000 + .80 × Cost of goods sold for next month)...................	64,800*	53,600	48,000	42,400***	
− Beginning inventory	(48,000)**	(64,800)	(53,600)	(48,000)	
= Purchases..................................	$51,800	$44,800	$36,400	$29,400	

* $20,000 + (.80 × $56,000) = $64,800   *** Assumed for illustrative purposes.
** Balance at March 31 (Fact 3, page 792)

To solidify your understanding of how this information fits into the master budget, trace the total budgeted cost of goods sold ($168,000) to the income statement in Exhibit 20-5. We will be using the budgeted inventory and purchases amounts later.

Step 3. Some budgeted operating expenses, like sales commissions and delivery expenses, fluctuate and thus vary with changing sales. Other expenses, like rent, depreciation, and insurance, are the same each month (fixed) and do not vary with sales. Schedule C is the operating expense budget.

Schedule C—Operating Expenses Budget
(Facts 6 and 7, page 793)

	April	May	June	July	April–July Total
Wages, fixed amount	$ 2,500	$ 2,500	$ 2,500	$ 2,500	
Commission, 15% of sales from Schedule A	7,500	12,000	9,000	7,500	
Total wages and commissions	10,000	14,500	11,500	10,000	$46,000
Rent, fixed amount	2,000	2,000	2,000	2,000	8,000
Depreciation, fixed amount	500	500	500	500	2,000
Insurance, fixed amount	200	200	200	200	800
Miscellaneous, 5% of sales	2,500	4,000	3,000	2,500	12,000
Total operating expenses	$15,200	$21,200	$17,200	$15,200	$68,800

Trace the April–July totals (wages and commissions of $46,000, rent of $8,000, and so on) to the budgeted income statement in Exhibit 20-5.

Step 4. Steps 1 through 3 provide the information to determine income from operations on the budgeted income statement in Exhibit 20-5. (We explain computation of the interest expense as part of the cash budget.)

Preparing the Financial Budget

The second major section of the master budget is the financial budget, which consists of the budgeted statement of cash receipts and disbursements (cash budget) and the budgeted balance sheet.

Preparing the Cash Budget (Statement of Budgeted Cash Receipts and Disbursements). The **cash budget,** or **statement of budgeted cash receipts and disbursements,** details how the business intends to go from the beginning cash balance to the desired ending balance. Cash receipts and disbursements depend in part on revenues and expenses, which appear in the budgeted income statement. The cash budget, then, is usually prepared after the budgeted income statement.

The cash budget has the following major parts: cash collections from customers (Schedule D), cash disbursements for purchases (Schedule E), cash disbursements for operating expenses (Schedule F), and capital expenditures.

Schedule D—Budgeted Cash Collections from Customers

	April	May	June	July
Cash sales from Schedule A	$30,000	$48,000	$36,000	$30,000
Collection of last month's credit sales from Schedule A (Fact 4, page 793)...	16,000*	20,000	32,000	24,000
Total collections	$46,000	$68,000	$68,000	$54,000

*March 31 accounts receivable

Schedule E—Budgeted Cash Disbursements for Purchases

	April	May	June	July
50% of last month's purchases, from Schedule B	$16,800*	$25,900	$22,400	$18,200
50% of this month's purchases, from Schedule B	25,900	22,400	18,200	14,700
Total disbursements for purchases	$42,700	$48,300	$40,600	$32,900

*.50 × March purchases of $33,600 (amount assumed)

Schedule F—Budgeted Cash Disbursements for Operating Expenses

Expense amounts from Schedule C:	April	May	June	July
Wages and commissions:				
50% of last month's expenses from Schedule C (Fact 6, page 793)...	$ 4,250*	$ 5,000	$ 7,250	$ 5,750
50% of this month's expenses from Schedule C..................	5,000	7,250	5,750	5,000
Total wages and commissions	9,250	12,250	13,000	10,750
Rent (Fact 7, page 793)......................................	2,000	2,000	2,000	2,000
Miscellaneous (5% of sales, Schedule A)	2,500	4,000	3,000	2,500
Total disbursements for operating expenses......................	$13,750	$18,250	$18,000	$15,250

*March 31 wages and commissions payable

OBJECTIVE 4
Budget cash receipts and disbursements

The cash receipt and disbursement data in Schedules D, E, and F and the $3,000 capital expenditure to acquire the truck appear in the cash budget, Exhibit 20-6. Acquisitions of long-term assets like the truck are based on a decision process called *capital budgeting*. We cover this management tool in Chapter 26.

In preparing the cash budget (Exhibit 20-6) you must first determine the cash available before financing. (This amount is $61,000 for April.) Add total disbursements ($59,450) to the minimum desired cash balance ($10,000) to find the total cash needed during April—$69,450. If cash available exceeds cash needed, an excess occurs. If cash needed is greater, a deficiency results. During April, you budget an $8,450 deficiency. The company then borrows $9,000 on a six-month note payable. (The loan exceeds the deficiency because Whitewater borrows in even $1,000 amounts.) Compute the budgeted cash balance at the end of each month by subtracting total disbursements from the cash available before financ-

EXHIBIT 20-6 *Cash Budget*

Whitewater Sporting Goods Store No. 18
Statement of Budgeted Cash Receipts and Disbursements
Four Months Ending July 31, 19X5

		April	May	June	July
	Beginning cash balance	$15,000	$10,550	$10,410	$18,235
	Cash receipts, collections from customers (Schedule D)	46,000	68,000	68,000	54,000
(1)	Cash available before financing	$61,000	$78,550	$78,410	$72,235
	Cash disbursements:				
	Purchases of inventory (Schedule E).	$42,700	$48,300	$40,600	$32,900
	Operating expenses (Schedule F)	13,750	18,250	18,000	15,250
	Purchase of truck (Fact 8, page 793).	3,000	—	—	—
(2)	Total disbursements.	59,450	66,550	58,600	48,150
	Minimum cash balance desired.	10,000	10,000	10,000	10,000
(3)	Total cash needed	69,450	76,550	68,600	58,150
	Cash excess (deficiency), (1) − (3).	$ (8,450)	$ 2,000	$ 9,810	$14,085
	Financing of cash deficiency (See Notes b–d below):				
	Borrowing (at end of month).	$ 9,000			
	Principal payments (at end of month)		$ (1,500)	$ (1,500)	$ (1,500)
	Interest expense (at 12% annually).		(90)	(75)	(60)
(4)	Total effects of financing.	9,000	(1,590)	(1,575)	(1,560)
	Ending cash balance (1) − (2) + (4)	$10,550	$10,410	$18,235	$22,525

Notes: a. Insurance expense is the expiration of prepaid insurance, and depreciation is the expensing of the cost of a plant
asset. Therefore, these expenses do not require cash outlays in the current accounting period.
b. Borrowing occurs in multiples of $1,000 and only for the amount needed to maintain a minimum cash balance of
$10,000.
c. Monthly principal payments: $9,000/6 = $1,500.
d. Interest expense: May: $9,000 × (.12 × 1/12) = $90.
June: ($9,000 − $1,500) × (.12 × 1/12) = $75.
July: ($9,000 − $1,500 − $1,500) × (.12 × 1/12) = $60.
Total: $90 + $75 + $60 = $225

OBJECTIVE 5
Prepare a cash budget

ing and then adding the total projected effects of financing.[1] Exhibit 20-6 shows
that Whitewater expects to end April with $10,550 of cash. The exhibit also shows
the budgeted cash balance at the end of May, June, and July.

Interest expense for the four months totals $225 ($90 + $75 + $60). This item
is listed on the budgeted income statement in Exhibit 20-5.

Preparing the Budgeted Balance Sheet.   The final step in preparing the master
budget is to complete the balance sheet. You project each asset, liability, and
owner equity account based on the plans outlined in the previous schedules and
exhibits. Exhibit 20-7 presents the budgeted balance sheet. If desired, you can
prepare separate schedules to show the computations of accounts receivable,
plant assets, and so on.

The **master budget** has now been completed. It consists of the budgeted
financial statements and all supporting schedules.

---

[1] In the case of loan payments, you will be adding a negative amount.

EXHIBIT 20-7 *Budgeted Balance Sheet*

Whitewater Sporting Goods Store No. 18		
Budgeted Balance Sheet		
July 31, 19X5		
Assets		
Current assets:		
Cash (Exhibit 20-6)	$ 22,525	
Accounts receivable, net (.40 × July sales of $50,000; Schedule A)	20,000	
Inventory (Schedule B)	42,400	
Prepaid insurance (beginning balance of $1,800–$800 for four months' expiration; fact 7 on page 793)	1,000	$ 85,925
Plant assets:		
Equipment and fixtures (beginning balance of $32,000 + $3,000 truck acquisition; item 8 on page 793)	35,000	
Accumulated depreciation (beginning balance of $12,800 + $500 depreciation for each of four months; fact 7 on page 793)	(14,800)	20,200
Total assets		$106,125
Liabilities		
Current liabilities:		
Short-term note payable ($9,000 − $4,500 paid back; Exhibit 20-6)	$ 4,500	
Accounts payable (.50 × July purchases of $29,400; Schedule B).................	14,700	
Wages and commissions payable (.50 × July expense of $10,000; Schedule C)........	5,000	
Total liabilities		$ 24,200
Owners' Equity		
Owners' equity (beginning balance of $78,950 + $2,975 net income; Exhibit 20-5)......		81,925
Total liabilities and owners' equity...........................		$106,125

OBJECTIVE 6
Prepare a budgeted
balance sheet

Summary of Budgeting Procedures

The most important budget documents are the budgeted income statement (Exhibit 20-5), the budgeted statement of cash receipts and disbursements (Exhibit 20-6), and the budgeted balance sheet (Exhibit 20-7). Top management analyzes these statements to ensure that all the budgeted figures are consistent with company goals. As the business strives to reach these goals, management controls operations by comparing actual results with the forecasted performance (as shown in Exhibit 20-3, the performance report).

Importance of Sales Forecasting _____

The Whitewater Sporting Goods illustration began with the sales budget, which is the foundation of a master budget. Managers—under the direction of the top marketing executive—invest ample resources in accurately forecasting sales. Factors considered in projecting sales include:

1. *Patterns of past sales.* By learning from past sales activity, a company can fine tune its sales budget. This includes breaking sales down by product line, geographical region, and salesperson. The more detailed the budget, the more helpful it is likely to be.

2. *Predictions of marketing personnel.* These people are calling on customers on a regular basis and can provide the most reliable, current information for forecasting sales. They conduct market research to learn which customers prefer certain products.

3. *Analysis of general and industry economic conditions.* In an economic recession, consumers usually delay expenditures on leisure-time products like Whitewater's sporting goods. What is the outlook for the economy next year?

4. *Strength of competitors.* A business must stay informed about what competitors are doing. For example, an effective advertising campaign by Chrysler can lure customers away from Ford and General Motors and decrease Ford and GM profits. An effective budget must consider the activity of competitors.

5. *Future changes in prices.* Budgeted sales equal the budgeted quantity multiplied by the expected future selling price. Any changes in prices affect the sales budget.

6. *Development of new product lines and phasing out of old product lines.* The budget must include the sales of new products expected to be introduced and eliminate old products that will be phased out. This ensures that the budget is based on an up-to-date product line.

7. *Plans for advertising and sales promotion.* Advertising stimulates sales, so plans for upcoming promotional efforts will affect the budgeted level of sales.

The importance of the sales forecast is not limited to profit-seeking organizations. For example, the revenue forecast is critical to hospitals, churches and synagogues, universities, cities, and states. Unless these organizations budget revenues accurately, they risk spending too much and running out of money just like profit-seeking businesses. All types of organizations base their budgets on general economic and industry data plus information that is specific to the entity. An entire industry exists to provide economic forecasting data. All types of organizations subscribe to forecasting newsletters, primarily to aid their budgeting efforts.

Budgeting and Short-Term Financing _____

The cash budget in Exhibit 20-6 illustrates the usual pattern of **short-term, self-liquidating financing.** This term refers to debt incurred to buy inventories that will be sold on credit. Cash collections are used to pay the debt:

This diagram shows the financing plan budgeted in Exhibit 20-6. Whitewater had a temporary need for $9,000. The company borrowed this amount and paid it back from cash generated by operations.

Many companies have seasonal peaks of high sales volume and valleys of low activity. For example, retailers like Sears, J. C. Penney, and K mart make most of their sales during November, December, and January. June, July, and August are slow months. Companies use the slow months to stock up on inventory for the rush near the end of the year and to remodel stores and make repairs. By increasing a store's attractiveness and efficiency, the company can attract more customers and increase sales.

When monthly sales fluctuate seasonally, companies often borrow on short-term, self-liquidating loans. A cash budget can help managers avoid a cash shortage. By planning ahead, the manager can shop around for the best interest rate on a short-term loan. Then, if a cash shortage looms in some months, the company is prepared. A carefully mapped budget keeps the cash balance well matched to cash needs.

Continuous (Rolling) Budgets

A **continuous,** or **rolling, budget** systematically adds a month as the month just ended is deleted. This budget keeps managers thinking ahead, with a steady planning horizon. Suppose Whitewater Sporting Goods prepared the following six-month sales budget:

> **OBJECTIVE 7**
> Use a continuous budget

	March	April	May	June	July	August
Budgeted sales	$40,000	$50,000	$80,000	$60,000	$50,000	$30,000

The first budget covers March through August. Roll 1 deletes March and adds September; roll 2 then deletes April and adds October; and so on.

Roll 1:	March	April	May	June	July	August	September	October
Budgeted sales	—	$50,000	$80,000	$60,000	$50,000	$40,000	$25,000	—
Roll 2:								
Budgeted sales	—	—	$80,000	$60,000	$50,000	$30,000	$25,000	$20,000

When managers desire, the sales budgets for individual months can be combined into quarterly or semiannual totals.

Budget Models, What-If Questions, and Microcomputer Applications

The master budget models the entire organization's objectives, inputs, and outputs. When we combine the budget's broad coverage with the speed and ease of microcomputers, we have a powerful tool for management analysis, planning, and control.

Many software programs allow preparation of the master budget on an electronic spreadsheet. The manager or the accountant can then ask "what-if" questions by changing any figure. *What* net income can we expect *if* we increase advertising by 20 percent? *What* will the cash balance be *if* we prepay the full cost of the advertising campaign at the beginning of the next period? When the accountant changes one amount, the computer prepares a new budget that includes all the effects of that change. Computers make possible this nearly instant analysis of changes in the company's forecast. Managers can then study the answers to these questions.

The first draft of a budget is seldom the final draft. Answers to what-if questions can provide revenue, expense, and income data on a wide range of possible sales levels. Managers can then respond to changes in the business with information rather than hunches. Suppose the budget—based on the best possible forecast—shows a poor year ahead. Managers can examine various patterns of sales and net income, and cash receipts and disbursements. They can study ways to cut costs and develop marketing strategies to increase demand for the company's products. The master budget may then be revised. Chapter 24 examines flexible budgets—those based on various levels of activity—in greater detail.

The computer's speed also enables managers to react promptly to new and unexpected situations as they arise. For example, an executive of a New Jersey utility, Public Service Electric and Gas Company, has commented on the company's plans if an oil embargo were announced tomorrow. Within 24 hours management would know from the master budget the major financial effects of the embargo. Without having to wait for monthly or quarterly financial statements, they could begin reacting to its effects immediately. Microcomputers and user-friendly software give these capabilities to many employees who are not expert computer programmers. Knowing what to expect is a result of a successful budgeting system. Chapter 28 shows how to prepare a budget with a popular electronic spreadsheet.

Summary Problem for Your Review

Review the Whitewater Sporting Goods illustration in the chapter. Suppose you think that July sales might be $40,000 instead of the projected $50,000 in Schedule A, page 794. You draw up a new budget to learn what effect the change in the sales amount will have on the store.

Required

1. Revise schedules A, B, and C. Prepare a revised budgeted income statement for the four months ended July 31, 19X5.
2. Revise schedules D, E, and F. Prepare a revised cash budget for July and a revised budgeted balance sheet at July 31, 19X5.

Note: You need not repeat the parts of the revised schedules that do not change.

SOLUTION TO REVIEW PROBLEM

Note: Although not required, for completeness this solution repeats the budgeted amounts for April, May, and June.

Requirement 1

Revised Schedule A—Sales Budget

	April	May	June	July	April–July Total
Cash sales, 60%	$30,000	$48,000	$36,000	$24,000	
Credit sales, 40%	20,000	32,000	24,000	16,000	
Total sales, 100%	$50,000	$80,000	$60,000	$40,000	$230,000

Revised Schedule B—Purchases, Cost of Goods Sold, and Inventory Budget

	April	May	June	July	April–July Total
Cost of goods sold (.70 × sales from Revised Schedule A)................................	$ 35,000	$ 56,000	$ 42,000	$ 28,000	$161,000
+ Desired ending inventory ($20,000 + .80 × cost of goods sold for next month.....................	64,800	53,600	42,400	42,400	
− Beginning inventory	(48,000)	(64,800)	(53,600)	(42,400)	
= Purchases	$ 51,800	$ 44,800	$ 30,800	$ 28,000	

Revised Schedule C—Operating Expenses Budget

	April	May	June	July	April–July Total
Wages, fixed amount	$ 2,500	$ 2,500	$ 2,500	$ 2,500	
Commission, 15% of sales from Revised Schedule A	7,500	12,000	9,000	6,000	
Total wages and commissions	10,000	14,500	11,500	8,500	$44,500
Rent, fixed amount...................................	2,000	2,000	2,000	2,000	8,000
Depreciation, fixed amount...........................	500	500	500	500	2,000
Insurance, fixed amount	200	200	200	200	800
Miscellaneous, 5% of sales	2,500	4,000	3,000	2,000	11,500
Total operating expenses.............................	$15,200	$21,200	$17,200	$13,200	$66,800

REVISED EXHIBIT 20-5   *Budgeted Income Statement*

Whitewater Sporting Goods Store No. 18
Budgeted Income Statement
Four Months Ending July 31, 19X5

		Amount	Source
Sales		$230,000	Revised Schedule A
Cost of goods sold		161,000	Revised Schedule B
Gross margin		69,000	
Operating expenses:			
Wages and commissions	$44,500		
Rent	8,000		
Depreciation	2,000		
Insurance	800		
Miscellaneous	11,500	66,800	Revised Schedule C
Income from operations		2,200	
Interest expense		225	Revised Exhibit 20-6
Net income		$ 1,975	

Requirement 2

Revised Schedule D — Budgeted Cash Collections from Customers

	April	May	June	July
Cash sales from Revised Schedule A	$30,000	$48,000	$36,000	$24,000
Collection of last month's credit sales, from Revised Schedule A	16,000	20,000	32,000	24,000
Total collections	$46,000	$68,000	$68,000	$48,000

Revised Schedule E — Budgeted Disbursements for Purchases

	April	May	June	July
50% of last month's purchases, from Revised Schedule B	$16,800	$25,900	$22,400	$15,400
50% of this month's purchases, from Revised Schedule B	25,900	22,400	15,400	14,000
Total disbursements for purchases	$42,700	$48,300	$37,800	$29,400

Revised Schedule F — Budgeted Disbursements for Operating Expenses

Expense amounts from Revised Schedule C:	April	May	June	July
Wages and commissions:				
50% of last month's expenses from Revised Schedule C	$ 4,250	$ 5,000	$ 7,250	$ 5,750
50% of this month's expenses from Revised Schedule C	5,000	7,250	5,750	4,250
Total wages and commissions	9,250	12,250	13,000	10,000
Rent	2,000	2,000	2,000	2,000
Miscellaneous	2,500	4,000	3,000	2,000
Total disbursements for operating expenses	$13,750	$18,250	$18,000	$14,000

REVISED EXHIBIT 20-6 *Cash Budget*

Whitewater Sporting Goods Store No. 18
Statement of Budgeted Cash Receipts and Disbursements
Four Months Ending July 31, 19X5

		April	May	June	July
	Beginning cash balance	$15,000	$10,550	$10,410	**$21,035**
	Cash receipts, collections from customers (Revised Schedule D)	46,000	68,000	68,000	**48,000**
(1)	Cash available before financing	$61,000	$78,550	$78,410	**$69,035**
	Cash disbursements:				
	Purchases of inventory (Revised Schedule E)	$42,700	$48,300	**$37,800**	**$29,400**
	Operating expenses (Revised Schedule F)	13,750	18,250	18,000	**14,000**
	Purchase of truck	3,000	—	—	**—**
(2)	Total disbursements	59,450	66,550	**55,800**	**43,400**
	Minimum cash balance desired	10,000	10,000	10,000	**10,000**
(3)	Total cash needed	69,450	76,550	65,800	**53,400**
	Cash excess (deficiency), (1) − (3)	$ (8,450)	$ 2,000	**$12,610**	**$12,835**
	Financing of cash deficiency:				
	Borrowing (at end of month)	$ 9,000			
	Principal payments (at end of month)		$ (1,500)	$ (1,500)	**$ (1,500)**
	Interest expense (at 12% annually)		(90)	(75)	**(60)**
(4)	Total effects of financing	9,000	(1,590)	(1,575)	**(1,560)**
	Ending cash balance (1) − (2) + (4)	$10,550	$10,410	**$21,035**	**$24,075**

REVISED EXHIBIT 20-7 *Budgeted Balance Sheet*

Whitewater Sporting Goods Store No. 18
Budgeted Balance Sheet
July 31, 19X5

Assets

Current assets:		
Cash (Revised Exhibit 20-6)	**$24,075**	
Accounts receivable, net (.40 × July sales of $40,000; Revised Schedule A)	**16,000**	
Inventory (Revised Schedule B)	42,400	
Prepaid insurance	1,000	$ 83,475
Plant assets:		
Equipment and fixtures	35,000	
Accumulated depreciation	(14,800)	20,200
Total assets		$103,675

Liabilities

Current liabilities:		
Short-term note payable	$ 4,500	
Accounts payable (.50 × July purchases of **$28,000**; Revised Schedule B)	**14,000**	
Wages and commissions payable (.50 × July expense of $8,500; Revised Schedule C)	4,250	
Total liabilities		$ 22,750

Owners' Equity

Owners' equity (beginning balance of $78,950 + **$1,975** net income; Revised Exhibit 20-5)		80,925
Total liabilities and owners' equity		$103,675

Summary _____

Management accounting helps managers plan and control the operations of their organizations. A major element of the management plan is the *budget,* which expresses the business's goals for earning income and for asset, liability, and owner equity position. The master budget consists of the budgeted financial statements and supporting schedules.

The budget forces managers to set specific goals for the future. Such goals provide direction for the organization and meaning to the work of individual employees. The budget coordinates the various activities of the organization and aids performance evaluation. Comparisons of budgeted and actual amounts reveal areas of the business that need improvement.

Many organizations have a *budget committee,* which includes representatives of all departments, to prepare the budget. The *budget period* usually coincides with the accounting period to ease the comparison of actual and budgeted amounts.

The components of the master budget that cover operations include *sales, purchases, cost of goods sold, inventory,* and *operating expenses.* These budgets are usually prepared in this order and are combined into the *budgeted income statement.* Sales comes first because most expenses, assets, and liabilities depend on sales volume. A second component of the master budget is the *capital expenditures budget,* which includes plans for purchasing long-term capital assets. The third main component is the financial budget, consisting of the *cash budget,* which is a statement of budgeted cash receipts and disbursements, and the *budgeted balance sheet.*

Many companies use *continuous,* or *rolling, budgets* that systematically add a future month as the month just ended is deleted. Continuous budgets keep managers thinking ahead with a steady planning horizon.

Microcomputers and electronic spreadsheets are ideally suited for use in budgeting because they allow managers to answer what-if questions. Analyzing data over a wide range of outcomes enables managers to meet the challenges brought about by changes in the business.

Self-Study Questions

Test your understanding of the chapter by marking the best answer for each of the following questions.

1. The budget is *(pp. 787, 788)*
    a. A general, not specific, statement of the business's goals
    b. Not used by most successful businesses
    c. A major tool of financial, rather than management, accounting
    d. None of the above
2. For the budget to be most effective, it should be prepared *(pp. 787, 788)*
    a. From the bottom up, with participation from employees at all levels
    b. From the top down, with managers developing goals based on their own experience
    c. Without reference to results obtained in past periods
    d. None of the above
3. Which of the following is *not* a benefit of a budgeting system? *(pp. 788, 789)*
    a. Coordinates activities   c. Aids performance evaluation
    b. Automatically fires lazy   d. Provides direction to the business
        employees
4. Chewning Corporation's actual revenues are $90,000, and expenses are $50,000. Budgeted revenues were $86,000, and budgeted expenses were $51,000. What is the relationship between actual net income and budgeted net income? *(p. 790)*
    a. Actual exceeds budget by $40,000   c. Actual exceeds budget by $5,000
    b. Budget exceeds actual by $35,000   d. Budget exceeds actual by $5,000

5. The master budget starts with *(p. 791)*
   a. Cash
   b. Owners' equity
   c. Sales
   d. Inventory
6. The operating budget ends with *(pp. 791, 794)*
   a. Budgeted sales
   b. The budgeted income statement
   c. The cash budget
   d. The budgeted balance sheet
7. The most complex single part of the master budget is preparation of *(p. 798)*
   a. Budgeted sales
   b. The budgeted income statement
   c. The cash budget
   d. The budgeted balance sheet
8. The master budget usually ends with *(p. 798)*
   a. Budgeted sales
   b. The budgeted income statement
   c. The cash budget
   d. The budgeted balance sheet
9. A continuous (rolling) budget *(p. 801)*
   a. Adds a month and deletes the month just ended
   b. Keeps managers thinking ahead
   c. Maintains a steady planning horizon
   d. All of the above
10. Managers can use a microcomputer along with a master budget to *(pp. 801, 802)*
    a. Develop strategies for dealing with a variety of possible situations
    b. Eliminate all the uncertainty of the business environment
    c. Prepare the budget correctly on the first attempt
    d. Set near-perfect goals for the company

Answers to the self-study questions are at the end of the chapter.

Accounting Vocabulary

budget *(p. 787)*, budget committee *(p. 787)*, capital expenditures budget *(p. 790)*, cash budget *(p. 796)*, continuous budget *(p. 801)*, financial budget *(p. 790)*, master budget *(p. 787)*, operating budget *(p. 790)*, rolling budget *(p. 801)*, short-term, self-liquidating financing *(p. 800)*, statement of budgeted cash receipts and disbursements *(p. 796)*

ASSIGNMENT MATERIAL _____

Questions

1. How does management accounting differ from financial accounting?
2. Identify two types of goals set by managers.
3. Briefly discuss three components of a budgeting system.
4. What are four benefits of using a budgeting system?
5. Draw a diagram that shows how managers use a budgeting system.
6. How does a manager use a performance report?
7. List the components of a master budget.
8. A Ford dealer sets a goal of selling more Ford automobiles than any other dealer in the city. Does this goal represent a budget? Give your reason.
9. Taft Corporation installs a budgeting system in which the president sets all the goals for the company. The vice-president checks up on all 90 employees to ensure that they are meeting top management's budget goals. What is the weakness in this budgeting system? How can the system be improved?

10. In most successful budgeting systems, who or what group in the organization prepares the budget? What makes this approach successful?

11. Why should the capital expenditures budget be prepared before the cash budget and the budgeted balance sheet?

12. How does a company budget inventory purchases? In your answer, show the relationships among purchases, cost of goods sold, and inventories.

13. What is the first step in preparing the master budget? Why does this step come first?

14. Outline the four steps in preparing an operating budget.

15. Identify the last item (prior to net income) to compute for the budgeted income statement. Where is this item computed initially, and why does it come last?

16. What is another name for the cash budget? Identify six subtotals or totals listed on the cash budget.

17. What is the last document to prepare for the master budget? Why does it come last?

18. Is sales forecasting important only to a profit-seeking business, or is it used by nonprofit organizations like hospitals and colleges? Give your reason.

19. Suppose you are the marketing vice-president of a company. What factors would you consider in forecasting the company's sales for the coming year?

20. Describe how short-term, self-liquidating financing works.

21. Tick-Tock Clocks is a chain of specialty shops operating in resort areas. During some periods, the managers of the company's 42 stores budget for the coming quarter, and during other periods they budget for the coming year. What type of budget should top management use to keep store managers looking ahead with a steady planning horizon? How does this budget work?

22. Why are microcomputers and electronic spreadsheets well suited for budgeting?

Exercises

Exercise 20-1 *Preparing a performance report*

During August Ogden Publishing Company's actual revenues were $126,000 compared to budgeted revenues of $142,000. Monthly operating expenses were $122,000, and budgeted expenses were $137,000. The company also incurred interest expense of $5,000, which was not included in the budget.

Prepare a performance report for Ogden to show the differences between actual income and budgeted income for August.

Exercise 20-2 *Budgeting sales, cost of goods sold, and gross profit*

Melissa Mueller operates Twin Oaks Gift Shop. She expects cash sales of $2,000 for October and a $500 monthly increase during November and December. Credit card sales of $1,000 during October should be followed by 20 percent increases during November and December. Sales returns can be ignored. Credit card companies like VISA, Master-Card, and American Express charge 5 percent on credit card sales, so Twin Oaks will net 95 percent. Cost of goods sold averages 60 percent of net sales.

Melissa asks you to prepare a schedule of budgeted sales, cost of goods sold, and gross profit for each month of the last quarter of 19X3. Also show totals for the quarter.

Exercise 20-3 *Budgeting quarterly income for a year*

Century 21 is a nationwide real estate firm. Suppose a suburban Kansas City office of the firm projects that Year 2 quarterly sales will increase by 3 percent in quarter one, 3 percent in quarter two, 5 percent in quarter three, and 5 percent in quarter four. Management expects total operating expenses to be 80 percent of revenues during each of the first two quarters, 82 percent of revenues during the third quarter, and 85 percent during the fourth.

The office manager expects to borrow $100,000 on July 1, with quarterly principal payments of $10,000 beginning on September 30 and interest paid at the annual rate of 12 percent. Year 1 last quarter sales were $520,000.

Required

Prepare a budgeted income statement for each of the four quarters of Year 2 and for the entire year. Present the Year 2 budget as follows:

Quarter 1   Quarter 2   Quarter 3   Quarter 4   Full Year

Exercise 20-4   *Budgeting purchases, cost of goods sold and inventory*

The sales budget of Lancer International, Inc., for the nine months ended September 30 follows.

| | **Quarter Ended** | | | **Nine-Month** |
	March 31	**June 30**	**Sept. 30**	**Total**
Cash sales, 20%	$18,000	$ 28,000	$ 21,000	$ 67,000
Credit sales, 80%	72,000	112,000	84,000	268,000
Total sales, 100%	$90,000	$140,000	$105,000	$335,000

In the past, cost of goods sold has been 65 percent of total sales. The director of marketing, the production manager, and the financial vice-president agree that ending inventory should not go below $15,000 plus 10 percent of cost of goods sold for the following quarter. Lancer expects sales of $100,000 during the fourth quarter. The January 1 inventory was $22,000.

Required

Prepare a purchases, cost of goods sold, and inventory budget for each of the first three quarters of the year. Compute the cost of goods sold for the entire nine-month period. (Use Schedule B, page 795, as a model.)

Exercise 20-5   *Identifying amounts of purchases, inventory, and cost of goods sold*

Compute the missing amount for each of the following independent situations:

	A	B	C	D	E
Beginning inventory	$18,000	$?	$24,800	$ 8,800	$?
Purchases	?	91,200	?	45,300	77,900
Available	73,000	118,800	97,100	?	?
Ending inventory	11,000	?	?	13,700	22,600
Cost of goods sold	$?	$87,700	$69,300	$?	$69,400

Exercise 20-6   *Identifying amounts in a cash budget*

Dulock Sales Corporation has completed its cash budget for May and June. The budget is presented with missing amounts identified by a question mark (?). Dulock's plan for eliminating any cash deficiency is to borrow the exact amount needed from its bank. The current annual interest rate is 12 percent. Dulock pays back all borrowed amounts less than $2,000 within one month.

Dulock Sales Corporation
Cash Budget
May and June

		May	June
	Beginning cash balance.............................	$14,900	$?
	Cash collections from customers	65,700	74,800
	Sale of plant assets	?	900
(1)	Cash available before financing	$92,800	$?
	Cash disbursements:		
	Purchases of inventory	$52,400	$41,100
	Operating expenses..............................	31,900	30,500
(2)	Total disbursements	84,300	71,600
	Minimum cash balance desired	10,000	?
(3)	Total cash needed	?	81,600
	Cash excess (deficiency), (1) − (3)	$ (1,500)	$?
	Financing of cash deficiency:		
	Borrowing (at end of month)	$?	
	Principal payments (at end of month)		$?
	Interest expense (at .010 monthly)..................		?
(4)	Total effects of financing...........................	?	(1,515)
	Ending cash balance (1) − (2) + (4)	$?	$12,585

Interest expense: June: ?

Required

Fill in each amount identified by a question mark.

Exercise 20-7   *Preparing a cash budget*

Phillips Manor, a family-owned furniture store, began October with $8,400 cash. Management forecasts that collections from credit customers will be $9,000 in October and $12,200 in November. The store is scheduled to receive $5,000 cash on a business note receivable in November. Projected cash disbursements include inventory purchases ($10,200 in October and $12,100 in November) and operating expenses ($3,000 each month).

Phillips's bank requires a $7,500 minimum balance in the store's checking account. At the end of any month when the account balance goes below $7,500, the bank automatically extends credit to the store in multiples of $1,000. Phillips Manor borrows as little as possible and pays back these loans in monthly installments of $1,000 plus 1.5 percent monthly interest on the entire unpaid principal. The first payment occurs at the end of the month following the loan.

Required

Prepare the store's cash budget for October and November.

Exercise 20-8   *Computing cash receipts and disbursements*

For each of the items a through d, compute the amount of cash receipts or disbursements Hernandez Company would budget for December. A solution to one item may depend on the answer to an earlier item.

a. Management expects to sell 4,000 units in November and 4,200 in December. Each unit sells for $6. Cash sales average 30 percent of the total sales, and credit sales make up the rest. One third of credit sales are collected in the month of sale, with the balance collected the following month.

b. Management has budgeted inventory purchases of $30,000 for November and $25,000 for December. Hernandez Company pays for 25 percent of its inventory at the time of purchase in order to get a 2 percent discount. The business pays the 75 percent balance the following month, with no further discount.

c. The company pays rent and property taxes of $6,000 each month. Commissions and other selling expenses average 20 percent of sales. Hernandez Company pays two thirds of these costs in the month incurred, with the balance paid in the following month.

d. Management expects to sell equipment that cost $14,100 at a gain of $2,000. Accumulated depreciation on this equipment is $6,000.

Exercise 20-9   *Preparing a budgeted balance sheet*

Use the following information to prepare a budgeted balance sheet for Bargain Book Store at July 31, 19X6. Show computations for cash and owners' equity amounts.

a. June 30 cash balance, $7,400.
b. July budgeted sales, $12,400.
c. July 31 accounts receivable balance, one fourth of July sales.
d. July cash receipts, $12,300.
e. July 31 inventory balance, $16,000.
f. July payments for inventory, $5,900.
g. July payments of June 30 accounts payable and accrued liabilities, $6,100.
h. July 31 accounts payable balance, $4,900.
i. June 30 furnitures and fixtures balance, $34,800; accumulated depreciation balance, $27,700.
j. July capital expenditures of $1,200 budgeted for cash purchase of furniture.
k. July operating expenses, including income tax, total $4,200, half of which will be paid during July and half accrued at July 31.
l. July depreciation, $300.
m. Cost of goods sold, 50 percent of sales.
n. June 30 owners' equity, $22,800.

Exercise 20-10   *Preparing a rolling budget for the income statement*

T Bar M Ranch budgets the following total revenues, total expenses, and net income for the first four months of the year:

	January	February	March	April
Budgeted total revenues	$175,000	$160,000	$170,000	$185,000
Budgeted total expenses	93,000	87,000	89,000	97,000
Budgeted net income.	$ 82,000	$ 73,000	$ 81,000	$ 88,000

Prepare T Bar M's rolling monthly income statement budget for the quarters ending on March 31 and April 30.

Problems   *(Group A)*

Problem 20-1A   *Budgeting income and evaluating income with a performance report*

The Rocky Mountain regional office of McIntosh Products divides its annual budget into semiannual periods. The regional manager forecast that sales would increase during the first half of the current year by 2.5 percent over the first half of the preceding year. The manager also believed that second-half sales of the current year would exceed second-half sales of the preceding year by 10 percent. Cost of goods sold was budgeted at 56 percent of budgeted sales. Total operating expenses, including income taxes, were expected to be 30 percent of revenues during the first six-month period and 32 percent during the second period.

Actual quarterly sales, operating expenses, and net income for the four most recent semiannual periods follow.

	Preceding Year		**Current Year**	
	Semiannual Period		**Semiannual Period**	
	1	**2**	**1**	**2**
Sales	$32,000	$27,000	$34,000	$36,000
Cost of goods sold	19,000	14,000	16,000	17,000
Gross margin	13,000	13,000	18,000	19,000
Operating expenses	10,000	9,000	11,000	13,000
Net income (loss)	$ 3,000	$ 4,000	$ 7,000	$ 6,000

Required

1. Prepare a budgeted income statement for each semiannual period of the current year. Round all amounts to the nearest $1,000.

2. Prepare a summarized income statement performance report for the same period. Present the actual and the budgeted income statement side by side. Show the differences between them. Round all amounts to the nearest $1,000.

Problem 20-2A   *Budgeting income for three months*

Representatives of the various departments of Fadal Firestone Tire Co. have assembled the following data. You are the business manager, and you must prepare the budgeted income statements for July, August, and September 19X6.

1. Sales in June were $18,400. You forecast that monthly sales will increase 2 percent in July and 2 percent in August, then decrease by 3 percent in September.

2. Fadal maintains inventory of $5,000 plus 20 percent of sales budgeted for the following month. Monthly purchases average 65 percent of sales. The inventory on June 30 is $8,000. Sales budgeted for October are $19,500.

3. Monthly salaries amount to $1,200. Sales commissions equal 6 percent of sales. Combine salaries and commissions as a single figure on the income statements.

4. Other monthly expenses are

Rent expense	$1,200, paid as incurred
Depreciation expense	300
Insurance expense	100, expiration of prepaid
Miscellaneous expense	5% of sales
Income tax	20% of income from operations

Required

Prepare Fadal's budgeted income statements for July, August, and September. Show cost of goods sold computations. Round *all* amounts to the nearest $100. For example, budgeted July sales are $18,800 ($18,400 × 1.02), August sales are $19,200 ($18,800 × 1.02), and September sales are $18,600 ($19,200 × .97).

Problem 20-3A   *Preparing a cash budget for three months*

AltaVista Development Company is considering opening an office in a suburb of San Diego during September of the current year. The business estimates that the office opening will cost $17,000. To finance start-up, Guaranty Bank has agreed to loan AltaVista, in multiples of $1,000, the amount needed to keep AltaVista's cash balance above $12,000. The loan begins on the last day of any month in which AltaVista's cash balance goes below $12,000. The company will repay the loan in monthly installments of $1,000 each, beginning two months after the loan starts. AltaVista will also pay monthly interest of 1 percent on the entire unpaid balance until the loan is repaid.

Management expects AltaVista's operations to generate the following figures:

	August	September	October
Sales	$41,000	$44,000	$52,000
Cost of goods sold	17,000	21,000	26,000
Cash operating expenses	19,000	22,000	24,000
Collection of note receivable		25,000	

On August 1 AltaVista expects to have $7,000 cash and $7,000 of inventory. Inventory is expected to increase by $3,000 each month. Monthly cash receipts average 95 percent of sales. The company purchases inventory through cash disbursements.

Required

Prepare AltaVista's cash budgets for the months of August, September, and October.

Problem 20-4A *Preparing a rolling budget for the income statement*

The budgeted income statements of Polonski, Inc., for the six most recent quarters follow.

Polonski, Inc.
Budgeted Income Statements
For the Quarters Ended September 30, 19X5, through December 31, 19X6

	19X5		19X6			
	Sep. 30	Dec. 31	Mar. 31	June 30	Sep. 30	Dec. 31
Sales...........	$50,000	$100,000	$60,000	$80,000	$ 40,000	$130,000
Cost of goods sold..........	25,000	55,000	35,000	50,000	25,000	75,000
Gross margin....	25,000	45,000	25,000	30,000	15,000	55,000
Operating expenses......	22,000	20,000	22,000	23,000	25,000	24,000
Net income (loss).........	$ 3,000	$25,000	$ 3,000	$ 7,000	$(10,000)	$ 31,000

Required

1. Combine the quarterly totals necessary to prepare Polonski's rolling budgeted income statement for the last semiannual period in 19X5 and for the four semiannual periods ending in 19X6. (The first semiannual period in 19X6 ends March 31, the second June 30, and so on.)
2. Based on the comparison of the last half of 19X6 with the last half of 19X5, does Polonski management appear to expect increasing or decreasing sales and net income for 19X6?

Problem 20-5A *Preparing a budgeted balance sheet*

Mazeroski, Inc., has applied for a loan. The bank, RepublicBank, has requested a budgeted balance sheet at June 30, 19X4. As the controller (chief accounting officer) of Mazeroski, you have assembled the following information:

a. May 31 cash balance, $15,900.

b. June budgeted sales, $50,000, 40 percent of which is for cash. Of the remaining 60 percent, half will be collected in June and half in July.

c. June cash collections on May sales, $14,900.

d. June cash payments of May 31 liabilities, $10,700.

e. May 31 inventory balance, $7,300.

f. June purchases of inventory, $11,000 for cash and $21,400 on credit. Half of the credit purchases will be paid in June and half in July.

g. May 31 equipment balance, $60,600; accumulated depreciation, $11,700.

h. June capital expenditures of $15,800 budgeted for cash purchase of equipment.

i. June operating expenses, including income tax, total $18,800, 75 percent of which will be paid in cash and the remainder accrued at June 30.

j. June depreciation, $400.

k. Cost of goods sold, 45 percent of sales.

l. May 31 owners' equity, $76,300.

Required

Prepare the budgeted balance sheet of Mazeroski, Inc., at June 30, 19X4. Show separate computations for cash, inventory, and owners' equity balances.

Problem 20-6A   *Preparing all the components of a master budget*

Copeland & Holtizer's balance sheet at September 30, 19X4, follows.

Copeland & Holtizer
Balance Sheet
September 30, 19X4

Assets		Liabilities	
Current assets:		Current liabilities:	
Cash	$ 7,000	Accounts payable.	$ 32,000
Accounts receivable, net	25,000	Salaries and commissions payable	8,000
Inventory	67,000	Total liabilities	40,000
Prepaid insurance	2,000		
	101,000	**Owners' Equity**	
Plant assets:		Owners' equity	90,000
Furniture and fixtures	48,000		
Accumulated depreciation.	(19,000)		
	29,000	Total liabilities	
Total assets.	$130,000	and owners' equity	$130,000

Additional budget information follows.

a. Sales in September were $50,000. Management projects these monthly sales: October $60,000; November $70,000; December $90,000; January $80,000.

  Sales are half for cash and half on credit. All accounts receivable are collected in the month following sale. Uncollectible accounts are insignificant and can be ignored.

b. Management wishes to maintain inventory of $40,000 plus 75 percent of the cost of goods sold in the following month. Cost of goods sold averages 60 percent of sales.

Copeland & Holtizer pays for inventory as follows: 20 percent of each month's purchases in the month of purchase and the remaining 80 percent in the next month.

c. Payroll is made up of fixed salaries of $3,000 and sales commissions equal to 10 percent of sales. The monthly payroll is accrued at the end of the month and paid early the following month.

h. Other monthly expenses are

Advertising expense	$1,500, paid as incurred
Rent expense	900, paid as incurred
Depreciation expense	600
Insurance expense	200, expiration of prepaid amount
Miscellaneous expense	2% of sales, paid as incurred

e. Management has budgeted $8,000 cash for the acquisition of furniture in October.

f. The company keeps a minimum cash balance of $5,000 at the end of each month. The company may borrow on short-term notes payable in multiples of $1,000. Management borrows no more than necessary. The company repays the notes in three equal monthly installments that begin one month after the company borrows. The notes also carry monthly interest of 1 percent on the entire unpaid principal. Borrowing and all principal and interest payments occur at the end of the month.

g. In September purchases were $40,000, and salaries and commissions were $8,000.

h. The business is a partnership. The partners, therefore, pay personal income tax on their earnings. The business itself incurs no income tax liability, so income taxes do not enter into the computations.

Required

Prepare Copeland & Holtizer's master budget for the fourth quarter of 19X4. Include the following statements and schedules:

Statements:

Budgeted income statement for the quarter ending December 31, 19X4

Statement of budgeted cash receipts and disbursements for the quarter ending December 31, 19X4

Budgeted balance sheet at December 31, 19X4

Schedules:

Sales

Purchases, cost of goods sold, and inventory

Operating expenses

Cash collections from customers

Disbursements for purchases

Disbursements for operating expenses

(Group B)

Problem 20-1B *Budgeting income and evaluating income with a performance report*

The Mid-Atlantic district office of Galvan Sales Company divides its annual budget into semiannual periods. The district manager forecast that sales would increase during the first half of the current year by 8.1 percent over the first half of the preceding year. The manager also believed that second-half sales of the current year would exceed second-half sales of the preceding year by 4.5 percent. Cost of goods sold was budgeted at 43 percent of budgeted sales. Total operating expenses, including income taxes, were expected to be 36 percent of revenues during the first six-month period and 37 percent during the second period.

Actual quarterly sales, operating expenses, and net income for the four most recent semiannual periods follow.

	Preceding Year		Current Year	
	Semiannual Period		Semiannual Period	
	1	2	1	2
Sales........................	$113,000	$134,000	$124,000	$165,000
Cost of goods sold..............	40,000	63,000	66,000	81,000
Gross margin...................	73,000	71,000	58,000	84,000
Operating expenses.............	52,000	49,000	39,000	47,000
Net income (loss)..............	$ 21,000	$ 22,000	$ 19,000	$ 37,000

Required

1. Prepare a budgeted income statement for each semiannual period of the current year. Round all amounts to the nearest $1,000.

2. Prepare a summarized income statement performance report for the same period. Present the actual and budgeted income statements side by side. Show the differences between them. Round all amounts to the nearest $1,000.

Problem 20-2B   *Budgeting income for three months*

The budget committee of Scott Rubin & Company has assembled the following data. You are the business manager, and you must prepare the budgeted income statements for April, May, and June 19X3.

1. Sales in March were $31,300. You forecast that monthly sales will increase 1.3 percent in each of the three months.

2. The company maintains inventory of $8,000 plus 20 percent of sales budgeted for the following month. Monthly purchases average 55 percent of sales. Budgeted inventory on March 31 is $12,000. Sales budgeted for July are $30,600.

3. Monthly salaries amount to $3,000. Sales commissions equal 5 percent of sales. Combine salaries and commissions as a single figure.

4. Other monthly expenses are

Rent expense	$2,700, paid as incurred
Depreciation expense	500
Insurance expense....................	100, expiration of prepaid
Miscellaneous expense	3% of sales
Income tax	30% of income from operations

Required

Prepare Scott Rubin's budgeted income statements for April, May, and June. Show cost of goods sold computations. Round *all* amounts to the nearest $100. For example, budgeted April sales are $31,700 ($31,300 × 1.013), May sales are $32,100 ($31,700 × 1.013), and June sales are $32,500 ($32,100 × 1.013).

Problem 20-3B   *Preparing a cash budget for three months*

Sutfin Recreational Vehicles is considering opening a sales office in a suburb of Indianapolis during May of the current year. The business estimates the office opening will cost $92,000. To finance start-up, Interstate Bank has agreed to loan Sutfin, in multiples of $10,000, the amount needed to keep Sutfin's cash balance above $7,000. The loan begins on the last day of any month in which Sutfin's cash balance goes below $7,000. The company will repay the loan in monthly installments of $10,000 each, beginning one month after the loan starts. Sutfin will also pay monthly interest of 1.5 percent on the entire unpaid balance until the loan is fully repaid.

Management expects Sutfin's operations to generate the following figures:

	May	June	July
Sales	$63,000	$71,000	$74,000
Cost of goods sold	45,000	51,000	52,000
Cash operating expenses.......................	6,000	9,000	9,000
Sale of land		13,000	

On May 1 Sutfin expects to have $9,000 cash and $36,000 of inventory. Inventory is expected to decrease by $4,000 each month. Monthly cash receipts average 95 percent of sales. The company purchases inventory through cash disbursements.

Required

Prepare Sutfin's cash budgets for the months of May, June, and July.

Problem 20-4B *Preparing a rolling budget for the income statement*

The budgeted income statements of Goetz Company for the six most recent quarters follow.

Goetz Company
Budgeted Income Statements
For the Quarters Ended September 30, 19X2, through December 31, 19X3

	19X2		19X3			
	Sep. 30	Dec. 31	Mar. 31	June 30	Sep. 30	Dec. 31
Sales..............	$20,000	$80,000	$50,000	$60,000	$30,000	$90,000
Cost of goods sold...	8,000	30,000	22,000	23,000	11,000	30,000
Gross margin	12,000	50,000	28,000	37,000	19,000	60,000
Operating expenses..	5,000	21,000	12,000	17,000	10,000	28,000
Net income (loss)....	$ 7,000	$29,000	$16,000	$20,000	$ 9,000	$32,000

Required

1. Combine the quarterly totals necessary to prepare Goetz's rolling budgeted income statement for the last semiannual period in 19X2 and for the four semiannual periods ending in 19X3. (The first semiannual period in 19X3 ends March 31, the second June 30, and so on.)
2. Based on the comparison of the last half of 19X2 with the last half of 19X3, does Goetz management appear to expect increasing or decreasing sales and net income for 19X3?

Problem 20-5B *Preparing a budgeted balance sheet*

Pesco Leather Goods, Inc., has applied for a loan. The bank, Commerce Bank, has requested a budgeted balance sheet at April 30, 19X8. As the controller (chief accounting officer) of Pesco, you have assembled the following information:

a. March 31 cash balance, $26,200.
b. April budgeted sales, $70,000, 60 percent of which is for cash sales. Of the remaining 40 percent, half will be collected in April and half in May.
c. April cash collections on March sales, $31,200.
d. April cash payments of March 31 liabilities, $17,300.
e. March 31 inventory balance, $18,400.
f. April purchases of inventory, $9,000 for cash and $37,400 on credit. Half of the credit purchases will be paid in April and half in May.

g. March 31 equipment balance, $35,200; accumulated depreciation, $22,800.

h. April capital expenditures of $41,700 budgeted for cash purchase of equipment.

i. April operating expenses, including income tax, total $9,600, 25 percent of which will be paid in cash and the remainder accrued at April 30.

j. April depreciation, $700.

k. Cost of goods sold, 60 percent of sales.

l. March 31 owners' equity, $70,900.

Required

Prepare the budgeted balance sheet of Pesco Leather Goods, Inc., at April 30, 19X8. Show separate computations for cash, inventory, and owners' equity balances.

Problem 20-6B   *Preparing all the components of a master budget*

Noble & Barnes's balance sheet at September 30, 19X4, follows.

Noble & Barnes
Balance Sheet
September 30, 19X4

Assets		Liabilities	
Current assets:		Current liabilities:	
Cash	$ 11,000	Accounts payable.....................	$ 40,000
Accounts receivable, net	45,000	Salaries and commissions payable	10,000
Inventory	62,000	Total liabilities	50,000
Prepaid insurance	4,000		
	122,000	**Owners' Equity**	
Plant assets:		Owners' equity	140,000
Furniture and fixtures	96,000		
Accumulated depreciation.............	(28,000)		
	68,000	Total liabilities	
Total assets.........................	$190,000	and owners' equity	$190,000

Additional budget information follows.

a. Sales in September were $90,000. Management projects these monthly sales: October $80,000; November $70,000; December $80,000; January $60,000.

   Sales are half for cash and half on credit. All accounts receivable are collected in the month following sale. Uncollectible accounts are insignificant and can be ignored.

b. Management wishes to maintain inventory of $22,000 plus 75 percent of the cost of goods to be sold in the following month. Cost of goods sold averages 60 percent of sales. Noble & Barnes pays for inventory as follows: 20 percent in the month of purchase and 80 percent in the next month.

c. Payroll is made up of fixed salaries of $1,000 and sales commissions equal to 10 percent of sales. The monthly payroll is accrued at the end of the month and paid early the next month.

d. Other monthly expenses are

Advertising expense	$3,600, paid as incurred
Rent expense....................	1,300, paid as incurred
Depreciation expense	1,000
Insurance expense	400, expiration of prepaid amount
Miscellaneous expense	2% of sales, paid as incurred

e. Management has budgeted $26,000 cash for the acquisition of furniture in October.

f. The company is required by its bank to maintain a minimum cash balance of $8,000 at the end of each month. Money can be borrowed in multiples of $1,000. Management borrows no more than what is needed to maintain the $8,000 minimum balance and pays back all debts less than $5,000 at the end of the next month. Short-term notes payable greater than $5,000 are paid back in three equal monthly principal payments. The monthly interest rate on all notes payable is 1 percent on the entire unpaid principal. Borrowing and all principal and interest payments occur at the end of the month.

g. In September purchases were $50,000, and salaries and commissions were $10,000.

h. The business is a partnership. The partners, therefore, pay personal income tax on their earnings. The business itself incurs no income tax liability, so income taxes do not enter into the computations.

Required

Prepare Noble & Barnes's master budget for the fourth quarter of 19X4. Include the following statements and schedules:

Statements:

Budgeted income statement for the quarter ending December 31, 19X4

Statement of budgeted cash receipts and disbursements for the quarter ending December 31, 19X4

Budgeted balance sheet at December 31, 19X4

Schedules:

Sales

Purchases, cost of goods sold, and inventory

Operating expenses

Cash collections from customers

Disbursements for purchases

Disbursements for operating expenses

Decision Problem

Preparing a cash budget to analyze a loan request

Twin Sisters, a women's boutique, is requesting a $40,000 loan to finance the remodeling of its store. The bank requires a statement of budgeted cash receipts and disbursements to support the loan application.

The Twin Sisters cash balance at February 28 is $7,100. During March the store expects to collect $3,900 from sales made in January and February. Also, in February the store sold an old display case for $700, and the owners expect to receive that amount during March. During March the business will pay off accounts payable of $2,100 and a note payable of $6,000 plus $540 interest.

The store expects monthly sales of $9,500 for March, April, and May. Experience indicates that the store will collect 60 percent of sales in the month of sale, 30 percent in the month following sale, and 7 percent in the second month after sale. The remaining 3 percent is uncollectible.

The February 28 inventory is $37,800. Purchases average one half of sales. The store owners keep a minimum inventory of $25,000 plus 20 percent of purchases for the next month. The owners pay all accounts payable arising from inventory purchases in time to receive a 2 percent discount, 80 percent in the month of purchase and 20 percent the next month.

Budgeted operating expenses for March are rent (8 percent of sales), advertising ($500), utilities ($330), depreciation ($240), and insurance ($120). Depreciation and insurance are recorded as the assets expire. Half of the advertising expense is paid as incurred, and half is accrued at the end of the month. During March Twin Sisters will pay advertising of $160 that was accrued at February 28.

In order to make the loan, the bank requires that Twin Sisters's cash balance be at least $2,000 before any effects of financing.

Required

Prepare a cash budget (a statement of budgeted cash receipts and disbursements) for Twin Sisters Boutique for March. As the bank loan officer, decide if the store qualifies for the loan.

Financial Statement Problem

Preparing a budgeted income statement and comparing the budget to actual

Suppose Gulf+Western managers had based their fiscal 1987 budget on these figures for the income statement:

	Increase over 1986
a. Net revenues	10%
b. Earnings of unconsolidated finance subsidiary	20
c. Cost of goods sold.	15
d. Selling, general and administrative expenses	12
e. Other expense	10
f. Interest expense—net	5
g. Provision for income taxes (Income tax expense)	12

Use the company's actual data in Appendix C to prepare the budgeted income statement for fiscal 1987. Follow the Gulf+Western format, showing amounts in millions rounded to the nearest $100,000. Compare the actual and budgeted figures as shown in Exhibit 20-3 to report the difference for each item through net income. You can ignore extraordinary items because they are not expected to recur. Was 1987 better or worse than management predicted? Give the reason for your answer.

Answers to Self-Study Questions

1. d
2. a
3. b
4. c Actual: $90,000 − $50,000 = $40,000
   Budget: 86,000 − 51,000 = 35,000
   Actual over budget . . . . . . $ 5,000

5. c
6. b
7. c
8. d
9. d
10. a

21

Cost-Volume-Profit Relationships and the Contribution Margin Approach to Decision Making

LEARNING OBJECTIVES

After studying this chapter, you should be able to

1 Identify different cost behavior patterns

2 Compute break-even sales

3 Compute the sales level needed to earn a target net income

4 Graph a set of cost-volume-profit relationships

5 Compute a margin of safety

6 Separate a mixed expense into variable and fixed components

7 Use a contribution margin income statement to make business decisions

How much additional income does General Motors earn when it sells 5,000 more Oldsmobile Cutlasses? How much in additional expense does the sale of these 5,000 cars cost GM? How many Cutlasses must GM sell for the Oldsmobile Division to break even—earn zero profit?

Many questions in business—on the number of cars sold, the number of passengers transported by an airline, and so on—boil down to this general question: *What effects does a change in volume have on profits?* To answer these questions, managers study the links among cost, volume, and profit.

Cost-volume-profit (CVP) analysis helps managers to predict the outcome of their decisions by expressing the relationships among a business's costs, volume, and profit or loss. It is an important part of the budgeting system. We begin our discussion of this valuable decision-making tool by looking at costs.

Cost behavior describes how costs change—indeed, if they change—in response to a shift in the volume of business activity. For example, office rent does not usually change with the volume of business. The company may sell one million, one thousand, one, or none of its products and must still pay the same monthly rent. Sales commission paid to a salesperson, on the other hand, varies directly with sales volume. The higher the sales, the higher the sales commission expense.

Cost Behavior Patterns _____

OBJECTIVE 1

Identify different cost
behavior patterns

Costs follow one of three behavior patterns: variable, fixed, or mixed. **Variable costs (variable expenses)** change in total in direct proportion to changes in volume or activity. Variable costs include cost of goods sold, sales commission expense, and delivery expense. Each of these expenses rises or falls directly with any increase or decrease in sales volume. Suppose a clothing merchandiser pays $2 for each T-shirt purchased for resale to customers. The more T-shirts sold, the higher the cost of goods sold. Cost of goods sold varies directly with sales.

Exhibit 21-1 shows three graphs of three different variable costs. The first graph presents the cost behavior of a product that costs $2 an item. The sloped line in the first graph indicates the 3,000 T-shirts cost $6,000 (3,000 × $2). We see that 4,500 T-shirts cost $9,000 (4,500 × $2).

The higher the cost of an item, the steeper the graph of its variable cost. For example, the second graph in Exhibit 21-1 is based on each item costing $3. Study this graph to confirm that 2,000 T-shirts cost $6,000 (2,000 × $3) and that 4,000 T-shirts cost $12,000 (4,000 × $3). The third variable cost graph, showing the cost behavior of designer T-shirts that cost $10 each, is steeper yet.

A variable cost graph always passes through the origin (where the cost and volume axes intersect) because at zero volume, the variable cost is zero. As volume increases, variable cost increases in a straight line that leads out from the origin. The steepness of the graph's slope depends on the variable cost per unit. A higher variable unit cost results in a steeper slope. A lower variable unit cost has a lower slope.

Fixed costs (fixed expenses) do not change in total as volume changes. Rent, depreciation, and property taxes, for example, remain at a set amount whether sales volume rises, falls, or stays steady. These expenses occur even if the com-

EXHIBIT 21-1   *Variable Cost Pattern*

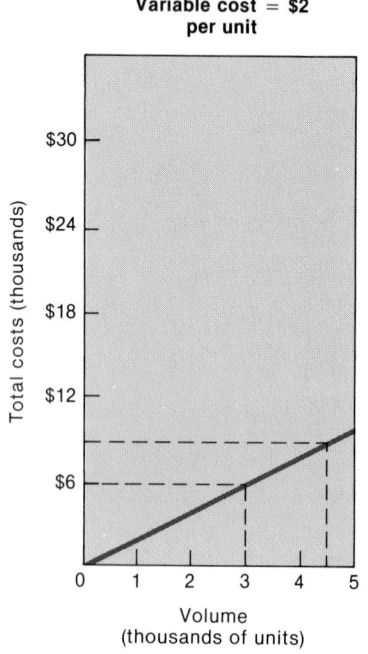

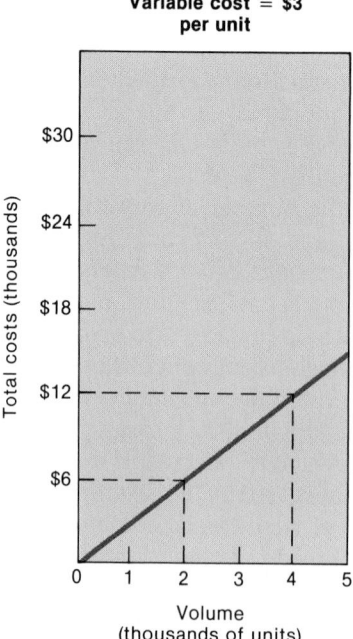

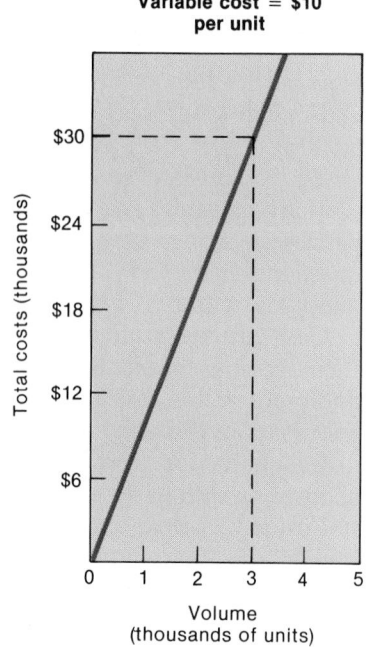

EXHIBIT 21-2 *Fixed Cost Pattern*

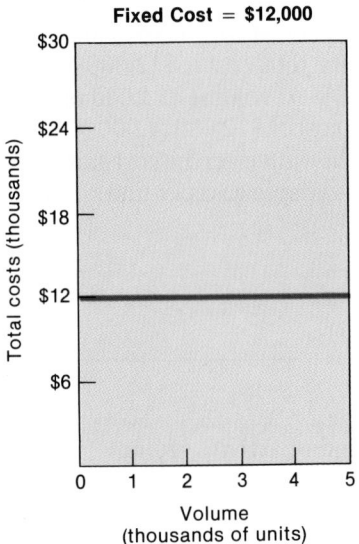

pany makes no sales, for this is the nature of a *fixed* cost. Exhibit 21-2 graphs a fixed cost, which is always a horizontal line intersecting the cost axis at the level of the fixed cost. In the graph, fixed cost is $12,000, not changing with any shift in the volume of activity.

Mixed costs (mixed expenses) are part variable and part fixed. They are also called semivariable costs. Consider a utility expense like electricity, for example. The company must pay a minimum charge regardless of how much electricity it uses. In our illustrations, this fixed cost is $6,000. In addition, the company must

EXHIBIT 21-3 *Mixed Cost Pattern*

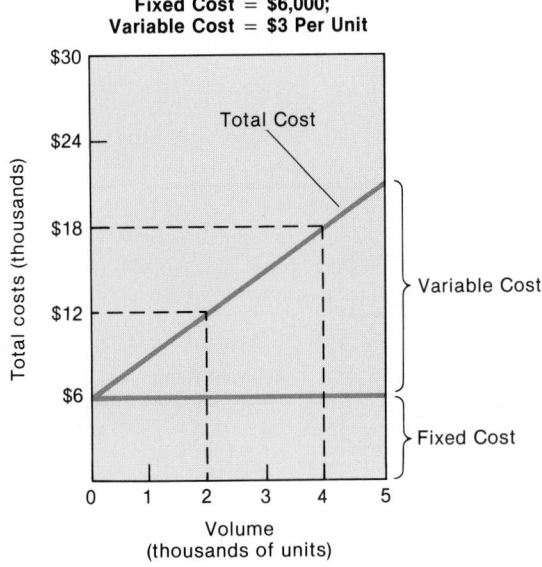

pay a variable cost, which works out to be $3 for every product it sells. Exhibit 21-3 shows this mixed cost graph.

In a mixed cost graph, total cost is the sum of fixed cost plus the variable cost. At sales volume of 2,000 units, total cost is $12,000 [fixed cost of $6,000 + variable cost of $6,000 (2,000 × $3)]. At volume of 4,000 units, total cost is $18,000 [fixed cost of $6,000 + variable cost of $12,000 (4,000 × $3)]. All graphs of mixed costs show the same pattern. They intersect the cost axis at the fixed cost point, and the slope of the graph is the variable cost per unit.

Relevant Range

A **relevant range** is a band of activity (volume) in which actual operations are likely to occur. Within this range, a particular relationship exists between revenue and expenses. For example, a fixed cost is fixed only within a given relevant range. Exhibit 21-4 shows a fixed cost level of $50,000 for the volume range of 0 to 10,000 units. Between 10,000 and 20,000 units, fixed expenses may be $80,000, and they may increase to $100,000 for volume above 20,000 units.

Companies use the relevant range concept in budgeting their costs. Suppose the business in Exhibit 21-4 expects sales volume of 12,000 during the year. For this period the relevant range is between 10,000 and 20,000 units, and managers would budget fixed expenses of $80,000. If actual sales for the year exceed 20,000 units, the company will consider hiring additional employees and perhaps open a new store, increasing rent expense. Fixed expenses will increase as the relevant range shifts to a new band of activity.

Fixed costs change from year to year, and so does the relevant range. Expecting sales of only 8,000 units next year, the business would budget fixed expenses in a lower relevant range. The company may have to shut down a sales office, lay off employees, and eliminate other fixed expenses.

EXHIBIT 21-4 *Relevant Range*

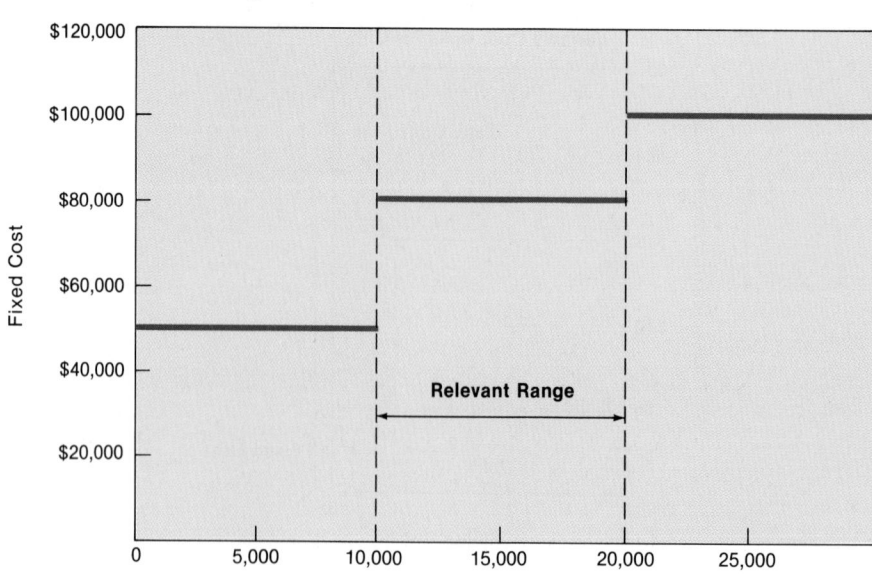

The relevant range concept also applies to variable costs. Some variable expenses may behave differently at different levels of volume. For example, utility expenses for water and electricity often cost less per unit as usage increases. Also, a company may pay higher sales commission rates for higher levels of sales to encourage extra selling effort. Therefore, businesses need to consider cost behavior — both fixed and variable — over the full range of sales volumes that are likely to occur during the budget period.

Cost behavior is one of the most challenging aspects of budgeting. After managers finalize the business's sales goal for the next period, accountants estimate costs. The behavior of various costs affects the expense budget. If budgeted expenses are too high, top managers may revise budgets for sales or expenses before setting the profit goal for the period.

In cost-volume-profit analysis, which we discuss next, we begin by classifying each cost as either variable or fixed. Later in this chapter, we show how to separate a mixed cost into its variable and fixed components.

Cost-Volume-Profit Analysis _____

The easiest way to learn cost-volume-profit analysis is with an example. Suppose Maria Martinez is considering renting a booth at a county fair. Maria plans to sell travel posters for $3.50 each. She can purchase the posters for $2.10 each and can return all unsold items for a full refund. Rent for the booth will cost $700. Using this information, let's answer six questions about Maria's business.

Question 1: What is Maria's Break-Even Sales Level?

The study of cost-volume-profit analysis is often called **break-even analysis.** Why? CVP analysis allows us to compute an amount in unit sales or dollar sales at which revenue equals expenses. This sales level is called the **break-even point.** In other words, we may calculate the sales volume at which the business breaks even. Revenue must reach the break-even point to cover costs. Sales below the break-even point mean a loss. Sales above break-even bring a profit. CVP, or break-even, analysis answers the questions, How many units must the business sell to cover expenses? and How much in sales must we reach before we earn a profit? The break-even point is often only incidental to managers because their focus is on the sales level needed to earn a target net income. However, the break-even point is a useful place to start the analysis of CVP relationships.

Two popular methods in cost-volume-profit analysis are the equation approach and the contribution margin approach.

Equation Approach.   In the equation approach, we start by dividing total expenses into variable expenses and fixed expenses.

For Maria Martinez, the variable cost is her cost of goods sold. This expense will equal the number of posters sold multiplied by her $2.10 cost to purchase each item. Her fixed cost is the $700 rent expense. A large company would have numerous variable expenses and fixed expenses. Such a business would combine all variable expenses into a single total and compute a single total for fixed expenses.

Our next step is to express income in equation form:

Sales − Variable expenses − Fixed expenses = Net income

We find it useful to rearrange the equation:

$$\textbf{Sales} - \textbf{Variable expenses} = \textbf{Fixed expenses} + \textbf{Net income}$$

At the break-even point, income equals expenses, so net income is zero. Sales equals the unit selling price multiplied by the number of units sold. Variable expenses equals variable cost per unit times the number of units sold. We substitute these terms into the equation and enter the dollar amounts that we have:

Sales − Variable expenses	= Fixed expenses + Net income
$\left(\begin{array}{c}\text{Unit}\\\text{sale}\\\text{price}\end{array}\cdot \text{Units sold}\right) - \left(\begin{array}{c}\text{Variable}\\\text{unit}\\\text{cost}\end{array}\cdot \text{Units sold}\right)$	= Fixed expenses + Net income
($3.50 · Units sold) − ($2.10 · Units sold) =	$700 + $0
($3.50 − $2.10) · Units sold =	$700 + $0
$1.40 · Units sold =	$700
Units sold =	$700/$1.40
Break-even sales in units =	**500 units**

Maria must sell 500 units to break even. Her break-even sales in dollars is the 500 units times their selling price of $3.50. Break-even dollar sales are $1,750 (500 units × $3.50).

Another form of the equation approach determines dollar sales first and unit sales second. We divide the variable expense, $2.10, by the selling price, $3.50, to determine the ratio of the variable expense to the selling price:

$$\frac{\textbf{Variable expense}}{\textbf{Selling price}} = \frac{\$2.10}{\$3.50} = .60$$

We use this ratio in the equation, as follows:

Sales − Variable expense = Fixed expenses + Net income	
Sales − (.60 · Sales) =	$700 + $0
Sales − (.60 · Sales) =	$700
.40 · Sales =	$700
Sales =	$700/.40
Break-even sales in dollars =	$1,750
Break-even sales in units =	500 ($1,750/$3.50)

Contribution Margin Approach.   A second way to do CVP analysis is the contribution margin approach. Each unit sold has a **contribution margin,** which is the excess of the sale price over variable expenses. The contribution margin can be expressed per unit, as a percentage, or as a ratio. Sales revenue "contributes" this excess, so to speak, to the recovery of fixed costs, with any remaining excess going to profit, as follows for Maria Martinez's business:

	Per Unit	Percent	Ratio
Sale price	$ 3.50	100%	1.00
Variable expense	−2.10	−60	−.60
Contribution margin	$ 1.40	40%	.40

In percentage terms, sales of 100 percent minus the variable expense percentage equals the **contribution margin percentage.** Likewise, 100 percent minus the contribution margin percentage equals the variable expense percentage. These relationships can be diagrammed:

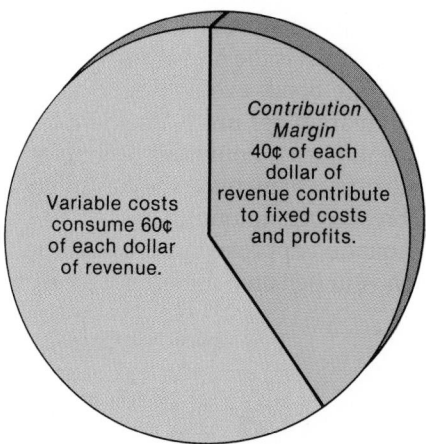

Breakdown of $1 of Revenue

In our illustration, the contribution margin *per unit* is $1.40 ($3.50 − $2.10). To compute break-even sales in units sold, divide fixed expenses by the contribution margin per unit:

$$\textbf{Break-even sales in units} = \frac{\textbf{Fixed expenses}}{\textbf{Contribution margin per unit}}$$

$$= \frac{\$700}{\$1.40}$$

$$= \textbf{500 units}$$

We may use percentages in the contribution margin approach. In our example, the contribution margin percentage is $1.40/$3.50, or 40 percent. Earlier we subtracted the variable cost percentage (60 percent) from sales (100 percent) to compute the 40 percent contribution margin percentage. The contribution margin percentage equals the contribution margin divided by the sale price.

We may use the sale price and variable cost of a single item, or we may use the total sales figure and the total variable cost amount of the entire product line in our computations. For example, consider the figures that arise from Maria's selling 500 items. Total sales equals $1,750 ($3.50 × 500), and the total contribution margin is $700 ($1.40 × 500). We see that $700/$1,750 equals .40, or 40 percent.

$$\textbf{Break-even sales in dollars} = \frac{\textbf{Fixed expenses}}{\textbf{Contribution margin ratio}}$$

$$= \frac{\$700}{.40}$$

$$= \textbf{\$1,750}$$

If variable costs rise, then the amount needed to reach break-even sales increases. Why? A higher variable cost lowers the contribution margin. In contrast, a lower variable cost means a higher contribution margin, which leads to lower break-even sales.

If sales increase, so does net income. To find the increase in net income, we can multiply the increase in sales by the contribution margin ratio. For example, Maria's contribution margin ratio is .40. If sales increase by $1,000, for example, then net income grows by $400.

The business press often refers to break-even sales, or break-even revenues. For example, a news story might report that "the Big Three auto makers have slashed their sales break-even point in North America from 12.2 million cars and trucks to only 9.1 million this year." The companies could accomplish this by decreasing fixed expenses, which is the numerator of the break-even formula. As the numerator decreases, the break-even amount decreases too. Similarly, increasing the contribution margin per unit—the denominator in the formula—will also decrease the break-even amount. For example, a reduction in variable expenses like tires or radiators will increase the contribution margin per automobile and so reduce the break-even amount.

Should you use the equation approach or the contribution margin approach? Use either, depending on your personal preference. We return to questions about Maria's business.

Question 2. If A Fixed Cost (Such As Rent Expense) Is Changed, What Would Break-Even Sales Be?

Suppose the rental on the booth were $1,050 instead of $700. What is Maria's break-even point in units sold and dollar sales?

Use the formula discussed in the contribution margin approach:

$$\text{Break-even sales in units} = \frac{\text{Fixed expenses}}{\text{Contribution margin per unit}}$$

$$= \frac{\$1,050}{\$1.40}$$

$$= 750 \text{ units}$$

$$\text{Break-even sales in dollars} = \frac{\text{Fixed expenses}}{\text{Contribution margin ratio}}$$

$$= \frac{\$1,050}{.40}$$

$$= \$2,625$$

The $1,050 in fixed expenses is an increase of $350, or 50 percent, in excess of $700. Note that the break-even point also rises by 50 percent, from 500 to 750 units. This match in percentage between the increase in fixed expenses and the increase in the break-even point always exists (if other factors are held constant). Maria must sell more posters to cover the higher fixed costs. Similarly, a decrease in fixed expenses means that she can sell less and still cover these costs.

Question 3. If the Sale Price is Changed, What Would Break-Even Sales Be?

Suppose the sale price per poster is $3.85 rather than $3.50. Variable expense per unit remains at $2.10, and fixed expenses stay at $700. What are Maria's revised break-even sales in units and in dollars? The unit contribution margin becomes $1.75 ($3.85 − $2.10) and the new contribution margin ratio is .4545 ($1.75/$3.85).

Compute break-even in units and in dollars as follows:

$$\text{Break-even sales in units} = \frac{\textbf{Fixed expenses}}{\textbf{Contribution margin per unit}}$$

$$= \frac{\$700}{\$1.75}$$

$$= \textbf{400 units}$$

$$\text{Break-even sales in dollars} = \frac{\textbf{Fixed expenses}}{\textbf{Contribution margin ratio}}$$

$$= \frac{\$700}{.4545}$$

$$= \textbf{\$1,540}$$

Note that an increase in sale price reduces break-even sales, in units and in dollars. This occurs because the contribution margin per unit increases. Consequently, it takes fewer sales at the higher price to break even. Conversely, a reduction in sale price would decrease the contribution margin and force Maria to increase sales just to break even.

Question 4. If a Variable Cost Is Changed, What Would Break-Even Sales Be?

Suppose that variable cost per unit is $2.38 instead of $2.10. The unit sale price remains $3.50, and fixed costs stay at $700. Compute break-even sales in units and in dollars.

The new unit contribution margin is $1.12 ($3.50 − $2.38), and the new contribution margin ratio is .32 ($1.12/$3.50). Break-even sales are

$$\text{Break-even sales in units} = \frac{\textbf{Fixed expenses}}{\textbf{Contribution margin per unit}}$$

$$= \frac{\$700}{\$1.12}$$

$$= \textbf{625 units}$$

$$\text{Break-even sales in dollars} = \frac{\textbf{Fixed expenses}}{\textbf{Contribution margin ratio}}$$

$$= \frac{\$700}{.32}$$

$$= \textbf{\$2,187.50}$$

An increase in variable cost per unit decreases the contribution margin and means that Maria must increase sales in units and in dollars to break even. A decrease in variable cost per unit would lower the break-even point.

Question 5. How Many Units Must Be Sold To Earn A Target Net Income?

Suppose Maria would be content with net income of $490 for a week's work in the booth. Assuming a unit sale price of $3.50, variable expense of $2.10 per unit, and fixed expenses of $700, how many posters must Maria sell to earn a profit of $490?

Until now, we have concentrated on break-even sales, the point where net income is zero. How should we consider a target net income greater than zero? The contribution margin must be sufficient to cover the fixed expenses plus the target net income. Our contribution margin approach is basically unchanged. However, the numerator now contains both fixed expenses and the target net income.

OBJECTIVE 3

Compute the sales level needed to earn a target net income

$$\text{Target sales in units} = \frac{\text{Fixed expenses} + \text{Target net income}}{\text{Contribution margin per unit}}$$

$$= \frac{\$700 + \$490}{\$1.40}$$

$$= \frac{\$1,190}{\$1.40}$$

$$= \textbf{850 units}$$

$$\text{Target sales in dollars} = \frac{\text{Fixed expenses} + \text{Target net income}}{\text{Contribution margin ratio}}$$

$$= \frac{\$700 + \$490}{.40}$$

$$= \frac{\$1,190}{.40}$$

$$= \textbf{\$2,975}$$

The minimum level needed to earn net income of $490 is 850 units, or $2,975 (850 × $3.50).

Question 6. What Net Income Is Expected At Various Sales Levels?

A convenient way to answer this question is to graph the cost-volume-profit relationships, as shown in Exhibit 21-5.

To set up the graph, we place units on the horizontal axis and dollars on the vertical axis. We label each axis appropriately. (We have chosen to place labels every 100 units and every $500. These labels offer enough detail for ease in understanding the graph but do not clutter it. Labels on the graphs depend on the data in the problem. The labels should be helpful but not crowd the information.) We use Maria Martinez's data (as originally given) and follow five steps:

EXHIBIT 21-5 *Cost-Volume-Profit Graph*

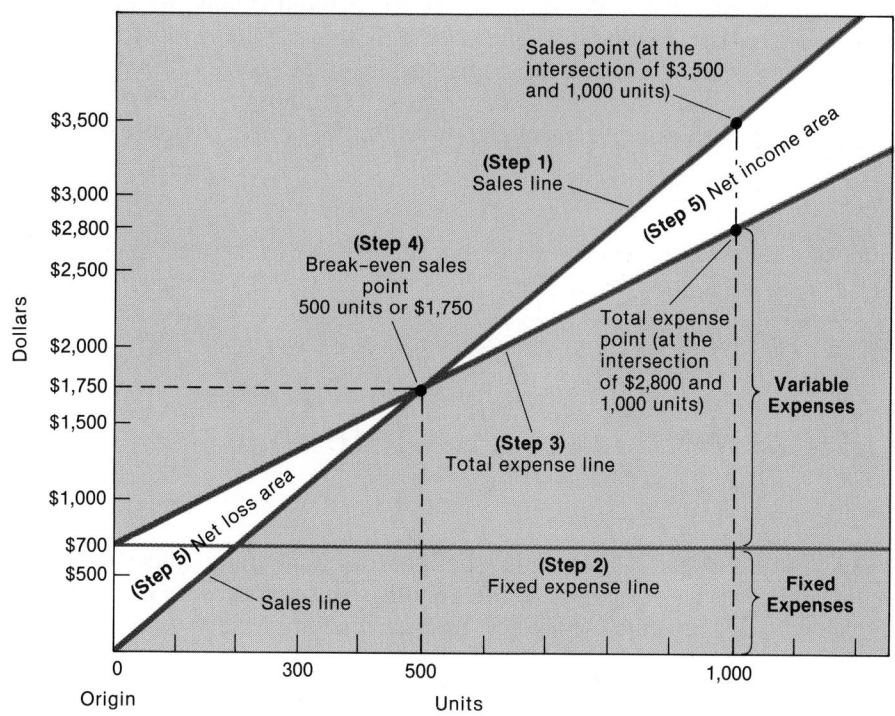

OBJECTIVE 4

Graph a set of cost-volume-profit relationships

Step 1. Choose a relevant sales volume, such as 1,000 units. Plot the point for sales dollars at that volume: 1,000 units × $3.50 per unit = sales of $3,500. Draw the *sales line* from the origin through the $3,500 point.

Step 2. Draw the *fixed expense line,* which intersects the dollar amount axis at $700 and runs across the graph horizontally.

Step 3. Compute variable expense at a relevant sales volume, such as 1,000 units: 1,000 units × $2.10 per unit = variable expense of $2,100. Add variable expense to fixed expense: $2,100 + $700 = $2,800. Plot the total expense point ($2,800) for 1,000 units. Then draw a line through this point from the $700 fixed expenses intercept on the dollar amount axis. This is the *total expense line.*

Step 4. Identify the *break-even point.* The break-even point is the spot where the sales line intersects the total expense line. The equations we used earlier told us that Maria's break-even point was 500 units, or $1,750 in sales. The graph gives us the same information visually.

Step 5. Mark the *net income* and the *net loss area* on the graph. To the left of the break-even point, expenses exceed sales. Consider unit sales of 300, which provide dollar sales of $1,050 (300 × $3.50). Total expenses are $1,330 [(300 × $2.10) + $700]. Therefore, the graph point for sales of 300 units lies in the net loss area. The vertical distance between the total expense line and the sales line equals the net loss. For sales of 300 units, the loss is $280 (sales of $1,050 minus total expenses of $1,330).

To the right of the break-even point, Maria earns a profit. The vertical distance between the sales line and the total expense line equals the amount of net income.

We can tell from the graph whether net loss, break-even, or net income results from a given sales figure. We can also see the amount of any net loss or net income. By contrast, the equation approach indicates income or loss for a single sales amount. Many computer programs display graphs for CVP analysis. The CVP graph is a valuable budgeting tool because it can show expected net income or net loss for all sales levels, from zero units to the company's upper limit.

Summary Problem for Your Review

Grady Nutt is considering opening a booth at the county fair. Grady's booth is smaller and not as well located as Maria's booth, so his rent expense will be $600. He plans to sell souvenirs, which cost $.95 each, at an average selling price of $1.75.

Required

1. Use the contribution margin approach to compute Grady's break-even sales in units and in dollars. Round the contribution margin ratio to three decimal places.
2. How many units must he sell to earn net income of $720? What are dollar sales at this level? Round to the nearest dollar.
3. Prepare a graphic solution to the break-even problem, showing net income and net loss areas from 0 to 2,000 units. Mark the break-even sales level and the sales level needed to earn net income of $720.

SOLUTION TO SUMMARY PROBLEM

Requirement 1

The unit contribution margin is $.80 ($1.75 − $.95). The contribution margin ratio is .457 ($.80/$1.75)

$$\text{Break-even sales in units} = \frac{\text{Fixed expenses}}{\text{Contribution margin per unit}} = \frac{\$600}{\$.80} = 750 \text{ units}$$

$$\text{Break-even sales in dollars} = \frac{\text{Fixed expenses}}{\text{Contribution margin ratio}} = \frac{\$600}{.457} = \$1,313$$

Requirement 2

$$\text{Target sales in units} = \frac{\text{Fixed expenses} + \text{Net income}}{\text{Contribution margin per unit}} = \frac{\$600 + \$720}{\$.80} = \frac{\$1,320}{\$.80} = 1,650 \text{ units}$$

Target sales in dollars = $2,888 (1,650 units × $1.75)

Requirement 3

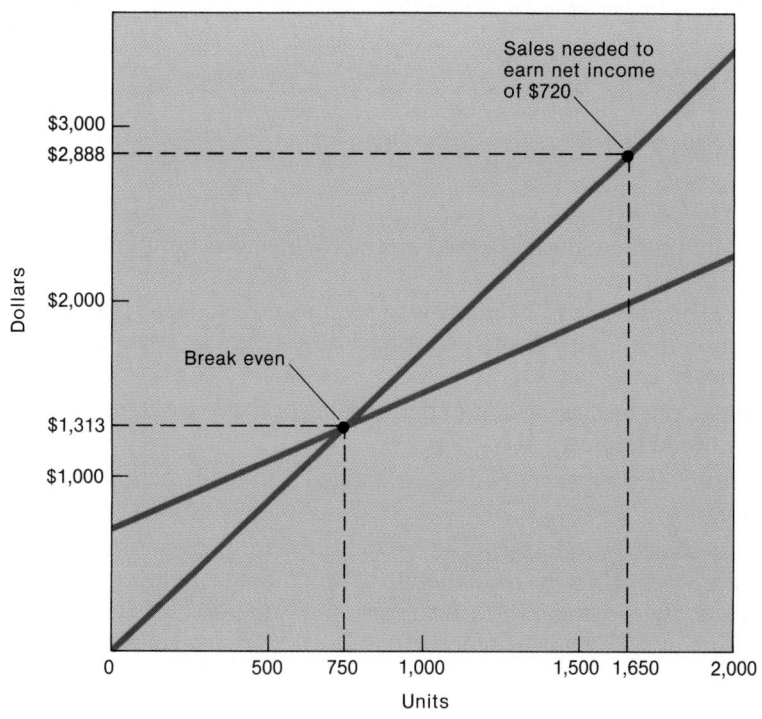

Margin of Safety —————————————————

The **margin of safety** is the excess of expected sales over break-even sales. In other words, the margin of safety is the drop in sales dollars that the company can absorb before incurring a net loss. A high margin of safety serves as a cushion. A low margin of safety is a warning. Managers use the margin of safety to evaluate current operations or to measure the risk of a new business plan. The lower the margin, the higher the risk. The higher the margin, the lower the risk.

Suppose the break-even point is 375 units and the company expects to sell 825 units during the period. Assuming a sale price of $3.50 per unit, we compute the margin of safety as follows:

Margin of safety in units = Expected sales in units − Break-even sales in units

$$= 825 - 375 = 450$$

Margin of safety in dollars = Margin of safety in units × Sale price per unit

$$= 450 \text{ units} \times \$3.50 = \$1,575$$

OBJECTIVE 5
Compute a margin of safety

Sales can drop by 450 units, or $1,575, before the company incurs a loss.

For any level of sales, managers can compute the margin of safety as a percentage. We divide the margin of safety in units (450) by sales in units (825), which equals 55 percent. We reach the same percentage by dividing the margin of safety in dollars ($1,575) by sales in dollars (825 × $3.50 = $2,888).

Assumptions Underlying CVP Analysis _____

Cost-volume-profit analysis is based on the following assumptions:

1. The cost-volume-profit relationships are linear over a wide range of production and sales. Linear relationships can be graphed as straight lines (like all the lines in Exhibit 21-5).
2. Expenses can be classified as either variable or fixed (we discuss mixed costs later in this chapter).
3. Sale prices and expenses will be unchanged during the period under consideration.
4. The sales mix of products will be unchanged during the period under consideration. **Sales mix** is the combination of products that make up total sales. For example, the sales mix of a furniture store may be 70 percent household furniture and 30 percent office furniture. We discuss sales mix in the next section.

When these conditions are met, CVP analysis is precise. Most actual business conditions do not perfectly correspond to these assumptions, and the resulting analysis becomes an approximation. The next three sections discuss how to deal with these real-world situations.

Sales Mix _____

Our illustrations thus far have focused on a single product, travel posters. Most companies sell more than one product, so sales mix must be considered in figuring CVP relationships. Sales mix has an important effect on profits. For example, the business earns more income selling high-margin products than by selling an equal number of low-margin items.

We may perform CVP analysis for a company that sells more than one product by using the same equations that we have discussed in analyzing a company selling a single product. However, we must first express the number of units in terms of a single product.

Let's return to the Maria Martinez example. Suppose Maria plans to sell two types of posters instead of one. The second, larger, poster costs $3.92 and will sell for $6.00. Recall that the basic poster costs $2.10 and sells for $3.50.

An ongoing business uses its experience to compute its sales mix. Maria, on the other hand, is starting a new venture. Suppose she estimates that she will sell 500 large posters and 400 regular posters, a ratio of 1.25 large posters for each regular poster (500/400 = 1.25).

Break-even sales in units is computed as follows:

Let A = number of *regular* posters in break-even sales mix

1.25A = number of *large* posters in break-even sales mix

We use the equation approach to CVP analysis. Sales equals the number of regular posters at $3.50 ($3.50A) plus the number of large posters at $6.00 ($6.00 × 1.25A). Similarly, variable expenses equal the number of regular posters times $2.10 ($2.10A) plus the number of large posters times $3.92 ($3.92 × 1.25A). We use these amounts in the break-even equation.

Sales	−	**Variable expenses**		**= Fixed expenses**	**+ Net income**
$3.50A + $6.00(1.25A)	−	[$2.10A + $3.92(1.25A)] =		$700	+ $0
$3.50A + $7.50A	−	[$2.10A + $4.90A]	=	$700	
$11.00A	−	$7.00A	=	$700	
		$4.00A =		$700	

$$A = \$700/\$4 = 175 \text{ regular posters in the}$$
$$\text{break-even sales mix}$$

$$1.25A = 1.25(175) = 219 \text{ large posters in the}$$
$$\text{break-even sales mix}$$

The overall break-even point in dollar sales is $1,927: 175 regular posters (175 × $3.50 = $613) plus 219 large posters (219 × $6 = $1,314). At break-even, Maria's net income can be computed:

	Regular	Large	Total
Sales (175 × $3.50) and (219 × $6.00)	$613	$1,314	$1,927
Variable expenses (175 × $2.10) and (219 × $3.92)......	368	859	1,227
Contribution margin............................	$245	$ 455	700
Fixed expenses			700
Net income			$ -0-

After performing a CVP analysis, prepare an income statement as a check on your analysis. If the CVP analysis focuses on breaking even, as in the preceding example, the income statement should show net income of zero. If the CVP analysis shows the sales level needed to earn a target net income, the income statement should report that income amount.

If Maria's sales mix changes, planned net income will differ from these estimates. For example, if she sells a higher proportion of large posters, she stands a chance of earning more money because the large posters generate a higher contribution margin.

Management's discussion of income statements often refers to sales mix. For example, an annual report of Deere and Company, a manufacturer of farm equipment, stated that profits decreased because of "a less favorable mix of products sold." What is a "less favorable mix of products"? It is the selling of items with low contribution margins.

CVP sales-mix analysis enters the budgeting system. Suppose a company's profits have decreased. Analysis of the sales mix in the past may indicate that this decrease resulted from concentrating on low-margin products. This information can be used to budget a campaign to try to sell products with a higher contribution margin.

Separating a Mixed Cost into its Variable and Fixed Components

An assumption of CVP analysis is that each cost is either variable or fixed. As mentioned previously, some expenses are mixed, combining variable expenses and fixed expenses. We cited utility expense as an example of a mixed cost. Similarly, businesses often pay sales personnel a set monthly salary (a fixed expense) plus a sales commission based on their sales (a variable expense). The salesperson's overall compensation is a mixed cost to the employer. Mixed expenses, also called semivariable costs, must be separated into their variable and fixed components for CVP analysis.

A number of methods exist for separating mixed expenses into variable and fixed expenses. The more sophisticated methods use statistical computations that are covered in more advanced accounting courses and statistics courses. To introduce you to the concept of separating mixed costs, we present the *high-low* method.

Assume Baylor Drug Store keeps few accounting records. The available records show total monthly revenues and expenses only. Total expenses must be separated into fixed and variable components. See Exhibit 21-6. To use the **high-low method,** pick the highest and the lowest monthly expense figures. Do the

EXHIBIT 21-6   *CVP Graph for High-Low Method*

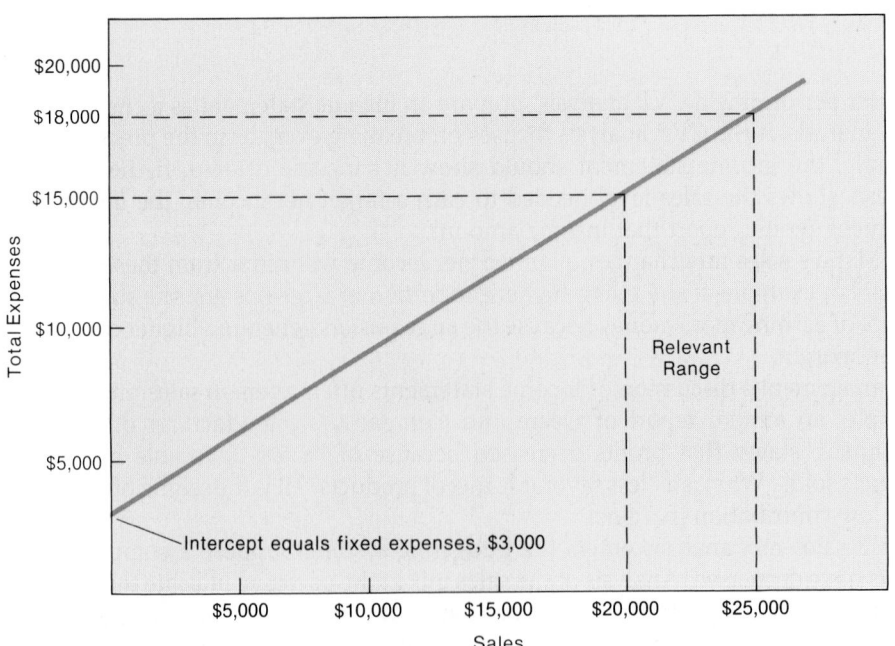

$$\text{Variable expense percentage} = \frac{\text{Change in total expenses}}{\text{Change in sales}} = \frac{\$18{,}000 - \$15{,}000}{\$25{,}000 - \$20{,}000} = \frac{\$3{,}000}{\$5{,}000} = .60 \text{ of sales}$$

Fixed expenses = Total expense − Variable expenses
 at high point: $18,000 − ($25,000 × .60) = $3,000
 at low point: $15,000 − ($20,000 × .60) = $3,000

Intercept equals fixed expenses, $3,000

same for sales. For both expenses and sales, subtract the lower amount from the higher amount. Baylor Drug's records show:

	Total Expenses	Sales
High..............	$18,000	$25,000
Low	15,000	20,000
Change	$ 3,000	$ 5,000

OBJECTIVE 6

Separate a mixed cost into its variable and fixed components

Exhibit 21-6 graphs the CVP relationships for the relevant range, which is between sales of $20,000 and $25,000.

Divide the difference in total expenses (in our example, $3,000) by the difference in sales ($5,000). The result is the ratio of variable expenses to sales. Multiply this ratio ($3,000/$5,000 = .60) by the high sales amount to determine variable expenses:

Variable expenses = .60 of sales

$$= \$25,000 \times .60$$

$$= \$15,000$$

By subtracting variable expenses from total expenses, we arrive at fixed expenses:

Fixed expenses = Total expenses − Variable expenses

$$= \$18,000 - \$15,000$$

$$= \$3,000$$

Alternatively, we can multiply the .60 ratio by the lower sales amount ($20,000) to compute variable expenses ($12,000) at that sales level. Subtract variable expenses from the corresponding total expense amount ($15,000) to compute fixed expenses:

Fixed expenses = Total expenses − Variable expenses

$$= \$15,000 - (\$20,000 \times .60)$$

$$= \$15,000 - \$12,000$$

$$= \$3,000$$

Baylor Drug's cost behavior can be described as fixed monthly expenses of $3,000 plus variable monthly expenses that average 60 percent of sales. These data can be used for analyzing the store's CVP relationships, for example, to prepare a cost budget. Because budget estimates are usually based on historical data from the past, the method can be applied to actual past costs in order to estimate budgeted amounts. Exhibit 21-6 summarizes these computations.

Contribution Margin Approach to Decision Making _____

An income statement can be prepared using two fundamentally different methods. The early part of this book focused on accounting from the perspective of external users of the financial statements. That emphasis leads to the conventional income statement.

The present focus on management's use of accounting information calls for a different format for the income statement. In the management focus, the nature of an expense is important. Whether a cost is variable or fixed affects management decisions.

Managers, then, want an income statement format that identifies the different types of costs. The contribution margin income statement provides this information.

The **contribution margin income statement** separates expenses into variable costs and fixed costs and highlights the contribution margin, which is the excess of sales over variable expenses. Exhibit 21-7 presents a contribution margin income statement alongside a conventional income statement for comparison.

Income from operations is the same on both income statements. However, the contribution margin of $9,000 differs from the gross margin of $16,000. The primary categories of expenses on the contribution margin statement are variable expenses and fixed expenses. By contrast, the conventional income statement contains no such distinctions. Instead, its primary categories of expenses are cost of goods sold and operating expenses.

Recall that the contribution margin receives its name because the excess of revenues over variable expenses "contributes" to the payment of fixed expenses. The amount of revenues left over "contributes" to profit. Management's goal, of course, is to make the contribution margin as large as possible.

Suppose that Reynolds Company managers are considering expanding operations to increase sales by $20,000 (50 percent), from $40,000 to $60,000. Management, in drawing up the company budget, must know the impact of this possible sales increase on income from operations. If sales increase by 50 percent, variable expenses can be expected to increase by the same percentage. Fixed expenses will remain at $3,000 because sales of $40,000 and $60,000 are both within the same relevant range.

We compute the income from operations resulting from the sales increase as follows:

Increase in sales revenue	$20,000
Increase in expenses:	
Fixed expenses	-0-
Variable expenses	
$\dfrac{\text{Increase in sales}}{\text{Current sales}} \times$ Current variable expenses	
$\dfrac{\$20,000}{\$40,000} \times \$31,000$	15,500
Increase in contribution margin	4,500
Income from operations before sales increase	6,000
Income from operations after sales increase	$10,500

OBJECTIVE 7

Use a contribution margin income statement to make business decisions

Management can use this information to decide whether to expand operations.

Important points about the analysis are that (1) fixed expenses do not change and (2) variable expenses increase proportionately with sales. That is, sales are expected to increase by 50 percent ($20,000/$40,000 = .50), and so variable expenses and the contribution margin also increase by 50 percent.

Similar analysis using the conventional income statement is not possible. Managers cannot use the conventional income statement to accurately predict the change in income from an increase in sales because this statement does not show which expenses are variable and which are fixed.

EXHIBIT 21-7 *Contribution Margin Income Statement*

Reynolds Company Contribution Margin Income Statement Month Ended December 31, 19XX			Reynolds Company Conventional Income Statement Month Ended December 31, 19XX		
Sales revenue..................		$40,000	Sales revenue..................		$40,000
Variable expenses:			Cost of goods sold.............		24,000
Cost of goods sold...........	$24,000		**Gross margin**		16,000
Selling	4,000		Operating expenses:		
General and administrative....	3,000	31,000	Selling....................	$6,000	
Contribution margin..........		9,000	General and administrative....	4,000	10,000
Fixed expenses:					
Selling	2,000				
General and administrative....	1,000	3,000			
Income from operations		$ 6,000	Income from operations		$ 6,000

Computer Spreadsheet Analysis of CVP Relationships

Computer spreadsheets are ideally suited for cost-volume-profit analysis because computers can be programmed to show income for any number of sales levels. Spreadsheet programs answer as many "what-if" questions as managers wish to ask: What will variable expenses be if sales rise by a certain amount? By a certain number of units? What if sales fall? If we cut fixed expenses, how many units of each product must we sell to reach a certain level of profits? Computer spreadsheet programs allow managers to analyze the results of any one change or the results of many changes in the business's figures.

Suppose Hyden Company wishes to expand its operations by opening two new stores. The business has received two bids from outside contractors for the construction job. The first bid is $100,000, and the second bid is $140,000. Variable expenses fluctuate between 40 percent and 50 percent of its sales. Fixed costs are expected to be from $280,000 to $420,000. Managers need to know the sales level that the business must reach to earn net income of $100,000, net income of $150,000, and net income of $200,000. A computer spreadsheet program provides the answers to these questions, as shown in Exhibit 21-8, which gives management the information it needs to make an informed decision.

The person who writes the spreadsheet program uses a single formula based on the CVP relationships. The computer places the varying input amounts in the formula and computes the 27 amounts that appear in the exhibit. The computer handles this job in seconds and figures the amounts without computational error.

Managers can insert new figures for fixed expenses, variable expenses, net income — whatever they wish to change — in order to evaluate the financial results of the various situations. Managers use the computer output — which covers the wide range of cost, volume, and profit patterns — to plan their best course of action. As discussed in the preceding chapter, the spreadsheet is a valuable budgeting tool. Chapter 28 assignment materials include an exercise and problems that will develop your ability to write such a spreadsheet program.

EXHIBIT 21-8   *Spreadsheet Analysis of CVP Relationships*

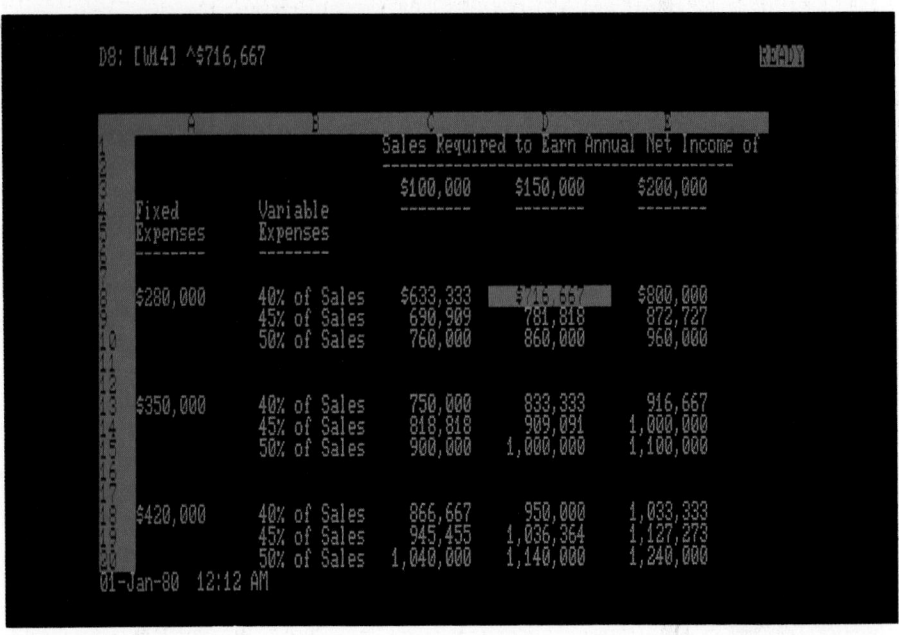

Summary Problem for Your Review

Part A.   Chambers Company sells its product for $8. Management expects October sales to be between 12,000 units and 20,000 units. The business will incur expenses of $58,000 in selling 12,000 units and expenses of $90,000 in selling 20,000 units.

Required

1. Use the high-low method to separate total expenses into variable and fixed components.
2. Use both the equation approach and the contribution margin approach to compute the company's break-even monthly sales in units and in dollars.
3. Compute the monthly sales level needed to earn net income of $14,000. Use either the equation approach or the contribution margin approach.

Part B.   Chambers's sales reach 18,000 units during October. Cost of goods sold makes up 60 percent of variable expenses. Operating expenses are the other 40 percent of variable expenses and all of fixed expenses.

Required

1. Prepare a contribution margin income statement for Chambers for the month of October.
2. Compute income from operations if sales decrease by 10 percent.

SOLUTION TO SUMMARY PROBLEM

Part A — Requirement 1

	Total Expenses	Sales	
High	$90,000	$160,000	(20,000 × $8)
Low.................	58,000	96,000	(12,000 × $8)
Change..............	$32,000	$ 64,000	

$$\text{Variable expense percentage} = \frac{\text{Change in total expenses}}{\text{Change in sales}} = \frac{\$32,000}{\$64,000} = .50 \text{ of sales}$$

Fixed expenses = Total expenses − Variable expenses

At high point: $90,000 − ($160,000 × .50) = $10,000

At low point: $58,000 − ($96,000 × .50) = $10,000

Requirement 2
Equation approach:

$$\underbrace{\text{Sales}}_{\begin{pmatrix} \text{Unit} \\ \text{sale} \\ \text{price} \end{pmatrix} \cdot \text{Units sold}} - \underbrace{\text{Variable expenses}}_{\begin{pmatrix} \text{Variable} \\ \text{unit} \\ \text{cost} \end{pmatrix} \cdot \text{Units sold}} = \text{Fixed expenses} + \text{Net income}$$

$$($8 \cdot \text{Units sold}) - ($8 \cdot .50) \cdot \text{Units sold} = $10,000 \quad + \quad $0$$
$$($8 - $4) \cdot \text{Units sold} = $10,000 \quad + \quad $0$$
$$$4 \cdot \text{Units sold} = $10,000$$
$$\text{Units sold} = $10,000/$4$$

Break-even sales in units = 2,500 units

Break-even sales in dollars = 2,500 units × $8 = $20,000

Contribution margin approach:

$$\text{Break-even sales in units} = \frac{\text{Fixed expense} + \text{Net income}}{\text{Contribution margin per unit}}$$

$$= \frac{($10,000 + $0)}{($8 - $4)}$$

$$= \frac{$10,000}{$4}$$

$$= 2,500 \text{ units}$$

Break-even sales in dollars = 2,500 units × $8 = $20,000

Requirement 3
Equation approach:

$$\left(\begin{array}{c}\text{Unit}\\ \text{sale}\\ \text{price}\end{array} \cdot \text{Units sold}\right) - \left(\begin{array}{c}\text{Variable}\\ \text{unit}\\ \text{cost}\end{array} \cdot \text{Units sold}\right) = \text{Fixed expenses} + \begin{array}{c}\text{Target}\\ \text{net income}\end{array}$$

$$(\$8 \cdot \text{Units sold}) - (\$8 \cdot .50) \cdot \text{Units sold} = \$10,000 + \$14,000$$

$$(\$8 - \$4) \cdot \text{Units sold} = \$10,000 + \$14,000$$

$$\$4 \cdot \text{Units sold} = \$24,000$$

$$\text{Units sold} = \$24,000/\$4$$

$$\text{Target sales in units} = 6,000 \text{ units}$$

$$\text{Target sales in dollars} = 6,000 \text{ units} \times \$8 = \$48,000$$

Contribution margin approach:

$$\text{Break-even sales in units} = \frac{\text{Fixed expense} + \begin{array}{c}\text{Target}\\ \text{net income}\end{array}}{\text{Contribution margin per unit}}$$

$$= \frac{(\$10,000 + \$14,000)}{(\$8 - \$4)}$$

$$= \frac{\$24,000}{\$4}$$

$$= 6,000 \text{ units}$$

$$\text{Break-even sales in dollars} = 6,000 \text{ units} \times \$8 = \$48,000$$

Part B — Requirement 1

Chambers Company
Contribution Margin Income Statement
Month of October 19XX

Sales revenue (18,000 × $8)		$144,000
Variable expenses:		
Cost of goods sold ($144,000 × .50 × .60)	$43,200	
Operating expenses ($144,000 × .50 × .40)	28,800	72,000
Contribution margin		72,000
Fixed expenses:		
Operating expenses		10,000
Income from operations.		$ 62,000

Requirement 2

Decrease in sales revenue ($144,000 × .10)	$14,440
Decrease in expenses:	
Fixed expenses.	$ -0-
Variable expenses ($72,000 × .10)	7,200
Decrease in contribution margin	(7,200)
Income from operations before sales decrease	62,000
Income from operations after sales decrease.	$54,800

Summary

Cost-volume-profit (CVP) analysis examines the relationships among a company's expenses, revenues, and income. These relationships depend on cost behavior. We classify costs as *fixed, variable,* or *mixed.*

Two popular ways to use cost-volume-profit analysis are the *equation approach* and the *contribution margin approach.* The contribution margin is the excess of the sale price over variable expenses. The contribution margin ratio is the contribution margin divided by the sale price.

CVP analysis yields an amount in unit sales or in dollar sales at which income equals expenses, which is the *break-even point.* Management can also project target sales using CVP analysis. *Graphic* displays of CVP relationships present information over a wide range of sales levels, not just at the break-even point. CVP analysis is widely used in budgeting.

The *margin of safety* is the excess of actual or expected sales over the sales figure at breakeven. The larger the margin, the lower the risk of a given plan.

CVP analysis has certain limitations. For example, we must restrict analysis to the span of volume over which fixed costs remain unchanged, which we call the *relevant range.* Also, mixed costs must be separated into fixed costs and variable costs. We can use the *high-low method* to achieve this separation.

The *contribution margin income statement* reports variable expenses and fixed expenses separately. This format allows management to analyze costs. Computer spreadsheet programs can be programmed to measure CVP relationships across a wide range of conditions.

Self-Study Questions

Test your understanding of the chapter by marking the best answer for each of the following questions.

1. Cost-volume-profit analysis is most directly useful to *(p. 821)*
   a. Managers for predicting the outcome of their decisions
   b. Investors for deciding how much to pay for a company's stock
   c. Lenders for analyzing a loan request
   d. Tax authorities for setting income tax rates

2. The graph of a mixed cost *(p. 823)*
   a. Passes through the origin and slopes upward
   b. Is horizontal from the point marking the level of fixed costs
   c. Has a steeper slope than the graph of a fixed cost or a variable cost
   d. Slopes upward from the point marking the level of fixed costs

3. At the break-even point *(p. 825)*
   a. Sales equal fixed expenses
   b. Sales equal variable expenses
   c. Sales equal total expenses
   d. Sales exactly equal net income

4. Variable expenses consume 70 percent of sales, and fixed expenses total $420,000. The break-even point in dollars is *(p. 826)*
   a. $140,000
   b. $600,000
   c. $1,260,000
   d. $1,400,000

5. What happens to the break-even point if both variable expenses and fixed expenses increase? *(pp. 828, 829)*
   a. Break-even sales increase
   b. Break-even sales decrease
   c. Break-even sales are unchanged because the two changes offset each other
   d. The effect on breakeven cannot be determined from the information given

6. William Thomas Corporation's monthly sales have averaged $480,000 for the past year. The monthly break-even point is $400,000. The company's margin of safety percentage is *(p. 833)*
   a. 16⅔%
   b. 20%
   c. 62½%
   d. 100%

7. Raj Mujadeen sells Oriental rugs—handmade for $1,000 each, machine-made for $300 each. Customers buy five times as many machine-made rugs as handmade rugs. Variable expenses consume 80 percent of sales, and monthly fixed expenses total $2,000. How many of each type of rug must Raj sell to earn monthly net income of $3,000? *(p. 835)*

   a. 8 handmade and 40 machine made   c. 12 handmade and 60 machine made
   b. 10 handmade and 50 machine made   d. 20 handmade and 100 machine made

8. Separating mixed costs into fixed and variable components is useful for *(p. 836)*

   a. Budgeting costs   c. Computing break-even sales
   b. Analyzing cost-volume-profit relationships   d. All of the above

9. Refer to Exhibit 21-4, page 824. If sales are 21,000 units, the business can expect fixed expenses of *(pp. 824, 825)*

   a. $50,000   c. $100,000
   b. $80,000   d. Cannot be determined from the information given

10. Refer to Exhibit 21-7, page 839. What will income from operations be if sales increase by 25 percent? *(pp. 838, 839)*

   a. $7,500   c. $10,000
   b. $8,250   d. $12,750

Answers to the self-study questions are at the end of the chapter.

Accounting Vocabulary

break-even analysis *(p. 825)*, break-even point *(p. 825)*, contribution margin *(p. 826)*, contribution margin income statement *(p. 838)*, contribution margin percentage *(p. 827)*, cost behavior *(p. 821)*, cost-volume-profit (CVP) analysis *(p. 821)*, fixed cost *(p. 822)*, fixed expense *(p. 822)*, high-low method (p. 836), margin of safety *(p. 833)*, mixed cost *(p. 823)*, mixed expense *(p. 823)*, relevant range *(p. 824)*, sales mix *(p. 834)*, variable cost *(p. 822)*, variable expense *(p. 822)*

ASSIGNMENT MATERIAL _____

Questions

1. How is cost-volume-profit analysis used in budgeting?
2. Define the three types of cost behavior patterns.
3. Draw graphs of the three types of costs.
4. What are six questions cost-volume-profit analysis can answer?
5. What is the break-even point? What is its significance to a business?
6. Give the contribution margin formulas for break-even sales in units and in dollars.
7. How does an increase in fixed expenses affect the break-even point? How does a decrease in fixed expenses affect break-even sales? Give the reason for each answer.
8. How does an increase in variable expenses affect the break-even point? How does a decrease in variable expenses affect break-even sales? Give the reason for each answer.
9. How does an increase in selling price affect the break-even point? How does a decrease in selling price affect break-even sales? Give the reason for each answer.
10. Briefly outline two ways to compute the target sales in dollars needed to earn a given net income.
11. Give the contribution margin formula for target sales in units needed to earn a given net income. Do the same for target sales in dollars.

12. Identify the steps in the preparation of a cost-volume-profit graph.
13. What advantages does a CVP graph have over the equation approach and the contribution margin approach?
14. How does the margin of safety serve as a measure of risk?
15. Give the assumptions underlying cost-volume-profit analysis.
16. Briefly describe how to perform CVP analysis when a company sells more than one product.
17. McMillan Corporation's expenses are mixed. Management wishes to know its break-even point and seeks your advice. How can you separate total expenses into variable and fixed components?
18. Why is the concept of the relevant range important to cost-volume-profit analysis?
19. Draw a graph of fixed expenses from 0 to 50,000 units. The relevant range lies between 20,000 and 35,000 units, where fixed expenses are $300,000. Below the relevant range, fixed expenses are $200,000. Above the relevant range, fixed expenses are $400,000.
20. How does a contribution margin income statement differ from a conventional income statement? Which income statement is more useful for predicting the income effect of a change in sales? Why?
21. Why are computer spreadsheets useful for CVP analysis?

Exercises

Exercise 21-1 *Graphing cost behaviors*

Graph each of the following cost behavior patterns over a relevant range from 0 to 10,000 units:

a. Variable expenses of $5 per unit.
b. Fixed expenses of $25,000.
c. Mixed expenses made up of fixed costs of $10,000 and variable costs of $3 per unit.

Exercise 21-2 *Computing break-even sales by the contribution margin approach*

BentTree Associates has fixed expenses of $40,000 and variable expenses of $3 per unit of its product, which it sells for $5.50 per unit.

Required

1. Compute the company's contribution margin per unit and its contribution margin ratio to six decimal places.
2. Determine the break-even point in units and in dollars, using the contribution margin approach.

Exercise 21-3 *Computing break-even sales under different CVP relationships*

For several years, Chin's Chinese Restaurant has offered a lunch special for $4.50. Monthly fixed expenses have been $3,000. The variable cost of a meal has been $1.50. Rudy Chin, the owner, believes that by remodeling the restaurant and upgrading the food services, he can increase the price of the lunch special to $5.25. Monthly fixed expenses would increase to $4,200, and the variable expenses would increase to $1.75 per meal.

Required

Use the equation approach to compute Chin's monthly break-even sales in dollars before and after remodeling.

Exercise 21-4 *Computing break-even sales and net income or loss under different conditions*

Transco Truck Lines delivers freight through Indiana, Ohio, and Kentucky. The company has monthly fixed expenses of $350,000 and a contribution margin of 70 percent of revenues.

Required

1. Compute Transco's monthly break-even sales in dollars. Use the contribution margin approach.
2. Compute Transco's monthly net income or net loss if revenues are $400,000 and if they are $700,000.

Exercise 21-5 *Computing break-even sales and sales needed to earn a given net income; sales-mix considerations*

A. Dale's Auto Supply has fixed monthly expenses of $3,600 and a contribution margin ratio of 30 percent. What must monthly sales be for the business to break even? to earn net income of $3,000?

B. Barb's Boutique sells two product lines, one with a contribution margin ratio of 40 percent, the other with a contribution margin ratio of 50 percent. Each product line makes up one half of sales. If monthly fixed expenses are $2,700, what must monthly sales be for the business to break even? to earn net income of $3,600? Hint: Average the contribution margin ratios of the two product lines, and use the average contribution margin ratio in the analysis.

Exercise 21-6 *Graphing cost-volume-profit relationships*

Suppose that Veterans Stadium, the home field for the Philadelphia Phillies baseball team, earns total revenue that averages $9 for every ticket sold. Assume that annual fixed expenses are $8 million and that variable expenses are $1 per ticket.

Required

Prepare the ballpark's cost-volume-profit graph under these assumptions. Show the break-even point in dollars and in tickets. Label fixed expenses, variable expenses, net loss area, and net income area on the graph.

Exercise 21-7 *Analyzing a cost-volume-profit graph*

The top managers of Bronson Stoker, Inc., are planning the budget for 19X6. The accountant who prepared the following cost-volume-profit graph forgot to label the lines:

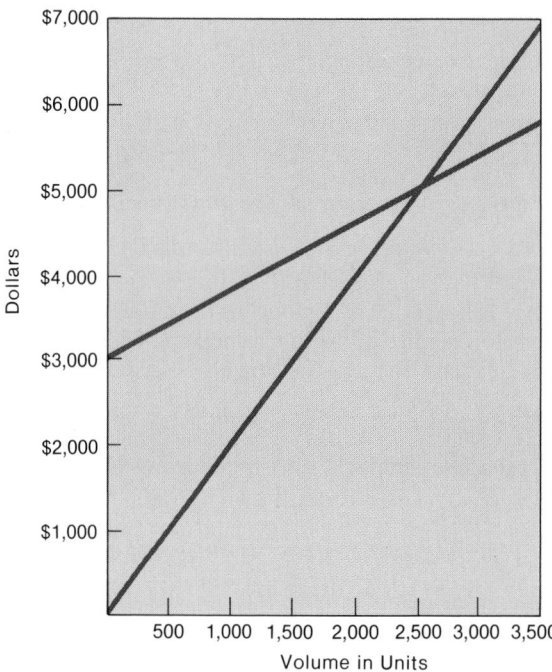

Required

Answer the following questions asked by the managers:

1. What do the lines mean?
2. Where is the net income area? The net loss area?
3. What is break-even sales in units and in dollars?
4. What will net income (or net loss) be if sales are 1,700 units?
5. What sales level in dollars is needed to earn net income of $1,000?

Exercise 21-8   *Computing a margin of safety*

Pyle's Pac-Sac convenience store has a monthly profit goal of $4,000. Variable expenses are 60 percent of sales, and fixed monthly expenses are $6,000. Compute the monthly margin of safety in dollars if the store achieves its profit goal. Express Pyle's margin of safety as a percent of target sales.

Exercise 21-9   *Cost-volume-profit analysis with a sales mix*

Three college friends open an off-campus shop named Big Bear T-Shirts. They plan to sell a standard T-shirt for $6 and a fancier version for $7.50. The $6 shirt costs them $3, and the $7.50 shirt costs them $3.50. The friends expect to sell two fancy T-shirts for each standard T-shirt. Their monthly fixed expenses are $1,650. How many of each type of T-shirt must they sell monthly to break even? to earn $2,200?

Exercise 21-10   *Analyzing cost behavior by the high-low method*

Hillcrest Hospital is struggling to break even. Its management has decided to install a new accounting system. Management wishes to know the behavior of the hospital's costs. The lowest and highest expected monthly revenues are $225,000 and $300,000. Corresponding total expenses are $270,000 and $300,000.

Required

Separate total expenses into variable and fixed components. Express the hospital's cost behavior as follows: Total monthly expenses = Fixed expenses + Variable expenses as a percent of revenues.

Exercise 21-11   *Computing break-even revenue by the equation approach*

Use the answer to Exercise 21-10 to compute Hillcrest Hospital's break-even monthly revenues in dollars. Follow the equation approach.

Exercise 21-12   *Preparing a contribution margin income statement*

Salazar, Inc., reported the following income statement for April:

Salazar, Inc. Income Statement April 19XX		
Sales revenue		$637,000
Cost of goods sold		448,000
Gross margin		189,000
Operating expenses:		
Selling	$72,000	
General and administrative (including income tax)	34,000	106,000
Net income		$ 83,000

Salazar accounting records indicate that cost of goods sold is a variable expense and that selling expense is 20 percent fixed and 80 percent variable. General and administrative expense is half fixed and half variable.

Required

Prepare Salazar's contribution margin income statement for April. Compute the expected increase in net income to the nearest $1,000 if sales increase by $100,000.

Problems

(Group A)

Problem 21-1A   *Contribution margin analysis*

The accounting records of four different companies yield the following information:

	A	B	C	D
Target sales	$	$500,000	$	$70,000
Variable expenses	104,000		100,000	20,000
Fixed expenses			80,000	38,000
Net income (loss)	$ 35,000	$ 60,000	$	$
Units sold		100,000	5,000	
Unit contribution margin	$6	$2		$200
Contribution margin ratio	.600		.200	

Required

Fill in the blanks for each company. Show your work, and round contribution margin ratios to three decimal places.

Problem 21-2A   *Computing break-even revenue and the revenue needed to earn a given net income; preparing a contribution margin income statement*

The Mystic Clipper is a schooner that sails from Annapolis, Maryland, during the spring and fall. During the summer the ship leaves from Mystic, Connecticut. The average cruise has 45 tourists on board, and each person pays $50 for a day sail. The ship sails 80 days each year.

The Clipper has a crew of 8. Each member earns an average of $100 per cruise. The crew is paid only when the ship sails. The other variable expenses are for refreshments, which average $10 per passenger per cruise. Fixed annual expenses total $44,000.

Required

1. Compute revenue and variable expenses for each cruise.
2. Use the equation approach to compute the number of cruises the Clipper must take each year to break even. Replace "Sales" in the equation with "Revenue."
3. Use the contribution margin approach to compute the number of cruises needed each year to earn $70,000. Is this profit goal realistic? Give your reason.
4. Prepare the Clipper's contribution margin income statement for 80 cruises for the year. Report only two categories of expenses: variable and fixed.

Problem 21-3A   *CVP analysis under different conditions*

Suppose Louisville Clip-Quick imprints ballpoint pens with company logos. The company has fixed expenses of $286,000 each month plus variable expenses of $1.60 per box of pens. For each box of pens sold, the company earns revenue of $2.90.

Required

1. Use the equation approach to compute the number of boxes of pens Louisville must sell each month to break even.

2. Use the contribution margin approach to compute the dollar amount of monthly revenue Louisville needs in order to earn $22,000 in net income. Round the contribution margin ratio to six decimal places.
3. Prepare Louisville's contribution margin income statement for August for sales of 240,000 boxes of pens. Cost of goods sold is 80 percent of variable expenses. Operating expenses make up the rest of variable expenses and all of fixed expenses.
4. The company is considering an expansion that will increase fixed expenses by 30 percent and variable expenses by 10¢ per box of pens. What will the new break-even point be in units and in dollars? Use either the equation approach or the contribution margin approach. (Round the contribution margin ratio to six decimal places.)

Problem 21-4A   *Computing break-even sales and sales needed to earn a given net income; graphing cost-volume-profit relationships*

Air & Sea Travel is opening an office in Oklahoma City. Fixed monthly expenses are office rent ($3,000), depreciation of office furniture ($200), utilities ($110), a special telephone line ($520), a connection with the airlines' computerized reservation service ($380), and the salary of a travel agent ($1,400). Variable expenses are utilities (2 percent of sales), incentive compensation for the employee (5 percent of sales), advertising (4 percent of sales), supplies and postage (1 percent of sales), and a usage fee for the telephone line and computerized reservation service (3 percent of sales). The business is a proprietorship, so it pays no business income tax.

Required

1. Use the contribution margin approach to compute Air & Sea's break-even sales in dollars. If the average sale is a $300 plane ticket, how many units does it take to break even?
2. Use the equation approach to compute dollar sales needed to earn monthly net income of $4,000.
3. Graph the travel agency's cost-volume-profit relationships. Assume an average sale is a $300 plane ticket. Show the break-even point, fixed expenses, variable expenses, net loss area, net income area, and the sales in units and dollars where monthly net income of $4,000 is earned. The graph should range from 0 to 50 units.
4. Assume that the average sale price increases to $400. Use the contribution margin approach to figure the new break-even point in units. What is the effect of the sale price increase on the break-even point?

Problem 21-5A   *Using a contribution margin income statement for break-even analysis; sales mix, margin of safety, and changes in the CVP relationship*

The contribution margin income statement of Mario's Pizza for May 19X6 is as follows:

Mario's Pizza
Contribution Margin Income Statement
May 19X6

Sales revenue		$160,000
Variable expenses:		
Cost of goods sold	$32,000	
Selling	25,000	
General and administrative	3,000	60,000
Contribution margin		100,000
Fixed expenses:		
Selling	27,000	
General and administrative	9,000	36,000
Income from operations		$ 64,000

Mario's sells three small pizzas for every large pizza. The sale price for a small pizza is $10. A large pizza sells for $20.

Required

1. Compute the contribution margin ratio.
2. Use the contribution margin approach to determine Mario's monthly break-even point in the numbers of small pizzas and large pizzas. Prove the correctness of your computation by preparing a summary contribution margin income statement at breakeven. You need show only two categories of expenses: variable and fixed.
3. Compute Mario's margin of safety in dollars.
4. If Mario can increase monthly sales by 15 percent above $160,000, what will income from operations be?
5. Mario's hopes to decrease monthly fixed expenses by $20,000 to scale back operations. Use the contribution margin approach to determine the new break-even sales in dollars.

Problem 21-6A *Analyzing cost behavior; computing break-even sales and net income under different CVP relationships; preparing a contribution margin income statement*

Galindo Baking Company accounting records summarize the fiscal year ended November 30, 19X2:

Quarter ended	Sales	Total expenses
Feb. 28, 19X2	$161,000	$115,000
May 31, 19X2	138,000	109,000
Aug. 31, 19X2	111,000	93,000
Nov. 30, 19X2	119,000	101,000

Required

1. Categorize total expenses as fixed, variable, or mixed. Give your reasoning.
2. Use the high-low method to separate total quarterly expenses into fixed and variable components. Multiply quarterly fixed expenses by 4 to compute annual fixed expenses.
3. Compute break-even sales in dollars for the year. Use the contribution margin approach.
4. Prepare Galindo's contribution margin income statement at the break-even point for the year ended November 30, 19X2. Cost of goods sold is 71 percent of total variable expenses. The remainder of variable expenses is 19 percent selling and 10 percent general. Fixed expenses are evenly divided between selling and general.
5. Compute net income if sales increase by $50,000 above the break-even point.

(Group B)

Problem 21-1B *Contribution margin analysis*

The accounting records of four different companies yield the following information:

	A	B	C	D
Target sales	$48,000	$	$560,000	$280,000
Variable expenses	32,000	130,000		
Fixed expenses			312,000	120,000
Net income (loss)	$ 7,000	$ 25,000	$	$
Units sold		8,000	112,000	11,000
Unit contribution margin	$4	$15		$12
Contribution margin ratio			.30	

Required

Fill in the blanks for each company. Show your work, and round contribution margin ratios to three decimal places.

Problem 21-2B *Computing break-even revenue and the revenue needed to earn a given net income; preparing a contribution margin income statement*

Windjammer Cruises sails a schooner from Miami. The average cruise has 80 tourists on board. Each person pays $75 for a day sail in the Caribbean. The ship sails 100 days each year.

The schooner has a crew of 12. Each member earns an average of $85 per cruise. The crew is paid only when the ship sails. Other variable expenses are for refreshments, which average $14 per passenger per cruise. Fixed annual expenses total $80,000.

Required

1. Compute revenue and variable expenses for each cruise.
2. Use the equation approach to compute the number of cruises needed annually to break even. Replace "Sales" in the equation with "Revenues."
3. Use the contribution margin approach to compute the number of cruises needed annually to earn $100,000. Is this profit goal realistic? Give the reason.
4. Prepare Windjammer's contribution margin income statement for 100 cruises each year. Report only two categories of expenses: variable and fixed.

Problem 21-3B *CVP analysis under different conditions*

Suppose Denver Ballpoint Pen Distributors imprints pens with company names. The company has fixed expenses of $360,000 each month plus variable expense of $2 per box of pens. For each box of pens sold, Denver earns revenue of $3.20.

Required

1. Use the equation approach to compute the number of boxes of pens Denver must sell each month to break even.
2. Use the contribution margin approach to compute the dollar amount of monthly revenue Denver needs in order to earn $30,000 in net income.
3. Prepare Denver's contribution margin income statement for June for sales of 400,000 boxes of pens. Cost of goods sold is 70 percent of variable expenses. Operating expenses make up the rest of variable and all of fixed expenses.
4. The company is considering an expansion that will increase fixed expenses by 40 percent and variable expenses by 10 percent. What will the new break-even point be in units and in dollars? Use either the equation approach or the contribution margin approach. Compute the contribution margin ratio to four decimal places.

Problem 21-4B *Computing break-even sales and sales needed to earn a given net income; graphing cost-volume-profit relationships*

Bon Voyage Travel is opening an office in New Orleans. Fixed monthly expenses are office rent ($3,400), depreciation of office furniture ($190), utilities ($140), a special telephone line ($390), a connection with the airlines' computerized reservation service ($480), and the salary of a travel agent ($1,800). Variable expenses are utilities (3 percent of sales), incentive compensation of the employee (6 percent of sales), advertising (6 percent of sales), supplies and postage (1 percent of sales), and a usage fee for the telephone line and computerized reservation service (4 percent of sales). The business is a partnership, so it pays no business income tax.

Required

1. Use the contribution margin approach to compute the travel agency's break-even sales in dollars. If the average sale is a $400 plane ticket, how many units does it take to break even?

2. Use the equation approach to compute dollar sales needed to earn monthly net income of $3,500.
3. Graph the travel agency's cost-volume-profit relationships. Assume an average sale is a $400 plane ticket. Show the break-even point, fixed expenses, variable expenses, net loss area, net income area, and the sales in units and dollars where monthly net income of $3,500 is earned. The graph should range from 0 to 40 units.
4. Assume that the average sale price increases to $500. Use the contribution margin approach to compute the new break-even point in units. What is the effect of the sale price increase on the break-even point?

Problem 21-5B   *Using a contribution margin income statement for break-even analysis; sales mix, margin of safety, and changes in the CVP relationship*

The contribution margin income statement of Robinette Men's Store for November 19X5 is as follows:

Robinette Men's Store
Contribution Margin Income Statement
November 19X5

Sales revenue		$60,000
Variable expenses:		
Cost of goods sold	$22,000	
Selling	13,000	
General and administrative	7,000	42,000
Contribution margin		18,000
Fixed expenses:		
Selling	11,000	
General and administrative	1,000	12,000
Income from operations		$ 6,000

Robinette sells two ties for every belt. The ties sell for $7, and the belts sell for $6.

Required

1. Compute the contribution margin ratio.
2. Use the contribution margin approach to determine Robinette's monthly break-even point in the numbers of ties and belts. Prove the correctness of your computation by preparing a summary contribution income statement at break even. You need show only two categories of expenses: variable and fixed.
3. Compute Robinette's margin of safety in dollars.
4. If Robinette increases monthly sales by 15 percent above $60,000, what will income from operations be?
5. Robinette may expand the store and increase monthly fixed expenses by $2,100. Use the contribution margin approach to determine the new break-even sales in dollars.

Problem 21-6B   *Analyzing cost behavior; computing break-even sales and net income under different CVP relationships; preparing a contribution margin income statement*

Everglades Manufacturing Company accounting records summarize the fiscal year ended February 28, 19X3:

Quarter ended	Sales	Total expenses
May 31, 19X2	$230,500	$210,000
Aug. 31, 19X2	185,000	186,500
Nov. 30, 19X2	199,500	187,000
Feb. 28, 19X3	265,000	218,500

Required

1. Categorize total expenses as fixed, variable, or mixed. Give your reasoning.
2. Use the high-low method to separate total quarterly expenses into fixed and variable components. Multiply quarterly fixed expenses by 4 to compute annual fixed expenses.
3. Compute break-even sales in dollars for the year. Use the contribution margin approach.
4. Prepare Everglades's contribution margin income statement at the break-even point for the year ended February 28, 19X3. Cost of goods sold is 83 percent of total variable expenses. The remainder of variable expenses is 11 percent selling and 6 percent general. Fixed expenses are 40 percent selling and 60 percent general.
5. Compute net income if sales increase by $100,000 above the break-even point.

Decision Problem

Using A Contribution Margin Income Statement To Make Business Decisions

Biltrite Toy Company markets three lines of toys. Each line is manufactured by a different company, and each line has a different set of cost-volume-profit relationships.

	Newborns	Toddlers	Preschoolers
Sales	$320,000	$150,000	$270,000
Variable expenses	64,000	75,000	108,000
Contribution margin	256,000	75,000	162,000
Fixed expenses	188,000	120,000	126,000
Income (loss) before tax	$ 68,000	$ (45,000)	$ 36,000

Average sale prices are $2 for toys for newborns, $3 for toys for toddlers, and $5 for preschoolers' toys.

Required

1. Which product line is the least profitable?
2. Use the equation approach to compute break-even sales in units for the company as a whole.
3. Prepare a contribution margin income statement—for each product line—at the break-even point.
4. Prepare a contribution margin income statement assuming that sales of toddler toys are eliminated altogether.
5. Would it be wise to drop the toddler toy line? What would explain the overall net loss that would result if the company did drop the toddler toy line?

Financial Statement Problem

CVP Relationships for an Actual Company

Gulf+Western's income statement in Appendix C can be summarized as follows for fiscal years 1987 and 1986 (amounts in millions):

	1987	**1986**
Total net revenues	$3,227.7	$2,383.3
Total expenses	2,871.6	2,154.6
Earnings before extraordinary items	$ 356.1	$ 228.7

Assume that managers are budgeting for fiscal 1988. Suppose they view the 1986 amounts as a low level of activity and the 1987 amounts as a high level.

Required

1. Use the high-low method to separate total expenses into fixed and variable components. Round the variable expense percentage to six decimal places, and show all dollar amounts in millions rounded to the nearest $100,000.
2. Compute break-even net revenues in dollars. Use the contribution margin approach.
3. Suppose managers' profit goal for fiscal 1988 is $400 million. Compute the target net revenues needed to achieve this goal.

Answers to Self-Study Questions

1. a
2. d
3. c
4. d   Sales $-$ .70 Sales = $420,000; .30 Sales = $420,000;
   Break-even sales = $420,000/.30 = $1,400,000
5. a
6. a   Margin of safety in dollars = $80,000 ($480,000 $-$ $400,000)
   Margin of safety as a percentage = $16\frac{2}{3}$% ($80,000/$480,000)
7. b   Let A = number of $1,000 rugs
      5A = number of $300 rugs
   $1,000 A + $300(5A) $-$ .8[$1,000 A + $300(5A)] = $2,000 + $3,000
         $2,500 A $-$ $2,000 A   = $5,000
                                   $500 A = $5,000
                                   A = $5,000/$500 = 10
                                   5A = 5(10)   = 50
8. d
9. c
10. b   Increase in contribution margin ($9,000 $\times$ .25) $2,250
    Income from operations before sales increase 6,000
    Income from operations after sales increase $8,250

Manufacturing Accounting and Job Order Costing

The Sportster specializes in athletic shoes. Like all merchandisers, The Sportster buys its inventory ready for resale to customers. Determining the cost of the shoes is relatively easy. Cost is the price that the merchandiser pays for the goods plus the freight and insurance charges incurred in transporting them to the store.

How do we account for the companies — Nike, Reebok, Adidas, and others — that make the shoes The Sportster sells? Manufacturers use their labor force and factory assets to shape raw materials into finished products. Their manufacturing processes begin with materials — cloth, rubber, plastics, and related items. These materials are cut, glued, stitched, and formed into athletic shoes. The process of converting these materials into finished products makes it more difficult to measure a manufacturer's inventory cost than that of a merchandiser.

In this and the next chapter we turn our attention to manufacturers, with emphasis on their cost accounting systems. The first part of this chapter introduces manufacturing accounting. The second part discusses a particular system for controlling and determining a manufacturer's costs — job order costing.

Objectives of a Manufacturing Cost System

Manufacturers need a special accounting system — called a cost accounting system — to determine and control the cost of their manufactured inventory. Exhibit 22-1 illustrates the dual objectives of *cost control* and *product costing* for a shoe manufacturer like Nike, Inc.

EXHIBIT 22-1 *Dual Objectives of a Cost Accounting System*

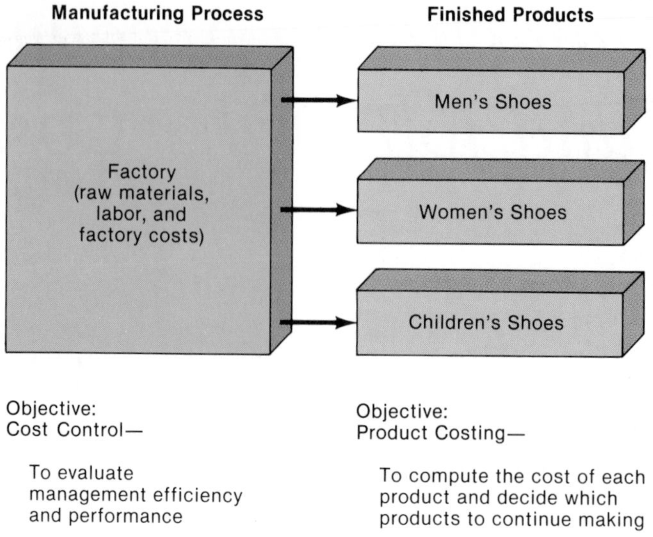

OBJECTIVE 1

Identify the dual objectives of a cost accounting system

An important focus of cost accounting is the control of cost. Businesses achieve cost control through the evaluation of management efficiency and performance. Managers strive for the maximum output of finished products at the minimum cost. The company's actual product cost and output provide the information the company needs to measure performance—how well a manager succeeds in controlling costs while manufacturing goods.

Product costing—determining the cost to the manufacturer of each of its products—is a primary objective in cost accounting. The manufacturer must know its product costs in order to measure inventory values (and so the cost of goods sold) and profitability (revenues minus expenses, which include the cost of goods sold).

Product costs frequently help managers decide on pricing: How much does the manufacturer charge the merchandiser for its goods? The answer depends in large part on how much it costs the manufacturer to produce these goods. Also, managers must determine which products to continue manufacturing and which to phase out. For example, Nike managers may learn that the company is losing money on children's shoes, and this information may lead the company to drop that product line. This decision depends on accurate product cost data for each product.

Our discussion in this chapter centers on product costing. We turn now to a closer look at manufacturing inventory.

Manufacturing Accounts

Inventory Accounts—Materials, Work in Process, and Finished Goods

Inventory considerations differ between merchandiser and manufacturer. Merchandisers need only one category of inventory for the finished goods they buy and sell. By contrast, manufacturers have three inventory accounts, as we discuss in a moment. Exhibit 22-2 compares the inventory accounts of a manufacturing company and a merchandising company. *Note that the two types of business have identical balance sheets except for the inventory accounts.*

EXHIBIT 22-2   *Inventory Accounts of a Manufacturing Firm and a Merchandising Firm*

Manufacturing Firm			Merchandising Firm	
Current assets:			Current assets:	
Cash		$ X,XXX	Cash	$ X,XXX
Short-term invest-			Short-term invest-	
ments		X,XXX	ments	X,XXX
Receivables		X,XXX	Receivables	X,XXX
Inventories:			**Inventories . . . .**	**10,000**
Materials	$1,000		Prepaid expenses . . .	X,XXX
Work in process . .	4,000			
Finished goods . . .	8,000			
Total inventories .		13,000		
Prepaid expenses . . .		X,XXX		
Total current assets . .		$XX,XXX	Total current assets . .	$XX,XXX

The **Materials Inventory,** also called **Raw Materials Inventory,** account holds the cost of materials on hand and intended for use in the manufacturing process. A shoe manufacturer's materials include leather, glue, plastics, cloth, and thread. Raw materials for Bethlehem Steel include iron ore, coal, and chemicals. Materials—kept in vats, bins, or other storage areas—are collectively called *stores.*

The **Work in Process Inventory** account gives the cost of the goods that are in the manufacturing process and not yet complete. For a shoe manufacturer, partially completed shoes make up its work in process inventory. For a petroleum refiner, work in process is the crude oil being distilled into gasoline, different grade oils, and other products. Work in process inventory is also called *work in progress* and *goods in process.*

The completed goods that have not yet been sold make up the **Finished Goods Inventory** account. Manufacturers store finished goods in warehouses, tanks, or whatever storage facility is appropriate to the particular type of inventory. Finished goods are what the manufacturer sells to a merchandising business. For example, Procter and Gamble manufactures soap and toothpaste, which it sells to Safeway, K mart, and other stores. The Finished Goods account of a manufacturer, then, becomes the Inventory account of a merchandiser.

Materials, work in process, and finished goods are assets to the manufacturer and so are reported as current assets on the balance sheet, as Exhibit 22-2 shows. Our goal is to take the information in these inventory accounts to compute the cost of goods manufactured.

Cost of Goods Manufactured

You know the merchandiser's computation of cost of goods sold: beginning inventory + purchases − ending inventory = cost of goods sold. All of a merchandiser's inventory is finished goods. The merchandiser has no materials or work in process inventory. A manufacturer, however, produces its own inventory. **Cost of goods manufactured** is the manufacturer's counterpart to the merchandiser's Purchases account. Therefore, cost of goods manufactured represents the cost of *finished* goods that the business has produced. Exhibit 22-3 shows that

EXHIBIT 22-3 *Cost of Goods Manufactured on the Income Statement*

Manufacturing Firm		Merchandising Firm	
Sales revenue	$XX,XXX	Sales revenue	$XX,XXX
Cost of goods sold:		Cost of goods sold:	
Beginning finished goods inventory	$ 6,000	Beginning inventory	$ 6,000
Cost of goods manufactured	**42,000**	**Purchases . . . .**	**42,000**
Goods available for sale	48,000	Goods available for sale	48,000
Ending finished goods inventory	(8,000)	Ending inventory	(8,000)
Cost of goods sold	40,000	Cost of goods sold	40,000
Gross margin	X,XXX	Gross margin	X,XXX
Operating expenses:		Operating expenses:	
Selling	X,XXX	Selling	X,XXX
General	X,XXX	General	X,XXX
Total operating expenses	X,XXX	Total operating expenses	X,XXX
Net income	$ X,XXX	Net income	$ X,XXX

Cost of Goods Manufactured takes the place of Purchases in computing cost of goods sold. *Otherwise, a manufacturer's income statement is identical to the income statement of a merchandiser.*

Purchases, for a merchandiser, is simply the total cost of all goods bought for resale during the current period. Cost of goods manufactured is more complex. Before we illustrate how to compute this amount, we must introduce some new terms.

Definitions of Key Manufacturing Terms

Direct Materials. To be considered **direct materials,** materials must meet two requirements: (1) the materials must become a physical part of the finished product, and (2) the cost of the materials must be separately and conveniently traceable through the manufacturing process to finished goods. Consider again the athletic-shoe manufacturer. The leather uppers, the rubber and plastic soles, and the laces are among the direct materials. We can trace them *directly* to the finished shoe. Also, we can follow their costs from the purchase of raw materials through work in process to finished goods.

Direct Labor. **Direct labor** is the cost of salaries and wages for the employees who physically convert materials into the company's products. For a shoe manufacturer, direct labor includes the wages of the machine operators and the persons who actually assemble the shoes. For General Motors, direct labor is the pay of employees who work on production lines manufacturing automobiles. The efforts of these persons can be traced *directly* to finished goods.

Factory Overhead. **Factory overhead** includes all manufacturing costs other than direct materials and direct labor. Examples include indirect materials, indirect labor, and other costs, such as factory utilities, repairs, maintenance, rent, insurance, and property taxes and depreciation on the factory building and equipment. Factory overhead is also called *manufacturing overhead* and *indirect manufacturing cost.*

Indirect Materials. The glue and the thread used in the athletic shoes are also materials that become physical parts cf the finished product. However, compared to the cost of the leather uppers and the rubber soles, the glue and thread costs are minor. Measuring the cost of these low-priced materials is difficult for a single pair of shoes. How would a supervisor figure the cost of a brushful of glue? Of the thread used in a shoe? And how useful would this detailed information be? We call the material whose cost cannot conveniently be traced directly to particular finished products **indirect material.** Indirect materials are accounted for as part of factory overhead cost.

Indirect Labor. Other factory labor costs are classified as **indirect labor.** These costs are difficult to trace to specific products. Examples include the pay of forklift operators, janitors, and plant guards. Forklift operators move a wide variety of materials and finished goods around the factory. Plant guards provide security for the entire building. Indirect labor, like indirect materials, is a part of factory overhead.

Two of the major cost elements are sometimes combined in cost terminology as follows. **Prime costs** consist of direct materials plus direct labor. **Conversion costs** consist of direct labor plus factory overhead.

$$\text{Prime costs} \begin{cases} \text{Direct materials} \\ \text{Direct labor} \\ \text{Factory overhead} \end{cases} \text{Conversion costs}$$

Exhibit 22-4 shows the computation of cost of goods manufactured. This statement of cost of goods manufactured is an internal statement, prepared by cost accountants for the business's managers.

EXHIBIT 22-4 *Statement of Cost of Goods Manufactured*

OBJECTIVE 2
Compute cost of goods manufactured

Shoes Unlimited
Statement of Cost of Goods Manufactured
Year Ended December 31, 19X3

Beginning work in process inventory			$ 5,000
Add: Direct materials used:			
Beginning balance	$ 9,000		
Purchases of materials	27,000		
Materials available for use..............	36,000		
Ending balance........................	(22,000)		
Direct materials used......................		$14,000	
Direct labor		19,000	
Factory overhead:			
Indirect materials	$ 1,500		
Indirect labor	3,500		
Depreciation–factory building	2,000		
Depreciation–factory equipment..........	1,000		
Utilities	2,500		
Insurance..............................	1,000		
Property tax	500	12,000	
Total manufacturing costs..................			45,000
Less: Ending work in process inventory			(4,000)
Cost of goods manufactured................			$46,000

OBJECTIVE 3

Diagram the flow of
inventory costs through a
manufacturing company

EXHIBIT 22-5   *Flow of Costs Through a Manufacturing Company—Three Similar Computations*

Direct Materials	Work in Process	Finished Goods
Beginning inventory + Purchases	Beginning inventory + Direct materials used Direct labor Factory overhead	Beginning inventory + Cost of goods manufactured
Direct materials available for use − Ending inventory	Subtotal − Ending inventory	Goods available for sale − Ending inventory
Direct materials used	Cost of goods manufactured	Cost of goods sold ⟶

The authors are indebted to Judith Cassidy for this presentation.

Computation of cost of goods manufactured starts with the work in process inventory ($5,000) at the beginning of the period. These goods become complete in the manufacturing process during the current period, so their cost becomes part of cost of goods manufactured. To this amount we add the three components of manufacturing cost: direct materials used ($14,000), direct labor ($19,000), and factory overhead cost ($12,000). Exhibit 22-4 looks closely at direct materials used. Direct labor is simply the total direct labor cost incurred during the period. Factory overhead is the sum of various costs. Direct materials used, direct labor, and factory overhead total $45,000, which is the **total manufacturing cost** incurred during the period. We subtract ending work in process inventory—because cost of goods manufactured refers to the cost of *finished goods manufactured*—to get $46,000.

Exhibit 22-5 diagrams the flow of costs through a manufacturing system. It reveals a similar computational format at all three stages—direct materials, work in process, and finished goods. Observe that the final amount at each stage flows into the next stage.

The cost of direct materials used is simply beginning direct materials plus purchases minus the ending balance. The cost of direct materials used becomes part of cost of goods manufactured, which is included in cost of goods sold. Study the exhibit carefully. It should ease the computational burden of manufacturing accounting.

Product Costs and Period Costs

A manufacturer's operations revolve around its inventory and its production process. To keep inventory costs separate from all the other costs of running a business, accountants often distinguish between *product costs* and *period costs*.

Product costs are identified with goods purchased or manufactured for resale. These costs are also called *inventoriable costs* because they arise as the business creates inventory. Product costs include materials, direct labor, and factory overhead. Materials are clearly a product cost because materials are assets that go into the manufacture of inventory. Direct labor may not look like a product cost because it includes wages, which merchandisers account for as an expense. But to a manufacturer, direct labor is a product cost because factory labor goes into the production of inventory. Likewise, factory overhead appears to be an expense because it includes depreciation, insurance, utilities, and property taxes on the factory building. However, because the factory is used to produce inventory, factory overhead is a product cost. Product costs become expense (cost of goods sold) when the inventory is sold.

Period costs are never traced through the inventory accounts. Instead, we account for them as operating expenses—selling expenses or general and administrative expenses—during the current period, without ever being classified as inventory. Examples of period costs include sales commission expense, delivery expense, advertising expense, and income tax expense. The distinction between the two categories of costs is illustrated as follows:

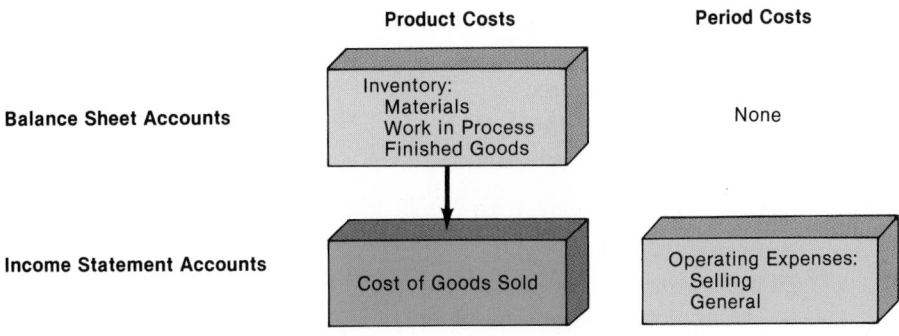

Perpetual and Periodic Inventory Systems _____

Chapter 9 compared the accounting for inventories under the periodic system and the perpetual system. Most manufacturers use the perpetual system because they need a continuous record of materials, work in process, and finished goods on hand. The perpetual records help managers control operations and also provide the data for interim financial statements. Physical counts of inventories are taken at least annually to check the accuracy of the records.

Manufacturers that use a periodic inventory system follow the general accounting procedures that merchandisers use, as discussed in Chapter 9. In this chapter we concentrate on the perpetual system because it is more commonly used by manufacturers.

Summary Questions for Your Review

1. What inventory accounts does a manufacturer have that a merchandising entity does not need?

2. What is the manufacturer's counterpart to a merchandiser's Purchases account?

3. Show how to compute cost of goods manufactured. Use single amounts for direct materials used, direct labor, and factory overhead.

4. Diagram the flow of costs through a manufacturing company.
5. Identify the following as either a product cost or a period cost:
    a. Depreciation on factory equipment
    b. Depreciation on salespersons' automobiles
    c. Insurance on factory building
    d. Factory manager's salary
    e. Marketing manager's salary

ANSWERS TO REVIEW QUESTIONS

1. Materials Inventory, Work in Process Inventory, and Finished Goods Inventory
2. Cost of goods manufactured
3. Cost of goods manufactured:

Beginning work in process inventory		$ 5,000
Add: Direct materials used	$14,000	
Direct labor	19,000	
Factory overhead	8,000	41,000
Total manufacturing costs		46,000
Less: Ending work in process inventory		(4,000)
Cost of goods manufactured		$42,000

4. Flow of costs through a manufacturing company:

Direct Materials	Work in Process	Finished Goods
Beginning inventory + Purchases	Beginning inventory → + Direct materials used Direct labor Factory overhead	Beginning inventory → + Cost of goods manufactured
Direct materials available for use − Ending inventory	Subtotal − Ending inventory	Goods available for sale − Ending inventory
Direct materials used ┘	Cost of goods manufactured ┘	Cost of goods sold ⟶

5. a. Product cost; b. Period cost; c. Product cost; d. Product cost;
   e. Period cost

Cost Accounting and Its Uses by Management _____

As mentioned previously, managers use cost accounting (1) in *controlling costs* and (2) in *product costing* — determining the manufacturing cost of its products. Tight control is an obvious feature of good management. Product costing is important because managers want to know about the relative profitability of the company's various products.

Consider two companies that manufacture the same product. Company A has an inadequate cost accounting system. Its managers make decisions by hunches and guesses. Company B has a carefully designed cost system, and its managers keep tight reins on the cost of the manufacturing process. Company B budgets the costs of products for control purposes, and its managers compare budgeted amounts to actual results. Where actual costs exceed the budget, managers make the adjustments necessary to correct the situation. Company B, then, probably produces goods at lower cost than Company A. As a result, B is likely to be more profitable than A. Indeed, the managers of Company A may not even be able to pinpoint the cost of manufacturing their inventory. This is true more often than you might imagine. *The Wall Street Journal, Business Week,* and other publications include articles about companies that have failed because of inadequate cost accounting.

There are two main types of accounting systems for product costing: *job order costing* and *process costing.* This chapter discusses job order costing, and the next chapter covers process costing. Because these chapters deal primarily with inventory costs, our discussions emphasize product costs, not period costs. *Manufacturers account for and control period costs the same way that merchandisers do.*

Job Order Costing

Job order costing is an accounting system used by companies that manufacture products (1) as individual units or (2) in distinct batches that receive varying degrees of attention and skill. Industries using job order costing include aircraft, furniture, construction, and machinery. Their inventory items are unique or few of a kind, differing from the identical products that roll off a production line, such as tubes of toothpaste, boxes of cereal, and rolls of carpet. Mass-produced inventories are accounted for by the process costing system, discussed in the next chapter.

The essential feature of job order costing (often shortened to *job costing*) is the allocation of costs to a specific job. (The job may be a production order, work order, project, or batch.) The job may consist of a single unit, like a bridge built by a construction contractor, or a group of similar units in a distinct batch, like 10 recliner chairs built by a furniture manufacturer. We illustrate job order costing for a manufacturing situation, but the system applies to other types of business, such as an auto-repair shop (the job is one automobile needing repair), a research organization (the job is a research project), and an accounting firm (the job is a tax return).

In a job cost system, the job is the focus, so the manufacturer accumulates materials, labor, and overhead costs by job. Cost control is the key to earning a profit on each job. If cost is too high, profit is reduced or eliminated. Managers monitor each job to help ensure that its cost stays within the budgeted limits.

OBJECTIVE 4
Describe a job order costing system

Job Costing Illustrated

Consider the Ramirez Furniture Company, which has a job order costing system with the following inventories on December 31, 19X4:

Materials inventory (many kinds)	$20,000
Work in process inventory (5 jobs)	29,000
Finished goods inventory (unsold units from 2 jobs)	12,000

The following is a summary of relevant transactions for the year 19X5:

1.	Materials purchased on account	$320,000
2.	Direct materials requisitioned for manufacturing	285,000
	Indirect materials requisitioned for manufacturing	40,000
3.	Factory wages incurred	335,000
4.	Direct labor on jobs	250,000
	Indirect labor to support factory activities	85,000
5.	Factory overhead (depreciation on plant and equipment)	50,000
6.	Factory overhead (factory utilities)	20,000
7.	Factory overhead (factory insurance)	5,000
8.	Factory overhead (property taxes – factory)	10,000
9.	Factory overhead applied to jobs	200,000
10.	Cost of goods completed and transferred to finished goods inventory	740,000
11.	Sales on account	996,000
	Cost of goods sold	734,000

The accounting for these transactions will now be explained, step by step.

Job Cost Record

The bulk of the work in cost accounting is a detailed recording and summarization of source documents such as requisitions, time tickets, and invoices. The document used to accumulate and control cost in a job order system is a **job cost record.** This cost record lists the materials, labor, and overhead costs charged to the job. It is the basic internal document used by management to control costs in this system. Exhibit 22-6 illustrates a job cost record. It includes sections for direct materials, direct labor, and overhead costs.

This cost record shows that for Job 293, the direct materials cost $300, direct labor cost $500, and factory overhead cost $400, for a total of $1,200. Each chair cost the manufacturer $120 ($1,200/10). Managers would use this information by comparing these actual costs to budgeted amounts. Suppose the direct materials budget for this job was $270. The $300 actual cost of direct materials exceeds budget, so managers would determine the reason for the cost overrun and seek to improve future performance. The remainder of the chapter discusses how to account for the direct materials, direct labor, and factory overhead costs.

The job cost record in Exhibit 22-6 is the basic record for product costing. A file of current job cost records is the subsidiary ledger for the general ledger account, Work in Process Inventory. As each job begins, a job cost record is prepared. As units are worked on, costs are applied to the products. We now illustrate these accounting procedures.

Accounting for Materials in a Job Cost System

Manufacturing companies that use job order costing tend to have relatively low inventories. Only when they receive an order do they acquire the added materials needed to fill the order, produce the goods, and deliver the merchandise. Suppose Ramirez, our furniture manufacturer, receives an order for 10 recliner chairs. The company may need to buy additional lumber, so Ramirez sends a *purchase order* to a lumber supplier.

EXHIBIT 22-6 *Job Cost Record*

Job Cost Record

Job No. 293

Customer Name and Address Macy's New York City

Job Description 10 recliner chairs

Date Promised 7-31	Date Started 7-24	Date Completed 7-29

Date	Direct Materials — Requisition Numbers	Amount	Direct Labor — Time Ticket Numbers	Amount	Date	Rate	Amount
19X5 7-24	334	$ 90	236,251,258	$150	7-29	80% of Direct labor	$400
25	338	180	264,269,273,291	300			
28	347	30	305	50			

Overall Cost Summary

Direct materials ...... $ 300
Direct labor 500
Factory overhead 400

| Totals | | $300 | | $500 | Total Job Cost ...... $1,200 |

In practice, general ledger entries are made monthly. To offer a sweeping overview, however, we use a summary entry for the entire year 19X5. Our first entry is for purchases of materials (data from top of page 864):

OBJECTIVE 5
Account for materials in a job order costing system

1. Materials Inventory 320,000
   Accounts Payable............................ 320,000

Ramirez receives the lumber and stores it. Control over materials in storage is established with a subsidiary materials ledger. This ledger holds perpetual inven-

EXHIBIT 22-7 *Materials Ledger Record*

Materials Ledger Record

Item No. B-220   Description Lumber/Recliner chairs

Date	Received — Rec. Report No.	Units	Price	Total Price	Used — Mat. Req. No.	Units	Price	Total Price	Balance — Units	Price	Total Price
19X5 7-20									30	$9.00	$270
7-23	678	20	$9.00	$180					50	9.00	450
7-24					334	10	$9.00	$90	40	9.00	360

EXHIBIT 22-8 *Materials Inventory Accounts*

General Ledger

Subsidiary Ledger
Materials Ledger

Materials Inventory

XXX

Lumber			
Date	Received	Used	Balance
7-24			$360

Padding			
Date	Received	Used	Balance
7-24			$160

Upholstery Fabric			
Date	Received	Used	Balance
7-24			$390

Nails			
Date	Received	Used	Balance
7-24			$40

Thread			
Date	Received	Used	Balance
7-24			$20

Other Materials			
Date	Received	Used	Balance
7-24			$XX

$XXX

Total balances equal the balance
in the general ledger account.

tory records, which list the quantity and the cost of manufacturing materials received and used. They show the cost of materials on hand at all times. Exhibit 22-7 shows a materials ledger record for the lumber (only) that goes into the manufacture of chairs.

Materials received are logged in by receiving report number (abbreviated as *Rec. Report No.* in Exhibit 22-7). Materials used in the product are recorded by materials requisition number *(Mat. Req. No.)*. Management can use these underlying data to follow the flow of materials through the production process and so control operations on a day-to-day basis.

The general ledger has a Materials Inventory account. This account is supported by a subsidiary ledger—the materials ledger—that includes a separate record for each raw material. Exhibit 22-8 illustrates the general ledger account and the materials ledger for Ramirez. The balance of Materials Inventory in the general ledger equals the sum of the balances in the materials ledger.

After materials are purchased and stored, the manufacturing process is set in motion by a document called a **materials requisition,** the formal title for a request prepared by manufacturing personnel. In effect, they ask that the lumber be moved from storage to the factory so work can begin. Exhibit 22-9 illustrates a

EXHIBIT 22-9 *Material Requisition*

	Materials Requisition No. 334			
Date 7-24-X5			Job No. 293	
Item No.	Item	Quantity	Unit Price	Amount
B-220	Lumber/Recliner chairs	10	$9.00	$90

materials requisition for the lumber needed to manufacture the 10 recliner chairs that make up Job 293. (See the job description in Exhibit 22-6 and the "Used" section in Exhibit 22-7.) The details in materials requisitions are posted to job cost records.

Direct and Indirect Materials

To introduce the main points of manufacturing accounting, the first half of this chapter omitted some of the detailed procedures. One such step is the way to account for *direct* materials separately from *indirect* materials. Recall that the cost of indirect materials is part of Factory Overhead. The flow of materials costs is diagrammed as follows (data from the top of page 864):

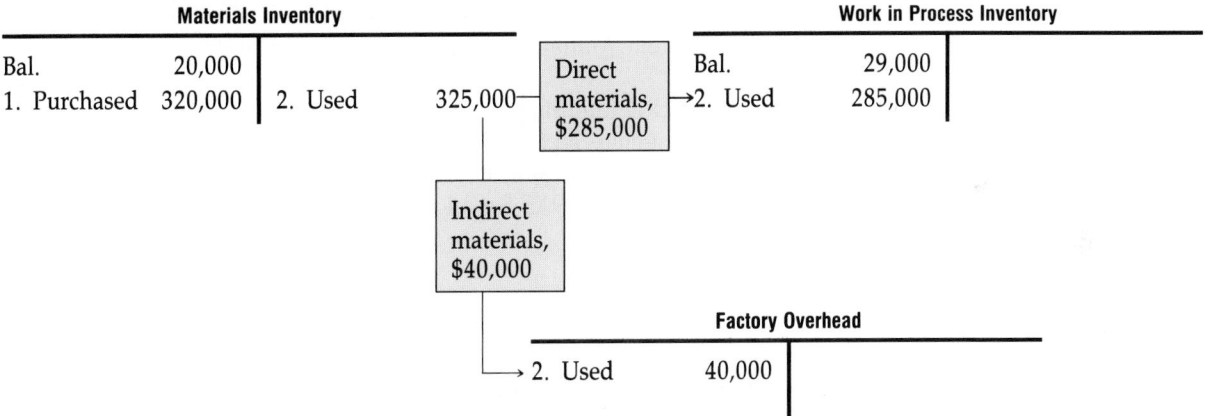

Materials Inventory is debited for the cost of all materials purchased, direct *and* indirect. Observe that the Materials Inventory account in Exhibit 22-8 includes the cost of direct materials—lumber, padding, and upholstery fabric—and the cost of indirect materials—nails and thread. When either type of materials is used in production, Materials Inventory is credited. For direct materials, the debit is made directly to Work in Process Inventory. For indirect materials, the debit is made to Factory Overhead. (Recall that factory overhead includes all manufacturing costs other than direct materials and direct labor.)

Of course, the furniture manufacturer will work on many jobs over the course of the accounting period. At regular intervals (commonly a month but for our illustration a year), accountants collect the data from the materials requisitions to make a single journal entry, like the following 19X5 entry for Ramirez:

2.	Work in Process Inventory	285,000	
	Factory Overhead	40,000	
	Materials Inventory		325,000

As Exhibit 22-9 indicates, $90 of the direct materials relates to Job 293. The Ramirez computer would enter the $90 on the job cost record.

Job Cost Record

Job. No. 293

Customer Name and Address   Macy's New York City

Job Description   10 recliner chairs

| Date Promised 7-31 | Date Started 7-24 | Date Completed |

Date	Direct Materials		Direct Labor		Factory Overhead Costs		
	Requisition No.	Amount	Time Ticket No.	Amount	Date	Rate	Amount
19X5							
7-24	334	$90					

Overall Cost Summary

Direct materials ...... $
Direct labor ....
Factory overhead .....

| Totals | | | | | Total Job Cost .... $ |

Accounting for Labor in a Job Cost System

Control over labor cost in a job cost system is established through time tickets and payroll registers, as discussed in Chapter 11. Exhibit 22-10 illustrates a time ticket used in a job cost system. Managers use its data to charge labor cost to a particular job.

The **labor time ticket** identifies the employee, the hours spent on a particular job, and the labor cost charged to the job. Time tickets are accumulated by job to determine the labor cost to be allocated to each job.

The company's entry for 19X5 for all factory wages for all jobs is

3. Factory Wages 335,000
    Wages Payable 335,000

OBJECTIVE 6

Account for labor in a job order costing system

This entry records the actual labor cost incurred. The separation of direct labor and indirect labor is accomplished as shown in the diagram on the following page:

EXHIBIT 22-10 *Labor Time Ticket*

Labor Time Ticket   No. 251

EMPLOYEE Jay Barlow   Date 7-24

JOB   293

Time:		Rate $8.00
Started	1:00	Cost of labor
Stopped	8:30	charged to job $60.00
Elapsed	7:30	

Employee   Jay Barlow

Supervisor   G. Dean Childres

Direct and Indirect Labor

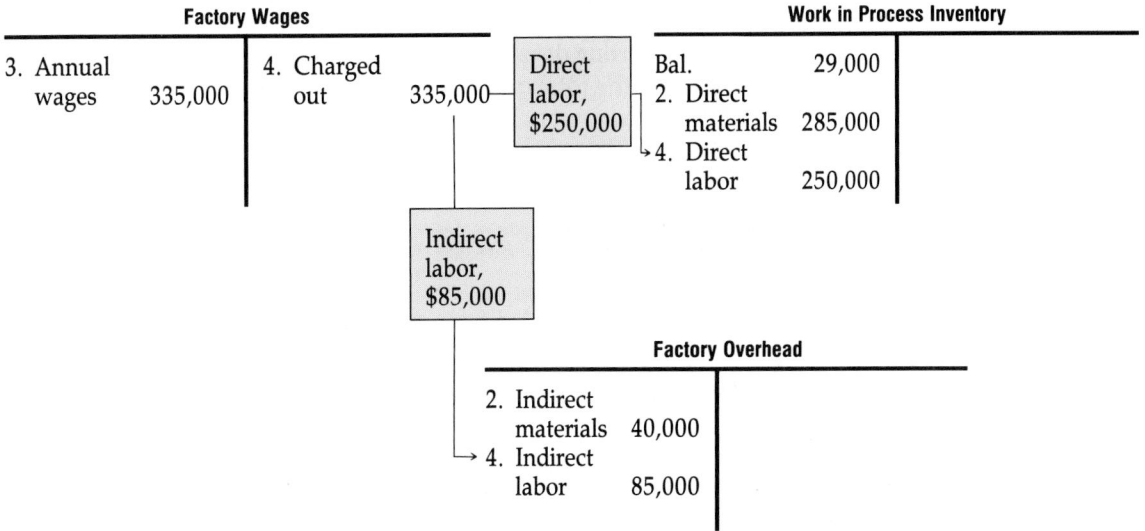

After the factory wages have been recorded, direct labor is debited directly to Work in Process Inventory. Indirect labor passes through the Factory Overhead account en route to Work in Process Inventory. The transfer of labor cost to production results in a credit to the Factory Wages account. The following entry allocates factory wages to Work in Process Inventory and Factory Overhead:

4.	Work in Process Inventory	250,000	
	Factory Overhead.................................	85,000	
	Factory Wages		335,000

This entry brings the balance in Factory Wages to zero, its transferred balance now allocated between Work in Process Inventory (direct labor) and Factory Overhead (indirect labor).

Assume that $150 of the direct labor cost relates to Job 293. The Ramirez computer would enter Job 293's direct labor on the job cost record. The $150 amount in the accompanying job cost record includes Jay Barlow's wages of $60 (ticket 251, Exhibit 22-10) and the labor costs entered onto time tickets 236 and 258.

Job Cost Record

Job No. 293

Customer Name and Address   Macy's New York City

Job Description   10 recliner chairs

Date Promised 7-31	Date Started 7-24	Date Completed

Date	Direct Materials		Direct Labor		Factory Overhead Costs		
	Requisition No.	Amount	Time Ticket No.	Amount	Date	Rate	Amount
19X5 7-24	334	$ 90	236,251,258	$150			

Overall Cost Summary

Direct materials..... $
Direct labor........
Factory overhead....

Totals

Total Job Cost...... $

The Work in Process Inventory account now contains the cost of direct materials and direct labor charged to Job 293—and the costs of many other jobs as well. Work in Process Inventory serves as a control account, with the job cost records giving the supporting details for each job. The balance in Work in Process Inventory should equal the total of the individual job costs, in the same manner illustrated for Materials Inventory in Exhibit 22-8. The job cost records thus serve as a subsidiary ledger for the general ledger balance in Work in Process Inventory.

We summarize the accounting for materials and labor just illustrated:

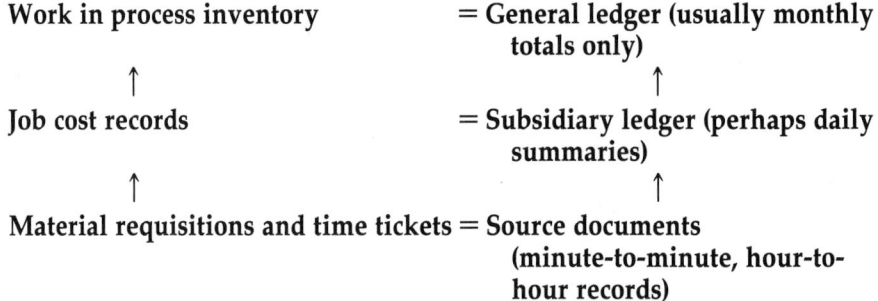

Work in process inventory   **= General ledger (usually monthly totals only)**

↑   ↑

Job cost records   **= Subsidiary ledger (perhaps daily summaries)**

↑   ↑

Material requisitions and time tickets = Source documents (minute-to-minute, hour-to-hour records)

We see that accounting data are most condensed in the general ledger and most detailed in the source documents.

In practice, the daily accounting duties are carried out using source documents and subsidiary ledgers. Copies of the source documents are independently summarized and are usually journalized and posted to the general ledger only once a month.

Accounting for Factory Overhead in a Job Cost System

Materials requisitions and labor time tickets make it easy to identify direct materials and direct labor with a specific job. Factory overhead, on the other hand, includes a variety of costs that cannot be linked to a particular job. How do we allocate overhead cost to jobs?

Overhead costs are recorded as incurred. The following entries—depreciation on plant and equipment, factory utilities, insurance, and property taxes—are typical. Note that all these overhead costs are debited to a single account—Factory Overhead in the general ledger. The account titles in parentheses in the following entries indicate the subsidiary accounts that are debited in an overhead subsidiary ledger. Budgeting these individual items and then keeping track of their actual amounts help managers control overhead costs.

OBJECTIVE 7

Account for factory overhead in a job order costing system

5.	Factory Overhead (Depreciation–Plant and Equipment)	50,000	
	Accumulated Depreciation–Plant and Equipment.		50,000
6.	Factory Overhead (Factory Utilities)	20,000	
	Cash		20,000
7.	Factory Overhead (Factory Insurance)	5,000	
	Prepaid Insurance–Factory		5,000
8.	Factory Overhead (Property Taxes–Factory)	10,000	
	Property Tax Payable.		10,000

The Factory Overhead account now contains all the overhead costs of the period:

Factory Overhead

2.	Indirect materials	40,000	
4.	Indirect labor	85,000	
5.	Depreciation–		
	plant and equipment	50,000	
6.	Factory utilities	20,000	
7.	Factory insurance	5,000	
8.	Property taxes-factory	10,000	
	Total actual overhead cost	210,000	

It would be virtually impossible to say that a specific amount of overhead (for example, the cost of heating the factory) was incurred on any particular job. Yet factory overhead costs certainly add to the costs of producing goods. We now discuss how accountants apply overhead in job costing.

The Budgeted Rate in Applying Overhead

Management wants to tie overhead cost to the costs of manufacturing the business's different products. After all, indirect materials, indirect labor, and all the other individual accounts that make up factory overhead contribute to product costs. And if product costs are to help management in product pricing, income determination, and inventory valuation, they must be timely as well as accurate.

The most accurate application of overhead could be made only at the end of the year, after actual results are determined. However, this timing would be too late. Managers want product-cost information throughout the year, not only at the end of the period. To meet these needs, accountants usually budget overhead application rates — that is, they compute a rate in advance of production. The usual steps in applying factory overhead using an annual averaging process follow.

1. Select a **cost application base,** which is a common denominator linking costs among all products. This application base should be the best available measure of the cause-and-effect relationship between overhead costs and production volume. Direct labor costs generally rise and fall proportionately with changes in production volume, and direct labor dollars are often chosen as the cost application base. Other examples include machine hours and direct labor hours.

2. Prepare a budget for the planning period, ordinarily a year. The two key items are (a) budgeted total overhead and (b) budgeted total volume of the cost application base, which is direct labor cost in our Ramirez illustration.

3. Compute the **budgeted factory overhead rate** by dividing the total budgeted overhead by the cost application base.

4. Obtain the actual application base data (such as direct labor cost) as the year unfolds.

5. Apply the budgeted overhead to the jobs by multiplying the budgeted rate times the actual application base data.

6. At the end of the year, account for any differences between the amount of overhead actually incurred and overhead applied to products.

The Ramirez forecast is based on a volume of activity expressed in direct labor cost. Assume detailed forecasts predict total overhead of $212,000 for the next year at an anticipated $265,000 direct-labor-cost level of activity. The budgeted factory overhead rate is computed as follows:

$$\text{Budgeted factory overhead rate} = \frac{\text{Total budgeted overhead}}{\text{Total budgeted direct labor cost}} = \frac{\$212,000}{\$265,000} = .80 \text{ or } 80\%$$

The 80 percent rate would be used for costing job orders.

To *apply overhead* means to debit Work in Process Inventory for the cost of overhead and to credit the Factory Overhead account. The overhead application rate is used to compute the amount of overhead to apply to a specific job. In our example, for each dollar of direct labor debited to Work in Process Inventory, 80¢ in overhead cost is also debited to that account. If the actual direct labor cost of a job is $800 (see Step 4), 80 percent of that amount, or $640, is debited to Work in Process Inventory as factory overhead.

The budgeted factory overhead rate is applied to all jobs uniformly throughout the year. After the direct materials and direct labor costs have been applied to a job, the overhead is applied, as shown in the accompanying record for Job 293. Recall that total direct labor cost for the job is $500. With an overhead application rate of 80 percent of direct labor, the amount of overhead to charge to Job 293 is $400 ($500 × .80).

Job Cost Record

Job No.   293

Customer Name and Address   Macy's, New York City

Job Description   10 recliner chairs

Date Promised 7-31	Date Started 7-24	Date Completed 7-29

Date	Direct Materials		Direct Labor		Factory Overhead Costs		
	Requisition No.	Amount	Time Ticket Nos.	Amount	Date	Rate	Amount
19X5 7-24 25 28	334 338 347	$ 90 180 30	236,251,258 264,269,273,291 305	$150 300 50	7-29	80% of Direct labor	$400
					Overall Cost Summary		
					Direct materials..... $ 300 Direct labor.......... 500 Factory overhead..... 400		
Totals		$300		$500	Total Job Cost...... $1,200		

The job cost record for Job 293 is complete. It provides the detailed subsidiary ledger support for the debits to the general ledger account, Work in Process Inventory.

Of course, similar applications of overhead have been made for other jobs in 19X5. The total overhead applied to all jobs worked on during 19X5 was 80 percent of $250,000 direct labor, .80 × $250,000 = $200,000. The journal entry to apply overhead to production is

9. Work in Process Inventory 200,000
        Factory Overhead............................ 200,000

Trace this application of Factory Overhead to Work in Process Inventory.

Factory Overhead						Work in Process Inventory		
2.	40,000	9. Applied	200,000			Bal.	29,000	
4.	85,000					2.	285,000	
5.	50,000			Factory		4.	250,000	
6.	20,000			Overhead →9.		9.	200,000	
7.	5,000			Applied				
8.	10,000							
Actual costs	210,000							
Bal.	10,000							

An additional detail exists in accounting for overhead cost. First, however, we need to discuss accounting for finished goods and the sale of inventory.

Accounting for Finished Goods, Sales, and Cost of Goods Sold

As each job is completed, its cost is transferred from Work in Process Inventory to Finished Goods Inventory. The completion date is written on the job cost record, which is compared to the budget and filed away. Then, sales of finished goods are recorded as they occur.

A summary entry for goods completed in 19X5 follows:

10. Finished Goods Inventory 740,000
        Work in Process Inventory 740,000

In turn, familiar entries would be made for sales and cost of goods sold.

11. Accounts Receivable 996,000
        Sales Revenue................................ 996,000
    Cost of Goods Sold 734,000
        Finished Goods Inventory..................... 734,000

The second entry is needed to maintain the perpetual inventory record. (Only the first entry is needed as sales are made in a periodic inventory system.)

The key accounts for product costs now show:

Work in Process Inventory				Finished Goods Inventory				Cost of Goods Sold	
Bal.	29,000	10.	740,000	Bal.	12,000	11.	734,000 →11.	734,000	
2.	285,000		→10.	740,000					
4.	250,000								
9.	200,000		Bal.	18,000					
Bal.	24,000								

Disposing of Overapplied and Underapplied Overhead

The application of factory overhead cost to production will usually not bring to zero the balance in the Factory Overhead account. This account is debited for *actual cost* and credited for *estimated amounts*—equal to the budgeted factory overhead rate multiplied by the actual direct labor cost.

The total debits to Factory Overhead for the year may not equal the total credits to the account. A *debit* balance remaining in the Factory Overhead account is called **underapplied overhead.** In our illustration, actual overhead ($210,000 debited to the account) exceeded the amount applied to jobs ($200,000 credited to the account) during the period, which resulted in $10,000 in underapplied overhead. Conversely, a *credit* balance, called **overapplied overhead,** results when applied overhead exceeds the actual amount. Accountants usually ignore over- and underapplied overhead during the year and dispose of it at year end. The entry to close the Factory Overhead account adjusts the records to account for the actual overhead cost incurred during the year. The more accurate the budgeted overhead rate, the less the difference between actual and applied amounts of factory overhead for the year.

If the amount of over- or underapplied overhead is *significant,* it often is allocated to Work in Process, Finished Goods, and Cost of Goods Sold based on their relative balances before the allocation. For example, suppose 15 percent of the year's production is still in process, 25 percent is finished but unsold, and the remaining 60 percent has been sold. If *overapplied* overhead at the end of the period is $50,000—a significant amount—the Factory Overhead Account will have a $50,000 credit balance. The entry to dispose of this credit balance debits Factory Overhead as follows:

Dec. 31	Factory Overhead	50,000	
	Work in Process Inventory ($50,000 × .15).....		7,500
	Finished Goods Inventory ($50,000 × .25)		12,500
	Cost of Goods Sold ($50,000 × .60)...........		30,000

This entry removes the $50,000 credit balance from Factory Overhead. It also adjusts Work in Process, Finished Goods, and Cost of Goods Sold to actual costs.

If the over- or underapplied amount is *insignificant,* it can be closed to Cost of Goods Sold without seriously affecting the financial statements. Suppose actual overhead cost exceeded the amount of overhead applied to jobs. In our illustration the year's production resulted in the following summary activity in the Factory Overhead account:

Factory Overhead

Actual	210,000	Applied	200,000
Balance—Underapplied	10,000		

The $10,000 is minor relative to the $210,000 of actual overhead cost for the year. Moreover, the Cost of Goods Sold balance ($734,000) dwarfs the Work in Process Inventory and Finished Goods Inventory balances ($24,000 and $18,000, respectively). This means that an allocation of $10,000 to the three accounts would have tiny effects on the balances in ending work in process and finished goods. Therefore, we may close this underapplied overhead to Cost of Goods Sold as follows:

Dec. 31	Cost of Goods Sold	10,000	
(Entry 12)	Factory Overhead		10,000

Overview of Illustration

Exhibit 22-11 provides an overview of the Ramirez job order costing illustration. The key Inventory accounts and Cost of Goods Sold are displayed at the top. Accounts for Factory Wages and Factory Overhead also are shown. The relationships of subsidiary material records to Materials Inventory and of subsidiary job cost records to Work in Process Inventory are also illustrated.

As Exhibit 22-11 makes clear, the ending balance sheet accounts would be

Materials Inventory......................	$15,000
Work in Process Inventory................	24,000
Finished Goods Inventory	18,000

The condensed income statement for 19X5 would report the following through gross margin:

Sales	$996,000
Cost of goods sold	734,000
Gross margin (or gross profit)	$262,000

As mentioned previously, the remainder of the manufacturer's income statement (operating expenses, other revenue and expense, and net income) is the same as for a merchandising entity.

Summary Problem for Your Review

Hillis Incorporated had the following inventories at the end of 19X4:

Materials	$20,000
Work in Process	17,000
Finished Goods.........................	11,000

During January 19X5 Hillis completed the following transactions:

1. Purchased materials on account, $31,000.
2. Requisitioned (placed into production) direct materials, $39,000.
3. Factory payroll incurred, $40,000.
4. Allocated factory labor as follows: direct labor, 90 percent; indirect labor, 10 percent.
5. Requisitioned (placed into production) indirect materials, $3,000.
6. Incurred other factory overhead, $13,000 (credit Accounts Payable).
7. Applied factory overhead to product as 50 percent of direct labor.
8. Completed production, $99,000.
9. Sold goods on account, $172,000; cost of goods sold, $91,400.
10. Closed ending balance of Factory Overhead to Cost of Goods Sold.

EXHIBIT 22-11 Job Order Costing, General Flow of Costs *(in thousands)*

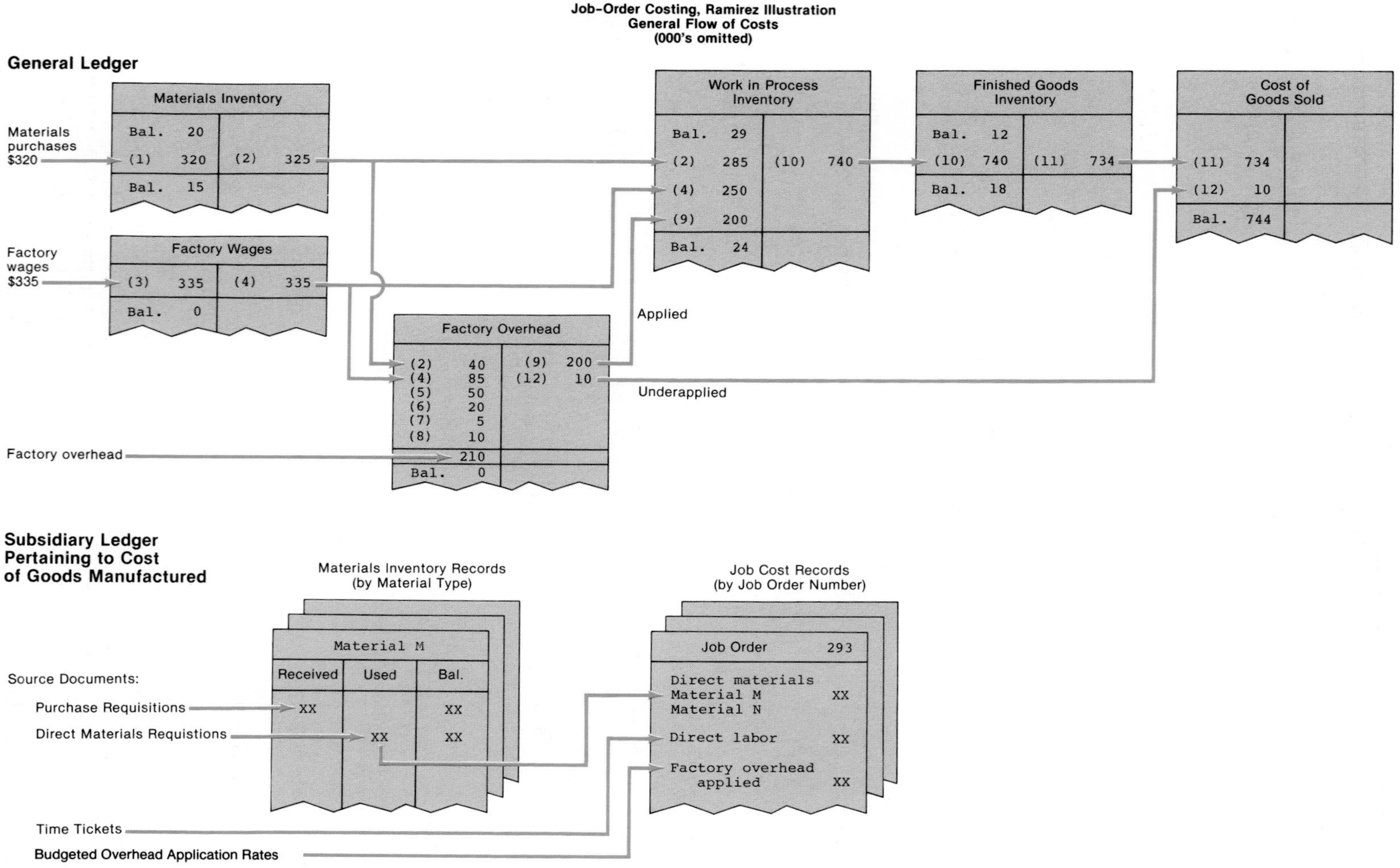

Job–Order Costing, Ramirez Illustration
General Flow of Costs
(000's omitted)

General Ledger

Materials Inventory

Bal. 20	
(1) 320	(2) 325
Bal. 15	

Materials purchases $320

Factory Wages

(3) 335	(4) 335
Bal. 0	

Factory wages $335

Work in Process Inventory

Bal. 29	
(2) 285	(10) 740
(4) 250	
(9) 200	
Bal. 24	

Finished Goods Inventory

Bal. 12	
(10) 740	(11) 734
Bal. 18	

Cost of Goods Sold

(11) 734	
(12) 10	
Bal. 744	

Factory Overhead

(2) 40	(9) 200
(4) 85	(12) 10
(5) 50	
(6) 20	
(7) 5	
(8) 10	
210	0
Bal.	

Applied

Underapplied

Factory overhead

Subsidiary Ledger Pertaining to Cost of Goods Manufactured

Materials Inventory Records (by Material Type)

Material M

Received	Used	Bal.
XX		XX
	XX	XX

Job Cost Records (by Job Order Number)

Job Order 293

Direct materials	
Material M	XX
Material N	XX
Direct labor	XX
Factory overhead applied	XX

Source Documents:

Purchase Requisitions

Direct Materials Requistions

Time Tickets

Budgeted Overhead Application Rates

Required

1. Record the transactions in the general journal.
2. Determine the ending balances in the three inventory accounts and Cost of Goods Sold.

SOLUTION TO REVIEW PROBLEM

Requirement 1 (Journal entries)

1.	Materials Inventory...............................	31,000	
	Accounts Payable		31,000
2.	Work in Process Inventory.......................	39,000	
	Materials Inventory.........................		39,000
3.	Factory Wages....................................	40,000	
	Wages Payable		40,000
4.	Work in Process Inventory ($40,000 × .90)...........	36,000	
	Factory Overhead ($40,000 × .10).................	4,000	
	Factory Wages.............................		40,000
5.	Factory Overhead	3,000	
	Materials Inventory.........................		3,000
6.	Factory Overhead	13,000	
	Accounts Payable		13,000
7.	Work in Process Inventory ($36,000 × .50)...........	18,000	
	Factory Overhead		18,000
8.	Finished Goods Inventory	99,000	
	Work in Process Inventory		99,000
9.	Accounts Receivable	172,000	
	Sales Revenue		172,000
	Cost of Goods Sold.............................	91,400	
	Finished Goods Inventory		91,400
10.	Cost of Goods Sold.............................	2,000	
	Factory Overhead		2,000

Balance in Factory Overhead for entry 10:

Factory Overhead

(4)	4,000	(7)	18,000
(5)	3,000		
(6)	13,000		
Bal.	2,000		

Requirement 2 (Ending balances)

Materials Inventory

Bal.	20,000	(2)	39,000
(1)	31,000	(5)	3,000
Bal.	9,000		

Work in Process Inventory

Bal.	17,000	(8)	99,000
(2)	39,000		
(4)	36,000		
(7)	18,000		
Bal.	11,000		

Finished Goods Inventory				Cost of Goods Sold		
Bal.	11,000	(9)	91,400	(9)	91,400	
(8)	99,000			(10)	2,000	
Bal.	18,600			Bal.	93,400	

Summary

Manufacturing companies use separate inventory accounts for raw materials, work in process, and finished goods. The *Materials Inventory* account carries the cost of direct and indirect materials that are held for use in production. The *Work in Process Inventory* account shows the cost of goods that are still in the manufacturing process and not yet complete. *Finished Goods Inventory* represents completed goods that have not yet been sold. This account corresponds to the single inventory account of a merchandising business.

A manufacturer obtains inventory for resale by producing the goods. The manufacturer's *Cost of Goods Manufactured* account replaces the purchases account of a merchandiser. Otherwise, a manufacturer's income statement resembles the income statement of a merchandiser.

Direct materials include all the important materials used to make the product. *Direct labor* is the cost of employing people who physically produce the company's product. These two costs are traced directly to finished goods. *Factory overhead* includes all other manufacturing costs, including *indirect materials* and *indirect labor*.

Manufacturers keep inventory costs separate from all the other costs of running the business. *Product costs* are those identified with inventory. *Period costs* are accounted for as operating expenses and are never traced through the inventory accounts.

Cost accounting provides information for controlling operations and for product costing. In a *job order costing system*—designed to account for products manufactured as individual units or in batches—costs are accumulated for specific jobs. A *job cost record* lists the materials, labor, and overhead costs of completing the job. In a job cost system this document is the basic internal management device for accumulating and controlling costs. It serves as the subsidiary record for Work in Process Inventory. The cost of materials is traced via materials ledger cards. Labor costs are traced by time tickets.

The Factory Overhead account, which includes many different costs, is debited for actual costs incurred. Overhead cost is applied to product at a budgeted rate usually stated as a percentage of direct labor cost. At the end of the period, any *underapplied* or *overapplied overhead* is closed.

Self-Study Questions

Test your understanding of the chapter by marking the best answer for each of the following questions.

1. Which of the following is an inventory account of a manufacturer but not of a merchandiser? *(p. 857)*
   a. Cost of goods manufactured
   b. Merchandise inventory
   c. Work in process
   d. Direct labor

2. Cost of goods manufactured is used to compute *(p. 858)*
   a. Cost of goods sold
   b. Factory overhead applied
   c. Direct materials used
   d. Finished goods inventory

3. Beginning work in process inventory is $35,000; manufacturing costs for the period total $140,000; and ending work in process inventory is $20,000. What is the cost of goods manufactured? *(p. 859)*

a. $125,000   c. $175,000

b. $155,000   d. $195,000

4. Which of the following is a period cost? *(p. 861)*
   a. Materials inventory   c. Factory overhead
   b. Direct labor   d. Selling expense

5. Job order costing would be an appropriate system to account for the manufacture of *(p. 863)*
   a. Aircraft   c. Zippers
   b. Matches   d. Cardboard boxes

6. What purpose does a job cost record serve? *(p. 864)*
   a. Lists total materials, labor, and overhead costs charged to a job
   b. Is management's basic internal document that helps to control cost in a job cost system
   c. Both of the above
   d. Neither of the above

7. Using direct materials in production and charging direct labor costs to a job result in a debit to *(pp. 867, 869)*
   a. Direct materials and direct labor c. Finished goods inventory
   b. Work in process inventory   d. Materials inventory and factory wages

8. Which documents serve as a subsidiary ledger for the general ledger balance in Work in Process Inventory? *(pp. 864, 870)*
   a. Job cost records   c. Labor time tickets
   b. Materials requisitions   d. Materials ledger accounts

9. Why is direct labor often used as a basis for applying overhead cost to jobs? *(p. 871)*
   a. Overhead is very similar to direct labor
   b. Overhead includes direct labor
   c. Overhead occurs before direct labor is charged to a job
   d. Overhead occurs in relation to the incurrence of direct labor cost

10. At the end of the period, after overhead has been applied to all jobs, Factory Overhead has a credit balance of $900. We would say that overhead has been *(p. 874)*
    a. Misstated   c. Overapplied
    b. Incorrectly applied   d. Underapplied

Answers to the self-study questions are at the end of the chapter.

Accounting Vocabulary

budgeted factory overhead rate *(p. 871)*, conversion costs *(p. 859)*, cost of goods manufactured *(p. 857)*, direct labor *(p. 858)*, direct materials *(p. 858)*, factory overhead *(p. 858)*, finished goods inventory *(p. 857)*, indirect labor *(p. 859)*, indirect materials *(p. 859)*, job cost record *(p. 864)*, job order costing *(p. 863)*, labor time ticket *(p. 868)*, materials inventory *(p. 857)*, materials requisition *(p. 866)*, overapplied overhead *(p. 874)*, period cost *(p. 861)*, prime costs *(p. 859)*, product cost *(p. 860)*, raw materials inventory *(p. 857)*, total manufacturing cost *(p. 860)*, underapplied overhead *(p. 874)*, work in process inventory *(p. 857)*.

ASSIGNMENT MATERIAL ________________________

Questions

1. How do manufacturing companies differ from merchandisers? What inventory accounts does a manufacturer use that a merchandiser does not need?

2. What is the manufacturer's counterpart to the Purchases account of a merchandiser?

3. Distinguish direct materials from indirect materials and direct labor from indirect labor. Direct materials and direct labor are debited directly to what inventory account when placed in production? What account do indirect materials and indirect labor pass through en route to this inventory account?

4. Give examples of direct material and indirect material for a home builder.

5. Identify six or more components of factory overhead. Is overhead an asset or an expense account to a manufacturer?

6. Outline the flow of inventory costs through a manufacturing company's accounting system.

7. Distinguish between product costs and period costs. Which represents an asset, and which is used to account for expenses?

8. Name two benefits of a perpetual inventory system.

9. Briefly discuss two purposes of cost accounting.

10. What do the terms "charged to a job" and "applied to jobs" mean? What account is debited when a cost is applied to a job?

11. What is the essential nature of a job order costing system? How can companies that use a job cost system operate with low levels of inventories?

12. What document is used to control costs in a job cost system? Identify the three categories of costs listed on this document.

13. Name three documents or records used to account for raw materials, control them, and move them through the production process. Give the function served by each document.

14. Use T-accounts to outline how the costs of materials and labor are transferred to Work in Process Inventory. Include both direct and indirect materials and direct and indirect labor.

15. What document is used to charge labor cost to specific jobs? Briefly describe how the document is used.

16. Is factory overhead cost applied to jobs by a precise identification of the overhead cost of each job or by an estimation process? Briefly discuss the process.

17. Is Factory Overhead debited for actual overhead cost or the amount of overhead applied to product? Which amount is credited to Factory Overhead?

18. How can factory overhead be underapplied? How can it be overapplied?

19. Insignificant amounts of over- or underapplied overhead are closed to what account? Significant amounts are closed to what three accounts?

20. Which of the following accounts have their balances brought to zero at the end of the period? Which keep their ending balances to start the next period — Materials Inventory, Factory Overhead, Finished Goods Inventory, Factory Wages?

21. What three categories of manufacturing costs are listed on a statement of cost of goods manufactured?

22. Summarize the computation of cost of goods manufactured. You can use your own dollar amounts.

Exercises

Exercise 22-1   *Reporting current assets of a manufacturer*

The following selected accounts of Frostex Foods are listed in alphabetical order:

Accounts receivable	$ 73,000	Factory overhead	$26,000
Cash	9,000	Finished goods inventory	58,000
Cost of goods manufactured	94,000	Materials inventory	14,000
Cost of goods sold	101,000	Prepaid expenses	5,000
Direct labor	47,000	Selling expense	39,000
Direct materials	25,000	Work in process inventory	32,000

Required

Show how Frostex would report current assets. Not all accounts are used.

Exercise 22-2 *Computing cost of goods manufactured*

Compute cost of goods manufactured from the following account balances:

	Beginning of Year	End of Year
Materials inventory	$22,000	$ 26,000
Work in process inventory	31,000	30,000
Finished goods inventory	18,000	23,000
Purchases of raw materials		75,000
Direct labor		103,000
Indirect labor		15,000
Factory insurance		9,000
Depreciation–factory building and equipment		11,000
Repairs and maintenance–factory		4,000
Selling expenses		63,000
General and administrative expenses		29,000
Income tax expense		30,000

Exercise 22-3 *Preparing a manufacturer's income statement*

Prepare an income statement for the company in Exercise 22-2, assuming it sold 27,000 units of its product at a price of $14 during the current year.

Exercise 22-4 *Computing cost of goods manufactured and cost of goods sold*

Compute cost of goods manufactured and cost of goods sold for the following situation:

Property tax on factory building	$ 3,000
Selling expenses	37,000
Beginning finished goods inventory	27,000
Factory utilities	17,000
Ending work in process inventory	26,000
Depreciation of factory building	9,000
Nonfactory administrative expenses	43,000
Direct materials used	67,000
Ending finished goods inventory	34,000
Depreciation of factory equipment	11,000
Factory repairs and maintenance	16,000
Beginning work in process inventory	19,000
Direct labor	54,000
Indirect labor	23,000
Indirect materials	13,000
Miscellaneous factory overhead	4,000

Exercise 22-5 *Computing gross margin for a manufacturer*

Supply the missing amounts from the following computation of gross margin:

Sales revenue.		$473,000
Cost of goods sold:		
Beginning finished goods inventory . . .		$ 95,000
Cost of goods manufactured:		
Beginning work in process inventory	$ 57,000	
Direct materials used $84,000		
Direct labor. X		
Factory overhead 51,000		
Total manufacturing cost.	231,000	
Ending work in process inventory . .	(40,000)	
Cost of goods manufactured		X
Goods available for sale		X
Ending finished goods inventory		(107,000)
Cost of goods sold		X
Gross margin		$ X

Exercise 22-6   *Journalizing manufacturing transactions*

Record the following transactions in the general journal:

a. Purchased materials on account, $8,900.
b. Paid factory wages, $6,000.
c. Used in production: direct materials, $9,000, and indirect materials, $2,000.
d. Applied factory labor to jobs: direct labor, 80 percent; indirect labor, 20 percent.
e. Recorded factory overhead: depreciation, $13,000; insurance, $1,000; property tax, $4,000 (credit Property Tax Payable).
f. Applied factory overhead to jobs, 150% percent of direct labor.
g. Completed production, $16,000.
h. Sold inventory on account, $22,000; cost of goods sold, $14,000.
i. Paid selling expenses, $2,000.

Exercise 22-7   *Identifying manufacturing transactions*

Describe the transactions indicated by the letters in the following manufacturing accounts:

Materials Inventory		Work in Process Inventory		Finished Goods Inventory	
(a)	(b)	(b)	(h)	(h)	(i)
	(e)	(d)	(j)		(j)
		(g)			

Factory Wages		Factory Overhead		Cost of Goods Sold	
(c)	(d)	(d)	(g)	(i)	(j)
		(e)			
		(f)			
		(j)			

Exercise 22-8   *Accounting for overhead cost*

Selected cost data for Henderson & Tipton are presented below:

Budgeted factory overhead cost for the year	$27,000
Budgeted direct labor cost for the year	81,000
Actual factory overhead cost for the year.	25,700
Actual direct labor cost for the year	78,000

Required

1. Compute the budgeted factory overhead rate.
2. Journalize the application of overhead cost for the year.
3. By what amount is factory overhead over- or underapplied? Is this amount significant or insignificant?
4. Based on your answer to (3), journalize disposition of the overhead balance.

Exercise 22-9   *Using the Work in Process Inventory account*

August production generated the following activity in the Work in Process Inventory account of Bronstadt Manufacturing Company:

Work in Process Inventory

August 1 Bal.	8,000
Direct materials used	23,000
Direct labor charged to jobs	31,000
Factory overhead applied to jobs	11,000

Completed production, not yet recorded, consists of Jobs B-78, G-65, and Y-11, with total costs of $3,000, $19,000, and $39,000, respectively.

Required

1. Compute the cost of work in process at August 31.
2. Journalize completed production for August.
3. Journalize the credit sale of Job G-65 for $41,000. Also make the cost of goods sold entry.

Exercise 22-10   *Analyzing job cost data*

Bancroft Publishing Company job cost records yielded the following information:

Job No.	Dates Started	Finished	Sold	Total Cost of Job at July 31
1	June 19	July 14	July 15	$ 4,100
2	June 29	July 21	July 26	17,000
3	July 3	Aug. 11	Aug. 13	6,500
4	July 7	July 29	Aug. 1	8,800
5	July 9	July 30	Aug. 2	2,700
6	July 22	Aug. 11	Aug. 13	900
7	July 23	July 27	July 29	1,300

Compute Bancroft's cost of (a) work in process inventory at July 31, (b) finished goods inventory at July 31, and (c) cost of goods sold for July.

Problems   (Group A)

Problem 22-1A   *Completing a manufacturer's income statement*

Certain item descriptions and amounts are missing from the income statement of Lakewood Manufacturing Company.

Lakewood Manufacturing Company
Income Statement
For the Year Ended June 30, 19X9

Sales revenue			$ ✕
Cost of goods sold:			
Beginning _____ inventory		$ 101,000	
Cost of goods _____:			
Beginning _____ inventory		$ 28,000	
Direct _____:			
Beginning materials inventory	$ ✕		
Purchases of materials	62,000		
Materials available for use	79,000		
Ending materials inventory	(23,000)		
Direct _____	$ ✕		
Direct _____	✕		
_____	38,000		
Total _____ cost		166,000	
Ending _____ inventory		(31,000)	
Cost of goods _____		163,000	
Goods available for sale		✕	
Ending _____ inventory		(✕)	
Cost of goods _____			168,000
Gross margin			224,000
Operating expenses:			
Selling		99,000	
General		✕	
Total operating expense			144,000
Income before income tax			80,000
Income tax expense (40%)			✕
Net income			$ ✕

Required

Supply the missing item descriptions (_____) and the missing amounts (✕).

Problem 22-2A *Analyzing job cost data*

Burleson and Schmidt Manufacturing Company job cost records yielded the following information. The company has a perpetual inventory system.

Job No.	Dates			Total Cost of Job at June 30	Total Manufacturing Cost Added in July
	Started	Finished	Sold		
1	5/26	6/ 7	6/ 9	$ 700	
2	6/ 3	6/12	6/13	3,100	
3	6/ 3	6/30	7/ 1	1,800	
4	6/17	7/24	7/27	100	$ 500
5	6/29	7/29	8/ 3	400	1,600
6	7/ 8	7/12	7/14		800
7	7/23	8/ 6	8/ 9		300
8	7/30	8/22	8/26		2,900

Required

1. Compute Burleson and Schmidt's cost of (a) work in process inventory at June 30 and July 31, (b) finished goods inventory at June 30 and July 31, and (c) cost of goods sold for June and July.

2. Make summary journal entries to record the transfer of completed units from work in process to finished goods for June and July.

3. Record the sale of Job 4 for $850.

Problem 22-3A   *Computing manufacturing cost amounts for the financial statements*

Stride-Rite Shoe Company makes the Sperry Top-Sider deck shoe. Assume Stride-Rite accounting records include the following cost information on jobs for the manufacture of the basic brown leather Top-Sider.

During the most recent year Stride-Rite incurred total manufacturing cost of $22.6 million on materials, labor, and factory overhead, of which $4.6 million represented overhead applied. Beginning balances for the year were materials inventory, $500,000; work in process inventory, $700,000; and finished goods inventory, $400,000. The company applies overhead to work in process (and finished goods) based on the relationship between overhead and direct labor costs. At year end the inventory account showed these balances:

	Materials	Direct Labor	Factory Overhead
Materials inventory	$600,000	$ -0-	$ -0-
Work in process inventory.............	300,000	450,000	150,000
Finished goods inventory	100,000	150,000	50,000

Required

1. Prepare Stride-Rite's statement of cost of goods manufactured for the brown leather Top-Sider shoe.

2. Compute cost of goods sold for the Top-Sider product.

3. Compute the cost of materials purchased during the year. Hint: Use a T-account for Materials Inventory.

Problem 22-4A   *Accounting for manufacturing transactions*

Nash-Phillips-Copus, Inc. (NPC), located in Austin, Texas, has been one of the largest home builders in the United States. Assume NPC uses a perpetual inventory system and a job cost system in which each house represents a job. Because it constructs houses on-site rather than in a factory, the company uses accounts titled Construction Wages (not Factory Wages), Overhead (not Factory Overhead), and Supervisory Salaries for indirect labor. The following transactions and events were completed during August:

(a)   Purchases of materials on account, $385,600.

(b)   Requisitions of direct materials and direct labor used in manufacturing:

	Direct Materials	Direct Labor
House #302	$36,800	$19,100
House #303	39,100	17,400
House #304	45,600	20,500
House #305	22,400	11,000
House #306	63,900	33,700
House #307	52,800	27,500

(c)   Depreciation of equipment used on different houses, $5,800.

(d)   Other overhead costs incurred on houses #302–#307:

Supervisory salaries	$17,000
Equipment rentals paid	7,300
Liability insurance expired	5,100

(e)   Applied overhead to jobs at the budgeted overhead rate of 20% of direct labor excluding supervision.

(f)   Houses completed: #302, #304, #305, #307.

(g)   Houses sold: #305 for $41,500; #307 for $115,000.

Required

1.   Record the foregoing transactions and events in the general journal.
2.   Open T-accounts for Work in Process Inventory and Finished Goods Inventory. Post the appropriate entries to these accounts, identifying the entry by letter. Determine the ending account balances assuming the beginning balances were zero.
3.   List the costs of unfinished houses, and show that this total amount equals the ending balance in the Work in Process Inventory account.
4.   List the costs of completed houses that have not yet been sold, and show that this total amount equals the ending balance in the Finished Goods Inventory account.

Problem 22-5A   *Preparing and using a job cost record*

Maxell Magnetic Tape Company manufactures diskettes for use in reproducing sound. Maxell has a job cost system and a perpetual inventory system.

On November 2 Maxell began production of 10,000 diskettes, assigned job number 378, to be sold to music stores for $1.25 each. The company incurred the following costs in completing the job:

Date	Materials Requisition No.	Description	Amount
11-2	36	55 lbs. polypropylene @ $8	$440
11-2	37	68 lbs. magnetic filament @ $13	884
11-3	42	7 lbs. bucylic acid @ $48	336
	Time Ticket No.	Description	Amount
11-2	556	12 hours @ $10	$120
11-3	557	24.5 hours @ $8	196

Maxell charges overhead to jobs based on the relationship between estimated overhead ($560,000) and estimated direct labor ($448,000). The job was completed on November 3 and shipped to music stores when ordered.

Required

1.   Prepare a job cost record similar to Exhibit 22-6.
2.   Journalize the requisition of direct materials and the application of direct labor and factory overhead to Job 378.
3.   Journalize completion of the job and sale of 500 diskettes.

Problem 22-6A   *Comprehensive accounting treatment of manufacturing transactions*

 Columbia Telecommunications manufactures specialized parts used in its business. Initially, the company manufactured the parts for its own use, but it gradually began selling them to other companies as well. Columbia's trial balance on April 1, the beginning of the current fiscal year, follows.

Columbia Telecommunications
Trial Balance
April 1, 19XX

Cash	$ 19,160	
Accounts receivable	74,290	
Inventories:		
Materials	6,780	
Work in process	35,880	
Finished goods	18,960	
Plant assets	244,570	
Accumulated depreciation		$103,680
Accounts payable		26,770
Wages payable		3,670
Common stock		120,000
Retained earnings		145,520
Sales revenue		—
Cost of goods sold	—	
Factory wages	—	
Factory overhead	—	
Selling and general expenses	—	
	$399,640	$399,640

April 1 balances in the subsidiary ledgers:

Materials ledger: Steel, $1,580; Petrochemicals, $2,810; Electronic parts, $1,960; Indirect materials, $430.

Work in process ledger: Job 145, $35,880.

Finished goods ledger: Transformers, $5,310; Transmissions lines, $4,780; Switches, $8,870.

April transactions are summarized as follows:

(a) Materials purchased on credit: Steel, $5,540; Petrochemicals, $9,690; Electronic parts, $15,830; Indirect materials, $3,590.

(b) Materials used in production (requisitioned):
Job 145: Steel, $340, Petrochemicals, $1,770.
Job 146: Steel, $3,570, Petrochemicals, $5,720; Electronic parts, $3,980.
Job 147: Steel, $1,970, Petrochemicals, $3,610; Electronic parts, $3,730.
Indirect materials, $2,380.

(c) Factory wages incurred during April, $31,930, of which $30,520 was paid. Wages payable at March 31 were paid during April, $3,670.

(d) Labor time tickets for the month: Job 145, $3,000; Job 146, $12,050; Job 147, $9,940; Indirect labor, $6,940.

(e) Factory overhead incurred on account, $4,630.

(f) Depreciation recorded on factory plant and equipment, $3,450.

(g) Payments on account, $36,040.

(h) Factory overhead applied at the budgeted rate of 70 percent of direct labor.

(i) Jobs completed during the month: Job 145, two transformers at total cost of $43,090; Job 146, 200 switches at total cost of $33,755.

(j) Selling and general expenses paid, $27,470.

(k) Credit sales on account: All of Job 145 for $91,640 (cost $43,090); Job 146, 120 switches for $31,600 (cost, $20,253).

(l) Collections on account, $127,470.

Required

1. Open T-accounts for the general ledger, the materials ledger, the work in process ledger, and the finished goods ledger. Insert each account balance as given, and use the reference *Bal.*
2. Record the April transactions directly in the accounts, using the letters as references. Columbia has a perpetual inventory system.
3. Prepare a trial balance at April 30 of the current year.
4. Prepare a multiple-step income statement through income from operations for April of the current year, assuming any balance in Factory Overhead is insignificant. Take amounts directly from the trial balance, and report cost of goods sold as a single amount.

Problem 22-7A   *Using a manufacturing system to account for overhead cost*

Selected accounts of Weimar & Martinez, a partnership, follow.

Accounts Receivable

Nov. 1	Balance	28,900	Nov. 30	Collections	54,600
30	Sales	(1)			

Materials Inventory

Nov. 1	Balance	8,400	Nov. 30	Requisitions	(2)
30	Purchases	41,700			

Work in Process Inventory

Nov. 1	Balance	24,600	Nov. 30	Jobs completed	(5)
30	Direct materials	(3)			
30	Direct labor	68,000			
30	Factory overhead	(4)			

Finished Goods Inventory

Nov. 1	Balance	104,700	Nov. 30	Sales	(7)
30	Jobs completed	(6)			

Factory Overhead

Nov. 30	Costs incurred: indirect materials of $9,000, indirect labor, etc. Total amount	75,200	Nov. 1	Balance	1,100
			30	Applied at rate of 110% of direct labor cost	(8)

Cost of Goods Sold

Nov. 30	Sales	(9)		

Sales Revenue

			Nov. 30	Sales	(10)

Selected balances at Nov. 30 are

Accounts receivable $31,400
Materials inventory 10,100

Work in process inventory...............	21,900	
Finished goods inventory...............	89,800	

Required

1. Determine the amounts of the numbered items in the accounts.
2. a. Was factory overhead under- or overapplied at November 1?
    b. What is the November 30 balance in Factory Overhead? Is factory overhead under-
       or overapplied at November 30?
    c. Assume November 30 is the end of the company's fiscal year. Give the year-end
       entry to close the Factory Overhead account depending on whether the November
       30 balance is significant or insignificant. You must make this judgment.

(Group B)

Problem 22-1B *Completing a manufacturer's income statement*

Certain item descriptions and amounts are missing from the income statement of Rocky
Mountain Construction Company.

Rocky Mountain Construction Company
Income Statement
For the Month Ended March 31, 19X6

Sales revenue			$247,000
Cost of goods sold:			
Beginning ——— inventory..................		$ X	
Cost of goods ———:			
Beginning ——— inventory.................		$ X	
Direct ———:			
Beginning materials inventory	$34,000		
Purchases of materials...................	70,000		
Materials available for use	X		
Ending materials inventory...............	(26,000)		
Direct ———......................		$ X	
Direct ———......................		83,000	
———		19,000	
Total ——— cost.......................		X	
Ending ——— inventory		(49,000)	
Cost of goods ———			163,000
Goods available for sale			192,000
Ending ——— inventory			(54,000)
Cost of goods ———			X
Gross margin................................			109,000
Operating expenses:			
Selling		23,000	
General		26,000	
Total operating expense			X
Income before income tax			X
Income tax expense (30%)			X
Net income			$ X

Required

Supply the missing item descriptions (———) and the missing amounts (X).

Problem 22-2B   *Analyzing job cost data*

Atchison and Topeka Fabricating Company job cost records yielded the following information. The company has a perpetual inventory system.

Job No.	Dates			Total Cost of Job at March 31	Total Manufacturing Cost Added in April
	Started	Finished	Sold		
1	2/26	3/ 7	3/ 9	$2,200	
2	2/ 3	3/12	3/13	500	
3	3/29	3/31	4/ 3	300	
4	3/31	4/ 1	4/ 1	100	$ 200
5	3/17	4/24	4/27	1,400	2,200
6	4/ 8	4/12	4/14		700
7	4/23	5/ 6	5/ 9		1,200
8	4/30	5/22	5/26		600

Required

1. Compute Atchison and Topeka's cost of (a) work in process inventory at March 31 and
   April 30, (b) finished goods inventory at March 31 and April 30, and (c) cost of goods
   sold for March and April.
2. Make summary journal entries to record the transfer of completed units from work in
   process to finished goods for March and April.
3. Record the sale of Job 5 for $7,000.

Problem 22-3B   *Computing manufacturing cost amounts for the financial statements*

Assume Levi Strauss & Company accounting records include the following cost information on jobs for the manufacture of a line of jeans. During the most recent year Levi Strauss
incurred total manufacturing cost of $168.8 million on materials, labor, and factory over-
head, of which $33.8 million represented direct materials used. Beginning balances for the
year were materials inventory, $3.4 million; work in process inventory, $2.6 million; and
finished goods inventory, $7.4 million. The company applies overhead to work in process
(and finished goods) based on the relationship between overhead and direct labor costs. At
year end the inventory accounts showed these balances (millions):

	Materials	Direct Labor	Factory Overhead
Materials inventory.	$0.9	$0.0	$0.0
Work in process inventory	1.5	2.0	2.5
Finished goods inventory	2.4	3.2	4.0

Required

1. Prepare Levi Strauss's statement of cost of goods manufactured for the line of jeans.
2. Compute cost of goods sold for the product.
3. Record the transfer from Work in Process Inventory to Finished Goods Inventory and
   the transfer from Finished Goods Inventory to Cost of Goods Sold during the year.

Problem 22-4B   *Accounting for manufacturing transactions*

Monarch Homes builds prefabricated houses in a factory. The company uses a perpetual
inventory system and a job cost system in which each house represents a job. The following transactions and events were completed during May:

(a) Purchases of materials on account, $204,900.
(b) Requisitions of direct materials and direct labor used in manufacturing:

	Direct Materials	Direct Labor
House #613	$24,600	$11,600
House #614	41,700	22,500
House #615	31,000	14,700
House #616	54,000	23,800
House #617	43,900	20,700
House #618	32,800	14,600

(c)   Depreciation of equipment used on different houses, $14,300.

(d)   Other overhead costs incurred on houses #613–#618:

Factory wages............................	$21,600
Equipment rentals paid....................	6,000
Liability insurance expired	3,900

(e)   Applied overhead to jobs at the budgeted overhead rate of 30 percent of direct labor excluding supervision.

(f)   Houses completed: #613, #615, #616.

(g)   Houses sold: #615 for $59,900; #616 for $103,900.

Required

1.   Record the foregoing transactions and events in the general journal.

2.   Open T-accounts for Work in Process Inventory and Finished Goods Inventory. Post the appropriate entries to these accounts, identifying the entry by letter. Determine the ending account balances assuming the beginning balances were zero.

3.   List the costs of unfinished houses, and show that this total amount equals the ending balance in the Work in Process Inventory account.

4.   List the costs of completed houses that have not yet been sold, and show that this total amount equals the ending balance in the Finished Goods Inventory account.

Problem 22-5B   *Preparing and using a job cost record*

Manhattan Belt Company produces conveyor belts used by other companies in their manufacturing processes. Manhattan has a job cost system and a perpetual inventory system.

On September 22 Manhattan received an order for 50 industrial-grade belts from Ogden Jones Corporation at a price of $56 each. The job, assigned number 449, was promised for October 15. After purchasing the materials, Manhattan began production on September 30 and incurred the following costs in completing the order:

Date	Materials Requisition No.	Description	Amount
9-30	593	40 lbs. rubber @ $9	$360
10-2	598	30 meters polyester fabric @ $7	210
10-3	622	12 meters steel cord @ $12	144

Date	Time Ticket No.	Description	Amount
9-30	1754	8 hours @ $9	$ 72
10-3	1805	31 hours @ $8	248

Manhattan charges overhead to jobs based on the relationship between estimated overhead ($375,000) and estimated direct labor ($250,000). The job was completed on October 3 and shipped to Ogden Jones on October 5.

Required

1. Prepare a job cost record similar to Exhibit 22-6.
2. Journalize the requisition of direct materials and the application of direct labor and factory overhead to Job 449.
3. Journalize completion of the job and sale of the goods.

Problem 22-6B   *Comprehensive accounting treatment of manufacturing transactions*

Nebraska Public Service Company (NPS) manufactures specialized parts used in the generation of power. Initially, the company manufactured the parts for its own use, but it gradually began selling them to other public utilities as well. The trial balance of NPS's manufacturing operation on January 1 of the current year follows.

Nebraska Public Service Company—Manufacturing Operation
Trial Balance
January 1, 19XX

Cash	$ 32,740	
Accounts receivable	65,860	
Inventories:		
Materials...	18,910	
Work in process	43,350	
Finished goods	78,550	
Plant assets...	342,860	
Accumulated depreciation.............................		$145,960
Accounts payable....................................		88,650
Wages payable		5,700
Common stock......................................		200,000
Retained earnings....................................		141,960
Sales revenue		—
Cost of goods sold	—	
Factory wages.......................................	—	
Factory overhead	—	
Selling and general expenses...........................	—	
	$582,270	$582,270

January 1 balances in the subsidiary ledgers:

Materials ledger: Steel, $4,730; Petrochemicals, $5,280; Electronic parts, $7,800; Indirect materials, $1,100.

Work in process ledger: Job 86, $43,350.

Finished goods ledger: Transformers, $35,770; Transmissions lines, $21,910; Switches, $20,870.

January transactions are summarized as follows:

(a)   Materials purchased on credit: Steel, $12,660; Petrochemicals, $19,570; Electronic parts, $28,360; Indirect materials, $6,130.

(b)   Materials used in production (requisitioned):
    Job 86: Steel, $1,580, Petrochemicals, $3,400.
    Job 87: Steel, $10,580, Petrochemicals, $9,870; Electronic parts, $4,690.
    Job 88: Steel, $2,930, Petrochemicals, $7,680; Electronic parts, $29,920.
    Indirect materials, $4,760.

(c) Factory wages incurred during January, $51,730, of which $49,560 was paid. Wages payable at December 31 were paid during January, $5,700.

(d) Labor time tickets for the month: Job 86, $3,650; Job 87, $19,880; Job 88, $16,560; Indirect labor, $11,640.

(e) Factory overhead incurred on account, $27,660.

(f) Depreciation recorded on factory plant and equipment, $6,710.

(g) Payments on account, $79,330.

(h) Factory overhead applied at the budgeted rate of 120 percent of direct labor.

(i) Jobs completed during the month: Job 86, one transformer at total cost of $56,360; Job 87, 620 switches at total cost of $68,876.

(j) Selling and general expenses paid, $21,660.

(k) Credit sales on account: All of Job 86 for $96,490 (cost $56,360); Job 87, 480 switches for $88,230 (cost, $53,323).

(l) Collections on account, $177,880.

Required

1. Open T-accounts for the general ledger, the materials ledger, the work in process ledger, and the finished goods ledger. Insert each account balance as given, and use the reference *Bal.*

2. Record the January transactions directly in the accounts, using the letters as references. NPS has a perpetual inventory system.

3. Prepare a trial balance at January 31 of the current year.

4. Prepare a multiple-step income statement through income from operations for January of the current year, assuming any balance in Factory Overhead is insignificant. Take amounts directly from the trial balance, and report cost of goods sold as a single amount.

Problem 22-7B *Using a manufacturing system to account for overhead cost*

Selected accounts of Kwang & Foster, a partnership, follow.

Accounts Receivable

| Aug. 1 | Balance | 122,400 | Aug. 31 | Collections | 165,900 |
| 31 | Sales | (1) | | | |

Materials Inventory

| Aug. 1 | Balance | 31,500 | Aug. 31 | Requisitions | (2) |
| 31 | Purchases | 94,600 | | | |

Work in Process Inventory

Aug. 1	Balance	73,200	Aug. 31	Jobs completed	(5)
31	Direct materials	(3)			
31	Direct labor	104,000			
31	Factory overhead	(4)			

Finished Goods Inventory

| Aug. 1 | Balance | 59,500 | Aug. 31 | Sales | (7) |
| 31 | Jobs completed | (6) | | | |

Factory Overhead

Aug. 1	Balance	800	Aug. 31	Applied at rate of 80% of direct labor cost	(8)
31	Costs incurred: indirect materials of $31,400, indirect labor, etc.				
	Total amount	81,900			

Cost of Goods Sold

Aug. 31	Sales	(9)

Sales Revenue

	Aug. 31 Sales	(10)

Selected balances at August 31 are

Accounts receivable	$103,700
Materials inventory	28,400
Work in process inventory	43,700
Finished goods inventory	72,900

Required

1. Determine the amounts of the numbered items in the accounts.
2. a. Was factory overhead under- or overapplied at August 1?
    b. What is the August 31 balance in Factory Overhead? Is factory overhead under- or overapplied at August 31?
    c. Assume August 31 is the end of the company's fiscal year. Give the year-end entry to close the Factory Overhead account, depending on whether the August 31 balance is significant or insignificant. You must make this judgment.

Decision Problem

Using cost data to price a new product

MultiMedia, Inc., is experimenting with a new process for manufacturing special telephone equipment in an attempt to lower the cost and sale price of its products. The goal is to capture a larger share of the telephone equipment market. The new process uses laser technology that decreases the amount of raw material needed to make a telephone. The *current* manufacturing process requires the following inputs per 1,000 telephones:

Direct materials:			
Material A	20 lbs. @ $	11
Material B	130 lbs. @	9
Material C	8 lbs. @	106
Direct labor:			
Fabricating	80 hrs. @ $	10
Assembling	20 hrs. @	12
Testing	50 hrs. @	13

Factory overhead @ 150% of direct labor cost

The *new technology* would decrease the amounts of material A by 20 percent and of material C by 40 percent. It would also require three pounds of material D, which costs $22 per pound. Fabricating and testing would require 10 percent less time, but purchase of the laser machine would increase overhead to 175 percent of direct labor cost.

MultiMedia sells its products for 70 percent above cost but would need to increase this margin to 72 percent for telephone equipment manufactured by the new process to compensate for the lower selling price. Market analysis shows that customer demand for telephones is extremely sensitive to price. MultiMedia personnel believe any sale price reduction more than 50¢ per telephone will increase sales volume enough to warrant using the new production process.

Required

Compute the current selling price of a telephone and the price of a telephone using the laser technology to decide whether to proceed with the new process. Make a recommendation to the company.

Financial Statement Problem

Answer these questions about the cost accounting system of Gulf+Western Inc., whose financial statements appear in Appendix C.

1. Gulf+Western (G+W) segment data—immediately after the income statement—indicate that entertainment and publishing/information are two of the company's main lines of business. Study the *Management Discussion and Analysis of Financial Condition and Results of Operations,* which appears on the next page of Appendix C. Identify, by name, five entertainment jobs and five publishing jobs that passed through G+W's job cost accounting system.
2. Identify individual items that make up the direct materials, direct labor, and overhead costs in G+W's entertainment and publishing businesses. Example:

    Entertainment—Movie
    Direct materials: Motion picture film

3. Suppose the Paramount Pictures unit of G+W engages former President Reagan to star in a movie about his presidency. Assume the company estimates 2,000 showings of the movie will bring in average revenue of $2,500 per showing. Estimated manufacturing costs include direct materials of $.2 million, direct labor, excluding the former president's fee, of $1.3 million, and overhead of $1.1 million. How much can Paramount afford to pay Mr. Reagan and still earn income before income tax, equal to 12 percent of net revenue? Show amounts in millions rounded to the nearest $100,000.
4. Use the G+W income statement and Note D inventory data to compute cost of goods manufactured for fiscal 1987. Hint: Use the cost of goods sold model, substituting cost of goods manufactured for purchases.

Answers to Self-Study Questions

1.	c	6.	c
2.	a	7.	b
3.	b ($35,000 + $140,000 − $20,000 = $155,000)	8.	a
4.	d	9.	d
5.	a	10.	c

23

Process Costing, Operation Costing, and Joint Products

LEARNING OBJECTIVES

After studying this chapter, you should be able to

1 Distinguish process costing from job order costing

2 Compute equivalent units of production

3 Perform the steps in a process costing system

4 Record process costing transactions

5 Account for process costing in a second department

6 Account for an operation costing system

7 Allocate cost to joint products and byproducts

Job order costing and process costing are the two major accounting systems for determining the costs of products. Chapter 22 discussed job order costing. This chapter explains process costing. It also covers the related subjects of operation costing and accounting for joint products and byproducts.

Process Costing: An Overview

Process costing is a system for assigning costs to goods that are mass-produced in a continuous sequence of steps called *processes*. Companies in manufacturing industries—chemicals, petroleum, cosmetics, food, and beverages, for example—use process costing systems. Each of several departments is responsible for one specific process, although a single department may perform more than one process.

In the manufacturing process, the physical form of the product often changes as it passes from one process to another (and so from one department to another). For example, corn flake cereal starts as raw corn. The corn is cleaned and cooked before being packaged as corn flakes and shipped for sale to consumers. A company that produces corn flakes—like Kellogg's or General Mills—may have one department for cleaning, one department for cooking, one department for packaging, and one department for shipping.

A mass-production manufacturing process produces large numbers of identical units—boxes of cereal, gallons of paint, and cases of Coca-Cola. In contrast, a job system produces custom goods. In a process system the flow of goods through

OBJECTIVE 1

Distinguish process costing from job order costing

EXHIBIT 23-1 *Comparison of Process Costing and Job Order Costing*

Job-Order Costing: Examples include aircraft, construction, furniture, auditing, repairing, and jewelry

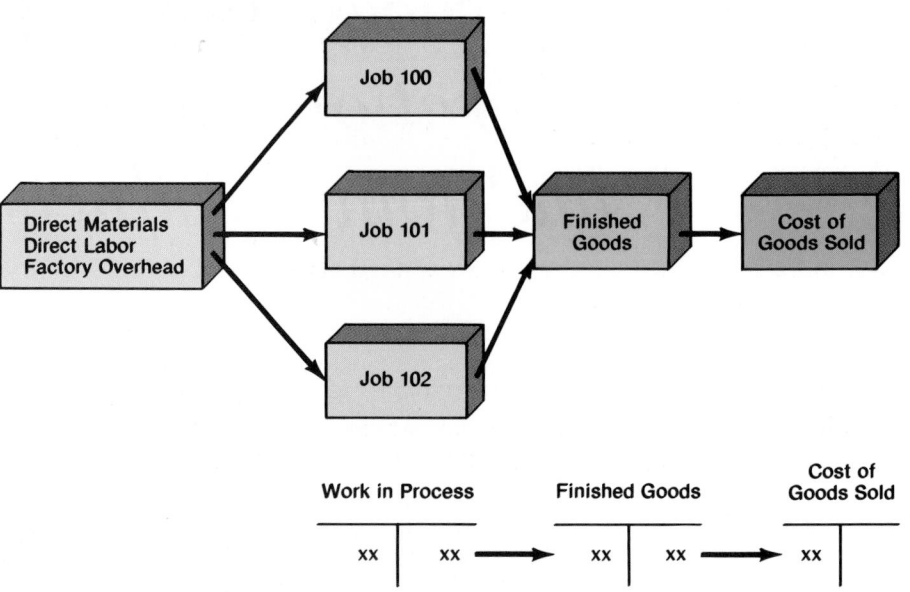

Process Costing: Examples include flour, glass, paint, paper, and silicon wafers

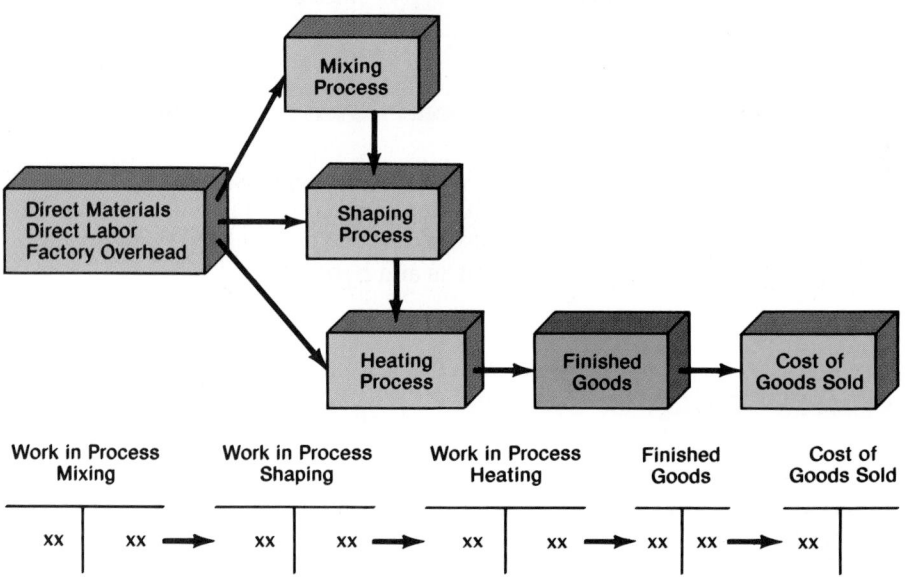

the factory is continuous and repetitive. Job cost records are not used. Instead, cost is accumulated in each department for a week or a month. At the end of the period, total manufacturing cost is the sum of the costs added in the processing departments. Unit cost is computed by dividing total manufacturing cost by the number of units produced. For example, if it cost $600,000 to produce 150,000 units during July, unit cost is $4.00 ($600,000/150,000 units).

Consider a manufacturing company that produces its goods in three steps. The business mixes materials to produce ceramic blocks, shapes the blocks into figurines, and heats the figures for hardness. The company has a Mixing Department, a Shaping Department, and a Heating Department. To account for the costs that make up the finished products, accountants use three work in process inventory accounts—one for mixing, one for shaping, and one for heating. Exhibit 23-1 shows the flow of costs in this three-step process.

Note in the exhibit that mixing costs accumulate in the Work in Process Inventory—Mixing account. After mixing is completed, the blocks are transferred to the Shaping Department, and so are the costs. When shaping has been completed, product costs flow to Work in Process–Heating and then on to Finished Goods Inventory. When the figurines are sold, the cost of the inventory is transferred into Cost of Goods Sold. For comparison, the exhibit also diagrams the flow of costs through a job order costing system, which has only one Work in Process account.

Exhibit 23-2 uses dollar amounts to illustrate costs flowing through a process system. Each Work in Process account lists direct materials and conversion costs, a term defined as direct labor plus overhead.

You will notice that each of the Work in Process accounts has a nonzero ending balance. Why? Because the manufacturing process is ongoing. No department ever sits idle. At any time, the Mixing Department will be carrying on its function while the Shaping Department and the Heating Department are handling their tasks. Before the Mixing Department ships off the most recent batch of ceramic blocks, it has already begun preparing the next batch. In Exhibit 23-2, we see that the Mixing Department has forwarded goods costing $10,000 to the Shaping Department. At the start of the next period, the Mixing Department is working on goods costing $2,000, which are left over from the preceding period.

Likewise, as the Shaping Department is completing one batch of figurines, it may be starting to shape a second batch. Since any department at any time will be engaged in the manufacturing process, its Work in Process Inventory account will carry a nonzero balance.

Recording Costs

The journal entries for a process cost accounting system are like those for a job order costing system. That is, direct materials, direct labor, and factory overhead are recorded as follows (all amounts are assumed for illustrative purposes):

To purchase materials and incur labor and overhead cost (amounts in thousands):

Materials Inventory	11	
Accounts Payable		11
Factory Wages	3	
Wages Payable		3
Factory Overhead	5	
Accumulated Depreciation		1
Property Tax Payable		1
Accounts Payable, and so on		3

To requisition materials, assign labor cost, and assign overhead cost to the Mixing Department. (These entries are posted to Work in Process–Mixing in Exhibit 23-2, amounts in thousands):

Work in Process Inventory–Mixing	7	
Materials Inventory		7
Work in Process Inventory–Mixing	2	
Factory Wages		2
Work in Process Inventory–Mixing	3	
Factory Overhead		3

EXHIBIT 23-2 *Flow of Costs Through a Process Costing System (amounts in thousands)*

Work in Process Inventory – Mixing	
Direct materials 7	Transfer cost of
Conversion costs:	goods ready for
Direct labor 2	shaping process 10
Factory overhead 3	
Ending balance 2	

Finished Goods Inventory	
Cost of goods completed from heating department 12	Cost of goods sold 8
Ending balance 4	

Work in Process Inventory – Shaping	
Cost tranferred in from mixing 10	Transfer cost of
Conversion costs:	goods ready for
Direct labor 1	heating process 9
Factory overhead 2	
Ending balance 4	

Cost of Goods Sold	
Cost of goods sold 8	

Work in Process Inventory – Heating	
Cost tranferred in from shaping 9	Transfer cost of
Conversion costs:	goods completed
Direct labor 1	to finished goods
Factory overhead 5	
Ending balance 3	

The following entry transfers cost from one processing department to the next:

To transfer cost from the Mixing Department to the Shaping Department (amounts in thousands):

Work in Process Inventory – Shaping	10	
Work in Process Inventory – Mixing		10

Remaining entries for adding cost in the Shaping Department, transferring costs on to finished goods, and accounting for cost of goods sold follow.

To record the additional labor and overhead cost of the Shaping Department. (These entries affect the Work in Process Inventory – Shaping account in Exhibit 23-2, amounts in thousands.)

Work in Process Inventory – Shaping	1	
Factory Wages		1
Work in Process Inventory – Shaping	2	
Factory Overhead		2

Entries for the Heating Department parallel those for the Shaping Department.

To transfer cost of goods completed from the Heating Department to Finished Goods (amounts in thousands):

Finished Goods Inventory	12	
Work in Process Inventory–Heating		12

To account for the cost of goods sold (amounts in thousands):

Cost of Goods Sold	8	
Finished Goods Inventory		8

Unlike a job order costing system, a process costing system is likely to have a separate work in process account for each processing department. In a job order system the work in process account is supported by job cost records for the various jobs.

Tracing the Flow of Costs

In process costing, the accounting task is to trace the flow of costs through the production process. This task has two parts. First, we must account for the cost of goods that have been completed in one department and sent to the second department. Second, we must account for the cost of incomplete units, which remain within a department.

Let's look at a sports company that manufactures swimming masks. This company's Shaping Department shapes the body of the swim masks. The direct material is the plastic that is formed into the masks. The partially completed masks then move to the Finishing Department, where the clear faceplate is inserted in the body and sealed in place.

Assume that during October, the Shaping Department incurs the following costs in processing 50,000 masks:

Direct materials		$140,000
Conversion costs:		
Direct labor	$21,250	
Factory overhead	46,750	68,000
Cost to account for		$208,000

If the shaping process is complete for all 50,000 masks, the cost to be transferred to Work in Process Inventory–Finishing is the full $208,000. The unit cost is $208,000 divided by the 50,000 units, which equals $4.16. But suppose that shaping is complete for only 40,000 units. At October 31 the Shaping Department still has 10,000 masks in process. How do we compute unit cost when the total cost applies to finished units *and* unfinished units? Accountants answer this question by using the concept of *equivalent units of production.*

Equivalent Units of Production

Equivalent units of production—often called simply equivalent units—is a measure of the number of complete units that *could* have been manufactured from start to finish using the costs incurred during the period.

Let's assume that the 10,000 unfinished units still in the Shaping Department are one-quarter complete. The number of equivalent units equals the number of partially complete units times the percentage of completion: 10,000 units × 25% complete = 2,500 units. The number 2,500 tells us how many whole units are represented by the partially complete units. We add the 2,500 units to the number of finished units — 40,000 — to arrive at the period's equivalent units of production: 42,500.

The idea of equivalent units is not confined to manufacturing situations. It is a basic common denominator for measuring activities, output, and workload. For example, colleges and universities measure student enrollments in "full-time equivalents." Suppose a full-time class load is 12 hours per term. Assume 1,000 students are taking a full load and an additional 1,000 students are taking an average of 6 hours in classes. This school has a full-time equivalent enrollment of 1,500 students [1,000 + (1,000 × 6/12)].

Steps in Process Cost Accounting _____

Using the data from the swimming mask example, we will discuss the five-step application of process costing.

Step 1: Summarize the Flow of Production in Physical Units

The left part of Exhibit 23-3 tabulates the movement of swimming masks into and out of the Shaping Department. We assume for clarity that work began October 1, so the Work in Process account had no balance at September 30.

Step 2: Compute Equivalent Units of Production

Cost accountants compute equivalent units separately for the two types of costs incurred in manufacturing: direct materials and conversion costs. The Shaping Department has 10,000 units unfinished at October 31. We assume that all direct materials have been added (the chemicals have been added to begin shaping the bodies of the swimming masks) but that three quarters of the conversion costs (direct labor and factory overhead) remain to be applied. Thus all 50,000 units are finished in terms of direct material. We must compute equivalent units for the conversion costs. Since 25 percent of conversion costs have already been added, we multiply the 10,000 unfinished units by .25, which gives us 2,500 units. Added to the 40,000 finished units, the equivalent units for conversion costs come to 42,500.

Exhibit 23-3 combines the data for Step 1 and Step 2. Note that the number of equivalent units for direct materials and conversion costs are different. This is often the case.

Step 3: Summarize Total Cost to Account For

Exhibit 23-4 summarizes the total costs to account for in the Shaping Department (cost data are assumed). These costs are the total debits in Work in Process Inventory – Shaping, including any beginning balance. The Shaping Department has 50,000 units and $208,000 of cost to account for.

EXHIBIT 23-3 *Step 1: Flow of Production in Physical Units and*
Step 2: Equivalent Units of Production

Shaping Department
For the Month Ended October 31, 19XX

		Step 2 Equivalent Units of Production	
Flow of Production	**Step 1 Flow of Physical Units**	**Direct Materials**	**Conversion Costs**
Units to account for:			
Work in process, September 30	—		
Started production during October	50,000		
Total physical units to account for	50,000		
Units accounted for:			
Completed and transferred out during October	40,000	40,000	40,000
Work in process, October 31	10,000	10,000	2,500*
Total physical units accounted for	50,000		
Equivalent units of production		50,000	42,500

* 10,000 units each 25% complete = 2,500 equivalent units

Step 4: Compute Unit Costs

In Step 2 we computed the number of equivalent units for direct materials (50,000) and conversion costs (42,500). Because their equivalent units differ, a separate cost per unit must be computed for materials cost and for conversion costs. Exhibit 23-4 provides the data. The direct materials cost is $140,000. Conversion costs are $68,000, the sum of direct labor ($21,250) and factory overhead ($46,750).

We now have all the data needed to apply process costing in this example. We divide the direct materials cost by the equivalent units for direct materials:

EXHIBIT 23-4 *Step 3: Summary of Total Costs to Account For*

Shaping Department
For the Month Ended October 31, 19XX

Work in Process–Shaping

	Physical Units	Dollars		Physical Units	Dollars
Inventory, September 30	-0-	$ -0-	Transferred out	40,000	$?
Production started:	50,000		Ending inventory	10,000	?
Direct materials		140,000	Total accounted for	50,000	
Conversion costs:					
Direct labor		21,250			
Factory overhead		46,750			
Total to account for	50,000	$208,000			

EXHIBIT 23-5   *Step 4: Computation of Unit Costs*

Shaping Department
For the Month Ended October 31, 19XX

	Direct Materials	Conversion Costs	Total
Work in process, September 30	$ -0-	$ -0-	$ -0-
Costs added during October	$140,000	$ 68,000	$208,000
Divide by equivalent units of production	÷50,000	÷42,500	
Cost per equivalent unit.	$ 2.80 +	$ 1.60 =	$ 4.40

$140,000/50,000 = $2.80. The $2.80 is the unit price for direct materials. We compute unit price for conversion cost in a similar manner: $68,000/42,500 = $1.60. Exhibit 23-5 shows the computation of unit costs.

Step 5: Apply Total Cost to Units Completed and Units in Ending Work in Process Inventory

Exhibit 23-6 shows how the units costs computed in Step 4 are applied to units completed and to units in ending work in process. With Step 5 we account for the cost of the shaping process during the period.

The 40,000 units completed and transferred out of the shaping department bear a unit cost of $4.40 (direct materials of $2.80 + conversion cost of $1.60). The 10,000 units still in process at the end of the period have 10,000 equivalent units of *direct materials* (at $2.80 per unit) and 2,500 equivalent units of *conversion cost* (at $1.60 per unit). Observe that the sum of these two unit costs ($2.80 and $1.60) is the same as total unit cost of the completed units ($4.40), from Step 4. Also, total cost accounted for ($208,000) must agree with the total from Step 3.

October production in the Shaping Department would be recorded as follows:

OBJECTIVE 4

Record process costing transactions

To requisition materials and apply labor and overhead cost to the shaping department. (Exhibit 23-4)

EXHIBIT 23-6   *Step 5: Application of Total Cost to Units Completed and Units in Ending Work in Process Inventory*

Shaping Department
For the Month Ended October 31, 19XX

	Direct Materials	Conversion Costs	Total
Units completed and transferred out (40,000)	40,000 × $4.40		= $176,000
Units in ending work in process inventory (10,000):			
Direct materials	10,000 × $2.80		= 28,000
Conversion costs		2,500 × $1.60 =	4,000
Total cost of work in process.			32,000
Total cost accounted for			$208,000

Work in Process Inventory–Shaping....................	140,000	
Materials Inventory.............................		140,000
Work in Process Inventory–Shaping....................	21,250	
Factory Wages.................................		21,250
Work in Process Inventory–Shaping....................	46,750	
Factory Overhead...............................		46,750

The entry to transfer the cost of completed units from the Shaping Department to the Finishing Department is (Exhibit 23-6)

Work in Process Inventory–Finishing....................	176,000	
Work in Process Inventory–Shaping.................		176,000

After these entries are posted, the Work in Process Inventory–Shaping account appears as follows:

Work in Process Inventory–Shaping

Balance, September 30	—	Transferred to Finishing	176,000
Direct materials	140,000		
Direct labor	21,250		
Factory overhead	46,750		
Balance, October 31	32,000		

    With Shaping Department costs accounted for, we proceed to the Finishing Department. First, however, let's reinforce what you have learned with a Summary Problem for Your Review.

Summary Problem for Your Review

Identify the missing amounts X and Y in the following production cost report prepared by Jacobs-Webster, Inc., for May:

Painting Department
Production Cost Report
For the Month Ended May 31, 19XX

	Physical Units	Total Costs
Work in process, April 30	—	$ —
Started in production during May..............................	20,000	43,200*
Total to account for	20,000	$43,200
Completed and transferred to Finishing Department during May	17,000	$ X
Work in process, May 31 (0% complete as to direct materials, 40% complete as to conversion cost)...	3,000	Y
Total accounted for	20,000	$43,200

   * Includes direct materials of $6,800 and conversion costs of $36,400.

SOLUTION TO REVIEW PROBLEM

Step 1: Flow of Production in Physical Units
and
Step 2: Equivalent Units of Production

Painting Department
For the Month Ended May 31, 19XX

Flow of Production	Step 1 Flow of Physical Units	Step 2 Equivalent Units of Production Direct Materials	Conversion Costs
Units to account for:			
Work in process, April 30	—		
Started production during May	20,000		
Total physical units to account for	20,000		
Units accounted for:			
Completed and transferred out during May	17,000	17,000	17,000
Work in process, May 31	3,000	— *	1,200*
Total physical units accounted for	20,000		
Equivalent units of production		17,000	18,200

* Direct materials: 3,000 units each 0% complete = 0 equivalent units
Conversion costs: 3,000 units each 40% complete = 1,200 equivalent units

Step 3: Summary of Total Costs to Account For

Painting Department
For the Month Ended May 31, 19XX

Work in Process – Painting

	Physical Units	Dollars
Inventory, April 30	-0-	$ -0-
Production started:	20,000	
Direct materials		6,800
Conversion costs		36,400
Total to account for	20,000	$43,200

Step 4: Computation of Unit Costs

Painting Department
For the Month Ended May 31, 19XX

	Direct Materials	Conversion Costs	Total
Work in process, April 30.	$ -0-	$ -0-	$ -0-
Costs added during May	$ 6,800	$ 36,400	$43,200
Divide by equivalent units of production	÷17,000	÷18,200	
Cost per equivalent unit.	$ .40 +	$ 2.00 =	$ 2.40

Step 5: Allocation of Total Cost to Units Completed and Units in Ending Work in Process Inventory

Painting Department
For the Month Ended May 31, 19XX

		Direct Materials	Conversion Costs	Total
X	Units completed and transferred out (17,000)	17,000 × $2.40		= $40,800
	Units in ending work in process inventory (3,000):			
	Direct materials	-0- × $.40		= -0-
	Conversion costs		1,200 × $2.00 =	2,400
Y	Total cost of work in process.			2,400
	Total cost accounted for			$43,200

Process Costing Extended to a Second Department _____

Most manufacturing systems include multiple processing steps. In this section, we introduce a second processing department to complete the picture of process costing. We continue with the manufacture of swim masks. The Finishing Department adds the faceplate and sealant to the shaped swim masks. The faceplate is the direct material added in the finishing process. It is important to keep in mind that *direct materials* in the Finishing Department refers to the faceplates added *in that department* and not to the materials (the chemicals) added in the previous Shaping Department. Likewise, *conversion cost* in the Finishing Department refers to the labor and overhead of that department only.

We assume 5,000 units were in process in the Finishing Department on October 1. These units were 60 percent complete as to Finishing Department conversion costs but 0 percent complete as to direct materials because the faceplates are added near the end of the finishing process. These facts, used throughout

OBJECTIVE 5

Account for process costing in a second department

EXHIBIT 23-7 *Finishing Department Facts for October*

Units:		
Work in process, September 30 (0% complete as to direct materials, 60% complete as to conversion costs).............................		5,000 units
Transferred in from Shaping Department during October............................		40,000 units
Completed during October.....................		38,000 units
Work in process, October 31 (0% complete as to direct materials, 30% complete as to conversion costs)..		7,000 units
Costs:		
Work in process, September 30		$ 24,000
Transferred in from Shaping Department during October............................		176,000
Direct materials added during October		19,000
Conversion costs added during October:		
Direct labor................................	$ 3,710	
Factory overhead..........................	11,130	14,840

discussion of the accounting for the Finishing Department, are summarized in Exhibit 23-7. (Refer to Exhibit 23-6, page 904.)

Equivalent Units in a Second Department

The major accounting task in dealing with a second department is the computation of equivalent units. Exhibit 23-8 summarizes the flow of physical units (Step 1) in order to compute the equivalent units of production (Step 2) for the Finishing Department. Note that there are three categories of equivalent units. In addition to equivalent units for *direct materials* and *conversion costs* added in the Finishing Department, we must also compute equivalent units for those units that were *transferred in* from the preceding department. Whenever there is a second department, it will always have units and costs transferred in from the preceding department. In our illustration, 40,000 units were transferred into the Finishing Department during October. Of these transferred-in units, 33,000 units were completed, and 7,000 units remained in ending inventory. For transferred-in costs, equivalent units include the full total (33,000 + 7,000 = 40,000).

Equivalent units of *direct materials* have three components: beginning work-in-process inventory, units transferred in and completed during the month, and ending work-in-process inventory. Exhibit 23-7 indicates that beginning inventory contained 5,000 units that were 0 percent complete as to direct materials. The first-in, first-out (FIFO) method is employed in Exhibit 23-7 in accounting for work in process inventories. Under FIFO, the computation of equivalent units is confined to the work done during the current period—October in this example. Therefore, the $24,000 beginning balance is kept separate from the costs added during the current period. The $24,000 is *not* included in the computation of the unit costs of equivalent units for the work done in October. The major advantage of the FIFO method is that the efficiency of performance in October can be judged independently from the performance in September. In brief, the work done during the current period is key information for planning and control purposes as well as for FIFO inventory valuation.[1]

---

[1] Other methods, such as weighted-average cost, can also be used. They are explored in cost accounting textbooks.

Under the FIFO cost method, beginning inventory is completed first. During October the Finishing Department added the faceplates (100 percent of the direct materials that the Finishing Department adds) to complete these 5,000 units. The 33,000 units that were transferred in and completed are automatically part of equivalent units. Ending inventory is 0 percent complete as to direct materials (faceplates have not yet been added). Consequently ending inventory accounts for no equivalent units. Altogether, equivalent production for direct materials is 38,000 units (5,000 units from beginning inventory + 33,000 units transferred in during the month).

Equivalent units of *conversion costs* also have three components: beginning work-in-process inventory, units transferred in and completed during the month, and ending work-in-process inventory. The Finishing Department's beginning inventory of 5,000 units was 60 percent complete as to conversion costs when the last period ended. During October the Finishing Department completed these 5,000 units by adding the remaining 40 percent of conversion costs. For beginning inventory, equivalent production is 2,000 units (5,000 × .40). Units transferred in and completed during the month (33,000 units) are the second component of equivalent production. Ending inventory is the third component. At October 31 the inventory of 7,000 units still in process in the Finishing Department is 30 percent complete as to conversion costs, so equivalent production includes 2,100 units (7,000 × .30). Altogether, equivalent production for conversion costs totals 37,100 units (2,000 + 33,000 + 2,100). Exhibit 23-8 summarizes the equivalent unit computations for the Finishing Department.

EXHIBIT 23-8   Step 1: Flow of Production in Physical Units and
Step 2: Equivalent Units of Production

Finishing Department
For the Month Ended October 31, 19XX

Flow of Production	Step 1 Flow of Physical Units	Step 2 Equivalent Units of Production		
		Transferred In	Direct Materials	Conversion Costs
Units to account for:				
Work in process, September 30	5,000			
Transferred in during October	40,000			
Total physical units to account for	45,000			
Units accounted for:				
Completed and transferred out during October:				
From beginning inventory	5,000	—	5,000*	2,000*
Transferred in and completed during October				
(38,000 − 5,000)	33,000	33,000	33,000	33,000
Work in process, October 31	7,000	7,000	— **	2,100**
Total physical units accounted for.	45,000			
Equivalent units of production		40,000	38,000	37,100

* Direct materials: 5,000 units each 100% completed in Finishing Department during October = 5,000 equivalent units.
  Conversion costs: 5,000 units each 40% completed in Finishing Department during October = 2,000 equivalent units.
** Direct materials: 7,000 units each 0% completed in Finishing Department during October = 0 equivalent units.
  Conversion costs: 7,000 units each 30% completed in Finishing Department during October = 2,100 equivalent units.

EXHIBIT 23-9 *Steps 3 and 4: Computation of Unit Costs*

	Transferred-In Costs	Direct Materials	Conversion Costs	Total
Finishing Department				
For the Month Ended October 31, 19XX				
Work in process, September 30 (from Exhibit 23-7)........	Work done before October			$ 24,000
Costs added during October (from Exhibit 23-7)..........	$176,000	$ 19,000	$ 14,840	209,840
Divide by equivalent units (from Exhibit 23-8)...........	÷40,000	÷38,000	÷37,100	
Cost per equivalent unit...............................	$4.40	$.50	$.40	
Total cost to account for...............................				$233,840

Unit Costs in a Second Department

The October costs of the Finishing Department are accumulated as shown in Exhibit 23-9. The exhibit shows how equivalent units are used to compute the unit costs in the Finishing Department process.

Application of Total Cost in a Second Department

Exhibit 23-10 shows how to apply total cost of the Finishing Department to units completed and transferred to finished goods and to units still in process at the end of the period.

EXHIBIT 23-10 *Step 5: Application of Total Cost to Units Completed and Units in Ending Work in Process Inventory*

	Transferred-In Costs	Direct Materials	Conversion Costs	Total
Finishing Department				
For the Month Ended October 31, 19XX				
Units completed and transferred out to Finished Goods Inventory:				
From work in process, September 30:				$ 24,000
Costs added during October:				
Direct materials	—	5,000 × $.50		2,500
Conversion costs	—		2,000 × $.40	800
Total completed from September 30 inventory.........				27,300
Units transferred in and completed during October.......	33,000 × ($4.40 + $.50 + $.40)			174,900
Total costs transferred out				$202,200
Work in process, October 31:				
Transferred-in costs...............................	7,000 × $4.40			$ 30,800
Direct materials..................................		—		—
Conversion costs.................................			2,100 × $.40	840
Total work in process, October 31				31,640
Total cost accounted for				$233,840

The entries for the Shaping Department were recorded on page 905. The following entries record Finishing Department activity during October.

To transfer in cost of completed units from the Shaping Department (repeat of the last entry in the Shaping Department, page 905):

Work in Process Inventory – Finishing.....................	176,000	
Work in Process Inventory – Shaping................		176,000

To requisition materials and apply labor and overhead cost to the Finishing Department (amounts from Exhibit 23-7):

Work in Process Inventory – Finishing.....................	19,000	
Materials Inventory................................		19,000
Work in Process Inventory – Finishing.....................	3,710	
Factory Wages.....................................		3,710
Work in Process Inventory – Finishing.....................	11,130	
Factory Overhead..................................		11,130

The entry to transfer the cost of completed units from the Finishing Department to finished goods is based on the dollar amount taken from Exhibit 23-10 and listed on the production report in Exhibit 23-11.

Finished Goods Inventory	202,200	
Work in Process Inventory – Finishing................		202,200

After posting, the key accounts appear as follows. Observe the accumulation of costs as debits to Work in Process and the transfer of costs from one account to the next.

Work in Process Inventory – Shaping

(Exhibit 23-4)		(Exhibit 23-6)	
Balance, September 30	—	Transferred to finishing	176,000
Direct materials	140,000		
Direct labor	21,250		
Factory overhead	46,750		
Balance, October 31	32,000		

Work in Process Inventory – Finishing

(Exhibit 23-7)		(Exhibit 23-10)	
Balance, September 30	24,000	Transferred to finished goods	202,200
Transferred from shaping	176,000		
Direct materials	19,000		
Direct labor	3,710		
Factory overhead	11,130		
Balance, October 31	31,640		

Finished Goods Inventory

Balance, September 30	—	
Transferred from finishing	202,200	

EXHIBIT 23-11 Production Cost Report

Finishing Department
Production Cost Report
For the Month Ended October 31, 19XX

	Physical Units	Total Costs
Work in process, September 30	5,000	$ 24,000
Transferred in from Shaping Department during October. . .	40,000	176,000
Cost added in Finishing Department during October:		
Direct materials	—	19,000
Conversion costs ($3,710 + $11,130).	—	14,840
Total to account for.	45,000	$233,840
Completed and transferred to finished goods		
during October	38,000	$202,200
Work in process, October 31	7,000	31,640
Total accounted for.	45,000	$233,840

Production Cost Report

A **production cost report** summarizes the activity in a processing department for the period. Exhibit 23-11 is a production cost report for the Finishing Department for October. It shows the department's beginning inventory, the number of units and the cost transferred in during the month, and the costs added. These amounts make up the totals to account for. The production report also shows the units completed and the costs transferred out of the department and the ending inventory.

These reports vary from company to company, depending on the level of detail desired by the managers. If managers want more detail, some or all of the additional information in Exhibits 23-8, 23-9, and 23-10 can be included. For example, Exhibit 23-12 provides more detail than Exhibit 23-11.

How is the production report used for decision making? Managers compare direct materials and conversion costs to budgeted amounts for the department. If these costs are too high, corrective action is taken. If costs are below budget, the employees responsible may receive incentive awards. The number of units produced can be compared to budgeted production. Production that is too low can be investigated and corrected. If production in excess of budget is welcomed, such performance may lead to pay raises for responsible employees.

Operation Costing

We have discussed and illustrated the job order cost system in Chapter 22 and the process cost system in this chapter. These costing methods do not fit all companies' manufacturing situations. Each company designs its cost system to meet its own needs. Some businesses use hybrid cost systems that combine features from job costing and process costing.

EXHIBIT 23-12 *Production Cost Report (Expanded)*

Finishing Department
Production Cost Report (Expanded)
For the Month Ended October 31, 19XX

		Transferred-in Costs	Direct Materials	Conversion Costs	Total
	Work in process, September 30				$ 24,000
	Cost added during October	$176,000	$ 19,000	$ 14,840	209,840
(Step 3)	Total costs to account for				$233,840
	Equivalent units for work during October (Steps 1 and 2 in Exhibit 23-8)	÷40,000	÷38,000	÷37,100	
(Step 4)	Cost per equivalent unit.	$ 4.40	$ .50	$ .40	
(Step 5)	Application of total costs:				
	From work in process, September 30				$ 24,000
	Costs added during October.		5,000 × $.50 = $2,500	2,000 × $.40 = $800	3,300
	Total completed from September 30 inventory				27,300
	Units transferred in and completed during October.	33,000 × ($4.40 + $.50 + $.40)			174,900
					202,200
	Work in process, October 31:				
	Transferred-in costs	7,000 × $4.40			30,800
	Direct materials.		—		—
	Conversion costs.			2,100 × $.40	840
	Total work in process, October 31				31,640
	Total costs accounted for				$233,840

The most popular hybrid costing system is called *operation costing.* For example, a textile manufacturer like Burlington may mass-produce cotton into fabric of a certain weave and pattern. This part of the work calls for a *process* costing system.

Suppose, however, market research indicates that some consumers want the fabric to be water repellant, so Burlington divides the fabric into two groups. One half of the fabric receives additional chemical treatment. Because the two halves of fabric receive different treatments, a *job order* costing system is appropriate. **Operation costing** is a hybrid cost system used to account for the manufacture of goods that have some common features plus some individual characteristics.

The textile, clothing, shoe, and semiconductor industries use operation costing systems. We may also consider the automakers' cost systems as operation systems. All cars undergo common processing steps, but certain operations—for instance, installing electric windows—are performed on some autos but not on others.

Products pass through the various operations in groups identified by *work orders* or *production orders.* The work order—similar to a job cost record in a job order system—lists the direct materials and the step-by-step procedures needed to make a finished product. A Zenith appliance factory may specify that standard televisions receive one test for quality control. However, deluxe models may be tested twice. Work orders for various models differ in the materials and/or the operations they require.

Suppose a clothing manufacturer like L. L. Bean produces two lines of blazers. The deluxe blazers use better materials and undergo more operations than the standard blazers, as the following data indicate:

	Work Order 1 Deluxe Blazers	Work Order 2 Standard Blazers
Direct materials	Wool Satin lining Bone buttons	Polyester Rayon lining Plastic buttons
Operations (conversion costs).....	1. Cutting cloth 2. Checking edges 3. Sewing body 4. Checking seams 6. Sewing collars and lapels by *hand*	1. Cutting cloth 3. Sewing body 5. Sewing collars and lapels by *machine*

The costs of the blazers are compiled by work order. The direct materials—different for each group—must be specifically identified with the appropriate order. Conversion costs—direct labor and factory overhead—are not tied to separate orders. Instead, conversion costs are accumulated by operation. An average conversion cost for each unit of operation time (a minute or an hour, for example) is applied to each work order in a manner similar to the application of overhead in a *job cost system*. The similarity of this operation costing system to *process costing* is that certain steps apply to all items. In our example, all blazers undergo cutting the cloth and sewing the body. This blending of the two types of cost systems makes up this operation costing system.

Suppose L. L. Bean has work orders for 100 deluxe wool blazers and for 200 standard polyester blazers, as shown in Exhibit 23-13 (amounts are assumed):

EXHIBIT 23-13   *Cost Summary—Operation Costing System*

	Work Order 1 100 Deluxe Blazers	Work Order 2 200 Standard Blazers
Direct materials....................	$2,000	$3,100
Conversion costs:		
Operation 1.....................	580	1,160
Operation 2...................	300	
Operation 3.....................	500	1,000
Operation 4.................	600	
Operation 5....................		800
Operation 6....................	700	
Total manufacturing costs	$4,680	$6,060

Direct labor and overhead vanish as separate classifications in an operation costing system. These costs are added together, and their sum is applied to production based on the company's budgeted rate for conversion cost of performing each operation. For example, the conversion costs of Operation 1 might be budgeted for the year as follows (amounts are assumed):

Budgeted application rate for conversion cost in Operation 1 $=$ $\dfrac{\text{Budgeted conversion cost of Operation 1 for the year}}{\text{Budgeted machine hours for the year in Operation 1}}$

(Budgeted direct labor + Budgeted factory overhead)

$$= \frac{\$180{,}000 + \$400{,}000}{20{,}000 \text{ hours}} = \$29 \text{ per machine hour}$$

As goods are produced, conversion costs are applied to the work orders by multiplying the hourly application rate ($29) times the number of machine hours used in that operation. Suppose it takes 20 machine hours to work on the 100 wool blazers in Operation 1. The conversion cost of Operation 1 is $580 (20 hours × $29 per hour) for the wool blazers. For the 200 polyester blazers, the conversion cost of Operation 1 is twice as much, $1,160 (40 hours × $29), because there are twice as many polyester blazers. Likewise, Operation 3 costs twice as much for the polyester blazers as for the wool blazers. Operations 2, 4, and 6 are performed on the wool blazers only—Operation 5 on the polyester blazers only.

Summary journal entries for applying costs to the polyester blazers follow. Entries for the wool blazers would be similar.

The entry to requisition materials for the 200 polyester blazers is as follows (amount is taken from Exhibit 23-13):

Work in Process Inventory–Standard Blazers..................	3,100	
Materials Inventory.....................................		3,100

Because direct labor and factory overhead lose their separate identities in an operation costing system, these costs are combined in a single Conversion Cost account, as follows (amounts are assumed):

Conversion Cost	3,080	
Factory Wages.......................................		1,730
Factory Overhead		1,350

In an operation costing system, conversion cost is applied to work in process based on the budgeted application rate. To apply conversion cost to the 200 polyester blazers, the business can make the following summary entry for Operations 1, 3, and 5 (amounts from Exhibit 23-13):

Work in Process Inventory–Standard Blazers		
($1,160 + $1,000 + $800)...............................	2,960	
Conversion Cost		2,960

After posting, Work in Process Inventory–Standard Blazers has a $6,060 debit balance as follows:

Work in Process Inventory–Standard Blazers

Direct materials	3,100	
Conversion costs	2,960	
Balance	6,060	

When the blazers are finished, their cost is transferred to Finished Goods Inventory in the usual manner.

Any over- or underapplication of conversion cost is disposed of at the end of the year in the same manner as over- or underapplied overhead in a job order costing system. In this case, Conversion Cost has been debited for actual cost of $3,080 and credited for cost applied of $2,960. The debit balance of $120 indicates that conversion costs are underapplied:

Conversion Cost			
Actual cost	3,080	Cost applied	2,960
Balance — cost underapplied	120		

Joint Product Cost

A manufacturing process that produces more than one product simultaneously is called a joint process. **Joint products** are goods that are specifically identified as individual products only after a juncture in the production process called the **split-off point.** To be called a joint product, the item must have a sales value that is significant in relation to the other item produced. For example, refining crude oil produces gasoline and natural gas as joint products. Exhibit 23-14 diagrams this joint process.

Many industries have manufacturing processes that create joint products. Soap making, for example, produces lanolin and other oils for cosmetics, in addition to soap. Refining copper also produces ammonia, which has many uses.

How do we assign costs to individual products that are manufactured by a joint process? After the split-off point, costs are easily assigned. For example, after gasoline and natural gas are separated in the refining process, further costs can be separately identified with the two products. But what costs incurred *before* split-off are assigned to the individual joint products? For example, how should we allocate the cost of exploring and drilling for oil to final products (gasoline and natural gas)? These *joint processing costs* may be allocated using the *relative sales value* method.

Assume the joint cost of processing 65,000 gallons of gasoline and liquid natural gas is $72,000. Exhibit 23-15 shows how to allocate this joint cost to the two products.

The relative sales value of each joint product is computed by dividing its individual sales value by the total sales value. In the exhibit, the gasoline sales value is $60,000 (50,000 × $1.20), and liquid natural gas's sales value is $30,000 (15,000 × $2). Total sales value of the two products is $90,000. Gasoline makes up ⅔ ($60,000/$90,000) of the total sales value, and liquid natural gas makes up the remaining ⅓ ($30,000/$90,000). Multiplying joint cost of $72,000 by these fractions gives the two products' individual costs of $48,000 and $24,000. Any

EXHIBIT 23-14   *Joint Products*

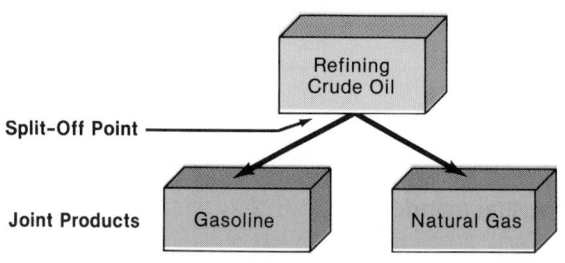

EXHIBIT 23-15 *Allocation of Joint Cost to Joint Products*

OBJECTIVE 7

Allocate cost to joint products and byproducts

cost of processing gasoline after split-off is added to $48,000 to determine the total cost of the gasoline. The cost of liquid natural gas is computed similarly.

Byproduct Cost

The difference between a joint product and a byproduct depends on the relative sales values of the products. **Byproducts** are those outputs of joint processes with minor sale value in comparison to the main products. Sawdust is a byproduct of a lumber company. Meat packing yields byproducts that are used as pet food.

Accounting for the cost of byproducts is straightforward. Byproducts are assigned an accounting value called **net realizable value,** which is their sales value, less the cost of selling them. Suppose a lumber company's Work in Process–Milling account has a balance of $229,000. This amount includes the estimated sales value of the byproduct sawdust, $5,600. It will cost the company $600 to sell the sawdust, so the net realizable value of the sawdust is $5,000 ($5,600 − $600). The entry to record the net realizable value of the sawdust is

Byproducts Inventory	5,000	
Work in Process–Milling		5,000

Sale of the byproduct is accounted for in the usual manner. Because its cost is embedded in the cost of the main product, the accounting value of the byproduct is subtracted from the main product's cost. In this illustration, the cost assigned to lumber is $224,000 ($229,000 − $5,000).

Summary Problem for Your Review

This problem extends the Summary Problem for Your Review on page 905 to a second processing department. Jacobs-Webster, Inc., had the following activity in its Finishing Department during May.

Finishing Department Facts for May

Units:

Work in process, April 30 (20% complete as to direct materials, 70% complete as to conversion costs)............................ 4,000 units

Transferred in from Painting Department during May............. 17,000 units

Completed during May....................................... 15,000 units

Work in process, May 31 (30% complete as to direct materials, 80% complete as to conversion costs)............................ 6,000 units

Costs:

Work in process, April 30................................... $18,000

Transferred in from Painting Department during May............. 40,800

Direct materials added during May........................... 6,400

Conversion costs added during May........................... 25,500

Required

Show the allocation of total cost to units completed and units in ending work in process inventory in the Finishing Department during May.

SOLUTION TO REVIEW PROBLEM

Step 1: Flow of Production in Physical Units and
Step 2: Equivalent Units of Production

Finishing Department
For the Month Ended May 31, 19XX

Flow of Production	Step 1 Flow of Physical Units	Step 2 Equivalent Units of Production Transferred In	Direct Materials	Conversion Costs
Units to account for:				
Work in process, April 30	4,000			
Transferred in during May	17,000			
Total physical units to account for	21,000			
Units accounted for:				
Completed and transferred out during May:				
From beginning inventory..............................	4,000	—	3,200*	1,200*
Transferred in and completed during May (17,000 − 6,000) ..	11,000	11,000	11,000	11,000
Work in process, May 31..............................	6,000	6,000	1,800**	4,800**
Total physical units accounted for	21,000			
Equivalent units of production............................		17,000	16,000	17,000

* Direct materials: 4,000 units each 80% completed = 3,200 equivalent units.
  Conversion costs: 4,000 units each 30% completed = 1,200 equivalent units.
** Direct materials: 6,000 units each 30% completed = 1,800 equivalent units.
   Conversion costs: 6,000 units each 80% completed = 4,800 equivalent units.

Steps 3 and 4: Computation of Unit Costs

Finishing Department
For the Month Ended May 31, 19XX

	Transferred-In Costs	Direct Materials	Conversion Costs	Total
Work in process, April 30	Work done before May			$18,000
Costs added during May	$ 40,800	$ 6,400	$ 25,500	72,700
Divide by equivalent units.............................	÷ 17,000	÷ 16,000	÷ 17,000	
Cost per equivalent unit................................	$ 2.40	$ .40	$ 1.50	
Total cost to account for................................				$90,700

Step 5: Application of Total Cost to Units Completed and Units in Ending Work in Process Inventory

Finishing Department
For the Month Ended October 31, 19XX

	Transferred-In Costs	Direct Materials	Conversion Costs	Total
Units completed and transferred out to Finished Goods Inventory:				
From work in process, April 30.........................				$18,000
Costs added during May:				
Direct materials.....................................	—	3,200 × $.40		1,280
Conversion costs....................................	—		1,200 × $1.50	1,800
Total completed from April 30 inventory................				21,080
Units transferred in and completed during May	11,000 × ($2.40 + $.40 + $1.50)			47,300
Total costs transferred out.............................				$68,380
Work in process, May 31:				
Transferred-in costs..................................	6,000 × $2.40			$14,400
Direct materials		1,800 × $.40		720
Conversion costs			4,800 × $1.50	7,200
Total work in process, May 31				22,320
Total cost accounted for				$90,700

Summary

Process costing is a system for assigning costs to products that are mass-produced in continuous fashion through a sequence of production steps. In a process costing system costs are accumulated by processes (departments) and flow from one department to another until the product is completed.

The main accounting problem in process costing is determining the cost of the work in process transferred from one department to the next. This complication arises because the goods in process may be in various stages of completion. For example, they may be 40 percent complete as to direct materials but only 25 percent complete as to conversion costs (direct labor and factory overhead). Cost accountants compute the number of *equivalent units* of production that could have been manufactured from start to finish with the costs that were incurred in each department during the period. Cost divided by the number of equivalent units equals unit cost. This unit cost, multiplied by the number of units transferred out of the department, determines the cost entering the next department. Unit cost, multiplied by the number of units remaining in Work in Process Inventory, measures the department's ending inventory. Companies summarize the activity in each processing department for the period on a production cost report.

Five steps in process cost accounting are

Step 1. Summarize the flow of production in physical units.

Step 2. Compute equivalent units of production.

Step 3. Summarize total costs to account for.

Step 4. Compute unit costs.

Step 5. Apply unit costs to units completed and units in ending work in process inventory.

A number of hybrid costing systems include elements of process costing and job order costing. *Operation costing* is a system used for the manufacture of goods that have some common features but also some individual characteristics.

Joint products are those items with significant value that are not identified as specific products until after a split-off point in the production process. Cost is allocated to joint products based on their relative sales values. *Byproducts* are insignificant relative to the main item being produced. The value assigned to a byproduct is its *net realizable value* (expected sale price less the cost of selling the byproduct).

Self-Study Questions

Test your understanding of the chapter by marking the best answer to each of the following questions.

1. For which of the following products is a process costing system most appropriate? *(p. 897)*
   a. Breakfast cereal
   b. Automobiles
   c. Houses
   d. Furniture

2. A key difference between job order costing and process costing is that *(p. 898)*
   a. Costs are assigned to direct materials in job costing and to indirect materials in process costing.
   b. Job costing uses a single work in process account and process costing uses a separate work in process account for each department.
   c. Job order costing, but not process costing, uses conversion costs.
   d. Factory overhead is used in process costing but not in job order costing.

3. During August the Assembly Department of Fisk Manufacturing Company completed and transferred 20,000 intercom units to the Finishing Department. The Assembly Department's August 31 inventory included 6,000 units, 90 percent complete as to direct materials and 75 percent complete as to conversion costs. August equivalent units of the Assembly Department total *(p. 902)*
   a. 20,000
   b. 24,500
   c. 25,400
   d. 25,400 as to direct materials and 24,500 as to conversion costs

4. The concept of equivalent units is useful for *(p. 903)*
   a. Measuring the cost of direct materials and conversion costs incurred in a processing department
   b. Measuring the unit costs of direct materials and conversion costs to compute the cost of goods transferred from one processing department to the next

    c. Separating the cost of a manufacturing *process* from the cost of a manufacturing *operation*

    d. Dividing ending inventory between finished goods and work in process

5. The entry to record the transfer of goods from the Heating Department to the Drying Department is *(p. 905)*

    a. Finished Goods   XXX

            Work in Process – Drying.   XXX

    b. Work in Process – Heating.   XXX

            Work in Process – Drying.   XXX

    c. Work in Process – Heating.   XXX

            Finished Goods   XXX

    d. Work in Process – Drying.   XXX

            Work in Process – Heating.   XXX

6. The costs to account for in a second processing department include those associated with *(p. 910)*

    a. Beginning work in process and goods transferred in during the period

    b. Beginning work in process and costs added during the period

    c. Beginning work in process, goods transferred in, and costs added during the period.

    d. Beginning work in process and ending work in process

7. Refer to the production cost report in Exhibit 23-11, page 912. The unit cost of goods completed and transferred to finished goods during October was *(p. 912)*

    a. $4.40   c. $4.90

    b. $4.80   d. $5.32

8. In an operation costing system, conversion cost is accounted for in a manner similar to *(p. 914)*

    a. Overhead in a job cost system

    b. Overhead in a process cost system

    c. Direct materials in a process cost system

    d. Direct labor in a job cost system

9. The joint cost of manufacturing Products A and B is $160,000. Product A can be sold for $240,000 and Product B for $80,000. The costs of Products A and B are *(p. 916)*

    a. $240,000 and $80,000   c. $120,000 and $40,000

    b. $160,000 and $80,000   d. Cannot be determined from the information given

10. The accounting value assigned to byproducts is called *(p. 917)*

    a. Sales value   c. Net realizable value

    b. Net value   d. Selling cost

Answers to the self-study questions are at the end of the chapter.

Accounting Vocabulary

byproduct *(p. 917)*,   equivalent units *(p. 901)*,   joint product *(p. 916)*,   net realizable value *(p. 917)*,   operation costing *(p. 913)*,   process costing *(p. 897)*,   production cost report *(p. 912)*,   split-off point *(p. 916)*.

ASSIGNMENT MATERIAL ⎯⎯⎯⎯⎯⎯⎯⎯⎯⎯⎯⎯⎯⎯⎯⎯⎯⎯⎯⎯

Questions

1. Distinguish a process cost accounting system from a job order system.

2. Which type of costing system—job order, process costing, or operation costing—

would be better suited to account for manufacture of each of the following products: (a) chemicals, (b) automobiles, (c) lumber, (d) hand-held calculators, (e) custom lampshades?

3. Why does a process costing system use multiple work in process accounts but a job order system use only one such account?

4. Give the entries (accounts only) to record the following: (a) purchase of materials; (b) incurrence of labor; (c) overhead cost; (d) requisition of materials and application of labor and overhead to Work in Process Inventory–Department 1 (combine in one entry); (e) transfer of cost of work in process inventory from Department 1 to Department 2; (f) transfer of cost of completed units to finished goods; (g) cost of goods sold.

5. What is an equivalent unit of production? Give an example of equivalent units.

6. Montague Manufacturing Company completed and transferred 35,000 units of its product to a second department during the period. At the end of the period, another 10,000 units were in work in process inventory, 20 percent complete. How many equivalent units did Montague produce during the period?

7. Outline the five steps to account for a process costing system.

8. How are equivalent units used in Exhibits 23-5 and 23-6?

9. Why might a company have different numbers of equivalent units for direct materials and conversion costs?

10. What information does a production cost report give? Why does the format of the report differ from company to company?

11. What is the major accounting challenge in a process costing system that has more than one processing department? Why is this such a challenge?

12. Compute the equivalent units of production for direct materials and for conversion costs in Department 2 during July:

Units:
Work in process, June 30 (10% complete as to direct materials, 40% complete as to conversion costs) . . . .   1,000 units
Transferred in from Department 1 during July. . . . . 25,000 units
Completed during July . . . . 22,000 units
Work in process, July 31 (20% complete as to direct materials, 70% complete as to conversion costs) . . . .   4,000 units

13. Briefly describe an operation costing system, indicating the role that work orders play.

14. Distinguish joint products from byproducts.

15. How is the cost of a joint product determined?

16. How is an accounting value assigned to a byproduct? Give the entry to record the value of a byproduct.

Exercises

Exercise 23-1 *Diagramming flows through a process costing system*

Mueller & Martinez, Inc., manufactures furniture in a three-stage process that includes milling, assembling, and finishing, in that order. Direct materials are added in the milling and finishing departments, and direct labor and overhead are applied in all three departments. The company's general ledger includes the following accounts:

Work in Process Inventory–Finishing   Factory Wages
Raw Materials Inventory   Work in Process Inventory–Milling
Finished Goods Inventory   Cost of Goods Sold
Factory Overhead   Work in Process Inventory–Assembling

Required

Outline the flow of costs through the company's accounts. Include a T-account for each account title given. Follow the pattern of Exhibit 23-2, and use X in place of dollar amounts.

Exercise 23-2 *Journalizing process costing transactions*

Record the following selected process cost accounting transactions in the general journal:

a. Purchase of raw materials on account, $3,500.
b. Payment of factory labor, $11,000.
c. Incurrence of factory overhead costs: depreciation, $600; insurance, $500; utilities paid, $900.
d. Requisition of direct materials to Processing Department 1, $800.
e. Application of conversion costs to Processing Department 1: direct labor, $1,900; factory overhead, $2,850.
f. Transfer of cost from Processing Department 1 to Department 2, $4,100.
g. Application of conversion costs to Processing Department 2: direct labor, $700; factory overhead, $1,050.
h. Transfer of cost from Processing Department 2 to finished goods, $5,200.

Exercise 23-3 *Transferring costs between processing departments*

The Mixing Department of a chemical company began February with no work in process inventory. During the month, production that cost $37,000 (direct materials, $9,000, and conversion costs, $28,000) was started on 22,000 units. A total of 18,000 units were completed and transferred to the Heating Department. The ending work in process inventory was 50 percent complete as to direct materials and 75 percent complete as to conversion costs.

Required

1. Journalize the transfer of cost from the Mixing Department to the Heating Department. Round unit costs to five places.
2. What is the balance in Work in Process–Mixing on February 28?
3. Account for the total cost incurred during February.

Exercise 23-4 *Computing processing costs and journalizing cost transfers*

The following information was taken from the ledger of Carnegie Polyvinyl Products. Ending inventory is 100 percent complete as to direct materials but only 37.5 percent complete as to conversion costs.

Work in Process–Forming

	Physical Units	Dollars		Physical Units	Dollars
Inventory, November 30	-0-	$ -0-	Transferred to Painting	72,000	?
Production started:	80,000		Ending inventory	8,000	
1. Direct materials		340,000	Total accounted for	80,000	
2. Conversion costs		225,000			
Total to account for	80,000	$565,000			

Required

Journalize the transfer of cost to the Painting Department.

Exercise 23-5 *Computing equivalent units in a single department*

Insert the missing values:

		Equivalent Units of Production	
Flow of Production	**Flow of Physical Units**	**Direct Materials**	**Conversion Costs**
Units to account for:			
Work in process, November 30	12,000		
Started production during December	X		
Total physical units to account for...............................	67,000		
Units accounted for:			
Completed and transferred out during December:			
From beginning inventory	12,000	X *	X *
Started and completed during December	47,000	X	X
Work in process, December 31	X	X **	X **
Total physical units accounted for...............................	67,000		
Equivalent units of production		X	X

  * Direct materials: 40% completed during December
     Conversion costs: 50% completed during December
** Direct materials: 30% completed during December
     Conversion costs: 20% completed during December

Exercise 23-6 *Computing equivalent units in two departments*

Selected production and cost data of Gulig Enterprises follow for May 19X5.

	Flow of Physical Units	
Flow of Production	**Heating Department**	**Finishing Department**
Units to account for:		
Work in process, April 30..........................	10,000	6,000
Transferred in during May..........................	80,000	75,000
Total physical units to account for....................	90,000	81,000
Units accounted for:		
Completed and transferred out during May:		
From beginning inventory	10,000*	6,000***
Transferred in and completed during May	65,000	70,000
Work in process, May 31	15,000**	5,000****
Total physical units accounted for...................	90,000	81,000

    * Direct materials: 20 percent completed during May
      Conversion costs: 30 percent completed during May
   ** Direct materials: 50 percent completed during May
      Conversion costs: 40 percent completed during May
 *** Direct materials: $2/3$ completed during May
      Conversion costs: 40 percent completed during May
**** Direct materials: 50 percent completed during May
      Conversion costs: 60 percent completed during May

Required

Compute equivalent units for goods transferred in, direct materials, and conversion costs for each department.

Exercise 23-7 *Computing equivalent units and applying cost to completed units and work in process*

Leslie Production Co. experienced the following activity in its Finishing Department during December.

Units:

Work in process, November 30 (60% complete as to direct materials, 80% complete as to conversion costs)	8,000 units
Transferred in from Heating Department during December	31,000 units
Completed during December	26,000 units
Work in process, December 31 (60% complete as to direct materials, 80% complete as to conversion costs)	13,000 units

Costs:

Work in process, November 30	$ 19,000
Transferred in from Heating Department during December	108,500
Direct materials added during December	72,500
Conversion costs added during December	102,000

Required

1. Compute the number of equivalent units produced by the Finishing Department during December.
2. Compute unit costs, and apply total cost to (a) units completed and transferred to finished goods and (b) units in December 31 work in process inventory.

Exercise 23-8 *Using a production cost report*

Cost accountants for Wucker, Inc., prepared the following production cost report for February:

Finishing Department
Production Cost Report
For the Month Ended February 28, 19XX

	Physical Units	Total Costs
Work in process, January 31	14,000	$ 82,000
Transferred in from Grinding Department during February	90,000	439,000
Cost added in Finishing Department during February:		
Direct materials	—	66,000
Conversion costs:		
Direct labor	—	106,000
Factory overhead	—	83,000
Total to account for	104,000	$776,000
Completed and transferred to finished goods during February	95,000	$727,000
Work in process, February 28	9,000	49,000
Total accounted for	104,000	$776,000

Required

Journalize all February activity in the Finishing Department.

Exercise 23-9   *Computing manufacturing cost in an operation costing system*

Hagman, Inc., uses an operation costing system to account for the manufacture of western wear. The company's two main products, slacks and shirts, are manufactured in four operations. During the most recent full year, the costs for operations on these two products were $720,000 for direct labor and $300,000 for factory overhead. Management expects labor cost to remain constant during the current year, but the budget contains a 20 percent increase for overhead cost. Budgeted machine hours are 60,000 for the year. During the current quarter, actual direct material costs are $2,300,000 for slacks and $410,000 for shirts, with 12,000 machine hours used on slacks and 3,000 hours used on shirts.

Required

Compute the total manufacturing costs of slacks and shirts during the current quarter.

Exercise 23-10   *Determining the cost of joint products and byproducts*

Part A. Pineville Paper Mill manufactures cardboard and linerboard by a joint process that costs $270,000 on average each month. Cardboard sells for $32 per ton and linerboard for $12 per ton. Each month the manufacturing process generates 5,000 tons of cardboard and 20,000 tons of linerboard. Use the relative sales value method to determine the cost of each ton of the two products.

Part B. Herald Chair Company makes recliner chairs. The manufacturing process leaves byproducts including scrap wood and upholstery remnants with resale value averaging $1 per chair. Two percent of this amount is consumed by the cost of disposing of byproducts. Herald manufactures 5,000 chairs per year. Make the general journal entry to record the byproduct inventory.

Problems   *(Group A)*

Problem 23-1A   *Computing equivalent units and applying cost to completed units and work in process; no beginning inventory or cost transferred in*

Bristol Printing, Inc., is an engraving company in Wilmington, Delaware, that engraves and prints specialty books for publishers all over the United States. Production occurs in three processes: engraving, printing, and binding. The Engraving Department was empty on May 31. In mid-June Bristol started production on 65,000 books. Of this number, 52,600 books were engraved during June. The June 30 work in process in the Engraving Department was 31 percent complete as to direct materials and 54 percent complete as to conversion costs. Direct materials costing $129,600 were placed in production in the Engraving Department during June, and direct labor of $45,300 and factory overhead of $62,700 were applied in this department.

Required

1. Compute the number of equivalent units of production and unit costs (rounded to five decimal places) in the Engraving Department for June.
2. Show the application of total cost in the Engraving Department to (a) units completed and transferred to finished goods during June and (b) units still in process at June 30.
3. Prepare a T-account for Work in Process Inventory–Engraving to show its activity during June, including the June 30 balance.

Problem 23-2A   *Computing equivalent units, applying cost to completed units and work in process, and journalizing transactions; no beginning inventory or cost transferred in*

Waco Newsprint, Inc., manufactures newsprint (the paper stock on which newspapers are printed) by a four-stage process that includes mixing, cooking, rolling, and cutting. In the

Mixing Department, wood pulp and chemicals, the basic raw materials, are blended. The resulting mix is heated in the Cooking Department in much the same way food is prepared. Then the cooked mix is rolled to produce sheets. The final process, cutting, divides the sheets into large rolled units for shipment to newspaper companies.

Cost accumulation in the Mixing Department during August is summarized in the following account:

Work in Process Inventory – Mixing

Direct materials	26,600
Direct labor	7,400
Factory overhead	13,900

August activity in the Mixing Department consisted of completion of the mixing process for 1,800 rolls of newsprint plus partial completion of 300 additional rolls. These in-process units were 36 percent complete with respect to direct materials and 44 percent complete with respect to conversion costs.

Required

1. Compute the equivalent units of production and unit costs (rounded to four decimal places) in the Mixing Department for August.
2. Prove that the sum of (a) cost of goods transferred out of the Mixing Department and (b) ending Work in Process Inventory – Mixing equals the total cost accumulated in the department during August.
3. Journalize all transactions affecting the company's mixing process during August, including those already posted.

Problem 23-3A *Computing equivalent units for a second department with beginning inventory; applying cost to completed units and work in process*

Sequoyah Mills, Inc., manufactures broadloom carpet in seven processes: spinning, dyeing, plying, spooling, tufting, latexing, and shearing.

First, fluff nylon purchased from a company such as DuPont or Monsanto is spun into yarn that is dyed the desired color. Then two or more threads of the yarn are joined together, or plied, for added strength. The plied yarn is spooled for use in the actual carpet making. Tufting is the process by which yarn is added to burlap backing. After the backing is latexed to hold it together and make it skid resistant, the carpet is sheared to give it an even appearance and feel.

At March 31, before recording the transfer of cost from department to department, the Sequoyah Mills general ledger included the following account for one of its lines of carpet:

Work in Process Inventory – Dyeing

Feb. 28 Balance	5,900
Transferred in from Spinning	23,600
Direct materials	12,700
Direct labor	7,300
Factory overhead	42,900

Work in process inventory of the Dyeing Department on February 28 consisted of 75 rolls that were 60 percent complete as to direct materials and conversion costs. During March 560 rolls were transferred in from the Spinning Department. The Dyeing Department completed 500 rolls of the carpet in March, and 135 rolls were still in process on March 31. This ending inventory was 100 percent complete as to direct materials and 80 percent complete as to conversion costs.

Required

1. Compute the equivalent units of production, unit costs (rounded to three decimal places), and total cost to account for in the Dyeing Department for March.
2. Show the application of total Dyeing Department cost for March to (a) cost of goods transferred from Dyeing to Plying and (b) cost of ending Work in Process Inventory – Dyeing on March 31.

Problem 23-4A *Preparing a production cost report and recording transactions based on the information in the report*

Required

1. Prepare the March production cost report for the Dyeing Department in Problem 23-3A.
2. Journalize all transactions affecting the Dyeing Department during March, including those entries that have already been posted.

Problem 23-5A *Computing equivalent units for a second department with beginning inventory, applying cost to completed units and work in process, and accounting for byproducts and joint products*

Many products are developed from crude oil, including aviation fuel, gasoline, asphalt, and the wax used to make wax paper and automobile wax. This problem focuses on the wax products.

Wax is removed from crude oil by two basic processes, heating and cooling. Heating separates the lighter components, such as aviation fuel and gasoline, from the heavier components. The heavier residue is cooled, passed through a brine solution, and filtered to obtain wax. Therefore, the manufacture of wax consists of heating, cooling, mixing, and filtering processes, in that order.

 Suppose the accounting records of a Gulf Oil Corporation refinery yielded the following information about its Wax Filtering Department for a weekly period:

Gallons:

Work in process, beginning (30% complete as to direct materials, 40% complete as to conversion costs)	8,000 gallons
Transferred in from the Mixing Department during the week	62,000 gallons
Completed during the week	50,000 gallons
Work in process, ending (67% complete as to direct materials, 81% complete as to conversion costs)	20,000 gallons

Costs:

Work in process, beginning	$ 6,450
Transferred in from the Mixing Department during the week	80,600
Direct materials added during the week	13,420
Conversion costs added during the week	19,530

Required

1. Compute the number of equivalent gallons of wax produced during the week by the Wax Filtering Department.
2. Show the application of total cost in the Wax Filtering Department to (a) gallons completed and transferred to finished goods and (b) gallons in ending work in process inventory.
3. Assume a lower grade of wax is removed as a byproduct from the wax filtering process. Its sale price is 2 percent, and the cost of selling the byproduct is ¼ percent (.0025), of the total cost to be transferred to finished goods. Record the byproduct inventory.
4. After 4,000 gallons of the byproduct inventory (in Requirement 3) is removed, the finished goods inventory consists of 46,000 gallons of wax. The company will sell 15,000 gallons at $2.06 per gallon to a wax paper manufacturer and 31,000 gallons at

$5.91 per gallon to an automobile wax producer. Use the relative sales value method to compute the costs per gallon of these two joint products. Round relative sales value to the nearest percent.

Problem 23-6A *Computing equivalent units for a second department with beginning inventory, applying cost to completed units and work in process, and operation costing*

The manufacture of lawn mowers includes two processes: forming the blade housing from steel and assembling the parts of the mower. Two operations, lubricating the moving parts and testing the completed mowers, complete their manufacture. The completed mowers are transferred to finished goods prior to shipment to Sears, Montgomery Ward, Penney's, and other department stores.

Process costing information for the Assembling Department of Rocco Garden Machines, Inc., for a period follows. No direct materials are required.

Units:

Work in process, beginning (60% complete as to conversion costs).	2,000 units
Transferred in from the Forming Department during the period.	9,000 units
Completed during the period.	6,000 units
Work in process, ending (70% complete as to conversion costs).	5,000 units

Costs:

Work in process, beginning	$ 12,016
Transferred in from the Forming Department during the period.	369,270
Conversion costs added during the period	63,993

The cost of direct materials in the operation costing phase is the cost of the mowers transferred out of the Assembling Department. The lubricating operation is entirely automated and takes 30 seconds per mower. Testing each completed mower requires an average of five minutes of a technician's time. Conversion costs are $30 per machine hour for lubricating and $50 per man hour for testing. There is only one work order for the mowers in each production run.

Required

1. Compute the number of equivalent units (mowers) produced by the Assembling Department during the period.
2. Show the application of total cost to (a) units completed and transferred to finished goods and (b) units in ending work in process inventory.
3. Compute the total manufacturing cost of the mowers completed and transferred to finished goods. Also compute the unit cost of each complete mower (to the nearest cent).

(Group B)

Problem 23-1B *Computing equivalent units and applying cost to completed units and work in process; no beginning inventory or cost transferred in*

Matuzak Multigraph Manufacturers produce component parts that are used in hand-held calculators. One part, a diode generator, is manufactured in a single processing department. No diode generators were in process on May 31, and Matuzak started production on 12,000 units during June. Completed production for June totaled 9,900 units. The June 30 work in process was 22 percent complete as to direct materials and 34 percent complete as to conversion costs. Direct materials costing $6,700 were placed in production during June, and direct labor of $5,100 and factory overhead of $2,300 were applied to the manufacture of diode generators.

Required

1. Compute the number of equivalent units of production and the unit costs (rounded to five decimal places) for June.
2. Show the application of total cost to (a) units completed and transferred to finished goods and (b) units still in process at June 30.
3. Prepare a T-account for Work in Process Inventory to show its activity during June, including the June 30 balance.

Problem 23-2B   *Computing equivalent units, applying cost to completed units and work in process, and journalizing transactions; no beginning inventory or cost transferred in*

Clinkscale Wool Company produces wool fabric by a three-stage process: cleaning, spinning, and weaving, in that order. Costs incurred in the Cleaning Department during September are summarized as follows:

Work in Process Inventory – Cleaning

Direct materials	76,200
Direct labor	2,600
Factory overhead	8,700

September activity in the Cleaning Department included completion of 17,000 pounds of wool, which were transferred to the Spinning Department. Also, work on 3,000 pounds began, which on September 30 was 20 percent complete with respect to direct materials and 60 percent complete with respect to conversion costs.

Required

1. Compute the equivalent units of production and unit costs (rounded to five decimal places) in the Cleaning Department for September.
2. Prove that the sum of (a) cost of goods transferred out of the Cleaning Department and (b) ending Work in Process Inventory – Cleaning equals the total cost accumulated in the department during September.
3. Journalize all transactions affecting the company's cleaning process during September, including those already posted.

Problem 23-3B   *Computing equivalent units for a second department with beginning inventory; applying cost to completed units and work in process*

Maremont Fabricator Corporation manufactures auto bumpers in a two-stage process that includes shaping and plating. Steel alloy is the basic raw material of the shaping process. The steel is molded according to the design specifications of the automobile manufacturers (Chrysler, Ford, and General Motors). The Plating Department then adds a finish plate of chrome to give the new bumper a shiny appearance.

At March 31, before recording the transfer of cost from the Plating Department to Finished Goods Inventory, the Maremont general ledger included the following account:

Work in Process Inventory – Plating

Feb. 28 Balance	13,300
Transferred in from Shaping	32,600
Direct materials	28,000
Direct labor	17,100
Factory overhead	36,800

Work in process of the Plating Department on February 28 consisted of 600 bumpers that were 50 percent complete as to direct materials and conversion costs. During March 3,000 bumpers were transferred in from the Shaping Department. The Plating Department transferred 2,200 bumpers to finished goods in March, and 1,400 bumpers were still in process on March 31. This ending inventory was 40 percent complete as to direct materials and 70 percent complete as to conversion costs.

Required

1. Compute the equivalent units of production, unit costs (rounded to three decimal places), and total cost to account for in the Plating Department for March.
2. Show the application of total Plating Department cost for March to (a) cost of goods transferred out of the Plating Department and (b) cost of ending Work in Process Inventory–Plating on March 31.

Problem 23-4B *Preparing a production cost report and recording transactions based on the report's information*

Required

1. Prepare the March production cost report for the Plating Department in Problem 23-3B.
2. Journalize all transactions affecting the Plating Department during March, including those entries that have already been posted.

Problem 23-5B *Computing equivalent units for a second department with beginning inventory, applying cost to completed units and work in process, and accounting for byproducts and joint products*

Frito-Lay, Inc., manufactures convenience foods including potato chips and corn chips. Production of corn chips occurs in five steps: cleaning, mixing, cooking, drying, and packaging. Suppose the accounting records of a Frito-Lay plant yielded the following information for corn chips in its Packaging Department during a weekly period:

Cases:

Work in process, beginning (10% complete as to direct materials,	
0% complete as to conversion costs)	3,000 cases
Transferred in from the Drying Department during the week.	18,000 cases
Completed during the week.	15,000 cases
Work in process, ending (5% complete as to direct materials,	
0% complete as to conversion costs)	6,000 cases

Costs:

Work in process, beginning	$ 840
Transferred in from the Drying Department during the week.	11,700
Direct materials added during the week	6,750
Conversion costs added during the week	15,300

Required

1. Compute the number of equivalent cases of corn chips produced by the Packaging Department during the week.
2. Show the application of total cost in the Packaging Department to (a) cases completed and transferred to finished goods and (b) cases in ending work in process inventory.
3. Inventory ruined during packaging can be sold as a byproduct. Its sale price is 1.3 percent, and the cost of selling the byproduct is ¼ percent (.0025), of the total cost to be transferred to finished goods. Record the byproduct inventory.
4. After 300 cases of the byproduct inventory (in Requirement 3) are removed, the finished goods inventory consists of 20,700 cases. Of this finished goods inventory,

12,300 cases are Frito corn chips, sold at $5.40 per case, and 8,400 cases are Doritos, sold at $5.70 per case. Use the relative sales value method to compute the costs per case of these two joint products. Round relative sales value to the nearest percent.

Problem 23-6B *Computing equivalent units for a second department with beginning inventory, applying cost to completed units and work in process, and operation costing*

The manufacture of hand tools, such as pliers and screwdrivers, can be costed by an operation costing system. Consider screwdrivers with plastic handles. Manufacture of the handles includes mixing and heating the raw materials, shaping the mix by pouring it into molds, and drying. Production of the screwdrivers is then completed in two operations: assembling the handles and shanks, and packaging for shipment to retail outlets such as K mart, Target, and True Value hardware stores.

Process costing information for the Drying Department of Ward's Tool Manufacturing Company for a period follows. No direct materials are required.

Units:

Work in process, beginning (30% complete as to conversion costs)	7,000 units
Transferred in from the Molding Department during the period	32,000 units
Completed during the period	16,000 units
Work in process, ending (20% complete as to conversion costs)	23,000 units

Costs:

Work in process, beginning	$ 190
Transferred in from the Molding Department during the period	4,480
Conversion costs added during the period	555

The cost of direct materials in the operation costing phase includes the cost of the plastic handles transferred out of the Drying Department plus the cost of the metal shanks, which is $1,493. The assembling and packaging operations are entirely automated. Assembling occurs at the rate of 4,000 units per hour and packaging at 2,000 per hour. Conversion cost is allocated to the assembling operation at the predetermined rate of $25.00 per machine hour and to packaging at the rate of $27.50 per machine hour. There is only one work order for the screwdrivers.

Required

1. Compute the number of equivalent units (screwdrivers) produced by the Drying-Processing Department during the period.
2. Show the application of total cost to (a) units completed and transferred to finished goods and (b) units in ending work in process inventory.
3. Compute the total manufacturing cost of the screwdrivers completed and transferred to finished goods. Also compute the unit cost of each complete screwdriver.

Decision Problem

Preparing a production cost report and identifying decisions that would be based on the information.

Akron Manufacturing Company makes automobile parts. The following cost data for the company's Finishing Department are available for May.

Equivalent units of production:

Flow of Production	Flow of Physical Units	Transferred In	Direct Materials	Conversion Costs
		Equivalent Units of Production		
Units to account for:				
Beginning work in process inventory	12,000			
Transferred in during May	28,000			
Total units to account for	40,000			
Units accounted for:				
Completed and transferred out to finished goods during May:				
From beginning inventory	12,000	—	7,200	6,000
Transferred in from Molding and completed during May				
(36,000 − 12,000)	24,000	24,000	24,000	24,000
Work in process, May 31	4,000	4,000	800	1,200
Total physical units accounted for	40,000			
Equivalent units of production		28,000	32,000	31,200

Unit costs:

	Transferred-In Costs	Direct Materials	Conversion Costs	Total
Work in process, April 30	Work done before May			$ 73,000
Costs added during May	$ 64,400	$ 35,200	$ 49,920	149,520
Divide by equivalent units	÷28,000	÷32,000	÷31,200	
Cost per equivalent unit	$ 2.30	$ 1.10	$ 1.60	
Total cost to account for				$222,520

Allocation of total cost:

	Transferred-In Costs	Direct Materials	Conversion Costs	Total
Units completed and transferred out to finished goods:				
From work in process, April 30				$ 73,000
Costs added during May:				
Direct materials	—	7,200 × $1.10		7,920
Conversion costs	—		6,000 × $1.60	9,600
Total completed from April 30 inventory				90,520
Units transferred in from Molding and				
completed during May	24,000 × ($2.30 + $1.10 + $1.60)			120,000
Total costs transferred out				$210,520
Work in process, May 31:				
Transferred-in costs	4,000 × $2.30			$ 9,200
Direct materials		800 × $1.10		880
Conversion costs			1,200 × $1.60	1,920
Total work in process, May 31				12,000
Total cost accounted for				$222,520

Required

1. Prepare a production cost report for the Finishing Department for May.
2. Discuss specific decisions that would be based on the information in the report.

Answers to Self-Study Questions

1. a
2. b
3. d Direct materials: $20{,}000 + (6{,}000 \times .90) = 25{,}400$
   Conversion costs: $20{,}000 + (6{,}000 \times .75) = 24{,}500$
4. b
5. d
6. c
7. d $\$202{,}200/38{,}000 = \$5.32$
8. a
9. c A: $[\$240{,}000/(\$240{,}000 + \$80{,}000)] \times \$160{,}000 = \$120{,}000$
   B: $[\$80{,}000/(\$240{,}000 + \$80{,}000)] \times \$160{,}000 = \$40{,}000$
10. c

24

Flexible Budgets and Standard Costs

LEARNING OBJECTIVES
After studying this chapter, you should be able to

1 Prepare a flexible budget expense graph

2 Prepare an income statement performance report

3 Explain the benefits of standard costing

4 Compute direct materials cost variances

5 Compute direct labor cost variances

6 Compute production overhead cost variances

7 Prepare a standard cost income statement for management

Chapter 20 emphasized that budgets are a major help in planning and control. This chapter explores budgeting in more depth. The first half of the chapter covers flexible budgets, and the second half discusses standard costs. We begin by reviewing the cost behavior patterns introduced in Chapter 21.

Cost Behavior Patterns

Accountants define **cost** as resources given up to achieve a specific objective. For now, consider costs as dollars paid for goods and services. Examples are the costs of materials, factory wages, sales commissions, utilities, and interest expense. Distinctions among these categories of costs are important in many accounting situations. In budgeting, however, they can be treated similarly.

Cost behavior is the movement of a cost in response to a measure of volume such as sales. Two extreme types of cost behavior are variable and fixed. **Variable costs** are those whose total amount changes in direct proportion with changes in volume or activity. **Fixed costs** are costs whose total amount does not change during a given time period over a wide range of volume. Examples include depreciation, property taxes, insurance, and executive salaries.

Throughout this chapter, we assume that each cost is either variable or fixed or that it can be divided into variable and fixed portions. A **mixed cost** has both variable and fixed components. The compensation of a salesperson who is paid a

935

flat monthly salary plus a commission based on his or her sales is a mixed cost. Water expense computed as a fixed monthly amount plus a unit cost per 100 gallons used is also a mixed cost.

Note that the "variable" and "fixed" characteristics of a cost relate to its *total* amount, not its *unit* amount. A variable cost is variable with respect to its *total* amount. A fixed cost is fixed with respect to its *total* amount. The behavior of variable and fixed costs with respect to per-unit sales is different, as the following table shows.

	If Volume Increases (Decreases)	
Type of Cost	**Total Cost**	**Cost Per Unit**
Variable cost (example: sales commission)	Increases (decreases)	No change
Fixed cost (example: monthly rent)	No change	Decreases (increases)

Illustrations will clarify the difference between the total and the unit amounts of variable cost and fixed cost. Suppose a sales clerk in the shoe department of a J. C. Penney store is paid a sales commission of 5 percent, which is a variable cost. The commission on a $40 pair of shoes is $2. Weekly sales of 200 pairs generates total sales commission expense of $400. Unit selling cost—the commission— remains $2 ($40 × .05) per pair of shoes.

Now consider the fixed monthly rent of a cookie store in a shopping mall. Total monthly rent expense of $2,000 does not change in response to changes in volume. If the store sells 20,000 cookies each month, the rent cost per unit is $.10 ($2,000 rent/20,000 cookies). But if the store sells 40,000 cookies monthly, the unit cost of rent is only $.05 ($2,000/40,000). In either case, the total monthly rent is fixed at $2,000.

Relevant Range

The definition of a fixed cost has two underlying assumptions.

1. The total cost will not change for a given time period, which is the *budget period*. Fixed costs may change from budget year to budget year because of changes in salary levels, number of workers, rent levels, and property tax levels. But fixed costs are not expected to change within a given budget period.
2. The total cost will not change over a wide range of volume, which is the *relevant range.*

Fixed costs are based on an expected band of volume. For example, a toy manufacturer may have monthly fixed costs of $200,000 when it is producing 16,000 to 24,000 units per month. However, after the Christmas rush, sales fall below 16,000 units, and fixed costs decrease to $175,000. So "fixed" is a useful concept, but "fixed" does not mean forever or under all operating conditions. Instead, it relates to a relevant range of activity, as shown by the following graph of cost behavior:

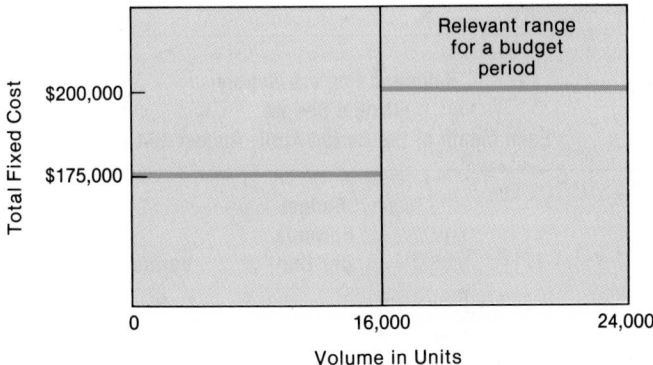

Having reviewed the necesary concepts and terms, let's turn to flexible budgets and their role in management decision making.

Flexible Budgets

The master budget in Chapter 20 is a **static budget,** which is prepared for only one level of activity. Consider a master budget based on a single target sales volume of 200,000 units. Assume actual volume turns out to be 180,000 units. The comparison of actual and budgeted results, which is an example of a **performance report,** follows (amounts assumed).

	Actual Results	Static (Master) Budget	Variance
Units	180,000	200,000	20,000 U
Sales...................	$540,000	$600,000	$60,000 U
Expenses	500,000	525,000	25,000 F
Operating income	$ 40,000	$ 75,000	$35,000 U

Variance is the difference between an actual amount and the corresponding budgeted amount. In this table, U = unfavorable variance and F = favorable variance.

This performance report is difficult to analyze because the budget is based on 200,000 units, but only 180,000 units were sold. Note the $25,000 expense variance. Why did it occur? Because of efficient cost control? Because of a lower sales volume? We are unsure. This performance report, based on a static budget, simply does not provide enough detail to answer these important management questions.

For a detailed analysis of performance, managers often use a **flexible budget,** which is a set of budgets covering a range of volume rather than a single level of volume. Flexible budgets are also called *variable budgets* because they present budgeted amounts for different levels of activity. Managers find flexible budgets helpful for studying the behavior of expenses as volume fluctuates. Microcomputers and electronic spreadsheets have placed this budgeting tool at the disposal of most middle and top managers in the United States.

EXHIBIT 24-1   *Flexible Budget*

Bellmead Pools & Supply
Flexible Budget
Each Month of the Period April–August 19X5

	Budget Formula per Unit	Various Levels of Volume		
		6	8	10
Units	—	6	8	10
Sales	$12,000	$72,000	$96,000	$120,000
Variable expenses	8,000	48,000	64,000	80,000
Fixed expenses	(see Note)	20,000	20,000	20,000
Total expenses.		68,000	84,000	100,000
Operating income (loss)		$ 4,000	$12,000	$ 20,000

Note: Fixed expenses are given as a total amount rather than as a cost per unit.

Exhibit 24-1 shows a condensed flexible budget for Bellmead Pools & Supply, which installs swimming pools.

In this example, the total variable cost of installing a $12,000 swimming pool is $8,000. A more detailed budget would list the individual variable costs, such as direct materials and direct labor. It might also detail the various fixed expenses, including depreciation on equipment, insurance, and administrative overhead. Total monthly fixed expenses are $20,000.

Flexible budgets are useful both before and after a budget period. As a planning tool, they can help managers identify the level of volume that will serve as the business's target level of activity for the coming period. As a control device, they help managers analyze actual results.

The **budget formula**—the heart of the flexible budget—shows how to compute the budget amounts:

$$\text{Revenues} - \text{Variable expenses} - \text{Fixed expenses} = \text{Operating income (loss)}$$

$$\left(\begin{array}{c} \text{Number of units sold} \\ \times \text{Unit sale price} \end{array} \right) - \left(\begin{array}{c} \text{Number of units sold} \\ \times \text{Variable cost per unit} \end{array} \right) - \text{Fixed expenses} = \text{Operating income (loss)}$$

In this illustration, Bellmead Pools' cost behavior is fixed expenses of $20,000 per month plus variable expenses of $8,000 per pool installed. Exhibit 24-1 shows the expected results for three operating levels. Other volume levels could be added for 7, 9, or any other number of pools per month, as the situation warrants. Keep in mind that expenses are unlikely to behave according to a set formula outside some volume range. A flexible budget relates to a specific relevant range only. A volume of 15 pools per month may not fall within the relevant range. In such cases, managers must develop a new budget formula.

Graphing the Budget Expense Formula _____

Another budgeting tool is a graph of the expense formula. With such a graph, the accountant can provide a budget customized to any volume level. The graph in Exhibit 24-2 shows total expenses for Bellmead Pools & Supply for all volume

EXHIBIT 24-2 *Bellmead Pools & Supply*
Graph of Monthly Flexible Expense Budget

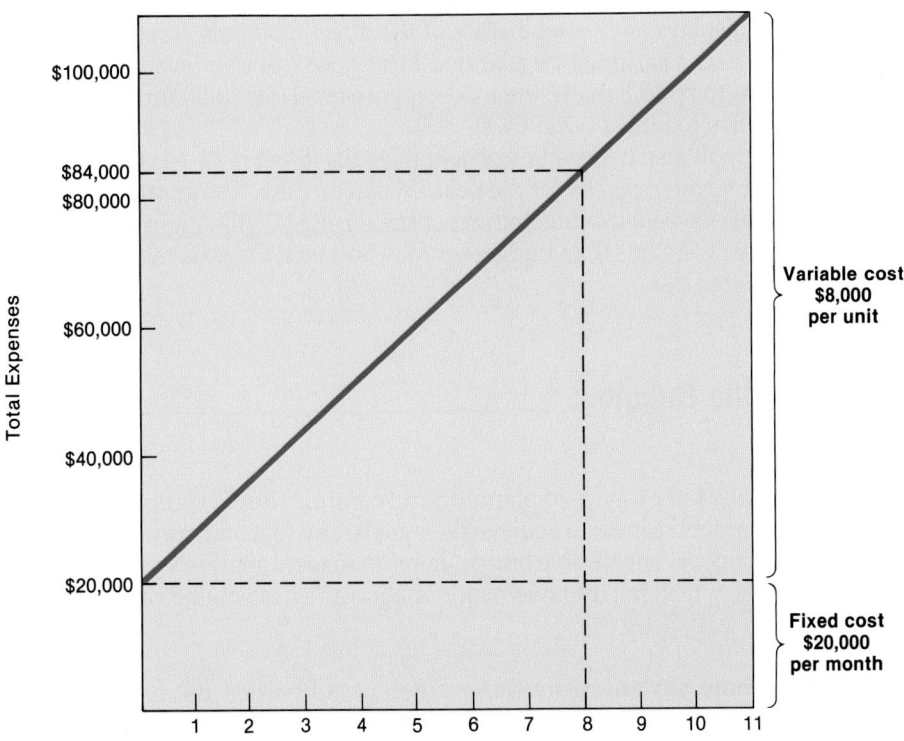

EXHIBIT 24-3 *Bellmead Pools & Supply*
Graph of Actual and Budgeted Monthly Total Expenses

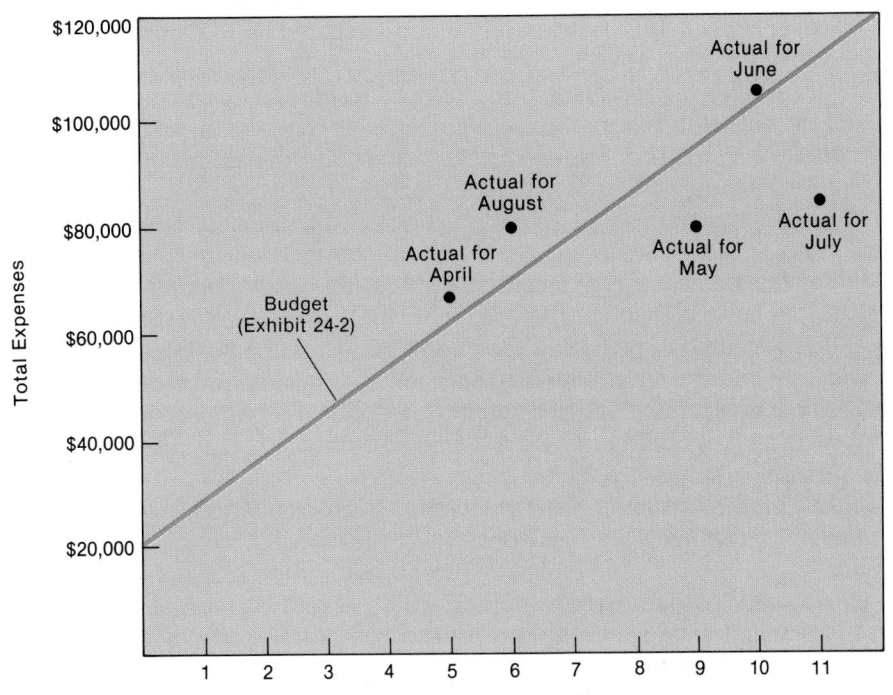

levels from 0 to 11 pool installations per month. Let us assume this span of activity is the relevant range. Also, we assume that management based the master budget — the static budget — on a projected sales volume of 8 pools per month.

The graph displays an overall picture of the direct materials, direct labor, and all other expenses that must be planned at various volume levels. When the company plans to build 8 pools, the total expense level ($84,000) for this volume is highlighted (as Exhibit 24-2 shows).

A budget graph also helps analyze actual results. Exhibit 24-3 is the graph of actual versus budgeted results for the peak season of 19X5. The graph shows that actual expenses exceeded budgeted expenses during April, August, and June. Actual expenses were less than budget for May and July. Overall, the budget and actual figures are close.

Analyzing the Results _____

Managers usually have a cycle of planning and control. They (1) prepare a master budget, (2) transact business to achieve their goals, and (3) compare actual results to the master budget. The flexible budget helps managers analyze variances from planned results, which fall into two major categories: sales volume variances and flexible budget variances.

1. **Sales volume variances** are those differences between the revenues, expenses, and operating income in the flexible budget and the revenues, expenses, and income in the static (master) budget. For example, assume Bellmead Pools & Supply set a goal of installing 8 pools each month during April–August 19X5 and budgeted accordingly. During June the company installs 10 pools. Exhibit 24-4, column 4, shows that the sales volume variance is the difference between the flexible budget for actual volume achieved and the static (master) budget (column 3 minus column 5).

2. **Flexible budget variances** are differences between actual results and the flexible budget. This category of variances is based on the actual sales level achieved. For example, Bellmead Pools & Supply budgeted total expenses of $100,000 for the installation of 10 pools. In June the company installs 10 pools, but total expenses exceed budget. This can be seen in Exhibit 24-3, where total expenses for June lie above the budget line. Exhibit 24-4 shows how to compute a flexible budget variance: actual results minus the flexible budget for actual volume achieved (column 1 minus column 3).

We have seen that mere comparison of a *static* (*master*) budget with *actual* results does not explain much, because the actual sales level may differ from the level that was used in preparing the master budget. But a flexible budget does provide the information needed to understand why actual revenues, expenses, and income differ from budgeted amounts. Exhibit 24-4 is an income statement performance report based on a flexible budget. Study it carefully, especially the two variance columns.

In Exhibit 24-4, column 3 information is taken from Exhibit 24-1. For the flexible budget amounts we match units sold to actual sales in units, which in this case is 10. Use of a flexible budget allows us, within the scope of the relevant range, to analyze results over a range of activity levels. Had actual sales been 6 units, we could have made the comparison based on 6 units by drawing the necessary data from Exhibit 24-1.

EXHIBIT 24-4 *Income Statement Performance Report*

Bellmead Pools & Supply
Income Statement Performance Report
For the Month Ended June 30, 19X5

	(1) Actual Results at Actual Prices	(2) (1)−(3) Flexible Budget Variances	(3) Flexible Budget for Actual Volume Achieved*	(4) (3)−(5) Sales Volume Variances	(5) Static (Master) Budget*
Units...............	10	-0-	10	2 F	8
Sales...............	$120,000	$ -0-	$120,000	$24,000 F	$96,000
Variable expenses	83,000	3,000 U	80,000	16,000 U	64,000
Fixed expenses........	22,000	2,000 U	20,000	-0-	20,000
Total expenses........	105,000	5,000 U	100,000	16,000 U	84,000
Operating income	$ 15,000	$5,000 U	$ 20,000	$ 8,000 F	$12,000

↑ Flexible budget variance, $5,000 U ↑   Sales volume variance, $8,000 F ↑

↑ Total variance from static budget, $3,000 F ↑

U = unfavorable variance; F = favorable variance
* Amounts from Exhibit 24-1

OBJECTIVE 2
Prepare an income
statement performance
report

Exhibit 24-4 shows that actual operating income ($15,000 in column 1) exceeded the static (master) budget amount ($12,000 in column 5) by $3,000. This difference is explained by an $8,000 favorable sales volume variance (column 4) and a $5,000 unfavorable flexible budget variance (column 2). Stated differently, strong sales caused actual income to exceed budget by $8,000. However, the company failed to control expenses as well as expected, resulting in an unfavorable flexible budget variance of $5,000.

How would the owners of the company use this information? Perhaps they would reward the sales staff, and they would certainly determine why expenses were too high. Our analysis of the performance report shows the unfavorable $5,000 variance, but it does not identify why expenses exceeded budget, nor does it identify the cure. Those answers depend on the specific situation. For example, Bellmead's higher-than-expected expenses might have resulted from an increase in the cost of gunite, the concrete derivative used to construct swimming pools. Such an increase might be unavoidable. However, the expense level might have resulted from wasting materials or mismanaging employees. If so, the owner would take corrective action. Variance information can direct a manager to areas of the business needing praise or improvement.

Managers can of course analyze expenses in a more detailed manner—by listing each expense separately. Also, the flexible budget variances can be analyzed further, as the next major section of the chapter explains. First, however, test your understanding of the coverage thus far by working the summary problem for review.

Summary Problem for Your Review

Exhibit 24-4 indicates that Bellmead Pools & Supply installed 10 swimming pools during June. Suppose June installations were 7 pools instead of 10. Suppose further that the price of each pool was $12,500 instead of the budgeted $12,000. Actual variable expenses were $57,400, and actual fixed expenses were $19,000.

Required

1. Given these new assumptions, prepare a revised income statement performance report like Exhibit 24-4.
2. Show that the flexible budget and the sales volume variances in operating income account for the difference between actual operating income and the static (master) budgeted income.
3. As the company owner, what specific employees would you praise or criticize after you analyze this performance report?

SOLUTION TO REVIEW PROBLEM

Requirement 1

Bellmead Pools & Supply
Income Statement Performance Report—Revised
For the Month Ended June 30, 19X5

	(1)	(2) (1)-(3)	(3)	(4) (3)-(5)	(5)
	Actual Results at Actual Prices	Flexible Budget Variances	Flexible Budget for Actual Volume Achieved	Sales Volume Variances	Static (Master) Budget
Units	7	-0-	7	1 U	8
Sales...................	$87,500	$3,500 F	$84,000	$12,000 U	$96,000
Variable expenses	57,400	1,400 U	56,000	8,000 F	64,000
Fixed expenses	19,000	1,000 F	20,000	—	20,000
Total expenses............	76,400	400 U	76,000	8,000 F	84,000
Operating income	$11,100	$3,100 F	$ 8,000	$ 4,000 U	$12,000

Flexible budget variance, $3,100 F ↑ Sales volume variance, $4,000 U ↑

Total variance from static budget, $900 U ↑

U = unfavorable variance; F = favorable variance

Requirement 2

Static (master) budgeted operating income	$12,000
Actual operating income at actual prices	11,100
Total difference to account for	$ 900 U
Sales volume variance	$ 4,000 U
Flexible budget variance	3,100 F
Total net variance	$ 900 U

Requirement 3

Management may praise the salespersons who sold pools more expensive than the budgeted sale price of $12,000 and the employees responsible for cutting fixed cost by $1,000.

Management may criticize the sales staff for not meeting the goal of selling 8 pools during the month. Also, construction or purchasing personnel were responsible for spending $1,400 more in variable costs than budget to construct the 7 pools.

Standard Costing

A **standard cost** is a carefully predetermined cost that is usually expressed on a per-unit basis. It is a target cost, a cost that should be attained. Standard costs are budgeted costs for a single unit of output. **Standard cost systems** help to build budgets, gauge performance, obtain product costs, and save bookkeeping costs. Such systems help managers analyze the relationships between what should have occurred (standard costs) and what did occur (actual costs).

OBJECTIVE 3
Explain the benefits of standard costing

Standard costs are used by a wide variety of organizations and in conjunction with any kind of product costing—job order, process, or a hybrid system such as operation costing. A construction company that builds tract houses uses a job cost system to accumulate the cost of each house. To measure performance, the company may compare actual cost for each house to the standard cost. Companies like General Mills use a process cost system for many of the foods they manufacture. To remain competitive, General Mills helps control costs by developing standard costs. Standard costing provides a concrete goal for manufacturing personnel. They strive to produce the product at standard cost or less. The difference between profits and losses often depends on controlling product cost.

Variances between actual and standard costs are divided into price and efficiency effects for direct materials and direct labor. A *price variance* measures how well a business keeps the unit prices of materials and labor within standards. An *efficiency variance* measures whether the quantity of materials or labor used to make a product is within the budget. By pinpointing price and efficiency effects, standard costing helps managers find ways of reducing costs. It also identifies those employees who deserve praise for controlling costs.

At first glance, standard cost systems might appear to be more costly to operate than other systems. Obviously, a startup investment is necessary to develop the standards. But the ongoing data-processing costs can be less than so-called actual cost systems. For example, it is more economical simply to carry all inventories at standard unit prices. In this way, the system avoids the extra data-collection costs and possible confusion of making cost-flow assumptions such as first-in, first-out or last-in, first-out.

This section of the chapter explains how standard costing divides flexible budget variances into price and efficiency effects. We continue using the Bellmead Pools & Supply example.

Relationship Between Standard Costs and Flexible Budgets

What standard of performance should be used? *Currently attainable standards* are the most popular. They are standards that can be achieved but with difficulty. Standard costs are set low enough that employees view their fulfillment as possible, though perhaps not probable. Variances tend to be unfavorable, but managers accept the standards as reasonable goals.

Does a standard cost differ from a budgeted cost? No, if the standards are attainable. However, the term *standard cost* usually refers to a unit cost, whereas *budgeted cost* refers to a total cost. For example, suppose the budgeted variable expenses in Exhibit 24-4 included direct materials as follows:

	Budget Formula Per Unit	Flexible Budget for Various Levels of Volume		
Finished swimming pools	1	6	8	10
Direct materials	$2,000	$12,000	$16,000	$20,000

The standard cost of direct materials is $2,000 *per unit.* Budgeted cost is the total cost for the installation of all pools sold during the period. For 8 pools, budgeted cost is $16,000. For 10 pools, budgeted cost is $20,000. But standard cost of direct materials remains $2,000 per unit regardless of changes in total outlays because of differences in sales volume. Think of a standard variable cost as a budget for a single unit.

Illustration of Standard Costing

Let's return to our Bellmead Pools example. Recall that 10 swimming pools were installed during June and that the static (master) budget had been drawn up for 8 pools per month. Exhibit 24-5 provides the cost data to be used throughout our discussion of standard costing applications.

To focus on the main points of standard costing, we assume the standard cost system applies to materials, labor, and production overhead, but not to selling and administrative expenses. We also assume purchases of direct materials equals materials used.

EXHIBIT 24-5 *Facts for Illustration of Standard Costing*

Bellmead Pools & Supply
Facts for Illustration of Standard Costing
Month of June

Panel A—Comparison of Actual Results with Flexible Budget:
   Installed 10 Swimming Pools:

	Actual Results at Actual Prices	Flexible Budget	Flexible Budget Variances
Variable expenses:			
Direct materials	$ 23,100[a]	$ 20,000[c]	$3,100 U
Direct labor	41,800[b]	42,000[c]	200 F
Variable production overhead...........	9,000	8,000[d]	1,000 U
Selling and administrative expenses......	9,100	10,000	900 F
Total variable expenses	83,000	80,000	3,000 U
Fixed expenses:			
Fixed production overhead.............	12,300	12,000[e]	300 U
Selling and administrative expenses......	9,700	8,000	1,700 U
Total fixed expenses.................	22,000	20,000	2,000 U
Total expenses........................	$105,000	$100,000	$5,000 U

[a] $23,100 = 11,969 cubic yards at actual price of $1.93 per cubic yard.
[b] $41,800 = 3,800 hours at actual price of $11.00 per hour.
[c] See Panel B.
[d] Variable production overhead was budgeted at $2.00 per direct labor hour:
   $8,000 = 4,000 direct labor hours (10 pools × 400 direct labor hours) × $2.00.
[e] Fixed production overhead was budgeted at $12,000 per month.

Panel B—Standards for Direct Material and Direct Labor Flexible Budget:
   10 Swimming Pools:

	(1) Standard Inputs Budgeted for 10 Finished Units (Swimming Pools Installed)	(2) Standard Price per Unit of Input	(1) × (2) Flexible Budget for 10 Finished Units of Output
Direct materials	1,000 cubic yards per pool × 10 pools = 10,000 cubic yards	$ 2.00	$20,000
Direct labor............	400 hours per pool × 10 pools = 4,000 hours	10.50	42,000

Direct Material and Direct Labor Variances

Flexible budget variances for direct material and direct labor are often subdivided into price and efficiency variances.

The **price variance** is the difference between actual unit prices of inputs and their standard unit prices, multiplied by the number of *actual inputs used:*

$$\text{PRICE VARIANCE} = \begin{pmatrix} \text{DIFFERENCE BETWEEN} \\ \text{ACTUAL AND BUDGETED} \\ \text{UNIT PRICES OF INPUTS} \end{pmatrix} \times \text{ACTUAL INPUTS USED}$$

The **efficiency variance**—also called the *usage variance* and the *quantity variance*—is the difference between the quantity of inputs actually used and the quantity that should have been used (the flexible budget) for the actual output achieved, multiplied by the *standard unit price:*

$$\text{EFFICIENCY VARIANCE} = \begin{pmatrix} \text{INPUTS} & \text{INPUTS THAT SHOULD} \\ \text{ACTUALLY} - & \text{HAVE BEEN USED} \\ \text{USED} & \text{FOR ACTUAL OUTPUT} \end{pmatrix} \times \begin{matrix} \text{STANDARD} \\ \text{UNIT PRICE} \\ \text{OF INPUT} \end{matrix}$$

Price variances are computed not only for their own sake but also to give managers a sharper focus on efficiency. In this way, efficiency can be measured by holding unit prices constant. Thus managers' judgments about efficiency are unaffected by price changes. Efficiency variances have an important underlying assumption: All unit prices are *standard* prices.

Direct Materials Variances
The relevant data for computing Bellmead Pools' direct materials variances are

	Actual Cost	Flexible Budget Standard Cost	Flexible Budget Variance
Cubic yards...........	11,969	10,000	
Unit price	× $1.93	× $2.00	
Total	$23,100	$20,000	$3,100 U

Managers seek to gain further insight by dividing this flexible budget variance into price and efficiency variances.

$$\text{PRICE VARIANCE} = \begin{pmatrix} \text{DIFFERENCE BETWEEN} \\ \text{ACTUAL AND BUDGETED} \\ \text{UNIT PRICES OF INPUTS} \end{pmatrix} \times \text{ACTUAL INPUTS USED}$$

OBJECTIVE 4
Compute direct materials cost variances

Price variance = ($1.93 − $2.00) × 11,969 cubic yards

= $838 F

$$\text{EFFICIENCY VARIANCE} = \begin{pmatrix} \text{INPUTS} & \text{INPUTS THAT SHOULD} \\ \text{ACTUALLY} - & \text{HAVE BEEN USED} \\ \text{USED} & \text{FOR ACTUAL OUTPUT} \end{pmatrix} \times \begin{matrix} \text{STANDARD} \\ \text{UNIT PRICE} \\ \text{OF INPUT} \end{matrix}$$

Efficiency variance = (11,969 cubic yards − 10,000 cubic yards) × $2.00 per cubic yard

= (11,969 − 10,000) × $2.00

= $3,938 U

The direct materials variances can be summarized as follows:

Price variance	$ 838 F
Efficiency variance	3,938 U
Total flexible budget variance explained	$3,100 U

EXHIBIT 24-6 *Bellmead Pools & Supply*
Direct Materials Variance Computations

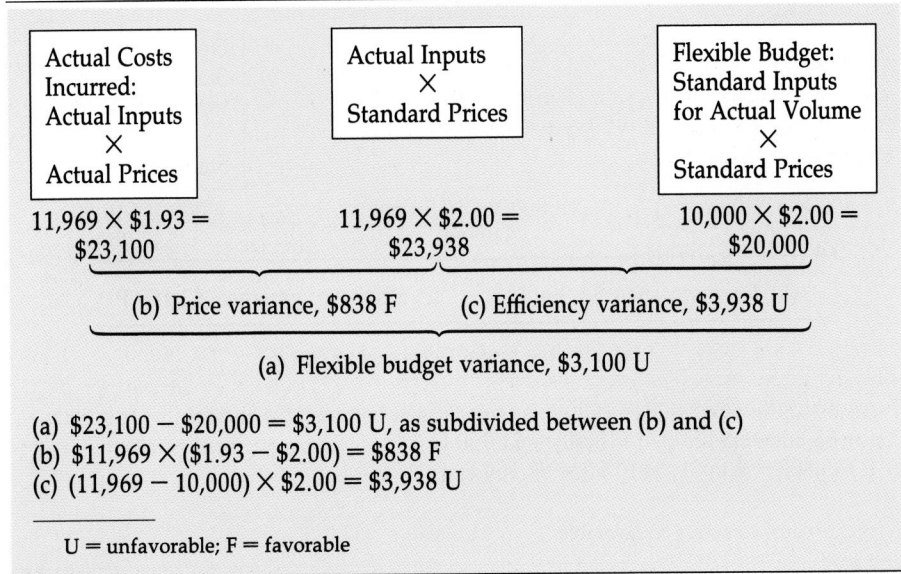

Exhibit 24-6 summarizes the direct materials cost variance computations. Variance analysis begins with a total variance to be explained—in this example, the $3,100 flexible budget variance.

Direct Labor Variances

The relevant data for computing Bellmead Pools' direct labor variances are

	Actual Cost	Flexible Budget Standard Cost	Flexible Budget Variance
Hours	3,800	4,000	
Hourly rate.	× $11.00	× $10.50	
Total	$41,800	$42,000	$200 F

> **OBJECTIVE 5**
> Compute direct labor cost variances

$$\text{PRICE VARIANCE} = \begin{array}{c} \text{DIFFERENCE BETWEEN} \\ \text{ACTUAL AND BUDGETED} \\ \text{UNIT PRICES OF INPUTS} \end{array} \times \begin{array}{c} \text{ACTUAL INPUTS USED} \end{array}$$

$$\text{Price variance} = (\$11.00 - \$10.50) \times 3{,}800 \text{ hours}$$

$$= \$1{,}900 \text{ U}$$

This variance is also called the direct labor *rate* variance.

$$\text{EFFICIENCY VARIANCE} = \left(\begin{array}{c} \text{INPUTS} \\ \text{ACTUALLY} \\ \text{USED} \end{array} - \begin{array}{c} \text{INPUTS THAT SHOULD} \\ \text{HAVE BEEN USED} \\ \text{FOR ACTUAL OUTPUT} \end{array} \right) \times \begin{array}{c} \text{STANDARD} \\ \text{UNIT PRICE} \\ \text{OF INPUT} \end{array}$$

$$\text{Efficiency variance} = (3{,}800 \text{ hours} - 4{,}000 \text{ hours}) \times \$10.50 \text{ per hour}$$

$$= \$2{,}100 \text{ F}$$

EXHIBIT 24-7 *Bellmead Pools & Supply*
Direct Labor Variance Computations

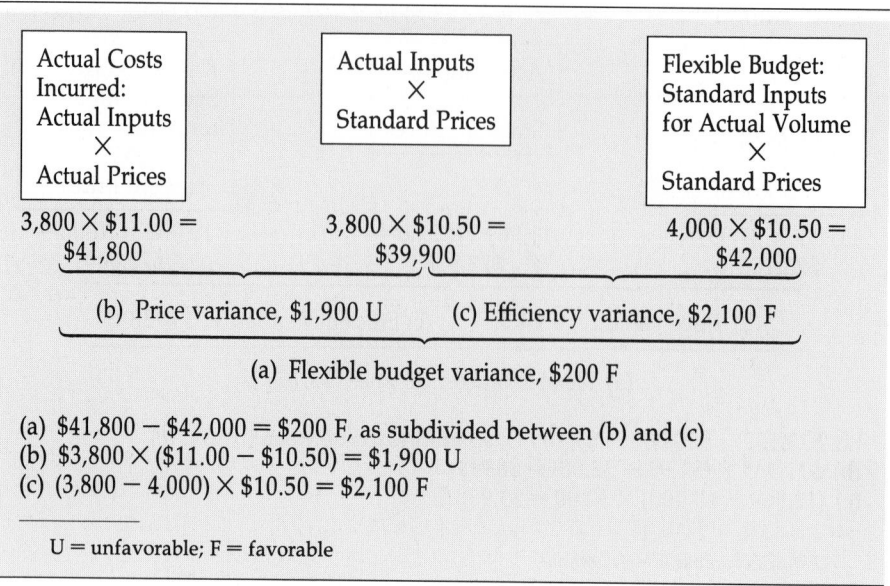

(a) $41,800 − $42,000 = $200 F, as subdivided between (b) and (c)
(b) $3,800 × ($11.00 − $10.50) = $1,900 U
(c) (3,800 − 4,000) × $10.50 = $2,100 F

U = unfavorable; F = favorable

The direct labor variances can be summarized as follows:

Price variance	$1,900 U
Efficiency variance	2,100 F
Total flexible budget variance explained	$ 200 F

To relate standard costing to the overall budget, trace these total flexible budget variances to Exhibit 24-5. In addition, Exhibit 24-7 summarizes the direct labor variance computations, providing an overall picture to aid your study.

Management Use of Variance Information

Variances do not identify problems or their solutions. But they often raise questions that deserve attention. For example, an unfavorable materials price variance may point to the need to shop around for a new supplier of raw materials. *Price* effects, though, may depend on market factors, which are hard or sometimes impossible to control. An unfavorable labor efficiency variance, however, directs management to examine employee performance. The company certainly has greater control over its own people than it has over outside markets.

Managers sometimes trade off price and efficiency effects, accepting an unfavorable variance in one area in order to achieve a favorable variance in the other. In our example, Bellmead's favorable materials price variance may have resulted from using cheaper material. The unfavorable materials efficiency variance may have arisen because employees had to use more material than standard, perhaps because of its inferior quality. Thus the company's strategy failed. The overall materials cost variance was unfavorable by $3,100.

In another trade-off between price and efficiency, Bellmead used more expensive labor than standard. But the company gained greater efficiency, and the company achieved a net labor cost saving of $200.

When should a variance be investigated? Most often the answer is based on personal judgment. For example, a manager may believe that a 5 percent variance in a $1 million materials cost deserves more attention than a 20 percent variance in a $10,000 budget. Rules of thumb—such as "Investigate all variances above $5,000" and "Investigate all variances 25 percent or more above standard cost" —are also common in practice.

Production Overhead Variances

Production overhead cost variances can be computed for individual overhead costs like property taxes, utilities, and insurance, but many companies compute variances on total overhead. The most common accounting practice is to split production overhead variances into two parts: a *flexible budget variance* and a *production volume variance*.

The *flexible budget variance* for production overhead shows whether managers are keeping total overhead cost within the budgeted amount for the actual production of the period. The *production volume variance* arises when actual production differs from the level in the static (master) budget. The two variances combine to explain the difference between actual overhead cost and standard overhead cost that has been applied to production. Before discussing the computation of overhead variances, let's review how overhead cost is applied to production.

Applying Overhead to Production

In a system that uses standard costs, overhead is applied to production at a budgeted rate, as discussed in the two preceding chapters. Companies develop overhead standards based on past experience and budgets that reflect the business's goals. Suppose Exhibit 24-8 is Bellmead Pools' flexible overhead budget, which shows activity levels for 6, 8, 9, and 10 pools per month. We have high-

EXHIBIT 24-8   *Flexible Monthly Production Overhead Cost Budget*

		Static (Master) Budget		Flexible Budget for Actual Production
Bellmead Pools & Supply **Flexible Monthly Production Overhead Cost Budget**				
Number of pools installed per month...............	6	8	9	10
Standard direct labor hours.......................	2,400	3,200	3,600	4,000
Budgeted production overhead cost:				
Variable.....................................	$ 4,800	$ 6,400	$ 7,200	$ 8,000
Fixed	12,000	12,000	12,000	12,000
Total	$16,800	$18,400	$19,200	$20,000
Standard variable overhead rate per direct labor hour ..		$6,400/3,200 = $2.00		
Standard fixed overhead rate per direct labor hour		$12,000/3,200 = $3.75		
Standard total overhead rate per direct labor hour		$18,400/3,200 = $5.75		

lighted the static (master) budget level of 8 pools and the actual production level of 10 pools because these levels are useful for computing the overhead variances.

Exhibit 24-8 indicates that Bellmead applies $5.75 of overhead cost to production for each direct labor hour spent installing a swimming pool. Of this amount, $2.00 is for variable overhead, and $3.75 is for fixed overhead. These standards can be based on any level of production that is consistent with company goals. In this case, Bellmead's goal is static (master) budget volume of 8 pools per month.

Bellmead accountants assemble the data in Exhibit 24-9 for computing the overhead cost variances associated with actual production of 10 pools.

The total production overhead cost variance is the difference between actual cost and standard overhead applied to production. For Bellmead Pools & Supply, the total overhead cost variance is favorable by $1,700 ($21,300 − $23,000). Accountants break the total variance down further for management use.

Flexible Budget (Controllable) Variance. The **flexible budget production overhead variance** is the difference between total actual overhead—fixed and variable—and the flexible budget amount for actual production volume. Bellmead Pools' flexible budget variance for June is computed as follows (data from Exhibit 24-9):

OBJECTIVE 6

Compute production overhead cost variances

Total actual overhead cost	$21,300
Total flexible budget overhead for actual production	20,000
Flexible budget variance	$ 1,300 U

Total June overhead was $21,300, compared to the flexible budget amount of $20,000. The unfavorable variance suggests that managers did not control costs very well. Often this variance is due more to variable costs than to fixed costs, and production managers exercise considerable control over variable overhead. Therefore, many accountants call this the *controllable variance.* We prefer to label it the flexible budget variance because it is the difference between actual production overhead and the production overhead cost in the flexible budget for actual production.

EXHIBIT 24-9 *Data for Computing Production Overhead Cost Variances*

Bellmead Pools & Supply
Data for Computing Production Overhead Cost Variances

	Actual Cost (Exhibit 24-5)	Flexible Budget for Actual Production (Exhibit 24-8)	Standard Overhead Applied to Production (Exhibit 24-8)
Variable overhead.	$ 9,000	$ 8,000	4,000 direct labor hours × $2.00 = $ 8,000
Fixed overhead . . .	12,300	12,000	4,000 direct labor hours × $3.75 = 15,000
Total overhead . . .	$21,300	$20,000	4,000 direct labor hours × $5.75 = $23,000

Total production overhead cost variance
$1,700 F

Production Volume Variance. The **production volume overhead variance** is the difference between the flexible budget for actual production and standard overhead applied to production (data from Exhibit 24-9):

Flexible budget overhead for actual production	$20,000
Standard overhead applied to production.	23,000
Production volume variance	$ 3,000 F

When the flexible overhead budget amount is less than the standard overhead applied to production, the variance is favorable, as shown for Bellmead Pools. The increase in volume from 8 pools to 10 pools was favorable because productive capacity was more fully utilized than expected. Had the flexible budget amount exceeded the standard overhead applied to production, the variance would have been unfavorable.

Exhibit 24-9 reveals that variable overhead is (always) the same for the flexible budget and the amount applied to production. Therefore, the production volume variance must be due solely to fixed cost effects. An alternative computation of this variance clarifies this point (all data from Exhibit 24-8):

Standard direct labor hours for actual production.	4,000
Standard direct labor hours for static (master) budget	3,200
Actual production in excess of static budget	800
Standard *fixed* overhead rate per direct labor hour	×$3.75
Production volume variance	$ 3,000 F

The production volume variance is favorable because Bellmead installed more pools than the static budget called for. The sum of the two overhead variances explains the total favorable production overhead variance of $1,700:

Flexible budget (controllable) variance	$1,300 U
Production volume variance	3,000 F
Total overhead cost variance explained.	$1,700 F

EXHIBIT 24-10 *Bellmead Pools & Supply*
Production Overhead Variance Computations

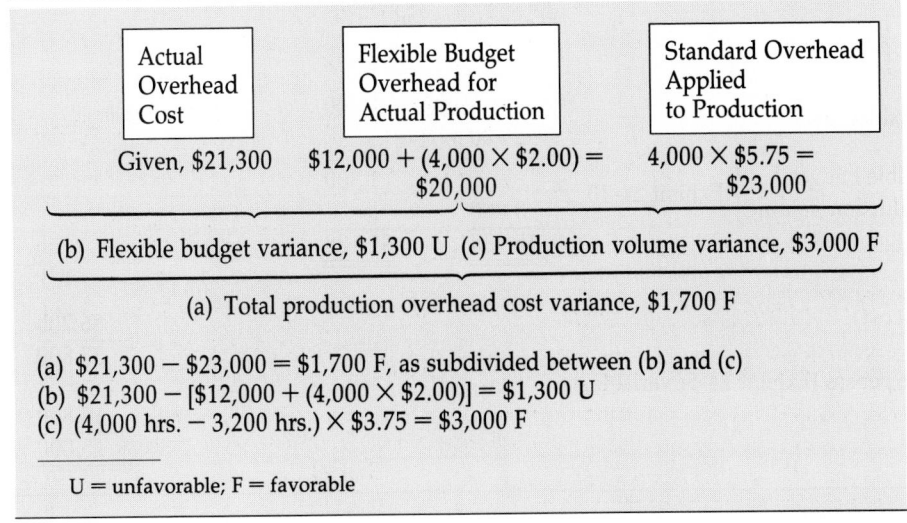

(a) $21,300 − $23,000 = $1,700 F, as subdivided between (b) and (c)
(b) $21,300 − [$12,000 + (4,000 × $2.00)] = $1,300 U
(c) (4,000 hrs. − 3,200 hrs.) × $3.75 = $3,000 F

U = unfavorable; F = favorable

Exhibit 24-10 summarizes the computation of overhead cost variances, with amounts shown for Bellmead Pools & Supply.

Two-variance analysis as just described is the most common in practice. Some companies, however, perform a three-variance analysis that splits the flexible budget variance into spending and efficiency effects. A few companies divide overhead cost variances into four parts. These topics are covered in managerial accounting and cost accounting courses.

Standard Costs in the Accounts

Some companies use standard costing for control purposes without entering the standards in the accounts. Others make special standard cost entries.

Accounting systems differ among those companies that do record standard costs in the accounts. For example, one practice is to debit actual costs to Materials Inventory and Wages. When materials are used, or when labor is applied to production, these accounts are credited for *actual* cost. However, Work in Process Inventory is debited for *standard* cost. Differences in these entries reveal the cost variances. In our Bellmead Pools illustration, Wage Cost has been credited for actual direct labor of $41,800. The entry to apply direct labor to production is

Work in Process Inventory (standard cost)	42,000	
Direct Labor Price Variance	1,900	
Direct Labor Efficiency Variance		2,100
Wage Cost (actual cost).............................		41,800
Application of direct labor to production.		

EXHIBIT 24-11   *Income Statement*

Bellmead Pools & Supply
Income Statement
For the Month Ended June 30, 19X5

	Favorable	Unfavorable		
Sales revenue (Exhibit 24-4: 10 pools at $12,000).........				$120,000
Cost of goods sold at standard cost (preceding section)			$85,000	
Cost variances:				
Direct materials: price } Exhibit 24-6 efficiency	$ 838			
		$3,938		
Direct labor: price } Exhibit 24-7 efficiency		1,900		
	2,100			
Production overhead: flexible budget } Exhibit 24-10 production volume		1,300		
	3,000			
	$5,938	$7,138		
Net cost variance		1,200 U		
Cost of goods sold at actual cost......................				86,200
Gross profit..				33,800
Selling and administrative expenses (Exhibit 24-5: variable, $9,100 + fixed, $9,700)				18,800
Operating income				$ 15,000

After posting, the variance accounts appear as follows:

Direct Labor Price Variance

Unfavorable variance 1,900	

Direct Labor Efficiency Variance

	Favorable variance.......... 2,100

A debit balance in a variance account is treated as expense, and a credit balance is handled as a contra expense, or a reduction in expense. In this example, Direct Labor Price Variance's debit balance is expense, and Direct Labor Efficiency Variance's credit balance is a reduction in expense. These variance accounts are closed to Income Summary in the usual manner. Accounting for materials and overhead parallel these entries for labor.

Assume Bellmead sold all 10 pools that were installed during June. The Work in Process Inventory account contains the following standard cost information:

Work in Process Inventory

Direct materials used (flexible budget *standard* cost Exhibit 24-5)...................	20,000	Goods finished...........	85,000
Direct labor applied (flexible budget *standard* cost Exhibit 24-5)...................	42,000		
Production overhead applied (*standard* cost for actual output: 4,000 direct labor hours × $5.75 per hour Exhibit 24-9)...............	23,000		
Total standard cost........	85,000		

Finished Goods Inventory

Goods finished...........	85,000	Cost of goods sold........	85,000

Cost of Goods Sold

Cost of goods sold........ 85,000	

Standard Cost Income Statement for Management

Standard costing is a management tool, so the company does not usually report variance information to investors, creditors, and other outsiders. Managers, however, are vitally interested in the cost variances. Exhibit 24-11 illustrates an income statement the Bellmead president might use for planning and control purposes. We assume that Bellmead's sales for June were the 10 pools installed during the month.

Summary Problem for Your Review

Exhibit 24-5 indicates that Bellmead Pools & Supply installed 10 swimming pools during June. Suppose that June installations and sales were 7 pools instead of 10 and that actual expenses for the month were as follows:

Direct materials......................	7,400 cubic yards @ $2.00 per cubic yard
Direct labor	2,740 hours @ $10.00 per hour
Variable production overhead	$5,400
Fixed production overhead..............	$11,900

Required

1. Given these new data, prepare two exhibits, similar to Exhibits 24-5 and 24-8. Ignore selling and administrative expenses in your first exhibit, and show budgeted overhead cost only for 7 and 8 pools per month in your second exhibit.
2. Compute the direct materials and direct labor price and efficiency variances.
3. Compute the total variance, the flexible budget variance, and the production volume variance for overhead.
4. Prepare a June income statement through operating income for the president of Bellmead Pools & Supply. Report all cost variances, and assume selling and administrative expenses for the month were $17,700.

SOLUTION TO REVIEW PROBLEM

Requirement 1

Bellmead Pools & Supply
Facts for Illustration of Standard Costing
Month of June

Panel A—Comparison of Actual Results with Flexible Budget:
 Installed 7 Swimming Pools

	Actual Results at Actual Prices	Flexible Budget	Flexible Budget Variances
Variable expenses:			
Direct materials	$14,800[a]	$14,000[c]	$ 800 U
Direct labor	27,400[b]	29,400[c]	2,000 F
Variable production overhead	5,400	5,600[d]	200 F
Total variable expenses	47,600	49,000	1,400 F
Fixed expenses:			
Fixed production overhead	11,900	12,000[e]	100 F
Total expenses	$59,500	$61,000	$1,500 F

[a] $14,800 = 7,400 cubic yards at actual price of $2.00 per cubic yard.
[b] $27,400 = 2,740 hours at actual price of $10.00 per hour.
[c] See Panel B.
[d] Variable production overhead was budgeted at $2.00 per direct labor hour:
  $5,600 = 2,800 direct labor hours (7 pools × 400 direct labor hours) × $2.00.
[e] Fixed production overhead was budgeted at $12,000 per month.

Panel B—Standards for Direct Material and Direct Labor Flexible Budget:
    7 Swimming Pools

	(1) **Standard Inputs Budgeted for 7 Finished Units (Swimming Pools Installed)**	(2) **Standard Price per Unit of Input**	(1) × (2) **Flexible Budget for 7 Finished Units of Output**
Direct materials	1,000 cubic yards × 7	$ 2.00	$14,000
Direct labor	400 hours × 7	10.50	29,400

Bellmead Pools & Supply
Flexible Monthly Production Overhead Cost Budget

Number of pools installed per month	7	8
Standard direct labor hours	2,800	3,200
Budgeted production overhead cost:		
Variable	$ 5,600	$ 6,400
Fixed	12,000	12,000
Total.	$17,600	$18,400

Standard variable overhead rate per direct labor hour. $6,400/3,200
                 = $2.00

Standard fixed overhead rate per direct labor hour $12,000/3,200
                 = $3.75

Standard total overhead rate per direct labor hour. $18,400/3,200
                 = $5.75

Requirement 2

$$\text{PRICE VARIANCE} = \begin{array}{c} \text{DIFFERENCE BETWEEN} \\ \text{ACTUAL AND BUDGETED} \\ \text{UNIT PRICES OF INPUTS} \end{array} \times \text{ACTUAL INPUTS USED}$$

Direct materials:
    Price variance =   ($2.00 − $2.00)   ×   7,400 cubic yards

               = $ 0

Direct labor:
    Price variance =   ($10.00 − $10.50)   ×   2,740 hours

               = $1,370 F

$$\text{EFFICIENCY VARIANCE} = \left(\begin{array}{c} \text{INPUTS} \\ \text{ACTUALLY} \\ \text{USED} \end{array} - \begin{array}{c} \text{INPUTS THAT SHOULD} \\ \text{HAVE BEEN USED} \\ \text{FOR ACTUAL OUTPUT} \end{array} \right) \begin{array}{c} \text{STANDARD} \\ \times \text{UNIT PRICE} \\ \text{OF INPUT} \end{array}$$

$$= \left(\begin{array}{c} \text{Actual cubic} \\ \text{yards or} \\ \text{hours used} \end{array} - \begin{array}{c} \text{Standard number of cubic} \\ \text{yards or hours allowed} \\ \text{for actual output} \end{array} \right) \begin{array}{c} \text{Standard} \\ \times \text{unit price} \\ \text{of input} \end{array}$$

Direct materials:

$$\text{Efficiency variance} = \begin{pmatrix} \begin{array}{c} 7,400 \\ \text{cubic} \\ \text{yards} \end{array} & - & \begin{array}{c} 1,000 \text{ cubic yards} \\ \times 7 \\ \text{swimming pools} \end{array} \end{pmatrix} \times \begin{array}{c} \$2.00 \\ \text{per} \\ \text{cubic yard} \end{array}$$

$$= \quad (7,400 \quad - \quad 7,000) \quad \times \quad \$2.00$$

$$= \$800 \text{ U}$$

Direct labor:

$$\text{Efficiency variance} = \begin{pmatrix} \begin{array}{c} 2,740 \\ \text{hours} \\ \text{used} \end{array} & - & \begin{array}{c} 400 \text{ hours} \\ \times 7 \text{ swimming} \\ \text{pools installed} \end{array} \end{pmatrix} \times \begin{array}{c} \$10.50 \\ \text{per} \\ \text{hour} \end{array}$$

$$= \quad (2,740 \quad - \quad 2,800) \quad \times \quad \$10.50$$

$$= \$630 \text{ F}$$

Requirement 3

Total actual overhead cost (variable, $5,400 + fixed, $11,900)	$17,300
Standard total overhead cost applied to production, 7 pools	
(2,800 direct labor hours × $5.75)	16,100
Total overhead cost variance	$ 1,200 U

Flexible Budget Variance:

Total actual overhead cost ($5,400 + $11,900)	$ 17,300
Total flexible budget overhead for actual production	
($5,600 + $12,000)	17,600
Flexible budget variance	$ 300 F

Production Volume Variance:

Flexible budget overhead for actual production	
(Requirement 1: variable, $5,600 + fixed, $12,000).	$ 17,600
Standard overhead applied to production	
[Requirement 1: 2,800 direct labor hours (for 7 pools) × $5.75].	16,100
Production volume variance.	$ 1,500 U

or

Standard direct labor hours for static (master) budget	
(Requirement 1: Flexible Budget)	3,200
Standard direct labor hours for actual production	
(Requirement 1: Flexible Budget)	2,800
Difference in direct labor hours between flexible budget and master	
budget.	400
Standard fixed overhead rate per direct labor hour	
(Requirement 1: Flexible Budget)	×$3.75
Production volume variance.	$ 1,500 U

Requirement 4

Bellmead Pools & Supply
Income Statement
For the Month Ended June 30, 19X5

Sales revenue (7 pools at $12,000)		$84,000
Cost of goods sold at standard cost [direct materials, $14,000 + direct labor, $29,400 + overhead, $16,100 (2,800 × $5.75)] . .	$59,500	

Cost variances:	Favorable	Unfavorable
Direct materials price	$ -0-	$ -0-
Direct materials efficiency		800
Direct labor price	1,370	
Direct labor efficiency.	630	
Overhead flexible budget.	300	
Overhead production volume		1,500
	$2,300	$2,300

Net cost variance	-0-	
Cost of goods sold at actual cost		59,500
Gross profit.		24,500
Selling and administrative expenses		17,700
Operating income.		$ 6,800

Summary

A *static budget* is prepared for only one level of activity, usually the volume level that management expects for the period. A *flexible budget* is a set of budgets covering a range of volume. *Performance reports* compare actual and budgeted results for the sales volume achieved. Differences between actual and budgeted revenues and expenses are called *variances*. A variance is *favorable* if actual revenue exceeds budgeted revenue, or if actual expense is less than budgeted expense. An *unfavorable* variance occurs when actual revenue is less than budget or actual expense exceeds budget.

Costs are classified as *variable, fixed,* or *mixed.* The total amount of a variable cost fluctuates in direct proportion to changes in volume. By contrast, the total amount of a fixed cost does not change during a given period over a wide range of volume. A mixed cost has both variable and fixed components. These distinctions are important to flexible budgeting, which identifies costs and income for different levels of volume.

The heart of a flexible budget is the *budget formula,* which expresses the behavior of costs. A *flexible budget graph* provides a customized budget for any volume level.

Standard costs are the predetermined costs that managers believe the business should incur in producing an item. The standards are set low enough to spur employees to improve their performance but not so low as to discourage workers. *Standard cost systems* are designed to control cost by analyzing differences between actual and standard cost. *Cost variances* are differences between actual cost and standard cost. In general, cost variances are divided into price and efficiency effects.

The *price variance* measures the effect price changes have on the cost of materials and labor. The *efficiency variance* gauges manager efficiency in using materials and labor.

Production overhead variances are divided two ways. The *flexible budget variance* is the difference between actual overhead cost and the flexible budget for actual output. It measures whether the company achieved its budgeted cost for the actual volume level achieved. The *production volume variance* arises when actual production differs from the level in the static (master) budget.

Some companies use standard costing for control purposes without recording standard costs in the accounts. Others journalize the standards and the related cost variances. The variance information is helpful in planning and control. It does not automatically identify problems or cures, but it points to areas of the business needing correction.

Self-Study Questions

Test your understanding of the chapter by marking the best answer for each of the following questions.

1. A flexible budget shows *(p. 937)*
   a. Expected results over a range of volume levels
   b. A single target level of volume
   c. Price variances
   d. Volume variances

2. Which is the most useful formula for budgeting expenses? *(p. 938)*
   a. Expenses = Sales − Income
   b. Expenses = Fixed + Variable
   c. Expenses = Fixed + (Variable X Number of Units)
   d. Expenses = Standard + Variances

3. Flexible budget variances are differences between *(p. 940)*
   a. Actual results and the static (master) budget
   b. Actual results and the flexible budget
   c. The static (master) budget and the flexible budget
   d. None of the above

4. Standard cost variances help managers identify *(p. 943)*
   a. Ways of reducing cost   c. Both of the above
   b. Employees who control cost   d. None of the above

5. Cost variances for direct materials and direct labor are divided into *(p. 945)*
   a. Flexible budget effects and production volume effects
   b. Efficiency effects and flexible budget effects
   c. Controllable effects and master budget effects
   d. Price effects and efficiency effects

6. Krakow, Inc., paid $3 per pound for 10,000 pounds of direct materials purchased and used. Standard cost was $2.80 per pound, and standard usage for actual production was 11,000 pounds. How much is the price variance? *(p. 946)*
   a. $800 favorable   c. $2,800 favorable
   b. $2,000 unfavorable   d. $3,000 favorable

7. How much is the efficiency variance in the preceding question? *(p. 946)*
   a. $800 favorable   c. $2,800 favorable
   b. $2,000 unfavorable   d. $3,000 favorable

8. Cost variances for production overhead are divided into *(p. 949)*
   a. Flexible budget effects and production volume effects
   b. Efficiency effects and flexible budget effects
   c. Controllable effects and master budget effects
   d. Price effects and efficiency effects

9. Actual overhead of Milstead Supply Company is $540,000. Overhead for static (master) budget volume is $500,000, and flexible budget overhead for actual production is $510,000. The production volume variance is *(p. 951)*
   a. $10,000 unfavorable   c. $40,000 unfavorable
   b. $30,000 unfavorable   d. Not determinable from the information given

10. Gonzalez Manufacturing made the following entry for the use of direct materials in production:

Work in Process	380,000	
Direct Materials Efficiency Variance	35,000	
Direct Materials Price Variance		6,000
Materials Inventory		409,000

Which of the following statements is true? *(p. 953)*
a. The price variance is unfavorable and the efficiency variance is favorable
b. The price variance is favorable and the efficiency variance is unfavorable
c. Both variances are favorable
d. Both variances are unfavorable

Answers to the self-study questions are at the end of the chapter.

Accounting Vocabulary

budget formula *(p. 938)*, controllable variance *(p. 950)*, efficiency variance *(p. 946)*, flexible budget *(p. 937)*, flexible budget overhead variance *(p. 950)*, flexible budget variance *(p. 940)*, price variance *(p. 945)*, production volume variance *(p. 951)*, production volume overhead variance *(p. 951)*, quantity variance *(p. 946)*, sales volume variance *(p. 940)*, standard cost *(p. 943)*, standard cost system *(p. 943)*, static budget *(p. 937)*, usage variance *(p. 946)*, variance *(p. 937)*.

ASSIGNMENT MATERIAL _____

Questions

1. Which costs in total amount move in direct proportion to changes in volume? Which costs do not fluctuate in total amount with volume changes? How do total and unit amounts behave for these two categories of costs?
2. What is the relevant range, and why must it be considered in preparing a flexible budget?
3. How does a static budget differ from a flexible budget?
4. Identify how managers use variance information from a performance report.
5. McLaren, Inc., prepared its static (master) budget for a sales level of 35,000 for the month. Actual sales totaled 46,000. Describe the problem of using the master budget to evaluate company performance for the month. Propose a better way to evaluate McLaren's performance for the period.
6. What advantage does a flexible expense budget graph offer over a flexible expense budget that shows four levels of volume?
7. What do the sales volume variance and the flexible budget variance measure?
8. Describe the purpose of a standard cost system.
9. What two general categories of cost variances do most standard cost systems provide?
10. Identify the similarities and differences between a standard cost and a budgeted cost.
11. Suppose your company is installing a standard cost system. What sort of standard cost is most popular? For employees, what purpose does a standard cost fulfill?
12. What does a price variance measure? How is it computed?
13. What does an efficiency variance measure? How is it computed?

14. Consider price variance and efficiency variance. How do they relate to the total variance between actual and budgeted cost for direct materials and direct labor?

15. Describe a tradeoff that a manager might make for labor cost.

16. When should a cost variance be investigated?

17. What causes a flexible budget overhead variance? What information does this variance provide?

18. What information is provided by the overhead production volume variance? How is this variance computed?

19. Scott & White, Inc., enters standard costs in the company accounts. The actual cost of direct materials used to manufacture inventory was $21,600. The direct materials price variance was $2,000 favorable, and the efficiency variance was $1,400 unfavorable. Make the journal entry to charge materials to production.

20. How does a standard cost income statement for management differ from an income statement reported to the public?

Exercises

Exercise 24-1 *Preparing a flexible budget for the income statement*

Antonelli & Salerno Company sells its main product for $6 per unit, and variable cost is $1.40 per unit. Fixed expenses are $180,000 per month for volumes up to 55,000 units of output. Above 55,000 units, monthly fixed expenses are $240,000.

Required

Prepare a monthly flexible budget for the product, showing sales, variable expenses, fixed expenses, and operating income or loss for volume levels of 40,000, 50,000, and 60,000 units.

Exercise 24-2 *Graphing expense behavior*

Graph the expense behavior of Antonelli & Salerno Company in Exercise 24-1. Show total expenses for volume levels of 40,000; 50,000; 55,000; and 60,000 units.

Exercise 24-3 *Completing a performance report*

Stonegate Manufacturing Company management received the following incomplete performance report:

Stonegate Manufacturing Company
Income Statement Performance Report
For the Year Ended April 30, 19X3

	Actual Results at Actual Prices	Flexible Budget Variances	Flexible Budget for Actual Volume Achieved	Sales Volume Variances	Static (Master) Budget
Units.................	24,000		24,000		22,000
Sales.................	$192,000		$192,000		$176,000
Variable expenses	68,000		72,000		66,000
Fixed expenses..........	109,000		100,000		100,000
Total expenses..........	177,000		172,000		166,000
Operating income	$ 15,000		$ 20,000		$ 10,000

Required

Complete the performance report by filling in the variance columns.

Exercise 24-4   *Preparing an income statement performance report*

Top managers of Black Bear Sporting Goods estimated 19X6 sales of 150,000 units of its product at a unit price of $6. Actual sales for the year were 140,000 units at $6.50. Variable expenses were budgeted at $2.20 per unit, and actual variable expenses were $2.25 per unit. Actual fixed expenses of $428,000 exceeded budgeted fixed expenses of $420,000.

Required

Prepare Black Bear's income statement performance report in a format similar to Exhibit 24-4. The bracketed amounts at the bottom are not required.

Exercise 24-5   *Computing price and efficiency cost variances for materials and labor*

Broadmoor Products, which uses a standard cost accounting system, manufactured 350,000 picture frames during the year, using 724,000 board feet of lumber at actual unit cost of $1.22. Production required 6,600 direct labor hours that cost $8.10 per hour. The materials standard was two board feet of lumber per frame, at standard cost of $1.20 per foot. The labor standard was .019 direct labor hour per frame, at standard cost of $8.00 per hour.

Required

Compute the price and efficiency variances for direct materials and direct labor.

Exercise 24-6   *Journalizing standard costing transactions*

Make the journal entries to charge direct materials and direct labor to production in Exercise 24-5.

Exercise 24-7   *Computing price and efficiency variances for direct materials*

The following direct materials variance computations are incomplete:

Price variance = ($7 − $?) × 3,560 pounds   = $712 U
Efficiency variance = (? − 3,600 pounds) × ? =   ?   F
Total materials cost variance . . . . $?

Required

Fill in the missing values and identify the total variance as favorable or unfavorable.

Exercise 24-8   *Computing overhead cost variances*

Matsuko, Inc., charges the following standard unit cost to production, based on master budget volume of 30,000 units per month:

Direct materials	$3.20
Direct labor	4.10
Overhead	1.00
Standard unit cost	$8.30

Matsuko used the following flexible overhead cost budget:

	Monthly Volume		
Number of units.	27,000	30,000	33,000
Standard direct labor hours.	2,700	3,000	3,300
Budgeted overhead cost:			
Variable.	$13,500	$15,000	$16,500
Fixed	15,000	15,000	15,000

Actual monthly production was 33,000 units. Actual overhead cost was variable, $19,700, and fixed, $15,200.

Required

Compute the total overhead cost variance, the flexible budget variance, and the production volume variance for overhead cost.

Exercise 24-9　*Preparing a standard cost income statement for management*

TriStar Corporation revenue and expense information for May follows.

	Revenue or Expense	
	Actual	**Standard**
Sales revenue	$135,000	$135,000
Cost of goods sold	?	71,000
Information regarding:		
Direct materials price variance	18,000	19,100
Direct materials efficiency variance.	19,000	19,600
Direct labor price variance.	46,000	43,400
Direct labor efficiency variance	42,000	42,300
Production overhead variance.	25,000	25,900

Required

Prepare a standard cost income statement through gross profit. Report all cost variances for use by management.

Exercise 24-10　*Explaining cost variances*

Walther Corporation managers are seeking explanations for the variances in the following report:

Walther Corporation
Income Statement for Managers
Year Ended December 31, 19X2

Sales revenue		$541,000
Cost of goods sold—standard	$310,000	
Cost variances:		
Materials: price.	4,000 F	
efficiency	6,000 U	
Labor: price.	8,000 U	
efficiency	3,000 F	
Overhead: flexible budget	9,000 U	
production volume.	10,000 U	
Net cost variance	26,000 U	
Cost of goods sold—actual.		336,000
Gross profit.		205,000
Selling and administrative expenses		181,000
Operating income.		$ 24,000

Required

Explain the meaning of each of Walther Corporation's materials variances and each of the overhead variances.

Problems   (Group A)

Preparing a flexible budget income statement and graphing cost behavior

Foster Kennedy Corporation manufactures solenoids for electronically controlled lawn sprinkler systems. The company's master budget income statement for 19X3 follows, based on expected sales volume of 36,000 units.

Foster Kennedy Corporation
Master Budget Income Statement
Year 19X3

Sales	$756,000
Variable expenses:	
Cost of goods sold	$288,000
Sales commissions	37,800
Shipping	18,000
Utilities	14,400
Fixed expenses:	
Salaries	110,000
Depreciation	53,000
Rent.............................	45,000
Insurance..........................	11,000
Utilities	9,000
Total operating expenses	586,200
Income before income tax	169,800
Income tax expense (25%)...............	42,450
Net income...........................	$127,350

Foster Kennedy's plant capacity is 38,000 units, so if actual volume exceeds 38,000 units it will be necessary to rent additional space. In that case, salaries will increase by 10 percent, rent will double, and insurance expense will increase by $2,000. Depreciation and fixed utilities will be unaffected by the increase in volume.

Required

1. Prepare a flexible budget income statement for the company, showing volume levels of 30,000, 36,000, 40,000, and 44,000 units.
2. Graph the total operating expense behavior of the company. Cost of goods sold is included.

Problem 24-2A   *Preparing an income statement performance report*

Refer to the Foster Kennedy Corporation situation of Problem 24-1A. The company sold 40,000 units during 19X3, and its actual income statement was as reported on the next page.

Required

Prepare an income statement performance report for 19X3.

Foster Kennedy Corporation
Income Statement
Year 19X3

Sales		$853,000
Variable expenses:		
Cost of goods sold	$354,000	
Sales commissions	45,000	
Shipping	17,000	
Utilities	18,000	
Fixed expenses:		
Salaries	107,000	
Depreciation	96,000	
Rent	62,000	
Insurance	14,000	
Utilities	9,000	
Total operating expenses		722,000
Income before income tax		131,000
Income tax expense (25%)		32,750
Net income		$ 98,250

Problem 24-3A *Computing cost variances and reporting to management*

Monarch Binder Company manufactures ring binders used by college students. During August the company produced and sold 78,000 binders and accumulated the following cost data:

	Standard Unit Cost	Total Actual Cost
Direct materials:		
Standard (1 lb. @ $.14 per lb.)	$.14	
Actual (74,900 lb. @ $.16 per lb.)		$11,984
Direct labor:		
Standard (.02 hr. @ $5.00 per hr.)	.10	
Actual (1,600 hr. @ $5.02 per hr.)		8,032
Overhead:		
Standard:		
Variable ($6.00 per direct labor hour)	$.12	
Fixed ($12,000 for master budget volume of 80,000 units and 1,600 direct labor hours)	.15	.27
Actual		21,840
Total	$.51	$41,856

Required

1. Compute the price and efficiency variances for direct materials and direct labor.
2. Compute the total variance, the flexible budget variance, and the production volume variance for overhead.
3. Prepare a standard cost income statement through gross profit to report all variances to management. Sale price of the binders to college bookstores was $1 each.

Problem 24-4A *Computing and journalizing cost variances*

White Rock, Inc., manufactures T-shirts that it sells to other companies for customizing with their own logos. White Rock prepares flexible budgets and uses a standard cost system to control manufacturing cost. The following standard unit cost of a basic white T-shirt is based on master budget volume of 20,000 T-shirts per month:

Direct materials (3 sq. yd. @ $.13 per sq. yd.)		$ .39
Direct labor (2 minutes @ $.15 per minute).......................		.30
Overhead:		
Variable.......................................	$.12	
Fixed (2 minutes @ $.16 per minute)	.32	.44
Total unit cost..		$1.13

Transactions during May of the current year included the following:

a. Actual production was 22,700 units.
b. Actual direct materials usage was 2.75 square yards per unit at actual cost of $.14 per square yard.
c. Actual direct labor usage of 47,200 minutes cost $7,316.
d. Total actual overhead cost was $10,107.

Required

1. Compute the price and efficiency variances for direct materials and direct labor. Carry amounts to three decimal places.
2. Journalize the usage of direct material and the application of direct labor, including the related cost variances.
3. Compute the total variance, the flexible budget variance, and the production volume variance for overhead.

Problem 24-5A *Preparing a flexible budget and computing cost variances*

MasterCraft Furniture manufactures recliner chairs and uses flexible budgeting and a standard cost system. The company's performance report includes the following selected data:

	Master Budget 4,000 Units	Actual Results 3,800 Units
Sales	$800,000	$729,600
Variable expenses:		
Cost of goods sold:		
Direct materials (160,000 lb. @ $.80)	$128,000	
(154,000 lb. @ $.78)......................		$120,120
Direct labor (20,000 hr. @ $6.00)	120,000	
(20,300 hr. @ $6.03).......................		122,409
Variable overhead (20,000 hr. @ $4.00).........	80,000	
(20,300 hr. @ $5.22).......................		105,966
Fixed expenses:		
Cost of goods sold:		
Fixed overhead.............................	112,000	107,000
Total cost of goods sold.........................	440,000	455,495
Gross profit.....................................	$360,000	$274,105

Required

1. Prepare a flexible budget based on actual volume.
2. Compute the price variance and the efficiency variance for direct materials and direct labor. Compute the total variance, the flexible budget variance, and the production volume variance for overhead.

3. Show that the sum of the price variance plus the efficiency variance equals the total cost variance for direct materials and for direct labor. Use Exhibit 24-6 as a guide.

Problem 24-6A   *Using incomplete cost and variance information to determine the number of direct labor hours worked*

The state of Minnesota has a shop that manufactures street signs used throughout the state. The manager of the shop uses standard costs to judge performance. Recently a clerk mistakenly threw away some of the records, and the manager has only partial data for April. She knows that the total direct labor variance for the month was $900—unfavorable and that the standard labor price was $6 per hour. A recent pay raise caused an unfavorable labor price variance of $.10 per hour. The standard direct labor hours for actual April output were 2,900.

Required

1. Find the actual number of direct labor hours worked during April. Hint: First, find the actual direct labor price per hour. Then determine the actual number of direct labor hours by setting up the computation of the total direct labor cost variance of $900: Actual labor cost *minus* standard labor cost for actual output *equals* $900.
2. Compute the direct labor price and efficiency variances.

(Group B)

Problem 24-1B   *Preparing a flexible budget income statement and graphing cost behavior*

Mueller Manufacturing Company produces and sells prepackaged tests for certain infectious diseases. The company's master budget income statement for 19X7 follows, based on expected sales volume of 110,000 units:

Mueller Manufacturing Company
Master Budget Income Statement
Year 19X7

Sales	$440,000
Variable expenses:	
Cost of goods sold	$121,000
Sales commissions	33,000
Shipping	24,200
Utilities	11,000
Fixed expenses:	
Salaries	73,000
Depreciation	48,000
Rent	23,000
Insurance	17,700
Utilities	12,400
Total operating expenses	363,300
Income before income tax	76,700
Income tax expense (30%)	23,010
Net income	$ 53,690

Mueller's plant capacity is 125,000 units, so if actual volume exceeds 125,000 units, it will be necessary to expand the plant. In that case, salaries will increase by 10 percent, depreciation by 20 percent, rent by $11,000 and insurance by $2,800. Fixed utilities will be unchanged by the volume increase.

Required

1. Prepare a flexible budget income statement for the company, showing volume levels of 100,000, 110,000, 120,000, and 130,000 units.

2. Graph the total operating expense behavior of the company. Cost of goods sold is included.

Problem 24-2B *Preparing an income statement performance report*

Refer to the Mueller Manufacturing Company situation of Problem 24-1B. The company sold 100,000 units during 19X7, and its actual income statement was as follows:

Mueller Manufacturing Company Income Statement Year 19X7	
Sales	$394,000
Variable expenses:	
Cost of goods sold	$103,000
Sales commissions	29,000
Shipping	27,000
Utilities	12,000
Fixed expenses:	
Salaries	76,000
Depreciation	48,000
Rent................................	11,000
Insurance...........................	15,000
Utilities	10,000
Total operating expenses	331,000
Income before income tax	63,000
Income tax expense (30%)...............	18,900
Net income	$ 44,100

Required

Prepare an income statement performance report for 19X7.

Problem 24-3B *Computing cost variances and reporting to management*

Finkelstein Company manufactures industrial plastics used in a variety of products. During April the company produced and sold 21,000 sheets of plastic and accumulated the following cost data:

	Standard Unit Cost	Total Actual Cost
Direct materials:		
Standard (3 lb. @ $1.22 per lb.).................	$3.66	
Actual (67,200 lb. @ $1.21 per lb.)		$ 81,312
Direct labor:		
Standard (.1 hr. @ $7.00 per hr.)................	.70	
Actual (2,100 hr. @ $6.90 per hr.)...............		14,490
Overhead;		
Standard:		
Variable ($12.00 per direct labor hour)	$1.20	
Fixed ($32,000 for master budget volume of 20,000		
units and 2,000 direct labor hours)...........	1.60 2.80	
Actual.......................................		55,440
Total.......................................	$7.16	$151,242

Required

1. Compute the price and efficiency variances for direct materials and direct labor.
2. Compute the total variance, the flexible budget variance, and the production volume variance for overhead.
3. Prepare a standard cost income statement through gross profit to report all variances to management. Sale price of the plastic was $11.31 per sheet.

Problem 24-4B *Computing and journalizing cost variances*

Blue Wing Boots, Inc., manufactures hiking boots. The company prepares flexible budgets and uses a standard cost system to control manufacturing cost. The following standard unit cost of a pair of high-top boots is based on master budget volume of 14,000 pairs per month:

Direct materials (2.3 sq. yd. @ $2.20 per sq. yd.)			$ 5.06
Direct labor (2 hours @ $9.15 per hour).			18.30
Overhead:			
Variable.		$1.22	
Fixed (2 hours @ $2.06 per hour)		4.12	5.34
Total unit cost.			$28.70

Transactions during November of the current year included the following:

a. Actual production was 11,400 units.
b. Actual direct materials usage was 2.44 square yards per pair at actual cost of $2.17 per pair.
c. Actual direct labor usage of 22,600 hours cost $208,372.
d. Total actual overhead cost was $69,980.

Required

1. Compute the price and efficiency variances for direct materials and direct labor. Carry amounts to two decimal places.
2. Journalize the usage of direct material and the application of direct labor, including the related cost variances.
3. Compute the total variance, the flexible budget variance, and the production volume variance for overhead.

Problem 24-5B *Preparing a flexible budget and computing cost variances*

Pathbreaker Stereo manufactures phonograph turntables and uses flexible budgeting and a standard cost system. The company's performance report includes the following selected data:

	Master Budget 12,000 Units	Actual Results 13,300 Units
Sales	$744,000	$811,300
Variable expenses:		
Cost of goods sold:		
Direct materials (18,000 lb. @ $7.00)	$126,000	
(17,800 lb. @ $7.03)		$125,134
Direct labor (24,000 hr. @ $6.20)	148,800	
(22,700 hr. @ $6.35)		144,145

Variable overhead (24,000 hr. @ $2.10)..........	50,400	
(22,700 hr. @ $2.22).....................		50,394
Fixed expenses:		
Cost of goods sold:		
Fixed overhead............................	93,600	104,000
Total cost of goods sold......................	418,800	423,673
Gross profit..................................	$325,200	$387,627

Required

1. Prepare a flexible budget based on actual volume.
2. Compute the price variance and the efficiency variance for direct materials and direct labor. Compute the total variance, the flexible budget variance, and the production volume variance for overhead.
3. Show that the sum of the price variance plus the efficiency variance equals the total cost variance for direct materials and for direct labor. Use Exhibit 24-6 as a guide.

Problem 24-6B   *Using incomplete cost and variance information to determine the number of direct labor hours worked*

The city of Dallas has a shop that manufactures street signs. The manager of the shop uses standard costs to judge performance. Recently a clerk mistakenly threw away some of the records, and the manager has only partial data for July. He knows that the total direct labor variance for the month was $650—favorable, and that the standard labor price was $6.70 per hour. A recent pay raise caused an unfavorable labor price variance of $.30 per hour. The standard direct labor hours for actual July output were 2,500.

Required

1. Find the actual number of direct labor hours worked during July. Hint: First, find the actual direct labor price per hour. Then, determine the actual number of direct labor hours by setting up the computation of the total direct labor cost variance of $650: Standard labor cost for actual output *minus* actual labor cost *equals* $650.
2. Compute the direct labor price and efficiency variances.

Decision Problem

Preparing a Performance Report and Using It to Evaluate Company Performance

The board of directors of Top Flite Golf Equipment Company is meeting to evaluate the company's performance for the year just ended. Suppose the report on the following page, which applies to Top Flite's basic line of golf clubs, has been prepared for use at the meeting.

The directors are disappointed at the net income results. They ask if the company maintained the price of its golf clubs at budgeted sale price of $120, and they are told yes. Moreover, the levels of beginning and ending inventories were unchanged.

Required

1. Use the above information to prepare a more informative performance report like the one in Exhibit 24-4. Hint: Begin by computing actual sales volume in units. Then prepare the flexible budget based on this actual volume.
2. A downturn in the economy was responsible for the company's inability to sell more golf clubs. How would you view company performance in light of this additional information? Would you decide to overhaul operations or keep the business operating on its present course? Consider how people adjust their spending on luxury items like golf clubs during a recession.

Top Flite Golf Equipment Co.
Performance Report
Year Ended June 30, 19X7

	Actual Results	Master Budget	Variance
Sales	$2,655,000	$3,240,000	$585,000 U
Variable expenses:			
Cost of goods sold	$1,189,000	$1,546,000	$357,000 F
Promotion expense	126,800	110,000	16,800 U
Sales commissions	116,900	166,000	49,100 F
Shipping	64,000	87,000	23,000 F
Utilities	13,000	14,000	1,000 F
Fixed expenses:			
Salaries	341,600	439,000	97,400 F
Depreciation	306,000	313,000	7,000 F
Rent	143,500	171,000	27,500 F
Utilities	11,200	13,000	1,800 F
Total operating expenses	2,312,000	2,859,000	547,000 F
Income before income tax	343,000	381,000	38,000 U
Income tax expense (30%)	102,900	114,300	11,400 F
Net income	$ 240,100	$ 266,700	$ 26,600 U

Answers to Self-Study Questions

1. a
2. c
3. b
4. c
5. d
6. b ($3.00 − $2.80) × 10,000 = $2,000 U
7. c (11,000 − 10,000) × $2.80 = $2,800 F
8. a
9. d
10. b

25

Responsibility Accounting: Departments and Branches

LEARNING OBJECTIVES
After studying this chapter, you should be able to

1 Define a responsibility accounting system

2 Identify different types of responsibility centers, and specify the information they report

3 Prepare a performance report for management by exception

4 Allocate indirect expenses to departments

5 Account for branch operations

Many companies, large and small alike, have operations scattered all over the world. For example, one company manufactures gas pumps for service stations. The corporation is chartered in Delaware, has its home office in Toronto, manufactures the gas pumps in New Jersey, and makes most of its sales in Europe. Its accounting is done in New Jersey, and its parent company is located in Dallas. Coordination of these activities is critical to the achievement of the company's profit goals. It is easy to see how the accounting system helps coordinate the operations of this firm by providing the information needed to measure performance. Managers are often judged based on whether revenues and expenses exceed or fall short of budgeted amounts.

If the manufacture of gas pumps occurs in two departments, who is responsible for the overall cost budget? This chapter discusses how accounting is used to evaluate managers by tracing costs and revenues to the activities for which the managers are responsible. This area of analysis is called responsibility accounting.

Responsibility Accounting

Many companies must divide the responsibility of management. Some companies, like the gas pump manufacturer, are geographically dispersed, and so it would be impossible for a single person to adequately oversee the entire operation. Other companies may have too many operations, have too many employees, or in some other way be so large that one person cannot handle all executive duties. The top executive—or executives—delegates the authority over a particular area to a middle-level manager. Depending on how complex or on how large the company is, this middle-level manager may in turn delegate authority to other employees to handle certain areas of operations under her responsibility.

OBJECTIVE 1

Describe a responsibility accounting system

How does the business measure each manager's performance? **Responsibility accounting** is a system for evaluating the progress of managers based on the activities under their supervision. Responsibility accounting is a key tool in managing large businesses, which may produce a wide variety of items or offer many different services. Global enterprises use responsibility accounting to help control their far-flung international operations.

Responsibility accounting also applies to small businesses. For example, automobile dealerships use responsibility accounting for separately measuring the performance of various activities such as new car sales, used car sales, parts sales, and the service department.

The basic unit in a responsibility accounting system is called a **responsibility center.** A center can be any subunit of an organization needing control. Each center works from a budget tailored to its particular activities. The three common types of responsibility centers are the cost center, the profit center, and the investment center.

OBJECTIVE 2

Identify different types of responsibility centers, and specify the information they report

1. *Cost center.* Reports costs only. Examples include a personnel department and a shipping department. It is important for these departments to control costs; they are not responsible for generating revenue. Consequently, only costs are reported for their activities. A shipping department manager is judged, for example, on the cost of shipping a certain volume of merchandise.

2. *Profit center.* Reports revenues, expenses, and income. Examples are a McDonald's restaurant and a jewelry department in a Macy's store. Managers of these concerns are responsible for generating income (revenues minus expenses). Both revenues and expenses are reported to show the income of a profit center.

3. *Investment center.* Reports revenues, expenses, income, and the investment needed to finance operations. Examples are a Hilton hotel and an Exxon exploration division. Investment in the business is reported in addition to revenues and expenses so that return on investment (income divided by investment) can be computed. Top managers, as well as investors, evaluate projects by comparing their returns on investment.

Illustration of Responsibility Accounting

The simplified organization chart in Exhibit 25-1 illustrates how companies may use responsibility accounting in the fast-food industry. At the top level, a district manager oversees the branch managers, who supervise the managers of the stores. Store managers have limited freedom to make operating decisions. They may decide on how to handle local advertising, the number of employees and their schedules, and the store hours. Branch managers oversee several stores, evaluate store managers' performance, and set store managers' compensation levels. In turn, district managers oversee several branches, evaluate branch managers' performance and compensation, and decide on district prices and sales promotions. District managers are accountable to regional managers, who answer to home-office vice-presidents.

Exhibit 25-2 provides a more detailed view of how responsibility accounting is used to evaluate profit centers. Examine the lowest level and move to the top. Follow how the reports are related through the three levels of responsibility. All variances may be subdivided for further analysis, either in these reports or in supporting schedules.

Trace the $54,000 operating income from the Store B manager report to the San Francisco branch manager report. The branch manager report summarizes the

EXHIBIT 25-1 McDonald's Corporation
Simplified Partial Organization Chart

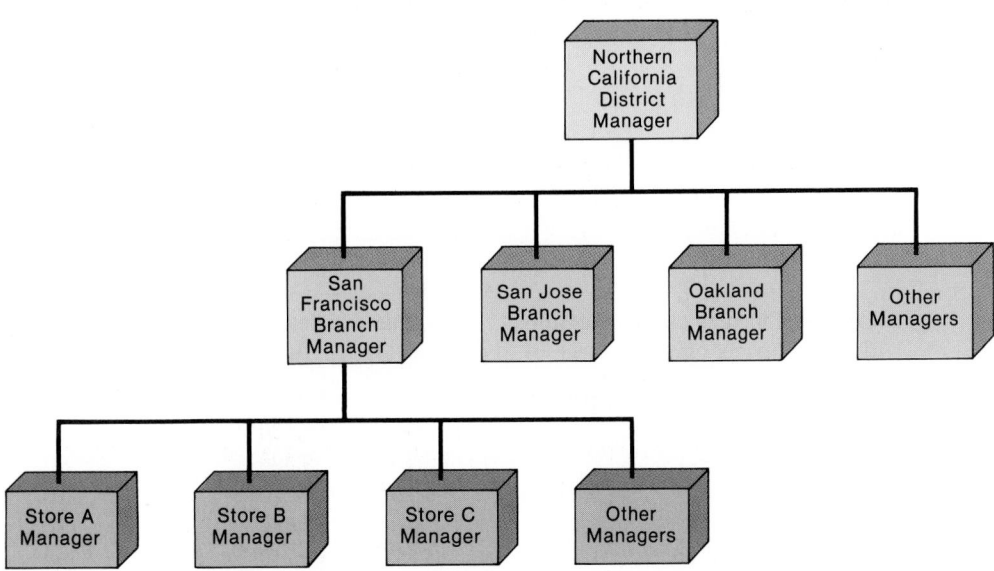

final results of the stores under his supervision. In addition, charges incurred by the branch manager office are included in this report.

Trace the $465,000 total from the San Francisco branch manager report to the northern California district manager report. The report of the district manager includes data for her own district office plus a summary of the entire district's operating income performance.

Performance Report Format

Exhibit 25-2 stresses variances. This focus is a highlight of **management by exception,** a management strategy in which executive attention is directed to the important deviations from budgeted amounts. For example, the San Francisco branch's operating income lagged behind the other branches during the current month and for the year to date. The district manager would concentrate her efforts on improving the San Francisco branch. Managers do not waste time investigating smoothly running operations.

The format for reporting operations used in Exhibit 25-2 may be expanded to highlight variances. The expanded performance report for the Store B manager follows.

OBJECTIVE 3
Prepare a performance report for management by exception

	Budget		Actual Results		Variance: Favorable (Unfavorable)		Variance: Percent of Budgeted Amount	
	This Month	Year to Date	This Month	Year to Date	This Month	Year to Date	This Month	Year to Date
Revenues ...	$170	$690	$178	$702	$8	$12	4.7%	1.7%

EXHIBIT 25-2 *Responsibility Accounting at Various Levels*

McDonald's Corporation
Responsibility Accounting at Various Levels
(in thousands of dollars)

Northern California District Manager Monthly Responsibility Report

Operating income of branches and district manager office expense:	Budget — This Month	Budget — Year to Date	Variance Favorable (Unfavorable) — This Month	Variance Favorable (Unfavorable) — Year to Date
District manager office expense ...	$ (150)	$ (600)	$ (8)	$ (20)
San Francisco branch	465	1,730	(5)	50
San Jose branch	500	1,800	19	90
Oakland branch.................	310	1,220	31	110
Others	600	2,560	47	130
Operating income	$1,725	$6,710	$84	$360

San Francisco Branch Manager Monthly Responsibility Report

Operating income of stores and branch manager office expense:	Budget — This Month	Budget — Year to Date	Variance Favorable (Unfavorable) — This Month	Variance Favorable (Unfavorable) — Year to Date
Branch manager office expense....	$ (20)	$ (306)	$ (5)	$ 4
Store A........................	48	148	(1)	(5)
Store B	54	228	7	16
Store C	38	160	4	10
Others	345	1,500	(10)	25
Operating income	$465	$1,730	$ (5)	$50

Store B Manager Monthly Responsibility Report

Revenue and expense:	Budget — This Month	Budget — Year to Date	Variance Favorable (Unfavorable) — This Month	Variance Favorable (Unfavorable) — Year to Date
Revenue	$170	$690	$ 8	$12
Food expense	50	198	5	14
Paper	15	62	(3)	(2)
Wages........................	24	98	(4)	(5)
Repairs	5	19	1	(1)
General.......................	12	45	—	(2)
Depreciation..................	10	40	—	—
Total expenses	116	462	(1)	4
Operating income	$ 54	$228	$ 7	$16

The complete performance report would likely include line-by-line presentations of other data. For example, a report for a restaurant will show the number of customers served and the average selling price per customer. In the hotel industry, managers report the percentage of rooms occupied and the average daily rental rate per room as performance measures.

No single format appeals to all users. Some managers prefer the greater detail shown in the eight-column format, but others prefer less detail. The choice is a matter of personal preference.

Design of a Responsibility Accounting System _____

A responsibility accounting system can be combined with whatever type of accounting system the company uses, such as a standard cost system, which highlights variances. The key to an effective accounting system is gathering and communicating information to assist the business in achieving its goals. Two factors are important: manager control over operations, and manager access to information.

Consider a furniture manufacturer that uses a standard cost system to measure an efficiency (usage) variance and a price variance for the cost of lumber. The production supervisor is responsible for the quantity of lumber used to manufacture chairs. Good work in the factory wastes little lumber and holds costs down. Careless work wastes lumber and increases production cost. The supervisor must control operations. Top managers communicate the efficiency (usage) variance to the supervisor, seeking reasons for an unfavorable variance and offering praise for a favorable variance.

Responsibility for the price variance is assigned to the purchasing manager who buys the lumber. The price of lumber may differ from standard cost because of droughts, crop disease, and forest fires, which are beyond the purchasing manager's control. Nevertheless, the price variance is the responsibility of the purchasing manager because he or she has access to more price information than anyone else in the business. The *reporting* responsibility of any manager is to explain the outcome of an action regardless of personal influence over the outcome.

Responsibility accounting, budgets, standards, and variances are aids to management. They permit top managers to delegate decision making to lower levels by assigning responsibility for action and establishing a way to evaluate performance. Such a system frees top managers to work on broad issues affecting the whole organization.

Responsibility accounting systems can also be misused as a way of finding fault and placing blame. The question should not be, Who should be blamed for an unfavorable variance? The question should be, Which individual is in the best position to explain why a specific variance occurred?

Departmental Accounting _____

Departments are the most widely encountered responsibility centers. The department store is a familiar illustration. Top managers of a department store want more information than the net income of the store as a whole. At a minimum, they want to know each department's gross margin (sales minus cost of goods sold). In addition, they usually want to know each department's operating income. With these data, managers can identify their most profitable and least profitable departments. This information aids decisions such as whether to expand some departments and phase out others.

Departmental gross margins are easy to measure because sales and cost of goods sold records are kept by department. Departmental operating income (gross margin minus operating expenses) is not as easy to measure. Why? Primarily because of indirect expenses.

Direct expenses are those that are conveniently identified with and traceable to the department. The wages of sales clerks, the salary of the department head, the advertising of the shoe department, and the depreciation of display cases within a department are direct expenses.

Indirect expenses are all those expenses other than direct expenses. Indirect expenses are not traceable to a single department. Examples are the costs of operating the receiving department and the stock room. Often these activities serve more than one department simultaneously. For example, an incoming truck may be delivering merchandise to several departments. How does the business allocate this shipping cost? To what department does the business assign the expense of operating the stock room, which holds inventory for several departments? How does the company allocate the expense of an advertising campaign that promotes the entire store, not just a single department?

Allocation of Service Department Expenses

Cost allocation is the assignment of various costs to departments. Cost allocation may also be called **expense allocation,** cost assignment, cost distribution, and cost apportionment. (As you learned in Chapters 22 and 23, the term *cost allocation* applies to the costs of products also. In our present discussion, we are allocating the costs of service departments, not manufacturing departments.)

To allocate expense, the business must first set an **allocation base,** which is a logical common denominator for assigning a given cost to two or more departments. Consider a store that sells furniture and appliances. These two departments share the expense of warehousing the store's inventory. The business could allocate the expense of warehousing on the basis of the ratio of space taken up by each department's goods. If furniture occupies 80 percent of the warehouse, then the furniture department might be assigned 80 percent of warehouse expense. Similarly, the cost of the receiving department may be divided between the two departments on the basis of the number of hours spent unloading each department's goods. If unloading appliances takes 30 percent of the receiving employees' time, then the appliance department could be allocated 30 percent of receiving department expense.

The costs of warehousing and receiving are examples of indirect expenses that are easy to assign to departments. Other indirect costs are more difficult to allocate. How do we assign factory overhead and home-office administrative costs to departments? The common denominator for allocating these expenses to departments is less clear. We will address this problem later in this chapter.

Companies use different allocation bases, and even within a single company several different bases may be used to allocate different expenses to the various departments. The list in Exhibit 25-3 offers common examples of allocation bases for selected costs and expenses.

Let us stress this point: The ideal guide for choosing an allocation base is a cause-and-effect relationship. For instance, as Exhibit 25-3 shows, generally the more square feet of space, the higher the cost of janitorial services. Choosing an

EXHIBIT 25-3 *Bases for Allocating Costs to Departments*

Cost or Expense	Base for Allocating Cost to Departments
Direct material	Separately traced
Merchandise	Separately traced
Packaging materials	Separately traced if feasible
Direct labor	Separately traced
Other labor	Time spent in each department
Supervision	Time spent, or number of employees, in each department
Equipment depreciation and rentals	Separately traced, hours used by each department
Building depreciation, property taxes, and rentals	Square feet of space. Sometimes heavier allocations are made to departments that experience higher customer traffic
Heat, light, and air conditioning	Square feet or cubic feet of space
Janitorial services	Square feet of space
Advertising	Separately traced if possible. Otherwise, in proportion to newspaper space or radio or TV time in advertisement, or in proportion to budgeted sales or actual sales
Payroll Department	Number of employees in each department
Personnel Department	Number of employees in each department
Purchasing Department	Number of orders or dollar amounts of purchases in each department

allocation base is largely a matter of common sense. No one "right" allocation base exists for each cost or expense. Companies use their experience and judgment in choosing these bases.

Illustration of Departmental Reporting

Exhibit 25-4 shows a simplified departmental income statement of a Computer Unlimited store.

Supporting details can be shown in various ways. For example, gross sales, sales returns and allowances, and sales discounts can appear in the body of the statement or in a separate schedule. Our discussion, however, focuses on the allocation of selected expenses to the store's two departments.

Salaries and wages.   These costs, which include each department manager's salary, are direct departmental expense.

Depreciation, equipment.   This expense is also direct departmental expense, related to the equipment used only by each specific department.

Supplies.   If each department may request supplies as needed, supplies are a direct cost. However, suppose the personnel from both departments help themselves to a companywide pool of supplies without recording usage. In this case, the company must establish a base for allocating supplies expense to the individ-

EXHIBIT 25-4 *Departmental Income Statement*

Computer Unlimited Store
Departmental Income Statement
For the Year Ended December 31, 19X1
(in thousands)

		Department	
	Total	Hardware	Software
Net sales..............................	$10,000	$7,000	$3,000
Cost of goods sold	5,500	4,000	1,500
Gross margin	4,500	3,000	1,500
Operating expenses:			
Salaries and wages..................	1,100	660	440
Depreciation, equipment	100	80	20
Supplies	200	140	60
Advertising.......................	1,000	400	600
Rent............................	600	480	120
Heat, light, air conditioning...........	60	40	20
Purchasing department	300	230	70
General administration department	200	160	40
Total operating expenses................	3,560	2,190	1,370
Operating income......................	$ 940	$ 810	$ 130

ual departments. The company may use percentage of sales, illustrated as follows for total supplies expense of $200:

OBJECTIVE 4

Allocate indirect expenses to departments

Department	Sales	Percent of Total Sales	Allocation of Supplies Expense of $200
Hardware.........................	$ 7,000	70%	.70 × $200 = $140
Software.........................	3,000	30%	.30 × 200 = 60
Total............................	$10,000	100%	1.00 × $200 = $200

Advertising. Consider a $960 computer store ad that takes up 24 square inches in the Sunday newspaper. Fifteen square inches advertise hardware, and 5 square inches promote software. The remaining 4 square inches carry information about the company as a whole (its address, hours, and so forth). How does the business allocate the overall cost of advertising to the two departments?

Suppose each square inch of advertising costs $40. Then the $960 total cost (24 inches × $40 = $960) may be allocated in two steps, as the accompanying table shows.

Department	Step (1): 20 Inches of Direct Advertising	Step (2): 4 Inches of General Advertising	Steps (1) + (2): 24 Inches of Total Advertising
Hardware	15 × $40 = $600 (75%)	75% × $160 = $120	$720
Software	5 × 40 = 200 (25%)	25% × 160 = 40	240
	$800 (100%)	$160	$960

Step 1 computes each department's direct cost, $600 and $200, respectively. Hardware's percentage of total direct costs is $600 ÷ $800, or 75 percent; Software's percentage is $200 ÷ $800, or 25 percent. Step 2 uses these percentages to allocate the $160 of general advertising costs ($960 − $800 = $160) to Hardware and Software.

If the computer store had three departments, we would simply total the individual departments' direct expense and use each department's percentage of that total to allocate the general advertising expense. We may allocate other general expenses, for example, salaries, wages, and depreciation, among departments in this way.

Rent.   Rent may be allocated on the basis of square footage, as follows:

Rent for entire store	$600,000
Total square feet.	25,000
Rent per square foot ($600,000/25,000).	$24

Suppose that the company considers each square foot of space in the store equally valuable and that the Hardware and Software Departments occupy 20,000 square feet and 5,000 square feet, respectively. The allocation of rent is

Hardware Department: 20,000 square feet × $24 per square foot = $480,000

Software Department: 5,000 square feet × $24 per square foot = 120,000

Total $600,000

However, space in certain parts of the store may have different values because of varying potential to generate sales. For example, the space near the entrance may be the most valuable space in the store. The rear of the store may be the least valuable. Managers use judgment, combined with outside consultants, to arrive at an appropriate allocation of rent. One approach is to weight the square footage. Suppose again that the Hardware and Software Departments occupy 20,000 and 5,000 square feet, respectively, and that Hardware's space is twice as valuable as Software's. In this case, rent of $600,000 is allocated to the two departments as follows:

Department	Space Occupied	Space Weighted By Value	Proportion of Weighted Space	Allocation of Rent of $600,000
Hardware	20,000	20,000 × 2 = 40,000	8/9	8/9 × $600,000 = $533,333
Software	5,000	5,000 × 1 = 5,000	1/9	1/9 × 600,000 = 66,667
Total	25,000	45,000	9/9	9/9 × $600,000 = $600,000

Heat, Light, Air Conditioning.   The most common allocation base is square feet of space occupied. Cubic feet is used if ceiling height varies in different parts of the building.

Purchasing Department.   Some of these expenses can be charged directly to specific departments. Any remaining expense is usually allocated in proportion to the dollar amount of purchases made on behalf of each department.

General Administrative Expenses.   This category includes depreciation on office furniture and equipment, office utilities, salaries of management and the office staff, and other expenses related to the organization as a whole. Some of these expenses may be charged directly. Others, such as payroll and personnel costs, may be allocated by the number of employees in various departments. The remainder is often allocated in proportion to departmental sales.

Managers may want expense allocations refined beyond those in Exhibit 25-4. For example, they may desire a statement with the following format to emphasize the difference between direct departmental expense and indirect expense:

Net sales..	$XXX
Cost of goods sold.............................	XXX
Gross margin...................................	XXX
Direct departmental expense	**XXX**
Margin before indirect expenses....................	XXX
Indirect expenses	**XXX**
Operating income	$XXX

The margin before indirect expenses may provide information for deciding whether to expand or cut back a department's operations. Accounting systems can be designed to fulfill these wishes.

Summary Problem for Your Review

Review the allocation of rent, as explained for the illustration of departmental reporting on page 979. Suppose the Hardware Department's space is three times as valuable as that of the Software Department. Total rent remains $600,000.

Required

1. Prepare an analysis to show how much total rent expense should be allocated to each department.
2. What is each department's rent expense per square foot?

SOLUTION TO REVIEW PROBLEM

Requirement 1

Department	Space Occupied	Space Weighted By Value	Proportion of Weighted Space	Allocation of Rent of $600,000
Hardware.....................	20,000	20,000 × 3 = 60,000	$12/13$	$12/13$ × $600,000 = $553,846
Software.....................	5,000	5,000 × 1 = 5,000	$1/13$	$1/13$ × 600,000 = 46,154
Total........................	25,000	65,000	$13/13$	$13/13$ × $600,000 = $600,000

Requirement 2

Rent expense per square foot:
   Hardware: $553,846/20,000 = $27.69   Software: $46,154/5,000 = $9.23

Note: Hardware's rent expense per square foot is indeed three times as high as Software's rent expense per square foot ($27.69 = $9.23 × 3).

14

Branch Accounting

Many companies diversify and establish branch offices or branch factories. Top managers may wish to take advantage of particular benefits that a certain geographical area offers. Materials and labor may be cheaper at a location removed from the home office. Or the company may want to open a new sales market. The example of the gas pump manufacturer at the beginning of this chapter illustrates how wide ranging a company's branches may be.

Branches are responsibility centers—often cost centers if the branch is devoted to manufacturing or warehousing with no sales responsibility. A branch manager has responsibility for certain aspects of a branch's operations. In turn, he must report the branch's successes and failures to his manager in the home office.

Who has the accounting responsibilities in a company that runs branch operations? The home office generally keeps most of the accounting records. The branch maintains only those records needed to manage its own operations. **Branch accounting** is a system for separating the accounts of a branch from those of the home office. The purpose is to establish accountability over the resources entrusted to the branch.

Consider a manufacturer that keeps cost records for direct materials, work in process inventory, and factory overhead at its branch factory. Receivables, finished goods inventory, plant assets, payables, depreciation, and other areas are accounted for in the corporate (home) office. This split of accounting between central headquarters and its branch means dividing the records between the two locations. With such a division, procedures are needed to ensure that all transactions are accounted for. Generally, two reciprocal accounts are used, one in the home office and one in the branch. **Reciprocal accounts** are two or more accounts that have exactly the same offsetting balances and are used to control a general ledger that is kept in two or more locations.

Branch Ledger and Journal

A **branch ledger** is that part of a general ledger kept by the branch, separate from the home-office ledger. The branch ledger contains only those accounts needed to manage its operations plus a special account used to handle its accountability to the home office. If the branch is a manufacturing plant, its ledger is often called a **factory ledger.** Each branch has its own branch or factory ledger.

The **home-office ledger** is that part of a general ledger kept by the home office, separate from the branch ledger. The home-office ledger is identical to the general ledger studied throughout this course except that it includes a special account for the branch and excludes the accounts kept by the branch. The home office and the branch also maintain separate journals for recording transactions.

Suppose Appliance Company of America is headquartered in Chicago but has its manufacturing plant in Indianapolis. The home office makes all purchases and sales, handles cash payments and cash receipts, and incurs all company liabilities. A separate factory ledger is maintained in Indianapolis for managing the branch plant.

When the factory completes inventory, it transfers the finished goods to warehouses, which are managed directly by the home office. Upon transfer of merchandise to the warehouses, the home office debits inventory and credits the factory account for shipments at cost.

The general ledger accounts of the company follow, showing the link between the reciprocal accounts.

Home-Office Accounts	Branch-Factory Accounts
Cash	Direct materials inventory
Accounts receivable	Work in process inventory
Finished goods inventory	Factory overhead
Plant and equipment	Home-office ledger control
Accumulated depreciation	
Branch-factory ledger control	
Accounts payable	
Wages payable	
Common stock	
Retained earnings	
Sales revenue	
Cost of goods sold	
Selling expenses	
Administrative expenses	

The home office's **branch-factory ledger control** account can be viewed as an *investment in,* or a *receivable from,* the branch. Similarly, the branch's **home-office ledger control** account represents an *owner equity of,* or a *payable to,* the home office.

Illustrative Transactions and Related Journal Entries

Entries for the following transactions illustrate accounting for branch operations:

1.	Direct materials purchased on credit	$230,000
2.	Direct materials used in production	150,000
3.	Factory payroll accrued.......................................	200,000
4.	Miscellaneous factory overhead cost incurred (credit Accounts Payable, $150,000; and Accumulated Depreciation, $18,000)................	168,000
5.	Factory overhead applied	165,000
6.	Cost of goods shipped to warehouse	425,000
7.	Cost of goods sold..	400,000
8.	Sales (on credit)...	600,000
9.	Cash collected on account.....................................	440,000

OBJECTIVE 5

Account for branch operations

Journal Entries.   Illustrative journal entries and postings to the reciprocal accounts are given in Exhibit 25-5 (in thousands of dollars). The entries that would be made in a regular, unified journal are given first in the exhibit. Relating each pair of home office/branch entries to the corresponding unified entry will help you see how branch accounting works. Keep in mind that the focus is on the home office and branch entries. The regular, unified entries are presented solely to aid your understanding. Let's consider the first transaction and related entry — the credit purchase of direct materials by the home office for the branch factory (amounts in thousands of dollars). (Discussion continues on page 984.)

Home-Office Journal			Branch-Factory Journal		
Branch-Factory Ledger Control	230		Direct Materials Inventory............	230	
Accounts Payable		230	Home-Office Ledger Control		230

EXHIBIT 25-5 Sample Journal Entries for Branch Accounting (in thousands of dollars)

Transaction	Entries That Would Be Made in a Regular, Unified Journal			Home-Office Journal			Branch-Factory Journal		

1. Direct materials purchases	Direct Materials Inventory
	  Accounts Payable
		230	230	Branch-Factory Ledger Control
				  Accounts Payable
					230	230	Direct Materials Inventory
							  Home-Office Ledger Control
								230	230

2. Direct materials uses	Work in Process Inventory
	  Direct Materials Inventory
		150	150	None			Work in Process Inventory
							  Direct Materials Inventory
								150	150

3. Factory payroll	Factory Wages
	  Wages Payable
		200	200	Branch-Factory Ledger Control
				  Wages Payable
					200	200	Factory Wages
							  Home-Office Ledger Control
								200	200

4. Miscellaneous overhead	Factory Overhead
	  Accounts Payable
	  Accumulated Depreciation
		168	150
			18
				Branch-Factory Ledger Control
				  Accounts Payable
				  Accumulated Depreciation
					168	150
						18
							Factory Overhead
							  Home-Office Ledger Control
								168	168

5. Overhead application	Work in Process Inventory
	  Factory Overhead
		165	165	None			Work in Process Inventory
							  Factory Overhead
								165	165

6. Shipments to warehouse	Finished Goods Inventory
	  Work in Process Inventory
		425	425	Finished Goods Inventory
				  Branch-Factory Ledger Control
					425	425	Home-Office Ledger Control
							  Work in Process Inventory
								425	425

7. Cost of goods sold	Cost of Goods Sold
	  Finished Goods Inventory
		400	400	Cost of Goods Sold
				  Finished Goods Inventory
					400	400	None		

8. Sales	Accounts Receivable
	  Sales Revenue
		600	600	Accounts Receivable
				  Sales Revenue
					600	600	None		

9. Collections on account	Cash
	  Accounts Receivable
		440	440	Cash
				  Accounts Receivable
					440	440	None		

Postings:

Branch-Factory Ledger Control

(1)	230	(6)	425	
(3)	200			
(4)	168			
Bal.	173			

Home-Office Ledger Control

(6)	425	(1)	230	
		(3)	200	
		(4)	168	
		Bal.	173	

The home office is responsible for paying the bill and so records the liability. The branch factory is responsible for using the direct materials and therefore records the inventory. Because accountability is split between the two locations, reciprocal accounts are used to assure that each transaction is fully accounted for. The home-office debit to the branch account counterbalances the branch's credit to the home-office account. We can regard the $230,000 debit in the first home-office entry as the home office's investment in, or receivable from, the factory. The branch's credit to the home-office account in the branch's entry shows the branch's obligation to the home office for the purchased materials.

Entries 2 and 5 are confined strictly to the branch-factory ledger because these transactions affect factory costs with no home-office involvement. Entries 3, 4, and 6 affect both home office and branch. Entries 7, 8, and 9 are recorded solely by the home office because the branch has no responsibility for sales, cost of sales, or collections of receivables.

Entry 6 deserves special comment. Factory shipments of finished goods transfer inventory from the factory to the warehouses, which are under direct home-office management. Such shipments reduce the home-office investment in the factory because the home office receives inventory. The effect is similar to collecting an account receivable. Likewise, the branch decreases the owner equity of the home office by transferring inventory to the warehouses.

Reciprocal Balances.   Exhibit 25-5 shows that the reciprocal accounts have identical, offsetting balances. Any difference between the balances signals the accountant to explain the imbalance. A common cause of imbalances is faulty communication. For example, a shipment of finished goods to the warehouse may be in transit at the balance sheet date. The home office may be unaware of the transaction until the goods arrive. At the same time, the factory may have already recorded the shipment. Progress in data processing via computers has reduced problems of this nature.

Accounting for a Sales Branch

Home-office and branch entries depend on the authority given to the branch. In the example shown in Exhibit 25-5, the home office pays branch bills, makes all sales, and collects all cash. Many companies use sales branches to enter new markets. For instance, IBM has sales offices throughout the United States. Sales branches may make sales, collect cash, and make some of their own cash disbursements. Often the home office keeps control of the revenue and expense accounts. Assume a sales branch completed the following transactions:

a.   Branch sold merchandise and received cash of $3,000.
b.   Branch transferred $3,000 cash to home office.
c.   Home office paid commission to salesperson who made the sale in *a*, $1,100.
d.   Branch paid water bill, $90.
e.   Branch recorded depreciation on office equipment, $300.

These transactions would be recorded by the home office and branch as follows:

Home-Office Journal			**Branch Journal**		
a. Branch Ledger Control.............	3,000		Cash	3,000	
Sales Revenue..............		3,000	Home-Office Ledger Control .		3,000
b. Cash	3,000		Home-Office Ledger Control	3,000	
Branch Ledger Control......		3,000	Cash		3,000
c. Sales Commission Expense	1,100		None		
Cash		1,100			
d. Utility Expense	90		Home-Office Ledger Control	90	
Branch Ledger Control......		90	Cash		90
e. Depreciation Expense............	300		Home-Office Ledger Control	300	
Branch Ledger Control......		300	Accumulated Depreciation – Office Furniture..........		300

After posting these entries, Branch Ledger Control's credit balance should equal the debit balance of Home-Office Ledger Control.

International Operations

International operations pose accounting challenges that are not encountered when all segments of the business are located in the same country. For example, customs, tax systems, and currencies vary from country to country. Because of these differences, parent companies usually organize foreign subsidiaries as separate companies. If the subsidiary has a full range of operations — manufacturing, sales, and so on — the parent may organize the subsidiary as a profit center. If the subsidiary only manufactures goods and has no responsibility for sales, the parent may treat the subsidiary as a cost center.

The parent company's financial statements usually include the statements of all its subsidiaries, including those located abroad. A French subsidiary's statements are prepared first in francs, a Japanese subsidiary's statements in yen. To prepare the consolidated financial statements of the U.S. parent company, these subsidiary statements must be translated into U.S. dollars. Exhibit 25-6 shows representative dollar values of some major foreign currencies. These values are called exchange rates because businesses exchange U.S. dollars for foreign currencies, and vice versa, the same way they buy and sell goods and services.

Appendix E provides added coverage of international accounting.

EXHIBIT 25-6   *Foreign Currency Exchange Rates*

Country	Monetary Unit	Dollar Value	Country	Monetary Unit	Dollar Value
Canada	Dollar	$ .81	Japan	Yen	$.0079
France	Franc	.17	Mexico	Peso	.0004
Great Britain	Pound	1.80	West Germany	Mark	.58

Source: *The Wall Street Journal*, June 3, 1988.

Summary Problem for Your Review

A general ledger may be divided between home office and branch in any manner whatsoever. Reconsider Exhibit 25-5. Suppose the branch factory, instead of the home office, keeps its plant and equipment accounts and the related depreciation records. The plant and equipment accounts would appear in the ledger of the factory but not the home office. Among the nine transactions in our example, what journal entry or entries would be changed? Prepare the changed entry or entries.

SOLUTION TO REVIEW PROBLEM

Entry 4 would be changed. Accumulated depreciation would appear in the branch-factory ledger but not in the home-office ledger. Moreover, the amounts recorded in the reciprocal accounts would be $150,000 instead of $168,000, as follows (amounts in thousands of dollars):

Home-Office Ledger		Branch-Factory Ledger		
4. Branch-Factory Ledger Control 150		Factory Overhead 168		
Accounts Payable	150	Accumulated Depreciation		18
		Home-Office Ledger Control . . .		150

Summary

Responsibility accounting is a system for evaluating the progress of managers based on activities under their supervision. This system is especially important in organizations with scattered operations. Most companies are organized into *responsibility centers* to establish accountability. There are different types of responsibility centers: *cost center, profit center,* and *investment center.* The most critical factor in designing a responsibility accounting system is gathering and communicating information to help the business achieve its goals.

Performance reports show deviations from budgeted amounts. By focusing on important variances, managers can direct their attention to operations needing improvement and avoid wasting time investigating successful operations. This practice is called *management by exception.*

Departments are the most widely encountered responsibility centers. Gross margin and operating income are important measures of their performance. *Direct expenses* are conveniently identified with and traceable to the department. *Indirect expenses* are all those expenses other than direct expenses. Direct expenses are easy to allocate to departments because of their natural link to a particular department. Indirect expenses are allocated based on some logical relationship between the expense and departments.

Branch accounting is a system for separating branch accounts from home-office accounts. Its key feature is a set of *reciprocal accounts.* The home office has a *Branch Ledger*

Control account for its investment in, or receivable from, the branch. The branch ledger has only those accounts needed to manage its own operations. Its special account, *Home-Office Ledger Control,* represents home-office equity in the branch, or the branch payable to the home office. The debit balance in the Branch Ledger Control account should equal the credit balance in Home-Office Ledger Control.

Self-Study Questions

Test your understanding of the chapter by marking the best answer for each of the following questions:

1. Responsibility accounting is *(p. 972)*
   a. An alternative to a standard cost system
   b. A system for assigning responsibility to managers and evaluating their progress
   c. A particular type of home-office/branch accounting system
   d. Designed without consideration of the business's organization structure

2. Which of the following departments is most likely to be a cost center? *(p. 972)*
   a. Personnel Department
   b. Housewares Department of a K mart store
   c. Sales office
   d. Manufacturing plant

3. Budgeted cost of goods sold was $30,000, and actual cost is $33,000. The variance is *(p. 973)*
   a. 110 percent favorable   c. 10 percent favorable
   b. 110 percent unfavorable   d. 10 percent unfavorable

4. The key to the design of an effective responsibility accounting system is *(p. 975)*
   a. Ability of the system to place blame when results are unfavorable
   b. Manager control over all aspects of the business in the department
   c. Gathering and communicating information to achieve the business's goals
   d. Use of a standard cost system

5. One of the more difficult accounting tasks in departmental accounting is *(p. 976)*
   a. Measuring departmental gross margin
   b. Allocating direct costs to departments
   c. Allocating indirect costs to departments
   d. Assigning responsibility to department managers

6. Which of the following costs is the most difficult to allocate to departments? *(p. 977)*
   a. Direct materials   c. Merchandise purchases
   b. Janitorial services   d. Direct labor

7. The most logical basis for allocating building depreciation to departments is *(p. 977)*
   a. Square feet of space
   b. Number of employees
   c. Hours used
   d. Building depreciation can be separately traced to each department

8. Which control device is a particular feature of branch accounting? *(p. 981)*
   a. Responsibility assignment   c. Departmental accounting
   b. Reciprocal accounts   d. Cost allocation

9. Which of these accounts would be the most likely to appear in a branch-factory ledger? *(p. 982)*
   a. Accounts Receivable   c. Common Stock
   b. Branch-Factory Ledger Control   d. Home-Office Ledger Control

10. A sales branch manages its own operations except for collections on account and cash payments for major expenses such as inventory purchases and salaries, which the home office pays. Which entry would the branch make to record its salary expense? *(p. 985)*

a. Salary Expense... XXX
       Cash XXX
b. Home-Office Ledger Control XXX
       Cash XXX
c. Salary Expense... XXX
       Branch Ledger Control XXX
d. None of the above. The entry would appear on the home-office books only.

Answers to the self-study questions are at the end of the chapter.

Accounting Vocabulary

allocation base *(p. 976)*, branch accounting *(p. 981)*, branch-factory ledger control *(p. 982)*, branch ledger *(p. 981)*, cost allocation *(p. 976)*, direct expense *(p. 976)*, expense allocation *(p. 976)*, factory ledger *(p. 981)*, home-office ledger *(p. 981)*, home-office ledger control *(p. 982)*, indirect expense *(p. 976)*, management by exception *(p. 973)*, reciprocal accounts *(p. 981)*, responsibility accounting *(p. 972)*, responsibility center *(p. 972)*.

ASSIGNMENT MATERIAL ─────────────────────

Questions

1. Briefly describe responsibility accounting, giving examples of how managers use it in operating a business.
2. Which manager will control expenses better: Grant, whose performance is measured by his departmental sales, or Bruns, whose performance is gauged by her departmental income? Give your reason.
3. Identify three types of responsibility centers, giving examples of each and stating the information they report.
4. A company owns 50 Burger King restaurants in Houston, Dallas, and El Paso, Texas. In each city a local manager oversees operations. Starting at the individual store level, describe a likely flow of information based on responsibility accounting. What information would be reported?
5. What are the goals of management by exception?
6. What is the key to effective design of a responsibility accounting system?
7. What main question is a responsibility accounting system designed to answer? How can a responsibility accounting system be abused?
8. Distinguish between direct expenses and indirect expenses, giving examples of each type.
9. Identify a reasonable allocation base for the following indirect expenses: heating expense, depreciation of equipment used to manufacture products for three separate departments, and advertising expense.
10. Which of the following are likely to be direct expenses? Which are likely to be indirect expenses?
    a. Manufacturing labor
    b. Supervisor labor
    c. Advertising of a specific toy
    d. Cost of goods sold
    e. Depreciation of home-office building
    f. Janitorial services for a manufacturing plant
    g. Expenses of personnel department
    h. Advertising of a storewide sale by a department store

11. Supplies are not charged to departments as used. Instead, supplies expense is allocated at the end of each period based on the period's sales. If a firm used supplies costing $900 and had sales of $5,000, $12,000, and $8,000 in departments X, Y, and Z, respectively, how much supplies expense would be charged to each department?

12. How might rent be allocated in a department store with three floors, one of which is on ground level and opens onto a busy street?

13. Describe a plan for allocating the various components of general administrative expenses.

14. How does branch accounting differ from departmental accounting?

15. What are the special features of a branch accounting system?

16. How does the general ledger of a company with a branch accounting system differ from an ordinary general ledger?

17. What special account does a branch ledger contain? What special account does a home-office ledger contain? Indicate which account normally has a debit balance and which normally has a credit balance.

18. Consider the Branch-Factory Ledger Control account and the Home-Office Ledger Control account. Which account is more like an investment or receivable? Which is more like an owner equity account or payable? Which account is in the ledger of the home office? Which is in the branch ledger?

19. Briefly describe a branch accounting system for a company with two manufacturing plants in distant locations. Identify the special account on the books of the home office and the special account on the books of the branches.

20. A company manufactures its products at three plants. Which of the following transactions is likely to be recorded by the home office only, by the branch only, or by both the home office and the branch?
    a. Use of materials in production
    b. Sale of merchandise
    c. Payment of manufacturing payroll
    d. Purchase of direct materials
    e. Incurrence of overhead cost
    f. Collection of accounts receivable
    g. Shipment of finished goods to home-office warehouse

Exercise 25-1   *Identifying different types of responsibility centers*

Identify each responsibility center as either a cost center, a profit center, or an investment center.

a. The legal department of an insurance company prepares its budget and subsequent performance report based on its expected expenses for the year.

b. A charter airline records revenues and expenses for each airplane for each month. The airplane's performance report shows its ratio of operating income to average book value.

c. The manager of an EXXON service station is evaluated based on the station's revenues and expenses.

d. A branch manager's performance is judged by the ratio of the branch's net income to the home office's cost of the branch.

e. Accountants compile the cost of surgical supplies for evaluating the purchasing department of a hospital.

f. The hospital pediatrics unit reports both revenues and expenses.

Exercise 25-2   *Using responsibility accounting to report on profit centers at three levels*

Computer Concepts, Inc., of Minnesota has city managers for its Minneapolis, Duluth, and Rochester operations. These managers report to a state manager, who reports to the manager of Midwest operations in Chicago. The Midwest manager has received the following data for June of the current year:

	Midwest		
	Minnesota		
	Duluth	**Minneapolis and Rochester**	**Midwest Totals excluding Minnesota**
Revenues, budget	$300,000	$1,800,000	$10,300,000
Expenses, budget	220,000	1,100,000	6,300,000
Revenues, actual	340,000	1,900,000	9,900,000
Expenses, actual	210,000	1,200,000	6,200,000

Required

Arrange the following data in a format similar to Exhibit 25-2. Show June results, in thousands of dollars, for Duluth, the state of Minnesota, and the Midwest.

Exercise 25-3 *Preparing a four-column performance report*

Using the data of Exercise 25-2, prepare a performance report for June in the format illustrated on page 973. Show June results, in thousands of dollars, for Duluth, the state of Minnesota, and the Midwest. In each case, format your answer in four columns:

Budget	**Actual**	**Variance Favorable (Unfavorable)**	**Variance: Percent of Budget**

Exercise 25-4 *Preparing a departmental income statement*

Taylor Enterprises, Inc., has two departments, electronics and industrial. Taylor's income statement for 19X7 appears as follows:

Net sales	$279,000
Cost of goods sold	105,000
Gross margin	174,000
Operating expenses:	
Salaries	72,000
Depreciation	15,000
Advertising	6,000
Other	10,000
Total operating expenses	103,000
Operating income	$ 71,000

Cost of goods sold is distributed $31,000 for electronics and $74,000 for industrial products. Salaries are allocated to departments based on sales: electronics, $93,000; industrial, $186,000. Two-thirds of advertising is spent on electronics. Depreciation is allocated based on square footage: electronics has 28,000 square feet; industrial has 42,000 square feet. Other expenses are allocated based on number of employees, with an equal number working in each department.

Required

Prepare a departmental income statement showing revenues, expenses, and operating income for Taylor's two departments.

Exercise 25-5 *Allocating costs to departments*

The cost records of Allegheny Manufacturing Company include the following selected indirect cost data for January of the current year:

Other labor.	$14,000
Equipment depreciation.	6,000
Building depreciation.	3,600
Utilities	2,700
Selling expenses	24,000

Data for cost allocations:

	Department		
	A	B	C
Sales	$70,000	$80,000	$50,000
Other labor—hours.	400	500	100
Machine hours	300	450	150
Building—square feet	9,000	3,000	1,500
Selling expense—allocate to departments in proportion to sales			

Required

Show the allocation of these expenses to departments A, B, and C for January.

Exercise 25-6 *Computing departmental rent expense*

Many department stores grant concessions to other companies to operate the store's shoe departments. Vogue Shoe Company markets its shoes this way. Vogue sells ladies' shoes in a space occupying 500 square feet near the front door of a Sax Third Avenue store. This location is three times as valuable as the average space in the store. Vogue's shoes for men occupy 200 square feet in a back corner of the ground floor, a space with average rental value. Children's shoes occupy 150 square feet on the third floor, which is only 30 percent as valuable as the average space in the store. The entire store has 50,000 square feet, and monthly rent is $400,000.

Required

Compute Vogue's monthly rent expense.

Exercise 25-7 *Recording home-office and branch manufacturing transactions*

McVey Lumber Company manages operations from its home office in Seattle. Company sawmills, located in the state of Washington, are organized as branches. McVey uses a branch accounting system. The home office makes all purchases and sales, handles cash payments and cash receipts, and incurs all company liabilities. When a sawmill completes a custom job, it transfers the inventory to central warehouses, which the home office controls. During August of the current year, the company completed the following transactions:

a. Direct materials purchased on account, $550.
b. Direct materials used in production, $1,090.
c. Sawmill payroll paid, $3,100.
d. Sawmill overhead applied, $4,600.
e. Goods shipped to central warehouse, $5,000.
f. Sales on account, $960.
g. Collections on account, $1,330.

Required

Journalize these transactions for the home office and the branch.

Exercise 25-8 *Recording home-office and branch sales-office transactions*

Nye & Wheeler, a partnership, has branch sales offices throughout Kentucky, Ohio, and Indiana. The company uses a branch accounting system. The branches purchase and sell goods, pay bills, collect cash from customers, and incur selling expenses. The home office, in Louisville, Kentucky, obtains outside financing as needed and advances cash to, and receives cash from, the branches. During a recent month, the company completed the following transactions:

a. Home office borrowed $2,500 from a bank, signing a note.
b. Home office advanced $2,250 to the Ohio branch.
c. Ohio branch purchased merchandise on account, $1,780 (debit Purchases).
d. Ohio branch paid selling expense, $60.
e. Ohio branch sold goods on account, $2,110.
f. Home office recorded depreciation of $740 on home-office building.
g. Ohio branch collected cash from customer, $930.
h. Ohio branch transferred $1,000 cash to home office.

Required

Journalize these transactions for the home office and the Ohio branch.

Problems *(Group A)*

Problem 25-1A *Identifying different types of responsibility centers*

Identify by letter each of the following as most likely being a cost center, a profit center, or an investment center:

a. Children's nursery in a church or synagogue
b. Lighting department in a Sears store
c. Personnel department of Coca-Cola, Inc.
d. Service department of an established automobile dealership
e. Proposed new office of a CPA firm
f. Branch offices of a bank
g. Police department of a city
h. Delta Air Lines, Inc.
i. Consumer Complaint Division of Procter and Gamble Co.
j. Quality-control department of a manufacturing company
k. Top management of a company
l. Southwest region of Pizza Inns, Inc.
m. Editorial department of *The Wall Street Journal*
n. A small clothing boutique
o. Payroll department of a university
p. Different product lines of a furniture manufacturer
q. Job superintendents of a home builder
r. A real estate firm
s. Fast-food restaurants under the supervision of a regional manager
t. European subsidiary of an American company

Problem 25-2A *Preparing a profit-center performance report*

EyeCare Specialists is a chain of optical shops that dispense eyeglasses. Each store has a manager who answers to a city manager, who in turn reports to a statewide manager. The income statements of Store No. 37, all stores in the Dallas area (including Store No. 37), and all stores in the state of Texas (including all Dallas stores) are summarized as follows for April:

	Store No. 37	Dallas	State of Texas
Revenue and expenses:			
Sales..............................	$39,900	$483,000	$3,261,500
Expenses:			
City/state manager office	—	16,000	41,000
Cost of goods sold..................	14,000	171,300	1,256,800
Salary expense.....................	5,300	37,500	409,700
Depreciation	3,000	26,100	334,000
Utilities..........................	2,700	19,300	245,600
Rent	1,900	16,400	186,000
Supplies	700	5,500	60,700
Total expenses.....................	27,600	292,100	2,533,800
Operating income	$12,300	$190,900	$ 727,700

Budgeted amounts for April are as follows:

	Store No. 37	Dallas	State of Texas
Revenue and expenses:			
Sales..............................	$42,000	$468,000	$3,143,000
Expenses:			
City/state manager office	—	15,000	43,000
Cost of goods sold..................	14,200	172,800	1,209,000
Salary expense.....................	5,600	37,900	412,000
Depreciation	3,500	25,400	320,000
Utilities..........................	2,100	17,000	240,000
Rent	1,600	15,700	181,000
Supplies	800	5,900	60,000
Total expenses.....................	27,800	289,700	2,465,000
Operating income	$14,200	$178,300	$ 678,000

Required

1. Prepare a report for April that shows the performance of Store No. 37, all the stores in the Dallas area, and all the stores in the state of Texas. Follow the format of Exhibit 25-2, using only two columns—one for the April budget and the other showing the variance for April.
2. Identify the responsibility centers whose operating income exceeds budget and those whose operating income falls short of budget.

Problem 25-3A *Preparing a profit-center performance report*

Software Designers is organized along product lines, with product managers reporting to division managers, who in turn report to the company vice-president. The vice-president, who has received the following data for November of the current year, needs a performance report to highlight the operating income of audio products, the audio-video division, and the company in total:

| | Company Totals | | |
| | Audio-Video Division | | |
	Audio Products	Video Products	Other Divisions
Revenues, actual	$163,000	$867,000	$788,000
Expenses, actual	138,000	516,000	374,000
Revenues, budget	218,000	907,000	760,000
Expenses, budget	147,000	505,000	368,000

Required

1. Prepare a performance report for November in a format similar to that on page 973. Show November operating income in thousands of dollars for audio products, the audio-video division, and the company as a whole.

2. Prepare a performance report in a format similar to Exhibit 25-2. Show November operating income in thousands of dollars for the same three responsibility centers reported in Requirement 1.

3. Which responsibility centers exceeded budget? Which performed below budget?

4. Do you prefer the format in Requirement 1 or in Requirement 2? Give your reason.

Problem 25-4A *Computing and allocating occupancy cost to a department*

Modern Electric Company occupies three floors in a building in downtown Atlanta. Occupancy cost for a recent quarter included the following items and amounts:

Rent	$36,000
Utilities	8,140
Janitorial services	4,200
Depreciation–building fixtures	3,500
Total	$51,840

Modern occupies 5,000 square feet on the street level, 3,000 square feet on the second floor, and 4,000 square feet of the basement. The company accountant computed the occupancy cost per square foot by dividing the total cost of $51,840 by 12,000 square feet. He charges occupancy to all company departments based on this $4.32 cost per square foot.

The manager of the industrial products department, located in the basement, objected. She cited an engineering study conducted for the company by a real estate firm. It estimated that space in the basement is one-half as valuable as second-floor space and one-fourth as valuable as space on the street level.

Required

1. Based on the engineering study, compute the occupancy cost of a square foot of space on each of Modern's three floors. Round decimals to three places, and round the cost per square foot to the nearest cent.

2. The industrial products department occupies 2,200 square feet of the basement. How much occupancy cost should be charged to this department each quarter?

Problem 25-5A *Preparing a departmental income statement*

Mistletoe Express is organized into a copy department and a printing department. At May 31, the end of Mistletoe's fiscal year, the bookkeeper prepared the following trial balance, which includes the effects of year-end adjusting entries:

Cash	$ 2,400	
Receivables	1,600	
Supplies	25,400	
Prepaid expenses	1,100	
Land	25,900	
Building	41,200	
Accumulated depreciation–building		$ 16,200
Printing equipment	33,700	
Accumulated depreciation–printing equipment		9,600
Other assets	4,700	
Accounts payable		3,200
Accrued liabilities		1,600
Unearned printing revenue		2,200
Long-term note payable		15,000
Owner equity		61,400
Copy revenue		54,900
Printing revenue		67,100
Salary expense–machine operators	23,600	
Salary expense–store manager	22,900	
Salary expense–bookkeeper	18,300	
Lease expense–copy equipment	12,000	
Supplies expense	9,000	
Depreciation expense–printing equipment	2,400	
Property tax expense	2,300	
Insurance expense	1,600	
Depreciation expense–building	1,400	
Interest expense	1,400	
Uncollectible account expense	300	
	$231,200	$231,200

Mistletoe owns its printing equipment and leases a copier from Xerox. Established printing customers do business with the company on a credit basis, but copy services are performed for cash only. Insurance expense is evenly divided between departments. The bookkeeper spends approximately two-thirds of his time on accounts receivable and other printing department matters and the remainder on general accounting. Interest expense relates to the note payable, which the company signed to purchase the printing equipment. The store manager spends 60 percent of her time on printing and 40 percent on copy services. The company allocates all other expenses based on service revenue.

Required

1. Prepare a departmental income statement through operating income.
2. Which department is more profitable? What factor contributes most to the profitability difference between departments?

Problem 25-6A   *Preparing a budgeted departmental income statement*

Goldwyn's is a neighborhood clothing store with two departments. The most recent annual report to management appears on the next page.

Goldwyn is considering opening a children's department early in fiscal 19X8. To plan for the coming year, the store owner seeks your help in preparing a budgeted income statement. Your conversation with the owner reveals the following:

1. Management expects annual sales of the new department to be $65,000, with a gross profit percentage (gross profits divided by sales) equal to that of the two existing departments, that is, 52 percent.

Goldwyn's
Departmental Income Statement
For the Year Ended January 31, 19X7

	Total	Men's	Women's
Sales revenue	$317,700	$141,800	$175,900
Expenses:			
Cost of goods sold	152,500	68,050	84,450
Sales salaries	44,300	20,800	23,500
Salary–store manager	32,900	16,450	16,450
Rent expense–building	14,000	7,000	7,000
Advertising	8,000	2,400	5,600
Property tax	2,000	1,000	1,000
Insurance	1,800	900	900
Depreciation–store fixtures	1,700	850	850
Supplies	1,000	500	500
Interest	600	300	300
Uncollectible accounts	300	150	150
Total expenses	259,100	118,400	140,700
Operating income	$ 58,600	$ 23,400	$ 35,200

2. Addition of a children's department will draw more women than men into the store and should increase sales of women's wear by 20 percent. Sales of men's wear are expected to increase by only 5 percent.

3. A salesperson can be hired for the children's department at an annual salary of $14,000. Other salaries will increase by 6 percent.

4. Thus far, the Goldwyn accountant has allocated all expenses except cost of goods sold, sales salaries, and advertising equally to the men's and women's departments. The store owner decides that the equal allocation of indirect expenses to the two departments is inappropriate.

5. The store manager expects to spend equal amounts of time in the three departments during the coming year.

6. The women's department is nearest the door and occupies 3,000 square feet of the most valuable space in the store. Men's wear also occupies 3,000 square feet, but its space is only two-thirds as valuable as that of women's wear. The new children's department will take up 1,000 square feet with the same value per square foot as the women's department. Total rent expense under the long-term lease will be unchanged in 19X8.

7. Advertising expense will remain unchanged for the two existing departments. The company will commit $3,000 to advertising the children's department.

8. Depreciation of new store fixtures for the children's department will be $900. Other depreciation amounts will be unchanged.

9. Interest expense needed to finance the children's department will be $1,000. The remaining 19X8 interest of $600 belongs equally to the other two departments.

10. All other expenses will increase by 10 percent and should be allocated to departments based on relative sales, except property tax, which is allocated on the same basis used for rent. Round percentages to three decimal places.

Required

Prepare a budgeted departmental income statement in multiple-step format for fiscal year 19X8 based on the preceding projections.

Problem 25-7A *Recording home-office and branch transactions*

South Side Realty has branch offices throughout the Boston area and uses a branch accounting system for control purposes. The home office has a separate Branch Ledger Control account for each branch, and the branches maintain branch ledgers. Branch ledgers contain asset, liability, and Home-Office Ledger-Control accounts.

The home office advances cash to the branches. Branch managers have the authority to purchase supplies and office furniture and equipment. They also pay utility and other branch-office expenses. However, only the home office records branch expenses. The branches collect commissions earned from their real estate sales and immediately transfer the cash to the home office. Only the home office records commissions revenue. The home office then pays a commission directly to the agent who made the sale. During a recent month the following transactions occurred at the Plymouth Branch of South Side Realty:

a. Home office advanced $3,000 to branch.
b. Branch purchased office supplies on account, $600.
c. Branch paid cash for a file cabinet, $400.
d. Branch paid account payable, $600.
e. Branch sold a house, earning a commission and receiving cash of $6,200.
f. Branch transferred $6,200 to home office.
g. Home office paid commission to agent making sale in *e*, $3,100.
h. Branch transferred $1,000 cash to home office.
i. Branch paid electricity expense, $300.
j. Branch recorded depreciation on office equipment, $900.

Required

1. Record these transactions in the home-office journal and in the branch journal.
2. Post the transactions to the reciprocal accounts. Show the balances of the reciprocal accounts after posting.

(Group B)

Problem 25-1B *Identifying different types of responsibility centers*

Identify by letter each of the following as being most likely a cost center, a profit center, or an investment center:

a. Eastern district of a salesperson's territory
b. Typesetting department of a printing company
c. Surgery unit of a privately owned hospital
d. Personnel department of Goodyear Tire and Rubber Company
e. Accounts payable section of an accounting department
f. Proposed new office of a real estate firm
g. Branch warehouse of a carpet manufacturer
h. Disneyland
i. Assembly-line supervisory employees
j. Service department of a stereo shop
k. Men's clothing in a department store
l. American subsidiary of a Japanese company
m. Music director of a church or synagogue
n. Catering operation of an established restaurant
o. Executive director of a United Way agency
p. Different product lines of a gift shop
q. The Empire State Building in New York City

r. Work crews of a painting contractor
s. Investments department of a bank
t. Accounting department of a company

Problem 25-2B   *Preparing a profit-center performance report*

San Fernando Gift Shops is organized with store managers reporting to a statewide manager, who in turn reports to the vice-president of marketing. The income statements of the
Sacramento store, all stores in California (including the Sacramento store), and the company as a whole (including California stores) are summarized as follows for 19X6:

	Sacramento	California	Companywide
Revenue and expenses:			
Sales........................	$137,800	$1,643,000	$3,884,000
Expenses:			
State manager/vice-president's office........................	—	59,000	116,000
Cost of goods sold..............	53,000	671,900	1,507,000
Salary expense..................	38,100	415,500	1,119,000
Depreciation	7,200	91,000	435,000
Utilities	3,800	46,200	260,000
Rent..........................	2,400	34,700	178,000
Supplies......................	1,100	15,600	86,000
Total expenses..................	105,600	1,333,900	3,701,000
Operating income.................	$ 32,200	$ 309,100	$ 183,000

Budgeted amounts for 19X6 are as follows:

	Sacramento	California	Companywide
Revenue and expenses:			
Sales........................	$151,300	$1,769,700	$4,400,000
Expenses:			
State manager/vice-president's office........................	—	65,600	118,000
Cost of goods sold	61,500	763,400	1,672,000
Salary expense	38,800	442,000	1,095,000
Depreciation....................	7,200	87,800	449,000
Utilities.......................	4,700	54,400	271,000
Rent	2,800	32,300	174,000
Supplies	900	16,100	93,000
Total expenses	115,900	1,461,600	3,872,000
Operating income	$ 35,400	$ 308,100	$ 528,000

Required

1. Prepare a report for 19X6 that shows the performance of the Sacramento store, all the
    stores in California, and the company as a whole. Follow the format of Exhibit 25-2,
    using only two columns—one for the annual budget and the other showing the
    variance for the year.
2. Identify the responsibility centers whose operating income exceeds budget and those
    whose operating income falls short of budget.

Problem 25-3B   *Preparing a profit-center performance report*

Maxwell Home Furnishings is organized along product lines, with product managers reporting to department managers, who in turn report to the company vice-president. The vice-president, who has received the following data for August of the current year, needs a performance report to highlight the operating income of bedspreads, the bedding department, and the company in total:

	Company Totals		
	Bedding Department		
	Bedspreads	**Linens**	**Other Departments**
Revenues, actual	$3,700	$1,500	$6,500
Expenses, actual	1,900	800	3,100
Revenues, budget	3,300	1,400	7,100
Expenses, budget.	1,600	700	3,600

Required

1. Prepare a performance report for August in a format similar to that on page 973. Show August operating income for bedspreads, the bedding department, and the company as a whole.

2. Prepare a performance report in a format similar to Exhibit 25-2. Show August operating income for the same three responsibility centers reported in Requirement 1.

3. Which responsibility centers exceeded budget? Which performed below budget?

4. Do you prefer the format in Requirement 1 or in Requirement 2? Give your reason.

Problem 25-4B   *Computing and allocating occupancy cost to a department*

Joske's occupies a six-story building (including the basement) in downtown Houston. Assume occupancy cost for a recent month included the following:

Depreciation – building.	$ 83,200
Utilities	11,300
Janitorial services	6,600
Rent – store fixtures.	4,700
Total	$105,800

Each floor of the building has 8,000 square feet, except for the second floor, which has 6,000 square feet. The company accountant computed the occupancy cost per square foot by dividing the total cost of $105,800 by 46,000 square feet. She charges occupancy to all company departments based on this $2.30 cost per square foot.

The manager of the Budget Buyer Department, located in the basement, objected. He cited a space-usage study conducted for the company by a real estate firm. It estimated that space in the basement is one-fourth as valuable as street level space, one-half as valuable as space on the second floor, and equal in value to the other floors.

Required

1. Based on the space-usage study, compute the occupancy cost of a square foot of space on each of Joske's floors. Round decimals to three places, and round the cost per square foot to the nearest cent.

2. The Budget Buyer Department occupies 5,500 square feet of the basement. How much occupancy cost should be charged to this department monthly?

Problem 25-5B *Preparing a departmental income statement*

Adventure Travel is organized into a custom department and a group discount department. At August 31, the end of Adventure's fiscal year, the bookkeeper prepared the following trial balance, which includes the effects of year-end adjusting entries:

Cash	$ 1,300	
Receivables	24,600	
Supplies	3,800	
Prepaid expenses	1,700	
Building	55,500	
Accumulated depreciation–building		$ 20,900
Office furniture	38,100	
Accumulated depreciation–office furniture		7,300
Other assets	3,100	
Accounts payable		11,400
Accrued liabilities		6,900
Unearned service revenue		5,800
Long-term note payable		22,000
Owner equity		19,200
Custom travel service revenue		69,300
Group discount travel service revenue		95,700
Salary expense–travel agents	29,600	
Commission expense–travel agents	26,000	
Salary expense–office manager	25,000	
Salary expense–bookkeeper	16,800	
Lease expense–computer equipment	15,000	
Supplies expense	6,300	
Depreciation expense–office furniture	2,500	
Property tax expense	2,200	
Depreciation expense–building	2,100	
Interest expense	2,000	
Insurance expense	1,700	
Advertising expense	1,200	
	$258,500	$258,500

In January, Adventure hired a group travel specialist at an annual salary of $20,000. Remaining agent salaries of $9,600 go to part-time agents that handle custom travel plans. The office manager spends 60 percent of her time on group discount plans and 40 percent on custom travel planning. The bookkeeper spends approximately two-thirds of his time on accounting for custom travel planning operations and the remainder on group discount plans. Adventure leases a computer that it uses 80 percent of the time for custom travel planning and 20 percent of the time for group discount packages. Insurance expense is evenly divided between the two departments. Interest expense relates to the note payable, which the company signed to purchase the building. The company allocates all other expenses based on relative service revenue.

Required

1. Prepare a departmental income statement through operating income.
2. Which department is more profitable? Was the decision to hire the group specialist wise? Give your reason.

Problem 25-6B *Preparing a budgeted departmental income statement*

Chicosky's is a suburban hardware store with two departments. The most recent annual report to management follows.

Chicosky's
Departmental Income Statement
For the Year Ended January 31, 19X2

	Total	Dept. A	Dept. B
Sales revenue.............................	$400,000	$300,000	$100,000
Expenses:			
Cost of goods sold........................	160,000	120,000	40,000
Sales salaries.............................	41,000	28,000	13,000
Salary–store manager.....................	35,000	17,500	17,500
Rent expense–building	16,000	8,000	8,000
Advertising...............................	5,000	3,500	1,500
Property tax	3,000	1,500	1,500
Insurance	2,400	1,200	1,200
Depreciation–store fixtures.................	1,200	600	600
Supplies	1,000	500	500
Interest	800	400	400
Uncollectible accounts.....................	600	300	300
Total expenses	266,000	181,500	84,500
Operating income	$134,000	$118,500	$ 15,500

The company is considering opening a third department early in fiscal 19X3. To plan for the coming year, the store owner seeks your help in preparing a budgeted income statement. Your conversation with the owner reveals the following:

1. Management expects annual sales of the new department to be $80,000, with a gross profit percentage (gross profit divided by sales) equal to that of the two existing departments, that is, 60 percent.
2. Addition of a third department will also draw customers into Department A and should increase Department A sales by 25 percent. Sales of Department B are expected to increase by only 10 percent.
3. A salesperson can be hired for the new department at an annual salary of $16,000. Other salaries will increase by 5 percent.
4. Thus far, the company accountant has allocated all expenses except cost of goods sold, sales salaries, and advertising equally to Departments A and B. The store owner decides that the equal allocation of indirect expenses to departments is inappropriate.
5. The store manager expects to spend equal amounts of time in the three departments during the coming year.
6. Department A is nearest the door and occupies 2,000 square feet of the most valuable space in the store. Department B also occupies 2,000 square feet, but its space is only half as valuable as that of Department A. The new department will take up 1,000 square feet with the same value per square foot as Department A. Total rent expense under the long-term lease will be unchanged in 19X3.
7. Advertising expense will remain unchanged for the two existing departments. The company will commit $2,000 to advertising Department C merchandise.
8. Depreciation of new store fixtures for Department C will be $900. Other depreciation amounts will be unchanged.
9. Interest expense needed to finance Department C will be $1,000. The remaining 19X3 interest of $500 belongs equally to the other two departments.
10. All other expenses will increase by 8 percent and should be allocated to departments based on relative sales, except property tax, which is allocated on the same basis used for rent. Round percentages to three decimal places.

Required

Prepare a budgeted departmental income statement in multiple-step format for fiscal year 19X3 based on the preceding projections.

Problem 25-7B *Recording home-office and branch transactions*

Cactus Realty has branch offices throughout the Phoenix area and uses a branch accounting system for control purposes. The home office has a separate Branch Ledger Control account for each branch, and the branches maintain branch ledgers. Branch ledgers contain only asset, liability, and Home-Office Ledger Control accounts.

The home office advances cash to the branches. Branch managers have authority to purchase supplies and office furniture and equipment. They also pay utility and other branch-office expenses. However, only the home office records branch expenses. The branches collect commissions earned from their real estate sales and immediately transfer the cash to the home office. Only the home office records commissions revenue. The home office then pays half the commission directly to the agent who made the sale. During a recent month the following transactions occurred at the Desert Branch of Cactus Realty:

a. Home office advanced $5,500 to branch.
b. Branch sold a house, earning a commission and receiving cash of $8,000.
c. Branch transferred $8,000 to home office.
d. Home office paid commission to agent making sale in b, $4,000.
e. Branch paid office cleaning expense, $220.
f. Branch purchased office furniture on account, $1,400.
g. Branch paid cash for office supplies, $160.
h. Branch paid account payable, $700.
i. Branch transferred $2,300 cash to home office.
j. Branch recorded depreciation on office equipment, $440.

Required

1. Record these transactions in the home-office journal and in the branch journal.
2. Post the transactions to the reciprocal accounts. Show the balances of the reciprocal accounts after posting.

Decision Problem

Using Departmental Operating Income to Decide on an Advertising Campaign
The accountant of Mazelli Oldsmobile-Cadillac has produced the following annual summary of revenue and expense information for management:

	Oldsmobiles	Cadillacs
Units sold.	200	80
Average selling price per unit.	$15,000	$22,000
Average cost per unit	12,200	17,300
Average direct expense per unit.	1,900	2,320
Average variable indirect expense per unit	500	1,200

Ron Mazelli, owner of the business, is considering an advertising campaign to increase sales and operating income. He estimates that additional advertising cost of $25,000 will increase sales by 30 automobiles each year. However, because Mazelli is the only Oldsmobile-Cadillac dealer in the area, any increase in Oldsmobile sales is likely to decrease sales of Cadillacs by an equal number. Likewise, an increase in Cadillac sales of 30 automobiles is likely to cause an equal decrease in Oldsmobile sales. Mazelli's fixed expenses, other than the $25,000 of advertising, will be unaffected by this decision.

Required

Prepare an analysis to show whether Mazelli should advertise Oldsmobiles or Cadillacs, or not undertake the advertising campaign at all. Base your decision on operating income (ignoring fixed expenses other than the $25,000 advertising) under three alternatives: (1) no new advertising, (2) advertise Oldsmobiles, and (3) advertise Cadillacs.

Answers to Self-Study Questions

1. b
2. a
3. d ($33,000 − $30,000 = $3,000; $3,000/$30,000 = 10 percent unfavorable)
4. c
5. c
6. b
7. a
8. b
9. d
10. d

Special Decisions and Capital Budgeting

Should we sell 50,000 units of our product for $9 each — a price slightly below our cost? Should we make a special part used in our manufacturing process, or should we buy the part from an outside supplier? Should we drop the women's clothing line altogether? These are examples of special decisions that managers make. They are more far-reaching than day-to-day decisions, like whether to work overtime, to accept a rush job, or to change the schedule for repairing equipment. This chapter shows how to use accounting data to make special decisions with long-run effects on the business.

Relevant Information for Decision Making

The main financial goals in business are to earn a profit and to have a strong financial position. Decisions center on how to achieve these goals. Decision making includes choosing among several courses of action, which means managers must make comparisons. The process has two steps: (1) identifying the information useful for making the decision and (2) analyzing the information to compare alternatives.

Relevant information is the expected future data that differ between the alternative courses of action. Which alternative will increase sales more? Which alternative will decrease expenses by a greater amount? By studying the expected future amounts resulting from the alternative actions, the manager can decide which action will help the business reach its goals.

Not all data influence a manager. Irrelevant data will not change a decision. For example, in some situations the cost of fixed overhead will not change regardless of the action the manager takes. The manager, then, need not consider fixed overhead in making the decision. Determining which information is relevant — which data make a difference — is as important a skill as being able to analyze the information.

Let's consider an illustration of decision analysis using relevant information. Suppose Pendleton Woolen Mills is deciding whether to use pure wool or a wool-polyester blend in the manufacture of a line of sweaters. Pendleton predicts the following costs under the two alternatives:

OBJECTIVE 1

Identify the relevant information for a special business decision

Expected manufacturing cost per sweater:	Wool	Wool Blend	Cost Difference
Direct material.............................	$10	$6	$4
Direct labor	2	2	0
Total cost of direct material and direct labor......	$12	$8	$4

Assume cost is the chief consideration in this decision. The cost of direct material is relevant to the decision because this cost differs between alternatives (the wool costs more than the wool blend). The labor cost is irrelevant because there is no difference in its cost whichever material is used.

We can compute the $4 cost difference between alternatives either from the cost of direct material only or from total cost. It is helpful to know that there is a $4 total cost difference between the two alternatives. But it is more helpful for managers to know that the $4 cost difference results from the materials, not from labor. Failure to identify the reason for the difference may lead managers to make an unwise decision.

Let us emphasize this important point about special decision analysis: relevant information is *expected future data* that differ between alternative courses of action. Managers should base their decisions on the expected future data rather than on historical data.

Historical data are usually supplied by the accounting system and are often useful guides to predictions. However, bear in mind that historical data by themselves are irrelevant. They are useful only to the extent that managers use them to help predict future data.

This approach to making decisions is called the *relevant information* approach. This approach applies to a wide variety of decisions, regardless of the specific characteristics of the particular situation. We turn now to a number of special decisions.

Special Sales Order

Torino Corporation, a manufacturer of automobile parts, ordinarily sells oil filters for $3.20 each. A mail-order company has offered Torino $35,000 for 20,000 oil filters. That works out to a special sale price of $1.75 per oil filter ($35,000/ 20,000 = $1.75). This sale will not affect regular business in any way, it will not change fixed costs, it will not require any additional variable selling and administrative expense, it will put idle manufacturing capacity to use, and it will violate no antitrust laws regarding pricing. Torino's total manufacturing cost of an oil filter is $2.00. Should Torino accept the special order and make the sale at $1.75? At first glance, the answer appears to be no, because each oil filter costs $2.00. But more thought must go into making this decision.

OBJECTIVE 2

Make seven types of special business decisions

To set the stage for the analysis, let's examine Torino's income statement.

EXHIBIT 26-1 *Functional Format and Contribution Margin Format for the Income Statement*

Torino Corporation
Income Statement
For the Year Ended December 31, 19X2

Functional Format		Contribution Margin Format		
Sales.............	$800,000	Sales.............		$800,000
Less manufacturing		Less variable expenses:		
cost of goods sold .	500,000	Manufacturing....	$300,000	
Gross margin.......	300,000	Selling and		
Less selling and		administrative ..	75,000	375,000
administrative ex-		Contribution margin .		425,000
penses...........	200,000	Less fixed expenses:		
		Manufacturing....	200,000	
		Selling and		
		administrative ..	125,000	325,000
Operating income ...	$100,000	Operating income ...		$100,000

Exhibit 26-1 presents the income statement in two different formats. The income statement on the left is the standard format presented to stockholders, creditors, and other parties outside the company. It is also called a *functional* income statement because it categorizes expenses by function: cost of goods sold and selling and administrative expenses. The contribution margin format on the right shows variable expenses and fixed expenses. The contribution margin format is more useful for special decision analysis because it highlights how costs and income are affected by decisions. Recall that the contribution margin is revenue minus all variable expenses.

In this illustration, assume that Torino made and sold 250,000 oil filters. Under the functional costing approach, the manufacturing cost per unit is $2.00 ($500,000/250,000 = $2.00). But the contribution margin approach shows that the variable manufacturing cost per unit is $1.20 ($300,000/250,000 = $1.20). We now answer the key question facing Torino: What difference would the special sale make to the company's operating income?

Correct Analysis: Contribution Margin Approach

The correct analysis concentrates on the differences in revenues, expenses, and operating income, as the quick summary in Exhibit 26-2 shows:

EXHIBIT 26-2 *Quick Summary of Special Sales Order Analysis*

Expected increase in revenues—sale of 20,000 oil filters × $1.75 each ..	$35,000
Expected increase in expenses—variable manufacturing expenses:	
20,000 oil filters × $1.20 each	24,000
Expected increase in operating income	$11,000

This special sale is expected to increase revenues by $35,000. The only cost affected by the sale is variable manufacturing expense, which is expected to increase by $24,000. Torino management predicts that the special sales order will increase operating income by $11,000. Fixed expenses do not enter the analysis because they do not change. Variable selling and administrative expenses are unchanged because Torino has to make no special effort to get the sale. To make the decision, Torino should compare the special sale price to total variable cost of producing and selling the goods. As long as the increase in revenues exceeds the increase in variable expenses, there is a contribution to fixed costs and profits.

Exhibit 26-3 gives Torino's income statements both without the special sales order (column 1) and with it (column 2). It shows operating income under both courses of action. Column 3 of the exhibit repeats the quick summary by showing the differences caused by the special sales order. The quick summary presents the result of accepting the special sales order, an $11,000 increase in operating income.

You have just seen two correct ways of deciding whether to accept or reject the special sales order at a price less than total cost per unit: (1) a quick summary of differences (Exhibit 26-2) and (2) total revenues, expenses, and operating income under both courses of action (Exhibit 26-3). Whether to use a quick summary or a total analysis depends on the question you are addressing. The summary answers this question: What will be the *difference* in revenues, expenses, and operating income if the business accepts the special order? The total analysis shows the summary of differences and answers an additional question: What will total revenues, expenses, and operating income be under the alternative courses of action? To accept or reject the special sales order can be decided from either analysis.

EXHIBIT 26-3   *Total Special Order Analysis—Income Statements Without and With the Special Order*

Torino Corporation
Income Statement
For the Year Ended December 31, 19X2

	(1) Without Special Order, 250,000 Units	(2) With Special Order, 270,000 Units	(3) Special-Order Difference, 20,000 Units Total	Per Unit
Sales....................	$800,000	$835,000	$35,000	$1.75
Variable expenses:				
Manufacturing..........	$300,000	$324,000	$24,000	$1.20
Selling and administrative.........	75,000	75,000	—	—
Total variable expenses ...	375,000	399,000	24,000	1.20
Contribution margin	425,000	436,000	11,000	.55
Fixed expenses:				
Manufacturing..........	200,000	200,000	—	—
Selling and administrative.........	125,000	125,000	—	—
Total fixed expenses......	325,000	325,000	—	—
Operating income	$100,000	$111,000	$11,000	$ .55

Incorrect Analysis: Ignoring the Nature of Fixed Costs

Let's look at an incorrect analysis of the Torino special sales order situation. Functional costing, shown on the left-hand side of Exhibit 26-1, leads to an incorrect measure of the change in expenses resulting from the sale.

Total manufacturing costs...................................	$500,000
Units produced	÷250,000
Total cost per unit ($500,000/250,000)	$2.00
Expected increase in revenues—sale of 20,000 oil filters × $1.75 each...	$ 35,000
Expected increase in expenses—*total* manufacturing expenses:	
20,000 oil filters × $2.00 each................................	40,000
Expected decrease in operating income	$ (5,000)

OBJECTIVE 3
Explain the difference between correct analysis and incorrect analysis of a particular business decision

A manager following this approach reasons that it costs $2.00 to make an oil filter. In this view, it is unprofitable to sell the product for less than $2.00. *The flaw in this analysis arises from treating a fixed cost as though it changes like a variable cost.* To manufacture one additional oil filter would increase Torino's cost by the variable manufacturing expense of $1.20. Fixed expenses are irrelevant to the decision analysis because Torino will incur the fixed expenses whether or not the company accepts the special sales order. The addition of 20,000 oil filters will *not* add to *total* fixed expenses. As volume changes, manufacturing costs will increase at the rate of $1.20 per unit, not $2.00 per unit. In this analysis, the variable expenses are relevant, and the fixed expenses are irrelevant.

Short-Run Versus Long-Run: Other Factors to Consider

The special sales order analysis focused on short-run factors—the expected effect on operating income. We must also consider long-run factors. What will be the impact on customers? Will acceptance of the order at $1.75 per unit hurt Torino's ability to make sales at the standard price of $3.20? Will regular customers find out about the special price and balk at paying the regular price? How will competitors react? Will they view this sale as the start of a price war?

Accepting the order yields an $11,000 advantage in operating income. Will potential disadvantages offset this $11,000? The sales manager may think so and reject the order. In turning away the business, the manager is saying that the company is better off passing up $11,000 now to protect its long-run market position. Rejecting the special sales order is like making an $11,000 "investment" in the company's long-run future.

Deletion of Products, Departments, Territories — Fixed Costs Unchanged

To analyze whether a company should drop a product line, a department, or a territory, let's use the Torino Corporation data. Assume that Torino is already operating at the 270,000-unit level, as shown in column 2 of Exhibit 26-3. Suppose Torino is considering dropping product line B, which makes up $35,000 (20,000 units) of the company's sales. A manager is given an income statement divided by product line as follows:

	Total	Product Line A	Product Line B
Units..	270,000	250,000	20,000
Sales.......................................	$835,000	$800,000	$ 35,000
Variable expenses	399,000	375,000	24,000
Contribution margin	436,000	425,000	11,000
Fixed expenses:			
Manufacturing	200,000	185,185*	14,815*
Selling and administrative...............	125,000	115,741**	9,259**
Total fixed expenses....................	325,000	300,926*	24,074
Operating income (loss)	$111,000	$124,074	$(13,074)

* $200,000 ÷ 270,000 units = $.74074 per unit; 250,000 units × $.74074 = $185,185; 20,000 units × $.74074 = $14,815

** $125,000 ÷ 270,000 units = $.46296 per unit; 250,000 units × $.46296 = $115,741; 20,000 units × $.46296 = $9,259

In determining cost per unit, Torino, like many companies, allocates fixed expenses to units in proportion to the number of units sold. For example, the data show that Torino sold 270,000 units of its products altogether. Total fixed manufacturing expenses of $200,000 divided by 270,000 units equals fixed manufacturing cost of $.74074 per unit. Applying this unit cost to the 250,000 units of Product Line A allocates fixed manufacturing cost of $185,185 to this product. The same procedure allocates fixed manufacturing cost of $14,815 to Product B. Fixed selling and administrative expenses are allocated in the same manner. Using this allocation method we see that Product Line B has an operating loss of $13,074. Should Product B be dropped?

This illustration is basically the same example we studied for the special sales order. The relevant items are the changes in revenues and expenses. But now we are considering a decrease in volume instead of an increase. The difference between the change in revenues and the change in expenses is the change in operating income, as shown in Exhibit 26-4. Again, only the variable expenses are relevant to the decision. In the short run, dropping Product Line B would decrease operating income by $11,000. This analysis suggests that Torino should *not* drop Product B.

The decision of whether to delete a product is based on the same analysis used for the special sales order. The only difference is that deleting products leads to decreases in revenues and expenses whereas accepting a special sales order leads to increased revenues and expenses. Decisions in both cases are based on the expected change in operating income.

EXHIBIT 26-4 *Deletion of a Product—Fixed Costs Unchanged*

Expected decrease in revenues:	
Deletion of sales of Product B—20,000 units × $1.75 each	$35,000
Expected decrease in expenses:	
Deletion of variable manufacturing expenses—	
20,000 units × $1.20 each.....................................	24,000
Expected decrease in operating income...........................	$11,000

EXHIBIT 26-5 *Deletion of a Product — Fixed Costs Changed*

Expected decrease in revenues:		
Deletion of sales of Product B		$35,000
Expected decrease in expenses:		
Variable manufacturing expenses	$24,000	
Fixed expenses — engineer salary.	12,000	
Expected decrease in total expenses.		36,000
Expected increase in operating income		$ 1,000

Deletion of Products, Departments, Territories — Fixed Costs Changed

In our two examples total fixed expenses have not changed. However, do not jump to the conclusion that fixed costs are always irrelevant. The following example illustrates the role of fixed costs in special decision analysis.

Suppose Torino Corporation employs a part-time engineer to work on Product B in a particular territory. This employee is paid a fixed annual salary of $12,000. The question facing management is whether to drop Product B and close the territory. To make this decision, Torino managers analyze all costs — fixed and variable affected by the decision. Exhibit 26-5 shows the analysis.

The analysis suggests that operating income will increase by $1,000 if Torino drops Product B and closes the territory. In this situation, fixed expenses are relevant, and so the change in the fixed cost must enter the analysis. Special decisions should consider all costs that management expects to be affected by the situation. Managers must ask, What costs — fixed *and* variable — will change?

Which Product to Emphasize

Companies must decide which products to emphasize and which to de-emphasize. This decision has a profound impact on profits. If salespersons push a product with a low profit margin, the company's operating income may decrease even though they succeed in selling the product. How should a manager decide which product to emphasize? Decisions like this are important because of limited sales staff, store display space, and advertising budgets.

Assume a clothing manufacturer has two products, shirts and slacks. The following data are relevant:

	Product	
	Shirts	**Slacks**
Per unit:		
Selling price	$15	$20
Variable expenses.	6	16
Contribution margin	$ 9	$ 4
Contribution margin ratio:		
Shirts — $9/$15	60%	
Slacks — $4/$20		20%

EXHIBIT 26-6   *Which Product to Emphasize*

		Product	
		Shirts	**Slacks**
(1)	Units that can be produced each hour	1	3
(2)	Contribution margin per unit	×$9	×$4
(3)	Contribution margin per hour (1) × (2)	$9	$12
	Capacity—Number of hours	×20,000	×20,000
	Total contribution margin for capacity	$180,000	$240,000

The data indicate that shirts are more profitable than slacks. But an important piece of information has been withheld—the time it takes to manufacture each product. This factor is called the *constraint,* or the *limiting factor.*

The **limiting factor,** or **constraint,** is the item that restricts production or sales. In some companies, the constraint is production. The factory or the labor force may be large enough to produce only so many units. This constraint—the limit to how much the labor force can produce—may be stated in terms of labor hours, machine hours, materials, or square feet of shelf space. (For example, storage may be limited to 50,000 square feet of space in a warehouse.) These factors vary from company to company, depending on its line of business. Other companies are constrained by sales. Competition may be stiff, and the business may be able to sell only so many units. In other companies, the constraint is time, as we see in the following example: Suppose the company can produce three pairs of slacks *or* one shirt per hour. This company has 20,000 hours of capacity. Which product should the company emphasize?

The way to maximize profits for a given capacity is to obtain the highest possible contribution margin per unit of the limiting factor—in our example, direct labor hours. The analysis includes two steps. First, determine the contribution margin per unit of the limiting factor. Second, multiply this unit contribution margin by the company's capacity, stated in the number of units of the limiting factor.

Exhibit 26-6 shows how to decide which product to emphasize when there is a limiting factor. Slacks should be emphasized because they contribute more profit per hour. When the limiting factor is a part of the analysis, it is clear that the business should push slacks.

Make or Buy

Manufactured goods often include specialized parts. Overhead garage doors, for example, are activated by electronic controls. A garage door manufacturer may face this question: Should we manufacture the control device ourselves or buy it from an outsider? A furniture company may ask: Should we stain, lacquer, and finish the furniture we manufacture or hire an outsider for the finish work? At the heart of the make-or-buy decision is *how best to use available facilities.*

Let's see how to answer the make-or-buy question. Torino Corporation's production process uses Part No. 4, which has the following manufacturing costs for 250,000 parts:

	Total Cost (250,000 Units)

Part No. 4 costs:

Direct material	$ 40,000
Direct labor...	20,000
Variable overhead	15,000
Fixed overhead...	50,000
Total manufacturing cost.................................	$125,000
Cost per unit of Part No. 4 ($125,000/250,000)	$.50

Another manufacturer offers to sell Torino the same part for $.37 a unit. Should Torino make Part No. 4 or buy it from the outside supplier? Torino's $.50 unit cost of manufacturing the part is $.13 higher than the $.37 cost of buying it outside. At first glance, it appears that Torino should purchase Part No. 4 from the outsider. But the correct answer to a make-or-buy question is rarely as clear as this comparison suggests. The key to making the correct decision lies in analyzing the difference in expected future costs between the alternatives. Which costs listed above will differ depending on whether Torino makes or buys Part No. 4?

Assume that by purchasing the part from an outsider, Torino can avoid all variable manufacturing costs and reduce the fixed overhead cost by $10,000. (Fixed overhead will decrease to $40,000.) Exhibit 26-7 shows the difference in cost between the make-and-buy alternatives.

It would be cheaper to make the part than to buy it outside. Fixed overhead represents a significant amount of cost even in the buy alternative. The total cost savings for 250,000 units of Part No. 4 is $7,500, which is $.03 per unit.

This example shows that *fixed costs are relevant to a special decision if fixed costs differ between the alternatives.* In this instance, fixed costs differ by $10,000. In these situations, this $10,000 amount is often called *avoidable* fixed overhead.

Best Use of Facilities

The cost data in the make-or-buy decision indicate that making the part is the right decision. As we mention in that discussion, the focus is on making the best use of available facilities. This decision is illustrated further with a make-or-buy decision that includes three alternative courses of action.

EXHIBIT 26-7 *Make or Buy*

	Make Part	Buy Part	Cost to Make minus Cost to Buy
Part No. 4 costs:			
Direct material	$ 40,000	$ —	$40,000
Direct labor..................	20,000	—	20,000
Variable overhead	15,000	—	15,000
Fixed overhead...............	50,000	40,000	10,000
Purchase price from outsider (250,000 × $.37).............	—	92,500	(92,500)
Total cost of Part No. 4	$125,000	$132,500	$ (7,500)
Cost per unit—250,000 units	$.50	$.53	$.03

EXHIBIT 26-8 *Best Use of Facilities*

	Make	Buy and Leave Facilities Idle	Buy and Use Facilities for Other Products
Expected cost of obtaining 250,000 units of Part No. 4 (amounts from Exhibit 26-7).	$125,000	$132,500	$132,500
Expected profit contribution from the other product	—	—	(18,000)
Expected *net* cost of obtaining 250,000 units of Part No. 4	$125,000	$132,500	$114,500

Assume that buying from an outside supplier releases factory facilities that can be used to manufacture another product. Suppose the expected annual profit contribution of this other product is $18,000. The three alternatives become (1) make, (2) buy and leave facilities idle, or (3) buy and use facilities to manufacture another product. The alternative with the lowest *net* cost indicates the best use of facilities. The comparison of *net* cost under the three alternatives is given in Exhibit 26-8.

This analysis of *net* cost indicates that buying the parts outside and using the vacated facilities to manufacture another product is the best choice. If the facilities remain idle, the company will forgo the opportunity to earn $18,000.

Special decisions often include nonquantitative factors. For example, Torino managers may believe they can better control the quality of Part No. 4 by manufacturing it themselves. Or they may fear that an outside supplier cannot deliver sufficient quantities of the part on time. These factors argue for Torino's making the part itself. However, Torino may not have the employees or the factory facilities to manufacture Part No. 4. Its manufacture may require rare materials that Torino cannot obtain economically, so Torino may decide to buy from the outside supplier. Managers consider nonquantitative factors as well as cost differences in making decisions.

Sell As-Is or Process Further

Inventories become obsolete. Should the company incur the additional manufacturing cost to rework the inventory, or should the company try to sell the inventory as is? Some companies hold inventory that is only partially finished. These businesses face the decision of whether to finish the inventory or sell it as is. Of course the finished inventory will bring a higher sale price, but management must consider the additional costs of completing the inventory. Whether the inventory is obsolete or incomplete, managers must decide if further work on it makes financial sense. For this decision, managers must know which costs to analyze. Historical costs are irrelevant to the "sell-or-process-further" decision.

Suppose a company has 1,000 obsolete computer parts that are carried in inventory at a manufacturing cost of $200,000. The alternatives facing the company are (1) process the inventory further at a cost of $40,000 with the expectation of selling it for $64,000, or (2) scrap the inventory for $17,000. Which alternative should the company select? The inventory's $200,000 historical cost is irrelevant

EXHIBIT 26-9 *Sell As-Is or Process Further*

	(1) Process Inventory Further	(2) Scrap Inventory (Sell As-Is)	Difference (1)−(2)
Expected revenue	$64,000	$17,000	$47,000
Expected costs	40,000	—	40,000
Expected net revenue	$24,000	$17,000	$ 7,000

to the decision. Such a cost is called a sunk cost. A **sunk cost** is an actual outlay that has been incurred in the past and is present under all alternatives. It is irrelevant because it makes no difference to a current decision.

Exhibit 26-9 shows how to make the decision of whether to sell an asset in its present condition or to process it further.

Based on the expected revenues and costs, it appears best to process the inventory further. The historical cost—the sunk cost—of the obsolete inventory makes no difference to the decision of whether to scrap the inventory or to rework it for sale at a higher price.

The decision whether to replace a plant asset is analyzed the same way. The asset's book value (cost less accumulated depreciation) is a sunk cost and, therefore, is irrelevant to the replacement decision. The relevant data are the expected revenues minus the expected costs from (1) using the old asset or (2) using a new asset.

Residual value, also called *scrap value* and *disposal value,* is *not* a sunk cost. Residual value is relevant to special decisions because it is the amount of cash to be received by selling the asset. During the asset's life, residual, or scrap, value is an expected *future* amount, which is why it enters the analysis shown in Exhibit 26-9.

Opportunity Cost

The concept of opportunity cost is often relevant to special decisions. An **opportunity cost** is the maximum available profit contribution forgone (rejected) by using limited resources for a particular purpose. It is the cost of the forsaken next-best alternative. This definition indicates that opportunity cost is not the usual outlay cost recorded in accounting. An outlay cost requires a cash disbursement sooner or later. It is the typical cost recorded by accountants.

A common example of an opportunity cost is the salary forgone by an engineer who quits his job with IBM to start his own business. Suppose this engineer analyzes the two job opportunities as follows:

OBJECTIVE 4
Use opportunity cost in decision making

	Open an Independent Business	Remain an IBM Employee
Expected salary income from IBM		$60,000
Expected revenue	$200,000	
Expected total expenses	120,000	
Expected net income	$ 80,000	$60,000

The opportunity cost of staying with IBM is the forgone $80,000 of net income that the independent business is expected to earn. The opportunity cost of starting a new business is the $60,000 salary that could be received from IBM for the next year.

The concept of opportunity cost applies to all business decisions that specify alternative courses of action. For example, in Exhibit 26-3 the opportunity cost of rejecting the special sales order is $11,000 of operating income. In Exhibit 26-6, the opportunity cost of manufacturing shirts is the $240,000 of contribution margin that could be earned on slacks. The opportunity cost of manufacturing slacks is the $180,000 contribution margin available on shirts. In Exhibit 26-9, the opportunity cost of scrapping the inventory in its present condition is the $24,000 that can be earned by processing the inventory further. The opportunity cost of processing the inventory further is $17,000, which can be received immediately by selling the inventory as-is.

Summary Problems for Your Review

1. A company has two products, H and J, with the following per-unit data:

	H	J
Selling price	$20	$30
Variable expenses.	16	21

The company has 15,000 hours of capacity available. Seven units of H can be produced in an hour, compared to three units of J per hour. Which product should the company emphasize?

2. Suppose Zenith Corporation has the following manufacturing costs for 20,000 of its television cabinets:

Direct material	$ 20,000
Direct labor.	80,000
Variable overhead	40,000
Fixed overhead	80,000
Total manufacturing cost	$220,000
Cost per cabinet ($220,000/20,000)	$11

Another manufacturer has offered to sell Zenith similar cabinets for $10, a total purchase cost of $200,000. By purchasing the cabinets outside, Zenith can save $50,000 of fixed overhead cost. The released facilities can be devoted to the manufacture of other products that will contribute $60,000 to profits. Identify and analyze the alternatives. What is Zenith's best decision?

SOLUTIONS TO REVIEW PROBLEMS

1. *Decision:* The company should emphasize Product H because its contribution margin at capacity is greater by $15,000:

	Product	
	H	**J**
(1) Units per hour that can be produced	7	3
(2) Contribution margin per unit	× $4*	× $9*
(3) Contribution margin per hour (1) × (2)	$28	$27
Capacity—Number of hours	× 15,000	× 15,000
Total contribution margin for capacity	$420,000	$405,000

* Contribution margins: H: $20 − $16 = $4; J: $30 − $21 = $9.

2.

	Alternatives		
	Make	**Buy and Leave Facilities Idle**	**Buy and Use Facilities for Other Products**
Cabinets for televisions:			
Direct material	$ 20,000	—	
Direct labor	80,000	—	
Variable overhead	40,000	—	
Fixed overhead	80,000	$ 30,000	$ 30,000
Purchase price from outsider			
(20,000 × $10)	—	200,000	200,000
Total cost of obtaining cabinets	$220,000	$230,000	$230,000
Profit contribution from other products			(60,000)
Net cost of obtaining 20,000 cabinets	$220,000	$230,000	$170,000

Decision: Zenith should buy the television cabinets from an outside supplier and use the released facilities to manufacture other products.

Capital Budgeting

A factory building may be used for 50 years. Equipment for successful products like Ivory soap and Coca-Cola may be used for decades. The term *capital asset* refers to an asset that is used over a long period of time. Plant assets like land, buildings, machinery, equipment, and furniture and fixtures are capital assets. The decisions for the purchase of such long-term assets often require long-range planning and large risks. Many uncertain factors—such as consumer preferences, manufacturing costs, and government legislation—enter into the decisions on the purchase of capital assets. Successful organizations quantify as many of these factors as they can before making long-range decisions. The method, or technique, for evaluating and choosing among alternative courses of action is called a **decision model.**

  Capital budgeting is a formal means of making long-range decisions for investments. Examples include plant locations, equipment purchases, additions of product lines, and territorial expansions. The following diagram shows where capital budgeting fits into the process of purchasing and using long-term assets:

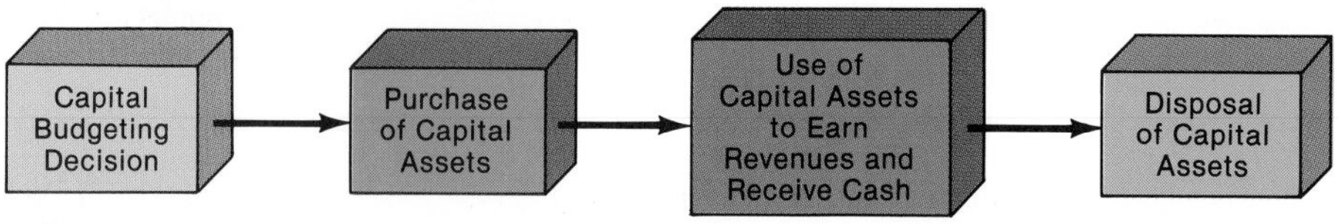

In the remainder of this chapter, we discuss three popular capital-budgeting decision models: payback, accounting rate of return, and net present value.

Payback—Equal Annual Cash Flows

Payback is the length of time it will take to recover, in net cash inflow from operations, the dollars of a capital outlay. Suppose a business pays $24,000 for a machine with an estimated useful life of six years and zero estimated residual value. Managers expect use of the machine to generate net cash inflow from operations of $6,000 annually. This increase in cash could result from an increase in revenues, a decrease in expenses, or a combination of the two.

Payback is expressed as a period of time, as shown in Exhibit 26-10.

The payback model measures how swiftly an investment dollar may be recovered. The shorter the payback period, the more attractive the asset.

A major criticism of the payback model is that it does *not* consider or measure profitability. Consequently, the payback technique can lead to an unwise decision. Suppose an alternative to the $24,000 machine is a comparable machine that also costs $24,000 but which will save $8,000 annually during its three-year life. The two machines' payback periods are computed as follows:

$$\text{Payback period for Machine 1} = \frac{\$24,000}{\$6,000} = 4 \text{ years}$$

$$\text{Payback period for Machine 2} = \frac{\$24,000}{\$8,000} = 3 \text{ years}$$

The payback criterion favors the second machine because it recovers the asset cost more quickly. But consider useful lives. Suppose the second machine's useful life is the same as its payback period—three years. Its use will merely cover cost and provide no profits. Machine 1, on the other hand, will be more profitable. It will generate net cash inflows for six years—two years beyond its payback period—which will give the company additional net cash inflow of $12,000 ($6,000 × 2 years).

EXHIBIT 26-10 *Payback—Equal Annual Net Cash Inflows*

OBJECTIVE 5

Evaluate and use three capital-budgeting models

$$\text{Payback period (P)} = \frac{\text{Amount invested (I)}}{\text{Expected annual net cash inflow from operations (0)}}$$

$$P = \frac{I}{O}$$

$$= \frac{\$24,000}{\$6,000} = 4 \text{ years}$$

Exhibit 26-11　*Payback—Unequal Annual Net Cash Inflows*

| | | Net Cash Inflow | |
| | Amount | | |
Year	Invested	Each Year	Accumulated
0	$24,000	—	—
1	—	$10,000	$10,000
2	—	8,000	18,000
3	—	5,000	23,000
3.2	—	1,000	24,000

Payback—Unequal Annual Cash Flows

The payback equation can be used only when net cash inflows are the same each period. When periodic cash flows are unequal, the payback computation has a cumulative form. Each year's net cash inflows are accumulated until the amount invested is recovered. Suppose Machine 1 in our example will produce annual net cash inflows of $10,000 in the first year, $8,000 in Year 2, and $5,000 in Years 3 through 6. Exhibit 26-11 shows the payback computation when annual cash flows are unequal.

Years 1, 2, and 3 bring in $23,000. Recovery of the amount invested ($24,000) occurs during Year 4. We can compute that payback occurs in 3.2 years:

$$P = 3 \text{ years} + \left(\frac{\substack{\text{\$1,000 needed to complete recovery} \\ \text{in Year 4}}}{\substack{\text{\$5,000 net cash inflow during the} \\ \text{year when recovery is completed}}} \times 1 \text{ year} \right) =$$

$$= 3 \text{ years} + \qquad\qquad .2 \text{ year} \qquad\qquad = 3.2 \text{ years}$$

How does a manager use the payback model in capital budgeting? Managers require that an asset or a project have a payback period shorter than its useful life. Let's take an extreme example. If a machine has a payback period of five years and a useful life of three years, the company will never earn a profit from using the asset. How much shorter than the useful life the payback period must be is a matter of personal preference. When the business is deciding between two or more assets, the asset with the shortest payback period is the most attractive—if all other factors are the same.

The payback method highlights cash flows, an important factor in business decisions. Moreover, payback is easily understood. Advocates view it as a way to eliminate proposals (with lengthy payback periods) where the project is unusually risky. A major weakness of payback is that it ignores profitability.

Accounting Rate of Return

A primary goal of business is to maximize profits. The most widely used measure of profitability is the accounting rate of return on investment. As we discussed in Chapter 19, a rate of return is computed by dividing income by the amount of the investment made to earn the income:

$$\text{Rate of Return} = \frac{\text{Income}}{\text{Investment}}$$

EXHIBIT 26-12 Accounting Rate of Return

$$\begin{array}{l} \text{Accounting} \\ \text{rate of} \\ \text{return (R)} \end{array} = \dfrac{\begin{array}{c}\text{Average annual} \\ \text{operating income} \\ \text{from investment}\end{array}}{\begin{array}{c}\text{Average} \\ \text{amount invested}\end{array}} = \dfrac{\begin{array}{c}\text{Average annual net cash} \\ \text{inflow from operations (O)}\end{array} - \begin{array}{c}\text{Annual} \\ \text{depreciation (D)}\end{array}}{\dfrac{\text{Amount invested (I)} + \text{Residual value (RV)}}{2}}$$

$$R = \frac{O - D}{\dfrac{(I + RV)}{2}}$$

$$= \frac{\$6,000 - \$4,000}{\dfrac{(\$24,000 + \$0)}{2}} = \frac{\$2,000}{\$12,000} = .167 = 16.7\%$$

In capital budgeting, the income amount is income from operations (operating income) that results from use of the asset. Operating income on an asset can be computed as net cash inflow minus depreciation on the asset. Accounting rate of return is computed in Exhibit 26-12 for the machine in the payback illustration. Recall that the machine cost $24,000 and has a useful life of six years with no estimated residual value. Annual straight-line depreciation is, therefore, $4,000 ($24,000/6 years). Use of the machine is expected to generate annual net cash inflows of $6,000.

Accounting rate of return is an *average*. It measures the average rate of return from using the asset over its entire life. The computation is average annual operating income divided by the average amount invested in the asset. If annual operating income varies by year (as in the preceding payback illustration), compute the average annual operating income over the asset's life and use this amount (as O) to compute the accounting return. Also, the book value of the asset decreases as it is used and depreciated. Thus the company's investment in the asset declines. Average investment in the asset is computed as the average of its cost and estimated residual value.

When the asset's residual value is not zero, the average amount invested will *not* be half the asset's cost. For example, assume the asset's residual value is $3,000. Annual depreciation is $3,500 [($24,000 − $3,000)/6]. The accounting rate of return computation becomes

$$R = \frac{\$6,000 - \$3,500}{\dfrac{(\$24,000 + \$3,000)}{2}} = \frac{\$2,500}{\$13,500} = .185 = 18.5\%$$

Suppose a company is purchasing a machine. The company can use the accounting rate of return in two ways to make the capital-budgeting decision. Let's assume the machine under consideration is the one in Exhibit 26-12, with an accounting rate of return of 16.7 percent. Many companies have a target rate of return that they demand of their investment projects. They invest only in assets with accounting rates of return equal to or greater than the target rate. Assume that the company's target rate is 20 percent. Would managers approve an investment in the illustrated machine, which is expected to generate an average return of 16.7 percent? No, because the asset's average annual return is less than the company's target rate.

Although the accounting rate of return model measures profitability, it has a major weakness. It does not recognize the time value of money. It fails to consider the timing of the cash outlay to purchase the asset and the timing of the annual net cash inflows. The net-present-value model is popular because it overcomes this weakness.

Net Present Value

The appendix to Chapter 16 on bonds introduced the concept of present value. The present value of $1 to be received in the future is less than $1 today. The logic is this: to receive $1 a year from now, we would pay less than $1 today. Why? Because if we pay $1 or more now to receive $1 a year later, we earn no income. Instead, we could deposit our $1 in a bank to earn interest of, say, $.08 during the year and have $1.08 a year later. We would rather have $1.08 than $1.00. The fact that we can earn income by investing money for a period of time is called the **time value of money.**

The present-value concept can be applied to the acquisition of capital assets. A company purchases an asset in order to earn revenues and receive cash. The timing of the net cash inflows from operations is important because of the time value of money. Consider two $10,000 investments. Both investments promise future cash receipts of $11,000. Investment 1 will bring in cash of $5,500 at the end of each of two years. Investment 2 will return the full $11,000 at the end of the second year. Which investment is better? Investment 1, because it brings cash home sooner, and so the cash can be invested for a longer period of time.

Net present value is a method of computing the expected net monetary gain or loss from a project by discounting all expected cash flows to the present value, using a desired rate of return. A zero or positive net present value indicates that the investment should be purchased. A negative net present value indicates that the investment should be rejected. If this model is used to compare several assets, the asset with the highest net present value is the best.

Assume that the business is considering the manufacture of two products, tape decks and VCRs. Each would require different specialized equipment costing the same amount, $1 million, and having zero residual value. Each piece of equipment is expected to have a five-year life. The two products have different patterns of expected net cash inflows:

	Annual Net Cash Inflows	
Year	Tape Decks	VCRs
1	$ 300,000	$ 500,000
2	300,000	350,000
3	300,000	300,000
4	300,000	250,000
5	300,000	40,000
Total	$1,500,000	$1,440,000

Total net cash inflows are greater if we invest in the manufacture of tape decks. However, these net cash inflows will occur in the future. In the net-present-value model, we base the capital budgeting decision on present value, not future values. In present-value language, we say that we *discount* these future cash flows to present value. Discounted cash flow is a representation of cash inflows and outflows at a common time so that they can be compared (added, subtracted, and so on) in an appropriate way for decision making.

Computation of present value requires an earnings rate. This rate, called the **discount rate,** is management's minimum desired rate of return on an investment. Synonyms are *hurdle rate, cutoff rate, required rate, cost of capital,* and *target rate.* The discount rate varies from company to company depending on the risks undertaken. The higher the risk, the higher the discount rate. Let's assume that an appropriate discount rate for these investments is 14 percent.

The manufacture and sale of tape decks is expected to generate $300,000 of net cash inflow each year — a total of $1,500,000. A stream of equal periodic amounts is called an **annuity.** The present value of an annuity is computed by multiplying the periodic amount ($300,000 annually, in this case) by the present value of an annuity of $1 from Table 2, page 652. The table indicates that the present value of an annuity of $1 for five periods discounted at 14 percent is 3.433. Exhibit 26-13 shows the computation of the present value of the net cash inflows from investing in the tape-deck project — $1,029,900.

The annual net cash inflows from investing in the manufacture of VCRs are unequal — $500,000 in Year 1, $350,000 in Year 2, and so on. Because these amounts vary by year, the present value of each annual amount is computed separately. For example, the present value of the Year 1 amount is determined by multiplying the $500,000 net cash inflow by the present value of $1 discounted at 14 percent for one period (.877 from Table 1, page 651). Year 2's net cash inflow of $350,000 is multiplied by the present value of $1 discounted at 14 percent for two periods (.769), and so on. Exhibit 26-13 shows these present-value computations.

The exhibit indicates that the VCR project has a net present value of $78,910, compared to $29,900 for the tape-deck project. The analysis favors VCRs because

EXHIBIT 26-13   *Net Present Value*

		Present Value at 14%		Net Cash Inflow		Present Value of Net Cash Inflows
Tape-Deck Project:						
Present value of equal annual net cash inflows for 5 years..........		3.433*	×	$300,000 per year	=	$ 1,029,900
Investment.........................						(1,000,000)
Net present value of the tape deck project...............						$ 29,900
VCR Project:						
Present value of net cash inflow by year:						
	Year					
	1	.877**	×	$500,000	=	$ 438,500
	2	.769	×	350,000	=	269,150
	3	.675	×	300,000	=	202,500
	4	.592	×	250,000	=	148,000
	5	.519	×	40,000	=	20,760
Total present value of net cash inflows ..						1,078,910
Investment.........................						(1,000,000)
Net present value of the VCR project ...						$ 78,910

* Present value of annuity of $1 for 5 years at 14%, Table 16-2, page 652.
** Present value of $1 for 1 year, 2 years, 3 years, and so on, at 14%, Table 16-1, page 651.

an investment in that project will earn the company's target return of 14 percent plus an additional $78,910. This expected excess is greater than the net present value of the tape-deck project, which also meets the target return of 14 percent but returns only an additional $29,900.

This example illustrates an important point about net-present-value analysis: the tape-deck project promises the greater total amount of net cash inflows. But the timing of the VCR cash flows—loaded near the beginning of the project—causes the VCR project to have a higher net present value. The VCR project is more attractive because of the time value of money. Its nearer dollars are worth more now than the more distant dollars of the tape-deck project.

Net Present Value of a Project with Residual Value

When the asset to be acquired is expected to have a residual value at the end of its useful life, that amount should also be considered in the net-present-value analysis. It must be discounted to its present value and added to the present value of the annual net cash inflows to determine the total present value of the project. The residual value is discounted as a single amount—not an annuity—because it will be received only at the end of the asset's useful life (for example, when the asset is sold).

Suppose the equipment to manufacture the tape decks (in Exhibit 26-13) is expected to be worth $100,000 at the end of its five-year life. To determine the tape-deck project's net present value, we discount $100,000 for five years at 14 percent and add the present value ($51,900), as shown in Exhibit 26-14.

Compare the tape-deck project's net present values in Exhibits 26-13 and 26-14. The residual amount raises the project's net present value to $1,081,800, which is slightly higher than the VCR project's net present value. If the VCR equipment is expected to have zero disposal value, then the tape-deck project is slightly more attractive. This illustrates the difference that residual value can make to a business decision. Although the amount may often be insignificant, it can change an investment decision.

There is a slightly different way to use present-value analysis for making capital-budgeting decisions. Suppose the company starts the decision process by determining the present values of the expected future net cash inflows from the two projects—$1,029,900 for tape decks and $1,078,910 for VCRs. Managers may ask, What is the most we can invest in the tape-deck project and still earn our target rate of return of 14 percent? With zero residual values, the answer is $1,029,900. Similarly, the maximum acceptable investment for VCRs is $1,078,910. Negotiations with the seller of the tape-deck manufacturing equipment may drive the required investment down to only $850,000. This would

EXHIBIT 26-14   *Net Present Value of a Project with Residual Value*

Tape-Deck Project	Present Value at 14%		Net Cash Inflow		Present Value of Net Cash Inflows
Present value of equal annual net cash inflows for 5 years (from Exhibit 26-13)	3.433	×	$300,000 per year	=	$1,029,900
Present value of residual value	.519*	×	$100,000	=	51,900
Present value of the project's net cash inflows					$ 1,081,800
Investment					(1,000,000)
Net present value of the tape-deck project....					$ 81,800

* Present value of $1 for 5 years at 14%, Table 16-1, page 651.

EXHIBIT 26-15   *Capital-Budgeting Decision Models*

Model	Strengths	Weaknesses
Payback	Easy to understand Based on cash flows Highlights risks	Ignores profitability and the time value of money
Accounting rate of return	Based on profitability	Ignores cash flows and the time value of money
Net present value	Based on cash flows, profitability, and the time value of money	None

increase the tape-deck project's attractiveness, especially if the cost of the VCR manufacturing equipment remains $1,000,000. In any event, managers would not want to pay more than $1,029,900 for the tape-deck equipment or more than $1,078,910 for the VCR equipment. At costs above these present-value amounts, the company would not be able to earn 14 percent on its investment.

The net-present-value model is the best of the three capital-budgeting models because it is based on cash flows and because it considers profitability and the time value of money. Each of the other two capital-budgeting models ignores two of these factors. In actual practice, managers often use more than one model to gain different perspectives on risks and returns. Exhibit 26-15 summarizes the strengths and weaknesses of the payback, accounting rate of return, and net-present-value techniques.

Computers in Business Decision Analysis _____

Computers are ideally suited for decision analysis. They can compute the outcomes of alternative courses of action instantly and without computational error. Consider the net-present-value analysis of three possible investments. Suppose the assets under consideration promise irregular net cash inflows for 20 years. The 60 (3 × 20) present-value computations would be time consuming and present a great possibility for error. However, a computer can be programmed to handle these multiple computations. The manager can then use the program over and over. He can alter the annual cash flows, the earnings (discount) rate, and the timing of the cash flows. With a computer, the manager simply enters the data, and the entire analysis is performed in seconds. Chapter 28 provides an exercise and problems of this nature.

Consider the special sales order decision. Many companies store their cost data in computers. The manager can enter the special sale price and call up the variable expenses and any fixed expenses that will change because of the special sale. The change in operating income is computed automatically. If the computed income is high enough, the manager can accept the order. If the income is too low, the manager can enter a revised sale price and compute the revised operating income. By trying different sale prices, she can come up with a range of acceptable options. Armed with this knowledge, the company may propose a different sale price to the buyer. More knowledge places the company in a stronger bargaining position. Microcomputers and spreadsheet programs like Lotus 1-2-3, AppleWorks, and SuperCalc bring this analytical power even to small companies.

Summary Problem for Your Review

The data for a machine follow.

Cost of machine $48,000
Estimated residual value. 6,000
Estimated annual net cash inflow 13,000
Estimated useful life . . . . 5 years
Annual rate of return required. 16%

Required

1. Compute the payback period.
2. Compute the accounting rate of return.
3. Compute the net present value (NPV).
4. Indicate whether each decision model leads to purchase or rejection of this investment. Would you decide to buy the machine? Give your reason.

SOLUTION TO REVIEW PROBLEM

Requirement 1

$$P = \frac{I}{O} = \frac{\$48,000}{\$13,000} = 3.7 \text{ years}$$

Requirement 2

$$R = \frac{O - D}{\dfrac{I + RV}{2}} = \frac{\$13,000 - \$8,400^*}{\dfrac{\$48,000 + \$6,000}{2}} = \frac{\$4,600}{\dfrac{\$54,000}{2}}$$

$$= \frac{\$4,600}{\$27,000} = .170 = 17\%$$

$$^* D = \frac{\$48,000 - \$6,000}{5 \text{ years}} = \$8,400$$

Requirement 3

Present value of equal annual net cash inflows ($13,000 × 3.274**) . . . . $ 42,562
Present value of residual value ($6,000 × .476***)   2,856
Present value of the machine   45,418
Investment   48,000
Net present value. . . . . $ (2,582)

** Present value of annuity of $1 for 5 years at 16%, Table 16-2, page 652.
*** Present value of $1 for 5 years at 16%, Table 16-1, page 651.

Requirement 4

Payback: Purchase machine because payback period (3.7 years) is less than useful life (5 years).

Accounting rate of return: Purchase machine because return on machine of 17 percent exceeds target rate of 16 percent.

Net present value: Reject machine because it has negative net present value.

Decision: Reject machine because of negative net present value. The net-present-value model considers cash flows, profitability, and the time value of money. Each of the other models ignores two of these factors.

Summary

Special decisions are those with long-term consequences. In making these decisions, managers focus on differences among the alternative courses of action. Often historical data are irrelevant, except for helping to develop the *expected future data* for the decision analysis. The approach to making special decisions is called the *relevant information approach.*

Whether to *delete a product, which product to emphasize,* whether to *make or buy* a part, how to make the *best use of facilities,* and whether to *sell inventory in its present condition or process it further* are decisions with long-range effects. In each decision, the best alternative is the one that will produce the largest increase in income from operations.

A *contribution margin income statement,* which shows variable expenses and fixed expenses, is helpful to decision analysis. The change in *variable expenses* is always a factor because variable expenses change in direct response to changes in volume. Fixed expenses may or may not change, depending on the circumstances. Failure to account for *fixed expenses* correctly is a common mistake. When fixed expenses do not change, they do not enter the analysis. But when they do change, their effect must be considered.

In making special decisions, managers also consider nonquantitative factors, like the long-run effect on customers and competitors. Opportunity cost is another factor in special decisions. *Opportunity cost* is the maximum profit forgone by following a specific course of action. Thus it differs from ordinary accounting costs.

Capital budgeting helps managers make long-range decisions. *Payback, accounting rate of return,* and *net present value* are three models for making capital budgeting decisions. Net present value is the best of these because it is based on cash flows and also considers profitability and the time value of money. Payback is the simplest. Companies may use more than one method in practice. Computers are ideally suited for special decision analysis because they can help predict the outcomes of various courses of action.

Self-Study Questions

Test your understanding of the chapter by marking the best answer for each of the following questions.

1. Relevant information for decision analysis (*pp. 1005, 1006*)
   a. Remains constant regardless of the alternative courses of action
   b. Is used in some but not all business decisions
   c. Varies with the alternative courses of action
   d. Excludes direct materials and direct labor because they are fixed
2. Assume fixed costs remain unchanged. To decide whether to make a sale at a special price, compare (*p. 1007*)
   a. Expected change in gross margin (sales minus cost of goods sold) with and without the sale
   b. Expected change in revenue with expected change in fixed expenses
   c. Expected change in revenue with expected change in selling expenses
   d. Expected change in revenue with expected change in variable expenses
3. To decide whether to delete a product, a manager should (*pp. 1009–1011*)

a. Consider all costs that change
b. Consider only variable costs
c. Consider all costs that remain unchanged
d. Consider only fixed costs

4. Pontchatrain's $.47 cost per unit (incurred in manufacturing its inventory) includes fixed cost of $.19. Another company offers to sell the product to Pontchatrain for $.35 per unit. The make-or-buy decision hinges on the comparison between Pontchatrain's $.47 manufacturing cost and the total cost if the products are purchased from the other company. That total cost is *(p. 1013)*
   a. $.28   c. $.54
   b. $.35   d. $.66

5. Sunk costs are *(p. 1015)*
   a. Relevant to most business decisions
   b. The cost of the next-best alternative
   c. Equal to the residual value of a plant asset
   d. Irrelevant to most business decisions

6. Capital budgeting is a (an) *(p. 1017)*
   a. Depreciation method   c. Alternative to the payback method
   b. Short-run decision   d. Way to make long-range investment decisions

7. A machine costs $45,000. It is expected to earn operating income of $6,000 and to generate $7,500 net cash inflow annually. Expected residual value is $5,000 at the end of five years. What is the asset's payback period? *(p. 1018)*
   a. 5 years   c. 7½ years
   b. 6 years   d. 9 years

8. The accounting rate of return of the machine in the preceding question is *(p. 1020)*
   a. 15 percent   c. 26.7 percent
   b. 24 percent   d. 37.5 percent

9. The time value of money is an important part of *(p. 1021)*
   a. Payback analysis   c. Net-present-value analysis
   b. Accounting rate of return analysis   d. All capital-budgeting methods

10. Payback analysis and net-present-value analysis indicate that a particular investment should be rejected, but the accounting rate of return is favorable. What is the wisest investment decision? Give your reason. *(p. 1024)*
    a. Reject because of net-present-value analysis
    b. Reject because of payback analysis
    c. Accept because of favorable accounting rate of return
    d. Cannot decide because of differences among the methods' results

Answers to the self-study questions are at the end of the chapter.

Accounting Vocabulary

accounting rate of return *(p. 1019)*, annuity *(p. 1022)*, capital budgeting *(p. 1017)*, constraint *(p. 1012)*, decision model *(p. 1017)*, discount rate *(p. 1022)*, limiting factor *(p. 1012)*, net present value *(p. 1021)*, opportunity cost *(p. 1015)*, payback *(p. 1018)*, relevant information *(p. 1005)*, sunk cost *(p. 1015)*, time value of money *(p. 1021)*.

ASSIGNMENT MATERIAL _____

Questions

1. How do special decisions differ from ordinary day-to-day business decisions? Give examples.

2. Briefly describe how relevant information is used in making special decisions.
3. Discuss the roles of expected future data and historical data in special decision analysis. On which set of data are special decisions based?
4. Identify two income statement formats. Which is more useful for deciding whether to accept a special sales order? Why?
5. Identify two income amounts on which special decisions are based.
6. What is "special" about a special sales order? How does a manager make a special sales order decision?
7. Identify two long-run factors to be considered in making a special sales order decision.
8. What is the similarity between a special sales order decision and a decision to delete a product? What is the difference?
9. Which type of cost is more likely to change in a special decision situation, a fixed cost or a variable cost? Can both costs change?
10. Outline how to decide which product to emphasize when there is a limiting factor. Give four examples of limiting factors.
11. Which is relevant to special decision analysis, an asset's sunk cost or its residual value? Give your reason.
12. What is opportunity cost? How does it differ from an ordinary accounting cost?
13. Give an example of a decision that would be based on opportunity cost. Discuss the role of opportunity cost in making this decision.
14. What are decision models? Why are they helpful in capital budgeting?
15. What is capital budgeting? Are capital-budgeting decisions made before or after long-term assets are purchased?
16. Name three capital-budgeting decision models. State the strengths and the weaknesses of each model. Which model is best? Why?
17. Name the capital-budgeting model that fits each description:
     a. based on operating income only; b. based on cash flows without regard for their timing or for profitability; c. based on the time value of money.
18. How is payback period computed? How does the estimated useful life of a capital asset affect the payback computation?
19. Your company is considering purchasing a manufacturing plant with an expected useful life of 15 years. What is the maximum acceptable payback period on this plant? Justify your answer.
20. How can managers use accounting rate of return in capital-budgeting decisions?
21. How can accounting rate of return be computed when the annual amounts of operating income are expected to vary each period?
22. State why a positive net present value indicates an attractive investment project and a negative net present value indicates an unattractive project.
23. Which capital-budgeting strategy is best? (1) Pick out the best model and use it exclusively. (2) Use all three models. Support your answer.
24. A company is investing in a 20-year project. The managers, who use the net-present-value model for capital-budgeting decisions, expect the net cash inflow amounts to vary considerably each year. How can a computer help the managers decide the amount to invest in this project?

Exercises

Exercise 26-1 *Accept or reject a special sales order?*

All-Star Marketing approaches McDade Manufacturing Company with a special offer. All-Star wishes to purchase 100,000 monogrammed golf balls for a special promotional campaign. All-Star offers $.37 per ball—a total of $37,000. McDade's total manufacturing cost per ball is $.42, broken down as follows:

Variable costs:	
Direct material	$.08
Direct labor	.03
Variable overhead.........................	.11
Total variable cost........................	.22
Fixed overhead cost	.20
Total cost.................................	$.42

Required

Prepare a quick summary to help determine whether McDade should accept the special sales order. Assume McDade has excess capacity.

Exercise 26-2   Retain or drop a product line (fixed costs unchanged)?

Top managers of Mercedes, Inc., are alarmed that operating income is so low. They are considering dropping the building materials product line. Company accountants have prepared the following analysis to help make this decision:

	Total	Hardware	Building Materials
Sales.....................................	$460,000	$280,000	$ 180,000
Variable expenses	240,000	140,000	100,000
Contribution margin	220,000	140,000	80,000
Fixed expenses:			
Manufacturing	120,000	70,000	50,000
Selling and administrative.................	90,000	55,000	35,000
Total fixed expenses......................	210,000	125,000	85,000
Operating income (loss)	$ 10,000	$ 15,000	$ (5,000)

Fixed costs will not change if the company stops selling building materials.

Required

Prepare a quick summary to show whether Mercedes should drop the building materials product line.

Exercise 26-3   Retain or drop a product line (fixed costs change)?

Refer to the data of Exercise 26-2. Assume that Mercedes can avoid $25,000 of fixed expenses by dropping the building materials product line. Prepare a quick summary to show whether Mercedes should stop selling building materials.

Exercise 26-4   Which product to emphasize?

Belvedere Fashions sells both designer and moderately priced women's wear. Profits have fluctuated recently, and top management is deciding which product line to emphasize. Accountants provide the following relevant data:

	Designer	Moderately Priced
Per item:		
Average sale price	$100	$60
Average variable expenses.............................	35	18
Average contribution margin..........................	$ 65	$42
Average contribution margin ratio	65%	70%

The store, in Montclair, New Jersey, has 8,000 square feet of floor space. If moderately priced goods are emphasized, 400 items can be displayed in the store. Only 300 designer items could be displayed for sale.

Required

Prepare an analysis to show which product to emphasize.

Exercise 26-5 *Make or buy?*

The production process of Ford Products Company uses an electronic control that has the following manufacturing cost per unit:

Direct material	$2.60
Direct labor.	.55
Variable overhead	.62
Fixed overhead.	2.04
Total manufacturing cost per unit.	$5.81

Another company has offered to sell Ford the electronic control for $4.19 per unit. If Ford buys the controls from the outside supplier, the manufacturing facilities that will be idle cannot be used for any other purpose in the business. Should Ford make or buy the electronic controls? Show how you made this decision.

Exercise 26-6 *Best use of facilities?*

Refer to Exercise 26-5. Assume that Ford needs 20,000 of the electronic controls. By purchasing them from the outside supplier, Ford could use its idle facilities to manufacture another product that can be sold for a $15,200 profit. Identify the *net* costs that Ford may incur to acquire 20,000 electronic controls under three alternative plans. Which alternative makes the best use of Ford's facilities? Support your answer with analysis.

Exercise 26-7 *Scrap inventory or process further?*

Rotan Cabinet Works has damaged some custom cabinets, which cost the company $6,000 to manufacture. Raphael Rotan, the owner, is considering two options for disposing of this inventory. One plan is to sell the cabinets as damaged inventory for $1,900. The alternative is to spend an additional $600 to repair the damage and expect to sell the cabinets for $3,100. How should Rotan dispose of this inventory? Support your decision with an analysis that shows expected net revenue under each alternative.

Exercise 26-8 *Identifying opportunity costs*

Identify the opportunity cost of each alternative in the following cases:

Case A: Lisa Malone's annual salary as an accountant with Eastman Kodak is $32,000. She has received a $37,000 offer from Procter & Gamble.
Case B: Dallas Country Club can rent its swimming pool for a private party at a rate of $2,500, which includes food and drinks. If the pool is left open for members only, the club expects to sell food and drinks totaling $2,000.
Case C: Obsolete inventory that cost $42,000 can be sold for $2,600 in its present condition or reworked at a cost of $1,400 and sold for $3,800.

Exercise 26-9 *Payback analysis of an investment—equal cash flows*

Chin & McQuade, Inc., is considering acquiring a manufacturing plant. The purchase price is $400,000. The owners believe the plant will generate net cash inflows of $65,000 annually. It will have to be replaced in five years. Use the payback model to determine whether Chin & McQuade should purchase this plant.

Exercise 26-10 *Payback analysis of an investment—unequal cash flows*

Skyhawk Manufacturing is adding a new product line that will require an investment of $870,000. Managers estimate that this investment will generate net cash inflows of $110,000 the first year, $180,000 the second year, and $200,000 each year thereafter. What is the payback period for this investment? Compute a fraction of a year if necessary.

Exercise 26-11 *Accounting rate of return analysis of investments*

FanMaster Corporation is shopping for new equipment. Managers are considering two investments. Equipment manufactured by Ling, Inc., costs $270,000 and will last for five years, with no residual value. The Ling equipment should generate annual operating income of $24,000. Equipment manufactured by Johnson Controls is priced at $310,000 and will remain useful for six years. It promises annual operating income of $32,000, and its expected residual value is $30,000.

Required

Which equipment offers the higher accounting rate of return?

Exercise 26-12 *Net present-value analysis of investments*

Use the net-present-value model to determine whether Rust Manufacturing should invest in the following projects:

Project A costs $550,000 and offers 10 annual net cash inflows of $100,000. Rust demands an annual return of 12 percent on investments of this nature.

Project B costs $330,000 and offers 7 annual net cash inflows of $75,000. Rust requires an annual return of 14 percent on projects like B.

Exercise 26-13 *Present-value analysis of investments*

Refer to the data of Exercise 26-12. What is the maximum acceptable price to pay for projects A and B?

Problems *(Group A)*

Problem 26-1A *Accept or reject a special sales order?*

Hillcrest Manufacturing Company's contribution margin income statement for the most recent month reports the following:

Sales—units.	38,000
Sales	$95,000
Variable expenses:	
Manufacturing	$19,000
Selling and administrative	27,000
Total variable expenses	46,000
Contribution margin	49,000
Fixed expenses:	
Manufacturing	29,000
Selling and administrative	8,000
Total fixed expenses	37,000
Income from operations.	$12,000

American Marketing Associates wishes to buy 7,000 industrial belts from Hillcrest. Acceptance of the offer will not increase selling and administrative expenses. American has offered $1.60 per belt, which is considerably below the normal sale price of $2.50.

Required

1. Prepare a quick summary to help determine whether Hillcrest should accept this special sales order.
2. Prepare a total analysis to show Hillcrest's operating income with and without the special sales order.
3. Identify long-run factors that Hillcrest should consider in deciding whether to accept the special sales order.

Problem 26-2A *Retain or drop a product line?*

The income statement of Mazzio's Pasta Company highlights the losses of the ravioli division:

	Total	All Other Products	Ravioli
Sales...............................	$920,000	$630,000	$290,000
Cost of goods sold:			
Variable	$170,000	$100,000	$ 70,000
Fixed................................	140,000	90,000	50,000
Total cost of goods sold..................	310,000	190,000	120,000
Gross margin............................	610,000	440,000	170,000
Selling and administrative expenses:			
Variable	410,000	270,000	140,000
Fixed................................	150,000	80,000	70,000
Total selling and administrative expenses	560,000	350,000	210,000
Operating income (loss)	$ 50,000	$ 90,000	$ (40,000)

Foge Mazzio, owner of the company, is considering deleting the ravioli product line. Accountants for the company estimate that dropping ravioli will decrease fixed cost of goods sold by $30,000 and decrease fixed selling and administrative expenses by $40,000.

Required

1. Prepare a quick summary to show whether Mazzio's should drop the ravioli product line.
2. Prepare a total analysis to show Mazzio's operating income with and without the ravioli division. Prepare the income statement in contribution margin format.

Problem 26-3A *Which product to emphasize?*

Copeland Appliances is located in Cody, Wyoming. The business specializes in washers/dryers and televisions. Jim and Mary Sue Copeland, the owners, are expanding the store, and they are deciding which product line to emphasize. To make this decision, they assemble the following data, which suggest that televisions, with the higher contribution margin ratio, are more profitable:

	Washers/Dryers	Televisions
Per unit:		
Sale price.....................................	$450	$320
Variable expenses.............................	235	136
Contribution margin...........................	$215	$184
Contribution margin ratio	47.8%	57.5%

After the renovation, the store will have 6,400 square feet of floor space. By devoting the new floor space to washers/dryers, the Copelands can display 40 units of merchandise in the store. If televisions are emphasized, they can display only 32 units.

Required

1. Identify the limiting factor for Copeland Appliances.
2. Prepare an analysis to show which product to emphasize. Round contribution margin per square foot to five decimal places.

Problem 26-4A *Make or buy/best use of facilities?*

Western Corporation manufactures snowmobiles. Currently the company makes the seats. The cost of producing 2,000 seats each year is

Direct material.	$ 3,900
Direct labor	2,800
Variable overhead.	1,040
Fixed overhead	5,110
Total manufacturing costs.	$12,850

Racine Corporation can make the seats for $5 each. Western would pay $.22 per unit to transport the seats to its manufacturing plant and add its own Western insignia at a cost of $.06 per unit.

Required

1. Western accountants estimate that purchasing the seats from Racine will enable the company to avoid $1,800 of fixed overhead. Prepare an analysis to show whether Western should make or buy the seats.
2. Assume the Western factory space freed up by the company's purchasing the seats from Racine can be used to manufacture another product that can be sold for a $2,360 profit. Fixed costs will not change. Prepare an analysis to show which alternative makes the best use of Western's factory space: (a) make, (b) buy and leave facilities idle, or (c) buy and make another product.

Problem 26-5A *Sell or process further?*

The refining of crude oil by Gulf Oil Corporation produces a variety of petroleum products. Assume that Gulf has spent $240,000 to refine 60,000 gallons of petroleum distillate. Suppose Gulf can sell the distillate for $5.75 a gallon. Alternatively, Gulf can process the distillate further and produce cleaner for tape heads in cassette decks. The additional processing will cost another $1.33 a gallon. The tape-head cleaner can be sold for $7.50 a gallon. To make this sale, Gulf must pay a sale commission of $.10 a gallon and a transportation charge of $.35 a gallon.

Required

1. Identify the sunk cost in this situation. Is the sunk cost relevant to Gulf's decision?
2. Using the three-column format of Exhibit 26-9, prepare an analysis to indicate whether Gulf should sell the distillate or process it into tape-head cleaner for cassette decks. Show the expected net revenue difference between the two alternatives.

Problem 26-6A *Capital budgeting decision by three methods*

Lakeway Resorts, Inc., west of Austin in the hill country of Texas, is considering an investment. The architectural plan calls for a purchase price of $1,850,000. Top managers of Lakeway believe the new facility will generate annual net cash inflows of $450,000 for eight years. Architects and engineers estimate that the facility will remain useful for eight years and have a residual value of $600,000. The stockholders of Lakeway Resorts demand an annual return of 16 percent on investments of this nature.

Required

1. Compute the payback period, the accounting rate of return, and the net present value of this investment.
2. Make a recommendation to Lakeway management as to whether the company should invest in this project.

Problem 26-7A   *Capital budgeting decision by three methods*

T. J. Cinnamon, Inc., features the original gourmet cinnamon roll. The company is considering two possible expansion plans. Plan A includes opening six stores at a cost of $2,100,000. This investment is expected to generate net cash inflows of $500,000 each year for seven years, which is the estimated life of the store properties. Because of the location, estimated residual value is zero. Under Plan B, Cinnamon would open four stores at a cost of $1,600,000. Expected annual net cash inflows are $350,000, with residual value of $200,000 at the end of seven years, the estimated useful life of these stores. Cinnamon's top managers require an annual return of 14 percent.

Required

1. Compute the payback period, the accounting rate of return, and the net present value of these two investment plans.
2. Make a recommendation to T. J. Cinnamon management as to whether the company should invest in these projects.

(Group B)

Problem 26-1B   *Accept or reject a special sales order?*

Martinez Fabricating Corporation manufactures toys in Monterrey, Mexico. Martinez's contribution margin income statement for the most recent month contains the following:

Sales—units	630,000
Sales	$ 63,000
Variable expenses:	
Manufacturing	$ 12,600
Selling and administrative	14,900
Total variable expenses	27,500
Contribution margin	35,500
Fixed expenses:	
Manufacturing	17,400
Selling and administrative	11,300
Total fixed expenses	28,700
Income from operations	$ 6,800

Pan American Promotions, Inc., wishes to buy 120,000 toys from Martinez. Acceptance of the offer will not increase selling and administrative expenses. Pan American has offered $.06 per toy, which is considerably below the normal sale price of $.10.

Required

1. Prepare a quick summary to help determine whether Martinez should accept this special sales order.
2. Prepare a total analysis to show Martinez's operating income with and without the special sales order.
3. Identify long-run factors that Martinez should consider in deciding whether to accept the special sales order.

Problem 26-2B   *Retain or drop a product line?*

Members of the board of directors of Smoke Detector Corporation have received the following income statement for the year just ended:

	Total	Industrial Products	Household Products
Sales	$866,000	$445,000	$421,000
Cost of goods sold:			
Variable	$119,000	$ 64,000	$ 55,000
Fixed......................................	327,000	241,000	86,000
Total cost of goods sold....................	446,000	305,000	141,000
Gross margin	420,000	140,000	280,000
Selling and administrative expenses:			
Variable	178,000	86,000	92,000
Fixed......................................	89,000	58,000	31,000
Total selling and administrative expenses	267,000	144,000	123,000
Operating income (loss).....................	$153,000	$ (4,000)	$157,000

Members of the board are alarmed that the industrial products division is losing money. They commission a study to determine whether the company should delete the industrial products line. Company accountants estimate that dropping industrial products will decrease fixed cost of goods sold by $46,000 and decrease fixed selling and administrative expenses by $19,000.

Required

1. Prepare a quick summary to show whether Smoke Detector should drop the industrial products line.
2. Prepare a total analysis to show Smoke Detector's operating income with and without industrial products. Prepare the income statement in contribution margin format.

Problem 26-3B   *Which product to emphasize?*

Sutfin Manufacturing produces two lines of household appliances in Seattle, Washington: deluxe and standard models. Art and Joan Sutfin, the owners, are expanding the plant, and they are deciding which product line to emphasize. To make this decision, they assemble the following data, which suggest that the two product lines with the same contribution margin ratio are equally profitable:

	Deluxe	Standard
Per unit:		
Sale price	$40	$25.00
Variable expenses	12	7.50
Contribution margin.....................	$28	$17.50
Contribution margin ratio................	70%	70%

After the plant expansion, the factory will have production capacity of 1,200 machine hours per month. By devoting the machine hours to deluxe appliances, the plant can manufacture six units of merchandise each hour. If standard appliances are emphasized, they can produce eight units per hour.

Required

1. Identify the limiting factor for Sutfin Manufacturing.
2. Prepare an analysis to show which product to emphasize.

Problem 26-4B   *Make or buy/best use of facilities?*

Glastron Company manufactures ski boats. Currently the company makes the seat covers. The cost of producing 1,000 seat covers each year is

Direct material.	$1,400
Direct labor	1,100
Variable overhead.	760
Fixed overhead	2,210
Total manufacturing cost per unit	$5,470

Belton Corporation can make the seat covers for $3 each. Glastron would pay $.14 per unit to transport the seat covers to its manufacturing plant and add its own Galstron label at a cost of $.05 per seat cover.

Required

1. Glastron accountants estimate that purchasing the seat covers from Belton will enable the company to avoid $700 of fixed overhead. Prepare an analysis to show whether Glastron should make or buy the seat covers.
2. Assume the Glastron factory space freed up by the company's purchasing the seat covers from Belton can be used to manufacture another product that can be sold for a $1,390 profit. Fixed costs will not change. Prepare an analysis to show which alternative makes the best use of Galstron's factory space: (a) make, (b) buy and leave facilities idle, or (c) buy and make another product.

Problem 26-5B   *Sell or process further?*

DuPont Corporation's manufacture of chemicals produces a wide variety of products. Assume that DuPont has spent $105,000 to refine 84,000 gallons of acetone, which can be sold for $3.16 a gallon. Alternatively, DuPont can process the acetone further and produce 77,000 gallons of lacquer thinner that can be sold for $4.80 a gallon. The additional processing will cost $.89 a gallon. To sell the lacquer thinner, DuPont must pay a transportation charge of $.23 a gallon and administrative expenses of $.16 a gallon.

Required

1. Identify the sunk cost in this situation. Is the sunk cost relevant to DuPont's decision?
2. Using the three-column format of Exhibit 26-9, prepare an analysis to indicate whether DuPont should sell the acetone or process it into lacquer thinner. Show the expected net revenue difference between the two alternatives.

Problem 26-6B   *Capital-budgeting decision by three methods*

Auburn Investments, Inc., operates a resort near Geneva in the Finger Lakes region of New York. The company is considering an expansion. The architectural plan calls for a construction cost of $5,200,000. Top managers of Auburn believe the expansion will generate annual net cash inflows of $500,000 for 10 years. Architects and engineers estimate that the new facilities will remain useful for 10 years and have a residual value of $2,400,000. The stockholders of Auburn Investments demand an annual return of 12 percent on investments of this nature.

Required

1. Compute the payback period, the accounting rate of return, and the net present value of this investment.
2. Make a recommendation to Auburn management as to whether the company should invest in this project.

Problem 26-7B *Capital budgeting decision by three methods*

Whole Foods, Inc., operates a chain of grocery stores that specialize in health foods. The company is considering two possible expansion plans. Plan A includes opening three stores at a cost of $4,800,000. This plan is expected to generate net cash inflows of $400,000 each year for 20 years, the estimated life of the store properties. Estimated residual value is $3,000,000. Under Plan B, Whole Foods would open eight smaller stores at a cost of $7,200,000. Expected annual net cash inflows are $750,000, with zero residual value at the end of 19 years. Whole Foods's top managers require an annual return of 8 percent.

Required

1. Compute the payback period, the accounting rate of return, and the net present value of these two investment plans.
2. Make a recommendation to Whole Foods owners as to whether the company should invest in these projects.

Decision Problem

Selecting Between Two Investment Projects

The capital-budgeting committee of McBride Corporation is evaluating two real estate investment projects. Project 1 is a shopping center in Sioux Falls, South Dakota, and Project 2 is a parking garage in Minneapolis. Estimated data for the two projects follow.

	Project 1			Project 2		
Year	Net Cash Inflow	Operating Income	Residual Value	Net Cash Inflow	Operating Income	Residual Value
1	$181,000	$105,000		$87,000	$68,000	
2	202,000	182,000		87,000	68,000	
3	234,000	203,000		87,000	68,000	
4	166,000	144,000		87,000	68,000	$31,000
5	116,000	98,000				
6	85,000	59,000	$93,000			

Project 1 requires an investment of $700,000, and Project 2 costs $250,000. McBride managers demand a 14 percent annual return on real estate investments.

Required

1. Compute the payback period, the accounting rate of return, and the net present value of the two investment projects.
2. Which capital-budgeting model is best? Give your reason.
3. McBride will invest in only one of these projects. Based on your analysis, make an investment recommendation to McBride managers.

Answers to Self-Study Questions

1. c
2. d

3. a
4. c Fixed cost ($.19) + Cost of outside units ($.35) = $.54
5. d
6. d
7. b $45,000/$7,500 = 6 years
8. b $\dfrac{\$6,000}{(\$45,000 + \$5,000)/2} = \dfrac{\$6,000}{\$25,000} = 24\%$
9. c
10. a

27

Income Taxes and Their Effects on Business Decisions

LEARNING OBJECTIVES
After studying this chapter, you should be able to

1 Identify the important components in determining taxable income

2 Compute the income tax of an individual

3 Use some special tax rules for corporations

4 Compute the income tax of a corporation

5 Record a corporation's income tax

6 Consider the effects of income taxes on business decisions

7 Discuss the use of microcomputers in tax work

Taxes are important to everyone. National tax policy affects business decisions, voting patterns, the rate of inflation, pollution control, and many other aspects of daily life. Most federal programs—social welfare, national defense, education, and the courts—are financed in some way by our tax dollars.

There are many kinds of taxes. For example, *property taxes* are levied on land, buildings, and other property. We pay retail *sales taxes* on most goods and many services. *Excise taxes* apply to a wide variety of items, including gasoline, beer, tires, fishing equipment, and air travel. Some taxes are levied by the federal government, others by states, cities, and counties. Some taxes are directed toward a special purpose. For example, property taxes may finance public education, and taxes on tires, trucks, trailers, and gasoline help support highway maintenance. Other taxes, like sales taxes, are more general purpose in nature. They are used to finance a host of state and city government functions.

The **income tax,** which is the subject of this chapter, is a general-purpose tax levied on the income of the taxpayer. Entirely separate from all other taxes, it is the federal government's largest source of revenue.

Accounting enters the tax picture by helping to determine the amount of income to be taxed. Many differences exist between *accounting income,* which we have discussed throughout this book, and *taxable income,* which is used to compute income tax. However, the starting points in determining accounting income and taxable income are similar, and many accountants specialize in income taxation. These specialists help taxpayers compute their income taxes and plan their activities so as to minimize their tax burden. In a landmark case, Judge Learned Hand wrote that "nobody owes any public duty to pay more [taxes] than the law demands." An understanding of income taxes, therefore, is an important part of financial planning.

This chapter discusses income taxes from the perspective of the taxpayer—people like you, your family and friends, the local automobile dealer, and corporations like Coca-Cola Company and IBM. Our discussion is a practical introduction to some of the steps in computing the amount of income tax that individuals and corporations pay to the government. This chapter provides a foundation for any future tax courses you may take.

History and Operation of the Income Tax

The federal government first used an income tax for a brief period during the Civil War. Our present income tax system began in 1913 with ratification of the Sixteenth Amendment to the United States Constitution. That amendment removed the requirement that a national income tax be based on state population. It opened the door for the federal government to base a tax on the personal income of individual citizens. Initially the purpose of the income tax was simply to raise money for national defense and the operation of government. Over the years, the goals of our tax system have broadened to include stimulating economic growth, curtailing inflation, and providing for the health and welfare of the aged and the disadvantaged.

From time to time, Congress passes new tax laws known as *revenue acts*. As these revenue acts and the related interpretations accumulate, they are summarized periodically in tax documents called *internal revenue codes*. Internal revenue codes were published in 1939, 1954, and 1986. Today we operate under the Internal Revenue Code of 1986.

Administration of the federal tax system is the responsibility of the Internal Revenue Service (IRS), a division of the Treasury Department of the United States government. Congress passes tax laws, and the Treasury Department publishes its interpretations of the tax law, called Treasury Regulations, and administers the tax system. The federal courts make final decisions on disputes between taxpayers and the government. (Interestingly, it is often easier to prosecute criminals for breaking income tax laws than for committing other offenses.)

In its most basic form, the amount of income tax is computed by multiplying taxable income by the tax rate. For example, a tax rate of 15 percent applied to taxable income of $20,000 results in income tax of $3,000. Income tax rates have varied over the years. Initially rates were quite low. The Underwood Act in 1913 set tax rates between 1 percent and 7 percent. A person with taxable income of $15,000 paid income tax of 1 percent, or $150. Today, a taxpayer with this same amount of taxable income pays income tax of 15 percent, or $2,250.

EXHIBIT 27-1 *Minimum and Maximum Income Tax Rates for Individual Taxpayers*

	Tax Rates	
	Minimum	**Maximum**
1913 tax law	1%	7%
During World War II	23	94
During most of the 1970s	14	70
Prior to 1986 tax law	11	50
1986 tax law	15	28

Generally, tax rates climb during wartime to help finance the war effort. Peace usually brings lower rates, although tax rates fluctuate. Some taxpayers want more government programs, which cause higher taxes. Others want lower taxes, which would mean cutting back government programs. The final result is the combination of government programs and income tax policy that reflects the will of the people. Exhibit 27-1 shows a sampling of income tax rates that have been in effect in the United States since 1913.

Most states and some cities have an income tax that is patterned in some way after the federal income tax. In this chapter, we focus on the *federal* income tax.

Classes and Filing Status of Taxpayers

Tax law identifies four major classes of taxpayers: individuals, corporations, estates, and trusts. In this chapter, we focus on the taxation of individuals and corporations.

Each taxpayer reports income and shows the computation of income tax on a document called a **tax return.** Submitting the completed document to the IRS is called *filing a tax return.* An individual must file his or her tax return within three and one-half months after the end of the tax year. A person who uses the calendar year (as most do) must file a 1990 income tax return by April 15, 1991. Corporations have only two and one-half months after the year's end to file their tax returns. A corporation with a fiscal year ending June 30, 1990, must file its 1990 tax return by September 15 of that year.

An individual taxpayer must use a particular *filing status.* This status determines the tax rates used to compute the amount of income tax. There are four filing statuses for individuals. Married couples may file a combined tax return, called a *joint return.* Alternatively, each marriage partner may file his or her own tax return separately, a practice called *separate returns. Single status* applies to a single individual who does not qualify as a head of household. The fourth filing status, called *head of household,* applies to a single individual with the opportunity to claim certain categories of dependents. **Dependents** are persons who receive more than half their support from another individual—in our discussion, from the taxpayer. Taxpayers who file joint returns pay at the lowest income tax rates, with increasing rates applying to head of household, single, and separate returns, in that order.

A business organized as a proprietorship pays no income tax. Its income is taxed directly to the proprietor. A partnership is taxed the same way. The business itself incurs no income tax, but each partner includes in personal taxable income his or her share of partnership income. Even though the partnership pays no income tax, it must file a tax return with the IRS to list the income of the business and of each partner. This *information tax return* permits the IRS to trace the income of the partnership to the tax returns of the individual partners. In addition to earnings from their business, proprietors and partners must pay tax on their other income, such as interest, dividends, and gains on the sale of investments.

In the eyes of income tax law, a corporation is a separate taxable entity. Corporations pay tax on their income directly to the IRS regardless of whether they distribute any dividends to their stockholders. If the corporation does pay dividends to its owners (the stockholders), the stockholders then pay individual income tax on this dividend income. Many people believe this "double taxation" of corporation income is unfair.

EXHIBIT 27-2   *An Individual's Income Tax Computation*

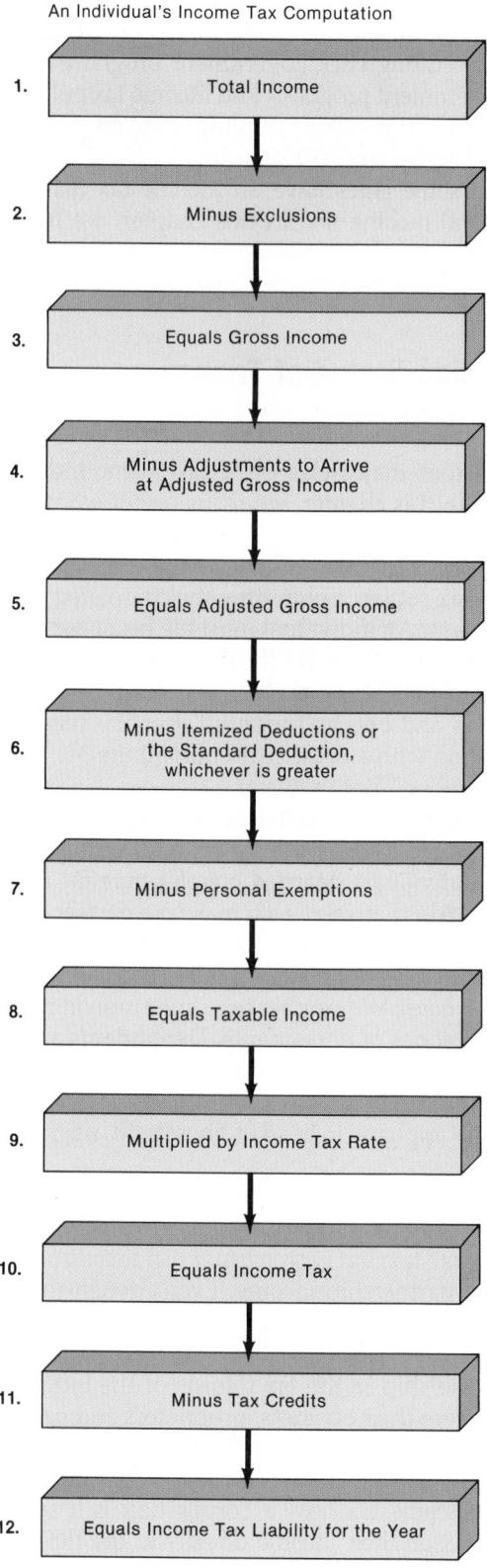

An Individual's Income Tax Computation

OBJECTIVE 1

Identify the important components in determining taxable income

1. Total Income

2. Minus Exclusions

3. Equals Gross Income

4. Minus Adjustments to Arrive at Adjusted Gross Income

5. Equals Adjusted Gross Income

6. Minus Itemized Deductions or the Standard Deduction, whichever is greater

7. Minus Personal Exemptions

8. Equals Taxable Income

9. Multiplied by Income Tax Rate

10. Equals Income Tax

11. Minus Tax Credits

12. Equals Income Tax Liability for the Year

Income Taxation of Individuals

In general, citizens of the United States must pay tax on all income from all sources. Tax laws permit certain *exclusions, deductions,* and *exemptions* to be subtracted from total income in arriving at taxable income. Multiplying the amount of taxable income by the appropriate tax rate yields the amount of income tax for the year. Tax credits are then subtracted, and the final result is the amount of income tax liability for the year. Exhibit 27-2 shows how to compute the income tax liability for an individual. Taxable income, Step 8 in Exhibit 27-2, is the focal point in our discussions.

Total Income, Exclusions, and Gross Income — Steps 1, 2, and 3

In income taxation, **total income** is all income from whatever source derived. Salary or wage income is the most common taxable income. A business proprietor includes in total income the net income of the business (net sales less cost of goods sold and less all business expenses — salaries and wages for employees, rent, insurance, depreciation, repairs, property taxes, supplies expense, and so on). Gains on the sale of business assets like buildings and delivery vehicles are included as income, and losses are deductible in arriving at total income.

Also part of total income are interest earned on a savings account whether or not the interest is withdrawn, dividend revenue from a stock investment, and a gain on the sale of an investment. Net rent income (income minus expenses) on rental property, royalties earned on minerals, commissions, bonuses, tips, and gains on the sale of assets are also included in total income. Even gambling profits and income from illegal sources appear in the tax code as taxable income.

From total income we subtract *exclusions,* which are types of income that the tax law specifically identifies as nontaxable. Common exclusions are interest revenue on tax-exempt state and municipal bonds, certain scholarships received, gifts and inheritances, life insurance benefits, and some Social Security benefits. Subtracting exclusions from total income gives us **gross income,** which is all income not excluded from taxation.

Adjustments to Arrive at Adjusted Gross Income — Step 4

The adjustments in Step 4 are deductions of a wide variety. Payments into a personal retirement plan, alimony payments, and penalty on early withdrawal of savings fall into this category. The total of these adjustments is subtracted from gross income.

Adjusted Gross Income — Step 5

Gross income minus the adjustments (deductions) described in the preceding section equals an amount that exists only in the tax law — **adjusted gross income.** Often abbreviated in the business press as AGI, this amount is important in taxation because several expenses are deductible only if they exceed a certain percentage of adjusted gross income, as we discuss in the next section.

Itemized Deductions and the Standard Deduction — Step 6

An individual can take a tax deduction for the greater of two amounts: the total of itemized deductions or the standard deduction. **Itemized deductions** make up a particular category that includes the following six types of expenditures:

1. *Medical expenses* include doctor fees, hospital expenses, and the cost of eyeglasses, medicine, and special treatment. Medical expenses can be deducted only to the extent that they exceed 7½ percent (.075) of adjusted gross income. A taxpayer with adjusted gross income of $40,000 and medical expenses of $3,300 can deduct only $300 of these expenses [$3,300 − (.075 × $40,000)]. If this individual's medical expenses are $3,000 or less, he or she gets no medical expense deduction.

2. *Interest expense* on a home mortgage is deductible up to a maximum of interest incurred on $1 million of mortgage debt. All other interest is classified as consumer interest. In 1989, 20 percent of consumer interest is deductible, and the deductible percentage drops to 10 percent in 1990. After 1990, consumer interest is not deductible.

3. *Charitable contributions* are gifts to charitable and religious organizations such as United Way, the Red Cross, churches, synagogues, hospitals, and colleges and universities. The IRS keeps a list of approved charitable entities. Contributions to these organizations are deductible. Gifts to friends and relatives are not.

4. *Taxes paid* may be deducted. State income tax and local property taxes are the most common taxes deducted. Sales taxes cannot be deducted.

5. *Casualty losses* are losses of property, such as by theft or by storm damage to one's home. Casualty losses can be deducted subject to certain limitations.

6. *Miscellaneous deductions* include such expenses as union dues, subscriptions to professional journals, investment expenses, and fees paid for the preparation of an income tax return. To get a miscellaneous deduction, the taxpayer totals the expenses in this category. If the total exceeds 2 percent of adjusted gross income (AGI), the taxpayer gets a deduction for the excess. If total miscellaneous expenses are 2 percent of AGI or less, no deduction is permitted. Suppose a taxpayer's adjusted gross income is $40,000 and miscellaneous expenses total $875. This person lists all miscellaneous expenses on the tax return and gets a miscellaneous deduction of $75 [$875 − (.02 × $40,000)]. Miscellaneous expenses of $800 or less would not appear on the tax return at all because their total does not exceed 2 percent of AGI.

Notice that personal living costs are *not* tax deductible. The cost of a home and expenditures for apartment or house rent, clothing, furniture, and an automobile may not be claimed as tax deductions.

An alternative to itemizing deductions is taking the **standard deduction,** a set amount of tax deduction that varies depending on the individual's filing status. In 1988 married taxpayers filing a joint return could deduct $5,000 for the standard deduction. A head of a household could deduct $4,400 and a single taxpayer, $3,000. Starting in 1989, these amounts are adjusted for the effects of inflation. Many taxpayers favor the standard deduction because it requires no receipts or other supporting documents. Thus it is much easier than itemizing. An individual who itemizes cannot take the standard deduction, and likewise, one who elects the standard deduction passes up the opportunity to itemize. Throughout this chapter and in the assignment material, we assume a standard deduction of $5,000 for a joint tax return, $4,400 for a head of household, and $3,000 for a single taxpayer.

Personal Exemptions—Step 7

Another type of income tax deduction is called a **personal exemption.** This deduction is a set amount allowed for the taxpayer, the taxpayer's spouse, and each person who qualifies as a dependent. A taxpayer who files a single return gets one exemption. A married couple with no children and who file a joint return may claim two exemptions. A married couple with two children take four exemptions if they file a joint return. If the husband and the wife with two children file separate returns, they must decide who will claim exemptions for the children. Their two separate returns will show four exemptions in total. A head of household receives one exemption for himself or herself plus an exemption for each dependent. For example, a single man who supports a parent may claim two exemptions, one for himself and one for the parent.

The amount of the personal exemption is $2,000 in 1989. Beginning in 1990, the amount is to be adjusted for inflation. For illustrative purposes and in all exercises and problems, we assume a personal exemption of $2,000.

Taxable Income—Step 8

Taxable income is the earnings amount on which the income tax is based. It is the figure that is multiplied by the tax rate to compute the amount of income tax.

A special category of gains and losses—defined in the tax law—enters the determination of taxable income. These items, called **capital gains and losses,** result from the disposal of property that the tax law labels as capital assets. Common examples include investments in stocks, bonds, real estate, and personal assets such as homes, automobiles, and jewelry. A capital gain results from selling the asset for a price that exceeds its tax basis. A capital loss occurs if the sale price is less than the asset's tax basis. The *tax basis* of an asset is generally its cost (reduced by accumulated depreciation if any).

Capital gains and losses receive special treatment in a tax computation. The individual first separates capital gains and losses from other types of income, then combines capital gains and losses to calculate a net capital gain or a net capital loss for the year. A net capital gain is fully taxable. However, only $3,000 of net capital losses can be deducted in any one year. Any excess may be carried forward to reduce taxes in future years.

Let's take an example to illustrate the tax treatment of capital gains and losses. Suppose a married taxpayer has performed a partial tax computation for 19X1 and has determined that taxable income from other sources is $42,000. This taxpayer also has a capital gain of $4,000 on the sale of a stock investment and a capital loss of $9,000 on the sale of land. This person's taxable income for 19X1 is $39,000, computed as follows:

Taxable income from other sources		$42,000
Net capital loss:		
Capital loss	$9,000	
Capital gain	4,000	
Net capital loss	$5,000	
Maximum net capital loss deductible in one year		(3,000)
Taxable income		$39,000

In the determination of 19X2 taxable income, this person can deduct the net capital loss of $2,000 remaining from 19X1 ($5,000 less the $3,000 deducted in 19X1).

The tax definition of a capital asset is different from the accounting definition. Tax courses cover capital assets and capital gains and losses in more detail. For example, buildings, equipment, furniture, and other depreciable assets that are used in a business are *not* capital assets under the tax law. A loss on disposal of such *business* assets is fully deductible in the determination of taxable income. The $3,000 limit does not apply.

Income Tax Rates and the Amount of Income Tax—Steps 9 and 10

Exhibit 27-3 shows the tax rates that are used to compute an individual's income tax.

Exhibit 27-3 shows that various tax rates apply to various levels of taxable income. Higher rates apply when income reaches specific higher levels. This is called a progressive income tax system. For example, a single (unmarried) person with taxable income of $16,000 is taxed at 15 percent. A single individual with income of $28,000 is taxed at 15 percent of the first $17,850 of income ($2,678) plus 28 percent of income in excess of $17,850.

A person's maximum tax rate is important for tax planning because it indicates how much of each additional dollar of income must be paid in taxes.

Consider two single taxpayers. The person in the 15 percent bracket pays fifteen cents of every taxable dollar earned. The person in the 28 percent bracket pays nearly double that amount, twenty-eight cents of every taxable dollar earned. Each additional dollar earned is thirteen cents less valuable—and less attractive—to the person in the 28 percent bracket, and so the incentive to earn additional income is less.

The **surtax** is an additional tax. It is often designed to shift more of the tax burden to high-income taxpayers. Exhibit 27-3 indicates that the surtax has two parts. Each part is computed separately and added to the individual's taxes computed at the 15 percent and the 28 percent rates. The sum of the 15 percent, the 28 percent, and the surtax amounts make up the individual's income tax. For a single taxpayer, the first part of the surtax equals 5 percent of taxable income

EXHIBIT 27-3 *Individual Income Tax Rates*

Single Taxpayer:

If taxable income is	The tax is
Up to $17,850	15% of taxable income
Over $17,850	$2,678 + 28% of the excess over $17,850
(See surtax below)	

Married Taxpayer:

If taxable income is	The tax is
Up to $29,750	15% of taxable income
Over $29,750	$4,463 + 28% of the excess over $29,750
(See surtax below)	

Surtax:

Taxpayers with higher incomes must pay an additional tax, called a *surtax*. The surtax has two parts as follows:

1. Single taxpayer—5% of taxable income between $43,150 and $89,560, a maximum of $2,321
   Married taxpayer—5% of taxable income between $71,900 and $149,250, a maximum of $3,868

Plus the smaller of:

2. Single taxpayer—5% of taxable income above $89,560
   Married taxpayer—5% of taxable income above $149,250
   Or
   $560 multiplied by the number of personal exemptions

EXHIBIT 27-4   *1989 Income Tax Computation for Ron and Sarah Marks and Daughter Carmen—*
Married Filing Jointly with Three Exemptions

Taxable Income of $44,000:

.15 × $29,750	$ 4,463
.28 × ($44,000 − $29,750)...............................	3,990
Income tax amount......................................	$ 8,453

Taxable Income of $190,000:

.15 × $29,750	$ 4,463
.28 × ($190,000 − $29,750).............................	44,870
Surtax:	
.05 × ($149,250 − $71,900)..............................	3,868
Smaller of:	
(a) .05 × ($190,000 − $149,250) = $2,038, or	
(b) $560 × 3 = $1,680	1,680
Income tax amount.......................................	$54,881

between $43,150 and $89,560. The maximum surtax amount thus computed is
$2,321 [.05 × ($89,560 − $43,150)]. If the individual's income exceeds $89,560,
an additional surtax must be paid. In 1989 this second part of the surtax is equal to
5 percent of taxable income above $89,560 *or* $560 multiplied by the number of
exemptions claimed on the tax return, whichever is less.

Let's work through examples to illustrate a simple and a complex tax computation. Suppose Ron and Sarah Marks have a daughter, Carmen, and they file a
joint tax return. Exhibit 27-4 shows their 1989 tax computation for two levels of
taxable income, $44,000 and $190,000. The tax rates come from Exhibit 27-3.

Tax Credits—Step 11

Tax credits are often confused with tax deductions. The two are very different.
Tax deductions are subtracted from adjusted gross income and so decrease the
taxable income amount in Step 8. By contrast, tax credits enter the tax computation after the amount of income tax has been computed. A **tax credit** is subtracted
directly from the amount of tax owed to the government. Thus a tax credit is
worth more to a taxpayer because it leads to a larger decrease in the amount of tax
owed. For example, a $1,000 tax *deduction* decreases income tax by $280
($1,000 × .28) for a taxpayer subject to the 28 percent rate. A $1,000 tax *credit*
decreases the amount of tax by the full $1,000 because the entire amount is
subtracted. Two prominent tax credits are the *earned income credit,* which applies
to low-income taxpayers, and the *credit for child-care expenses,* which applies to
parents who work outside the home and must pay for child care.

Income Tax Liability—Step 12

The process described in the preceding paragraphs concludes with determination
of the individual's income tax liability for the year. In this setting, *income tax
liability* refers to the total amount of tax the person owes for the entire year. The
taxpayer does not write a single check to pay this amount at the end of the year.
Taxes are paid during the year, as described in the next section.

Paying Income Tax Through Withholding and Quarterly Payments

Persons who earn salaries or wages and who are not self-employed pay taxes through payroll deductions that the business withholds from their weekly or monthly paychecks. The employer remits the withheld taxes to the IRS on behalf of the employees. Individuals who are self-employed or who have outside income make quarterly tax payments directly to the IRS. All taxpayers must settle with the IRS when they file their annual tax returns. If the income tax listed on the tax return exceeds the total payments during the year, the individual must pay the difference when filing the tax return. If the amount of income tax on the tax return is less than the total payments, the taxpayer claims a refund and receives a check from the government.

Summary Problem for Your Review

Chip Reed is a financial consultant in Austin, Texas. He and his wife, Linda, have a son, Paul, and a daughter, Jennifer. During 1989 Chip's business earned gross income of $147,000 and had expenses of $62,000. Chip paid $7,600 into his retirement program. Linda works part time as an interior decorator and received a salary of $19,000. She also received $5,000 as an inheritance from an uncle. The Reeds' investments earned interest of $6,000 and dividends of $1,600. They sold a stock investment at a gain of $4,400 and land at a loss of $8,000. Their charitable contributions for the year totaled $2,700, interest expense on their home mortgage was $13,100, and they paid property taxes of $2,400. During the year Chip made quarterly income tax payments totaling $13,200, and $3,600 was withheld from Linda's paychecks. The Reeds file a joint income tax return.

Required

Compute the Reeds' taxable income and income tax liability for the year. Show how much they must pay or will receive after filing their 1989 income tax return.

SOLUTION TO REVIEW PROBLEM

Chip and Linda Reed
Income Tax Computation
1989

Gross income (excluding inheritance):		
Chip's business gross income..........................	$147,000	
Less: Business expenses	62,000	
Net business income.................................		$ 85,000
Linda's salary income................................		19,000
Interest...		6,000
Dividends		1,600
Capital gains and losses:		
Capital loss	$ 8,000	
Capital gain	4,400	
Net capital loss	$ 3,600	
Maximum net capital loss deductible in one year		(3,000)
Gross income.......................................		108,600
Deductions to arrive at adjusted gross income:		
Payment into Chip's retirement program		7,600
Adjusted gross income		101,000
Itemized deductions or standard deduction ($5,000), whichever is greater—itemized deductions in this case:		
Mortgage interest	$ 13,100	
Charitable contributions............................	2,700	
Property tax..	2,400	
Personal exemptions (4 × $2,000)......................	8,000	26,200
Taxable income		**$ 74,800**
Tax computation:		
.15 × $29,750	$ 4,463	
.28 × ($74,800 − $29,750)	12,614	
Surtax: .05 × ($74,800 − $71,900)....................	145	
Income tax liability for the year		**$ 17,222**
Less tax payments:		
Chip's quarterly payments...........................	$ 13,200	
Linda's withholdings	3,600	
Total payments		16,800
Tax to be paid with return............................		$ 422

Income Taxation of Corporations

A corporation is a taxable entity entirely separate from its owners, the stockholders. In this chapter, we focus on the general business corporation. A corporation, like an individual, must file a tax return whether or not it earns taxable income. However, the concept of adjusted gross income does not apply to a corporation. Also, a corporation has no standard deduction and no personal exemptions. We compute the actual amount of income tax for a corporation, though, in much the same way as for an individual, multiplying taxable income by the appropriate tax rate.

Taxable Income of a Corporation

To compute a corporation's taxable income, we follow many of the generally accepted accounting principles studied throughout this book. Indeed the starting point for computing the taxable income of a corporation is its *accounting income before income tax* on the income statement (also called *pretax accounting income*). Most revenues are taxable, and most expenses are tax deductible. **Ordinary income** is total business revenues minus total business expenses, including gains and losses from the sale of business assets like buildings and equipment. Special rules govern the tax treatment of certain revenues, expenses, and other items. The following paragraphs discuss some of these special tax rules.

OBJECTIVE 3

Use some special tax rules for corporations

1. Dividends-received deduction. The dividends a corporation earns on its stock investments are included in income. For tax purposes, however, 80 percent of these dividends can be deducted from gross income. Thus only 20 percent of dividend revenue enters taxable income. This provision of the tax law provides relief from what would otherwise be triple taxation of such dividends. Suppose Corporation Y owns Corporation X and outside stockholders own Corporation Y. Further, assume that the only entity with operating income is Corporation X. The following diagram illustrates triple taxation.

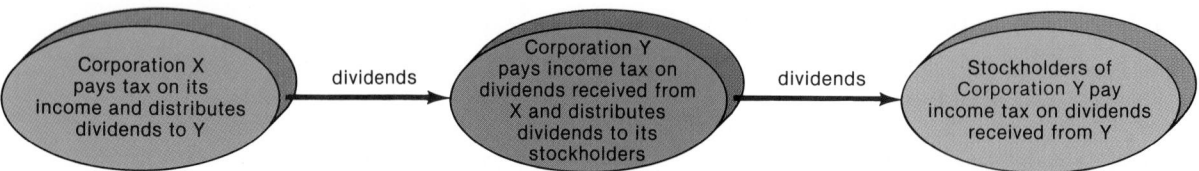

2. Net operating loss carryback and carryforward. In years when a corporation earns taxable income, it pays income tax. What is its tax situation when a loss occurs? Does the corporation get an income tax refund? Yes. The corporation can recover from the government the amount of taxes paid in other years. The tax law provides that an operating loss in a particular year can be offset against the income of the three preceding years, starting with the earliest year. If the loss is less than the corporation's total income during these three preceding years, the government mails a refund check to the company after its tax return is filed. If the loss exceeds the sum of the three preceding years' income, then the corporation can receive a refund and carry its excess loss forward for 15 years. This tax provision gives the corporation some tax relief from its operating losses. In effect, profitable years (in which the corporation paid taxes) absorb the shock of years when the corporation has a loss. Without this carryback/carryforward provision, a $500,000 loss before income tax would result in a $500,000 *net* loss on the income statement. But if the corporation has $500,000 or more of taxable income

EXHIBIT 27-5   *Corporate Income Tax Rates*

If taxable income is	The tax is
Up to $50,000	15% of taxable income
Between $50,000 and $75,000	$7,500 + 25% of taxable income in excess of $50,000
Over $75,000	$13,750 + 34% of taxable income in excess of $75,000

Surtax:

A corporation must pay a *surtax* equal to 5 percent of taxable income between $100,000 and $335,000, a maximum of $11,750.

and has paid taxes in the carryback/carryforward years, a pretax loss of $500,000 results in a *net* loss of $330,000 ($500,000 − the tax effect equal to 34 percent of $500,000).

3. *Capital gains and losses.* In taxation, corporations must separate capital gains and losses from ordinary income. Examples of capital gains and losses are gains and losses on the sale of investments such as stocks, bonds, and land. In the same manner as for individuals, capital gains are included in gross income. But a corporation may *not* offset capital losses against ordinary income. Instead, the corporation may carry net capital losses (capital losses in excess of capital gains) back three years and forward five years to be offset against capital gains in those carryback/carryforward years.

Corporate Income Tax Rates

Corporations have a tax rate schedule different from the tax rate schedule for individuals. Corporate income tax rates range from 15 percent to 34 percent, as shown in Exhibit 27-5.

There is a 5 percent surtax on corporate taxable income between $100,000 and $335,000. The maximum surtax is $11,750 [.05 × ($335,000 − $100,000)]. It is added to the amount of tax computed using the 15 percent to 34 percent tax rates.

Exhibit 27-6 illustrates a tax computation for two corporations, one with relatively low income ($100,000) and the other with high income ($1,000,000).

EXHIBIT 27-6   *Income Tax Computation for Two Corporations*

OBJECTIVE 4
Compute the income tax of a corporation

Corporation A—Taxable Income of $100,000:

.15 × $50,000	$ 7,500
.25 × ($75,000 − $50,000)	6,250
.34 × ($100,000 − $75,000)	8,500
Income tax amount	$ 22,250

Corporation B—Taxable Income of $1,000,000:

.15 × $50,000	$ 7,500
.25 × ($75,000 − $50,000)	6,250
.34 × ($1,000,000 − $75,000)	314,500
Surtax:	
.05* × ($335,000 − $100,000)	11,750
Income tax amount	$340,000

* 5% surtax on taxable income between $100,000 and $335,000.

The tax rate structure is designed to keep small companies from paying excessive taxes. Corporation A in Exhibit 27-6 pays income tax of $22,250 on taxable income of $100,000—an effective tax rate of 22.25 percent ($22,250/$100,000). A taxpayer's **effective tax rate** is computed by dividing the income tax amount by taxable income. In this case, Corporation A's effective rate is less than the top rate of 34 percent.

Corporation B has an effective tax rate of 34 percent ($340,000/$1,000,000). For high-income corporations such as B, the 5 percent surtax removes the benefit of the 15 percent and 25 percent rates applied to the $50,000 and $75,000 levels of income. Those with taxable income of $335,000 or more pay tax at the rate of 34 percent on all their income.

Corporations record their income taxes in journal entries like Corporation B's:

Income Tax Expense	340,000	
Income Tax Payable		340,000

Accounting for Income Taxes by Corporations

Income Tax Expense is based on pretax accounting income from the income statement. Income Tax Payable is based on taxable income from the income tax return filed with the Internal Revenue Service. In this example, we assume the two amounts are the same.

We have discussed some of the differences between the accounting income and the taxable income of a corporation. Some revenues and expenses enter the determination of accounting income in periods different from those in which they enter the determination of taxable income. Over a period of several years, total accounting income may equal total taxable income, but for any one year the two income amounts are likely to differ.

The most important difference between pretax accounting income and taxable income occurs when a corporation uses the straight-line method to compute depreciation for the financial statements and a special tax depreciation method for the tax return and the payment of taxes. The tax depreciation method is called the **modified accelerated cost recovery system,** abbreviated as MACRS. For any one year, MACRS depreciation listed on the tax return may differ from accounting depreciation on the income statement.

Suppose Krieg Corporation has accounting income, before income tax, of $500,000 in each of two years. The accounting issue is, What is the correct amount of income tax expense for the two years? By answering this question, we can complete Krieg's income statement:

Income Statement (partial)

	19X1	19X2
Income before income tax	$500,000	$500,000
Income tax expense	?	?
Net income	$?	$?

Suppose Krieg uses straight-line depreciation to compute income for the income statement. On the tax return, Krieg uses MACRS depreciation, and so the tax returns report taxable income of $400,000 in 19X1 and $600,000 in 19X2. Total taxable income for the two years combined—$1 million—is the same as total pretax accounting income. However, each year shows a difference between

EXHIBIT 27-7 *Income Tax Entries for a Corporation*

19X1	Income Tax Expense ($500,000 × .34)............	170,000	
	Income Tax Payable ($400,000 × .34)		136,000
	Deferred Income Tax ($100,000 × .34).........		34,000
19X2	Income Tax Expense ($500,000 × .34)............	170,000	
	Deferred Income Tax ($100,000 × .34)............	34,000	
	Income Tax Payable ($600,000 × .34)		204,000

OBJECTIVE 5

Record a corporation's income tax

accounting income and taxable income. With a 34 percent tax rate, income tax payable to the government is $136,000 ($400,000 × .34) in 19X1 and $204,000 ($600,000 × .34) in 19X2. Should Krieg report these amounts as income tax expense on the income statement? No, because this would amount to using the cash basis to account for income taxes.

Generally accepted accounting principles do *not* permit accounting for income tax using the cash basis. GAAP requires use of the accrual basis of accounting. Corporations account for income tax expense and all other expenses based on when the expense occurs, not on when it is paid. The process of accruing income taxes during the period that the related income occurs is called **income tax allocation.** The goal of income tax allocation is to match the period's expenses against its revenues. In this case, Krieg Corporation will record the same amount of income tax expense in both years because pretax accounting income is the same.

Corporations generally record Income Tax Expense based on the amount of *pretax accounting income* multiplied by the tax rate. Income Tax Payable is credited for an amount equal to *taxable income* multiplied by the tax rate. When these two amounts differ, a new account, Deferred Income Tax, is credited or debited to balance the entry. In Exhibit 27-7, Deferred Income Tax is credited in 19X1 because accounting income ($500,000) exceeds taxable income ($400,000). The reverse is true in 19X2, and Deferred Income Tax is debited. The 19X2 entry eliminates the preceding credit balance in Deferred Income Tax.

For other corporations, the 19X1 entry may include a debit to Deferred Income Tax. This occurs if taxable income exceeds pretax accounting income. In this case, the credit to Income Tax Payable is greater than the debit to Income Tax Expense, and the balancing amount is a debit to Deferred Income Tax. Entries in later years will include credits to eliminate the debit balance in Deferred Income Tax. Here is a way to remember whether to debit or credit Deferred Income Tax:

Debit: Income Tax Expense for the amount equal to *pretax accounting income* multiplied by the income tax rate.

Credit: Income Tax Payable for the amount equal to *taxable income* multiplied by the income tax rate.

Debit or Credit: Deferred Income Tax for the amount needed to balance the entry.

Exhibit 27-8 shows Krieg's comparative income statement for 19X1 and 19X2. Income Tax Expense comes directly from the entries recorded in Exhibit 27-7.

Net income is the same both years because pretax income is the same. Tax allocation thus matches income tax expense against income in accordance with the accrual basis of accounting. Income Tax Payable and Deferred Income Tax are reported on the balance sheet. Accounting for income tax by corporations is a controversial area that has received much FASB attention.

EXHIBIT 27-8   *Income Tax on a Corporation Income Statement*

Krieg Corporation Partial Income Statement For the Years Ended December 31, 19X1 and 19X2		
	19X1	**19X2**
Income before income tax	$500,000	$500,000
Income tax expense ($500,000 × .34 both years)	170,000	170,000
Net income	$330,000	$330,000

Tax Factors in Business Decisions

OBJECTIVE 6

Consider the effects of
income taxes on business
decisions

Tax planning is critical to making wise business decisions. Tax planning is the legitimate reduction of, and delay in, paying taxes within the legal system. Also called **tax avoidance,** it is the structuring of business transactions in order to pay the least amount of income tax at the latest possible time permitted by the law. Tax avoidance should not be confused with **tax evasion,** which is illegal activity designed to reduce tax. An example of tax planning (tax avoidance) is delaying revenue until a later year, when tax rates are scheduled to decrease. Failing to report the income on the tax return or reporting less than the full amount of income is tax evasion.

Corporations and individuals pay so much in taxes that intelligent financial strategies must consider the tax effects of transactions. The complexities of the federal tax laws demand specialized knowledge, so giant corporations like American Airlines and RJR Nabisco have tax specialists on the staff to advise them on major decisions. Proprietorships, partnerships, and private individuals often call on certified public accountants for advice. Many accountants earn a majority of their business income as tax consultants. In this section, we consider how tax factors affect business decisions by looking at the form of business organization, basis of accounting, methods of accounting, and compensation of employees.

Form of Business Organization

Suppose you are starting a new business. While working at a bank for the past five years, you have learned that the physicians in your area need help in organizing their office staffs, keeping their records, and managing their financial affairs. You decide to open an accounting and office management business for physicians. As you prepare to start up, your most basic question is how to organize the company. Should it be a proprietorship or a corporation?

A major factor in deciding the form of business organization is the amount of income tax you would pay under each alternative. You cannot be certain of what your income will be, but you can develop **pro forma data**—a carefully formulated expression of predicted results. These data would include projections of future income and income taxes.

Suppose you estimate that during the first year the business can earn pretax accounting income of $70,000. Assume that you are married with no children and take the standard deduction ($5,000) and the personal exemptions (2 ×

EXHIBIT 27-9 *Pro Forma Income and Tax Information*

	Corporation	Proprietorship
Business income	$70,000	$70,000
Less salary expense	36,000	—
Taxable income	34,000	70,000
Corporation income tax:		
.15 × $34,000	5,100	—
Business net income	$28,900	$70,000
Total income taxes:		
Corporation income tax	$ 5,100	
Individual income tax*—joint tax return:		
On taxable income of $27,000 (salary, $36,000, less deductions, $5,000, and exemptions, $4,000)	4,050	
On proprietor taxable income of $61,000 (business income, $70,000, less deductions, $5,000, and exemptions, $4,000)		$13,213
Total income taxes	$ 9,150	$13,213

* Income tax rates are given in Exhibit 27-3.

$2,000 = $4,000). You plan to withdraw $36,000 for living expenses. Exhibit 27-9 shows the total tax you can expect to pay in 1990 under the proprietorship and the corporation forms of business organization.

The proforma analysis indicates that incorporating the business leads to lower taxes, $9,150, compared to $13,213 if you organize as a proprietorship. The key to this advantage is leaving some of the corporation's income in the business. In this way you can arrange to have both yourself and the corporation pay taxes at the lowest rate, 15 percent. If you form a proprietorship, you pay some of your tax at 28 percent, and that increases your tax burden.

Let's consider another situation. Suppose you take all business earnings for personal use. In this case, the corporation has business income of $70,000, salary expense of $70,000, no income, and no taxes. The full $70,000 becomes taxable income to the owner. This places you in the same tax situation as you would be with a proprietorship.

The keys to the corporate advantage are twofold. (1) Through wise salary and dividend policy, you can divide the corporation's income between yourself and the business. Recall that the corporation is taxed as a separate legal entity. The total income, then, is split between two taxable entities—you and the corporation—and each entity's income is taxed at lower rates than if you reported all the income on your personal tax return. Of course, the tax savings resulting from leaving part of the income in the corporation comes at a price. In our example, you have only about half the personal income that you would have if you withdrew the total income from the business. (2) By leaving part of the corporation's income in the business, you can postpone the payment of taxes. However, this is only a delaying strategy. The owner must pay taxes on money taken out of the corporation. Sooner or later you must pay taxes in order to obtain income from the business, but the later you pay, the more time you have to earn income from investing your tax savings.

Using the corporate form of organization does *not* result in lower taxes in all situations. For example, if you organize as a corporation and take a relatively low salary and the remainder of your compensation in dividends, you will pay higher taxes than you would if organized as a proprietorship. Each situation requires a thorough analysis to determine what is best for the taxpayer.

Method of Financing

How a company finances operations has tax consequences. Two ways of obtaining funds are borrowing money and selling equity investments in the business. In a corporation, equity means stock. Borrowed funds must be repaid, with interest. Stockholders' equity does not have to be repaid, but stockholders demand returns in the form of dividends. Thus a corporation can expect to pay either interest or dividends for the funds it obtains from outsiders. Which form of financing has the tax advantage?

Business interest expense is tax deductible. Dividend payments to investors are not. Therefore, borrowing is less costly than selling ownership in the business, as an example will demonstrate.

Suppose you need $200,000 to finance a business expansion. You can borrow the money from a bank at 12 percent interest, an annual interest charge of $24,000. Alternatively, you can sell stock in the business. Assume that annual dividends on this stock are $18,000. Note that the dividends are $6,000 less than the interest. Before considering taxes, selling stock looks cheaper. However, if the corporation pays income tax at 34 percent, borrowing is less costly, as shown in Exhibit 27-10.

Basis of Accounting

Taxpayers, be they corporations or individuals, generally use the same basis for computing taxable income that they use for accounting purposes. For example, large corporations use the *accrual* basis for their accounting records, and they make any adjustments to those records to conform to tax law. Most corporations must use the accrual basis for computing their income taxes.

Almost all individuals and many service-oriented businesses keep their accounting records and prepare their income tax returns using the cash basis. In taxation, however, the cash basis is modified to include depreciation accounting. The costs of long-term business assets, such as buildings, equipment, and delivery vehicles, are capitalized and depreciated as in accrual accounting. Also, prepaid interest expense is deductible as it accrues rather than when it is paid. The cash basis for reporting to tax authorities is therefore really a modified cash basis.

The cash basis has several advantages. It is simpler than accrual accounting because it requires fewer records. By measuring taxable income by the amount of

EXHIBIT 27-10 *Financing With Debt Is Cheaper Than Issuing Stock*

	Alternative Ways to Raise $200,000	
	Borrow at 12%	Issue Stock That Pays Annual Dividends of 9%
Annual payment to providers of outside financing	$24,000	$18,000
Tax deduction (at 34%)	(8,160)	-0-
Net cost of outside financing	$15,840	$18,000

cash received rather than the amount of revenue earned, the taxpayer avoids having to pay taxes on revenues not yet collected in cash. Without this feature, a taxpayer might have to liquidate noncash assets to pay a tax liability. In general, tax law does not place this burden on taxpayers. Tax law is rather cash oriented. It is likely to link tax to an event that provides the taxpayer with the cash to pay it.

Let's take an extreme example. Suppose your new business has earned $25,000 but you have collected only $1,000 in cash. You would not have enough cash from the business to pay the income tax liability on total net income. However, you would be able to pay the tax on the $1,000 collected in cash.

The cash basis also allows the taxpayer some measure of control over the timing of income and expense. A lawyer with higher-than-expected income can delay billing a client in order to exclude this revenue from the current year. If this income would have caused the attorney to pay a surtax, a considerable savings results from this shifting of income. The lawyer can also pay expenses and charitable contributions on December 31 and receive an immediate deduction. Or if it helps the individual's tax situation, these expenses can be paid on January 1, and they become tax deductions in the next year.

The accounting basis chosen by the taxpayer—cash or accrual—must be followed consistently from period to period. The taxpayer may change accounting basis only with the approval of the IRS.

Methods of Accounting

A business in which inventory is a significant factor in computing income must use the accrual basis for revenue and cost of goods sold. This taxpayer cannot account for revenue on the cash basis for the purpose of determining taxable income. However, the taxpayer can elect the *last-in, first-out (LIFO)* method for inventories. This method assumes that the last costs into inventory are the first costs to pass into cost of goods sold (as opposed to first-in, first-out, FIFO). During a period of rising prices, LIFO causes gross profit to be lower than under the other inventory methods, thus reducing income taxes. If the company uses this method for income tax purposes, it generally must also use it for reporting to stockholders, creditors, and others. LIFO is the most popular inventory method, primarily because of its effect on taxes. Chapter 9 illustrates the income tax advantage of LIFO.

Another accounting choice with tax effects is *depreciation method.* A company may use one depreciation method for preparing the financial statements and a different method for preparing the tax return. For tax purposes, it is best to use the method that gives the largest depreciation amounts in the early years of the asset's life. By taking these deductions as soon as possible, the taxpayer reduces tax payments and saves cash that can be invested in the business. The only accelerated depreciation method permitted for tax purposes by the IRS is the Modified Accelerated Cost Recovery System (MACRS). Chapter 10 discusses depreciation in more detail and illustrates the tax advantage of accelerated depreciation.

Compensation of Employees

Businesses compensate their employees in a variety of ways. Salaries and wages are the most common. However, some contracts give the employee a choice among several forms of compensation. Many employees elect to take less salary in order to build retirement income. Under a typical arrangement, the employer makes payments into a pension account managed for the employee by an outside agency. The tax advantage is that the employer's pension contributions are *not* taxable income to the employee. Because no tax is paid currently, the full amount paid into the account earns retirement income for the employee. Furthermore, the pension fund pays no income tax while it is building up for the employee's retirement. Contrast this arrangement with paying the same amount to the employee as fully taxable salary and letting the employee set up her own retirement program. Suppose the employee's earnings are taxed at 15 percent. Of every dollar of salary earned, $.15 goes to pay taxes, leaving only $.85 to invest for retirement. And the employee must also pay tax on all income as it is earned by her retirement program.

Compensation plans that postpone the payment of taxes until the employee draws money from the retirement fund are called **tax-deferred,** or **tax-sheltered, compensation.** In many cases, the taxpayer will be subject to a lower tax rate during the retirement years and, therefore, will pay less in taxes than if the income were taken when the person was working and collecting a salary or wage. Self-employed persons can also shelter some of their income from taxes by making payments into a pension fund.

Another form of compensation with a tax advantage is noncash compensation. Many employers buy life, health, and disability insurance for their employees. Tax law does *not* levy a tax on the full amount of these forms of noncash compensation.

Income Taxes and Microcomputers

For many years, professionals have used computers for tax planning and the preparation of tax returns. Microcomputers have brought these capabilities within the reach of most individuals. Computer stores sell software programs that will perform tax calculations and prepare income tax returns. Many programs operate by use of a menu such as the one shown in Exhibit 27-11. All the taxpayer must do is answer questions and enter the data.

Menu-driven programs are easy to use. The computer takes the data, performs calculations, and enters the amounts in the correct place on the tax return. For example, suppose the taxpayer claims five exemptions. The program computes a total exemption of $10,000 (5 × $2,000), prints this amount on the exemption line of the tax return, and bases the tax calculation on this amount. A taxpayer who does not keep records of itemized deductions can elect the standard deduction. If the taxpayer does not know whether his itemized deductions exceed the standard deduction, he can enter the itemized amounts. The computer will total them, compare this amount to the standard deduction, and use the larger of the two. It

EXHIBIT 27-11 *Menu for a Tax-Return Preparation Program*

What is your status for filing this tax return?
_____ Single return
_____ Married person—joint return
_____ Married person—separate returns
_____ Head of household return

Enter the number of personal exemptions you are claiming _____

How do you wish to take deductions?
_____ Standard deduction
_____ Itemize deductions
_____ Compute itemized deductions. If itemized total exceeds standard deduction, itemize. If not, take the standard deduction.

EXHIBIT 27-12 *Spreadsheet Results of Business Financing Decision—Annual Cost of Alternative Ways to Raise $500,000*

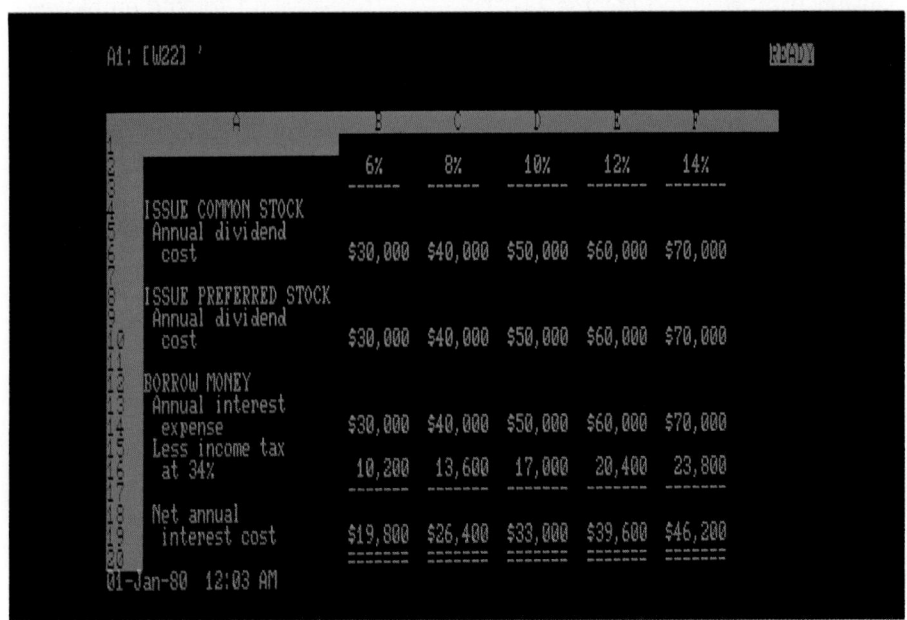

OBJECTIVE 7

Discuss the use of microcomputers in tax work

will also print the various itemized deductions in the appropriate places on the tax return.

Spreadsheet programs are ideal for tax planning. Suppose a business is raising $500,000 to purchase equipment. Should the company sell stock or borrow the money? What should be the dividend rate on the stock? At what interest rate should the money be borrowed? A spreadsheet can be written using Lotus 1-2-3, SuperCalc, Appleworks, or one of the other spreadsheet programs. Exhibit 27-12 shows how the output might look.

The exhibit shows, for example, that borrowing at 12 percent (with a net annual interest cost of $39,600) is a little cheaper than issuing stock with an 8 percent dividend rate ($40,000). Borrowing at 14 percent costs less ($46,200) than paying dividends of 10 percent ($50,000). With a spreadsheet program, this information is available for decision making immediately after it is entered in the computer. If interest rates or other data inputs change, the company can alter the information for an up-to-date analysis.

Summary Problem for Your Review

The bookkeeper for Highland Corporation provides the following data for computation of the company's income taxes for 19X7:

Ordinary income excluding dividend revenue	$440,000
Dividend revenue.	50,000
Capital gains.	32,000
Capital losses	(49,000)
Total business income	$473,000

Required

1. Compute Highland Corporation's taxable income and income tax liability for 19X7.
2. Journalize Highland's income taxes for 19X7, assuming pretax accounting income is $420,000.
3. What is Highland's effective income tax rate?

SOLUTION TO REVIEW PROBLEM

Requirement 1   (Taxable income and income tax liability)

Taxable income:

Ordinary income excluding dividend revenue	$440,000
Dividend revenue [$50,000 − (.80 × $50,000)]—Note 1..............	10,000
Capital gains	32,000
Capital losses—Note 2...	(32,000)
Taxable income	$450,000

Notes: 1. 80% of dividend revenue is deductible.
2. In any one year, capital losses can be deducted only to the extent of capital gains.

Tax liability—$450,000 × .34 = $153,000, or:

.15 × $50,000	$ 7,500
.25 × ($75,000 − $50,000)...............................	6,250
.34 × ($450,000 − $75,000).............................	127,500
Surtax:	
.05 × ($335,000 − $100,000)............................	11,750
Income tax amount	$153,000

Requirement 2   (Income tax entry for 19X7)

Income Tax Expense ($420,000 × .34)	142,800	
Deferred Income Tax ($30,000 × .34).....................	10,200	
Income Tax Payable ($450,000 × .34)...................		153,000

Requirement 3   (Effective income tax rate)
Effective tax rate = 34% ($153,000/$450,000)

Summary

The *income tax* is a general-purpose tax levied on the taxable earnings of the taxpayer. Individuals, corporations, estates, and trusts are the four classes of taxpayers. Single individuals may file a *single income tax return* or, if they support other persons, a *head-of-household return*. Married persons may file a *joint return*, which has the lowest rate, or the husband and the wife may file *separate returns*.

A business organized as a proprietorship or a partnership pays no income tax. Instead, its owners pay individual income tax on the earnings of the business. In tax law, a corporation is a separate taxable entity that pays its own income tax. Dividends that a corporation distributes to the stockholders are taxable to them as personal income. For all classes of taxpayers and forms of business organization the computation of income tax equals *taxable income multiplied by the tax rate.*

Individuals subtract exclusions from total income to determine *gross income. Deductions* and *exemptions* are subtracted to compute *taxable income.* After multiplying taxable income by the tax rate, *tax credits* are taken out to arrive at the *income tax liability* for the year. Individuals are taxed at 15 percent or 28 percent, and a surtax applies to high levels of income.

A corporation computes taxable income by making adjustments to pretax accounting income. Among these are the deduction for dividends received, the net operating loss carryback and carryforward, and the special treatment of capital gains and losses. Corporations are taxed at 15 percent, 25 percent, or 34 percent, and corporations with high levels of income must pay a surtax.

The *income tax expense* of a corporation is based on its pretax accounting income. *Income tax payable* is based on taxable income. These amounts are rarely the same for a given year. Differences between the expense and the payable are debited or credited to an account titled Deferred Income Tax. Using this account helps the taxpayer match income tax expense against revenue, a process called *income tax allocation.*

Income taxes influence many business decisions, among them choosing the form of business organization, the method of financing, the basis of accounting, the accounting methods that minimize taxes, and employee compensation.

Self-Study Questions

Test your understanding of the chapter by marking the best answer for each of the following questions.

1. A taxpayer's income tax is computed by multiplying the appropriate tax rate by *(p. 1040)*
   a. Net income
   b. Filing status
   c. Taxable income
   d. Total deductions

2. Which filing status of individual taxpayer pays income tax at the lowest rates? *(p. 1041)*
   a. Married filing jointly
   b. Married filing separately
   c. Head of household
   d. Single

3. Tax-exempt interest revenue is an example of a (an) *(p. 1043)*
   a. Personal exemption
   b. Itemized deduction
   c. Tax credit
   d. Exclusion

4. An individual has salary income of $37,000, capital gains of $4,000, and an $8,000 capital loss. How much is this person's taxable income? *(p. 1045)*
   a. $33,000
   b. $34,000
   c. $37,000
   d. $41,000

5. A married couple with one child has proprietorship income of $50,000 and itemized deductions of $7,000. How much is this family's income tax if they file a joint return as a married couple? *(p. 1047)*
   a. $6,493
   b. $7,053
   c. $8,040
   d. $8,600

6. Which is the most valuable to a taxpayer? *(p. 1047)*
   a. Itemized deduction
   b. Adjustment to arrive at adjusted gross income
   c. Tax credit
   d. Personal exemption

7. Why does a corporation with taxable income of $1 million pay more income tax than an individual with the same amount of income? *(pp. 1051, 1046)*
   a. The surtax rate is higher for corporations than for individuals
   b. The highest tax rate applicable to corporations is higher than the highest rate applicable to individuals
   c. Corporations must follow income tax allocation procedures
   d. Corporations but not individuals receive a dividends-received deduction

8. Modified Accelerated Cost Recovery is a tax system for computing *(p. 1052)*
   a. Dividends
   b. Salary
   c. Capital gains and losses
   d. Depreciation
9. Which statement is true? *(p. 1056)*
   a. An individual always pays less in tax by organizing a business as a proprietorship because the entity pays no business income tax.
   b. An individual always pays less in tax by organizing a business as a corporation because of the opportunity to split personal income between the individual and the corporation.
   c. Tax planning is useful to corporations but not to individuals.
   d. In some cases, it costs less in taxes to organize as a proprietorship. In other cases, organizing as a corporation has the tax advantage.
10. Which method of financing is less costly? *(p. 1056)*
    a. Borrowing
    b. Issuing common stock
    c. Issuing preferred stock
    d. Issuing stock and borrowing

Answers to the self-study questions are at the end of the chapter.

Accounting Vocabulary

adjusted gross income *(p. 1043)*,   capital gain *(p. 1045)*,   capital loss *(p. 1045)*,   dependent *(p. 1041)*,   effective tax rate *(p. 1052)*,   gross income *(p. 1043)*,   income tax *(p. 1039)*, income tax allocation *(p. 1053)*,   itemized deduction *(p. 1043)*,   modified accelerated cost recovery system (MACRS) *(p. 1052)*,   personal exemption *(p. 1044)*,   pro forma data *(p. 1054)*,   standard deduction *(p. 1044)*,   surtax *(p. 1046)*,   taxable income *(p. 1045)*,   tax avoidance *(p. 1054)*,   tax credit *(p. 1047)*,   tax-deferred compensation *(p. 1058)*,   tax evasion *(p. 1054)*,   tax return *(p. 1041)*,   tax-sheltered compensation *(p. 1058)*,   total income *(p. 1043)*.

ASSIGNMENT MATERIAL _____

Questions

1. Briefly describe four different kinds of taxes.
2. Does tax law in the United States state that each American has a patriotic responsibility to pay tax in a manner that goes beyond the call of duty?
3. When was the first income tax levied in the United States? When did our present tax structure begin? What government action opened the door for the income tax?
4. Identify the lowest and the highest income tax rates that have existed in the United States. What event triggered the highest rate?
5. Name the four filing statuses for an individual taxpayer, and rank them from lowest to highest in tax rate.
6. Enter the correct letter (or letters) from the right column in the blank spaces. More than one answer may apply.

_____ Files an information tax return only	a. Individual
_____ Pays no business income tax	b. Proprietorship
_____ Is viewed by tax law as a taxable business entity	c. Partnership
_____ Has four possible filing statuses	d. Corporation

7. Outline an individual's twelve-step computation of income tax liability.
8. How does total income of a taxpayer differ from gross income? Identify four types of income that are specifically listed as nontaxable.
9. Identify two tax deductions that depend on the amount of a taxpayer's adjusted gross income (AGI). Give the percentage relationship of these two items to AGI.
10. What is the alternative to taking the standard deduction? Identify the advantage and the disadvantage of the standard deduction.

11. What are capital gains and losses, and how are they treated for tax purposes by an individual? Give three examples of a capital asset.

12. Which is worth more to a taxpayer, a $400 tax deduction or a $400 tax credit? How much more (assume an income tax rate of 28 percent)?

13. Leslie B. Good's income tax liability for the year is $4,700. Describe how Leslie will pay this income tax if her earnings consist of salary. How will she pay her taxes on outside income?

14. Briefly describe three items that receive special tax treatments by corporations.

15. What income tax rates apply to single individuals and to corporations?

16. What is the effective tax rate of a corporation with taxable income of $70,000? Why is this effective rate below 25 percent?

17. Does a corporation's income tax expense depend on its pretax accounting income or on its taxable income? On which income amount does income tax payable depend?

18. Indicate whether each of the following statements is true or false.

   _____ a. Deferred Income Tax is an expense account.
   _____ b. Deferred Income Tax may have either a debit balance or a credit balance.
   _____ c. Deferred Income Tax is reported on the balance sheet.

19. Which method of financing—equity or debt—is usually cheaper for a business? Why?

20. Which basis of accounting do most individuals use for tax purposes? Why? Which basis do most corporations use? Why?

21. Name two accounting methods that result in lower income taxes.

22. Why do many taxpayers choose tax-sheltered compensation over salary income?

23. Briefly describe two aspects of tax work that can be aided by a microcomputer.

Exercises

Exercise 27-1 *Classifying tax items*

Listed below are eight tax terms discussed in this chapter.

Tax credit	Itemized deduction
Personal exemption	Capital gain or loss
Standard deduction	Adjustment to arrive at adjusted gross income
Surtax	Income excluded from gross income

Indicate which of these tax terms applies to the following descriptions.

a. Gain on the sale of a stock investment
b. Interest revenue earned on bonds issued by the city of St. Louis, Missouri
c. Medical expenses, charitable contributions, and casualty losses
d. $2,000 for the taxpayer and each dependent claimed on the tax return
e. Additional tax based on high levels of income
f. Child-care expenses
g. $5,000 for a married taxpayer filing a joint return, $4,400 for a head of a household, $3,000 for a single taxpayer
h. Penalty on early withdrawal of savings

Exercise 27-2 *Identifying items to include in gross income*

State whether each of the following items should be *included in* or *excluded from* gross income for the purpose of computing the income tax of an individual.

a. Inheritance of $10,000 received from the estate of a deceased relative
b. Rent income received from lease of personal residence while away on business
c. Tips received by the headwaiter of a restaurant
d. Gift of oil royalties received from a parent
e. Tax-deferred compensation received from employer
f. Gain from sale of investment in bonds
g. Profits earned from a partnership
h. Life insurance proceeds received
i. Income received during retirement from a pension plan. The earnings that went into the pension plan were tax-deferred in *e*
j. Interest revenue earned on state of Idaho bonds

Exercise 27-3 *Classifying tax items*

For each of the following expenditures by an individual taxpayer, indicate whether the item is a *deductible business expense,* an *adjustment to arrive at adjusted gross income,* an *itemized deduction,* or *not deductible.*

a. State income taxes paid
b. Wage expense paid to employees
c. Net capital losses in excess of $3,000
d. Insurance expense on rental property
e. Contribution to a personal retirement program
f. Charitable contributions
g. Sales tax paid
h. Medical expenses less than 7½ percent of adjusted gross income
i. Cost of adding a room to personal residence
j. Interest expense paid on home mortgage note payable

Exercise 27-4 *Computing adjusted gross income*

Chris Mendoza is single with no dependents. His personal income tax records reveal the following:

Gross income of Mendoza Floor Coverings, a proprietorship	$137,000
Operating expenses of Mendoza Floor Coverings	73,000
Capital loss on sale of personal (nonbusiness) investment	7,000
Gift received from Chris's parents	12,500
Rent income on a building adjacent to Mendoza Floor Coverings store	19,100
Medical expenses	4,600
Interest expense:	
Home mortgage note payable	7,400
Business debt	3,100
Personal exemption	2,000

Compute Mendoza's adjusted gross income and taxable income.

Exercise 27-5 *Computing an individual's income tax*

Case A: Compute the income tax of Chris Mendoza in the preceding exercise.

Case B: Assume that Chris Mendoza in the preceding exercise is married with one child. He and his wife, Maria, file a joint income tax return. During the year, the Mendozas made quarterly income tax payments totaling $14,000. Compute their *income tax* for the year. Also, show the amount of *income tax they owe* or the *refund* they may claim when they file their tax return.

Exercise 27-6 *Computing a single person's adjusted gross income and taxable income*

Margo Hayba's architecture firm, which she operates as a proprietorship, had gross fee revenue of $269,000 for the year just ended. Business expenses included salaries of $119,000, office depreciation of $4,000, and other operating expenses totaling $51,000. Ms. Hayba's personal investments earned dividend revenue of $4,000, and she sold General Electric stock at a gain of $2,000. She sold another personal investment at a loss of $7,000. Her itemized deductions for the year were $4,100. She received an inheritance of $6,000. Ms. Hayba is single, and she supports her two children.

Required

Compute Ms. Hayba's adjusted gross income and taxable income. Assume she files a head-of-household tax return.

Exercise 27-7 *Computing income tax for a family's joint tax return*

Assume Margo Hayba in the preceding exercise is married with two children. Her husband's salary income is $74,400. Compute the family's taxable income and income tax for the year, assuming she and her husband file a joint tax return.

Exercise 27-8 *Treatment of capital gains and losses by individuals and corporations*

A taxpayer had the following capital gains and losses during a year:

a. A capital gain of $6,000 and a capital loss of $5,000
b. A capital gain of $7,000 and a capital loss of $1,000
c. A capital gain of $2,000 and a capital loss of $8,000
d. No capital gain and a capital loss of $12,000

Required

1. Assume the taxpayer is an *individual.* For each situation, indicate the amount of net capital gain that will be included in, or the amount of net capital loss that will be deductible from, the individual's gross income.
2. Assume the taxpayer is a *corporation.* For each situation, indicate how the corporation should treat the capital gains and losses.

Exercise 27-9 *Computing a corporation's income tax and effective tax rate*

Impala Corporation's income tax records provide the following data:

Gross profit from sales (sales − cost of goods sold)	$393,000
Operating expenses	(274,000)
Dividend revenue	15,000
Gain on sale of equipment—not a capital gain	8,000
Capital loss	(27,000)
Total business income	$115,000

Required

1. Compute Impala Corporation's taxable income and income tax liability for the year.
2. Compute the corporation's effective income tax rate.

Exercise 27-10 *Recording a corporation's income tax*

Excel Corporation has pretax accounting income of $700,000 in 19X5 and $650,000 in 19X6. Taxable income is $680,000 in 19X5 and $670,000 in 19X6. Record the corporation's income taxes for both years. The tax rate is 34 percent.

Exercise 27-11 *Computing and recording a corporation's income tax*

The income tax records of Livesay Corporation provide the following data:

Service revenue...	$367,000
Operating expenses...	(113,000)
Dividend revenue	35,000
Loss on sale of building—not a capital loss	(92,000)
Capital gain..	6,000
Total business income......................................	$203,000

Required

1. Compute Livesay Corporation's taxable income and income tax liability for the year.
2. Record the corporation's income tax for the year. Assume that pretax accounting income is $160,000, and apply the same tax rates to pretax accounting income that are used on taxable income.

Exercise 27-12 *Pro forma analysis of income tax for a corporation*

Gerald and Patty Molitor own a Wendy's restaurant that they operate as a proprietorship in Kit Carson, Colorado. The business earns annual pretax accounting income of $110,000 before any compensation to the owners. The Molitors have no children, file a joint tax return, and take the standard deduction and the personal exemption. They withdraw $100,000 annually for living expenses. They are considering reorganizing the business as a corporation.

Required

1. Prepare a proforma analysis to indicate their total income taxes under the two forms of business organization.
2. Which form of business organization results in the lower total income tax for the owners? Compute the difference.

Problems (Group A)

Problem 27-1A *Computing income tax for a joint tax return*

Ron and Elisa Stern are married and have two children. Ron's salary is $44,000, and Elisa's investments earn interest of $13,000 annually. Ron contributes $2,000 to a pension plan. The Sterns have compiled the following income tax data to aid in the preparation of their joint income tax return:

Salary income..	$44,000
Interest income, of which $8,000 results from municipal bonds............	13,000
Rent income	11,000
Expense of operating rent property.............................	5,000
Itemized deductions..	5,300
Personal exemptions (4 × $2,000)...............................	8,000
Contribution to a retirement program............................	3,000
Income taxes withheld and paid directly to the IRS	7,000

Required (continued on next page)

1. Compute gross income.
2. Compute adjusted gross income.
3. Compute taxable income.

4. Compute income tax.
5. Compute the amount of tax to be paid or the refund to be claimed when the tax return is filed.

Problem 27-2A   *Computing adjusted gross income and taxable income*

The tax records of Monte Marconi, a single taxpayer with no dependents, reveal the following data for the current year:

Partner interest in:

Operating profits of Bon Voyage Travel Agency	$ 64,200
Gain on sale of travel agency building	31,800
Life insurance benefits received	150,000
Contribution to a retirement program	5,000
Capital gain on sale of personal investment in stock	3,200
Capital loss on sale of personal investment in land	7,700
Capital gain on sale of recreational vehicle	800
Medical expenses	4,775
Interest expense on home mortgage note payable	3,800
Sales tax paid	1,100
Property tax paid	2,200
Charitable contributions	1,900
Personal exemption	2,000

Compute Marconi's adjusted gross income and taxable income. Not all items are used.

Problem 27-3A   *Computing income tax for a joint tax return*

Walter and Lillian Khoury, a married couple with two children, have income, expenses, and other expenditures for the year as follows. They file a joint tax return.

Salaries ($35,000 each)	$70,000
Profit on a partnership interest in an office building	24,200
Interest income on:	
Bank deposit	3,500
City of San Antonio bonds	900
Gift received	2,500
Contribution to retirement program	3,000
Capital gain on sale of personal investment in stock	2,100
Unused capital loss carryover from preceding year	1,900
Capital gain on sale of stereo equipment	100
Clothing	2,600
Food	3,800
Medical expenses	1,400
Interest expense on home mortgage note payable	2,100
Cost of painting personal residence	6,700
State income tax paid	500
Property tax paid	1,800
Charitable contributions	2,200
Miscellaneous deductions	2,100
Personal exemptions	8,000
Income tax withheld	13,300
Total of quarterly tax payments	6,200

Required

1. Compute the Khourys' adjusted gross income and taxable income for the year. Identify each item not used in this computation, and state why the item is not used.
2. Compute the income tax liability for the year and show whether the Khourys will pay tax when they file their return or receive a refund. Show the amount.

Problem 27-4A   *Computing and recording a corporation's income tax*

Sharp Electronics Corporation is about to complete its first year of operations. To assess the company's income tax situation before year end, the company accountant prepares the following proforma income statement:

Revenue and gains:		
Sales revenue	$418,000	
Dividend revenue....................................	35,000	
Gain on sale of asset—a capital gain	8,000	
Total revenues and gains.............................		$461,000
Expenses:		
Cost of goods sold—		
FIFO method for inventories	196,000	
Operating expenses:		
Depreciation—straight-line method..................	22,000	
Other expenses.....................................	104,000	
Loss on payment of debt—a capital loss	9,000	
Total expenses and losses		331,000
Proforma pretax accounting income......................		$130,000

Rachel Sharp, the company president, is pleased with the successful operations of the first year. However, she is concerned about the high income taxes the corporation may have to pay. Sharp asks the accountant to consider ways to reduce income taxes. The accountant determines that the LIFO method would decrease ending inventory by $11,000 from the FIFO amount and that the MACRS depreciation method would increase depreciation expense by $6,000.

Required

1. Assume Sharp changes to LIFO and prepares its income tax return based on the LIFO method for inventories and the MACRS method for depreciation. Compute the corporation's taxable income and income tax payable, taking into account any special tax rules that apply to corporations.
2. Compute the corporation's effective income tax rate.
3. Record Sharp Electronics Corporation's income tax for the year. Compute income tax expense based on pretax accounting income of $108,000.

Problem 27-5A   *Computing and recording a corporation's income tax*

The accounting (not the income tax) records of Mertz Corporation provide the comparative income statement for 19X3 and 19X4:

	19X3	19X4
Total revenue	$660,000	$700,000
Expenses:		
Cost of goods sold	290,000	310,000
Operating expenses	180,000	190,000
Total expenses before tax............................	470,000	500,000
Pretax accounting income	$190,000	$200,000

Total revenue of 19X4 includes rent of $10,000 that was received late in 19X3. This rent is included in 19X4 total revenue because the rent was earned in 19X4. However, rent revenue that is collected in advance is included in taxable income when the cash is received. In calculating taxable income on the tax return, this rent revenue belongs in 19X3.

Also, the operating expenses of each year include depreciation of $40,000 computed under the straight-line method. In calculating taxable income on the tax return, Mertz Corporation uses the Modified Accelerated Cost Recovery System (MACRS). MACRS depreciation was $60,000 for 19X3 and $20,000 for 19X4.

Required

(Assume a corporate income tax rate of 34 percent.)

1. Compute taxable income for each year.
2. Journalize the corporation's income taxes for each year.
3. Prepare the corporation's single-step income statement for each year.

Problem 27-6A   *Computing total tax burden for a corporation and a proprietor*

Lisa Miller is opening a consulting firm. She expects business income—before any salary for herself—ranging between $50,000 and $120,000, and she plans to take an annual salary of $35,000 the first year. Concerned about the effects of income tax, she is considering the best way to organize the business.

Required

1. Prepare an analysis to show Miller's total annual income tax burden if she organizes the business as a corporation. Also show what Miller's total tax burden would be if the business were a proprietorship. Base your analysis on the range of business income Miller expects for the first year. She will file a single individual tax return and take the standard deduction. The business is her only source of income.
2. How should Miller organize the business to minimize her total tax burden?

(Group B)

Problem 27-1B   *Computing income tax for a joint tax return*

Brad and Jan Stokes are married and have one son. Brad's salary is $52,000, and Jan's investments earn annual dividends of $17,000. In addition, the couple has some capital gains and losses. Brad contributes $4,000 to a pension plan. During the current year, Jan received a gift of $3,000 from an aunt. The Stokes have compiled the following income tax data to aid in the preparation of their joint income tax return:

Salary income	$52,000
Dividend income	17,000
Capital gains	6,000
Capital losses	2,000
Itemized deductions	3,300
Personal exemptions (3 × $2,000)	6,000
Contribution to a retirement program	4,000
Income taxes withheld and paid directly to the IRS	12,000

Required   (continued on next page)

1. Compute gross income.
2. Compute adjusted gross income.
3. Compute taxable income.

4. Compute income tax.
5. Compute the amount of tax to be paid or the refund to be claimed when the tax return is filed.

Problem 27-2B   *Computing adjusted gross income and taxable income*

The tax records of Abner and Edna Page, a married couple with three children, reveal the following data for the current year. The Pages file a joint income tax return.

Partner interest in:	
Operating profits of Epicure Restaurant	$37,900
Loss on sale of restaurant building	8,300
Inheritance received	75,000
Rent income	6,000
Expense of operating rent property	1,600
Contribution to a retirement program	2,000
Capital gain on sale of personal investment in land	600
Capital loss on sale of personal investment in bonds	2,900
Gambling profits	300
Medical expenses	2,950
Interest expense on home mortgage note payable	2,700
Sales tax paid	700
Property tax paid	900
Charitable contributions	800
Personal exemptions	10,000

Compute the Pages' adjusted gross income and taxable income. Not all items are used.

Problem 27-3B   *Computing income tax for a joint tax return*

Carroll and Harriet Fadal, a married couple with one daughter, have income, expenses, and other expenditures for the year as follows. They file a joint tax return.

Salaries ($41,000 and $27,000)	$68,000
Loss on a partnership interest in an apartment building	9,600
Interest income on:	
City of El Paso bonds	1,800
Bank deposit	1,100
Consulting fee earned	600
Inheritance received	50,000
Contribution to retirement program	2,600
Capital gain on sale of personal investment in land	2,300
Unused capital loss carryover from preceding year	3,800
Clothing	3,100
Food	4,400
Medical expenses	4,400
Interest expense on home mortgage note payable	3,700
Cost of remodeling personal residence	9,300
State income tax paid	1,200
Property tax paid	1,000
Charitable contributions	3,300
Miscellaneous deductions	800
Personal exemptions	6,000
Income tax withheld	7,000
Total of quarterly tax payments	400

Required

1. Compute the Fadals' adjusted gross income and taxable income for the year. Identify each item not used in this computation, and state why the item is not used.
2. Compute the income tax liability for the year, and show whether filing their tax return will lead the Fadals to pay tax or receive a refund. Show the amount.

Problem 27-4B   *Computing and recording a corporation's income tax*

Lafferty Corporation is about to complete its first year of operations. To assess the company's income tax situation before year end, the company accountant prepares the following proforma income statement:

Revenues and gains:		
Sales revenue	$360,000	
Dividend revenue.	20,000	
Gain on sale of asset—a capital gain	14,000	
Total revenues and gains.		$394,000
Expenses:		
Cost of goods sold—		
FIFO method for inventories	150,000	
Operating expenses:		
Depreciation—straight-line method.	16,000	
Other expenses.	88,000	
Loss on payment of debt—a capital loss	19,000	
Total expenses and losses		273,000
Proforma pretax accounting income.		$121,000

Preston Lafferty, the company president, is pleased with the successful operations of the first year. However, he is concerned about the high income taxes the corporation may have to pay. Lafferty asks the accountant to consider ways to reduce income taxes. The accountant determines that the LIFO method would decrease ending inventory by $9,000 from the FIFO amount and the MACRS depreciation method would increase depreciation expense by $3,000.

Required

1. Assume Lafferty changes to LIFO and prepares its income tax return based on the LIFO method for inventories and the MACRS method for depreciation. Compute the corporation's taxable income and income tax payable, taking into account any special tax rules that apply to corporations.
2. Compute the corporation's effective income tax rate.
3. Record Lafferty Corporation's income tax for the year. Compute income tax expense based on pretax accounting income of $105,000.

Problem 27-5B   *Computing and recording a corporation's income tax*

The accounting (not the income tax) records of Jarman Corporation provide the comparative income statement for 19X7 and 19X8:

	19X7	19X8
Total revenue	$930,000	$990,000
Expenses:		
Cost of goods sold	410,000	460,000
Operating expenses	270,000	280,000
Total expenses before tax.	680,000	740,000
Pretax accounting income	$250,000	$250,000

Total revenue of 19X8 includes revenue of $5,000 that was received late in 19X7. This revenue is included in 19X8 total revenue because it was earned in 19X8. However, revenue that is collected in advance is included in the taxable income of the year when the cash is received. In calculating taxable income on the tax return, this revenue belongs in 19X7.

Also, the operating expenses of each year include depreciation of $50,000 computed on the straight-line method. In calculating taxable income on the tax return, Jarman Corporation uses the Modified Accelerated Cost Recovery System (MACRS). MACRS depreciation was $80,000 for 19X7 and $20,000 for 19X8.

Required

(Assume a corporate income tax rate of 34 percent.)

1. Compute taxable income for each year.
2. Journalize the corporation's income taxes for each year.
3. Prepare the corporation's single-step income statement for each year.

Problem 27-6B *Computing total tax burden for a corporation and a proprietor*

Dave Sneller operates a successful construction company. For the past several years, the business has had annual net income ranging from $200,000 to $300,000 before any deduction for Dave's $100,000 salary. This is his only source of income. The business is incorporated, but Dave is considering reorganizing as a proprietorship. He wonders whether his family's total tax burden would be less if the business were a proprietorship.

Required

1. Prepare an analysis to show the Snellers' total annual income tax burden with the business organized as a corporation. Also show what the Snellers' total tax burden would be if the business were *reorganized* as a proprietorship. Base your analysis on the range of business income in recent years. The Snellers will file a joint tax return with three exemptions and take the standard deduction.
2. Will reorganizing the business as a proprietorship reduce the Sneller family's total income tax burden?

Decision Problem

Tax Factors in Deciding How to Organize a Business

David and Angela Tekell own The Double Eagle, a restaurant in San Diego organized as a proprietorship. The business earns pretax income of $90,000 per year before any compensation to the Tekells. They are considering reorganizing the business as a corporation in order to avoid the unlimited personal liability of the proprietorship form of business. If they incorporate, the cost of the restaurant's liability insurance will increase by $2,000 per year over its present level. Operating as a corporation will increase other expenses by $500 each year. Revenues will be unchanged.

Under the proprietorship form, the Tekells withdraw $45,000 of business income each year for personal living expenses. They will need the same amount of personal family income if the business incorporates. They are considering two alternative ways of receiving $45,000 from the corporation: (1) $45,000 annually as salary or (2) $30,000 annually as salary, plus $15,000 as dividends.

David and Angela file a joint tax return and have itemized deductions of $7,000 each year. They have no children.

Required

1. Prepare a schedule showing the Tekells' total income taxes and additional expense each year under three alternative plans: (1) corporation—salary only; (2) corporation—salary and dividends; (3) proprietorship.
2. Which plan do you recommend? Give your reason.

Answers to Self-Study Questions

1. c
2. a
3. d
4. b $37,000 − net capital loss limited to $3,000 = $34,000
5. a Taxable income = $50,000 − personal exemptions of $6,000 ($2,000 × 3) − itemized deductions of $7,000 = $37,000. Tax on income of $37,000 = $6,493 [$4,463 + .28 × ($37,000 − $29,750)]
6. c
7. b
8. d
9. d
10. a

28

Accounting with Computers

Accounting has benefited more from computer technology than any other area of business. The application of computers to accounting is natural because the computer is ideally suited for repetitive calculations.

This chapter expands the Chapter 6 discussion of computer systems. It outlines a personal-computer (PC) system of accounting for general ledger, accounts receivable, accounts payable, and payroll transactions. The second half of the chapter discusses spreadsheet programs — giving specific commands and leading you through the preparation of a budgeted income statement. Learning these commands will equip you to use a spreadsheet program for a variety of accounting tasks. The exercises and problems are designed to be solved by hands-on use of a personal computer.

The first computerized accounting systems were developed in the 1950s. Only the largest organizations could afford the expensive computer equipment available at that time. Since then the price of computer equipment has dropped dramatically. Today even the smallest business can afford a computer capable of keeping its accounting records.

Advantages of Computer Systems

Computerized systems offer many advantages over manual systems:

Speed. A computerized system can provide information more quickly than a manual system because the computer can perform tasks instantaneously that are time-consuming when done manually.

Volume of output. A much larger volume of transactions can be handled using a computerized system because of its speed of processing.

Error protection.   Using a computer greatly reduces the number of errors because the computer does calculations more accurately than a human. Also, computerized accounting systems have many error-protection features. For example, most systems do not accept an entry that does not balance.

Automatic posting.   Posting is automatically performed in a computerized system —an enormous savings in time. Not only is the repetitive task of posting time-consuming, but it can create many errors in a manual accounting system. Using a computer ensures that each entry is posted accurately. This prevents such errors as double posting, posting to the wrong account, posting a debit as a credit (and vice versa), and posting the wrong amount.

Automatic report preparation.   Reports can be generated automatically in a computerized accounting system — journals, ledgers, the financial statements, and special reports to aid management in decision making.

Automatic document printing.   A computerized system can provide many of the documents used in a business — invoices, monthly statements for accounts receivable customers, payroll checks, and employee earnings statements, among others.

Accounting procedures are basically the same whether performed manually or on a computer. Exhibit 28-1 reviews the accounting cycle from Chapter 4 and lists the corresponding steps in a computerized system. Observe how many steps the computer performs automatically.

Computer Basics

A computer **program** is a set of instructions that tells the computer what to do. Without a program it cannot perform even the simplest tasks. This does not mean that you must become a programmer to use a computer for accounting. Since accounting is one of the computer's most important applications, many programs have been written to handle accounting data. To use the computer for accounting, a business can simply purchase a program that suits its needs and is compatible with its computer.

Hardware

Computers are classified according to their speed and the amount of data they can store. There are three basic classes of computers: mainframes, minicomputers, and microcomputers. In the 1950s the only type of computer available for accounting applications was the mainframe. A *mainframe* computer can handle a large volume of transactions very quickly, but its cost is prohibitive for most small businesses. In the late 1960s the *minicomputer* was developed. It was less powerful and less expensive than the mainframe.

As technology progressed, a new type of computer was developed — the **microcomputer,** which is small enough for each employee to have one. At first microcomputers were not very powerful and were used mostly for playing computer games. However, new ones were soon developed with more memory and speed. Some microcomputers today are more powerful than the mainframes of the 1950s and they are very affordable. A complete microcomputer system can be purchased for less than $2,000. Because of their low cost, programmers have a

EXHIBIT 28-1   *Comparison of the Accounting Cycle in a Manual System and in a Computerized System*

Accounting Cycle in a Manual System	Accounting Cycle in a Computerized System
1. Start with the account balances in the ledger at the beginning of the period.	1. Same
2. Analyze and journalize transactions as they occur.	2. Analyze transactions and enter them in the computer, which automatically prepares a journal that can be printed at any time.
3. Post journal entries to the ledger accounts.	3. The computer automatically posts from the journal to the ledger.
4. Compute the unadjusted balance in each account at the end of the period.	4. The computer automatically computes the balance in each account.
5. Enter the trial balance on the work sheet and complete the work sheet.	5. The computer automatically prepares a trial balance. Enter adjusting entries in the computer. No work sheet is needed.
6. Using the work sheet as a guide, a. Prepare the financial statements b. Journalize and post adjusting entries c. Journalize and post closing entries	6. The computer automatically prepares the financial statements and posts the adjusting and closing entries.
7. Prepare the post-closing trial balance.	7. The computer automatically prepares the post-closing trial balance.

OBJECTIVE 2

Compare the accounting cycle in a manual system and in a computerized system

large market for their software programs. Hundreds of software packages have been produced for the microcomputer, making it a valuable business tool. Some medium and large-size businesses still require mainframes and minicomputers, but microcomputer packages now provide virtually all of the features offered by larger computers and can easily meet the needs of small businesses.

Although we concentrate on accounting procedures for microcomputers, the basic procedures are the same no matter what type of computer is used. Exhibit 28-2 shows the hardware for a typical microcomputer system consisting of three main types of components:

Input devices (disk drive and keyboard)
Central processing unit (the "brain" of the computer)
Output devices (monitor, printer, and disk drive)

Input Devices.   Input devices are used to feed instructions and data into the computer. An input device usually found on a computer system is a **disk drive,** which reads data and instructions from magnetic disks. The most common form of disk is the floppy **diskette,** also called a floppy disk. This thin, 5¼-inch diameter round diskette, enclosed in a square plastic envelope, can store approximately 360,000 characters of data and costs under $3. Exhibit 28-3 is a picture of a floppy diskette.

To use the computer program or the data stored on a diskette, place the diskette in the disk drive, and the computer can read the information from it. Some computers use a hard disk. This type of disk is metal and can hold much more information than a floppy diskette. However, it is also more expensive.

EXHIBIT 28-2   *Microcomputer Hardware*

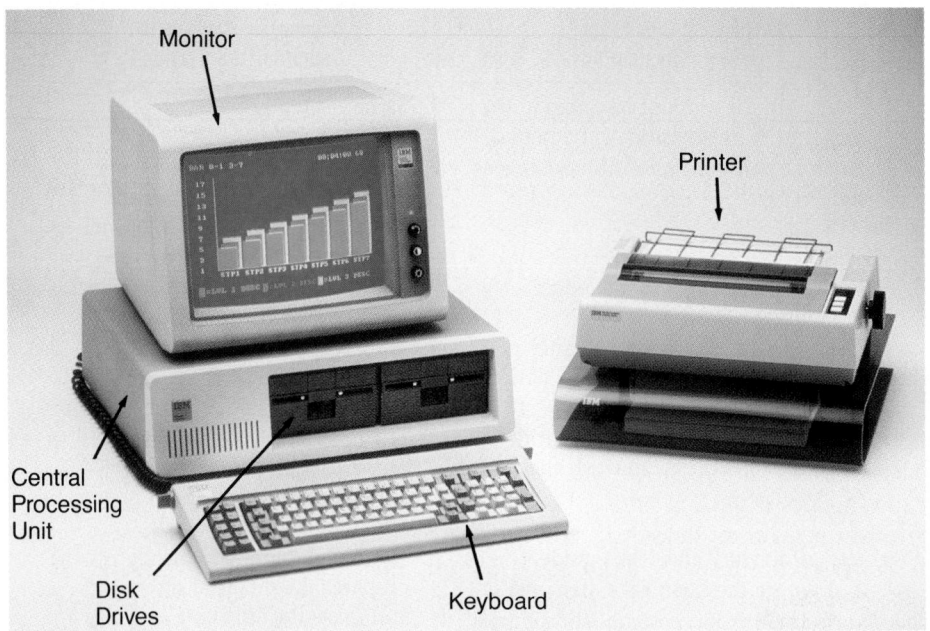

The other input device usually found in a microcomputer system is the *keyboard.* Much like a typewriter keyboard, this device is used to enter data and instructions.

Central Processing Unit.   The **central processing unit (CPU)** is the "brain" of the microcomputer. The CPU does the "thinking" for the computer. It performs mathematical and logical operations and controls all the other components of the system.

Output Devices.   *Output devices* give us the information we want to receive from the computer—in several ways. The **monitor** looks like a television screen and allows the user to view data being processed and to receive messages from the program being run.

EXHIBIT 28-3   *Floppy Diskette*

The *printer* can provide printed copies of the information after it has been processed. Examples of the printed copies (also called *hard copies*) in an accounting system include printouts of the balance sheet and income statement, payroll checks, and invoices for mailing to customers.

A third common output device is the disk drive (which we also listed as an input device). We can save the records that have been updated during processing by placing them on a diskette. When the computer is turned off at the end of a work session, the internal memory in the CPU "forgets" the data put into it. However, the diskette provides extra storage for later use.

Accounting Software Programs

Accounting packages are usually sold in *modules.* Each module handles a particular area of the accounting records — general ledger, accounts receivable, inventory, accounts payable, and payroll. Others are available for specific functions such as billing, budgeting, plant asset management, and job costing. Generally each module is written on a separate diskette, so that one module can be used alone or several modules can be used together.

Payroll procedures are often the first accounting function to be computerized. This area is ideally suited to computerization because of the repetitive nature of payroll activities and the large number of mathematical calculations. The accountant can save a great deal of time by putting a large payroll on the computer but still keep the other accounting records on a manual basis.

Many businesses can do their accounting more efficiently by computerizing several accounting functions. Bringing several modules together requires **integrated software,** which includes modules that handle different functions and coordinate the output of the various modules. For instance, to record a collection of cash on accounts receivable, you would use the accounts receivable module. The journal entry would be recorded in the cash receipts journal in this module, and the customer's account would automatically be updated. In an integrated system this information would also be posted to the Cash and Accounts Receivable accounts in the general ledger module.

Most computerized systems have common features. Virtually all accounting programs are **menu-driven.** This means that when you turn the computer on and insert the program diskette, a list of options will be displayed for you to choose from — in the same way you select food from a restaurant menu. To choose a particular computer function, simply highlight your choice and hit the enter key. **Menus** simplify the task of learning to use an accounting program. Each time the program is loaded onto the computer, a menu will come onto the screen listing the choice of functions. The first menu is called a master menu. It will guide you to the section of the program sought. When you choose an option, the computer will either perform the function or display a new set of menu choices to receive more instructions. A typical master menu is shown in Exhibit 28-4.

To work with a particular module of this program you would simply select from the menu. To use the general ledger section of this program you would type a "1."

Generally, in a computerized system (as in a manual system with a large volume of data), transactions are recorded in batches. Transactions are not recorded the instant they occur. Rather, similar transactions are recorded in groups. For example, instead of recording each sale or purchase immediately, we would record each day's sales at one time and then all of the purchases at one time. In the remainder of this section we discuss four common modules and explain how batches of transactions might be handled by a typical accounting software package.

EXHIBIT 28-4   Master Menu

```
MASTER MENU
COPYRIGHT © 1988 BY ACCT. SOFTWARE, INC.
ALL RIGHTS RESERVED


   1}  GENERAL LEDGER MODULE
   2}  ACCOUNTS RECEIVABLE MODULE
   3}  ACCOUNTS PAYABLE MODULE
   4}  PAYROLL MODULE
   5}  EXIT PROGRAM


   OPTION?
```

OBJECTIVE 3

Describe how a general ledger software program works

General Ledger Module

The general ledger module is the center of an integrated system. In this module all of the general ledger accounts are maintained. Exhibit 28-5 is a typical menu for using a general ledger module.

One option included in this module is the chart of accounts feature. The accountant sets up the chart of accounts by telling the computer each account's name, number, normal balance, and type (current asset, plant asset, and so on). Since the program will remember this information, it need be entered only once. This chart can be modified as necessary. Once the chart has been set up, the accountant can refer to an account simply by listing its account number. With this

EXHIBIT 28-5   Menu for General Ledger Module

```
ACCOUNTING SOFTWARE, INC.
GENERAL LEDGER MENU

   1}  SET UP CHART OF ACCOUNTS
   2}  EDIT/DELETE CHART OF ACCOUNTS
   3}  VIEW/PRINT CHART OF ACCOUNTS
   4}  ENTER TRANSACTIONS
   5}  PRINT JOURNAL
   6}  POST TRANSACTIONS
   7}  VIEW/PRINT GENERAL LEDGER
   8}  VIEW/PRINT TRIAL BALANCE
   9}  PRINT FINANCIAL STATEMENTS
  10}  PERFORM END-OF-PERIOD PROCESS


   OPTION?
```

information, the program can supply the account name and other information by referring back to the chart of accounts.

Journal entries can also be entered through this module. Just as in the manual system of Chapters 1–5, some businesses choose to use the general journal as their only book of original entry. In Chapter 6 we saw the advantages of special journals. The same option exists in a computerized system. The general ledger module can be used on a stand-alone basis, with the general journal as the only book of original entry. Other modules with their special journals can also be used in an integrated system.

To make a journal entry we list the number of each account affected (the computer will supply the account name), the amount of the transaction, and the choice of either debit or credit for that account. Once the transaction has been listed, the program will ask if the entry is correct before recording it. The computer will then check to see if the journal entry balances (debits equal credits).

After the entries have been recorded, the general journal can be printed. This print-out, commonly called a "hard copy," provides a permanent record of the journal entries. Most companies with computerized systems keep hard copies of all work to document the accounting records. Exhibit 28-6 shows a sample page of general journal entries.

Posting in a computer system is easy. In the system menu of Exhibit 28-5, choose menu option 6, "Post Transactions." The program will post and also enter posting references automatically. This represents a considerable time saving over

EXHIBIT 28-6 *General Journal Entries*

```
J&L OFFICE SUPPLY
GENERAL JOURNAL
PAGE 08
-------------------------------------------------------------------------
TRANS    DATE    ACCT NO.    ACCT. NAME                DR.          CR.
-------------------------------------------------------------------------
 32     4/20      1360      STORE EQUIP             1130.00
                  2200        ACCOUNTS PAYABLE                    1130.00
-------------------------------------------------------------------------
 33     4/20      5400      SALARY EXP              1900.00
                  2710        EMPLOYEE INCOME TAX PAY              399.00
                  2711        FICA TAX PAY                        135.85
                  2712        EMPLOYEE HEALTH INS. PAY             16.00
                  2713        EMPLOYEE UNION DUES PAY              35.00
                  2720        SALARIES PAY                       1314.15
-------------------------------------------------------------------------
 34     4/20      5410      PAYROLL TAX EXP          212.65
                  2711        FICA TAX PAY                        135.85
                  2718        STATE UNEMPL TAX PAY                 67.20
                  2719        FED UNEMPL TAX PAY                    9.60
-------------------------------------------------------------------------
 35     4/20      4130      SALES RET & ALL           86.40
                  2370      SALES TAX PAY              6.05
                  1200        ACCOUNTS REC                        92.45
-------------------------------------------------------------------------
 36     4/20      2200      ACCOUNTS PAYABLE         651.00
                  5130        PURCH RET & ALL                     651.00
-------------------------------------------------------------------------

-------------------------------------------------------------------------
 39     4/21      1360      STORE EQUIP              400.00
                  2200        ACCOUNTS PAY                        400.00
-------------------------------------------------------------------------
                            PAGE TOTALS             5056.10       5056.10
                                                    ======        ======
```

the manual method of posting. It is also more accurate, because the computer is unlikely to make a posting error.

Accountants may wish to see (on the screen or printed out) the whole general ledger — in order to check each account, for example. A printout of a few general ledger accounts is shown in Exhibit 28-7. Note that the posting references refer to other journals besides the general journal. These postings come from the other modules, as explained later.

At the end of the period, the program produces the trial balance as a basis for making the adjusting entries. Adjusting entries, like all other general journal entries, are recorded using the "Enter Transactions" option in Exhibit 28-5. These entries are posted using the posting option on the menu. Once this is done, the account balances are updated and ready to be reported on the financial statements.

An important feature of a computerized system is that a work sheet is unnecessary. The reason for a work sheet in a manual system is to organize data to prepare the financial statements and the adjusting and closing entries. On the work sheet ending balances are computed for the statements and the closing entries. Having the machine perform these steps automatically eliminates this time-consuming task. To print the financial statements, simply select this option from the menu, and the statements are created automatically.

Most accounting packages include an option allowing you to request that the temporary accounts be automatically closed at the end of the period. In Exhibit

EXHIBIT 28-7   *General Ledger Accounts*

```
J&L OFFICE SUPPLY
GENERAL LEDGER
AS OF 04-30-XX


CASH                                              ACCOUNT NO. 1100

DATE        EXPLANATION        REF        DR.          CR.         BALANCE

19XX
0401        BEG. BAL.          ---                                 35540.00 DR
0430        TOTAL              CR12       23671.00                 59211.00 DR
0430        TOTAL              CD7                     31437.23    27773.77 DR


PETTY  CASH                                       ACCOUNT NO. 1120

DATE        EXPLANATION        REF        DR.          CR.         BALANCE

0401        BEG. BAL.          ---                                  100.00 DR


ACCOUNTS RECEIVABLE                               ACCOUNT NO. 1200

DATE        EXPLANATION        REF        DR.          CR.         BALANCE

0401        BEG. BAL.          ---                                  8743.00 DR
0420                           J8                      92.45        8650.55 DR
0420                           J8                      107.00       8543.55 DR
0430        TOTAL              S16        19872.00                 28415.55 DR
0430        TOTAL              CR12                    25112.00      3303.55 DR
```

28-5, this menu option, "Perform End-of-Period Process," closes the accounts and prepares a post-closing trial balance. The post-closing trial balance can be printed by choosing the "View/Print Trial Balance" option in the general ledger menu. Just as in a manual system, this completes the accounting cycle, with balances updated and ready for use in the next accounting period.

Accounts Receivable Module

The accounts receivable module is used to keep track of the accounts receivable subsidiary ledger and to provide special journals for recording transactions that affect this asset account. In Chapter 6 we discussed the need for the sales journal and the cash receipts journal. A typical menu for the accounts receivable module is shown in Exhibit 28-8.

The sales for each day are recorded at one time using this module. In some programs the sales are entered in general journal format:

```
Apr. 19   Accounts Receivable—Customer Name . . . . . . . . . . . . . .    1,300
              Sales Revenue . . . . . . . . . . . . . . . . . . . . . . . . . . . . . . . .              1,300
```

Other programs allow the accountant to enter each sale in the form of a sales invoice. The program creates an entry for the sales journal and also prints out the actual sale invoice to be sent to the customer, eliminating the manual preparation of these invoices. An example of a computer-generated sale invoice is shown in Exhibit 28-9.

After the day's sales have been entered, a sales journal can be printed. The hard copy is checked for correctness and saved as a permanent record. This journal can now be posted. Just as in a manual system, the sales journal should be posted to

EXHIBIT 28-8   *Menu for Accounts Receivable Module*

```
ACCOUNTING SOFTWARE, INC.
ACCOUNTS RECEIVABLE MENU

   1)   SET UP ACCOUNTS RECEIVABLE LEDGER
   2)   MODIFY ACCTS REC LEDGER
   3)   VIEW/PRINT ACCTS REC LEDGER
   4)   ENTER/PRINT SALES INVOICES
   5)   VIEW/PRINT SALES JOURNAL
   6)   POST SALES JOURNAL TO GEN LEDGER
   7)   POST SALES JOURNAL TO ACCTS REC LEDGER
   8)   ENTER CASH RECEIPTS
   9)   VIEW/PRINT CASH RECEIPTS JOURNAL
  10)   POST CASH RECEIPTS JOURNAL TO GEN LEDGER
  11)   POST CASH RECEIPTS JOURNAL TO ACCTS REC LEDGER
  12)   AGE ACCTS. REC
  13)   PRINT REPORTS


OPTION?
```

EXHIBIT 28-9   *Computer-Generated Sales Invoice*

J&L Office Supply				**INVOICE**		INVOICE NO. 2081

J&L Office Supply   **INVOICE**   INVOICE NO.   2081
1200 Poydras Street   INVOICE DATE 4-23-XX
New Orleans, LA 70130   ACCOUNT NO.   H01000

PAGE 1

SOLD TO: Shaw Engineering Consultants   SHIP TO: Same
          1400 Veteran's Blvd.
          Metarie, LA 70123

PURCHASE ORDER NO.	SALESPERSON	SHIP VIA	FREIGHT	DATE SHIPPED	TERMS
628		Your Truck		April 23	2/10,N/30

QUANTITY	STOCK ITEM	UNIT	DESCRIPTION	UNIT PRICE	DISC %	AMOUNT
10	24X914		Staplers	7.00		70.00
50	87A827		Mechanical Pencils	1.25		62.50
20	24X820		Staples	1.50		30.00
100	42B191		Memo Pads	.25		25.00

	SALE AMOUNT	187.50
	MISC CHARGES SALES TAX FREIGHT	13.13
	TOTAL	200.63

ORIGINAL INVOICE

two ledgers, the accounts receivable ledger in the accounts receivable module and the general ledger in the general ledger module. See 6 and 7 in Exhibit 28-8.

The other journal in the accounts receivable module is the cash receipts journal, where all receipts of cash are recorded. A batch of cash receipt transactions is entered into the computer as it is in manual recording. As with the other journals, a hard copy is printed and checked for correctness. This journal is also posted to both the general ledger and the accounts receivable ledger.

Some programs will keep a running balance of the customer accounts in the accounts receivable subsidiary ledger and also can print monthly statements to be sent to customers. An example of a monthly statement is shown in Exhibit 28-10.

The accounts receivable module can perform an aging of the customer accounts to estimate uncollectible account expense. Using the computer for such tasks saves much time and money.

Exhibit 28-11 shows how information flows through the accounts receivable module and interacts with the general ledger module.

Accounts Payable Module

A business can use the accounts payable program to maintain its accounts payable ledger, issue checks to pay accounts payable, and generate both the purchases and cash payments journals. A typical accounts payable module menu is shown in Exhibit 28-12.

When a purchase invoice is received from a vendor, it is entered into the accounts payable module. For each batch of purchase invoices the program will create a purchases journal. Its entries can be posted to both the accounts payable ledger and the general ledger.

EXHIBIT 28-10 *Customer Monthly Statement*

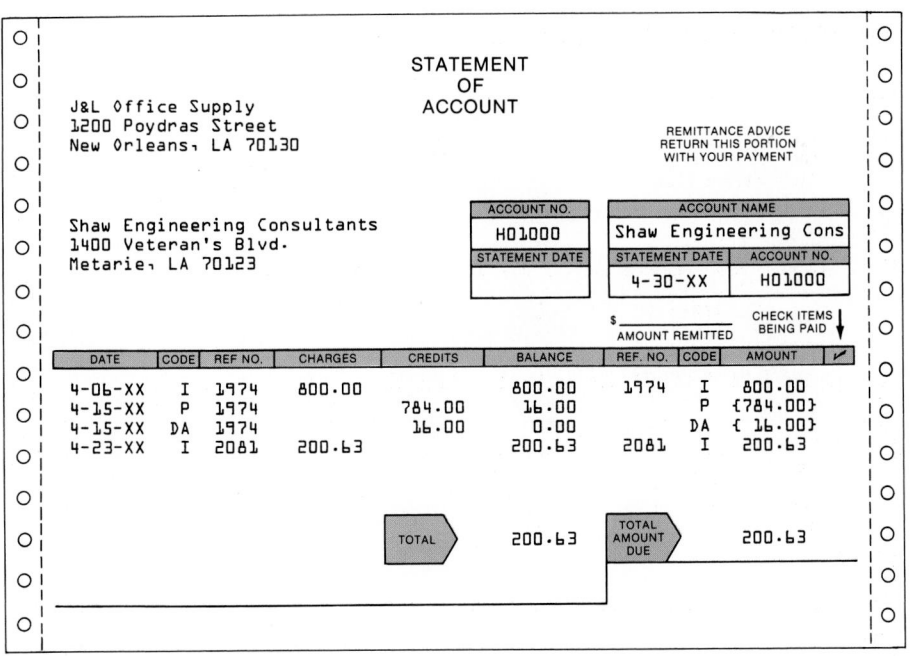

EXHIBIT 28-11 *Information Flow in the Accounts Receivable Module*

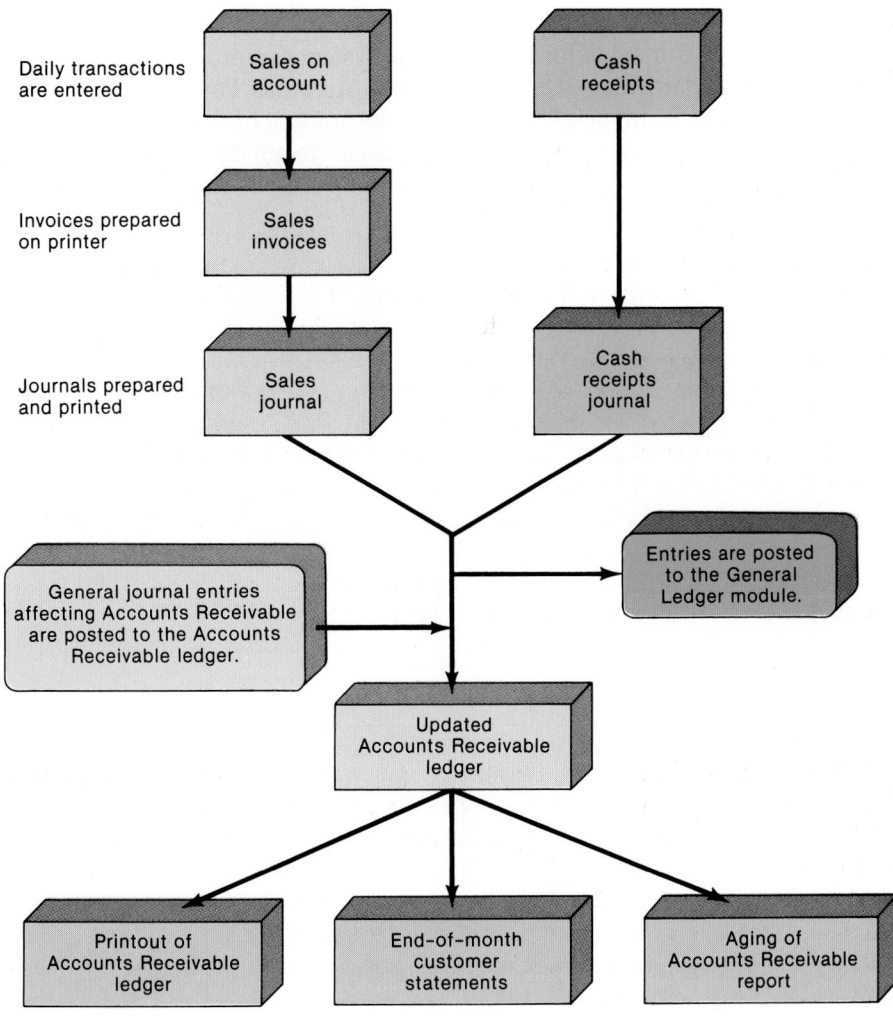

EXHIBIT 28-12   *Menu for Accounts Payable Module*

```
ACCOUNTING SOFTWARE, INC.
ACCOUNTS PAYABLE MENU

 1}   SET UP ACCOUNTS PAYABLE LEDGER
 2}   MODIFY ACCTS PAY LEDGER
 3}   VIEW/PRINT ACCTS PAY LEDGER
 4}   ENTER PURCHASE INVOICES
 5}   VIEW/PRINT PURCHASES JOURNAL
 6}   POST PURCHASES JOURNAL TO GEN LEDGER
 7}   POST PURCHASES JOURNAL TO ACCTS PAY LEDGER
 8}   VIEW/PRINT INVOICES DUE BY DATE
 9}   PRINT CHECKS
10}   VIEW/PRINT CASH DISBURS JOURNAL
11}   POST CASH DISBURS JOURNAL TO GEN LEDGER
12}   POST CASH DISBURS JOURNAL TO ACCTS PAY LEDGER
```

Before invoices come due for payment, the system can provide a list of each invoice due on a particular date (item 8 of the Accounts Payable menu). The accountant can list the invoice to be paid and the amount of the payment. Using preprinted forms, the computer can print the checks (menu item 9). Exhibit 28-13 is an example of a computer-generated check along with its stub showing information about the invoice paid.

EXHIBIT 28-13   *Check for Cash Payment*

GUARANTY NATIONAL BANK

J&L Office Supply
1200 Poydras Street
New Orleans, LA 70130

CHECK 005074

	DATE	CONTROL NO.	AMOUNT
	4-23-XX	4813	4471.60

FOUR THOUSAND FOUR HUNDRED SEVENTY ONE AND 60/100------------------

PAY TO THE ORDER OF   Franklin Paper Co.
2120 Essen Lane
Baton Rouge, LA 70810

J&L Office Supply

_____
AUTHORIZED SIGNATURE

J&L Office Supply—1200 Poydras Street—New Orleans, LA   CHECK 005074

OUR REF. NO.	YOUR INVOICE NO.	INVOICE DATE	INVOICE AMOUNT	AMOUNT PAID	DISCOUNT TAKEN	NET CHECK AMOUNT
P1028	5673	4-10-XX	3080.00	3080.00		3080.00
P1264	5823	4-17-XX	1420.00	1420.00	28.40	1391.60
					TOTAL	4471.60

EXHIBIT 28-14 *Information Flow in the Accounts Payable Module*

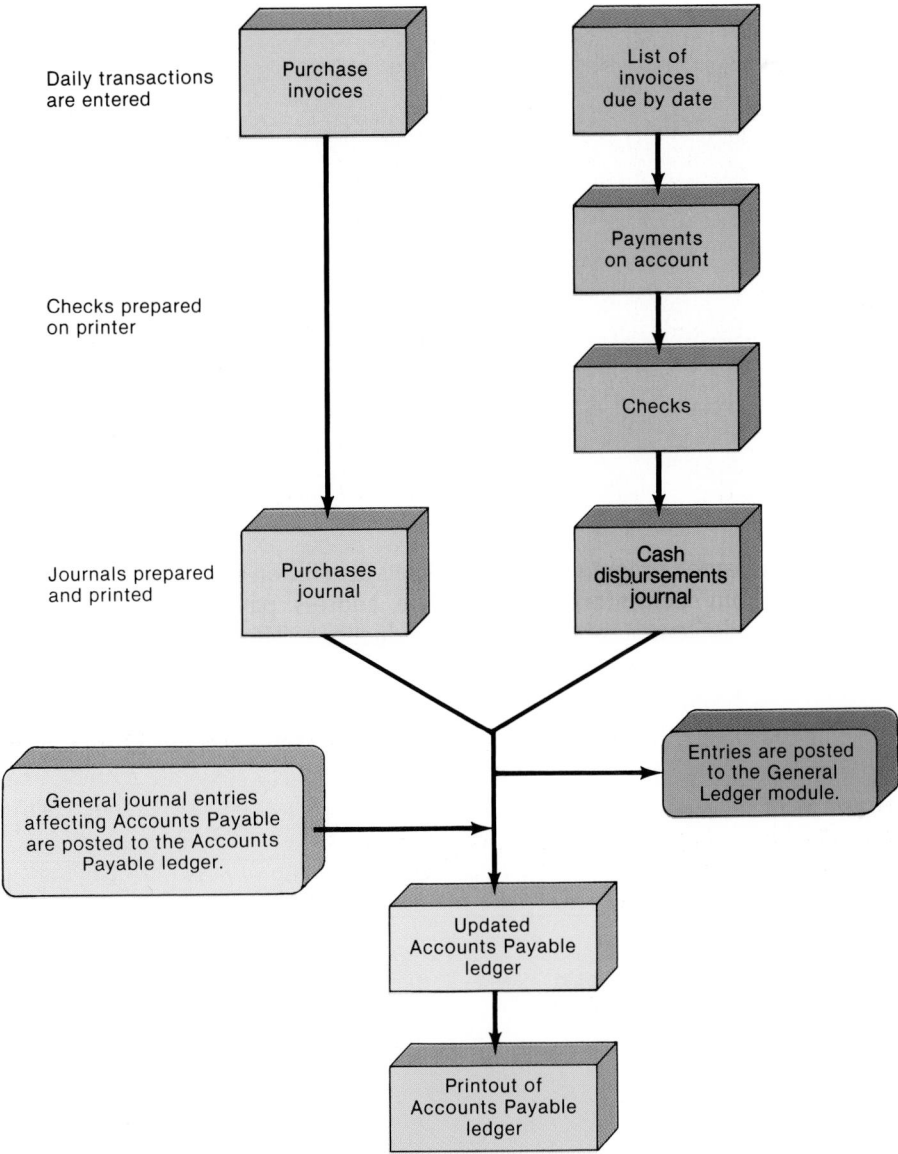

The program records each check in the cash disbursements journal. This journal can be posted to both the accounts payable and general ledgers. Paid invoices can be shown along with the date of payment. A business may wish to print a list of all paid invoices for the records and delete them from the computer files. This step can prevent paying an invoice twice, paying the wrong amount, or mistakenly paying too late to receive the discount. Also, if an inventory module is added to this system, each purchase of merchandise can automatically be added into the inventory list. Exhibit 28-14 shows how information flows in a system using an accounts payable module.

Payroll Module

As stated earlier, payroll accounting is ideally suited for a computerized system. A typical payroll module menu is shown in Exhibit 28-15.

EXHIBIT 28-15   *Menu for a Payroll Module*

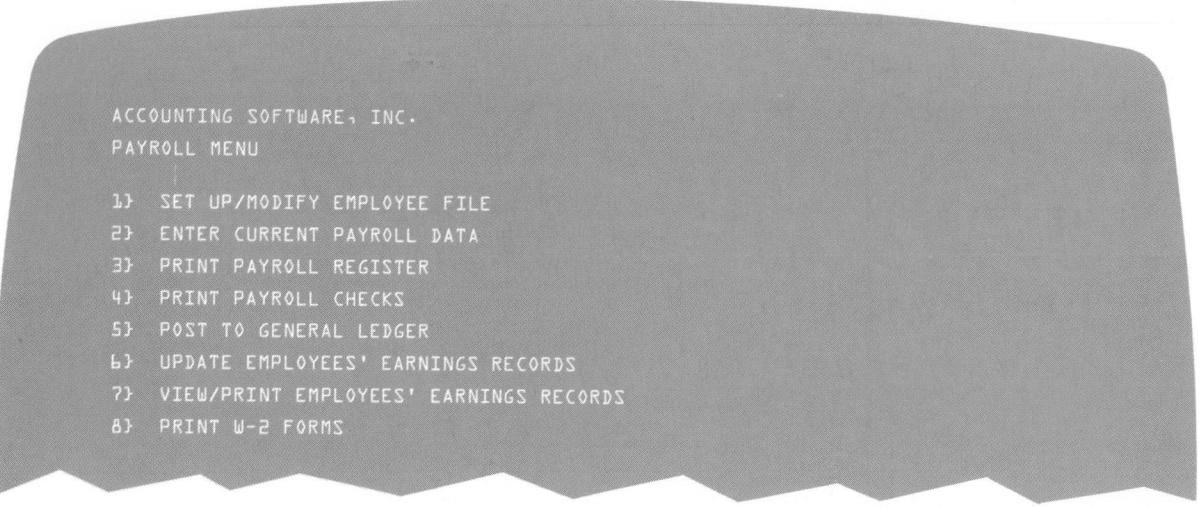

```
ACCOUNTING SOFTWARE, INC.
PAYROLL MENU

1}  SET UP/MODIFY EMPLOYEE FILE
2}  ENTER CURRENT PAYROLL DATA
3}  PRINT PAYROLL REGISTER
4}  PRINT PAYROLL CHECKS
5}  POST TO GENERAL LEDGER
6}  UPDATE EMPLOYEES' EARNINGS RECORDS
7}  VIEW/PRINT EMPLOYEES' EARNINGS RECORDS
8}  PRINT W-2 FORMS
```

To use the payroll program, the business sets up a file on each employee. These files will contain such information as name, address, pay rate, marital status, withholding allowances, and voluntary deductions. This information can be modified at any time (for example, when an employee moves or receives a raise, or when a new employee is hired).

For each pay period we will use the "Enter Current Payroll Data" option in the

EXHIBIT 28-16   *Paycheck*

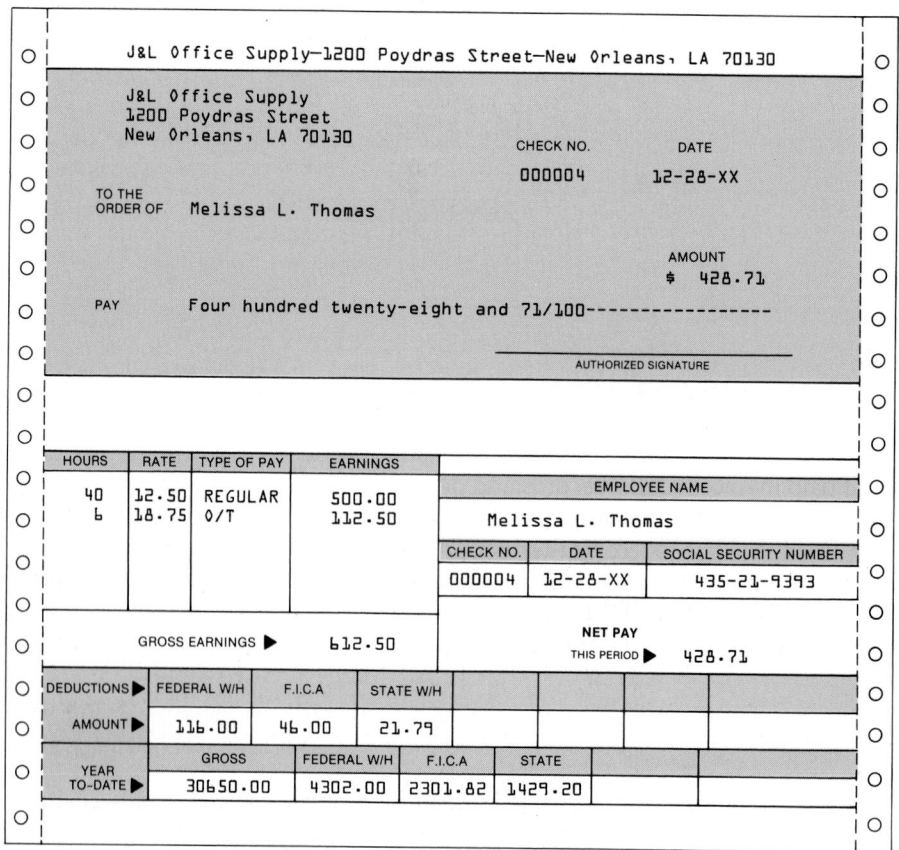

EXHIBIT 28-17   *W-2 Form*

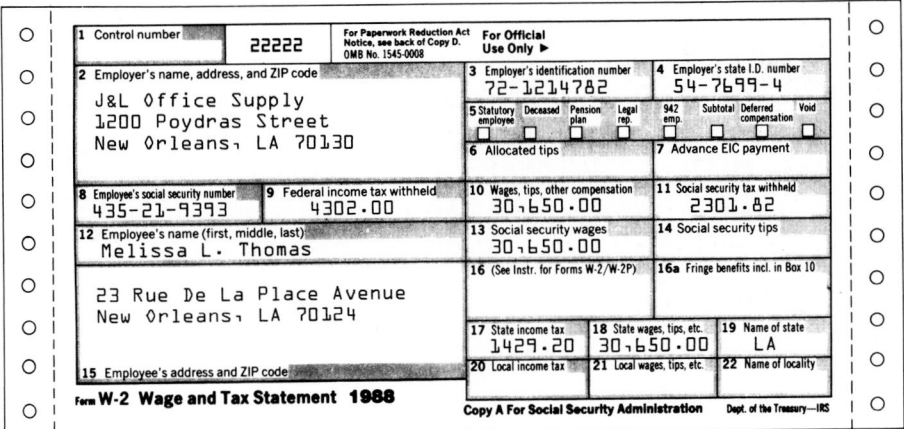

menu to calculate the period's payroll. The program will list each employee and show the current-period information—number of regular and overtime hours worked, bonuses or commissions to be received, and any voluntary deductions from this paycheck. For most employees this information does not change from pay period to pay period and will not have to be modified. After the information for the current payroll is entered, the computer will automatically calculate each paycheck. The program will calculate regular pay, overtime pay, gross pay, each deduction, and net pay. Current tax tables should be built into the program so that both federal and state taxes can be computed. Also, the computer keeps a record of year-to-date earnings for each employee and can calculate FICA taxes.

The program can print the payroll register. After the information is verified, the payroll checks are printed. Using preprinted checks, the program can print checks and the accompanying stubs, as illustrated in Exhibit 28-16.

After the payroll checks have been printed, the payroll register information is posted to the general ledger and the employee's individual earnings records are updated. Both tasks are performed by choosing the appropriate menu option.

At the end of the calendar year the business prepares a W-2 form for each employee. An example is shown in Exhibit 28-17.

Exhibit 28-18, on page 1091, shows how information flows in a system using a payroll module.

Spreadsheets

Spreadsheets are integrated software programs that can be used to solve many different problems. Spreadsheet programs replace the manual solution of problems. Typical accounting applications performed with a spreadsheet include budgets, depreciation schedules, debt amortization schedules, cost-volume-profit analysis, and capital budgeting.

The most popular of the spreadsheet programs is Lotus 1-2-3®, which includes an electronic spreadsheet with graphics and data-management capabilities. Lotus 1-2-3 runs on a variety of personal computers and IBM-compatible computers. Other spreadsheet programs on the market that are structured similarly to Lotus 1-2-3 include VP Planner and Quattro.

The spreadsheet of a 1-2-3 application is organized into a matrix of rows labeled by numbers and columns labeled by letters:

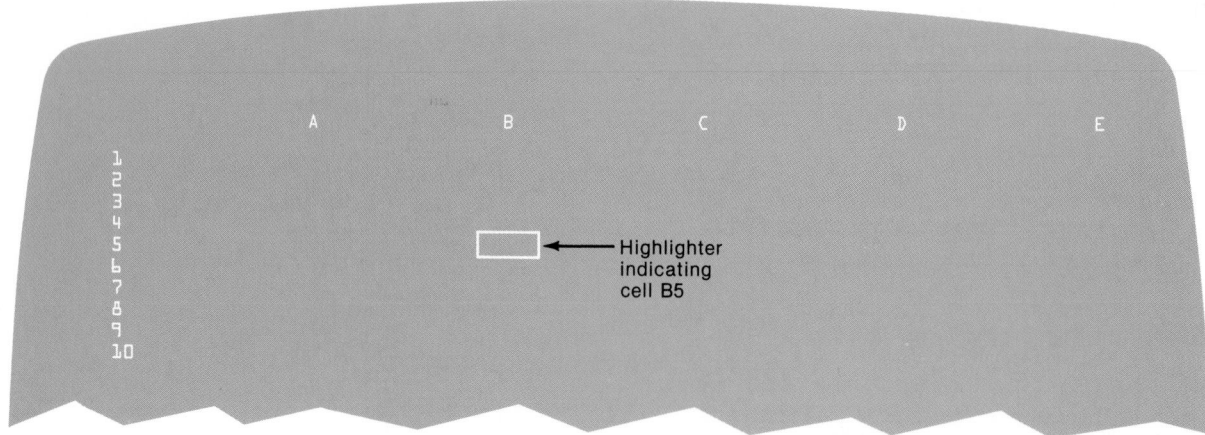

The intersections of the rows and columns represent entry positions called *cells*. The cells may be referenced by their column-row coordinates. Position B5 represents column B and row 5. The spreadsheet of Lotus 1-2-3, Release 2, has 256 columns and 8,192 rows. At each cell, you can type either a label (title) or a value. A value can be a number, a formula, or a 1-2-3 function. The highlighter must be moved to the cell in which you want to enter the label or value. A sample income statement follows.

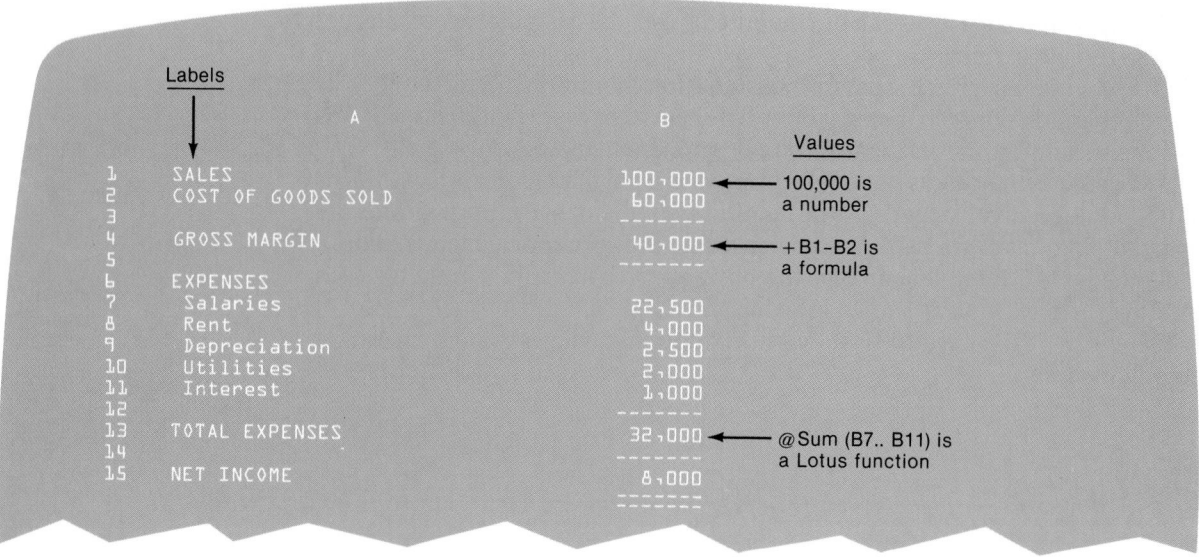

By creating labels and values on the spreadsheet, you can set up charts and tables. Through formatting commands, you control the appearance of the spreadsheet. It is easy to format the spreadsheet as a personal budget or as an income statement for a business. We illustrate formatting later in the chapter.

A powerful feature of a spreadsheet program is its ability to remember the formulas and calculations that have been entered into the spreadsheet. Suppose you want to change the sales in the preceding illustration from $100,000 to $150,000. You can simply make a change in the cell containing the sales amount, B1, and all other entries that depend on sales are automatically recalculated. For example, Gross Margin, in cell B4, would change automatically from $40,000 to

EXHIBIT 28-18 *Information Flow in the Payroll Module*

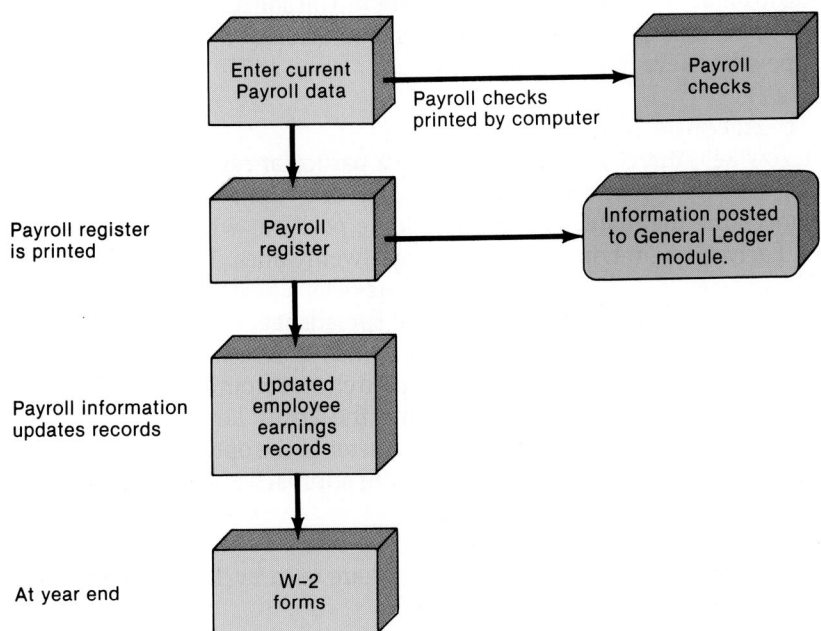

$90,000. This feature makes a spreadsheet very efficient for creating "what-if" analysis without the tedious recalculation by hand calculator and pencil.

Keyboard

The keyboard, an input device for entering data into the computer, includes four major parts: (1) typewriter section, (2) pointer-movement keys, (3) function keys, and (4) special keys. Exhibit 28-19 shows one version of an IBM PC keyboard. The position of the keys may vary slightly among similar keyboards.

Typewriter Section

The typewriter section acts just like a typewriter. Striking a key gives the lower-case character, for example, "g," not "G." Holding down the shift key, ⇧, and pressing any letter or special character results in the upper case of the key. For example, with the shift key depressed, striking the 8 key gives * (the asterisk). If

EXHIBIT 28-19 *IBM PC Keyboard*

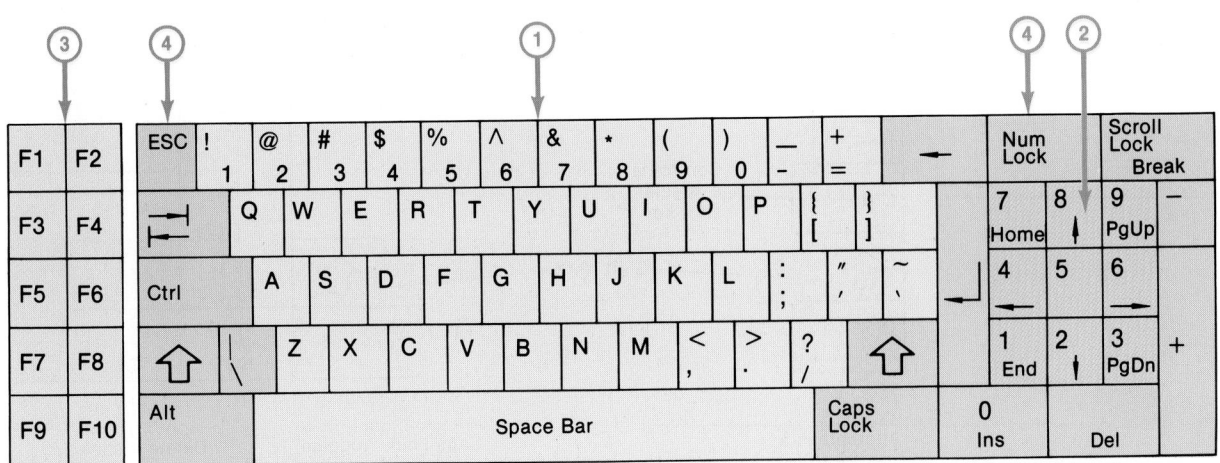

the [Caps Lock] key is ON, then you will get the upper case of the letters without having to depress the shift key in combination. You still must press the shift key to get the upper case of the special (nonletter) characters (+, <, >, ?, and so on). Use the typewriter keys to enter numbers.

Pointer-movement Keys

The arrow keys direct 1-2-3's attention to a particular cell in the spreadsheet by moving the highlighter cell up and down, left and right. Depressing the [Home] key moves the highlighter cell to the Home position, which is column A and row 1. Each screen in Lotus 1-2-3® displays twenty lines. The [PgUp] key moves the screen twenty lines closer to the spreadsheet's beginning. The [PgDn] key moves the screen twenty lines toward the spreadsheet's end.

Lotus 1-2-3 is a menu-driven system, which means that you are presented choices of commands and options to select. To choose from a 1-2-3 menu, you can highlight the appropriate choice by using the arrow keys and depressing ⏎. Alternatively, you can depress the first character of the option desired (for example, to copy a cell, type C for copy). The latter approach is more commonly used.

Function Keys

The ten function keys on the IBM keyboard are used by 1-2-3 as follows:

F1:	Help	Display Help screen	
F2:	Edit	Switch to/from Edit for current entry	
F3:	Name	(Point Mode)	Display menu of range names
F4:	Abs	(Point Mode)	Make/Unmake cell addresses absolute
F5:	GoTo	Move cell pointer to a particular cell	
F6:	Window	(Split screen only) Move cell pointer to other window	
F7:	Query	Repeat most recent Data Query operation	
F8:	Table	Repeat most recent Data Table operation	
F9:	Calc	Recalculates worksheet formulas in Ready Mode	
F10:	Graph	Draws current graph	

Special Keys

We look at some of the special keys in the following diagram.

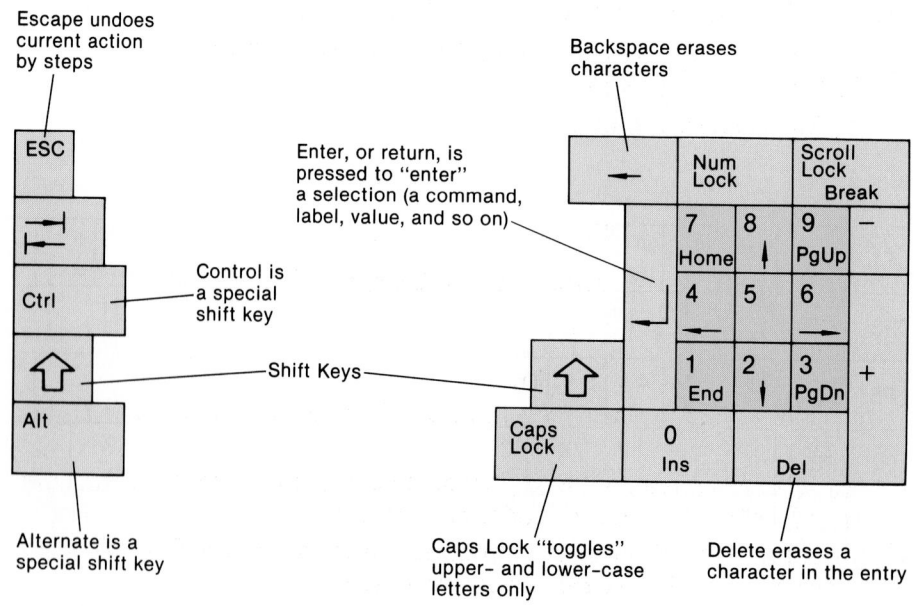

EXHIBIT 28-20 *The Spreadsheet*

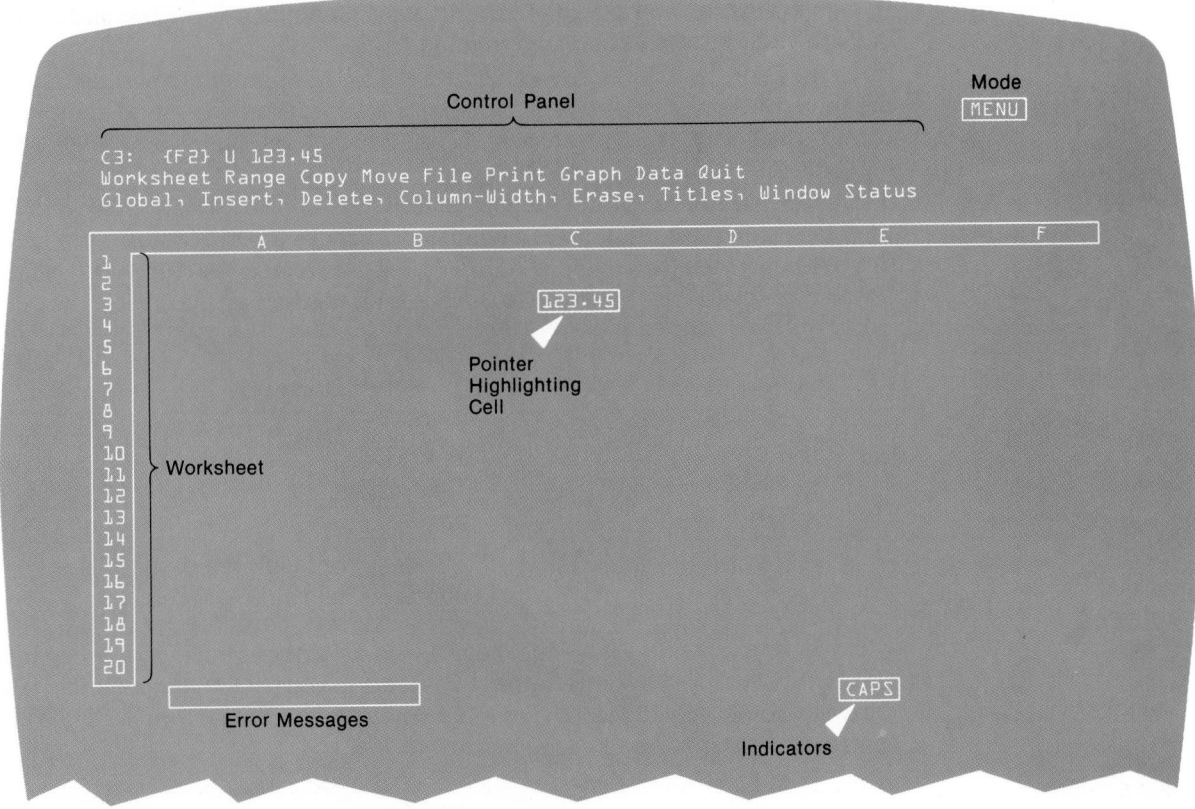

Exhibit 28-20 describes what you see on the monitor screen with 1-2-3.

Mode Indicators

The upper right corner of the 1-2-3 screen tells what is occurring at that time.

Ready   1-2-3 is waiting on you.
Value   You are typing a number, formula, or numeric function.
Label   You are typing a label.
Menu   You are selecting a menu choice.

Moving Around the Spreadsheet

You can move the highlighter cell around the spreadsheet by using one of the following methods:

1. Arrow keys on the numeric pad.
2. Function key, F5. When depressing F5, 1-2-3 will ask for the address (row and column) to seek.
3. The [Home] key returns you to position A1 at the top left-hand corner of the spreadsheet if the worksheet titles have been set.
4. [PgUp] and [PgDn] moves an entire screen up and down. The Tab key (⇥) allows horizontal movement across the screen.

Typing Cell Entries

In the spreadsheet, you can either directly type in numbers, formulas, and labels or use a Copy or Move command to fill in entries.

To type an entry, move the highlighter cell to the appropriate position. Type the entry, then press ↵. As you type, each letter appears on the second line of the control panel above the spreadsheet. If you type in a cell that you have already filled, the new entry replaces the old one.

If you begin an entry with a number-indicator, 1 2 3 4 5 6 7 8 9 0 + − . (@ # or $, then 1-2-3 interprets the entry as a number or formula. If you begin an entry with any other character (for example, A, L, or *), 1-2-3 interprets the entry as a label. A few of these characters have special purposes for positioning the label in the cell:

Special Label Prefix Symbols	Function	Example Cell
' (apostrophe)	left-aligns	123.45
" (quotation mark)	right-aligns	123.45
^ (caret)	centers	123.45
\ (backslash)	fills entire cell with the character following \	

If you want to enter a label that begins with a number-indicator, precede the entry with a special label prefix symbol. By doing so you tell the computer that the entry is a label and not a value. For example, if you want a column headed by a centered "1," begin the "1" with a caret.

Correcting Mistakes

If you make an incorrect entry before depressing ↵, you can correct the error two ways. Either blank out the entire entry by depressing [Esc] or use the backspace key, which erases the incorrect characters.

After storing an entry in a particular cell (by depressing ↵ after typing in the entry), you can use the Edit mode to correct the error. To Edit, locate the pointer at the cell in question and depress F2. Once in the Edit mode, the current contents of the cell will appear in the upper left corner of the screen with the cursor (the flashing underline symbol) at the end of the entry. The cursor indicates the position of the next character to be typed.

Deleting
[Backspace]   Delete character preceding the cursor
[Del]   Delete character at the cursor

Most personal computers have an auto-repeat feature that is particularly useful with these editing keys. When you hold a key down, it repeats its function at about 2 strokes per second.

Inserting
Just type new characters to be inserted at the cursor position. 1-2-3 always inserts new characters in the Edit mode. It does not "overstrike" or "replace" existing characters with newly added ones. Therefore, you must insert new characters after deleting old ones. For example, to change a cell, first delete the old characters. Then enter the new ones. When you are finished editing, depress ↵ to store the changed entry.

Formulas

A formula is a cell entry that instructs 1-2-3 to calculate a number. Often a formula uses cell addresses as values. For example, the formula +A1+A2 means to sum the values in cells A1 and A2 and enter that number in the highlighted cell.

The arithmetic operators used in formulas are listed in their order of precedence.

Arithmetic operator	Result
*	multiplication
/	division
+	addition
−	subtraction

In the formula +A1+A2/A3, the division would be carried out before the addition even though the "/" sign comes after the "+" sign. You can use parentheses to override the built-in order. Writing the above formula as (A1+A2)/A3 would cause the addition to take place first.

Start formulas with a "+" sign. This ensures that 1-2-3 will not think you are typing a label. Alternatively, you can place parentheses around the formula to guarantee that the entry will be interpreted as a value rather than as a label.

Cell Addresses in Formulas

A major benefit of spreadsheet software is the ability to enter a formula in one cell and then copy that formula into many other cells. Cell addresses are relative or absolute.

RELATIVE ADDRESSES.   A cell address that does not include a "$" character is relative. Assume the formula +B1−B2 is entered into B4. Relative to B4, cell B1 is 3 rows above and cell B2 is 2 rows above. We can, then, interpret the formula to mean "take the number in the cell 2 rows up (but in the same column) and subtract from it the number 3 rows up." The resulting amount is entered into the cell in which this formula appears. See cell B4 in the next display. We copy this formula to columns C, D, and E. Since the cell addresses are relative, the formula in cell C4 means to subtract the amount in C2 from the amount in C1. The formula shifts similarly as we copy +B1−B2 into columns D and E.

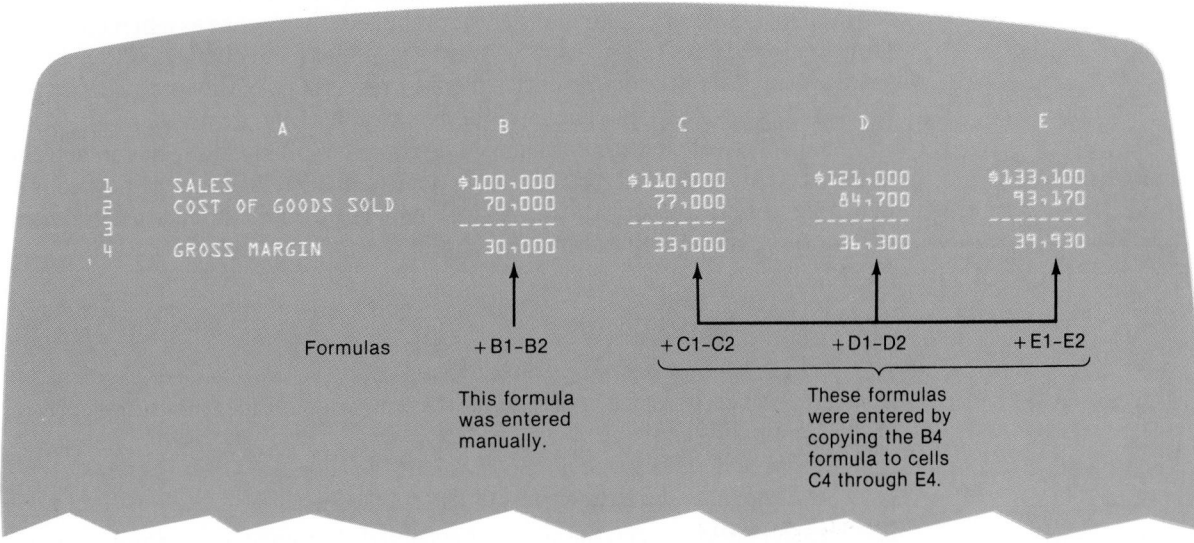

Notice in the above example how each B in the formula in cell B4 changed to a C, a D, and an E when the formula was copied to cells C4 through E4. When a formula with relative cell addresses is copied across columns, as in this example, the letter portion of the addresses will change relative to the new column. When a formula with relative cell addresses is copied down rows, the number portion of the addresses will change relative to the new row.

ABSOLUTE ADDRESSES (USED ONLY IN FORMULAS).   A cell address in which the symbol "$" precedes both the column letter and the row number is absolute, which means it will not change even if it is copied elsewhere. In a formula, an absolute cell address indicates the value's exact column/row location. The formula 12*$C$5 means "twelve times the value of cell C5." The result of this multiplication will be the same in however many cells to which this formula is copied. In a copied formula, all absolute cell addresses are the same as in the original formula (C5 in this case).

A formula may contain both relative and absolute addresses. "Mixed" addresses—part relative, part absolute—can also be used.

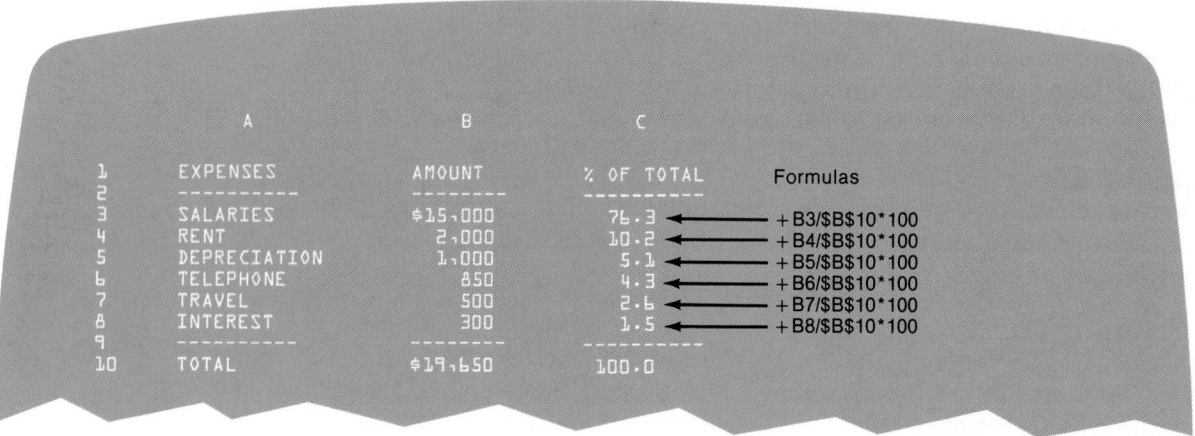

	A	B	C	
1	EXPENSES	AMOUNT	% OF TOTAL	Formulas
2	----------	--------	----------	
3	SALARIES	$15,000	76.3	+B3/$B$10*100
4	RENT	2,000	10.2	+B4/$B$10*100
5	DEPRECIATION	1,000	5.1	+B5/$B$10*100
6	TELEPHONE	850	4.3	+B6/$B$10*100
7	TRAVEL	500	2.6	+B7/$B$10*100
8	INTEREST	300	1.5	+B8/$B$10*100
9	----------	--------	----------	
10	TOTAL	$19,650	100.0	

The formula (B3/$B$10) in cell C3 was entered manually. The formulas in cells C4 through C8 were entered by copying this same formula from cell C3 to cells C4 through C8. Placing a "$" in front of the "B" and in front of the "10" in the formula in cell C3 keeps $B$10 constant in cells C4 through C8. Notice however that the "3" in B3 *does* change relative to the new rows. We want $B$10 to remain constant in the denominator in order to compute each expense as a percent of the same total—$19,650. However, we want the "3" in B3 to change relative to the new rows in order to compute each expense's percentage of the total. This is why we do not place a $ symbol around the B3 portion of the formula.

When you create a formula that is to be copied to other cells, ask yourself the question, "Do I want part of the formula not to change relative to the new cells in which the formula is copied?" If the answer is yes, you must place a "$" before each portion of the address that should not change.

1-2-3 Commands

During each 1-2-3 session, you can issue commands to operate on the spreadsheet. Commands can:

1.   Copy, move, and delete entries in the spreadsheet.
2.   Transfer data between the spreadsheet and disk storage (for example, to store

the spreadsheet on a diskette and to retrieve the spreadsheet from a storage diskette).

3. Print reports.

To use a command, depress the slash (/) key. A menu with the following choices on the first line will appear:

```
Worksheet Range Copy Move File Print Graph Data System Quit
```

You can choose one of these commands either by typing the first letter of the command or by pointing the highlighter to the command and depressing ↵. Most of the commands have submenus, from which you choose the next steps as necessary. If you want to interrupt a command, depress [Esc]. Each time you depress [Esc], you back up one level.

In general, when you want an option that affects the entire spreadsheet, you choose the Worksheet option. When you want a command that affects limited cells, you typically choose the Range option. The Copy command saves time by minimizing the manual entry of cells. The Move command is a "cut and paste" operation that allows you to "cut" out a portion of the spreadsheet and "paste" it to another area without having to retype the information. The File command is used to save or retrieve a file stored on a diskette. The Print command allows you to print a copy of your spreadsheet on paper. The Graph command is used to draw five different types of graphs. The Data command is used to sort data in a spreadsheet either alphabetically or numerically and also to select certain data from the spreadsheet. The System command (in a later release of 1-2-3) returns control of the computer to its operating system. The Quit commmand is used to stop operations in 1-2-3.

Application of Common 1-2-3 Commands

1. Changing column widths   Initially the widths of all 256 columns are 9 characters. This width can be decreased or increased as follows:

/Worksheet Global Column-Width
changes the width of all the columns.

/Worksheet Column-Width *Set*
changes the width of only the column in which the highlighter was positioned prior to issuing the command.

With either command, you will be asked what width you want. You can either type the width or use the left or right directional arrow key. The right arrow key increases the width, and the left arrow key decreases it. After you have selected the desired width, depress ↵ to enter the command.

2. Formatting the spreadsheet   Formatting, in computer language, determines how results are to be displayed. Lotus 1-2-3 provides several formats in a spreadsheet. You can use dollar signs, commas, a fixed number of decimal positions, and percent signs in numbers. You can format the entire spreadsheet with one command, or you can format selected cells. A format command does not affect cells that are labels, even if the labels are numbers. A format command does not affect what is actually stored in a cell. The command affects only the appearance of the cell, as follows:

/Worksheet Global *Format*
affects the appearance of the entire spreadsheet;

/Range Format
affects the appearance of selected cells.

With either selection, you are asked for the specific format of your choice. The following choices and their results are:

Format	Result of Format
1. Currency	Displays numbers with a leading $ and places commas where necessary.
2. , [Comma]	Produces same format as currency but omits the $.
3. Percent.....................	Multiplies the entry by 100 and places a % on the end of the display.

3. Erasing the contents of existing cells
/Worksheet Erase Yes
erases the contents of *all* the cells in the spreadsheet. Use this command with care.

/Range Erase
erases selected cells. At the end of the command, you will be asked which cells you want to erase. You can type the range. A range is specified by typing the first and last cell addresses in the range and separating them by a period. For example, A1. C1 specifies cells A1, B1, and C1. The range A1. C3 specifies cells A1, A2, A3, B1, B2, B3, and C1, C2, C3.

4. Inserting or deleting columns or rows Before issuing the following commands, you should place the highlighter in the column or row where you want to insert or delete.

/Worksheet Insert (Column or Row)
/Worksheet Delete (Column or Row)

5. Moving cells You can "cut" cells out of the spreadsheet and "paste" them into another area by specifying a FROM and a TO range. The FROM range specifies the cells you want to move, and the TO range specifies where you want the cells to be placed.

/Move From: Range (for example, B5.B8) To: Range (for example, C5.C8)

6. Copying cells You can copy (a) one cell to another cell, (b) one cell to many cells, and (c) many cells to many cells. In copying cells, you must specify a FROM range and a TO range for the command. You can specify these ranges by typing.
Copying examples:
   (a) One cell to another cell
       If you want to copy the contents of cell A1 to cell B1, you would issue the following command and ranges:
                    /Copy From: A1 To: B1
   (b) One cell to many cells
       If you want to copy the contents of cell A1 to cells B1 through H1, you would issue the following command and ranges:
                    /Copy From: A1 To: B1.H1

(c) Many cells to many cells

If you want to copy the contents of cells A10 through A15 to columns B through H, you would issue the command and ranges:

/Copy   From: A10.A15   To: B10.H15

7. Interacting with the storage diskette   To make a permanent copy of your active spreadsheet on a storage diskette or to retrieve a previously stored spreadsheet from the diskette and load it into the computer memory, issue a File command.

/*File Save*

copies the spreadsheet on the screen to your storage diskette. When you save a spreadsheet for the first time, you will be asked for a file name. This name can be as long as eight characters with no spaces in the name. The file name can be a combination of letters, numbers, and special characters. When you save a spreadsheet for the second time or thereafter, the original name you gave it will appear after you enter /File Save. If you depress ↵, you will be presented with the options Cancel or Replace. If you choose the option Replace, the old version stored on the diskette will be written over (replaced) by the new version. If you want to keep the old version on the diskette and also save the new version, change the name of the present file after issuing the command /File Save.

/*File Retrieve*

moves a previously stored spreadsheet into memory. A list of the stored spreadsheets will appear on the screen, and you can either type the name or highlight the desired spreadsheet and depress ↵. This operation does not affect the spreadsheet on the diskette. Before you can make changes to or print an existing spreadsheet, you must load it into memory.

8. Printing a 1-2-3 spreadsheet   In order to print a spreadsheet using Lotus 1-2-3, you must first have the spreadsheet loaded into memory and visible on the screen. You should also have the printer turned on, with the online light switched on and the paper positioned at the top of a fresh page.

(a) If you want to print the entire spreadsheet, depress the Home key to move the cursor to the top-left corner of the sheet.

(b) Depress /P for Print and P for Printer, and the following menu will appear:

```
Range  Line  Page  Options  Clear  Align  Go  Quit
```

(c) Select the *Range* option, and respond to the following question by typing the appropriate range:

Enter Print Range:

The cell addresses of the print range define the top left corner and the bottom right corner to be printed. After selecting the appropriate range, depress ↵.

(d) By depressing ↵ after setting the print range, you return to the menu listed in (b). Depress *Align* and then *Go*, and the spreadsheet will begin printing.

Functions

Lotus 1-2-3 includes many mathematical formulas referred to as functions. To use a function, specify its name and the factors that it uses. All function names are preceded by "@." Three important functions are shown in Exhibit 28-21.

EXHIBIT 28-21   *Three Important LOTUS 1-2-3 Functions*

Function Name	What It Does
@SUM(range or list)	Adds the values in the range or list
Examples:	
@SUM(B5.B9)	Adds values in B5 through B9.
@SUM(C8,D3,F2)	Adds values in C8, D3, and F2.
@NPV (interest rate, range)	Computes the present value of the amounts in the range at the specified interest rate.
Example:	
@NPV(.11,A6.A8)	Computes the present value of the amount in A6 for 1 period, the amount in A7 for 2 periods, the amount in A8 for 3 periods, all at 11%, and sums the three present values.
@IF (condition, calculation if true, calculation if false)	Tests a condition and performs the appropriate calculation.
Example:	
@IF(B5>5000,B5*.3,B5*.6)	Tests whether the value in cell B5 exceeds 5,000. If yes, multiply the value in B5 by .3. If no, multiply the value in B5 by .6.

Summary Problem for Your Review

The following spreadsheet is a budgeted income statement for Randolph-Macon Corporation with the following assumptions:

First quarter sales...............	$140,000
Quarterly sales growth	3%
Cost of goods sold..............	70% of sales
Operating expenses.............	as shown
Income tax rate	40%

Directions for Creating the Spreadsheet Model

1. In cell B1 begin typing the three-line heading. Don't worry that the heading will extend into columns D and E. You do not need to widen any of the columns.
2. In cell B5 begin typing the months, MAR, JUNE, SEP, and DEC. Use a ^ as a label prefix to center the months. Remember must depress the shift key in combination with the ^ key.
3. In cell F5 type TOTAL. This entry should be prefaced with a ^.

```
              A                B          C          D          E          F
   1                          Randolph-Macon Corporation
   2                          Budgeted Income Statement
   3               For the Four Quarters ended December 31,19X4
   4
   5                         MAR        JUNE       SEP        DEC       TOTAL
   6
   7     Sales             $140,000   $144,200   $148,526   $152,982   $585,708
   8     Cost of goods sold  98,000    100,940    103,968    107,087    409,995
   9                       --------   --------   --------   --------   --------
  10     Gross margin        42,000     43,260     44,558     45,895    175,713
  11     Operating expenses
  12       Salaries          20,000     20,000     20,000     20,000     80,000
  13       Depreciation       6,000      6,000      6,000      6,000     24,000
  14       Rent               5,000      5,000      5,000      5,000     20,000
  15       Utilities          4,500      4,500      4,500      4,500     18,000
  16       Insurance          1,500      1,500      2,000      2,000      7,000
  17                       --------   --------   --------   --------   --------
  18     Total expenses      37,000     37,000     37,500     37,500    149,000
  19                       --------   --------   --------   --------   --------
  20     Income from operations 5,000    6,260      7,058      8,395     26,713
  21     Income tax expense   2,000      2,504      2,823      3,358     10,685
  22                       --------   --------   --------   --------   --------
  23     Net income         $3,000     $3,756     $4,235     $5,037    $16,028
  24                       ========   ========   ========   ========   ========
```

4. In cell A7 begin typing the labels that define the rows (Sales, Cost of goods sold, and so on). The entries do not need any special label prefix symbols because they are to be left-aligned, which is the default (automatic) alignment for labels. Notice that the individual operating expenses are indented two spaces. You accomplish this by depressing the space bar twice before typing the entry. After typing each category, depress the down arrow key. This will drive the previous entry into its appropriate cell and move the highlighter to the next cell.

5. With the highlighter in cell A9, issue the command /WCS, type 22 over the default width of 9, and depress ↵. This sets the width of column A at 22 characters to accommodate the account titles and income captions.

6. In cell B7 type 140000. (Do not place commas or dollar signs in the number).

7. In cell B8 enter the formula .7*B7. This formula takes the amount in cell B7 and multiplies it by .7, which is 70 percent. This computes cost of goods sold for the first quarter.

8. In cell B9 type the label: ' -------- (eight spaces). Copy this single underlining to cells B17, B19, and B22. To copy it to B17, issue the command:
    /Copy   From: B9.B9 ↵   To: B17 ↵

9. In cell B10 type the formula +B7-B8. This computes gross margin.

10. Beginning in cell B12 enter the expenses for the first quarter. Do not type in the commas. We will use a formatting command to enter the commas later.

11. In cell B18 type the function @SUM(B12.B16). This totals the operating expenses.

12. In cell B20 type the formula +B10-B18. This subtracts total operating expenses from gross margin to compute income from operations.

13. In cell B21 type the formula .4*B20. This formula computes income tax expense.

14. In cell B23 type the formula +B20-B21. This computes net income.

15.   In cell B24 type the label: ' ======== (eight spaces).

16.   In cell C7 type the formula +B7+.03*B7. This formula increases sales by the 3 percent growth rate. Then copy this formula for the remaining 2 quarters with the following command:

   /Copy   From: C7.C7   To: D7.E7

17.   Move to cell B8 and copy column B, rows 8 through 24, across the remaining three quarters using the command:

   /Copy   From: B8.B24   To: C8.E24

18.   Enter the insurance expense for September and December. Delete 1500 and type 2000, or simply type 2000 over 1500.

19.   In cell F7 type the function: @SUM(B7.E7). Then copy this function to total the four quarters using the command:

   /Copy   From: F7.F7   TO: F8.F23

20.   With the highlighter in cell F11, issue the command
   /Range Erase to erase the unwanted sum function for the blank row.

21.   Copy the underlining in cell B9 to cells F9, F17, F19, and F22. Copy the double underlining in cell B24 to cell F24.

22.   Issue the command /WGF , 0 to format the values of the entire spreadsheet with commas and no decimal places.

23.   In cell B7 issue the command /RFC 0 and type the range of B7.F7 to format the SALES values with dollar signs, commas, and no decimal places. After both the 0 and the specified range, depress ↵. Repeat this procedure in cell B23 to place dollar signs on all the net income amounts.

24.   To save this worksheet to your storage diskette, insert your own diskette in disk drive B, depress the Home key, and issue the command /FS. Type the filename BUDGET. Your storage diskette in disk drive B will now have a copy of the spreadsheet. If you escape out of the active spreadsheet, you will still have a copy on your storage diskette that you can retrieve without having to create this spreadsheet model again.

25.   To print this worksheet, first advance the paper to the top of the next fresh page. Issue the command /P for Print, P for Printer, R for Range, and type the range A1.F24. Then depress A for align and G for go, and the program will begin printing the Randolph-Macon budgeted income statement. The printout should look like the budgeted income statement as shown. The amounts may vary slightly due to rounding.

Summary

Accounting with computers is exactly like manual accounting, except that the machine saves time by doing much of the work automatically. *Software programs* are available to perform a variety of accounting tasks. Often an accounting software program is divided into *modules*: general ledger, accounts receivable, accounts payable, payroll, and inventories. A business can select any or all of these modules to do its accounting by computer.

Spreadsheets are software programs that can be used to solve many different kinds of problems, including budgeting, depreciation schedules, what-if analysis, payroll computations, and cost-volume-profit analysis.

Self-Study Questions

Test your understanding of the chapter by marking the best answer for each of the following questions.

1. Which of the following statements is true? *(p. 1076)*
   a. Accounting with computers is fundamentally different from manual accounting.
   b. Computerized accounting is slower and more tedious than manual accounting.
   c. Accounting with computers and manual accounting are fundamentally alike.
   d. It takes extensive computer programming experience to use an accounting software program.
2. Which of the following is an input device? *(p. 1077)*
   a. Printer   c. Central processing unit
   b. Disk drive   d. Monitor
3. The device that actually does the computer's "thinking" is the *(p. 1078)*
   a. Printer   c. Central processing unit
   b. Disk drive   d. Monitor
4. A software menu is a *(p. 1079)*
   a. List of computer functions   c. Computer printout
   b. Group of input devices   d. Task with the most software programs
5. In an integrated accounting software program, the center is the *(p. 1080)*
   a. Accounts receivable module   c. Payroll module
   b. Inventory module   d. General ledger module
6. A key time saver in a spreadsheet program is the accountant's ability to *(p. 1090)*
   a. Enter amounts manually   c. Copy formulas and functions
   b. List amounts in order   d. Use the typewriter section of the keyboard
7. The function key used for editing with Lotus 1-2-3® is *(p. 1092)*
   a. F1   c. F3
   b. F2   d. F4
8. When the formula +A6/$C$3 is copied in a 1-2-3 program, *(p. 1096)*
   a. The value in A6 can change, but the value in C3 is constant
   b. The value in A6 is constant, but the value in C3 can change
   c. The values in A6 and in C3 can change
   d. The values in A6 and in C3 are constant
9. The 1-2-3 command /Copy From: A1.A3 To: B1.B3 copies *(p. 1098)*
   a. Rows B1 through B3 to rows A1 through A3
   b. Columns B1 through B3 to columns A1 through A3
   c. Rows A1 through A3 to rows B1 through B3
   d. Columns A1 through A3 to columns B1 through B3
10. To save a 1-2-3 file on a storage diskette, use the command *(p. 1099)*
    a. /SF   c. \SF
    b. /FS   d. \FS

Answers to the self-study questions are at the end of the chapter.

Accounting Vocabulary

central processing unit (CPU) *(p. 1078)*, disk drive *(p. 1077)*, diskette *(p. 1077)*, integrated software *(p. 1079)*, menu *(p. 1079)*, menu-driven *(p. 1079)*, microcomputer *(p. 1076)*, monitor *(p. 1078)*, program *(p. 1076)*, spreadsheet *(p. 1089)*.

ASSIGNMENT MATERIAL _____

Questions

1. Name six advantages that computers offer over manual accounting.
2. Briefly compare and contrast the accounting cycle in a manual accounting system and the cycle in a computerized system.
3. What is the difference between a minicomputer and a microcomputer?
4. How do input devices, the CPU, and output devices work together in a computer system?
5. A service business with 20 employees needs an integrated computerized accounting system. Identify a way for many businesses to acquire the needed system most efficiently?
6. Identify the advantage of a menu-driven computerized accounting system over a system in which accountants must write computer programs to do the work.
7. List the options that might appear on the monitor screen for a menu-driven general ledger software program.
8. Outline the flow of information in the accounts receivable module of an integrated accounting software program.
9. Why is payroll ideally suited for a computerized accounting system?
10. Compare and contrast a computer keyboard and a typewriter keyboard.
11. On a monitor screen in a spreadsheet program, what do C5 and D3 mean?
12. Suppose you make an error while using a spreadsheet program. How would you correct the error if you have not yet depressed the ↵ key? How would you correct the error if you have already depressed the ↵ key?
13. In a budget, the same formula is used in six places. How can a spreadsheet program handle this situation efficiently?
14. Suppose you type the formula +B1+B2 in cell B3 and copy the formula into cells C3 and D3. What values will be added in B3, C3, and D3?
15. Suppose you type the formula +$B$1+$B$2 in cell B3 and copy the formula into cells C3 and D3. What values will be added in B3, C3, and D3?
16. Suppose you type the formula +B1+$B$2 in cell B3 and copy the formula into cells C3 and D3. What values will be added in B3, C3, and D3?
17. What character comes first in 1-2-3 commands?
18. What is the name of the formatting command in 1-2-3 that is used to place dollar signs before amounts?
19. Write the copy command in 1-2-3 to copy data in cell G4 into cells H1 through H3.
20. What should you do at the end of a work session when you plan to update your spreadsheet at a later time? Write the appropriate 1-2-3 command.

Exercises   *(Note: Answers may contain rounding error.)*

Exercise 28-1   *Budgeted income statement*

Padgitt ComputerWorld is considering an expansion that would increase sales to $1,000,000 and operating expenses to $300,000. A spreadsheet program to prepare the company's actual 19X4 and budgeted 19X5 income statements appears on the next page.

The purpose of this exercise is to show the power of the computer in preparing a financial statement.

Required

1. Enter this material in a spreadsheet program. Set column A to be 25 characters wide, and columns B and C to be 15 characters wide.

2. Copy B7.B17 to C7.C17.
3. Insert 1000000 in C7 and 300000 in C11. Watch the budgeted 19X5 income statement appear instantly on the screen.
4. Format with dollar signs and commas.
5. Print the actual and budgeted income statements as they appear on the screen.

	A	B	C
1	Padgitt ComputerWorld		
2	Income Statements		
3	For the years Ended December 31,		
4			
5		Actual 19X4	Budgeted 19X5
6			
7	Sales	850000	$
8	Cost of goods sold (50%)	+B7*.50	
9		——————	——————
10	Gross margin	+B7-B8	
11	Total operating expenses	250000	
12		——————	——————
13	Income from operations	+B10-B11	
14	Income tax expense (40%)	+B13*.40	
15		——————	——————
16	Net income	+B13-B14	$
17		══════	══════

Exercise 28-2 *Sales budget*

The managers of Mid-Tex, Inc., are budgeting sales for the first six months of 19X3. January sales are expected to be $75,000. Each month thereafter, sales are expected to increase by ¼ percent (.0025) to ¾ percent (.0075).

Required

Create a spreadsheet model, and print Mid-Tex's sales budget for the six months ended June 30, 19X3, under both assumptions (¼ percent and ¾ percent) about the monthly increase. Round to the nearest dollar, and format your answer as follows:

	A	B	C	D	E	F	G	H
1				Mid-Tex, Inc.				
2				Sales Budget				
3			For the Six Months Ended June 30, 19X3					
4								
5				(.0025 Monthly Increase)				
6		JAN	FEB	MAR	APR	MAY	JUNE	TOTAL
7	Sales	$	$	$	$	$	$	$
8								
9								
10				(.0075 Monthly Increase)				
11		JAN	FEB	MAR	APR	MAY	JUNE	TOTAL
12	Sales	$	$	$	$	$	$	$

Exercise 28-3 *Gross margin budget*

Western Supply Company is budgeting gross margin for the four quarters of 19X7. Sales are estimated at $100,000 for the first quarter. Cost of goods sold is 55 percent of sales.

Required

Create a spreadsheet model for the gross margin budget under two separate assumptions about quarterly sales growth:

a. Quarterly sales are expected to increase by 1.5 percent (.015) during quarters 2, 3, and 4.

b. Quarterly sales are expected to increase by 2.5 percent (.025) during quarters 2, 3, and 4.

Round to the nearest dollar, and format your answer as follows:

	A	B	C	D	E	F
1		Western Supply Company				
2		Budgeted Gross Margin				
3		For the Four Quarters of 19X4				
4						
5			(Sales increase = .015)			
6		Q1	Q2	Q3	Q4	TOTAL
7	Sales	$	$	$	$	$
8						
9	Cost of goods sold					
10		——	——	——	——	——
11	Gross margin	$	$	$	$	$
12		══	══	══	══	══
13						
14						
15			(Sales increase = .025)			
16		Q1	Q2	Q3	Q4	TOTAL
17	Sales	$	$	$	$	$
18						
19	Cost of goods sold					
20		——	——	——	——	——
21	Gross margin	$	$	$	$	$
22		══	══	══	══	══

Exercise 28-4   *Change from LIFO to FIFO*

Dysan Corporation is considering a change from the last-in, first-out (LIFO) inventory method to the first-in, first-out (FIFO) method. Managers are concerned about the effect of this change on income tax expense and reported net income. If the change is made, it will become effective on March 1. Inventory on hand at February 28 is $63,000. During March, Dysan managers expect sales of $250,000, net purchases between $159,000 and $182,000, and operating expenses, excluding income tax, of $83,000. The income tax rate is 40 percent. Inventories at March 31 are budgeted as follows: FIFO, $85,000; LIFO, $78,000.

Required

Create a spreadsheet model to compute estimated net income for March under FIFO and LIFO. Format your answer as follows:

	A	B	C	D	E
1		Dysan Corporation			
2		Estimated Income Under FIFO and LIFO			
3		March 19XX			
4					
5		FIFO	LIFO	FIFO	LIFO
6					
7	Sales	$250,000	$250,000	$250,000	$250,000
8					
9	Cost of goods sold				
10	Beginning inventory	63,000	63,000	63,000	63,000
11	Net purchases	159,000	159,000	182,000	182,000
12					
13	Cost of goods available				
14	Ending inventory	85,000	78,000	85,000	78,000
15					
16	Cost of goods sold				
17					
18	Gross margin				
19	Operating expenses	83,000	83,000	83,000	83,000
20					
21	Income from operations				
22	Income tax expense				
23					
24	Net income	$	$	$	$
25					

Exercise 28-5 *Straight-line depreciation schedule*

Create a spreadsheet model to print a straight-line depreciation schedule for a machine that cost $694,206, has an estimated useful life of six years, and has an estimated residual value of $120,000. Round to the nearest dollar, and format your answer as follows:

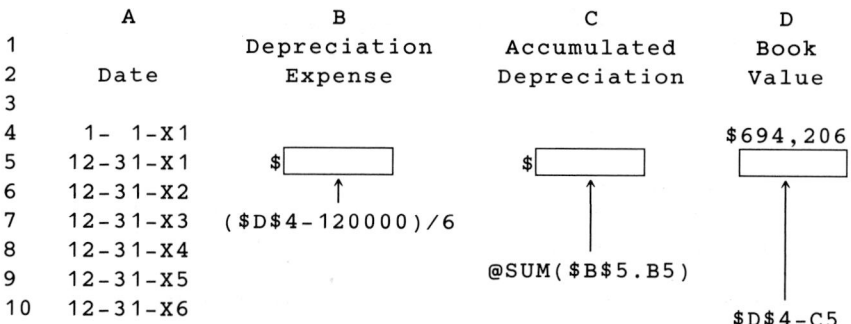

	A	B	C	D
1		Depreciation	Accumulated	Book
2	Date	Expense	Depreciation	Value
3				
4	1- 1-X1			$694,206
5	12-31-X1	$	$	
6	12-31-X2	↑		
7	12-31-X3	($D$4-120000)/6		
8	12-31-X4		@SUM($B$5.B5)	
9	12-31-X5			
10	12-31-X6			$D$4-C5

Exercise 28-6 *Dissolution of a partnership*

The partnership of Finn, Marks, and Hess is dissolving. Business assets include cash of $6,000 and noncash assets of $126,000. Liabilities total $77,000. The partners' capital accounts are Finn, $12,000; Marks, $37,000; and Hess, $6,000. The partners share profits and losses as follows: Finn, 25 percent; Marks, 55 percent; and Hess, 20 percent.

Required

Create a spreadsheet model to show the ending balances in all accounts after selling the noncash assets for $85,000; $107,000; and $140,000. Determine the unknown amounts (?):

	A	B	C	D	E	F
1			Finn, Marks, and Hess			
2			Sale of Noncash Assets			
3			(For $85,000)			
4						
5		Noncash		Finn	Marks	Hess
6	Cash	Assets	Liabilities	Capital	Capital	Capital
7						
8	$ 6,000	$126,000	$77,000	$12,000	$37,000	$ 6,000
9	85,000	(126,000)		?	?	?
10						
11	$91,000	$ 0	$77,000	$?	$?	$?
12						
13						
14						($A9 − $B8) * .25
15			(For $107,000)			
16						
17		Noncash		Finn	Marks	Hess
18	Cash	Assets	Liabilities	Capital	Capital	Capital
19						
20	$ 6,000	$126,000	$77,000	$12,000	$37,000	$ 6,000
21	107,000	(126,000)		?	?	?
22						
23	$113,000	$ 0	$77,000	$?	$?	$?
24						
25						
26						($A21 − $B20) * .25
27			(For $140,000)			
28						
29		Noncash		Finn	Marks	Hess
30	Cash	Assets	Liabilities	Capital	Capital	Capital
31						
32	$ 6,000	$126,000	$77,000	$12,000	$37,000	$ 6,000
33	140,000	(126,000)		?	?	?
34						
35	$146,000	$ 0	$77,000	$?	$?	$?
36						
						($A33 − $B32) * .25

Exercise 28-7   *Debt payment and discount amortization schedule*

McLain Company issued $500,000 of 8⅜ percent (.08375), 5-year bonds payable when the market interest rate was 9½ percent (.095). McLain pays interest annually at year end. The issue price of the bonds was $478,402.

Required

Create a spreadsheet model to prepare a schedule to amortize the discount on these bonds. Use the interest method of amortization. Round to the nearest dollar, and format your answer as follows:

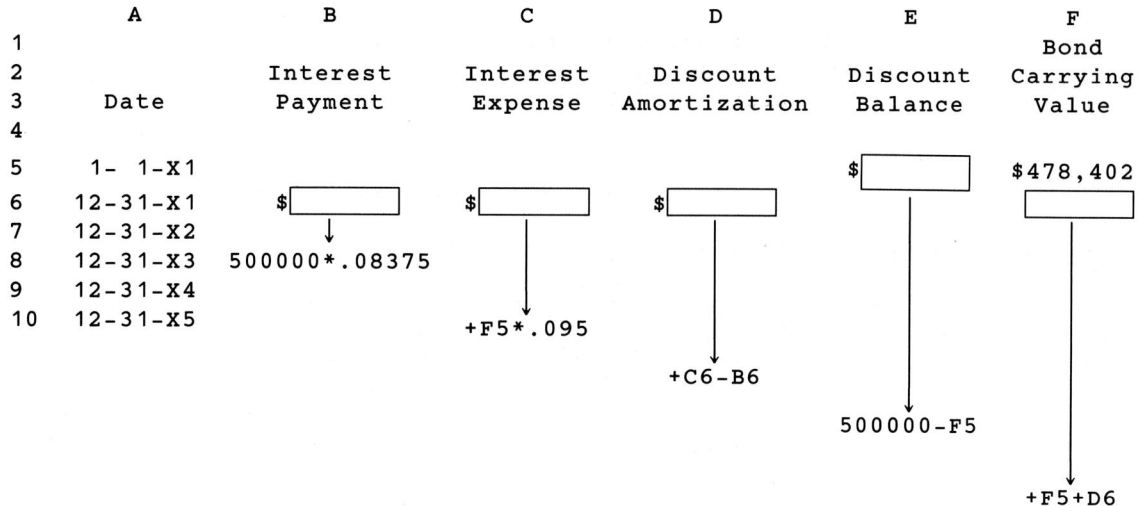

Exercise 28-8 *Budgeted income statement*

Grafton Sales, a wholesale grocery supplier, is preparing its budgeted income statement for the quarter ended March 31, 19X6. Lou Nettle, the proprietor, expects January sales of $50,000, followed by 2 percent increases in February and March. Cost of goods sold is 70 percent of sales, and the operating expenses are as shown in the solution format that follows. Salary expense is expected to increase by 5 percent in March. All other monthly operating expenses will remain at the January amounts.

	A	B	C	D	E
1		Grafton Sales			
2		Budgeted Income Statement			
3		For the Quarter Ended March 31, 19X6			
4					
5		JAN	FEB	MAR	TOTAL
6					
7	Sales	$50,000	$	$	$
8	Cost of goods sold				
9		_____	_____	_____	_____
10	Gross margin				
11	Operating expenses:				
12	Salaries	4,000			
13	Depreciation	2,000			
14	Rent	1,000			
15	Utilities	500			
16		_____	_____	_____	_____
17	Total expenses				
18		_____	_____	_____	_____
19	Net income	$	$	$	$
20		=======	=======	=======	=======

Required

Create a spreadsheet model to prepare and print Grafton Sales's budgeted income statement for the quarter, formatted as shown here.

Exercise 28-9 *Cost-volume-profit analysis*

Create a spreadsheet model to compute and print break-even sales and the dollar sales needed to earn target income from operations under the following conditions:

Fixed expenses	$183,000	$196,000	
Variable expenses	54% of sales	51% of sales	
Target income from operations	$90,000	$90,000	

Format your answer as follows:

	A	B	C	D	E
1	Fixed expenses	$183,000	$196,000	$183,000	$196,000
2	Variable expenses	.54	.51	.54	.51
3	Income from operations	0	0	$90,000	$90,000
4	Break-even sales	$ [?]	$ [?]		
5	Target sales	↓		$ [?]	$ [?]

$$(B1+B3)/(1-B2)$$

Hint: Copy the formula for B4 into C4, D5, and E5.

Exercise 28-10 *Net present value analysis*

A company is considering the purchase of two machines. The company's required rate of return on investments is 12½ percent (.125). The following data are applicable.

	A	B	C
1		Machine 1	Machine 2
2			
3	Cost	$396,000	$728,000
4			
5	Annual net cash inflow:		
6	Year 1	$180,000	$150,000
7	2	160,000	200,000
8	3	100,000	250,000
9	4	60,000	300,000
10	5	30,000	100,000
11	6	20,000	

Required

Create a spreadsheet model to help decide which machine has the higher net present value. Format the printout as above. Add three lines at the bottom to show present value of net cash inflows, investment, and net present value. The formula for computing the present value of the net cash inflows for machine 1 is @NPV(.125,B6.B11).

Exercise 28-11 *Income tax*

An accountant is preparing the income tax returns of clients with the following data presented in solution format. "AGI" is the abbreviation for *Adjusted Gross Income,* "Std Ded" abbreviates *Standard Deduction,* and "Exempt" stands for *Personal Exemptions.*

	A	B	C	D	E	F	G
1		Filing				Taxable	Income
2	Name	Status	AGI	Std Ded	Exempt	Income	Tax
3							
4	Lisa Gonzalez	Single	$22,100	$3,000	$2,000	$?	$?
5							
6	Tom Mendenhall	Single	20,000	3,000	2,000	?	?
7							
8	R. and K. Gray	Joint	51,500	4,400	8,000	?	?
9							
10	L. and T. Chin	Joint	83,000	4,400	6,000	?	?

Required

Create a spreadsheet model to compute the taxable income and the income tax liability of each client. Refer to Chapter 27 for the appropriate income tax rates. Format your answer as shown here.

Problems   (Note: Answers may contain certain rounding error.)   *(Group A)*

Problem 28-1A   *Budgeted income statement*

Dakota, Inc., is budgeting operations for the first quarter of 19X5. Income tax expense is 40 percent. Other data follow:

January sales	$100,000
Cost of goods sold percentage	60% of sales
Monthly sales growth rate	1.1%

	A	B	C	D	E
1		Dakota, Inc.			
2		Budgeted Income Statement			
3		For the Three Months Ended March 31, 19X5			
4					
5		JAN	FEB	MAR	TOTAL
6					
7	Sales	$100,000	$101,100	$102,212	$303,312
8	Cost of goods sold	60,000	60,660	61,327	181,987
9					
10	Gross margin	40,000	40,440	40,885	121,325
11	Operating expenses:				
12	Salaries	22,500	22,500	22,500	67,500
13	Rent	4,000	4,000	4,000	12,000
14	Depreciation	2,500	2,500	2,500	7,500
15	Utilities	2,000	2,000	2,000	6,000
16					
17	Total operating expenses	31,000	31,000	31,000	93,000
18					
19	Income from operations	9,000	9,440	9,885	28,325
20	Income tax expense	3,600	3,776	3,954	11,330
21					
22	Net income	$5,400	$5,664	$5,931	$16,995
23					

Required

Create a spreadsheet model to prepare and print the Dakota budgeted income statement for the quarter, formatted as shown here.

Problem 28-2A   *Budgeted gross profit*

Hulme TV Appliances is budgeting gross profit (gross margin) for the six months ended June 30, 19X4. Fred Hulme, the owner, expects January sales of $50,000 for TVs and $10,000 for VCRs. He is hoping for 1 percent monthly sales growth for TVs and 3 percent for VCRs. Cost of goods sold is 70 percent of sales for TVs and 60 percent for VCRs.

Required

Create a spreadsheet model to complete and print the following budget:

	A	B	C	D	E	F	G
1			Hulme TV Appliances				
2			Budgeted Gross Profit				
3			For the Six Months Ended June 30, 19X4				
4							
5		JAN	FEB	MAR	APR	MAY	JUN
6	Sales						
7	TVs	$50,000					
8	VCRs	10,000					
9	------						
10	Total						
11							
12	COGS						
13	TVs						
14	VCRs						
15	------						
16	Total						
17							
18	Gross Pft						
19	TVs						
20	VCRs						
21	------						
22	Total						

Problem 28-3A   *Budgeted income statement*

Using the six-month projections from Problem 28-2A for the sales, cost of goods sold, and gross profit (gross margin) for TVs and VCRs, complete Hulme's budgeted income statement by including expenses and totals for the 6 months. The business budgets expenses as follows:

Salaries	$14,000 per month
Rent	2,000 per month
Depreciation	1,000 per month
Insurance	500 per month
Travel	750 per quarter (in January and April only)
Utilities	500 per month
Income tax rate	40%

Required

Create a spreadsheet model to prepare Hulme's budgeted income statement for the six months ended June 30, 19X4. Show each expense, total operating expenses, income from operations, income tax expense, and net income.

Problem 28-4A   *Double-declining-balance depreciation schedule*

Create a spreadsheet model to print a double-declining-balance depreciation schedule for a building that cost $950,000, has an estimated useful life of 20 years, and has an estimated residual value of $120,000. Format your answer as follows, showing all years through 19X20.

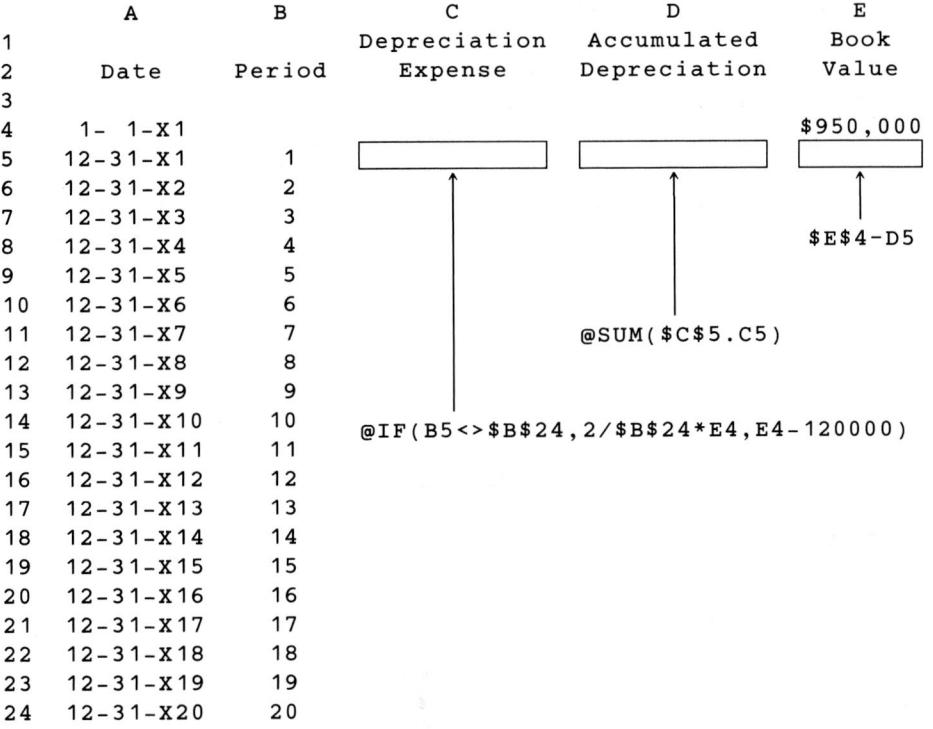

	A	B	C	D	E
1			Depreciation	Accumulated	Book
2	Date	Period	Expense	Depreciation	Value
3					
4	1- 1-X1				$950,000
5	12-31-X1	1			
6	12-31-X2	2			
7	12-31-X3	3			
8	12-31-X4	4			
9	12-31-X5	5			
10	12-31-X6	6			
11	12-31-X7	7			
12	12-31-X8	8			
13	12-31-X9	9			
14	12-31-X10	10			
15	12-31-X11	11			
16	12-31-X12	12			
17	12-31-X13	13			
18	12-31-X14	14			
19	12-31-X15	15			
20	12-31-X16	16			
21	12-31-X17	17			
22	12-31-X18	18			
23	12-31-X19	19			
24	12-31-X20	20			

$E$4-D5

@SUM($C$5.C5)

@IF(B5<>$B$24,2/$B$24*E4,E4-120000)

Problem 28-5A *Payroll*

Spann Pipe & Supply has a weekly payroll for its hourly employees. An employee's gross pay is determined by multiplying his/her straight-time pay rate times the number of hours worked for the first 40 hours. For every hour over 40, the employee receives 1.5 times the pay rate. Weekly deductions consist of FICA tax, withheld income tax, and United Way contribution. FICA tax is 7% of gross pay, withheld income tax is 12% of gross pay, and the United Way contribution varies by employee. Net pay is gross pay less total deductions.

	A	B	C	D	E	F	G	H
1			Spann Pipe & Supply					
2			Payroll Register					
3			For the Week Ended March 18, 19X4					
4								
5			Straight-			Deductions		
6			Time					
7	Employee		Hourly Pay	Gross		With.	United	Net
8	Name	Hours	Rate	Pay	FICA	Tax	Way	Pay
9								
10	Allen, D.	40	$5.50				5.00	
11	Brown, G.	35	7.50				10.00	
12	Chin, B.	45	5.00				3.50	
13	Olson, T.	38	5.25				6.00	
14	Reed, K.	20	6.00				5.00	
15	Tusa, R.	47	6.50				5.00	
16	Ward, R.	40	5.00				2.50	
17	Wills, C.	45	5.25				5.00	
18								
19	Totals							
20								

Required

Create a spreadsheet model to complete and print this payroll register for Spann Pipe & Supply. Your spreadsheet should be formatted as above.

Problem 28-6A *Cost-volume-profit analysis*

The Santos Corporation management team is planning for 19X7. Fixed expenses are expected to range from $120,000 to $150,000. Variable expenses will likely range from 60 percent of sales to 70 percent of sales. The company's target income from operations is $50,000.

Required

Prepare a spreadsheet that shows break-even sales in dollars and dollar sales needed to earn the target income from operations under all possible combinations being considered. The spreadsheet should be formatted as follows:

	A	B	C	D	E	F	G
1	Fixed exp	$120,000	$150,000	$120,000	$150,000	$120,000	$150,000
2	Variable exp	60%	60%	70%	70%	60%	70%
3	Income from oper	$0	$0	$0	$0	$50,000	$50,000
4	Break-even sales	?	?	?	?		
5	Target sales	↑				?	?
6		(+B1+B3)/(1-B2)					

Problem 28-7A *Net present value analysis*

Weems Rental Corporation is considering purchasing a truck to rent out to do-it-yourself movers. Weems Rental has a required rate of return of 10 percent (.10). The company is considering two trucks:

	A	B	C
1			
2		Truck 1	Truck 2
3	Cost	$90,000	$125,000
4			
5	Annual net cash inflows:		
6	Year 1	$28,000	$30,000
8	2	30,000	35,000
9	3	35,000	45,000
10	4	22,000	30,000
11	5	15,000	20,000
12	6		15,000
13	7		5,000
14			
15	Present value of net cash inflows		
16			
17	Investment		
18			
19	Net present value	$	$
20			

Required

Create a spreadsheet model to help decide which truck has the higher net present value and is, therefore, more attractive as an investment. Format the spreadsheet as above.

(Group B)

Problem 28-1B *Budgeted income statement*

Ward Foods, Inc., is budgeting operations for the first quarter of 19X5. Income tax expense is 40 percent. Other data follow:

January sales...................	$150,000
Cost of goods sold percentage......	65% of sales
Monthly sales growth rate.........	1.5%

	A	B	C	D	E
1		Ward Foods, Inc.			
2		Budgeted Income Statement			
3		For the Three Months Ended March 31, 19X5			
4					
5		JAN	FEB	MAR	TOTAL
6					
7	Sales	$150,000	$152,250	$154,534	$456,784
8	Cost of goods sold	97,500	98,963	100,447	296,909
9					
10	Gross margin	52,500	53,288	54,087	159,874
11	Operating expenses:				
12	Salaries	25,000	25,000	25,000	75,000
13	Rent	4,500	4,500	4,500	13,500
14	Depreciation	3,000	3,000	3,000	9,000
15	Utilities	1,800	1,800	1,800	5,400
16					
17	Total operating expenses	34,300	34,300	34,300	102,900
18					
19	Income from operations	18,200	18,988	19,787	56,974
20	Income tax expense	7,280	7,595	7,915	22,790
21					
22	Net income	$10,920	$11,393	$11,872	$34,185
23					

Required:

Create a spreadsheet model to prepare and print for Ward Foods a budgeted income statement for the quarter, formatted as shown here. The computer solution may contain an insignificant rounding error.

Problem 28-2B *Budgeted gross profit*

Advanced Information Systems, Inc., is budgeting gross profit (gross margin) for the six months ended June 30, 19X5. Lynn Bradshaw, the owner, expects January sales of $70,000 for computer hardware and $25,000 for software. She is hoping for 2 percent monthly sales growth for hardware and 4 percent for software. Cost of goods sold is 70 percent of sales for hardware and 50 percent for software.

Required

Create a spreadsheet model to complete and print the following budget:

```
              A           B        C        D        E        F        G        H
 1                     Advanced Information Systems, Inc.
 2                          Budgeted Gross Profit
 3                     For the Six Months Ended June 30, 19X5
 4
 5                        JAN      FEB      MAR      APR      MAY      JUN
 6   Sales
 7     Hardware    $70,000
 8     Software     25,000
 9                 _____
10   Total
11
12   COGS
13     Hardware
14     Software
15                 _____
16   Total
17
18   Gross Pft
19     Hardware
20     Software
21                 _____
22   Total
```

Problem 28-3B   *Budgeted income statement*

Using the six month projections from Problem 28-2B for the sales, cost of goods sold, and gross profit (gross margin) for hardware and software, complete Advanced Information Systems's budgeted income statement by including expenses and totals for the 6 months. The business budgets expenses as follows:

Salaries	$20,000 per month
Rent	2,500 per month
Depreciation	2,000 per month
Insurance	1,500 per month
Travel	900 per quarter (in January and April only)
Utilities	650 per month
Income tax rate	40%

Required

Create a spreadsheet model to prepare the Advanced Information Systems income statement for the six months ended June 30, 19X5. Show each expense, total operating expenses, income from operations, income tax expense, and net income.

Problem 28-4B   *Sum-of-years-digits depreciation schedule*

Create a spreadsheet model to print a sum-of-years-digits depreciation schedule for a building that cost $935,000, has an estimated useful life of 15 years, and has an estimated residual value of $120,000. Format your answer as follows, showing all years through 19X15.

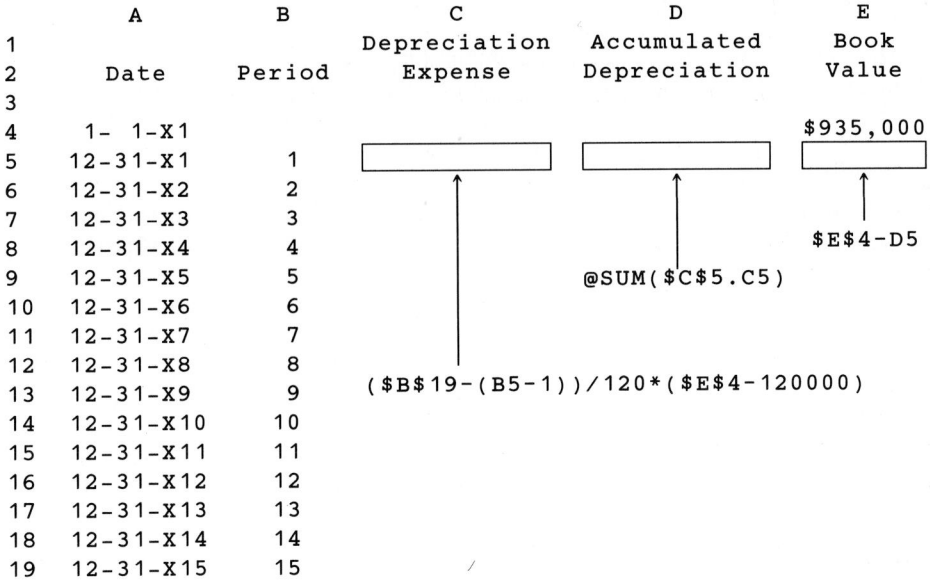

Problem 28-5B *Payroll*

Multi Fitness has a weekly payroll for its hourly employees. Debbie Rhoads, the owner/manager of Multi Fitness, currently processes the payroll manually. An employee's gross pay is determined by multiplying his/her straight-time pay rate times the number of hours worked for the first 40 hours. For every hour over 40, the employee receives 1.5 times the pay rate. Weekly deductions consist of FICA tax, withheld income tax, and United Way contribution. FICA tax is 7% of gross pay; withheld income tax is 12% of gross pay; and the United Way contribution varies by employee. Net pay is gross pay less total deductions.

	A	B	C	D	E	F	G	H
1			Multi Fitness					
2			Payroll Register					
3			For the Week Ended February 15, 19X6					
4								
5			Straight-			Deductions		
6			Time					
7	Employee		Hourly Pay	Gross		With.	United	Net
8	Name	Hours	Rate	Pay	FICA	Tax	Way	Pay
9								
10	Chang, H.	45	$6.50				5.00	
11	Craig, B.	35	5.00				10.00	
12	Lowe, B.	50	6.00				3.50	
13	Pita, N.	40	6.25				6.00	
14	Potts, F.	40	7.00				5.00	
15	Rawl, R.	20	6.50				5.00	
16	Tong, J.	45	5.50				2.50	
17	Ware, R.	38	5.75				5.00	
18								
19	Totals							
20								

Required

Create a spreadsheet model to complete and print this payroll register for Multi Fitness. Your spreadsheet should be formatted as above.

Problem 28-6B   *Cost-volume-profit analysis*

The Dobroski management team is planning for 19X2. Fixed expenses are expected to range from $150,000 to $180,000. Variable expenses will range from 65 percent of sales to 75 percent of sales. The company's target income from operations is $60,000.

Required

Prepare a spreadsheet that shows break-even sales in dollars and dollar sales needed to earn the target income from operations under all possible combinations being considered. The spreadsheet should be formatted as follows:

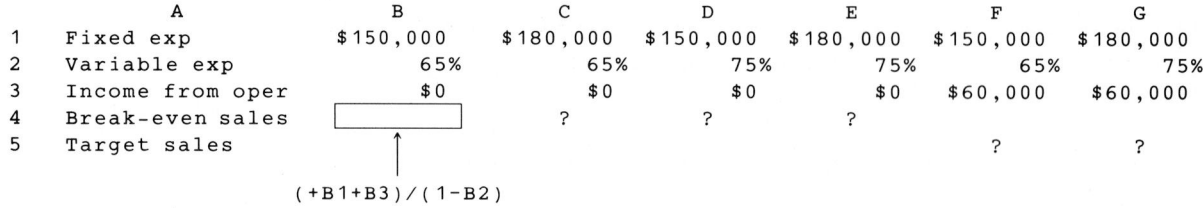

	A	B	C	D	E	F	G
1	Fixed exp	$150,000	$180,000	$150,000	$180,000	$150,000	$180,000
2	Variable exp	65%	65%	75%	75%	65%	75%
3	Income from oper	$0	$0	$0	$0	$60,000	$60,000
4	Break-even sales		?	?	?		
5	Target sales					?	?

(+B1+B3)/(1-B2)

Problem 28-7B   *Net present value analysis*

Advanced Information Systems, Inc., is considering starting a mainframe time-sharing business. AIS has a required rate of return of 10 percent (.10). The company is considering two computers:

	A			B	C
1				Computer 1	Computer 2
2					
3	Cost			$750,000	$600,000
4					
5	Annual net cash inflows:				
6					
7	Year		1	$180,000	$150,000
8			2	225,000	200,000
9			3	315,000	275,000
10			4	125,000	100,000
11			5	100,000	100,000
12			6	85,000	
13			7	50,000	
14					
15	Present value of net cash inflows				
16					
17	Investment				
18					
19	Net present value				
20				$	$

Required

Create a spreadsheet model to help decide which computer has a higher net present value and is, therefore, more attractive as an investment. Format the spreadsheet as above.

Answers to Self-Study Questions

1. c   6. c
2. b   7. b
3. c   8. a
4. a   9. d
5. d   10. b

A

Mathematical Presentations

This appendix reviews some of the mathematical presentations in the book. You may find it helpful to refer to this appendix as you use the text.

Fractions, Decimals, Percentages, and Ratios

There are four ways to describe mathematically a specific portion of something: as a fraction, a decimal, a percentage, and a ratio. These expressions are interchangeable, as the following discussion shows.

Delwood Plaza, a shopping center, consists of 40 stores. Thirty of the stores are occupied. Ten are vacant. We can describe the portions of the shopping center that are occupied and vacant in four ways:

	Portion of the Shopping Center	
	Occupied	**Vacant**
Fraction	$^{30}/_{40} = {}^3/_4$	$^{10}/_{40} = {}^1/_4$
Decimal	$^3/_4 = 3 \div 4 = .75$	$^1/_4 = 1 \div 4 = .25$
Percentage	$.75 = 75\%$	$.25 = 25\%$
Ratio	$3:4$	$1:4$

Fractions, decimals, percentages, and ratios are based on the relationship between two numbers. In this example, we are expressing the relationship between (a) the portion of the shopping center that is occupied (or vacant) and (b) the total shopping center.

As another example, suppose your daily drive to college is six miles. After driving two miles, you could describe your progress as $^2/_6 = {}^1/_3$, or as .333, or as $33^1/_3\%$, or as $1:3$. They all carry the same meaning. In this example, we are expressing the relationship between (a) the portion of the drive completed and (b) the total distance to be driven.

In all cases, there is a key question to ask before computing fractions, decimals, percentages, and ratios: What is the base amount? That is, what is the denominator in the computation? For example, if a percentage is to be computed, the base amount is the number that represents 100 percent (40 stores in the shopping center and 6 miles in the daily drive to college).

Percentage Changes

In business, percentage changes are widely used to measure achievement. For example, a company's total assets may increase from $200,000 to $240,000. This is a 20 percent increase, computed as follows:

Total assets now	$240,000	120%
Total assets previously...............	200,000	100
Increase in total assets	$ 40,000	20%
Percentage increase in total assets:		
Increase divided by previous amount		
($40,000 ÷ $200,000)		20%

Suppose that during the next period total assets decrease to $180,000. The decrease is 25 percent, computed in exactly the same manner:

Total assets now	$180,000	75%
Total assets previously	240,000	100
Decrease in total assets	$ 60,000	25%
Percentage decrease in total assets:		
Decrease divided by previous amount		
($60,000 ÷ $240,000)...............		25%

Dollar Signs and Double Underlines

In this book we show monetary figures by placing a dollar sign ($) with the first amount in each column and with each total that is underlined twice. This is the method used in companies' published annual reports. The preceding section, Percentage Changes, gives two examples.

Dollar signs are *not* used for amounts debited and credited in journals and ledgers. It is understood that these are monetary figures. However, we often use dollar signs in parenthetical explanations to aid your understanding of a particular entry. For example, two cash purchases of supplies for $50 and $40 could be combined into one entry:

	Amount	
	Debit	Credit
Supplies ($50 + $40)	90	
Cash.....................		90

The ledger also omits dollar signs:

Supplies	Cash
90	90

Double underlines indicate a final total, as presented in the Percentage Changes section.

Positive and Negative Amounts

In most mathematical presentations, the plus sign (+) denotes a positive amount, and the minus sign (−) denotes a negative amount: for example, $7 + 5 − 3 = 9$. In a columnar presentation it would be cumbersome to use a + or a − sign for each number. Accountants use a short-cut method that omits the plus sign for positive amounts and uses parentheses to denote negatives, as follows:

$$
\begin{array}{r}
7 \\
5 \\
\underline{(3)} \\
\underline{\underline{9}}
\end{array}
$$

Not all negative amounts are presented with parentheses, however. Parentheses are often omitted where the description clearly indicates that a subtraction occurs, as follows:

Males	7
Plus: Females	5
Less: Children	$\underline{3}$
Total adults	$\underline{\underline{9}}$

Reversing Entries

This appendix shows how accountants use a special technique called *reversing entries* to ease the burden of bookkeeping.

Accrued Expenses and the Related Liabilities _____

Some expenses accrue day by day (or even hour by hour), but they are paid at regular, longer intervals, often weekly or monthly. Many times the payment does not occur on the financial statement date. Therefore, at the end of the period the business must make an adjusting entry to record the expenses that have built up to that time but that will not be paid until later. Without an adjustment, the business's financial statements will overstate net income and owner's equity (because expenses and liabilities will be understated). These built-up expenses are called accrued expenses (or accrued liabilities because their recording includes a credit to a liability account). Examples include property taxes, interest on notes payable, and employee salaries and wages.

Assume that at December 27, 19X1 — near the end of the accounting period — Salary Expense has a debit balance of $185,000 from salaries paid during the year. At year end the business owes employees $3,000 for their service during the last three work days of the year. This amount will be paid on January 3, the next payday, along with $2,000 in salaries for the first two work days of the new year. The next weekly payroll amount will be $5,000. However, to present the complete financial picture, the $3,000 in salaries incurred in 19X1 must be included in the 19X1 statements. Accordingly, the business makes the following adjusting entry on December 31:

Adjusting Entries

19X1

Dec. 31 Salary Expense.................................... 3,000
    Salary Payable   3,000

After posting, the Salary Payable and Salary Expense accounts appear as follows:

Salary Payable

	19X1
	Dec. 31 Adj.* 3,000
	Dec. 31 Bal. 3,000

Salary Expense

19X1		
Year's total through		
Dec. 27	185,000	
Dec. 31 Adj.	3,000	
Dec. 31 Bal.	188,000	

After the adjusting entry, the 19X1 *income statement* reports salary expense of $188,000, and the *balance sheet* at December 31, 19X1, reports Salary Payable, a liability, of $3,000. The $188,000 debit balance of Salary Expense will be eliminated by a closing entry at December 31, 19X1, as follows:

Closing Entries

19X1

Dec. 31 Income Summary 188,000
    Salary Expense........................   188,000

After posting, Salary Expense appears as follows:

Salary Expense

Year's total through			
Dec. 27	185,000		
Dec. 31 Adj.	3,000		
Dec. 31 Bal.	188,000	Dec. 31 Clo.	188,000

* Entry explanations used throughout this appendix are
Adj. = Adjusting entry
Bal. = Balance
Clo. = Closing entry
CP = Cash payment entry
CR = Cash receipt entry
Rev. = Reversing entry, explained later in the appendix

Reversing Entries

Reversing entries are special types of entries that ease the burden of accounting after adjusting entries have been made in a preceding period. Let's see how reversing entries work. Suppose you are the accountant who records cash payments for salaries. In the normal course of recording salary payments during the year, you make the following payroll entry:

Salary Expense	5,000	
Cash.		5,000

However, suppose that payday does not land on the day the accounting period ends and that you have made an adjusting entry to accrue salary payable of $3,000, as we have just seen. On January 3, 19X2, you record the weekly payroll of $5,000. You credit Cash for $5,000, but what account—or accounts—do you debit? The cash payment entry is

19X2

Jan. 3	Salary Payable	3,000	
	Salary Expense	2,000	
	Cash.		5,000

This method of recording the cash payment is *inefficient* because you must refer back to the adjusting entries of December 31, 19X1. Otherwise, you do not know the amount of the required debit (in this example, $3,000) to Salary Payable. Searching the preceding year's adjusting entries takes time, and in business, time is money. To avoid having to analyze the payment entry and having to separate the debit into two accounts, accountants have devised a technique called reversing entries.

Making a Reversing Entry.   A **reversing entry** switches the debit and the credit of a previous adjusting entry. The reversing entry is dated the first day of the period following the adjusting entry.

Let's continue with our example of the end-of-period cash payment of $5,000 in salaries. On December 31, 19X1, the accountant made the following entry to accrue Salary Payable:

Adjusting Entries

19X1

Dec. 31	Salary Expense.	3,000	
	Salary Payable		3,000

The reversing entry simply flip-flops the position of the debit and the credit:

Reversing Entries

19X2

Jan. 1	Salary Payable	3,000	
	Salary Expense		3,000

> **OBJECTIVE 1**
> Make a reversing entry for an accrued expense

Notice that the reversing entry is dated the first day of the new period. It is the exact opposite of the December 31 adjusting entry. Ordinarily, the accountant who makes the adjusting entry also prepares the reversing entry at the same time.

She postdates the reversing entry to January 1 of the next period, however, so that it affects the new period. Note how the accounts appear after the accountant posts the reversing entry:

Salary Payable

19X2			19X1		
Jan. 1 **Rev.**	3,000		Dec. 31 Bal.		3,000

Zero balance

Salary Expense

19X1			19X1		
Dec. 31 Bal.	188,000		Dec. 31 Clo.	188,000

Zero balance

		19X2		
		Jan. 1 **Rev.**	3,000

The arrow shows the transfer of the $3,000 credit balance from Salary Payable to Salary Expense. This credit balance in Salary Expense does not mean that the entity has negative salary expense, as might be suggested by a credit balance in an expense account. Instead, the odd credit balance is merely a temporary result of the reversing entry. The credit balance is eliminated on January 3, 19X2, when the $5,000 cash payment for salaries is debited to Salary Expense in the customary manner:

19X2
Jan. 3   Salary Expense 5,000
                   Cash..   5,000

Then this cash payment entry is posted:

Salary Expense

19X2			19X2		
Jan. 3 CP	5,000		Jan. 1 Rev.	3,000
Jan. 3 Bal.	2,000			

Now Salary Expense has its correct debit balance of $2,000, which is the amount of salary expense incurred thus far in 19X2. The $5,000 cash disbursement also pays the liability for Salary Payable. Thus the Salary Payable account has a zero balance which is correct, as shown at the top of this page.

The adjusting and reversing process is repeated year after year. Cash payments for salaries are debited to Salary Expense, and these amounts accumulate in that account. At the end of the year, the accountant makes an adjusting entry to accrue salary expense incurred but not yet paid. At the same time, the accountant also makes a reversing entry, which allows her to record all payroll entries in the customary manner—by routinely debiting Salary Expense. Even in computerized systems, making reversing entries is more efficient than writing a program to locate the amount accrued from the preceding period and making the more complicated journal entry.

Reversing entries deserve emphasis. Accountants often must deal with hundreds or even thousands of repetitive transactions. With reversing entries, accountants don't have to worry that a cash payment might apply in part to an accrued liability recognized at the end of the preceding period. Reversing entries allow them to debit an expense for the full cash expense payment. Reversing entries may be made for all types of accrued expenses. However, they are optional, and some companies do not use them.

Accrued Revenues and the Related Assets _____

Certain revenues, such as interest earned on notes receivable, accrue with the passage of time, just as expenses do. However, a business usually does not record *accrued revenues* daily, weekly, or even monthly. Instead, it records them when it receives cash. Thus at the end of the accounting period, the business may have earned revenue that it has not yet recorded.

Assume the business has a note receivable on which it receives cash interest on February 1 and August 1. Interest accumulates at $200 per month. During 19X3 the business receives $1,200 of interest on August 1, and that amount is the balance in Interest Revenue at December 31, 19X3, before any adjustments. Suppose that between August 1 and December 31 the business has earned additional interest revenue of $1,000, which it will receive February 1, 19X4, along with $200 of interest revenue for January 19X4. The year-end adjusting entry on December 31, 19X3 is

Adjusting Entries

19X3
Dec. 31   Interest Receivable................................ 1,000
                    Interest Revenue   1,000

After posting, the accounts appear as follows:

Interest Receivable

19X3			
Dec. 31	Adj.	1,000	
Dec. 31	Bal.	1,000	

Interest Revenue

	19X3		
	Aug. 1	CR	1,200
	Dec. 31	Adj.	1,000
	Dec. 31	Bal.	2,200

The 19X3 income statement reports interest revenue of $2,200, and the balance sheet reports interest receivable of $1,000.

Receipt of $1,200 cash interest on February 1, 19X4, eliminates the $1,000 receivable. This receipt also includes $200 interest revenue earned during January 19X4. A reversing entry, dated January 1, 19X4, avoids having to account for these dual effects. The reversing entry is

Reversing Entries

OBJECTIVE 2

Make a reversing entry for an accrued revenue

19X4			
Jan. 1	Interest Revenue	1,000	
	Interest Receivable		1,000

After posting the reversing entry, Interest Receivable and Interest Revenue appear as follows:

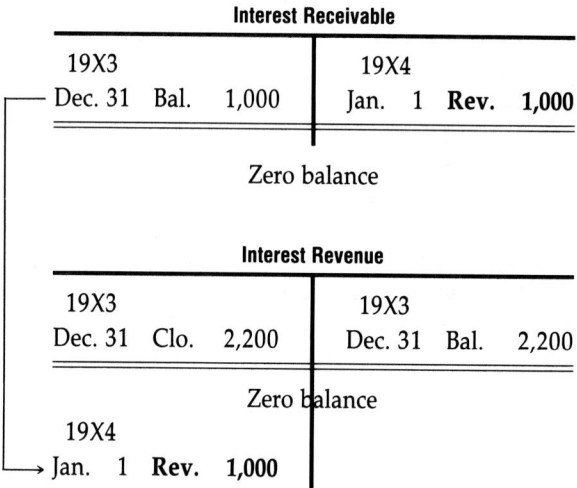

Interest Receivable

19X3				19X4			
Dec. 31	Bal.	1,000		Jan. 1	Rev.	1,000	

Zero balance

Interest Revenue

19X3				19X3			
Dec. 31	Clo.	2,200		Dec. 31	Bal.	2,200	

Zero balance

19X4			
Jan. 1	Rev.	1,000	

The arrow shows the transfer of the debit balance from Interest Receivable to Interest Revenue. This debit will be eliminated on February 1, 19X4, when the business receives cash interest of $1,200. The cash receipt entry is then routinely recorded:

19X4			
Feb. 1	Cash	1,200	
	Interest Revenue.............................		1,200

After posting, the Interest Revenue account has the correct credit balance of $200, which is the amount of interest revenue earned in 19X4:

Interest Revenue

19X4				19X4			
Jan. 1	Rev.	1,000		Feb. 1	CR	1,200	
				Feb. 1	Bal.	200	

Accountants use reversing entries for all types of accrued revenues, but they are optional.

Summary Problem for Your Review

The fiscal year accounting period of Blue Bell, Inc., maker of Wrangler jeans, ends on September 30. After going through the accounting process, including the adjusting entries, Blue Bell reported its *accrued liabilities* on a recent balance sheet as follows. These accrued liabilities resulted directly from the adjusting entries.

Liabilities

Notes payable—Banks and other	$135,419,000
Current maturities of long-term debt	3,664,000
Accounts payable, principally trade	120,697,000
Dividends payable	5,756,000
Accrued liabilities:	
Compensation [salaries and wages]	23,620,000
Pension and profit sharing	4,981,000
Income taxes	21,624,000
Taxes—Other than income	8,028,000
Interest	3,534,000
Other	7,983,000
Total	$335,306,000

The company's accrued liability for compensation is its unpaid compensation expense for the year ended September 30.

Required

1. Journalize adjusting entries like those that Blue Bell made at September 30 to record accrued compensation expense and accrued interest expense.
2. Journalize the related reversing entries. Date them appropriately.
3a. Set up ledger accounts for Compensation Payable and Compensation Expense, on September 30, prior to the adjusting entries in Requirement 1. Compensation Payable had a zero balance and Compensation Expense had a debit balance of $380,000,000.
 b. Journalize the closing entry for Compensation Expense at September 30.
 c. Assume Blue Bell paid compensation of $25 million on October 3. Journalize this cash payment, assuming a reversing entry was made.
 d. Post the adjusting, closing, reversing, and cash payment entries to Compensation Payable and Compensation Expense. Use the appropriate dates and label adjusting entries as Adj., closing entries as Clo., reversing entries as Rev., and cash payments as CP.
 e. After all postings, what is the balance in Compensation Payable? What does this mean? What is the balance in Compensation Expense? What does this balance mean?

SOLUTION TO REVIEW PROBLEM

1. Adjusting entries at September 30:

Adjusting Entries

Sep. 30	Compensation Expense	23,620,000	
	Compensation Payable.		23,620,000
30	Interest Expense	3,534,000	
	Interest Payable.		3,534,000

2. Reversing entries at October 1:

Reversing Entries

Oct. 1	Compensation Payable.	23,620,000	
	Compensation Expense.		23,620,000
1	Interest Payable.	3,534,000	
	Interest Expense		3,534,000

3a. Ledger accounts and balances prior to September 30 adjusting entries:

Compensation Payable

Compensation Expense

CP	⌇		
CP	⌇		
Sep. 30	Bal.	380,000,000	

b. Closing entry at September 30:

Closing Entries

Sep. 30	Income Summary ($380,000,000 +		
	$23,620,000).	403,620,000	
	Compensation Expense		403,620,000

c. Cash payment for compensation at October 3:

Oct. 3	Compensation Expense	25,000,000	
	Cash		25,000,000

d. Ledger accounts posted:

Compensation Payable

Oct. 1	Rev.	23,620,000		Sep. 30	Adj.	23,620,000

Zero balance

Compensation Expense

CP		≷				
CP		≷				
		380,000,000				
Sep. 30	Adj.	23,620,000				
Sep. 30	Bal.	403,620,000	Sep. 30	Clo.	403,620,000	
Oct. 3	CP	25,000,000	Oct. 1	Rev.	23,620,000	
Oct. 3	Bal.	1,380,000				

e. The balance in Compensation Payable is zero. This means Blue Bell has no compensation liability. The debit balance in Compensation Expense is $1,380,000. This amount is the portion of the October 3 payment that is compensation expense of the new year.

Prepaid Expenses

Prepaid expenses are advance payments of expenses. Prepaid Insurance, Prepaid Rent, Prepaid Advertising, and Prepaid Legal Cost are prepaid expenses. Supplies that will be used up in the current period or within one year are also accounted for as prepaid expenses.

When a business prepays an expense—rent, for example—it can debit an *asset* account (Prepaid Rent) as follows:

Prepaid Rent	XXX	
Cash		XXX

Alternatively, the accountant can debit an *expense* account in the entry to record this cash payment, as follows:

Rent Expense	XXX	
Cash		XXX

Regardless of the account debited, the business must adjust the accounts at the end of the period. Making the adjustment allows the business to report the correct amount of expense for the period and the correct amount of asset at the period's end.

Prepaid Expense Recorded Initially as an Asset

Prepayments of expenses provide a future benefit to the business, so it is logical to record the prepayment by debiting an *asset* account. Suppose on August 1, 19X6, the business prepays one year's rent of $6,000 ($500 per month). The cash payment is recorded:

19X6

Aug. 1	Prepaid Rent	6,000	
	Cash		6,000

On December 31, the end of the accounting period, five months' prepayment has expired and must be accounted for as *expense.* The adjusting entry is

Adjusting Entries

19X6
Dec. 31 Rent Expense ($6,000 × 5/12)...................... 2,500
              Prepaid Rent   2,500

The adjusting entry transfers $2,500 of the original $6,000 prepayment from Prepaid Rent to Rent Expense. This leaves a $3,500 debit balance in Prepaid Rent, which is seven months' rent still prepaid. After posting, the accounts appear as follows:

Prepaid Rent

19X6			19X6		
Aug. 1	CP	6,000	Dec. 31	Adj.	2,500
Dec. 31	Bal.	3,500			

Rent Expense

19X6			
Dec. 31	Adj.	2,500	
Dec. 31	Bal.	2,500	

The $2,500 balance of Rent Expense is closed to Income Summary, along with all other expenses and revenues, at the end of the accounting period.

No reversing entry is used under this approach. The asset account Prepaid Rent has a debit balance to start the new period. This is consistent with recording prepaid expenses initially as assets.

The balance sheet at December 31, 19X6, reports Prepaid Rent of $3,500 as an asset. The 19X6 income statement reports Rent Expense of $2,500 as an expense, which is the expired portion of the initial $6,000 rent prepayment. Keep this reporting result in mind as you study the next section.

Prepaid Expense Recorded Initially as an Expense

Prepaying an expense creates an asset. However, the asset may be so short-lived that it will expire in the current accounting period — within one year or less. Thus the accountant may decide to debit the prepayment to an expense account at the time of payment. Continuing with the rent example, the $6,000 cash payment on August 1 may be debited to Rent Expense:

19X6
Aug. 1 Rent Expense.................................. 6,000
              Cash......................................   6,000

At December 31 only five months' prepayment has expired, leaving seven months' rent still prepaid. In this case, the accountant must transfer 7/12 of the original prepayment of $6,000, or $3,500, to Prepaid Rent. The adjusting entry decreases the balance of Rent Expense to 5/12 of the original $6,000, or $2,500. The December 31 adjusting entry is

Adjusting Entries

19X6

Dec. 31   Prepaid Rent ($6,000 × $^7/_{12}$)   3,500

             Rent Expense   3,500

After posting, the two accounts appear as follows:

Prepaid Rent

19X6			
Dec. 31	Adj.	3,500	
Dec. 31	Bal.	3,500	

Rent Expense

19X6			19X6		
Aug. 1	CP	6,000	Dec. 31	Adj.	3,500
Dec. 31	Bal.	2,500			

The balance sheet for 19X6 reports Prepaid Rent of $3,500, and the income statement for 19X6 reports Rent Expense of $2,500. Whether the business initially debits the prepayment to an asset account or to an expense account, the financial statements report the same amounts for prepaid rent and rent expense. The Rent Expense's balance is closed at the end of the period.

During the next accounting period, the $3,500 balance in Prepaid Rent will expire and become expense. It is efficient on the beginning date of the new year to make a *reversing entry* that transfers the ending balance of Prepaid Rent back to Rent Expense:

Reversing Entries

19X7

Jan. 1   Rent Expense   3,500

            Prepaid Rent   3,500

OBJECTIVE 4
Reverse the adjustment for a prepaid expense recorded initially as an expense

This reversing entry avoids later worry about what prepayments become expenses. The arrow shows the transfer of the debit balance from Prepaid Rent to Rent Expense after posting:

Prepaid Rent

19X6			19X7			
Dec. 31	Bal.	3,500	Jan.	1	**Rev.**	**3,500**

Zero balance

Rent Expense

19X6			19X6			
Aug. 1	CP	6,000	Dec. 31	Adj.	3,500	
Dec. 31	Bal.	2,500	Dec. 31	Clo.	2,500	
19X7						
Jan.	1	**Rev.**	**3,500**			

After the reversing entry, the $3,500 amount is lodged in the expense account. This is consistent with recording prepaid expenses initially as expenses. Because this $3,500 amount will become expense during 19X7, no additional adjustment is needed. Subsequent expense prepayments are debited to Rent Expense and then adjusted at the end of the period as outlined here. Reversing entries ease the work of the accounting process for all types of prepaid expenses that are recorded initially as expenses. Reversing entries are *not* used for prepaid expenses that are recorded initially as assets.

Comparing the Two Approaches to Recording Prepaid Expenses

In summary, the two approaches to recording prepaid expenses are similar in that the asset amount reported on the balance sheet and the expense amount reported on the income statement are the same. They differ, however, in the prepayment entries and the adjusting entries. When a prepaid expense is recorded initially as an asset, (1) the adjusting entry transfers the *used* portion of the asset to the expense account and (2) no reversing entry is used. When a prepaid expense is recorded initially as an expense, (1) the adjusting entry transfers the *unused* portion of the expense to the asset account and (2) a reversing entry transfers the amount of the asset account back to the expense account to start the new accounting period.

Unearned (Deferred) Revenues _____

Unearned (deferred) revenues arise when a business collects cash in advance of earning the revenue. The recognition of revenue is *deferred* until later when it is earned. Unearned revenues are liabilities because the business that receives cash owes the other party goods or services to be delivered later.

Recall the prepaid expense examples listed on p. 1131—insurance, rent, advertising, and so on. Prepaid expenses create assets for the business that pays the cash. The business that receives the cash in advance, however, faces a liability. For example, the landlord who receives a tenant's rent in advance must provide future service to the tenant. This is a liability, and the cash the landlord receives is unearned rent revenue. Similarly, unearned revenue arises as magazine publishers sell subscriptions, colleges collect tuition, airlines sell tickets, and attorneys accept advance fees.

When a business receives cash before earning the related revenue, the business debits Cash. It can credit either a *liability* account or a *revenue* account. In either case, the business must make adjusting entries at the end of the period to report the correct amounts of liability and revenue on the financial statements.

Unearned (Deferred) Revenue Recorded Initially as a Liability

Receipt of cash in advance of earning revenue creates a liability, so it is logical to debit Cash and credit a *liability* account. Assume an attorney receives a $7,200 fee in advance from a client on October 1, 19X2. The attorney will earn this amount at the rate of $800 per month during the nine-month period ending June 30, 19X3. The attorney's cash receipt entry is

OBJECTIVE 5

Record unearned revenues in two ways

19X2			
Oct. 1	Cash	7,200	
	Unearned Legal Revenue......................		7,200

On December 31, 19X2, the end of the law firm's accounting period, three months of the fee agreement have elapsed. The attorney has earned $\frac{3}{9}$ of the $7,200, or $2,400. The adjusting entry to transfer $2,400 to the revenue account is

Adjusting Entries

19X2
Dec. 31   Unearned Legal Revenue ($7,200 $\times$ $\frac{3}{9}$).   2,400
                Legal Revenue   2,400

After posting, the liability and revenue accounts are

Unearned Legal Revenue

19X2			19X2		
Dec. 31	Adj.	2,400	Oct. 1	CR	7,200
			Dec. 31	Bal.	4,800

Legal Revenue

			19X2		
			Dec. 31	Adj.	2,400
			Dec. 31	Bal.	2,400

The law firm's 19X2 income statement reports legal revenue of $2,400, while its balance sheet reports unearned legal revenue of $4,800 as a liability. During 19X3 the attorney will earn the remaining $4,800 and will then make an adjusting entry to transfer $4,800 to the Legal Revenue account. No reversing entry is used. The balance in the liability account is consistent with recording the unearned revenue initially as a liability.

Unearned (Deferred) Revenue Recorded Initially as a Revenue

Receipt of cash in advance of earning the revenue can be credited initially to a *revenue* account. If the business has earned all the revenue within the period during which it received the cash, no adjusting entry is necessary. However, if the business earns only a part of the revenue at the end of the period, it must make adjusting entries.

Suppose on October 1, 19X2, the law firm records the nine-month advance fee of $7,200 as revenue. The cash receipt entry is

19X2
Oct. 1   Cash   7,200
                Legal Revenue   7,200

At December 31 the attorney has earned only $\frac{3}{9}$ of the $7,200, or $2,400. Accordingly, the firm makes an adjusting entry to transfer the unearned portion ($\frac{6}{9}$ of $7,200, or $4,800) from the revenue account to a liability account.

Adjusting Entries

19X2
Dec. 31   Legal Revenue ($7,200 $\times$ $\frac{6}{9}$).   4,800
                Unearned Legal Revenue   4,800

The adjusting entry leaves the earned portion (³/₉, or $2,400) of the original amount in the revenue account. After posting, the total amount ($7,200) is properly divided between the liability account ($4,800) and the revenue account ($2,400), as follows:

Unearned Legal Revenue

		19X2		
		Dec. 31	Adj.	4,800
		Dec. 31	Bal.	4,800

Legal Revenue

19X2			19X2		
Dec. 31	Adj.	4,800	Oct. 1	CR	7,200
			Dec. 31	Bal.	2,400

The attorney's 19X2 income statement reports legal revenue of $2,400, and the balance sheet at December 31, 19X2, reports as a liability the unearned legal revenue of $4,800. Whether the business initially credits a liability account or a revenue account, the financial statements report the same amounts for unearned legal revenue and legal revenue.

The law firm will earn the $4,800 during 19X3. On January 1, 19X3, it is efficient to make a reversing entry in order to transfer the liability balance back to the revenue account. By making the reversing entry, the accountant avoids having to reconsider the situation one year later, when the 19X3 adjusting entries will be made. The reversing entry is

OBJECTIVE 6

Reverse the adjustment for an unearned revenue recorded initially as a revenue

Reversing Entries

19X3			
Jan. 1	Unearned Legal Revenue	4,800	
	Legal Revenue.		4,800

After posting, the liability account has a zero balance. The $4,800 credit is now lodged in the revenue account because it will be earned during 19X3. The arrow in the following example shows the transfer from the liability account to the revenue account.

Unearned Legal Revenue

			19X2		
			Dec. 31	Adj.	4,800
19X3			19X2		
Jan. 1	**Rev.**	**4,800**	Dec. 31	Bal.	4,800

Zero balance

Legal Revenue

19X2			19X2		
Dec. 31	Adj.	4,800	Oct. 1	CR	7,200
Dec. 31	Clo.	2,400	Dec. 31	Bal.	2,400
			19X3		
			Jan. 1	**Rev.**	**4,800**

Subsequent advance receipts of revenue are credited to the Legal Revenue account. The year-end adjusting process is the same for every period.

Comparing the Two Approaches to Recording Unearned (Deferred) Revenues

The two approaches to recording unearned revenue are similar in that the liability amount reported on the balance sheet and the revenue amount reported on the income statement are the same. The approaches differ, though, in how adjustments are handled. When unearned revenues are recorded initially as liabilities, (1) the adjusting entry transfers to the revenue account the amount of the advance collection that has been *earned* during the period, and (2) *no* reversing entry is used. When unearned revenues are recorded initially as revenue, (1) the adjustment transfers to the liability account the amount of the advance collection that is still *unearned,* and (2) a reversing entry transfers the balance of the liability account to the revenue account to begin the next accounting period.

Summary Problem for Your Review

Pizza Time Theatre, Inc., reported prepaid expenses of $429,380 on a recent balance sheet. Assume that during the year the company paid cash in the amount of $1 million for prepaid insurance, rent, and so on.

Required

Record the company's prepaid expense transactions and related adjusting, closing, and reversing entries, assuming the company records prepaid expenses initially as (1) an asset and (2) an expense. Record entries in a single Prepaid Expense account and a single Expense account.

SOLUTION TO REVIEW PROBLEM

1. Prepaid expense recorded initially as an *asset*:
   Cash payment of $1,000,000:

Prepaid Expense............................	1,000,000	
Cash		1,000,000

   Year-end adjusting entry:

Expense ($1,000,000 − $429,380)...............	570,620	
Prepaid Expense........................		570,620

Year-end closing entry:

Income Summary.........................	570,620	
Expense..............................		570,620

Reversing entry: None

2. Prepaid expense recorded initially as an *expense*:
   Cash payment of $1,000,000:

Expense................................	1,000,000	
Cash		1,000,000

Year-end adjusting entry:

Prepaid Expense...........................	429,380	
Expense..............................		429,380

Year-end closing entry:

Income Summary.........................	570,620	
Expense..............................		570,620

Reversing entry dated January 1 of new year:

Expense................................	429,380	
Prepaid Expense......................		429,380

Summary

Accrual entries may be accompanied by *reversing entries,* which eliminate the need to refer back to the adjusting entries of the preceding period when recording the cash payments and receipts of a new period. They are the exact opposite of the related adjusting entry. An efficiency device, they eliminate the need to refer back to a preceding period's adjusting entries when making cash entries in the next period. However, they are optional.

Prepaid expenses may be recorded initially in an *asset* account or an *expense* account. When prepaid expenses are recorded initially as an asset, no need exists for a reversing entry because the asset account balance will be adjusted at the end of the next period. However, when prepaid expenses are recorded initially as an expense, a reversing entry eases accounting for the expense of the new period. Regardless of the approach taken, the financial statements should report the same amount of asset and expense.

Unearned (deferred) revenues may be recorded initially as a *liability* or a *revenue.* Recording unearned revenues initially as liabilities causes no need for a reversing entry. However, when recording them initially as revenues, a reversing entry eases accounting. Either recording approach is acceptable as long as the *financial statements* report the *correct* amounts.

Self-Study Questions

Test your understanding of this appendix by marking the best answer for each of the following questions.

1. The reversing entry for a $900 accrual of salary expense is *(p. 1125)*

a. Salary Expense.....................................	900	
Salary Payable..................................		900
b. Salary Expense.....................................	900	
Cash...		900
c. Salary Payable.....................................	900	
Cash...		900
d. Salary Payable.....................................	900	
Salary Expense.................................		900

2. Reversing entries are dated *(p. 1125)*
   a. The date on which the entry is made
   b. The beginning of the next period
   c. The end of the period
   d. Any of the above
3. The benefit of reversing entries is that they *(p. 1127)*
   a. Eliminate the need for adjusting entries
   b. Close out the balances in all the revenues and expenses
   c. Streamline the accounting for transactions in a period following an adjusting entry
   d. Increase the amounts of assets and decrease the amounts of liabilities reported on the balance sheet
4. Which of the following entries would it be helpful to reverse? *(pp. 1127–1128, 1133)*

a. Interest Receivable..................................	XXX	
Interest Revenue		XXX
b. Rent Expense	XXX	
Prepaid Rent		XXX
c. Cash..	XXX	
Interest Receivable..............................		XXX
d. Supplies	XXX	
Supplies Expense................................		XXX

   d. Both a and b
   e. Both a and d
   f. None of the above
5. Recording a prepaid expense initially as an asset *(pp. 1131, 1134)*
   a. Has no effect on the amount of asset and expense reported in the financial statements so long as the correct adjusting entry is made at the end of the period.
   b. Leads to reporting the correct amount of asset and expense in the financial statements.
   c. Leads to reporting an incorrect amount of asset and expense in the financial statements.
   d. Is illogical. It is more logical to record the prepaid expense initially as an expense.

Answers to the self-study questions are at the end of the appendix.

Accounting Vocabulary

reversing entry *(p. 1125)*.

ASSIGNMENT MATERIAL _____

Questions

1. What are the identifying characteristics of a reversing entry? What is the practical value of reversing entries?
2. The title Accrued Expenses does not include the word *liability* or *payable.* Why are accrued expenses liabilities?
3. What are the two ways to initially record a prepaid expense? How are they similar? How are they different?
4. Explain why recording a prepaid expense initially as an expense calls for a reversing entry.
5. Unearned revenues are also called deferred revenues. Why?
6. Suppose your company receives cash from customers in advance of earning the revenue. Which approach to recording the unearned revenue would you take and why?
7. Which approach to recording unearned (deferred) revenues calls for a reversing entry?
8. Each of the following adjusting entries is incomplete. Indicate the account debited or credited in the other half of the entry.

Accounts Receivable.	XXX	
a		XXX
b		XXX
Wage Payable		XXX
Supplies Expense	XXX	
c		XXX
Unearned Revenue.	XXX	
d		XXX

9. Indicate whether each of the following accounts is (a) an asset, (b) a liability, (c) a revenue, or (d) an expense: Unearned Legal Revenue, Interest Receivable, Prepaid Rent, Sales Revenue, Insurance Expense, Supplies, Salary Expense, Income Tax Expense, Property Tax Payable, Deferred Subscription Revenue, Service Fees Earned.
10. Where is the ultimate emphasis in financial accounting? How do adjusting entries tie into this emphasis?

Exercises

Exercise B-1 *Journalizing and posting wage payment and accrual transactions*

During 19X2 London Sales Company pays wages of $40,800 to its employees. At December 31, 19X2, the company owes accrued wages of $900 that will be included in the $1,200 weekly payroll payment on January 4, 19X3.

Required

1. Open T-accounts for Wage Expense and Wage Payable.
2. Journalize all wage transactions for the year, including adjusting, closing, and reversing entries. Record the $40,800 amount by a single debit to Wage Expense.
3. Post amounts to the two T-accounts, showing their balances at January 4, 19X3. Denote cash payment entries by CP, adjusting entries by Adj., closing entries by Clo., reversing entries by Rev., and balances by Bal.

Exercise B-2 *Recording supplies transactions two ways*

At the beginning of the year supplies of $1,490 were on hand. During the year the business paid $3,300 cash for supplies. At the end of the year the count of supplies indicates the ending balance is $1,260.

Required

1. Assume the business records supplies by initially debiting an *asset* account. Therefore, place the beginning balance in the Supplies T-account and record the above entries directly in the accounts without using a journal.

2. Assume the business records supplies by initially debiting an *expense* account. Therefore, place the beginning balance in the Supplies Expense T-account and record the above entries directly in the accounts without using a journal.

3. Compare the ending account balances under the two approaches. Are they the same or different? Why?

Exercise B-3 *Recording unearned revenues two ways*

At the beginning of the year the company owed customers $6,450 for unearned sales collected in advance. During the year the business received advance cash receipts of $10,000. At year end the unearned revenue liability is $3,900.

Required

1. Assume the company records unearned revenues by initially crediting a *liability* account. Open T-accounts for Unearned Sales Revenue and Sales Revenue and place the beginning balance in Unearned Sales Revenue. Journalize the cash collection and adjusting entries and post their dollar amounts. As references in the T-accounts, denote a balance by Bal., a cash receipt by CR, and an adjustment by Adj.

2. Assume the company records unearned revenues by initially crediting a *revenue* account. Open T-accounts for Unearned Sales Revenue and Sales Revenue and place the beginning balance in Sales Revenue. Journalize the cash collection and adjusting entries and post their dollar amounts. As references in the T-accounts, denote a balance by Bal., a cash receipt by CR, and an adjustment by Adj.

3. Compare the ending balances in the two accounts. Explain why they are the same or different.

Exercise B-4 *Using reversing entries to account for unearned revenues*

One approach to recording unearned revenue in Exercise B-3 calls for a reversing entry. Identify that approach. Journalize and post the entries required in Exercise B-3 and also the closing and reversing entries. The end of the current period is December 31, 19X1. Use dates for all entries and postings except the cash collection, which is a summary of the year's transactions. As references in the ledger accounts, denote a balance by Bal., cash receipts by CR, adjusting entries by Adj., closing entries by Clo., and reversing entries by Rev.

Exercise B-5 *Recording accrued revenues with and without reversing entries*

Columbus Corporation receives a note receivable on November 1, 19X5. During the remainder of the year, Columbus earns accrued interest revenue of $3,000. This amount will be collected on May 1, 19X6, along with $6,000 of interest revenue for 19X6.

Required

1. Open T-accounts for Interest Receivable and Interest Revenue. Journalize and post the interest accrual and cash collection transactions and the closing entry, assuming reversing entries are not used. As references in the ledger accounts, denote a balance by Bal., cash receipts by CR, adjusting entries by Adj., closing entries by Clo., and reversing entries by Rev.

2. Repeat requirement 1, assuming reversing entries are used.

3. Compare the account balances achieved in requirements 1 and 2.

Exercise B-6   *Identifying transactions from a ledger account*

McGraw Company makes its annual insurance payment on June 30. Identify each of the entries (a) through (e) to the Insurance Expense account as a cash payment, an adjusting entry, a closing entry, or a reversing entry. Also give the other account debited or credited in each entry.

Insurance Expense

Date	Item	Debit	Credit	Balance Debit	Balance Credit
19X4					
Jan. 1	(a)	800		800	
June 30	(b)	1,240		2,040	
Dec. 31	(c)		410	1,630	
Dec. 31	(d)		1,630	—	
19X5					
Jan. 1	(e)	410			410

Problems   (Group A)

Problem B-1A   *Recording prepaid rent and revenue collected in advance two ways*

DeGroot Sales and Service completes the following transactions during 19X4:

Aug. 31   Pays $9,000 store rent covering the six-month period ending February 28, 19X5.
Dec.   1   Collects $2,200 cash in advance from customers. The service revenue will be earned $550 monthly over the period ending March 30, 19X5.

Required

1. Journalize these entries by debiting an asset account for Prepaid Rent and by crediting a liability account for Unearned Service Revenue. Explanations are unnecessary.
2. Journalize the related adjustments at December 31, 19X4.
3. Post the entries to the ledger accounts and show their balances at December 31, 19X4. Posting references are unnecessary.
4. Repeat Requirements 1 through 3. This time debit Rent Expense for the rent payment and credit Service Revenue for the collection of revenue in advance.
5. Compare the account balances in Requirements 3 and 4. They should be equal.

Problem B-2A   *Journalizing adjusting and reversing entries*

Vidmar Company's accounting records reveal the following information before adjustments at December 31, 19X3, the end of the accounting period:

a. Wages owed to hourly employees total $3,400. Total salaries owed to salaried employees are $2,790. These amounts will be paid on the next scheduled payday in January 19X4.
b. On October 31 Vidmar loaned $40,000 to another business. The loan agreement requires the borrower to pay Vidmar interest of $2,400 on April 30, 19X4. One third of this interest is earned in 19X3.
c. Vidmar routinely debits Sales Supplies when it purchases supplies. At the beginning of 19X3 supplies of $800 were on hand, and during the year the company purchased supplies of $6,700. At year end the count of sales supplies on hand indicates the ending amount is $950.
d. Vidmar collects revenue in advance from customers and credits such amounts to Sales Revenue because the revenue is usually earned within a short time. At December 31,

19X3, however, the company has a liability of $6,840 to customers for goods they paid for in advance.

e. Rentals cost the company $1,000 per month. The company prepays rent of $6,000 each May 1 and November 1 and debits Rent Expense for such payments.

f. On December 23 Vidmar Company received a property tax bill from the city. The total amount, due on February 1, 19X4, is $4,600. Half of this amount is property tax expense for 19X3.

g. The company prepaid $3,500 for television advertising that will run daily for two weeks—December 27, 19X3 through January 9, 19X4. Vidmar debited Prepaid Advertising for the full amount on December 1.

Required

1. Journalize the adjusting entry needed for each situation at December 31, 19X3, identifying each entry by its corresponding letter.
2. Journalize reversing entries as needed. Use the corresponding letters for references. Date the entries appropriately.
3. Use the first situation that calls for a reversing entry to explain the practical value of the reversal.

Problem B-3A *Preparing an adjusted trial balance; journalizing reversing entries*

The year-end trial balance of Retton Company at July 31 of the current year appears as follows:

Retton Company
Trial Balance
July 31, 19XX

Account Title	Balance Debit	Balance Credit
Cash.	$ 3,960	
Accounts receivable	14,700	
Note receivable	78,330	
Prepaid rent.	6,000	
Prepaid insurance		
Furniture	9,600	
Accumulated depreciation		$ 4,200
Accounts payable		16,090
Wage payable		
Salary payable.		
Interest payable.		
Unearned service revenue		
Notes payable		30,000
M. L. Retton, capital		48,490
M. L. Retton, withdrawals	46,000	
Service revenue.		129,000
Advertising expense	3,000	
Wage expense	31,750	
Salary expense.	26,300	
Rent expense.		
Utilities expense	3,640	
Depreciation expense		
Insurance expense.	2,400	
Interest expense.	2,100	
Total.	$227,780	$227,780

The accounting records reveal the following additional data at July 31, 19XX.

a. Accrued wages of $1,400 and accrued salaries of $640 at July 31.
b. Retton records advance collections from customers by crediting Service Revenue. At July 31, $2,400 of the balance of Service Revenue has still not been earned. This amount of revenue will be earned early in August.
c. Prepaid rent expired during the year, $5,300. When Retton pays rent, he debits Prepaid Rent.
d. Insurance expense for the year, $2,100. When Retton pays insurance, he debits Insurance Expense.
e. Depreciation on furniture for the year, $1,200.
f. Accrued interest expense at July 31, $430.

Required

1. Write the trial balance on a sheet of paper, enter the adjustments in adjacent columns, and prepare the adjusted trial balance at July 31 of the current year.
2. Journalize the reversing entries, as appropriate, at August 1.

Problem B-4A   *Identifying adjustments and the related reversing entries*

The unadjusted and adjusted balances are shown below for selected accounts. Journalize the adjusting entries that were made and posted at May 31, 19X5, the end of the accounting period. Where appropriate, also journalize the reversing entries at June 1, 19X5.

	Unadjusted Balance	Adjusted Balance
Interest receivable...................	$ —	$ 1,465
Prepaid rent........................	4,500	1,500
Supplies............................	—	940
Accumulated depreciation	12,900	15,300
Salary payable......................	—	3,090
Property tax payable.................	—	1,300
Unearned sales revenue	—	790
Sales revenue.......................	98,870	98,080
Interest revenue.....................	3,590	5,055
Salary expense......................	49,550	52,640
Rent expense.......................	—	3,000
Supplies expense....................	5,560	4,620
Property tax expense.................	2,110	3,410
Depreciation expense	—	2,400

Problem B-5A   *Recording supplies and unearned revenue transactions two ways*

The accounting records of Stone Company reveal the following information about sales supplies and unearned sales revenue for 19X5:

Sales Supplies

19X5
Jan. 1	Beginning amount on hand......................	$	420
Mar. 16	Cash purchase of supplies......................		3,740
Dec. 31	Ending amount on hand		290

Unearned Sales Revenue

19X5

Jan. 1	Beginning amount on advance collections	6,590
July 22	Advance cash collection from customer	16,480
Nov. 4	Advance cash collection from customer	38,400
Dec. 31	Advance collections earned during the year.	52,160

Required

1. Assume Stone Company records (a) supplies by initially debiting an asset account and (b) advance collections from customers by initially crediting a liability account
   a. Open T-accounts for Sales Supplies, Sales Supplies Expense, Unearned Sales Revenue, and Sales Revenue. Insert the beginning balances in the appropriate accounts.
   b. Record the cash transactions during 19X5 directly in the accounts.
   c. Record the adjusting and closing entries at December 31, 19X5, directly in the accounts.
   d. If appropriate, record the reversing entries at January 1, 19X6, directly in the accounts.
2. Assume Stone Company records (a) supplies by initially debiting an expense account and (b) advance collections by initially crediting a revenue account. Perform Steps *a* through *d* as in Requirement 1.
3. Using the following format, compare the amounts that would be reported for the above accounts in the 19X5 balance sheet and income statement under the two recording approaches of Requirements 1 and 2. Explain any similarity or difference.

	Requirement 1	Requirement 2
Balance sheet at December 31, 19X5 reports:		
Sales supplies.	$_____	$_____
Unearned sales revenue	_____	_____
Income statement for year ended December 31, 19X5, reports:		
Sales revenue.	_____	_____
Sales supplies expense.	_____	_____

(Group B)

Problem B-1B *Recording prepaid rent and revenue collected in advance two ways*

McGraw Service Company completes the following transactions during 19X7:

Oct. 31 Pays $4,200 store rent covering the six-month period ending April 30, 19X8.
Nov. 1 Collects $1,800 cash in advance from customers. The service revenue will be earned $600 monthly over the period ending January 31, 19X8.

Required

1. Journalize these entries by debiting an asset account for Prepaid Rent and by crediting a liability account for Unearned Service Revenue. Explanations are unnecessary.
2. Journalize the related adjustments at December 31, 19X7.
3. Post the entries to the ledger accounts and show their balances at December 31, 19X7. Posting references are unnecessary.
4. Repeat Requirements 1 through 3. This time debit Rent Expense for the rent payment and credit Service Revenue for the collection of revenue in advance.
5. Compare the account balances in Requirements 3 and 4. They should be equal.

Problem B-2B   *Journalizing adjusting and reversing entries*

The accounting records of Conner Company reveal the following information before adjustments at December 31, 19X6, the end of the accounting period.

a. On December 29 the company prepaid $2,200 for newspaper advertising that will run for 10 days beginning December 29, 19X6. Conner debited Prepaid Advertising for the full amount.

b. On July 31 Conner deposited $25,000 in a savings account. The bank will pay Conner interest of $1,200 on January 31, 19X7. Of this amount, five sixths is earned in 19X6.

c. On November 29 Conner Company received a property tax bill from the city. The total amount, due on January 15, 19X7, is $3,900. Three fourths of this amount is property tax expense of 19X6.

d. Commissions owed to sales employees at December 31 are $2,565, and salaries owed to home office employees are $1,870.

e. Conner collected revenue of $12,400 in advance from customers during the year. The company expected to earn the revenue during the year, so it credited Sales Revenue for the full amount. However, at December 31, the company has not yet shipped $3,169 of these goods.

f. On December 1 the company paid $4,500 rent for December, January, and February. It is company practice to debit Rent Expense for such prepayments.

g. Conner routinely debits Sales Supplies when it purchases supplies. At the beginning of 19X6 supplies of $380 were on hand, and during the year the company paid $4,000 for supplies. At year end, supplies of $510 are on hand.

Required

1. Journalize the adjusting entry needed for each situation at December 31, 19X6, identifying each entry by its corresponding letter.

2. Journalize reversing entries as needed. Use the corresponding letters for references. Date the entries.

3. Use the first situation that calls for a reversing entry to explain the practical value of the reversal.

Problem B-3B   *Preparing an adjusted trial balance; journalizing reversing entries*

The year-end trial balance of Saxman Company at June 30 of the current year appears as shown on the following page.

The accounting records reveal the following additional data at June 30, 19XX:

a. Accrued wages of $970 and accrued salaries of $880 at June 30.

b. Saxman records advance collections from customers by crediting Service Revenue. At June 30, $1,780 of the balance of Service Revenue has still not been earned.

c. Prepaid rent expired during the year, $1,400. When Saxman pays rent, she debits Prepaid Rent.

d. Insurance expense for the year, $3,640. When Saxman pays insurance, she debits Insurance Expense.

e. Depreciation on furniture for the year, $2,600.

f. Accrued interest expense at June 30, $560.

Required

1. Write the trial balance on a sheet of paper, enter the adjustments in adjacent columns, and prepare the adjusted trial balance at June 30 of the current year.

2. Journalize the reversing entries, as appropriate, at July 1.

Saxman Company
Trial Balance
June 30, 19XX

Account Title	Balance	
	Debit	Credit
Cash............................	$ 4,120	
Accounts receivable	23,800	
Note receivable	91,030	
Prepaid insurance		
Prepaid rent........................	1,500	
Furniture	14,700	
Accumulated depreciation		$ 6,280
Accounts payable		24,630
Wage payable		
Salary payable......................		
Interest payable.....................		
Unearned service revenue		
Notes payable		42,000
Betty Saxman, capital		55,170
Betty Saxman, withdrawals	41,000	
Service revenue.....................		136,000
Advertising expense	3,750	
Wage expense	40,900	
Salary expense......................	31,200	
Rent expense.......................		
Utilities expense	4,200	
Depreciation expense		
Insurance expense...................	3,880	
Interest expense.....................	4,000	
Total.............................	$264,080	$264,080

Problem B-4B *Identifying adjustments and the related reversing entries*

The unadjusted and adjusted balances are shown below for selected accounts. Journalize the adjusting entries that were made and posted at January 31, 19X2, the end of the accounting period. Where appropriate, also journalize the reversing entries at February 1, 19X2.

	Unadjusted Balance	Adjusted Balance
Interest receivable...................	$ —	$ 780
Prepaid insurance	3,400	860
Supplies............................	—	1,195
Accumulated depreciation	32,600	39,100
Wage payable	—	2,285
Income tax payable...................	—	2,860
Unearned sales revenue	—	2,390
Sales revenue	134,670	132,280
Interest revenue.....................	3,300	4,080
Wage expense	24,660	26,945
Insurance expense...................	—	2,540
Depreciation expense	—	6,500
Supplies expense....................	7,990	6,795
Income tax expense.................	11,800	14,660

Problem B-5B   *Recording prepaid expense and unearned revenue transactions two ways*

The accounting records of Waco Publications reveal the following information about prepaid insurance and unearned subscription revenue for 19X7:

Prepaid Insurance

19X7

Jan. 1	Beginning prepaid amount......................	$ 2,000
Aug. 31	Cash payment of insurance premiums	4,050
Dec. 31	Ending prepaid amount	2,700

Unearned Subscription Revenue

19X7

Jan. 1	Beginning liability for unearned subscriptions	9,640
June 30	Advance cash collections from customers...........	48,500
Dec. 31	Advance cash collections from customers...........	51,980
Dec. 31	Subscription revenue earned during the year........	97,410

Required

1. Assume Waco records (a) prepaid insurance by initially debiting an asset account and (b) advance collections of subscriptions from customers by initially crediting a liability account.
   a. Open accounts for Prepaid Insurance, Insurance Expense, Unearned Subscription Revenue, and Subscription Revenue. Insert the beginning balances in the appropriate accounts.
   b. Record the cash transactions during 19X7 directly in the accounts.
   c. Record the adjusting and closing entries at December 31, 19X7, directly in the accounts.
   d. If appropriate, record the reversing entries at January 1, 19X8, directly in the accounts.

2. Assume Waco records (a) prepaid insurance by initially debiting an expense account and (b) advance collections on subscriptions by initially crediting a revenue account. Perform Steps *a* through *d* as in Requirement 1.

3. Using the following format, compare the amounts that would be reported for the above accounts in the 19X7 balance sheet and income statement under the two recording approaches of Requirements 1 and 2. Explain any similarity or difference.

	Requirement 1	Requirement 2
Balance sheet at December 31, 19X7, reports:		
Prepaid insurance	$_____	$_____
Unearned subscription revenue	_____	_____
Income statement for year ended December 31, 19X7, reports:		
Subscription revenue...........................	_____	_____
Insurance expense.............................	_____	_____

Answers to Self-Study Questions

1. d   2. b   3. c   4. e   5. a

C

Published
Financial Statements

Gulf+Western Inc.

1 9 8 7 SELECTED FINANCIAL DATA

The table below summarizes recent financial information for Gulf+Western. For further information, refer to the audited financial statements and the notes thereto contained elsewhere herein.

Year Ended or at October 31	1987	1986	1985	1984	1983
	(Dollar amounts in millions, except per share)				
Revenues	$4,681.1	$3,781.1	$3,320.7	$2,818.3	$2,522.3
Net revenues	2,903.6	2,093.8	1,860.8	1,582.3	1,436.5
Earnings from continuing operations before income taxes	608.7	386.3	235.2	213.3	277.7
Earnings from continuing operations before extraordinary items	356.1	228.7	151.6	137.4	185.5
Net earnings (loss)	356.1	267.4	247.8	235.9	(191.7)
Earnings (loss) per share					
From continuing operations before extraordinary items	5.76	3.66	2.15	1.93	2.39
Net earnings (loss)	5.76	4.28	3.51	3.32	(2.54)
Cash dividends declared per common share	1.125	.90	.90	.90	.788
Working capital	776.3	492.0	614.5	1,018.5	1,033.0
Total assets	4,928.9	4,243.4	4,064.1	4,202.6	4,553.7
Notes payable and current maturities of long-term debt	64.9	29.8	121.9	72.1	213.1
Long-term debt, net of current maturities	1,334.9	1,260.8	1,076.1	894.1	1,001.7
Stockholders' equity	2,106.6	1,902.1	1,737.7	1,875.7	1,958.0
Book value per common share	35.05	30.85	27.91	26.75	25.32
Capital expenditures	57.1	73.6	62.8	68.9	49.3
Number of stockholders					
Common Stock	31,000	34,000	39,000	46,000	49,000
Preferred stock	3,000	3,000	3,000	3,000	4,000

Reference is made to Note B to the consolidated financial statements for a description of the Company's discontinued operations.

24

Gulf+Western Inc.

CONSOLIDATED STATEMENT OF EARNINGS

Year Ended October 31	1987	1986	1985
	(In millions, except per share)		
Revenues.	**$4,681.1**	$3,781.1	$3,320.7
Less revenues of unconsolidated finance subsidiary — Note A	**1,777.5**	1,687.3	1,459.9
Net Revenues	**2,903.6**	2,093.8	1,860.8
Earnings of unconsolidated finance subsidiary before income taxes — Note A.	**324.1**	289.5	251.0
	3,227.7	2,383.3	2,111.8
Cost of goods sold	**1,753.5**	1,215.8	1,178.2
Selling, general and administrative expenses	**751.8**	671.3	576.2
	2,505.3	1,887.1	1,754.4
Operating Income	**722.4**	496.2	357.4
Other expense	**(1.0)**	(2.4)	(6.0)
Interest expense — net — Note J	**(112.7)**	(107.5)	(116.2)
Earnings from Continuing Operations Before Income Taxes	**608.7**	386.3	235.2
Provision for income taxes — Notes A and H.	**252.6**	157.6	83.6
Earnings from Continuing Operations Before Extraordinary Items	**356.1**	228.7	151.6
Extraordinary items — Note C		38.7	
Earnings from discontinued operations — Note B			96.2
Net Earnings	**$ 356.1**	$ 267.4	$ 247.8
Dividends on preferred stock	**$ 0.8**	$ 0.8	$ 0.8
Average common and common equivalent shares outstanding — Note A	**61.7**	62.3	70.3
Earnings per share — Note A			
From continuing operations before extraordinary items	**$ 5.76**	$ 3.66	$ 2.15
Net earnings.	**5.76**	4.28	3.51

See notes to consolidated financial statements.

Gulf+Western Inc.

1 9 8 7 FINANCIAL REPORTING BY BUSINESS SEGMENTS

A summary description of the Company's business segments and Consumer/Commercial Finance operations is as follows:

Entertainment

Produces, finances and distributes motion pictures, television programming and prerecorded videocassettes and operates motion picture theatres and sports and entertainment facilities.

Publishing/Information

Publishes and distributes hardcover, mass market and trade paperback books, consumer information and special interest books, educational textbooks and materials, and business and professional information and services.

Consumer/Commercial Finance

Provides consumer finance (including direct installment and revolving credit loans and other consumer finance services) and commercial finance (including transportation and industrial equipment financing) and related insurance products.

REVENUES AND OPERATING INCOME

	Revenues			Operating Income		
Year Ended October 31	**1987**	1986	1985	**1987**	1986	1985
	(In millions)					
Business Segments						
Entertainment	**$1,829.6**	$1,144.8	$1,062.6	**$297.3**	$128.8	$ 69.1
Publishing/Information	**1,074.0**	949.0	798.2	**161.5**	140.5	103.7
Total	**2,903.6**	2,093.8	1,860.8	**458.8**	269.3	172.8
Consumer/Commercial Finance	**1,777.5**	1,687.3	1,459.9	**324.1**	289.5	251.0
Corporate Expenses				**(60.5)**	(62.6)	(66.4)
	$4,681.1	$3,781.1	$3,320.7	**$722.4**	$496.2	$357.4

Net revenues by business segment include revenues that are directly associated with a particular segment. Revenues between business segments (amounts are insignificant), which are accounted for on substantially the same basis as revenues from unaffiliated customers, have been eliminated. No single customer accounts for 10% or more of the consolidated net revenues.

Export sales to unaffiliated customers were $365.8, $206.4 and $223.8 million, respectively, for the three years ended October 31, 1987, 1986 and 1985. These sales were principally made in the following foreign geographic areas: Europe, the Far East, Canada and Latin America.

See Note K for additional disclosures related to business segments.

26

Gulf+Western Inc.

MANAGEMENT'S DISCUSSION AND ANALYSIS OF FINANCIAL CONDITION AND RESULTS OF OPERATIONS

RESULTS OF OPERATIONS

Entertainment

Operating income increased in both fiscal 1987 and fiscal 1986 from fiscal 1985. Results for the current year reflected the box office success of *Beverly Hills Cop II, Fatal Attraction* and *The Untouchables,* the outstanding performances of *Top Gun, Star Trek IV: The Voyage Home, The Golden Child,* "*Crocodile" Dundee* and *Children of a Lesser God* in both theatrical release and the videocassette market, as well as videocassette sales of *Indiana Jones and the Temple of Doom* and *Ferris Bueller's Day Off.* Television operations increased significantly, primarily because of the domestic syndication of *Cheers* and *Family Ties.* In addition to the above, fiscal 1987 results benefited from the availability of *Witness* and *Ferris Bueller's Day Off* for pay cable and the gain from the sale of Hughes Television Network. Partially offsetting these results was a modest adjustment to domestic syndication bad debt reserves in the first quarter of 1987. The theatre operations reflected record revenues from the Canadian theatre chain due to higher attendance levels and concession sales as well as contributions to earnings from the acquired domestic theatre operations. Operating income for Madison Square Garden declined because of the absence of income earned in the prior-year period from Rangers' playoff games and Hughes Television Network.

Results for fiscal 1986 reflect increases from all operations. The substantial improvement in revenues from theatrical releases was attributable primarily to the blockbuster performance of *Top Gun* and the outstanding results of *Ferris Bueller's Day Off* and "*Crocodile" Dundee.* The recognition of income related to licensing of *Raiders of the Lost Ark, Trading Places, 48 Hours* and *Flashdance* to network television, network profits resulting from the higher domestic syndication sales levels and network license fees of *Family Ties, Cheers* and *Webster,* and the continued growth of the home video operations, which benefited from the strong sales of *Beverly Hills Cop, Witness* and the cassettes included in Paramount's holiday season promotion program, also contributed to the improved results. These increases more than offset the lower syndication income resulting from the timing of renewals of library products. In addition, Madison Square Garden Network and Madison Square Garden Center reported improved earnings. The MSG Network benefited from growth in subscriber revenues, the increased number of events televised, including Rangers' playoff games, and lower programming costs, while Madison Square Garden Center benefited from an expanded schedule of concerts and increased attendance at sporting events. Theatre operations showed improvement as a result of higher concession sales and increased attendance. Fiscal 1986 also reflects the absence of operating losses sustained in the prior year from the coin-operated video game business, which had been shut down.

Publishing/Information

Operating income increased in fiscal 1987 and fiscal 1986 compared with fiscal 1985. Results of the elementary and secondary groups increased in fiscal 1987 because of strong sales performances, which were partially offset by the inclusion in the first six months of fiscal 1987 of the expected seasonal losses of Silver Burdett Company, which was acquired in May 1986. The consumer publishing group registered a significant increase primarily in trade operations, which benefited from such titles as *The Closing of the American Mind, The Great Depression of 1990, Women Who Love Too Much, Dark Angel* and *Veil: The Secret Wars of the CIA 1981–1987.* The international group's operations increased principally as a result of growth in the Asian, Canadian and United Kingdom markets. The professional information group's operating income declined as a result of higher expenses related to tax reform act supplements and increased business development spending. The higher education group posted an increase in operating results due to strong college book sales.

Elementary and secondary publishing operations made the largest contribution to the fiscal 1986 increase as compared with fiscal 1985, benefiting from the acquisition of Silver Burdett Company. The higher education operations increased principally because of revenues from college book and technical publications, while the professional information group benefited from acquired product lines and product enhancements. The international operations' improvement is primarily a result of growth in both the Canadian and United Kingdom markets. These increases more than offset the decline in the consumer publishing operations, which benefited from growth of its direct marketing operations and strong sales of *Hollywood Husbands, A Matter Of Honor* and *The Road Less Traveled* but which were adversely affected by a sluggish market that reduced profit margins in the paperback operations.

Results for the above periods were augmented by the acquisitions of Prentice-Hall, Inc. in December 1984, Ginn & Company in June 1985 and Silver Burdett Company in May 1986 as well as by the operating efficiencies attained through the consolidation of these operations.

Consumer/Commercial Finance

Operating income increased in both fiscal 1987 and fiscal 1986 compared with fiscal 1985 because of the increase in finance charge revenue resulting from the growth of net finance receivables (15.6% in 1987 and 8.4% in 1986) and increases in insurance sales, primarily to commercial finance customers. Consumer operations benefited from increased real estate-secured lending and improved results in mortgage banking and related real estate services as well as from its strong credit card portfolio. Commercial finance gains were achieved primarily in the heavy-duty truck portfolio as a result of receivables growth, while both operations continued to benefit from strict control of operating costs. Interest expense increased for fiscal 1987 and 1986 as a result of the higher average debt outstanding, due to an increased finance receivables portfolio, which was partially offset by a decline in average interest rates. The average interest margin was 8.54%, 8.87% and 8.66% for the years ended October 31, 1987, 1986 and 1985, respectively. Like other consumer finance businesses, the consumer/commercial finance unit experienced a higher level of credit losses during fiscal 1987 compared with fiscal 1986. As a result of a recent Financial Accounting Standards Board pronouncement, the Company will be required to consolidate its consumer/commercial finance subsidiary beginning in fiscal 1989. Separate financial statements for these operations are presented elsewhere herein.

Interest Expense — Net

In addition to the results of the operating units, earnings for fiscal 1987 reflect an increase in interest costs after a decrease in fiscal 1986 versus fiscal 1985. The increase in fiscal 1987 results from an increase in average debt outstanding and a decrease in average short-term investments that more than offset the effect of lower interest rates. The decrease for fiscal 1986 reflects a lower average of debt outstanding during the year as well as lower average interest rates.

LIQUIDITY AND CAPITAL RESOURCES

The Company depended primarily upon internal cash flow and external borrowings to finance its operations during the three years ended October 31, 1987. During fiscal 1987, the Company borrowed $250 million under long-term revolving loan agreements and received $222 million from the sale of certain entertainment receivables with the proceeds used to reduce commercial paper borrowings. During the year ended October 31, 1987, the Company purchased an additional 1.8 million shares of its Common Stock under a 12-million share repurchase program announced in October 1985. Subsequent to October 31, 1987, the Company purchased an additional 1.1 million shares of its Common Stock through December 10, 1987, leaving 0.8 million remaining shares authorized under the program. The Company may authorize an additional share repurchase program in 1988. Total debt as a percentage of total capitalization was 40% at October 31, 1987 and 1986.

At October 31, 1987, available long-term revolving loan agreements were $564 million which were used to support outstanding commercial paper and long-term revolving loan agreement borrowings. In the past, the Company has been able to increase its borrowings as required and expects to be able to continue to do so.

Capital expenditures amounted to $57 million in 1987, $74 million in 1986 and $63 million in 1985.

Effects of Change in Accounting for Income Taxes

The Financial Accounting Standards Board has issued a rule which will materially change the accounting and reporting for income taxes. The Company will be required to comply with its provisions in fiscal 1990.

Recognition of the provisions of the rule may result in a reduction in stockholders' equity not exceeding $80 million depending on the ultimate effect of tax planning alternatives developed prior to the time of adoption. This charge would reflect the elimination of certain deferred tax assets which would not meet the asset recognition requirements of the rule. The rule provides that the reduction in stockholders' equity may be accounted for by a one-time charge to earnings in the year the rule becomes effective or by restatement of prior years' financial statements.

Effects of Inflation and Changing Prices

The Company has, as a result of a restructuring program launched in 1983, divested itself of capital-intensive businesses and has expanded, through acquisitions and internal growth, its non-capital-intensive operations in the entertainment, publishing/information and consumer/commercial finance fields. While inflation affects all companies, its impact on those that are not heavily invested in fixed assets is mitigated because there is less potential for earnings to be inflated by understated depreciation charges or for significant understatement of the current value of assets. Furthermore, the impact of inflation on entertainment and publishing inventories is generally less than that in other industries due to the rapidity of their turnover, the uniqueness of product and the manner in which they are produced.

Helping to offset inflation's impact is the Company's maintenance of a net monetary liability position, since these liabilities will be paid with dollars of decreased purchasing power during inflationary times. Management believes that as a result of its concentration in non-capital-intensive operations, along with various Company programs designed to ensure the efficient utilization of resources and the control of costs, it has taken the necessary steps to minimize the effects of inflation on its operations.

Gulf+Western Inc.

CONSOLIDATED BALANCE SHEET

October 31	1987	1986
ASSETS	(In millions)	
Current Assets		
Cash and cash equivalents	$ 365.0	$ 61.5
Trade receivables, net of allowance for doubtful accounts of $51.8 million in 1987 and $29.0 million in 1986	642.6	540.3
Inventories — Notes A and D	324.6	277.6
Prepaid expenses, income taxes and other — Note J	405.1	390.8
Total Current Assets	1,737.3	1,270.2
Property, Plant and Equipment — Note A		
Land	93.7	90.7
Buildings	244.1	231.2
Machinery, equipment and other	182.5	192.2
	520.3	514.1
Less allowance for depreciation	142.2	121.5
	378.1	392.6
Other Assets		
Investment in affiliated companies — Notes A, B and E	1,463.2	1,016.0
Noncurrent receivables and inventories — Notes A and D	286.2	369.5
Intangible assets, net of accumulated amortization of $67.0 million in 1987 and $43.2 million in 1986 — Note A	863.7	1,039.2
Deferred costs and other — Note A	200.4	155.9
	2,813.5	2,580.6
	$4,928.9	$4,243.4
LIABILITIES AND STOCKHOLDERS' EQUITY		
Current Liabilities		
Current maturities of long-term debt	$ 64.9	$ 29.8
Trade accounts payable	122.9	95.4
Accrued expenses and other liabilities — Note J	741.0	643.1
Income taxes payable	32.2	9.9
Total Current Liabilities	961.0	778.2
Deferred Liabilities	526.4	302.3
Long-Term Debt, net of current maturities — Notes A and F	1,334.9	1,260.8
Stockholders' Equity — Note G		
Common Stock, recorded at $1.00 par value; 300,000,000 shares authorized; shares outstanding, 60,110,377 at October 31, 1987 (excluding 28,126,877 shares held in treasury) and 61,657,498 at October 31, 1986 (excluding 26,339,687 shares held in treasury)	60.1	61.7
Paid-in surplus	505.8	508.1
Retained earnings — Notes E, F and H	1,548.0	1,363.7
Cumulative translation adjustments	(7.3)	(31.4)
	2,106.6	1,902.1
	$4,928.9	$4,243.4

See notes to consolidated financial statements.

Gulf+Western Inc.

1 9 8 7 CONSOLIDATED STATEMENT OF CHANGES IN STOCKHOLDERS' EQUITY

Three Years Ended October 31, 1987	Common Stock	Paid-in Surplus	Retained Earnings	Cumulative Translation Adjustments	Total Stockholders' Equity
			(In millions)		
Balance at October 31, 1984, net of treasury	$ 70.1	$ 534.9	$ 1,329.8	$ (59.1)	$ 1,875.7
Common Stock issued					
Exercise of stock options and grants to employees	1.0	28.8			29.8
Dividend reinvestment and stock purchase plan	0.1	2.3			2.4
Conversion of debentures	0.1	3.2			3.3
Acquisition of stock for the treasury	(9.0)	(71.0)	(317.2)		(397.2)
Cash dividends					
Common Stock ($.90 per share)			(63.1)		(63.1)
Preferred stock			(0.8)		(0.8)
Translation adjustments				6.0	6.0
Realization upon sale of businesses				33.8	33.8
Net earnings for the year			247.8		247.8
Balance at October 31, 1985, net of treasury	62.3	498.2	1,196.5	(19.3)	1,737.7
Common Stock issued					
Exercise of stock options and grants to employees	0.4	16.6			17.0
Dividend reinvestment and stock purchase plan	0.1	2.2			2.3
Acquisition of stock for the treasury	(1.1)	(8.9)	(43.8)		(53.8)
Cash dividends					
Common Stock ($.90 per share)			(55.6)		(55.6)
Preferred stock			(0.8)		(0.8)
Translation adjustments				(12.1)	(12.1)
Net earnings for the year			267.4		267.4
Balance at October 31, 1986, net of treasury	61.7	508.1	1,363.7	(31.4)	1,902.1
Common Stock issued					
Exercise of stock options and grants to employees	**0.2**	**10.5**			**10.7**
Dividend reinvestment and stock purchase plan		2.3			2.3
Acquisition of stock for the treasury	**(1.8)**	**(15.1)**	**(102.4)**		**(119.3)**
Cash dividends					
Common Stock ($1.125 per share)			**(68.6)**		**(68.6)**
Preferred stock			**(0.8)**		**(0.8)**
Translation adjustments				**24.1**	**24.1**
Net earnings for the year			**356.1**		**356.1**
Balance at October 31, 1987, net of treasury	**$60.1**	**$505.8**	**$1,548.0**	**$ (7.3)**	**$2,106.6**

See notes to consolidated financial statements.

Gulf+Western Inc.

CONSOLIDATED STATEMENT OF CASH FLOWS

Year Ended October 31	1987	1986	1985
	(In millions)		
Cash Flows from Continuing Operating Activities			
Earnings from continuing operations before extraordinary items	$ 356.1	$ 228.7	$ 151.6
Non-cash expenses			
Depreciation	30.0	25.8	23.3
Deferred income taxes	32.6	83.9	30.2
Amortization of intangible assets	24.0	21.6	20.2
Amortization of plate costs	30.1	24.1	23.7
Gross cash flows provided from continuing operating activities	472.8	384.1	249.0
Undistributed net earnings of unconsolidated affiliates	(135.7)	(104.7)	(72.2)
Theatrical and television inventories			
Gross additions	(477.5)	(381.0)	(366.0)
Amortization	503.8	314.6	324.2
Network features and syndication licenses	10.1	35.0	18.9
Net (increase) decrease in receivables, inventories (other than theatrical and television), payables and other	143.8	(116.5)	(178.2)
Net cash flows provided from (used for) continuing operating activities	517.3	131.5	(24.3)
Cash Flows from Investment and Other Activities			
Expenditures for property, plant and equipment	(57.1)	(73.6)	(62.8)
Proceeds on disposal of property, plant and equipment	8.8	107.5	1.4
Purchase price of acquired businesses	(107.0)	(398.0)	(808.5)
Increase in investment in affiliated companies	(20.6)	(40.6)	(28.2)
Proceeds on sale of businesses	17.6	100.1	1,113.7
Discontinued operations			74.1
Decrease in noncurrent receivables	28.9	11.5	13.9
Net cash flows provided from (used for) investment and other activities	(129.4)	(293.1)	303.6
Cash Flows from Financing Activities			
Proceeds of long-term debt		272.6	850.1
Payments of long-term debt	(51.0)	(241.2)	(691.6)
Increase in commercial paper and other borrowings classified as long-term debt	142.3	11.1	106.2
Issuance of Common Stock	13.0	19.3	32.2
Acquisition of stock for the treasury	(119.3)	(53.8)	(397.2)
Dividends	(69.4)	(56.4)	(63.9)
Net cash flows used for financing activities	(84.4)	(48.4)	(164.2)
Increase (Decrease) in Cash and Cash Equivalents	303.5	(210.0)	115.1
Cash and Cash Equivalents at Beginning of Year	61.5	271.5	156.4
Cash and Cash Equivalents at End of Year	$ 365.0	$ 61.5	$ 271.5

See notes to consolidated financial statements.

31

Gulf+Western Inc.

1 9 8 7 Notes to Consolidated Financial Statements

NOTE A — SIGNIFICANT ACCOUNTING POLICIES

Principles of Consolidation

The consolidated financial statements include the accounts of Gulf+Western Inc. ("Company") and its significant majority-owned affiliates other than its consumer/commercial finance subsidiary. The Company's investments in its unconsolidated finance subsidiary and 20–50% owned investees are carried on the equity basis. The income taxes of the unconsolidated finance subsidiary and investees are included in the provision for income taxes.

Certain amounts in the consolidated financial statements for periods prior to fiscal 1987 have been reclassified to conform to current presentation for comparative purposes.

Inventories

Inventories are generally determined using the lower of cost (first-in, first-out or average cost method) or net realizable value.

Theatrical and Television Inventories, Revenues and Costs

Feature films are produced or acquired for distribution normally first in the theatrical market followed by, in usual order of priority, videocassettes, pay cable, network television and syndicated television. On average, the length of the revenue cycle for feature films approximates four years. Television series produced for the networks are licensed first to television networks and foreign markets; the more successful ones are later syndicated in domestic markets. Television series produced for syndication or other non-network (first-run) markets are generally licensed to domestic and foreign markets concurrently. The length of the revenue cycle for television series will vary depending on the number of seasons a series remains in active production.

Theatrical revenues from domestic and foreign markets are recognized as films are exhibited. Revenues arising from television license agreements are recognized in the year that the films or television series are available for telecast. Revenues from the sale of videocassettes are recognized upon delivery of the merchandise.

Inventories related to theatrical and television product (which include direct production costs, production overhead, capitalized interest and acquisition costs) are stated at the lower of cost less amortization or net realizable value. Inventories are amortized and profit participations and residuals are accrued on an individual product basis in the proportion that current revenues bear to the estimated remaining total lifetime revenues. Estimates of total lifetime revenues and expenses are periodically reviewed. The costs of feature and television films are classified as current assets to the extent such costs are expected to be recovered through the respective primary markets. Other costs relating to film production are classified as noncurrent.

The Company estimates that approximately 95% of unamortized film costs at October 31, 1987 will be amortized within the next three years.

Property, Plant and Equipment

Property, plant and equipment are carried at cost. Provision for depreciation on substantially all depreciable assets is computed using the straight-line method over the estimated useful lives of the assets.

Intangible Assets

Intangible assets primarily arose from the excess of cost of purchased businesses over the value of their net underlying assets (goodwill) and are being amortized by the straight-line method over appropriate periods not exceeding forty years.

Deferred Costs and Other

Deferred costs and other includes plate costs, which consist of certain prepublication costs being amortized by the straight-line method over appropriate periods not exceeding four years.

Unamortized Debt Discount

Debt discount is amortized over the term of the related debt using the interest method.

Income Taxes

Provision for income taxes includes deferred taxes which represent future tax effects of items reported for income tax purposes in periods different than for financial purposes. Investment tax credits are recognized as a reduction in the income tax provision using the flow-through method.

Pension Plans

Pension expense includes amortization of prior service cost over periods of thirty to forty years. The Company's funding policy varies; however, it generally follows the requirements of government regulations.

Earnings Per Share

Earnings per share amounts are based on the weighted average common and dilutive common equivalent (stock options) shares outstanding during the respective periods. Earnings per share are computed by dividing the average common and, where dilutive, common equivalent shares outstanding into the earnings applicable to such shares.

NOTE B — ACQUISITION AND DISPOSITION OF BUSINESSES

Acquisitions

In December 1984, the Company completed the purchase of Prentice-Hall, Inc., one of the nation's largest publishers of books, business information services and educational materials, for approximately $710 million. In June 1985, the Company completed the purchase of Ginn & Company, a leading elementary and secondary textbook publisher, for approximately $110 million. In May 1986, the Company completed the purchase of Silver Burdett Company, an elementary textbook publisher, for approximately $125 million. In October 1986 and December 1986, the Company purchased Mann

Theatres Corporation and Festival Enterprises, motion picture theatre circuits, for approximately $220 million and $50 million, respectively. The acquisitions have been accounted for as purchases and the financial statements include the results of their operations from the dates of acquisition.

The following table summarizes, on a pro forma basis, the combined results of operations as though Silver Burdett, Mann Theatres and Festival Enterprises had been acquired on November 1, 1985. It includes estimated interest expense, amortization of intangible assets and related income taxes. These pro forma results do not necessarily reflect the actual results of operations had the acquisitions taken place on that date, nor are they necessarily indicative of future results.

Year Ended October 31	1987	1986
	(In millions, except per share) (Unaudited)	
Revenues.	**$4,681.1**	$3,918.0
Earnings from continuing operations before		
extraordinary items	**356.3**	200.9
Net earnings	**356.3**	239.6
Earnings per share		
From continuing operations before		
extraordinary items	**5.76**	3.21
Net earnings	**5.76**	3.83

Dispositions

In September 1985, the Company completed the sale of its Consumer and Industrial Products Group to Wickes Companies, Inc. for approximately $1 billion cash and a five-year option to purchase two million shares of Wickes common stock at $30.00 per share. The Consumer and Industrial Products Group comprised the Company's Apparel and Hosiery, Manufacturing, Bedding and Home Furnishings, and Automotive Parts Distribution segments. The sale resulted in a gain, net of taxes payable, of approximately $120 million. However, the elimination of previously deferred foreign exchange losses and tax benefits applicable to such businesses reduced the gain for accounting purposes to approximately $15 million.

Net revenues and operating results to date of disposition and gain on disposal of discontinued operations for the year ended October 31, 1985 are as follows (in millions):

Net revenues	$2,001.9
Earnings from operations before income taxes	$ 140.3
Provision for income taxes	(59.1)
	81.2
Gain on sale before income taxes	105.0
Provision for income taxes	(90.0)
	15.0
Earnings from discontinued operations	$ 96.2

In February 1987, the Company entered into an agreement in principle with Warner Communications Inc. ("Warner") under which Warner will acquire a 50% interest in the Company's domestic motion picture theatre operations for approximately half of the Company's purchase price. The transaction is expected to close in January 1988 and, after closing, is subject to the approval of the United States District Court for the Southern District of New York pursuant to the 1951 Warner consent judgment. Accordingly, the results of these operations have been deconsolidated.

During fiscal 1987, 1986 and 1985, the Company also acquired or sold certain other businesses, the results of which are included in continuing operations. The contributions of these businesses in the aggregate were not significant to the Company's results of operations for the years presented, nor are they expected to have a material effect on the Company's results on a continuing basis.

NOTE C — EXTRAORDINARY ITEMS

During the fourth quarter of fiscal 1986, the Company sold real estate, which was not used in its business, for cash of $100 million. This sale resulted in a gain of $58.9 million, net of applicable taxes of $30.6 million. In addition, the Company redeemed 80.5% of its 12³/₈% Subordinated Notes due 1995 for $1,202.50 per $1,000 principal amount and terminated an interest rate obligation due 1990 through a cash payment of $20.5 million. These financing transactions resulted in a loss of $20.2 million, net of income tax benefits of $17.2 million.

NOTE D — INVENTORIES

Inventories as described in Note A are stated as follows (in millions):

October 31	1987	1986
Current		
Lower of cost or net realizable value		
Finished goods	**$142.0**	$143.1
Work in process	**24.8**	14.1
Materials and supplies	**28.2**	22.5
	195.0	179.7
Theatrical and television productions	**129.6**	97.9
	324.6	277.6
Noncurrent		
Theatrical and television productions	**146.9**	204.9
	$471.5	$482.5

NOTE E — INVESTMENT IN AFFILIATED COMPANIES

Investment in affiliated companies at October 31, 1987 includes $1,074.2 million ($943.9 million at October 31, 1986) applicable to the Company's ownership of all of the outstanding capital stock of Associates First Capital Corporation (First Capital). Also included in this caption are net receivables from First Capital of approximately $22.1 million at October 31, 1987 ($6.0 million net payables at October 31, 1986). The Company's investment in First Capital is $141.5 million greater than the underlying equity in the net assets of such company. This difference, which arose prior to November 1, 1970, is not being amortized because, in the opinion of management, it is considered to have a continuing value. The Company received dividends of $84.0 million, $80.5 million and $82.5 million from First Capital in fiscal 1987, 1986 and 1985, respectively. Separate financial statements of First Capital are presented elsewhere herein.

In addition, investment in affiliated companies at October 31, 1987 includes $281.6 million applicable to the Company's domestic motion picture theatre operations (see Note B).

Included in consolidated retained earnings at October 31, 1987 is $714.5 million of undistributed earnings principally attributable to First Capital.

NOTE F — LONG-TERM DEBT

Long-term debt includes:

October 31	1987	1986
	(In millions)	
Notes payable to institutional investors, interest 8.75% to 9.55%, averaging 9.49%, due 1988 to 1999	$ 103.8	$ 114.8
8½% senior notes due 1996	99.5	99.4
9¾% senior debentures due 2016	173.3	173.3
11⅝% senior notes due 1992	124.6	124.5
12⅛% Eurodollar notes due 1989	100.0	100.0
7% subordinated debentures due 2003, net of unamortized discount of $66.0 million at October 31, 1987 and $67.5 million at October 31, 1986 (effective average interest rate of 11%)	165.5	163.9
12⅜% subordinated notes due 1995	19.4	19.4
6% subordinated debentures due 1988	12.1	26.0
Revolving loan agreement borrowings, interest at variable short-term market rates	250.0	
Commercial paper supported by unused long-term revolving loan agreements	235.6	343.3
Other notes and debentures, interest 4% to 12%, averaging 9.58%, due 1988 to 2002	51.2	65.6
Obligations under capital leases	64.8	60.4
	1,399.8	1,290.6
Less current maturities	64.9	29.8
	$1,334.9	$1,260.8

Maturities of long-term debt (including the present value of obligations under capital leases as set forth in Note I) during the five years ending October 31, 1992 are (in millions):

1988	$ 64.9
1989	117.5
1990	263.9[1]
1991	97.4[1]
1992	156.2[1]

[1]Includes $245.6, $75.0 and $15.0 million in 1990, 1991 and 1992, respectively, of unused long-term revolving loan agreements supporting commercial paper and revolving loan agreement borrowings, which are expected to be extended.

At October 31, 1987, the Company had $564 million of unused long-term revolving loan agreements used to support outstanding commercial paper and long-term revolving loan agreement borrowings.

The Company has complied with restrictions and limitations required under terms of various loan agreements. Consolidated retained earnings unrestricted as to the payment of cash dividends was $845 million at October 31, 1987.

At October 31, 1987, approximately $377 million of net assets of subsidiaries, including $299 million of the retained earnings of the Company's unconsolidated finance subsidiary, were restricted as to the payment of dividends and loans to the Company, primarily as the result of these subsidiaries' debt agreements.

NOTE G — CAPITAL STOCK

The authorized capital stock of the Company includes 10,000,000 shares of Cumulative Preferred Stock (nonconvertible), of which 600,000 shares are designated as Series A 12% (all issued and held by a subsidiary of the Company), 400,000 shares are designated as Series B 8% and 9,000,000 shares are undesignated. In addition, 20,000,000 shares of Cumulative Convertible Preferred Stock are authorized, all of which are undesignated.

The Company has outstanding $5.75 Sinking Fund Preferred Stock, which has an annual dividend rate of $5.75 a share. At October 31, 1987 and 1986, 471,981 and 479,262 shares, respectively, of $5.75 Sinking Fund Preferred Stock were authorized. At October 31, 1987, 145,611 shares, excluding 89,668 shares held in treasury, were outstanding and at October 31, 1986, 145,611 shares, excluding 96,949 shares held in treasury, were outstanding. The carrying value of such $5.75 Sinking Fund Preferred Stock was $14.6 million at October 31, 1987 and 1986.

Common Stock outstanding at October 31, 1987 does not include 86,377 shares reserved under the 1964 Stock Option Incentive Plan; 116,500 shares reserved under the 1973 Key Employees Stock Purchase Plan; 4,483,456 shares reserved under the 1984 Stock Option Plan; and 1,907,855 shares reserved under the Long-Term Performance Plan.

The Company's 1964 Stock Option Incentive Plan provided for the issuance of options to key employees to purchase Common Stock of the Company at a price not less than fair market value on the date of grant. Options granted under this plan were exercisable on a cumulative basis over a four-year period beginning one year from the date of grant at the rate of 25% of the original grant each year. In August 1985, the Company made all outstanding options under this plan immediately exercisable.

The Company's 1973 Key Employees Stock Purchase Plan provided for the issuance of options to key employees to purchase shares of the Company's Common Stock at a price not less than fair market value on the date of grant. Options granted under this plan are exercisable for a period of ten years from the date of grant.

The Company's 1984 Stock Option Plan provides for the issuance of options to key employees to purchase Common Stock of the Company at a price not less than fair market value on the date of grant. Options may not be granted under this plan that expire more than ten years from the date of grant. The Company may establish installment exercise terms for a stock option so that the option becomes fully exercisable in a series of cumulative portions. The Company may also accelerate the period for the exercise of any stock option or portion thereof. In December 1985, the Company made substantially all outstanding options under this plan immediately exercisable.

Transactions involving outstanding stock options under these plans were:

	Number of Common Shares			Option Price	
	1964 Plan	1973 Plan	1984 Plan	Per Share	Aggregate
					(in millions)
Outstanding at October 31, 1984	769,681	223,375	771,398	$ 8.88–$27.88	$45.2
Granted			483,256	27.25– 41.38	19.2
Upon exercise					
Issued	(430,072)	(78,725)	(140,210)	8.88– 34.50	(15.0)
Rescinded		(15,650)	(27,151)	8.88– 30.75	(1.0)
Rescinded	(58,239)		(28,347)	15.50– 40.38	(2.2)
Outstanding at October 31, 1985	281,370	129,000	1,058,946	9.40– 41.38	46.2
Granted			846,741	46.31– 63.38	52.7
Upon exercise					
Issued	(139,593)	(12,500)	(152,344)	12.46– 40.38	(8.8)
Rescinded			(2,125)	30.75– 40.38	(0.1)
Rescinded	(10,045)		(45,449)	13.13– 40.38	(1.8)
Outstanding at October 31, 1986	131,732	116,500	1,705,769	9.40– 63.38	88.2
Granted			48,836	63.44– 78.00	3.3
Issued	(45,355)		(194,714)	27.13– 63.38	(10.1)
Rescinded			(10,350)	30.75– 63.38	(0.6)
Outstanding at October 31, 1987	86,377	116,500	1,549,541	9.40– 78.00	$80.8
Exercisable at					
October 31, 1986	131,732	116,500	1,605,269		
October 31, 1987	86,377	116,500	1,457,124		
Reserved for future grants at					
October 31, 1986			2,972,401		
October 31, 1987			2,933,915		

In November 1987, the Company granted options under the 1984 Plan to purchase an additional 900,926 shares of the Company's Common Stock at a total price of $61.0 million.

The Company follows the practice of recording amounts received upon the exercise of options by crediting Common Stock and paid-in surplus. No charges are reflected in the consolidated statement of earnings as a result of the grant or exercise of stock options. The Company records compensation expense related to stock appreciation rights of the 1973 Plan and 1984 Plan and share unit features of the 1973 Plan based on the change in the quoted market price of the Common Stock for the period. The exercise prices of options are subject to anti-dilution provisions.

During fiscal 1985, 1986 and November 1987, 335,000, 50,000 and 100,000 shares, respectively, of Common Stock of the Company were granted to certain key employees subject to restrictions which will lapse on certain dates through fiscal 1993. The average market price of these shares on the date on which they were granted ranged from $27.25 to $67.75. Compensation expense is being recorded over the period during which services are to be performed.

During the year ended October 31, 1986, 92,415 shares of Common Stock of the Company were granted to employees at an average market price of $58.70 under the terms of the Company's Long-Term Performance Plan. At October 31, 1987 and 1986, there were 1,907,855 shares of Common Stock reserved for future grants under this plan.

NOTE H — INCOME TAXES

Provision (benefit) for income taxes on continuing operations includes (in millions):

Year Ended October 31	1987	1986	1985
Current			
Federal	**$142.8**	$ 26.7	$16.6
Foreign	**58.8**	35.1	20.2
State and other	**18.4**	11.9	16.6
	220.0	73.7	53.4
Deferred			
Federal	**33.4**	84.0	31.3
Foreign	**(0.8)**	(3.1)	4.7
State and other		3.0	(5.8)
	32.6	83.9	30.2
	$252.6	$157.6	$83.6

Deferred taxes of continuing operations reflect the tax effect of recognition of various income and expense items in different periods for financial reporting than for income tax purposes including charges (credits) of (in millions):

Year Ended October 31	1987	1986	1985
Costs of motion picture and television production	**$31.1**	$28.5	$44.7
Income on motion picture and television production	**(5.1)**	(10.7)	4.1
Valuation of inventories	**(15.4)**	4.6	(3.3)
One-time life insurance reserves adjustment			(8.0)
Leasing transactions	**31.4**	40.8	10.0
Employee compensation and other payroll related expenses	**(2.5)**	(7.2)	(6.1)
Income on consumer finance receivables	**(2.5)**	16.6	0.4
Provisions for bad debts	**(22.6)**	6.7	(4.9)
Other	**18.2**	4.6	(6.7)
	$32.6	$83.9	$30.2

The following summarizes the components of earnings from continuing operations before income taxes (in millions):

Year Ended October 31	1987	1986	1985
Domestic	**$528.8**	$330.1	$190.9
Foreign	**79.9**	56.2	44.3
	$608.7	$386.3	$235.2

A reconciliation between the statutory Federal income tax rate and the effective rate of income tax expense to earnings from continuing operations before income taxes for the three years ended October 31, 1987 is as follows:

	% of Earnings Before Income Taxes		
	1987	1986	1985
Statutory rate	**42.0%**	46.0%	46.0%
Increase (decrease) in taxes arising from effect of			
Foreign earnings	**0.7**	(3.1)	(2.0)
Investment tax credits	**(7.5)**	(5.0)	(7.5)
U.S. state and local income taxes	**1.8**	2.1	2.6
Special deductions relating to life insurance companies		(1.4)	(1.7)
One-time life insurance reserves adjustment			(4.2)
Other	**4.5**	2.2	2.3
Effective tax rate	**41.5%**	40.8%	35.5%

The Company's share of the undistributed earnings of subsidiaries not included in its consolidated Federal income tax return, which could be subject to additional income taxes if remitted, was approximately $530 million at October 31, 1987. No provision has been made for taxes which could result from the remittance of such undistributed earnings since the Company intends to reinvest these earnings indefinitely.

NOTE I — COMMITMENTS AND CONTINGENCIES

Total rental expense of continuing operations was $52.0, $48.3 and $48.3 million, respectively, for the three years ended October 31, 1987, 1986 and 1985. Contingent rental expense (primarily based on revenues) included therein for 1987, 1986 and 1985 was $10.7, $9.5 and $10.7 million, respectively.

At October 31, 1987, the minimum lease payments under capital leases and noncancellable operating leases were as follows (in millions):

Year Ending October 31	Capital Leases	Operating Leases
1988	$ 14.2	$ 35.5
1989	14.4	31.2
1990	13.8	27.1
1991	13.1	24.2
1992	12.9	22.0
Thereafter	49.1	188.6
Total minimum lease payments	117.5	$328.6
Less amounts representing interest	52.7	
Present value of net minimum lease payments	$ 64.8	

Many of the leases also require the lessee to pay property taxes, insurance and ordinary repairs and maintenance.

Effective January 1, 1987, the Company established a new pension plan to cover substantially all permanent employees. The assets and liabilities of the Company's former pension plans, including those of its unconsolidated finance subsidiary and those pension plans covering retired employees of certain of its discontinued operations that had been retained by the Company, were merged into this plan.

Pension expense from continuing operations excluding the Company's unconsolidated finance subsidiary was $24.8, $10.6 and $6.9 million, respectively, for the three years ended October 31, 1987, 1986 and 1985. As of the most recent valuation dates, the actuarially computed value of accumulated benefits under the Company's merged pension plans and the market value of net fund assets were as follows (in millions):

October 31	1987	1986
Accumulated benefits		
Vested	$279.0	$37.9
Nonvested	17.9	4.3
	$296.9	$42.2
Net fund assets available for benefits	$386.6	$67.8

The interest rate used in determining the actuarially computed value of accumulated benefits was primarily 8.5%.

In addition to providing pension benefits, the Company provides certain health care and life insurance benefits for retired employees. Substantially all of the Company's employees may become eligible for those benefits when they reach normal retirement age while working for the Company. The cost of health care and life insurance benefits is recognized as insurance premiums are paid or as claims are paid for those uninsured benefits. Such costs were not material.

The Company is a defendant in various lawsuits wherein substantial amounts are claimed. In the opinion of counsel, these suits should not result in judgments which in the aggregate would have a material adverse effect on the Company's financial condition.

NOTE J — SUPPLEMENTAL INFORMATION

The details of certain balance sheet accounts are as follows (in millions):

October 31	1987	1986
Prepaid expenses, income taxes and other		
Income taxes	$221.9	$240.5
Other	183.2	150.3
	$405.1	$390.8
Accrued expenses and other liabilities		
Accrued compensation and other employee benefit related items	$ 77.7	$ 67.4
Participations payable and accrued syndication expenses	226.9	203.8
Deferred television contracts income	62.3	43.8
Royalties	45.5	43.8
Unexpired subscriptions and advanced subscription payments	47.9	43.9
Other	280.7	240.4
	$741.0	$643.1

The details of interest expense — net are as follows (in millions):

Year Ended October 31	1987	1986	1985
Interest expense			
Interest on indebtedness and other	$143.5	$147.7	$155.5
Interest paid to unconsolidated finance subsidiary	3.8	5.4	9.0
Imputed interest on long-term liabilities	6.7	8.0	8.0
Less capitalized interest	(5.4)	(5.4)	(6.2)
	148.6	155.7	166.3
Interest income			
Interest on investments	17.8	24.5	26.4
Imputed interest on long-term receivables	18.1	23.7	23.7
	35.9	48.2	50.1
	$112.7	$107.5	$116.2

Imputed interest relates principally to network and syndication licenses of motion picture and television products.

Capitalized interest relates to projects under construction and theatrical and television productions in process, of which $5.9, $6.1 and $8.3 million was amortized as a charge to earnings in 1987, 1986 and 1985, respectively.

NOTE K — FINANCIAL REPORTING BY BUSINESS SEGMENTS

A summary description of the Company's business segments and their respective Revenues and Operating Income for 1987, 1986 and 1985 is set forth on page 26.

Depreciation, capital expenditures and identifiable assets were as follows (in millions):

Year Ended or at October 31	Depreciation 1987	1986	1985	Capital Expenditures 1987	1986	1985	Identifiable Assets 1987	1986	1985
Business Segments									
Entertainment	$17.8	$15.9	$13.1	$37.2	$57.7[1]	$51.5[2]	$1,360.9	$1,298.7	$ 925.6
Publishing/Information	9.3	7.1	7.2	16.6	10.6	8.1	1,706.4	1,537.8	1,489.2
Total	27.1	23.0	20.3	53.8	68.3	59.6	3,067.3	2,836.5	2,414.8
Investment in Consumer/Commercial Finance							1,096.3	937.9	811.7
Corporate and Other Non-Segment Items	2.9	2.8	3.0	3.3	5.3	3.2	765.3	469.0	815.8
	$30.0	$25.8	$23.3	$57.1	$73.6	$62.8	$4,928.9	$4,243.4	$4,042.3[3]

[1]Includes the purchase of various previously leased theatres in Canada.
[2]Includes the purchase of lease and related rights as well as the land under Madison Square Garden Center.
[3]In addition there were $21.8 million of identifiable assets related to discontinued operations.

Identifiable assets are those which can be directly identified or associated with the segments. Amounts reflected for consumer/commercial finance represent the Company's net investment in those operations. Corporate and other non-segment items principally include cash and cash equivalents, prepaid and deferred income taxes and corporate property and equipment.

NOTE L — QUARTERLY RESULTS (UNAUDITED)

The following summarizes the quarterly operating results of the Company for the fiscal years ended October 31, 1987 and 1986 (in millions, except per share):

	Quarter Ended January 31 1987	1986	April 30 1987	1986	July 31 1987	1986	October 31 1987	1986
Revenues	$1,087.7	$862.0	$989.9	$863.9	$1,150.1	$1,044.4	$1,453.4	$1,010.8
Net revenues	656.6	460.8	558.8	438.4	695.4	618.7	992.8	575.9
Cost of goods sold	418.1	286.2	339.2	250.9	388.4	343.1	607.8	335.6
Operating income	146.4	81.6	118.5	102.6	206.5	170.5	251.0	141.5
Earnings from continuing operations before income taxes	119.5	57.0	90.9	74.0	176.8	140.8	221.5	114.5
Earnings from continuing operations before extraordinary items	69.3	34.2	52.7	45.7	102.6	82.1	131.5	66.7
Extraordinary items								38.7
Net earnings	69.3	34.2	52.7	45.7	102.6	82.1	131.5	105.4
Earnings per share								
From continuing operations before extraordinary items	1.11	.55	.86	.73	1.66	1.31	2.13	1.07
Net earnings	1.11	.55	.86	.73	1.66	1.31	2.13	1.69

D

The Adjusting and Closing Process for a Merchandising Business: Adjusting-Entry Method

This appendix illustrates the adjusting-entry method for completing the accounting cycle of a merchandising business. In this approach we record the end-of-period inventory entries as adjustments rather than as closing entries. Except for this difference in handling inventory entries, the adjusting-entry method and the closing-entry method are identical. No other adjusting or closing entries are affected by the approach taken, and the financial statements that result from both methods are the same.

The Adjusting and Closing Process

To illustrate a merchandiser's adjusting and closing process, let's use Austin Sound's December 31, 19X6, trial balance in Exhibit 5-6, page 182. All the new accounts—Inventory, Freight In, and the contra accounts—are highlighted for emphasis. Inventory is the only new account that is affected by the adjusting procedures. Note that additional-data item *g* gives the ending inventory of $52,000.

Work Sheet of a Merchandising Business

The Exhibit D-1 work sheet is similar to the work sheets we have seen so far, but a few differences appear. Note that this work sheet does not include adjusted trial balance columns. In most accounting systems, a single operation combines trial balance amounts with the adjustments and extends the adjusted balances directly to the income statement and balance sheet columns. Therefore, to reduce clutter, the adjusted trial balance columns are omitted. A second difference is that the merchandiser's work sheet includes inventory and purchase amounts (which are highlighted). Let's examine the entire work sheet.

Account Title Columns. The trial balance lists a number of accounts without balances. Ordinarily, these accounts are affected by the adjusting process. Examples include Interest Receivable, Interest Payable, and Depreciation Expense. The accounts are listed in the order they appear in the ledger. This eases the preparation of the work sheet. Note that Income Summary—used for the inventory adjustments—is listed between the owner withdrawals and sales revenue. If additional accounts are needed, they can be written in at the bottom of the work

EXHIBIT D-1 Work Sheet

Austin Sound
Work Sheet
For the Year Ended December 31, 19X6

Account Title	Trial Balance Debit	Trial Balance Credit	Adjustments Debit	Adjustments Credit	Income Statement Debit	Income Statement Credit	Balance Sheet Debit	Balance Sheet Credit
Cash	4,850						4,850	
Accounts receivable	17,000						17,000	
Note receivable, current	10,000						10,000	
Interest receivable			(a) 400				400	
Inventory	50,500		(g2) 52,000	(g1) 50,500			52,000	
Supplies	650			(b) 550			100	
Prepaid insurance	1,200			(c) 1,000			200	
Furniture and fixtures	6,800						6,800	
Accumulated depreciation		2,400		(d) 600				3,000
Accounts payable		7,000						7,000
Unearned sales revenue		2,000	(e) 1,300					700
Interest payable				(f) 200				200
Note payable, long-term		12,600						12,600
C. Ernest, capital		65,900						65,900
C. Ernest, withdrawals	34,100						34,100	
Income summary			(g1) 50,500	(g2) 52,000	50,500	52,000		
Sales revenue		138,000		(e) 1,300		139,300		
Sales discounts	1,400				1,400			
Sales returns and allowances	2,000				2,000			
Interest revenue		600		(a) 400		1,000		
Purchases	89,300				89,300			
Purchase discounts		3,000				3,000		
Purchase returns and allowances		1,200				1,200		
Freight in	5,200				5,200			
Rent expense	8,400				8,400			
Depreciation expense			(d) 600		600			
Insurance expense			(c) 1,000		1,000			
Supplies expense			(b) 550		550			
Interest expense	1,300		(f) 200		1,500			
	232,700	232,700	106,550	106,550	160,450	196,500	125,450	89,400
Net income					36,050			36,050
					196,500	196,500	125,450	125,450

sheet before net income is determined. Simply move net income down to make room for the additional accounts.

Trial Balance Columns. Examine the Inventory account, $50,500 in the trial balance. This $50,500 is the cost of the beginning inventory. The work sheet is designed to replace this outdated amount with the new ending balance, which in our example is $52,000 (additional-data item *g* in Exhibit 5-6). As we shall see, this task is accomplished through the adjusting process.

Adjustments Columns. The adjustments are similar to those discussed in Chapters 3 and 4. They may be entered in any order desired. The debit amount of each entry should equal the credit amount, and total debits should equal total credits.

The inventory adjustments are new. At the end of the period, accountants replace the beginning Inventory balance with the ending Inventory balance. Entry g1 removes the beginning balance ($50,500) by crediting the Inventory account. The debit portion of entry g1 transfers the beginning inventory amount to the Income Summary. This is done because beginning inventory becomes part of cost of goods sold during the year. Entry g2 places the ending balance ($52,000) in the Inventory account with a debit. The credit to Income Summary signifies that the ending inventory amount is subtracted in computing cost of goods sold. Therefore, the two inventory adjustments prepare Inventory for the balance sheet and aid in computing cost of goods sold for the income statement.

Income Statement Columns. The income statement columns contain adjusted amounts for the revenues and the expenses. Sales Revenue, for example, is $139,300, which includes the $1,300 adjustment.

The two inventory amounts appear in the income statement columns alongside Income Summary because beginning inventory and ending inventory enter the computation of cost of goods sold. Recall that beginning inventory is added to purchases and ending inventory is subtracted. Even though the resulting cost-of-goods-sold amount does not appear on the work sheet, all the components of cost of goods sold are evident there. Placement of beginning inventory ($50,500) in the work sheet's income statement debit column has the effect of adding beginning inventory in computing cost of goods sold. Placing ending inventory ($52,000) in the credit column has the opposite effect.

Purchases and Freight In appear in the debit column because they are added in computing cost of goods sold. Purchase Discounts and Purchase Returns and Allowances appear as credits because they are subtracted. Together, all these items are used to compute cost of goods sold—$88,000 on the income statement in Exhibit 5-5, on page 179.

The income statement column subtotals on the work sheet indicate whether the business earned net income or incurred a net loss. If total credits are greater, the result is net income, as shown in the exhibit. Inserting the net income amount in the debit column brings total debits into agreement with total credits. If total debits are greater, a net loss has occurred. Inserting a net loss amount in the credit column would equalize total debits and total credits. Net income or net loss is then extended to the opposite column of the balance sheet.

Balance Sheet Columns. The only new item on the balance sheet is inventory. The balance listed is the ending amount of $52,000, which is determined by a physical count of inventory on hand at the end of the period. On the work sheet this amount comes from the $52,000 amount in the Adjustments Debit column.

Recall that the financial statements for a company are the same whether the adjusting-entry method or the closing-entry method is used. Exhibit 5-8, on page 185, presents Austin Sound's financial statements, which are based on the information in the work sheet. The text on page 184 discusses these financial statements in detail.

Adjusting and Closing Entries for a Merchandising Business

Exhibit D-2 presents Austin Sound's adjusting entries, which are similar to those you have seen previously. Adjustment g1 transfers the beginning Inventory balance to Income Summary. Entry g2 sets up the ending Inventory balance.

The first closing entry debits the revenue and expense accounts that have credit balances. For Austin Sound these accounts are Sales Revenue, Interest Revenue,

OBJECTIVE 5

Adjust and close the accounts of a merchandising business

Purchase Discounts, and Purchase Returns and Allowances. The offsetting credit of $144,500 transfers their sum to Income Summary.

The second closing entry credits the revenue and expense accounts with debit balances. These are Sales Discounts, Sales Returns and Allowances, Purchases, Freight In, and the expense accounts.

EXHIBIT D-2A   *Journalizing and Posting the Adjusting and Closing Entries*

Journal
Adjusting Entries

a. Dec. 31	Interest Receivable		400	
	Interest Revenue			400
b. 31	Supplies Expense ($650 − $100)		550	
	Supplies			550
c. 31	Insurance Expense		1,000	
	Prepaid Insurance			1,000
d. 31	Depreciation Expense		600	
	Accumulated Depreciation			600
e. 31	Unearned Sales Revenue		1,300	
	Sales Revenue			1,300
f. 31	Interest Expense		200	
	Interest Payable			200
g1 31	Income Summary		50,500	
	Inventory			50,500
g2 31	Inventory		52,000	
	Income Summary			52,000

Closing Entries

Dec. 31	Sales Revenue		139,300	
	Interest Revenue		1,000	
	Purchase Discounts		3,000	
	Purchase Returns and Allowances		1,200	
	Income Summary			144,500
31	Income Summary		109,950	
	Sales Discounts			1,400
	Sales Returns and Allowances			2,000
	Purchases			89,300
	Freight In			5,200
	Rent Expense			8,400
	Depreciation Expense			600
	Insurance Expense			1,000
	Supplies Expense			550
	Interest Expense			1,500
31	Income Summary ($196,500 − $160,450)*		36,050	
	C. Ernest, Capital			36,050
31	C. Ernest, Capital		34,100	
	C. Ernest, Withdrawals			34,100

* The $196,500 amount is the sum of the $144,500 credit in the closing entry and the $52,000 credit in the g1 adjusting entry. The $160,450 amount is the sum of the $109,950 debit in the closing entry and the $50,500 debit in the g2 adjusting entry.

EXHIBIT D-2B *Ledger Accounts of Austin Sound*

Assets

Cash	
4,850	

Accounts Receivable	
17,000	

Note Receivable	
10,000	

Interest Receivable	
(A) 400	

Inventory	
50,500	(A) 50,500
(A) 52,000	

Supplies	
650	(A) 550
100	

Prepaid Insurance	
1,200	(A) 1,000
200	

Furniture and Fixtures	
6,800	

Accumulated Depreciation	
	2,400
	(A) 600
	3,000

Liabilities

Accounts Payable	
	7,000

Unearned Sales Revenue	
(A) 1,300	2,000
	700

Interest Payable	
	(A) 200

Note Payable	
	12,600

Owner's Equity

C. Ernest, Capital	
(C) 34,100	65,900
	(C) 36,050
	67,850

C. Ernest, Withdrawals	
34,100	(C) 34,100

Income Summary	
(A) 50,500	(A) 52,000
(C) 109,950	(C) 144,500
(C) 36,050	

Owner's Equity

Sales Revenue	
	138,000
	(A) 1,300
(C) 139,300	139,300

Sales Discounts	
1,400	(C) 1,400

Sales Returns and Allowances	
2,000	(C) 2,000

Interest Revenue	
	600
	(A) 400
(C) 1,000	1,000

Expenses

Purchases	
89,300	(C) 89,300

Purchase Discounts	
(C) 3,000	3,000

Purchase Returns and Allowances	
(C) 1,200	1,200

Freight In	
5,200	(C) 5,200

Rent Expense	
8,400	(C) 8,400

Depreciation Expense	
(A) 600	(C) 600

Insurance Expense	
(A) 1,000	(C) 1,000

Supplies Expense	
(A) 550	(C) 550

Interest Expense	
1,300	
(A) 200	
1,500	(C) 1,500

A = Adjusting entry; C = Closing entry

The last two closing entries close net income from Income Summary and also close owner Withdrawals into the Capital account.

The entries to the Inventory account deserve additional explanation. Recall that before the adjusting process Inventory still has the period's beginning balance. At the end of the period, this balance is one year old and must be replaced with the ending balance in order to prepare the financial statements at December 31, 19X6. The adjusting entries give Inventory its correct ending balance of $52,000, as shown here:

Inventory

Beginning balance (same as last period's ending balance)	50,500	Adjusting entry to eliminate beginning balance	50,500
Adjusting entry to set up ending balance	52,000		
Ending balance for the current balance sheet	52,000		

The inventory amounts for these adjusting entries are taken directly from the Adjustments columns of the work sheet. The offsetting debits and credits to Income Summary in these adjusting entries also serve to record the dollar amount of cost of goods sold in the accounts. Income Summary contains the cost of goods sold amount after Purchases and its related contra accounts and Freight In are closed.

Study Exhibits D-1, D-2, and 5-8 carefully because they illustrate the entire end-of-period process that leads to the financial statements. As you progress through this book, you may want to refer to these exhibits to refresh your understanding of the adjusting and closing process for a merchandising business.

Return to the heading Income Statement Format on page 188.

ALTERNATE SOLUTION TO REVIEW PROBLEM

Requirement 1
Sales, purchases, and related discount and return and allowance entries:

19X3			
a.	Accounts Receivable	346,700	
	Sales Revenue.......................		346,700
b.	Sales Returns and Allowances...............	8,200	
	Accounts Receivable		8,200
c.	Cash	329,000	
	Sales Discounts.........................	10,300	
	Accounts Receivable		339,300
d.	Purchases	175,900	
	Accounts Payable.....................		175,900
e.	Accounts Payable........................	7,430	
	Purchase Returns and Allowances		7,430

f.	Accounts Payable.........................	194,400	
	Purchase Discounts		6,000
	Cash		188,400
g.	Freight In	9,300	
	Cash		9,300

Requirement 2

Jan King Distributing Company
Work Sheet
For the Year Ended December 31, 19X3

Account Title	Trial Balance Debit	Trial Balance Credit	Adjustments Debit	Adjustments Credit	Income Statement Debit	Income Statement Credit	Balance Sheet Debit	Balance Sheet Credit
Cash	5,670						5,670	
Accounts receivable	37,100						37,100	
Inventory	190,500		(g2) 195,800	(g1) 190,500			195,800	
Supplies	3,930			(a) 2,580			1,350	
Prepaid rent	6,000			(b) 5,000			1,000	
Furniture and fixtures	26,500						26,500	
Accumulated depreciation		21,200		(d) 2,650				23,850
Accounts payable		46,340						46,340
Salary payable				(e) 1,300				1,300
Interest payable				(f) 600				600
Unearned sales revenue		3,500	(c) 1,100					2,400
Note payable, long-term		35,000						35,000
J. King, capital		153,680						153,680
Jan King, withdrawals	48,000						48,000	
Income summary			(g1) 190,500	(g2) 195,800	190,500	195,800		
Sales revenue		346,700		(c) 1,100		347,800		
Sales discounts	10,300				10,300			
Sales returns and allowances	8,200				8,200			
Purchases	175,900				175,900			
Purchase discounts		6,000				6,000		
Purchase returns and allowances		7,430				7,430		
Freight in	9,300				9,300			
Salary expense	82,750		(e) 1,300		84,050			
Rent expense	7,000		(b) 5,000		12,000			
Depreciation expense			(d) 2,650		2,650			
Utilities expense	5,800				5,800			
Supplies expense			(a) 2,580		2,580			
Interest expense	2,900		(f) 600		3,500			
	619,850	619,850	399,530	399,530	504,780	557,030	315,420	263,170
Net income					52,250			52,250
					557,030	557,030	315,420	315,420

Requirement 3
Adjusting entries:

19X3			
Dec. 31	Supplies Expense...........................	2,580	
	Supplies		2,580
31	Rent Expense	5,000	
	Prepaid Rent		5,000

	31	Unearned Sales Revenue........................	1,100	
		Sales Revenue		1,100
	31	Depreciation Expense	2,650	
		Accumulated Depreciation		2,650
	31	Salary Expense..............................	1,300	
		Salary Payable...........................		1,300
	31	Interest Expense.............................	600	
		Interest Payable..........................		600
	31	Income Summary	190,500	
		Inventory		190,500
	31	Inventory	195,800	
		Income Summary		195,800

Closing entries:

19X3				
Dec. 31		Sales Revenue	347,800	
		Purchase Discounts..........................	6,000	
		Purchase Returns............................	7,430	
		Income Summary		361,230
	31	Income Summary	314,280	
		Sales Discounts		10,300
		Sales Returns and Allowances		8,200
		Purchases...............................		175,900
		Freight In		9,300
		Salary Expense..........................		84,050
		Rent Expense		12,000
		Depreciation Expense		2,650
		Utilities Expense		5,800
		Supplies Expense.........................		2,580
		Interest Expense.........................		3,500
	31	Income Summary ($557,030 − $504,780)	52,250	
		Jan King, Capital		52,250
	31	Jan King, Capital	48,000	
		Jan King, Withdrawals....................		48,000

	Income Summary			
Adj.	190,500	Adj.	195,800
Clo.	314,280	Clo.	361,230
Clo.	52,250	Bal.	52,250

Turn back to page 194 for the solution to requirement 4, which shows the financial statements for Jan King Distributing Company.

E

Accounting for International Operations

After studying this appendix, you should be able to

1 Define foreign currency exchange rate

2 Discuss strong and weak currencies

3 Record purchases and payments denominated in a foreign currency

4 Record sales and collections denominated in a foreign currency

5 Discuss techniques for hedging foreign currency transaction losses

6 Explain the translation adjustment reported on a balance sheet

Did you know that EXXON and Bank of America earn most of their revenue outside the United States? It is common for American companies to do a large part of their business abroad. IBM, Ford, Coca-Cola, Boeing, and Kraft (Foods), among many others, are very active in other countries.

Accounting for business activities across national boundaries makes up the field of *international accounting.* As communications and transportation improve and trade barriers fall, global integration makes international accounting more important.

Economic Structures and Their Impact on International Accounting

The business environment varies widely across the globe. New York reflects the diversity of the market-driven economy of the United States. Japan's economy is similar to ours, although Japanese business activity focuses more on imports and exports. The central government controls the economy of East Germany and other communist countries, so there are almost no private investors and no creditors. With no need for accounting information for making investment and credit decisions, accounting disclosure is relatively unimportant. In Brazil, extremely high rates of inflation have made historical-cost amounts meaningless. Accountants must continually adjust the price levels because of the rapid change in the value of the cruzeiro, Brazil's monetary unit. International accounting deals with these and other differences in economic structures.

Foreign Currencies and Foreign Currency Exchange Rates

Each country uses its own national currency. Assume Boeing, a United States company, sells a 747 jet to Air France. Will Boeing receive United States dollars or French francs? If the transaction takes place in dollars, Air France must exchange its francs for dollars in order to pay Boeing in U.S. currency. If the transaction takes place in francs, Boeing will receive francs, which it must exchange for dollars. In either case, a step has been added to the transaction: one company must convert domestic currency into foreign currency, or the other company must convert foreign currency into domestic currency.

The price of one nation's currency may be stated in terms of another country's monetary unit. This measure of one currency against another currency is called the *foreign currency exchange rate.* In Exhibit 25-6, page 985, the dollar value of a French franc is $.17. This means that one French franc could be bought for seventeen cents. Other currencies, such as the pound and the yen (also listed in Exhibit 25-6), are similarly bought and sold.

We use the exchange rate to convert the cost of an item given in one currency to its cost in a second currency. We call this conversion a *translation.* Suppose that an item costs two hundred French francs. To compute its cost in dollars, we multiply the amount in francs by the conversion rate: 200 French francs × $.17 = $34.

To aid the flow of international business, a market exists for foreign currencies. Traders buy and sell U.S. dollars, French francs, and other currencies in the same way they buy and sell other commodities like beef, cotton, and automobiles. And just as supply and demand cause the prices of these other commodities to shift, so supply and demand for a particular currency cause exchange rates to fluctuate daily. When the demand for a nation's currency exceeds the supply of that currency, its exchange rate rises. When supply exceeds demand, the currency's exchange rate falls.

Two main factors determine the supply and demand for a particular currency: (1) the ratio of a country's imports to its exports, and (2) the rate of return available in the country's capital markets.

The import/export ratio. Japanese exports far surpass its imports. Customers of Japanese companies must buy yen (the Japanese unit of currency) in the international currency market to pay for their purchases. This strong demand drives up the price—the foreign exchange rate—of the yen. France, on the other hand, imports more goods than it exports. French businesses must sell francs in order to buy the foreign currencies needed to acquire the foreign goods. This increases the supply of the French franc and so decreases its price.

The rate of return. The rate of return available in a country's capital markets affects the amount of investment funds flowing into the country. When rates of return are high in a politically stable country such as the United States, international investors buy stocks, bonds, and real estate in that country. This increases the demand for the nation's currency and drives up its exchange rate.

Currencies are often described in the financial press as "strong" or "weak." What do these terms mean? The exchange rate of a *strong currency* is rising relative to other nations' currencies. The exchange rate of a *weak currency* is falling relative to other currencies.

Suppose on June 3 *The Wall Street Journal* listed the exchange for the British pound as $1.80. On June 4 that rate has changed to $1.78. We would say that the dollar has risen against the British pound—the dollar is stronger than the pound

—because the pound has become less expensive, and so the dollar now buys more pounds. A stronger dollar would make travel to England more attractive to Americans.

Assume that *The Wall Street Journal* reports a rise in the exchange rate of the Japanese yen from $.0079 to $.0080. This indicates that the yen is stronger than the dollar. Japanese automobiles, cameras, and electronic products are more expensive because each dollar buys fewer yen.

In our example situation—in which the pound has dropped relative to the dollar and the yen has risen relative to the dollar—we would describe the yen as the strongest currency, the pound as the weakest currency, and the dollar as somewhere between the other two currencies.

Accounting for International Transactions _____

When an American company transacts business with a foreign company, the transaction price can be stated either in dollars or in the national currency of the other company. If the price is stated in dollars, the American company has no special accounting difficulties. The transaction is recorded and reported in dollars exactly as though the other company were also American.

Purchases on Account

If the transaction price is stated in units of the foreign currency, the American company encounters two accounting steps. First, the transaction price must be translated into dollars for recording in the accounting records. Second, credit transactions (the most common international transaction) usually cause the American company to experience a *foreign currency transaction gain or loss.* This type of gain or loss occurs when the exchange rate changes between the date of the purchase on account and the date of the subsequent payment of cash.

The credit purchase creates an Account Payable that is recorded at the prevailing exchange rate. Later, when the buyer pays cash, the exchange rate has almost certainly changed. Accounts Payable is debited for the amount recorded earlier, and Cash is credited for the amount paid at the current exchange rate. A debit difference is a loss, and a credit difference is a gain.

Suppose on April 1, Macy's Department Store imports Shalimar perfume from a French supplier at a price of 200,000 francs. The exchange rate is $.17 per French franc. Macy's records this credit purchase as follows:

> **OBJECTIVE 3**
> Record purchases and payments denominated in a foreign currency

Apr. 1	Purchases......................................	34,000	
	Accounts Payable (200,000 × $.17)............		34,000

Macy's translates the French franc price of the merchandise (200,000 Fr) into dollars ($34,000) for recording the purchase and the related account payable.

If Macy's were to pay this account immediately—which is unlikely in international commerce—Macy's would debit Accounts Payable and credit Cash for $34,000. Suppose, however, that the credit terms specify payment within 60 days. On May 20, when Macy's pays this debt, the exchange rate has fallen to $.16 per French franc. Macy's payment entry is

May 20	Accounts Payable	34,000	
	Cash (200,000 × $.16).....................		32,000
	Foreign Currency Transaction Gain...........		2,000

Macy's has a gain because the company has settled the debt with fewer dollars than the amount of the original account payable. If on the payment date the exchange rate of the French franc had exceeded $.17, Macy's would have paid more dollars than the original $34,000. The company would have recorded a loss on the transaction as a debit to Foreign Currency Transaction Loss.

Sales on Account

International sales on account also may be measured in foreign currency. Suppose IBM sells a small computer to the West German government on October 9. The price of the computer is 140,000 West German marks, and the exchange rate is $.58 per West German mark. IBM's sale entry is

OBJECTIVE 4

Record sales and collections denominated in a foreign currency

| Oct. 9 | Accounts Receivable (140,000 × $.58) .... | 81,200 | |
| | Sales Revenue.............................. | | 81,200 |

Assume IBM collects from West Germany on November 30, when the exchange rate has fallen to $.57 per West German mark. IBM receives fewer dollars than the recorded amount of the receivable and so experiences a foreign currency transaction loss. The collection entry is

Nov. 30	Cash (140,000 × $.57)	79,800	
	Foreign Currency Transaction Loss	1,400	
	Accounts Receivable.......................		81,200

Foreign Currency Transaction Gains and Losses are combined for each accounting period. The net amount of gain or loss can be reported as Other Revenue and Expense on the income statement.

Hedging—A Strategy to Avoid Foreign Currency Transaction Losses

One approach to avoiding foreign currency transaction losses is to insist that international transactions be settled in dollars, which puts the burden of currency translation on the foreign party. However, that strategy may alienate customers and result in lost sales, or it may cause suppliers to demand unreasonable credit terms. Another way for a company to insulate itself from the effects of fluctuating foreign currency exchange rates is called hedging.

OBJECTIVE 5

Discuss techniques for hedging foreign currency transaction losses

Hedging means to protect oneself from losing by engaging in a counterbalancing transaction. An American company selling goods measured in Mexican pesos expects to receive a fixed number of pesos in the future. If the peso is weak, the American company would expect the pesos to be worth fewer dollars than the amount of the receivable—an expected loss situation.

The American company may have accumulated payables stated in Mexican pesos in the normal course of its business. Losses on the receipt of pesos would be approximately offset by gains on the payment of pesos to Mexican suppliers. Most companies do not have equal amounts of receivables and payables in the same foreign currency. However, buying futures contracts in the foreign currency effectively creates a payable to offset a receivable and vice versa. Many companies that do business internationally use hedging techniques.

Consolidation of Foreign Subsidiaries _____

An American company with a foreign subsidiary must consolidate the subsidiary's financial statements into its own statements for reporting to the public. The consolidation of a foreign subsidiary poses two special challenges. Many countries outside the United States specify accounting treatments that differ from American accounting principles. For the purpose of reporting to the American public, accountants for the parent company must first bring the subsidiary's statements into conformity with American GAAP.

The second accounting challenge arises when the subsidiary statements are expressed in a foreign currency. A preliminary step in the consolidation process is to translate the subsidiary statements into dollars. Then the dollar-value statements of the subsidiary can be combined with the parent statements in the usual manner, as illustrated in Chapter 17.

The process of translating a foreign subsidiary's financial statements into dollars may create a *translation adjustment.* This item appears in the financial statements of most multinational companies and is reported as part of stockholders' equity, as shown in this material from IBM's December 31, 1988, balance sheet:

	Dollars in millions	
Stockholders' Equity:		
Capital stock, par value $1.25 per share..................	$ 6,442	
Shares authorized: 750,000,000		
Issued: 1988–590,037,328; 1987–597,326,059		
Retained earnings.....................................	31,186	
Translation adjustments.............................	**1,917**	
	39,545	
Less: Treasury stock, at cost...........................	36	
Shares: 1988–296,820; 1987–274,315		39,509

A translation adjustment arises because of changes in the foreign exchange rate over time. *Assets* and *liabilities* in the foreign subsidiaries' financial statements are translated into dollars at the exchange rate in effect on the date of the statements, which in the IBM example is December 31, 1988. However, *stockholders' equity* is translated into dollars at older, different exchange rates. This difference in exchange rates creates an out-of-balance condition on the balance sheet. The translation adjustment amount brings the balance sheet back into balance. The translation adjustment can be positive, as it is for IBM, or negative.

OBJECTIVE 6

Explain the translation adjustment recorded on the balance sheet

International Accounting Standards ⎯⎯⎯⎯⎯⎯⎯⎯⎯⎯⎯⎯

For the most part, accounting principles are similar from country to country. However, some important differences exist. For example, some countries, such as Italy, require financial statements to conform closely to income tax laws. In other countries, such as Brazil and Argentina, high inflation rates dictate that companies make price-level adjustments to report amounts in units of common purchasing power. Neither practice is followed as closely in the United States.

Several organizations are working to achieve worldwide harmony of accounting standards. Chief among these is the International Accounting Standards Committee (IASC). Headquartered in London, the IASC operates much as the Financial Accounting Standards Board in the United States. It has the support of the accounting professions in the United States, most of the British Commonwealth countries, Japan, France, West Germany, the Netherlands, and Mexico. However, the IASC has no authority to require compliance with its accounting standards. It must rely on cooperation by the various national accounting professions. Since its creation in 1973, the IASC has succeeded in narrowing some differences in international accounting standards.

Summary ⎯⎯⎯⎯⎯⎯⎯⎯⎯⎯⎯⎯⎯⎯⎯⎯⎯⎯⎯⎯⎯⎯⎯

International accounting deals with accounting for business activities across national boundaries. A key issue is the translation of foreign currency amounts into dollars, accomplished through a *foreign currency exchange rate.* Changes in exchange rates cause companies to experience *foreign currency transaction gains and losses* on credit transactions.

Consolidation of a foreign subsidiary's financial statements into the parent-company statements requires adjusting the subsidiary statements to American accounting principles and then translating the foreign-company statements into dollars. The translation process creates a *translation adjustment* that is reported in stockholders' equity. The International Accounting Standards Committee is working to harmonize accounting principles worldwide.

Self-Study Questions

Test your understanding of this appendix by marking the best answer for each of the following questions.

1. On May 16, the exchange rate of a West German mark was $.58. On May 20, the exchange rate is $.57. Which of the following statements is true? *(p. 1174)*
   a. The dollar has risen against the mark
   b. The dollar has fallen against the mark
   c. The dollar is weaker than the mark
   d. The dollar and the mark are equally strong
2. A strong dollar encourages *(p. 1175)*
   a. Travel to the United States by foreigners
   b. Purchase of American goods by foreigners
   c. Americans to travel abroad
   d. Americans to save dollars
3. Ford Motor Company purchased auto accessories from an English supplier at a price of 500,000 British pounds. On the date of the credit purchase the exchange rate of the

British pound was $1.80. On the payment date the exchange rate of the pound is $1.82. If payment is in dollars, Ford experiences *(p. 1175)*
 a. A foreign currency transaction gain of $10,000
 b. A foreign currency transaction loss of $10,000
 c. Neither a transaction gain nor a loss because the debt is paid in dollars
 d. A translation adjustment to stockholders' equity

4. If the payment in the preceding question is made in British pounds, Ford will experience *(p. 1175)*
 a. A foreign currency transaction gain of $10,000
 b. A foreign currency transaction loss of $10,000
 c. Neither a transaction gain nor a loss because the debt is paid in pounds
 d. A $10,000 translation adjustment to stockholders' equity

5. The translation adjustment in stockholders' equity *(p. 1177)*
 a. Arises from foreign currency transaction gains and losses
 b. Represents a cash excess or deficiency
 c. Represents a gain or loss that is reported on the income statement
 d. Is a figure needed to bring the balance sheet into balance.

Accounting Vocabulary

foreign currency exchange rate *(p. 1174)*, foreign currency transaction gain or loss *(p. 1175)*, hedging *(p. 1176)*, international accounting *(p. 1173)*, strong currency *(p. 1174)*, translation adjustment *(p. 1177)*, weak currency *(p. 1174)*

ASSIGNMENT MATERIAL _____

Questions

1. Explain the difference between a foreign currency transaction gain or loss and a translation adjustment. Indicate the specific location in the financial statements where each item is reported.
2. Which situation results in a foreign currency transaction gain? Which situation results in a loss?
 a. Credit purchase denominated in pesos, followed by weakness in the peso
 b. Credit purchase denominated in pesos, followed by weakness in the dollar
 c. Credit sale denominated in pesos, followed by weakness in the peso
 d. Credit sale denominated in pesos, followed by weakness in the dollar

Exercises and Problems

Exercise E-1   *Journalizing foreign currency transactions*

Journalize the following foreign currency transactions:

1. Purchased goods on account from a Japanese company. The price was 200,000 yen, and the exchange rate of the yen was $.0080.
2. Paid the Japanese supplier when the exchange rate was $.0081.
3. Sold merchandise on account to a French company at a price of 60,000 French francs. The exchange rate was $.16.
4. Collected from the French company. The exchange rate was $.17.

Problem E-1A *Journalizing foreign currency transactions and reporting the transaction gain or loss.*

Suppose Xerox Corporation completed the following transactions.

July 1 Sold a photocopy machine on account to Pirelli Tire Company for $70,000. The exchange rate of the Italian lire is $.0007, and Pirelli agrees to pay in dollars.

10 Purchased supplies on account from a Canadian company at a price of Canadian $50,000. The exchange rate of the Canadian dollar is $.80, and payment will be in Canadian dollars.

Aug. 7 Sold a photocopy machine on account to an English firm for 100,000 British pounds. Payment will be in pounds, and the exchange rate of the pound is $1.80.

12 Collected from Pirelli.

18 Paid the Canadian company. The exchange rate of the Canadian dollar is $.77.

Sep. 14 Collected from the English firm. The exchange rate of the British pound is $1.79.

Record these transactions in Xerox's general journal, and show how to report the transaction gain or loss on the income statement.

Problem E-1B *Journalizing foreign currency transactions and reporting the transaction gain or loss*

Suppose Coca-Cola Company completed the following transactions.

Feb. 4 Sold soft-drink syrup on account to a Mexican company for $36,000. The exchange rate of the Mexican peso is $.0004, and the customer agrees to pay in dollars.

13 Purchased inventory on account from a Canadian company at a price of Canadian $100,000. The exchange rate of the Canadian dollar is $.80, and payment will be in Canadian dollars.

Mar. 10 Sold goods on account to an English firm for 70,000 British pounds. Payment will be in pounds, and the exchange rate of the pound is $1.80.

15 Collected from the Mexican company.

21 Paid the Canadian company. The exchange rate of the Canadian dollar is $.78.

Apr. 17 Collected from the English firm. The exchange rate of the British pound is $1.77.

Record these transactions in Coca-Cola's general journal, and show how to report the transaction gain or loss on the income statement.

Answers to Self-Study Questions

1. a
2. c
3. c
4. b [500,000 × ($1.82 − $1.80)]
5. d

Glossary

Accelerated depreciation. A type of depreciation method that writes off a relatively larger amount of the asset's cost nearer the start of its useful life than does the straight-line method *(p. 389)*.

Account. The detailed record of the changes that have occurred in a particular asset, liability, or owner equity during a period *(p. 39)*.

Account format of the balance sheet. Format that lists the assets at the left, with liabilities and owner equity at the right *(p. 143)*.

Account payable. A liability that is not written out. Instead, it is backed by the reputation and credit standing of the debtor *(p. 11)*.

Account receivable. An asset, a promise to receive cash from customers to whom the business has sold goods *(p. 11)*.

Accounting. The system that measures business activities, processes that information into reports and financial statements, and communicates the findings to decision makers *(p. 2)*.

Accounting controls. Methods and procedures that safeguard assets, authorize transactions, and ensure the accuracy of the financial records *(p. 265)*.

Accounting cycle. Process by which accountants produce an entity's financial statements for a specific period *(p. 125)*.

Accounting information system. The combination of personnel, records, and procedures that a business uses to meet its need for financial data *(p. 215)*.

Accounting rate of return. The remainder of average annual net cash inflow from operations minus annual depreciation, divided by average amount invested in the business. This is the most widely used measure of profitability. The higher the accounting rate of return, the better the investment *(p. 1020)*.

Accounts receivable turnover. Ratio of net credit sales to average net accounts receivable. Measures ability to collect cash from credit customers *(p. 753)*.

Accrual-basis accounting. Accounting that recognizes (records) the impact of a business event as it occurs, regardless of whether the transaction affected cash *(p. 86)*.

Accrued expense. An expense that has been incurred but not yet paid in cash *(p. 94)*.

Accrued revenue. A revenue that has been earned but not yet received in cash *(p. 95)*.

Accumulated depreciation. The cumulative sum of all depreciation expense from the date of acquiring a plant asset *(p. 93)*.

Acid-test ratio. Ratio of the sum of cash plus short-term investments plus net current receivables to current liabil-

ities. Tells whether the entity could pay all its current liabilities if they came due immediately. Also called the quick ratio *(p. 751)*.

Additional paid-in capital. Another name for Paid-in capital in excess of par *(p. 543)*.

Adjusted gross income. Total income minus specified adjustments (deductions) equals adjusted gross income, an amount that exists only in the tax law *(p. 1043)*.

Adjusted trial balance. A list of all the ledger accounts with their adjusted balances *(p. 99)*.

Adjusting entry. Entry made at the end of the period to assign revenues to the period in which they are earned and expenses to the period in which they are incurred. Adjusting entries help measure the period's income and bring the related asset and liability accounts to correct balances for the financial statements *(p. 89)*.

Administrative controls. Plan of organization, methods, and procedures that help managers achieve operational efficiency and adherence to company policies *(p. 265)*.

Aging of accounts receivable. A way to estimate bad debts by analyzing individual accounts receivable according to the length of time they have been due *(p. 316)*.

Allocation base. Logical common denominator for assigning a given cost to two or more departments of a business *(p. 976)*.

Allowance for doubtful accounts. A contra account, related to accounts receivable, that holds the estimated amount of collection losses. Also called Allowance for uncollectible accounts *(p. 313)*.

Allowance for uncollectible accounts. Another name for Allowance for doubtful accounts *(p. 313)*.

Allowance method. A method of recording collection losses based on estimates prior to determining that the business will not collect from specific customers *(p. 312)*.

Amortization. Expense that applies to intangible assets in the same way depreciation applies to plant assets and depletion applies to natural resources *(p. 401)*.

Annuity. Stream of equal periodic amounts *(p. 1022)*.

Appropriation of retained earnings. Restriction of retained earnings that is recorded by a formal journal entry *(p. 584)*.

Articles of partnership. Agreement that is the contract between partners specifying such items as the name, location, and nature of the business, the name, capital investment, and duties of each partner, and the method of sharing profits and losses by the partners. Also called the partnership agreement *(p. 496)*.

Asset. An economic resource a business owns that is expected to be of benefit in the future *(p. 10)*.

Auditing. The examination of financial statements by outside accountants, the most significant service that CPAs perform. The conclusion of an audit is the accountant's professional opinion about the financial statements *(p. 7)*.

Authorization of stock. Provision in a corporate charter that gives the state's permission for the corporation to issue — that is, to sell — a certain number of shares of stock *(p. 542)*.

Average cost method. Inventory costing method based on the average cost of inventory during the period. Average cost is determined by dividing the cost of goods available for sale by the number of units available *(p. 348)*.

Bad debt expense. Another name for Uncollectible accounts expense *(p. 311)*.

Balance sheet. List of an entity's assets, liabilities, and owner equity as of a specific date. Also called the statement of financial position *(p. 18)*.

Balancing the ledgers. Establishing the equality of (a) total debits and total credits in the general ledger, (b) the balance of the accounts receivable control account in the general ledger and the sum of individual customer accounts in the accounts receivable subsidiary ledger, or (c) the balance of the accounts payable control account in the general ledger and the sum of individual creditor accounts in the accounts payable subsidiary ledger *(p. 238)*.

Bank collection. Collection of money by the bank on behalf of a depositor *(p. 273)*.

Bank reconciliation. Process of explaining the reasons for the difference between a depositor's records and the bank's records about the depositor's bank account *(p. 273)*.

Bank statement. Document for a particular bank account showing its beginning and ending balances and listing the month's transactions that affected the account *(p. 271)*.

Batch processing. Computerized accounting for similar transactions in a group or batch *(p. 220)*.

Beginning inventory. Goods left over from the preceding period *(p. 345)*.

Board of directors. Group elected by the stockholders to set policy for a corporation and to appoint its officers *(p. 537)*.

Bond discount. Excess of a bond's maturity (par) value over its issue price *(p. 611)*.

Bond indenture. Contract under which bonds are issued *(p. 624)*.

Bond premium. Excess of a bond's issue price over its maturity (par) value *(p. 611)*.

Bond sinking fund. Group of assets segregated for the purpose of retiring bonds payable at maturity *(p. 624)*.

Bonds payable. Groups of notes payable (bonds) issued to multiple lenders called bondholders *(p. 609)*.

Bonus. Amount over and above regular compensation *(p. 431)*.

Book value of a plant asset. The asset's cost less accumulated depreciation *(p. 93)*.

Book value of stock. Amount of owners' equity on the company's books for each share of its stock *(p. 554)*.

Book value per share of common stock. Common stockholders' equity divided by the number of shares of common stock outstanding *(p. 760)*.

Branch accounting. System for separating the accounts of a branch of a business from the accounts of the home office *(p. 981)*.

Branch-factor ledger control. Account in the home office ledger that represents the home office investment in, or receivable from, a branch of the business *(p. 982)*.

Branch ledger. The part of a general ledger kept by a branch of the business, separate from the home office ledger *(p. 981)*.

Break-even analysis. Another name for Cost-volume-profit analysis *(p. 825)*.

Break-even point. Amount of unit sales or dollar sales at which revenue equals expenses *(p. 825)*.

Budget. Management's tool for forecasting a business's future in amounts, including the quantities of products to be sold and their expected selling prices, the numbers of employees and their pay, and a host of other amounts that are ultimately expressed in dollars *(p. 787)*.

Budget committee. Group that prepares the master budget; includes representatives from all departments of the business *(p. 787)*.

Budget formula. The heart of a flexible budget, shows how to compute the budget amounts *(p. 938)*.

Budgeted factory overhead rate. Budgeted total overhead cost divided by the budgeted rate base *(p. 871)*.

Budgeting. Setting of goals for a business, such as its sales and profits, for a future period *(p. 7)*.

Bylaws. Constitution for governing a corporation *(p. 537)*.

Byproduct. Output of a joint production process with minor sales value in comparison to the main product *(p. 917)*.

Callable bonds. Bonds that the issuer may call or pay off at a specified price whenever the issuer wants *(p. 625)*.

Capital. Another name for the owner equity of a business *(p. 11)*.

Capital budgeting. Formal means of making long-range decisions for investments such as plant locations, equipment purchases, additions of product lines, and territorial expansions *(p. 1017)*.

Capital deficiency. Debit balance in a partner's capital account *(p. 516)*.

Capital expenditure. Expenditure that increases the capacity or efficiency of an asset or extends its useful life. Capital expenditures are debited to an asset account *(p. 404)*.

Capital expenditures budget. Plan for purchases of property, plant, and equipment and other assets that management uses to produce revenues over a long time *(p. 790)*.

Capital gain. Special category of gain (or loss) defined in the tax law that results from the disposal of property such as investments in stocks, bonds, and real estate, and personal assets *(p. 1045)*.

Capital lease. Lease agreement that meets any one of four criteria: (1) The lease transfers title of the leased asset to the lessee. (2) The lease contains a bargain purchase option. (3) The lease term is 75 percent or more of the estimated useful life of the leased asset. (4) The present value of the lease payments is 90 percent or more of the market value of the leased asset *(p. 629)*.

Capital loss. Special category of loss (or gain) defined in the tax law that results from the disposal of property such as investments in stocks, bonds, and real estate, and personal assets *(p. 1045)*.

Cash-basis accounting. Accounting that records only transactions in which cash is received or paid *(p. 86).*

Cash budget. Details the way a business intends to go from the beginning cash balance to the desired ending balance. Also called the Statement of budgeted cash receipts and disbursements *(p. 796).*

Cash disbursements journal. Special journal used to record cash disbursements by check *(p. 232).*

Cash equivalent. Highly liquid short-term investments that can be converted into cash with little delay *(p. 698).*

Cash flows. Cash receipts and cash payments (disbursements) *(p. 695).*

Cash receipts journal. Special journal used to record cash receipts *(p. 225).*

Central processing unit (CPU). The brain of a computer. It performs mathematical and logical operations and controls the other components of the computer system *(p. 1078).*

Certified Public Accountant (CPA). A professional accountant who earns this title through a combination of education, experience, and an acceptable score on a written national examination *(p. 4).*

Chairperson of the board. Elected person on a corporation's board of directors, usually the most powerful person in the corporation *(p. 537).*

Change in accounting estimate. A change that occurs in the normal course of business as a company alters earlier expectations. Decreasing uncollectible account expense from 2 percent to 1½ percent of sales and changing the estimated useful life of a plant asset are examples *(p. 472).*

Change in accounting principle. A change in accounting method, such as from the LIFO method to the FIFO method for inventories and a switch from the sum-of-years-digits depreciation method to the straight-line method *(p. 472).*

Chart of accounts. List of all the accounts and their account numbers in the ledger *(p. 56).*

Charter. Document that gives the state's permission to form a corporation *(pp. 535, 537).*

Check. Document that instructs the bank to pay the designated person or business the specified amount of money *(p. 271).*

Check register. Special journal used to record all checks issued in a voucher system *(p. 287).*

Closing entries. Entries that transfer the revenue, expense, and owner withdrawal balances from these respective accounts to the capital account *(p. 138).*

Closing the accounts. Step in the accounting cycle at the end of the period that prepares the accounts for recording the transactions of the next period. Closing the accounts consists of journalizing and posting the closing entries to set the balances of the revenue, expense, and owner withdrawal accounts to zero *(p. 136).*

Collection method. Method of applying the revenue principle by which the seller waits until cash is received to record the sale. This method is used only if the receipt of cash is uncertain *(p. 468).*

Commission. Employee compensation computed as a percentage of the sales that the employee has made *(p. 431).*

Common-size statement. A financial statement that reports only percentages (no dollar amounts); a type of vertical analysis *(p. 745).*

Common stock. The most basic form of capital stock. In describing a corporation, the common stockholders are the owners of the business *(p. 541).*

Comparability principle. Specifies that accounting information must be comparable from business to business and that a single business's financial statements must be comparable from one period to the next *(p. 466).*

Completed-contract method. Method of applying the revenue principle by a construction company by which all revenue earned on the project is recorded in the period when the project is completed *(p. 470).*

Conservatism. Concept that underlies presenting the gloomiest possible figures in the financial statements *(p. 356).*

Consignment. Transfer of goods by the owner (consignor) to another business (consignee) who, for a fee, sells the inventory on the owner's behalf. The consignee does not take title to the consigned goods *(p. 347).*

Consistency principle. A business must use the same accounting methods and procedures from period to period *(p. 353).*

Consolidation method for investments. A way to combine the financial statements of two or more companies that are controlled by the same owners *(p. 661).*

Constraint. Item that restricts production or sales. Also called the Limiting factor *(p. 1012).*

Contingent liability. A potential liability *(p. 325).*

Continuous budget. Systematically adds a month or a quarter as the month or quarter just ended is deleted. Also called a Rolling budget *(p. 801).*

Contra account. An account with two distinguishing characteristics: (1) it always has a companion account, and (2) its normal balance is opposite that of the companion account *(p. 93).*

Contra asset. An asset account with a credit balance. A contra account always has a companion account and its balance is opposite that of the companion account *(p. 93).*

Contract interest rate. Interest rate that determines the amount of cash interest the borrower pays and the investor receives each year. Also called the Stated interest rate *(p. 612).*

Contributed capital. Another name for Paid-in capital *(p. 539).*

Contribution margin. Excess of sale price over variable expenses *(p. 826).*

Contribution margin income statement. Separates expenses into variable costs and fixed costs and highlights the contribution margin, which is the excess of sales over variable expenses *(p. 838).*

Contribution margin percentage. Sales of 100 percent minus the variable expense percentage *(p. 827)*

Control account. An account whose balance equals the sum of the balances in a group of related accounts in a subsidiary ledger *(p. 224).*

Controllable overhead variance. Another name for the Flexible budget overhead variance *(p. 950).*

Controlling (majority) interest. Ownership of more than 50 percent of an investee company's voting stock *(p. 661).*

Conversion cost. Short-hand term that includes direct labor and overhead *(p. 859).*

Convertible bonds. Bonds that may be converted into the common stock of the issuing company at the option of the investor *(p. 626).*

Convertible preferred stock. Preferred stock that may be exchanged by the preferred stockholders, if they choose, for another class of stock in the corporation *(p. 552).*

Copyright. Exclusive right to reproduce and sell a book, musical composition, film, or other work of art. Issued by the federal government, copyrights extend 50 years beyond the author's life (*p. 402*).

Corporation. A business owned by stockholders that begins when the state approves its articles of incorporation. A corporation is a legal entity, an "artificial person," in the eyes of the law (*p. 9*).

Cost accounting. The branch of accounting that determines and controls a business's costs (*p. 7*).

Cost allocation. Assignment of various costs to the departments of a business. (*p. 976*).

Cost behavior. Description of how costs change in response to a shift in the volume of business activity (*p. 821*).

Cost method for investments. The method used to account for short-term investments in stock and for long-term investments when the investor holds less than 20 percent of the investee's voting stock. Under the cost method, investments are recorded at cost and reported at the lower of their cost or market value (*p. 658*).

Cost of a plant asset. Purchase price, sales tax, purchase commission, and all other amounts paid to acquire the asset and to ready it for its intended use (*p. 384*).

Cost of goods manufactured. Manufacturers' counterpart to the Purchases account. Cost of goods manufactured takes the place of purchases in the computation of cost of goods sold (*p. 857*).

Cost of goods sold. The cost of the inventory that the business has sold to customers, the largest single expense of most merchandising businesses. Also called Cost of sales (*p. 177*).

Cost of sales. Another name for Cost of goods sold (*p. 177*).

Cost principle. States that assets and services are recorded at their purchase cost and that the accounting record of the asset continues to be based on cost rather than current market value (*p. 467*).

Cost-volume-profit analysis. Expresses the relationships among a business's costs, volume, and profit or loss. An important part of a budgeting system that helps managers predict the outcome of their decisions (*p. 821*).

Coupon bonds. Bonds for which the owners receive interest by detaching a perforated coupon (which states the interest due and the date of payment), from the bond and depositing it in a bank for collection (*p. 610*).

CPU. Abbreviation of Central processing unit (*p. 1078*).

Credit. The right side of an account (*p. 43*).

Credit memorandum. Document issued by a seller to indicate having credited a customer's account receivable account (*p. 234*).

Creditor. The party to a credit transaction who sells a service or merchandise and obtains a receivable (*p. 309*).

Cumulative preferred stock. Preferred stock whose owners must receive all dividends in arrears before the corporation pays dividends to the common stockholders (*p. 551*).

Current asset. An asset that is expected to be converted to cash, sold, or consumed during the next twelve months, or within the business's normal operating cycle if longer than a year (*p. 142*).

Current cost. Present cost of replacing an asset's particular service potential or usefulness (*p. 669*).

Current cost accounting. Accounting model that uses the current cost of a company's assets and expenses in place of their historical cost (*p. 670*).

Current liability. A debt due to be paid within one year or one of the entity's operating cycles if the cycle is longer than a year (*p. 143*).

Current portion of long-term debt. Amount of the principal that is payable within one year (*p. 426*).

Current ratio. Current assets divided by current liabilities (*p. 751*).

CVP analysis. Abbreviation of Cost-volume-profit analysis (*p. 821*).

Date of record. Date on which the owners of stock to receive a dividend are identified (*p. 573*).

Days' sales in receivables. Ratio of average net accounts receivable to one day's sales. Tells how many days' sales remain in Accounts Receivable awaiting collection (*p. 754*).

Debentures. Unsecured bonds, backed only by the good faith of the borrower (*p. 611*).

Debit. The left side of an account (*p. 42*).

Debit memorandum. Business document issued by a buyer to state that the buyer no longer owes the seller for the amount of returned purchases (*p. 236*).

Debt ratio. Ratio of total liabilities to total assets. Tells the proportion of a company's assets that it has financed with debt (*p. 755*).

Debtor. The party to a credit transaction who makes a purchase and creates a payable (*p. 309*).

Decision model. A method or technique for evaluating and choosing among alternative courses of action (*p. 1017*).

Declaration date. Date on which the board of directors announce the intention to pay a dividend. The declaration creates a liability for the corporation (*p. 573*).

Default on a note. Failure of the maker of a note to pay at maturity. Also called Dishonor of a note (*p. 326*).

Deferred revenue. Another name for Unearned revenue (*p. 427*).

Deficit. Debit balance in the retained earnings account (*p. 540*).

Dependent. Person who receives more than half of his or her support from another taxpayer (*p. 1041*).

Depletion. That portion of a natural resource's cost that is used up in a particular period. Depletion expense is computed in the same way as units of production depreciation (*p. 401*).

Deposit in transit. A deposit recorded by the company but not yet by its bank (*p. 273*).

Depreciation. Expense associated with spreading (allocating) the cost of a plant asset over its useful life (*p. 92*).

Direct expense. Expense that is conveniently identified with and traceable to a particular department of a business (*p. 976*).

Direct labor. Cost of salaries and wages for the employees who physically convert materials into the company's products (*p. 858*).

Direct material. Material that becomes a physical part of a finished product and whose cost is separately and conveniently traceable through the manufacturing process to finished goods (*p. 858*).

Direct method. Format of the operating activities section of the statement of cash flows that lists the major categories of operating cash receipts (collections from customers and receipts of interest and dividends) and cash disbursements (payments to suppliers, to employees, for interest and income taxes) (*p. 698*).

Direct write-off method. A method of accounting for bad

debts by which the company waits until the credit department decides that a customer's account receivable is uncollectible and then records uncollectible account expense and credits the customer's account receivable *(p. 311).*

Disclosure principle. Holds that a company's financial statements should report enough information for outsiders to make knowledgeable decisions about the company *(p. 471).*

Discount on stock. Excess of the par value of stock over its issue price *(p. 543).*

Discount rate. Management's minimum desired rate of return on an investment, used in a present value computation *(p. 1022).*

Discounting a note payable. A borrowing arrangement in which the bank subtracts the interest amount from the note's face value. The borrower receives the net amount *(p. 424).*

Discounting a note receivable. Selling a note receivable before its maturity *(p. 324).*

Dishonor of a note. Another name for Default on a note *(p. 326).*

Disk drive. Computer input device that reads data and instructions from magnetic disks *(p. 1077).*

Diskette. Thin 5¼-inch diameter round magnetic disk enclosed in a square plastic envelope. Also called a Floppy diskette *(p. 1077).*

Dissolution. Ending of a partnership *(p. 496).*

Dividend yield. Ratio of dividends per share of stock to the stock's market price per share *(p. 760).*

Dividends. Distributions by a corporation to its stockholders *(p. 540).*

Dividends in arrears. Cumulative preferred dividends that the corporation has failed to pay *(p. 551).*

Donated capital. Special category of stockholders' equity created when a corporation receives a donation (gift) from a donor who receives no ownership interest in the company *(p. 548).*

Double-declining-balance (DDB) method. An accelerated depreciation method that computes annual depreciation by multiplying the asset's decreasing book value by a constant percentage, which is two times the straight-line rate *(p. 389).*

Double taxation. Corporations pay their own income taxes on corporate income. Then, the stockholders pay personal income tax on the cash dividends that they receive from corporations *(p. 537).*

Doubtful account expense. Another name for Uncollectible account expense *(p. 311).*

Earnings per share (EPS). Amount of a company's net income per share of its outstanding common stock *(p. 588).*

Effective interest rate. Another name for market interest rate *(p. 612).*

Effective tax rate. A taxpayer's income tax amount divided by taxable income *(p. 1052).*

Efficiency variance. Difference between the quantity of inputs (materials and labor) actually used and the quantity that should have been used (the flexible budget) for the actual output achieved, multiplied by the standard unit price of the input. Also called the Usage variance and the Quantity variance *(p. 946).*

Electronic fund transfer. System that accounts for cash transactions by electronic impulses rather than paper documents *(p. 289).*

Ending inventory. Goods still on hand at the end of the period *(p. 345).*

Entity. An organization or a section of an organization that, for accounting purposes, stands apart from other organizations and individuals as a separate economic unit. This is the most basic concept in accounting *(p. 9).*

EPS. Abbreviation of Earnings per share of common stock *(p. 588).*

Equity. A legal and economic claim to the assets of a business. Equities are divided between outsider claims (liabilities) and insider claims (owner equity or capital) *(p. 11).*

Equity method for investments. The method used to account for investments in which the investor can significantly influence the decisions of the investee. Under the equity method, investments are recorded initially at cost. The investment account is debited (increased) for ownership in the investee's net income and credited (decreased) for ownership in the investee's dividends *(p. 660).*

Equivalent units. Measure of the number of complete units that could have been manufactured from start to finish using the costs incurred during the period *(p. 901).*

Estimated residual value. Expected cash value of an asset at the end of its useful life. Also called Residual value, Scrap value and Salvage value *(p. 387).*

Estimated useful life. Length of the service that a business expects to get from an asset, may be expressed in years, units of output, miles, or other measures *(p. 387).*

Expense. Decrease in owner equity that occurs in the course of delivering goods or services to customers or clients *(p. 14).*

Expense allocation. Assignment of various expenses to the departments of a business *(p. 976).*

Extraordinary item. A gain or loss that is both unusual for the company and infrequent *(p. 588).*

Extraordinary repair. Repair work that generates a capital expenditure *(p. 404).*

Factory ledger. A branch ledger for a manufacturing plant *(p. 981).*

Factory overhead. All manufacturing costs other than direct materials and direct labor *(p. 858).*

FICA tax. Federal Insurance Contributions Act (FICA) or Social Security tax which is withheld from employees' pay *(p. 433).*

FIFO. The First-in, first-out inventory method *(p. 348).*

Financial accounting. The branch of accounting that provides information to people outside the business *(p. 8).*

Financial budget. Projects the means of raising money from stockholders and creditors and plans cash management *(p. 790).*

Financial statements. Business documents that report financial information about an entity to persons and organizations outside the business *(p. 18).*

Financing activity. Activity that obtains the funds from investors and creditors needed to launch and sustain the business. A section of the statement of cash flows *(p. 697).*

Finished goods inventory. Completed goods that have not yet been sold *(p. 857).*

First-in, first-out (FIFO) method. Inventory costing

method by which the first costs into inventory are the first costs out to cost of goods sold. Ending inventory is based on the costs of the most recent purchases (p. 348).

Fixed cost. Cost that does not change in total as volume changes (p. 822).

Fixed expense. Expense that does not change in total as volume changes (p. 822).

Flexible budget. Set of budgets covering a range of volume rather than a single level of volume (p. 937).

Flexible budget overhead variance. Difference between total actual overhead (fixed and variable) and the flexible budget amount for actual production volume. Also called the Controllable variance (p. 950).

Flexible budget variance. Difference between an amount in the flexible budget and the actual results for the corresponding item (p. 940).

FOB destination. Terms of a transaction that govern when the title to the inventory passes from the seller to the purchaser—when the goods arrive at the purchaser's location (p. 347).

FOB shipping point. Terms of a transaction that govern when the title to the inventory passes from the seller to the purchaser—when the goods leave the seller's place of business (p. 347).

Franchises and licenses. Privileges granted by a private business or a government to sell a product or service in accordance with specified conditions (p. 402).

Fringe benefits. Employee compensation, like health and life insurance and retirement pay, which the employee does not receive immediately in cash (p. 432).

Gain. An increase in owner equity that does not result from a revenue or an investment by an owner in the business (p. 476).

Generally accepted accounting principles (GAAP). Accounting guidelines, formulated by the Financial Accounting Standards Board, that govern how businesses report their financial statements to the public (p. 6).

General journal. Journal used to record all transactions that do not fit one of the special journals (p. 222).

General ledger. Ledger of accounts that are reported in the financial statements (p. 223).

Going concern concept. Accountants' assumption that the business will continue operating in the foreseeable future (p. 464).

Goods available for sale. Beginning inventory plus net purchases (p. 345).

Goodwill. Excess of the cost of an acquired company over the sum of the market values of its net assets (assets minus liabilities) (p. 403).

Gross income. In taxation, total income minus exclusions (p. 1043).

Gross margin. Excess of sales revenue over cost of goods sold. Also called gross profit (p. 169).

Gross margin method. A way to estimate inventory based on a rearrangement of the cost of goods sold model: Beginning inventory + Net purchases = Cost of goods available for sale. Cost of goods available for sale − Cost of goods sold = Ending inventory. Also called the Gross profit method (p. 359).

Gross pay. Total amount of salary, wages, commissions, or any other employee compensation before taxes and other deductions are taken out (p. 432).

Gross profit. Excess of sales revenue over cost of goods sold. Also called gross margin (p. 169).

Gross profit method. Another name for the gross margin method of estimating inventory cost (p. 359).

Hardware. Equipment that makes up a computer system (p. 219).

High-low method. Method of separating a mixed cost into its variable and fixed components (p. 836).

Home office ledger. The part of a general ledger kept by the home office, separate from the branch ledger, which the branch keeps (p. 981).

Home-office ledger control. Account in the branch ledger that represents an owner equity of, or branch payable to, the home office (p. 982).

Horizontal analysis. Study of percentage changes in comparative financial statements (p. 740).

Imprest system. A way to account for petty cash by maintaining a constant balance in the petty cash account, supported by the fund (cash plus disbursement tickets) totalling the same amount (p. 283).

Income from operations. Gross margin (sales revenue minus cost of goods sold) minus operating expenses. Also called Operating income (p. 184).

Income statement. List of an entity's revenues, expenses, and net income or net loss for a specific period. Also called the Statement of operations (p. 18).

Income summary. A temporary "holding tank" account into which the revenues and expenses are transferred prior to their final transfer to the capital account (p. 139).

Income tax. A general-purpose tax levied on the income of a taxpayer. Entirely separate from all other taxes, it is the federal government's largest source of revenue (p. 1039).

Income tax allocation. Process of accruing income taxes during the period that the related income occurs, with the goal of matching the period's expenses—including income tax expense—against the period's revenues, regardless of when the income tax is paid (p. 1053).

Incorporators. Persons who organize a corporation (p. 537).

Indirect expense. Expense that is not traceable to a single department of a business; an expense other than a direct expense. Often indirect expenses arise from activities that serve more than one department simultaneously (p. 976).

Indirect labor. Factory labor costs other than direct labor. Indirect labor costs, which are difficult to trace to specific products, include the pay of forklift operators, janitors, and plant guards (p. 859).

Indirect materials. Manufacturing materials whose cost cannot easily be traced directly to particular finished products (p. 859).

Indirect method. Format of the operating activities section of the statement of cash flows that starts with net income and shows the reconciliation from net income to operating cash flows. Also called the Reconciliation method (p. 713).

Inflation. Increase in the general price level (p. 669).

Information system design. Identification of an organization's information needs, and development and implementation of the system to meet those needs (p. 7).

Installment method. Method of applying the revenue principle in which gross profit (sales revenue minus cost of goods sold) is recorded as cash is collected (p. 468).

Intangible asset. An asset with no physical form, a special right to current and expected future benefits (p. 383).

Integrated software. Computer program that includes modules handling different functions. Coordinates the output of the various modules *(p. 1079)*.

Interest. The revenue to the payee for loaning out the principal, and the expense to the maker for borrowing the principal *(p. 322)*.

Interest coverage ratio. Another name for the Times-interest-earned ratio *(p. 756)*.

Interest period. The period of time during which interest is to be computed, extending from the original date of the note to the maturity date *(p. 322)*.

Interest rate. The percentage rate that is multiplied by the principal amount to compute the amount of interest on a note *(p. 322)*.

Internal auditing. Auditing that is performed by a business's own accountants to evaluate the firm's accounting and management systems. The aim is to improve operating efficiency and to ensure that employees follow management's procedures and plans *(p. 7)*.

Internal control. Organizational plan and all the related measures adopted by an entity to safeguard assets, ensure accurate and reliable accounting records, promote operational efficiency, and encourage adherence to company policies *(p. 265)*.

Inventory cost. Price paid to acquire inventory—not the selling price of the goods. Inventory cost includes its invoice price, less all discounts, plus sales tax, tariffs, transportation fees, insurance while in transit, and all other costs incurred to make the goods ready for sale *(p. 347)*.

Inventory profit. Difference between gross margin figured on the FIFO basis and gross margin figured on the LIFO basis *(p. 352)*.

Inventory turnover. Ratio of cost of goods sold to average inventory. Measures the number of times a company sells its average level of inventory during a year *(p. 752)*.

Investing activity. Activity that increases and decreases the assets that the business has to work with. A section of the statement of cash flows *(p. 697)*.

Invoice. Seller's request for payment from a purchaser. Also called a bill *(p. 171)*.

Itemized deduction. In taxation, a particular category that includes medical expenses, interest expense, charitable contributions, taxes paid, casualty losses, and miscellaneous deductions *(p. 1043)*.

Job cost record. Document used to accumulate and control cost in a job order system *(p. 864)*.

Job order costing. Accounting system used by companies that manufacture products as individual units or in batches, each of which receives varying degrees of attention and skill *(p. 863)*.

Joint product. Goods identified as individual products only after a juncture in the production process called the split-off point *(p. 916)*.

Journal. The chronological accounting record of an entity's transactions *(p. 45)*.

Labor time ticket. Document that identifies an employee, the amount of time the employee spent on a particular job, and the employee's labor cost charged to the job *(p. 868)*.

Large stock dividend. A stock dividend of 25 percent or more of the corporation's issued stock *(p. 575)*.

Last-in, first-out (LIFO) method. Inventory costing method by which the last costs into inventory are the first costs out to cost of goods sold. This leaves the oldest costs—those of beginning inventory and the earliest purchases of the period—in ending inventory *(p. 348)*.

LCM rule. The Lower-of-cost-or-market rule *(p. 356)*.

Lease. Rental agreement in which the tenant (lessee) agrees to make rent payments to the property owner (lessor) in exchange for the use of the asset *(p. 627)*.

Leasehold. Prepayment that a lessee (renter) makes to secure the use of an asset from a lessor (landlord) *(p. 402)*.

Ledger. The book of accounts *(p. 39)*.

Lessee. Tenant in a lease agreement *(p. 627)*.

Lessor. Property owner in a lease agreement *(p. 627)*.

Leverage. Another name for Trading on the equity *(p. 758)*.

Liability. An economic obligation (a debt) payable to an individual or an organization outside the business *(p. 11)*.

LIFO. The Last-in, first-out inventory method *(p. 348)*.

Limited liability. No personal obligation of a stockholder for corporation debts. The most that a stockholder can lose on an investment in a corporation's stock is the cost of the investment *(p. 536)*.

Limiting factor. Item that restricts production or sales. Also called the Constraint *(p. 1012)*.

Liquidation. The process of going out of business by selling the entity's assets and paying its liabilities. The final step in liquidation of a business is the distribution of any remaining cash to the owners *(p. 513)*.

Liquidation value of stock. Amount a corporation agrees to pay a preferred stockholder per share if the company liquidates *(p. 554)*.

Liquidity. Measure of how quickly an item may be converted to cash *(p. 142)*.

Long-term asset. An asset other than a current asset *(p. 142)*.

Long-term investment. Separate asset category reported on the balance sheet between current assets and plant assets *(p. 632)*.

Long-term liability. A liability other than a current liability *(p. 143)*.

Loss. A decrease in owner equity that does not result from an expense or a distribution to an owner of the business *(p. 477)*.

Lower-of-cost-or-market (LCM) rule. Requires that an asset be reported in the financial statements at the lower of its historical cost or its market value (current replacement cost) *(p. 356)*.

Mainframe. Computer system characterized by a single computer *(p. 219)*.

Majority interest. Another name for a Controlling ownership interest in another business *(p. 661)*.

Maker of a note. The person or business that signs the note and promises to pay the amount required by the note agreement. The maker is the debtor *(p. 321)*.

Management accounting. The branch of accounting that generates confidential information for internal decision makers of a business, such as top executives *(p. 8)*.

Management by exception. Management strategy by which executive attention is directed to the important deviations from budgeted amounts *(p. 973)*.

Margin of safety. Excess of expected sales over break-even sales *(p. 833)*.

Market interest rate. Interest rate that investors demand in order to loan their money. Also called the Effective interest rate *(p. 612)*.

Market value of stock. Price for which a person could buy or sell a share of stock (*p. 553*).

Marketable security. Another name for Short-term investment, one that may be sold any time the investor wishes (*p. 657*).

Master budget. Budget that includes the major financial statements and supporting schedules. The master budget can be divided into the operating budget, the capital expenditures budget, and the financial budget (*p. 787*).

Matching principle. The basis for recording expenses. Directs accountants to identify all expenses incurred during the period, to measure the expenses, and to match them against the revenues earned during that same span of time (*p. 88*).

Materiality concept. States that a company must perform strictly proper accounting only for items and transactions that are significant to the business's financial statements (*p. 475*).

Materials inventory. Materials on hand and intended for use in the manufacturing process. Also called Raw materials inventory (*p. 857*).

Materials requisition. Request for materials prepared by manufacturing personnel, the document that sets a manufacturing process in motion (*p. 866*).

Maturity date. The date on which the final payment of a note is due. Also called the Due date (*p. 322*).

Maturity value. The sum of the principal and interest due at the maturity date of a note (*p. 322*).

Menu. List of options for choosing computer functions (*p. 1079*).

Menu-driven. Type of computer software that offers a list of options for doing various functions (*p. 1079*).

Microcomputer. A computer small enough for each employee (work station) to have its own (*p. 219*).

Minicomputer. Small computer that operates like a large system but on a smaller scale (*p. 219*).

Minority interest. A subsidiary company's equity that is held by stockholders other than the parent company (*p. 665*).

Mixed cost. Cost that is part variable and part fixed (*p. 823*).

Mixed expense. Expense that is part variable and part fixed (*p. 823*).

Modified Accelerated Cost Recovery System (MACRS). Special tax depreciation method (*p. 1052*).

Monetary asset. Asset whose value is stated in a fixed number of dollars. This amount does not change, regardless of inflation (*p. 672*).

Monetary liability. Liability stated in a fixed number of dollars. This amount does not change, regardless of inflation (*p. 672*).

Monitor. Computer output device that resembles a television and allows the user to view data being processed and to receive messages from the program being run (*p. 1078*).

Mortgage. Borrower's promise to transfer the legal title to certain assets to the lender if the debt is not paid on schedule (*p. 627*).

Multiple-step income statement. Format that contains subtotals to highlight significant relationships. In addition to net income, it also presents gross margin and income from operations (*p. 188*).

Mutual agency. Every partner can bind the business to a contract within the scope of the partnership's regular business operations (*p. 496*).

Net earnings. Another name for Net income or Net profit (*p. 15*).

Net income. Excess of total revenues over total expenses. Also called Net earnings or Net profit (*p. 15*).

Net loss. Excess of total expenses over total revenues (*p. 15*).

Net monetary assets. Excess of monetary assets over monetary liabilities (*p. 672*).

Net monetary liabilities. Excess of monetary liabilities over monetary assets (*p. 672*).

Net pay. Gross pay minus all deductions, the amount of employee compensation that the employee actually takes home (*p. 432*).

Net present value. Method of computing the expected net monetary gain or loss from a project by discounting all expected cash flows to the present value, using a desired rate of return. A zero or positive net present value indicates that the investment should be purchased. A negative net present value indicates that the investment should be rejected (*p. 1021*).

Net profit. Another name for Net income or Net earnings (*p. 15*).

Net purchases. Purchases less purchase discounts and purchase returns and allowances (*p. 174*).

Net realizable value. Sales value less the cost of selling the item (*p. 917*).

Net sales. Sales revenue less sales discounts and sales returns and allowances (*p. 177*).

Nominal account. Another name for a temporary account —revenues and expenses—that are closed at the end of the period. In a proprietorship the owner withdrawal account is also nominal (*p. 137*).

Nonmonetary asset. Asset whose price may change during inflation, such as inventory, land, buildings, and equipment (*p. 672*).

Non-sufficient funds check. A "hot" check, one for which the payer's bank account has insufficient money to pay the check (*p. 273*).

Note payable. A liability evidenced by a written promise to make a future payment (*p. 11*).

Note receivable. An asset evidenced by another party's written promise that entitles you to receive cash in the future (*pp. 11, 310*).

NSF check. A non-sufficient funds check (*p. 273*).

Objectivity principle. Another name for the Reliability principle (*p. 466*).

Off-balance-sheet financing. Acquisition of assets or services with debt that is not reported on the balance sheet (*p. 629*).

On-line processing. Computerized accounting for transaction data on a continuous basis, often from various locations, rather than in batches at a single location (*p. 220*).

Operating activity. Activity that creates revenue or expense in the entity's major line of business. Operating activities affect the income statement. A section of the statement of cash flows (*p. 697*).

Operating budget. Sets the target revenues and expenses, and thus net income, for the period (*p. 790*).

Operating expenses. Expenses, other than cost of goods sold, that are incurred in the entity's major line of business—rent, depreciation, salaries, wages, utilities, property tax, and supplies expense (*p. 184*).

Operating income. Another name for Income from operations (p. 184).

Operating lease. Usually a short-term or cancelable rental agreement (p. 627).

Operation costing. The most popular hybrid costing system, combining features from job costing and process costing, used to account for the manufacture of goods that have some common features plus some individual characteristics (p. 913).

Opportunity cost. Maximum available profit contribution forgone (rejected) by using limited resources for a particular purpose. It is the cost of the forsaken next best alternative (p. 1015).

Ordinary repair. Repair work that creates a revenue expenditure, which is debited to an expense account (p. 404).

Organization cost. The costs of organizing a corporation, including legal fees, taxes and fees paid to the state, and charges by promoters for selling the stock. Organization cost is an intangible asset (p. 549).

Other expense. Expense that is outside the main operations of a business, such as a loss on the sale of plant assets (p. 184).

Other receivables. A miscellaneous category that includes loans to employees and branch companies, usually long-term assets reported on the balance sheet after current assets and before plant assets. Other receivables can be current assets (p. 310).

Other revenue. Revenue that is outside the main operations of a business, such as a gain on the sale of plant assets (p. 184).

Outstanding check. A check issued by the company and recorded on its books but not yet paid by its bank (p. 273).

Outstanding stock. Stock in the hands of a stockholder (p. 538).

Overapplied overhead. Credit balance in the factory overhead account, results when applied overhead exceeds the actual overhead cost (p. 874).

Owner equity. The claim of an owner of a business to the assets of the business. Also called Capital (p. 11).

Paid-in capital. A corporation's capital from investments by the stockholders. Also called Contributed capital (p. 539).

Par value. Arbitrary amount assigned to a share of stock (p. 541).

Parent company. An investor company that owns more than 50 percent of the voting stock of a subsidiary company (p. 661).

Participating preferred stock. Preferred stock whose owners may receive—that is participate in—dividends beyond the stated amount or stated percentage (p. 552).

Partnership. A business with two or more owners (p. 8).

Partnership agreement. Another name for the Articles of partnership (p. 496).

Patent. A federal government grant giving the holder the exclusive right for 17 years to produce and sell an invention (p. 402).

Payback. Length of time it will take to recover, in net cash inflow from operations, the dollars of a capital outlay. The shorter the payback period the better the investment, and vice versa (p. 1018).

Payee of a note. The person or business to whom the maker of a note promises future payment. The payee is the creditor (p. 321).

Payroll. Employee compensation, a major expense of many businesses (p. 431).

Pension. Employee compensation that will be received during retirement (p. 629).

Percentage-of-completion method. Method of applying the revenue principle by a construction company by which revenue is recorded as the work is performed (p. 470).

Period cost. Operating expenses which are never traced through the inventory accounts (p. 861).

Periodic inventory system. The business does not keep a continuous record of the inventory on hand. Instead, at the end of the period the business makes a physical count of the on-hand inventory and applies the appropriate unit costs to determine the cost of the ending inventory (p. 360).

Permanent accounts. The assets, liabilities, and capital accounts. These accounts are *not* closed at the end of the period because their balances are not used to measure income (p. 138).

Perpetual inventory system. The business keeps a continuous record for each inventory item to show the inventory on hand at all times (p. 361).

Personal exemption. A tax deduction that is a set amount allowed for a taxpayer, the taxpayer's spouse, and each person who qualifies as a dependent (p. 1044).

Petty cash. Fund containing a small amount of cash that is used to pay minor expenditures (p. 282).

Plant asset. Long-lived assets, like land, buildings, and equipment, used in the operation of the business (pp. 92, 383).

Postclosing trial balance. List of the ledger accounts and their balances at the end of the period after the journalizing and posting of the closing entries. The last step of the accounting cycle, the postclosing trial balance ensures that the ledger is in balance for the start of the next accounting period (p. 141).

Posting. Transferring of amounts from the journal to the ledger (p. 46).

Preemptive right. A stockholder's right to maintain a proportionate ownership in a corporation (p. 541).

Preferred stock. Stock that gives its owners certain advantages over common stockholders, such as the priority to receive dividends before the common stockholders and the priority to receive assets before the common stockholders if the corporation liquidates (p. 541).

Premium on stock. Excess of the issue price of stock over its par value (p. 542).

Prepaid expense. A category of miscellaneous assets that typically expire or get used up in the near future. Examples include prepaid rent, prepaid insurance, and supplies (p. 90).

Present value. Amount a person would invest now to receive a greater amount at a future date (p. 612).

President. Chief operating officer in charge of managing the day-to-day operations of a corporation (p. 537).

Price/earnings ratio. Ratio of the market price of a share of common stock to the company's earnings per share (p. 759).

Price variance. Difference between the actual unit price of an input (materials and labor) and a standard unit price, multiplied by the actual quantity of inputs used (pp. 945–946).

Prime costs. Direct materials plus direct labor (p. 859).

Principal amount. The amount loaned out by the payee and borrowed by the maker of a note *(p. 321)*.

Prior period adjustment. Correction to retained earnings for an error of an earlier period is a prior period adjustment *(p. 591)*.

Private accountant. Accountant who works for a single business, such as a department store or General Motors *(p. 4)*.

Process costing. System for assigning costs to goods that are mass-produced in a continuous sequence of steps *(p. 897)*.

Product cost. Cost identified with goods purchased or manufactured for resale *(p. 860)*.

Production cost report. Summary of the activity in a processing department for a period *(p. 912)*.

Production volume overhead variance. Difference between the flexible budget for actual production and standard overhead applied to production *(p. 951)*.

Pro forma data. Carefully formulated expression of predicted results, such as projections of future income and income tax *(p. 1054)*.

Program. Set of instructions that tell the computer what to do *(p. 1076)*.

Promissory note. A written promise to pay a specified amount of money at a particular future date *(p. 321)*.

Proprietorship. A business with a single owner *(p. 8)*.

Proxy. Legal document that expresses a stockholder's preference and appoints another person to cast the vote *(p. 537)*.

Public accountant. Accountant who serves the general public and collects fees for work, which includes auditing, income tax planning and preparation, and management consulting *(p. 4)*.

Purchase discount. Reduction in the cost of inventory that is offered by a seller as an incentive for the customer to pay promptly. A contra account to purchases *(p. 173)*.

Purchase returns and allowances. Decrease in a buyer's debt from returning merchandise to the seller or from receiving from the seller an allowance from the amount owed. A contra account to purchases *(p. 174)*.

Purchases. The cost of inventory that a firm buys to resell to customers in the normal course of business *(p. 170)*.

Purchases journal. Special journal used to record all purchases of inventory, supplies, and other assets on account *(p. 230)*.

Purchasing power gain (or loss). A purchasing power gain occurs during inflation because a company is able to pay its liabilities with dollars that are cheaper than the dollars borrowed. A purchasing power loss occurs during inflation when a creditor receives dollars that are worth less than the dollars lent *(p. 672)*.

Quantity variance. Another name for the efficiency variance used to control materials and labor costs in a standard cost system *(p. 946)*.

Quick ratio. Another name for the Acid-test ratio *(p. 751)*.

Rate of return on common stockholders' equity. Net income minus preferred dividends, divided by average common stockholders' equity. A measure of profitability. Also called return on common stockholders' equity *(p. 758)*.

Rate of return on net sales. Ratio of net income to net sales.

A measure of profitability. Also called Return on sales *(p. 756)*.

Rate of return on total assets. The sum of net income plus interest expense divided by average total assets. This ratio measures the success a company has in using its assets to earn a profit. Also called Return on assets *(p. 757)*.

Raw materials inventory. Another name for Materials inventory *(p. 857)*.

Real account. Another name for a Permanent account—asset, liability, and capital—that are *not* closed at the end of the period *(p. 138)*.

Receivable. A monetary claim against a business or an individual, acquired mainly by selling goods and services and by lending money *(p. 309)*.

Reciprocal accounts. Two or more accounts that have the same offsetting balances and are used to control a general ledger that is kept in two or more locations *(p. 981)*.

Reconciliation method. Another name for the indirect method of formatting the operating activities section of the statement of cash flows *(p. 713)*.

Redemption value of stock. Price a corporation agrees to pay for stock, which is set when the stock is issued *(p. 553)*.

Registered bonds. Bonds for which the owners receive interest checks from the issuing company *(p. 610)*.

Relative sales value method. Allocation technique for identifying the cost of each asset purchased in a group for a single amount *(p. 385)*.

Relevant information. Expected future data that differ between alternative courses of action *(p. 1005)*.

Relevant range. Band of activity or volume in which actual operations are likely to occur. Within this range, a particular relationship exists between revenue and expenses *(p. 824)*.

Reliability principle. Requires that accounting information be dependable (free from error and bias). Also called the Objectivity principle *(p. 466)*.

Report format of the balance sheet. Format that lists the assets at the top, with the liabilities and owner equity below *(p. 143)*.

Residual value. Same as Estimated residual value *(p. 387)*.

Responsibility accounting. System for evaluating the progress of managers based on activities under their supervision *(p. 972)*.

Responsibility center. Any subunit of an organization needing control, the basic unit in a responsibility accounting system. The three common types of responsibility center are the cost center, the profit center, and the investment center *(p. 972)*.

Retail method. A way to estimate inventory cost based on the cost of goods sold model. The retail method requires that the business record inventory purchases both at cost and at retail. Multiply ending inventory at retail by the cost ratio to estimate the ending inventory's cost *(p. 359)*.

Retained earnings. A corporation's capital that is earned through profitable operation of the business *(p. 539)*.

Return on assets. Another name for Rate of return on total assets *(p. 757)*.

Return on common stockholders' equity. Another name for Rate of return on common stockholders' equity *(p. 758)*.

Return on sales. Another name for Rate of return on net sales *(p. 756)*.

Revenue. Increase in owner equity that is earned by delivering goods or services to customers or clients (*p. 13*).

Revenue expenditure. Expenditure that merely maintains an asset in its existing condition or restores the asset to good working order. Revenue expenditures are expensed (matched against revenue) (*p. 404*).

Revenue principle. The basis for recording revenues, tells accountants when to record revenue and the amount of revenue to record (*p. 87*).

Reversing entry. An entry that switches the debit and the credit of a previous adjusting entry. The reversing entry is dated the first day of the period following the adjusting entry (*p. 1125*).

Rolling budget. Another name for a continuous budget (*p. 801*).

Salary. Employee compensation stated at a yearly, monthly, or weekly rate (*p. 431*).

Sales discount. Reduction in the amount receivable from a customer, offered by the seller as an incentive for the customer to pay promptly. A contra account to Sales revenue (*p. 176*).

Sales journal. Special journal used to record credit sales (*p. 222*).

Sales method. Method of applying the revenue principle in which revenue is recorded at the point of sale. This method is used for most sales of goods and services (*p. 468*).

Sales mix. Combination of products that make up total sales (*p. 834*).

Sales returns and allowances. Decrease in the seller's receivable from a customer's return of merchandise or from granting the customer an allowance from the amount the customer owes the seller. A contra account to Sales revenue (*p. 176*).

Sales revenue. Amount that a merchandiser earns from selling inventory before subtracting expenses (*p. 169*).

Sales volume variance. Difference between a revenue, expense, or operating income amount in the flexible budget and the corresponding revenue, expense, or income amount in the static (master) budget (*p. 940*).

Salvage value. Another name for residual value or estimated residual value (*p. 387*).

Segment of a business. A significant part of a company (*p. 587*).

Serial bonds. Bonds that mature in installments over a period of time (*p. 610*).

Sevice charge. Bank's fee for processing a depositor's transactions (*p. 273*).

Shareholder. Another name for stockholder (*p. 535*).

Short presentation. A way to report contingent liabilities in the body of the balance sheet, after total liabilities but with no amount given (*pp. 429, 430*).

Short-term note payable. Note payable due within one year, a common form of financing (*p. 424*).

Short-term self-liquidating financing. Debt incurred to buy inventories that will be sold and with the cash collections used to pay the debt (*p. 800*).

Single-step income statement. Format that groups all revenues together and then lists and deducts all expenses together without drawing any subtotals (*p. 188*).

Slide. An accounting error that results from adding one or more zeroes to a number, or from dropping a zero. For example, writing $500 as $5,000 or as $50 is a slide. A slide is evenly divisible by 9. (*p. 145*).

Small stock dividend. A stock dividend of less than 25 percent of the corporation's issued stock (*p. 525*).

Social Security tax. Another name for FICA tax (*p. 433*).

Software. Set of programs or instructions that cause the computer to perform the work desired (*pp. 145, 219*).

Specific cost method. Inventory cost method based on the specific cost of particular units of inventory (*p. 348*).

Split-off point. Juncture in the production process after which joint products are specifically identified (*p. 916*).

Spreadsheet. Integrated software program that can be used to solve many different kinds of problems. An electronically prepared work sheet (*p. 145*).

Stable monetary unit concept. Accountants' basis for ignoring the effect of inflation and making no adjustments for the changing value of the dollar (*p. 465*).

Standard cost. Predetermined cost that management believes the business should incur in producing an item (*p. 943*).

Standard cost system. Designed to control costs by analyzing the relationship between actual costs and standard costs (*p. 943*).

Standard deduction. A set amount of tax deduction that varies depending on the individual's filing status: single, married filing jointly, or head of household. The standard deduction is an alternative to itemizing tax deductions (*p. 1044*).

Stated interest rate. Another name for the Contract interest rate (*p. 612*).

Statement of budgeted cash receipts and disbursements. Another name for the Cash budget (*p. 796*).

Statement of cash flows. Reports cash receipts and cash disbursements classified according to the entity's major activities: operating, investing, and financing (*p. 695*).

Statement of financial position. Another name for the Balance sheet (*p. 18*).

Statement of operations. Another name for the Income statement (*p. 18*).

Statement of owner equity. Summary of the changes in the owner equity of an entity during a specific period (*p. 18*).

Static budget. A budget prepared for only one level of activity (*p. 937*).

Stock. Shares into which the owners' equity of a corporation is divided (*p. 536*).

Stock dividend. A proportional distribution by a corporation of its own stock to its stockholders (*p. 573*).

Stock split. An increase in the number of outstanding shares of stock coupled with a proportionate reduction in the par value of the stock (*p. 573*).

Stock subscription. Contract that obligates an investor to purchase the corporation's stock at a later date (*p. 544*).

Stockholder. A person who owns the stock of a corporation (*p. 9*).

Stockholders' equity. Owners' equity of a corporation (*p. 538*).

Straight-line method. Depreciation method in which an equal amount of depreciation expense is assigned to each year (or period) of asset use (*p. 387*).

Subsequent event. An event that occurs after the end of a company's accounting period but before publication of its financial statements and which may affect the interpretation of the information in those statements (*p. 473*).

Subsidiary company. An investee company in which a parent company owns more than 50 percent of the voting stock *(p. 661).*

Subsidiary ledger. Book of accounts that provides supporting details on individual balances, the total of which appears in a general ledger account *(p. 224).*

Sum-of-years-digits (SYD) method. An accelerated depreciation method by which depreciation is figured by multiplying the depreciable cost of the asset by a fraction. The denominator of the SYD fraction is the sum of the years' digits of the asset's life. The numerator of the SYD fraction starts with the asset life in years and decreases by one each year thereafter *(p. 390).*

Sunk cost. Actual outlay incurred in the past and is present under all alternative courses of action. Sunk cost is irrelevant because it makes no difference to a current decision *(p. 1015).*

Surtax. An additional tax often designed to shift more of the tax burden to high-income taxpayers *(p. 1046).*

Tax avoidance. Structuring of business transactions in order to pay the least amount of income tax at the latest possible time permitted by the law *(p. 1054).*

Tax credit. Amount that is subtracted directly from the amount of tax owed to the government *(p. 1047).*

Tax-deferred compensation. Compensation that postpones the payment of taxes until the employee draws the money. Also called Tax-sheltered compensation *(p. 1058).*

Tax evasion. Illegal activity designed to reduce tax *(p. 1054).*

Tax return. Document on which each taxpayer reports income and shows the computation of income tax *(p. 1041).*

Tax-sheltered compensation. Another name for Tax-deferred compensation *(p. 1058).*

Taxable income. Earnings amount on which the income tax is based. It is the figure that is multiplied by the tax rate to compute the amount of income tax *(p. 1045).*

Temporary accounts. The revenue and expense accounts which relate to a particular accounting period are closed at the end of the period. For a proprietorship, the owner withdrawal account is also temporary *(p. 137).*

Term bonds. Bonds that all mature at the same time for a particular issue *(p. 610).*

Time and a half. Overtime pay computed as 150 percent (1.5 times) the straight-time rate *(p. 432).*

Time period concept. Ensures that accounting information is reported at regular intervals *(p. 465).*

Time value of money. The fact that one can earn income by investing money for a period of time *(p. 1021).*

Times-interest-earned ratio. Ratio of income from operations to interest expense. Measures the number of times that operating income can cover interest expense. Also called the Interest-coverage ratio *(p. 756).*

Total income. In taxation, all income from whatever source derived *(p. 1043).*

Total manufacturing cost. Sum of direct materials used, direct labor, and factory overhead. Total manufacturing cost is used to compute cost of goods manufactured, which is part of cost of goods sold *(p. 860).*

Trade discount. A purchase discount that provides a lower price per item the larger the quantity purchased *(p. 173).*

Trademarks and trade names. Distinctive identifications of a product or service *(p. 402).*

Trading on the equity. Earning more income than the borrowed amount, which increases the earnings for the owners of a business. Also called leverage *(p. 631).*

Transaction. An event that affects the financial position of a particular entity and may be reliably recorded *(p. 11).*

Transposition. An accounting error that occurs when digits are flip-flopped. For example, $85 is a transposition of $58. A transposition is evenly divisible by 9 *(p. 145).*

Treasury stock. A corporation's own stock that it has issued and later reacquired *(p. 578).*

Trial balance. A list of all the ledger accounts with their balances *(p. 50).*

Uncollectible account expense. Cost to the seller of extending credit. Arises from the failure to collect from credit customers *(p. 311).*

Underapplied overhead. Debit balance remaining in the factory overhead account after overhead is applied, means that actual overhead cost exceeded the amount applied to jobs *(p. 874).*

Underwriter. Organization that purchases the bonds from an issuing company and resells them to its clients, or sells the bonds for a commission, agreeing to buy all unsold bonds *(p. 610).*

Unearned revenue. A liability created when a business collects cash from customers in advance of doing work for the customer. The obligation is to provide a product or a service in the future. Also called deferred revenue *(p. 96).*

Unemployment compensation tax. Payroll tax paid by employers to the government, which uses the money to pay unemployment benefits to people who are out of work *(p. 435).*

Units-of-production (UOP) method. Depreciation method by which a fixed amount of depreciation is assigned to each unit of output produced by the plant asset *(p. 389).*

Unlimited personal liability. When a partnership (or a proprietorship) cannot pay its debts with business assets, the partners (or the proprietor) must use personal assets to meet the debt *(p. 497).*

Usage variance. Another name for the Efficiency variance used to control materials and labor costs in a standard cost system *(p. 946).*

Useful life. Same as Estimated useful life *(p. 387).*

Variable cost. Cost that changes in total in direct proportion with changes in volume or activity *(p. 822).*

Variable expense. Expense that changes in total in direct proportion with changes in volume or activity *(p. 822).*

Variance. Difference between an actual amount and the corresponding budget amount *(p. 937).*

Vertical analysis. Analysis of a financial statement that reveals the relationship of each statement item to the total, which is the 100-percent figure *(p. 743).*

Voucher. Document authorizing a cash disbursement *(p. 284).*

Voucher register. Special journal used to record all expenditures in a voucher system, similar to but more comprehensive than the purchases journal *(p. 287).*

Voucher system. A way to record cash payments that enhances internal control by formalizing the process of approving and recording invoices for payment *(p. 283)*.

Wages. Employee pay stated at an hourly figure *(p. 431)*.

Withheld income tax. Income tax deducted from employees' gross pay *(p. 432)*.

Work in process inventory. Cost of the goods that are in the manufacturing process and not yet complete *(p. 857)*.

Work sheet. A columnar document designed to help move data from the trial balance to the financial statements *(p. 126)*.

Working capital. Current assets minus current liabilities, measures a business's ability to meet its short-term obligations with its current assets *(p. 750)*.

Index

Boldface indicates an Accounting Vocabulary term and the page in the text where it is defined. These terms are also defined in the Glossary.

(continued from front cover)

17-1A Feb. 6, Gain on Sale of Investment, Cr. $5,513

17-2A Investments in Affiliates, Dec. 31 balance, $84,643,000

17-3A Total consolidated assets, $756,000

17-4A Total consolidated assets, $973,000

17-5A Total assets, current cost/constant dollar, $900,000

17-6A Purchasing power gain, $28,000

17-1B Jan. 14, Gain on Sale of Investment, Cr. $20,350

17-2B Investment in Affiliates, Dec. 31 balance, $11,829,000

17-3B Total consolidated assets, $762,000

17-4B Total consolidated assets, $925,000

17-5B Total assets, current cost/constant dollar, $597,000

17-6B Purchasing power gain, $33,000

DP No check figure

FSP No check figure

All amounts in Chapter 18 are net cash inflows from operating activities

18-1A $31,000

18-2A $117,100

18-3A $74,400

18-4A $60,900

18-5A $32,700

18-6A $46,400

18-1B $78,200

18-2B $98,200

18-3B $48,800

18-4B $79,100

18-5B $70,800

18-6B $62,200

DP $170,000

FSP No check figure

19-1A 19X5: 1. Net sales, 94%; 2. .141

19-2A 2. Better; 3. Worse

19-3A Buy TransPacific

19-4A Transaction a: current ratio, 1.38; debt ratio, .60; EPS $1.78

19-5A 2.a. Improved; 2.b. Increased

19-6A Buy Hutton

19-1B 19X2: 1. Net sales, 105%; 2. .055

19-2B 2. Worse; 3. Worse

19-3B Buy Mid America

19-4B Transaction a: current ratio, 1.91; debt ratio, .50; EPS $3.72

19-5B 2.a. Deteriorated; 2.b. Decreased

19-6B Buy AgriCorp

DP No check figure

FSP No check figure

20-1A Net income, Period 2, actual — budget, $3,000

20-2A Net income, Sept., $1,500

20-3A Ending cash balance, Oct., $12,030

20-4A Net income, quarter ended Dec. 31, 19X6, $21,000

20-5A Total assets, $100,000; total liabilities, $15,400

20-6A Net income, $42,950; ending cash balance, Dec., $27,950; total assets, $185,550

20-1B Net income, Period 2, actual — budget, $9,000

20-2B Net income, June, $3,700

20-3B Ending cash balance, July, $25,350

20-4B Net income, quarter ended Dec. 31, 19X3, $41,000

20-5B Total assets, $114,500; total liabilities, $25,900

20-6B Net income, $42,470; ending cash balance, $39,870; total assets, $222,670

DP Cash balance before financing, $3,578

FSP Net earnings, actual — budget, $147.6 mil.

21-1A A: $260,000; $121,000; 26,000 units

21-2A Break-even number of cruises, 44

21-3A 4. Break-even sales in dollars, $898,516

21-4A 4. Break-even sales in units, 16.5

21-5A 5. New break-even sales, $25,600

21-6A 5. Net income, $28,000

21-1B A: $9,000; 4,000 units; .333

21-2B Break-even number of cruises, 21

21-3B 4. Break-even sales in dollars, $1,612,800

21-4B 4. Break-even sales in units, 16

21-5B 5. New break-even sales, $47,000

21-6B 5. Net income, $60,000

DP 2. Break-even sales mix: 44,016, toddler; 140,851, newborn; 47,537, pre-schooler. 4. Without toddler contribution margin, $66,027 net loss

FSP Break-even net revenues in dollars, $867.6 mil.; target net revenues in dollars, $3,518.8 mil.

22-1A Net income, $48,000

22-2A Cost of goods sold, July 31, $3,200

22-3A 2. Cost of goods sold, $22,500,000

22-4A Finished Goods Inventory, balance, $129,920

22-5A Total job cost, $2,371

22-6A Income from operations, $32,520

22-7A Cost of goods sold, $191,400

22-1B Net income, $42,000

22-2B Cost of goods sold, Apr. 30, $4,900

22-3B 2. Cost of goods sold, $163.2 mil.

22-4B Finished Goods Inventory, balance, $39,680

22-5B Total job cost, $1,514

22-6B Income from operations, $50,715

22-7B Cost of goods sold, $269,600

DP Sales price per unit under current process, $10.98; sales price per unit under new process, $10.61

FSP 3. $1.8 mil.; 4. Cost of goods manuf., $1,752.4 mil.

23-1A Total cost of each completed unit, $4.11745; balance in Work in Process at June 30, $21,022

23-2A Total cost of each completed unit, $24.9661; balance in Work in Process at Aug., 31, $2,961

23-3A Equivalent units: Transferred in, 560; Direct materials, 590; Conversion costs, 563. Cost per equivalent unit: Transferred in $42.143; Direct materials, $21.525; Conversion costs, $89.165

23-4A Completed and transferred to Plying Dept. during March: physical units, 500; total costs, $74,175

23-5A Equivalent units: Transferred in, 62,000; Direct materials, 61,000; Conversion costs, 63,000. Cost per equivalent unit: Transferred in, $1.30; Direct materials, $.22; Conversion costs, $.31. Cost per gallon: wax for wax paper, $.79; auto wax, $2.34

23-6A Equivalent units: Transferred in, 9,000; Conversion costs, 8,300. Cost per equivalent unit: Transferred in, $41.03; Conversion costs, $7.71. Unit cost per mower, $39.94

23-1B Total cost of each completed unit, $1.34378; balance in Work in Process at June 30, $797

23-2B Total cost of each completed unit, $4.93061; balance in Work in Process at Sept. 30, $3,680

23-3B Equivalent units: Transferred in, 3,000; Direct materials, 2,460; Conversion costs, 2,880. Cost per equivalent unit: Transferred in, $10.867; Direct materials, $11.382; Conversion costs, $18.715

23-4B Completed and transferred to finished goods during March: physical units, 2,200; total costs, $87,871

23-5B Equivalent units: Transferred in, 18,000; Direct materials, 15,000; Conversion costs, 15,000. Cost per equivalent unit: Transferred in, $.65; Direct materials, $.45; Conversion costs, $1.02. Cost per case: Frito, $1.43; Dorito, $1.51

23-6B Equivalent units: Transferred in, 32,000; Conversion costs, 18,500. Cost per equivalent unit: Transferred in, $.14; Conversion costs, $.03. Unit cost per screwdriver, $.23

DP Cost completed and transferred out, $210,520; cost of ending work in process, $12,000

24-1A Net income: at 30,000 units, $77,625; at 40,000 units, $117,000; at 44,000 units, $150,150

24-2A Net income: flexible budget variances, $18,750 U; sales volume variances, $10,350 U

24-3A Direct materials price variance, $1,498 U; direct labor price variance, $32 U; direct materials efficiency variance, $434 F; direct labor efficiency variance, $200 U; total flexible budget variance, $480 U; production volume variance, $300 U; gross profit, $36,144

24-4A Direct materials price variance, $624.25 U; direct labor price variance, $236 U; direct materials efficiency variance, $737.75 F; direct labor efficiency variance, $270 U; total flexible budget variance, $983 U; production volume variance, $864 F

24-5A Gross profit, $336,400; direct materials price variance, $3,080 F; direct